JESUS THE CHRIST:

A Study of the Messiah and His Mission according to Holy Scriptures both Ancient and Modern

By

JAMES E. TALMAGE

One of the Twelve Apostles of the Church of Jesus Christ of Latter-day Saints

Published by
The Jaredite Publication Society

PUBLISHER'S PREFACE

Jesus the Christ: A Study of the Messiah and His Mission According to the Holy Scriptures Both Ancient and Modern is a 1915 book by James E. Talmage. The book is doctrinal study on the life and ministry of Jesus Christ and is widely appreciated by members of The Church of Jesus Christ of Latter-day Saints (LDS Church). The book consists of 42 chapters, each focusing on important aspects of the life and mission of Jesus as the Messiah.

Since it was first published in September 1915, Jesus the Christ has been viewed by LDS Church as a classic text on its teachings and beliefs concerning the life and ministry of Jesus. Marion G. Romney said, "One who gets the understanding, the vision, and the spirit of the resurrected Lord through a careful study of the text Jesus the Christ by Elder James E. Talmage will find that he has greatly increased his moving faith in our glorified Redeemer."

In his preface to the first edition, Talmage wrote: "The author has departed from the course usually followed by writers on the Life of Jesus Christ, which course, as a rule, begins with the birth of Mary's Babe and ends with the ascension of the slain and risen Lord from Olivet. The treatment embodied in these pages, in addition to the narrative of the Lord's life in the flesh, comprises the antemortal existence and activities of the world's Redeemer, the revelations and personal manifestations of the glorified and exalted Son of God during the apostolic period of old and in modern times, the assured nearness of the Lord's second advent, and predicted events beyond-all so far as the Holy Scriptures make it plain. It is particularly congruous and appropriate that The Church of Jesus Christ of Latter-day Saints—the only Church that affirms authority based on specific revelation and commission to use the Lord's Holy Name as a distinctive designation—should set forth her doctrines concerning the Messiah and His mission."

Talmage first presented his study on the Savior as a series of lectures delivered under the auspices of the Deseret Sunday School Union Board at the LDS University in Salt Lake City from September 1904 to April 1906. He was subsequently asked by the First Presidency of the church to publish the lectures in book form. Because of other commitments, he was unable to complete this assignment for several years.

On December 8, 1911, Dr. Talmage was ordained a member of the Quorum of the Twelve Apostles of LDS Church. Less than three years later he was able at last to continue his work on the manuscript, writing in longhand, in a council room on the fourth floor of the Salt Lake Temple (known as the Study Room today). As chapters were completed, he presented them to the First Presidency, members of the Twelve, and Sunday School board members.

In his journal under date of April 19, 1915, Talmage wrote: "Finished the actual writing on the book Jesus the Christ, to which I have devoted every spare hour since settling down to the work of composition on September 14th last. Had it not been that I was privileged to do this work in the Temple it would be at present far from completion. I have felt the inspiration of the place and have appreciated the privacy and quietness incident thereto. I hope to proceed with the work of revision without delay."[citation needed]

Published more than eight decades ago and translated into many languages, Jesus the Christ has become a classic volume in Mormon literature.

CONTENTS.

AUTHOR'S PREFACE.

The scope of the subject presented in this work is expressed on the title page. It will be readily seen that the author has departed from the course usually followed by writers on the Life of Jesus Christ, which course, as a rule, begins with the birth of Mary's Babe and ends with the ascension of the slain and risen Lord from Olivet. The treatment embodied in these pages, in addition to the narrative of the Lord's life in the flesh comprizes the antemortal existence and activities of the world's Redeemer, the revelations and personal manifestations of the glorified and exalted Son of God during the apostolic period of old and in modern times, the assured nearness of the Lord's second advent, and predicted events beyond--all so far as the Holy Scriptures make plain.

It is particularly congruous and appropriate that the Church of Jesus Christ of Latter-day Saints--the only Church that affirms authority based on specific revelation and commission to use the Lord's Holy Name as a distinctive designation--should set forth her doctrines concerning the Messiah and His mission.

The author of this volume entered upon his welcome service under request and appointment from the presiding authorities of the Church; and the completed work has been read to and is approved by the First Presidency and the Council of the Twelve. It presents, however, the writer's personal belief and profoundest conviction as to the truth of what he has written. The book is published by the Church of Jesus Christ of Latter-day Saints.

A characteristic feature of the work is the guidance afforded by modern scriptures and the explication of the Holy Writ of olden times in the light of present day revelation, which, as a powerful and well directed beam, illumines many dark passages of ancient construction.

The spirit of the sacredness inherent in the subject has been a constant companion of the writer throughout his pleasing labor, and he reverently invokes the same as a minister to the readers of the volume.

JAMES E. TALMAGE.

Salt Lake City, Utah, September, 1915.

Jesus the Christ

CHAPTER 1. INTRODUCTION.

It is a matter of history that, at or near the beginning of what has since come to be known as the Christian era, the Man Jesus, surnamed the Christ, was born in Bethlehem of Judea.[1] The principal data as to His birth, life, and death are so well attested as to be reasonably indisputable; they are facts of record, and are accepted as essentially authentic by the civilized world at large. True, there are diversities of deduction based on alleged discrepancies in the records of the past as to circumstantial details; but such differences are of strictly minor importance, for none of them nor all taken together cast a shadow of rational doubt upon the historicity of the earthly existence of the Man known in literature as Jesus of Nazareth.

As to who and what He was there are dissensions of grave moment dividing the opinions of men; and this divergence of conception and belief is most pronounced upon those matters to which the greatest importance attaches. The solemn testimonies of millions dead and of millions living unite in proclaiming Him as divine, the Son of the Living God, the Redeemer and Savior of the human race, the Eternal Judge of the souls of men, the Chosen and Anointed of the Father—in short, the Christ. Others there are who deny His Godhood while extolling the transcendent qualities of His unparalleled and unapproachable Manhood.

To the student of history this Man among men stands first, foremost, and alone, as a directing personality in the world's progression. Mankind has never produced a leader to rank with Him. Regarded solely as a historic personage He is unique. Judged by the standard of human estimation, Jesus of Nazareth is supreme among men by reason of the excellence of His personal character, the simplicity, beauty, and genuine worth of His precepts, and the influence of His example and doctrines in the advancement of the race. To these distinguishing characteristics of surpassing greatness the devout Christian soul adds an attribute that far exceeds the sum of all the others—the divinity of Christ's origin and the eternal reality of His status as Lord and God.

Christian and unbeliever alike acknowledge His supremacy as a Man, and respect the epoch-making significance of His birth. Christ was born in the meridian of time;[2] and His life on earth marked at once the culmination of the past and the inauguration of an era distinctive in human hope, endeavor, and achievement. His advent determined a new order in the reckoning of the years; and by common consent the centuries antedating His birth have been counted backward from the pivotal event and are designated accordingly. The rise and fall of dynasties, the birth and dissolution of nations, all the cycles of history as to war and peace, as to prosperity and adversity, as to health and pestilence, seasons of plenty and of famine, the awful happenings of earthquake and storm, the triumphs of invention and discovery, the epochs of man's development in godliness and the long periods of his dwindling in unbelief—all the occurrences that make history—are chronicled throughout Christendom by reference to the year before or after the birth of Jesus Christ.

His earthly life covered a period of thirty-three years; and of these but three were spent by Him as an acknowledged Teacher openly engaged in the activities of public ministry. He was brought to a violent death before He had attained what we now regard as the age of manhood's prime. As an individual He was personally known to but few; and His fame as a world character became general only after His death.

Brief account of some of His words and works has been preserved to us; and this record, fragmentary and incomplete though it be, is rightly esteemed as the world's greatest treasure. The earliest and most extended history of His mortal existence is embodied within the compilation of scriptures known as the New Testament; indeed but little is said of Him by secular historians of His time. Few and short as are the allusions to Him made by non-scriptural writers in the period immediately following that of His ministry, enough is found to corroborate the sacred record as to the actuality and period of Christ's earthly existence.

No adequate biography of Jesus as Boy and Man has been or can be written, for the sufficing reason that a fulness of data is lacking. Nevertheless, man never lived of whom more has been said and sung, none to whom is devoted a greater proportion of the world's literature. He is extolled by Christian, Mohammedan and Jew, by skeptic and infidel, by the world's greatest poets, philosophers, statesmen, scientists, and historian. Even the profane sinner in the foul, sacrilege of his oath acclaims the divine supremacy of Him whose name he desecrates.

The purpose of the present treatise is that of considering the life and mission of Jesus _as_ the Christ. In this undertaking we shall be guided by the light of both ancient and modern scriptures; and, thus led, we shall discover, even in the early stages of our course, that the word of God as revealed in latter days is effective in illuming and making plain the Holy Writ of ancient times, and this, in many matters of the profoundest imports.[3]

Instead of beginning our study with the earthly birth of the Holy Babe of Bethlehem, we shall consider the part taken by the Firstborn Son of God in the primeval councils of heaven, at the time when He was chosen and ordained to be the Savior of the unborn race of mortals, the Redeemer of a world then in its formative stages of development. We are to study Him as the Creator of the world, as the Word of Power, through whom the purposes of the Eternal Father were realized in the preparation of the earth for the abode of His myriad spirit-children during the appointed period of their mortal probation. Jesus Christ was and is Jehovah, the God of Adam and of Noah, the God of Abraham, Isaac, and Jacob, the God of Israel, the God at whose instance the prophets of the ages have spoken, the God of all nations, and He who shall yet reign on earth as King of kings and Lord of lords.

His wondrous yet natural birth, His immaculate life in the flesh, and His voluntary death as a consecrated sacrifice for the sins of mankind, shall claim our reverent attention; as shall also His redeeming service in the world of disembodied spirits; His literal resurrection from bodily death to immortality; His several appearings to men and His continued ministry as the Resurrected Lord on both continents; the reestablishment of His Church through His personal presence and that of the Eternal Father in the latter days; and His coming to His temple in the current dispensation. All these developments in the ministration of the Christ are already of the past. Our proposed course of investigation will lead yet onward, into the future concerning which the word of divine revelation is of record. We shall consider the conditions incident to the Lord's return in power and glory to inaugurate the dominion of the Kingdom of Heaven on earth, and to usher in the predicted Millennium of peace and righteousness. And yet beyond we shall follow Him, through the post-Millennial conflict between the powers of heaven and the forces of hell, to the completion of His victory over Satan, sin, and death, when He shall present the glorified earth and its sanctified hosts, spotless and celestialized, unto the Father.

The Church of Jesus Christ of Latter-day Saints affirms her possession of divine authority for the use of the sacred name, Jesus Christ, as the essential part of her distinctive designation. In view of this exalted claim, it is pertinent to inquire as to what special or particular message the Church has to give to the world concerning the Redeemer and Savior of the race, and as to what she has to say in justification of her solemn affirmation, or in vindication of her exclusive name and title. As we proceed with our study, we shall find that among the specific teachings of the Church respecting the Christ are these:

(1) The unity and continuity of His mission in all ages--this of necessity involving the verity of His preexistence and foreordination. (2) The fact of His antemortal Godship. (3) The actuality of His birth in the flesh as the natural issue of divine and mortal parentage. (4) The reality of His death and physical resurrection, as a result of which the power of death shall be eventually overcome. (5) The literalness of the atonement wrought by Him, including the absolute requirement of individual compliance with the laws and ordinances of His gospel as the means by which salvation may be attained. (6) The restoration of His Priesthood and the reestablishment of His Church in the current age, which is verily the Dispensation of the Fulness of Times. (7) The certainty of His return to earth in the near future, with power and great glory, to reign in Person and bodily presence as Lord and King.

FOOTNOTES:

[1] As to the year of Christ's birth, see chapter 8.

[2] See chapter 6.

[3] The Holy Bible, the Book of Mormon, the Doctrine and Covenants, and the Pearl of Great Price constitute the standard works of the Church of Jesus Christ of Latter-day Saints. These will be cited alike as Scriptures in the following pages, for such they are.

CHAPTER 2. PREEXISTENCE AND FOREORDINATION OF THE CHRIST.

We affirm, on the authority of Holy Scripture, that the Being who is known among men as Jesus of Nazareth, and by all who acknowledge His Godhood as Jesus the Christ, existed with the Father prior to birth in the flesh; and that in the preexistent state He was chosen and ordained to be the one and only Savior and Redeemer of the human race. Foreordination implies and comprizes preexistence as an essential condition; therefore scriptures bearing upon the one are germane to the other; and consequently in this presentation no segregation of evidence as applying specifically to the preexistence of Christ or to His foreordination will be attempted.

John the Revelator beheld in vision some of the scenes that had been enacted in the spirit-world before the beginning of human history. He witnessed strife and contention between loyalty and rebellion, with the hosts defending the former led by Michael the archangel, and the rebellious forces captained by Satan, who is also called the devil, the serpent, and the dragon. We read: "And there was war in heaven; Michael and his angels fought against the dragon; and the dragon fought against his angels."[4]

In this struggle between unembodied hosts the forces were unequally divided; Satan drew to his standard only a third part of the children of God, who are symbolized as the "stars of heaven";[5] the majority either fought with Michael, or at least refrained from active opposition, thus accomplishing the purpose of their "first estate"; while the angels who arrayed themselves on the side of Satan "kept not their first estate",[6] and therefore rendered themselves ineligible for the glorious possibilities of an advanced condition or "second estate".[7] The victory was with Michael and his angels; and Satan or Lucifer, theretofore a "son of the morning", was cast out into heaven, yea "he was cast out into the earth, and his angels were cast out with him".[8] The prophet Isaiah, to whom these momentous occurrences had been revealed about eight centuries prior to the time of John's writings, laments with inspired pathos the fall of so great a one; and specifies selfish ambition as the occasion: "How art thou fallen from heaven, O Lucifer, son of the morning! how art thou cut down to the ground, which didst weaken the nations! For thou hast said in thine heart, I will ascend into heaven, I will exalt my throne above the stars of God: I will sit also upon the mount of the congregation, in the sides of the north: I will ascend above the heights of the clouds; I will be like the most High. Yet thou shalt be brought down to hell, to the sides of the pit."[9]

Justification for citing these scriptures in connection with our present consideration will be found in the cause of the great contention--the conditions that led to this war in heaven. It is plain from the words of Isaiah that Lucifer, already of exalted rank, sought to aggrandize himself without regard to the rights and agency of others. The matter is set forth, in words that none may misapprehend, in a revelation given to Moses and repeated through the first prophet of the present dispensation: "And I, the Lord God, spake unto Moses, saying: That Satan, whom thou hast commanded in the name of mine Only Begotten, is the same which was from the beginning, and he came before me, saying--Behold, here am I, send me, I will be thy son, and I will redeem all mankind, that one soul shall not be lost, and surely I will do it; wherefore give me thine honor. But, behold, my Beloved son, which was my Beloved and Chosen from the beginning, said unto me--Father, thy will be done, and the glory be thine forever. Wherefore, because that Satan rebelled against me, and sought to destroy the agency of man, which I, the Lord God, had given him, and also, that I should give unto him mine own power; by the power of mine Only Begotten, I caused that he should be cast down; and he became Satan, yea, even the devil, the father of all lies, to deceive and to blind men, and to lead them captive at his will, even as many as would not hearken unto my voice."[10]

Thus it is shown that prior to the placing of man upon the earth, how long before we do not know, Christ and Satan, together with the hosts of the spirit-children of God, existed as intelligent individuals,[11] possessing power and opportunity to choose the course they would pursue and the leaders whom they would follow and obey.[12] In that great concourse of spirit-intelligences, the Father's plan, whereby His children would be advanced to their second estate, was submitted and doubtless discussed. The opportunity so placed within the reach of the spirits who were to be privileged to take bodies upon the earth was so transcendently glorious that those heavenly multitudes burst forth into song and shouted for joy.[13]

Satan's plan of compulsion, whereby all would be safely conducted through the career of mortality, bereft of freedom to act and agency to choose, so circumscribed that they would be compelled to do right--that one soul would not be lost--was rejected; and the humble offer of Jesus the First-born--to assume mortality and live among men as their Exemplar and Teacher, observing the sanctity of man's agency but teaching men to use aright that divine heritage--was accepted. The decision brought war, which resulted in the vanquishment of Satan and his angels, who were cast out and deprived of the boundless privileges incident to the mortal or second estate.

In that august council of the angels and the Gods, the Being who later was born in flesh as Mary's Son, Jesus, took prominent part, and there was He ordained of the Father to be the Savior of mankind. As to time, the term being used in the sense of all duration past, this is our earliest record of the Firstborn among the sons of God; to us who read, it marks the beginning of the written history of Jesus the Christ.[14]

Old Testament scriptures, while abounding in promises relating to the actuality of Christ's advent in the flesh, are less specific in information concerning His antemortal existence. By the children of Israel, while living under the law and still unprepared to receive the gospel, the Messiah was looked for as one to be born in the lineage of Abraham and David, empowered to deliver them from personal and national burdens, and to vanquish their enemies. The actuality of the Messiah's status as the chosen Son of God, who was with the Father from the beginning, a Being of preexistent power and glory, was but dimly perceived, if conceived at all, by the people in general; and although to prophets specially commissioned in the authorities and privileges of the Holy Priesthood, revelation of the great truth was given,[15] they transmitted it to the people rather in the language of imagery and parable than in words of direct plainness. Nevertheless the testimony of the evangelists and the apostles, the attestation of the Christ Himself while in the flesh, and the revelations given in the present dispensation leave us without dearth of scriptural proof.

In the opening lines of the Gospel book written by John the apostle, we read: "In the beginning was the Word, and the word was with God, and the word was God. The same was in the beginning with God. All things were made by him; and without him was not anything made that was made.... And the Word was made flesh, and dwelt among us, (and we beheld his glory, the glory as of the only begotten of the Father), full of grace and truth."[16]

The passage is simple, precise and unambiguous. We may reasonably give to the phrase "In the beginning" the same meaning as attaches thereto in the first line of Genesis; and such signification must indicate a time antecedent to the earliest stages of human existence upon the earth. That the Word is Jesus Christ, who was with the Father in that beginning and who was Himself invested with the powers and rank of Godship, and that He came into the world and dwelt among men, are definitely affirmed. These statements are corroborated through a revelation given to Moses, in which he was permitted to see many of the creations of God, and to hear the voice of the Father with respect to the things that had been made: "And by the word of my power, have I created them, which is mine Only Begotten Son, who is full of grace and truth."[17]

John the apostle repeatedly affirms the preexistence of the Christ and the fact of His authority and power in the antemortal state.[18] To the same effect is the testimony of Paul[19] and of Peter. Instructing the saints concerning the basis of their faith, the last-named apostle impressed upon them that their redemption was not to be secured through corruptible things nor by the outward observance of traditional requirements, "But with the precious blood of Christ, as of a lamb without blemish and without spot: who verily was foreordained before the foundation of the world, but was manifest in these last times for you."[20]

Even more impressive and yet more truly conclusive are the personal testimonies of the Savior as to His own pre-existent life and the mission among men to which He had been appointed. No one who accepts Jesus as the Messiah can consistently reject these evidences of His eternal nature. When, on a certain occasion, the Jews in the synagogue disputed among themselves and murmured because of their failure to understand aright His doctrine concerning Himself, especially as touching His relationship with the Father, Jesus said unto them: "For I came down from heaven, not to do mine own will, but the will of him that sent me." And then, continuing the lesson based upon the contrast between the manna with which their fathers had been fed in the wilderness and the bread of life which He had to offer, He added: "I am the living bread which came down from heaven," and again declared "the living Father hath sent me." Not a few of the disciples failed to comprehend His teachings; and their complaints drew from Him these words: "Doth this offend you? What and if ye shall see the Son of man ascend up where he was before?"[21]

To certain wicked Jews, wrapped in the mantle of racial pride, boastful of their descent through the lineage of Abraham, and seeking to excuse their sins through an unwarranted use of the great patriarch's name, our Lord thus proclaimed His own preeminence: "Verily, verily, I say unto you, Before Abraham was, I am."[22] The fuller significance of this remark will be treated later; suffice it in the present connection to consider this scripture as a plain avowal of our Lord's seniority and supremacy over Abraham. But as Abraham's birth had preceded that of Christ by more than nineteen centuries, such seniority must have reference to a state of existence antedating that of mortality.

When the hour of His betrayal was near, in the last interview with the apostles prior to His agonizing experience in Gethsemane, Jesus comforted them saying: "For the Father himself loveth you, because ye have loved me, and have believed that I came out from God. I came forth from the Father, and am come into the world again, I leave the world, and go to the Father."[23] Furthermore, in the course of upwelling prayer for those who had been true to their testimony of His Messiahship, He addressed the Father with this solemn invocation: "And this is the life eternal, that they might know thee the only true God, and Jesus Christ, whom thou hast sent. I have glorified thee on the earth: I have finished the work which thou gavest me to do. And now, O Father glorify thou with thine own self with the glory which I had with thee before the world was."[24]

Book of Mormon scriptures are likewise explicit in proof of the preexistence of the Christ and of His foreappointed mission. One only of the many evidences therein found will be cited here. An ancient prophet, designated in the record as the brother of Jared,[25] once pleaded with the Lord in special supplication: "And the Lord said unto him, Believest thou the words which I shall speak? And he answered, Yea, Lord, I know that thou speakest the truth, for thou art a God of truth, and canst not lie. And when he had said these words, behold, the Lord shewed himself unto him, and said, Because thou knowest these things, ye are redeemed from the fall: therefore ye are brought back into my presence; therefore I shew myself unto you. Behold, I am he who was prepared from the foundation of the world to redeem my people. Behold, I am Jesus Christ. I am the Father and the Son. In me shall all mankind have light, and that eternally, even they who shall believe on my name; and they shall become my sons and my daughters. And never have I shewed myself unto man whom I have created, for never has man believed in me as thou hast. Seest thou that ye are created after mine own image? Yea, even all men were created in the beginning, after mine own image. Behold, this body, which ye now behold, is the body of my spirit; and man have I created after the body of my spirit; and even as I appear unto thee to be in the spirit, will I appear unto my people in the flesh."[26] The main facts attested by this scripture as having a direct bearing upon our present subject are those of the Christ manifesting Himself while yet in His antemortal state, and of His declaration that He had been chosen from the foundation of the world as the Redeemer.

Revelation given through the prophets of God in the present dispensation is replete with evidence of Christ's appointment and ordination in the primeval world; and the whole tenor of the scriptures contained in the Doctrine and Covenants may be called in witness. The following instances are particularly in point. In a communication to Joseph Smith the prophet, in May, 1833, the Lord declared Himself as the One who had previously come into the world from the Father, and of whom John had borne testimony as the Word; and the solemn truth is reiterated that He, Jesus Christ, "was in the beginning, before the world was", and further, that He was the Redeemer who "came into the world, because the world was made by him, and in him was the life of men and the light of men." Again, He is referred to as "the Only Begotten of the Father, full of grace and truth, even the Spirit of truth, which came and dwelt in the flesh." In the course of the same revelation the Lord said: "And now, verily I say unto you, I was in the beginning with the Father and am the firstborn."[27] On an earlier occasion, as the modern prophet testifies, he and an associate in the priesthood were enlightened by the Spirit so that they were able to see and understand the things of God--"Even those things which were from the beginning before the world was, which were ordained of the Father, through his Only Begotten Son, who was in the bosom of the Father, even from the beginning, of whom we bear record, and the record which we bear is the fulness of the gospel of Jesus Christ, who is the Son, whom we saw and with whom we conversed in the heavenly vision."[28] The testimony of scriptures written on both hemispheres, that of records both ancient and modern, the inspired utterances of prophets and apostles, and the words of the Lord Himself, are of one voice in proclaiming the preexistence of the Christ and His ordination as the chosen Savior and Redeemer of mankind--in the beginning, yea, even before the foundation of the world.

NOTES TO CHAPTER 2.

1. Graded Intelligences in the Antemortal State.--That the spirits of men existed as individual intelligences, of varying degrees of ability and power, prior to the inauguration of the mortal state upon this earth and even prior to the creation of the world as a suitable abode for human beings, is shown in great plainness through a divine revelation to Abraham: "Now the Lord had shown unto me, Abraham, the intelligences that were organized before the world was; and among all these there were many of the noble and great ones; and God saw these souls that they were good, and he stood in the midst of them, and he said: These I will make my rulers; for he stood among those that were spirits, and he saw that they were good; and he said unto me: Abraham, thou art one of them; thou wast chosen before thou wast born." (P. of G.P., Abraham 3:22, 23.)

That both Christ and Satan were among those exalted intelligences, and that Christ was chosen while Satan was rejected as the future Savior of mankind, are shown by the portions of the revelation immediately following that above quoted: "And there stood one among them that was like unto God, and he said unto those who were with him: We will go down, for there is space there, and we will take of these materials, and we will make an earth whereon these may dwell; and we will prove them herewith, to see if they will do all things whatsoever the Lord their God shall command them; and they who keep their first estate shall be added upon, and they who keep not their first estate shall not have glory in the same kingdom with those who keep their first estate; and they who keep their second estate shall have glory added upon their heads forever and ever. And the Lord said: Whom shall I send? And one answered like unto the Son of Man: Here am I, send me. And another answered and said: Here am I, send me. And the Lord said: I will send the first. And the second was angry, and kept not his first estate; and, at that day, many followed after him" (verses 24-28).

2. The Primeval Council in the Heavens.--"It is definitely stated in the Book of Genesis that God said, 'Let us make man in our image, after our likeness;' and again, after Adam had taken of the forbidden fruit the Lord said, 'Behold, the man has become as one of us;' and the inference is direct that in all that related to the work of the creation of the world there was a consultation; and though God spake as it is recorded in the Bible, yet it is evident He counseled with others. The scriptures tell us there are 'Gods many and Lords many. But to us there is but one God, the Father' (1 Cor. 8:5). And for this reason, though there were others engaged in the creation of the worlds, it is given to us in the Bible in the shape that it is; for the fulness of these truths is only revealed to highly favored persons for certain reasons known to God; as we are told in the scriptures: 'The secret of the Lord is with them that fear him; and he will show them his covenant.'--Psalms 25:14.

"It is consistent to believe that at this Council in the heavens the plan that should be adopted in relation to the sons of God who were then spirits, and had not yet obtained tabernacles, was duly considered. For, in view of the creation of the world and the placing of men upon it, whereby it would be possible for them to obtain tabernacles, and in those tabernacles obey laws of life, and with them again be exalted among the Gods, we are told that at that time, 'the morning stars sang together, and all the sons of God shouted for joy.' The question then arose, how, and upon what principle, should the salvation, exaltation and eternal glory of God's sons be brought about? It is evident that at that Council certain plans had been proposed and discussed, and that after a full discussion of those principles, and the declaration of the Father's will pertaining to His design, Lucifer came before the Father with a plan of his own, saying, 'Behold [here am] I; send me, I will be thy son, and I will redeem all mankind, that one soul shall not be lost, and surely I will do it; wherefore, give me thine honor.' But Jesus, on hearing this statement made by Lucifer, said, 'Father, thy will be done, and the glory be thine forever.' From these remarks made by the well beloved Son, we should naturally infer that in the discussion of this subject the Father had made known His will and developed His plan and design pertaining to these matters, and all that His well beloved Son wanted to do was to carry out the will of His Father, as it would appear had been before expressed. He also wished the glory to be given to His Father, who, as God the Father, and the originator and designer of the plan, had a right to all the honor and glory. But Lucifer wanted to introduce a plan contrary to the will of his Father, and then wanted His honor, and said: 'I will save every soul of man, wherefore give me thine honor.' He wanted to go contrary to the will of his Father, and presumptuously sought to deprive man of his free agency, thus making him a serf, and placing him in a position in which it was impossible for him to obtain that exaltation which God designed should be man's, through obedience to the law which He had suggested; and again, Lucifer wanted the honor and power of his Father, to enable him to carry out principles which were contrary to the Father's wish."--John Taylor--_Mediation and Atonement_, pp. 93, 94.

3. The Jaredites.--"Of the two nations whose histories constitute the Book of Mormon, the first in order of time consisted of the people of Jared, who followed their leader from the Tower of Babel at the time of the confusion of tongues. Their history was written on twenty-four plates of gold by Ether, the last of their prophets, who, foreseeing the destruction of his people because of their wickedness, hid away the historical plates. They were afterward found, B.C. 123, by an expedition sent out by King Limhi, a Nephite ruler. The record engraved on these plates was subsequently abridged by Moroni, and the condensed account was attached by him to the Book of Mormon record; it appears in the modern translation under the name of the Book of Ether.

"The first and chief prophet of the Jaredites is not mentioned by name in the record as we have it; he is known only as the brother of Jared. Of the people, we learn that, amid the confusion of Babel, Jared and his brother importuned the Lord that He would spare them and their associates from the impending disruption. Their prayer was heard, and the Lord led them with a considerable company, who, like themselves, were free from the taint of idolatry, away from their homes, promising to conduct them to a land choice above all other lands. Their course of travel is not given with exactness; we learn only that they reached the ocean, and there constructed eight vessels, called barges, in which they set out upon the waters. These vessels were small and dark within; but the Lord made luminous certain stones, which gave light to the imprisoned voyagers. After a passage of three hundred and forty-four days, the colony landed on the western shore of North America, probably at a place south of the Gulf of California, and north of the Isthmus of Panama.

"Here they became a flourishing nation; but, giving way in time to internal dissensions, they divided into factions, which warred with one another until the people were totally destroyed. This destruction, which occurred near the hill Ramah, afterward known among the Nephites as Cumorah, probably took place at about the time of Lehi's landing in South America--590 B.C."--The author, _Articles of Faith_, xiv:10-12.

FOOTNOTES:

[4] Rev. 12:7; see also verses 8 and 9.

[5] Rev. 12:4; see also Doc. and Cov. 29:36-38; and 76:25-27.

[6] Jude 6.

[7] P. of G.P., Abraham 3:26.

[8] Rev. 12:9.

[9] Isa. 14:12-15; compare Doc. and Cov. 29:36-38; and 76:23-27.

[10] P. of G.P., Moses 4:1-4; see also Abraham 3:27, 28.

[11] For a further treatment of the preexistence of spirits see the author's "Articles of Faith" x:21-30.

[12] Note 1, end of chapter.

[13] Job 38:7.

[14] Note 2, end of chapter.

[15] Psalm 25:14; Amos 3:7.

[16] John 1:1-3, 14; see also 1 John 1:1; 5: 7; Rev. 19:13; compare Doc. and Cov. 93:1-17, 21.

[17] P. of C.P., Moses 1:32, 33; see also 2:5.

[18] 1 John 1:1-3; 2:13, 14; 4:9; Rev. 3:14.

[19] 2 Tim. 1:9, 10; Rom. 16:25; Eph. 1:4; 3:9, 11; Titus 1:2. See especially Rom. 3:25; and note the marginal rendering--"foreordained"-- making the passage read: "Whom God hath foreordained to be a propitiation."

[20] 1 Peter 1:19, 20.

[21] John 6:38, 51, 57, 61, 62.

[22] John 8:58; see also 17:5, 24; and compare Exo. 3:14. Page 37.

[23] John 16:27, 28; see also 13:3.

[24] John 17:3-5; see also verses 24, 25.

[25] Note 3, end of chapter.

[26] B. of M., Ether 3:11-16. See also 1 Nephi 17:30; 19:7; 2 Nephi 9:5; 11:7; 25:12; 26:12; Mosiah 3:5; 4:2; 7:27; 13:34; 15:1; Alma 11:40; Hela. 14:12; 3 Nephi 9:15.

[27] Doc. and Cov. 93:1-17, 21.

[28] Doc. and Cov. 76:13, 14.

CHAPTER 3. THE NEED OF A REDEEMER.

We have heretofore shown that the entire human race existed as spirit-beings in the primeval world, and that for the purpose of making possible to them the experiences of mortality this earth was created. They were endowed with the powers of agency or choice while yet but spirits; and the divine plan provided that they be free-born in the flesh, heirs to the inalienable birthright of liberty to choose and to act for themselves in mortality. It is undeniably essential to the eternal progression of God's children that they be subjected to the influences of both good and evil, that they be tried and tested and proved withal, "to see if they will do all things whatsoever the Lord their God shall command them."[29] Free agency is an indispensable element of such a test.

The Eternal Father well understood the diverse natures and varied capacities of His spirit-offspring; and His infinite foreknowledge made plain to Him, even in the beginning, that in the school of life some of His children would succeed and others would fail; some would be faithful, others false; some would choose the good, others the evil; some would seek the way of life while others would elect to follow the road to destruction. He further foresaw that death would enter the world, and that the possession of bodies by His children would be of but brief individual duration. He saw that His commandments would be disobeyed and His law violated; and that men, shut out from His presence and left to themselves, would sink rather than rise, would retrograde rather than advance, and would be lost to the heavens. It was necessary that a means of redemption be provided, whereby erring man might make amends, and by compliance with established law achieve salvation and eventual exaltation in the eternal worlds. The power of death was to be overcome, so that, though men would of necessity die, they would live anew, their spirits clothed with immortalized bodies over which death could not again prevail.

Let not ignorance and thoughtlessness lead us into the error of assuming that the Father's foreknowledge as to what _would be_, under given conditions, determined that such _must be_. It was not His design that the souls of mankind be lost; on the contrary it was and is His work and glory, "to bring to pass the immortality and eternal life of man."[30] Nevertheless He saw the evil into which His children would assuredly fall; and with infinite love and mercy did He ordain means of averting the dire effect, provided the transgressor would elect to avail himself thereof.[31] The offer of the firstborn Son to establish through His own ministry among men the gospel of salvation, and to sacrifice Himself, through labor, humiliation and suffering even unto death, was accepted and made the foreordained plan of man's redemption from death, of his eventual salvation from the effects of sin, and of his possible exaltation through righteous achievement.

In accordance with the plan adopted in the council of the Gods, man was created as an embodied spirit; his tabernacle of flesh was composed of the elements of earth.[32] He was given commandment and law, and was free to obey or disobey--with the just and inevitable condition that he should enjoy or suffer the natural results of his choice.[33] Adam, the first man[34] placed upon the earth in pursuance of the established plan, and Eve who was given unto him as companion and associate, indispensable to him in the appointed mission of peopling the earth, disobeyed the express commandment of God and so brought about the "fall of man", whereby the mortal state, of which death is an essential element, was inaugurated.[35] It is not proposed to consider here at length the doctrine of the fall; for the present argument it is sufficient to establish the fact of the momentous occurrence and its portentous consequences.[36] The woman was deceived, and in direct violation of counsel and commandment partook of the food that had been forbidden, as a result of which act her body became degenerate and subject to death. Adam realized the disparity that had been brought between him and his companion, and with some measure of understanding followed her course, thus becoming her partner in bodily degeneracy. Note in this matter the words of Paul the apostle: "Adam was not deceived, but the woman being deceived was in the transgression."[37] ⟶ Nope.

The man and the woman had now become mortal; through indulgence in food unsuited to their nature and condition and against which they had been specifically warned, and as the inevitable result of their disobeying the divine law and commandment, they became liable to the physical ailments and bodily frailties to which mankind has since been the natural heir.[38] Those bodies, which before the fall had been perfect in form and function, were now subjects for eventual dissolution or death. The arch-tempter through whose sophistries, half-truths and infamous falsehoods, Eve had been beguiled, was none other than Satan, or Lucifer, that rebellious and fallen "son of the morning", whose proposal involving the destruction of man's liberty had been rejected in the council of the heavens, and who had been "cast out into the earth", he and all his angels as unbodied spirits, never to be tabernacled in bodies of their own.[39] As an act of diabolic reprisal following his rejection in the council, his defeat by Michael and the heavenly hosts, and his ignominious expulsion from heaven, Satan planned to destroy the bodies in which the faithful spirits--those who had kept their first estate--would be born; and his beguilement of Eve was but an early stage of that infernal scheme.

Death has come to be the universal heritage; it may claim its victim in infancy or youth, in the period of life's prime, or its summons may be deferred until the snows of age have gathered upon the hoary head; it may befall as the result of accident or disease, by violence, or as we say, through natural causes; but come it must, as Satan well knows; and in this knowledge is his present though but temporary triumph. But the purposes of God, as they ever have been and ever shall be, are infinitely superior to the deepest designs of men or devils; and the Satanic machinations to make death inevitable, perpetual and supreme were provided against even before the first man had been created in the flesh. The atonement to be wrought by Jesus the Christ was ordained to overcome death and to provide a means of ransom from the power of Satan.

As the penalty incident to the fall came upon the race through an individual act, it would be manifestly unjust, and therefore impossible as part of the divine purpose, to make all men suffer the results thereof without provision for deliverance.[40] Moreover, since by the transgression of one man sin came into the world and death was entailed upon all, it is consistent with reason that the atonement thus made necessary should be wrought by one.[41] "Wherefore, as by one man sin entered into the world, and death by sin; and so death passed upon all men, for that all have sinned ... Therefore as by the offence of one judgment came upon all men to condemnation; even so by the righteousness of one the free gift came upon all men unto justification of life."[42] So taught the apostle Paul; and, further: "For since by man came death, by man came also the resurrection of the dead. For as in Adam all die, even so in Christ shall all be made alive."[43]

The atonement was plainly to be a vicarious sacrifice, voluntary and love-inspired on the Savior's part, universal in its application to mankind so far as men shall accept the means of deliverance thus placed within their reach. For such a mission only one who was without sin could be eligible. Even the altar victims of ancient Israel offered as a provisional propitiation for the offenses of the people under the Mosaic law had to be clean and devoid of spot or blemish; otherwise they were unacceptable and the attempt to offer them was sacrilege.[44] Jesus Christ was the only Being suited to the requirements of the great sacrifice:

1--As the one and only sinless Man;

2--As the Only Begotten of the Father and therefore the only Being born to earth possessing in their fulness the attributes of both Godhood and manhood;

3--As the One who had been chosen in the heavens and foreordained to this service.

What other man has been without sin, and therefore wholly exempt from the dominion of Satan, and to whom death, the wage of sin, is not naturally due? Had Jesus Christ met death as other men have done--the result of the power that Satan has gained over them through their sins--His death would have been but an individual experience, expiatory in no degree of any faults or offenses but His own. Christ's absolute sinlessness made Him eligible, His humility and willingness rendered Him acceptable to the Father, as the atoning sacrifice whereby propitiation could be made for the sins of all men.

What other man has lived with power to withstand death, over whom death could not prevail except through his own submission? Yet Jesus Christ could not be slain until His "hour had come", and that, the hour in which He voluntarily surrendered His life, and permitted His own decease through an act of will. Born of a mortal mother He inherited the capacity to die; begotten by an immortal Sire He possessed as a heritage the power to withstand death indefinitely. He literally gave up His life; to this effect is His own affirmation: "Therefore doth my Father love me, because I lay down my life, that I might take it again. No man taketh it from me, but I lay it down of myself. I have power to lay it down, and I have power to take it again."[45] And further: "For as the Father hath life in himself; so hath he given to the Son to have life in himself."[46] Only such a One could conquer death; in none but Jesus the Christ was realized this requisite condition of a Redeemer of the world.

What other man has come to earth with such appointment, clothed with the authority of such foreordination? The atoning mission of Jesus Christ was no self-assumption. True, He had offered Himself when the call was made in the heavens; true, He had been accepted, and in due time came to earth to carry into effect the terms of that acceptance; but He was chosen by One greater than Himself. The burden of His confession of authority was ever to the effect that He operated under the direction of the Father, as witness these words: "I came down from heaven, not to do mine own will, but the will of him that sent me."[47] "My meat is to do the will of him that sent me, and to finish his work."[48] "I can of mine own self do nothing: as I hear, I judge: and my judgment is just; because I seek not mine own will but the will of the Father which hath sent me."[49]

Through the atonement accomplished by Jesus Christ--a redeeming service, vicariously rendered in behalf of mankind, all of whom have become estranged from God by the effects of sin both inherited and individually incurred--the way is opened for a reconciliation whereby man may come again into communion with God, and be made fit to dwell anew and forever in the presence of his Eternal Father. This basal thought is admirably implied in our English word, "atonement," which, as its syllables attest, is _at-one-ment_, "denoting reconciliation, or the bringing into agreement of those who have been estranged."[50] The effect of the atonement may be conveniently considered as twofold:

1--The universal redemption of the human race from death invoked by the fall of our first parents; and,

2--Salvation, whereby means of relief from the results of individual sin are provided.

The victory over death was made manifest in the resurrection of the crucified Christ; He was the first to pass from death to immortality and so is justly known as "the first fruits of them that slept."[51] That the resurrection of the dead so inaugurated is to be extended to every one who has or shall have lived is proved by an abundance of scriptural evidence. Following our Lord's resurrection, others who had slept in the tomb arose and were seen of many, not as spirit-apparitions but as resurrected beings possessing immortalized bodies: "And the graves were opened; and many bodies of the saints which slept arose, and came out of the graves after his resurrection, and went into the holy city, and appeared unto many."[52]

Those who thus early came forth are spoken of as "the saints"; and other scriptures confirm the fact that only the righteous shall be brought forth in the earlier stages of the resurrection yet to be consummated; but that all the dead shall in turn resume bodies of flesh and bones is placed beyond doubt by the revealed word. The Savior's direct affirmation ought to be conclusive: "Verily, verily, I say unto you, The hour is coming, and now is, when the dead shall hear the voice of the Son of God: and they that hear shall live.... Marvel not at this: for the hour is coming, in the which all that are in the graves shall hear his voice, and shall come forth; they that have done good, unto the resurrection of life; and they that have done evil, unto the resurrection of damnation.."[53] The doctrine of a universal resurrection was taught by the apostles of old,[54] as also by the Nephite prophets;[55] and the same is confirmed by revelation incident to the present dispensation.[56] Even the heathen who have not known God shall be brought forth from their graves; and, inasmuch as they have lived and died in ignorance of the saving law, a means of making the plan of salvation known unto them is provided. "And then shall the heathen nations be redeemed, and they that knew no law shall have part in the first resurrection."[57]

Jacob, a Nephite prophet, taught the universality of the resurrection, and set forth the absolute need of a Redeemer, without whom the purposes of God in the creation of man would be rendered futile. His words constitute a concise and forceful summary of revealed truth directly bearing upon our present subject:

"For as death hath passed upon all men, to fulfil the merciful plan of the great Creator, there must needs be a power of resurrection, and the resurrection must needs come unto man by reason of the fall; and the fall came by reason of transgression; and because man became fallen, they were cut off from the presence of the Lord; wherefore it must needs be an infinite atonement; save it should be an infinite atonement, this corruption could not put on incorruption. Wherefore, the first judgment which came upon man, must needs have remained to an endless duration. And if so, this flesh must have laid down to rot and to crumble to its mother earth, to rise no more. O the wisdom of God! his mercy and grace! For behold, if the flesh should rise no more, our spirits must become subject to that angel who fell from before the presence of the eternal God, and became the devil, to rise no more. And our spirits must have become like unto him, and we become devils, angels to a devil, to be shut out from the presence of our God, and to remain with the father of lies, in misery, like unto himself; yea, to that being who beguiled our first parents; who transformeth himself nigh unto an angel of light, and stirreth up the children of men unto secret combinations of murder, and all manner of secret works of darkness. O how great the goodness of our God, who prepareth a way for our escape from the grasp of this awful monster; yea, that monster, death and hell, which I call the death of the body, and also the death of the spirit. And because of the way of deliverance of our God, the Holy One of Israel, this death, of which I have spoken, which is the temporal, shall deliver up its dead; which death is the grave. And this death of which I have spoken, which is the spiritual death, shall deliver up its dead; which spiritual death is hell; wherefore, death and hell must deliver up their dead, and hell must deliver up its captive spirits, and the grave must deliver up its captive bodies, and the bodies and the spirits of men will be restored one to the other; and it is by the power of the resurrection of the Holy One of Israel. O how great the plan of our God! For on the other hand, the paradise of God must deliver up the spirits of the righteous, and the grave deliver up the body of the righteous; and the spirit and the body is restored to itself again, and all men become incorruptible, and immortal, and they are living souls, having a perfect knowledge like unto us in the flesh; save it be that our knowledge shall be perfect."[58]

The application of the atonement to individual transgression, whereby the sinner may obtain absolution through compliance with the laws and ordinances embodied in the gospel of Jesus Christ, is conclusively attested by scripture. Since forgiveness of sins can be secured in none other way, there being either in heaven or earth no name save that of Jesus Christ whereby salvation shall come unto the children of men,[59] every soul stands in need of the Savior's mediation, since all are sinners. "For all have sinned and come short of the glory of God", said Paul of old,[60] and John the apostle added his testimony in these words: "If we say that we have no sin we deceive ourselves, and the truth is not in us."[61]

Who shall question the justice of God, which denies salvation to all who will not comply with the prescribed conditions on which alone it is declared obtainable? Christ is "the author of eternal salvation unto all them that obey him",[62] and God "will render to every man according to his deeds: to them who by patient continuance in well doing seek for glory and honor and immortality, eternal life: but unto them that are contentious, and do not obey the truth, but obey unrighteousness, indignation and wrath, tribulation and anguish, upon every soul of man that doeth evil."[63]

Such then is the need of a Redeemer, for without Him mankind would forever remain in a fallen state, and as to hope of eternal progression would be inevitably lost.[64] The mortal probation is provided as an opportunity for advancement; but so great are the difficulties and the dangers, so strong is the influence of evil in the world, and so weak is man in resistance thereto, that without the aid of a power above that of humanity no soul would find its way back to God from whom it came. The need of a Redeemer lies in the inability of man to raise himself from the temporal to the spiritual plane, from the lower kingdom to the higher. In this conception we are not without analogies in the natural world. We recognize a fundamental distinction between inanimate and living matter, between the inorganic and the organic, between the lifeless mineral on the one hand and the living plant or animal on the other. Within the limitations of its order the dead mineral grows by accretion of substance, and may attain a relatively perfect condition of structure and form as is seen in the crystal. But mineral matter, though acted upon favorably by the forces of nature-- light, heat, electric energy and others--can never become a living organism; nor can the dead elements, through any process of chemical combination dissociated from life, enter into the tissues of the plant as essential parts thereof. But the plant, which is of a higher order, sends its rootlets into the earth, spreads its leaves in the atmosphere, and through these organs absorbs the solutions of the soil, inspires the gases of the air, and from such lifeless materials weaves the tissue of its wondrous structure. No mineral particle, no dead chemical substance has ever been made a constituent of organic tissue except through the agency of life. We may, perhaps with profit, carry the analogy a step farther. The plant is unable to advance its own tissue to the animal plane. Though it be the recognized order of nature that the "animal kingdom" is dependent upon the "vegetable kingdom" for its sustenance, the substance of the plant may become part of the animal organism only as the latter reaches down from its higher plane and by its own vital action incorporates the vegetable compounds with itself. In turn, animal matter can never become, even transitorily, part of a human body, except as the living man assimilates it, and by the vital processes of his own existence lifts, for the time being, the substance of the animal that supplied him food to the higher plane of his own existence. The comparison herein employed is admittedly defective if carried beyond reasonable limits of application; for the raising of mineral matter to the plane of the plant, vegetable tissue to the level of the animal, and the elevation of either to the human plane, is but a temporary change; with the dissolution of the higher tissues the material thereof falls again to the level of the inanimate and the dead. But, as a means of illustration the analogy may not be wholly without value.

So, for the advancement of man from his present fallen and relatively degenerate state to the higher condition of spiritual life, a power above his own must cooperate. Through the operation of the laws obtaining in the higher kingdom man may be reached and lifted; himself he cannot save by his own unaided effort.[65] A Redeemer and Savior of mankind is beyond all question essential to the realization of the plan of the Eternal Father, "to bring to pass the immortality and eternal life of man";[66] and that Redeemer and Savior is Jesus the Christ, beside whom there is and can be none other.

NOTES TO CHAPTER 3.

1. God's Foreknowledge Not a Determining Cause.--"Respecting the foreknowledge of God, let it not be said that divine omniscience is of itself a determining cause whereby events are inevitably brought to pass. A mortal father, who knows the weaknesses and frailties of his son, may by reason of that knowledge sorrowfully predict the calamities and sufferings awaiting his wayward boy. He may foresee in that son's future a forfeiture of blessings that could have been won, loss of position, self-respect, reputation and honor; even the dark shadows of a felon's cell and the night of a drunkard's grave may appear in the saddening visions of that fond father's soul; yet, convinced by experience of the impossibility of bringing about that son's reform, he foresees the dread developments of the future, and he finds but sorrow and anguish in his knowledge. Can it be said that the father's foreknowledge is a cause of the son's sinful life? The son, perchance, has reached his maturity; he is the master of his own destiny; a free agent unto himself. The father is powerless to control by force or to direct by arbitrary command; and, while he would gladly make any effort or sacrifice to save his son from the fate impending, he fears for what seems to be an awful certainty. But surely that thoughtful, prayerful, loving parent does not, because of his knowledge, contribute to the son's waywardness. To reason otherwise would be to say that a neglectful father, who takes not the trouble to study the nature and character of his son, who shuts his eyes to sinful tendencies, and rests in careless indifference as to the probable future, will by his very heartlessness be benefitting his child, because his lack of forethought cannot operate as a contributory cause to dereliction.

"Our Heavenly Father has a full knowledge of the nature and disposition of each of His children, a knowledge gained by long observation and experience in the past eternity of our primeval childhood; a knowledge compared with which that gained by earthly parents through mortal experience with their children is infinitesimally small. By reason of that surpassing knowledge, God reads the future of child and children, of men individually and of men collectively as communities and nations; He knows what each will do under given conditions, and sees the end from the beginning. His foreknowledge is based on intelligence and reason. He foresees the future as a state which naturally and surely will be; not as one which must be because He has arbitrarily willed that it shall be."--From the author's _Great Apostasy_, pp. 19, 20.

2. Man Free to Choose for Himself.--"The Father of souls has endowed His children with the divine birthright of free agency; He does not and will not control them by arbitrary force; He impels no man toward sin; He compels none to righteousness. Unto man has been given freedom to act for himself; and, associated with this independence, is the fact of strict responsibility and the assurance of individual accountability. In the judgment with which we shall be judged, all the conditions and circumstances of our lives shall be considered. The inborn tendencies due to heredity, the effect of environment whether conducive to good or evil, the wholesome teachings of youth, or the absence of good instruction--these and all other contributory elements must be taken into account in the rendering of a just verdict as to the soul's guilt or innocence. Nevertheless, the divine wisdom makes plain what will be the result with given conditions operating on known natures and dispositions of men, while every individual is free to choose good or evil within the limits of the many conditions existing and operative."--_Great Apostasy_, p. 21; see also _Articles of Faith_, iii:1, 2.

3. The Fall a Process of Physical Degeneracy.--A modern revelation given to the Church in 1833 (Doc. and Cov. Sec. 89), prescribes rules for right living, particularly as regards the uses of stimulants, narcotics, and foods unsuited to the body. Concerning the physical causes by which the fall was brought about, and the close relation between those causes and current violations of the Word of Wisdom embodied in the revelation referred to above, the following is in point. "This, [the Word of Wisdom] like other revelations that have come in the present dispensation, is not wholly new. It is as old as the human race. The principle of the Word of Wisdom was revealed unto Adam. All the essentials of the Word of Wisdom were made known unto him in his immortal state, before he had taken into his body those things that made of it a thing of earth. He was warned against that very practise. He was not told to treat his body as something to be tortured. He was not told to look upon it as the fakir of India has come to look upon his body, or professes to look upon it, as a thing to be utterly contemned; but he was told that he must not take into that body certain things which were there at hand. He was warned that, if he did, his body would lose the power which it then held of living for ever, and that he would become subject to death. It was pointed out to him, as it has been pointed out to you, that there are many good fruits to be plucked, to be eaten, to be enjoyed. We believe in enjoying good food. We think that these good things are given us of God. We believe

in getting all the enjoyment out of eating that we can; and, therefore, we should avoid gluttony, and we should avoid extremes in all our habits of eating; and as was told unto Adam, so is it told unto us: Touch not these things; for in the day that thou doest it thy life shall be shortened and thou shalt die.

"Here let me say that therein consisted the fall--the eating of things unfit, the taking into the body of the things that made of that body a thing of earth: and I take this occasion to raise my voice against the false interpretation of scripture, which has been adopted by certain people, and is current in their minds, and is referred to in a hushed and half-secret way, that the fall of man consisted in some offense against the laws of chastity and of virtue. Such a doctrine is an abomination. What right have we to turn the scriptures from their proper sense and meaning? What right have we to declare that God meant not what He said? The fall was a natural process, resulting through the incorporation into the bodies of our first parents of the things that came from food unfit, through the violation of the command of God regarding what they should eat. Don't go around whispering that the fall consisted in the mother of the race losing her chastity and her virtue. It is not true; the human race is not born of fornication. These bodies that are given unto us are given in the way that God has provided. Let it not be said that the patriarch of the race, who stood with the gods before he came here upon the earth, and his equally royal consort, were guilty of any such foul offense. The adoption of that belief has led many to excuse departures from the path of chastity and the path of virtue, by saying that it is the sin of the race, that it is as old as Adam. It was not introduced by Adam. It was not committed by Eve. It was the introduction of the devil and came in order that he might sow the seeds of early death in the bodies of men and women, that the race should degenerate as it has degenerated whenever the laws of virtue and of chastity have been transgressed.

"Our first parents were pure and noble, and when we pass behind the veil we shall perhaps learn something of their high estate, more than we know now. But be it known that they were pure; they were noble. It is true that they disobeyed the law of God, in eating things they were told not to eat; but who amongst you can rise up and condemn?"--From an address by the author at the Eighty-fourth Semiannual Conference of the Church, Oct. 6, 1913; published in the Proceedings of the Conference, pp. 118, 119.

4. Christ Wrought Redemption from the Fall.--"The Savior thus becomes master of the situation--the debt is paid, the redemption made, the covenant fulfilled, justice satisfied, the will of God done, and all power is now given into the hands of the Son of God--the power of the resurrection, the power of the redemption, the power of salvation, the power to enact laws for the carrying out and accomplishment of this design. Hence life and immortality are brought to light, the gospel is introduced, and He becomes the author of eternal life and exaltation. He is the Redeemer, the Resurrector, the Savior of man and the world; and He has appointed the law of the gospel as the medium which must be complied with in this world or the next, as He complied with His Father's law; hence 'he that believeth shall be saved, and he that believeth not shall be damned.' The plan, the arrangement, the agreement, the covenant was made, entered into and accepted before the foundation of the world; it was prefigured by sacrifices, and was carried out and consummated on the cross. Hence being the mediator between God and man, He becomes by right the dictator and director on earth and in heaven for the living and for the dead, for the past, the present and the future, pertaining to man as associated with this earth or the heavens, in time or eternity, the Captain of our salvation, the Apostle and High-Priest of our profession, the Lord and Giver of life."--John Taylor, _Mediation and Atonement_, p. 171.

5. Redemption from the Effect of the Fall.--"'Mormonism' accepts the doctrine of the fall, and the account of the transgression in Eden, as set forth in Genesis; but it affirms that none but Adam is or shall be answerable for Adam's disobedience; that mankind in general are absolutely absolved from responsibility for that 'original sin,' and that each shall account for his own transgressions alone; that the fall was foreknown of God, that it was turned to good effect by which the necessary condition of mortality should be inaugurated; and that a Redeemer was provided before the world was; that general salvation, in the sense of redemption from the effects of the fall, comes to all without their seeking it; but that individual salvation or rescue from the effects of personal sins is to be acquired by each for himself by faith and good works through the redemption wrought by Jesus Christ."--From the author's _Story and Philosophy of 'Mormonism,'_ p. 111.

FOOTNOTES:

[29] P. of G.P., Abraham 3:25. For a fuller treatment of man's Free Agency, see the author's "Articles of Faith," iii:1-10, and the numerous references there given.

[30] P. of G.P., Moses 1:39; compare 6:59. Note 1, end of chapter.

[31] Note 2, end of chapter.

[32] Gen. 1:26, 27; 2:7; compare P. of G.P., Moses 2:26, 27; 3:7; Abraham 4:26-28; 5:7.

[33] Gen. 1:28-31; 2:16, 17; compare P. of G.P., Moses 2:28-31; 3:16, 17; Abraham 4:28-31; 5:12, 13.

[34] Gen. 2:8; compare statement in verse 5--that prior to that time there was "not a man to till the ground"; see also P. of G.P., Moses 3:7; Abraham 1:3; and B. of M., 1 Nephi 5:11.

[35] Gen. chap. 3; compare P. of G.P., Moses chap. 4.

[36] See "Articles of Faith," iii:21-32.

[37] 1 Tim. 2:14; see also 2 Cor. 11:3.

[38] Note 3, end of chapter.

[39] See page 7.

[40] Note 4, end of chapter.

[41] Note 5, end of chapter.

[42] Rom. 5:12, 18.

[43] 1 Cor. 15:21, 22.

[44] Lev. 22:20; Deut. 15:21; 17:1; Mal. 1:8, 14; compare Heb. 9:14; 1 Peter 1:19.

[45] John 10:17-18

[46] John 5:26

[47] John 6:38

[48] John 4:34

[49] John 5:30; see also verse 19; also Matt. 26:42; compare Doc. and Cov. 19:2; 20:24.

[50] New Standard Dictionary under "propitiation."

[51] 1 Cor. 15:20; see also Acts 26:23; Col. 1:18; Rev. 1:5.

[52] Matt. 27:52, 53.

[53] John 5:25, 28, 29. A modern scripture attesting the same truth reads: "They who have done good in the resurrection of the just; and they who have done evil in the resurrection of the unjust."--Doc. and Cov. 76:17.

[54] For instances see Acts 24:15; Rev. 20:12, 13.

[55] For instances see B. of M., 2 Nephi 9:6, 12, 13, 21, 22; Helaman 14:15-17; Mosiah 15:20-24; Alma 40:2-16; Mormon 9:13, 14.

[56] For instances see Doc. and Cov. 18:11, 12; 45:44, 45; 88:95-98.

[57] Doc. and Cov. 45:54.

[58] B. of M., 2 Nephi 9:6-13; read the entire chapter.

[59] P. of G.P., Moses 6:52; compare B. of M., 2 Nephi 25:20; Mosiah 3:17; 5:8; Doc. and Cov. 76:1.

[60] Rom. 3:23; see also verse 9; Gal. 3:22.

[61] 1 John 1:8.

[62] Heb. 5:9.

[63] Rom. 2:6-9.

[64] No special treatment relating to the Fall, the Atonement, or the Resurrection has been either attempted or intended in this chapter. For such the student is referred to doctrinal works dealing with these subjects. See the author's "Articles of Faith," lectures iii, iv, and xxi.

[65] A comparison related to that given in the text is treated at length by Henry Drummond in his essay, "Biogenesis," which the reader may study with profit.

[66] P. of G.P., Moses 1:39.

Jesus the Christ

CHAPTER 4. THE ANTEMORTAL GODSHIP OF CHRIST.

It now becomes our purpose to inquire as to the position and status of Jesus the Christ in the antemortal world, from the period of the solemn council in heaven, in which He was chosen to be the future Savior and Redeemer of mankind, to the time at which He was born in the flesh.

We claim scriptural authority for the assertion that Jesus Christ was and is God the Creator, the God who revealed Himself to Adam, Enoch, and all the antediluvial patriarchs and prophets down to Noah; the God of Abraham, Isaac and Jacob; the God of Israel as a united people, and the God of Ephraim and Judah after the disruption of the Hebrew nation; the God who made Himself known to the prophets from Moses to Malachi; the God of the Old Testament record; and the God of the Nephites. We affirm that Jesus Christ was and is Jehovah, the Eternal One.

The scriptures specify three personages in the Godhead; (1) God the Eternal Father, (2) His Son Jesus Christ, and (3) the Holy Ghost. These constitute the Holy Trinity, comprizing three physically separate and distinct individuals, who together constitute the presiding council of the heavens.[67] At least two of these appear as directing participants in the work of creation; this fact is instanced by the plurality expressed in Genesis: "And God said, Let us make man in our image, after our likeness"; and later, in the course of consultation concerning Adam's act of transgression, "the Lord God said, Behold, the man is become as one of us."[68] From the words of Moses, as revealed anew in the present dispensation, we learn more fully of the Gods who were actively engaged in the creation of this earth: "And I, God, said unto mine Only Begotten, which was with me from the beginning: Let us make man in our image, after our likeness." Then, further, with regard to the condition of Adam after the fall: "I, the Lord God, said unto mine Only Begotten: Behold, the man is become as one of us."[69] In the account of the creation recorded by Abraham, "the Gods" are repeatedly mentioned.[70]

As heretofore shown in another connection, the Father operated in the work of creation through the Son, who thus became the executive through whom the will, commandment, or word of the Father was put into effect. It is with incisive appropriateness therefore, that the Son, Jesus Christ, is designated by the apostle John as the Word; or as declared by the Father "the word of my power".[71] The part taken by Jesus Christ in the creation, a part so prominent as to justify our calling Him the Creator, is set forth in many scriptures. The author of the Epistle to the Hebrews refers in this wise distinctively to the Father and the Son as separate though associated Beings: "God, who at sundry times and in divers manners spake in time past unto the fathers by the prophets, hath in these last days spoken unto us by his Son, whom he hath appointed heir of all things, by whom also he made the worlds."[72] Paul is even more explicit in his letter to the Colossians, wherein, speaking of Jesus the Son, he says: "For by him were all things created, that are in heaven, and that are in earth, visible and invisible, whether they be thrones, or dominions, or principalities, or powers: all things were created by him, and for him: and he is before all things, and by him all things consist."[73] And here let be repeated the testimony of John, that by the Word, "who was with God, and who was God even in the beginning, all things were made; and without him was not anything made that was made."[74]

That the Christ who was to come was in reality God the Creator was revealed in plainness to the prophets on the western hemisphere. Samuel, the converted Lamanite, in preaching to the unbelieving Nephites justified his testimony as follows: "And also that ye might know of the coming of Jesus Christ, the Son of God, the Father of heaven and of earth, the Creator of all things, from the beginning; and that ye might know of the signs of his coming, to the intent that ye might believe on his name."[75]

To these citations of ancient scripture may most properly be added the personal testimony of the Lord Jesus after He had become a resurrected Being. In His visitation to the Nephites He thus proclaimed Himself: "Behold, I am Jesus Christ the Son of God. I created the heavens and the earth, and all things that in them are. I was with the Father from the beginning. I am in the Father, and the Father in me; and in me hath the Father glorified his name."[76] To the Nephites, who failed to comprehend the relation between the gospel declared unto them by the Resurrected Lord, and the Mosaic law which they held traditionally to be in force, and who marveled at His saying that old things had passed away, He explained in this wise: "Behold I say unto you, that the law is fulfilled that was given unto Moses. Behold, I am he that gave the law, and I am he who covenanted with my people Israel: therefore, the law in me is fulfilled, for I have come to fulfil the law; therefore it hath an end."[77]

Through revelation in the present or last dispensation the voice of Jesus Christ, the Creator of heaven and earth, has been heard anew: "Hearken, O ye people of my church to whom the kingdom has been given--hearken ye and give ear to him who laid the foundation of the earth, who made the heavens and all the hosts thereof, and by whom all things were made which live, and move, and have a being."[78] And again, "Behold, I am Jesus Christ the Son of the living God, who created the heavens and the earth; a light which cannot be hid in darkness."[79]

The divinity of Jesus Christ is indicated by the specific names and titles authoritatively applied to Him. According to man's judgment there may be but little importance attached to names; but in the nomenclature of the Gods every name is a title of power or station. God is righteously zealous of the sanctity of His own name[80] and of names given by His appointment. In the case of children of promise names have been prescribed before birth; this is true of our Lord Jesus and of the Baptist, John, who was sent to prepare the way for the Christ. Names of persons have been changed by divine direction, when not sufficiently definite as titles denoting the particular service to which the bearers were called, or the special blessings conferred upon them.[81]

Jesus is the individual name of the Savior, and as thus spelled is of Greek derivation; its Hebrew equivalent was _Yehoshua_ or _Yeshua_, or, as we render it in English, _Joshua_. In the original the name was well understood as meaning "Help of Jehovah", or "Savior". Though as common an appellation as John or Henry or Charles today, the name was nevertheless divinely prescribed, as already stated. Thus, unto Joseph, the espoused husband of the Virgin, the angel said, "And thou shalt call his name JESUS: for he shall save his people from their sins."[82]

Christ is a sacred title, and not an ordinary appellation or common name; it is of Greek derivation, and in meaning is identical with its Hebrew equivalent _Messiah_ or _Messias_, signifying the _Anointed One_.[83] Other titles, each possessing a definitive meaning, such as _Emmanuel_, _Savior_, _Redeemer_, _Only Begotten Son_, _Lord_, _Son of God_, _Son of Man_, and many more, are of scriptural occurrence; the fact of main present importance to us is that these several titles are expressive of our Lord's divine origin and Godship. As seen, the essential names or titles of Jesus the Christ were made known before His birth, and were revealed to prophets who preceded Him in the mortal state.[84]

Jehovah is the Anglicized rendering of the Hebrew, _Yahveh_ or _Jahveh_, signifying the _Self-existent One_, or _The Eternal_. This name is generally rendered in our English version of the Old Testament as LORD, printed in capitals.[85] The Hebrew, _Ehyeh_, signifying _I Am_, is related in meaning and through derivation with the term _Yahveh_ or _Jehovah_; and herein lies the significance of this name by which the Lord revealed Himself to Moses when the latter received the commission to go into Egypt and deliver the children of Israel from bondage: "Moses said unto God, Behold, when I come unto the children of Israel, and shall say unto them, The God of your fathers hath sent me unto you; and they shall say to me, What is his name? what shall I say unto them? And God said unto Moses, I AM THAT I AM: and he said, Thus shalt thou say unto the children of Israel, I AM hath sent me unto you."[86] In the succeeding verse the Lord declares Himself to be "the God of Abraham, the God of Isaac, and the God of Jacob." While Moses was in Egypt, the Lord further revealed Himself, saying "I am the LORD: and I appeared unto Abraham, unto Isaac, and unto Jacob, by the name of God Almighty, but by my name JEHOVAH was I not known to them."[87] The central fact connoted by this name, _I Am_, or _Jehovah_, the two having essentially the same meaning, is that of existence or duration that shall have no end, and which, judged by all human standards of reckoning, could have had no beginning; the name is related to such other titles as _Alpha and Omega_, the first and the last, the beginning and the end.[88]

Jesus, when once assailed with question and criticism from certain Jews who regarded their Abrahamic lineage as an assurance of divine preferment, met their abusive words with the declaration: "Verily, verily, I say unto you, Before Abraham was, I am".[89] The true significance of this saying would be more plainly expressed were the sentence punctuated and pointed as follows: "Verily, verily, I say unto you, Before Abraham, was I AM;" which means the same as had He said--Before Abraham, was I, Jehovah. The captious Jews were so offended at hearing Him use a name which, through an erroneous rendering of an earlier scripture,[90] they held was not to be uttered on pain of death, that they immediately took up stones with the intent of killing Him. The Jews regarded _Jehovah_ as an ineffable name, not to be spoken; they substituted for it the sacred, though to them the not-forbidden name, _Adonai_, signifying _the Lord_. The original of the terms _Lord_ and _God_ as they appear in the Old Testament, was either _Yahveh_ or _Adonai_; and the divine Being designated by these sacred names was, as shown by the scriptures cited, Jesus Christ. John, evangelist and apostle, positively identifies Jesus Christ with Adonai, or the Lord who spoke through the voice of Isaiah,[91] and with Jehovah who spoke through Zechariah.[92]

The name _Elohim_ is of frequent occurrence in the Hebrew texts of the Old Testament, though it is not found in our English versions. In form the word is a Hebrew plural noun;[93] but it connotes the plurality of excellence or intensity, rather than distinctively of number. It is expressive of supreme or absolute exaltation and power. _Elohim_, as understood and used in the restored Church of Jesus Christ, is the name-title of God the Eternal Father, whose firstborn Son in the spirit is _Jehovah_--the Only Begotten in the flesh, Jesus Christ.

Jesus of Nazareth, who in solemn testimony to the Jews declared Himself the _I Am_ or _Jehovah_, who was God before Abraham lived on earth, was the same Being who is repeatedly proclaimed as the God who made covenant with Abraham, Isaac, and Jacob; the God who led Israel from the bondage of Egypt to the freedom of the promised land, the one and only God known by direct and personal revelation to the Hebrew prophets in general.

The identity of Jesus Christ with the Jehovah of the Israelites was well understood by the Nephite prophets, and the truth of their teachings was confirmed by the risen Lord who manifested Himself unto them shortly after His ascension from the midst of the apostles at Jerusalem. This is the record: "And it came to pass that the Lord spake unto them saying, Arise and come forth unto me, that ye may thrust your hands into my side, and also that ye may feel the prints of the nails in my hands and in my feet, that ye may know that I am the God of Israel, and the God of the whole earth, and have been slain for the sins of the world."[94]

It would appear unnecessary to cite at greater length in substantiating our affirmation that Jesus Christ was a God even before He assumed a body of flesh. During that antemortal period there was essential difference between the Father and the Son, in that the former had already passed through the experiences of mortal life, including death and resurrection, and was therefore a Being possessed of a perfect, immortalized body of flesh and bones, while the Son was yet unembodied. Through His death and subsequent resurrection Jesus the Christ is today a Being like unto the Father in all essential characteristics.

A general consideration of scriptural evidence leads to the conclusion that God the Eternal Father has manifested Himself to earthly prophets or revelators on very few occasions, and then principally to attest the divine authority of His Son, Jesus Christ. As before shown, the Son was the active executive in the work of creation; throughout the creative scenes the Father appears mostly in a directing or consulting capacity. Unto Adam, Enoch, Noah, Abraham and Moses the Father revealed Himself, attesting the Godship of the Christ, and the fact that the Son was the chosen Savior of mankind.[95] On the occasion of the baptism of Jesus, the Father's voice was heard, saying, "This is my beloved Son, in whom I am well pleased";[96] and at the transfiguration a similar testimony was given by the Father.[97] On an occasion yet later, while Jesus prayed in anguish of soul, submitting Himself that the Father's purposes be fulfilled and the Father's name glorified, "Then came there a voice from heaven, saying, I have both glorified it, and will glorify it again."[98] The resurrected and glorified Christ was announced by the Father to the Nephites on the western hemisphere, in these words: "Behold my beloved Son, in whom I am well pleased, in whom I have glorified my name: hear ye him."[99] From the time of the occurrence last noted, the voice of the Father was not heard again among men, so far as the scriptures aver, until the spring of 1820, when both the Father and the Son ministered unto the prophet Joseph Smith, the Father saying, "This is my beloved Son, hear him!"[100] These are the instances of record in which the Eternal Father has been manifest in personal utterance or other revelation to man apart from the Son. God the Creator, the Jehovah of Israel, the Savior and Redeemer of all nations, kindreds and tongues, are the same, and He is Jesus the Christ.

NOTES TO CHAPTER 4.

1. Names Given of God.--The significance of names when given of God finds illustration in many scriptural instances. The following are examples: "Jesus" meaning _Savior_ (Matt. 1:21; Luke 1:31); "John," signifying _Jehovah's gift_, specifically applied to the Baptist, who was sent to earth to prepare the way for Jehovah's coming in the flesh (Luke 1:13); "Ishmael," signifying _God shall hear him_ (Gen. 16:11); "Isaac," meaning _laughter_ (Gen. 17:19, compare 18:10-15). As instances of names changed by divine authority to express added blessings, or special callings, consider the following: "Abram," which connoted _nobility_ or _exaltation_ and as usually rendered, _father of elevation_, was changed to "Abraham," _father of a multitude_ which expressed the reason for the change as given at the time thereof, "for a father of many nations have I made thee" (Gen. 17:5). "Sarai," the name of Abraham's wife, and of uncertain distinctive meaning, was substituted by "Sarah" which signified _the princess_ (Gen 17:15). "Jacob," a name given to the son of Isaac with reference to a circumstance attending his birth, and signifying _a supplanter_, was superseded by "Israel" meaning _a soldier of God, a prince of God_; as expressed in the words effecting the change, "Thy name shall be called no more Jacob, but Israel, for as a prince hast thou power with God and with men, and hast prevailed." (Gen. 32:28; compare 35:9, 10.) "Simon," meaning _a hearer_, the name of the man who became the chief apostle of Jesus Christ, was changed by the Lord to "Cephas" (Aramaic) or "Peter" (Greek) meaning _a rock_ (John 1:42; Matt 16:18; Luke 6:14). On James and John the sons of Zebedee, the Lord conferred the name or title "Boanerges" meaning _sons of thunder_ (Mark 3:17).

The following is an instructive excerpt: "_Name_ in the scriptures not only = that by which a person is designated, but frequently = all that is known to belong to the person having this designation, and the person himself. Thus 'the name of God' or 'of Jehovah,' etc., indicates His authority (Deut. 18:20; Matt. 21:9, etc.), His dignity and glory (Isa. 48:9, etc.), His protection and favor (Prov. 18:10, etc.), His character (Exo. 34:5, 14, compare 6, 7, etc.), His divine attributes in general (Matt. 6:9, etc.), etc. The Lord is said to set or put His name where the revelation or manifestation of His perfections is made (Deut. 12:5, 14:24, etc.). To believe in or on the name of Christ is to receive and treat Him in accordance with the revelation which the scriptures make of Him (John 1:12; 2:23), etc."--Smith's _Comprehensive Dictionary of the Bible_, article "Name." 2. Jesus Christ, the God of Israel.--"That Jesus Christ was the same Being who called Abraham from his native country, who led Israel out of the land of Egypt with mighty miracles and wonders, who made known to them His law amid the thunderings of Sinai, who delivered them from their enemies, who chastened them for their disobedience, who inspired their prophets, and whose glory filled Solomon's temple, is evident from all the inspired writings, and in none more so than in the Bible.

"His lamentation over Jerusalem evidences that, in His humanity, He had not forgotten His former exalted position: 'O Jerusalem, Jerusalem, thou that killest the prophets, and stonest them which are sent unto thee, how often would I have gathered thy children together ... and ye would not!' (Matt. 23:37). It was this Creator of the world, this mighty Ruler, this Controller of the destinies of the human family, who, in His last moments, cried out in the agony of His soul, 'My God, my God, why hast thou forsaken me?'" (Mark 15:34.)--From _Compendium of the Doctrines of the Gospel_, by Franklin D. Richards and James A. Little.

3. "Jehovah" a Name Not Uttered by the Jews.--Long prior to the time of Christ, certain schools among the Jews, ever intent on the observance of the letter of the law, though not without disregard of its spirit, had taught that the mere utterance of the name of God was blasphemous, and that the sin of so doing constituted a capital offense. This extreme conception arose from the accepted though uninspired interpretation of Lev. 24:16, "And he that blasphemeth the name of the Lord, he shall surely be put to death, and all the congregation shall certainly stone him: as well the stranger, as he that is born in the land, when he blasphemeth the name of the Lord, shall be put to death." We take the following from Smith's _Comprehensive Dictionary of the Bible_, article "Jehovah": "The true pronunciation of this name, [Yehovah] by which God was known to the Hebrews, has been entirely lost, the Jews themselves scrupulously avoiding every mention of it, and substituting in its stead one or other of the words with whose proper vowel-points it may happen to be written [_Adonai_, Lord, or _Elohim_, God].... According to Jewish tradition it was pronounced but once a year by the high priest on the day of atonement when he entered the Holy of Holies; but on this point there is some doubt."

FOOTNOTES:

[67] See "God and the Godhead," in the author's "Articles of Faith," lecture ii.
[68] Gen. 1:26; and 3:22.
[69] P. of G.P., Moses 2:26; and 4:28.
[70] P. of G.P., Abraham, chaps. 4 and 5.
[71] See page 10; John 1:1; and P. of G.P., Moses 1:32.
[72] Heb. 1:1, 2; see also 1 Cor. 8:6.
[73] Colos. 1:16, 17.
[74] John 1:1-3.
[75] B. of M., Helaman 14:12; see also Mosiah 3:8; 4:2: Alma 11:39.
[76] B. of M., 3 Nephi 9:15.
[77] B. of M., 3 Nephi 15:4, 5.
[78] Doc. and Cov. 45:1.
[79] Doc. and Cov. 14:9; see also 29:1, 31; 76:24.
[80] Exo. 20:7; Lev. 19:12; Deut. 5:11.
[81] Note 1, end of chapter.
[82] Matt. 1:21; see also verses 23, 25; Luke 1:31.
[83] John 1:41; 4:25.
[84] Luke 1:31; 2:21; Matt. 1:21, 25; see also verse 23 and compare Isa. 7:14; Luke 2:11. See further P. of G.P., Moses 6:51, 57; 7:20; 8:24. B. of M., 1 Nephi 10:4; 2 Nephi 10:3; Mosiah 3:8.
[85] The name appears thus in Gen. 2:5; see also Exo. 6:2-4; and read for comparison Gen. 17:1; 35:11.
[86] Exo. 3:13, 14; compare with respect to the fact of eternal duration expressed in this name, Isa. 44:6; John 8:58; Colos. 1:17; Heb. 13:8; Rev. 1:4; see also P. of G.P., Moses 1:3 and the references there given.
[87] Exo. 6:2, 3. Note 2, end of chapter.
[88] Rev. 1:11, 17; 2:8; 22:13; compare Isa. 41:4; 44:6; 48:12.
[89] John 8:58.
[90] Lev. 24:16. Note 3, end of chapter.
[91] Isa. 6:8-11; and compare John 12:40, 41.
[92] Zech. 12:10; compare John 19:37.
[93] The singular, "Eloah," appears only in poetic usage.
[94] B. of M., 3 Nephi 11:13, 14; also 1 Nephi 17:40 and observe from verse 30 that the Redeemer is here spoken of as the God who delivered Israel. See further Mosiah 7:19. Chapter 39 herein.
[95] P. of G.P., Moses 1:6, 31-33; 2:1; 4:2, 3; 6:57; compare 7:35, 39, 47, 53-59; 8:16, 19, 23, 24; Abraham 3:22-28. See chapter 5 herein.
[96] Matt. 3:17; also Mark 1:11; Luke 3:22.
[97] Matt. 17:5; Luke 9:35.
[98] John 12:28.
[99] B. of M., 3 Nephi 11:7.
[100] P. of G.P. Joseph Smith 2:17.

CHAPTER 5. EARTHLY ADVENT OF THE CHRIST PREDICTED.

The coming of Christ to earth to tabernacle in the flesh was no unexpected or unheralded event. For centuries prior to the great occurrence the Jews had professed to be looking for the advent of their King; and, in the appointed ceremonials of worship as in private devotions, the coming of the promised Messiah was prominent as a matter of the supplication of Israel to Jehovah. True, there was much diversity in lay opinion and in rabbinical exposition as to the time and manner of His appearing; but the certainty thereof was fundamentally established in the beliefs and hopes of the Hebrew nation.

The records known to us as the books of the Old Testament, together with other inspired writings once regarded as authentic but excluded from later compilations as not strictly canonical, were current among the Hebrews at and long before the time of Christ's birth. These scriptures had their beginning in the proclamation of the law through Moses,[101] who wrote the same, and delivered the writing into the official custody of the priests with an express command that it be read in the assemblies of the people at stated times. To these earlier writings were added the utterances of divinely commissioned prophets, the records of appointed historians, and the songs of inspired poets, as the centuries passed; so that at the time of our Lord's ministry the Jews possessed a great accumulation of writings accepted and revered by them as authoritative.[102] These records are rich in prediction and promise respecting the earthly advent of the Messiah, as are other scriptures to which the Israel of old had not access.

Adam, the patriarch of the race, rejoiced in the assurance of the Savior's appointed ministry, through the acceptance of which, he, the transgressor, might gain redemption. Brief mention of the plan of salvation, the author of which is Jesus Christ, appears in the promise given of God following the fall—that though the devil, represented by the serpent in Eden, should have power to bruise the heel of Adam's posterity, through the seed of the woman should come the power to bruise the adversary's head.[103] It is significant that this assurance of eventual victory over sin and its inevitable effect, death, both of which were introduced to earth through Satan the arch-enemy of mankind, was to be realized through the offspring of woman; the promise was not made specifically to the man, nor to the pair. The only instance of offspring from woman dissociated from mortal fatherhood is the birth of Jesus the Christ, who was the earthly Son of a mortal mother, begotten by an immortal Father. He is the Only Begotten of the Eternal Father in the flesh, and was born of woman.

Through scriptures other than those embodied in the Old Testament we learn with greater fulness of the revelations of God to Adam respecting the coming of the Redeemer. As a natural and inevitable result of his disobedience, Adam had forfeited the high privilege he once enjoyed—that of holding direct and personal association with his God; nevertheless in his fallen state he was visited by an angel of the Lord, who revealed unto him the plan of redemption: "And after many days an angel of the Lord appeared unto Adam, saying: Why dost thou offer sacrifices unto the Lord? And Adam said unto him: I know not, save the Lord commanded me. And then the angel spake, saying: This thing is a similitude of the sacrifice of the Only Begotten of the Father, which is full of grace and truth. Wherefore, thou shalt do all that thou doest in the name of the Son, and thou shalt repent and call upon God in the name of the Son for evermore. And in that day the Holy Ghost fell upon Adam, which beareth record of the Father and the Son, saying: I am the Only Begotten of the Father from the beginning, henceforth and for ever, that as thou hast fallen thou mayest be redeemed, and all mankind, even as many as will."[104]

The Lord's revelation to Adam making known the ordained plan whereby the Son of God was to take upon Himself flesh in the meridian of time, and become the Redeemer of the world, was attested by Enoch, son of Jared and father of Methuselah. From the words of Enoch we learn that to him as to his great progenitor, Adam, the very name by which the Savior would be known among men was revealed—"which is Jesus Christ, the only name which shall be given under heaven, whereby salvation shall come unto the children of men."[105] The recorded covenant of God with Abraham, and the reiteration and confirmation thereof with Isaac and in turn with Jacob—that through their posterity should all nations of the earth be blessed—presaged the birth of the Redeemer through that chosen lineage.[106] Its fulfilment is the blessed heritage of the ages.

In pronouncing his patriarchal blessing upon the head of Judah, Jacob prophesied: "The sceptre shall not depart from Judah, nor a lawgiver from between his feet, until Shiloh come; and unto him shall the gathering of the people be."[107] That by Shiloh is meant the Christ is evidenced by the fulfilment of the conditions set forth in the prediction, in the state of the Jewish nation at the time of our Lord's birth. [108]

Moses proclaimed the coming of a great Prophet in Israel, whose ministry was to be of such importance that all men who would not accept Him would be under condemnation; and that this prediction had sole reference to Jesus Christ is conclusively shown by later scriptures. Thus spake the Lord unto Moses: "I will raise them up a Prophet from among their brethren, like unto thee, and will put my words in his mouth; and he shall speak unto them all that I shall command him. And it shall come to pass, that whosoever will not hearken unto my words which he shall speak in my name, I will require it of him."[109] The system of sacrifice expressly enjoined in the Mosaic code was essentially a prototype of the sacrificial death to be accomplished by the Savior on Calvary. The blood of countless altar victims, slain by Israel's priests in the course of prescribed ritual, ran throughout the centuries from Moses to Christ as a prophetic flood in similitude of the blood of the Son of God appointed to be shed as an expiatory sacrifice for the redemption of the race. But, as already shown, the institution of bloody sacrifice as a type of the future death of Jesus Christ dates from the beginning of human history; since the offering of animal sacrifices through the shedding of blood was required of Adam, to whom the significance of the ordinance, as "a similitude of the sacrifice of the Only Begotten of the Father", was expressly defined.[110]

The paschal lamb, slain for every Israelitish household at the annually recurring feast of the Passover, was a particular type of the Lamb of God who in due time would be slain for the sins of the world. The crucifixion of Christ was effected at the Passover season; and the consummation of the supreme Sacrifice, of which the paschal lambs had been but lesser prototypes, led Paul the apostle to affirm in later times: "For even Christ our passover is sacrificed for us."[111]

Job in the day of dire affliction rejoiced in his testimony of the coming Messiah, and declared with prophetic conviction: "I know that my redeemer liveth, and that he shall stand at the latter day upon the earth."[112] The songs of David the psalmist abound in oft-recurring allusion to the earthly life of Christ, many circumstances of which are described in detail, and, as to these, corroboration of the utterances is found in New Testament scriptures.[113]

Isaiah, whose prophetic office was honored by the personal testimony of Christ and the apostles, manifested in numerous passages the burden of his conviction relating to the great event of the Savior's advent and ministry on earth. With the forcefulness of direct revelation he told of the Virgin's divine maternity, whereof Immanuel should be born, and his prediction was reiterated by the angel of the Lord, over seven centuries later.[114] Looking down through the ages the prophet saw the accomplishment of the divine purposes as if already achieved, and sang in triumph: "For unto us a child is born, unto us a son is given: and the government shall be upon his shoulder: and his name shall be called Wonderful, Counselor, The mighty God, The everlasting Father, The Prince of Peace. Of the increase of his government and peace there shall be no end, upon the throne of David, and upon his kingdom, to order it, and to establish it with judgment and with justice from henceforth even forever."[115]

Immediately prior to its fulfilment, the blessed promise was repeated by Gabriel, sent from the presence of God to the chosen Virgin of Nazareth.[116] As made known to the prophet and by him proclaimed, the coming Lord was the living Branch that should spring from the undying root typified in the family of Jesse;[117] the foundation Stone insuring the stability of Zion;[118] the Shepherd of the house of Israel;[119] the Light of the world,[120] to Gentile as well as Jew; the Leader and Commander of His people. [121] The same inspired voice predicted the forerunner who should cry in the wilderness: "Prepare ye the way of the Lord, make straight in the desert a highway for our God."[122]

Isaiah was permitted to read the scroll of futurity as to many distinguishing conditions to attend the Messiah's lowly life and atoning death. In Him the prophet saw One who would be despized and rejected of men, a Man of sorrows, acquainted with grief, One to be wounded and bruised for the transgressions of the race, on whom would be laid the iniquity of us all--a patient and willing Sacrifice, silent under affliction, as a lamb brought to the slaughter. The Lord's dying with sinners, and His burial in the tomb of the wealthy were likewise declared with prophetic certainty.[123]

Unto Jeremiah came the word of the Lord in terms of plainness, declaring the sure advent of the King by whom the safety of both Judah and Israel should be assured;[124] the Prince of the House of David, through whom the divine promise to the son of Jesse should be realized.[125] Under the same spirit prophesied Ezekiel,[126] Hosea,[127] and Micah.[128] Zechariah broke off in the midst of fateful prediction to voice the glad song of thanksgiving and praise as he beheld in vision the simple pageantry of the King's triumphal entry into the city of David.[129] Then the prophet bewailed the grief of the conscience-smitten nation, by whom, as was foreseen, the Savior of humankind would be pierced, even unto death;[130] and showed that, when subdued by contrition His own people would ask, "What are these wounds in thy hands?", the Lord would answer: "Those with which I was wounded in the house of my friends."[131] The very price to be paid for the betrayal of the Christ to His death was foretold as in parable.[132]

The fact, that these predictions of the Old Testament prophets had reference to Jesus Christ and to Him only, is put beyond question by the attestation of the resurrected Lord. To the assembled apostles He said: "These are the words which I spake unto you, while I was yet with you, that all things must be fulfilled, which were written in the law of Moses, and in the prophets, and in the psalms, concerning me. Then opened he their understanding, that they might understand the scriptures, and said unto them, Thus it is written, and thus it behoved Christ to suffer, and to rise from the dead the third day."[133]

John the Baptist, whose ministry immediately preceded that of the Christ, proclaimed the coming of One mightier than himself, One who should baptize with the Holy Ghost, and specifically identified Jesus of Nazareth as that One, the Son of God, the Lamb who should assume the burden of the world's sins.[134]

The predictions thus far cited as relating to the life, ministry, and death of the Lord Jesus, are the utterances of prophets who, excepting Adam and Enoch, lived and died on the eastern hemisphere. All save John the Baptist are of Old Testament record, and he, a contemporary of the Christ in mortality, figures in the early chapters of the Gospels. It is important to know that the scriptures of the western hemisphere are likewise explicit in the declaration of the great truth that the Son of God would be born in the flesh. The Book of Mormon contains a history of a colony of Israelites, of the tribe of Joseph, who left Jerusalem 600 B.C., during the reign of Zedekiah, king of Judah, on the eve of the subjugation of Judea by Nebuchadnezzar and the inauguration of the Babylonian captivity. This colony was led by divine guidance to the American continent, whereon they developed into a numerous and mighty people; though, divided by dissension, they formed two opposing nations known respectively as Nephites and Lamanites. The former cultivated the arts of industry and refinement, and preserved a record embodying both history and scripture, while the latter became degenerate and debased. The Nephites suffered extinction about 400 A.D., but the Lamanites lived on in their degraded course, and are today extant upon the land as the American Indians.[135]

The Nephite annals from the beginning thereof down to the time of our Lord's birth abound in prediction and promise of the Christ; and this chronicle is followed by a record of the actual visitation of the resurrected Savior to the Nephites, and the establishment of His Church among them. Unto Lehi, the leader of the colony, the Lord revealed the time, place, and manner of Christ's then future advent, together with many important facts of His ministry, and the preparatory work of John the forerunner. This revelation was given while the company was journeying in the wilderness of Arabia, prior to their crossing the great waters. The prophecy is thus written by Nephi, a son of Lehi and his successor in the prophetic calling: "Yea, even six hundred years from the time that my father left Jerusalem, a prophet would the Lord God raise up among the Jews; even a Messiah; or, in other words, a Savior of the world. And he also spake concerning the prophets, how great a number had testified of these things concerning this Messiah, of whom he had spoken, or this Redeemer of the world. Wherefore all mankind were in a lost and in a fallen state, and ever would be, save they should rely on this Redeemer. And he spake also concerning a prophet who should come before the Messiah, to prepare the way of the Lord; yea, even he should go forth and cry in the wilderness. Prepare ye the way of the Lord, and make his paths straight; for there standeth one among you whom ye know not; and he is mightier than I, whose shoe's latchet I am not worthy to unloose. And much spake my father concerning this thing. And my father said he should baptize in Bethabara, beyond Jordan; and he also said he should baptize with water; even that he should baptize the Messiah with water. And after he had baptized the Messiah with water, he should behold and bear record, that he had baptized the Lamb of God, who should take away the sins of the world. And it came to pass after my father had spoken these words, he spake unto my brethren concerning the gospel which should be preached among the Jews; and also concerning the dwindling of the Jews in unbelief. And after they had slain the Messiah, who should come, and after he had been slain, he should rise from the dead, and should make himself manifest, by the Holy Ghost, unto the Gentiles."[136]

At a later time Nephi writes, not as his father's scribe, but as a prophet and revelator voicing the word of God as made known to himself. He was permitted to behold in vision and to declare to his people the circumstances of the Messiah's birth, His baptism by John and the ministration of the Holy Ghost with its accompanying sign of the dove; he beheld our Lord moving as a Teacher of righteousness among the people, healing the afflicted and rebuking spirits of evil; he saw and bore record of the dread scenes of Calvary; he beheld and predicted the calling of the chosen Twelve, the apostles of the Lamb, for so these were designated by Him who vouchsafed the vision. Moreover he told of the iniquity of the Jews, who were seen in contention with the apostles; and thus concludes the portentous prophecy: "And the angel of the Lord spake unto me again, saying, Thus shall be the destruction of all nations, kindreds, tongues, and people, that shall fight against the twelve apostles of the Lamb."[137] Soon after the defection whereby the distinction between Nephites and Lamanites was established, Jacob, a brother of Nephi, continued in prophecy of the assured coming of the Messiah, specifically declaring that He would minister at Jerusalem and affirming the necessity of His atoning death as the ordained means of human redemption.[138] The prophet Abinadi, in his fearless denunciation of sin to the wicked king Noah, preached the Christ who was to come;[139] and righteous Benjamin, who was at once prophet and king, proclaimed the same great truth to his people about 125 B.C. So taught Alma[140] in his inspired admonition to his wayward son, Corianton; and so also Amulek[141] in his contention with Zeezrom. So proclaimed the Lamanite prophet, Samuel, only five years prior to the actual occurrence; furthermore he specified the signs by which the birth of Jesus in Judea would be made known to the people of the western world. Said he: "Behold, I give unto you a sign; for five years more cometh, and behold, then cometh the Son of God to redeem all those who shall believe on his name. And behold, this will I give unto you for a sign at the time of his coming; for behold, there shall be great lights in heaven, insomuch that in the night before he cometh there shall be no darkness, insomuch that it shall appear unto man as if it was day, therefore there shall be one day and a night, and a day, as if it were one day, and there were no night; and this shall be unto you for a sign; for ye shall know of the rising of the sun, and also of its setting; therefore they shall know of a surety that there shall be two days and a night; nevertheless the night shall not be darkened; and it shall be the night before he is born. And behold there shall a new star arise, such an one as ye never have beheld; and this also shall be a sign unto you. And behold this is not all, there shall be many signs and wonders in heaven."[142]

Thus the scriptures of both hemispheres and in all ages of ante-meridian time bore solemn testimony to the certainty of Messiah's advent; thus the holy prophets of old voiced the word of revelation predicting the coming of the world's King and Lord, through whom alone is salvation provided, and redemption from death made sure. It is a characteristic of prophets sent of God that they possess and proclaim a personal assurance of the Christ, "for the testimony of Jesus is the spirit of prophecy."[143] Not a word of inspired prophecy relating to the great event has been found void. The literal fulfilment of the predictions is ample attestation of their origin in divine revelation, and proof conclusive of the divinity of Him whose coming was so abundantly foretold.

NOTES TO CHAPTER 5.

1. The Antiquity of Sacrifice as a Prototype of Christ's Atoning Death.--While the Biblical record expressly attests the offering of sacrifices long prior to Israel's exodus from Egypt--e.g. by Abel and by Cain (Gen. 4:3, 4); by Noah after the deluge (Gen. 8:20); by Abraham (Gen. 22:2, 13); by Jacob (Gen. 31:54; 46:1)--it is silent concerning the divine origin of sacrifice as a propitiatory requirement prefiguring the atoning death of Jesus Christ. The difficulty of determining time and circumstance, under which the offering of symbolical sacrifices originated amongst mankind, is recognized by all investigators save those who admit the validity of modern revelation. The necessity of assuming early instruction from God to man on the subject has been asserted by many Bible scholars. Thus, the writer of the article "Sacrifice" in the

Cassell _Bible Dictionary_ says: "The idea of sacrifice is prominent throughout the scriptures, and one of the most ancient and widely recognized in the rites of religion throughout the world. There is also a remarkable similarity in the developments and applications of the idea. On these and other accounts it has been judiciously inferred that sacrifice formed an element in the primeval worship of man; and that its universality is not merely an indirect argument for the unity of the human race, but an illustration and confirmation of the first inspired pages of the world's history. The notion of sacrifice can hardly be viewed as a product of unassisted human nature, and must therefore be traced to a higher source and viewed as a divine revelation to primitive man."

Smith's _Dic. of the Bible_ presents the following: "In tracing the history of sacrifice from its first beginning to its perfect development in the Mosaic ritual, we are at once met by the long-disputed question as to the origin of sacrifice, whether it arose from a natural instinct of man, sanctioned and guided by God, or was the subject of some distinct primeval revelation. There can be no doubt that sacrifice was sanctioned by God's Law, with a special, typical reference to the Atonement of Christ; its universal prevalence, independent of, and often opposed to, man's natural reasonings on his relation to God, shows it to have been primeval, and deeply rooted in the instincts of humanity. Whether it was first enjoined by an external command, or was based on that sense of sin and lost communion with God, which is stamped by His hand on the heart of man--is an historical question, perhaps insoluble."

The difficulty vanishes, and the "historical question" as to the origin of sacrifice is definitely solved by the revelations of God in the current dispensation, whereby parts of the record of Moses--not contained in the Bible--have been restored to human knowledge. The scripture quoted in the text (pp. 43, 44) makes clear the fact that the offering of sacrifices was required of Adam after his transgression, and that the significance of the divinely established requirement was explained in fulness to the patriarch of the race. The shedding of the blood of animals in sacrifice to God, as a prototype "of the sacrifice of the Only Begotten of the Father," dates from the time immediately following the fall. Its origin is based on a specific revelation to Adam. See P. of G.P., Moses 5:5-8.

2. Jacob's Prophecy Concerning "Shiloh."--The prediction of the patriarch Jacob--that the sceptre should not depart from Judah before the coming of Shiloh--has given rise to much disputation among Bible students. Some insist that "Shiloh" is the name of a place and not that of a person. That there was a place known by that name is beyond question (see Josh. 18:1; 19:51; 21:2; 22:9; 1 Sam. 1:3; Jer. 7:12); but the name occurring in Gen. 49:10 is plainly that of a person. It should be known that the use of the word in the King James or authorized version of the Bible is held to be correct by many eminent authorities. Thus, in Dummelow's _Commentary on the Holy Bible_, we read: "This verse has always been regarded by both Jews and Christians as a remarkable prophecy of the coming of the Messiah.... On the rendering given above, the whole verse foretells that Judah would retain authority until the advent of the rightful ruler, the Messiah, to whom all peoples would gather. And, broadly speaking, it may be said that the last traces of Jewish legislative power (as vested in the Sanhedrin) did not disappear until the coming of Christ and the destruction of Jerusalem, from which time His kingdom was set up among men."

Adam Clarke, in his exhaustive Bible Commentary, briefly analyzes the objections urged against the admissibility of this passage as applying to the Messiah's advent, and dismisses them all as unfounded. His conclusion as to the meaning of the passage is thus worded: "Judah shall continue a distinct tribe until the Messiah shall come; and it did so; and after His coming it was confounded with the others, so that all distinction has been ever since lost."

Prof. Douglas, as cited in Smith's Dictionary, "claims that something of Judah's sceptre still remained, a total eclipse being no proof that the day is at an end--that the proper fulfilment of the prophecy did not begin till David's time, and is consummated in Christ according to Luke 1:32, 33."

The accepted meaning of the word by derivation is "Peaceable," and this is applicable to the attributes of the Christ, who in Isa. 9:6, is designated the Prince of Peace.

Eusebius, who lived between 260 and 339 A.D., and is known in ecclesiastical history as Bishop of C├ªsarea, wrote: "At the time that Herod was king, who was the first foreigner that reigned over the Jewish people, the prophecy recorded by Moses received its fulfilment, viz. 'That a prince should not fail of Judah, nor a ruler from his loins, until He should come for whom it is reserved, the expectation of nations.'" (The quoted passage is founded on the Septuagint rendering of Genesis 49:10).

Some critics have held that in Jacob's use of the word "Shiloh" he did not intend it as a name or proper noun at all. The writer of the article "Shiloh" in Cassell's _Bible Dictionary_ says: "The preponderance of evidence is in favor of the Messianic interpretation, but opinions are very divided respecting the retention of the word 'Shiloh' as a proper name.... Notwithstanding all the objections that are urged against it being so regarded, we are of the opinion that it is rightly considered to be a proper name, and that the English version represents the true sense of the passage. We recommend those who wish to enter more fully into a question which cannot well be discussed without Hebrew criticism, to the excellent notes upon Gen. 49:10 in the 'Commentary on the Pentateuch' by Keil and Delitzsch. Here the text is thus rendered: 'The sceptre shall not depart from Judah, nor the ruler's staff from between his feet, till Shiloh come, and the willing obedience of the nations be to him.'

"Notwithstanding the slight put upon the Messianic interpretation by some writers, even those from whom we should scarcely expect it, we see this explanation confirmed and not weakened in the events of history. The text is not taken to mean that Judah should at no time be without a royal ruler of his own, but that the regal power should not finally cease from Judah until Shiloh had come. The objections founded on the Babylonian captivity, and similar intermissions, are of no force, because it is the complete and final termination which is pointed out, and that only happened after the time of Christ." See further _The Book of Prophecy_, by G. Smith, LL.D., p. 320. See also _Compendium of the Doctrines of the Gospel_, by Franklin

D. Richards and James A. Little, article "Christ's First Coming."

3. Nephites and Lamanites.--The progenitors of the Nephite nation were led from Jerusalem, 600 B.C., by Lehi, a Jewish prophet of the tribe of Manasseh. His immediate family, at the time of their departure from Jerusalem, comprized his wife Sariah, and their sons, Laman, Lemuel, Sam, and Nephi; at a later stage of the history, daughters are mentioned, but whether any of these were born before the family exodus we are not told. Beside his own family, the colony of Lehi included Zoram, and Ishmael, the latter an Israelite of the tribe of Ephraim. Ishmael, with his family, joined Lehi in the wilderness; and his descendants were numbered with the nation of whom we are speaking. The company journeyed somewhat east of south, keeping near the borders of the Red Sea; then, changing their course to the eastward, crossed the peninsula of Arabia; and there, on the shores of the Arabian Sea, built and provisioned a vessel in which they committed themselves to divine care upon the waters. Their voyage carried them eastward across the Indian Ocean, then over the south Pacific Ocean to the western coast of South America, whereon they landed (590 B.C.).... The people established themselves on what to them was the land of promise; many children were born, and in the course of a few generations a numerous posterity held possession of the land. After the death of Lehi, a division occurred, some of the people accepting as their leader, Nephi, who had been duly appointed to the prophetic office; while the rest proclaimed Laman, the eldest of Lehi's sons, as their chief. Henceforth the divided people were known as Nephites and Lamanites respectively. At times they observed toward each other fairly friendly relations; but generally they were opposed, the Lamanites manifesting implacable hatred and hostility toward their Nephite kindred. The Nephites advanced in the arts of civilization, built large cities and established prosperous commonwealths; yet they often fell into transgression; and the Lord chastened them by allowing their foes to become victorious. They spread northward, occupying the northern part of South America; then, crossing the Isthmus, they extended their domain over the southern, central and eastern portions of what is now the United States of America. The Lamanites, while increasing in numbers, fell under the curse of darkness; they became dark in skin and benighted in spirit, forgot the God of their fathers, lived a wild nomadic life, and degenerated into the fallen state in which the American Indians--their lineal descendants--were found by those who rediscovered the western continent in later times. See the author's _Articles of Faith_ xiv:7, 8.

4. The First Gospel Dispensation.--The gospel of Jesus Christ was revealed to Adam. Faith in God the Eternal Father, and in His Son the Savior of Adam and all his posterity, repentance of sin, water baptism by immersion, and the reception of the Holy Ghost as a divine bestowal were proclaimed in the beginning of human history as the essentials to salvation. The following scriptures attest this fact. "And thus the Gospel began to be preached, from the beginning, being declared by holy angels sent forth from the presence of God, and by his own voice and by the gift of the Holy Ghost" (Moses 5:58). The prophet Enoch thus testified: "But God hath made known unto our fathers that all men must repent. And he called upon our father Adam by his own voice, saying: I am God; I made the world, and men before they were in the flesh. And he also said unto him: If thou wilt turn unto me, and hearken unto my voice, and believe, and repent of all thy transgressions, and be baptized, even in water, in the name of mine Only Begotten Son, who is full of grace and truth, which is Jesus Christ, the only name which shall be given under heaven, whereby salvation shall come unto the children of men, ye shall receive the gift of the Holy Ghost, asking all things in his name, and whatsoever ye shall ask, it shall be given you" (Moses 6:50-52; read also 53-61). "And now, behold, I say unto you: This is the plan of salvation unto all men, through the blood of mine Only Begotten, who shall come in the meridian of time" (62). "And it came to pass, when the Lord had spoken with Adam, our father, that Adam cried unto the Lord, and he was caught away by the Spirit of the Lord, and was carried down into the water, and was laid under the water, and was brought forth out of the water. And thus he was baptized, and the Spirit of God descended upon him, and thus he was born of the Spirit and became quickened in the inner man. And he heard a voice out of heaven, saying: Thou art baptized with fire, and with the Holy Ghost. This is the record of the Father, and the Son, from henceforth and for ever" (64-66). Compare Doc. and Cov 29:42.

FOOTNOTES:

[101] Deut. 31:9, 24-26; compare 17:18-20.

[102] "Articles of Faith," xiii:7-10.

[103] Gen. 3:15; compare Heb. 2:14; Rev, 12:9; 20:3.

[104] P. of G.P., Moses 5:6-9. Note 1, end of chapter.

[105] P. of G.P., Moses 6:52; study paragraphs 50-56; see also Gen. 5:18, 21-24; Jude 14. Note 4, end of chapter.

[106] Gen. 12:3; 18:18; 22:18; 26:4; 28:14; compare Acts 3:25; Gal. 3:8.

[107] Gen. 49:10.

[108] Note 2, end of chapter.

[109] Deut. 18:15-19; compare John 1:45; Acts 3:22; 7:37; see also a specific confirmation by our Lord after His resurrection, 3 Nephi 20:23.

[110] Note 1, end of chapter.

[111] 1 Cor. 5:7. For references to Christ as the Lamb of God, see John 1:29, 36; 1 Peter 1:19; Rev. chaps. 5, 6, 7, 12, 13, 14, 15, 17, 19, 21, 22; also B. of M., 1 Nephi 10:10, and chaps. 11, 12, 13, 14; 2 Nephi 31:4, 5, 6; 33:14; Alma 7:14; Mormon 9:2, 3; Doc. and Cov. 58:11; 132:19.

[112] Job 19:25; see also verses 26-27.

[113] Instances: Psalm 2:7; compare Acts 13:33; Heb. 1:5; 5:5. Psa. 16:10; compare Acts 13:34-37. Psa. 22:18; compare Matt. 27:35; Mark 15:24; Luke 23:34; John 19:24. Psa. 41:9; compare John 13:18.

Psa. 69:9 and 21; compare Matt. 27:34, 48; Mark 15:23; John 19:29; and John 2:17. Psa. 110:1 and 4; compare Matt. 22:44; Mark 12:35-37; Luke 20:41-44; and Heb. 5:6. Psa. 118:22, 23; compare Matt. 21:42; Mark 12:10; Luke 20:17; Acts 4:11; Eph. 2:20; 1 Peter 2:4, 7. The following are known specifically as Messianic Psalms: 2, 21, 22, 45, 67, 69, 89, 96, 110, 132; in them the psalmist extols in poetic measure the excellencies of the Messiah, and the certainty of His coming.

[114] Isa. 7:14; compare Matt. 1:21-23.
[115] Isa. 9:6,7.
[116] Luke 1:26-33.
[117] Isa. 11:1 and 10; compare Rom. 15:12; Rev. 5:5; 22:16; see also Jer. 23:5, 6.
[118] Isa. 28:16; compare Psa. 118:22; Matt. 21:42; Acts 4:11; Rom. 9:33; 10:11; Eph. 2:20; 1 Peter 2:6-8.
[119] Isa. 40:9-11; compare John 10:11, 14; Heb. 13:20; 1 Peter 2:25; 5:4; see also Ezek. 34:23.
[120] Isa. 42-1; see also 9:2; 49:6; 60:3; compare Matt. 4:14-16; Luke 2:32; Acts 13:47; 26:18; Eph. 5:8, 14.
[121] Isa. 55:4; compare John 18:37.
[122] Isa. 40:3; compare Matt. 3:3; Mark 1:3; Luke 3:4; John 1:23.
[123] Isa. 53; study the entire chapter; compare Acts 8:32-35.
[124] Jer. 23:5, 6; see also 33:14-16.
[125] Jer. 30:9.
[126] Ezek. 34:23; 37:24, 25.
[127] Hos. 11:11; compare Matt. 2:15.
[128] Mic. 5:2; compare Matt 2:6; John 7:42.
[129] Zech. 9:9; compare Matt. 21:4-9.
[130] Zech. 12:10; compare John 19:37.
[131] Zech. 13:6.
[132] Zech. 11:12, 13; compare Matt. 26:15; 27:3-10.
[133] Luke 24:44, 46; see also verses 25-27.
[134] Matt. 3:11; Mark 1:8; Luke 3:16; John 1:15, 26, 27, 29-36; see also Acts 1:5, 8; 11:16; 19:4.
[135] Note 3, end of chapter.
[136] B. of M., 1 Nephi 10:4-11.
[137] B. of M., 1 Nephi chapters 11 and 12; see also 19:10.
[138] B. of M., 2 Nephi 9:5, 6; 10:3. See also Nephi's prophecy 25:12-14; and chap. 26.
[139] B. of M., Mosiah 13:33-35; 15:1-13.
[140] B. of M., Alma 39:15; 40:1-3.
[141] B. of M., Alma 11:31-44.
[142] B. of M., Helaman 14:1-6; compare 3 Nephi 1:4-21.
[143] Rev. 19:10.

CHAPTER 6. THE MERIDIAN OF TIME.

Unto Moses, with whom the Lord spake "face to face, as a man speaketh unto his friend,"[144] the course of the human race, both as then past and future, was made known; and the coming of the Redeemer was recognized by him as the event of greatest import in all the happenings to which the earth and its inhabitants would be witness. The curse of God had aforetime fallen upon the wicked, and upon the earth because of them, "For they would not hearken unto his voice, nor believe on his Only Begotten Son, even him whom he declared should come in the meridian of time, who was prepared from before the foundation of the world."[145] In this scripture appears the earliest mention of the expressive and profoundly significant designation of the period in which the Christ should appear--the meridian of time. If the expression be regarded as figurative, be it remembered the figure is the Lord's.

The term "meridian", as commonly used, conveys the thought of a principal division of time or space[146] thus we speak of the hours before the daily noon as ante-meridian (a.m.) and those after noon as post-meridian (p.m.). So the years and the centuries of human history are divided by the great event of the birth of Jesus Christ. The years preceding that epoch-making occurrence are now designated as time _Before Christ_ (B.C.); while subsequent years are each specified as a certain _Year of our Lord_, or, as in the Latin tongue, _Anno Domini_ (A.D.). Thus the world's chronology has been adjusted and systematized with reference to the time of the Savior's birth; and this method of reckoning is in use among all Christian nations. It is instructive to note that a similar system was adopted by the isolated branch of the house of Israel that had been brought from the land of Palestine to the western continent; for from the appearance of the promised sign among the people betokening the birth of Him who had been so abundantly predicted by their prophets, the Nephite reckoning of the years, starting with the departure of Lehi and his colony from Jerusalem, was superseded by the annals of the new era.[147]

The occasion of the Savior's advent was preappointed; and the time thereof was specifically revealed through authorized prophets on each of the hemispheres. The long history of the Israelitish nation had unfolded a succession of events that found a relative culmination in the earthly mission of the Messiah. That we may the better comprehend the true significance of the Lord's life and ministry while in the flesh, some consideration should be given to the political, social, and religious condition of the people amongst whom He appeared and with whom He lived and died. Such consideration involves at least a brief review of the antecedent history of the Hebrew nation. The posterity of Abraham through Isaac and Jacob had early come to be known by the title in which they took undying pride and found inspiring promise, Israelites, or the children of Israel.[148] Collectively they were so designated throughout the dark days of their bondage in Egypt;[149] so during the four decades of the exodus and the return to the land of promise,[150] and on through the period of their prosperity as a mighty people under the administration of the judges, and as a united monarchy during the successive reigns of Saul, David, and Solomon.[151]

Immediately following the death of Solomon, about 975 B.C. according to the most generally accepted chronology, the nation was disrupted by revolt. The tribe of Judah, part of the tribe of Benjamin, and small remnants of a few other tribes remained true to the royal succession, and accepted Rehoboam, son of Solomon, as their king; while the rest, usually spoken of as the Ten Tribes, broke their allegiance to the house of David, and made Jeroboam, an Ephraimite, their king. The Ten Tribes retained the title Kingdom of Israel though also known as Ephraim.[152] Rehoboam and his adherents were distinctively called the Kingdom of Judah. For about two hundred and fifty years the two kingdoms maintained their separate autonomy; then, about 722 or 721 B.C., the independent status of the Kingdom of Israel was destroyed, and the captive people were transported to Assyria by Shalmanezer and others. Subsequently they disappeared so completely as to be called the Lost Tribes. The Kingdom of Judah was recognized as a nation for about one hundred and thirty years longer; then, about 588 B.C., it was brought into subjection by Nebuchadnezzar, through whom the Babylonian captivity was inaugurated. For three score years and ten Judah was kept in exile and virtual bondage, in consequence of their transgression as had been predicted through Jeremiah.[153] Then the Lord softened the hearts of their captors, and their restoration was begun under the decree of Cyrus the Persian, who had subdued the Babylonian kingdom. The Hebrew people were permitted to return to Judea, and to enter upon the work of rebuilding the temple at Jerusalem.[154]

A great company of the exiled Hebrews availed themselves of this opportunity to return to the lands of their fathers, though many elected to remain in the country of their captivity, preferring Babylon to Israel. The "whole congregation" of the Jews who returned from the Babylonian exile were but "forty and two thousand three hundred and three score, beside their servants and their maids, of whom there were seven thousand three hundred thirty and seven." The relatively small size of the migrating nation is further shown by the register of their beasts of burden.[155] While those who did return strove valiantly to reestablish themselves as the house of David, and to regain some measure of their former prestige and glory, the Jews were never again a truly independent people. In turn they were preyed upon by Greece, Egypt, and Syria; but about 164-163 B.C., the people threw off, in part at least, the alien yoke, as a result of the patriotic revolt led by the Maccabees, the most prominent of whom was Judas Maccabeus. The temple service, which had been practically abolished through the proscription of victorious foes, was reestablished.[156] In the year 163 B.C., the sacred structure was rededicated, and the joyful occasion was thereafter celebrated in annual festival as the Feast of Dedication.[157] During the reign of the Maccabees, however, the temple fell into an almost ruinous condition, more as a result of the inability of the reduced and impoverished people to maintain it than through any further decline of religious zeal. In the hope of insuring a greater measure of national protection, the Jews entered into an unequal alliance with the Romans and eventually became tributary to them, in which condition the Jewish nation continued throughout the period of our Lord's ministry. In the meridian of time Rome was virtually mistress of the world. When Christ was born Augustus

C⊦ªsar[158] was emperor of Rome, and the Idumean, Herod,[159] surnamed the Great, was the vassal king of Judea.

Some semblance of national autonomy was maintained by the Jews under Roman dominion, and their religious ceremonials were not seriously interfered with. The established orders in the priesthood were recognized, and the official acts of the national council, or Sanhedrin,[160] were held to be binding by Roman law; though the judicial powers of this body did not extend to the infliction of capital punishment without the sanction of the imperial executive. It was the established policy of Rome to allow to her tributary and vassal peoples freedom in worship so long as the mythological deities, dear to the Romans, were not maligned nor their altars desecrated.[161]

Needless to say, the Jews took not kindly to alien domination, though for many generations they had been trained in that experience, their reduced status having ranged from nominal vassalage to servile bondage. They were already largely a dispersed people. All the Jews in Palestine at the time of Christ's birth constituted but a small remnant of the great Davidic nation. The Ten Tribes, distinctively the aforetime kingdom of Israel, had then long been lost to history, and the people of Judah had been widely scattered among the nations.

In their relations with other peoples the Jews generally endeavored to maintain a haughty exclusiveness, which brought upon them Gentile ridicule. Under Mosaic law Israel had been required to keep apart from other nations; they attached supreme importance to their Abrahamic lineage as children of the covenant, "an holy people unto the Lord," whom He had chosen "to be a special people unto himself, above all people that are upon the face of the earth".[162] Judah had experienced the woful effects of dalliance with pagan nations, and, at the time we are now considering, a Jew who permitted himself unnecessary association with a Gentile became an unclean being requiring ceremonial cleansing to free him from defilement. Only in strict isolation did the leaders find hope of insuring the perpetuity of the nation.

It is no exaggeration to say that the Jews hated all other peoples and were reciprocally despized and contemned by all others. They manifested especial dislike for the Samaritans, perhaps because this people persisted in their efforts to establish some claim of racial relationship. These Samaritans were a mixed people, and were looked upon by the Jews as a mongrel lot, unworthy of decent respect. When the Ten Tribes were led into captivity by the king of Assyria, foreigners were sent to populate Samaria.[163] These intermarried with such Israelites as had escaped the captivity; and some modification of the religion of Israel, embodying at least the profession of Jehovah worship, survived in Samaria. The Samaritan rituals were regarded by the Jews as unorthodox, and the people as reprobate. At the time of Christ the enmity between Jew and Samaritan was so intense that travelers between Judea and Galilee would make long detours rather than pass through the province of Samaria which lay between. The Jews would have no dealings with the Samaritans.[164]

The proud feeling of self-sufficiency, the obsession for exclusiveness and separation--so distinctively a Jewish trait at that time--was inculcated at the maternal knee and emphasized in synagog and school. The Talmud,[165] which in codified form post-dates the time of Christ's ministry, enjoined all Jews against reading the books of alien nations, declaring that none who so offended could consistently hope for Jehovah's favor.[166] Josephus gives his endorsement to similar injunction, and records that wisdom among the Jews meant only familiarity with the law and ability to discourse thereon.[167] A thorough acquaintanceship with the law was demanded as strongly as other studies were discountenanced. Thus the lines between learned and unlearned came to be rigidly drawn; and, as an inevitable consequence those who were accounted learned, or so considered themselves, looked down upon their unscholarly fellows as a class distinct and inferior.[168]

Long before the birth of Christ, the Jews had ceased to be a united people even in matters of the law, though the law was their chief reliance as a means of maintaining national solidarity. As early as four score years after the return from the Babylonian exile, and we know not with accuracy how much earlier, there had come to be recognized, as men having authority, certain scholars afterward known as scribes, and honored as rabbis[169] or teachers. In the days of Ezra and Nehemiah these specialists in the law constituted a titled class, to whom deference and honor were paid. Ezra is designated "the priest, the scribe, even a scribe of the words of the commandments of the Lord, and of his statutes to Israel".[170] The scribes of those days did valuable service under Ezra, and later under Nehemiah, in compiling the sacred writings then extant; and in Jewish usage those appointed as guardians and expounders of the law came to be known as members of the Great Synagog, or Great Assembly, concerning which we have little information through canonical channels. According to Talmudic record, the organization consisted of one hundred and twenty eminent scholars. The scope of their labors, according to the admonition traditionally perpetuated by themselves, is thus expressed: _Be careful in judgment; set up many scholars, and make a hedge about the law_. They followed this behest by much study and careful consideration of all traditional details in administration; by multiplying scribes and rabbis unto themselves; and, as some of them interpreted the requirement of setting up many scholars, by writing many books and tractates; moreover, they made a fence or hedge about the law by adding numerous rules, which prescribed with great exactness the officially established proprieties for every occasion.

Scribes and rabbis were exalted to the highest rank in the estimation of the people, higher than that of the Levitical or priestly orders; and rabbinical sayings were given precedence over the utterances of the prophets, since the latter were regarded as but messengers or spokesmen, whereas the living scholars were of themselves sources of wisdom and authority. Such secular powers as Roman suzerainty permitted the Jews to retain were vested in the hierarchy, whose members were able thus to gather unto themselves practically all official and professional honors. As a natural result of this condition, there was practically no distinction between Jewish civil and ecclesiastical law, either as to the code or its administration.

Rabbinism comprized as an essential element the doctrine of the equal authority of oral rabbinical tradition with the written word of the law. The aggrandizement implied in the application of the title "Rabbi" and the self-pride manifest in welcoming such adulation were especially forbidden by the Lord, who proclaimed Himself the one Master; and, as touching the interpretation of the title held by some as "father", Jesus proclaimed but one Father and He in heaven: "But be not ye called Rabbi: for one is your Master, even Christ; and all ye are brethren. And call no man your father upon the earth: for one is your Father, which is in heaven. Neither be ye called masters: for one is your Master, even Christ."[171]

The scribes, whether so named or designated by the more distinguishing appellation, rabbis, were repeatedly denounced by Jesus, because of the dead literalism of their teachings, and the absence of the spirit of righteousness and virile morality therefrom; and in such denunciations the Pharisees are often coupled with the scribes. The judgment of the Christ upon them is sufficiently expressed by His withering imprecation: "Woe unto you, scribes and Pharisees, hypocrites!"[172]

The origin of the Pharisees is not fixed by undisputed authority as to either time or circumstance; though it is probable that the sect or party had a beginning in connection with the return of the Jews from the Babylonian captivity. New ideas and added conceptions of the meaning of the law were promulgated by Jews who had imbibed the spirit of Babylon; and the resulting innovations were accepted by some and rejected by others. The name "Pharisee" does not occur in the Old Testament, nor in the Apocrypha, though it is probable that the Assideans mentioned in the books of the Maccabees[173] were the original Pharisees. By derivation the name expresses the thought of separatism; the Pharisee, in the estimation of his class, was distinctively set apart from the common people, to whom he considered himself as truly superior as the Jews regarded themselves in contrast with other nations. Pharisees and scribes were one in all essentials of profession, and rabbinism was specifically their doctrine.

In the New Testament the Pharisees are often mentioned as in opposition to the Sadducees; and such were the relations of the two parties that it becomes a simpler matter to contrast one with the other than to consider each separately. The Sadducees came into existence as a reactionary organization during the second century B.C., in connection with an insurgent movement against the Maccabean party. Their platform was that of opposition to the ever-increasing mass of traditional lore, with which the law was not merely being fenced or hedged about for safety, but under which it was being buried. The Sadducees stood for the sanctity of the law as written and preserved, while they rejected the whole mass of rabbinical precept both as orally transmitted and as collated and codified in the records of the scribes. The Pharisees formed the more popular party; the Sadducees figured as the aristocratic minority. At the time of Christ's birth the Pharisees existed as an organized body numbering over six thousand men, with Jewish women very generally on their side in sympathy and effort;[174] while the Sadducees were so small a faction and of such limited power that, when they were placed in official positions, they generally followed the policy of the Pharisees as a matter of incumbent expediency. The Pharisees were the Puritans of the time, unflinching in their demand for compliance with the traditional rules as well as the original law of Moses. In this connection note Paul's confession of faith and practise when arraigned before Agrippa--"That after the most straitest sect of our religion I lived a Pharisee."[175] The Sadducees prided themselves on strict compliance with the law, as they construed it, irrespective of all scribes or rabbis. The Sadducees stood for the temple and its prescribed ordinances, the Pharisees for the synagog and its rabbinical teachings. It is difficult to decide which were the more technical if we judge each party by the standard of its own profession. By way of illustration: the Sadducees held to the literal and full exaction of the Mosaic penalty--an eye for an eye and a tooth for a tooth[176]--while the Pharisees contended on the authority of rabbinical dictum, that the wording was figurative, and that therefore the penalty could be met by a fine in money or goods.

Pharisees and Sadducees differed on many important if not fundamental matters of belief and practise, including the preexistence of spirits, the reality of a future state involving reward and punishment, the necessity for individual self-denial, the immortality of the soul, and the resurrection from the dead; in each of which the Pharisees stood for the affirmative while the Sadducees denied.[177] Josephus avers--the doctrine of the Sadducees is that the soul and body perish together; the law is all that they are concerned to observe.[178] They were "a skeptical school of aristocratic traditionalists; adhering only to the Mosaic law."[179]

Among the many other sects and parties established on the ground of religious or political differences, or both, are the Essenes, the Nazarites, the Herodians and the Galileans. The Essenes were characterized by professions of ultra-piety; they considered even the strictness of Pharisaic profession as weak and insufficient; they guarded membership in their order by severe exactions extending through a first and a second novitiate; they were forbidden even to touch food prepared by strangers; they practised strict temperance and rigid self-denial, indulged in hard labor--preferably that of agriculture, and were forbidden to trade as merchants, to take part in war, or to own or employ slaves.[180] Nazarites are not named in the New Testament, though of specific record in the earlier scriptures;[181] and from sources other than scriptural we learn of their existence at and after the time of Christ. The Nazarite was one of either sex who was bound to abstinence and sacrifice by a voluntary vow for special service to God; the period of the vow might be limited or for life. While the Essenes cultivated an ascetic brotherhood, the Nazarites were devoted to solitary discipline.

The Herodians constituted a politico-religious party who favored the plans of the Herods under the professed belief that through that dynasty alone could the status of the Jewish people be maintained and a reestablishment of the nation be secured. We find mention of the Herodians laying aside their partisan antipathies and acting in concert with the Pharisees in the effort to convict the Lord Jesus and bring Him to death.[182] The Galileans or people of Galilee were distinguished from their fellow Israelites of Judea by greater simplicity and less ostentatious devotion in matters pertaining to the law. They were opposed to innovations, yet were generally more liberal or less bigoted than some of the professedly devout Judeans. They were prominent as able defenders in the wars of the people, and won for themselves a reputation for bravery and patriotism. They are mentioned in connection with certain tragical occurrences during our Lord's lifetime.[183]

The authority of the priesthood was outwardly acknowledged by the Jews at the time of Christ; and the appointed order of service for priest and Levite was duly observed. During the reign of David, the descendants of Aaron, who were the hereditary priests in Israel, had been divided into twenty-four courses, [184] and to each course the labors of the sanctuary were alloted in turn. Representatives of but four of these courses returned from the captivity, but from these the orders were reconstructed on the original plan. In the days of Herod the Great the temple ceremonies were conducted with great display and outward elaborateness, as an essential matter of consistency with the splendor of the structure, which surpassed in magnificence all earlier sanctuaries.[185] Priests and Levites, therefore, were in demand for continuous service, though the individuals were changed at short intervals according to the established system. In the regard of the people the priests were inferior to the rabbis, and the scholarly attainments of a scribe transcended in honor that pertaining to ordination in the priesthood. The religion of the time was a matter of ceremony and formality, of ritual and performance; it had lost the very spirit of worship, and the true conception of the relationship between Israel and Israel's God was but a dream of the past.

Such in brief were the principal features of the world's condition, and particularly as concerns the Jewish people, when Jesus the Christ was born in the meridian of time.

NOTES TO CHAPTER 6.

1. The Sanhedrin.--This, the chief court or high council of the Jews, derives its name from the Greek _sunedrion_, signifying "a council." In English it is sometimes though inaccurately, written "Sanhedrim." The Talmud traces the origin of this body to the calling of the seventy elders whom Moses associated with himself, making seventy-one in all, to administer as judges in Israel (Numb. 11:16, 17). The Sanhedrin in the time of Christ, as also long before, comprized seventy-one members, including the high-priest who presided in the assembly. It appears to have been known in its earlier period as the Senate, and was occasionally so designated even after Christ's death (Josephus, Antiquities xii, 3:3; compare Acts 5:21); the name "Sanhedrin" came into general use during the reign of Herod the Great; but the term is not of Biblical usage; its equivalent in the New Testament is "council" (Matt. 5:22; 10:17; 26:59) though it must be remembered that the same term is applied to courts of lesser jurisdiction than that of the Sanhedrin, and to local tribunals. (Matt 5:22; 10:17; 26:59; Mark 13:9; see also Acts 25:12.)

The following, from the _Standard Bible Dictionary_, is instructive: "Those qualified to be members were in general of the priestly house and especially of the Sadducean nobility. But from the days of Queen Alexandra (69-68 B.C.) onward, there were with these chief priests also many Pharisees in it under the name of scribes and elders. These three classes are found combined in Matt. 27:41; Mark 11:27; 14:43, 53; 15:1. How such members were appointed is not entirely clear. The aristocratic character of the body and the history of its origin forbid the belief that it was by election. Its nucleus probably consisted of the members of certain ancient families, to which, however, from time to time others were added by the secular rulers. The presiding officer was the high priest, who at first exercized in it more than the authority of a member, claiming a voice equal to that of the rest of the body. But after the reduction of the high priesthood from a hereditary office to one bestowed by the political ruler according to his pleasure, and the frequent changes in the office introduced by the new system, the high priest naturally lost his prestige. Instead of holding in his hands the 'government of the nation,' he came to be but one of many to share this power; those who had served as high priests being still in esteem among their nation, and having lost their office not for any reason that could be considered valid by the religious sense of the community, exerted a large influence over the decisions of the assembly. In the New Testament they are regarded as the rulers (Matt. 26:59; 27:41; Acts 4:5, 8; Luke 23:13, 35; John 7:26), and Josephus' testimony supports this view. The functions of the Sanhedrin were religious and moral, and also political. In the latter capacity they further exercized administrative as well as judicial functions. As a religious tribunal, the Sanhedrin wielded a potent influence over the whole of the Jewish world (Acts 9:2); but as a court of justice, after the division of the country upon the death of Herod, its jurisdiction was limited to Judea. Here, however, its power was absolute even to the passing of sentence of death (Josephus, Ant. xiv, 9:3, 4; Matt. 26:3; Acts 4:5; 6:12; 22:30), although it had no authority to carry the sentence into execution except as approved and ordered by the representative of the Roman government. The law by which the Sanhedrin governed was naturally the Jewish, and in the execution of it this tribunal had a police of its own, and made arrests at its discretion (Matt 26:47).... While the general authority of the Sanhedrin extended over the whole of Judea, the towns in the country had local councils of their own (Matt. 5:22; 10:17; Mark 13:9; Josephus, B. J. ii, 14:1), for the administration of local affairs. These were constituted of elders (Luke 7:3), at least seven in number, (Josephus, Ant. iv, 8:14; B. J. ii, 20:5), and in some of the largest towns as many as twenty-three. What the relation of these to the central council in Jerusalem was does not appear clearly.... Some sort of mutual recognition existed among them; for whenever the judges of the local court could not agree it seems that they were in the habit of referring their cases to the Sanhedrin in Jerusalem. (Josephus, Ant. iv, 8:14; Mishna, Sanh. 11:2)."

2. Talmud.--"The body of Jewish civil and religious law (and discussion directly or remotely relating thereto) not comprized in the Pentateuch, commonly including the _Mishna_ and the _Gemara_, but sometimes limited to the latter; written in Aramaic. It exists in two great collections, the _Palestinian Talmud_, or _Talmud of the Land of Israel_, or _Talmud of the West_, or, more popularly, _Jerusalem

Talmud_, embodying the discussions on the Mishna of the Palestinian doctors from the 2d to the middle of the 5th century; and the _Babylonian_, embodying those of the Jewish doctors in Babylonia, from about 190 to the 7th century."--_New Standard Dict._ The Mishna comprizes the earlier portions of the Talmud; the Gemara is made up of later writings and is largely an exposition of the Mishna. An edition of the Babylonian Talmud alone (issued at Vienna in 1682) comprized twenty-four tomes. (Geikie.)

3. Rabbis.--The title Rabbi is equivalent to our distinctive appellations Doctor, Master, or Teacher. By derivation it means Master or my Master, thus connoting dignity and rank associated with politeness of address. A definite explanation of the term is given by John (1:38), and the same meaning attaches by implication to its use as recorded by Matthew (23:8). It was applied as a title of respect to Jesus on several occasions (Matt. 23:7, 8; 26:25, 49; Mark 9:5; 11:21; 14:45; John 1:38, 49; 3:2, 26; 4:31; 6:25; 9:2; 11:8). The title was of comparatively recent usage in the time of Christ, as it appears to have first come into general use during the reign of Herod the Great, though the earlier teachers, of the class without the name of Rabbis, were generally reverenced, and the title was carried back to them by later usage. Rab was an inferior title and Rabban a superior one to Rabbi. Rabboni was expressive of most profound respect, love and honor (see John 20:16). At the time of our Lord's ministry the Rabbis were held in high esteem, and rejoiced in the afflations of precedence and honor among men. They were almost exclusively of the powerful Pharisaic party.

The following is from Geikie's _Life and Words of Christ_, vol. I, chap. 6: "If the most important figures in the society of Christ's day were the Pharisees, it was because they were the Rabbis or teachers of the Law. As such they received superstitious honor, which was, indeed, the great motive, with many, to court the title or join the party. The Rabbis were classed with Moses, the patriarchs, and the prophets, and claimed equal reverence. Jacob and Joseph were both said to have been Rabbis. The Targum of Jonathan substitutes Rabbis, or Scribes, for the word 'prophets' where it occurs. Josephus speaks of the prophets of Saul's day as Rabbis. In the Jerusalem Targum all the patriarchs are learned Rabbis.... They were to be dearer to Israel than father or mother--because parents avail only in this world [as was then taught] but the Rabbi forever. They were set above kings, for is it not written 'Through me kings reign'? Their entrance into a house brought a blessing; to live or to eat with them was the highest good fortune.... The Rabbis went even further than this in exalting their order. The Mishna declares that it is a greater crime to speak anything to their discredit, than to speak against the words of the Law.... Yet in form, the Law received boundless honor. Every saying of the Rabbis had to be based on some words of it, which were, however, explained in their own way. The spirit of the times, the wild fanaticism of the people, and their own bias, tended alike to make them set value only on ceremonies and worthless externalisms, to the utter neglect of the spirit of the sacred writings. Still it was held that the Law needed no confirmation, while the words of the Rabbis did. So far as the Roman authority under which they lived left them free, the Jews willingly put all power in the hands of the Rabbis. They or their nominees filled every office, from the highest in the priesthood to the lowest in the community. They were the casuists, the teachers, the priests, the judges, the magistrates, and the physicians of the nation.... The central and dominant characteristic of the teaching of the Rabbis was the certain advent of a great national Deliverer--the Messiah or Anointed of God or in the Greek translation of the title, the Christ. In no other nation than the Jews has such a conception ever taken such root or shown such vitality.... It was agreed among the Rabbis that His birthplace must be Bethlehem, and that He must rise from the tribe of Judah."

Individual rabbis gathered disciples about them, and, inevitably, rivalry became manifest. Rabbinical schools and academies were established, each depending for its popularity on the greatness of some rabbi. The most famous of these institutions in the time of Herod I. were the school of Hillel and that of his rival Shammai. Later, tradition invested these with the title "the fathers of old." It appears from the trifling matters over which the followers of these two disagreed, that only by opposition could either maintain a distinguishing status. Hillel is reputed as the grandfather of Gamaliel, the rabbi and doctor of the law at whose feet Saul of Tarsus, afterward Paul the apostle, received his early instruction (Acts 22:3). So far as we have historic record of the views, principles or beliefs advocated by the rival schools of Hillel and Shammai, it appears that the former stood for a greater degree of liberality and tolerance, while the later emphasized a strict and possibly narrow interpretation of the law and its associated traditions. The dependence of the rabbinical schools on the authority of tradition is illustrated by an incident of record to the effect that even the prestige of the great Hillel did not insure him against uproar when once he spoke without citing precedent; only when he added that so had his masters Abtalion and Shemajah spoken did the tumult subside.

4. Sadducean Denial of the Resurrection.--As set forth in the text, the Sadducees formed an association numerically small as compared with the more popular and influential Pharisees. In the Gospels the Pharisees are of frequent mention, and very commonly in connection with the scribes, while the Sadducees are less frequently named. In the Acts of the Apostles, the Sadducees appear frequently as opponents of the Church. This condition was doubtless due to the prominence given the resurrection from the dead among the themes of the apostolic preaching, the Twelve continually bearing testimony to the actual resurrection of Christ. Sadducean doctrine denied the actuality and possibility of a bodily resurrection, the contention resting mainly on the ground that Moses, who was regarded as the supreme mortal lawgiver in Israel, and the chief mouthpiece of Jehovah, had written nothing concerning life after death. The following is taken from Smith's _Dictionary of the Bible_, article "Sadducees," as touching this matter: "The denial of man's resurrection after death followed in the conception of the Sadducees as a logical conclusion from their denial that Moses had revealed to the Israelites the Oral Law. For on a point so momentous as a second life beyond the grave, no religious party among the Jews would have deemed themselves bound to accept any doctrine as an article of faith, unless it had been proclaimed by Moses,

their great legislator; and it is certain that in the written Law of the Pentateuch there is a total absence of any assertion by Moses of the resurrection of the dead. This fact is presented to Christians in a striking manner by the well-known words of the Pentateuch which are quoted by Christ in argument with the Sadducees on this subject (Exo. 3:6, 16; Mark 12:26, 27; Matt. 22:31, 32; Luke 20:37). It cannot be doubted that in such a case Christ would quote to His powerful adversaries the most cogent text in the Law; and yet the text actually quoted does not do more than suggest an inference on this great doctrine. It is true that passages in other parts of the Old Testament express a belief in the resurrection (Isa. 26:19; Dan. 12:2; Job 19:26; and in some of the Psalms); and it may at first sight be a subject of surprize that the Sadducees were not convinced by the authority of those passages. But although the Sadducees regarded the books which contained these passages as sacred, it is more than doubtful whether any of the Jews regarded them as sacred in precisely the same sense as the written Law. To the Jews Moses was and is a colossal form, preeminent in authority above all subsequent prophets."

5. The Temple of Herod.--"Herod's purpose in the great undertaking [that of restoring the temple, and of enlarging it on a plan of unprecedented magnificence] was that of aggrandizing himself and the nation, rather than the rendering of homage to Jehovah. His proposition to rebuild or restore the temple on a scale of increased magnificence was regarded with suspicion and received with disfavor by the Jews, who feared that were the ancient edifice demolished, the arbitrary monarch might abandon his plan and the people would be left without a temple. To allay these fears the king proceeded to reconstruct and restore the old edifice, part by part, directing the work so that at no time was the temple service seriously interrupted. So little of the ancient structure was allowed to stand, however, that the temple of Herod must be regarded as a new creation. The work was begun about sixteen years before the birth of Christ; and while the Holy House itself was practically completed within a year and a half, this part of the labor having been performed by a body of one thousand priests specially trained for the purpose, the temple area was a scene of uninterrupted building operations down to the year 63 A.D. We read that in the time of Christ's ministry the temple had been forty-six years in building; and at that time it was unfinished.

"The Biblical record gives us little information regarding this the last and the greatest of ancient temples; for what we know concerning it we are indebted, mainly to Josephus, with some corroborative testimony found in the Talmud. In all essentials the Holy House, or Temple proper, was similar to the two earlier houses of sanctuary, though externally far more elaborate and imposing than either; but in the matter of surrounding courts and associated buildings, the Temple of Herod preeminently excelled.... Yet its beauty and grandeur lay in architectural excellence rather than in the sanctity of its worship or in the manifestation of the Divine Presence within its walls. Its ritual and service were largely man-prescribed; for while the letter of the Mosaic Law was professedly observed, the law had been supplemented and in many features supplanted by rule and priestly prescription. The Jews professed to consider it holy, and by them it was proclaimed as the House of the Lord. Devoid though it was of the divine accompaniments of earlier shrines accepted of God, and defiled as it was by priestly arrogance and usurpation, as also by the selfish interest of traffic and trade, it was nevertheless recognized even by our Lord the Christ as His Father's House. (Matt. 21:12; compare Mark 11:15; Luke 19:45.).... For thirty or more years after the death of Christ, the Jews continued the work of adding to and embellishing the temple buildings. The elaborate design conceived and projected by Herod had been practically completed; the temple was well-nigh finished, and, as soon afterward appeared, was ready for destruction. Its fate had been definitely foretold by the Savior Himself."--From the author's _House of the Lord_, pp. 54-61.

6. State of the World at the Time of the Savior's Birth.--At the beginning of the Christian era, the Jews, in common with most other nations, were subjects of the Roman empire. They were allowed a considerable degree of liberty in maintaining their religious observances and national customs generally, but their status was far from that of a free and independent people. The period was one of comparative peace--a time marked by fewer wars and less dissension than the empire had known for many years. These conditions were favorable for the mission of the Christ, and for the founding of His Church on earth. The religious systems extant at the time of Christ's earthly ministry may be classified in a general way as Jewish and Pagan, with a minor system--the Samaritan--which was essentially a mixture of the other two. The children of Israel alone proclaimed the existence of the true and living God; they alone looked forward to the advent of the Messiah, whom mistakenly they awaited as a prospective conqueror coming to crush the enemies of their nation. All other nations, tongues, and peoples, bowed to pagan deities, and their worship comprized nought but the sensual rites of heathen idolatry. Paganism was a religion of form and ceremony, based on polytheism--a belief in the existence of a multitude of gods, which deities were subject to all the vices and passions of humanity, while distinguished by immunity from death. Morality and virtue were unknown as elements of heathen service; and the dominant idea in pagan worship was that of propitiating the gods, in the hope of averting their anger and purchasing their favor.--See the author's _The Great Apostasy_, 1:2-4, and notes following the chapter cited.

FOOTNOTES:

[144] Exo. 33:11; see also Numb. 12:8; Deut. 34:10; compare P. of G.P., Moses 1:2, 11, 31.
[145] P. of G.P., Moses 5:57; for later mention of the "meridian of time," see 6:56-62; and 7:46; and compare Doc. and Cov. 20:26; 39:3.
[146] "Meridian: ... figuratively, the highest point or culminating-point of anything; the zenith; as the meridian of life."--"New Stand. Dict."
[147] B. of M., 3 Nephi 2:8; compare 4 Nephi 1:1, 21; Mormon 8:6; Moroni 10:1.
[148] Gen. 32:28; 35:10.

[149] Exo. 1:1, 7; 9:6, 7; 12:3, etc.
[150] Exo. 12:35, 40; 13:19; 15:1; Numb. 20:1, 19, 24, etc.
[151] See mention throughout the books of Judges, 1 and 2 Samuel, 1 and 2 Kings, and references therein.
[152] Isa. 11:13; 17:3; Ezek. 37:16-22; Hos. 4:17.
[153] Jer. 25:11, 12; see also 29:10.
[154] Ezra 1:1-4; the author, "House of the Lord," pp. 47-53; also "Articles of Faith" xvii:1-22.
[155] Ezra 2:64-67.
[156] "House of the Lord," pp. 51-53.
[157] Josephus, Ant. xii:6 and 7; 2 Maccabees 2:19; 10:1-8; also John 10:22.
[158] Luke 2:1.
[159] Matt. 2:1. Page 106.
[160] Note 1, end of chapter.
[161] Deut. 7:6; see also 10:15; Exo. 19:5, 6; Psa. 135:4; Isa. 41:8; 45:4; compare 1 Peter 2:9.
[162] Note 6, end of chapter.
[163] 2 Kings 17:24.
[164] John 4:9; Luke 9:51-53. Pages 172, 183 herein.
[165] Note 2, end of chapter.
[166] Bab. Talmud, Sanhedrin, 90.
[167] Josephus, Ant. xx, 11:2.
[168] Note the emphasis given to this distinction in John 7:45-49; see also 9:34.
[169] Note 3, end of chapter.
[170] Ezra 7:11; see also verses 6, 10, 12.
[171] Matt. 23:8-10; see also John 1:38; 3:2.
[172] Matt. 23:13, 14, 15, 23. etc., read the entire chapter; compare Mark 12:38-40; Luke 20:46; see also as instances of special denunciation of the Pharisees Luke 11:37-44. Note also that the lawyers, who were professionally associated with the scribes, are included in the sweeping criticism: verses 45-54. See pages 552-560 herein.
[173] 1 Maccabees 2:42; 7:13-17; 2 Maccabees 14:6.
[174] Josephus, Antiquities, xvii, 2:4.
[175] Acts 26:5; see also 23:6; Philip. 3:5.
[176] Exo. 21:23-35; Lev. 24:20; Deut. 19:21; contrast Matt 5:38-44.
[177] Note 4, end of chapter.
[178] Josephus, Antiquities xviii, 1:4.
[179] "New Stand. Dict.," under "Sadducees."
[180] Josephus, Antiquities xviii, 1:5.
[181] Numb. 6:2-21; Judges 13:5, 7; 16:17; Amos. 2:11, 12. Page 87.
[182] Matt. 22:15, 16; Mark 12:13.
[183] Luke 13:1, 2; see also John 4:45; Mark 14:70; Acts 2:7.
[184] 1 Chron. 24:1-18.
[185] Note 5, end of chapter.

CHAPTER 7. GABRIEL'S ANNUNCIATION OF JOHN AND OF JESUS.

JOHN THE FORERUNNER.

Associated with the prophecies of the birth of Christ are predictions concerning one who should precede Him, going before to prepare the way. It is not surprizing that the annunciation of the immediate advent of the forerunner was speedily followed by that of the Messiah; nor that the proclamations were made by the same heavenly embassador--Gabriel, sent from the presence of God.[186]

About fifteen months prior to the Savior's birth, Zacharias, a priest of the Aaronic order, was officiating in the functions of his office in the temple at Jerusalem. His wife, Elisabeth, was also of a priestly family, being numbered among the descendants of Aaron. The couple had never been blessed with children; and at the time of which we speak they were both well stricken in years and had sorrowfully given up hope of posterity. Zacharias belonged to the course of priests named after Abijah, and known in later time as the course of Abia. This was the eighth in the order of the twenty-four courses established by David the king, each course being appointed to serve in turn a week at the sanctuary.[187] It will be remembered that on the return of the people from Babylon only four of the courses were represented; but of these four each averaged over fourteen hundred men.[188]

During his week of service each priest was required to maintain scrupulously a state of ceremonial cleanliness of person; he had to abstain from wine, and from food except that specifically prescribed; he had to bathe frequently; he lived within the temple precincts and thus was cut off from family association; he was not allowed to come near the dead, nor to mourn in the formal manner if death should rob him of even his nearest and dearest of kin. We learn that the daily selection of the priest who should enter the Holy Place, and there burn incense on the golden altar, was determined by lot;[189] and furthermore we gather, from non-scriptural history, that because of the great number of priests the honor of so officiating seldom fell twice to the same person.

On this day the lot had fallen to Zacharias. It was a very solemn occasion in the life of the humble Judean priest--this one day in his life on which the special and particularly sacred service was required of him. Within the Holy Place he was separated by the veil of the temple only from the Oracle or Holy of Holies--the inner sanctuary into which none but the high priest might enter, and he only on the Day of Atonement, after long ceremonial preparation.[190] The place and the time were conducive to the highest and most reverential feelings. As Zacharias ministered within the Holy Place, the people without bowed themselves in prayer, watching for the clouds of incense smoke to appear above the great partition which formed the barrier between the place of general assembly and the Holy Place, and awaiting the reappearance of the priest and his pronouncement of the benediction.

Before the astonished gaze of Zacharias, at this supreme moment of his priestly service, there appeared, standing on the right of the golden altar of incense, an angel of the Lord. Many generations had passed in Jewry since any visible presence other than mortal had been manifest within the temple, either in the Holy Place or the Holy of Holies; the people regarded personal visitations of heavenly beings as occurrences of the past; they had come almost to believe that there were no longer prophets in Israel. Nevertheless, there was always a feeling of anxiety, akin to that of troubled expectancy, whenever a priest approached the inner sanctuary, which was regarded as the particular abode of Jehovah should He ever again condescend to visit His people. In view of these conditions we read without surprize that this angelic presence troubled Zacharias and caused fear to fall upon him. The words of the heavenly visitant, however, were comforting though of startling import, embodying as they did the unqualified assurance that the man's prayers had been heard, and that his wife should bear him a son, who must be named John.[191] The promise went even further, specifying that the child to be born of Elisabeth would be a blessing to the people; many would rejoice at his birth; he would be great in the sight of the Lord, and must be guarded against wine and strong drink;[192] he would be filled with the Holy Ghost, would be the means of turning many souls to God, and would go before to make ready a people prepared to receive the Messiah.

Doubtless Zacharias recognised in the predicted future of the yet unborn child the great forerunner, of whom the prophets had told and the psalmist had sung; but that such a one should be offspring of himself and his aged wife seemed impossible despite the angel's promise. The man doubted, and asked whereby he should know that what his visitant had spoken was true: "And the angel answering said unto him, I am Gabriel, that stand in the presence of God; and am sent to speak unto thee, and to show thee these glad tidings. And, behold, thou shalt be dumb, and not able to speak, until the day that these things shall be performed, because thou believest not my words, which shall be fulfilled in their season."[193] When the highly blessed though sorely smitten priest at length came from within and appeared before the expectant congregation, already made anxious by his delayed return, he could but mutely dismiss the assembly and by signs indicate that he had seen a vision. The penalty for doubt was already operative; Zacharias was dumb.

In due time the child was born, there in the hill country of Judea[194] where Zacharias and Elisabeth had their home; and, on the eighth day following the birth the family assembled in accordance with custom and Mosaic requirement, to name the babe in connection with the rite of circumcision.[195] All suggestions that he be called after his father were overruled by Zacharias, who wrote with decisive finality: "His name is John." Thereupon the dumb[196] priest's tongue was loosed, and being filled with the Holy Ghost he burst forth in prophecy, praise and song; his inspired utterances have been set to music and are sung in worship by many Christian congregations as the Benedictus:

"Blessed be the Lord God of Israel; for he hath visited and redeemed his people, and hath raised up an horn of salvation for us in the house of his servant David; as he spake by the mouth of his holy prophets, which have been since the world began: that we should be saved from our enemies, and from the hand of   all that hate us; to perform the mercy promised to our fathers,   and to remember his holy covenant; the oath which he sware to   our father Abraham, that he would grant unto us, that we being   delivered out of the hand of our enemies might serve him without   fear, in holiness and righteousness before him, all the days of   our life. And thou, child, shalt be called the prophet of the Highest: for thou shalt go before the face of the Lord to   prepare his ways; to give knowledge of salvation unto his people   by the remission of their sins, through the tender mercy of our   God; whereby the dayspring from on high hath visited us, to give   light to them that sit in darkness and in the shadow of death,   to guide our feet into the way of peace."[197]

The last words Zacharias had uttered prior to the infliction of dumbness were words of doubt and unbelief, words in which he had called for a sign as proof of authority of one who came from the presence of the Almighty; the words with which he broke his long silence were words of praise unto God in whom he had all assurance, words that were as a sign to all who heard, and the fame whereof spread throughout the region.

The unusual circumstances attending the birth of John, notably the months of dumbness passed by the father and his sudden recovery of speech on the bestowal of the fore-appointed name, caused many to marvel and some to fear, as they asked: "What manner of child shall this be?" When, a man grown, John raised his voice in the wilderness, again in fulfillment of prophecy, the people questioned as to whether he was not the Messiah.[198] Of his life between infancy and the beginning of his public ministry, a period of approximately thirty years, we have of record but a single sentence: "And the child grew, and waxed strong in spirit, and was in the deserts till the day of his shewing unto Israel."[199]

THE ANNUNCIATION TO THE VIRGIN.

Six months after the visitation of Gabriel to Zacharias, and three months prior to the birth of John, the same heavenly messenger was sent to a young woman named Mary, who lived at Nazareth, a town in Galilee. She was of the lineage of David; and though unmarried was betrothed or espoused to a man named Joseph, who also was of royal descent through the Davidic line. The angel's salutation, while full of honor and blessing, caused Mary to wonder and to feel troubled. "Hail, thou that art highly favoured, the Lord is with thee: blessed art thou among women";[200] thus did Gabriel greet the virgin. In common with other daughters of Israel, specifically those of the tribe of Judah and of known descent from David, Mary had doubtless contemplated, with holy joy and ecstasy, the coming of the Messiah through the royal line; she knew that some Jewish maiden was yet to become the mother of the Christ. Was it possible that the angel's words to her had reference to this supreme expectation and hope of the nation? She had little time to turn these things in her mind, for the angel continued: "Fear not, Mary: for thou hast found favour with God. And, behold, thou shalt conceive in thy womb, and bring forth a son, and shalt call his name JESUS. He shall be great, and shall be called the Son of the Highest: and the Lord God shall give unto him the throne of his father David: and he shall reign over the house of Jacob for ever; and of his kingdom there shall be no end."[201]

Even yet she comprehended but in part the import of this momentous visitation. Not in the spirit of doubt such as had prompted Zacharias to ask for a sign, but through an earnest desire for information and explanation, Mary, conscious of her unmarried status and sure of her virgin condition, asked: "How shall it be, seeing I know not a man?" The answer to her natural and simple inquiry was the announcement of a miracle such as the world had never known--not a miracle in the sense of a happening contrary to nature's law, nevertheless a miracle through the operation of higher law, such as the human mind ordinarily fails to comprehend or regard as possible. Mary was informed that she would conceive and in time bring forth a Son, of whom no mortal man would be the father:--"And the angel answered and said unto her, The Holy Ghost shall come upon thee, and the power of the Highest shall overshadow thee: therefore also that holy thing which shall be born of thee shall be called the Son of God."[202]

Then the angel told her of the blessed condition of her cousin Elisabeth, who had been barren; and by way of sufficient and final explanation added: "For with God nothing shall be impossible." With gentle submissiveness and humble acceptance, the pure young virgin replied: "Behold the handmaid of the Lord; be it unto me according to thy word."

His message delivered, Gabriel departed, leaving the chosen Virgin of Nazareth to ponder over her wondrous experience. Mary's promised Son was to be "The Only Begotten" of the Father in the flesh; so it had been both positively and abundantly predicted. True, the event was unprecedented; true also it has never been paralleled; but that the virgin birth would be unique was as truly essential to the fulfilment of prophecy as that it should occur at all. That Child to be born of Mary was begotten of Elohim, the Eternal Father, not in violation of natural law but in accordance with a higher manifestation thereof; and, the offspring from that association of supreme sanctity, celestial Sireship, and pure though mortal maternity, was of right to be called the "Son of the Highest." In His nature would be combined the powers of Godhood with the capacity and possibilities of mortality; and this through the ordinary operation of the fundamental law of heredity, declared of God, demonstrated by science, and admitted by philosophy, that living beings shall propagate--after their kind. The Child Jesus was to inherit the physical, mental, and spiritual traits, tendencies, and powers that characterized His parents--one immortal and glorified--God, the other human--woman.

Jesus Christ was to be born of mortal woman, but was not directly the offspring of mortal man, except so far as His mother was the daughter of both man and woman. In our Lord alone has been fulfilled the word of God spoken in relation to the fall of Adam, that the _seed of the woman_ should have power to overcome Satan by bruising the serpent's head.[203]

In respect to place, condition, and general environment, Gabriel's annunciation to Zacharias offers strong contrast to the delivery of his message to Mary. The prospective forerunner of the Lord was announced to his father within the magnificent temple, and in a place the most exclusively sacred save one other in the Holy House, under the light shed from the golden candlestick, and further illumined by the glow of living coals on the altar of gold; the Messiah was announced to His mother in a small town far from the capital and the temple, most probably within the walls of a simple Galilean cottage.

MARY'S VISIT TO HER COUSIN ELISABETH.

It was natural that Mary, left now to herself with a secret in her soul, holier, greater, and more thrilling than any ever borne before or since, should seek companionship, and that of some one of her own sex, in whom she could confide, from whom she might hope to derive comfort and support, and to whom it would be not wrong to tell what at that time was probably known to no mortal save herself. Her heavenly visitant had indeed suggested all this in his mention of Elisabeth, Mary's cousin, herself a subject of unusual blessing, and a woman through whom another miracle of God had been wrought. Mary set out with haste from Nazareth for the hill country of Judea, on a journey of about a hundred miles if the traditional account be true that the little town of Juttah was the home of Zacharias. There was mutual joy in the meeting between Mary the youthful virgin, and Elisabeth, already well advanced in life. From what of Gabriel's words her husband had communicated, Elisabeth must have known that the approaching birth of her son would soon be followed by that of the Messiah, and that therefore the day for which Israel had waited and prayed through the long dark centuries was about to dawn. When Mary's salutation fell upon her ears, the Holy Ghost bore witness that the chosen mother of the Lord stood before her in the person of her cousin; and as she experienced the physical thrill incident to the quickening spirit of her own blessed conception, she returned the greeting of her visitor with reverence: "Blessed art thou among women, and blessed is the fruit of thy womb. And whence is this to me, that the mother of my Lord should come to me?"[204] Mary responded with that glorious hymn of praise, since adopted in the musical ritual of churches as the Magnificat:

"My soul doth magnify the Lord, and my spirit hath rejoiced in   God my Saviour. For he hath regarded the low estate of his   handmaiden: for, behold, from henceforth all generations shall   call me blessed. For he that is mighty hath done to me great   things; and holy is his name. And his mercy is on them that fear   him from generation to generation. He hath shewed strength with   his arm; he hath scattered the proud in the imagination of their   hearts. He hath put down the mighty from their seats, and exalted them of low degree. He hath filled the hungry with good   things; and the rich he hath sent empty away. He hath holpen his   servant Israel, in remembrance of his mercy; as he spake to our   fathers, to Abraham, and to his seed for ever."[205]

MARY AND JOSEPH.

The visit lasted about three months, after which time Mary returned to Nazareth. The real embarrassment of her position she had now to meet. At the home of her cousin she had been understood; her condition had served to confirm the testimony of Zacharias and Elisabeth; but how would her word be received at her own home? And especially, how would she be regarded by her espoused husband?[206] Betrothal, or espousal, in that time was in some respects as binding as the marriage vow, and could only be set aside by a ceremonial separation akin to divorce; yet an espousal was but an engagement to marry, not a marriage. When Joseph greeted his promised bride after her three months' absence, he was greatly distressed over the indications of her prospective maternity. Now the Jewish law provided for the annulment of a betrothal in either of two ways--by public trial and judgment, or by private agreement attested by a written document signed in the presence of witnesses. Joseph was a just man, a strict observer of the law, yet no harsh extremist; moreover he loved Mary and would save her all unnecessary humiliation, whatever might be his own sorrow and suffering. For Mary's sake he dreaded the thought of publicity; and therefore determined to have the espousal annulled with such privacy the law allowed. He was troubled and thought much of his duty in the matter, when, "behold, the angel of the Lord appeared unto him in a dream, saying, Joseph, thou son of David, fear not to take unto thee Mary thy wife: for that which is conceived in her is of the Holy Ghost. And she shall bring forth a son, and thou shalt call his name JESUS: for he shall save his people from their sins."[207]

Great was Joseph's relief of mind; and great his joy in the realization that the long predicted coming of the Messiah was at hand; the words of the prophets would be fulfilled; a virgin, and she the one in the world most dear to him, had conceived, and in due time would bring forth that blessed Son, Emmanuel, which name by interpretation means "God with us."[208] The angel's salutation was significant; "Joseph, thou son of David," was the form of address; and the use of that royal title must have meant to Joseph that, though he was of kingly lineage, marriage with Mary would cast no shadow upon his family status. Joseph waited not; to insure Mary all possible protection and establish his full legal right as her lawful guardian he hastened the solemnization of the marriage, and "did as the angel of the Lord had bidden him, and took unto him his wife: and knew her not till she had brought forth her firstborn son: and he called his name JESUS."[209]

The national hope of a Messiah based on promise and prophecy had become confused in the Jewish mind, through the influence of rabbinism with its many vagaries, and its "private interpretation"[210] made to appear authoritative by the artificially sustained prestige of the expositors; yet certain conditions had been emphasized as essential, even by the rabbis, and by these essentials would be judged the claim of any Jew who might declare himself to be the long expected One. It was beyond question that the Messiah was to be born within the tribe of Judah and through the line of descent from David, and, being of David He must of necessity be of the lineage of Abraham, through whose posterity, according to the covenant, all nations of the earth were to be blessed.[211]

Two genealogical records, purporting to give the lineage of Jesus are found in the New Testament, one in the first chapter of Matthew, the other in the third chapter of Luke. These records present several apparent discrepancies, but such have been satisfactorily reconciled by the research of specialists in Jewish genealogy. No detailed analysis of the matter will be attempted here; but it should be borne in mind that the consensus of judgment on the part of investigators is that Matthew's account is that of the royal lineage, establishing the order of sequence among the legal successors to the throne of David, while the account given by Luke is a personal pedigree, demonstrating descent from David without adherence to the line of legal succession to the throne through primogeniture or nearness of kin.[212] Luke's record is regarded by many, however, as the pedigree of Mary, while Matthew's is accepted as that of Joseph. The all important fact to be remembered is that the Child promised by Gabriel to Mary, the virginal bride of Joseph, would be born in the royal line. A personal genealogy of Joseph was essentially that of Mary also, for they were cousins. Joseph is named as son of Jacob by Matthew, and as son of Heli by Luke; but Jacob and Heli were brothers, and it appears that one of the two was the father of Joseph and the other the father of Mary and therefore father-in-law to Joseph. That Mary was of Davidic descent is plainly set forth in many scriptures; for since Jesus was to be born of Mary, yet was not begotten by Joseph, who was the reputed, and, according to the law of the Jews, the legal, father, the blood of David's posterity was given to the body of Jesus through Mary alone. Our Lord, though repeatedly addressed as Son of David, never repudiated the title but accepted it as rightly applied to Himself.[213] Apostolic testimony stands in positive assertion of the royal heirship of Christ through earthly lineage, as witness the affirmation of Paul, the scholarly Pharisee: "Concerning his Son Jesus Christ our Lord, which was made of the seed of David according to the flesh;" and again: "Remember that Jesus Christ of the seed of David was raised from the dead."[214]

In all the persecutions waged by His implacable haters, in all the false accusations brought against Him, in the specific charges of sacrilege and blasphemy based on His acknowledgment of the Messiahship as His own, no mention is found of even an insinuation that He could not be the Christ through any ineligibility based on lineage. Genealogy was assiduously cared for by the Jews before, during, and after the time of Christ; indeed their national history was largely genealogical record; and any possibility of denying the Christ because of unattested descent would have been used to the fullest extent by insistent Pharisee, learned scribe, haughty rabbi, and aristocratic Sadducee.

At the time of the Savior's birth, Israel was ruled by alien monarchs. The rights of the royal Davidic family were unrecognized; and the ruler of the Jews was an appointee of Rome. Had Judah been a free and independent nation, ruled by her rightful sovereign, Joseph the carpenter would have been her crowned king; and his lawful successor to the throne would have been Jesus of Nazareth, the King of the Jews.

Gabriel's annunciation to Mary was that of the Son of David, on whose coming the hope of Israel rested as on a sure foundation. The One, thus announced, was Emmanuel, even God who was to dwell in flesh with His people,[215] the Redeemer of the world, Jesus the Christ.

NOTES TO CHAPTER 7.

1. John the Baptist Regarded as a Nazarite.--The instruction of the angel Gabriel to Zacharias, that the promised son, John, was to "drink neither wine nor strong drink," and the adult life of John as a dweller in the desert, together with his habit of wearing rough garb, have led commentators and Biblical specialists to assume that he was a "Nazarite for life." It is to be remembered, however, that nowhere in scripture extant is John the Baptist definitely called a Nazarite. A Nazarite, the name signifying _consecrated_ or _separated_, was one, who by personal vow or by that made for him by his parents, was set apart to some special labor or course of life involving self denial. (See page 67). Smith's _Comp. Dict, of the Bible_ says: "There is no notice in the Pentateuch of Nazarites for life; but the regulations for the vow of a Nazarite of days are given (Numb. 6:1-2). The Nazarite, during the term of his consecration, was bound to abstain from wine, grapes, and every production of the vine, and from every kind of intoxicating drink. He was forbidden to cut the hair of his head, or to approach any dead body, even that of his nearest relation." The sole instance of a Nazarite for life named in the scriptures is that of Samson, whose mother was required to put herself under Nazarite observances prior to his birth, and the child was to be a Nazarite to God from his birth (Judges 13:3-7, 14). In the strictness of his life, John the Baptist is to be credited with all the personal discipline required of Nazarites whether he was under voluntary or parental vows or was not so bound.

2. Circumcision, while not exclusively a Hebrew or an Israelitish practise, was made a definite requirement through the revelations of God to Abraham, as the sign of the covenant between Jehovah and the patriarch. (Gen. 17:9-14.) This covenant was made to include the establishment of Abraham's posterity as a great nation, and provided that through his descendants should all nations of the earth be blessed (Gen. 22:18)--a promise which has been proved to mean that through that lineage should the Messiah be born. Circumcision was a binding condition; and its practise therefore became a national characteristic. Every male was to be circumcized eight days after birth (Gen. 17:12; Lev. 12:3). This requirement as to age came to be so rigidly enforced, that even if the eighth day fell on a Sabbath the rite had to be performed on that day (John 7:22, 23). All male slaves had to be circumcized (Gen. 17:12, 13) and even strangers who

sojourned with the Hebrews and desired to partake of the Passover with them had to submit to the requirement (Exo. 12:48). From the _Standard Bible Dictionary_ we take the following: "The ceremony indicated the casting off of uncleanness as a preparation for entrance into the privileges of membership in Israel. In the New Testament, with its transfer of emphasis from the external and formal to the inner and spiritual side of things, it was first declared unnecessary for Gentile converts to the gospel to be circumcized (Acts 15:28), and afterward the rite was set aside even by Jewish Christians." It became customary to name a child at the time it was circumcized, as is instanced in the case of John, son of Zacharias (Luke 1:59).

3. Zacharias' Affliction.--The sign for which Zacharias asked was thus given by the angel: "Behold, thou shalt be dumb, and not able to speak, until the day that these things shall be performed, because thou believest not my words, which shall be fulfilled in their season." (Luke 1:20.) From the account of the circumcision and naming of the boy, John, it is held by some that the afflicted father was also deaf, as the company "made signs" to him as to how he would have his son named (verse 62).

4. Jewish Betrothal.--The vow of espousal, or betrothal, has always been regarded as sacred and binding in Jewish law. In a manner it was as binding as a marriage ceremony, though it carried none of the particular rights of marriage. The following succinct statements are taken from Geikie's _Life and Words of Christ_, vol. I. p. 99: "Among the Jews of Mary's day it was even more of an actual engagement [than it later came to be]. The betrothal was formally made with rejoicings in the house of the bride under a tent or slight canopy raised for the purpose. It was called the 'making sacred' as the bride thenceforth was sacred to her husband in the strictest sense. To make it legal, the bridegroom gave his betrothed a piece of money, or the worth of it, before witnesses, with the words, 'Lo, thou art betrothed unto me,' or by a formal writing in which similar words and the maiden's name were given, and this in the same way was handed to her before witnesses."

5. Genealogies of Joseph and Mary.--"It is now almost certain that the genealogies in both Gospels are genealogies of Joseph, which if we may rely on early traditions of their consanguinity involve genealogies of Mary also. The Davidic descent of Mary is implied in Acts 2:30; 13:23; Rom. 1:3; Luke 1:32, etc. St. Matthew gives the legal descent of Joseph through the elder and regal line, as heir to the throne of David; St. Luke gives the natural descent. Thus, the real father of Salathiel was heir of the house of Nathan, but the childless Jeconiah (Jer. 22:30) was the last lineal representative of the elder kingly line. The omission of some obscure names and the symmetrical arrangement, into tesseradecads were common Jewish customs. It is not too much to say that after the labors of Mill (_On the Mythical Interpretation of the Gospels_, pp. 147-217) and Lord A. C. Hervey (_On the Genealogies of Our Lord_, 1853) scarcely a single difficulty remains in reconciling the apparent divergencies. And thus in this as in so many other instances, the very discrepancies which appear to be most irreconcilable, and most fatal to the historic accuracy of the four evangelists, turn out, on closer and more patient investigation, to be fresh proofs that they are not only entirely independent, but also entirely trustworthy."--Farrar, _Life of Christ_, p. 27, note.

The writer of the article "Genealogy of Jesus Christ" in Smith's _Bible Dict_, says: "The New Testament gives us the genealogy of but one person, our Savior (Matt. 1; Luke 3).... The following propositions will explain the true construction of these genealogies (so Lord A. C. Hervey): 1. They are both the genealogies of Joseph, i.e. of Jesus Christ, as the reputed and legal son of Joseph and Mary. 2. The genealogy of Matthew is, as Grotius asserted, Joseph's genealogy as legal successor to the throne of David. That of Luke is Joseph's private genealogy, exhibiting his real birth, as David's son, and thus showing why he was heir to Solomon's crown. The simple principle that one evangelist exhibits that genealogy which contained the successive heirs to David's and Solomon's throne, while the other exhibits the paternal stem of him who was the heir, explains all the anomalies of the two pedigrees, their agreements as well as their discrepancies, and the circumstance of there being two at all. 3. Mary, the mother of Jesus, was probably the daughter of Jacob, and first cousin to Joseph her husband."

A valuable contribution to the literature of this subject appears in the _Journal of the Transactions of the Victoria Institute, or Philosophical Society of Great Britain_, 1912, vol. 44, pp. 9-36, as an article, "The Genealogies of our Lord," by Mrs. A. S. Lewis, and discussion thereof by many scholars of acknowledged ability. The author, Mrs. Lewis, is an authority on Syriac manuscripts, and is one of the two women who, in 1892, discovered in the library of St. Catherine's monastery on Mount Sinai, the Syriac palimpsest MS. of the four Gospels. The gifted author holds that Matthew's account attests the royal pedigree of Joseph, and that Luke's genealogical table proves the equally royal descent of Mary. Mrs. Lewis says: "The Sinai Palimpsest also tells us that Joseph and Mary went to Bethlehem, to be enrolled there, because they were both of the house and lineage of David."

Canon Girdlestone, in discussing the article, says in pertinent emphasis of Mary's status as a princess of royal blood through descent from David: "When the angel was foretelling to Mary the birth of the Holy Child, he said, 'The Lord God shall give Him the throne of His father David.' Now if Joseph, her betrothed, had alone been descended from David, Mary would have answered, 'I am not yet married to Joseph,' whereas she did answer simply, 'I am an unmarried woman,' which plainly implies--if I were married, since I am descended from David, I could infuse my royal blood into a son, but how can I have a royal son while I am a virgin?'"

After brief mention of the Jewish law relating to adoption, wherein it is provided (according to Hammurabi's Code, section 188), that if a man teach his adopted son a handicraft, the son is thereby confirmed in all the rights of heirship, Canon Girdlestone adds: "If the crown of David had been assigned to his successor in the days of Herod it would have been placed on the head of Joseph. And who would have been the legal successor to Joseph? Jesus of Nazareth would have been then the King of the Jews, and the title on the cross spoke the truth. God had raised Him up to the house of David."

6. The Inner Sanctuary of the Temple.--The Holy of Holies in the Temple of Herod retained the

form and dimensions of the Oracle in the Temple of Solomon; it was therefore a cube, twenty cubits in each principal measurement. Between this and the Holy Place hung a double veil, of finest material, elaborately embroidered. The outer of the two veils was open at the north end, the inner at the south; so that the high priest who entered at the appointed time once a year could pass between the veils without exposing the Holy of Holies. The sacred chamber was empty save for a large stone upon which the high priest sprinkled the sacrificial blood on the Day of Atonement; this stone occupied the place of the Ark and its Mercy Seat. Outside the veil, in the Holy Place, stood the altar of incense, the seven-branched candlestick, and the table of shewbread.--_The House of the Lord_, p. 59.

FOOTNOTES:

[186] Luke 1:19, 26; see also Dan. 8:16; 9:21-23.

[187] Luke 1:5; compare 1 Chron. 24:10.

[188] Ezra 2:36-39.

[189] Luke 1:8, 9; read the entire chapter.

[190] Lev. chap. 16; Heb. 9:1-7; see also "House of the Lord," p. 59, and compare pp. 24 and 39. Note 6, end of chapter.

[191] Page 45. For other instances of children promised in spite of barrenness due to age or other causes, see Isaac (Gen. 17:16, 17 and 21:1-3); Samson, (Judges, chap. 13); Samuel (1 Sam. chap. 1); son of the Shunammite (2 Kings 4:14-17).

[192] Note 1, end of chapter.

[193] Luke 1:19, 20.

[194] Luke 1:57; compare verse 39.

[195] Note 2, end of chapter.

[196] Note 3, end of chapter.

[197] Luke 1:68-79.

[198] Luke 1:65, 66; see also 3:15.

[199] Luke 1:80.

[200] Luke 1:28.

[201] Luke 1:30-33.

[202] Luke 1:35; see also preceding verses, 31-33.

[203] Page 43; and Gen. 3:15.

[204] Luke 1:42; read verses 39-56.

[205] Luke 1:46-55.

[206] Note 4, end of chapter.

[207] Matt. 1:20, 21; read 18-25.

[208] Matt. 1:22-23; compare Isa. 7:14; see also 9:6.

[209] Matt. 1:24, 25.

[210] 2 Peter 1:20.

[211] Gen. 12:3; 18:18; 22:18; 26:4; compare Acts 3:25; Gal. 3:8.

[212] Note 5, end of chapter.

[213] For instances see Matt. 9:27; 15:22; 21:9; 20:30, 31, with which compare Luke 18:38, 39.

[214] Rom. 1:3; 2 Tim. 2:8; see also Acts 2:30; 13:23; compare Psa. 132:11; see also Luke 1:32.

[215] Matt. 1:23.

CHAPTER 8. THE BABE OF BETHLEHEM.

THE BIRTH OF JESUS.

Equally definite with the prophecies declaring that the Messiah would be born in the lineage of David are the predictions that fix the place of His birth at Bethlehem, a small town in Judea. There seems to have been no difference of opinion among priests, scribes, or rabbis on the matter, either before or since the great event. Bethlehem, though small and of little importance in trade or commerce, was doubly endeared to the Jewish heart as the birthplace of David and as that of the prospective Messiah. Mary and Joseph lived in Nazareth of Galilee, far removed from Bethlehem of Judea; and, at the time of which we speak, the maternity of the Virgin was fast approaching.

At that time a decree went out from Rome ordering a taxing of the people in all kingdoms and provinces tributary to the empire; the call was of general scope, it provided "that all the world should be taxed."[216] The taxing herein referred to may properly be understood as an enrolment,[217] or a registration, whereby a census of Roman subjects would be secured, upon which as a basis the taxation of the different peoples would be determined. This particular census was the second of three such general registrations recorded by historians as occurring at intervals of about twenty years. Had the census been taken by the usual Roman method, each person would have been enrolled at the town of his residence; but the Jewish custom, for which the Roman law had respect, necessitated registration at the cities or towns claimed by the respective families as their ancestral homes. As to whether the requirement was strictly mandatory that every family should thus register at the city of its ancestors, we need not be specially concerned; certain it is that Joseph and Mary went to Bethlehem, the city of David, to be inscribed under the imperial decree.[218]

The little town was crowded at the time, most likely by the multitude that had come in obedience to the same summons; and, in consequence, Joseph and Mary failed to find the most desirable accommodations and had to be content with the conditions of an improvised camp, as travelers unnumbered had done before, and as uncounted others have done since, in that region and elsewhere. We cannot reasonably regard this circumstance as evidence of extreme destitution; doubtless it entailed inconvenience, but it gives us no assurance of great distress or suffering.[219] It was while she was in this situation that Mary the Virgin gave birth to her firstborn, the Son of the Highest, the Only Begotten of the Eternal Father, Jesus the Christ.

But few details of attendant circumstances are furnished us. We are not told how soon the birth occurred after the arrival of Mary and her husband at Bethlehem. It may have been the purpose of the evangelist who made the record to touch upon matters of purely human interest as lightly as was consistent with the narration of fact, in order that the central truth might neither be hidden nor overshadowed by unimportant incident. We read in Holy Writ this only of the actual birth: "And so it was, that, while they were there, the days were accomplished that she should be delivered. And she brought forth her firstborn son, and wrapped him in swaddling clothes, and laid him in a manger; became there was no room for them at the inn."[220]

In vivid contrast with the simplicity and brevity of the scriptural account and of its paucity of incidental details, is the mass of circumstance supplied by the imagination of men, much of which is wholly unsupported by authoritative record and in many respects is plainly inconsistent and untrue. It is the part of prudence and wisdom to segregate and keep distinctly separate the authenticated statements of fact, in so momentous a matter, from the fanciful commentaries of historians, theologians, and writers of fiction, as also from the emotional rhapsodies of poets and artistic extravaganzas wrought by chisel or brush.

From the period of its beginning, Bethlehem had been the home of people engaged mostly in pastoral and agricultural pursuits. It is quite in line with what is known of the town and its environs to find at the season of Messiah's birth, which was in the springtime of the year, that flocks were in the field both night and day under the watchful care of their keepers. Unto certain of these humble shepherds came the first proclamation that the Savior had been born. Thus runs the simple record: "And there were in the same country shepherds abiding in the field, keeping watch over their flock by night. And, lo, the angel of the Lord came upon them, and the glory of the Lord shone round about them: and they were sore afraid. And the angel said unto them, Fear not: for, behold, I bring you good tidings of great joy, which shall be to all people. For unto you is born this day in the city of David a Saviour, which is Christ the Lord. And this shall be a sign unto you: Ye shall find the babe wrapped in swaddling clothes, lying in a manger. And suddenly there was with the angel a multitude of the heavenly host praising God, and saying, Glory to God in the highest, and on earth peace, good will toward men."[221]

Tidings of such import had never before been delivered by angel or received by man--good tidings of great joy, given to but few and those among the humblest of earth, but destined to spread to all people. There is sublime grandeur in the scene, as there is divine authorship in the message, and the climax is such as the mind of man could never have conceived--the sudden appearance of a multitude of the heavenly host, singing audibly to human ears the briefest, most consistent and most truly complete of all the songs of peace ever attuned by mortal or spirit choir. What a consummation to be wished--Peace on earth! But how can such come except through the maintenance of good will toward men? And through what means could glory to God in the highest be more effectively rendered?

The trustful and unsophisticated keepers of sheep had not asked for sign or confirmation; their faith was in unison with the heavenly communication; nevertheless the angel had given them what he called a sign, to guide them in their search. They waited not, but went in haste, for in their hearts they believed, yea, more than believed, they knew, and this was the tenor of their resolve: "Let us now go even unto

Bethlehem, and see this thing which is come to pass, which the Lord hath made known unto us."[222] They found the Babe in the manger, with the mother and Joseph near by; and, having seen, they went out and testified to the truth concerning the Child. They returned to their flocks, glorifying and praising God for all they had heard and seen.

There is meaning as deep as the pathos that all must feel in the seemingly parenthetical remark by Luke. "But Mary kept all these things, and pondered them in her heart."[223] It is apparent that the great truth as to the personality and mission of her divine Son had not yet unfolded itself in its fulness to her mind. The whole course of events, from the salutation of Gabriel to the reverent testimony of the shepherds concerning the announcing angel and the heavenly hosts, was largely a mystery to that stainless mother and wife.

REQUIREMENTS OF THE LAW STRICTLY OBSERVED.

The Child was born a Jew; the mother was a Jewess, and the reputed and legal father, Joseph, was a Jew. The true paternity of the Child was known to but few, perhaps at that time to none save Mary, Joseph, and possibly Elisabeth and Zacharias; as He grew He was regarded by the people as Joseph's son. [224] The requirements of the law were carried out with exactitude in all matters pertaining to the Child. When eight days old He was circumcized, as was required of every male born in Israel;[225] and at the same time He received as an earthly bestowal the name that had been prescribed at the annunciation. He was called JESUS, which, being interpreted is Savior; the name was rightfully His for He came to save the people from their sins.[226]

Part of the law given through Moses to the Israelites in the wilderness and continued in force down through the centuries, related to the procedure prescribed for women after childbirth.[227] In compliance therewith, Mary remained in retirement forty days following the birth of her Son; then she and her husband brought the Boy for presentation before the Lord as prescribed for the male firstborn of every family. It is manifestly impossible that all such presentations could have taken place in the temple, for many Jews lived at great distances from Jerusalem; it was the rule, however, that parents should present their children in the temple when possible. Jesus was born within five or six miles from Jerusalem; He was accordingly taken to the temple for the ceremonial of redemption from the requirement applying to the firstborn of all Israelites except Levites. It will be remembered that the children of Israel had been delivered from the bondage of Egypt with the accompaniment of signs and wonders. Because of Pharaoh's repeated refusals to let the people go, plagues had been brought upon the Egyptians, one of which was the death of the firstborn throughout the land, excepting only the people of Israel. In remembrance of this manifestation of power, the Israelites were required to dedicate their firstborn sons to the service of the sanctuary.[228] Subsequently the Lord directed that all males belonging to the tribe of Levi should be devoted to this special labor instead of the firstborn in every tribe; nevertheless the eldest son was still claimed as particularly the Lord's own, and had to be formally exempted from the earlier requirement of service by the paying of a ransom.[229]

In connection with the ceremony of purification, every mother was required to furnish a yearling lamb for a burnt offering, and a young pigeon or dove for a sin offering; but in the case of any woman who was unable to provide a lamb, a pair of doves or pigeons might be offered. We learn of the humble circumstances of Joseph and Mary from the fact that they brought the less costly offering, two doves or pigeons, instead of one bird and a lamb.

Among the righteous and devout Israelites were some who, in spite of traditionalism, rabbinism, and priestly corruption, still lived in righteous expectation of inspired confidence, awaiting patiently the consolation of Israel.[230] One of these was Simeon, then living in Jerusalem. Through the power of the Holy Ghost he had gained the promise that he should not see death until he had looked upon the Lord's Christ in the flesh. Prompted by the Spirit he repaired to the temple on the day of the presentation of Jesus, and recognized in the Babe the promised Messiah. In the moment of realization that the hope of his life had found glorious consummation, Simeon raised the Child reverently in his arms, and, with the simple but undying eloquence that comes of God uttered this splendid supplication, in which thanksgiving, resignation and praise are so richly blended:

"Lord, now lettest thou thy servant depart in peace, according   to thy word: for mine eyes have seen thy salvation, which thou   hast prepared before the face of all people; a light to lighten   the Gentiles, and the glory of thy people Israel."[231]

Then under the spirit of prophecy, Simeon told of the greatness of the Child's mission, and of the anguish that the mother would be called to endure because of Him, which would be even like unto that of a sword piercing her soul. The Spirit's witness to the divinity of Jesus was not to be confined to a man. There was at that time in the temple a godly woman of great age, Anna, a prophetess who devoted herself exclusively to temple service; and she, being inspired of God, recognized her Redeemer, and testified of Him to all about her. Both Joseph and Mary marveled at the things that were spoken of the Child; seemingly they were not yet able to comprehend the majesty of Him who had come to them through so miraculous a conception and so marvelous a birth.

WISE MEN SEARCH FOR THE KING.

Some time after the presentation of Jesus in the temple, though how long we are not told, possibly but a few days, possibly weeks or even months, Herod, king of Judea, was greatly troubled, as were the people of Jerusalem in general, over the report that a Child of Prophecy--one destined to become King of the Jews--had been born. Herod was professedly an adherent of the religion of Judah, though by birth an Idumean, by descent an Edomite or one of the posterity of Esau, all of whom the Jews hated; and of all Edomites not one was more bitterly detested than was Herod the king. He was tyrannical and merciless, sparing neither foe nor friend who came under suspicion of being a possible hindrance to his ambitious designs. He had his wife and several of his sons, as well as others of his blood kindred, cruelly murdered; and he put to death nearly all of the great national council, the Sanhedrin. His reign was one of revolting cruelty and unbridled oppression. Only when in danger of inciting a national revolt or in fear of incurring the displeasure of his imperial master, the Roman emperor, did he stay his hand in any undertaking.[232]

Rumors of the birth of Jesus reached Herod's ears in this way. There came to Jerusalem certain men from afar, wise men they were called, and they asked, "Where is he that is born King of the Jews? for we have seen his star in the east, and are come to worship him."[233] Herod summoned "all the chief priests and scribes of the people," and demanded of them where, according to the prophets, Christ should be born. They answered him: "In Bethlehem of Judea: for thus it is written by the prophet, And thou Bethlehem, in the land of Juda, art not the least among the princes of Juda: for out of thee shall come a Governor, that shall rule my people Israel."[234]

Herod sent secretly for the wise men, and inquired of them as to the source of their information, and particularly as to the time at which the star, to which they attached such significance, had appeared. Then he directed them to Bethlehem, saying: "Go and search diligently for the young child; and when ye have found him, bring me word again, that I may come and worship him also." As the men set out from Jerusalem on the last stage of their journey of inquiry and search, they rejoiced exceedingly, for the new star they had seen in the east was again visible. They found the house wherein Mary was living with her husband and the Babe, and as they recognized the royal Child they "fell down, and worshipped him: and when they had opened their treasures, they presented unto him gifts; gold, and frankincense, and myrrh."[235] Having thus gloriously accomplished the purpose of their pilgrimage, these devout and learned travelers prepared to return home, and would have stopped at Jerusalem to report to the king as he had requested, but "being warned of God in a dream that they should not return to Herod, they departed into their own country another way."[236]

Much has been written, beyond all possible warrant of scriptural authority, concerning the visit of the magi, or wise men, who thus sought and found the infant Christ. As a matter of fact, we are left without information as to their country, nation, or tribal relationship; we are not even told how many they were, though unauthenticated tradition has designated them as "the three wise men," and has even given them names; whereas they are left unnamed in the scriptures, the only true record of them extant, and may have numbered but two or many. Attempts have been made to identify the star whose appearance in their eastern sky had assured the magi that the King was born; but astronomy furnishes no satisfactory confirmation. The recorded appearance of the star has been associated by both ancient and modern interpreters with the prophecy of Balaam, who, though not an Israelite had blessed Israel, and under divine inspiration had predicted: "there shall come a Star out of Jacob, and a Sceptre shall rise out of Israel."[237] Moreover, as already shown, the appearance of a new star was a predicted sign recognized and acknowledged among the people of the western world as witness of Messiah's birth.[238]

THE FLIGHT INTO EGYPT.

Herod's perfidy in directing the magi to return and report to him where the royal Infant was to be found, falsely professing that he wished to worship Him also, while in his heart he purposed taking the Child's life, was thwarted by the divine warning given to the wise men as already noted. Following their departure, the angel of the Lord appeared to Joseph, saying: "Arise, and take the young child and his mother, and flee into Egypt, and be thou there until I bring thee word: for Herod will seek the young child to destroy him."[239] In obedience to this command, Joseph took Mary and her Child, and set out by night on the journey to Egypt; and there the family remained until divinely directed to return. When it was apparent to the king that the wise men had ignored his instructions, he was exceedingly angry; and, estimating the earliest time at which the birth could have occurred according to the magis' statement of the star's appearing, he ruthlessly ordered the slaughter of "all the children that were in Bethlehem, and in all the coasts thereof, from two years old and under."[240] In this massacre of the innocents, the evangelist found a fulfilment of Jeremiah's fateful voicing of the word of the Lord, spoken six centuries earlier and expressed in the forceful past tense as though then already accomplished: "In Rama was there a voice heard, lamentation, and weeping, and great mourning, Rachel weeping for her children, and would not be comforted, because they are not."[241]

BIRTH OF JESUS MADE KNOWN TO THE NEPHITES.

As heretofore shown, the prophets of the western hemisphere had foretold in great plainness the earthly advent of the Lord, and had specifically set forth the time, place, and circumstances of His birth. [242] As the time drew near the people were divided by conflicting opinions concerning the reliability of these prophecies; and intolerant unbelievers cruelly persecuted those, who, like Zacharias, Simeon, Anna, and other righteous ones in Palestine, had maintained in faith and trust their unwavering expectation of the coming of the Lord. Samuel, a righteous Lamanite, who, because of his faithfulness and sacrificing devotion had been blessed with the spirit and power of prophecy, fearlessly proclaimed the birth of Christ as near: "And behold, he said unto them, Behold I give unto you a sign; for five years more cometh, and behold, then cometh the Son of God to redeem all those who shall believe on his name."[243] The prophet told of many signs and wonders, which were to mark the great event. As the five years ran their course, the believers grew more steadfast, the unbelievers more violent, until the last day of the specified period dawned; and this was the "day set apart by the unbelievers, that all those who believed in those traditions should be put to death, except the sign should come to pass which had been given by Samuel the prophet."[244]

Nephi, a prophet of the time, cried unto the Lord in anguish of soul because of the persecution of which his people were the victims; "and behold, the voice of the Lord came unto him, saying, Lift up your head and be of good cheer, for behold, the time is at hand, and on this night shall the sign be given, and on the morrow come I into the world, to shew unto the world that I will fulfil all that which I have caused to be spoken by the mouth of my holy prophets. Behold, I come unto my own, to fulfil all things which I have made known unto the children of men, from the foundation of the world, and do the will, both of the Father, and of the Son; of the Father, because of me, and of the Son, because of my flesh. And behold, the time is at hand, and this night shall the sign be given."[245]

The words of the prophet were fulfilled that night; for though the sun set in its usual course there was no darkness; and on the morrow the sun rose on a land already illumined; a day and a night and another day had been as one day; and this was but one of the signs. A new star appeared in the firmament of the west, even as was seen by the magi in the east; and there were many other marvelous manifestations as the prophets had predicted. All these things occurred on what is now known as the American continent, six hundred years after Lehi and his little company had left Jerusalem to come hither.

THE TIME OF THE BIRTH OF JESUS.

The time of Messiah's birth is a subject upon which specialists in theology and history, and those who are designated in literature "the learned," fail to agree. Numerous lines of investigation have been followed, only to reach divergent conclusions, both as to the year and as to the month and day within the year at which the "Christian era" in reality began. The establishment of the birth of Christ as an event marking a time from which chronological data should be calculated, was first effected about 532 A.D. by Dionysius Exiguus; and as a basis for the reckoning of time this method has come to be known as the Dionysian system, and takes for its fundamental datum A.U.C. 753, that is to say 753 years after the founding of Rome, as the year of our Lord's birth. So far as there exists any consensus of opinion among later scholars who have investigated the subject, it is to the effect that the Dionysian calculation is wrong, in that it places the birth of Christ between three and four years too late; and that therefore our Lord was born in the third or fourth year before the beginning of what is designated by the scholars of Oxford and Cambridge, "the Common Account called Anno Domini."[246]

Without attempting to analyze the mass of calculation data relating to this subject, we accept the Dionysian basis as correct with respect to the year, which is to say that we believe Christ to have been born in the year known to us as B.C. 1, and, as shall be shown, in an early month of that year. In support of this belief we cite the inspired record known as the "Revelation on Church Government, given through Joseph the Prophet, in April, 1830," which opens with these words: "The rise of the Church of Christ in these last days, being one thousand eight hundred and thirty years since the coming of our Lord and Saviour Jesus Christ in the flesh."[247]

Another evidence of the correctness of our commonly accepted chronology is furnished by the Book of Mormon record. Therein we read that "in the commencement of the first year of the reign of Zedekiah, king of Judah," the word of the Lord came to Lehi at Jerusalem, directing him to take his family and depart into the wilderness.[248] In the early stages of their journey toward the sea, Lehi prophesied, as had been shown him of the Lord, concerning the impending destruction of Jerusalem and the captivity of the Jews. Furthermore, he predicted the eventual return of the people of Judah from their exile in Babylon, and the birth of the Messiah, which latter event he definitely declared would take place six hundred years from the time he and his people had left Jerusalem.[249] This specification of time was repeated by later prophecy;[250] and the signs of the actual fulfilment are recorded as having been realized "six hundred years from the time that Lehi left Jerusalem."[251] These scriptures fix the time of the beginning of Zedekiah's reign as six hundred years before the birth of Christ. According to the commonly accepted reckoning, Zedekiah was made king in the year 597 B.C.[252] This shows a discrepancy of about three years between the commonly accepted date of Zedekiah's inauguration as king and that given in the Book of Mormon statement; and, as already seen, there is a difference of between three and four years between the Dionysian reckoning and the nearest approach to an agreement among scholars concerning the beginning of the current era. Book of Mormon chronology therefore sustains in general the correctness of the common or Dionysian system.

As to the season of the year in which Christ was born, there is among the learned as great a diversity of opinion as that relating to the year itself. It is claimed by many Biblical scholars that December 25th, the day celebrated in Christendom as Christmas, cannot be the correct date. We believe April 6th to be the birthday of Jesus Christ as indicated in a revelation of the present dispensation already cited,[253] in which that day is made without qualification the completion of the one thousand eight hundred and thirtieth year since the coming of the Lord in the flesh. This acceptance is admittedly based on faith in modern revelation, and in no wise is set forth as the result of chronological research or analysis. We believe that Jesus Christ was born in Bethlehem of Judea, April 6, B.C. 1.

NOTES TO CHAPTER 8.

1. The "Taxing."--Regarding the presence of Joseph and Mary in Bethlehem, far from their

Galilean home, and the imperial decree by compliance with which they were led there, the following notes are worthy of consideration. Farrar (_Life of Christ_, p. 24, note), says: "It appears to be uncertain whether the journey of Mary with her husband was obligatory or voluntary.... Women were liable to a capitation tax, if this enrolment also involved taxation. But, apart from any legal necessity, it may easily be imagined that at such a moment Mary would desire not to be left alone. The cruel suspicion of which she had been the subject, and which had almost led to the breaking off of her betrothal (Matt. 1:19) would make her cling all the more to the protection of her husband." The following excerpt is from Geikie's _Life and Words of Christ_, vol. 1, chap. 9; p. 108: "The Jewish nation had paid tribute to Rome through their rulers, since the days of Pompey; and the methodical Augustus, who now reigned, and had to restore order and soundness to the finances of the empire, after the confusion and exhaustion of the civil wars, took good care that this obligation should neither be forgotten nor evaded. He was accustomed to require a census to be taken periodically in every province of his vast dominions, that he might know the number of soldiers he could levy in each, and the amount of taxes due to the treasury.... In an empire embracing the then known world, such a census could hardly have been made simultaneously, or in any short or fixed time; more probably it was the work of years, in successive provinces or kingdoms. Sooner or later, however, even the dominions of vassal kings like Herod had to furnish the statistics demanded by their master. He had received his kingdom on the footing of a subject, and grew more entirely dependent on Augustus as years passed, asking his sanction at every turn for steps he proposed to take. He would, thus, be only too ready to meet his wish, by obtaining the statistics he sought, as may be judged from the fact that in one of the last years of his life, just before Christ's birth, he made the whole Jewish nation take a solemn oath of allegiance to the emperor as well as to himself.

"It is quite probable that the mode of taking the required statistics was left very much to Herod, at once to show respect to him before his people, and from the known opposition of the Jews to anything like a general numeration, even apart from the taxation to which it was designed to lead. At the time to which the narrative refers, a simple registration seems to have been made, on the old Hebrew plan of enrolling by families in their ancestral districts, of course for future use; and thus it passed over quietly.... The proclamation having been made through the land, Joseph had no choice but to go to Bethlehem, the city of David, the place in which his family descent, from the house and lineage of David, required him to be inscribed."

2. Jesus Born Amidst Poor Surroundings.--Undoubtedly the accommodations for physical comfort amidst which Jesus was born were few and poor. But the environment, considered in the light of the customs of the country and time, was far from the state of abject deprivation which modern and western ways would make it appear. "Camping out" was no unusual exigency among travelers in Palestine at the time of our Lord's birth; nor is it considered such to-day. It is, however, beyond question that Jesus was born into a comparatively poor family, amidst humble surroundings associated with the inconveniences incident to travel. Cunningham Geikie, _Life and Words of Christ_, chap. 9, pp. 112, 113, says: "It was to Bethlehem that Joseph and Mary were coming, the town of Ruth and Boaz, and the early home of their own great forefather David. As they approached it from Jerusalem they would pass, at the last mile, a spot sacred to Jewish memory, where the light of Jacob's life went out, when his first love, Rachel, died, and was buried, as her tomb still shows, 'in the way to Ephrath, which is Bethlehem.' ... Traveling in the East has always been very different from Western ideas. As in all thinly-settled countries, private hospitality, in early times, supplied the want of inns, but it was the peculiarity of the East that this friendly custom continued through a long series of ages. On the great roads through barren or uninhabited parts, the need of shelter led, very early, to the erection of rude and simple buildings, of varying size, known as khans, which offered the wayfarer the protection of walls and a roof, and water, but little more. The smaller structures consisted of sometimes only a single empty room, on the floor of which the traveler might spread his carpet for sleep; the larger ones, always built in a hollow square, enclosing a court for the beasts, with water in it for them and their masters. From immemorial antiquity it has been a favorite mode of benevolence to raise such places of shelter, as we see so far back as the times of David, when Chimham built a great khan near Bethlehem, on the caravan road to Egypt."

Canon Farrar (_Life of Christ_, chap, 1) accepts the traditional belief that the shelter within which Jesus was born was that of one of the numerous limestone caves which abound in the region, and which are still used by travelers as resting places. He says: "In Palestine it not infrequently happens that the entire khan, or at any rate the portion of it in which the animals are housed, is one of those innumerable caves which abound in the limestone rocks of its central hills. Such seems to have been in the case at the little town of Bethlehem-Ephratah, in the land of Judah. Justin Martyr, the Apologist, who, from his birth at Shechem, was familiar with Palestine, and who lived less than a century after the time of our Lord, places the scene of the nativity in a cave. This is, indeed, the ancient and constant tradition both of the Eastern and the Western Churches, and it is one of the few to which, though unrecorded in the Gospel history, we may attach a reasonable probability."

3. Herod the Great.--The history of Herod I, otherwise known as Herod the Great, must be sought in special works, in which the subject is treated at length. Some of the principal facts should be considered in our present study, and for the assistance of the student a few extracts from works regarded as reliable are presented herewith.

Condensed from part of article in the _Standard Bible Dictionary_, edited by Jacobus, Nourse, and Zenos; published by Funk and Wagnalls Co., 1909:--Herod I, the son of Antipater, was early given office by his father, who had been made procurator of Judea. The first office which Herod held was that of governor of Galilee. He was then a young man of about twenty-five, energetic and athletic. Immediately he set about the eradication of the robber bands that infested his district, and soon was able to execute the robber chief Hezekiah and several of his followers. For this he was summoned to Jerusalem by the Sanhedrin, tried and condemned, but with the connivance of Hyrcanus II [the high priest and ethnarch] he escaped by night.--He went to Rome where he was appointed King of Judea by Antony and Octavius.--For the next two years he was engaged in fighting the forces of Antigonus, whom he finally defeated, and in 37 B.C. gained possession of Jerusalem.--As king, Herod confronted serious difficulties. The Jews objected to him because of his birth and reputation. The Asmonean family regarded him as a usurper, notwithstanding the fact that he had married Mariamne. The Pharisees were shocked at his Hellenistic sympathies, as well as at his severe methods of government. On the other hand the Romans held him responsible for the order of his kingdom, and the protection of the eastern frontier of the Republic. Herod met these various difficulties with characteristic energy and even cruelty, and generally with cold sagacity. Although he taxed the people severely, in times of famine he remitted their dues and even sold his plate to get means to buy them food. While he never became actually friendly with the Pharisees, they profited by his hostility to the party of the Asmoneans, which led at the beginning of his reign to the execution of a number of Sadducees who were members of the Sanhedrin.

From Smith's _Comprehensive Dictionary of the Bible_: The latter part "of the reign of Herod was undisturbed by external troubles, but his domestic life was embittered by an almost uninterrupted series of injuries and cruel acts of vengeance. The terrible acts of bloodshed which Herod perpetrated in his own family were accompanied by others among his subjects equally terrible, from the number who fell victims to them. According to the well-known story, he ordered the nobles whom he had called to him in his last moments to be executed immediately after his decease, that so at least his death might be attended by universal mourning. It was at the time of his fatal illness that he must have caused the slaughter of the infants at Bethlehem" (Matt. 2:16-18).

The mortal end of the tyrant and multi-murderer is thus treated by Farrar in his _Life of Christ_, pp. 54, 55:--"It must have been very shortly after the murder of the innocents that Herod died. Only five days before his death he had made a frantic attempt at suicide, and had ordered the execution of his eldest son Antipater. His death-bed, which once more reminds us of Henry VIII., was accompanied by circumstances of peculiar horror; and it has been asserted that he died of a loathsome disease, which is hardly mentioned in history, except in the case of men who have been rendered infamous by an atrocity of persecuting zeal. On his bed of intolerable anguish, in that splendid and luxurious palace which he had built for himself, under the palms of Jericho, swollen with disease and scorched by thirst, ulcerated externally and glowing inwardly with a 'soft slow fire,' surrounded by plotting sons and plundering slaves, detesting all and detested by all, longing for death as a release from his tortures yet dreading it as the beginning of worse terrors, stung by remorse yet still unslaked with murder, a horror to all around him yet in his guilty conscience a worse terror to himself, devoured by the premature corruption of an anticipated grave, eaten of worms as though visibly smitten by the finger of God's wrath after seventy years of successful villainy, the wretched old man, whom men had called the Great, lay in savage frenzy awaiting his last hour. As he knew that none would shed one tear for him, he determined that they should shed many for themselves, and issued an order that, under pain of death, the principal families of the kingdom and the chiefs of the tribes should come to Jericho. They came, and then, shutting them in the hippodrome, he secretly commanded his sister Salome that at the moment of his death they should all be massacred. And so, choking as it were with blood, devising massacres in its very delirium, the soul of Herod passed forth into the night."

For mention of the Temple of Herod see Note 5, following Chapter 6.

4. Gifts from the Wise Men to the Child Jesus.--The scriptural account of the visit of the wise men to Jesus and His mother states that they "fell down and worshipped him," and furthermore that "when they had opened their treasures, they presented unto him gifts; gold, and frankincense, and myrrh." The offering of gifts to a superior in rank, either as to worldly status or recognized spiritual endowment, was a custom of early days and still prevails in many oriental lands. It is worthy of note that we have no record of these men from the east offering gifts to Herod in his palace; they did, however, impart of their treasure to the lowly Infant, in whom they recognized the King they had come to seek. The tendency to ascribe occult significance to even trifling details mentioned in scripture, and particularly as regards the life of Christ, has led to many fanciful suggestions concerning the gold and frankincense and myrrh specified in this incident. Some have supposed a half-hidden symbolism therein--gold a tribute to His royal estate, frankincense an offering in recognition of His priesthood, and myrrh for His burial. The sacred record offers no basis for such conjecture. Myrrh and frankincense are aromatic resins derived from plants indigenous to eastern lands, and they have been used from very early times in medicine and in the preparation of perfumes and incense mixtures. They were presumably among the natural productions of the lands from which the magi came, though probably even there they were costly and highly esteemed. Such, together with gold, which is of value among all nations, were most appropriate as gifts for a king. Any mystical significance one may choose to attach to the presents must be remembered as his own supposition or fancy, and not as based on scriptural warrant.

5. Testimonies from Shepherds and Magi.--The following instructive note on the testimonies relating to Messiah's birth, is taken from the _Young Men's Mutual Improvement Association Manual_ for 1897-8: "It will be observed that the testimonies concerning the birth of the Messiah are from two extremes, the lowly shepherds in the Judean field, and the learned magi from the far east. We cannot think this is the result of mere chance, but that in it may be discerned the purpose and wisdom of God. All Israel was looking forward to the coming of the Messiah, and in the birth of Jesus at Bethlehem, the hope of Israel-- though unknown to Israel--is fulfilled. Messiah, of whom the prophet spake, is born. But there must be those who can testify of that truth, and hence to the shepherds who watched their flocks by night an angel

was sent to say: 'Fear not, behold I bring you good tidings of great joy, which shall be to all people; for unto you is born this day, in the city of David, a Saviour, which is Christ, the Lord.' And for a sign of the truth of the message, they were to find the child wrapped in swaddling clothes, lying in a manger in Bethlehem. And they went with haste and found Mary and Joseph, and the babe lying in a manger; and when they had seen it, they made known abroad the saying which was told them concerning this child. God had raised up to Himself witnesses among the people to testify that Messiah was born, that the hope of Israel was fulfilled. But there were classes of people among the Jews whom these lowly shepherd witnesses could not reach, and had they been able to reach them, the story of the angel's visit, and the concourse of angels singing the magnificent song of 'Peace on earth, good will to men,' would doubtless have been accounted an idle tale of superstitious folk, deceived by their own over-wrought imaginations or idle dreams. Hence God raised up another class of witnesses--the 'wise men from the east'--witnesses that could enter the royal palace of proud King Herod and boldly ask: 'Where is he that is born king of the Jews? for we have seen his star in the east, and are come to worship him'; a testimony that startled Herod and troubled all Jerusalem. So that indeed God raised up witnesses for Himself to meet all classes and conditions of men--the testimony of angels for the poor and the lowly; the testimony of wise men for the haughty king and proud priests of Judea. So that of the things concerning the birth of Messiah, no less than of the things of His death and resurrection from the dead, His disciples could say, 'these things were not done in a corner.'"

6. The Year of Christ's Birth.--In treating this topic Dr. Charles F. Deems (_The Light of the Nations_, p. 28), after giving careful consideration of the estimates, calculations, and assumptions of men who have employed many means in their investigation and reach only discordant results says: "It is annoying to see learned men use the same apparatus of calculation and reach the most diverse results. It is bewildering to attempt a reconciliation of these varying calculations." In an appended note the same author states: "For example: the birth of our Lord is placed in B.C. 1 by Pearson and Hug; B.C. 2 by Scalinger; B.C. 3 by Baronius and Paulus; B.C. 4 by Bengel, Wieseler, and Greswell; B.C. 5 by Usher and Petavius; B.C. 6 by Strong, Luvin, and Clark; B.C. 7 by Ideler and Sanclemente."

FOOTNOTES:

[216] Luke 2:1; see also verses 2-4. Note 1, end of chapter.
[217] Note marginal reading, Oxford and Bagster Bibles.
[218] Note 1, end of chapter.
[219] Note 2, end of chapter.
[220] Luke 2:6, 7.
[221] Luke 2:8-14.
[222] Luke 2:15.
[223] Luke 2:19.
[224] Luke 4:22; Matt. 13:55; Mark 6:3.
[225] Gen. 17:12, 13; Lev. 12:3; compare John 7:22. Page 88.
[226] Luke 2:21; compare 1:31; Matt. 1:21, 25.
[227] Lev. chap. 12.
[228] Exo. 12:29; 13:2, 12; 22:29, 30.
[229] Numb. 8:15-18; 18:15, 16.
[230] Luke 2:25; see also verse 38; Mark 15:43; compare Psa. 40:1.
[231] Luke 2:29-32. These verses are known in Christian hymnology as the Nunc Dimittis; the name has reference to the first two words of the Latin version.
[232] Note 3, end of chapter.
[233] Matt. 2:2; read 1-10.
[234] Matt. 2:5, 6; compare Micah 5:2; John 7:42.
[235] Note 4, end of chapter.
[236] Note 5, end of chapter.
[237] Numb. 24:17.
[238] B. of M., Helaman 14:5; 3 Nephi 1:21. Pp. 52, 101 and 721 herein.
[239] Matt. 2:13.
[240] Matt. 2:16.
[241] Matt. 2:17, 18; compare Jer. 31:15.
[242] Page 49.
[243] B. of M., Helaman 14:2; read 1-9.
[244] B. of M., 3 Nephi 1:9; read verses 4-21.
[245] B. of M., 3 Nephi 1:12-21.
[246] Marginal reading, Oxford and Bagster Bibles, Matt. 2:1.
[247] Doc. and Cov. 20:1; compare 21:3. Note 6, end of chapter.
[248] B. of M., 1 Nephi 1:4; 2:2-4.
[249] B. of M., 1 Nephi 10:4.
[250] B. of M., 1 Nephi 19:8; 2 Nephi 25:19.
[251] B. of M., 3 Nephi 1:1.
[252] "Standard Bible Dictionary," edited by Jacobus, Nourse, and Zenos, pub. by Funk & Wagnalls Co., New York and London, 1909, p. 915, article "Zedekiah."
[253] Doc. and Cov. 20:1; compare 21:2

CHAPTER 9. THE BOY OF NAZARETH.

Joseph, Mary, and her Son remained in Egypt until after the death of Herod the Great, which event was made known by another angelic visitation. Their stay in the foreign land was probably brief, for Herod did not long survive the babes he had slain in Bethlehem. In the return of the family from Egypt the evangelist finds a fulfilment of Hosea's prophetic vision of what should be: "Out of Egypt have I called my son."[254]

It appears to have been Joseph's intention to make a home for the family in Judea, possibly at Bethlehem--the city of his ancestors and a place now even more endeared to him as the birthplace of Mary's Child--but, learning on the way that Herod's son Archelaus ruled in the place of his wicked father, Joseph modified his purpose; and, "being warned of God in a dream, he turned aside into the parts of Galilee: and he came and dwelt in a city called Nazareth: that it might be fulfilled which was spoken by the prophets, He shall be called a Nazarene."[255]

While Archelaus, who appears to have been a natural heir to his infamous father's wickedness and cruelty, ruled in Judea,[256] for a short time as king, then with the less exalted title of ethnarch, which had been decreed to him by the emperor, his brother Antipas governed as tetrarch in Galilee. Herod Antipas was well nigh as vicious and reprobate as others of his unprincipled family, but he was less aggressive in vindictiveness, and in that period of his reign was comparatively tolerant.[257]

Concerning the home life of Joseph and his family in Nazareth, the scriptural record makes but brief mention. The silence with which the early period of the life of Jesus is treated by the inspired historians is impressive; while the fanciful accounts written in later years by unauthorized hands are full of fictitious detail, much of which is positively revolting in its puerile inconsistency. None but Joseph, Mary, and the other members of the immediate family or close associates of the household could have furnished the facts of daily life in the humble home at Nazareth; and from these qualified informants Matthew and Luke probably derived the knowledge of which they wrote. The record made by those who knew is marked by impressive brevity. In this absence of detail we may see evidence of the genuineness of the scriptural account. Inventive writers would have supplied, as, later, such did supply, what we seek in vain within the chapters of the Gospels. With hallowed silence do the inspired scribes honor the boyhood of their Lord; he who seeks to invent circumstances and to invest the life of Christ with fictitious additions, dishonors Him. Read thoughtfully the attested truth concerning the childhood of the Christ: "And the child grew, and waxed strong in spirit, filled with wisdom: and the grace of God was upon him."[258]

In such simplicity is the normal, natural development of the Boy Jesus made clear. He came among men to experience all the natural conditions of mortality; He was born as truly a dependent, helpless babe as is any other child; His infancy was in all common features as the infancy of others; His boyhood was actual boyhood, His development was as necessary and as real as that of all children. Over His mind had fallen the veil of forgetfulness common to all who are born to earth, by which the remembrance of primeval existence is shut off. The Child grew, and with growth there came to Him expansion of mind, development of faculties, and progression in power and understanding. His advancement was from one grace to another, not from gracelessness to grace; from good to greater good, not from evil to good; from favor with God to greater favor, not from estrangement because of sin to reconciliation through repentance and propitiation.[259]

Our knowledge of Jewish life in that age justifies the inference that the Boy was well taught in the law and the scriptures, for such was the rule. He garnered knowledge by study, and gained wisdom by prayer, thought, and effort. Beyond question He was trained to labor, for idleness was abhorred then as it is now; and every Jewish boy, whether carpenter's son, peasant's child, or rabbi's heir, was required to learn and follow a practical and productive vocation. Jesus was all that a boy should be, for His development was unretarded by the dragging weight of sin; He loved and obeyed the truth and therefore was free.[260]

Joseph and Mary, devout and faithful in all observances of the law, went up to Jerusalem every year at the feast of the Passover. This religious festival, it should be remembered, was one of the most solemn and sacred among the many ceremonial commemorations of the Jews; it had been established at the time of the peoples' exodus from Egypt, in remembrance of the outstretched arm of power by which God had delivered Israel after the angel of destruction had slain the firstborn in every Egyptian home and had mercifully passed over the houses of the children of Jacob.[261] It was of such importance that its annual recurrence was made the beginning of the new year. The law required all males to present themselves before the Lord at the feast. The rule was that women should likewise attend if not lawfully detained; and Mary appears to have followed both the spirit of the law and the letter of the rule, for she habitually accompanied her husband to the annual gathering at Jerusalem.

When Jesus had attained the age of twelve years He was taken by His mother and Joseph to the feast as the law required; whether the Boy had ever before been present on such an occasion we are not told: At twelve years of age a Jewish boy was recognized as a member of his home community; he was required then to enter with definite purpose upon his chosen vocation; he attained an advanced status as an individual in that thereafter he could not be arbitrarily disposed of as a bond-servant by his parents; he was appointed to higher studies in school and home; and, when accepted by the priests, he became a "son of the law." It was the common and very natural desire of parents to have their sons attend the feast of the Passover and be present at the temple ceremonies as recognized members of the congregation when of the prescribed age. Thus came the Boy Jesus to the temple.

The feast proper lasted seven days, and in the time of Christ was annually attended by great concourses of Jews; Josephus speaks of such a Passover gathering as "an innumerable multitude."[262] The people came from distant provinces in large companies and caravans, as a matter of convenience and as a means of common protection against the marauding bands which are known to have infested the country. As members of such a company Joseph and his family traveled.

When, following the conclusion of the Passover, the Galilean company had gone a day's journey toward home, Joseph and Mary discovered to their surprize and deep concern that Jesus was not with their company. After a fruitless search among their friends and acquaintances, they turned back toward Jerusalem seeking the Boy. Their inquiries brought little comfort or assistance until three days had passed; then "they, found him in the temple, sitting in the midst of the doctors, both hearing them and asking them questions."[263] It was no unusual thing for a twelve year old boy to be questioned by priests, scribes, or rabbis, nor to be permitted to ask questions of these professional expounders of the law, for such procedure was part of the educational training of Jewish youths; nor was there anything surprizing in such a meeting of students and teachers within the temple courts, for the rabbis of that time were accustomed to give instruction there; and people, young and old, gathered about them, sitting at their feet to learn; but there was much that was extraordinary in this interview as the demeanor of the learned doctors showed, for never before had such a student been found, inasmuch as "all that heard him were astonished at his understanding and answers." The incident furnishes evidence of a wellspent boyhood and proof of unusual attainments.[264]

The amazement of Mary and her husband on finding the Boy in such distinguished company, and so plainly the object of deference and respect, and the joy of seeing again the beloved One who to them had been lost, did not entirely banish the memory of the anguish His absence had caused them. In words of gentle yet unmistakable reproof the mother said: "Son, why hast thou thus dealt with us? behold, thy father and I have sought thee sorrowing." The Boy's reply astonished them, in that it revealed, to an extent they had not before realized, His rapidly maturing powers of judgment and understanding. Said He: "How is it that ye sought me? wist ye not that I must be about my Father's business?"

Let us not say that there was unkind rebuke or unfilial reproof in the answer of this most dutiful of sons to His mother. His reply was to Mary a reminder of what she seems to have forgotten for the moment--the facts in the matter of her Son's paternity. She had used the words "thy father and I;" and her Son's response had brought anew to her mind the truth that Joseph was not the Boy's father. She appears to have been astonished that One so young should so thoroughly understand His position with respect to herself. He had made plain to her the inadvertent inaccuracy of her words; His Father had not been seeking Him; for was He not even at that moment in His Father's house, and particularly engaged in His Father's business, the very work to which His Father had appointed Him?

He had in no wise intimated a doubt as to Mary's maternal relationship to Himself; though He had indisputably shown that He recognized as His Father, not Joseph of Nazareth, but the God of Heaven. Both Mary and Joseph failed to comprehend the full import of His words. Though He understood the superior claim of duty based on His divine Sonship, and had shown to Mary that her authority as earthly mother was subordinate to that of His immortal and divine Father, nevertheless He obeyed her. Interested as were the doctors in this remarkable Boy, much as He had given them to ponder over through His searching questions and wise answers, they could not detain Him, for the very law they professed to uphold enjoined strict obedience to parental authority. "And he went down with them, and came to Nazareth, and was subject unto them: but his mother kept all these sayings in her heart."

What marvelous and sacred secrets were treasured in that mother's heart; and what new surprizes and grave problems were added day after day in the manifestations of unfolding wisdom displayed by her more than mortal Son! Though she could never have wholly forgotten, at times she seemingly lost sight of her Son's exalted personality. That such conditions should exist was perhaps divinely appointed. There could scarcely have been a full measure of truly human experience in the relationship between Jesus and His mother, or between Him and Joseph, had the fact of His divinity been always dominant or even prominently apparent. Mary appears never to have fully understood her Son; at every new evidence of His uniqueness she marveled and pondered anew. He was hers, and yet in a very real sense not wholly hers. There was about their relation to each other a mystery, awful yet sublime, a holy secret which that chosen and blessed mother hesitated even to tell over to herself. Fear must have contended with joy within her soul because of Him. The memory of Gabriel's glorious promises, the testimony of the rejoicing shepherds, and the adoration of the magi must have struggled with that of Simeon's portentous prophecy, directed to herself in person: "Yea, a sword shall pierce through thy own soul also."[265]

As to the events of the eighteen years following the return of Jesus from Jerusalem to Nazareth, the scriptures are silent save for one rich sentence of greatest import: "And Jesus increased in wisdom and stature, and in favor with God and man."[266] Plainly this Son of the Highest was not endowed with a fulness of knowledge, nor with the complete investiture of wisdom, from the cradle.[267] Slowly the assurance of His appointed mission as the Messiah, of whose coming He read in the law, the prophets, and the psalms, developed within His soul; and in devoted preparation for the ministry that should find culmination on the cross He passed the years of youth and early manhood. From the chronicles of later years we learn that He was reputed without question to be the son of Joseph and Mary, and was regarded as the brother of other and younger children of the family. He was spoken of both as a carpenter and a carpenter's son; and, until the beginning of His public ministry He appears to have been of little prominence even in the small home community.[268]

He lived the simple life, at peace with His fellows, in communion with His Father, thus increasing in favor with God and men. As shown by His public utterances after He had become a man, these years of seclusion were spent in active effort, both physical and mental. Jesus was a close observer of nature and men. He was able to draw illustrations with which to point His teachings from the varied occupations, trades and professions; the ways of the lawyer and the physician, the manners of the scribe, the Pharisee and the rabbi, the habits of the poor, the customs of the rich, the life of the shepherd, the farmer, the vinedresser and the fisherman--were all known to Him. He considered the lilies of the field, and the grass in meadow and upland, the birds which sowed not nor gathered into barns but lived on the bounty of their Maker, the foxes in their holes, the petted house dog and the vagrant cur, the hen sheltering her brood beneath protecting wings--all these had contributed to the wisdom in which He grew, as had also the moods of the weather, the recurrence of the seasons, and all the phenomena of natural change and order.

Nazareth was the abode of Jesus until He was about thirty years of age; and, in accordance with the custom of designating individuals by the names of their home towns as additions to their personal names,[269] our Lord came to be generally known as Jesus of Nazareth.[270] He is also referred to as a Nazarene, or a native of Nazareth, and this fact is cited by Matthew as a fulfilment of earlier prediction, though our current compilation of scriptures constituting the Old Testament contains no record of such prophecy. It is practically certain that this prediction was contained in some one of the many scriptures extant in earlier days but since lost.[271] That Nazareth was an obscure village, of little honor or renown, is evidenced by the almost contemptuous question of Nathanael, who, on being informed that the Messiah had been found in Jesus of Nazareth, asked: "Can there any good thing come out of Nazareth?"[272] The incredulous query has passed into a proverb current even today as expressive of any unpopular or unpromising source of good. Nathanael lived in Cana, but a few miles from Nazareth, and his surprize at the tidings brought by Philip concerning the Messiah incidentally affords evidence of the seclusion in which Jesus had lived.

So passed the boyhood, youth, and early manhood of the Savior of mankind.

NOTES TO CHAPTER 9.

1. Archelaus Reigned in Herod's Stead.--"At his death Herod [the Great] left a will according to which his kingdom was to be divided among his three sons. Archelaus was to have Judea, Idumea, and Samaria, with the title of king (Matt 2:22). Herod Antipas was to receive Galilee and Perea, with the title of tetrarch; Philip was to come into possession of the trans-Jordan territory with the title of tetrarch (Luke 3:1). This will was ratified by Augustus with the exception of the title given to Archelaus. Archelaus, after the ratification of Herod's will by Augustus, succeeded to the rule of Judea, Samaria, and Idumea, having the title of ethnarch, with the understanding that, if he ruled well, he was to become king. He was, however, highly unpopular with the people, and his reign was marked by disturbances and acts of oppression. The situation became finally so intolerable that the Jews appealed to Augustus, and Archelaus was removed and sent into exile. This accounts for the statement in Matt. 2:22, and possibly also suggested the point of the parable (Luke 19:12, etc.)."--_Standard Bible Dictionary_, Funk and Wagnalls Co., article "Herod." Early in his reign he wreaked summary vengeance on the people who ventured to protest against a continuation of his father's violence, by slaughtering three thousand or more; and the awful deed of carnage was perpetrated in part within the precincts of the temple. (Josephus, Antiquities xvii, 9:1-3.)

2. Herod Antipas.--Son of Herod I (the Great) by a Samaritan woman, and full brother to Archelaus. By the will of his father he became tetrarch of Galilee and Perea (Matt. 14:1; Luke 3:19; 9:7; Acts 13:1; compare Luke 3:1). He repudiated his wife, a daughter of Aretas, king of Arabia Petrea, and entered into an unlawful union with Herodias, the wife of his half-brother Herod Philip I (not the tetrarch Philip). John the Baptist was imprisoned and finally put to death, through the anger of Herodias over his denunciation of her union with Herod Antipas. Herodias urged Antipas to go to Rome and petition Cæsar for the title of king (compare Mark 6:14, etc.). Antipas is the Herod most frequently mentioned in the New Testament (Mark 6:17; 8:15; Luke 3:1; 9:7; 13:31; Acts 4:27; 13:1). He was the Herod to whom Pilate sent Jesus for examination, taking advantage of Christ being known as a Galilean, and of the coincident fact of Herod's presence in Jerusalem at the time in attendance at the Passover (Luke 23:6, etc.). For further details see Smith's, Cassell's, or the Standard Bible Dictionary.

3. Testimony of John the Apostle Concerning Christ's Development in Knowledge and Grace.--In a modern revelation, Jesus the Christ has confirmed the record of John the apostle, which record appears but in part in our compilation of ancient scriptures. John thus attests the actuality of natural development in the growth of Jesus from childhood to maturity: "And I, John, saw that he received not of the fullness at the first, but received grace for grace; and he received not of the fullness at first, but continued from grace to grace, until he received a fullness; and thus he was called the Son of God, because he received not of the fullness at the first." (Doc. and Cov. 93:12-14). Notwithstanding this graded course of growth and development after His birth in the flesh, Jesus Christ had been associated with the Father from the beginning, as is set forth in the revelation cited. We read therein: "And he [John] bore record, saying, I saw his glory that he was in the beginning before the world was; therefore in the beginning the Word was, for he was the Word, even the messenger of salvation, the light and the Redeemer of the world; the Spirit of truth, who came into the world, because the world was made by him, and in him was the life of men and the light of men. The worlds were made by him: men were made by him: all things were made by him, and through him, and of him. And I, John, bear record that I beheld his glory, as the glory of the Only Begotten of the Father, full of grace and truth, even the Spirit of truth, which came and dwelt in the flesh, and dwelt among us" (verses 7-11).

4. Missing Scripture.--Matthew's commentary on the abode of Joseph, Mary and Jesus at Nazareth, "and he came and dwelt in a city called Nazareth: that it might be fulfilled which was spoken by the prophets, he shall be called a Nazarene" (2:23), with the fact that no such saying of the prophets is found in any of the books contained in the Bible, suggests the certainty of lost scripture. Those who oppose

the doctrine of continual revelation between God and His Church, on the ground that the Bible is complete as a collection of sacred scriptures, and that alleged revelation not found therein must therefore be spurious, may profitably take note of the many books not included in the Bible, yet mentioned therein, generally in such a way as to leave no doubt that they were once regarded as authentic. Among these extra-Biblical scriptures, the following may be named; some of them are in existence to-day, and are classed with the Apocrypha; but the greater number are unknown. We read of the Book of the Covenant (Exo. 24:7); Book of the Wars of the Lord (Numb. 21:14); Book of Jasher (Josh. 10:13); Book of the Statutes (1 Sam. 10:25); Book of Enoch (Jude 14); Book of the Acts of Solomon (1 Kings 11:41); Book of Nathan the Prophet, and that of Gad the Seer (1 Chron. 29:29); Book of Ahijah the Shilonite, and visions of Iddo the Seer (2 Chron. 9:29); Book of Shemaiah (2 Chron. 12:15); Story of the Prophet Iddo (2 Chron. 13:22); Book of Jehu (2 Chron. 20:34); the Acts of Uzziah, by Isaiah, the son of Amoz (2 Chron. 26:22); Sayings of the Seers (2 Chron. 33:19); a missing epistle of Paul to the Corinthians (1 Cor. 5:9); a missing epistle to the Ephesians (Eph. 3:3); missing epistle to the Colossians, written from Laodicea (Col. 4:16); a missing epistle of Jude (Jude 3).

5. Nazareth.--A town or "city" in Galilee, of which Biblical mention is found in the New Testament only. Josephus says nothing concerning the place. The name of the existing village, or the Nazareth of to-day, is _En-Nazirah_. This occupies an upland site on the southerly ridge of Lebanon, and "commands a splendid view of the Plain of Esdraelon and Mount Carmel, and is very picturesque in general" (Zenos). The author of the article "Nazareth" in Smith's _Bible Dict._ identifies the modern En-Nazirah, with the Nazareth of old on the following grounds: "It is on the lower declivities of a hill or mountain (Luke 4:29); it is within the limits of the province of Galilee (Mark 1:9); it is near Cana (John 2:1, 2, 11); a precipice exists in the neighborhood (Luke 4:29); and a series of testimonials reaching back to Eusebius represent the place as having occupied the same position." The same writer adds: "Its population is 3000 or 4000; a few are Mohammedans, the rest Latin and Greek Christians. Most of the houses are well built of stone, and appear neat and comfortable. The streets or lanes are narrow and crooked, and after rain are so full of mud and mire as to be almost impassable." At the time of Christ's life the town was not only regarded as unimportant by the Judeans who professed but little respect for Galilee or the Galileans, but as without honor by the Galileans themselves, as appears from the fact that the seemingly contemptuous question, "Can there any good thing come out of Nazareth?" was uttered by Nathanael (John 1:46), who was a Galilean and a native of Cana, a neighboring town to Nazareth (John 21:2). Nazareth owes its celebrity to its association with events in the life of Jesus Christ (Matt. 2:23; 13:54; Mark 1:9; 6:1; Luke 1:26; 2:4; 4:23,34; John 1:45,46; 19:19; Acts 2:22).

FOOTNOTES:

[254] Matt. 2:15; compare Hos. 11:1.
[255] Matt. 2:19-23. Note 5, end of chapter.
[256] Note 1, end of chapter.
[257] Note 2, end of chapter.
[258] Luke 2:40.
[259] Note 3, end of chapter.
[260] Compare His teachings after He had reached manhood, e.g. John 8:32.
[261] Deut. 16:1-6; compare Exo. 12:2.
[262] Josephus; Wars of the Jews, ii, 1:3.
[263] Luke 2:46; read 41-52.
[264] Compare Matt. 7:28, 29; 13:54; Mark 6:2; Luke 4:22.
[265] Luke 2:35.
[266] Luke 2:52.
[267] Note 3, end of chapter.
[268] Matt. 13:55, 56; Mark 6:3; Luke 4:22; compare Matt. 12:46, 47; Gal. 1:19.
[269] For illustrative examples see Joseph of Arimathea (Mark 15:43); Mary Magdalene, so known from her native town of Magdala (Matt. 27:56); Judas Iscariot, possibly named after his home in Kerioth (Matt. 10:4; see page 225 herein.)
[270] Matt. 21:11; John 18:5; 19:19; Acts 2:22; 3:6; see also Luke 4:16.
[271] Note 4, end of chapter.
[272] John 1:45, 46.

CHAPTER 10. IN THE WILDERNESS OF JUDEA.

THE VOICE IN THE WILDERNESS.

At a time definitely stated as the fifteenth year of the reign of Tiberius C├ªsar, emperor of Rome, the people of Judea were greatly aroused over the strange preaching of a man theretofore unknown. He was of priestly descent, but untrained in the schools; and, without authorization of the rabbis or license from the chief priests, he proclaimed himself as one sent of God with a message to Israel. He appeared not in the synagogs nor within the temple courts, where scribes and doctors taught, but cried aloud in the wilderness. The people of Jerusalem and of adjacent rural parts went out in great multitudes to hear him. He disdained the soft garments and flowing robes of comfort, and preached in his rough desert garb, consisting of a garment of camel's hair held in place by a leathern girdle. The coarseness of his attire was regarded as significant. Elijah the Tishbite, that fearless prophet whose home had been the desert, was known in his day as "an hairy man, and girt with a girdle of leather about his loins;"[273] and rough garments had come to be thought of as a distinguishing characteristic of prophets.[274] Nor did this strange preacher eat the food of luxury and ease, but fed on what the desert supplied, locusts and wild honey.[275]

The man was John, son of Zacharias, soon to be known as the Baptist. He had spent many years in the desert, apart from the abodes of men, years of preparation for his particular mission. He had been a student under the tutelage of divine teachers; and there in the wilderness of Judea the word of the Lord reached him;[276] as in similar environment it had reached Moses[277] and Elijah[278] of old. Then was heard "The voice of one crying in the wilderness, Prepare ye the way of the Lord, make his paths straight."[279] It was the voice of the herald, the messenger who, as the prophets had said, should go before the Lord to prepare His way.[280] The burden of his message was "Repent ye, for the kingdom of heaven is at hand." And to such as had faith in his words and professed repentance, confessing their sins, he administered baptism by immersion in water--proclaiming the while, "I indeed baptize you with water unto repentance: but he that cometh after me is mightier than I, whose shoes I am not worthy to bear: he shall baptize you with the Holy Ghost, and with fire."[281]

Neither the man nor his message could be ignored; his preaching was specific in promise to the repentant soul, and scathingly denunciatory to the hypocrite and the hardened sinner. When Pharisees and Sadducees came to his baptism, prating of the law, the spirit of which they ceased not to transgress, and of the prophets, whom they dishonored, he denounced them as a generation of vipers, and demanded of them: "Who hath warned you to flee from the wrath to come?" He brushed aside their oft-repeated boasts that they were the children of Abraham, saying, "Bring forth therefore fruits meet for repentance: and think not to say within yourselves, We have Abraham to our father: for I say unto you, that God is able of these stones to raise up children unto Abraham."[282] The ignoring of their claims to preferment as the children of Abraham was a strong rebuke, and a cause of sore affront alike to aristocratic Sadducee and rule-bound Pharisee. Judaism held that the posterity of Abraham had an assured place in the kingdom of the expected Messiah, and that no proselyte from among the Gentiles could possibly attain the rank and distinction of which the "children" were sure. John's forceful assertion that God could raise up, from the stones on the river bank, children to Abraham, meant to those who heard that even the lowest of the human family might be preferred before themselves unless they repented and reformed.[283] Their time of wordy profession had passed; fruits were demanded, not barren though leafy profusion; the ax was ready, aye, at the very root of the tree; and every tree that produced not good fruit was to be hewn down and cast into the fire.

The people were astonished; and many, seeing themselves in their actual condition of dereliction and sin, as John, with burning words laid bare their faults, cried out: "What shall we do then?"[284] His reply was directed against ceremonialism, which had caused spirituality to wither almost to death in the hearts of the people. Unselfish charity was demanded--"He that hath two coats, let him impart to him that hath none; and he that hath meat, let him do likewise." The publicans or tax-farmers and collectors, under whose unjust and unlawful exactions the people had suffered so long, came asking: "Master, what shall we do? And he said unto them, Exact no more than that which is appointed you." To the soldiers who asked what to do he replied: "Do violence to no man, neither accuse any falsely; and be content with your wages."[285]

The spirit of his demands was that of a practical religion, the only religion of any possible worth--the religion of right living. With all his vigor, in spite of his brusqueness, notwithstanding his forceful assaults on the degenerate customs of the times, this John was no agitator against established institutions, no inciter of riot, no advocate of revolt, no promoter of rebellion. He did not assail the tax system but the extortions of the corrupt and avaricious publicans; he did not denounce the army, but the iniquities of the soldiers, many of whom had taken advantage of their position to bear false witness for the sake of gain and to enrich themselves by forcible seizure. He preached, what in the now current dispensation we call the first or fundamental principles of the gospel--"the beginning of the gospel of Jesus Christ, the Son of God,"[286] comprizing faith, which is vitalized belief, in God; genuine repentance, which comprizes contrition for past offenses and a resolute determination to turn from sin; baptism by immersion in water at his hands as the hands of one having authority; and the higher baptism by fire or the bestowal of the Holy Ghost by an authority greater than that possessed by himself. His preaching was positive, and in many respects opposed to the conventions of the times; he made no appeal to the people through the medium of miraculous manifestations;[287] and though many of his hearers attached themselves to him as disciples,[288] he established no formal organization, nor did he attempt to form a cult. His demand for repentance was an individual call, as unto each acceptable applicant the rite of baptism was individually administered.

To the Jews, who were living in a state of expectancy, waiting for the long-predicted Messiah, the words of this strange prophet in the wilderness were fraught with deep portent. Could it be that he was the Christ? He spoke of One yet to come, mightier than himself, whose shoe-latchet he was not worthy to loosen,[289] One who would separate the people as the thresher, fan in hand, blew the chaff from the wheat; and, he added, that mightier One "will gather the wheat into his garner; but the chaff he will burn with fire unquenchable."[290]

In such wise did the predicted herald of the Lord deliver his message. Himself he would not exalt; his office, however, was sacred to him, and with its functions he brooked no interference from priest, Levite, or rabbi. He was no respecter of persons; sin he denounced, sinners he excoriated, whether in priestly vestments, peasant garb, or royal robes. All the claims the Baptist had made for himself and his mission were later confirmed and vindicated by the specific testimony of Christ.[291] John was the harbinger not alone of the kingdom but of the King; and to him the King in person came.

THE BAPTISM OF JESUS--TO FULFIL ALL RIGHTEOUSNESS.

When Jesus "began to be about thirty years of age," He journeyed from His home in Galilee "to Jordan unto John, to be baptized of him. But John forbad him, saying, I have need to be baptized of thee, and comest thou to me? And Jesus answering said unto him, Suffer it to be so now; for thus it becometh us to fulfil all righteousness. Then he suffered him."[292]

John and Jesus were second cousins; as to whether there had existed any close companionship between the two as boys or men we are not told. It is certain, however, that when Jesus presented Himself for baptism, John recognized in Him a sinless Man who stood in no need of repentance; and, as the Baptist had been commissioned to baptize for the remission of sins, he saw no necessity of administering the ordinance to Jesus. He who had received the confessions of multitudes now reverently confessed to One whom he knew was more righteous than himself. In the light of later events it appears that at this time John did not know that Jesus was the Christ, the Mightier One for whom he waited and whose forerunner he knew himself to be. When John expressed his conviction that Jesus needed no baptismal cleansing, our Lord, conscious of His own sinlessness, did not deny the Baptist's imputation, but nevertheless pressed His application for baptism with the significant explanation: "Thus it becometh us to fulfil all righteousness." If John was able to comprehend the deeper meaning of this utterance, he must have found therein the truth that water baptism is not alone the means provided for gaining remission of sins, but is also an indispensable ordinance established in righteousness and required of all mankind as an essential condition for membership in the kingdom of God.[293]

Jesus Christ thus humbly complied with the will of the Father, and was baptized of John by immersion in water. That His baptism was accepted as a pleasing and necessary act of submission was attested by what immediately ensued: "And Jesus, when he was baptized, went up straightway out of the water: and, lo, the heavens were opened unto him, and he saw the Spirit of God descending like a dove, and lighting upon him: and lo a voice from heaven, saying, This is my beloved Son, in whom I am well pleased."[294] Then John knew his Redeemer.

The four Gospel-writers record the descent of the Holy Ghost upon the baptized Jesus as accompanied by a visible manifestation "like a dove;" and this sign had been indicated to John as the foreappointed means by which the Messiah should be made known to him; and to that sign, before specified, was now added the supreme testimony of the Father as to the literal Sonship of Jesus. Matthew records the Father's acknowledgment as given in the third person, "This is my beloved Son;" while both Mark and Luke give the more direct address, "Thou art my beloved Son." The variation, slight and essentially unimportant as it is though bearing on so momentous a subject, affords evidence of independent authorship and discredits any insinuation of collusion among the writers.

The incidents attending the emergence of Jesus from the baptismal grave demonstrate the distinct individuality of the three Personages of the Godhead. On that solemn occasion Jesus the Son was present in the flesh; the presence of the Holy Ghost was manifest through the accompanying sign of the dove, and the voice of the Eternal Father was heard from heaven. Had we no other evidence of the separate personality of each member of the Holy Trinity, this instance should be conclusive; but other scriptures confirm the great truth.[295]

THE TEMPTATIONS OF CHRIST.

Soon after His baptism, immediately thereafter as Mark asserts, Jesus was constrained by the promptings of the Spirit to withdraw from men and the distractions of community life, by retiring into the wilderness where He would be free to commune with His God. So strong was the influence of the impelling force that He was led thereby, or, as stated by the evangelist, driven, into solitary seclusion, in which He remained during forty days, "with the wild beasts" of the desert. This remarkable episode in our Lord's life is described, though not with equal fulness, in three of the Gospels;[296] John is silent thereon.

The circumstances attending this time of exile and test must have been related by Jesus Himself, for of other human witnesses there were none. The recorded narratives deal principally with events marking the close of the forty-day period, but considered in their entirety they place beyond doubt the fact that the season was one of fasting and prayer. Christ's realization that He was the chosen and foreordained Messiah came to Him gradually. As shown by His words to His mother on the occasion of the memorable interview with the doctors in the temple courts, He knew, when but a Boy of twelve years, that in a particular and personal sense He was the Son of God; yet it is evident that a comprehension of the full purport of His earthly mission developed within Him only as He progressed step by step in wisdom. His acknowledgment by the Father, and the continued companionship of the Holy Ghost, opened His soul to the glorious fact of His divinity. He had much to think about, much that demanded prayer and the communion with God that prayer alone could insure. Throughout the period of retirement, he ate not, but chose to fast, that His mortal body might the more completely be subjected to His divine spirit.

Then, when He was hungry and physically weak, the tempter came with the insidious suggestion that He use His extraordinary powers to provide food. Satan had chosen the most propitious time for his evil purpose. What will mortals not do, to what lengths have men not gone, to assuage the pangs of hunger? Esau bartered his birthright for a meal. Men have fought like brutes for food. Women have slain and eaten their own babes rather than endure the gnawing pangs of starvation. All this Satan knew when he came to the Christ in the hour of extreme physical need, and said unto Him: "If thou be the Son of God, command that these stones be made bread." During the long weeks of seclusion, our Lord had been sustained by the exaltation of spirit that would naturally attend such all-absorbing concentration of mind as His protracted meditation and communion with the heavens undoubtedly produced; in such profound devotion of spirit, bodily appetites were subdued and superseded; but the reaction of the flesh was inevitable.

Hungry as Jesus was, there was a temptation in Satan's words even greater than that embodied in the suggestion that He provide food for His famishing body--the temptation to put to proof the possible doubt implied in the tempter's "If." The Eternal Father had proclaimed Jesus as His Son; the devil tried to make the Son doubt that divine relationship. Why not prove the Father's interest in His Son at this moment of dire necessity? Was it proper that the Son of God should go hungry? Had the Father so soon forgotten as to leave His Beloved Son thus to suffer? Was it not reasonable that Jesus, faint from long abstinence, should provide for Himself, and particularly so since He could provide, and that by a word of command, _if_ the voice heard at His baptism was that of the Eternal Father. _If_ thou be in reality the Son of God, demonstrate thy power, and at the same time satisfy thy hunger--such was the purport of the diabolical suggestion. To have yielded would have been to manifest positive doubt of the Father's acknowledgment.

Moreover, the superior power that Jesus possessed had not been given to Him for personal gratification, but for service to others. He was to experience all the trials of mortality; another man, as hungry as He, could not provide for himself by a miracle; and though by miracle such a one might be fed, the miraculous supply would have to be given, not provided by himself. It was a necessary result of our Lord's dual nature, comprizing the attributes of both God and man, that He should endure and suffer as a mortal while possessing at all times the ability to invoke the power of His own Godhood by which all bodily needs could be supplied or overcome. His reply to the tempter was sublime and positively final: "It is written, Man shall not live by bread alone, but by every word that proceedeth out of the mouth of God."[297] The word that had proceeded from the mouth of God, upon which Satan would have cast mistrust, was that Jesus was the Beloved Son with whom the Father was well pleased. The devil was foiled; Christ was triumphant.

Realizing that he had utterly failed in his attempt to induce Jesus to use His inherent power for personal service, and to trust in Himself rather than rely upon the Father's providence, Satan went to the other extreme and tempted Jesus to wantonly throw Himself upon the Father's protection.[298] Jesus was standing upon one of the high parts of the temple, a pinnacle or battlement, overlooking the spacious courts, when the devil said unto Him: "If thou be the Son of God, cast thyself down: for it is written, He shall give his angels charge concerning thee: and in their hands they shall bear thee up, lest at any time thou dash thy foot against a stone." Again appears the implication of doubt.[299] _If_ Jesus was in fact the Son of God, could He not trust His Father to save Him, and particularly so as it was written[300] that angels would guard Him and bear Him up? Christ's reply to the tempter in the wilderness had embodied a scriptural citation, and this He had introduced with the impressive formula common to expounders of sacred writ--"It is written." In the second attempt, the devil tried to support his suggestion by scripture, and employed a similar expression--"for it is written." Our Lord met and answered the devil's quotation with another, saying: "It is written again, Thou shalt not tempt the Lord thy God."[301]

Beside the provocation to sin by wantonly placing Himself in danger, so that the Father's love might be manifested in a miraculous rescue, or by refusing so to challenge the Father's interposition demonstrate that He doubted His status as the Beloved Son, there lurked an appeal to the human side of Christ's nature, in thought of the fame which an astounding exploit, such as that of leaping from the dizzy height of the temple turrets and alighting unhurt, would surely bring. We cannot resist the thought, though we be not justified in saying that any such had even momentary place in the Savior's mind, that to act upon Satan's suggestion, provided of course the outcome proved to be such as he had indicated, would have been to insure public recognition of Jesus as a Being superior to mortals. It would have been a sign and a wonder indeed, the fame of which would have spread as fire in the dry grass; and all Jewry would have been aflame with excitement and interest in the Christ.

The glaring sophistry of Satan's citation of scripture was unworthy a categorical reply; his doctrine deserved neither logic nor argument; his misapplication of the written word was nullified by scripture that was germane; the lines of the psalmist were met by the binding fiat of the prophet of the exodus, in which he had commanded Israel that they should not provoke nor tempt the Lord to work miracles among them. Satan tempted Jesus to tempt the Father. It is as truly a blasphemous interference with the prerogatives of Deity to set limitations or make fixations of time or place at which the divine power shall be made manifest as it is to attempt to usurp that power. God alone must decide when and how His wonders shall be wrought. Once more the purposes of Satan were thwarted and Christ again was victor.

In the third temptation the devil refrained from further appeal to Jesus to put either His own power or that of the Father to the test. Twice completely foiled, the tempter abandoned that plan of assault;

and, discarding all disguise of purpose, submitted a definite proposition. From the top of a high mountain Jesus looked over the land with its wealth of city and field, of vineyard and orchard, of flocks and of herds; and in vision He saw the kingdoms of the world and contemplated the wealth, the splendor, the earthly glory of them all. Then saith Satan unto Him: "All these things will I give thee, if thou wilt fall down and worship me." So wrote Matthew; the more extended version by Luke follows: "And the devil said unto him, All this power will I give thee, and the glory of them: for that is delivered unto me; and to whomsoever I will I give it. If thou therefore wilt worship me, all shall be thine." We need not concern ourselves with conjecture as to whether Satan could have made good his promise in the event of Christ's doing him homage; certain it is Christ could have reached out, and have gathered to Himself the wealth and glory of the world had He willed so to do, and thereby have failed in His Messianic mission. This fact Satan knew full well. Many men have sold themselves to the devil for a kingdom and for less, aye, even for a few paltry pence.

The effrontery of his offer was of itself diabolical. Christ, the Creator of heaven and earth, tabernacled as He then was in mortal flesh, may not have remembered His preexistent state, nor the part He had taken in the great council of the Gods,[302] while Satan, an unembodied spirit--he the disinherited, the rebellious and rejected son--seeking to tempt the Being through whom the world was created by promising Him part of what was wholly His, still may have had, as indeed he may yet have, a remembrance of those primeval scenes. In that distant past, antedating the creation of the earth, Satan, then Lucifer, a son of the morning, had been rejected; and the Firstborn Son had been chosen. Now that the Chosen One was subject to the trials incident to mortality, Satan thought to thwart the divine purpose by making the Son of God subject to himself. He who had been vanquished by Michael and his hosts and cast down as a defeated rebel, asked the embodied Jehovah to worship him. "Then saith Jesus unto him, Get thee hence, Satan for it is written, Thou shalt worship the Lord thy God, and him only shalt thou serve. Then the devil leaveth him, and behold, angels came and ministered unto him."[303]

It is not to be supposed that Christ's victorious emergence from the dark clouds of the three specified temptations exempted Him from further assaults by Satan, or insured Him against later trials of faith, trust, and endurance. Luke closes his account of the temptations following the forty-day fast as follows: "And when the devil had ended all the temptation, he departed from him for a season."[304] This victory over the devil and his wiles, this triumph over the cravings of the flesh, the harassing doubts of the mind, the suggested reaching out for fame and material wealth, were great but not final successes in the struggle between Jesus, the embodied God, and Satan, the fallen angel of light. That Christ was subject to temptation during the period of His association with the apostles He expressly affirmed.[305] That His temptations extended even to the agony in Gethsemane will appear as we proceed with this study. It is not given to the rest of us, nor was it given to Jesus, to meet the foe, to fight and overcome in a single encounter, once for all time. The strife between the immortal spirit and the flesh, between the offspring of God on the one hand, the world and the devil on the other, is persistent through life.

Few events in the evangelical history of Jesus of Nazareth have given rise to more discussion, fanciful theory, and barren speculation, than have the temptations. All such surmizes we may with propriety ignore. To any believer in the holy scriptures, the account of the temptations therein given is sufficiently explicit to put beyond doubt or question the essential facts; to the unbeliever neither the Christ nor His triumph appeals. What shall it profit us to speculate as to whether Satan appeared to Jesus in visible form, or was present only as an unseen spirit; whether he spoke in audible voice, or aroused in the mind of his intended victim the thoughts later expressed by the written lines; whether the three temptations occurred in immediate sequence or were experienced at longer intervals? With safety we may reject all theories of myth or parable in the scriptural account, and accept the record as it stands; and with equal assurance may we affirm that the temptations were real, and that the trials to which our Lord was put constituted an actual and crucial test. To believe otherwise, one must regard the scriptures as but fiction.

A question deserving some attention in this connection is that of the peccability or impeccability of Christ--the question as to whether He was capable of sinning. Had there been no possibility of His yielding to the lures of Satan, there would have been no real test in the temptations, no genuine victory in the result. Our Lord was sinless yet peccable; He had the capacity, the ability to sin had He willed so to do. Had He been bereft of the faculty to sin, He would have been shorn of His free agency; and it was to safeguard and insure the agency of man that He had offered Himself, before the world was, as a redeeming sacrifice. To say that He could not sin because He was the embodiment of righteousness is no denial of His agency of choice between evil and good. A thoroughly truthful man cannot culpably lie; nevertheless his insurance against falsehood is not that of external compulsion, but of internal restraint due to his cultivated companionship of the spirit of truth. A really honest man will neither take nor covet his neighbor's goods, indeed it may be said that he cannot steal; yet he is capable of stealing should he so elect. His honesty is an armor against temptation; but the coat of mail, the helmet, the breastplate, and the greaves, are but an outward covering; the man within may be vulnerable if he can be reached.

But why proceed with labored reasoning, which can lead to but one conclusion, when our Lord's own words and other scriptures confirm the fact? Shortly before His betrayal, when admonishing the Twelve to humility, He said: "Ye are they which have continued with me in my temptations."[306] While here we find no exclusive reference to the temptations immediately following His baptism, the exposition is plain that He had endured temptations, and by implication, these had continued throughout the period of His ministry. The writer of the epistle to the Hebrews expressly taught that Christ was peccable, in that He was tempted "in all points" as are the rest of mankind. Consider the unambiguous declaration: "Seeing then that we have a great high priest, that is passed into the heavens, Jesus the Son of God, let us hold fast our profession. For we have not an high priest which cannot be touched with the feeling of our infirmities; but was in all points tempted like as we are, yet without sin."[307] And further: "Though he were a Son, yet learned he obedience by the things which he suffered."[308]

NOTES TO CHAPTER 10.

1. Raiment of Camel's Hair.--Through the prophet Zechariah (13:4) a time was foretold in which professing prophets would no longer "wear a rough garment to deceive." Of the raiment of camel's hair worn by John the Baptist, the Oxford and other marginal readings render the expression "a garment of hair" as more literal than the Bible text. Deems (_Light of the Nations_, p. 74, note) says: "The garment of camel's hair was not the camel's skin with the hair on, which would be too heavy to wear, but raiment woven of camel's hair, such as Josephus speaks of (B. J. i, 24:3)."

2. Locusts and Wild Honey.--Insects of the locust or grasshopper kind were specifically declared clean and suitable for food in the law given to Israel in the wilderness. "Yet these may ye eat of every flying creeping thing that goeth upon all four, which have legs above their feet, to leap withal upon the earth; even these of them ye may eat; the locust after his kind, and the bald locust after his kind, and the beetle after his kind, and the grasshopper after his kind." (Lev. 11:21, 22.) At the present time locusts are used as food by many oriental peoples, though usually by the poorer classes only. Of the passage referring to locusts as part of the Baptist's food while he lived as a recluse in the desert, Farrar (_Life of Christ_, p. 97, note,) says: "The fancy that it means the pods of the so-called locust tree (carob) is a mistake. Locusts are sold as articles of food in regular shops for the purpose at Medina; they are plunged into salt boiling water, dried in the sun, and eaten with butter, but only by the poorest beggars." Geikie (_Life and Words of Christ_, vol. 1, pp. 354, 355) gives place to the following as applied to the Baptist's life: "His only food was the locusts which leaped or flew on the bare hills, and the honey of wild bees which he found, here and there, in the clifts of the rocks, and his only drink a draught of water from some rocky hollow. Locusts are still the food of the poor in many parts of the East. 'All the Bedouins of Arabia, and the inhabitants of towns in Nedj and Hedjaz, are accustomed to eat them,' says Burckhardt. 'I have seen at Medina and Tayi, locust shops, where they are sold by measure. In Egypt and Nubia they are eaten only by the poorest beggars. The Arabs, in preparing them for eating, throw them alive into boiling water, with which a good deal of salt has been mixed, taking them out after a few minutes, and drying them in the sun. The head, feet, and wings, are then torn off, the bodies cleansed from the salt, and perfectly dried. They are sometimes eaten boiled in butter, or spread on unleavened bread mixed with butter.' In Palestine, they are eaten only by the Arabs on the extreme frontiers; elsewhere they are looked on with disgust and loathing, and only the very poorest use them. Tristram, however, speaks of them as 'very palatable.' 'I found them very good,' says he, 'when eaten after the Arab fashion, stewed with butter. They tasted somewhat like shrimps, but with less flavour.' In the wilderness of Judea, various kinds abound at all seasons, and spring up with a drumming sound, at every step, suddenly spreading their bright hind wings, of scarlet, crimson, blue, yellow, white, green, or brown, according to the species. They were 'clean,' under the Mosaic Law, and hence could be eaten by John without offence."

Concerning the mention of wild honey as food used by John, the author last quoted says in a continuation of the same paragraph: "The wild bees in Palestine are far more numerous than those kept in hives, and the greater part of the honey sold in the southern districts is obtained from wild swarms. Few countries, indeed, are better adapted for bees. The dry climate, and the stunted but varied flora, consisting largely of aromatic thymes, mints, and other similar plants, with crocuses in the spring, are very favourable to them, while the dry recesses of the limestone rocks everywhere afford them shelter and protection for their combs. In the wilderness of Judea, bees are far more numerous than in any other part of Palestine, and it is, to this day, part of the homely diet of the Bedouins, who squeeze it from the combs and store it in skins."

3. John's Inferiority to the Mightier One He Proclaimed.--"One mightier than I cometh, the latchet of whose shoes I am not worthy to unloose" (Luke 3:16), or "whose shoes I am not worthy to bear" (Matt. 3:11); this was the way by which the Baptist declared his inferiority to the Mightier One, who was to succeed and supersede him; and a more effective illustration would be difficult to frame. To loosen the shoe latchet or sandal thong, or to carry the shoes of another, "was a menial office betokening great inferiority on the part of the person performing it." (Smith's _Dict. of the Bible_.) A passage in the Talmud (_Tract. Kidduschin xxii:2_) requires a disciple to do for his teacher whatever a servant might be required to do for his master, except the loosing of his sandal thong. Some teachers urged that a disciple should carry his humility even to the extreme of carrying his master's shoes. The humility of the Baptist, in view of the widespread interest his call aroused, is impressive.

4. The Order in which the Temptations Were Presented.--But two of the Gospel-writers specify the temptations to which Christ was subjected immediately after His baptism; Mark merely mentions the fact that Jesus was tempted. Matthew and Luke place first the temptation that Jesus provide for Himself by miraculously creating bread; the sequence of the later trials is not the same in the two records. The order followed in the text is that of Matthew.

5. The Devil's "If."--Note the later taunting use of that diabolical _if_ as the Christ hung upon the cross. The rulers of the Jews, mocking the crucified Jesus in His agony said, "Let him save himself _if_ he be the Christ." And the soldier, reading the inscription at the head of the cross derided the dying God, saying: "_If_ thou be the king of the Jews, save thyself." And yet again, the unrepentant malefactor by His side cried but, "_If_ thou be Christ, save thyself and us." (Luke 23:35-39.) How literally did those railers and mockers quote the very words of their father the devil (see John 8:44). See further, page 658 herein.

6. Baptism Required of All.--Baptism is required of all persons who live to the age of accountability in the flesh. None are exempt. Jesus Christ, who lived as a Man without sin in the midst of a

sinful world, was baptized "to fulfil all righteousness." Six centuries before this event, Nephi, prophesying to the people on the western continent, foretold the baptism of the Savior, and thus drew therefrom the necessity of baptism as a universal requirement: "And now, if the Lamb of God, he being holy, should have need to be baptized by water, to fulfil all righteousness, O then, how much more need have we, being unholy, to be baptized, yea, even by water.... Know ye not that he was holy? But notwithstanding he being holy, he sheweth unto the children of men, that according to the flesh, he humbleth himself before the Father, and witnesseth unto the Father that he would be obedient unto him in keeping his commandments" (B. of M., 2 Nephi 31:5, 7). See _The Articles of Faith_, vi:18-29.

FOOTNOTES:

[273] 2 Kings 1:8.
[274] Note 1, end of chapter.
[275] Matt. 3:1-5; compare Lev. 11:22; see also Mark 1:1-8. Note 2, end of chapter.
[276] Luke 3:2.
[277] Exo. 3:1, 2.
[278] 1 Kings 17:2-7.
[279] Mark 1:3.
[280] Mark 1:2; compare Isa. 40:3; Mal. 3:1; Matt. 11:10; Luke 7:27.
[281] Matt. 3:11.
[282] Matt. 3:7-10; see also Luke 3:3-9.
[283] Compare a later instance, in which Christ similarly taught (John 8:33-59).
[284] Luke 3:10; compare Acts 2:37.
[285] Luke 3:10-15.
[286] Mark 1:1.
[287] John 10:41.
[288] John 1:35, 37; Matt. 11:2; Luke 7:18.
[289] Note 3, end of chapter.
[290] Luke 3:17; see also Matt. 3:12; compare Mal. 3:2.
[291] Matt. 11:11-14; 17:12; Luke 7:24-30.
[292] Luke 3:23.
[293] For treatment of Baptism as a universal requirement, see the author's "Articles of Faith" vi:18-29. Note 6, end of chapter.
[294] Matt. 3:16, 17; compare Mark 1:9-11; Luke 3:21, 22.
[295] Shortly before His death, the Savior promised the apostles that the Father would send unto them the Comforter, which is the Holy Ghost (John 14:26, and 15:26). See the author's "Articles of Faith" ii:20-24.
[296] Matt. 4:1-11; Mark 1:12, 13; Luke 4:1-13.
[297] Matt. 4:4; compare Deut. 8:3.
[298] Note 4, end of chapter.
[299] Note 5, end of chapter. Page 658 herein.
[300] Matt. 4:6; Psalm 91:11, 12.
[301] Matt. 4:5-7; compare Deut. 6:16.
[302] Pages 6-9.
[303] Matt. 4:10, 11; compare Exo. 20:3; Deut. 6:13; 10:20; Josh. 24:14; 1 Sam. 7:3.
[304] Luke 4:13.
[305] Luke 22:28.
[306] Luke 22:28.
[307] Heb. 4:14, 15.
[308] Heb. 5:8.

CHAPTER 11. FROM JUDEA TO GALILEE.

THE BAPTIST'S TESTIMONY OF JESUS.

During the period of our Lord's retirement in the wilderness the Baptist continued his ministry, crying repentance to all who would pause to hear, and administering baptism to such as came duly prepared and asking with right intent. The people generally were greatly concerned over the identity of John; and as the real import of the voice[309] dawned upon them, their concern deepened into fear. The ever recurring question was, Who is this new prophet? Then the Jews, by which expression we may understand the rulers of the people, sent a delegation of priests and Levites of the Pharisaic party to personally question him. He answered without evasion, "I am not the Christ," and with equal decisiveness denied that he was Elias, or more accurately, Elijah, the prophet who, the rabbis said through a misinterpretation of Malachi's prediction, was to return to earth as the immediate precursor of the Messiah.[310] Furthermore, he declared that he was not "that prophet," by which was meant the Prophet whose coming Moses had foretold,[311] and who was not universally identified in the Jewish mind with the expected Messiah. "Then said they unto him, Who art thou? that we may give an answer to them that sent us. What sayest thou of thyself? He said, I am the voice of one crying in the wilderness, Make straight the way of the Lord, as said the prophet Esaias."[312] The Pharisaic envoys then demanded of him his authority for baptizing; in reply he affirmed that the validity of his baptisms would be attested by One who even then was amongst them, though they knew Him not, and averred: "He it is, who coming after me is preferred before me, whose shoe's latchet I am not worthy to unloose."[313]

John's testimony, that Jesus was the Redeemer of the world, was declared as boldly as had been his message of the imminent coming of the Lord. "Behold the Lamb of God, which taketh away the sin of the world," he proclaimed; and, that none might fail to comprehend his identification of the Christ, he added: "This is he of whom I said, After me cometh a man which is preferred before me: for he was before me. And I knew him not: but that he should be made manifest to Israel, therefore am I come baptizing with water."[314] That the attestation of the ministering presence of the Holy Ghost through the material appearance "like a dove" was convincing to John is shown by his further testimony: "And John bare record saying, I saw the Spirit descending from heaven like a dove, and it abode upon him. And I knew him not: but he that sent me to baptize with water, the same said unto me, Upon whom thou shalt see the spirit descending, and remaining on him, the same is he which baptizeth with the Holy Ghost. And I saw, and bare record that this is the Son of God."[315] On the day following that of the utterance last quoted, John repeated his testimony to two of his disciples, or followers, as, Jesus passed, saying again: "Behold the Lamb of God."[316]

THE FIRST DISCIPLES OF JESUS.[317]

Two of the Baptist's followers, specifically called disciples, were with him when for the second time he expressly designated Jesus as the Lamb of God. These were Andrew and John; the latter came to be known in after years as the author of the fourth Gospel. The first is mentioned by name, while the narrator suppresses his own name as that of the second disciple. Andrew and John were so impressed by the Baptist's testimony that they immediately followed Jesus; and He, turning toward them asked: "What seek ye?" Possibly somewhat embarrassed by the question, or with a real desire to learn where He might be found later, they replied by another inquiry: "Rabbi, where dwellest thou?" Their use of the title Rabbi was a mark of honor and respect, to which Jesus did not demur. His courteous reply to their question assured them that their presence was no unwelcome intrusion. "Come and see," said He.[318] The two young men accompanied Him, and remained with Him to learn more. Andrew, filled with wonder and joy over the interview so graciously accorded, and thrilled with the spirit of testimony that had been enkindled within his soul, hastened to seek his brother Simon, to whom he said: "We have found the Messias." He brought Simon to see and hear for himself; and Jesus, looking upon Andrew's brother, called him by name and added an appellation of distinction by which he was destined to be known throughout all later history: "Thou art Simon the son of Jona; thou shalt be called Cephas." The new name thus bestowed was the Aramaic or Syro-Chaldaic equivalent of the Greek "Petros," and of the present English "Peter," meaning "a stone."[319]

On the following day Jesus set out for Galilee, possibly accompanied by some or all of his newly-made disciples; and on the way He found a man named Philip, in whom He recognized another choice son of Israel. Unto Philip He said: "Follow me." It was customary with rabbis and other teachers of that time to strive for popularity, that many might be drawn to them to sit at their feet and be known as their disciples. Jesus, however, selected His own immediate associates; and, as He found them and discerned in them the spirits who, in their preexistent state had been chosen for the earthly mission of the apostleship, He summoned them. They were the servants; He was the Master.[320]

Philip soon found his friend Nathanael, to whom he testified that He of whom Moses and the prophets had written had at last been found; and that He was none other than Jesus of Nazareth. Nathanael, as his later history demonstrates, was a righteous man, earnest in his hope and expectation of the Messiah, yet seemingly imbued with the belief common throughout Jewry--that the Christ was to come in royal state as seemed befitting the Son of David. The mention of such a One coming from Nazareth, the reputed son of a humble carpenter, provoked wonder if not incredulity in the guileless mind of Nathanael, and he exclaimed: "Can there any good thing come out of Nazareth?" Philip's answer was a repetition of Christ's words to Andrew and John--"Come and see." Nathanael left his seat under the fig tree,[321] where

Philip had found him, and went to see for himself. As he approached, Jesus said: "Behold an Israelite indeed, in whom is no guile." Nathanael saw that Jesus could read his mind, and asked in surprize: "Whence knowest thou me?" In reply Jesus showed even greater powers of penetration and perception under conditions that made ordinary observation unlikely if not impossible: "Before that Philip called thee, when thou wast under the fig tree, I saw thee." Nathanael replied with conviction: "Rabbi, thou art the Son of God; thou art the King of Israel." Earnest as the man's testimony was, it rested mainly on his recognition of what he took to be a supernatural power in Jesus; our Lord assured him that he should see yet greater things: "And he saith unto him, Verily, verily, I say unto you, Hereafter ye shall see heaven open, and the angels of God ascending and descending upon the Son of man."

THE SON OF MAN.

In the promise and prediction made by Christ to Nathanael, we find the significant title--The Son of Man--appearing for the first time, chronologically speaking, in the New Testament. It recurs, however, about forty times, excluding repetitions in parallel accounts in the several Gospels. In each of these passages it is used by the Savior distinctively to designate Himself. In three other instances the title appears in the New Testament, outside the Gospels; and in each case it is applied to the Christ with specific reference to His exalted attributes as Lord and God.[322]

In the Old Testament, the phrase "son of man" occurs in ordinary usage, denoting any human son[323] and it appears over ninety times as an appellation by which Jehovah addressed Ezekiel, though it is never applied by the prophet to himself.[324] The context of the passages in which Ezekiel is addressed as "son of man" indicates the divine intention of emphasizing the human status of the prophet as contrasted with the divinity of Jehovah.

The title is used in connection with the record of Daniel's vision,[325] in which was revealed the consummation, yet future, when Adam--the Ancient of Days--shall sit to judge his posterity;[326] on which great occasion, the Son of Man is to appear and receive a dominion that shall be everlasting, transcendently superior to that of the Ancient of Days, and embracing every people and nation, all of whom shall serve the Lord, Jesus Christ, the Son of Man.[327]

In applying the designation to Himself, the Lord invariably uses the definite article. "_The_ Son of Man" was and is, specifically and exclusively, Jesus Christ. While as a matter of solemn certainty He was the only male human being from Adam down who was not the son of a mortal man, He used the title in a way to conclusively demonstrate that it was peculiarly and solely His own. It is plainly evident that the expression is fraught with a meaning beyond that conveyed by the words in common usage. The distinguishing appellation has been construed by many to indicate our Lord's humble station as a mortal, and to connote that He stood as the type of humanity, holding a particular and unique relationship to the entire human family. There is, however, a more profound significance attaching to the Lord's use of the title "The Son of Man"; and this lies in the fact that He knew His Father to be the one and only supremely exalted Man,[328] whose Son Jesus was both in spirit and in body--the Firstborn among all the spirit-children of the Father, the Only Begotten in the flesh--and therefore in sense applicable to Himself alone, He was and is the Son of the "Man of Holiness," Elohim,[329] the Eternal Father. In His distinctive titles of Sonship, Jesus expressed His spiritual and bodily descent from, and His filial submission to, that exalted Father.

As revealed to Enoch the Seer, "Man of Holiness" is one of the names by which God the Eternal Father is known; "and the name of his Only Begotten is the Son of Man, even Jesus Christ." We learn further that the Father of Jesus Christ thus proclaimed Himself to Enoch: "Behold, I am God; Man of Holiness is my name; Man of Counsel is my name; and Endless and Eternal is my name, also."[330] "The Son of Man" is in great measure synonymous with "The Son of God," as a title denoting divinity, glory, and exaltation; for the "Man of Holiness," whose Son Jesus Christ reverently acknowledges Himself to be, is God the Eternal Father.

THE MIRACLE AT CANA IN GALILEE.

Soon after the arrival of Jesus in Galilee we find Him and His little company of disciples at a marriage party in Cana, a neighboring town to Nazareth. The mother of Jesus was at the feast; and for some reason not explained in John's narrative,[331] she manifested concern and personal responsibility in the matter of providing for the guests. Evidently her position was different from that of one present by ordinary invitation. Whether this circumstance indicates the marriage to have been that of one of her own immediate family, or some more distant relative, we are not informed.

It was customary to provide at wedding feasts a sufficiency of wine, the pure though weak product of the local vineyards, which was the ordinary table beverage of the time. On this occasion the supply of wine was exhausted, and Mary told Jesus of the deficiency. Said He: "Woman, what have I to do with thee? mine hour is not yet come." The noun of address, "Woman," as applied by a son to his mother may sound to our ears somewhat harsh, if not disrespectful; but its use was really an expression of opposite import.[332] To every son, the mother ought to be preeminently the woman of women; she is the one woman in the world to whom the son owes his earthly existence; and though the title "Mother" belongs to every woman who has earned the honors of maternity, yet to no child is there more than one woman whom by natural right he can address by that title of respectful acknowledgment. When, in the last dread scenes of His mortal experience, Christ hung in dying agony upon the cross, He looked, down upon the weeping Mary, His mother, and commended her to the care of the beloved apostle John, with the words: "Woman, behold thy son!"[333] Can it be thought that in this supreme moment, our Lord's concern for the mother from whom He was about to be separated by death was associated with any emotion other than that of honor, tenderness and love?[334]

Nevertheless, His words to Mary at the marriage feast may have conveyed a gentle reminder of her position as the mother of a Being superior to herself; even as on that earlier occasion when she had found her Boy, Jesus, in the temple, He had brought home to her the fact that her jurisdiction over Him was not supreme. The manner in which she told Him of the insufficiency of wine probably suggested an intimation that He use His more than human power, and by such means supply the need. It was not her function to direct or even to suggest the exercize of the power inherent in Him as the Son of God; such had not been inherited from her. "What have I to do with thee?" He asked; and added: "Mine hour is not yet come." Here we find no disclaimer of the ability to do what she apparently wanted Him to do, but the plain implication that He would act only when the time was right for the purpose, and that He, not she, must decide when that time had come. She understood His meaning, in part at least, and contented herself by instructing the servants to do whatsoever He directed. Here again is evidence of her position of responsibility and domestic authority at the social gathering.

The time for His intervention soon arrived. There stood within the place six water pots;[335] these He directed the servants to fill with water. Then, without audible command or formula of invocation, as best we know, He caused to be effected a transmutation within the pots, and when the servants drew therefrom, it was wine, not water that issued. At a Jewish social gathering, such as was this wedding festival, some one, usually a relative of the host or hostess, or some other one worthy of the honor, was made governor of the feast, or, as we say in this day, chairman, or master of ceremonies. To this functionary the new wine was first served; and he, calling the bridegroom, who was the real host, asked him why he had reserved his choice wine till the last, when the usual custom was to serve the best at the beginning, and the more ordinary later. The immediate result of this, the first recorded of our Lord's miracles, is thus tersely stated by the inspired evangelist: "This beginning of miracles did Jesus in Cana of Galilee, and manifested forth his glory; and his disciples believed on him."[336]

The circumstances incident to the miraculous act are instructive to contemplate. The presence of Jesus at the marriage, and His contribution to the successful conduct of the feast, set the seal of His approval upon the matrimonial relationship and upon the propriety of social entertainment. He was neither a recluse nor an ascetic; He moved among men, eating and drinking, as a natural, normal Being.[337] On the occasion of the feast He recognized and heeded the demands of the liberal hospitality of the times, and provided accordingly. He, who but a few days before had revolted at the tempter's suggestion that He provide bread for His impoverished body, now used His power to supply a luxury for others. One effect of the miracle was to confirm the trust of those whose belief in Him as the Messiah was yet young and untried. "His disciples believed on him"; surely they had believed in some measure before, otherwise they would not have followed Him; but their belief was now strengthened and made to approach, if indeed it did not attain, the condition of abiding faith in their Lord. The comparative privacy attending the manifestation is impressive; the moral and spiritual effect was for the few, the inauguration of the Lord's ministry was not to be marked by public display.

MIRACLES IN GENERAL

The act of transmutation whereby water became wine was plainly a miracle, a phenomenon not susceptible of explanation, far less of demonstration, by what we consider the ordinary operation of natural law. This was the beginning of His miracles, or as expressed in the revized version of the New Testament, "his signs." In many scriptures miracles are called signs, as also wonders, powers, works, wonderful works, mighty works,[338] etc. The spiritual effect of miracles would be unattained were the witnesses not caused to inwardly wonder, marvel, ponder and inquire; mere surprize or amazement may be produced by deception and artful trickery. Any miraculous manifestation of divine power would be futile as a means of spiritual effect were it unimpressive. Moreover, every miracle is a sign of God's power; and signs in this sense have been demanded of prophets who professed to speak by divine authority, though such signs have not been given in all cases. The Baptist was credited with no miracle, though he was pronounced by the Christ as more than a prophet;[339] and the chronicles of some earlier prophets[340] are devoid of all mention of miracles. On the other hand, Moses, when commissioned to deliver Israel from Egypt, was made, to understand that the Egyptians would look for the testimony of miracles, and he was abundantly empowered therefore.[341]

Miracles cannot be in contravention of natural law, but are wrought through the operation of laws not universally or commonly recognized. Gravitation is everywhere operative, but the local and special application of other agencies may appear to nullify it--by muscular effort or mechanical impulse a stone is lifted from the ground, poised aloft, or sent hurtling through space. At every stage of the process, however, gravity is in full play, though its effect is modified by that of other and locally superior energy. The human sense of the miraculous wanes as comprehension of the operative process increases. Achievements made possible by modern invention of telegraph and telephone with or without wires, the transmutation of mechanical power into electricity with its manifold present applications and yet future possibilities, the development of the gasoline motor, the present accomplishments in aerial navigation--these are no longer miracles in man's estimation, because they are all in some degree understood, are controlled by human agency, and, moreover, are continuous in their operation and not phenomenal. We arbitrarily classify as miracles only such phenomena as are unusual, special, transitory, and wrought by an agency beyond the power of man's control.

In a broader sense, all nature is miracle. Man has learned that by planting the seed of the grape in suitable soil, and by due cultivation, he may conduce to the growth of what shall be a mature and fruitful vine; but is there no miracle, even in the sense of inscrutable processes, in that development? Is there less of real miracle in the so-called natural course of plant development--the growth of root, stem, leaves, and fruit, with the final elaboration of the rich nectar of the vine--than there was in what appears supernatural in the transmutation of water into wine at Cana?

In the contemplation of the miracles wrought by Christ, we must of necessity recognize the operation of a power transcending our present human understanding. In this field, science has not yet advanced far enough to analyze and explain. To deny the actuality of miracles on the ground that, because we cannot comprehend the means, the reported results are fictitious, is to arrogate to the human mind the attribute of omniscience, by implying that what man cannot comprehend cannot be, and that therefore he is able to comprehend all that is. The miracles of record in the Gospels are as fully supported by evidence as are many of the historical events which call forth neither protest nor demand for further proof. To the believer in the divinity of Christ, the miracles are sufficiently attested; to the unbeliever they appear but as myths and fables.[342]

To comprehend the works of Christ, one must know Him as the Son of God; to the man who has not yet learned to know, to the honest soul who would inquire after the Lord, the invitation is ready; let him "Come and see."

NOTES TO CHAPTER 11.

1. Misunderstanding of Malachi's Prediction.--In the closing chapter of the compilation of scriptures known to us as the Old Testament, the prophet Malachi thus describes a condition incident to the last days, immediately preceding the second coming of Christ: "For, behold, the day cometh, that shall burn as an oven, and all the proud, yea, and all that do wickedly, shall be stubble: and the day that cometh shall burn them up, saith the Lord of hosts, that it shall leave them neither root nor branch. But unto you that fear my name shall the Sun of righteousness arise with healing in his wings." The fateful prophecy concludes with the following blessed and far-reaching promise: "Behold, I will send you Elijah the prophet before the coming of the great and dreadful day of the Lord: and he shall turn the heart of the fathers to the children, and the heart of the children to their fathers, lest I come and smite the earth with a curse." (Malachi 4:1, 2, 5, 6.) It has been held by theologians and Bible commentators that this prediction had reference to the birth and ministry of John the Baptist, (compare Matt. 11:14; 17:11; Mark 9:11; Luke 1:17), upon whom rested the spirit and power of Elias (Luke 1:17). However, we have no record of Elijah having ministered unto the Baptist, and furthermore, the latter's ministry, glorious though it was, justifies no conclusion that in him did the prophecy find its full realization. In addition, it should be remembered, that the Lord's declaration through Malachi, relative to the day of burning in which the wicked would be destroyed as stubble, yet awaits fulfilment. It is evident, therefore, that the commonly accepted interpretation is at fault, and that we must look to a later date than the time of John for the fulfilment of Malachi's prediction. The later occasion has come; it belongs to the present dispensation, and marks the inauguration of a work specially reserved for the Church in these latter days. In the course of a glorious manifestation to Joseph Smith and Oliver Cowdery, in the temple at Kirtland, Ohio, April 3d, 1836, there appeared unto them Elijah, the prophet of old, who had been taken from earth while still in the body. He declared unto them: "Behold, the time has fully come, which was spoken of by the mouth of Malachi, testifying that he (Elijah) should be sent before the great and dreadful day of the Lord come, to turn the hearts of the fathers to the children, and the children to the fathers, lest the whole earth be smitten with a curse. Therefore the keys of this dispensation are committed into your hands, and by this ye may know that the great and dreadful day of the Lord is near, even at the doors." (Doc. and Cov. 110:13-16.) See also _The House of the Lord_, pp. 82-83.

2. The Sign of the Dove.--"John the Baptist ... had the privilege of beholding the Holy Ghost descend in the form of a dove, or rather in the _sign_ of the dove, in witness of that administration. The sign of the dove was instituted before the creation of the world, a witness for the Holy Ghost, and the devil cannot come in the sign of a dove. The Holy Ghost is a personage, and is in the form of a personage. It does not confine itself to the _form_ of the dove, but in _sign_ of the dove. The Holy Ghost cannot be transformed into a dove; but the sign of a dove was given to John to signify the truth of the deed, as the dove is an emblem or token of truth and innocence."--From Sermon by Joseph Smith, _History of the Church_, vol. 5, pp. 260-261.

3. The Testimony of John the Baptist.--Observe that the Baptist's testimony to the divinity of Christ's mission is recorded as having been given after the period of our Lord's forty-day fast and temptations, and therefore approximately six weeks subsequent to the baptism of Jesus. To the deputation of priests and Levites of the Pharisaic party, who visited him by direction of the rulers, probably by appointment from the Sanhedrin, John, after disavowing that he was the Christ or any one of the prophets specified in the inquiry, said: "There standeth one among you whom ye know not; he it is who coming after me is preferred before me." On the next day, and again on the day following that, he bore public testimony to Jesus as the Lamb of God; and on the third day after the visit of the priests and Levites to John, Jesus started on the journey to Galilee (John 1:19-43).

John's use of the designation "Lamb of God" implied his conception of the Messiah as One appointed for sacrifice, and his use of the term is the earliest mention found in the Bible. For later Biblical applications, direct or implied, see Acts 8:32; 1 Peter 1:19; Rev. 5:6, 8, 12, 13; 6:1, 16; 7:9, 10, 17; etc.

4. "Come and See."--The spirit of our Lord's invitation to the young truth seekers, Andrew and John, is manifest in a similar privilege extended to all. The man who would know Christ must come to Him,

to see and hear, to feel and know. Missionaries may carry the good tidings, the message of the gospel, but the response must be an individual one. Are you in doubt as to what that message means to-day? Then come and see for yourself. Would you know where Christ is to be found? Come and see.

5. The Eternal Father a Resurrected, Exalted Being.--"As the Father hath power in himself, so hath the Son power in himself, to lay down his life and take it again, so he has a body of his own. The Son doeth what he hath seen the Father do: then the Father hath some day laid down his life and taken it again; so he has a body of his own; each one will be in his own body."--Joseph Smith; see _Hist, of the Church_, vol. 5, p. 426.

"God himself was once as we are now, and is an exalted Man, and sits enthroned in yonder heavens! That is the great secret. If the veil was rent to-day, and the Great God who holds this world in its orbit, and who upholds all worlds and all things by his power, was to make himself visible,--I say, if you were to see him to-day, you would see him like a man in form--like yourselves in all the person, image, and very form as a man; for Adam was created in the very fashion, image, and likeness of God, and received instruction from, and walked, talked and conversed with him, as one man talks and communes with another."--Joseph Smith; see _Compendium_, p. 190.

6. Waterpots for Ceremonial Cleansing.--In the house at Cana there stood in a place specially reserved, six waterpots of stone "after the manner of the purifying of the Jews." Vessels of water were provided as a matter of prescribed order in Jewish homes, to facilitate the ceremonial washings enjoined by the law. From these pots or jars the water was drawn off as required; they were reservoirs holding the supply, not vessels used in the actual ablution.

7. "The Attitude of Science Towards Miracles" is the subject of a valuable article by Prof. H. L. Orchard, published in _Journal of the Transactions of the Victoria Institute, or Philosophical Society of Great Britain_, 1910, Vol. 42, pp. 81-122. This article was the Gunning Prize Essay for 1909. After a lengthy analytical treatment of his subject, the author presents the following summation, which was concurred in by those who took part in the ensuing discussions: "We here complete our scientific investigation of Bible Miracles. It has embraced (1) the _nature_ of the phenomenon; (2) the _conditions_ under which it is alleged to have occurred; (3) the character of the _testimony_ to its occurrence. To the inquiry--Were the Bible miracles probable? science answers in the affirmative. To the further inquiry--Did they actually occur? the answer of science is again, and very emphatically, in the affirmative. If we liken them to gold, she has made her assay and says the gold is pure. Or the Bible miracles may be compared to a string of pearls. If science seeks to know whether the pearls are genuine, she may apply chemical and other tests to the examination of their _character_; she may search into the _conditions and circumstances_ in which the alleged pearls were found. Were they first found in an oyster, or in some manufacturing laboratory? And she may investigate the _testimony_ of experts. Should the result of any one of these examinations affirm the genuineness of the pearls, science will be slow to believe that they are 'paste'; if all the results declare their genuineness, science will not hesitate to say that they are true pearls. This, as we have seen, is the case of the Bible miracles. Science, therefore, affirms _their actual occurrence_."

8. The Testimony of Miracles.--The Savior's promise in a former day (Mark 16:17-18), as in the present dispensation (Doc. and Cov. 84:65-73), is definite, to the effect that specified gifts of the Spirit are to follow the believer as signs of divine favor. The possession and exercize of such gifts may be taken therefore as essential features of the Church of Christ. Nevertheless we are not justified in regarding the evidence of miracles as infallible testimony of authority from heaven; on the other hand, the scriptures furnish abundant proof that spiritual powers of the baser sort have wrought miracles, and will continue so to do, to the deceiving of many who lack discernment. If miracles be accepted as infallible evidence of godly power, the magicians of Egypt, through the wonders which they accomplished in opposition to the ordained plan for Israel's deliverance, have as good a claim to our respect as has Moses (Exo. 7:11). John the Revelator saw in vision a wicked power working miracles, and thereby deceiving many; doing great wonders, even bringing fire from heaven (Rev. 13:11-18). Again, he saw three unclean spirits, whom he knew to be "the spirits of devils working miracles" (Rev. 16:13-14). Consider, in connection with this, the prediction made by the Savior:--There shall arise false Christs, and false prophets, and shall show great signs and wonders, insomuch that, if it were possible, they shall deceive the very elect (Matt. 24:24). The invalidity of miracles as a proof of righteousness is indicated in an utterance of Jesus Christ regarding the events of the great judgment:--"Many will say to me in that day, Lord, Lord, have we not prophesied in thy name? and in thy name have cast out devils? and in thy name done many wonderful works? And then will I profess unto them, I never knew you; depart from me, ye that work iniquity" (Matt. 7:22-23). The Jews, to whom these teachings were addressed, knew that wonders could be wrought by evil powers; for they charged Christ with working miracles by the authority of Beelzebub the prince of devils (Matt. 12:22-30; Mark 3:22; Luke 11:15).--From the author's _The Articles of Faith_, xii:25, 26.

FOOTNOTES:

[309] Luke 3:4.
[310] John 1:21; compare Mal. 4:5. Note 1, end of chapter.
[311] Deut. 18:15, 18; see page 45 herein.
[312] John 1:22, 23; compare Isa. 40:3.
[313] John 1:25-27.
[314] John 1:29-31.
[315] John 1:32, 34; also verses 35, 36. Note 2, end of chapter.
[316] Note 3, end of chapter.
[317] John 1:35-51.

[318] Note 4, end of chapter.

[319] The name thus given was afterward confirmed, with accompaniments of promise; Matt. 16:18.

[320] To the apostles the Lord said on a subsequent occasion: "Ye have not chosen me, but I have chosen you" (John 15:16; see also 6:70).

[321] A favorite situation for rest, meditation, and study; 1 Kings 4:25; Micah 4:4.

[322] Acts 7:56; Rev. 1:13; 14:14.

[323] Job 25:6; Psalms 144:3; 146:3; see also 8:4 and compare Heb. 2:6-9.

[324] Ezek. 2:1, 3, 6, 8; 3:1, 3, 4; 4:1; etc.

[325] Dan. 7:13.

[326] Doc. and Cov. 27:11; 78:15, 16; 107:54-57; 116.

[327] Doc. and Cov. 49:6; 58:65; 65:5; 122:8. Observe that in modern revelation the title is used only as applying to the Christ in His resurrected and glorified state.

[328] Note 5, end of chapter.

[329] Page 38.

[330] P. of G.P., Moses 6:57; 7:35; see also 7:24, 47, 54, 56, 59, 65. Observe that Satan addressed Moses as "son of man" in a blasphemous attempt to coerce Moses into worshiping him by emphasizing the mortal weakness and inferiority of the man in contrast with his own false pretension of godship. (Moses 1:12.)

[331] John 2:1-11.

[332] "The address 'Woman' was so respectful that it might be and was, addressed to the queenliest."--(Farrar, "The Life of Christ," p. 134.)

[333] John 19:26.

[334] On a few occasions Jesus used the address "Woman" in a general way: Matt. 15:28; Luke 13:12; John 4:21; 8:10; etc.

[335] Note 6, end of chapter.

[336] John 2:11.

[337] The absence of all false austerity and outward show of abnormal abstinence in His life furnished an imagined excuse for unfounded charges of excess, through which He was said to be a glutton and a winebibber. (Matt. 11:19; Luke 7:34.)

[338] Matt. 7:22; 11:20; 12:38; 16:1; 24:24; Mark 6:14; Luke 10:13; John 2:18; 7:21; 10:25; 14:11; Acts 6:8; 8:6; 14:3; 19:11; Rom. 15:19; Rev. 13:13; etc.

[339] John 10:41; Matt. 11:9.

[340] For example Zechariah and Malachi.

[341] Exo. 3:20; 4:1-9. Note 8, end of chapter.

[342] Note 7, end of chapter.

CHAPTER 12. EARLY INCIDENTS IN OUR LORD'S PUBLIC MINISTRY.

FIRST CLEARING OF THE TEMPLE.

Soon after the marriage festivities in Cana, Jesus, accompanied by His disciples, as also by His mother and other members of the family, went to Capernaum, a town pleasantly situated near the northerly end of the Sea of Galilee or Lake of Gennesaret[343] and the scene of many of our Lord's miraculous works; indeed it came to be known as His own city.[344] Because of the unbelief of its people it became a subject of lamentation to Jesus when in sorrow He prefigured the judgment that would befall the place.[345] The exact site of the city is at present unknown. On this occasion Jesus tarried but a few days at Capernaum; for the time of the annual Passover was near, and in compliance with Jewish law and custom He went up to Jerusalem.

The synoptic Gospels,[346] which are primarily devoted to the labors of Christ in Galilee, contain no mention of His attendance at the paschal festival between His twelfth year and the time of His death; to John alone are we indebted for the record of this visit at the beginning of Christ's public ministry. It is not improbable that Jesus had been present at other Passovers during the eighteen years over which the evangelists pass in complete and reverent silence; but at any or all such earlier visits, He, not being thirty years old, could not have assumed the right or privilege of a teacher without contravening established customs.[347] It is worth our attention to note that on this, the first recorded appearance of Jesus in the temple subsequent to His visit as a Boy, He should resume His "Father's business" where He had before been engaged. It was in His Father's service that He had been found in discussion with the doctors of the law,[348] and in His Father's cause He was impelled to action on this later occasion.

The multitudinous and mixed attendance at the Passover celebration has already received passing mention;[349] some of the unseemly customs that prevailed are to be held in mind. The law of Moses had been supplemented by a cumulative array of rules, and the rigidly enforced requirements as to sacrifices and tribute had given rise to a system of sale and barter within the sacred precincts of the House of the Lord. In the outer courts were stalls of oxen, pens of sheep, cages of doves and pigeons; and the ceremonial fitness of these sacrificial victims was cried aloud by the sellers, and charged for in full measure. It was the custom also to pay the yearly poll tribute of the sanctuary at this season--the ransom offering required of every male in Israel, and amounting to half a shekel[350] for each, irrespective of his relative poverty or wealth. This was to be paid "after the shekel of the sanctuary," which limitation, as rabbis had ruled, meant payment in temple coin. Ordinary money, varieties of which bore effigies and inscriptions of heathen import, was not acceptable, and as a result, money-changers plied a thriving trade on the temple grounds.

Righteously indignant at what He beheld, zealous for the sanctity of His Father's House, Jesus essayed to clear the place;[351] and, pausing not for argument in words, He promptly applied physical force almost approaching violence--the one form of figurative language that those corrupt barterers for pelf could best understand. Hastily improvizing a whip of small cords, He laid about Him on every side, liberating and driving out sheep, oxen, and human traffickers, upsetting the tables of the exchangers and pouring out their heterogeneous accumulations of coin. With tender regard for the imprisoned and helpless birds He refrained from assaulting their cages; but to their owners He said: "Take these things hence;" and to all the greedy traders He thundered forth a command that made them quail: "Make not my Father's house an house of merchandise." His disciples saw in the incident a realization of the psalmist's line: "The zeal of thine house hath eaten me up."[352]

The Jews, by which term we mean the priestly officials and rulers of the people, dared not protest this vigorous action on the ground of unrighteousness; they, learned in the law, stood self-convicted of corruption, avarice, and of personal responsibility for the temple's defilement. That the sacred premises were in sore need of a cleansing they all knew; the one point upon which they dared to question the Cleanser was as to why He should thus take to Himself the doing of what was their duty. They practically submitted to His sweeping intervention, as that of one whose possible investiture of authority they might be yet compelled to acknowledge. Their tentative submission was based on fear, and that in turn upon their sin-convicted consciences. Christ prevailed over those haggling Jews by virtue of the eternal principle that right is mightier than wrong, and of the psychological fact that consciousness of guilt robs the culprit of valor when the imminence of just retribution is apparent to his soul.[353] Yet, fearful lest He should prove to be a prophet with power, such as no living priest or rabbi even professed to be, they timidly asked for credentials of His authority--"What sign shewest thou unto us, seeing that thou doest these things?" Curtly, and with scant respect for this demand, so common to wicked and adulterous men,[354] Jesus replied: "Destroy this temple and in three days I will raise it up."[355]

Blinded by their own craft, unwilling to acknowledge the Lord's authority, yet fearful of the possibility that they were opposing one who had the right to act, the perturbed officials found in the words of Jesus reference to the imposing temple of masonry within whose walls they stood. They took courage; this strange Galilean, who openly flouted their authority, spoke irreverently of their temple, the visible expression of the profession they so proudly flaunted in words--that they were children of the covenant, worshipers of the true and living God, and hence superior to all heathen and pagan peoples. With seeming indignation they rejoined: "Forty and six years was this temple in building, and wilt thou rear it up in three days?"[356] Though frustrated in their desire to arouse popular indignation against Jesus at this time, the Jews refused to forget or forgive His words. When afterward He stood an undefended prisoner, undergoing an illegal pretense of trial before a sin-impeached court, the blackest perjury uttered against Him was that of the false witnesses who testified: "We heard him say, I will destroy this temple that is made with hands, and within three days I will build another made without hands."[357] And while He hung in mortal suffering, the scoffers who passed by the cross wagged their heads and taunted the dying Christ with "Ah, thou that destroyest the temple, and buildest it in three days, save thyself, and come down from the cross."[358] Yet His words to the Jews who had demanded the credentials of a sign had no reference to the colossal Temple of Herod, but to the sanctuary of His own body, in which, more literally than in the man-built Holy of Holies, dwelt the ever living Spirit of the Eternal God. "The Father is in me" was His doctrine. [359]

"He spake of the temple of His body," the real tabernacle of the Most High.[360] This reference to the destruction of the temple of His body, and the renewal thereof after three days, is His first recorded prediction relating to His appointed death and resurrection. Even the disciples did not comprehend the profound meaning of His words until after His resurrection from the dead; then they remembered and understood. The priestly Jews were not as dense as they appeared to be, for we find them coming to Pilate while the body of the crucified Christ lay in the tomb, saying: "Sir, we remember that that deceiver said, while he was yet alive, After three days I will rise again."[361] Though we have many records of Christ having said that He would die and on the third day would rise again, the plainest of such declarations were made to the apostles rather than openly to the public. The Jews who waited upon Pilate almost certainly had in mind the utterance of Jesus when they had stood, nonplussed before Him, at the clearing of the temple courts.[362]

Such an accomplishment as that of defying priestly usage and clearing the temple purlieus by force could not fail to impress, with varied effect, the people in attendance at the feast; and they, returning to their homes in distant and widely separated provinces, would spread the fame of the courageous Galilean Prophet. Many in Jerusalem believed on Him at the time, mainly because they were attracted by the miracles He wrought; but He refused to "commit himself unto them," realizing the insecure foundation of their professions. Popular adulation was foreign to His purpose; He wanted no motley following, but would gather around Him such as received the testimony of His Messiahship from the Father. "He knew all men, and needed not that any should testify of man: for he knew what was in man."[363]

The incident of Christ's forcible clearing of the temple is a contradiction of the traditional conception of Him as of One so gentle and unassertive in demeanor as to appear unmanly. Gentle He was, and patient under affliction, merciful and long-suffering in dealing with contrite sinners, yet stern and inflexible in the presence of hypocrisy, and unsparing in His denunciation of persistent evil-doers. His mood was adapted to the conditions to which He addressed Himself; tender words of encouragement or burning expletives of righteous indignation issued with equal fluency from His lips. His nature was no poetic conception of cherubic sweetness ever present, but that of a Man, with the emotions and passions essential to manhood and manliness. He, who often wept with compassion, at other times evinced in word and action the righteous anger of a God. But of all His passions, however gently they rippled or strongly surged, He was ever master. Contrast the gentle Jesus moved to hospitable service by the needs of a festal party in Cana, with the indignant Christ plying His whip, and amidst commotion and turmoil of His own making, driving cattle and men before Him as an unclean herd.

JESUS AND NICODEMUS.[364]

That the wonderful deeds wrought by Christ at and about the time of this memorable Passover had led some of the learned, in addition to many of the common people, to believe in Him, is evidenced by the fact that Nicodemus, who was a Pharisee in profession and who occupied a high place as one of the rulers of the Jews, came to Him on an errand of inquiry. There is significance in the circumstance that this visit was made at night. Apparently the man was impelled by a genuine desire to learn more of the Galilean, whose works could not be ignored; though pride of office and fear of possible suspicion that he had become attached to the new Prophet led him to veil his undertaking with privacy.[365] Addressing Jesus by the title he himself bore, and which he regarded as one of honor and respect, he said: "Rabbi, we know that thou art a teacher come from God: for no man can do these miracles that thou doest, except God be with him."[366] Whether his use of the plural pronoun "we" indicates that he was sent by the Sanhedrin, or by the society of Pharisees--the members of which were accustomed to so speak, as representatives of the order--or was employed in the rhetorical sense as indicating himself alone, is of little importance. He acknowledged Jesus as a "teacher come from God," and gave reasons for so regarding Him. Whatever of feeble faith might have been stirring in the heart of the man, such was founded on the evidence of miracles, supported mainly by the psychological effect of signs and wonders. We must accord him credit for sincerity and honesty of purpose.

Without waiting for specific questions, "Jesus answered and said unto him, Verily, verily, I say unto thee, Except a man be born again, he cannot see the kingdom of God." Nicodemus appears to have been puzzled; he asked how such a rejuvenation was possible. "How can a man be born when he is old? can he enter the second time into his mother's womb, and be born?" We do Nicodemus no injustice in assuming that he as a rabbi, a man learned in the scriptures, ought to have known that there was other meaning in the words of Jesus than that of a mortal, literal birth. Moreover, were it possible that a man could be born a second time literally and in the flesh, how could such a birth profit him in spiritual growth? It would be but a reentrance on the stage of physical existence, not an advancement. The man knew that the figure of a new birth was common in the teachings of his day. Every proselyte to Judaism was spoken of at the time of his conversion as one new-born.

The surprize manifested by Nicodemus was probably due, in part at least, to the universality of the requirement as announced by Christ. Were the children of Abraham included? The traditionalism of centuries was opposed to any such view. Pagans had to be born again through a formal acceptance of Judaism, if they would become even small sharers of the blessings that belonged as a heritage to the house of Israel; but Jesus seemed to treat all alike, Jews and Gentiles, heathen idolaters and the people who with their lips at least called Jehovah, God.

Jesus repeated the declaration, and with precision, emphasizing by the impressive "Verily, verily," the greatest lesson that had ever saluted the ears of this ruler in Israel: "Verily, verily, I say unto thee, Except a man be born of water and of the Spirit, he cannot enter into the kingdom of God." That the new birth thus declared to be absolutely essential as a condition of entrance into the kingdom of God, applicable to every man, without limitation or qualification, was a spiritual regeneration, was next explained to the wondering rabbi: "That which is born of the flesh is flesh; and that which is born of the Spirit is spirit. Marvel not that I said unto thee, Ye must be born again." Still the learned Jew pondered yet failed to comprehend. Possibly the sound of the night breeze was heard at that moment; if so, Jesus was but utilizing the incident as a skilful teacher would do to impress a lesson when He continued: "The wind bloweth where it listeth, and thou hearest the sound thereof, but canst not tell whence it cometh, and whither it goeth: so is every one that is born of the Spirit." Plainly stated, Nicodemus was given to understand that his worldly learning and official status availed him nothing in any effort to understand the things of God; through the physical sense of hearing he knew that the wind blew; by sight he could be informed of its passage: yet what did he know of the ultimate cause of even this simple phenomenon? If Nicodemus would really be instructed in spiritual matters, he had to divest himself of the bias due to his professed knowledge of lesser things.

Rabbi and eminent Sanhedrist though he was, there at the humble lodging of the Teacher from Galilee, he was in the presence of a Master. In the bewilderment of ignorance he asked, "How can these things be?" The reply must have been humbling if not humiliating to the man: "Art thou a master of Israel, and knowest not these things?" Plainly a knowledge of some of the fundamental principles of the gospel had been before accessible; Nicodemus was held in reproach for his lack of knowledge, particularly as he was a teacher of the people. Then our Lord graciously expounded at greater length, testifying that He spoke from sure knowledge, based upon what He had seen, while Nicodemus and his fellows were unwilling to accept the witness of His words. Furthermore, Jesus averred His mission to be that of the Messiah, and specifically foretold His death and the manner thereof--that He, the Son of Man, must be lifted up, even as Moses had lifted the serpent in the wilderness as a prototype, whereby Israel might escape the fatal plague.[367]

The purpose of the foreappointed death of the Son of Man was: "That whosoever believeth in him should not perish, but have eternal life"; for to this end, and out of His boundless love to man had the Father devoted His Only Begotten Son. And further, while it was true that in His mortal advent the Son had not come to sit as a judge, but to teach, persuade and save, nevertheless condemnation would surely follow rejection of that Savior, for light had come, and wicked men avoided the light, hating it in their preference for the darkness in which they hoped to hide their evil deeds. Here again, perhaps, Nicodemus experienced a twinge of conscience, for had not he been afraid to come in the light, and had he not chosen the dark hours for his visit? Our Lord's concluding words combined both instruction and reproof: "But he that doeth truth cometh to the light, that his deeds may be made manifest, that they are wrought in God."

The narrative of this interview between Nicodemus and the Christ constitutes one of our most instructive and precious scriptures relating to the absolute necessity of unreserved compliance with the laws and ordinances of the gospel, as the means indispensable to salvation. Faith in Jesus Christ as the Son of God, through whom alone men may gain eternal life; the forsaking of sin by resolute turning away from the gross darkness of evil to the saving light of righteousness; the unqualified requirement of a new birth through baptism in water, and this of necessity by the mode of immersion, since otherwise the figure of a birth would be meaningless; and the completion of the new birth through baptism by the Spirit--all these principles are taught herein in such simplicity and plainness as to make plausible no man's excuse for ignorance.

If Jesus and Nicodemus were the only persons present at the interview, John, the writer, must have been informed thereof by one of the two. As John was one of the early disciples, afterward one of the apostles, and as he was distinguished in the apostolic company by his close personal companionship with the Lord, it is highly probable that he heard the account from the lips of Jesus. It was evidently John's purpose to record the great lesson of the occasion rather than to tell the circumstantial story. The record begins and ends with equal abruptness; unimportant incidents are omitted; every line is of significance; the writer fully realized the deep import of his subject and treated it accordingly. Later mention of Nicodemus tends to confirm the estimate of the man as he appears in this meeting with Jesus--that of one who was conscious of a belief in the Christ, but whose belief was never developed into such genuine and virile faith as would impel to acceptance and compliance irrespective of cost or consequence.[368]

FROM CITY TO COUNTRY.

Leaving Jerusalem, Jesus and His disciples went into the rural parts of Judea, and there tarried, doubtless preaching as opportunity was found or made; and those who believed on Him were baptized.[369] The prominent note of His early public utterances was that of His forerunner in the wilderness: "Repent: for the kingdom of heaven is at hand."[370] The Baptist continued his labors; though doubtless, since his recognition of the Greater One for whose coming he had been sent to prepare, he considered the baptism he administered as of somewhat different significance. He had at first baptized in preparation for One who was to come; now he baptized repentant believers unto Him who had come.

Disputation had arisen between some of John's zealous adherents and one or more Jews[371] concerning the doctrine of purifying. The context[372] leaves little room for doubt that a question was involved as to the relative merits of John's baptism and that administered by the disciples of Jesus. With excusable ardor and well-intended zeal for their master, the disciples of John, who had been embroiled in the dispute, came to him saying: "Rabbi, he that was with thee beyond Jordan, to whom thou bearest witness, behold, the same baptizeth, and all men come to him." John's supporters were concerned at the success of One whom they regarded in some measure as a rival to their beloved teacher. Had not John given to Jesus His first attestation? "He to whom thou bearest witness" said they, not deigning even to designate Jesus by name. Following the example of Andrew, and of John the future apostle, the people were leaving the Baptist and gathering about the Christ. John's reply to his ardent followers constitutes a sublime instance of self-abnegation. His answer was to this effect: A man receives only as God gives unto him. It is not given to me to do the work of Christ. Ye yourselves are witnesses that I disclaimed being the Christ, and that I said I was one sent before Him. He is as the Bridegroom; I am only as the friend of the bridegroom, [373] His servant; and I rejoice greatly in being thus near Him; His voice gives me happiness; and thus my joy is fulfilled. He of whom you speak stands at the beginning of His ministry; I near the end of mine. He must increase but I must decrease. He came from heaven and therefore is superior to all things of earth; nevertheless men refuse to receive His testimony. To such a One, the Spirit of God is not apportioned; it is His in full measure. The Father loveth Him, the Son, and hath given all things into His hand, and: "He that believeth on the Son hath everlasting life; and he that believeth not the Son shall not see life; but the wrath of God abideth on him."[374]

In such a reply, under the existent conditions, is to be found the spirit of true greatness, and of a humility that could rest only on a conviction of divine assurance to the Baptist as to himself and the Christ. In more than one sense was John great among all who are born of women.[375] He had entered upon his work when sent of God so to do;[376] he realized that his work had been in a measure superseded, and he patiently awaited his release, in the meantime continuing in the ministry, directing souls to his Master. The beginning of the end was near. He was soon seized and thrown into a dungeon; where, as shall be shown, he was beheaded to sate the vengeance of a corrupt woman whose sins he had boldly denounced. [377]

The Pharisees observed with increasing apprehension the growing popularity of Jesus, evidenced by the fact that even more followed after Him and accepted baptism at the hands of His disciples than had responded to the Baptist's call. Open opposition was threatened; and as Jesus desired to avert the hindrance to His work which such persecution at that time would entail, He withdrew from Judea and retired to Galilee, journeying by way of Samaria. This return to the northern province was effected after the Baptist had been cast into prison.[378]

NOTES TO CHAPTER 12.

1. Sea of Galilee.--This, the largest body of fresh water in Palestine, is somewhat pear-shape in outline and measures approximately thirteen miles in extreme length on a northerly-southerly line and between six and seven miles in greatest width. The river Jordan enters it at the northeast extremity and flows out at the south-west; the lake may be regarded, therefore, as a great expansion of the river, though the water-filled depression is about two hundred feet in depth. The outflowing Jordan connects the sea of Galilee with the Dead Sea, the latter a body of intensely saline water, which in its abundance of dissolved salts and in the consequent density of its brine is comparable to the Great Salt Lake in Utah, though the chemical composition of the waters is materially different. The sea of Galilee is referred to by Luke, in accordance with its more appropriate classification as a lake (Luke 5:1, 2; 8:22, 23, 33). Adjoining the lake on the north-west is a plain, which in earlier times was highly cultivated: this was known as the land of Gennesaret (Matt. 14:34; Mark 6:53); and the water body came to be known as the sea or lake of Gennesaret (Luke 5:1). From the prominence of one of the cities on its western shore, it was known also as the sea of Tiberias (John 6:1,23; 21:1). In the Old Testament it is called the sea of Chinnereth (Numb. 34:11) or Chinneroth (Josh. 12:3) after the name of a contiguous city (Josh. 19:35). The surface of the lake or sea is several hundred feet below normal sea-level, 681 feet lower than the Mediterranean according to Zenos, or 700 feet as stated by some others. This low-lying position gives to the region a semi-tropical climate. Zenos, in the _Standard Bible Dictionary_, says: "The waters of the lake are noted for abundant fish. The industry of fishing was accordingly one of the most stable resources of the country round about.... Another feature of the sea of Galilee is its susceptibility to sudden storms. These are occasioned partly by its lying so much lower than the surrounding tableland (a fact that creates a difference of temperature and consequent disturbances in the atmosphere), and partly by the rushing of gusts of wind down the Jordan valley from the heights of Hermon. The event recorded in Matt. 8:24 is no extraordinary case. Those who ply boats on the lake are obliged to exercize great care to avoid peril from such storms. The shores of the sea of Galilee as well as the lake itself were the scenes of many of the most remarkable events recorded in the Gospels."

2. The Four Gospels.--All careful students of the New Testament must have observed that the books of Matthew, Mark, and Luke, treat the events of the Savior's sayings and doings in Galilee with greater fulness than they accord to His work in Judea; the book or Gospel of John, on the other hand, treats particularly the incidents of our Lord's Judean ministry, without excluding, however, important events that occurred in Galilee. In style of writing and method of treatment, the authors of the first three Gospels (evangelists as they and John are collectively styled in theologic literature) differ more markedly from the author of the fourth Gospel than among themselves. The events recorded by the first three can be more readily classified, collated, or arranged, and in consequence the Gospels written by Matthew, Mark, and Luke are now commonly known as the Synoptics, or Synoptic Gospels.

3. Thirty Years of Age.--According to Luke (3:23) Jesus was about thirty years of age at the time of His baptism, and we find that soon thereafter, He entered publicly upon the work of His ministry. The law provided that at the age of thirty years the Levites were required to enter upon their special service (Numb. 4:3). Clarke, _Bible Commentary_, treating the passage in Luke 3:23, says: "This was the age required by the law to which the priests must arrive before they could be installed in their office." Jesus may possibly have had regard for what had become a custom of the time, in waiting until He had attained that age before entering publicly on the labors of a Teacher among the people. Not being of Levitical descent He was not eligible to priestly ordination in the Aaronic order, and therefore, certainly did not wait for such before beginning His ministry. To have taught in public at an earlier age would have been to arouse criticism, and objection, which might have resulted in serious handicap or hindrance at the outset.

4. Throngs and Confusion at the Passover Festival.--While it is admittedly impossible that even a reasonably large fraction of the Jewish people could be present at the annual Passover gatherings at Jerusalem, and in consequence provision was made for local observance of the feast, the usual attendance at the temple celebration in the days of Jesus was undoubtedly enormous. Josephus calls the Passover throngs "an innumerable multitude" (Wars, ii, 1:3), and in another place (Wars, vi, 9:3) states that the attendance reached the enormous aggregate of three millions of souls; such is the record, though many modern writers treat the statement as an exaggeration. Josephus says that for the purpose of giving the emperor Nero information as to the numerical strength of the Jewish people, particularly in Palestine, the chief priests were asked by Cestius to count the number of lambs slain at the feast, and the number reported was 256,500, which on the basis of between ten and eleven persons to each paschal table would indicate the presence, he says, of at least 2,700,200, not including visitors other than Jews, and such of the people of Israel as were debarred from participation in the paschal meal because of ceremonial unfitness.

The scenes of confusion, inevitable under the conditions then prevailing, are admirably summarized by Geikie (_Life and Words of Christ_, chap. 30), who cites many earlier authorities for his statements: "The streets were blocked by the crowds from all parts, who had to make their way to the Temple, past flocks of sheep, and droves of cattle, pressing on in the sunken middle part of each street reserved for them, to prevent contact and defilement. Sellers of all possible wares beset the pilgrims, for the great feasts were, as has been said, the harvest time of all trades at Jerusalem, just as, at Mecca, even at this day, the time of the great concourse of worshippers at the tomb of the Prophet, is that of the busiest trade among the merchant pilgrims, who form the caravans from all parts of the Mohammedan world.

"Inside the Temple space, the noise and pressure were, if possible, worse. Directions were posted up to keep to the right or the left, as in the densest thoroughfares of London. The outer court, which others than Jews might enter, and which was, therefore, known as the Court of the Heathen, was in part, covered with pens for sheep, goats, and cattle, for the feast and the thank-offerings. Sellers shouted the merits of their beasts, sheep bleated, and oxen lowed. It was, in fact, the great yearly fair of Jerusalem, and the crowds added to the din and tumult, till the services in the neighboring courts were sadly disturbed. Sellers of doves, for poor women coming for purification from all parts of the country, and for others, had a space set apart for them. Indeed, the sale of doves was, in great measure, secretly, in the hands of the priests themselves: Hannas, the high priest, especially, gaining great profits from his dove cotes on Mount Olivet. The rents of the sheep and cattle pens, and the profits on the doves, had led the priests to sanction the incongruity of thus turning the Temple itself into a noisy market. Nor was this all. Potters pressed on the pilgrims their clay dishes and ovens for the Passover lamb; hundreds of traders recommended their wares aloud; shops for wine, oil, salt, and all else needed for sacrifices, invited customers; and, in addition, persons going across the city, with all kinds of burdens, shortened their journey by crossing the Temple grounds. The provision for paying the tribute, levied on all, for the support of the Temple, added to the distraction. On both sides of the east Temple gate, stalls had for generations been permitted for changing foreign money. From the fifteenth of the preceding month money-changers had been allowed to set up their tables in the city, and from the twenty-first,--or twenty days before the Passover,--to ply their trade in the Temple itself. Purchasers of materials for offerings paid the amount at special stalls, to an officer of the Temple, and received a leaden cheque for which they got what they had bought, from the seller. Large sums, moreover, were changed, to be cast, as free offerings, into one of the thirteen chests which formed the Temple treasury. Every Jew, no matter how poor, was, in addition, required to pay yearly a half-shekel-- about eighteen pence--as atonement money for his soul, and for the support of the Temple. As this would not be received except in a native coin, called the Temple shekel, which was not generally current, strangers had to change their Roman, Greek, or Eastern money, at the stalls of the money-changers, to get the coin required. The trade gave ready means for fraud, which was only too common. Five per cent. exchange was charged, but this was indefinitely increased by tricks and chicanery, for which the class had everywhere earned so bad a name, that like the publicans, their witness would not be taken before a court."

Touching the matter of the defilement to which the temple courts had been subjected by traffickers acting under priestly license, Farrar, (_Life of Christ_, p. 152), gives us the following: "And this was the entrance-court to the Temple of the Most High! The court which was a witness that that house should be a House of Prayer for all nations had been degraded into a place which, for foulness, was more like shambles, and for bustling commerce more like a densely-crowded bazaar; while the lowing of oxen, the bleating of sheep, the Babel of many languages, the huckstering and wrangling, and the clinking of money and of balances (perhaps not always just), might be heard in the adjoining courts, disturbing the chant of the Levites and the prayers of priests!"

5. The Servility of the Jews in the Presence of Jesus.--The record of the achievement of Jesus, in ridding the temple courts of those who had made the House of the Lord a market place, contains nothing to suggest the inference that He exercized superhuman strength or more than manly vigor. He employed a

whip of His own making, and drove all before Him. They fled helter-skelter. None are said to have voiced an objection until the expulsion had been made complete. Why did not some among the multitude object? The submission appears to have been abject and servile in the extreme. Farrar, (_Life of Christ_, pp. 151, 152) raises the question and answers it with excellent reasoning and in eloquent lines: "Why did not this multitude of ignorant pilgrims resist? Why did these greedy chafferers content themselves with dark scowls and muttered maledictions, while they suffered their oxen and sheep to be chased into the streets and themselves ejected, and their money flung rolling on the floor, by one who was then young and unknown, and in the garb of despised Galilee? Why, in the same way we might ask, did Saul suffer Samuel to beard him in the very presence of his army? Why did David abjectly obey the orders of Joab? Why did Ahab not dare to arrest Elijah at the door of Naboth's vineyard? Because sin is weakness; because there is in the world nothing so abject as a guilty conscience, nothing so invincible as the sweeping tide of a Godlike indignation against all that is base and wrong. How could these paltry sacrilegious buyers and sellers, conscious of wrongdoing, oppose that scathing rebuke, or face the lightnings of those eyes that were enkindled by an outraged holiness? When Phinehas the priest was zealous for the Lord of Hosts, and drove through the bodies of the prince of Simeon and the Midianitish woman with one glorious thrust of his indignant spear, why did not guilty Israel avenge that splendid murder? Why did not every man of the tribe of Simeon become a Goel to the dauntless assassin? Because Vice cannot stand for one moment before Virtue's uplifted arm. Base and grovelling as they were, these money-mongering Jews felt, in all that remnant of their souls which was not yet eaten away by infidelity and avarice, that the Son of Man was right.

"Nay, even the Priests and Pharisees, and Scribes and Levites, devoured as they were by pride and formalism, could not condemn an act which might have been performed by a Nehemiah or a Judas Maccabaeus, and which agreed with all that was purest and best in their traditions. But when they had heard of this deed, or witnessed it, and had time to recover from the breathless mixture of admiration, disgust, and astonishment which it inspired, they came to Jesus, and though they did not dare to condemn what He had done, yet half indignantly asked Him for some sign that He had a right to act thus."

6. Jewish Regard for the Temple.--The Jews professed high regard for the temple. "An utterance of the Savior, construed by the dark-minded as an aspersion upon the temple, was used against Him as one of the chief accusations on which His death was demanded. When the Jews clamored for a sign of His authority He predicted His own death and subsequent resurrection, saying, 'Destroy this temple, and in three days I will raise it up,' (John 2:19-22; see also Matt. 26:61; 27:40; Mark 14:58; 15:29). They blindly regarded this remark as a disrespectful allusion to their temple, a structure built by human hands, and they refused to forget or forgive. That this veneration continued after the crucifixion of our Lord is evident from accusations brought against Stephen, and still later against Paul. In their murderous rage the people accused Stephen of disrespect for the temple, and brought false witnesses who uttered perjured testimony saying, 'This man ceaseth not to speak blasphemous words against this holy place.' (Acts 6:13.) And Stephen was numbered with the martyrs. When it was claimed that Paul had brought with him into the temple precincts, a Gentile, the whole city was aroused, and the infuriated mob dragged Paul from the place and sought to kill him. (Acts 21:26-31.)"--The author; _House of the Lord_, pp. 60, 61.

7. Some of the "Chief Rulers" Believed.--Nicodemus was not the only one among the ruling classes who believed in Jesus; but of most of these we learn nothing to indicate that they had sufficient courage to come even by night to make independent and personal inquiry. They feared the result in loss of popularity and standing. We read in John 12:42, 43: "Nevertheless among the chief rulers also many believed on him; but because of the Pharisees they did not confess him, lest they should be put out of the synagogue: for they loved the praise of men more than the praise of God." Note also the instance of the scribe who proffered to become a professed disciple, but, probably because of some degree of insincerity or unfitness, was rather discouraged than approved by Jesus. (Matt. 8:19, 20.)

8. Nicodemus.--The course followed by this man evidences at once that he really believed in Jesus as one sent of God, and that his belief failed of development into a condition of true faith, which, had it but been realized, might have led to a life of devoted service in the Master's cause. When at a later stage than that of his interview with Christ the chief priests and Pharisees upbraided the officers whom they had sent to take Jesus into custody and who returned to report their failure, Nicodemus, one of the council, ventured to mildly expostulate against the murderous determination of the rulers, by stating a general proposition in interrogative form: "Doth our law judge any man before it hear him and know what he doeth?" He was answered by his colleagues with contempt, and appears to have abandoned his well-intended effort (John 7:50-53; read preceding verses 30-49). We next hear of him bringing a costly contribution of myrrh and aloes, about a hundred-weight, to be used in the burial of Christ's then crucified body; but even in this deed of liberality and devotion, in which his sincerity of purpose cannot well be questioned, he had been preceded by Joseph of Arimathea, a man of rank, who had boldly asked for and secured the body for reverent burial (John 19:38-42). Nevertheless Nicodemus did more than did most of his believing associates among the noble and great ones; and to him let all due credit be given; he will not fail of his reward.

9. "The Jews" or "A Jew."--We read that "there arose a question between some of John's disciples and the Jews about purifying" (John 3:25). Bearing in mind that the expression "the Jews" is very commonly used by the author of the fourth Gospel to designate the officials or rulers among the people, the passage quoted may be understood to mean that the Baptist's disciples were engaged in disputation with the priestly rulers. It is held, however, by Biblical scholars generally, that "the Jews" in this passage is a mistranslation, and that the true rendering is "a Jew." The disputation concerning purifying appears to have arisen between some of the Baptist's followers and a single opponent; and the passage as it appears in the

King James version of the Bible is an instance of scripture not translated correctly.

10. Friend of the Bridegroom.--Judean marriage customs in the days of Christ required the appointing of a chief grooms-man, who attended to all the preliminaries and made arrangements for the marriage feast, in behalf of the bridegroom. He was distinctively known as the friend of the bridegroom. When the ceremonial requirements had been complied with, and the bride had been legally and formally given unto her spouse, the joy of the bridegroom's friend was fulfilled inasmuch as his appointed duties had been successfully discharged. (John 3:29.) According to Edersheim, (_Life and Times of Jesus the Messiah_, vol. 1, p. 148), by the simpler customs prevalent in Galilee a "friend of the bridegroom" was not often chosen; and (pp. 663-4) the expression "children of the bridechamber" (Matt. 9:15; Mark 2:19; Luke 5:34, in all of which citations the expression is used by Jesus), was applied collectively to all the invited guests at a wedding festival. He says: "As the institution of 'friends of the bridegroom' prevailed in Judea, but not in Galilee, this marked distinction of the 'friend of the bridegroom' in the mouth of the Judean John, and 'sons (children) of the bridechamber' in that of the Galilean Jesus, is itself evidential of historic accuracy."

11. The Atonement Money.--In the course of the exodus, the Lord required of every male in Israel who was twenty years old or older at the time of a census the payment of a ransom, amounting to half a shekel (Exo. 30:12-16). See pages 383 and 396 herein. As to the use to which this money was to be put, the Lord thus directed Moses: "And thou shalt take the atonement money of the children of Israel, and shalt appoint it for the service of the tabernacle of the congregation; that it may be a memorial unto the children of Israel before the Lord, to make an atonement for your souls" (Exo. 30:16; see also 38:25-31). In time, the tax of half a shekel, equivalent to a bekah (Exo. 38:26), was collected annually, though for this exaction no scriptural authority is of record. This tax must not be confused with the redemption money, amounting to five shekels for every firstborn male, the payment of which exempted the individual from service in the labors of the sanctuary. In place of the firstborn sons in all the tribes, the Lord designated the Levites for this special ministry; nevertheless He continued to hold the firstborn males as peculiarly His own, and required the payment of a ransom as a mark of their redemption from the duties of exclusive service. See Exo. 13:12, 13-15; Numb. 3:13, 40-51; 8:15-18; 18:15, 16; also pages 95, 96 herein.

FOOTNOTES:

[343] Note 1, end of chapter.
[344] John 2:12; compare Matt. 4:13; 9:1.
[345] Matt. 11:23; Luke 10:15.
[346] Note 2, end of chapter.
[347] Note 3, end of chapter.
[348] Page 114; Luke 2:46-49.
[349] Page 113. Note 4, end of chapter.
[350] Exo. 30:11-16. Note 11, end of chapter.
[351] John 2:14-17.
[352] Compare Psalm 69:9.
[353] Note 5, end of chapter.
[354] Matt. 12:38, 39; compare 16:1; Mark 8:11; John 6:30; 1 Cor. 1:22.
[355] John 2:19; read verses 18-22.
[356] Note 6, end of chapter.
[357] Mark 14:58. Page 624 herein.
[358] Mark 15:29, 30.
[359] John 10:38; 17:21.
[360] John 2:19-22; compare 1 Cor. 3:16, 17; 6:19; 2 Cor. 6:16; see further Col. 2:9; Heb. 8:2.
[361] Matt. 27:63. Page 665.
[362] As Canon Farrar has tersely written, "Unless the 'we remember' was a distinct falsehood, they could have been referring to no other occasion than this." ("Life of Christ," p. 155.)
[363] John 2:23-25.
[364] John 3:1-21.
[365] Note 7, end of chapter.
[366] John 3:2; read verses 1-21.
[367] Numb. 21:7-9.
[368] Note 8, end of chapter. See "Articles of Faith," v:1-5.
[369] John 3:22; compare 4:2.
[370] Matt. 4:17; compare Mark 1:15.
[371] Note 9, end of chapter.
[372] John 3:25-36.
[373] Note 10, end of chapter.
[374] John 3:27-36.
[375] Matt. 11:11.
[376] Luke 3:2,3.
[377] Matt. 14:3-12.
[378] Matt. 4:12.

CHAPTER 13. HONORED BY STRANGERS, REJECTED BY HIS OWN.

JESUS AND THE SAMARITAN WOMAN.

The direct route from Judea to Galilee lay through Samaria; but many Jews, particularly Galileans, chose to follow an indirect though longer way rather than traverse the country of a people so despized by them as were the Samaritans. The ill-feeling between Jews and Samaritans had been growing for centuries, and at the time of our Lord's earthly ministry had developed into most intense hatred.[379] The inhabitants of Samaria were a mixed people, in whom the blood of Israel was mingled with that of the Assyrians and other nations; and one cause of the animosity existing between them and their neighbors both on the north and the south was the Samaritans' claim for recognition as Israelites; it was their boast that Jacob was their father; but this the Jews denied. The Samaritans had a version of the Pentateuch, which they revered as the law, but they rejected all the prophetical writings of what is now the Old Testament, because they considered themselves treated with insufficient respect therein.

To the orthodox Jew of the time a Samaritan was more unclean than a Gentile of any other nationality. It is interesting to note the extreme and even absurd restrictions then in force in the matter of regulating unavoidable relations between the two peoples. The testimony of a Samaritan could not be heard before a Jewish tribunal. For a Jew to eat food prepared by a Samaritan was at one time regarded by rabbinical authority as an offense as great as that of eating the flesh of swine. While it was admitted that produce from a field in Samaria was not unclean, inasmuch as it sprang directly from the soil, such produce became unclean if subjected to any treatment at Samaritan hands. Thus, grapes and grain might be purchased from Samaritans, but neither wine nor flour manufactured therefrom by Samaritan labor. On one occasion the epithet "Samaritan" was hurled at Christ as an intended insult. "Say we not well that thou art a Samaritan, and hast a devil?"[380] The Samaritan conception of the mission of the expected Messiah was somewhat better founded than was that of the Jews, for the Samaritans gave greater prominence to the spiritual kingdom the Messiah would establish, and were less exclusive in their views as to whom the Messianic blessings would be extended.

In His journey to Galilee Jesus took the shorter course, through Samaria; and doubtless His choice was guided by purpose, for we read that "He must needs go" that way.[381] The road led through or by the town called Sychar,[382] "near to the parcel of ground that Jacob gave to his son Joseph."[383] There was Jacob's well, which was held in high esteem, not only for its intrinsic worth as an unfailing source of water, but also because of its association with the great patriarch's life. Jesus, travel-warn and weary, rested at the well, while His disciples went to the town to buy food. A woman came to fill her water-jar, and Jesus said to her: "Give me to drink." By the rules of oriental hospitality then prevailing, a request for water was one that should never be denied if possible to grant; yet the woman hesitated, for she was amazed that a Jew should ask a favor of a Samaritan, however, great the need. She expressed her surprize in the question "How is it that thou, being a Jew, askest drink of me, which am a woman of Samaria? for the Jews have no dealings with the Samaritans." Jesus, seemingly forgetful of thirst in His desire to teach, answered her by saving: "If thou knewest the gift of God, and who it is that saith to thee, Give me to drink; thou wouldest have asked of him, and he would have given thee living water." The woman reminded Him that He had no bucket or cord with which to draw from the deep well, and inquired further as to His meaning, adding: "Art thou greater than our father Jacob, which gave us the well, and drank thereof himself, and his children, and his cattle?"

Jesus found in the woman's words a spirit similar to that with which the scholarly Nicodemus had received His teachings; each failed alike to perceive the spiritual lesson He would impart. He explained to her that water from the well would be of but temporary benefit; to one who drank of it thirst would return. "But," he added, "whosoever drinketh of the water that I shall give him shall never thirst; but the water that I shall give him shall be in him a well of water springing up into everlasting life." The woman's interest was keenly aroused, either from curiosity or as an emotion of deeper concern, for she now became the petitioner, and, addressing Him by a title of respect, said: "Sir, give me this water, that I thirst not, neither come hither to draw." She could see nothing beyond the material advantage attaching to water that would once and for all quench thirst. The result of the draught she had in mind would be to give her immunity from one bodily need, and save her the labor of coming to draw from the well.

The subject of the conversation was abruptly changed by Jesus bidding her to go, call her husband, and return. To her reply that she had no husband Jesus revealed to her His superhuman powers of discernment, by telling her she had spoken truthfully, inasmuch as she had had five husbands, while the man with whom she was then living was not her husband. Surely no ordinary being could have so read the unpleasing story of her life; she impulsively confessed her conviction, saying: "Sir, I perceive that thou art a prophet." She desired to turn the conversation, and, pointing to Mount Gerizim, upon which the sacrilegious priest Manasseh had erected a Samaritan temple, she remarked with little pertinence to what had been said before: "Our fathers worshipped in this mountain; and ye say, that in Jerusalem is the place where men ought to worship." Jesus replied in yet deeper vein, telling her that the time was near when neither that mountain nor Jerusalem would be preeminently a place of worship; and He clearly rebuked her presumption that the traditional belief of the Samaritans was equally good with that of the Jews; for, said He: "Ye worship ye know not what: we know what we worship: for salvation is of the Jews." Changed and corrupted as the Jewish religion had become, it was better than that of her people; for the Jews did accept the prophets, and through Judah the Messiah had come. But, as Jesus expounded the matter to her, the place of worship was of lesser importance than the spirit of the worshiper. "God is a Spirit: and they that worship him must worship him in spirit and in truth."

Unable or unwilling to understand Christ's meaning, the woman sought to terminate the lesson by a remark that probably was to her but casual: "I know that Messias cometh, which is called Christ: when he is come, he will tell us all things." Then, to her profound amazement, Jesus rejoined with the awe-inspiring declaration: "I that speak unto thee am he." The language was unequivocal, the assertion one that required no elucidation. The woman must regard Him thereafter as either an imposter or the Messiah. She left her pitcher at the well, and hastening to the town told of her experience, saying: "Come, see a man, which told me all things that ever I did: is not this the Christ?"

Near the conclusion of the interview between Jesus and the woman, the returning disciples arrived with the provisions they had gone to procure. They marveled at finding the Master in conversation with a woman, and a Samaritan woman at that; yet none of them asked of Him an explanation. His manner must have impressed them with the seriousness and solemnity of the occasion. When they urged Him to eat He said: "I have meat to eat that ye know not of." To them His words had no significance beyond the literal sense, and they queried among themselves as to whether some one had brought Him food during their absence; but He enlightened them in this way: "My meat is to do the will of him that sent me, and to finish his work."

A crowd of Samaritans appeared, coming from the city. Looking upon them and upon the grain fields nearby, Jesus continued: "Say not ye, There are yet four months, and then cometh harvest? behold, I say unto you, Lift up your eyes, and look on the fields; for they are white already to harvest." The import of the saying seems to be that while months would elapse before the wheat and the barley were ready for the sickle, the harvest of souls, exemplified by the approaching crowd, was even then ready; and that from what He had sown the disciples might reap, to their inestimable advantage, since they would have wages for their hire and would gather the fruits of other labor than their own.

Many of the Samaritans believed on Christ, at first on the strength of the woman's testimony, then because of their own conviction; and they said to the woman at whose behest they had at first gone to meet Him: "Now we believe, not because of thy saying: for we have heard him ourselves, and know that this is indeed the Christ, the Saviour of the world." Graciously He acceded to their request to remain, and tarried with them two days. It is beyond question that Jesus did not share in the national prejudice of the Jews against the people of Samaria; an honest soul was acceptable to Him come whence he may. Probably the seed sown during this brief stay of our Lord among the despized people of Samaria was that from which so rich a harvest was reaped by the apostles in after years.[384]

JESUS AGAIN IN GALILEE: AT CANA AND NAZARETH.

Following the two days' sojourn among the Samaritans, Jesus, accompanied by the disciples who had traveled with Him from Judea, resumed the journey northward into Galilee, from which province He had been absent several months. Realizing that the people of Nazareth, the town in which He had been brought up, would be probably loath to acknowledge Him as other than the carpenter, or, as He stated, knowing that "a prophet hath no honour in his own country,"[385] He went first to Cana. The people of that section, and indeed the Galileans generally, received Him gladly; for many of them had attended the last Passover and probably had been personal witnesses of the wonders He had wrought in Judea. While at Cana He was visited by a nobleman, most likely a high official of the province, who entreated Him to proceed to Capernaum and heal his son, who was then lying at the point of death. With the probable design of showing the man the true condition of his mind, for we cannot doubt that Jesus could read his thoughts, our Lord said to him: "Except ye see signs and wonders, ye will not believe."[386] As observed in earlier instances, notably in the refusal of Jesus to commit Himself to the professing believers at Jerusalem, whose belief rested solely on their wonder at the things He did,[387] our Lord would not regard miracles, though wrought by Himself, as a sufficient and secure foundation for faith. The entreating nobleman, in anguish over the precarious state of his son, in no way resented the rebuke such as a captious mind may have found in the Lord's reply; but with sincere humility, which showed his belief that Jesus could heal the boy, he renewed and emphasized his plea: "Sir, come down ere my child die."

Probably the man had never paused to reason as to the direct means or process by which death might be averted and healing be insured through the words of any being; but in his heart he believed in Christ's power, and with pathetic earnestness besought our Lord to intervene in behalf of his dying son. He seemed to consider it necessary that the Healer be present, and his great fear was that the boy would not live until Jesus could arrive. "Jesus saith unto him, Go thy way; thy son liveth. And the man believed the word that Jesus had spoken unto him, and he went his way." The genuineness of the man's trust is shown by his grateful acceptance of the Lord's assurance, and by the contentment that he forthwith manifested. Capernaum, where his son lay, was about twenty miles away; had he been still solicitous and doubtful he would probably have tried to return home that day, for it was one o'clock in the afternoon when Jesus spoke the words that had given to him such relief; but he journeyed leisurely, for on the following day he was still on the road, and was met by some of his servants who had been sent to cheer him with the glad word of his son's recovery. He inquired when the boy had begun to amend, and was told that at the seventh hour on the yesterday the fever had left him. That was the time at which Christ had said, "Thy son liveth." The man's belief ripened fast, and both he and his household accepted the gospel.[388] This was the second miracle wrought by Jesus when in Cana, though in this instance the subject of the blessing was in Capernaum.

Our Lord's fame spread through all the region round about. During a period not definitely stated, He taught in the synagogs of the towns and was received with favor, being glorified of all.[389] He then returned to Nazareth, His former home, and as was his custom, attended the synagog on the Sabbath day. Many times as boy and man He had sat in that house of worship, listening to the reading of the law and the prophets and to the commentaries or Targums[390] relating thereto, as delivered by appointed readers; but now, as a recognized teacher of legal age He was eligible to take the reader's place. On this occasion He stood up to read, when the service had reached the stage at which extracts from the prophetical books were to be read to the congregation. The minister in charge handed Him the roll, or book, of Isaiah; He turned to the part known to us as the beginning of the sixty-first chapter, and read: "The Spirit of the Lord is upon me, because he hath anointed me to preach the gospel to the poor; he hath sent me to heal the broken-hearted, to preach deliverance to the captives, and recovering of sight to the blind, to set at liberty them that are bruised, to preach the acceptable year of the Lord."[391] Handing the book to the minister, He sat down. It was allowable for the reader in the service of the Jewish synagog to make comments in explanation of what had been read; but to do so he must sit. When Jesus took His seat the people knew that He was about to expound the text, and "the eyes of all them that were in the synagogue were fastened on him." The scripture He had quoted was one recognized by all classes as specifically referring to the Messiah, for whose coming the nation waited. The first sentence of our Lord's commentary was startling; it involved no labored analysis, no scholastic interpretation, but a direct and unambiguous application: "This day is this scripture fulfilled in your ears." There was such graciousness in His words that all wondered, and they said, "Is not this Joseph's son?"[392]

Jesus knew their thoughts even if He heard not their words, and, forestalling their criticism, He said: "Ye will surely say unto me this proverb, Physician, heal thyself: whatsoever we have heard done in Capernaum, do also here in thy country. And he said, Verily I say unto you, No prophet is accepted in his own country." In their hearts the people were eager for a sign, a wonder, a miracle. They knew that Jesus had wrought such in Cana, and a boy in Capernaum had been healed by His word; at Jerusalem too He had astonished the people with mighty works. Were they, His townsmen, to be slighted? Why would He not treat them to some entertaining exhibition of His powers? He continued His address, reminding them that in the days of Elijah, when for three years and a half no rain had fallen, and famine had reigned, the prophet had been sent to but one of the many widows, and she a woman of Sarepta in Sidon, a Gentile, not a daughter of Israel. And again, though there had been many lepers in Israel in the days of Elisha, but one leper, and he a Syrian, not an Israelite, had been cleansed through the prophet's ministration, for Naaman alone had manifested the requisite faith.

Then great was their wrath. Did He dare to class them with Gentiles and lepers? Were they to be likened unto despized unbelievers, and that too by the son of the village carpenter, who had grown from childhood in their community? Victims of diabolical rage, they seized the Lord and took Him to the brow of the hill on the slopes of which the town was built, determined to avenge their wounded feelings by hurling Him from the rocky cliffs. Thus early in His ministry did the forces of opposition attain murderous intensity. But our Lord's time to die had not yet come. The infuriated mob was powerless to go one step farther than their supposed victim would permit. "But he passing through the midst of them went his way." Whether they were overawed by the grace of His presence, silenced by the power of His words, or stayed by some more appalling intervention, we are not informed. He departed from the unbelieving Nazarenes, and thenceforth Nazareth was no longer His home.

IN CAPERNAUM.

Jesus wended His way to Capernaum,[393] which became to Him as nearly a place of abode as any He had in Galilee. There He taught, particularly on Sabbath days; and the people were astonished at His doctrine, for He spoke with authority and power.[394] In the synagog, on one of these occasions, was a man who was a victim of possession, and subject to the ravages of an evil spirit, or, as the text so forcefully states, one who "had a spirit of an unclean devil." It is significant that this wicked spirit, which had gained such power over the man as to control his actions and utterances, was terrified before our Lord and cried out with a loud voice, though pleadingly: "Let us alone; what have we to do with thee, thou Jesus of Nazareth? art thou come to destroy us? I know thee who thou art; the Holy One of God." Jesus rebuked the unclean spirit, commanding him to be silent, and to leave the man; the demon obeyed the Master, and after throwing the victim into violent though harmless paroxysm, left him. Such a miracle caused the beholders to wonder the more, and they exclaimed: "What a word is this! for with authority and power he commandeth the unclean spirits, and they come out. And the fame of him went out into every place of the country round about."[395]

In the evening of the same day, when the sun had set, and therefore after the Sabbath had passed[396], the people flocked about Him, bringing their afflicted friends and kindred; and these Jesus healed of their divers maladies whether of body or of mind. Among those so relieved were many who had been possessed of devils, and these cried out, testifying perforce of the Master's divine authority: "Thou art Christ the Son of God."[397]

On these as on other occasions, we find evil spirits voicing through the mouths of their victims their knowledge that Jesus was the Christ; and in all such instances the Lord silenced them with a word; for He wanted no such testimony as theirs to attest the fact of His Godship. Those spirits were of the devil's following, members of the rebellious and defeated hosts that had been cast down through the power of the very Being whose authority and power they now acknowledged in their demoniac frenzy. Together with Satan himself, their vanquished chief, they remained unembodied, for to all of them the privileges of the second or mortal estate had been denied;[398] their remembrance of the scenes that had culminated in their expulsion from heaven was quickened by the presence of the Christ, though He stood in a body of flesh.

Many modern writers have attempted to explain the phenomenon of demoniacal possession;

and beside these there are not a few who deny the possibility of actual domination of the victim by spirit personages. Yet the scriptures are explicit in showing the contrary. Our Lord distinguished between this form of affliction and that of simple bodily disease in His instructions to the Twelve: "Heal the sick, cleanse the lepers, raise the dead, cast out devils."[399] In the account of the incidents under consideration, the evangelist Mark observes the same distinction, thus: "They brought unto him all that were diseased, and them that were possessed with devils." In several instances, Christ, in rebuking demons, addressed them as individuals distinct from the human being afflicted,[400] and in one such instance commanded the demon to "come out of him, and enter no more into him."[401]

In this matter as in others the simplest explanation is the pertinent truth; theory raised on other than scriptural foundation is unstable. Christ unequivocally associated demons with Satan, specifically in His comment on the report of the Seventy whom He authorized and sent forth, and who testified with joy on their return that even the devils had been subject unto them through His name; and to those faithful servants He said: "I beheld Satan as lightning fall from heaven."[402] The demons that take possession of men, overruling their agency and compelling them to obey Satanic bidding, are the unembodied angels of the devil, whose triumph it is to afflict mortals, and if possible to impel them to sin. To gain for themselves the transitory gratification of tenanting a body of flesh, these demons are eager to enter even into the bodies of beasts.[403]

Possibly it was during the interval between the rebuking of the evil spirit in the synagog and the miracles of healing and casting out devils in the evening of that Sabbath, that Jesus went to the house of Simon, whom He had before named Peter, and there found the mother-in-law of His disciple lying ill of fever. Acceding to the request of faith He rebuked the disease; the woman was healed forthwith, rose from her bed, and ministered the hospitality of her home unto Jesus and those who were with Him.[404]

NOTES TO CHAPTER 13.

1. Animosity Between Jews and Samaritans.--In any consideration of the Samaritans, it must be kept in mind that a certain city and the district or province in which it was situated were both known as Samaria. The principal facts pertaining to the origin of the Samaritans and the explanation of the mutual animosity existing between that people and the Jews in the time of Christ, have been admirably summarized by Geikie (_Life and Words of Christ_, vol. i, pp. 495-6). Omitting his citation of authorities, we quote: "After the deportation of the Ten Tribes to Assyria, Samaria had been repeopled by heathen colonists from various provinces of the Assyrian empire, by fugitives from the authorities of Judea, and by stragglers of one or other of the Ten Tribes, who found their way home again. The first heathen settlers, terrified at the increase of wild animals, especially lions, and attributing it to their not knowing the proper worship of the God of the country, sent for one of the exiled priests, and, under his instructions, added the worship of Jehovah to that of their idols--an incident in their history from which later Jewish hatred and derision taunted them as 'proselytes of the lions,' as it branded them, from their Assyrian origin, with the name of Cuthites. Ultimately, however, they became even more rigidly attached to the Law of Moses than the Jews themselves. Anxious to be recognized as Israelites, they set their hearts on joining the Two Tribes, on their return from captivity, but the stern Puritanism of Ezra and Nehemiah admitted no alliance between the pure blood of Jerusalem and the tainted race of the north. Resentment at this affront was natural, and excited resentment in return, till, in Christ's day, centuries of strife and mutual injury, intensified by theological hatred on both sides, had made them implacable enemies. The Samaritans had built a temple on Mount Gerizim, to rival that of Jerusalem, but it had been destroyed by John Hyrcanus, who had also levelled Samaria to the ground. They claimed for their mountain a greater holiness than that of Moriah; accused the Jews of adding to the word of God, by receiving the writings of the prophets, and prided themselves on owning only the Pentateuch as inspired; favoured Herod because the Jews hated him, and were loyal to him and the equally hated Romans; had kindled false lights on the hills, to vitiate the Jewish reckoning by the new moons, and thus throw their feasts into confusion, and, in the early youth of Jesus, had even defiled the very Temple itself, by strewing human bones in it, at the Passover.

"Nor had hatred slumbered on the side of the Jews. They knew the Samaritans only as Cuthites, or heathens from Cuth. 'The race that I hate is no race,' says the son of Sirach. It was held that a people who once had worshipped five gods could have no part in Jehovah. The claim of the Samaritans that Moses had buried the Tabernacle and its vessels on the top of Gerizim, was laughed to scorn. It was said that they had dedicated their temple, under Antiochus Epiphanes, to the Greek Jupiter. Their keeping the commands of Moses even more strictly than the Jews, that it might seem they were really of Israel, was not denied; but their heathenism, it was said, had been proved by the discovery of a brazen dove, which they worshipped, on the top of Gerizim. It would have been enough that they boasted of Herod as their good king, who had married a daughter of their people; that he had been free to follow, in their country, his Roman tastes, so hated in Judea; that they had remained quiet, after his death, when Judea and Galilee were in uproar, and that for their peacefulness a fourth of their taxes had been remitted and added to the burdens of Judea. Their friendliness to the Romans was an additional provocation. While the Jews were kept quiet only by the sternest severity, and strove to the utmost against the introduction of anything foreign, the Samaritans rejoiced in the new importance which their loyalty to the empire had given them. Shechem flourished: close by, in Cæsarea, the procurator held his court: a division of cavalry, in barracks at Sebaste--the old Samaria--had been raised in the territory. The Roman strangers were more than welcome to while away the summer in their umbrageous valleys.

"The illimitable hatred, rising from so many sources, found vent in the tradition that a special curse had been uttered against the Samaritans, by Ezra, Zerubbabel, and Joshua. It was said that these great ones assembled the whole congregation of Israel in the Temple, and that three hundred priests, with three hundred trumpets, and three hundred books of the Law, and three hundred scholars of the Law, had been employed to repeat, amidst the most solemn ceremonial, all the curses of the Law against the Samaritans. They had been subjected to every form of excommunication; by the incommunicable name of Jehovah; by the Tables of the Law, and by the heavenly and earthly synagogues. The very name became a reproach. 'We know that Thou art a Samaritan, and hast a devil,' said the Jews, to Jesus, in Jerusalem.... A Samaritan egg, as the hen laid it, could not be unclean, but what of a boiled egg? Yet interest and convenience strove, by subtle casuistry, to invent excuses for what intercourse was unavoidable. The country of the Cuthites was clean, so that a Jew might, without scruple, gather and eat its produce. The waters of Samaria were clean, so that a Jew might drink them or wash in them. Their dwellings were clean, so that he might enter them, and eat or lodge in them. Their roads were clean, so that the dust of them did not defile a Jew's feet. The Rabbis even went so far in their contradictory utterances, as to say that the victuals of the Cuthites were allowed, if none of their wine or vinegar were mixed with them, and even their unleavened bread was to be reckoned fit for use at the Passover. Opinions thus wavered, but, as a rule, harsher feeling prevailed."

That the hostile sentiment has continued unto this day, at least on the part of the Jews, is affirmed by Frankl and others. Thus, as quoted by Farrar (p. 166 note): "'Are you a Jew?' asked Salameh Cohen, the Samaritan high priest, of Dr. Frankl; 'and do you come to us, the Samaritans, who are despised by the Jews?' (_Jews in the East_, ii, 329). He added that they would willingly live in friendship with the Jews, but that the Jews avoided all intercourse with them. Soon after, visiting Sepharedish Jews of Nablous, Dr. Frankl asked one of that sect, 'if he had any intercourse with the Samaritans?' The women retreated with a cry of horror, and one of them said, 'Have you been among the worshipers of the pigeons?' I said that I had. The women again fell back with the same expression of repugnance and one of them said, 'Take a purifying bath!'" (idem, p. 334). Canon Farrar adds, "I had the pleasure of spending a day among the Samaritans encamped on Mount Gerizim, for their annual passover, and neither in their habits nor apparent character could I see any cause for all this horror and hatred."

2. Sychar.--The town where dwelt the Samaritan woman with whom Jesus conversed at Jacob's well, is named Sychar in John 4:5; the name occurs nowhere else in the Bible. Attempts have been made to identify the place with Shechem, a city dear to the Jewish heart because of its prominence in connection with the lives of the early patriarchs. It is now generally admitted, however, that Sychar was a small village on the site of the present Askar, which is, says Zenos, "a village with a spring and some ancient rock-hewn tombs, about five eighths of a mile north of Jacob's well."

3. The Nobleman of Capernaum.--The name of the nobleman whose son was healed by the word of Jesus is not given. Attempts to identify him with Chuza, the steward of Herod Antipas, are based on unreliable tradition. The family of the nobleman accepted the teachings of Christ. "Joanna the wife of Chuza Herod's steward" (Luke 8:3) was among the grateful and honorable women who had been recipients of our Lord's healing ministry, and who contributed of their substance for the furtherance of His work. Unconfirmed tradition should not be confounded with authentic history.

4. The Targums are ancient Jewish paraphrases on the scriptures, which were delivered in the synagogs in the languages of the common people. In the time of Christ the language spoken by the Jews was not Hebrew, but an Aramaic dialect. Edersheim states that pure Hebrew was the language of scholars and of the synagog, and that the public readings from the scriptures had to be rendered by an interpreter. "In earliest times indeed," says he, "it was forbidden to the Methurgeman [interpreter] to read his translation, or to write down a Targum, lest the paraphrase should be regarded as of equal authority with the original." The use of written targums was "authoritatively sanctioned before the end of the second century after Christ. This is the origin of our two oldest extant Targumim--that of Onkelos (as it is called) on the Pentateuch; and that on the Prophets, attributed to Jonathan the son of Uzziel. These names do not indeed, accurately represent the authorship of the oldest Targumim, which may more correctly be regarded as later and authoritative recensions of what, in some form, had existed before. But although these works had their origin in Palestine, it is noteworthy that in the form in which at present we possess them, they are the outcome of the schools of Babylon." (_Life and Times of Jesus the Messiah_, vol. i, pp. 10, 11.)

5. Capernaum.--"The name Capernaum signifies, according to some authorities, 'the Village of Nahum,' according to others, 'the Village of Consolation.' As we follow the history of Jesus we shall discover that many of His mighty works were wrought, and many of His most impressive words were spoken in Capernaum. The infidelity of the inhabitants, after all the discourses and wonderful works which He had done among them, brought out the saying of Jesus, 'And thou, Capernaum, which art exalted unto heaven, shalt be cast down to hell.' (Matt. 11:23.) So thoroughly has this prediction been fulfilled that no trace of the city remains, and the very site which it occupied is now a matter of conjecture, there being even no ecclesiastical tradition of the locality. At the present day two spots have claims which are urged, each with such arguments of probability as to make the whole question the most difficult in sacred topography.... We shall probably never be able to know the exact fact. Jesus damned it to oblivion, and there it lies. We shall content ourselves with the New Testament notices as bearing on the work of Jesus.

"We learn that it was somewhere on the borders of Zabulun and Nephtali, on the western shore of the Sea of Galilee, (compare Matt 4:13, with John 6:24). It was near or in 'the land of Gennesaret' (compare Matt 14:34, with John 6:17, 21, 24), a plain about three miles long and one mile wide, which we learn from Josephus was one of the most prosperous and crowded districts of Palestine. It was probably on the great road leading from Damascus to the south, 'by the way of the sea,' (Matt. 4:15.) There was great wisdom in selecting this as a place to open a great public ministry. It was full of a busy population. The exceeding richness of the wonderful plain of Gennesaret supported the mass of inhabitants it attracted.

Josephus (B. J., iii, 10:8) gives a glowing description of this land."--Deems _Light of the Nations_, pp. 167, 168.

6. Knowledge Does Not Insure Salvation.--James of old chided his brethren for certain empty professions (James 2:19). Said he in effect: You take pride and satisfaction in declaring your belief in God; you boast of being distinguished from the idolaters and the heathen because you accept one God; you do well to so profess, and so believe; but, remember, others do likewise; even the devils believe; and, we may add, so firmly that they tremble at thought of the fate which that belief makes sure. Those confessions of the devils, that Christ was the Son of God, were founded on knowledge; yet their knowledge of the great truth did not change their evil natures. How different was their acknowledgment of the Savior from that of Peter, who, to the Master's question "Whom say ye that I am?" replied in practically the words used by the unclean spirits before cited, "Thou art the Christ, the Son of the living God" (Matt. 16:15-16; see also Mark 8:29; Luke 9:20). Peter's faith had already shown its vital power; it had caused him to forsake much that had been dear, to follow his Lord through persecution and suffering, and to put away worldliness with all its fascinations, for the sacrificing godliness which his faith made so desirable. His knowledge of God as the Father, and of the Son as the Redeemer, was perhaps no greater than that of the unclean spirits; but while to them that knowledge was but an added cause of condemnation, to him it was a means of salvation.--Abridged from _The Articles of Faith_.

FOOTNOTES:

[379] Note 1, end of chapter.
[380] John 8:48.
[381] John 4:4; for incidents following see verses 5-43.
[382] Note 2, end of chapter.
[383] Gen. 33:19; and Josh. 24:32.
[384] Acts 8:5; 9:31; 15:3.
[385] John 4:44; compare Matt. 13:57; Mark 6:4; Luke 4:24.
[386] John 4:48; read verses 46-54.
[387] John 2:23, 24.
[388] Note 3, end of chapter.
[389] Luke 4:14, 15; read verses 16-32.
[390] Note 4, end of chapter.
[391] Luke 4:18, 19; compare Isa. 61:1, 2.
[392] Luke 4:22; compare Matt. 13:55-57; Mark 6:3; John 6:42.
[393] Note 5, end of chapter.
[394] Luke 4:32; compare Matt. 7:28, 29; 13:54; Mark 1:22.
[395] Luke 4:33-37; and Mark 1:23-28. Note 6, end of chapter.
[396] The Jews' Sabbath began at sunset Friday and ended with the setting of the sun on Saturday.
[397] Luke 4:41; compare Mark 1:34; 3:11, 12; 5:1-18; Matt. 8:28-34.
[398] Pages 6, 7.
[399] Matt. 10:8; see verse 1; compare 4:24; Mark 1:32; 16:17, 18; Luke 9:1
[400] Matt. 8:32; Mark 1:25; Luke 4:35.
[401] Mark 9:25.
[402] Luke 10:17, 18; compare Rev. 12:7-9.
[403] Matt. 8:29-33; Mark 5:11-14; Luke 8:32-34.
[404] Matt. 8:14, 15; Mark 1:29-31; Luke 4:38, 39.

CHAPTER 14. CONTINUATION OF OUR LORD'S MINISTRY IN GALILEE.

A LEPER MADE CLEAN.

Early in the morning following that eventful Sabbath in Capernaum, our Lord arose "a great while before day" and went in quest of seclusion beyond the town. In a solitary place He gave Himself to prayer, thus demonstrating the fact that, Messiah though He was, He was profoundly conscious of His dependence upon the Father, whose work He had come to do. Simon Peter and other disciples found the place of His retirement, and told Him of the eager crowds who sought Him. Soon the people gathered about Him, and urged that He remain with them; but "he said unto them, I must preach the kingdom of God to other cities also: for therefore am I sent."[405] And to the disciples He said: "Let us go into the next towns, that I may preach there also: for therefore came I forth."[406] Thence He departed, accompanied by the few whom He had already closely associated with Himself, and ministered in many towns of Galilee, preaching in the synagogs, healing the sick, and casting out devils.

Among the afflicted seeking the aid that He alone could give came a leper,[407] who knelt before Him, or bowed with his face to the ground, and humbly professed his faith, saying: "If thou wilt, thou canst make me clean." The petition implied in the words of this poor creature was pathetic; the confidence he expressed is inspiring. The question in his mind was not--Can Jesus heal me? but--Will He heal me? In compassionate mercy Jesus laid His hand upon the sufferer, unclean though he was, both ceremonially and physically, for leprosy is a loathsome affliction, and we know that this man was far advanced in the disease since we are told that he was "full of leprosy." Then the Lord said: "I will: be thou clean." The leper was immediately healed. Jesus instructed him to show himself to the priest, and make the offerings prescribed in the law of Moses for such cases as his.[408]

In this instruction we see that Christ had not come to destroy the law, but, as He affirmed at another time, to fulfil it;[409] and at this stage of His work the fulfilment was incomplete. Moreover, had the legal requirements been disregarded in as serious a matter as that of restoring an outcast leper to the society of the community from which he had been debarred, priestly opposition, already waxing strong and threatening against Jesus, would have been augmented, and further hindrance to the Lord's work might have resulted. There was to be no delay in the man's compliance with the Master's instruction; Jesus "straitly charged him, and forthwith sent him away." Furthermore He explicitly directed the man to tell nobody of the manner of his healing. There was perhaps good reason for this injunction of silence, aside from the very general course of our Lord in discountenancing undesirable notoriety; for, had word of the miracle preceded the man's appearing before the priest, obstacles might have been thrown in the way of his Levitical recognition as one who was clean. The man, however, could not keep the good word to himself, but went about "and began to publish it much, and to blaze abroad the matter, insomuch that Jesus could no more openly enter into the city, but was without in desert places: and they came to him from every quarter."[410]

A PALSIED MAN HEALED AND FORGIVEN.

It must be borne in mind that no one of the evangelists attempts to give a detailed history of all the doings of Jesus, nor do all follow the same order in relating the incidents with which they associate the great lessons of the Master's teachings. There is much uncertainty as to the actual sequence of events.

"Some days" after the healing of the leper, Jesus was again in Capernaum. The details of His employment during the interval are not specified; but, we may be sure that His work continued, for His characteristic occupation was that of going about doing good.[411] His place of abode in Capernaum was well known, and word was soon noised about that He was in the house.[412] A great throng gathered, so that there was no room to receive them; even the doorway was crowded, and later comers could not get near the Master. To all who were within hearing Jesus preached the gospel. A little party of four approached the house bearing a litter or pallet on which lay a man afflicted with palsy, a species of paralysis which deprived the subject of the power of voluntary motion and usually of speech; the man was helpless. His friends, disappointed at finding themselves unable to reach Jesus because of the press, resorted to an unusual expedient, which exhibited in an unmistakable way their faith in the Lord as One who could rebuke and stay disease, and their determination to seek the desired blessing at His hands.

By some means they carried the afflicted man to the flat roof of the house, probably by an outside stairway or by the use of a ladder, possibly by entering an adjoining house, ascending the stairs to its roof and crossing therefrom to the house within which Jesus was teaching. They broke away part of the roof, making an opening, or enlarging that of the trapdoor such as the houses of that place and time were usually provided with; and, to the surprize of the assembled crowd, they then let down through the tiling the portable couch upon which the palsied sufferer lay. Jesus was deeply impressed by the faith and works[413] of those who had thus labored to place a helpless paralytic before Him; doubtless, too, He knew of the trusting faith in the heart of the sufferer; and, looking compassionately upon the man, He said: "Son, thy sins be forgiven thee."

Among the people there assembled were scribes, Pharisees, and doctors of the law, not only representatives of the local synagog but some who had come from distant towns in Galilee, and some from Judea, and even from Jerusalem. The official class had opposed our Lord and His works on earlier occasions, and their presence in the house at this time boded further unfriendly criticism and possible obstruction. They heard the words spoken to the paralytic, and were angered thereat. In their hearts they accused Jesus of the awful offense of blasphemy, which consists essentially in claiming for human or demon power the prerogatives of God, or in dishonoring God by ascribing to Him attributes short of perfection.[414] These unbelieving scholars, who incessantly wrote and talked of the coming of the Messiah, yet rejected Him when He was there present, murmured in silence, saying to themselves: "Who can forgive sins but God only?" Jesus knew their inmost thoughts,[415] and made reply thereto, saying: "Why reason ye these things in your hearts? Whether is it easier to say to the sick of the palsy, Thy sins be forgiven thee; or to say, Arise, and take up thy bed, and walk?" And then to emphasize, and to put beyond question His possession of divine authority, He added: "But that ye may know that the Son of man hath power on earth to forgive sins, (he saith to the sick of the palsy,) I say unto thee, Arise, and take up thy bed, and go thy way into thine house." The man arose, fully restored; and, taking up the mattress upon which he had been brought, walked out before them. The amazement of the people was mingled with reverence, and many glorified God, of whose power they were witnesses.

The incident demands our further study. According to one of the accounts, the Lord's first words to the afflicted one were: "Son, be of good cheer;" followed directly by the comforting and authoritative assurance: "Thy sins be given thee."[416] The man was probably in a state of fear; he may have known that his ailment was the result of wicked indulgences; nevertheless, though he may have considered the possibility of hearing only condemnation for his transgression, he had faith to be brought. In this man's condition there was plainly a close connection between his past sins and his present affliction; and in this particular his case is not unique, for we read that Christ admonished another, whom He healed, to sin no more lest a worse thing befall him.[417] We are not warranted, however, in assuming that all bodily ills are the result of culpable sin; and against such a conception stands the Lord's combined instruction and rebuke to those who, in the case of a man born blind, asked who had sinned, the man or his parents to bring so grievous an affliction upon him, to which inquiry our Lord replied that the man's blindness was due neither to his own sin nor to that of his parents.[418]

In many instances, however, disease is the direct result of individual sin. Whatever may have been the measure of past offense on the part of the man suffering from palsy, Christ recognized his repentance together with the faith that accompanied it, and it was the Lord's rightful prerogative to decide upon the man's fitness to receive remission of his sins and relief from his bodily affliction. The interrogative response of Jesus to the muttered criticism of the scribes, Pharisees, and doctors, has been interpreted in many ways. He inquired which was easier, to say, "Thy sins be forgiven thee," or to say, "Arise, and take up thy bed, and walk." Is it not a rational explanation that, when spoken authoritatively by Him, the two expressions were of allied meaning? The circumstance should have been a sufficient demonstration to all who heard, that He, the Son of Man, claimed and possessed the right and the power to remit both physical and spiritual penalties, to heal the body of visible disease, and to purge the spirit of the no less real malady of sin. In the presence of people of all classes Jesus thus openly asserted His divinity, and affirmed the same by a miraculous manifestation of power.

The charge of blasphemy, which the rabbinical critics formulated in their minds against the Christ, was not to end as a mental conception of theirs, nor to be nullified by our Lord's later remarks. It was through perjured testimony that He finally received unrighteous condemnation and was sent to His death.[419] Already, in that house at Capernaum, the shadow of the cross had fallen athwart the course of His life.

PUBLICANS AND SINNERS.

From the house Jesus repaired to the seaside, whither the people followed Him; there He taught them again. At the close of His discourse He walked farther and saw a man named Levi, one of the publicans[420] or official collectors of taxes, sitting at the custom-house where the tariff levied under Roman law had to be paid. This man was known also as Matthew, a name less distinctively Jewish than is Levi.[421] He afterward became one of the Twelve and the author of the first of the evangelical Gospels. To him Jesus said, "Follow me." Matthew left his place and followed the Lord. Some time later the new disciple provided a great feast at his house, in honor of the Master; and other disciples were present. So obnoxious to the Jews was the power of Rome to which they were subject, that they regarded with aversion all officials in Roman employ. Particularly humiliating to them was the system of compulsory taxation, by which they, the people of Israel, had to pay tribute to an alien nation, which in their estimation was wholly pagan and heathen.

Naturally, the collectors of these taxes were abhorred; and they, known as publicans, probably resented the discourteous treatment by inconsiderate enforcement of the tax requirements, and, as affirmed by historians, often inflicted unlawful extortion upon the people. If publicans in general were detested, we can readily understand how bitter would be the contempt in which the Jews would hold one of their own nation who had accepted appointment as such an official. In this unenviable status was Matthew when Jesus called him. The publicans formed a distinct social class, for from the community in general they were practically ostracized. All who associated with them were made to share in the popular odium, and "publicans and sinners" became a common designation for the degraded caste. To Matthew's feast many of his friends and some of his fellow officials were invited, so that the gathering was largely made up of these despised "publicans and sinners." And to such an assemblage went Jesus with His disciples.

The scribes and Pharisees could not let pass such an opportunity for faultfinding and caustic criticism. They hesitated to address themselves directly to Jesus, but of the disciples they asked in disdain: "Why eateth your Master with publicans and sinners?" The Master heard, and replied with edifying incisiveness mingled with splendid irony. Citing one of the common aphorisms of the day, He said: "They that be whole need not a physician, but they that are sick." To this He added: "I am not come to call the righteous, but sinners to repentance." The hypercritical Pharisees were left to make their own application of the rejoinder, which some may have understood to mean that their self-righteousness was arraigned and their claims to superiority derided. Aside from the veiled sarcasm in the Master's words, they ought to have perceived the wisdom enshrined in His answer and to have profited thereby. Is not the physician's place among the afflicted ones? Would he be justified in keeping aloof from the sick and the suffering? His profession is that of combating disease, preventing when possible, curing when necessary, to the full extent of his ability. If the festive assembly at Matthew's house really did comprize a number of sinners, was not the occasion one of rare opportunity for the ministrations of the Physician of Souls? The righteous need no call to repentance; but are the sinners to be left in sin, because those who profess to be spiritual teachers will not condescend to extend a helping hand?

THE OLD AND THE NEW.

Shortly after the entertainment provided by Matthew, the Pharisees were ready with another criticism, and in this they were associated with some of the Baptist's adherents. John was in prison; but many of those who had been drawn to his baptism, and had professed discipleship to him, still clung to his teachings, and failed to see that the Greater One of whom he had testified was then ministering amongst them. The Baptist had been a scrupulous observer of the law; his strict asceticism vied with the rigor of Pharisaic profession. His non-progressive disciples, now left without a leader, naturally fell in with the Pharisees. Some of John's disciples came to Jesus, and questioned Him concerning His seeming indifference in the matter of fasting. They propounded a plain question: "Why do the disciples of John and of the Pharisees fast, but thy disciples fast not?"[422] To the friends of the now imprisoned Baptist our Lord's reply must have brought memories of their beloved leader's words, when he had compared himself to the Bridegroom's friend, and had plainly told them who was the real Bridegroom.[423] "Jesus said unto them, Can the children of the bridechamber fast, while the bridegroom is with them? as long as they have the bridegroom with them, they cannot fast. But the days will come, when the bridegroom shall be taken away from them, and then shall they fast in those days."[424]

If the questioners were able to comprehend the true import of this reply, they could not fail to find therein an implied abrogation of purely ceremonial observances comprized in the code of rabbinical rules and the numerous traditions associated with the law. But to make the subject clearer to their biased minds, Jesus gave them illustrations, which may be classed as parabolic. "No man also," said He, "seweth a piece of new cloth on an old garment: else the new piece that filled it up taketh away from the old, and the rent is made worse. And no man putteth new wine into old bottles: else the new wine doth burst the bottles, and the wine is spilled, and the bottles will be marred: but new wine must be put into new bottles."[425]

In such wise did our Lord proclaim the newness and completeness of His gospel. It was in no sense a patching up of Judaism. He had not come to mend old and torn garments; the cloth He provided was new, and to sew it on the old would be but to tear afresh the threadbare fabric and leave a more unsightly rent than at first. Or to change the figure, new wine could not safely be entrusted to old bottles. The bottles here referred to were really bags, made of the skins of animals, and of course they deteriorated with age. Just as old leather splits or tears under even slight strain, so the old bottle-skins would burst from the pressure of fermenting juice, and the good wine would be lost. The gospel taught by Christ was a new revelation, superseding the past, and marking the fulfilment of the law; it was no mere addendum, nor was it a reenactment of past requirements; it embodied a new and an everlasting covenant. Attempts to patch the Judaistic robe of traditionalism with the new fabric of the covenant could result in nothing more sightly than a rending of the fabric. The new wine of the gospel could not be held in the old time-worn containers of Mosaic libations. Judaism would be belittled and Christianity perverted by any such incongruous association.[426]

FISHERS OF MEN.

It is improbable that the disciples who followed Jesus in the early months of His ministry had remained with Him continuously down to the time now under consideration. We find that some of those who were later called to the apostleship were following their vocation as fishermen even while Jesus was actively engaged as a Teacher in their own neighborhood. One day, as the Lord stood by the lake or sea of Galilee, the people pressed about Him in great numbers, eager to hear more of the wondrous words He was wont to speak.[427] Near the place were two fishing boats drawn in upon the beach; the owners were close by, washing and mending their nets. One of the boats belonged to Simon Peter, who had already become identified with the Master's work; this boat Jesus entered, and then asked Simon to thrust out a little from the land. Seating Himself, as teachers of that time usually did in delivering discourses, the Lord preached from this floating pulpit to the multitude on shore. The subject of the address is not given us.

When the sermon was ended, Jesus directed Simon to launch out into deep water and then let down the nets for a draught. Presumably Andrew was with his brother and possibly other assistants were in the boat. Simon replied to Jesus: "Master, we have toiled all the night, and have taken nothing: nevertheless at thy word I will let down the net." It was soon filled with fishes; so great was the haul that the net began to break, and the busy fishermen signalled to those in the other boat to come to their assistance. The catch filled both boats so that they appeared to be in danger of sinking. Simon Peter was overcome with this new evidence of the Master's power, and, falling at the feet of Jesus, he exclaimed: "Depart from me; for I am a sinful man, O Lord." Jesus answered graciously and with promise: "Fear not; from henceforth thou shalt catch men."[428] The occupants of the second boat were Zebedee and his two sons James and John, the last named being he who with Andrew had left the Baptist to follow Jesus at the Jordan.[429] Zebedee and his sons were partners with Simon in the fishing business. When the two boats were brought to land, the brothers Simon and Andrew, and Zebedee's two sons James and John, left their boats and accompanied Jesus.

The foregoing treatment is based on Luke's record; the briefer and less circumstantial accounts given by Matthew and Mark omit the incident of the miraculous draught of fishes, and emphasize the calling of the fishermen. To Simon and Andrew Jesus said: "Come ye after me, and I will make you to become fishers of men." The contrast thus presented between their former vocation and their new calling is strikingly forceful. Theretofore they had caught fish, and the fate of the fish was death; thereafter they were to draw men--to a life eternal. To James and John the call was no less definite; and they too left their all to follow the Master.

NOTES TO CHAPTER 14.

1. Leprosy.--In Biblical usage this name is applied to several diseases, all, however having some symptoms in common, at least in the earlier stages of the malady. The real leprosy is a scourge and a plague in many oriental lands to-day. Zenos, in _Standard Bible Dict._, says: "True leprosy, as known in modern times, is an affection characterized by the appearance of nodules in the eye-brows, the cheeks, the nose, and the lobes of the ears, also in the hands and feet, where the disease eats into the joints, causing the falling off of fingers and toes. If nodules do not appear, their place is taken by spots of blanched or discolored skin (Mascular leprosy). Both forms are based upon a functional degeneration of the nerves of the skin. Its cause was discovered by Hansen in 1871 to be a specific bacillus. Defective diet, however, seems to serve as a favorable condition for the culture of the bacillus. Leprosy was one of the few abnormal conditions of the body which the Levitical law declared unclean. Elaborate provision was therefore made for testing its existence and for the purification of those who were cured of it."

Deems, _Light of the Nations_, p. 185, summing up the conditions incident to the advanced stages of the dread disease, writes: "The symptoms and the effects of this disease are very loathsome. There comes a white swelling or scab, with a change of the color of the hair on the part from its natural hue to yellow; then the appearance of a taint going deeper than the skin, or raw flesh appearing in the swelling. Then it spreads and attacks the cartilaginous portions of the body. The nails loosen and drop off, the gums are absorbed, and the teeth decay and fall out; the breath is a stench, the nose decays; fingers, hands, feet, may be lost, or the eyes eaten out. The human beauty has gone into corruption, and the patient feels that he is being eaten as by a fiend, who consumes him slowly in a long remorseless meal that will not end until he be destroyed. He is shut out from his fellows. As they approach he must cry, 'Unclean! unclean!' that all humanity may be warned from his precincts. He must abandon wife and child. He must go to live with other lepers, in disheartening view of miseries similar to his own. He must dwell in dismantled houses or in the tombs. He is, as Trench says, a dreadful parable of death. By the laws of Moses (Lev. 13:45; Numb. 6:9; Ezek. 24:17) he was compelled, as if he were mourning for his own decease, to bear about him the emblems of death, the rent garments; he was to keep his head bare and his lip covered, as was the custom with those who were in communion with the dead. When the Crusaders brought the leprosy from the East, it was usual to clothe the leper in a shroud, and to say for him the masses for the dead.... In all ages this indescribably horrible malady has been considered incurable. The Jews believed that it was inflicted by Jehovah directly, as a punishment for some extraordinary perversity or some transcendent act of sinfulness, and that only God could heal it. When Naaman was cured, and his flesh came back like that of a little child, he said, 'Now I know that there is no God in all the earth but in Israel,' (2 Kings 5:14, 15.)"

The fact that leprosy is not ordinarily communicable by mere outward contact is accentuated by Trench, _Notes on the Miracles_, pp. 165-168, and the isolation of lepers required by the Mosaic law is regarded by him as an intended object lesson and figure to illustrate spiritual uncleanness. He says: "I refer to the mistaken assumption that leprosy was catching from one person to another; and that the lepers were so carefully secluded from their fellowmen lest they might communicate the disease to others, as in like manner that the torn garment, the covered lip, the cry, 'Unclean, unclean' (Lev. 13:45) were warnings to all that they should keep aloof, lest unawares touching a leper, or drawing unto too great a nearness, they should become partakers of this disease. So far from any danger of the kind existing, nearly all who have looked closest into the matter agree that the sickness was incommunicable by ordinary contact from one person to another. A leper might transmit it to his children, or the mother of a leper's children might take it from him; but it was by no ordinary contact communicable from one person to another. All the notices in the Old Testament, as well as in other Jewish books, confirm the statement that we have here something very much higher than a mere sanitary regulation. Thus, when the law of Moses was not observed, no such exclusion necessarily found place; Naaman the leper commanded the armies of Syria (2 Kings 5:1); Gehazi, with his leprosy that never should be cleansed, (2 Kings 5:27) talked familiarly with the king of apostate Israel (2 Kings 8:5).... How, moreover, should the Levitical priests, had the disease been this creeping infection, have ever themselves escaped it, obliged as they were by their very office to submit the leper to actual handling and closest examination?... Leprosy was nothing short of a living death, a corrupting of all the humors, a poisoning of the very springs, of life; a dissolution, little by little, of the whole body, so that one limb after another actually decayed and fell away. Aaron exactly describes the appearance which the leper presented to the eyes of the beholders, when, pleading for Miriam, he says, 'Let her not be as one dead, of whom the flesh is half consumed when he cometh out of his mother's womb.' (Numb. 12:12.) The disease, moreover, was incurable by the art and skill of man; not that the leper might not return to health; for, however rare, such cases are contemplated in the Levitical law.... The leper, thus fearfully bearing about the body the outward and visible tokens of sin in the soul, was treated throughout as a sinner, as one in whom sin had reached its climax, as one dead in trespasses and sins. He was himself a dreadful parable of death. He bore about him the emblems of death (Lev. 13:45); the rent garments, mourning for himself as one dead; the head bare as they were wont to have it who were defiled by communion with the dead (Numb. 6:9; Ezek. 24:27); and the lip covered (Ezek. 24:17).... But the leper was as one dead, and as such was shut out of the camp (Lev. 13:46; Numb. 5:2-4). and the city (2 Kings 7:3), this law being so strictly enforced that even the sister of Moses might not be exempted from it (Numb. 12:14, 15); and kings themselves, as Uzziah (2 Chron. 26:21; 2 Kings 15:5) must submit to it; men being by this exclusion taught that what here took place in a figure, should take place in the reality with every one who was found in the death of sin."

For the elaborate ceremonies incident to the cleansing of a recovered leper see Lev. chap. 14.

2. Blasphemy.--The essence of the deep sin of blasphemy lies not, as many suppose, in profanity alone, but as Dr. Kelso, _Stand. Bible Dict._, summarizes: "Every improper use of the divine name (Lev. 24:11), speech derogatory to the Majesty of God (Matt. 26:65), and sins with a high hand--i.e. premeditated transgressions of the basal principles of the theocracy (Numb. 9:13; 15:30; Exo. 31:14)--were regarded as blasphemy; the penalty was death by stoning (Lev. 24:16)." _Smith's Bible Dict._ states: "Blasphemy, in its technical English sense, signifies the speaking evil of God, and in this sense it is found in Psalm 74:18; Isa. 52:5; Rom. 2:24, etc.... On this charge both our Lord and Stephen were condemned to death by the Jews. When a person heard blasphemy he laid his hand on the head of the offender, to symbolize his sole responsibility for the guilt, and rising on his feet, tore his robe, which might never again be mended." (See Matt. 26:65.)

3. Publican.--"A word originally meaning a contractor for public works or supplies, or a farmer of public lands, but later applied to Romans who bought from the government the right to collect taxes in a given territory. These buyers, always knights (senators were excluded by their rank), became capitalists and formed powerful stock companies, whose members received a percentage on the capital invested. Provincial capitalists could not buy taxes, which were sold in Rome to the highest bidders, who to recoup themselves sublet their territory (at a great advance on the price paid the government) to the native (local) publicans, who in their turn had to make a profit on their purchase money, and being assessors of property as well as collectors of taxes, had abundant opportunities for oppressing the people, who hated them both for that reason and also because the tax itself was the mark of their subjection to foreigners."--J. R. Sterrett in _Stand. Bible Dict._

4. Fishers of Men.--"Follow me, and I will make you fishers of men," said Jesus to fishermen who afterward became His apostles (Matt. 4:19). Mark's version is nearly the same (1:17), while that of Luke (5:10) reads: "From henceforth thou shalt catch men." The correct translation is, as commentators practically agree, "From henceforth thou shalt take men alive." This reading emphasizes the contrast given in the text--that between capturing fish to kill them and winning men to save them. Consider in this connection the Lord's prediction through Jeremiah (16:16), that in reaching scattered Israel, "Behold, I will send for many fishers, saith the Lord, and they shall fish them;" etc.

5. "Thy Sins Be Forgiven Thee."--The following commentary by Edersheim (_Life and Times of Jesus the Messiah_, vol. i, pp. 505, 506) on the incident under consideration is instructive: "In this forgiveness of sins He presented His person and authority as divine, and He proved it such by the miracle of healing which immediately followed. Had the two been inverted, [i.e. had Christ first healed the man and afterward told him that his sins were forgiven] there would have been evidence, indeed, of His power, but not of His divine personality, nor of His having authority to forgive sins; and this, not the doing of miracles, was the object of His teaching and mission, of which the miracles were only secondary evidence. Thus the inward reasoning of the scribes, which was open and known to Him who readeth all thoughts, issued in quite the opposite of what they could have expected. Most unwarranted, indeed, was the feeling of contempt which we trace in their unspoken words, whether we read them: 'Why does this one thus speak blasphemies?' or, according to a more correct transcript of them: 'Why does this one speak thus? He blasphemeth!' Yet from their point of view they were right, for God alone can forgive sins; nor has that power ever been given or delegated to man. But was He a mere man, like even the most honored of God's servants? Man, indeed; but 'the Son of Man.' ... It seemed easy to say: 'Thy sins have been forgiven.' But to Him, who had authority to do so on earth, it was neither more easy nor more difficult than to say: 'Rise, take up thy bed, and walk.' Yet this latter, assuredly, proved the former, and gave it in the sight of all men unquestioned reality. And so it was the thoughts of these scribes, which, as applied to Christ, were 'evil'--since they imputed to Him blasphemy--that gave occasion for offering real evidence of what they would have impugned and denied. In no other manner could the object alike of miracles and of this special miracle have been so attained as by the 'evil thoughts' of these scribes, when, miraculously brought to light, they spoke out the inmost possible doubt, and pointed to the highest of all questions concerning the Christ. And so it was once more the wrath of man which praised Him."

FOOTNOTES:

[405] Luke 4:42-44.
[406] Mark 1:38.
[407] Mark 1:40-45; Matt. 8:2-4; Luke 5:12-15.
[408] Lev. 14:2-10. Note 1, end of chapter.
[409] Matt. 5:17.
[410] Mark 1:45.
[411] Acts 10:38.

[412] Mark 2:1-12; compare Matt. 9:2-8; Luke 5:17-24.
[413] Compare James 2:14-18.
[414] Note 2, end of chapter.
[415] See another instance of our Lord reading unuttered thoughts. Luke 7:39-50.
[416] Matt. 9:2. Note 5, end of chapter.
[417] John 5:14. Page 208.
[418] John 9:1-3.
[419] Compare John 10:33, and 5:18; Matt. 26:65, 66.
[420] Note 3, end of chapter.
[421] Matt. 9:9-13; Mark 2:13-17; Luke 5:27-32.
[422] Mark 2:18-22; Matt. 9:14-17; Luke 5:33-39.
[423] Page 164.
[424] Mark 2:19, 20.
[425] Mark 2:21, 22.
[426] See "The Great Apostasy" 7:5.
[427] Luke 5:1-11; compare Matt. 4:18-22; Mark 1:16-20.
[428] Note 4, end of chapter.
[429] Page 140.

CHAPTER 15. LORD OF THE SABBATH.

THE SABBATH DISTINCTIVELY SACRED TO ISRAEL.

The observance of the Sabbath as a holy day was prominent among the Lord's requirements of His people, Israel, from a very early period in their history as a nation. Indeed, the keeping of the Sabbath as a day of surcease from ordinary toil was a national characteristic, by which the Israelites were distinguished from pagan peoples, and rightly so, for the holiness of the Sabbath was made a mark of the covenant between the chosen people and their God. The sanctity of the Sabbath had been prefigured in the account of the creation, antedating the placing of man upon the earth, as shown by the fact that God rested after the six periods or days of creative work, and blessed the seventh day and hallowed it.[430] In the course of Israel's exodus, the seventh day was set apart as one of rest, upon which it was not allowed to bake, seethe, or otherwise cook food. A double supply of manna had to be gathered on the sixth day, while on other days the laying-by of a surplus of this daily bread sent from heaven was expressly forbidden. The Lord observed the sacredness of the holy day by giving no manna thereon.[431]

The commandment to celebrate the Sabbath in strictness was made definite and explicit in the decalog, written by the hand of God amidst the awful glory of Sinai; and the injunction was kept before the people through frequent proclamation.[432] It was unlawful to kindle a fire on that day; and record is made of a man who was put to death for gathering sticks on the seventh day.[433] Under the administration of later prophets, the holiness of the Sabbath, the blessings promised to those who sanctified the day unto themselves, and the sin of Sabbath desecration were reiterated in words of inspired forcefulness.[434] Nehemiah admonished and reproved in the matter, and attributed the affliction of the nation to the forfeiture of Jehovah's favor through Sabbath violation.[435] By the mouth of Ezekiel the Lord affirmed that the institution of the Sabbath was a sign of the covenant between Himself and the people of Israel; and with stern severity He upbraided those who heeded not the day.[436] To the separate branch of the Israelitish nation that had been colonized on the western hemisphere, regard for the sanctity of the Sabbath was no less an imperative requirement.[437]

The observance demanded, however, was the very opposite of affliction and burden; the Sabbath was consecrated to rest and righteous enjoyment, and was to be a day of spiritual feasting before the Lord. It was not established as a day of abstinence; all might eat, but both mistress and maid were to be relieved from the work of preparing food; neither master nor man was to plow, dig or otherwise toil; and the Weekly day of rest was as much the boon of the cattle as of their owners.

In addition to the weekly Sabbath, the Lord in mercy prescribed also a sabbatic year; in every seventh year the land was to rest, and thereby its fertility was enhanced.[438] After seven times seven years had passed, the fiftieth was to be celebrated throughout as a year of jubilee, during which the people should live on the accumulated increase of the preceding seasons of plenty, and rejoice in liberality by granting to one another redemption from mortgage and bond, forgiveness of debt, and general relief from burdens--all of which had to be done in mercy and justice.[439] The Sabbaths established by the Lord, whether of days, of years, or of weeks of years, were to be times of refreshing, relief, blessing, bounty, and worship.

To the many who profess to regard the necessity of toil as a part of the curse evoked through Adam's fall, the Sabbath should appeal as a day of temporary reprieve, a time of exemption from labor, and as affording blessed opportunity of closer approach to the Presence from which mankind has been shut out through sin. And to those who take the higher view of life, and find in work both happiness and material blessing, the periodical relief brings refreshment and gives renewed zest for the days that follow.

But long before the advent of Christ, the original purpose of the Sabbath had come to be largely ignored in Israel; and the spirit of its observance had been smothered under the weight of rabbinical injunction and the formalism of restraint. In the time of the Lord's ministry, the technicalities prescribed as rules appended to the law were almost innumerable; and the burden thus forced upon the people had become well nigh unbearable. Among the many wholesome requirements of the Mosaic law, which the teachers and spiritual rulers of the Jews had made thus burdensome, that of Sabbath observance was especially prominent. The "hedge," which by unwarranted assumption they professedly set about the law, [440] was particularly thorny in the sections devoted to the Jewish Sabbath. Even trifling infractions of traditional rules were severely punished, and the capital penalty was held before the eyes of the people as a supreme threat for extreme desecration.[441]

THE HEALING OF A CRIPPLE ON THE SABBATH.

In view of these conditions, we are not surprized to find our Lord confronted with charges of Sabbath violation relatively early in the course of His public work. An instance attended with many great developments is recorded by John,[442] whose narrative covers the incident of a very impressive miracle. Jesus was again in Jerusalem at the time of one of the Jewish festivals.[443] There was a pool of water, called Bethesda, near the sheep market in the city. From the recorded description, we may understand this to have been a natural spring; possibly the water was rich in dissolved solids or gases, or both, making it such as we would call today a mineral spring; for we find that the water was reputed to possess curative virtues, and many afflicted folk came to bathe therein. The spring was of the pulsating variety; at intervals its waters rose with bubbling disturbance, and then receded to the normal level. Mineral springs of this kind are known today in many parts of the world. Some believed that the periodical upwelling of the Bethesda waters was the result of supernatural agency; and it was said that "whosoever then first after the troubling of the water stepped in was made whole of whatsoever disease he had." The Bethesda pool was wholly or partly enclosed; and five porches had been built for the shelter of those who waited at the spring for the intermittent bubbling up of the water.

On a certain Sabbath day, Jesus visited the pool and saw many afflicted folk thus waiting. Among them lay a man who for thirty-eight years had been grievously afflicted. From the man's statement of his helplessness we may infer that his malady was paralysis, or possibly an extreme form of rheumatism; whatever his affliction, it was so disabling as to give him little chance of getting into the pool at the critical time, for others less crippled crowded him away; and, according to the legends regarding the curative properties of the spring, only the first to enter the pool after the agitation of the water might expect to be healed.

Jesus recognized in the man a fit subject for blessing, and said to him: "Wilt thou be made whole?" The question was so simple as almost to appear superfluous. Of course the man wanted to be made well, and on the small chance of being able to reach the water at the right moment was patiently yet eagerly waiting. There was purpose, however, in these as in all other words of the Master. The man's attention was drawn to Him, fixed upon Him; the question aroused in the sufferer's heart renewed yearning for the health and strength of which he had been bereft since the days of his youth. His answer was pitiful, and revealed his almost hopeless state of mind; he thought only of the rumored virtues of Bethesda pool as he said: "Sir, I have no man, when the water is troubled, to put me into the pool: but while I am coming, another steppeth down before me." Then spake Jesus: "Rise, take up thy bed, and walk." Immediately strength returned to the man, who for nearly four decades had been a helpless invalid; he obeyed the Master, and, taking up the little mattress or pallet on which he had rested, walked away.

He had not gone far, before the Jews, that is to say, some of the official class, for so the evangelist John employs the term, saw him carrying his bed; and it was the Sabbath day. To their peremptory reprimand he replied out of the gratitude and honest simplicity of his heart, that He who had healed him had told him to take up his bed and walk. The interest of the inquisitors was instantly turned from the man toward Him who had wrought the miracle; but the erstwhile cripple could not name his Benefactor, as he had lost sight of Jesus in the crowd before he had found opportunity for question or thanks. The man who had been healed went to the temple, possibly impelled by a desire to express in prayer his gratitude and joy. There Jesus found him, and said unto him: "Behold, thou art made whole: sin no more, lest a worse thing come unto thee."[444] The man had probably brought about his affliction through his own sinful habits. The Lord decided that he had suffered enough in body, and terminated his physical suffering with the subsequent admonition to sin no more.

The man went and told the rulers who it was that had healed him. This he may have done with a desire to honor and glorify the Giver of his boon; we are not justified in ascribing to him any unworthy purpose, though by his act he was instrumental in augmenting the persecution of his Lord. So intense was the hatred of the priestly faction that the rulers sought a means of putting Jesus to death, under the specious pretense of His being a Sabbath-breaker. We may well ask of what act they could possibly have hoped to convict Him, even under the strictest application of their rules. There was no proscription against speaking on the Sabbath; and Jesus had but spoken to heal. He had not carried the man's bed, nor had He attempted even the lightest physical labor. By their own interpretation of the law they had no case against Him.

OUR LORD'S REPLY TO THE ACCUSING JEWS.

Nevertheless, the Jewish officials confronted Jesus with accusations. Whether the interview took place within the temple walls, on the open street, at the market place, or in the judgment hall, matters not. His reply to their charges is not confined to the question of Sabbath observance; it stands as the most comprehensive sermon in scripture on the vital subject of the relationship between the Eternal Father and His Son, Jesus Christ.

His first sentence added to the already intense anger of the Jews. Referring to the work He had done on the holy day, He said: "My Father worketh hitherto, and I work." This remark they construed to be a blasphemy.[445] "Therefore the Jews sought the more to kill him, because he not only had broken the Sabbath, but said also that God was his Father, making himself equal with God." To their spoken or unuttered protest, Jesus replied, that He, the Son, was not acting independently, and in fact could do nothing except what was in accordance with the Father's will, and what He had seen the Father do; that the Father so loved the Son as to show unto Him the Father's works.

Be it observed that Jesus in no way attempted to explain away their construction of His words; on the contrary He confirmed their deductions as correct. He did associate Himself with the Father, even in a closer and more exalted relationship than they had conceived. The authority given to Him by the Father was not limited to the healing of bodily infirmities; He had power even to raise the dead--"For as the Father raiseth up the dead, and quickeneth them; even so the Son quickeneth whom he will." Moreover, the judgment of men had been committed unto Him; and no one could honor the Father except by honoring the Son. Then followed this incisive declaration: "Verily, verily, I say unto you, He that heareth my word, and believeth on him that sent me, hath everlasting life, and shall not come into condemnation; but is passed from death unto life."

Christ's realm was not bounded by the grave; even the dead were wholly dependent upon Him for their salvation; and to the terrified ears of His dumbfounded accusers He proclaimed the solemn truth, that even then the hour was near in which the dead should hear the voice of the Son of God. Ponder His profound affirmation: "Verily, verily, I say unto you, The hour is coming, and now is, when the dead shall hear the voice of the Son of God: and they that hear shall live." The murderous rage of the Jews was rebuffed by the declaration that without His submission they could not take His life: "For as the Father hath life in himself; so hath he given to the Son to have life in himself." Another utterance was equally portentous: "And hath given him authority to execute judgment also, because he is the Son of man." He, the Son of the exalted and glorified Man of Holiness and now Himself a mortal Man,[446] was to be the judge of men.

No wonder they marveled; such doctrine they had never before heard nor read; it was not of the scribes nor of the rabbis, of neither the Pharisaic nor Sadducean schools. But He reproved their amazement, saying: "Marvel not at this: for the hour is coming, in the which all that are in the graves shall hear his voice, And shall come forth; they that have done good, unto the resurrection of life; and they that have done evil, unto the resurrection of damnation."[447]

This enunciation of the resurrection, so plainly made that the most unlettered could understand, must have offended any Sadducees present, for they emphatically denied the actuality of the resurrection. The universality of a resurrection is here unquestionably affirmed; not only the righteous but even those who merit condemnation are to come forth from their graves in their bodies of flesh and bones. [448]

Then, renewing His solemn asseveration of the unity of His Father's will and His own, Christ discussed the matter of witnesses to His work. He admitted what was a recognized tenet of the time, that no man's unsupported witness of himself was sufficient; but, He added: "There is another that beareth witness of me; and I know that the witness which he witnesseth of me is true." He cites John the Baptist, and reminds them that they had sent a delegation to him, and that John had answered them by bearing testimony of the Messiah; and John had been a burning and a shining light, in whose illuminating ministry many had temporarily rejoiced. The hostile Jews were left to see that the witness of John was valid under their strictest construction of the rules of evidence; "But," He continued, "I receive not testimony from man ... But I have greater witness than that of John: for the works which the Father hath given me to finish, the same works that I do, bear witness of me, that the Father hath sent me. And the Father himself, which hath sent me, hath borne witness of me."

Then in terms of unqualified condemnation, He told them they were devoid of the Father's word, for they refused to accept Himself whom the Father had sent. With humiliating directness He admonished these learned men of the law, these interpreters of the prophets, these professional expounders of sacred writ, to betake themselves to reading and study. "Search the scriptures," said He, "for in them ye think ye have eternal life: and they are they which testify of me." Convictingly He continued--that they who admitted and taught that in the scriptures lay the way to eternal life, refused to come to Him, of whom those same scriptures testified, though by coming they might obtain eternal life. "I receive not honour from men," He added, "But I know you, that ye have not the love of God in you." They knew that they sought for honor among men, received honors from one another, were made rabbis and doctors, scribes and teachers, by the bestowal of titles and degrees--all of men; but they rejected Him who came in the name of One infinitely greater than all their schools or societies--He had come in the supreme name of the Father. The cause of their spiritual ignorance was pointed out--they relied upon the honors of men, and sought not the honor of real service in the cause of God.

He had spoken of the authority of judgment that had been committed to Himself; now He explained that they should not think He would accuse them before the Father; a lesser one than He would accuse, even Moses, another of His witnesses in whom they professed such trust--Moses whom they all were said to believe--and, driving home the full effect of His powerful arraignment, the Lord continued: "For had ye believed Moses, ye would have believed me: for he wrote of me. But if ye believe not his writings, how shall ye believe my words?" Such was the illuminating instruction combined with burning denunciation that these men had called forth by their futile attempt to convict Jesus on the charge of Sabbath desecration. This was but one of many evil machinations by which they so determinedly plotted, and strove to attach the stigma and invoke the penalty of Sabbath-breaking upon the very One who had ordained the Sabbath and was in truth and verity the one and only Lord thereof.

THE DISCIPLES CHARGED WITH SABBATH-BREAKING.

We may profitably consider in this connection other instances of good work done by our Lord on Sabbath days; and this we may do without undue regard to the order of the events in time. We again find Jesus in Galilee, whether prior to or after His visit to Jerusalem at the time of the unidentified feast, on which occasion He wrought the miracle of healing at the Bethesda pool, matters not. On a certain Sabbath, He and the disciples walked through a field of grain,[449] and, being hungry, the disciples began to pluck some of the ripening ears; rubbing out the kernels between their hands, they ate. There was no element of theft in what they did, for the Mosaic law provided that in passing through another's vineyard or corn field one might pluck grapes or corn to relieve hunger; but it was forbidden to use a sickle in the field, or to carry away any of the grapes in a vessel.[450] The permission extended only to the relief of present need. When the disciples of Jesus availed themselves of this lawful privilege, there were Pharisees on the watch, and these came at once to the Master, saying: "Behold, thy disciples do that which is not lawful to do upon the sabbath day." The accusers doubtless had in mind the rabbinical dictum that rubbing out an ear of grain in the hands was a species of threshing; that blowing away the chaff was winnowing; and that it was unlawful to thresh or winnow on the Sabbath. Indeed, some learned rabbis had held it to be a sin to walk on grass during the Sabbath, inasmuch as the grass might be in seed, and the treading out of the seed would be as the threshing of grain.

Jesus defended the disciples by citing a precedent applicable to the case, and of much greater import. The instance was that of David, who with a small company of men had asked bread of the priest Ahimelech; for they were hungry and in haste. The priest had none but consecrated bread, the loaves of shewbread which were placed in the sanctuary at intervals, and which none but the priests were allowed to eat. In view of the condition of urgent need the priest had given the shewbread to the hungry men.[451] Jesus also reminded the critical Pharisees that the priests in the temple regularly did much work on the Sabbath in the slaughtering of sacrificial victims and in altar service generally, yet were held blameless because of the higher requirements of worship which rendered such labor necessary; and added with solemn emphasis: "But I say unto you, That in this place is one greater than the temple." He cited the word of God spoken through Hosea, "I will have mercy, and not sacrifice,"[452] and reproved at once their ignorance and their unrighteous zeal by telling them that had they known what that scripture meant they would not have condemned the guiltless. Be it remembered, "The sabbath was made for man, and not man for the sabbath."[453]

His reproof was followed by the affirmation of His personal supremacy: "_For the Son of man is Lord even of the sabbath day!_" What can we gather from that declaration but that He, Jesus, there present in the flesh, was the Being through whom the Sabbath had been ordained, that it was He who had given and written in stone the decalog, including "Remember the sabbath day, to keep it holy," and, "the seventh day is the sabbath of the Lord thy God"?

A PHARISAICAL PLOT.

Again on a Sabbath, Jesus went into a synagog, and saw in the congregation a man whose right hand was withered.[454] There were Pharisees present, and they watched to see whether Jesus would heal the man, their purpose being to accuse Him if He did so. The Pharisees asked: "Is it lawful to heal on the sabbath days?" Our Lord countered their poorly veiled purpose by asking: "Is it lawful to do good on the sabbath days?" and extended the question, "or to do evil? to save life, or to kill?" They held their peace, for the question was double-edged. To reply in the affirmative would have been to justify the work of healing; a negative answer would have stultified them. He put another question: "What man shall there be among you, that shall have one sheep, and if it fall into a pit on the sabbath day, will he not lay hold on it, and lift it out? How much then is a man better than a sheep?"

As the Pharisees could not or would not reply, He summed up the whole matter thus: "Wherefore it is lawful to do well on the sabbath days." He called upon the man with the withered hand to stand forth before the congregation. Grief and anger were mingled in His penetrating and sweeping glance; but, turning with compassion toward the afflicted one, He commanded him to stretch forth his hand; the man obeyed, and lo! the hand "was restored whole, like as the other."

The discomfited Pharisees were furious, "filled with madness" Luke says; and they went out to plot anew against the Lord. So bitter was their hatred that they allied themselves with the Herodians, a political party generally unpopular among the Jews.[455] The rulers of the people were ready to enter into any intrigue or alliance to accomplish their avowed purpose of bringing about the death of the Lord Jesus. Aware of the wicked determination against Him, Jesus withdrew Himself from the locality. Other accusations of Sabbath-breaking, brought against Christ by Jewish casuists, will be considered later.[456]

NOTES TO CHAPTER 15.

1. Rabbinical Requirements Concerning Sabbath Observance.--"No feature of the Jewish system was so marked as their extraordinary strictness in the outward observance of the Sabbath, as a day of entire rest. The Scribes had elaborated from the command of Moses, a vast array of prohibitions and injunctions, covering the whole of social, individual, and public life, and carried it to the extreme of ridiculous caricature. Lengthened rules were prescribed as to the kinds of knots which might legally be tied on the Sabbath. The camel-driver's knot and the sailor's were unlawful, and it was equally illegal to tie or to loose them. A knot which could be untied with one hand might be undone. A shoe or sandal, a woman's cup, a wine or oil-skin, or a flesh-pot might be tied. A pitcher at a spring might be tied to the body-sash, but not with a cord.... To kindle or extinguish a fire on the Sabbath was a great desecration of the day, nor was even sickness allowed to violate Rabbinical rules. It was forbidden to give an emetic on the Sabbath--to set a broken bone, or put back a dislocated joint, though some Rabbis, more liberal, held that whatever endangered life made the Sabbath law void, 'for the commands were given to Israel only that they might live by them.' One who was buried under ruins on the Sabbath, might be dug for and taken out, if alive, but, if dead, he was to be left where he was, till the Sabbath was over."--Geikie, _Life and Words of Christ_, chap. 38.

2. The Unnamed Feast.--There has been no little discussion as to the particular festival referred to in John 5:1, at the time of which Jesus healed the cripple at the pool of Bethesda. Many writers hold that it was the Passover, others that it was the feast of Purim, or some other Jewish celebration. The only semblance of importance attaching to the question is the possibility of learning from the fact, if it could be proved, something of the chronological order of events at this period of our Lord's life. We are not told which feast this was, neither the year nor the time of the year when it occurred. The miracle wrought on the occasion, and the doctrinal discourse delivered as a result thereof, depend for their value in no degree on the determination of date.

3. Shewbread.--The name means "bread of the presence," signifying that it was placed in the presence of Jehovah. The bread so sanctified consisted of twelve loaves, made without leaven. They were to be deposited in the Holy Place in two columns of six loaves each. Zenos, in _Stand. Bible Dict._ writes: "They

were allowed to remain there for a whole week, at the end of which period they were removed, and eaten by the priest upon holy ground, i.e. within the precincts of the sanctuary. For other persons than priests to eat of the loaves of the shewbread was regarded as sacrilegious, for they were 'holy.'" See Exo. 25:30; Lev. 24:5-9; 1 Sam. 21:1-6.

4. The Sabbath Was Made for Man and Not Man for the Sabbath.--Edersheim (vol. i, pp. 57, 58) says: "When on his flight from Saul, David had, 'when an hungered,' eaten of the shewbread and given it to his followers, although, by the letter of the Levitical law, it was only to be eaten by the priests. Jewish tradition vindicated his conduct on the plea that 'danger to life superseded the Sabbath law,' and hence, all laws connected with it.... In truth, the reason why David was blameless in eating the shewbread was the same as that which made the Sabbath labor of the priests lawful. The Sabbath law was not one merely of rest, but of rest for worship. The service of the Lord was the object in view. The priests worked on the Sabbath, because this service was the object of the Sabbath; and David was allowed to eat of the shewbread, not [solely] because there was danger to life from starvation, but because he pleaded that he was on the service of the Lord, and needed this provision. The disciples, when following the Lord, were similarly on the service of the Lord; ministering to Him was more than ministering in the temple, for He was greater than the temple. If the Pharisees had believed this, they would not have questioned their conduct, nor in so doing have themselves infringed that higher law which enjoined mercy, not sacrifice."

FOOTNOTES:

[430] Gen. 2:3.
[431] Exo. 16:16-31.
[432] Exo. 20:8-11; 23:12; 31:13-15; 34:21; Lev. 19:3; 23:3; Deut. 5:12-14.
[433] Exo. 35:3; Numb. 15:32-36.
[434] Isa. 56:2; 58:13; Jer. 17:21-24.
[435] Neh. 8:9-12; 13:15-22.
[436] Ezek. 20:12-24.
[437] B. of M., Jarom 1:5; Mosiah 13:16-19; 18:23.
[438] Lev. 25:1-8; compare 26:34, 35.
[439] Lev. 25:10-55.
[440] Page 64.
[441] Note 1, end of chapter.
[442] John, chapter 5.
[443] Note 2, end of chapter.
[444] See another instance, pages 190-192.
[445] Pages 191 and 201. For further justification of this act of healing on the Sabbath, see John 7:21-24.
[446] Page 142.
[447] Compare Doc. and Cov. 76:16, 17. See page 24 herein.
[448] Page 25.
[449] Matt. 12:1-8; compare Mark 2:23-28; Luke 6:1-5.
[450] Deut. 23:24, 25.
[451] Note 3, end of chapter. [452] Hos. 6:6; compare Micah 6:6-9.
[453] Mark 2:27. Note 4, end of chapter.
[454] Matt. 12:10-13; Mark 3:1-6; Luke 6:6-8.
[455] Page 68.
[456] For instances, see Luke 13:14-16; 14:3-6; John 9:14-16.

CHAPTER 16. THE CHOSEN TWELVE.

THEIR CALL AND ORDINATION.[457]

The night preceding the morn on which the Twelve Apostles were called and ordained was spent by the Lord in solitary seclusion; He had "continued all night in prayer to God."[458] Then, when day had come, and while many people were gathering to hear more of the new and wonderful gospel of the kingdom, He called to come closer some who had theretofore been devotedly associated together as His disciples or followers, and from among them He chose twelve, whom he ordained and named apostles.[459] Prior to that time none of these had been distinguished by any special delegation of authority or appointment; they had been numbered with the disciples in general, though, as we have seen, seven had received a preliminary call, and had promptly responded thereto by abandoning wholly or in part their business affairs, and had followed the Master. These were Andrew, John, Simon Peter, Philip, Nathanael, James, and Levi Matthew. Prior to this eventful day, however, none of the Twelve had been ordained or set apart to their sacred office.

The three Gospel-writers who make record of the organization of the Twelve place Simon Peter first and Judas Iscariot last in the category; they agree also in the relative position of some but not of all the others. Following the order given by Mark, and this may be the most convenient since he names as the first three those who later became most prominent, we have the following list: Simon Peter, James (son of Zebedee), John (brother of the last-named), Andrew (brother of Simon Peter), Philip, Bartholomew (or Nathanael), Matthew, Thomas, James (son of Alpheus), Judas (also known as Lebbeus or Thaddeus), Simon (distinguished by his surname Zelotes, also known as the Canaanite), and Judas Iscariot.

TWELVE CONSIDERED INDIVIDUALLY.

Simon, named as the first apostle, is more commonly known as _Peter_--the appellation given him by the Lord on the occasion of their first meeting, and afterward confirmed.[460] He was the son of Jona, or Jonas, and by vocation was a fisherman. He and his brother Andrew were partners with James and John, the sons of Zebedee; and apparently the fishing business was a prosperous one with them, for they owned their boats and gave employment to other men.[461] Peter's early home had been at the little fishery town of Bethsaida,[462] on the west shore of the Sea of Galilee; but about the time of his first association with Jesus, or soon thereafter, he, with others of his family, removed to Capernaum, where he appears to have become an independent householder.[463] Simon Peter was a married man before his call to the ministry. He was well to do in a material way; and when he once spoke of having left all to follow Jesus, the Lord did not deny that Peter's sacrifice of temporal possessions was as great as had been implied. We are not justified in regarding him as unlettered or ignorant. True, both he and John were designated by the council of rulers as "unlearned and ignorant men,"[464] but this was spoken of them as indicating their lack of training in the schools of the rabbis; and it is worthy of note, that the members of that same council were amazed at the wisdom and power manifested by the two apostles, whom they professed to despise.

In temperament Peter was impulsive and stern, and, until trained by severe experience, was lacking in firmness. He had many human weaknesses, yet in spite of them all he eventually overcame the temptations of Satan and the frailties of the flesh, and served his Lord as the appointed and acknowledged leader of the Twelve. Of the time and place of his death the scriptures do not speak; but the manner thereof was prefigured by the resurrected Lord,[465] and in part has foreseen by Peter himself.[466] Tradition, originating in the writings of the early Christian historians other than the apostles, states that Peter met death by crucifixion as a martyr during the persecution incident to the reign of Nero, probably between A.D. 64 and 68. Origen states that the apostle was crucified with his head downward. Peter, with James and John, his associates in the presidency of the Twelve, has ministered as a resurrected being in the present dispensation, in restoring to earth the Melchizedek Priesthood, including the Holy Apostleship, which had been taken away because of the apostasy and unbelief of men.[467]

James and _John_, brothers by birth, partners in business as fishermen, brethren in the ministry, were associated together and with Peter in the apostolic calling. The Lord bestowed upon the pair a title in common--Boanerges, or Sons of Thunder[468]--possibly with reference to the zeal they developed in His service, which, indeed, at times had to be restrained, as when they would have had fire called from heaven to destroy the Samaritan villagers who had refused hospitality to the Master.[469] They and their mother aspired to the highest honors of the kingdom, and asked that the two be given places, one on the right the other on the left of Christ in His glory. This ambition was gently reproved by the Lord, and the request gave offense to the other apostles.[470] With Peter these two brothers were witnesses of many of the most important incidents in the life of Jesus; thus, the three were the only apostles admitted to witness the raising of the daughter of Jairus from death to life;[471] they were the only members of the Twelve present at the transfiguration of Christ;[472] they were nearest the Lord during the period of His mortal agony in Gethsemane;[473] and, as heretofore told, they have ministered in these modern days in the restoration of the Holy Apostleship with all its ancient authority and power of blessing.[474] James is commonly designated in theological literature as James I, to distinguish him from the other apostle bearing the same name. James, the son of Zebedee, was the first of the apostles to meet a martyr's violent death; he was beheaded by order of the king, Herod Agrippa.[475] John had been a disciple of the Baptist, and had demonstrated his confidence in the latter's testimony of Jesus by promptly turning from the forerunner and following the Lord.[476] He became a devoted servant, and repeatedly refers to himself as the disciple "whom Jesus loved."[477] At the last supper John sat next to Jesus leaning his head upon the Master's breast;[478] and next day as he stood beneath the cross he received from the dying Christ the special charge to care for the Lord's mother;[479] and to this he promptly responded by conducting the weeping Mary to his own house. He was the first to recognize the risen Lord on the shores of Galilee, and received from His immortal lips encouragement of his hope that his life would be continued in the body, in order that he might minister among men until the Christ shall come in His glory.[480] The realization of that hope has been attested by revelation in modern days.[481]

Andrew, son of Jona and brother of Simon Peter, is mentioned less frequently than the three already considered. He had been one of the Baptist's followers, and with John, the son of Zebedee, left the Baptist to learn from Jesus; and having learned he went in search of Peter, solemnly averred to him that the Messiah had been found, and brought his brother to the Savior's feet.[482] He shared with Peter in the honor of the call of the Lord on the sea shore, and in the promise "I will make you fishers of men."[483] In one instance we read of Andrew as present with Peter, James and John, in a private interview with the Lord; [484] and he is mentioned in connection with the miraculous feeding of the five thousand,[485] and as associated with Philip in arranging an interview between certain inquiring Greeks and Jesus.[486] He is named with others in connection with our Lord's ascension.[487] Tradition is rife with stories about this man, but of the extent of his ministry, the duration of his life, and the circumstances of his death, we have no authentic record.

Philip may have been the first to receive the authoritative call "Follow me" from the lips of Jesus, and we find him immediately testifying that Jesus was the long expected Messiah. His home was in Bethsaida, the town of Peter, Andrew, James, and John. It is said that Jesus found him,[488] whereas the others concerned in that early affiliation seem to have come of themselves severally to Christ. We find brief mention of him at the time the five thousand were fed, on which occasion Jesus asked him "Whence shall we buy bread, that these may eat?" This was done to test and prove him, for Jesus knew what would be done. Philip's reply was based on a statement of the small amount of money at hand, and showed no expectation of miraculous intervention.[489] It was to him the Greeks applied when they sought a meeting with Jesus as noted in connection with Andrew. He was mildly reproved for his misunderstanding when he asked Jesus to show to him and the others the Father--"Have I been so long time with you, and yet hast thou not known me, Philip?"[490] Aside from incidental mention of his presence as one of the Eleven after the ascension, the scriptures tell us nothing more concerning him.

Bartholomew is mentioned in scripture by this name only in connection with his ordination to the apostleship, and as one of the Eleven after the ascension. The name means son of Tolmai. It is practically certain, however, that he is the man called Nathanael in John's Gospel--the one whom Christ designated as "an Israelite indeed, in whom is no guile."[491] He is named again as among those who went fishing with Peter after the resurrection of Christ.[492] His home was in Cana of Galilee. The reasons for assuming that Bartholomew and Nathanael are the same persons are these: Bartholomew is named in each of the three synoptic Gospels as an apostle, but Nathanael is not mentioned. Nathanael is named twice in John's Gospel, and Bartholomew not at all; Bartholomew and Philip, or Nathanael and Philip, are mentioned together.

Matthew, or _Levi_, son of Alpheus, was one of the seven who received a call to follow Christ before the ordination of the Twelve. He it was who gave a feast, for attending which Jesus and the disciples were severely criticized by the Pharisees,[493] on the charge that it was unseemly for Him to eat with publicans and sinners. Matthew was a publican; he so designates himself in the Gospel he wrote;[494] but the other evangelists omit the mention when including him with the Twelve. His Hebrew name, Levi, is understood by many as an indication of priestly lineage. Of his ministry we have no detailed account; though he is the author of the first Gospel, he refrains from special mention of himself except in connection with his call and ordination. He is spoken of by other than scriptural writers as one of the most active of the apostles after Christ's death, and as operating in lands far from Palestine.

Thomas, also known as Didymus, the Greek equivalent of his Hebrew name, meaning "a twin," is mentioned as a witness of the raising of Lazarus. His devotion to Jesus is shown by his desire to accompany the Lord to Bethany, though persecution in that region was almost certain. To his fellow apostles Thomas said: "Let us also go, that we may die with him."[495] Even as late in his experience as the night before the crucifixion, Thomas had failed to comprehend the impending necessity of the Savior's sacrifice; and when Jesus referred to going away and leaving the others to follow, Thomas asked how they could know the way. For his lack of understanding he stood reproved.[496] He was absent when the resurrected Christ appeared to the assembled disciples in the evening of the day of His rising; and on being informed by the others that they had seen the Lord, he forcefully expressed his doubt, and declared he would not believe unless he could see and feel for himself the wounds in the crucified body. Eight days later the Lord visited the apostles again, when, as on the earlier occasion, they were within closed doors; and to Thomas the Lord said: "Reach hither thy finger, and behold my hands; and reach hither thy hand, and thrust it into my side." Then Thomas, no longer doubting but with love and reverence filling his soul, exclaimed "My Lord and my God." The Lord said unto him: "Thomas, because thou hast seen me, thou hast believed: blessed are they that have not seen, and yet have believed."[497] Of Thomas no further record appears in the New Testament aside from that of his presence with his fellows after the ascension.

James, son of Alpheus, is mentioned in the Gospels only in the matter of his ordination to the apostleship; and but once elsewhere in the New Testament by the appellation "son of Alpheus."[498] In writings other than scriptural he is sometimes designated as James II to avoid confusing him with James the son of Zebedee. There is acknowledged uncertainty concerning the identity of James the son of Alpheus as the James or one of the James's referred to in the Acts and the Epistles;[499] and a plenitude of controversial literature on the subject is extant.[500]

Judas is called _Lebbeus Thaddeus_ by Matthew, _Thaddeus_ by Mark, and _Judas the brother of James_ by Luke.[501] The only other specific reference to this apostle is made by John, and is incident to the last long interview between Jesus and the apostles, when this Judas, "not Iscariot," asked how or why Jesus would manifest Himself to His chosen servants and not to the world at large. The man's question shows that the really distinguishing character of the apostleship was not fully comprehended by him at that time.

Simon Zelotes, so designated in Acts,[502] and as _Simon called Zelotes_ in Luke's Gospel, is distinguished by both Matthew and Mark as the _Canaanite_. The last designation has no reference to the town of Cana, nor to the land of Canaan, neither is it in any sense of geographical signification; it is the Syro-Chaldaic equivalent of the Greek word which is rendered in the English translation "Zelotes." The two names, therefore, have the same fundamental meaning, and each refers to the Zealots, a Jewish sect or faction, known for its zeal in maintaining the Mosaic ritual. Doubtless Simon had learned moderation and toleration from the teachings of Christ; otherwise he would scarcely have been suited to the apostolic ministry. His zealous earnestness, properly directed, may have developed into a most serviceable trait of character. This apostle is nowhere in the scriptures named apart from his colleagues.

Judas Iscariot is the only Judean named among the Twelve; all the others were Galileans. He is generally understood to have been a resident of Kerioth, a small town in the southerly part of Judea, but a few miles west from the Dead Sea, though for this tradition, as also for the signification of his surname, we lack direct authority. So too we are uninformed as to his lineage, except that his father's name was Simon.[503] He served as treasurer or agent of the apostolic company, receiving and disbursing such offerings as were made by disciples and friends, and purchasing supplies as required.[504] That he was unprincipled and dishonest in the discharge of this trust is attested by John. His avaricious and complaining nature revealed itself in his murmuring against what he called a waste of costly spikenard, in the anointing of the Lord by Mary but a few days before the crucifixion; he hypocritically suggested that the precious ointment could have been sold and the proceeds given to the poor.[505] The crowning deed of perfidy in the career of Iscariot was his deliberate betrayal of his Master to death; and this the infamous creature did for a price, and accomplished the foul deed with a kiss. He brought his guilty life to a close by a revolting suicide and his spirit went to the awful fate reserved for the sons of perdition.[506]

GENERAL CHARACTERISTICS OF THE TWELVE.

A survey of the general characteristics and qualifications of this body of twelve men reveals some interesting facts. Before their selection as apostles they had all become close disciples of the Lord; they believed in Him; several of them, possibly all, had openly confessed that He was the Son of God; and yet it is doubtful that any one of them fully understood the real significance of the Savior's work. It is evident by the later remarks of many of them, and by the instructions and rebuke they called forth from the Master, that the common Jewish expectation of a Messiah who would reign in splendor as an earthly sovereign after He had subdued all other nations, had a place even in the hearts of these chosen ones. After long experience, Peter's concern was: "Behold, we have forsaken all, and followed thee; what shall we have therefore?"[507] They were as children to be trained and taught; but they were mostly willing pupils, receptive of soul, and imbued with a sincere eagerness to serve. To Jesus they were His little ones, His children, His servants, and His friends, as they merited.[508] They were all of the common people, not rabbis, scholars, nor priestly officials. Their inner natures, not their outward accomplishments, were taken into prime account in the Lord's choosing. The Master chose them; they did not choose themselves; by Him they were ordained,[509] and they could in consequence rely the more implicitly upon His guidance and support. To them much was given; much of them was required. With the one black exception they all became shining lights in the kingdom of God, and vindicated the Master's selection. He recognized in each the characteristics of fitness developed in the primeval world of spirits.[510]

DISCIPLES AND APOSTLES.

Discipleship is general; any follower of a man or devotee to a principle may be called a disciple. The Holy Apostleship is an office and calling belonging to the Higher or Melchizedek Priesthood, at once exalted and specific, comprizing as a distinguishing function that of personal and special witness to the divinity of Jesus Christ as the one and only Redeemer and Savior of mankind.[511] The apostleship is an individual bestowal, and as such is conferred only through ordination. That the Twelve did constitute a council or "quorum" having authority in the Church established by Jesus Christ, is shown by their ministrations after the Lord's resurrection and ascension. Their first official act was that of filling the vacancy in their organization occasioned by the apostasy and death of Judas Iscariot; and in connection with this procedure, the presiding apostle, Peter, set forth the essential qualifications of the one who would be chosen and ordained, which comprized such knowledge of Jesus, His life, death, and resurrection, as would make the new apostle one with the Eleven as special witnesses of the Lord's work.[512]

The ordination of the Twelve Apostles marked the inauguration of an advanced epoch in the earthly ministry of Jesus, an epoch characterized by the organization of a body of men invested with the authority of the Holy Priesthood, upon whom would rest, more particularly after the Lord's departure, the duty and responsibility of continuing the work He had begun, and of building up the Church established by Him.

The word "apostle" is an Anglicized form derived from the Greek _apostolos_, meaning literally "one who is sent," and connoting an envoy or official messenger, who speaks and acts by the authority of one superior to himself. In this sense Paul afterward applied the title to Christ as one specially sent and commissioned of the Father.[513]

The Lord's purpose in choosing and ordaining the Twelve is thus enunciated by Mark: "And he ordained twelve, that they should be with him, and that he might send them forth to preach, and to have power to heal sicknesses, and to cast out devils."[514] For a season following their ordination the apostles remained with Jesus, being specially trained and instructed by Him for the work then before them; afterward they were specifically charged and sent forth to preach and to administer in the authority of their priesthood, as shall be hereafter considered.

NOTES TO CHAPTER 16.

1. Judas Lebbeus Thaddeus.--This Judas (not Iscariot) is designated in the authorized version of Luke 6:16, and Acts 1:13, as "_the brother_ of James." That the words "the brother" are an addition to the original text is indicated by italics. The revised version of these passages reads in each instance "_the son_ of James," with italics of corresponding significance. The original reads "Judas of James." We are uninformed as to which James is referred to, and as to whether the Judas here mentioned was the son, the brother, or some other relative of the unidentified James.

2. The Meaning of "Apostle."--"The title 'Apostle' is likewise one of special significance and sanctity; it has been given of God, and belongs only to those who have been called and ordained as 'special witnesses of the name of Christ in all the world, thus differing from other officers in the Church in the duties of their calling' (Doc. and Cov. 107:23). By derivation the word 'apostle' is the English equivalent of the Greek _apostolos_, indicating a messenger, an ambassador, or literally 'one who is sent'. It signifies that he who is rightly so called, speaks and acts not of himself, but as the representative of a higher power whence his commission issued; and in this sense the title is that of a servant, rather than that of a superior. Even the Christ, however, is called an Apostle with reference to His ministry in the flesh (Hebrews 3:1), and this appellation is justified by His repeated declaration that He came to earth to do not His own will but that of the Father by whom _He was sent_.

"Though an apostle is thus seen to be essentially an envoy, or ambassador, his authority is great, as is also the responsibility associated therewith, for he speaks in the name of a power greater than his own--the name of Him whose special witness he is. When one of the Twelve is sent to minister in any stake, mission or other division of the Church, or to labor in regions where no Church organization has been effected, he acts as the representative of the First Presidency, and has the right to use his authority in doing whatever is requisite for the furtherance of the work of God. His duty is to preach the Gospel, administer the ordinances thereof, and set in order the affairs of the Church, wherever he is sent. So great is the sanctity of this special calling, that the title 'Apostle' should not be used lightly as the common or ordinary form of address applied to living men called to this office. The quorum or council of the Twelve Apostles as existent in the Church to-day may better be spoken of as the 'Quorum of the Twelve,' the 'Council of the Twelve,' or simply as the 'Twelve,' than as the 'Twelve Apostles,' except as particular occasion may warrant the use of the more sacred term. It is advized that the title 'Apostle' be not applied as a prefix to the name of any member of the Council of the Twelve; but that such a one be addressed or spoken of as 'Brother ----,' or 'Elder ----,' and when necessary or desirable, as in announcing his presence in a public assembly, an explanatory clause may be added, thus, 'Elder ----, one of the Council of the Twelve,'"--From "The Honor and Dignity of Priesthood," by the author, _Improvement Era_, Vol. 17, No. 5, pp. 409-410.

3. "Of Alpheus;" or "Son of Alpheus".--In all Bible passages specifying "James son of Alpheus" (Matt. 10:3; Mark 3:18; Luke 6:15; Acts 1:13) the word _son_ has been supplied by the translators, and therefore properly appears in _Italics_. The phrase in the Greek reads "James of Alpheus." This fact must not be given undue weight in support of the thought that the James spoken of was not the son of Alpheus; for the word _son_ has been similarly added in the translation of other passages, in all of which _Italics_ are used to indicate the words supplied, e.g. "James _the son_ of Zebedee" (Matt. 10:2; see also Mark 3:17). Read in this connection Note 1 on the opposite page.

FOOTNOTES:

[457] Matt. 10:1-4; Mark 3:13-19; Luke 6:12-16.
[458] Luke 6:12.
[459] Luke 3:13; compare John 15:16; see also Acts 1:22.
[460] John 1:42; compare Matt. 16:18.
[461] Mark 1:16-20; Luke 5:10.
[462] John 1:44; 12:21.
[463] Matt. 8:14; Mark 1:29; Luke 4:38.
[464] Acts 4:13.
[465] John 21:18, 19.
[466] 2 Peter 1:14.
[467] Doc. and Cov. 27:12. Page 768 herein.
[468] Mark 3:17.
[469] Luke 9:54. See also Mark 9:38, for instance of John's impulsive zeal.
[470] Mark 10:35-41; compare Matt. 20:20-24.
[471] Mark 5:37; Luke 8:51.
[472] Matt. 17:1-2; Luke 9:28-29.
[473] Matt. 26:36, 37.

[474] Doc. and Cov. 27:12. Page 768 herein.
[475] Acts 12:1, 2.
[476] John 1:35-40; see page 140.
[477] John 13:23; 19:26; 20:2.
[478] John 13:23, 25.
[479] John 19:25-27.
[480] John 21:7, 21-23.
[481] Doc. and Cov. Sec. 7; compare B. of M., 3 Nephi 28:1-12.
[482] John 1:35-40. [483] Matt. 4:18, 19.
[484] Mark 13:3.
[485] John 6:8.
[486] John 12:20-22.
[487] Acts 1:13.
[488] John 1:43-45.
[489] John 6:5-7.
[490] John 14:8, 9.
[491] John 1:45-51; see page 141.
[492] John 21:2, 3.
[493] Page 194.
[494] Matt. 10:3.
[495] John 11:16.
[496] John 14:1-7.
[497] John 20:24-29. Note 3, end of chapter.
[498] Acts 1:13. Note 3, end of chapter.
[499] Acts 12:17; 15:13-21; 21:18; 1 Cor. 15:7; Gal. 1:19; 2:9, 12; and the Epistle of James.
[500] Concerning the James's mentioned in the New Testament, the opinion of Bible scholars is divided, the question being as to whether two or three individuals are indicated. Those who hold that there were three men of this name distinguish them as follows: (1) James the son of Zebedee and brother of John the apostle; all scriptural references to him are explicit; (2) James the son of Alpheus; and (3) James the brother of the Lord (Matt. 13:55; Mark 6:3; Gal. 1:19). If we accept this classification, the references given in the previous footnote on this page apply to James the Lord's brother. Both the Oxford and Bagster Bible "Helps" treat James the son of Alpheus and James the Lord's brother as one person, the expression "son of" being understood in its general sense only (see page 280). The Bagster designation is: "James II, apostle, son of Alpheus, brother or cousin to Jesus." (See Note 3, end of chapter.) The Nave "Student's Bible" states (page 1327) that the question as to whether James the Lord's brother "is identical with James the son of Alpheus is one of the most difficult questions in the biographical history of the Gospels." Faussett (in his "Cyclopedia Critical and Expository") supports the contention that but one James is meant; and other acknowledged authorities treat the two as one. For detailed consideration of the subject the reader is referred to special works.
[501] Note 1, end of chapter.
[502] Acts 1:13; compare Luke 6:15.
[503] John 6:71; 12:4; 13:26.
[504] John 12:6; 13:29.
[505] John 12:1-7; compare Matt. 26:6-13; Mark 14:3-9.
[506] Matt. 27:5; compare Acts 1:18; see also John 17:12; Doc. and Cov. 76; 31-48; 132:27.
[507] Matt. 19:27.
[508] Matt. 10:42; John 21:5; 13:16. compare verse 13; 15:14, 15.
[509] John 15:16.
[510] Pages 8 and 17.
[511] Doc. and Cov. 18:27-33; 20:38-44; 107:1-9, 23, 24, 39.
[512] Acts 1:15-26.
[513] Heb. 3:1; see Note 2, end of chapter.
[514] Mark 3:14, 15.

Jesus the Christ

CHAPTER 17. THE SERMON ON THE MOUNT.

At some time very near that of the ordination of the Twelve, Jesus delivered a remarkable discourse, which, in reference to the place where it was given, has come to be known as the Sermon on the Mount. Matthew presents an extended account occupying three chapters of the first Gospel; Luke gives a briefer synopsis.[515] Circumstantial variations appearing in the two records are of minor importance;[516] it is the sermon itself to which we may profitably devote attention. Luke introduces in different parts of his writings many of the precious precepts given as parts of the sermon recorded as a continuous discourse in the Gospel written by Matthew. In our present study we shall be guided principally by Matthew's account. Some portions of this comprehensive address were expressly directed to the disciples, who had been or would be called to the apostleship and in consequence be required to renounce all their worldly interests for the labors of the ministry; other parts were and are of general application. Jesus had ascended the mountain side, probably to escape the crowds that thronged Him in or near the towns.[517] The disciples gathered about Him, and there He sat and taught them.[518]

THE BEATITUDES.[519]

The opening sentences are rich in blessing, and the first section of the discourse is devoted to an explanation of what constitutes genuine blessedness; the lesson, moreover, was made simple and unambiguous by specific application, each of the blessed being assured of recompense and reward in the enjoyment of conditions directly opposite to those under which he had suffered. The blessings particularized by the Lord on this occasion have been designated in literature of later time as the Beatitudes. The poor in spirit are to be made rich as rightful heirs to the kingdom of heaven; the mourner shall be comforted for he shall see the divine purpose in his grief, and shall again associate with the beloved ones of whom he has been bereft; the meek, who suffer spoliation rather than jeopardize their souls in contention, shall inherit the earth; those that hunger and thirst for the truth shall be fed in rich abundance; they that show mercy shall be judged mercifully; the pure in heart shall be admitted to the very presence of God; the peacemakers, who try to save themselves and their fellows from strife, shall be numbered among the children of God; they that suffer persecution for the sake of righteousness shall inherit the riches of the eternal kingdom. To the disciples the Lord spake directly, saying: "Blessed are ye, when men shall revile you, and persecute you, and shall say all manner of evil against you falsely, for my sake. Rejoice, and be exceeding glad: for great is your reward in heaven: for so persecuted they the prophets which were before you."[520]

It is evident that the specified blessings and the happiness comprized therein are to be realized in their fulness only beyond the grave; though the joy that comes from the consciousness of right living brings, even in this world, a rich return. An important element in this splendid elucidation of the truly blessed state is the implied distinction between pleasure and happiness.[521] Mere pleasure is at best but fleeting; happiness is abiding, for in the recollection thereof is joy renewed. Supreme happiness is not an earthly attainment; the promised "fulness of joy" lies beyond death and the resurrection.[522] While man exists in this mortal state he needs some of the things of the world; he must have food and clothing and provision for shelter; and beside these bare necessities he may righteously desire the facilities of education, the incidentals of advancing civilization, and the things that are conducive to refinement and culture; yet all of these are but aids to achievement, not the end to attain which man was made mortal.

The Beatitudes are directed to the duties of mortal life as a preparation for a greater existence yet future. In the kingdom of heaven, twice named in this part of the Lord's discourse, are true riches and unfailing happiness to be found. The kingdom of heaven was the all-comprizing text of this wonderful sermon; the means of reaching the kingdom and the glories of eternal citizenship therein are the main divisions of the treatise.

DIGNITY AND RESPONSIBILITY IN THE MINISTRY.[523]

The Master next proceeded to instruct with particular directness those upon whom would devolve the responsibility of the ministry as His commissioned representatives. "Ye are the salt of the earth," said He. Salt is the great preservative; as such it has had practical use since very ancient times. Salt was prescribed as an essential addition to every meat offering under the Mosaic law.[524] Long before the time of Christ, the use of salt had been accorded a symbolism of fidelity, hospitality, and covenant.[525] To be of use salt must be pure; to be of any saving virtue as salt, it must be salt indeed, and not the product of chemical alteration or of earthy admixture, whereby its saltiness or "savor" would be lost;[526] and, as worthless stuff, it would be fit only to be thrown away. Against such change of faith, against such admixture with the sophistries, so-called philosophies, and heresies of the times, the disciples were especially warned. Then, changing the figure, Jesus likened them to the light of the world, and enjoined upon them the duty of keeping their light before the people, as prominently as stands a city built upon a hill, to be seen from all directions, a city that cannot be hid. Of what service would a lighted candle be if hidden under a tub or a box? "Let your light so shine before men," said He, "that they may see your good works, and glorify your Father which is in heaven."

That they should make no error as to the relationship of the ancient law and the gospel of the kingdom which He was elucidating, Jesus assured them that He had not come to destroy the law nor to nullify the teachings and predictions of the prophets, but to fulfil such and to establish that for which the developments of the centuries gone had been but preparatory. The gospel may be said to have destroyed the

Mosaic law only as the seed is destroyed in the growth of the new plant, only as the bud is destroyed by the bursting forth of the rich, full, and fragrant flowers, only as infancy and youth pass forever as the maturity of years develops. Not a jot or a tittle of the law was to be void. A more effective analogy than the last could scarcely have been conceived; the jot or yod, and the tittle, were small literary marks in the Hebrew script; for present purposes we may regard them as equivalent to the dot of an "i" or the cross of a "t"; with the first, the jot, our English word "iota," signifying a trifle, is related. Not even the least commandment could be violated without penalty; but the disciples were admonished to take heed that their keeping of the commandments was not after the manner of the scribes and Pharisees, whose observance was that of ceremonial externalism, lacking the essentials of genuine devotion; for they were assured that by such an insincere course they could "in no case enter into the kingdom of heaven."

THE LAW SUPERSEDED BY THE GOSPEL.[527]

The next section of the sermon deals with the superiority of the gospel of Christ over the law of Moses, and contrasts the requirements of the two in particular instances. Whereas the law forbade murder, and provided a just penalty for the crime, Christ taught that one's giving way to anger, which might possibly lead to violence or even murder, was of itself a sin. To maliciously use an offensive epithet such as "Raca" laid one liable to punishment under the decree of the council, and to call another a fool placed one "in danger of hell fire." These objectionable designations were regarded at that time as especially opprobrious and were therefore expressive of hateful intent. The murderer's hand is impelled by the hatred in his heart. The law provided penalty for the deed; the gospel rebuked the evil passion in its incipiency. To emphasize this principle, the Master showed that hatred was not to be atoned by a material sacrifice; and that if one came to make an offering at the altar, and remembered that he was at enmity with his brother, he should first go to that brother and be reconciled, even though such a course involved the interruption of the ceremonial, which was a particularly grievous incident according to the judgment of the priests. Differences and contentions were to be adjusted without delay.

The law forbade the awful sin of adultery; Christ said that the sin began in the lustful glance, the sensual thought; and He added that it was better to become blind than to look with evil eye; better to lose a hand than to work iniquity therewith. Touching the matter of divorcement, in which great laxity prevailed in that day, Jesus declared that except for the most serious offense of infidelity to marriage vows, no man could divorce his wife without becoming himself an offender, in that she, marrying again while still a wife not righteously divorced, would be guilty of sin, and so would be the man to whom she was so married.

Of old it had been forbidden to swear or take oaths except in solemn covenant before the Lord; but in the gospel dispensation the Lord forbade that men swear at all; and the heinousness of wanton oaths was expounded. Grievously sinful indeed it was and is to swear by heaven, which is the abode of God; or by earth, which is His creation and by Him called His footstool; or by Jerusalem, which was regarded by those who swore as the city of the great King; or by one's own head, which is part of the body God has created. Moderation in speech, decision and simplicity were enjoined, to the exclusion of expletives, profanity and oaths.

Of old the principle of retaliation had been tolerated, by which one who had suffered injury could exact or inflict a penalty of the same nature as the offense. Thus an eye was demanded for the loss of an eye, a tooth for a tooth, a life for a life.[528] In contrast, Christ taught that men should rather suffer than do evil, even to the extent of submission without resistance under certain implied conditions. His forceful illustrations--that if one were smitten on one cheek he should turn the other to the smiter; that if a man took another's coat by process of law, the loser should allow his cloak to be taken also; that if one was pressed into service to carry another's burden a mile, he should willingly go two miles; that one should readily give or lend as asked--are not to be construed as commanding abject subserviency to unjust demands, nor as an abrogation of the principle of self-protection. These instructions were directed primarily to the apostles, who would be professedly devoted to the work of the kingdom to the exclusion of all other interests. In their ministry it would be better to suffer material loss or personal indignity and imposition at the hands of wicked oppressors, than to bring about an impairment of efficiency and a hindrance in work through resistance and contention. To such as these the Beatitudes were particularly applicable--Blessed are the meek, the peace-makers, and they that are persecuted for righteousness' sake.

Of old it had been said: "Love thy neighbour, and hate thine enemy";[529] but the Lord now taught: "Love your enemies, bless them that curse you, do good to them that hate you, and pray for them which despitefully use you, and persecute you." This was a new doctrine. Never before had Israel been required to love their foes. Friendship for enemies had found no place in the Mosaic code: indeed the people had grown to look upon Israel's enemies as God's enemies; and now Jesus required that tolerance, mercy, and even love be meted out to such! He supplemented the requirement by an explanation--through the course indicated by Him men may become children of God, like unto their Heavenly Father to the extent of their obedience; for the Father is kind, long-suffering and tolerant, causing His sun to shine on the evil and on the good, and sending rain for the sustenance of both just and unjust.[530] And further, what excellence has the man who gives only as he receives, acknowledges only those who salute him with respect, loves only as he is loved? Even the publicans[531] did that much. Of the disciples of Christ much more was expected. The admonition closing this division of the discourse is an effective and comprehensive summary of all that had preceded: "_Be ye therefore perfect, even as your Father which is in heaven is perfect._"[532]

SINCERITY OF PURPOSE.[533]

In the matter of alms-giving the Master warned against, and inferentially denounced, ostentation and hypocritical display. To give to the needy is praiseworthy; but to give for the purpose of winning the praise of men is rank hypocrisy. The tossing of alms to a beggar, the pouring of offerings into the temple treasure chests, to be seen of men,[534] and similar displays of affected liberality, were fashionable among certain classes in the time of Christ; and the same spirit is manifest today. Some there be now who cause a trumpet to be sounded, through the columns of the press perchance, or by other means of publicity, to call attention to their giving, that they may have glory of men--to win political favor, to increase their trade or influence, to get what in their estimation is worth more than that from which they part. With logical incisiveness the Master demonstrated that such givers have their reward. They have received what they bid for; what more can such men demand or consistently expect? _"But" said the Lord, "when thou doest alms, let not thy left hand know what thy right hand doeth: That thine alms may be in secret: and thy Father which seeth in secret himself shall reward thee openly!"_

In the same spirit did the Preacher denounce hypocritical prayers--the saying of prayers in place of praying. There were many who sought places of public resort, in the synagogs, and even on the street-corners, that they might be seen and heard of men when saying their prayers. They secured the publicity they sought; what more could they ask? "Verily I say unto you, They have their reward," He who would really pray--pray as nearly as possible as Christ prayed, pray in actual communion with God to whom the prayer is addressed--will seek privacy, seclusion, isolation; if opportunity permits he will retire to his chamber, and will shut the door, that none may intrude; there he may pray indeed, if the spirit of prayer be in his heart; and this course was commended by the Lord. Wordy supplications, made up largely of iterations and repetitions such as the heathen use, thinking that their idol deities will be pleased with their much speaking, were forbidden.

It is well to know that prayer is not compounded of words, words that may fail to express what one desires to say, words that so often cloak inconsistencies, words that may have no deeper source than the physical organs of speech, words that may be spoken to impress mortal ears. The dumb may pray, and that too with the eloquence that prevails in heaven. Prayer is made up of heart throbs and the righteous yearnings of the soul, of supplication based on the realization of need, of contrition and pure desire. If there lives a man who has never really prayed, that man is a being apart from the order of the divine in human nature, a stranger in the family of God's children. Prayer is for the uplifting of the suppliant. God without our prayers would be God; but we without our prayers cannot be admitted to the kingdom of God. So did Christ instruct: "your Father knoweth what things ye have need of, before ye ask him."

Then gave He unto those who sought wisdom at His feet, a model prayer, saying: "After this manner therefore pray ye:

"Our Father which art in heaven, Hallowed by thy name." In this we acknowledge the relation we bear to our Heavenly Father, and while reverencing His great and holy Name, we avail ourselves of the inestimable privilege of approaching Him, less with the thought of His infinite glory as the Creator of all that is, the Supreme Being above all creation, than with the loving realization that He is Father, and that we are His children. This is the earliest Biblical scripture giving instruction, permission, or warrant, for addressing God directly as "Our Father". Therein is expressed the reconciliation which the human family, estranged through sin, may attain by the means provided through the well beloved Son. This instruction is equally definite in demonstrating the brotherhood between Christ and humanity. As He prayed so pray we to the same Father, we as brethren and Christ as our Elder Brother.

"Thy kingdom come. Thy will be done in earth, as it is in heaven." The kingdom of God is to be a kingdom of order, in which toleration and the recognition of individual rights shall prevail. One who really prays that this kingdom come will strive to hasten its coming by living according to the law of God. His effort will be to keep himself in harmony with the order of the kingdom, to subject the flesh to the spirit, selfishness to altruism, and to learn to love the things that God loves. To make the will of God supreme on earth as it is in heaven is to be allied with God in the affairs of life. There are many who profess belief that as God is omnipotent, all that is is according to His will. Such a supposition is unscriptural, unreasonable, and untrue.[535] Wickedness is not in harmony with His will; falsehood, hypocrisy, vice and crime are not God's gifts to man. By His will these monstrosities that have developed as hideous deformities in human nature and life shall be abolished, and this blessed consummation shall be reached when by choice, without surrender or abrogation of their free agency, men shall do the will of God.

"Give us this day our daily bread." Food is indispensable to life. As we need it we should ask for it. True, the Father knows our need before we ask, but by asking we acknowledge Him as the Giver, and are made humble, grateful, contrite, and reliant by the request. Though the sun shines and the rain falls alike upon the just and the unjust, the righteous man is grateful for these blessings; the ungodly man receives the benefits as a matter of course with a soul incapable of gratitude. The capacity to be grateful is a blessing, for the possession of which we should be further grateful. We are taught to pray day by day for the food we need, not for a great store to be laid by for the distant future. Israel in the desert received manna as a daily supply[536] and were kept in mind of their reliance upon Him who gave. The man with much finds it easier to forget his dependence than he who must ask with each succeeding day of need.

"And forgive us our debts, as we forgive our debtors." He who can thus pray with full intent and unmixed purpose merits forgiveness. In this specification of personal supplication we are taught to expect only as we deserve. The selfish and sinful would rejoice in exemption from their lawful debts, but being selfish and sinful would exact the last farthing from those who owe them.[537] Forgiveness is too precious a pearl to be cast at the feet of the unforgiving;[538] and, without the sincerity that springs from a contrite heart, no man may justly claim mercy. If others owe us, either in actual money or goods as suggested by debts and debtors, or through some infringement upon our rights included under the broader designation as a trespass, our mode of dealing with them will be taken into righteous account in the judgment of our own offenses.

"And lead us not into temptation, but deliver us from evil:" The first part of this petition has occasioned comment and question. We are not to understand that God would ever lead a man into temptation except, perhaps, by way of wise permission, to test and prove him, thereby affording him opportunity of overcoming and so of gaining spiritual strength, which is the only true advancement in man's eternal course of progress. The one purpose of providing bodies for the preexistent spirits of the race, and of advancing them to the mortal state, was to "prove them herewith, to see if they will do all things whatsoever the Lord their God shall command them."[539] The plan of mortality involved the certainty of temptation. The intent of the supplication appears to be that we be preserved from temptation beyond our weak powers to withstand; that we be not abandoned to temptation without the divine support that shall be as full a measure of protection as our exercize of choice will allow.

How inconsistent then to go, as many do, into the places where the temptations to which we are most susceptible are strongest; for the man beset with a passion for strong drink to so pray and then resort to the dramshop; for the man whose desires are lustful to voice such a prayer and then go where lust is kindled; for the dishonest man, though he say the prayer, to then place himself where he knows the opportunity to steal will be found! Can such souls as these be other than hypocrites in asking God to deliver them from the evils they have sought? Temptation will fall in our way without our seeking, and evil will present itself even when we desire most to do right; for deliverance from such we may pray with righteous expectation and assurance.

"For thine is the kingdom, and the power, and the glory, for ever. Amen." Herein we acknowledge the supremacy of the Being whom we addressed at the beginning as Father. He is the Almighty in whom and through whose provision we live and move and have our existence.[540] To assert independence of God is both sacrilege and blasphemy; to acknowledge Him is a filial duty and a just confession of His majesty and dominion. The Lord's Prayer is closed with a solemn "Amen," set as a seal to the document of the supplication, attesting its genuineness as the true expression of the suppliant's soul; gathering within the compass of a word the meaning of all that has been uttered or thought. _So let it be_ is the literal signification of _Amen_.

From the subject of prayer the Master turned to that of fasting, and emphasized the important truth that to be of avail fasting must be a matter between the man and his God, not between man and his kind. It was a common thing in the Master's day to see men parading the fact of their abstinence as an advertisement of their assumed piety.[541] That they might appear haggard and faint, this class of hypocrites disfigured their faces, went with unkempt hair, gazed about with sad countenances. Of these also the Lord said, "Verily I say unto you, They have their reward." Believers were admonished to fast secretly, with no outward display, and to fast unto God, who could see in secret and would heed their sacrifice and prayer.

TREASURES OF EARTH AND OF HEAVEN.[542]

The transitory character of worldly wealth was next contrasted with the enduring riches of eternity. Many there were and many there are whose principal effort in life has been that of amassing treasures of earth, the mere possession of which entails responsibility, care, and disturbing anxiety. Some kinds of wealth are endangered by the ravages of moths, such as silks and velvets, satins and furs; some are destroyed by corrosion and rust--silver and copper and steel; while these and others are not infrequently made the booty of thieves. Infinitely more precious are the treasures of a life well spent, the wealth of good deeds, the account of which is kept in heaven, where the riches of righteous achievement are safe from moth, rust, and robbers. Then followed the trenchant lesson: _"For where your treasure is, there will your heart be also."_

Spiritual light is shown to be greater than any product of physical illuminants. What does the brightest light avail the man who is blind? It is the bodily eye that discerns the light of the candle, the lamp, or the sun; and the spiritual eye sees by spiritual light; if then man's spiritual eye be single, that is, pure and undimmed by sin, he is filled with the light that shall show him the way to God; whereas if his soul's eye be evil, he will be as one full of darkness. Solemn caution is expressed in the summary, "If therefore the light that is in thee be darkness, how great is that darkness!" Those whom the Master was addressing had received of the light of God; the degree of belief they had already professed was proof of that. Should they turn from the great emprise on which they had embarked, the light would be lost, and the succeeding darkness would be denser than that from which they had been relieved.[543] There was to be no indecision among the disciples. No one of them could serve two masters; if he professed so to do he would be an untrue servant to the one or the other. Then followed another profound generalization: _"Ye cannot serve God and mammon."_[544]

They were told to trust the Father for what they needed, taking no thought of food, drink, clothing, or even of life itself, for all these were to be supplied by means above their power to control. With the wisdom of a Teacher of teachers, the Master appealed to their hearts and their understanding by citing the lessons of nature, in language of such simple yet forceful eloquence that to amplify or condense it is but to mar:

"Behold the fowls of the air: for they sow not, neither do they reap, nor gather into barns; yet your heavenly Father feedeth them. Are ye not much better than they? Which of you by taking thought can add one cubit unto his stature? And why take ye thought for raiment? Consider the lilies of the field, how they grow; they toil not, neither do they spin: And yet I say unto you, That even Solomon in all his glory was not arrayed like one of these."

The weakness of faith was reproved in the reminder that the Father who cared even for the grass of the field, which one day flourishes and on the next is gathered up to be burned, would not fail to remember His own. Therefore the Master added: _"Seek ye first the kingdom of God, and his righteousness; and all these things shall be added unto you."_

HYPOCRISY FURTHER CONDEMNED.[545]

Men are prone to judge their fellows and to praise or censure without due consideration of fact or circumstance. On prejudiced or unsupported judgment the Master set His disapproval. "Judge not, that ye be not judged," He admonished, for, according to one's own standard of judging others, shall he himself be judged. The man who is always ready to correct his brother's faults, to remove the mote from his neighbor's eye so that that neighbor may see things as the interested and interfering friend would have him see, was denounced as a hypocrite. What was the speck in his neighbor's vision to the obscuring beam in his own eye? Have the centuries between the days of Christ and our own time made us less eager to cure the defective vision of those who cannot or will not assume our point of view, and see things as we see them?

These disciples, some of whom were soon to minister in the authority of the Holy Apostleship, were cautioned against the indiscreet and indiscriminate scattering of the sacred truths and precepts committed to them. Their duty would be to discern the spirits of those whom they essayed to teach, and to impart unto them in wisdom. The words of the Master were strong: "Give not that which is holy unto the dogs, neither cast ye your pearls before, swine, lest they trample them under their feet, and turn again and rend you."[546]

PROMISE AND REASSURANCE[547]

That their supplications would be heard and answered followed as a rich promise. They were to ask and they would receive; they were to knock and the door would be opened. Surely the Heavenly Father would not be less considerate than a human parent; and what father would answer his son's plea for bread by giving him a stone, or who would give a serpent when a fish was desired? With greater certainty would God bestow good gifts upon those who asked according to their need, in faith. "_Therefore all things whatsoever ye would that men should do to you, do ye even so to them: for this is the law and the prophets."_

The straight and narrow way by which man may walk in Godliness was compared with the broad highway leading to destruction. False prophets were to be shunned, such as were then among the people, comparable in their pretense to sheep, and in their reality to ravening wolves. These were to be recognized by their works and the results thereof, even as a tree to be judged as good or bad according to its fruit. A thorn bush does not produce grapes, nor can thistles bear figs. Conversely, it is as truly impossible for a good tree to produce evil fruit as for a useless and corrupt tree to bring forth good fruit.

Religion is more than the confession and profession of the lips. Jesus averred that in the day of judgment many would pretend allegiance to Him, saying: "Lord, Lord, have we not prophesied in thy name? and in thy name have cast out devils? and in thy name done many wonderful works? And then will I profess unto them, I never knew you: depart from me, ye that work iniquity." Only by doing the will of the Father is the saving grace of the Son obtainable. To assume to speak and act in the name of the Lord without the bestowal of authority, such as the Lord alone can give, is to add sacrilege to hypocrisy. Even miracles wrought will be no vindication of the claims of those who pretend to minister in the ordinances of the gospel while devoid of the authority of the Holy Priesthood.[548]

HEARING AND DOING.[549]

The Sermon on the Mount has stood through all the years since its delivery without another to be compared with it. No mortal man has ever since preached a discourse of its kind. The spirit of the address is throughout that of sincerity and action, as opposed to empty profession and neglect. In the closing sentences the Lord showed the uselessness of hearing alone, as contrasted with the efficacy of doing. The man who hears and acts is likened unto the wise builder who set the foundation of his house upon a rock; and in spite of rain and hurricane and flood, the house stood. He that hears and obeys not is likened unto the foolish man who built his house upon the sand; and when rain fell, or winds blew, or floods came, behold it fell, and great was the fall thereof.

Such doctrines as these astonished the people. For His distinctive teachings the Preacher had cited no authority but His own. His address was free from any array of rabbinical precedents; the law was superseded by the gospel: _"For he taught them as one having authority, and not as the scribes!"_

NOTES TO CHAPTER 17.

1. Time and Place of the Sermon on the Mount.--Matthew gives the address early mention, placing it even before the record of his own call from the seat of custom--which call certainly preceded the ordination of the Twelve as a body--and before his account of many sayings and doings of the Lord already

considered in these pages. Luke's partial summary of the sermon follows his record of the ordination of the apostles. Matthew tells us that Jesus had gone up the mountain and that He sat while speaking; Luke's account suggests the inference that Jesus and the Twelve first descended from the mountain heights to a plain, where they were met by the multitude, and that Jesus preached unto them, standing. Critics who rejoice in trifles, often to the neglect of weightier matters, have tried to make much of these seeming variations. Is it not probable that Jesus spoke at length on the mountain-side to the disciples then present, and from whom He had chosen the Twelve, and that after finishing His discourse to them He descended with them to the plain where a multitude had assembled, and that to these He repeated parts of what He had before spoken? The relative fulness of Matthew's report may be due to the fact that he, as one of the Twelve, was present at the first and more extended delivery.

2. Pleasure Versus Happiness.--"The present is an age of pleasure-seeking, and men are losing their sanity in the mad rush for sensations that do but excite and disappoint. In this day of counterfeits, adulterations, and base imitations, the devil is busier than he has ever been in the course of human history, in the manufacture of pleasures, both old and new; and these he offers for sale in most attractive fashion, falsely labeled, _Happiness_. In this soul-destroying craft he is without a peer; he has had centuries of experience and practise, and by his skill he controls the market. He has learned the tricks of the trade, and knows well how to catch the eye and arouse the desire of his customers. He puts up the stuff in bright-colored packages, tied with tinsel string and tassel; and crowds flock to his bargain counters, hustling and crushing one another in their frenzy to buy.

"Follow one of the purchasers as he goes off gloatingly with his gaudy packet, and watch him as he opens it. What finds he inside the gilded wrapping? He has expected fragrant happiness, but uncovers only an inferior brand of pleasure, the stench of which is nauseating.

"Happiness includes all that is really desirable and of true worth in pleasure, and much beside. Happiness is genuine gold, pleasure but gilded brass, which corrodes in the hand, and is soon converted into poisonous verdigris. Happiness is as the genuine diamond, which, rough or polished, shines with its own inimitable luster; pleasure is as the paste imitation that glows only when artificially embellished. Happiness is as the ruby, red as the heart's blood, hard and enduring; pleasure, as stained glass, soft, brittle, and of but transitory beauty.

"Happiness is true food, wholesome, nutritious and sweet; it builds up the body and generates energy for action, physical, mental and spiritual; pleasure is but a deceiving stimulant which, like spirituous drink, makes one think he is strong when in reality enfeebled; makes him fancy he is well when in fact stricken with deadly malady.

"Happiness leaves no bad after-taste, it is followed by no depressing reaction; it calls for no repentance, brings no regret, entails no remorse; pleasure too often makes necessary repentance, contrition, and suffering; and, if indulged to the extreme, it brings degradation and destruction.

"True happiness is lived over and over again in memory, always with a renewal of the original good; a moment of unholy pleasure may leave a barbed sting, which, like a thorn in the flesh, is an ever-present source of anguish.

"Happiness is not akin with levity, nor is it one with light-minded mirth. It springs from the deeper fountains of the soul, and is not infrequently accompanied by tears. Have you never been so happy that you have had to weep? I have." From an article by the author, _Improvement Era_, vol. 17, No. 2, pp. 172, 173.

3. Salt of the Earth.--Dummelow's _Commentary_, on Matt. 5:13, states: "Salt in Palestine, being gathered in an impure state, often undergoes chemical changes by which its flavor is destroyed while its appearance remains." Perhaps a reasonable interpretation of the expression, "if the salt have lost his savor," may be suggested by the fact that salt mixed with insoluble impurities may be dissolved out by moisture, leaving the insoluble residue but slightly salty. The lesson of the Lord's illustration is that spoiled salt is of no use as a preservative. The corresponding passage in the sermon delivered by Jesus to the Nephites after His resurrection reads: "Verily, verily, I say unto you, I give unto you to be the salt of the earth; but if the salt shall lose its savor, wherewith shall the earth be salted? The salt shall be thenceforth good for nothing, but to be cast out, and to be trodden under foot of men." (3 Nephi 12:13.)

4. Reference to Publicans.--Observe that Matthew, who had been a publican, frankly records this reference (5:46, 47) to his despized class. Luke writes "sinners" instead of "publicans" (6:32-34). Of course, if the accounts of the two writers refer to separate addresses (see Note 1, above), both may be accurate. But we find Matthew's designation of himself as a publican in his list of the apostles (10:3) and the considerate omission of the unenviable title by the other evangelists (Mark 3:18; Luke 6:15).

5. Relative Perfection.--Our Lord's admonition to men to become perfect, even as the Father is perfect (Matt. 5:48) cannot rationally be construed otherwise than as implying the possibility of such achievement. Plainly, however, man cannot become perfect in mortality in the sense in which God is perfect as a supremely glorified Being. It is possible, though, for man to be perfect in his sphere in a sense analogous to that in which superior intelligences are perfect in their several spheres; yet the relative perfection of the lower is infinitely inferior to that of the higher. A college student in his freshman or sophomore year may be perfect as freshman or sophomore; his record may possibly be a hundred per cent on the scale of efficiency and achievement; yet the honors of the upper classman are beyond him, and the attainment of graduation is to him remote, but of assured possibility, if he do but continue faithful and devoted to the end.

[515] Matt. chaps. 5, 6, 7; Luke 6:20-49. See also the version of the Sermon as delivered by Jesus Christ after His resurrection, to the Nephites on the western continent; B. of M., 3 Nephi, chaps. 12, 13, 14. See also chapter 39 herein.

[516] Note 1, end of chapter.
[517] Matt. 4:23-25; read these verses in connection with 5:1; see also Luke 6:17-19.
[518] Note 1, end of chapter.
[519] Matt. 5:3-12; compare Luke 6:20-26; and B. of M., 3 Nephi 12:1-12.
[520] Matt. 5:11,12; compare Luke 6:26; B. of M., 3 Nephi 12:11,12.
[521] Note 2, end of chapter.
[522] Doc. and Cov. 93:33.
[523] Matt. 5:13-20; compare Luke 14:34-35; B. of M., 3 Nephi 12:13-20.
[524] Lev. 2:13; compare Ezra 6:9; Ezek. 43:24.
[525] Note the expression "covenant of salt," indicating the covenant between Jehovah and Israel, Lev. 2:13; Numb. 18:19; compare 2 Chron. 13:5.
[526] Note 3, end of chapter.
[527] Matt. 5:21-48; Luke 6:27-36; compare B. of M., 3 Nephi 12:21-48.
[528] Exo. 21:23-25; Lev. 24:17-22; Deut. 19:21.
[529] Compare Lev. 19:18; Deut. 23:6; and Psa. 41:10.
[530] Compare the lesson taught in the Parable of the Tares, Matt. 13:24-30.
[531] Note 4, end of chapter; see also pages 193 and 201.
[532] Note 5, end of chapter.
[533] Matt. 6:1-18; compare Luke 11:2-4; B. of M., 3 Nephi 13:1-18.
[534] Consider the incident of the gifts of the rich and the widow's mite, Mark 12:41-44; Luke 21:1-4.
[535] Page 18.
[536] Exo. 16:16-21.
[537] Note the lesson of the parable of the Unmerciful Servant, Matt. 18:33-25.
[538] Compare Matt. 7:6.
[539] P. of G.P., Abraham 3:25; see pages 14, 15, herein.
[540] Acts 17:28.
[541] Compare the instance connected with the parable of the Pharisee and the Publican, Luke 18:10-14.
[542] Matt. 6:19-34; compare Luke 12:24-34; 16:13; 18:22; B. of M., 3 Nephi 13:19-34.
[543] Luke 11:34-36.
[544] Compare Gal. 1:10; 1 Tim. 6:17; James 4:4; 1 John 2:15.
[545] Matt. 7:1-5; Luke 6:37, 38, 41, 42; compare B, of M., 3 Nephi 14:1-5.
[546] Matt. 7:6; compare B. of M., 3 Nephi 14:6.
[547] Matt. 7:7-23; Luke 6:43-44, 46; 11:9-13; 13:24-30; compare B. of M., 3 Nephi 14:7-23.
[548] "Articles of Faith," x:1-20; and xii:1-30.
[549] Matt. 7:24-29; Luke 6:46-49; compare B. of M., 3 Nephi 14:24-27.

CHAPTER 18. AS ONE HAVING AUTHORITY.

Matthew's account of the invaluable address, known to us as the Sermon on the Mount, is closed with a forceful sentence of his own, referring to the effect of the Master's words upon the people: "For he taught them as one having authority, and not as the scribes."[550] A striking characteristic of Christ's ministry was the entire absence of any claim of human authority for His words or deeds; the commission He professed to have was that of the Father who sent Him. His addresses, whether delivered to multitudes or spoken in relative privacy to few, were free from the labored citations in which the teachers of the day delighted. His authoritative "I say unto you" took the place of invocation of authority and exceeded any possible array of precedent commandment or deduction. In this His words differed essentially from the erudite utterances of scribes, Pharisees and rabbis. Throughout His ministry, inherent power and authority were manifest over matter and the forces of nature, over men and demons, over life and death. It now becomes our purpose to consider a number of instances in which the Lord's power was demonstrated in divers mighty works.

THE CENTURION'S SERVANT HEALED.[551]

From the Mount of Beatitudes Jesus returned to Capernaum, whether directly or by a longer way marked by other works of power and mercy is of little importance. There was at that time a Roman garrison in the city. A military officer, a centurion or captain of a hundred men, was stationed there. Attached to the household of this officer was an esteemed servant, who was ill, "and ready to die." The centurion had faith that Christ could heal his servant, and invoked the intercession of the Jewish elders to beg of the Master the boon desired. These elders implored Jesus most earnestly, and urged the worthiness of the man, who, though a Gentile, loved the people of Israel and out of his munificence had built for them a synagog in the town. Jesus went with the elders, but the centurion, probably learning of the approach of the little company, hastily sent other envoys to say that he did not consider himself worthy to have Jesus enter his home, from which sense of unworthiness he had not ventured to make his request in person.[552] "But," ran the message of supplication, "say in a word, and my servant shall be healed." We may well contrast this man's conception of Christ's power with that of the nobleman of the same town, who had requested Jesus to hasten in person to the side of his dying son.[553]

The centurion seems to have reasoned in this way: He himself was a man of authority, though under the direction of superior officers. To his subordinates he gave orders which were obeyed. He did not find it necessary to personally attend to the carrying out of his instructions. Surely One who had such power as Jesus possessed could command and be obeyed. Moreover, the man may have heard of the marvelous restoration of the nobleman's dying son, in accomplishing which the Lord spoke the effective word when miles away from the sufferer's bed. That the centurion's trust and confidence, his belief and faith, were genuine, is not to be doubted, since Jesus expressly commended the same. The afflicted one was healed. Jesus is said to have marveled[554] at the centurion's manifestation of faith, and, turning to the people who followed, He thus spake: "I say unto you, I have not found so great faith, no, not in Israel." This remark may have caused some of the listeners to wonder; the Jews were unaccustomed to hear the faith of a Gentile so extolled, for, according to the traditionalism of the day, a Gentile, even though an earnest proselyte to Judaism, was accounted essentially inferior to even the least worthy of the chosen people. Our Lord's comment plainly indicated that Gentiles would be preferred in the kingdom of God if they excelled in worthiness. Turning to Matthew's record we find this additional teaching, introduced as usual with "I say unto you"--"That many shall come from the east and west, and shall sit down with Abraham, and Isaac, and Jacob, in the kingdom of heaven. But the children of the kingdom shall be cast out into outer darkness: there shall be weeping and gnashing of teeth."[555] This lesson, that the supremacy of Israel can be attained only through excellence in righteousness, is reiterated and enlarged upon in the Lord's teachings, as we shall see.

A YOUNG MAN OF NAIN RAISED FROM THE DEAD.[556]

On the day after that of the miracle last considered, Jesus went to the little town of Nain, and, as usual, many people accompanied Him. This day witnessed what in human estimation was a wonder greater than any before wrought by Him. He had already healed many, sometimes by a word spoken to afflicted ones present, and again when He was far from the subject of His beneficent power; bodily diseases had been overcome, and demons had been rebuked at His command; but, though the sick who were nigh unto death had been saved from the grave, we have no earlier record of our Lord having commanded dread death itself to give back one it had claimed.[557] As Jesus and His followers approached the town, they met a funeral cortege of many people; the only son of a widow was being borne to the tomb; the body was carried according to the custom of the day on an open bier. Our Lord looked with compassion upon the sorrowing mother, now bereft of both husband and son; and, feeling in Himself[558] the pain of her grief, He said in gentle tone, "Weep not." He touched the stretcher upon which the dead man lay, and the bearers stood still. Then addressing the corpse He said: "Young man, I say unto thee, Arise." And the dead heard the voice of Him who is Lord of all,[559] and immediately sat up and spoke. Graciously Jesus delivered the young man to his mother. We read without wonder that there came a fear on all who were present, and that they glorified God, testifying that a great prophet was amongst them and that God has visited His people. Reports of this miracle were carried throughout the land, and even reached the ears of John the Baptist, who was confined in the prison of Herod. The effect of the information conveyed to John concerning this and other mighty works of Christ, now claims our attention.

JOHN BAPTIST'S MESSAGE TO JESUS.

Even before Jesus had returned to Galilee after His baptism and the forty days of solitude in the wilderness, John the Baptist had been imprisoned by order of Herod Antipas, tetrarch of Galilee and Perea. [560] During the subsequent months of our Lord's activities, in preaching the gospel, teaching the true significance of the kingdom, reproving sin, healing the afflicted, rebuking evil spirits and even raising the dead to life, His forerunner, the God-fearing, valiant John, had lain a prisoner in the dungeons of Mach├ᵉrus, one of the strongest of Herod's citadels.[561]

The tetrarch had some regard for John, having found him to be a holy man; and many things had Herod done on the direct advice of the Baptist or because of the influence of the latter's general teaching. Indeed, Herod had listened to John gladly, and had imprisoned him through a reluctant yielding to the importunities of Herodias, whom Herod claimed as a wife under cover of an illegal marriage. Herodias had been and legally was still the wife of Herod's brother Philip, from whom she had never been lawfully divorced; and her pretended marriage to Herod Antipas was both adulterous and incestuous under Jewish law. The Baptist had fearlessly denounced this sinful association; to Herod he had said: "It is not lawful for thee to have thy brother's wife." Though Herod might possibly have ignored this stern rebuke, or at least might have allowed it to pass without punishment, Herodias would not condone. It was she, not the tetrarch, who most hated John; she "had a quarrel against him," and succeeded in inducing Herod to have the Baptist seized and incarcerated as a step toward the consummation of her vengeful plan of having him put to death.[562] Moreover, Herod feared an uprising of the people in the event of John being slain by his order.[563]

In the course of his long imprisonment John had heard much of the marvelous preaching and works of Christ; these things must have been reported to him by some of his disciples and friends who were allowed to visit him.[564] Particularly was he informed of the miraculous raising of the young man at Nain; [565] and forthwith he commissioned two of his disciples to bear a message of inquiry to Jesus.[566] These came to Christ and reported the purpose of their visit thus: "John Baptist hath sent us unto thee, saying, Art thou he that should come? or look we for another?" The messengers found Jesus engaged in beneficent ministrations; and, instead of giving an immediate reply in words, He continued His labor, relieving in that same hour many who were afflicted by blindness or infirmities, or who were troubled by evil spirits. Then, turning to the two who had communicated the Baptist's question, Jesus said: "Go your way, and tell John what things ye have seen and heard; how that the blind see, the lame walk, the lepers are cleansed, the deaf hear, the dead are raised, to the poor the gospel is preached. And blessed is he, whosoever shall not be offended in me."

The words of John's inquiring disciples were answered by wondrous deeds of beneficence and mercy. When the reply was reported to John, the imprisoned prophet could scarcely have failed to remember the predictions of Isaiah, that by those very tokens of miracle and blessing should the Messiah be known;[567] and the reproof must have been convincing and convicting as he called to mind his own citations of Isaiah's prophecies, when he had proclaimed in fiery, withering eloquence the fulfilment of those earlier predictions in his own mission and in that of the Mightier One to whom he had borne personal testimony.[568]

The concluding sentence of our Lord's answer to John was the climax of what had preceded, and a further though yet gentle rebuke of the Baptist's defective comprehension of the Messiah's mission. "Blessed is he, whosoever shall not be offended in me," said the Lord. Misunderstanding is the prelude to offense. Gaged by the standard of the then current conception of what the Messiah would be, the work of Christ must have appeared to many as failure; and those who were looking for some sudden manifestation of His power in the conquest of Israel's oppressors and the rehabilitation of the house of David in worldly splendor, grew impatient, then doubtful; afterward they took offense and were in danger of turning in open rebellion against their Lord. Christ has been an offender to many because they, being out of harmony with His words and works, have of themselves taken offense.[569]

John's situation must be righteously considered by all who assume to render judgment as to his purpose in sending to inquire of Christ, "Art thou he that should come?" John thoroughly understood that his own work was that of preparation; he had so testified and had openly borne witness that Jesus was the One for whom he had been sent to prepare. With the inauguration of Christ's ministry, John's influence had waned, and for many months he had been shut up in a cell, chafing under his enforced inactivity, doubtless yearning for the freedom of the open, and for the locusts and wild honey of the desert. Jesus was increasing while he decreased in popularity, influence, and opportunity; and he had affirmed that such condition was inevitable.[570]

But, left in prison, he may have become despondent, and may have permitted himself to wonder whether that Mightier One had forgotten him. He knew that were Jesus to speak the word of command the prison of Mach├ᵉrus could no longer hold him; nevertheless Jesus seemed to have abandoned him to his fate, which comprized not only confinement but other indignities, and physical torture.[571] It may have been a part of John's purpose to call Christ's attention to his pitiable plight; and in this respect his message was rather a reminder than a plain inquiry based on actual doubt. Indeed, we have good grounds for inference that John's purpose in sending disciples to inquire of Christ was partly, and perhaps largely, designed to confirm in these disciples an abiding faith in the Christ. The commission with which they were charged brought them into direct communication with the Lord, whose supremacy they could not well fail to comprehend. They were personal witnesses of His power and authority.

Our Lord's commentary on John's message indicated that the Baptist had no full understanding of what the spiritual kingdom of God comprized. After the envoys had departed, Jesus addressed Himself to the people who had witnessed the interview. He would not have them underrate the importance of the Baptist's service.[572] He reminded them of the time of John's popularity, when some of those then present, and multitudes of others, had gone into the wilderness to hear the prophet's stern admonition; and they had found him to be no reed, shaken by the wind, but a firm and unbending oak. They had not gone to see a man in fashionable attire; those who wore soft raiment were to be looked for in the court of the king, not in the wilderness, nor in the dungeon where John now lay. They had found in John a prophet indeed, yea, more than a prophet; "For," affirmed the Lord, "I say unto you, Among those that are born of women there is not a greater prophet than John the Baptist: but he that is least in the kingdom of God is greater than he."[573] What stronger testimony of the Baptist's integrity is needed? Other prophets had told of the Messiah's coming, but John had seen Him, had baptized Him, and had been to Jesus as a body servant to his master. Nevertheless from the day of John's preaching to the time at which Christ then spoke, the kingdom of heaven had been rejected with violence, and this even though all the prophets and even the fundamental law had told of its coming, and though both John and Christ had been abundantly predicted.

Concerning John, the Lord continued: "And if ye will receive it, this is Elias, which was for to come. He that hath ears to hear, let him hear."[574] It is important to know that the designation, Elias, here applied by Jesus to the Baptist, is a title rather than a personal name, and that it has no reference to Elijah, the ancient prophet called the Tishbite.[575] Many of those who heard the Lord's eulogy on the Baptist rejoiced, for they had accepted John, and had turned from him to Jesus as from the lesser to the Greater; as from the priest to the great High Priest, as from the herald to the King. But Pharisees and lawyers were present, those of the class that John had so vehemently denounced as of a generation of vipers, and those who had rejected the counsel of God in refusing to heed the Baptist's call to repentance.[576]

At this point the Master resorted to analogy to make His meaning clearer. He compared the unbelieving and dissatisfied generation to fickle children at play, disagreeing among themselves. Some wanted to enact the pageantry of a mock wedding, and though they piped the rest would not dance; then they changed to a funeral procession and essayed the part of mourners, but the others would not weep as the rules of the game required. Ever critical, ever skeptical, by nature fault-finders and defamers, hard of hearing and of heart, they grumbled. John the Baptist had come amongst them like the eremitic prophets of old, as strict as any Nazarite, refusing to eat with the merry-makers or drink with the convivial, and they had said "He hath a devil." Now came the Son of Man,[577] without austerity or hermit ways, eating and drinking as a normal man would do, a guest at the houses of the people, a participant in the festivities of a marriage party, mingling alike with the publicans and the Pharisees--and they complained again, saying: "Behold a gluttonous man, and a winebibber, a friend of publicans and sinners!" The Master explained that such inconsistency, such wicked trifling with matters most sacred, such determined opposition to truth, would surely be revealed in their true light, and the worthlessness of boasted learning would appear. "But," said He, "wisdom is justified of all her children."

From reproof for unbelieving individuals He turned to unappreciative communities, and upbraided the cities in which He had wrought so many mighty works, and wherein the people repented not: "Woe unto thee, Chorazin! woe unto thee, Bethsaida! for if the mighty works, which were done in you, had been done in Tyre and Sidon, they would have repented long ago in sackcloth and ashes. But I say unto you, It shall be more tolerable for Tyre and Sidon at the day of judgment, than for you. And thou, Capernaum, which art exalted unto heaven, shalt be brought down to hell: for if the mighty works which have been done in thee, had been done in Sodom, it would have remained until this day. But I say unto you, That it shall be more tolerable for the land of Sodom in the day of judgment, than for thee."[578]

Seemingly faint at heart over the unbelief of the people, Jesus sought strength in prayer.[579] With the eloquence of soul for which one looks in vain save in the anguish-laden communion of Christ with His Father, He voiced His reverent gratitude that God had imparted a testimony of the truth to the humble and simple rather than to the learned and great; though misunderstood by men He was known for what He really was by the Father. Turning again to the people, He urged anew their acceptance of Him and His gospel, and His invitation is one of the grandest outpourings of spiritual emotion known to man: "Come unto me, all ye that labour and are heavy laden, and I will give you rest. Take my yoke upon you, and learn of me; for I am meek and lowly in heart: and ye shall find rest unto your souls. For my yoke is easy, and my burden is light."[580] He invited them from drudgery to pleasant service; from the well-nigh unbearable burdens of ecclesiastical exactions and traditional formalism, to the liberty of truly spiritual worship; from slavery to freedom; but they would not. The gospel He offered them was the embodiment of liberty, but not of license; it entailed obedience and submission; but even if such could be likened unto a yoke, what was its burden in comparison with the incubus under which they groaned?

DEATH OF JOHN THE BAPTIST.

Reverting to John Baptist in his dungeon solitude, we are left without information as to how he received and understood the reply to his inquiry, as brought by his messengers. His captivity was destined soon to end, though not by restoration to liberty on earth. The hatred of Herodias increased against him. An opportunity for carrying into effect her fiendish plots against his life soon appeared.[581] The king celebrated his birthday by a great feast, to which his lords, high captains, and the principal officials of Galilee were bidden. To grace the occasion, Salome, daughter of Herodias though not of Herod, came in and danced before the company. So enchanted were Herod and his guests that the king bade the damsel ask whatever she would, and he swore he would give it unto her, even though the gift were half of his kingdom.

She retired to consult her mother as to what she should ask, and, being instructed, returned with the appalling demand: "I will that thou give me by and by in a charger the head of John the Baptist." The king was astounded; his amazement was followed by sorrow and regret; nevertheless, he dreaded the humiliation that would follow a violation of the oath he had sworn in the presence of his court; so, summoning an executioner, he immediately gave the fatal order; and John was forthwith beheaded in the dungeon. The headsman returned, carrying a dish in which lay the ghastly trophy of the corrupt queen's vengeance. The bloody gift was delivered to Salome, who carried it with inhuman triumph to her mother. Some of John's disciples came, secured the corpse, laid it in a tomb; and bore the tidings of his death to Jesus. Herod was sorely troubled over the murder he had ordered; and when, later, the marvels wrought by Jesus were reported to him, he was afraid, and said: "That John the Baptist was risen from the dead, and therefore mighty works do shew forth themselves in him." To those who dissented, the terrified king replied: "It is John, whom I beheaded: he is risen from the dead."[582]

So ended the life of the prophet-priest, the direct precursor of the Christ; thus was stilled the mortal voice of him who had cried so mightily in the wilderness: "Prepare ye the way of the Lord." After many centuries his voice has been heard again, as the voice of one redeemed and resurrected; and the touch of his hand has again been felt, in this the dispensation of restoration and fulness. In May, 1829, a resurrected personage appeared to Joseph Smith and Oliver Cowdery, announced himself as John, known of old as the Baptist, laid his hands upon the two young men, and conferred upon them the priesthood of Aaron, which comprizes authority to preach and minister the gospel of repentance and of baptism by immersion for the remission of sins.[583]

IN THE HOUSE OF SIMON THE PHARISEE.

"And one of the Pharisees desired him that he would eat with him. And he went into the Pharisee's house, and sat down to meat."[584]

From the place of this incident in Luke's narration of events, it appears that it may have occurred on the day of the visit of John's messengers. Jesus accepted the Pharisee's invitation, as He had accepted the invitations of others, including even publicans, and those called by the rabbis, sinners. His reception at Simon's house appears to have been somewhat lacking in warmth, hospitality and honorable attendance. The narrative suggests an attitude of condescension on the part of the host. It was the custom of the times to treat a distinguished guest with marked attention; to receive him with a kiss of welcome, to provide water for washing the dust from his feet, and oil for anointing the hair of the head and the beard. All these courteous attentions were omitted by Simon. Jesus took His place, probably on one of the divans or couches on which it was usual to partly sit, partly recline, while eating.[585] Such an attitude would place the feet of the person outward from the table. In addition to these facts relating to the usages of the time it should be further remembered that dwellings were not protected against intrusion by such amenities of privacy as now prevail. It was not unusual at that time in Palestine for visitors and even strangers, usually men however, to enter a house at meal time, observe the procedure and even speak to the guests, all without bidding or invitation.

Among those who entered Simon's house while the meal was in progress, was a woman; and the presence of a woman, though somewhat unusual, was not strictly a social impropriety and could not well be forbidden on such an occasion. But this woman was one of the fallen class, a woman who had been unvirtuous, and who had to bear, as part of the penalty for her sins, outward scorn and practical ostracism from those who professed to be morally superior. She approached Jesus from behind, and bent low to kiss His feet as a mark of humility on her part and of respectful homage to Him. She may have been one of those who had heard His gracious words, spoken possibly that day: "Come unto me, all ye that labour and are heavy laden, and I will give you rest." Whatever her motive in coming, she had certainly come in a repentant and deeply contrite state. As she leaned over the feet of Jesus her tears rained upon them. Seemingly oblivious of her surroundings and of disapproving eyes watching her movements, she shook out her tresses and wiped the Lord's feet with her hair. Then, opening an alabaster box of ointment, she anointed them, as a slave might do to his master. Jesus graciously permitted the woman to proceed unrebuked and uninterrupted in her humble service inspired by contrition and reverent love.

Simon had observed the whole proceeding; by some means he had knowledge as to the class to which this woman belonged; and though not aloud, within himself he said: "This man, if he were a prophet, would have known who and what manner of woman this is that toucheth him: for she is a sinner." Jesus read the man's thoughts, and thus spake: "Simon, I have somewhat to say unto thee," to which the Pharisee replied, "Master, say on." Jesus continued, "There was a certain creditor which had two debtors: the one owed five hundred pence, and the other fifty. And when they had nothing to pay, he frankly forgave them both. Tell me therefore, which of them will love him most?" But one answer could be given with reason, and that Simon gave, though apparently with some hesitation or reserve. He possibly feared that he might involve himself. "I suppose" he ventured, "that he, to whom he forgave most." Jesus said, "Thou hast rightly judged," and proceeded: "Seest thou this woman? I entered into thine house, thou gavest me no water for my feet; but she hath washed my feet with tears, and wiped them with the hairs of her head. Thou gavest me no kiss: but this woman since the time I came in hath not ceased to kiss my feet. My head with oil thou didst not anoint: but this woman hath anointed my feet with ointment."

The Pharisee could not fail to note so direct a reminder of his having omitted the ordinary rites of respect to a specially invited guest. The lesson of the story had found its application in him, even as Nathan's parable had drawn from David the king a self-convicting answer.[586] "Wherefore," Jesus continued, "I say unto thee, her sins, which are many, are forgiven; for she loved much: but to whom little is forgiven, the same loveth little." Then to the woman He spake the words of blessed relief: "Thy sins are forgiven." Simon and the others at table murmured within themselves, "Who is this that forgiveth sins also?" Understanding their unspoken protest, Christ addressed the woman again, saying, "Thy faith hath saved thee; go in peace."

The latter part of the narrative brings to mind another occasion on which Christ granted remission of sins, and because of opposition in the minds of some hearers, opposition none the less real because unvoiced, had supplemented His authoritative utterance by another pronouncement.[587]

The name of the woman who thus came to Christ, and whose repentance was so sincere as to bring to her grateful and contrite soul the assurance of remission, is not recorded. There is no evidence that she figures in any other incident recorded in scripture. By certain writers she has been represented as the Mary of Bethany who, shortly before Christ's betrayal, anointed the head of Jesus with spikenard;[588] but the assumption of identity is wholly unfounded,[589] and constitutes an unjustifiable reflection upon the earlier life of Mary, the devoted and loving sister of Martha and Lazarus. Equally wrong is the attempt made by others to identify this repentant and forgiven sinner with Mary Magdalene, no period of whose life was marked by the sin of unchastity so far as the scriptures aver. The importance of guarding against mistakes in the identity of these women renders advisable the following addition to the foregoing treatment.

In the chapter following that in which are recorded the incidents last considered, Luke[590] states that Jesus went throughout the region, visiting every city and village, preaching the gospel of the kingdom and showing the glad tidings thereof. With Him on this tour were the Twelve, and also "certain women, which had been healed of evil spirits and infirmities, Mary called Magdalene, out of whom went seven devils, and Joanna the wife of Chuza Herod's steward, and Susanna, and many others, which ministered unto him of their substance." Further reference is made to some or all of these honorable women in connection with the death, burial, and resurrection of our Lord, and of Mary Magdalene particular mention appears.[591] Mary Magdalene, whose second name is probably derived from her home town, Magdala, had been healed through the ministrations of Jesus from both physical and mental maladies, the latter having been associated with possession by evil spirits. Out of her we are told Christ cast seven devils,[592] but even such grievous affliction affords no warrant for the assertion that the woman was unvirtuous or unchaste.

Mary Magdalene became one of the closest friends Christ had among women; her devotion to Him as her Healer and as the One whom she adored as the Christ, was unswerving; she stood close by the cross while other women tarried afar off in the time of His mortal agony; she was among the first at the sepulchre on the resurrection morning, and was the first mortal to look upon and recognize a resurrected Being--the Lord whom she had loved with all the fervor of spiritual adoration. To say that this woman, chosen from among women as deserving of such distinctive honors, was once a fallen creature, her soul seared by the heat of unhallowed lust, is to contribute to the perpetuating of an error for which there is no excuse. Nevertheless the false tradition, arising from early and unjustifiable assumption, that this noble woman, distinctively a friend of the Lord, is the same who, admittedly a sinner, washed and anointed the Savior's feet in the house of Simon the Pharisee and gained the boon of forgiveness through contrition, has so tenaciously held its place in the popular mind through the centuries, that the name, Magdalene, has come to be a generic designation for women who fall from virtue and afterward repent. We are not considering whether the mercy of Christ could have been extended to such a sinner as Mary of Magdala is wrongly reputed to have been; man cannot measure the bounds nor fathom the depths of divine forgiveness; and if it were so that this Mary and the repentant sinner who ministered to Jesus as He sat at the Pharisee's table were one and the same, the question would stand affirmatively answered, for that woman who had been a sinner was forgiven. We are dealing with the scriptural record as a history, and nothing said therein warrants the really repellent though common imputation of unchastity to the devoted soul of Mary Magdalene.

CHRIST'S AUTHORITY ASCRIBED TO BEELZEBUB.[593]

At the time of our Lord's earthly ministry, the curing of the blind, deaf, or dumb was regarded as among the greatest possible achievements of medical science or spiritual treatment; and the subjection or casting out of demons was ranked among the attainments impossible to rabbinical exorcism. Demonstrations of the Lord's power to heal and restore, even in cases universally considered as incurable, had the effect of intensifying the hostility of the sacerdotal classes; and they, represented by the Pharisaic party, evolved the wholly inconsistent and ridiculous suggestion that miracles were wrought by Jesus through the power of the prince of devils, with whom He was in league.[594]

While the Lord was making His second missionary tour through Galilee, going about through "all the cities and villages, teaching in their synagogues, and preaching the gospel of the kingdom, and healing every sickness and every disease among the people,"[595] the absurd theory that Christ was Himself a victim of demoniacal possession, and that He operated by the power of the devil, was urged and enlarged upon until it became the generally accepted explanation among the Pharisees and their kind. Jesus had withdrawn Himself for a time from the more populous centers, where He was constantly watched by emissaries, whom the ruling classes had sent from Jerusalem into Galilee; for the Pharisees were in conspiracy against Him, seeking excuse and opportunity to take His life; but even in the smaller towns and rural districts He was followed and beset by great multitudes, to whom He ministered for both physical and spiritual ailments.[596]

He urged the people to refrain from spreading His fame; and this He may have done for the reason that at that stage of His work an open rupture with the Jewish hierarchy would have been a serious

Page 105

hindrance; or possibly He desired to leave the rulers, who were plotting against Him, time and opportunity to brew their bitter enmity and fill to the brim the flagons of their determined iniquity. Matthew sees in the Lord's injunctions against publicity a fulfilment of Isaiah's prophecy that the chosen Messiah would not strive nor cry out on the street to attract attention, nor would He use His mighty power to crush even a bruised reed, or to quench even the smoking flax; He would not fail nor be discouraged, but would victoriously establish just judgment upon the earth for the Gentiles, as well as, by implication, for Israel. [597] The figure of the bruised reed and the smoking flax is strikingly expressive of the tender care with which Christ treated even the weakest manifestation of faith and genuine desire to learn the truth, whether exhibited by Jew or Gentile.

Soon after His return from the missionary tour referred to, an excuse for the Pharisees to assail Him was found in His healing of a man who was under the influence of a demon, and was both blind and dumb. This combination of sore afflictions, affecting body, mind, and spirit, was rebuked, and the sightless, speechless demoniac was relieved of his three-fold burden.[598] At this triumph over the powers of evil the people were the more amazed and said: "Is not this the son of David?" in other words, Can this be any other than the Christ we have been so long expecting? The popular judgment so voiced maddened the Pharisees, and they told the almost adoring people: "This fellow doth not cast out devils, but by Beelzebub the prince of devils." Jesus took up the malicious charge and replied thereto, not in anger but in terms of calm reason and sound logic. He laid the foundation of His defense by stating the evident truth that a kingdom divided against itself cannot endure but must surely suffer disruption. If their assumption were in the least degree founded on truth, Satan through Jesus would be opposing Satan. Then, referring to the superstitious practises and exorcisms of the time, by which some such effects as we class today under mind cures were obtained, He asked: "If I by Beelzebub cast out devils, by whom do your children cast them out? therefore they shall be your judges." And to make the demonstration plainer by contrast, He continued: "But if I cast out devils by the Spirit of God, then the kingdom of God is come upon you." By the acceptance of either proposition, and surely one was true, for the fact that Jesus did cast out devils was known throughout the land and was conceded in the very terms of the charge now brought against Him, the accusing Pharisees stood defeated and condemned.

But the illustration went further. Jesus continued: "Or else how can one enter into a strong man's house, and spoil his goods, except he first bind the strong man? and then he will spoil his house." Christ had attacked the stronghold of Satan, had driven his evil spirits from the human tabernacles of which they had unwarrantably taken possession; how could Christ have done this had He not first subdued the "strong man," the master of devils, Satan himself? And yet those ignorant scholars dared to say in the face of such self-evident refutation of their own premises, that the powers of Satan were subdued by Satanic agency. There could be no agreement, no truce nor armistice between the contending powers of Christ and Satan. Offering a suggestion of self-judgment to His accusers, that they might severally decide on which side they were aligned, Jesus added: "He that is not with me is against me; and he that gathereth not with me scattereth abroad."

Then, the demonstration being complete, and the absurdity of His opponents' assumption proved, Christ directed their thoughts to the heinous sin of condemning the power and authority by which Satan was overcome. He had proved to them on the basis of their own proposition that He, having subdued Satan, was the embodiment of the Spirit of God, and that through Him the kingdom of God was brought to them. They rejected the Spirit of God, and sought to destroy the Christ through whom that Spirit was made manifest. What blasphemy could be greater? Speaking as one having authority, with the solemn affirmation "I say unto you," He continued: "All manner of sin and blasphemy shall be forgiven unto men: but the blasphemy against the Holy Ghost shall not be forgiven unto men. And whosoever speaketh a word against the Son of man, it shall be forgiven him: but whosoever speaketh against the Holy Ghost, it shall not be forgiven him, neither in this world, neither in the world to come."

Who among men can word a more solemn and awful warning against the danger of committing the dread unpardonable sin?[599] Jesus was merciful in His assurance that words spoken against Himself as a Man, might be forgiven; but to speak against the authority He possessed, and particularly to ascribe that power and authority to Satan, was very near to blasphemy against the Holy Ghost, for which sin there could be no forgiveness. Then, in stronger terms, which developed into cutting invective, He told them to be consistent--if they admitted that the result of His labors was good, as the casting out of devils surely was, to be likened unto good fruit--why did they not acknowledge that the power by which such results were attained, in other words that the tree itself, was good? "Either make the tree good, and his fruit good; or else make the tree corrupt, and his fruit corrupt: for the tree is known by his fruit." With burning words of certain conviction He continued: "O generation of vipers, how can ye, being evil, speak good things? for out of the abundance of the heart the mouth speaketh." By the truths He had made so plain it was evident that their accusing words were drawn from hearts stored with evil treasure. Moreover their words were shown to be not only malicious but foolish, idle and vain, and therefore doubly saturated with sin. Another authoritative declaration followed: "But I say unto you, That every idle word that men shall speak, they shall give account thereof in the day of judgment."

SEEKERS AFTER SIGNS?[600]

The Master's lesson, enforced though it was by illustration and analogy, by direct application, and by authoritative avowal, fell on ears that were practically deaf to spiritual truth, and found no place in hearts already stuffed with great stores of evil. To the profound wisdom and saving instruction of the word of God to which they had listened, they responded with a flippant request: "Master, we would see a sign from thee." Had they not already seen signs in profusion? Had not the blind and the deaf, the dumb and the infirm, the palsied and the dropsical, and people afflicted with all manner of diseases, been healed in their houses, on their streets, and in their synagogs; had not devils been cast out and their foul utterances been silenced by His word; and had not the dead been raised, and all by Him whom they now importuned for a sign? They would have some surpassing wonder wrought, to satisfy curiosity, or perhaps to afford them further excuse for action against Him--they wanted signs to waste on their lust.[601] Small wonder, that "he sighed deeply in his spirit" when such demands were made.[602] To the scribes and Pharisees who had shown such inattention to His words, He replied: "An evil and adulterous generation[603] seeketh after a sign; and there shall no sign be given to it, but the sign of the prophet Jonas."

The sign of Jonas (or Jonah) was that for three days he had been in the belly of the fish and then had been restored to liberty; so would the Son of Man be immured in the tomb, after which He would rise again. That was the only sign He would give them, and by that would they stand condemned. Against them and their generation would the men of Nineveh rise in judgment, for they, wicked as they were, had repented at the preaching of Jonas; and behold a greater than Jonas was among them.[604] The queen of Sheba would rise in judgment against them, for she had journeyed far to avail herself of Solomon's wisdom; and behold a greater than Solomon stood before them.[605]

Then, reverting to the matter of unclean and evil spirits, in connection with which they had spread the accusation that He was one of the devil's own, He told them, that when a demon is cast out, he tries after a season of loneliness to return to the house or body from which he had been expelled; and, finding that house in order, sweet and clean since his filthy self had been forced to vacate it, he calls other spirits more wicked than himself, and they take possession of the man, and make his state worse than it was at first.[606] In this weird example is typified the condition of those who have received the truth, and thereby have been freed from the unclean influences of error and sin, so that in mind and spirit and body they are as a house swept and garnished and set in cleanly order, but who afterward renounce the good, open their souls to the demons of falsehood and deceit, and become more corrupt than before. "Even so," declared the Lord, "shall it be also unto this wicked generation."

Though the scribes and Pharisees were mostly unconvinced, if at all really impressed by His teachings, our Lord was not entirely without appreciative listeners. A woman in the company raised her voice in an invocation of blessing on the mother who had given birth to such a Son, and on the breasts that had suckled Him. While not rejecting this tribute of reverence, which applied to both mother and Son, Jesus answered: "Yea rather, blessed are they that hear the word of God, and keep it."[607]

CHRIST'S MOTHER AND BRETHREN COME TO SEE HIM.[608]

While Jesus was engaged with the scribes and Pharisees, and a great number of others, possibly at or near the conclusion of the teachings last considered, word was passed to Him that His mother and His brethren were present and desired to speak with Him. On account of the press of people they had been unable to reach His side. Making use of the circumstance to impress upon all the fact that His work took precedence over the claims of family and kinship, and thereby explaining that He could not meet His relatives at that moment, He asked, "Who is my mother? and who are my brethren?" Answering His own question and expressing in the answer the deeper thought in His mind, He said, pointing toward His disciples: "Behold my mother and my brethren! For whosoever shall do the will of my Father which is in heaven, the same is my brother, and sister, and mother."

The incident reminds one of the answer He made to His mother, when she and Joseph had found Him in the temple after their long and anxious search: "How is it that ye sought me? wist ye not that I must be about my Father's business?"[609] In that business He was engaged when His mother and brethren desired to speak with Him as He sat amidst the crowd. The superior claims of His Father's work caused Him to let all minor matters wait. We are not justified in construing these remarks as evidence of disrespect, far less of filial and family disloyalty. Devotion, similar in kind at least, was expected by Him of the apostles, who were called to devote without reserve their time and talents to the ministry.[610] The purpose on which the relatives of Jesus had come to see Him is not made known; we may infer, therefore, that it was of no great importance beyond the family circle.[611]

NOTES TO CHAPTER 18.

1. The Two Accounts of the Miracle.--In the commentary on the miraculous healing of the centurion's servant, as given in the text, we have followed in the main Luke's more circumstantial account. Matthew's briefer statement of the officer's petition, and the Lord's gracious compliance therewith, represents the man as coming in person to Jesus; while Luke refers to the elders of the local synagog as presenting the request. There is here no real discrepancy. It was then allowable, as in our time it is, to speak of one who causes something to be done as doing that thing himself. One may properly be said to notify another, when he sends the notification by a third party. A man may say he has built a house, when in reality others did the work of building though at his instance. An architect may with propriety be said to have constructed a building, when as a matter of fact he made the design, and directed others who actually reared the structure.

2. Jesus Marveled.--Both Matthew and Luke tell us that Jesus marveled at the faith shown by the centurion, who begged that his beloved servant be healed (Matt. 8:10; Luke 7:9). Some have queried how Christ, whom they consider to have been omniscient during His life in the flesh, could have marveled at anything. The meaning of the passage is evident in the sense that when the fact of the centurion's faith was

brought to His attention, He pondered over it, and contemplated it, probably as a refreshing contrast to the absence of faith He so generally encountered. In similar way, though with sorrow in place of joy, He is said to have marveled at the peoples' unbelief (Mark 6:6).

3. Sequence of the Miracles of Raising the Dead.--As stated and reiterated in the text the chronology of the events in our Lord's ministry, as recorded by the Gospel-writers, is uncertain. Literature on the subject embodies much disputation and demonstrates absence of any near approach to agreement among Biblical scholars. We have record of three instances of miraculous restoration of the dead to life at the word of Jesus--the raising of the son of the widow of Nain, the raising of the daughter of Jairus, and the raising of Lazarus; and on the sequence of two of these there is difference of opinion. Of course the placing of the raising of Lazarus as the latest of the three is based on certainty. Dr. Richard C. Trench, in his scholarly and very valuable _Notes on the Miracles of our Lord_ definitely asserts that the raising of the daughter of Jairus is the first of the three works of restoration to life. Dr. John Laidlaw, in _The Miracles of our Lord_, treats this first among the miracles of its class though without affirming its chronological precedence; many other writers make it the second of the three. The incentive to arrange the three miracles of this group in the sequence indicated may, perhaps, be found in the desire to present them in the increasing order of apparent greatness--the raising of the damsel being an instance of recalling to life one who had but just died, ("hardly dead" as some wrongly describe her condition), the raising of the young man of Nain being the restoration of one on the way to the tomb, and the raising of Lazarus an instance of recalling to life one who had lain four days in the sepulchre. We cannot consistently conceive of these cases as offering grades of greater or lesser difficulty to the power of Christ; in each case His word of authority was sufficient to reunite the spirit and body of the dead person. Luke, the sole recorder of the miracle at Nain, places the event before that of the raising of the daughter of Jairus, with many incidents between. The great preponderance of evidence is in favor of considering the three miracles in the order followed herein, (1) the raising of the young man of Nain, (2) that of the daughter of Jairus, and (3) that of Lazarus.

4. Tetrarch.--This title by derivation of the term and as originally used was applied to the ruler of a fourth part, or one of four divisions of a region that had formerly been one country. Later it came to be the designation of any ruler or governor over a part of a divided country, irrespective of the number or extent of the fractions. Herod Antipas is distinctively called the tetrarch in Matt. 14:1; Luke 3:1, 19; 9:7; and Acts 13:1; and is referred to as king in Matt. 14:9; Mark 6:14, 22, 25, 26.

5. Mach├ªrus.--According to the historian Josephus (Antiquities xviii; 5:2), the prison to which John the Baptist was consigned by Herod Antipas was the strong fortress Mach├ªrus.

6. Christ an Offender to Many.--The concluding part of our Lord's message to the imprisoned Baptist, in answer to the latter's inquiry, was, "Blessed is he whosoever is not offended in me." In passing it may be well to observe that whatever of reproof or rebuke these words may connote, the lesson was given in the gentlest way and in the form most easy to understand. As Deems has written, "Instead of saying 'Woe to him who is offended in me,' He puts it in the softer way 'Blessed is he who is not offended.'" In our English version of the Holy Bible the word "offend" and its cognates, are used in place of several different expressions which occur in the original Greek. Thus, actual infractions of the law, sin, and wickedness in general are all called offenses, and the perpetrators of such are guilty offenders who deserve punishment. In other instances even the works of righteousness are construed as causes of offense to the wicked; but this is so, not because the good works were in any way offenses against law or right, but because the law-breaker takes offense thereat. The convicted felon, if unrepentant and still of evil mind, is offended and angry at the law by which he has been brought to justice; to him the law is a cause of offense. In a very significant sense Jesus Christ stands as the greatest offender in history; for all who reject His gospel, take offense thereat. On the night of His betrayal Jesus told the apostles that they would be offended because of Him (Matt. 26:31; see also verse 33). The Lord's personal ministry gave offense not alone to Pharisees and priestly opponents, but to many who had professed belief in Him (John 6:61; compare 16:1). The gospel of Jesus Christ is designated by Peter as "a stone of stumbling and a rock of offense, even to them which stumble at the word, being disobedient" (1 Peter 2:8; compare Paul's words, Romans 9:33). Indeed blessed is he to whom the gospel is welcome, and who finds therein no cause for offense.

7. The Greatness of the Baptist's Mission.--The exalted nature of the mission of John the Baptist was thus testified to by Jesus: "Verily I say unto you, Among them that are born of women there hath not risen a greater than John the Baptist: notwithstanding he that is least in the kingdom of heaven is greater than he" (Matt. 11:11; compare Luke 7:28). In elucidation of the first part of this testimony, the prophet Joseph Smith said, in the course of a sermon delivered May 24, 1843, (_Hist. of the Church_, under date named): "It could not have been on account of the miracles John performed, for he did no miracles; but it was--First, because he was trusted with a divine mission of preparing the way before the face of the Lord. Who was trusted with such a mission before or since? No man. Second, he was trusted and it was required at his hands, to baptise the Son of Man. Who ever did that? Who ever had so great a privilege or glory? Who ever led the Son of God into the waters of baptism, beholding the Holy Ghost descend upon Him in the sign of a dove? No man. Third, John at that time was the only legal administrator holding the keys of power there was on earth. The keys, the kingdom, the power, the glory had departed from the Jews; and John, the son of Zacharias, by the holy anointing and decree of heaven, held the keys of power at that time."

The latter part of our Lord's statement--"notwithstanding he that is least in the kingdom of heaven is greater than he" (John), has given rise to diverse interpretations and comment. The true meaning may be, that surpassingly great as was John's distinction among the prophets, he had not learned, at the time of the incident under consideration, the full purpose of the Messiah's mission, and such he would surely have to learn before he became eligible for admission into the kingdom of heaven; therefore, the least of those who through knowledge gained and obedience rendered, would be prepared for a place in the kingdom of which Jesus taught, was greater than was John the Baptist at that time. Through latter-day inspiration we learn that "it is impossible for a man to be saved in ignorance" (Doc. and Cov. 131:6), and that "The glory of God in intelligence, or, in other words, light and truth" (Doc. and Cov. 93:36). The Baptist's inquiry showed that he was then lacking in knowledge, imperfectly enlightened and unable to comprehend the whole truth of the Savior's appointed death and subsequent resurrection as the Redeemer of the world. But we must not lose sight of the fact, that Jesus in no wise intimated that John would remain less than the least in the kingdom of heaven. As he increased in knowledge of the vital truths of the kingdom, and rendered obedience thereto, he would surely advance, and become great in the kingdom of heaven as he was great among the prophets of earth.

8. John the Baptist the Elias that was to Come.--In the days of Christ the people clung to the traditional belief that the ancient prophet Elijah was to return in person. Concerning this tradition the Dummelow _Commentary_ says, on Matt. 11:14: "It was supposed that his [Elijah's] peculiar activity would consist in settling ceremonial and ritual questions, doubts and difficulties and that he would restore to Israel (1) the golden pot of manna, (2) the vessel containing the anointing oil, (3) the vessel containing the waters of purification, (4) Aaron's rod that budded and bore fruit." For this belief there was no scriptural affirmation. That John was to go before the Messiah in the spirit and power of Elias was declared by the angel Gabriel in his announcement to Zacharias (Luke 1:17); and our Lord made plain the fact that John was that predicted Elias. "Elias" is both a name and a title of office. Through revelation in the present dispensation we learn of the separate individuality of Elias and Elijah, each of whom appeared in person and committed to modern prophets the particular powers pertaining to his respective office (Doc. and Cov. 110:12, 13). We learn that the office of Elias is that of restoration (Doc. and Cov. 27:6, 7; 76:100; 77:9, 14). Under date of March 10, 1844, the following is recorded (_Hist. of Church_) as the testimony of the prophet Joseph Smith:--

"The spirit of Elias is to prepare the way for a greater revelation of God, which is the Priesthood of Elias, or the Priesthood that Aaron was ordained unto. And when God sends a man into the world to prepare for a greater work, holding the keys of the power of Elias, it was called the doctrine of Elias, even from the early ages of the world.

"John's mission was limited to preaching and baptizing; but what he did was legal; and when Jesus Christ came to any of John's disciples, He baptized them with fire and the Holy Ghost.

"We find the apostles endowed with greater power than John: their office was more under the spirit and power of Elijah than Elias.

"In the case of Philip, when he went down to Samaria, when he was under the spirit of Elias, he baptized both men and women. When Peter and John heard of it, they went down and laid hands upon them, and they received the Holy Ghost. This shows the distinction between the two powers.

"When Paul came to certain disciples, he asked if they had received the Holy Ghost? They said, No. Who baptized you, then? We were baptized unto John's baptism. No, you were not baptized unto John's baptism, or you would have been baptized by John. And so Paul went and baptized them, for he knew what the true doctrine was, and he knew that John had not baptized them. And these principles are strange to me, that men who have read the Scriptures of the New Testament are so far from it.

"What I want to impress upon your minds is the difference of power in the different parts of the Priesthood, so that when any man comes among you, saying, 'I have the spirit of Elias,' you can know whether he be true or false; for any man that comes having the spirit and power of Elias, he will not transcend his bounds.

"John did not transcend his bounds, but faithfully performed that part belonging to his office; and every portion of the great building should be prepared right and assigned to its proper place; and it is necessary to know who holds the keys of power, and who does not, or we may be likely to be deceived.

"That person who holds the keys of Elias hath a preparatory work.

    *   *   *   *   *

"This is the Elias spoken of in the last days, and here is the rock upon which many split, thinking the time was past in the days of John and Christ, and no more to be. But the spirit of Elias was revealed to me, and I know it is true; therefore I speak with boldness, for I know verily my doctrine is true."

9. At the Pharisee's Table.--The expression "sat at meat," as in Luke 7:37 and in other instances, is stated by good authority to be a mistranslation; it should be rendered "lay" or "reclined" (see Smith's _Comp. Dict. of the Bible_, article "Meals"). That sitting was the early Hebrew posture at meals is not questioned (Gen. 27:19; Judges 19:6; 1 Sam. 16:11; 20:5, 18, 24; 1 Kings 13:20); but the custom of reclining on couches set around the table seems to date back long before the days of Jesus (Amos 3:12; 6:4). The Roman usage of arranging the tables and adjoining couches along three sides of a square, leaving the fourth side open for the passage of the attendants who served the diners was common in Palestine. Tables and couches so placed constituted the _triclinium_. In reference to the ceremonial of the Pharisees in the matter of prescribed washing of articles used in eating, Mark (7:4) specifies "tables"; this mention is conceded to be a mistranslation, as couches or literally beds, are meant by the Greek expression. (See marginal reading, "beds" in Oxford Bible, and others.) A person reclining at table would have the feet directed outward. Thus it was a simple matter for the contrite woman to approach Jesus from behind and anoint His feet without causing disturbance to others at the table.

10. The Woman's Identity not Specified.--The attempt to identify the contrite sinner who anointed the feet of Jesus in the house of Simon the Pharisee with Mary of Bethany is thus strongly condemned by Farrar (p. 228, note): "Those who identify this feast at the house of Simon the Pharisee, in Galilee, with the long-subsequent feast at the house of Simon the leper, at Bethany, and the anointing of the feet by 'a woman that was a sinner' in the city, with the anointing of the head by Mary the sister of

Martha, adopt principles of criticism so reckless and arbitrary that their general acceptance would rob the Gospels of all credibility, and make them hardly worth study as truthful narratives. As for the names Simon and Judas, which have led to so many identifications of different persons and different incidents, they were at least as common among the Jews of that day as Smith and Jones among ourselves. There are five or six Judes and nine Simons mentioned in the New Testament, and two Judes and two Simons among the Apostles alone; Josephus speaks of some ten Judes and twenty Simons in his writings, and there must, therefore, have been thousands of others who at this period had one of these two names. The incident (of anointing with ointment) is one quite in accordance with the customs of the time and country, and there is not the least improbability in its repetition under different circumstances. (Eccles. 9:8; Cant. 4:10; Amos 6:6.) The custom still continues."

The learned canon is fully justified in his vigorous criticism; nevertheless he endorses the commonly-accepted identification of the woman mentioned in connection with the meal in the house of Simon the Pharisee with Mary Magdalene, although he admits that the foundation of the assumed identification is "an ancient tradition,--especially prevalent in the Western Church, and followed by the translation of our English version" (p. 233). As stated in our text, there is an entire absence of trustworthy evidence that Mary Magdalene was ever tainted with the sin for which the repentant woman in the Pharisee's house was so graciously pardoned by our Lord.

11. The Unpardonable Sin.--The nature of the awful sin against the Holy Ghost, against which the Lord warned the Pharisaic accusers who sought to ascribe His divine power to Satan, is more fully explained, and its dread results are more explicitly set forth in modern revelation. Concerning them and their dreadful fate, the Almighty has said:--"I say that it had been better for them never to have been born, for they are vessels of wrath, doomed to suffer the wrath of God, with the devil and his angels in eternity; concerning whom I have said there is no forgiveness in this world nor in the world to come.... They shall go away into everlasting punishment, which is endless punishment, which is eternal punishment, to reign with the devil and his angels in eternity, where their worm dieth not, and the fire is not quenched, which is their torment; and the end thereof, neither the place thereof, nor their torment, no man knows, neither was it revealed, neither is, neither will be revealed unto man, except to them who are made partakers thereof: nevertheless I, the Lord, show it by vision unto many, but straightway shut it up again; wherefore the end, the width, the height, the depth, and the misery thereof, they understand not, neither any man except them who are ordained unto this condemnation." (Doc. and Cov. 76:31-48; see also Heb. 6:4-6; B. of M., Alma 39:6.)

12. An Adulterous Generation Seeking after Signs.--Our Lord's reply to those who clamored for a sign, that "An evil and adulterous generation seeketh after a sign" (Matt. 12:39; see also 16:4; Mark 8:38) could only be interpreted by the Jews as a supreme reproof. That the descriptive designation "adulterous" was literally applicable to the widespread immorality of the time, they all knew. Adam Clarke in his commentary on Matt. 12:39, says of this phase of our topic: "There is the utmost proof from their [the Jews'] own writings, that in the time of our Lord, they were most literally an adulterous race of people; for at this very time Rabbi Jachanan ben Zacchi abrogated the trial by the bitter waters of jealousy, because so many were found to be thus criminal." For the information concerning the trial of the accused by the bitter waters, see Numb. 5:11-31. Although Jesus designated the generation in which He lived as adulterous, we find no record that the Jewish rulers, who by their demand for a sign had given occasion for the accusation, ventured to deny or attempt to repel the charge. The sin of adultery was included among capital offenses (Deut. 22:22-25). The severity of the accusation as applied by Jesus, however, was intensified by the fact that the older scriptures represented the covenant between Jehovah and Israel as a marriage bond (Isa. 54:5-7; Jer. 3:14; 31:32; Hos. 2:19, 20); even as the later scriptures typify the Church as a bride, and Christ as the husband (2 Cor. 11:2; compare Rev. 21:2). To be spiritually adulterous, as the rabbis construed the utterances of the prophets, was to be false to the covenant by which the Jewish nations claimed distinction, as the worshipers of Jehovah, and to be wholly recreant and reprobate. Convicted on such a charge those sign-seeking Pharisees and scribes understood that Jesus classed them as worse than the idolatrous heathen. The words "adultery" and "idolatry" are of related origin, each connoting the act of unfaithfulness and the turning away after false objects of affection or worship.

13. The Mother and the Brethren of Jesus.--The attempt of Mary and some members of her family to speak with Jesus on the occasion referred to in the text has been construed by many writers to mean that the mother and sons had come to protest against the energy and zeal with which Jesus was pursuing His work. Some indeed have gone so far as to say that the visiting members of the family had come to put Him under restraint, and to stem, if they could, the tide of popular interest, criticism, and offense, which surged about Him. The scriptural record furnishes no foundation for even a tentative conception of the kind. The purpose of the desired visit is not intimated. It is a fact as will be shown in pages to follow, that some members of Mary's household had failed to understand the great import of the work in which Jesus was so assiduously engaged; and we are told that some of His friends (marginal rendering, "kinsmen,") on one occasion set out with the purpose of laying hold on Him and stopping His public activities by physical force, for they said "He is beside himself." (Mark 3:21); furthermore we learn that His brethren did not believe on Him (John 7:5). These facts, however, scarcely warrant the assumption that the desire of Mary and her sons to speak with Him on the occasion referred to was other than peaceful. And to assume that Mary, His mother, had so far forgotten the wondrous scenes of the angelic annunciation, the miraculous conception, the heavenly accompaniments of the birth, the more than human wisdom and power exhibited in youth and manhood, as to believe her divine Son an unbalanced enthusiast, whom she ought to restrain, is to assume responsibility for injustice to the character of one whom the angel Gabriel declared was blessed among women, and highly favored of the Lord.

The statement that the brethren of Jesus did not believe on Him at the time referred to by the recorder (John 7:5) is no proof that some or even all of those same brethren did not later believe on their divine Brother. Immediately after the Lord's ascension, Mary, the mother of Jesus, and His brethren were engaged in worship and supplication with the Eleven and other disciples (Acts 1:14). The attested fact of Christ's resurrection converted many who had before declined to accept Him as the Son of God. Paul records a special manifestation of the resurrected Christ to James (1 Cor. 15:7) and the James here referred to may be the same person elsewhere designated as "the Lord's brother" (Gal. 1:19); compare Matt. 13:55; Mark 6:3. It appears that "brethren of the Lord" were engaged in the work of the ministry in the days of Paul's active service (1 Cor. 9:5). The specific family relationship of our Lord to James, Joses, Simon, Judas and the sisters referred to by Matthew (13:55, 56), and Mark (6:3), has been questioned; and several theories have been invented in support of divergent views. Thus, the Eastern or Epiphanian hypothesis holds, on no firmer basis than assumption, that the brethren of Jesus were children of Joseph of Nazareth by a former wife, and not the children of Mary the Lord's mother. The Levirate theory assumes that Joseph of Nazareth and Clopas (the latter name, it is interesting to note, is regarded as the equivalent of Alpheus, see footnote page 224) were brothers; and that, after the death of Clopas or Alpheus, Joseph married his brother's widow according to the levirate law (page 548). The Hieronymian hypothesis is based on the belief that the persons referred to as brethren and sisters of Jesus were children of Clopas (Alpheus) and Mary the sister of the Lord's mother, and therefore cousins to Jesus. (See Matt. 27:56; Mark 15:40; John 19:25.) It is beyond reasonable doubt that Jesus was regarded by those, who were acquainted with the family of Joseph and Mary as a close blood relative of other sons and daughters belonging to the household. If these others were children of Joseph and Mary, they were all juniors to Jesus, for He was undoubtedly His mother's firstborn child. The acceptance of this relationship between Jesus and His "brethren" and "sisters" mentioned by the synoptists constitutes what is known in theological literature as the Helvidian view.

FOOTNOTES:

[550] Matt. 7:29; compare Luke 4:32; John 7:46.
[551] Luke 7:1-10; compare Matt. 8:5-13.
[552] Note 1, end of chapter.
[553] John 4:46-53; see page 177.
[554] Note 2, end of chapter.
[555] Matt. 8:11, 12; see also Luke 13:28, 29; compare Acts 10:45.
[556] Luke 7:11-17.
[557] Note 3, end of chapter.
[558] Matt. 8:17; compare Isa. 53:4.
[559] Luke 20:36, 38; compare Acts 10:42; 2 Tim. 4:1; 1 Peter 4:5; Rom. 14:9.
[560] Matt. 4:12; Mark 1:14; Luke 3:19, 20; see Note 2, chap. 9, page 119, and Note 4, end of this chapter.
[561] Note 5, end of chapter.
[562] Mark 6:17-20.
[563] Matt. 14:5.
[564] Matt. 11:2. Note a similar liberty allowed to Paul when in durance, Acts 24:23.
[565] Luke 7:18; Matt. 11:2.
[566] Matt. 11:2-6; Luke 7:18-23.
[567] Isa. 35:5, 6.
[568] Matt. 3:3; compare Isa. 40:3; Matt. 3:7; compare Isa. 59:5; Luke 3:6; compare Isa. 52:10.
[569] Matt. 13:57; 24:10; 26:31; Mark 6:3; 14:27; John 6:61. Note 6, end of chapter.
[570] John 3:30.
[571] Note that Jesus compared the sufferings of John while in prison as in part comparable to those He would Himself have to endure, in that they did unto John "whatsoever they listed" (Matt. 17:12; Mark 9:13).
[572] Luke 7:24-30; see also Matt. 11:7-14; compare Christ's testimony of John Baptist delivered at Jerusalem, John 5:33-35.
[573] Luke 7:28; see Note 7, end of chapter.
[574] Matt. 11:12-15; compare 17:12; Luke 1:17.
[575] Note 8, end of chapter.
[576] Matt. 3:7; Luke 7:30.
[577] Page 142.
[578] Matt. 11:20-24; compare Luke 10:13-15.
[579] Matt. 11:25-27; compare Luke 10:21, 22.
[580] Matt. 11:28-30.
[581] Mark 6:21-29.
[582] Mark 6:14-16.
[583] "Articles of Faith," x:18; also chapter 41, herein.
[584] Luke 7:36; see further, verses 37-50.
[585] Note 9, end of chapter.
[586] 2 Sam. 12:1-7.
[587] Matt. 9:2-6; Mark 2:5-7; page 191 herein.
[588] Matt. 26:6, 7; Mark 14:3; John 11:2.

[589] Note 10, end of chapter.
[590] Luke 8:1-3.
[591] Matt. 27:55, 56, 61; 28:1, 5; Mark 15:40, 47; 16:1, 9; Luke 23:49, 55; 24:10, 22; John 19:25; 20:1, 13, 18.
[592] Mark 16:9; Luke 8:2.
[593] Matt. 12:24-45; compare 9:33, 34: see also Mark 3:22-30; Luke 11:14-26.
[594] Matt. 9:34.
[595] Matt. 9:35.
[596] Matt. 12:14-15.
[597] Matt. 12:17-20; compare Isa. 42:1.
[598] Matt. 12:22, 23.
[599] Note 11, end of chapter.
[600] Matt. 12:38-45; compare 16:1; Mark 8:11; Luke 11:16, 29; John 2:18; 1 Cor. 1:22.
[601] Doc. and Cov. 46:9; compare 63:7-12.
[602] Mark 8:12.
[603] Note 12, end of chapter.
[604] Jonah chaps. 1-4.
[605] Kings 10:1; 2 Chron. 9:1; compare Luke 11:31.
[606] Matt. 12:43-45; Luke 11:24-26.
[607] Luke 11:27, 28.
[608] Matt. 12:46-50; Mark 3:31-35; Luke 8:19-21.
[609] Luke 2:49. Page 114 herein.
[610] Matt. 10:37; compare Luke 14:26.
[611] Note 13, end of chapter.

Jesus the Christ

CHAPTER 19. HE SPAKE MANY THINGS UNTO THEM IN PARABLES.

Throughout the period of Christ's ministry with which we have thus far dealt, His fame had continuously increased, because of the authority with which He spoke and of the many mighty works He did; His popularity had become such that whenever He moved abroad great multitudes followed Him. At times the people so thronged as to impede His movements, some with a desire to hear more of the new doctrine, others to plead at His feet for relief from physical or other ills; and many there were who had faith that could they but reach Him, or even touch the border of His robe, they would be healed.[612] One effect of the people's eagerness, which led them to press and crowd around Him, was to render difficult if not impossible at times the effective delivery of any discourse. His usual place for open-air teaching while He tarried in the vicinity of the sea, or lake, of Galilee was the shore; and thither flocked the crowds to hear Him. At His request, the disciples had provided a "small ship," which was kept in readiness on the beach; [613] and it was usual with Him to sit in the boat a short distance off shore, and preach to the people, as He had done when in the earlier days He called the chosen fishermen to leave their nets and follow Him.[614]

On one such occasion He employed a means of instruction, which, prior to that time, had not been characteristic of His teaching; this consisted in the use of parables,[615] simple stories to illustrate His doctrines. Some of these we shall here consider briefly, in the order most advantageous for treatment, and as best we know, in what may have been the sequence in which they were given.

A SOWER WENT FORTH TO SOW.

First in the order of delivery is the Parable of the Sower. It is a splendid type of our Lord's parables in general, and is particularly valuable for its great intrinsic worth and because we possess a comprehensive interpretation of it by the divine Author. This is the story:

"Behold, a sower went forth to sow; and when he sowed, some seeds fell by the way side, and the fowls came and devoured them up: some fell upon stony places, where they had not much earth: and forthwith they sprung up, because they had no deepness of earth: and when the sun was up, they were scorched; and because they had no root, they withered away. And some fell among thorns; and the thorns sprung up, and choked them: but other fell into good ground, and brought forth fruit, some an hundredfold, some sixtyfold, some thirtyfold. Who hath ears to hear, let him hear."[616]

This new way of teaching, this departure from the Master's earlier method of doctrinal exposition, caused even the most devoted of the disciples to marvel. The Twelve and a few others came to Jesus when He was apart from the multitude, and asked why He had spoken to the people in this manner, and what was the meaning of this particular parable. Our Lord's reply to the first part of the inquiry we shall consider presently; concerning the second, He asked "Know ye not the parable? and how then will ye know all parables?"[617] Thus did He indicate the simplicity of this the first of His parables, together with its typical and fundamental character, and at the same time intimate that other parables would follow in the course of His teaching. Then He gave the interpretation:

"Hear ye therefore the parable of the sower. When anyone heareth the word of the kingdom, and understandeth it not, then cometh the wicked one, and catcheth away that which was sown in his heart. This is he which received seed by the way side. But he that received the seed into stony places, the same is he that heareth the word, and anon with joy receiveth it; yet hath he not root in himself, but dureth for a while: for when tribulation or persecution ariseth because of the word, by and by he is offended. He also that received seed among the thorns is he that heareth the word; and the care of this world, and the deceitfulness of riches, choke the word, and he becometh unfruitful. But he that received seed into the good ground is he that heareth the word, and understandeth it; which also beareth fruit, and bringeth forth, some an hundredfold, some sixty, some thirty."[618]

Further exposition may appear superfluous; some suggestion as to the individual application of the contained lessons may be in place, however. Observe that the prominent feature of the story is that of the prepared or unprepared condition of the soil. The seed was the same whether it fell on good ground or bad, on mellow mold or among stones and thistles. The primitive method of sowing still followed in many countries, consists in the sower throwing the grain by handfuls against the wind, thus securing a widespread scattering. Running through the Galilean fields, were pathways, hard trodden by feet of men and beasts. Though seed should fall on such tracts, it could not grow; birds would pick up the living kernels lying unrooted and uncovered and some of the grains would be crushed and trodden down. So with the seed of truth falling upon the hardened heart; ordinarily it cannot take root, and Satan, as a marauding crow, steals it away, lest a grain of it perchance find a crack in the trampled ground, send down its rootlet, and possibly develop.

Seed falling in shallow soil, underlain by a floor of unbroken stone or hard-pan, may strike root and flourish for a brief season; but as the descending rootlets reach the impenetrable stratum they shrivel, and the plant withers and dies, for the nutritive juices are insufficient where there is no depth of earth.[619] So with the man whose earnestness is but superficial, whose energy ceases when obstacles are encountered or opposition met; though he manifest enthusiasm for a time persecution deters him; he is offended,[620] and endures not. Grain sown where thorns and thistles abound is soon killed out by their smothering growth; even so with a human heart set on riches and the allurements of pleasure--though it receive the living seed of the gospel it will produce no harvest of good grain, but instead, a rank tangle of noxious weeds. The abundant yield of thorny thistles demonstrates the fitness of the soil for a better crop, were it only free from the cumbering weeds. The seed that falls in good deep soil, free from weeds and prepared for the sowing, strikes root and grows; the sun's heat scorches it not, but gives it thrift; it matures and yields to the harvester according to the richness of the soil, some fields producing thirty, others sixty, and a few even a hundred times as much grain as was sown.

Even according to literary canons, and as judged by the recognized standards of rhetorical construction and logical arrangement of its parts, this parable holds first place among productions of its class. Though commonly known to us as the Parable of the Sower, the story could be expressively designated as the Parable of the Four Kinds of Soil. It is the ground upon which the seed is cast, to which the story most strongly directs our attention, and which so aptly is made to symbolize the softened or the hardened heart, the clean or the thorn-infested soil. Observe the grades of soil, given in the increasing order of their fertility: (A) the compacted highway, the wayside path, on which, save by a combination of fortuitous circumstances practically amounting to a miracle, no seed can possibly strike root or grow; (B) the thin layer of soil covering an impenetrable bed-rock, wherein seed may sprout yet can never mature; (C) the weed-encumbered field, capable of producing a rich crop but for the jungle of thistles and thorns; and (D) the clean rich mold receptive and fertile. Yet even soils classed as good are of varying degrees of productiveness, yielding an increase of thirty, sixty, or even a hundred fold, with many inter-gradations.

Some Bible expositors have professed to find in this splendid parable evidence of decisive fatalism in the lives of individuals, so that those whose spiritual state is comparable to the hardened pathway or wayside ground, to the shallow soil on stony floor, or to the neglected, thorn-ridden tract, are hopelessly and irredeemably bad; while the souls who may be likened unto good soil are safe against deterioration and will be inevitably productive of good fruit. Let it not be forgotten that a parable is but a sketch, not a picture finished in detail; and that the expressed or implied similitude in parabolic teaching cannot logically and consistently be carried beyond the limits of the illustrative story. In the parable we are considering, the Teacher depicted the varied grades of spiritual receptivity existing among men, and characterized with incisive brevity each of the specified grades. He neither said nor intimated that the hard-baked soil of the wayside might be plowed, harrowed, fertilized, and so be rendered productive; nor that the stony impediment to growth might not be broken up and removed, or an increase of good soil be made by actual addition; nor that the thorns could never be uprooted and their former habitat be rendered fit to support good plants. The parable is to be studied in the spirit of its purpose; and strained inferences or extensions are unwarranted. A strong metaphor, a striking simile, or any other expressive figure of speech, is of service only when rationally applied; if carried beyond the bounds of reasonable intent, the best of such may become meaningless or even absurd.

THE WHEAT AND THE TARES.

Another parable, somewhat closely related to the foregoing as to the actual story, dealing again with seed and sowing, and, like the first, accompanied by an interpretation, was delivered by the Master as follows:

"The kingdom of heaven is likened unto a man which sowed good seed in his field: but while men slept, his enemy came and sowed tares among the wheat, and went his way. But when the blade was sprung up, and brought forth fruit, then appeared the tares also. So the servants of the householder came and said unto him, Sir, didst not thou sow good seed in thy field? from whence then hath it tares? He said unto them, An enemy hath done this. The servants said unto him, Wilt thou then that we go and gather them up? But he said, Nay; lest while ye gather up the tares, ye root up also the wheat with them. Let both grow together until the harvest: and in the time of harvest I will say to the reapers, Gather ye together first the tares, and bind them in bundles to burn them: but gather the wheat into my barn."[621]

When Jesus had retired to the house in which He lodged, the disciples came, saying: "Declare unto us the parable of the tares of the field."

"He answered and said unto them, He that soweth the good seed is the Son of man; the field is the world; the good seed are the children of the kingdom; but the tares are the children of the wicked one; the enemy that sowed them is the devil; the harvest is the end of the world; and the reapers are the angels. As therefore the tares are gathered and burned in the fire; so shall it be in the end of this world. The Son of man shall send forth his angels, and they shall gather out of his kingdom all things that offend, and them which do iniquity; and shall cast them into a furnace of fire: there shall be wailing and gnashing of teeth. Then shall the righteous shine forth as the sun in the kingdom of their Father. Who hath ears to hear, let him hear."[622]

By the Author's explication, the sower was Himself, the Son of Man; and, as the condition of wheat and tares growing together was one that shall continue until "the end of the world," those who were ordained to carry on the ministry after Him are by direct implication also sowers. The seed as here represented is not, as in the last parable, the gospel itself, but the children of men, the good seed typifying the honest in heart, righteous-minded children of the kingdom; while the tares are those souls who have given themselves up to evil and are counted as children of the wicked one. Inspired by zeal for their Master's profit, the servants would have forcibly rooted up the tares, but were restrained, for their unwise though well-intended course would have endangered the wheat while yet tender, since in the early stages of growth it would have been difficult to distinguish the one from the other, and the intertwining of the roots would have caused much destruction of the precious grain.

One cardinal lesson of the parable, apart from the representation of actual conditions present and future, is that of patience, long-suffering, and toleration--each an attribute of Deity and a trait of character that all men should cultivate. The tares mentioned in the story may be considered as any kind of noxious weed, particularly such as in early growth resembles the wholesome grain.[623] Over-sowing with the seed of weeds in a field already sown with grain is a species of malignant outrage not unknown even in the present day.[624] The certainty of a time of separation, when the wheat shall be garnered in the store-house of the Lord, and the tares be burned, that their poisonous seed may reproduce no more, is placed beyond question by the Lord's own exposition.

So important is the lesson embodied in this parable, and so assured is the literal fulfilment of its contained predictions, that the Lord has given a further explication through revelation in the current dispensation, a period in which the application is direct and immediate. Speaking through Joseph Smith the Prophet in 1832, Jesus Christ said:

"But behold, in the last days, even now while the Lord is   beginning to bring forth the word, and the blade is springing up   and is yet tender. Behold, verily I say unto you, the angels are   crying unto the Lord day and night, who are ready and waiting to   be sent forth to reap down the fields; but the Lord saith unto   them, pluck not up the tares while the blade is yet tender, (for   verily your faith is weak,) lest you destroy the wheat also.   Therefore, let the wheat and the tares grow together until the harvest is fully ripe, then ye shall first gather out the wheat   from among the tares, and after the gathering of the wheat,   behold and lo! the tares are bound in bundles, and the field   remaineth to be burned."[625]

THE SEED GROWING SECRETLY.

Matthew records the Parable of the Tares as immediately following that of the Sower; Mark places in the same position of sequence a parable found in his writings alone. It is presented in outline form, and by critical expositors would be classed rather as a simple analogy than a typical parable. Read it:

"And he said, So is the kingdom of God, as if a man should cast   seed into the ground; and should sleep, and rise night and day,   and the seed should spring and grow up, he knoweth not how. For the earth bringeth forth fruit of herself; first the blade, then   the ear, after that the full corn in the ear. But when the fruit   is brought forth, immediately he putteth in the sickle, because   the harvest is come."[626]

We have no record of the disciples asking nor of the Master giving any interpretation of this, or of any later parable.[627] In this story we find effectively illustrated the fact of the vitality of the seed of truth, though the secret processes of its growth be a mystery to all save God alone. A man having planted seed must needs leave it alone. He may tend the field, removing weeds, protecting the plants as best he may, but the growth itself is dependent upon conditions and forces beyond his power to ultimately control. Though it were Paul who planted and Apollos who watered, none but God could insure the increase.[628] The one who sowed may go about his other affairs, for the field does not demand continuous or exclusive attention; nevertheless, under the influences of sunshine and shower, of breeze and dew, the blade develops, then the ear, and in due time the full corn in the ear. When the grain is ripe the man gladly harvests his crop.

The sower in this story is the authorized preacher of the word of God; he implants the seed of the gospel in the hearts of men, knowing not what the issue shall be. Passing on to similar or other ministry elsewhere, attending to his appointed duties in other fields, he, with faith and hope, leaves with God the result of his planting. In the harvest of souls converted through his labor, he is enriched and made to rejoice.[629] This parable was probably directed more particularly to the apostles and the most devoted of the other disciples, rather than to the multitude at large; the lesson is one for teachers, for workers in the Lord's fields, for the chosen sowers and reapers. It is of perennial value, as truly applicable today as when first spoken. Let the seed be sown, even though the sower be straightway called to other fields or other duties; in the gladsome harvest he shall find his recompense.

THE MUSTARD SEED.

"Another parable put he forth unto them, saying, The kingdom of   heaven is like to a grain of mustard seed, which a man took, and   sowed in his field: which indeed is the least of all seeds: but when it is grown, it is the greatest among herbs, and becometh a   tree, so that the birds of the air come and lodge in the   branches thereof."[630]

This little story, addressed to the assembled multitude, must have set many thinking, because of the simplicity of the incident related and the thoroughly un-Jewish application made of it. To the mind taught by teachers of the time the kingdom was to be great and glorious from its beginning; it was to be ushered in by blare of trumpets and tramp of armies, with King Messiah at the head; yet this new Teacher spoke of it as having so small a beginning as to be comparable to a mustard seed. To make the illustration more effective He specified that the seed spoken of was "the least of all seeds." This superlative expression was made in a relative sense; for there were and are smaller seeds than the mustard, even among garden plants, among which rue and poppy have been named; but each of these plants is very small in maturity, while the well-cultivated mustard plant is one of the greatest among common herbs, and presents a strong contrast of growth from tiny seed to spreading shrub.

Moreover, the comparison "as small as a mustard seed" was in every-day use among Jews of the time. The comparison employed by Jesus on another occasion evidences the common usage, as when He said: "If ye have faith as a grain of mustard seed ... nothing shall be impossible unto you."[631] It should be known that the mustard plant attains in Palestine a larger growth than in more northerly climes.[632] The lesson of the parable is easy to read. The seed is a living entity. When rightly planted it absorbs and assimilates the nutritive matters of soil and atmosphere, grows, and in time is capable of affording lodgment and food to the birds. So the seed of truth is vital, living, and capable of such development as to furnish spiritual food and shelter to all who come seeking. In both conceptions, the plant at maturity produces seed in abundance, and so from a single grain a whole field may be covered.

THE LEAVEN.

"Another parable spake he unto them; The kingdom of heaven is   like unto leaven, which a woman took, and hid in three measures   of meal, till the whole was leavened."[633]
Points of both similarity and contrast between this parable and the last are easily discerned. In each the inherent vitality and capacity for development, so essentially characteristic of the kingdom of God, are illustrated. The mustard seed however, typifies the effect of vital growth in gathering the substance of value from without; while the leaven or yeast disseminates and diffuses outward its influence throughout the mass of otherwise dense and sodden dough. Each of these processes represents a means whereby the Spirit of Truth is made effective. Yeast is no less truly a living organism than a mustard seed. As the microscopic yeast plant develops and multiplies within the dough, its myriad living cells permeate the lump, and every bit of the leavened mass is capable of affecting likewise another batch of properly prepared meal. The process of leavening, or causing dough "to rise," by the fermentation of the yeast placed in the mass, is a slow one, and moreover as quiet and seemingly secret as that of the planted seed growing without the sower's further attention or concern.[634]

THE HIDDEN TREASURE.

"Again, the kingdom of heaven is like unto treasure hid in a   field; the which when a man hath found, he hideth, and for joy   thereof goeth and selleth all that he hath, and buyeth that field."[635]
This and the two parables following are recorded by Matthew only; and the place assigned them in his narrative indicates that they were spoken to the disciples alone, in the house, after the multitude had departed. The quest for treasure-trove is always fascinating. Instances of finding buried valuables were not uncommon in the time of which we speak, since the practise of so concealing treasure was usual with people exposed to bandit incursions and hostile invasion. Observe that the fortunate and happy man is represented as finding the treasure seemingly by accident rather than as a result of diligent search. He gladly sold all that he possessed to make possible his purchase of the field. The hidden treasure is the kingdom of heaven; when a man finds that, he ought to be ready to sacrifice all that he has, if by so doing he may gain possession. His joy in the new acquisition will be unbounded; and, if he but remain a worthy holder, the riches thereof shall be his beyond the grave.[636]
Casuists have raised the question of propriety as to the man's course of action in the story, inasmuch as he concealed the fact of his discovery from the owner of the field, to whom the treasure, they say, rightly belonged. Whatever opinion one may hold as to the ethics of the man's procedure, his act was not illegal, since there was an express provision in Jewish law that the purchaser of land became the legal owner of everything the ground contained.[637] Assuredly Jesus commended no dishonest course; and had not the story been in every detail probable, its effect as a parable would have been lost. The Master taught by this illustration that when once the treasure of the kingdom is found, the finder should lose no time nor shrink from any sacrifice needful to insure his title thereto.

THE PEARL OF GREAT PRICE.

"Again, the kingdom of heaven is like unto a merchant man,   seeking goodly pearls: who, when he had found one pearl of great   price, went and sold all that he had, and bought it."[638]
Pearls have always held high place among gems, and long before, as indeed ever since, the time of Christ, pearl-merchants have been active and diligent in seeking the largest and richest to be had. Unlike the man in the last parable, who found a hidden treasure with little or no search, the merchant in this story devoted his whole energy to the quest for goodly pearls, to find and secure which was his business. When at last he beheld the pearl that excelled all others, though it was, as of right it ought to have been, held at high cost, he gladly sold all his other gems; indeed he sacrificed "all that he had"--gems and other possessions--and purchased the pearl of great price. Seekers after truth may acquire much that is good and desirable, and not find the greatest truth of all, the truth that shall save them. Yet, if they seek persistently and with right intent, if they are really in quest of pearls and not of imitations, they shall find. Men who by search and research discover the truths of the kingdom of heaven may have to abandon many of their cherished traditions, and even their theories of imperfect philosophy and "science falsely so called,"[639] if they would possess themselves of the pearl of great price. Observe that in this parable as in that of the hidden treasure, the price of possession is one's all. No man can become a citizen of the kingdom by partial surrender of his earlier allegiances; he must renounce everything foreign to the kingdom or he can never be numbered therein. If he willingly sacrifices all that he has, he shall find that he has enough. The cost of the hidden treasure, and of the pearl, is not a fixed amount, alike for all; it is all one has. Even the poorest may come into enduring possession; his all is a sufficient purchase price.

THE GOSPEL NET.

"Again, the kingdom of heaven is like unto a net, that was cast   into the sea, and gathered of every kind: which, when it was full, they drew to shore, and sat down, and gathered the good into vessels, but cast the bad away. So shall it be at the end of the world: the angels shall come forth, and sever the wicked from among the just, and shall cast them into the furnace of fire: there shall be wailing and gnashing of teeth."[640]

Men of many minds, men good and bad, all nationalities and races, are affected by the gospel of the kingdom. The "fishers of men"[641] are skilful, active, and comprehensive in their haul. The sorting takes place after the net is brought to shore; and, as the fisherman discards every bad fish while he saves the good, so shall the angels who do the bidding of the Son of Man separate the just and the wicked, preserving the one kind to life eternal; consigning the other to destruction. Unwise efforts to carry the application of the parable beyond the Author's intent have suggested the criticism that whether the fish be good or bad they die. The good, however, die to usefulness, the bad to utter waste. Though all men die, they die not alike; some pass to rest, and shall come forth in the resurrection of the just; others go to a state of sorrow and disquiet there to anxiously and with dread await the resurrection of the wicked.[642] Similarity of application in the present parable as in that of the tares, is apparent in the emphasis given to the decreed separation of the just from the unjust, and in the awful fate of those who are fit subjects for condemnation. A further parallelism is noticed in the postponement of the judgment until the "end of the world," by which expression we may understand the consummation of the Redeemer's work, subsequent to the Millennium and the final resurrection of all who have had existence on earth.[643]

Following His delivery of this, the last of the group of parables recorded in the thirteenth chapter of Matthew, Jesus asked the disciples, "Have ye understood all these things?" They answered, "Yea, Lord." He impressed upon them that they should be ready, like well-taught teachers, to bring, from the store-house of their souls, treasures of truth both old and new, for the edification of the world.[644]

CHRIST'S PURPOSE IN USING PARABLES.

As before stated, the Twelve and other disciples were surprized at the Lord's innovation of parabolic instruction. Prior to that time His doctrines had been set forth in unveiled plainness, as witness the explicit teachings in the Sermon on the Mount. It is noticeable that the introduction of parables occurred when opposition to Jesus was strong, and when scribes, Pharisees, and rabbis were alert in maintaining a close watch upon His movements and His works, ever ready to make Him an offender for a word. The use of parables was common among Jewish teachers; and in adopting this mode of instruction Jesus was really following a custom of the time; though between the parables He spake and those of the scholars there is possible no comparison except that of most pronounced contrast.[645]

To the chosen and devoted followers who came asking the Master why He had changed from direct exposition to parables, He explained[646] that while it was their privilege to receive and understand the deeper truths of the gospel, "the mysteries of the kingdom of heaven" as He expressed it, with people in general, who were unreceptive and unprepared, such fulness of understanding was impossible. To the disciples who had already gladly accepted the first principles of the gospel of Christ, more should be given; while from those who had rejected the proffered boon, even what they had theretofore possessed should be taken away.[647] "Therefore," said He, "speak I to them in parables: because they seeing see not; and hearing they hear not, neither do they understand." That the state of spiritual darkness then existing among the Jews had been foreseen was instanced by a citation of Isaiah's words, in which the ancient prophet had told of the people becoming blind, deaf, and hard of heart respecting the things of God, whereby though they would both hear and see in a physical sense yet should they not understand.[648]

There is plainly shown an element of mercy in the parabolic mode of instruction adopted by our Lord under the conditions prevailing at the time. Had He always taught in explicit declaration, such as required no interpretation, many among His hearers would have come under condemnation, inasmuch as they were too weak in faith and unprepared in heart to break the bonds of traditionalism and the prejudice engendered by sin, so as to accept and obey the saving word. Their inability to comprehend the requirements of the gospel would in righteous measure give Mercy some claim upon them, while had they rejected the truth with full understanding, stern Justice would surely demand their condemnation.[649]

That the lesson of the parables was comprehensible through study, prayer and search was intimated in the Teacher's admonishment: "Who hath ears to hear, let him hear."[650] To the more studious inquirers, the Master added: "Take heed what ye hear: with what measure ye mete, it shall be measured to you: and unto you that hear shall more be given. For he that hath, to him shall be given: and he that hath not, from him shall be taken even that which he hath."[651] Two men may hear the same words; one of them listens in indolence and indifference, the other with active mind intent on learning all that the words can possibly convey; and, having heard, the diligent man goes straightway to do the things commended to him, while the careless one neglects and forgets. The one is wise, the other foolish; the one has heard to his eternal profit, the other to his everlasting condemnation.[652]

Another example of the merciful adaptation of the word of truth to the varied capacities of the people who heard the parables is found in the psychological fact, that the incidents of an impressive though simple story will live, even in minds which for the time being are incapable of comprehending any meaning beyond that of the common-place story itself. Many a peasant who had heard the little incident of the sower and the four kinds of soil, of the tares sown by an enemy at night, of the seed that grew though the planter had temporarily forgotten it, would be reminded by the recurring circumstances of his daily work; the gardener would recollect the story of the mustard seed whenever he planted afresh, or when he looked upon the umbrageous plant with birds nesting in its branches; the housewife would be impressed anew by the story of the leaven as she mixed and kneaded and baked; the fisherman at his nets would think again of the good fish and the bad and compare the sorting of his catch with the judgment to come. And then, when time and experience, including suffering perhaps, had prepared them for deeper thought, they would find the living kernel of gospel truth within the husk of the simple tale.

PARABLES IN GENERAL.

The essential feature of a parable is that of comparison or similitude, by which some ordinary, well-understood incident is used to illustrate a fact or principle not directly expressed in the story. The popular thought that a parable necessarily rests on a fictitious incident is incorrect; for, inasmuch as the story or circumstance of the parable must be simple and indeed common-place, it may be real. There is no fiction in the parables we have thus far studied; the fundamental stories are true to life and the given circumstances are facts of experience. The narrative or incident upon which a parable is constructed may be an actual occurrence or fiction; but, if fictitious, the story must be consistent and probable, with no admixture of the unusual or miraculous. In this respect the parable differs from the fable, the latter being imaginative, exaggerated and improbable as to fact; moreover, the intent is unlike in the two, since the parable is designed to convey some great spiritual truth, while the so-called moral of the fable is at best suggestive only of worldly achievement and personal advantage. Stories of trees, animals and inanimate things talking together or with men are wholly fanciful; they are fables or apologues whether the outcome be depicted as good or bad; to the parable these show contrast, not similarity. The avowed purpose of the fable is rather to amuse than to teach. The parable may embody a narrative as in the instances of the sower and the tares, or merely an isolated incident, as in those of the mustard seed and the leaven.

Allegories are distinguished from parables by greater length and detail of the story, and by the intimate admixture of the narrative with the lesson it is designed to teach; these are kept distinctly separate in the parable. Myths are fictitious stories, sometimes with historic basis of fact, but without symbolism of spiritual worth. A proverb is a short, sententious saying, in the nature of a maxim, connoting a definite truth or suggestion by comparison. Proverbs and parables are closely related, and in the Bible the terms are sometimes used interchangeably.[653] The Old Testament contains two parables, a few fables and allegories, and numerous proverbs; of the last-named we possess an entire book.[654] Nathan the prophet reproved King David by the parable of the poor man's ewe lamb, and so effective was the story that the king decreed punishment for the wealthy offender, and was overcome by sorrow and contrition when the prophet made application of his parable by the fateful words, "Thou art the man."[655] The story of the vineyard, which though fenced and well-tended yet brought forth only wild, useless fruit, was used by Isaiah to portray the sinful state of Israel in his attempt to awaken the people to lives of righteousness.[656]

The parables of the New Testament, spoken by the Teacher of teachers, are of such beauty, simplicity, and effectiveness, as to stand unparalleled in literature.

NOTES TO CHAPTER 19.

1. The First Group of Parables.--Many Bible scholars hold that the seven parables recorded in the thirteenth chapter of Matthew were spoken at different times and to different people, and that the writer of the first Gospel grouped them for convenience in recording and with prime consideration of their subjective interest. Some color is found for this claim in Luke's mention of some of these parables in different relations of both time and place; thus, the parables of the Mustard Seed and the Leaven are given (Luke 13:18, 21) as directly following the healing of the infirm woman in the synagog, and the rebuke to the hypocritical ruler. While we must admit that Matthew may have grouped with the parables spoken on that particular day some of other dates, it is probable that Jesus repeated some of His parables, as He certainly did other teachings, and thus presented the same lesson on more occasions than one. As a matter of fact each parable is a lesson in itself, and holds its high intrinsic value whether considered as an isolated story or in connection with related teachings. Let us give heed to the lesson of each whatever opinions men may promulgate as to the circumstances of its first delivery.

2. Local Setting for the Parable of the Sower.--Dr. R. C. Trench, in his excellent work _Notes on the Parables of our Lord_ (p. 57, note), quotes Dean Stanley's description of existing conditions in the place where the Parable of the Sower was given by Jesus; and as there is reason to believe that the environment has changed but little since the days of Christ, the account is here reproduced: "A slight recess in the hillside close upon the plain disclosed at once in detail, and with a conjunction which I remember nowhere else in Palestine, every feature of the great parable. There was the undulating corn-field descending to the water's edge. There was the trodden pathway running through the midst of it, with no fence or hedge to prevent the seed falling here or there on either side of it, or upon it--itself hard with the constant tramp of horse and mule and human feet. There was the 'good' rich soil, which distinguishes the whole of that plain and its neighborhood from the bare hills elsewhere, descending into the lake, and which, where there is no interruption, produces one vast mass of corn. There was the rocky ground of the hillside protruding here and there through the corn-fields, as elsewhere, through the grassy slopes. There were the large bushes of thorn, the 'nabk' ... springing up, like the fruit-trees of the more inland parts, in the very midst of the waving wheat."

3. Tares.--This term occurs nowhere within the Bible except in this instance of the parable. Plainly any kind of weed, particularly a poisonous sort, such as would seriously depreciate the garnered crop, would serve the Master's purpose in the illustration. The traditional belief commonly held is that the plant referred to in the parable is the darnel weed, known to botanists as _Lolium temulenium_, a species of bearded rye-grass. This plant closely resembles wheat in the early period of growth, and exists as a pest to

the farmers in Palestine to-day; it is called by the Arabians "Zowan" or "Zawan" which name, says Arnot, citing Thompson, "bears some resemblance to the original word in the Greek text." The writer of the article "Tares" in Smith's Dictionary says: "Critics and expositors are agreed that the Greek plural _zizania_, A.V. 'tares,' of the parable (Matt 13:25) denotes the weed called 'bearded darnel' (_Lolium temulentum_), a widely-distributed grass, and the only species of the order that has deleterious properties. The bearded darnel before it comes into ear is very similar in appearance to wheat, and the roots of the two are often intertwined; hence the command that the 'tares' should be left till the harvest, lest while men plucked up the tares 'they should root up also the wheat with them.' This darnel is easily distinguishable from the wheat and barley when headed out, but when both are less developed, 'the closest scrutiny will often fail to detect it. Even the farmers, who in this country generally weed their fields, do not attempt to separate the one from the other ... The taste is bitter, and, when eaten separately, or even when diffused in ordinary bread, it causes dizziness, and often acts as a violent emetic.'" The secondary quotation is from Thompson's _The Land and the Book_, ii, 111, 112. It has been asserted that the darnel is a degenerated kind of wheat; and attempts have been made to give additional significance to our Lord's instructive parable by injecting this thought; there is no scientific warrant for the strained conception, however, and earnest students will not be misled thereby.

4. The Wickedness of the Sower of Tares.--Attempts have been made to disparage the Parable of the Tares on the ground that it rests on an unusual if not unknown practise. Trench thus meets the criticism (_Notes on the Parables_, pp. 72, 73): "Our Lord did not imagine here a form of malice without example, but adduced one which may have been familiar enough to His hearers, one so easy of execution, involving so little risk, and yet effecting so great and lasting a mischief, that it is not strange, where cowardice and malice meet, that this should have been often the shape in which they displayed themselves. We meet traces of it in many quarters. In Roman law the possibility of this form of injury is contemplated; and a modern writer, illustrating Scripture from the manners and habits of the East, with which he had become familiar through a sojourn there, affirms the same to be now practised in India." In a subjoined note the author adds: "We are not without this form of malice nearer home. Thus in Ireland I have known an outgoing tenant, in spite at his eviction, to sow wild oats in the fields which he was leaving. These, like the tares in the parable, ripening and seeding themselves before the crops in which they were mingled, it became next to impossible to extirpate.";

5. The Parable of the Seed Growing Secretly.--This parable has given rise to much discussion among expositors, the question being as to who is meant by the man who cast seed into the ground. If, as in the parables of the Sower and the Tares, the Lord Jesus be the planter, then, some ask, how can it be said "that the seed should spring and grow up, he knoweth not how," when all things are known unto Him? If on the other hand the planter represents the authorized teacher or preacher of the gospel, how can it be said that at the harvest time "he putteth in the sickle," since the final harvesting of souls is the prerogative of God? The perplexities of the critics arise from their attempt to find in the parable a literalism never intended by the Author. Whether the seed be planted by the Lord Himself, as when He taught in Person, or by any one of His authorized servants, the seed is alive and will grow. Time is required; the blade appears first and is followed by the ear, and the ear ripens in season, without the constant attention which a shaping of the several parts by hand would require. The man who figures in the parable is presented as an ordinary farmer, who plants, and waits, and in due time reaps. The lesson imparted is the vitality of the seed as a living thing, endowed by its Creator with the capacity to both grow and develop.

6. The Mustard Plant.--The wild mustard, which in the temperate zone seldom attains a height of more than three or four feet, reaches in semitropical lands the height of a horse and its rider (Thompson, _The Land and the Book_ ii, 100). Those who heard the parable evidently understood the contrast between size of seed and that of the fully developed plant. Arnot, (_The Parables_, p. 102), aptly says: "This plant obviously was chosen by the Lord, not on account of its absolute magnitude, but because it was, and was recognized to be, a striking instance of increase from very small to very great. It seems to have been in Palestine, at that time, the smallest seed from which so large a plant was known to grow. There were, perhaps, smaller seeds, but the plants which sprung from them were not so great; and there were greater plants, but the seeds from which they sprung were not so small." Edersheim (i, p. 593) states that the diminutive size of the mustard seed was commonly used in comparison by the rabbis, "to indicate the smallest amount such as the least drop of blood, the least defilement, etc." The same author continues, in speaking of the grown plant: "Indeed, it looks no longer like a large garden-herb or shrub, but 'becomes' or rather appears like 'a tree'--as St. Luke puts it, 'a great tree,' of course, not in comparison with other trees, but with garden-shrubs. Such growth of mustard seed was also a fact well known at the time, and, indeed, still observed in the East.... And the general meaning would the more easily be apprehended, that a tree, whose wide-spreading branches afforded lodgment to the birds of heaven, was a familiar Old Testament figure for a mighty kingdom that gave shelter to the nations (Ezek. 31:6, 12; Dan. 4:12, 14, 21, 22). Indeed, it is specifically used as an illustration of the Messianic Kingdom (Ezek. 17:23)."

7. The Symbolism of Leaven.--In the parable, the kingdom of heaven is likened unto leaven. In other scriptures, leaven is figuratively mentioned as representing evil, thus, "the leaven of the Pharisees and of the Sadducees" (Matt. 16:6, see also Luke 12:1), "the leaven of Herod" (Mark 8:15). These instances, and others (1 Cor. 5:7, 8) are illustrative of the contagion of evil. In the incident of the woman using leaven in the ordinary process of bread-making, the spreading, penetrating vital effect of truth is symbolized by the leaven. The same thing in different aspects may very properly be used to represent good in one instance and evil in another.

8. Treasure Belonging to the Finder.--As to the justification of the man who found a treasure hidden in another's field and then, concealing the fact of his discovery, bought the field that he might

possess the treasure, Edersheim (i, p. 595-6) says: "Some difficulty has been expressed in regard to the morality of such a transaction. In reply it may be observed, that it was, at least, in entire accordance with Jewish law. If a man had found a treasure in loose coins among the corn it would certainly be his if he bought the corn. If he had found it on the ground, or in the soil, it would equally certainly belong to him if he could claim ownership of the soil, and even if the field were not his own, unless others could prove their right to it. The law went so far as to adjudge to the purchaser of fruits anything found among these fruits. This will suffice to vindicate a question of detail, which, in any case, should not be too closely pressed in a parabolic history."

9. Superiority of our Lord's Parables.--"Perhaps no other mode of teaching was so common among the Jews as that by parables. Only in their case, they were almost entirely illustrations of what had been said or taught; while in the case of Christ, they served as the foundation for His teaching.... In the one case it was intended to make spiritual teaching appear Jewish and national, in the other to convey spiritual teaching in a form adapted to the stand-point of the hearers. This distinction will be found to hold true, even in instances where there seems the closest parallelism between a Rabbinic and an Evangelic parable.... It need scarcely be said that comparison between such parables, as regards their spirit, is scarcely possible, except by way of contrast" (Edersheim, i, pp. 580-1). Geikie tersely says: "Others have uttered parables, but Jesus so far transcends them, that He may justly be called the creator of this mode of instruction" (ii, p. 145).

10. Parables and Other Forms of Analogy.--"The parable is also clearly distinguishable from the proverb, though it is true that, in a certain degree, the words are used interchangeably in the New Testament, and as equivalent the one to the other. Thus 'Physician, heal thyself (Luke 4:23) is termed a parable, being more strictly a proverb; so again, when the Lord had used that proverb, probably already familiar to His hearers 'If the blind lead the blind, both shall fall into the ditch'; Peter said 'Declare unto us this parable' (Matt. 15:14, 15); and Luke 5:36 is a proverb or proverbial expression, rather than a parable, which name it bears.... So, upon the other hand, those are called 'proverbs' in St. John, which if not strictly parables, yet claim much closer affinity to the parable than to the proverb, being in fact allegories; thus Christ's setting forth of His relations to His people under those of a shepherd to his sheep is termed a 'proverb,' though our translators, holding fast to the sense rather than to the letter, have rendered it a 'parable' (John 10:6; compare 16:25, 29). It is easy to account for this interchange of words. Partly it arose from one word in Hebrew signifying both parable and proverb."--Trench, _Notes on the Parables_, pp. 9, 10.

For the convenience of readers who may not have a dictionary at hand as they read, the following definitions are given:

Allegory.--The setting forth of a subject under the guise of some other subject or aptly suggestive likeness.

Apologue.--A fable or moral tale, especially one in which animals or inanimate things speak or act, and by which a useful lesson is suggested or taught.

Fable.--A brief story or tale feigned or invented to embody a moral, and introducing animals and sometimes even inanimate things as rational speakers and actors; a legend or myth.

Myth.--A fictitious or conjectural narrative presented as historical, but without any basis of fact.

Parable.--A brief narrative or descriptive allegory founded on real scenes or events such as occur in nature and human life, and usually with a moral or religious application.

Proverb.--A brief, pithy saying, condensing in witty or striking form the wisdom of experience; a familiar and widely known popular saying in epigrammatic form.

11. Old Testament Parables, Etc.--"Of parables in the strictest sense the Old Testament contains only two" (2 Sam. 12:1-; and Isa. 5:1-). "Other stories, such as that of the trees assembled to elect a king (Judges 9:8), and of the thistle and cedar (2 Kings 14:9), are more strictly fables. Still others, such as Ezekiel's account of the two eagles and the vine (17:2-), and of the caldron (24:3-) are allegories. The small number of parabolic narratives to be found in the Old Testament must not, however, be taken as an indication of indifference toward this literary form as suitable for moral instruction. The number is only apparently small. In reality, similitudes, which, though not explicitly couched in the terms of fictitious narrative, suggest and furnish the materials for such narrative, are abundant."--Zenos, _Stand. Bible Dict._, article "Parables."

By applying the term "parable" in its broadest sense, to include all ordinary forms of analogy, we may list the following as the most impressive parables of the Old Testament. Trees electing a king (Judges 9:7-); the poor man's ewe lamb (2 Sam. 12:1-); the contending brothers and the avengers (2 Sam. 14:1-); story of the escaped captive (1 Kings 20:35-); the thistle and the cedar (2 Kings 14:9); the vineyard and its wild grapes (Isa. 5:1-); the eagles and the vine (Ezek. 17:3-); the lion's whelps (Ezek. 19:2-); the seething pot (Ezek. 24:3-).

FOOTNOTES:

[612] Mark 3:10; compare Matt. 9:20, 21; 14:36; Mark 6:56; Luke 6:19
[613] Mark 3:9.
[614] Luke 5:10; page 197 herein.
[615] Note 1, end of chapter.
[616] Matt. 13:3-9; compare Mark 4:3-9; Luke 8:5-8.
[617] Mark 4:13.
[618] Matt. 13:18-23; compare Mark 4:13-20; Luke 8:11-15.

[619] Note 2, end of chapter.
[620] Pages 254 and 274.
[621] Matt. 13:24-30.
[622] Verses 36-43.
[623] Note 3, end of chapter.
[624] Note 4, end of chapter.
[625] Doc. and Cov. 86:4-7; read the entire section.
[626] Mark 4:26-29.
[627] Note 5, end of chapter.
[628] 1 Cor. 3:6.
[629] Read the Lord's early promise of souls as the hire of the appointed harvesters: John 4:35-38; see also Matt. 9:37, 38; Luke 10:2.
[630] Matt. 13:31, 32; compare Mark 4:30-32; Luke 13:18, 19.
[631] Matt. 17:20; compare Luke 17:6.
[632] Note 6, end of chapter.
[633] Matt. 13:33; compare Luke 13:20, 21.
[634] Page 288. Note 7, end of chapter.
[635] Matt. 13:44.
[636] Compare Matt. 6:19, 20.
[637] Note 8, end of chapter.
[638] Matt. 13:45, 48.
[639] 1 Tim. 6:20.
[640] Matt. 13:47-50.
[641] Matt. 4:19; Mark 1:17; Luke 5:10.
[642] John 5:29; see also B. of M., Alma 40:11-14; and the author, "Articles of Faith," xxi:24-39.
[643] See chapter 42.
[644] Matt. 13:51, 52.
[645] Note 9, end of chapter.
[646] Matt. 13:10-17; compare Mark 4:10-13; Luke 8:9, 10.
[647] Matt. 13:12; compare 25:29; Mark 4:25; Luke 8:18; 19:26.
[648] Isa. 6:9; see also 42:20; 43:8; Ezek. 12:2; John 12:40; Acts 28:26, 27.
[649] See the author's "Articles of Faith," iii:12, 13; B. of M., 2 Nephi 9:25-27; Rom. 2:12; Doc. and Cov. 45:54; 76:72.
[650] Matt. 13:9, 43; see also 11:15; Mark 4:9.
[651] Mark 4:24, 25.
[652] Read again Matt. 7:24-27; Luke 6:46-49.
[653] Note 10, end of chapter.
[654] Note 11, end of chapter.
[655] 2 Sam. 12:1-7, 13.
[656] Isa. 5:1-7.

Jesus the Christ

CHAPTER 20. PEACE, BE STILL.

INCIDENTS PRELIMINARY TO THE VOYAGE.

Near the close of the day on which Jesus had taught the multitudes for the first time by parables, He said to the disciples, "Let us pass over unto the other side."[657] The destination so indicated is the east side of the sea of Galilee. While the boat was being made ready, a certain scribe came to Jesus and said: "Master, I will follow thee whithersoever thou goest." Prior to that time, few men belonging to the titled or ruling class had offered to openly ally themselves with Jesus. Had the Master been mindful of policy and desirous of securing official recognition, this opportunity to attach to Himself as influential a person as a scribe would have received careful consideration if not immediate acceptance; but He, who could read the minds and know the hearts of men, chose rather than accepted. He had called men who were to be thenceforth His own, from their fishing boats and nets, and had numbered one of the ostracized publicans among the Twelve; but He knew them, every one, and chose accordingly. The gospel was offered freely to all; but authority to officiate as a minister thereof was not to be had for the asking; for that sacred labor, one must be called of God.[658]

In this instance, Christ knew the character of the man, and, without wounding his feelings by curt rejection, pointed out the sacrifice required of one who would follow whithersoever the Lord went, saying: "The foxes have holes, and the birds of the air have nests; but the Son of man hath not where to lay his head." As Jesus had no fixed place of abode, but went wherever His duty called Him, so was it necessary that they who represented Him, men ordained or set apart to His service, be ready to deny themselves the enjoyment of their homes and the comfort of family associations, if the duties of their calling so demanded. We do not read that the aspiring scribe pressed his offer.

Another man indicated his willingness to follow the Lord, but asked first for time to go and bury his father; to him Jesus said: "Follow me; and let the dead bury their dead." Some readers have felt that this injunction was harsh, though such an inference is scarcely justified. While it would be manifestly unfilial for a son to absent himself from his father's funeral under ordinary conditions, nevertheless, if that son had been set apart to service of importance transcending all personal or family obligations, his ministerial duty would of right take precedence. Moreover, the requirement expressed by Jesus was no greater than that made of every priest during his term of active service, nor was it more afflicting than the obligation of the Nazarite vow,[659] under which many voluntarily placed themselves. The duties of ministry in the kingdom pertained to spiritual life; one dedicated thereto might well allow those who were negligent of spiritual things, and figuratively speaking, spiritually dead, to bury their dead.

A third instance is presented; a man who wanted to be a disciple of the Lord asked that, before entering upon his duties, he be permitted to go home and bid farewell to his family and friends. The reply of Jesus has become an aphorism in life and literature: "No man, having put his hand to the plough, and looking back, is fit for the kingdom of God."[660]

From Matthew's record we draw the inference that the first two of these candidates for discipleship offered themselves to our Lord as He stood on the shore or in the boat ready to begin the evening voyage across the lake. Luke places the instances in a different connection, and adds to the offers of the scribe and the man who would first bury his father, that of the one who wished to go home and then return to Christ. The three incidents may be profitably considered together, whether all occurred in the evening of that same eventful day or at different times.

STILLING THE STORM.[661]

The instruction to launch forth and cross to the opposite side of the lake was given by Jesus, who probably desired a respite after the arduous labors of the day. No time had been lost in unnecessary preparation; "they took him, even as he was, into the ship," and set out without delay. Even on the water some of the eager people tried to follow; for a number of small boats, "little ships" as Mark styles them, accompanied the vessel on which Jesus was embarked; but these lesser craft may have turned back, possibly on account of the approaching storm; anyway, we do not hear of them further.

Jesus found a resting place near the stern of the ship and soon fell asleep. A great storm arose, [662] and still He slept. The circumstance is instructive as it evidences at once the reality of the physical attributes of Christ, and the healthy, normal condition of His body. He was subject to fatigue and bodily exhaustion from other causes, as are all men; without food He grew hungry; without drink He thirsted; by labor He became weary. The fact that after a day of strenuous effort He could calmly sleep, even amidst the turmoil of a tempest, indicates an unimpaired nervous system and a good state of health. Nowhere do we find record of Jesus having been ill. He lived according to the laws of health, yet never allowed the body to rule the spirit; and His daily activities, which were of a kind to make heavy demands on both physical and mental energy, were met with no symptoms of nervous collapse nor of functional disturbance. Sleep after toil is natural and necessary. The day's work done, Jesus slept.

Meanwhile the storm increased in fury; the wind rendered the boat unmanageable; waves beat over the side; so much water was shipped that the vessel seemed about to founder. The disciples were terror-stricken; yet through it all Jesus rested peacefully. In their extremity of fear, the disciples awakened Him, crying out, according to the several independent accounts, "Master, Master, we perish"; "Lord, save us: we perish"; and, "Master, carest thou not that we perish?" They were abjectly frightened, and at least partly forgetful that there was with them One whose voice even death had to obey. Their terrified appeal was not wholly devoid of hope nor barren of faith: "Lord, save us" they cried. Calmly He replied to their piteous call,

"Why are ye fearful, O ye of little faith?"

Then He arose; and out through the darkness of that fearsome night, into the roaring wind, over the storm-lashed sea, went the voice of the Lord as He "rebuked the wind, and said unto the sea, Peace, be still. And the wind ceased, and there was a great calm." Turning to the disciples, He asked in tones of gentle yet unmistakable reproof: "Where is your faith?" and "How is it that ye have no faith?" Gratitude for rescue from what but a moment before had seemed impending death was superseded by amazement and fear. "What manner of man is this," they asked one of another, "that even the wind and the sea obey him?"

Among the recorded miracles of Christ, none has elicited greater diversity in comment and in attempt at elucidation than has this marvelous instance of control over the forces of nature. Science ventures no explanation. The Lord of earth, air, and sea spoke and was obeyed. He it was who, amidst the black chaos of creation's earliest stages, had commanded with immediate effect--Let there be light; Let there be a firmament in the midst of the waters; Let the dry land appear--and, as He had decreed, so it was. The dominion of the Creator over the created is real and absolute. A small part of that dominion has been committed to man[663] as the offspring of God, tabernacled in the very image of his divine Father. But man exercizes that delegated control through secondary agencies, and by means of complicated mechanism. Man's power over the objects of his own devizing is limited. It is according to the curse evoked by Adam's fall, which came through transgression, that by the strain of his muscles, by the sweat of his brow, and by stress of his mind, shall he achieve. His word of command is but a sound-wave in air, except as it is followed by labor. Through the Spirit that emanates from the very Person of Deity, and which pervades all space, the command of God is immediately operative.

Not man alone, but also the earth and all the elemental forces pertaining thereto came under the Adamic curse[664] and as the soil no longer brought forth only good and useful fruits, but gave of its substance to nurture thorns and thistles, so the several forces of nature ceased to be obedient to man as agents subject to his direct control. What we call natural forces--heat, light, electricity, chemical affinity--are but a few of the manifestations of eternal energy through which the Creator's purposes are subserved; and these few, man is able to direct and utilize only through mechanical contrivance and physical adjustment. But the earth shall yet be "renewed and receive its paradisaical glory"; then soil, water, air, and the forces acting upon them, shall directly respond to the command of glorified man, as now they obey the word of the Creator.[665]

QUIETING THE DEMONS.[666]

Jesus and the disciples with Him landed on the eastern or Perean side of the lake, in a region known as the country of the Gadarenes or Gergesenes. The precise spot has not been identified, but it was evidently a country district apart from the towns.[667] As the party left the boat, two maniacs, who were sorely tormented by evil spirits, approached. Matthew states there were two; the other writers speak of but one; it is possible that one of the afflicted pair was in a condition so much worse than that of his companion that to him is accorded greater prominence in the narrative; or, one may have run away while the other remained. The demoniac was in a pitiful plight. His frenzy had become so violent and the physical strength incident to his mania so great that all attempts to hold him in captivity had failed. He had been bound in chains and fetters, but these he had broken asunder by the aid of demon power; and he had fled to the mountains, to the caverns that served as tombs, and there he had lived more like a wild beast than a man. Night and day his weird, terrifying shrieks had been heard, and through dread of meeting him people traveled by other ways rather than pass near his haunts. He wandered about naked, and in his madness often gashed his flesh with sharp stones.

Seeing Jesus, the poor creature ran toward Him, and, impelled by the power of his demon control, prostrated himself before Christ, the while crying out with a loud voice: "What have I to do with thee, Jesus, thou Son of the most high God?" As Jesus commanded the evil spirits to leave, one or more of them, through the voice of the man, pleaded to be left alone, and with blasphemous presumption exclaimed: "I adjure thee by God, that thou torment me not." Matthew records the further question addressed to Jesus: "Art thou come hither to torment us before the time?" The demons, by whom the man was possessed and controlled, recognized the Master, whom they knew they had to obey; but they pleaded to be left alone until the decreed time of their final punishment would come.[668]

Jesus asked, "What is thy name?" and the demons within the man answered, "My name is Legion, for we are many." The fact of the man's dual consciousness or multi-personality is here apparent. So complete was his possession by wicked spirits that he could no longer distinguish between his individual personality and theirs. The devils implored that Jesus would not banish them from that country; or as Luke records in words of awful import, "that he would not command them to go out into the deep."[669] In their wretched plight, and out of diabolical eagerness to find abode in bodies of flesh even though of beasts, they begged that, being compelled to leave the man they be allowed to enter a herd of hogs feeding nearby. Jesus gave permission; the unclean demons entered the swine; and the whole herd, numbering about two thousand, went wild, stampeded in terror, ran violently down a steep place into the sea, and were drowned. The swineherds were frightened, and, hastening to the town, told what had happened to the hogs. People came out in crowds to see for themselves; and all were astounded to behold the once wild man of whom they had all been afraid, now clothed, and restored to a normal state of mind, sitting quietly and reverently at the feet of Jesus. They were afraid of One who could work such wonders, and, conscious of their sinful unworthiness, begged Him to leave their country.[670]

The man who had been rid of the demons feared not; in his heart love and gratitude superseded all other feelings; and as Jesus returned to the boat he prayed that he might go also. But Jesus forbade, saying: "Go home to thy friends, and tell them how great things the Lord hath done for thee, and hath had compassion on thee." The man became a missionary, not alone in his home town but throughout Decapolis, the region of the ten cities; wherever he went he told of the marvelous change Jesus had wrought on him.

The testimony of wicked and unclean spirits to the divinity of Christ as the Son of God is not confined to this instance. We have already considered the case of the demoniac in the synagog at Capernaum;[671] and another instance appeared, when Jesus, withdrawing from the towns in Galilee, betook Himself to the sea shore, and was followed by a great multitude comprizing Galileans and Judeans, and people from Jerusalem and Idumea, and from beyond Jordan (i.e. from Perea), and inhabitants of Tyre and Sidon, amongst whom He had healed many of divers diseases; and those who were in bondage to unclean spirits had fallen down and worshiped Him; while the demons cried out: "Thou art the Son of God."[672]

In the course of the short journey considered in this chapter, the power of Jesus as Master of earth, men and devils, was manifest in miraculous works of the most impressive kind. We cannot classify the Lord's miracles as small and great, nor as easy and difficult of accomplishment; what one may consider the least is to another of profound import. The Lord's word was sufficient in every instance. To the wind and the waves, and to the demon-ridden mind of the man possessed, He had but to speak and be obeyed. "Peace, be still."

THE RAISING OF THE DAUGHTER OF JAIRUS.[673]

Jesus and His attendants recrossed the lake from the land of Gadara to the vicinity of Capernaum, where He was received with acclamation by a multitude of people, "for they were all waiting for him." Immediately after landing, Jesus was approached by Jairus, one of the rulers of the local synagog, who "besought him greatly, saying, My little daughter lieth at the point of death: I pray thee, come and lay thy hands on her, that she may be healed; and she shall live."

The fact of this man's coming to Jesus, with the spirit of faith and supplication, is an evidence of the deep impression the ministry of Christ had made even in priestly and ecclesiastical circles. Many of the Jews, rulers and officials as well as the people in common, believed in Jesus;[674] though few belonging to the upper classes were willing to sacrifice prestige and popularity by acknowledging their discipleship. That Jairus, one of the rulers of the synagog, came only when impelled by grief over the impending death of his only daughter, a girl of twelve years, is no evidence that he had not before become a believer; certainly at this time his faith was genuine and his trust sincere, as the circumstances of the narrative prove. He approached Jesus with the reverence due One whom he considered able to grant what he asked, and fell at the Lord's feet, or as Matthew says, worshiped Him. When the man had started from his home to seek aid of Jesus, the maiden was at the point of death; he feared lest she had died in the interval. In the very brief account given in the first Gospel, he is reported as saying to Jesus: "My daughter is even now dead: but come and lay thy hand upon her and she shall live."[675] Jesus went with the imploring father, and many followed.

On the way to the house an incident occurred to hinder progress. A sorely afflicted woman was healed, under circumstances of peculiar interest; this occurrence we shall consider presently. No intimation is given that Jairus showed impatience or displeasure over the delay; he had placed trust in the Master and awaited His time and pleasure; and while Christ was engaged in the matter of the suffering woman, messengers came from the ruler's house with the saddening word that the girl was dead. We may infer that even these dread tidings of certainty failed to destroy the man's faith; he seems to have still looked to the Lord for help, and those who had brought the message asked, "Why troublest thou the Master any further?" Jesus heard what was said, and sustained the man's sorely-taxed faith by the encouraging behest: "Be not afraid, only believe." Jesus permitted none of His followers save three of the apostles to enter the house with Himself and the bereaved but trusting father. Peter and the two brothers James and John were admitted.

The house was no place of such respectful silence or subdued quiet as we now consider appropriate to the time and place of death; on the contrary it was a scene of tumult, but that condition was customary in the orthodox observances of mourning at the time.[676] Professional mourners, including singers of weird dirges, and minstrels who made great noise with flutes and other instruments, had already been summoned to the house. To all such Jesus said, on entering: "Why make ye this ado, and weep? the damsel is not dead but sleepeth." It was in effect a repetition of His command uttered on a then recent occasion--Peace, be still. His words drew scorn and ridicule from those who were paid for the noise they made, and who, if what He said proved true, would lose this opportunity of professional service. Moreover, they knew the maid was dead; preparations for the funeral, which custom required should follow death as speedily as possible, were already in progress. Jesus ordered these people out, and restored peace to the house.[677] He then entered the death chamber, accompanied only by the three apostles and the parents of the girl. Taking the dead maiden by the hand He "said unto her, Talitha cumi; which is, being interpreted, Damsel, I say unto thee, arise." To the astonishment of all but the Lord, the girl arose, left her bed, and walked. Jesus directed that food be given her, as bodily needs, suspended by death, had returned with the girl's renewal of life.

The Lord imposed an obligation of secrecy, charging all present to refrain from telling what they had seen. The reasons for this injunction are not stated. In some other instances a similar instruction was given to those who had been blessed by Christ's ministrations; while on many occasions of healing no such instructions are recorded, and in one case at least the man who had been relieved of demons was told to go and tell how great a thing had been done for him.[678] In His own wisdom Christ knew when to prudently forbid and when to permit publication of His doings. Though the grateful parents, the girl herself, and the three apostles who had been witnesses of the restoration, may all have been loyal to the Lord's injunction of silence, the fact that the maiden had been raised to life could not be kept secret, and the means by which so great a wonder had been wrought would certainly be inquired into. The minstrels and the wailers who had been expelled from the company while it was yet a house of mourning, and who had scornfully laughed at the Master's assertion that the maiden was asleep and not dead as they thought, would undoubtedly, spread reports. It is not surprizing, therefore, to read in Matthew's short version of the history, that the fame of the miracle "went abroad into all that land."

RESTORATION TO LIFE AND RESURRECTION.

The vital distinction between a restoration of the dead to a resumption of mortal life, and the resurrection of the body from death to a state of immortality, must be thoughtfully heeded. In each of the instances thus far considered--that of the raising of the dead man of Nain,[679] and that of the daughter of Jairus, as also the raising of Lazarus to be studied later--the miracle consisted in reuniting the spirit and the body in a continuation of the interrupted course of mortal existence. That the subject of each of these miracles had to subsequently die is certain. Jesus Christ was the first of all men who have lived on earth to come forth from the tomb an immortalized Being; He is therefore properly designated as "the first fruits of them that slept."[680]

Though both Elijah and Elisha, many centuries prior to the time of Christ, were instrumental in restoring life to the dead, the former to the widow's son in Zareptha, the latter to the child of the Shunammite woman,[681] in these earlier miracles the restoration was to mortal existence, not to immortality. It is instructive to observe the difference in the procedure of each of the Old Testament prophets mentioned as compared with that of Christ in analogous miracles. By both Elijah and Elisha the wonderful change was brought about only after long and labored ministrations, and earnest invocation of the power and intervention of Jehovah; but Jehovah, embodied in flesh as Jesus Christ, did nothing outwardly but command, and the bonds of death were immediately broken. He spoke in His own name and by inherent authority, for by the power with which He was invested He held control of both life and death.

A REMARKABLE HEALING BY THE WAY.[682]

While Jesus was walking to the house of Jairus with a great crowd of people thronging about Him, the progress of the company was arrested by another case of suffering. In the throng was a woman who for twelve years had been afflicted with a serious ailment involving frequent hemorrhage. She had spent in medical treatment all she had owned, and "had suffered many things of many physicians," but had steadily grown worse. She worked her way through the crowd, and, approaching Jesus from behind, touched His robe; "For she said, If I may touch but his clothes I shall be whole." The effect was more than magical; immediately she felt the thrill of health throughout her body, and knew that she had been healed of her affliction. Her object attained, the blessing being now secured, she tried to escape notice, by hastily dropping back into the crowd. But her touch was not unheeded by the Lord. He turned to look over the throng and asked, "Who touched my clothes?" or as Luke puts it, "Who touched me?" As the people denied, the impetuous Peter speaking for himself and the others said: "Master, the multitude throng thee and press thee, and sayest thou, Who touched me?" But Jesus answered: "Somebody hath touched me: for I perceive that virtue is gone out of me."

The woman, finding that she could not escape identification, came tremblingly forward, and, kneeling before the Lord, confessed what she had done, her reason for so doing, and the beneficent result. If she had expected censure her fears were promptly set at rest, for Jesus, addressing her by a term of respect and kindness, said: "Daughter, be of good comfort: thy faith hath made thee whole; go in peace," and as Mark adds, "be whole of thy plague."

This woman's faith was sincere and free from guile, nevertheless it was in a sense defective. She believed that the influence of Christ's person, and even that attaching to His raiment, was a remedial agency, ample to cure her malady; but she did not realize that the power to heal was an inherent attribute to be exercized at His will, and as the influence of faith might call it forth. True, her faith had already been in part rewarded, but of greater worth to her than the physical cure of her illness would be the assurance that the divine Healer had granted the desire of her heart, and that the faith she had manifested was accepted by Him. To correct her misapprehension and to confirm her faith, Jesus gently subjected her to the necessary ordeal of confession, which must have been made easier through her consciousness of the great relief already experienced. He confirmed the healing and let her depart with the comforting assurance that her recovery was permanent.

In contrast with the many cases of healing in connection with which the Lord charged the beneficiaries that they should tell none how or by whom they had been relieved, we see here that publicity was made sure by His own action, and that too, when secrecy was desired by the recipient of the blessing. The purposes and motives of Jesus may be but poorly understood by man; but in this woman's case we see the possibility of stories strange and untrue getting afloat, and it appears to have been the wiser course to make plain the truth then and there. Moreover the spiritual worth of the miracle was greatly enhanced by the woman's confession and by the Lord's gracious assurance.

Observe the significant assertion, "Thy faith hath made thee whole." Faith is of itself a principle of power;[683] and by its presence or absence, by its fulness or paucity, even the Lord was and is influenced, and in great measure controlled, in the bestowal or withholding of blessings; for He ministers according to law, and not with caprice or uncertainty. We read that at a certain time and place Jesus "could there do no mighty work" because of the people's unbelief.[684] Modern revelation specifies that faith to be healed is one of the gifts of the Spirit, analogous to the manifestations of faith in the work of healing others through the exercize of the power of the Holy Priesthood.[685]

Our Lord's inquiry as to who had touched Him in the throng affords us another example of His asking questions in pursuance of a purpose, when He could readily have determined the facts directly and without aid from others. There was a special purpose in the question, as every teacher finds a means of instruction in questioning his pupils.[686] But there is in Christ's question, "Who touched me?" a deeper significance than could inhere in a simple inquiry as to the identity of an individual; and this is implied in the Lord's further words: "Somebody hath touched me: for I perceive that virtue is gone out of me." The usual external act by which His miracles were wrought was a word or a command, sometimes accompanied by the laying on of hands, or by some other physical ministration as in anointing the eyes of a blind man. [687] That there was an actual giving of His own strength to the afflicted whom He healed is evident from the present instance. Passive belief on the part of a would-be recipient of blessing is insufficient; only when it is vitalized into active faith is it a power; so also of one who ministers in the authority given of God, mental and spiritual energy must be operative if the service is to be effective.

THE BLIND SEE AND THE DUMB SPEAK.[688]

Two other instances of miraculous healing are chronicled by Matthew as closely following the raising of the daughter of Jairus. As Jesus passed down the streets of Capernaum, presumably on His departure from the house of the ruler of the synagog, two blind men followed Him, crying out: "Thou son of David, have mercy on us." This title of address was voiced by others at sundry times, and in no case do we find record of our Lord disclaiming it or objecting to its use.[689] Jesus paused not to heed this call of the blind, and the two sightless men followed Him, even entering the house after Him. Then He spoke to them, asking: "Believe ye that I am able to do this?" And they replied, "Yea, Lord." Their persistency in following the Lord was evidence of their belief that in some way, though to them unknown and mysterious, He could help them; and they promptly and openly confessed that belief. Our Lord touched their eyes, saying: "According to your faith be it unto you." The effect was immediate; their eyes were opened. They were explicitly instructed to say nothing of the matter to others; but, rejoicing in the inestimable blessing of sight, they "spread abroad his fame in all that country." So far as we can unravel the uncertain threads of sequence in the works of Christ, this is the earliest instance, recorded with attendant details, of His giving sight to the blind. Many remarkable cases follow.[690]

It is worthy of note that in blessing the sightless by the exercize of His healing power, Jesus usually ministered by some physical contact in addition to uttering the authoritative words of command or assurance. In this instance, as also in that of two blind men who sat by the wayside, He touched the sightless eyes; in the giving of sight to the blind indigent in Jerusalem He anointed the man's eyes with clay; to the eyes of another He applied saliva.[691] An analogous circumstance is found in the healing of one who was deaf and defective of speech, in which instance the Lord put His fingers into the man's ears and touched his tongue.[692] In no case can such treatment be regarded as medicinal or therapeutic. Christ was not a physician who relied upon curative substances, nor a surgeon to perform physical operations; His healings were the natural results of the application of a power of His own. It is conceivable that confidence, which is a stepping-stone to belief, as that in turn is to faith, may have been encouraged by these physical ministrations, strengthened, and advanced to a higher and more abiding trust in Christ, on the part of the afflicted who had not sight to look upon the Master's face and derive inspiration therefrom, nor hearing to hear His uplifting words. There is apparent not alone an entire absence of formula and formalism in His ministration, but a lack of uniformity of procedure quite as impressive.

As the two men, once sightless but now seeing, departed, others came, bringing a dumb friend whose affliction seems to have been primarily due to the malignant influence of an evil spirit rather than to any organic defect. Jesus rebuked the wicked spirit--cast out the demon that had obsessed the afflicted one and held him in the tyranny of speechlessness. The man's tongue was loosened, he was freed from the evil incubus, and was no longer dumb.[693]

NOTES TO CHAPTER 20.

1. Storms on the Lake of Galilee.--It is a matter of record that sudden and violent storms are common on the lake or sea of Galilee; and the tempest that was quieted by the Lord's word of command was of itself no unusual phenomenon, except perhaps in its intensity. Another incident connected with a storm on this small body of water is of scriptural record, and will be considered later in the text (Matt. 14:22-26; Mark 6:45-56; John 6:15-21). Dr. Thompson (_The Land and the Book_ ii:32) gives a description founded on his personal experience on the shores of the lake: "I spent a night in that Wady Shukaiyif, some three miles up it, to the left of us. The sun had scarcely set when the wind began to rush down toward the lake, and it continued all night long with constantly increasing violence, so that when we reached the shore next morning the face of the lake was a huge boiling caldron. The wind howled down every wady from the north-east and east with such fury that no efforts of rowers could have brought a boat to shore at any point along that coast.... To understand the causes of these sudden and violent tempests, we must remember that the lake lies low--six hundred feet lower than the ocean; that the vast and naked plateaus of the Jaulan rise to a great height, spreading backward to the wilds of the Hauran, and upward to snowy Hermon; and that the water-courses have cut out profound ravines and wild gorges, converging to the head of this lake, and that these act like gigantic funnels to draw down the cold winds from the mountains."

2. The Earth Before and After Its Regeneration.--That the earth itself fell under the curse incident to the fall of the first parents of the race, and that even as man shall be redeemed so shall the earth be regenerated, is implied in Paul's words: "Because the creature itself also shall be delivered from the bondage of corruption into the glorious liberty of the children of God. For we know that the whole Creation groaneth and travaileth in pain together until now. And not only they, but ourselves also, which have the firstfruits of the Spirit, even we ourselves groan within ourselves, waiting for the adoption, to wit, the redemption of our body" (Rom. 8:21-23). The present author has written elsewhere: "According to the scriptures, the earth has to undergo a change analogous to death, and to be regenerated in a manner comparable to a resurrection. References to the elements melting with heat, and to the earth being consumed and passing away, such as occur in many scriptures already cited, are suggestive of death; and the new earth, really the renewed or regenerated planet, which is to result, may be compared with a resurrected organism. The change has been likened unto a transfiguration (Doc. and Cov. 63:20, 21). Every created thing has been made for a purpose; and everything that fills the measure of its creation is to be advanced in the scale of progression, be it an atom or a world, an animalcule, or man--the direct and literal offspring of Deity. In speaking of the degrees of glory provided for His creations, and of the laws of regeneration and sanctification, the Lord, in a revelation dated 1832, speaks plainly of the approaching death and subsequent quickening of the earth. These are his words:--'And again, verily I say unto you, the earth abideth the law of a celestial kingdom, for it filleth the measure of its creation, and transgresseth not the law. Wherefore it shall be sanctified; yea, notwithstanding it shall die, it shall be quickened again, and shall abide the power by which it is quickened, and the righteous shall inherit it.' (Doc. and Cov. 88:25-26.)"

The vital Spirit that emanates from God and is coextensive with space, may operate directly and with as positive effect upon inanimate things, and upon energy in its diverse manifestations known to us as the forces of nature, as upon organized intelligences, whether yet unembodied, in the flesh, or disembodied. Thus, the Lord may speak directly to the earth, the air, the sea, and be heard and obeyed, for the divine affluence, which is the sum of all energy and power may and does operate throughout the universe. In the course of a revelation from God to Enoch, the earth is personified, and her groans and lamentations over the wickedness of men were heard by the prophet: "And it came to pass that Enoch looked upon the earth; and he heard a voice from the bowels thereof, saying: Wo, wo is me, the mother of men; I am pained, I am weary, because of the wickedness of my children. When shall I rest, and be cleansed from the filthiness which is gone forth out of me? When will my Creator sanctify me, that I may rest, and righteousness for a season abide upon my face?" Enoch pleaded: "O Lord, wilt thou not have compassion upon the earth?" Following further revelation as to the then future course of mankind in sin and in the rejection of the Messiah who was to be sent, the prophet wept with anguish, and asked of God "When shall the earth rest?" It was then shown unto him that the crucified Christ shall return to earth and establish a millennial reign of peace: "And the Lord said unto Enoch: As I live, even so will I come in the last days, in the days of wickedness and vengeance, to fulfil the oath which I have made unto you concerning the children of Noah; and the day shall come that the earth shall rest, but before that day the heavens shall be darkened, and a veil of darkness shall cover the earth; and the heavens shall shake, and also the earth; and great tribulations shall be among the children of men." And the glorious assurance followed "that for the space of a thousand years the earth shall rest." (P. of G.P., Moses 7:48, 49, 58, 60, 61, 64.)

A partial description of the earth in its regenerated state has been given through the prophet Joseph Smith in the present dispensation: "This earth, in its sanctified and immortal state, will be made like unto crystal and will be a Urim and Thummim to the inhabitants who dwell thereon, whereby all things pertaining to an inferior kingdom, or all kingdoms of a lower order, will be manifest to those who dwell on it; and this earth will be Christ's." (Doc. and Cov. 130:9).

That Jesus Christ, in the exercize of His powers of Godship, should speak directly to the wind or the sea and be obeyed, is no less truly in accord with the natural law of heaven, than that He should effectively command a man or an unembodied spirit. That through faith even mortal man may set in operation the forces that act upon matter and with assurance of stupendous results has been explicitly declared by Jesus Christ: "For verily I say unto you, If ye have faith as a grain of mustard seed, ye shall say unto this mountain, Remove hence to yonder place; and it shill remove; and nothing shall be impossible unto you" (Matt. 17:20; compare Mark 11:23; Luke 17:6).

3. The Land of the Gergesenes.--Attempts have been made to discredit the account of Christ's healing the demoniac in "the country of the Gadarenes" (Mark 5:1; Luke 8:26) on the claim that the ancient town of Gadara the capital of the district (see Josephus, Wars, iii, 7:1), was too far inland to make possible the precipitous dash of the swine into the sea from that place. Others lay stress on the fact that Matthew differs from the two other Gospel-historians, in specifying "the country of the Gergesenes" (8:28). As stated in the text, a whole region or section is referred to, not a town. The keepers of the swine ran off to the towns to report the disaster that had befallen their herd. In that district of Perea there were at the time towns named respectively Gadara, Gerasa, and Gergesa; the region in general, therefore, could properly be called the land of the Gadarenes or of the Gergesenes. Farrar (_Life of Christ_, p. 254 note) says: "After the researches of Dr. Thompson (_The Land and the Book_, ii:25), there can be no doubt that Gergesa ... was the name of a little town nearly opposite Capernaum, the ruined site of which is still called Kerza or Gersa by the Bedawin. The existence of this little town was apparently known both to Origen, who first introduced the reading, and to Eusebius and Jerome; and in their day a steep declivity near it, where the hills approach to within a little distance from the lake, was pointed out as the scene of the miracle."

4. Jesus Entreated to Leave the Country.--The people were frightened over the power possessed by Jesus, as demonstrated in the cure of the demoniac, and in the destruction of the swine, which latter occurrence, however, was not in pursuance of His command. It was the fear that sinful men feel in the

presence of the Righteous. They were not prepared for other manifestations of divine power, and they dreaded to think who among them might be directly affected thereby should it be exerted. We must judge the people mercifully, however, if at all. They were in part heathen, and had but superstitious conceptions of Deity. Their prayer that Jesus leave them brings to mind the ejaculation of Simon Peter in his witnessing one of Christ's miracles: "Depart from me: for I am a sinful man, O Lord" (Luke 5:8).

5. "Dead," or "At the Point of Death."--According to Luke (8:42) the daughter of Jairus "lay a dying" when the grief-stricken father sought help of the Lord; Mark (5:23) reports the man as stating that the girl lay "at the point of death." These two accounts agree; but Matthew (9:18) represents the father as saying: "My daughter is even now dead." Unbelieving critics have dwelt at length on what they designate an inconsistency if not a contradiction in these versions; and yet both accounts embodied in the three records are plainly true. The maid was seemingly breathing her last, she was in the very throes of death, when the father hurried away. Before he met Jesus he felt that the end had probably come; nevertheless his faith endured. His words attest his trust, that even had his daughter actually died since he left her side, the Master could recall her to life. He was in a state of frenzied grief, and still his faith held true.

6. Mourning Customs Among Orientals.--Observances that to us seem strange, weird, and out of place, prevailed from very early times among oriental peoples, some of which customs were common to the Jews in the days of Christ. Noise and tumult, including screeching lamentations by members of the bereaved family and by professional mourners, as also the din of instruments, were usual accompaniments of mourning. Geikie, citing Buxtorf's quotation from the Talmud, gives place to the following: "Even a poor Israelite was required to have not fewer than two flute players and one mourning woman at the death of his wife; but if he be rich all things are to be done according to his quality." In Smith's _Dictionary of the Bible_, we read: "The number of words (about eleven Hebrew and as many Greek) employed in scripture to express the various actions characteristic of mourning, shows in a great degree the nature of Jewish customs in this respect. They appear to have consisted chiefly in the following particulars: (1) Beating upon the breast or other parts of the body. (2) Weeping and screaming in an excessive degree. (3) Wearing sad-colored garments. (4) Songs of lamentation. (5) Funeral feasts. (6) Employment of persons, especially women, to lament. One marked feature of oriental mourning is what may be called its studied publicity, and the careful observance of prescribed ceremonies (Gen. 23:2; Job 1:20; 2:8; Isa. 15:3; etc.)."

7. "Not Dead, but Sleepeth."--That the daughter of Jairus was dead is placed beyond reasonable doubt by the scriptural record. Our Lord's statement to the noisy mourners that "the damsel is not dead but sleepeth" told that her sleep was to be of short duration. It was a rabbinical and common custom of the time to speak of death as a sleep, and those who laughed Jesus to scorn for His statement chose to construe His words in a sense of such literalism as the context scarcely warrants. It is noticeable that the Lord used a strictly equivalent expression with respect to the death of Lazarus. "Our friend Lazarus sleepeth," said He, "but I go that I may awake him out of sleep." The literal construction placed upon these words by the apostles evoked the plain declaration "Lazarus is dead" (John 11:11, 14). In the Talmud death is repeatedly designated as sleep--hundreds of times says Lightfoot, a recognized authority on Hebrew literature.

8. Why Did Jesus Make Inquiries?--We have already considered many instances of Christ's possession of what man would call superhuman knowledge, extending even to the reading of unuttered thoughts. Some people find difficulty in reconciling this superior quality with the fact that Jesus often asked questions even on matters of minor circumstance. We should realize that even complete knowledge may not preclude the propriety of making inquiries, and, moreover, that even omniscience does not imply ever-present consciousness of all that is. Undoubtedly through his paternal heritage of divine attributes, Jesus had the power of ascertaining for Himself, by means not possessed by others, any facts He might have desired to know; nevertheless we find Him repeatedly asking questions on circumstantial detail (Mark 9:21; 8:27; Matt. 16:13; Luke 8:45); and this He did even after His resurrection (Luke 24:41; John 21:5; B. of M., 3 Nephi 17:7).

That catechization is one of the most effective means of mind development is exampled in the methods followed by the best of human teachers. Trench (_Notes on the Miracles_, pp. 148-9), thus instructively points the lesson as illustrated by our Lord's question concerning the woman who was healed of her issue of blood: With little force "can it be urged that it would have been inconsistent with absolute truth for the Lord to profess ignorance, and to ask the question which He did ask, if all the while He perfectly knew what He thus seemed implicitly to say that He did not know. A father among his children, and demanding Who committed this fault? himself conscious, even while he asks, but at the same time willing to bring the culprit to a full confession, and so to put him in a pardonable state, can he be said, in any way to violate the law of the highest truth? The same offense might be found in Elisha's 'Whence comest thou, Gehazi?' (2 Kings 5:25) when his heart went with his servant all the way that he had gone; and even in the question of God Himself to Adam, 'Where art thou?' (Gen. 3:9), and to Cain, 'Where is Abel thy brother?' (Gen. 4:9). In every case there is a moral purpose in the question, an opportunity given even at the latest moment for making good at least a part of the error by its unreserved confession."

9. The Blind See.--In his treatment of the miraculous healing of the two blind men who had followed Jesus into the house, Trench (_Notes on the Miracles of our Lord_, p. 152) says: "We have here the first of those many healings of the blind recorded (Matt. 12:22; 20:30; 21:14; John 9) or alluded to (Matt. 11:5) in the Gospels; each of them a literal fulfilment of that prophetic word of Isaiah concerning the days of Messiah: 'Then the eyes of the blind shall be opened' (35:5). Frequent as these miracles are, they yet will none of them be found without distinguishing features of their own. That they should be so numerous is nothing wonderful, whether we regard the fact from a natural or spiritual point of view. Regarded naturally they need not surprize us if we keep in mind how far commoner a calamity is blindness in the East than with us. Regarded from a spiritual point of view we have only to remember how commonly sin is

contemplated in Scripture as a moral blindness (Deut. 28:29; Isa. 59:10; Job 12:25; Zeph. 1:17), and deliverance from sin as a removal of this blindness (Isa. 6:9, 10; 43:8; Eph. 1:18; Matt. 15:14); and we shall at once perceive how fit it was that He who was the 'light of the world' should often accomplish works which symbolized so well that higher work which He came into the world to accomplish."

10. Imputation of Satanic Agency.--Observe that in the matter of healing the dumb demoniac referred to in the text, Christ was charged with being in league with the devil. Although the people, impressed by the manifestation of divine power in the healing, exclaimed in reverence, "It was never so seen in Israel," the Pharisees, intent on counteracting the good effect of the Lord's miraculous ministration, said "He casteth out devils through the prince of the devils." (Matt. 9:32-34.) For further treatment of this inconsistent and, strictly speaking blasphemous charge, see pages 265-269.

FOOTNOTES:

[657] Mark 4:35.
[658] "Articles of Faith," x:1-20--"Men called of God."
[659] Page 87.
[660] Luke 9:57-62; see also Matt. 8:19-22.
[661] Matt 8:23-27; Mark 4:35-41; Luke 8:22-25.
[662] Note 1, end of chapter.
[663] Gen. 1:28; P. of G.P., Moses 2:26; 5:1.
[664] Gen. 3:17-19.
[665] Note 2, end of chapter.
[666] Matt. 8:28-34; Mark 5:1-19; Luke 8:26-39.
[667] Note 3, end of chapter.
[668] Compare Rev. 20:3.
[669] Revised version, "abyss" instead of "deep."
[670] Note 4, end of chapter.
[671] Mark 1:24; Luke 4:34, also verse 41; see page 181 herein.
[672] Mark 3:7-11; compare Luke 6:17-19. See page 187.
[673] Mark 5:22-24, 35-43; Luke 8:41, 42, 49-56; Matt. 9:18, 19, 23-26.
[674] John 11:45; compare 8:30; 10:42.
[675] Note 5, end of chapter.
[676] Note 6, end of chapter.
[677] Note 7, end of chapter.
[678] Mark 5:19-20; Luke 8:39. Page 312.
[679] Page 251.
[680] 1 Cor. 15:20, 23; see also Acts 26:23; Col. 1:18; Rev. 1:5; and "Articles of Faith," xxi:24-27.

[681] 1 Kings 17:17-24; 2 Kings 4:31-37.
[682] Mark 5:25-34; Matt. 9:20-22; Luke 8:43-48.
[683] "Articles of Faith," v:11-13.
[684] Mark 6:5, 6; compare Matt. 13:58.
[685] Doc. and Cov. 46:19; compare Matt. 8:10; 9:28, 29. Acts 14:9.
[686] Note 8, end of chapter.
[687] Matt. 8:3; Luke 4:40; 13:13; John 9:6; compare Mark 6:5; 7:33; 8:23.
[688] Matt. 9:27-35.
[689] Matt. 15:22; 20:30, 31; Mark 10:47, 48; Luke 18:38, 39.
[690] Note 9, end of chapter.
[691] Matt. 20:30-34; John 9:6; Mark 8:23.
[692] Mark 7:32-37.
[693] Matt. 9:32, 33. Note 10, end of chapter.

CHAPTER 21. THE APOSTOLIC MISSION, AND EVENTS RELATED THERETO.

JESUS AGAIN IN NAZARETH.[694]

It will be remembered that, in the early days of His public ministry, Jesus had been rejected by the people of Nazareth, who thrust Him out from their synagog and tried to kill Him.[695] It appears that subsequent to the events noted in our last chapter, He returned to the town of His youth, and again raised His voice in the synagog, thus mercifully affording the people another opportunity to learn and accept the truth. The Nazarenes, as they had done before, now again openly expressed their astonishment at the words He spoke, and at the many miraculous works He had wrought; nevertheless they rejected Him anew, for He came not as they expected the Messiah to come; and they refused to know Him save as "the carpenter, the son of Mary, the brother of James, and Joses, and of Juda, and Simon;" all of whom were common folk as were also His sisters. "And they were offended at him."[696] Jesus reminded them of the proverb then current among the people, "A prophet is not without honour, but in his own country, and among his own kin, and in his own house." Their unbelief was so dense as to cause Him to marvel;[697] and because of their lack of faith He was unable to accomplish any great work except to heal a few exceptional believers upon whom He laid His hands. Leaving Nazareth, He entered upon His third tour of the Galilean towns and villages, preaching and teaching as He went.[698]

THE TWELVE CHARGED AND SENT.[699]

About this time, also, Jesus inaugurated a notable expansion of the ministry of the kingdom, by sending forth the Twelve on assigned missions. Since their ordination the apostles had been with their Lord, learning from Him by public discourse and private exposition, and acquiring invaluable experience and training through that privileged and blessed companionship. The purpose of their ordination was specified--"that they should be with him, and that he might send them forth to preach."[700] They had been pupils under the Master's watchful guidance for many months; and now they were called to enter upon the duties of their calling as preachers of the gospel and individual witnesses of the Christ. By way of final preparation they were specifically and solemnly charged.[701] Some of the instructions given them on this occasion had particular reference to their first mission, from which they would in due time return and report; other directions and admonitions were to be of effect throughout their ministry, even after the Lord's ascension.

They were directed to confine their ministrations for the time being "to the lost sheep of the house of Israel," and not to open a propaganda among the Gentiles,[702] nor even in Samaritan cities. This was a temporary restriction, imposed in wisdom and prudence; later, as we shall see, they were directed to preach among all nations, with the world for their field.[703] The subject of their discourses was to be that upon which they had heard the Master preach--"the kingdom of heaven is at hand." They were to exercise the authority of the Holy Priesthood as conferred upon them by ordination; it was a specified part of their mission to "heal the sick, cleanse the lepers, raise the dead, cast out devils," as occasion presented itself; and they were commanded to give freely, even as they had freely received. Personal comfort and bodily needs they were not to provide for; the people were to be proved as to their willingness to receive and assist those who came in the name of the Lord; and the apostles themselves were to learn to rely upon a Provider more to be trusted than man; therefore money, extra clothing, and things of mere convenience were to be left behind. In the several towns they entered they were to seek entertainment and leave their blessing upon every worthy family into which they were received. If they found themselves rejected by a household or by a town as a whole, they were to shake the dust from their feet on leaving, as a testimony against the people; [704] and it was decreed that, in the day of judgment, the place so denounced would fare worse than wicked Sodom and Gomorrha upon which fire from heaven had descended.

The apostles were told to be prudent, to give no needless offense, but to be wise as serpents, and harmless as doves; for they were sent forth as sheep into the midst of wolves. They were not to recklessly entrust themselves to the power of men; for wicked men would persecute them, seek to arraign them before councils and courts, and to afflict them in the synagogs. Moreover they might expect to be brought before governors and kings, under which extreme conditions, they were to rely upon divine inspiration as to what they should say, and not depend upon their own wisdom in preparation and premeditation; "For," said the Master, "it is not ye that speak, but the Spirit of your Father which speaketh in you."[705]

They were not to trust even the claims of kinship for protection, for families would be divided over the truth, brother against brother, children against parents, and the resulting strife would be deadly. These servants of Christ were told that they would be hated of all men, but were assured that their sufferings were to be for His name's sake. They were to withdraw from the cities that persecuted them, and go to others; and the Lord would follow them, even before they would be able to complete the circuit of the cities of Israel. They were admonished to humility, and were always to remember that they were servants, who ought not to expect to escape when even their Master was assailed. Nevertheless they were to be fearless, hesitating not to preach the gospel in plainness; for the most their persecutors could do was to kill the body, which fate was as nothing compared to that of suffering destruction of the soul in hell.

Assurance of the Father's watchful care was impressed upon them by the simple reminder that though sparrows were sold two for a farthing, and yet not a sparrow could be sacrificed without the Father's concern, they, who were of more value than many sparrows, would not be forgotten. They were solemnly warned that whosoever would freely confess the Christ before men would be acknowledged by Him in the

Father's presence, while they who denied Him before men would be denied in heaven. And again they were told that the gospel would bring strife, whereby households would be disrupted; for the doctrine the Lord had taught would be as a sword to cut and divide. The duties of their special ministry were to supersede the love for kindred; they must be willing to leave father, mother, son, or daughter, whatever the sacrifice; for, said Jesus "He that taketh not his cross, and followeth after me, is not worthy of me."

The significance of this figure must have been solemnly impressive, and actually terrifying; for the cross was a symbol of ignominy, extreme suffering, and death. However, should they lose their lives for His sake, they would find life eternal; while he who was not willing to die in the Lord's service should lose his life in a sense at once literal and awful. They were never to forget in whose name they were sent; and were comforted with the assurance that whoever received them would be rewarded as one who had received the Christ and His Father; and that though the gift were only that of a cup of cold water, the giver should in no wise lose his reward.

Thus charged and instructed, the twelve special witnesses of the Christ set out upon their mission, traveling in pairs,[706] while Jesus continued His personal ministry.

THE TWELVE RETURN.

We are without definite information as to the duration of the apostles' first mission, and as to the extent of the field they traversed. The period of their absence was marked by many important developments in the individual labors of Jesus. It is probable that during this time our Lord visited Jerusalem, on the occasion mentioned by John as coincident with the unnamed feast of the Jews.[707] While the apostles were absent, Jesus was visited by the Baptist's disciples, as we have already seen[708] and the return of the Twelve occurred near the time of the infamous execution of John the Baptist in prison. [709]

The missionary labors of the apostles greatly augmented the spread of the new doctrine of the kingdom, and the name and works of Jesus were proclaimed throughout the land. The people of Galilee were at that time in a state of discontent threatening open insurrection against the government; their unrest had been aggravated by the murder of the Baptist. Herod Antipas, who had given the fatal order, trembled in his palace. He heard, with fear due to inward conviction of guilt, of the marvelous works wrought by Jesus, and in terror averred that Christ could be none other than John Baptist returned from the tomb. His fawning courtiers essayed to allay his fears by saying that Jesus was Elijah, or some other of the prophets whose advent had been predicted; but the conscience-stricken Herod said: "It is John whom I beheaded: he is risen from the dead." Herod desired to see Jesus; perhaps through the fascination of fear, or with the faint hope that sight of the renowned Prophet of Nazareth might dispel his superstitious dread that the murdered John had returned to life.

Upon the completion of their missionary tour, the apostles rejoined the Master and reported to Him both what they had taught and what they had done by way of authoritative ministration. They had preached the gospel of repentance in all the cities, towns, and villages to which they had gone; they had anointed with oil many afflicted ones, and the power of their priesthood had been attested by consequent healings; even unclean spirits and devils had been subject unto them.[710] They found Jesus attended by great multitudes; and they had little opportunity of private conference with Him; "for there were many coming and going, and they had no leisure so much as to eat." The apostles must have heard in gladness the Lord's invitation: "Come ye yourselves apart into a desert place, and rest awhile." In quest of seclusion, Jesus and the Twelve withdrew from the throng, and privately entered a boat in which they crossed to a rural spot adjacent to the city of Bethsaida.[711] Their departure had not been unobserved, however, and eager crowds hastened along the shore, and partly around the northerly end of the lake, to join the party at the landing place. From John's account we are led to infer that, before the arrival of great numbers, Jesus and His companions had ascended the hillside near the shore, where, for a short time they had rested. As the multitude gathered on the lower slopes, our Lord looked upon them as upon sheep without a shepherd; and, yielding to their desire and to His own emotions of divine pity, He taught them many things, healed their afflicted ones, and comforted their hearts with compassionate tenderness.

FIVE THOUSAND FED IN THE DESERT.[712]

So intent were the people on hearing the Lord's words, and so concerned in the miraculous relief resulting from His healing ministrations, that they remained in the wilderness, oblivious to the passing of the hours, until the evening approached. It was the springtime, near the recurrence of the annual Passover festival, the season of grass and flowers.[713] Jesus, realizing that the people were hungry, asked Philip, one of the Twelve, "Whence shall we buy bread, that these may eat?" The purpose of the question was to test the apostle's faith; for the Lord had already determined as to what was to be done. Philip's reply showed surprize at the question, and conveyed his thought that the suggested undertaking was impossible. "Two hundred pennyworth of bread is not sufficient for them, that every one of them may take a little," said he. Andrew added that there was a lad present who had five barley loaves, and two small fishes, "But," said he, "what are they among so many?"

Such is John's account; the other writers state that the apostles reminded Jesus of the lateness of the hour, and urged that He send the people away to seek for themselves food and lodging in the nearest towns. It appears most probable that the conversation between Jesus and Philip occurred earlier in the afternoon;[714] and that as the hours sped, the Twelve became concerned and advized that the multitude be dismissed. The Master's reply to the apostles was: "They need not depart; give ye them to eat." In amazed wonder they replied: "We have here but five loaves and two fishes;" and Andrew's despairing comment is implied again--What are they among so many?

Jesus gave command, and the people seated themselves on the grass in orderly array; they were grouped in fifties and hundreds; and it was found that the multitude numbered about five thousand men, beside women and children. Taking the loaves and the fishes, Jesus looked toward heaven and pronounced a blessing upon the food; then, dividing the provisions, He gave to the apostles severally, and they in turn distributed to the multitude. The substance of both fish and bread increased under the Master's touch; and the multitude feasted there in the desert, until all were satisfied. To the disciples Jesus said: "Gather up the fragments that remain, that nothing be lost;" and twelve baskets were filled with the surplus.

As to the miracle itself, human knowledge is powerless to explain. Though wrought on so great a scale, it is no more nor less inexplicable than any other of the Lord's miraculous works. It was a manifestation of creative power, by which material elements were organized and compounded to serve a present and pressing need. The broken but unused portion exceeded in bulk and weight the whole of the original little store. Our Lord's direction to gather up the fragments was an impressive object-lesson against waste; and it may have been to afford such lesson that an excess was supplied. The fare was simple, yet nourishing, wholesome and satisfying. Barley bread and fish constituted the usual food of the poorer classes of the region. The conversion of water into wine at Cana was a qualitative transmutation; the feeding of the multitude involved a quantitative increase; who can say that one, or which, of these miracles of provision was the more wonderful?

The multitude, now fed and filled, gave some consideration to the miracle. In Jesus, by whom so great a work had been wrought, they recognized One having superhuman powers. "This is of a truth the prophet that should come into the world," said they--the Prophet whose coming had been foretold by Moses and who should be like unto himself. Even as Israel had been miraculously fed during the time of Moses, so now was bread provided in the desert by this new Prophet. In their enthusiasm the people proposed to proclaim Him king, and forcibly compel Him to become their leader. Such was their gross conception of Messianic supremacy. Jesus directed His disciples to depart by boat, while He remained to dismiss the now excited multitude. The disciples hesitated to leave their Master; but He constrained them and they obeyed. His insistence, that the Twelve depart from both Himself and the multitude, may have been due to a desire to protect the chosen disciples against possible infection by the materialistic and unrighteous designs of the throng to make Him king. By means that are not detailed, He caused the people to disperse; and, as night came on, He found that for which He had come in quest, solitude and quiet. Ascending the hill, He chose a secluded place, and there remained in prayer during the greater part of the night.

IT IS I; BE NOT AFRAID."[715]

The return by boat proved to be a memorable journey for the disciples. They encountered a boisterous head-wind, which of course rendered impossible the use of sails; and though they toiled heavily at the oars the vessel became practically unmanageable and wallowed in the midst of the sea.[716] Though they had labored through the night they had progressed less than four miles on their course; to turn and run before the wind would have been to invite disastrous wreck; their sole hope lay in their holding the vessel to the wind by sheer power of muscle. Jesus, in His place of solitary retirement, was aware of their sad plight, and along in the fourth watch,[717] that is, between three and six o'clock in the morning, He came to their assistance, walking upon the storm-tossed water as though treading solid ground. When the voyagers caught sight of Him as He approached the ship in the faint light of the near-spent night, they were overcome by superstitious fears, and cried out in terror, thinking that they saw a ghostly apparition. "But straightway Jesus spake unto them, saying, Be of good cheer; it is I; be not afraid."

Relieved by these assuring words, Peter, impetuous and impulsive as usual, cried out: "Lord, if[718] it be thou, bid me come unto thee on the water." Jesus assenting, Peter descended from the ship and walked toward his Master; but as the wind smote him and the waves rose about him, his confidence wavered and he began to sink. Strong swimmer though he was,[719] he gave way to fright, and cried, "Lord, save me." Jesus caught him by the hand, saying: "O thou of little faith, wherefore didst thou doubt?"

From Peter's remarkable experience, we learn that the power by which Christ was able to walk the waves could be made operative in others, provided only their faith was enduring. It was on Peter's own request that he was permitted to attempt the feat. Had Jesus forbidden him, the man's faith might have suffered a check; his attempt, though attended by partial failure, was a demonstration of the efficacy of faith in the Lord, such as no verbal teaching could ever have conveyed. Jesus and Peter entered the vessel; immediately the wind ceased, and the boat soon reached the shore. The amazement of the apostles, at this latest manifestation of the Lord's control over the forces of nature, would have been more akin to worship and less like terrified consternation had they remembered the earlier wonders they had witnessed; but they had forgotten even the miracle of the loaves, and their hearts had hardened.[720] Marveling at the power of One to whom the wind-lashed sea was a sustaining floor, the apostles bowed before the Lord in reverent worship, saying: "Of a truth thou art the Son of God."[721]

Aside from the marvelous circumstances of its literal occurrence, the miracle is rich in symbolism and suggestion. By what law or principle the effect of gravitation was superseded, so that a human body could be supported upon the watery surface, man is unable to affirm. The phenomenon is a concrete demonstration of the great truth that faith is a principle of power, whereby natural forces may be conditioned and controlled.[722] Into every adult human life come experiences like unto the battling of the storm-tossed voyagers with contrary winds and threatening seas; ofttimes the night of struggle and danger is far advanced before succor appears; and then, too frequently the saving aid is mistaken for a greater terror. As came unto Peter and his terrified companions in the midst of the turbulent waters, so comes to all who toil in faith, the voice of the Deliverer--"It is I; be not afraid."

IN THE LAND OF GENNESARET.

The night voyage, in the course of which Jesus had reached the boat with its frightened occupants while "in the midst of the sea," ended at some point within the district known as the land of Gennesaret, which, as generally believed, embraced the rich and fertile region in the vicinity of Tiberias and Magdala. Of the natural beauties, for which the region was famed much has been written.[723] Word of our Lord's presence there spread rapidly, and, from "all that country round about" the people flocked to Him, bringing their afflicted to receive of His beneficence by word or touch. In the towns through which He walked, the sick were laid in the streets that the blessing of His passing might fall upon them; and many "besought him that they might touch if it were but the border of his garment; and as many as touched him were made whole."[724] Bounteously did He impart of His healing virtue to all who came asking with faith and confidence. Thus, accompanied by the Twelve, He wended His way northward to Capernaum, making the pathway bright by the plentitude of His mercies.

IN SEARCH OF LOAVES AND FISHES.[725]

The multitude who, on the yesterday, had partaken of His bounty on the other side of the lake, and who dispersed for the night after their ineffectual attempt to force upon Him the dignity of earthly kingship, were greatly surprized in the morning to discover that He had departed. They had seen the disciples leave in the only boat there present, while Jesus had remained on shore; and they knew that the night tempest had precluded the possibility of other boats reaching the place. Nevertheless their morning search for Him was futile; and they concluded that He must have returned by land round the end of the lake. As the day advanced some boats were sighted, bound for the western coast; these they hailed, and, securing passage, crossed to Capernaum.

Their difficulty in locating Jesus was at an end, for His presence was known throughout the town. Coming to Him, probably as He sat in the synagog, for on this day He taught there, some of the most intrusive of the crowd asked, brusquely and almost rudely, "Rabbi, when camest thou hither?" To this impertinent inquiry Jesus deigned no direct reply; in the miracle of the preceding night the people had no part, and no account of our Lord's movements was given them. In tone of impressive rebuke Jesus said unto them: "Verily, verily, I say unto you, Ye seek me, not because ye saw the miracles, but because ye did eat of the loaves, and were filled." Their concern was for the bread and fishes. One who could supply them with victuals as He had done must not be lost sight of.

The Master's rebuke was followed by admonition and instruction: "Labour not for the meat which perisheth, but for that meat which endureth unto everlasting life, which the Son of man shall give unto you: for him hath God the Father sealed." This contrast between material and spiritual food they could not entirely fail to understand, and some of them asked what they should do to serve God as Jesus required. The answer was: "This is the work of God, that ye believe on him whom he hath sent." That Jesus was referring to Himself, none could doubt; and straightway they demanded of Him further evidence of His divine commission; they would see greater signs. The miracle of the loaves and fishes was nearly a day old; and its impressiveness as evidence of Messianic attributes was waning. Moses had fed their fathers with manna in the desert, they said; and plainly they regarded a continued daily supply as a greater gift than a single meal of bread and fish, however much the latter may have been appreciated in the exigency of hunger. Moreover, the manna was heavenly food;[726] whereas the bread He had given them was of earth, and only common barley bread at that. He must show them greater signs, and give them richer provender, before they would accept Him as the One whom they at first had taken Him to be and whom He now declared Himself to be.

CHRIST, THE BREAD OF LIFE.[727]

"Then Jesus said unto them, Verily, verily, I say unto you, Moses gave you not that bread from heaven; but my Father giveth you the true bread from heaven. For the bread of God is he which cometh down from heaven, and giveth life unto the world." They were mistaken in assuming that Moses had given them manna; and after all, the manna had been but ordinary food in that those who ate of it hungered again; but now the Father offered them bread from heaven such as would insure them life.

As the Samaritan woman at the well, on hearing the Lord speak of water that would satisfy once for all, had begged impulsively and with thought only of physical convenience, "Sir, give me this water, that I thirst not, neither come hither to draw,"[728] so these people, eager to secure so satisfying a food as that of which Jesus spake, implored: "Lord, evermore give us this bread." Perhaps this request was not wholly gross; there may have been in the hearts of some of them at least a genuine desire for spiritual nourishment. Jesus met their appeal with an explanation: "I am the bread of life: he that cometh to me shall never hunger; and he that believeth on me shall never thirst." He reminded them that though they had seen Him they believed not His words; and assured them that those who really accepted Him would do as the Father directed. Then, without metaphor or symbolism, He affirmed: "I came down from heaven, not to do mine own will, but the will of him that sent me." And the Father's will was that all who would accept the Son should have everlasting life.

There were present in the synagog some of the rulers--Pharisees, scribes, rabbis--and these, designated collectively as the Jews, criticized Jesus, and murmured against Him because He had said, "I am the bread which came down from heaven." They averred that He could do nothing more than any man could do; He was known to them as the son of Joseph, and as far as they knew was of ordinary earthly parentage, and yet He had the temerity to declare that He had come down from heaven. Chiefly to this class rather than to the promiscuous crowd who had hastened after Him, Jesus appears to have addressed the remainder of His discourse. He advized them to cease their murmurings; for it was a certainty that they could not apprehend His meaning, and therefore would not believe Him, unless they had been "taught of God" as the prophets had written;[729] and none could come to Him in the sense of accepting His saving gospel unless the Father drew them to the Son; and none save those who were receptive, willing, and prepared, could be so drawn.[730] Yet belief in the Son of God is an indispensable condition to salvation, as Jesus indicated in His affirmation: "Verily, verily, I say unto you, he that believeth on me hath everlasting life."

Then, reverting to the symbolism of the bread, He reiterated: "I am the bread of life." In further elucidation He explained that while their fathers did truly eat manna in the wilderness, yet they were dead; whereas the bread of life of which He spake would insure eternal life unto all who partook thereof. That bread, He averred, was His flesh. Against this solemn avowal the Jews complained anew, and disputed among themselves, some asking derisively: "How can this man give us his flesh to eat." Emphasizing the doctrine, Jesus continued: "Verily, verily, I say unto you, Except ye eat the flesh of the Son of man, and drink his blood, ye have no life in you. Whoso eateth my flesh, and drinketh my blood, hath eternal life; and I will raise him up at the last day. For my flesh is meat indeed, and my blood is drink indeed. He that eateth my flesh, and drinketh my blood, dwelleth in me, and I in him. As the living Father hath sent me, and I live by the Father: so he that eateth me, even he shall live by me. This is that bread which came down from heaven: not as your fathers did eat manna, and are dead: he that eateth of this bread shall live forever."

There was little excuse for the Jews pretending to understand that our Lord meant an actual eating and drinking of His material flesh and blood. The utterances to which they objected were far more readily understood by them than they are by us on first reading; for the representation of the law and of truth in general as bread, and the acceptance thereof as a process of eating and drinking, were figures in every-day use by the rabbis of that time.[731] Their failure to comprehend the symbolism of Christ's doctrine was an act of will, not the natural consequence of innocent ignorance. To eat the flesh and drink the blood of Christ was and is to believe in and accept Him as the literal Son of God and Savior of the world, and to obey His commandments. By these means only may the Spirit of God become an abiding part of man's individual being, even as the substance of the food he eats is assimilated with the tissues of his body.

It is not sufficing to accept the precepts of Christ as we may adopt the doctrines of scientists, philosophers, and savants, however great the wisdom of these sages may be; for such acceptance is by mental assent or deliberate exercize of will, and has relation to the doctrine only as independent of the author. The teachings of Jesus Christ endure because of their intrinsic worth; and many men respect His aphorisms, proverbs, parables, and His profoundly philosophical precepts, who yet reject Him as the Son of God, the Only Begotten in the flesh, the God-Man in whom were united the attributes of Deity with those of humanity, the chosen and foreordained Redeemer of mankind, through whom alone may salvation be attained. But the figure used by Jesus--that of eating His flesh and drinking His blood as typical of unqualified and absolute acceptance of Himself as the Savior of men, is of superlative import; for thereby are affirmed the divinity of His Person, and the fact of His pre-existent and eternal Godship. The sacrament of the Lord's supper, established by the Savior on the night of His betrayal, perpetuates the symbolism of eating His flesh and drinking His blood, by the partaking of bread and wine in remembrance of Him.[732] Acceptance of Jesus as the Christ implies obedience to the laws and ordinances of His gospel; for to profess the One and refuse the other is but to convict ourselves of inconsistency, insincerity, and hypocrisy.

A CRUCIAL TEST--MANY TURN AWAY.[733]

The truth respecting Himself, as taught by the Lord in this, His last, discourse in the synagog at Capernaum, proved to be a test of faith through which many fell away. Not alone critical Jews of the official class, whose hostility was openly avowed, but those who had professed some measure of belief in Him were affected. "Many therefore of his disciples, when they had heard this, said, This is an hard saying; who can hear it?" Jesus, cognizant of their disaffection, asked: "Doth this offend you?" and added: "What and if ye shall see the Son of man ascend up where he was before?" His ascension, which was to follow His death and resurrection, is here definitely implied. The spiritual significance of His teachings was put beyond question by the explanation that only through the Spirit could they comprehend; "Therefore," He added, "said I unto you, that no man can come unto me except it were given unto him of my Father."

Many deserted Him, and from that time sought Him no more. The occasion was crucial; the effect was that of sifting and separation. The portentous prediction of the Baptist-prophet had entered upon the stage of fulfilment: "One mightier than I cometh ... Whose fan is in his hand, and he will thoroughly purge his floor, and gather his wheat into the garner; but he will burn up the chaff with unquenchable fire."[734] The fan was in operation, and much chaff was blown aside.

It appears that even the Twelve were unable to comprehend the deeper meaning of these latest teachings; they were puzzled, though none actually deserted. Nevertheless, the state of mind of some was such as to evoke from Jesus the question: "Will ye also go away?" Peter, speaking for himself and his brethren, answered with pathos and conviction: "Lord, to whom shall we go? thou hast the words of eternal life."[735] The spirit of the Holy Apostleship was manifest in this confession. Though they were unable to comprehend in fulness the doctrine, they knew Jesus to be the Christ, and were faithful to Him while others turned away into the dark depths of apostasy.

While Peter spoke for the apostolic body as a whole, there was among them one who silently revolted; the treacherous Iscariot, who was in worse plight than an openly avowed apostate, was there. The Lord knew this man's heart, and said: "Have not I chosen you twelve, and one of you is a devil?" The historian adds: "He spake of Judas Iscariot the son of Simon: for he it was that should betray him, being one of the twelve."

NOTES TO CHAPTER 21.

1. Jesus at Nazareth.--As no one of the Gospel-writers records two occasions of our Lord's ministry in Nazareth, and as the separate accounts appearing in the synoptic Gospels closely resemble one another in a few particulars, some commentators hold that our Lord preached to His townsmen in Nazareth and was rejected by them but once. Luke's account (4:14-30) refers to an occasion immediately following the first return of Jesus to Galilee after His baptism and temptations, and directly preceding the preliminary call of the fishermen-disciples, who afterward were numbered among the apostles. Matthew (13:53-58) and Mark (6:1-6) chronicle a visit of Jesus to Nazareth later than the occasion of the first teaching in parables, and the events immediately following the same. We have good reason for accepting Luke's record as that of an early incident, and the accounts given by Matthew and Mark as those of a later visit.

2. Gentiles.--In a general way the Jews designated all other peoples as Gentiles; though the same Hebrew word is rendered in the Old Testament variously, as "Gentiles" (Gen. 10:5; Judg. 4:2, 13, 16; Isa. 11:10; etc.), "nations" (Gen. 10:5, 20, 31, 32; 14:1, 9; etc.), and "heathen" (Neh. 5:8; Psa. 2:1, 8, etc.), the essential element of designation being that of foreigners. In Smith's _Dict. of the Bible_, we read "It [the name 'Gentiles'] acquired an ethnographic and also an invidious meaning, as other nations were idolatrous, rude, hostile, etc., yet the Jews were able to use it in a purely technical, geographical sense, when it was usually translated 'nations.'" Dr. Edward E. Nourse, writing for the _Standard Bible Dictionary_, says: "In New Testament times, the Jew divided mankind into three classes, (1) Jews, (2) Greeks (Hellenes, made to include Romans, thus meaning the civilized peoples of the Roman Empire, often rendered 'Gentiles' in Authorized Version), and (3) barbarians (the uncivilized, Acts 28:4; Rom. 1:14; 1 Cor. 14:11)." The injunction laid by Jesus upon the Twelve--"Go not into the way of the Gentiles"--was to restrain them for the time being from attempting to make converts among the Romans and Greeks, and to confine their ministry to the people of Israel.

3. Shaking the Dust from the Feet.--To ceremonially shake the dust from one's feet as a testimony against another was understood by the Jews to symbolize a cessation of fellowship and a renunciation of all responsibility for consequences that might follow. It became an ordinance of accusation and testimony by the Lord's instructions to His apostles as cited in the text. In the current dispensation, the Lord has similarly directed His authorized servants to so testify against those who wilfully and maliciously oppose the truth when authoritatively presented (see Doc. and Cov. 24:15; 60:15; 75:20; 84:92; 99:4). The responsibility of testifying before the Lord by this accusing symbol is so great that the means may be employed only under unusual and extreme conditions, as the Spirit of the Lord may direct.

4. The Two Bethsaidas.--It is held by many Bible students that Bethsaida, in the desert region adjoining which Jesus and the Twelve sought rest and seclusion, was the town of that name in Perea, on the eastern side of the Jordan, and known more specifically as Bethsaida Julias to distinguish it from Bethsaida in Galilee, which latter was close to Capernaum. The Perean village of Bethsaida had been enlarged and raised to the rank of a town by the tetrarch, Philip, and by him had been named Julias in honor of Julia, daughter of the reigning emperor. The Gospel narratives of the voyage by which Jesus and His companions reached the place, and of the return therefrom, are conformable to the assumption that Bethsaida Julias in Perea and not Bethsaida in Galilee, was the town to which the "desert place" referred to was an outlying district.

5. The Earlier and the Later Evening.--Matthew specifies two evenings of the day on which the five thousand were fed; thus "when it was evening" the disciples asked Jesus to send away the multitude; and later, after the miraculous feeding and after the disciples had left by boat, and after the crowds had departed, "when the evening was come" Jesus was alone on the mountain (Matt. 14:15, 23; compare Mark 6:35, 47). Trench _Notes on the Miracles_, (p. 217) says: "St. Matthew and St. Mark with him, makes two evenings to this day--one which had already commenced before the preparations for the feeding of the multitude had begun (verse 15), the other now, when the disciples had entered into the ship and set forth on their voyage (verse 23). And this was an ordinary way of speaking among the Jews, the first evening being very much our afternoon ... the second evening being the twilight, or from six o'clock to twilight, on which absolute darkness followed." See Smith's _Dict._, article "Chronology," from which the following excerpt is taken: "'Between the two evenings' (margin of Exo. 12:6; Numb. 9:3; 28:4) is a natural division between the late afternoon when the sun is low, and the evening when his light has not wholly disappeared, the two evenings into which the natural evening would be cut by the commencement of the civil day if it began at sunset."

6. Watches of the Night.--During the greater part of Old Testament time, the people of Israel divided the night into three watches, each of four hours, such a period being that of individual sentinel duty. Before the beginning of the Christian era, however, the Jews had adopted the Roman order of four night-watches, each lasting three hours. These were designated numerically, e.g. the fourth watch mentioned in the text (see Matt. 14:25), or as even, midnight, cock-crowing, and morning (see Mark 13:35). The fourth watch was the last of the three-hour periods between sunset and sunrise, or between 6 p.m. and 6 a.m. and therefore extended from 3 to 6 o'clock in the morning.

7. The Hem of the Garment.--The faith of those who believed that if they could but touch the border of the Lord's garment they would be healed, is in line with that of the woman who was healed of her long-standing malady by so touching His robe (see Matt. 9:21; Mark 5:27, 28; Luke 8:44). The Jews regarded the border or hem of their outer robes as of particular importance, because of the requirement made of Israel in earlier days (Numb. 15:38, 39) that the border be fringed and supplied with a band of blue, as a reminder to them of their obligations as the covenant people. The desire to touch the hem of Christ's robe may have been associated with this thought of sanctity attaching to the hem or border.

8. Traditions Concerning Manna.--The supplying of manna to the Israelites incident to the exodus and the long travel in the wilderness, was rightly regarded as a work of surpassing wonder (Exo. 16:14-36; Numb. 11:7-9; Deut. 8:3, 16; Josh. 5:12; Psa. 78:24, 25). Many traditions, some of them perniciously erroneous, gathered about the incident, and were transmitted with invented additions from generation to generation. In the time of Christ the rabbinical teaching was that the manna on which the fathers had fed was literally the food of the angels, sent down from heaven; and that it was of diverse taste and flavor to suit all ages, conditions, or desires; to one it tasted like honey, to another as bread, etc.; but in all Gentile mouths it was bitter. Moreover it was said that the Messiah would give an unfailing supply of manna to Israel when He came amongst them. These erroneous conceptions in part explain the demand of those who had been fed on barley loaves and fishes, for a sign that would surpass the giving of manna in the olden days, as evidence of the Messiahship of Jesus.

9. Faith a Gift of God.--"Though within the reach of all who diligently strive to gain it, faith is nevertheless a divine gift, and can be obtained only from God (Matt. 16:17; John 6:44, 65; Eph. 2:8; 1 Cor. 12:9; Rom. 12:3; Moroni 10:11). As is fitting for so priceless a pearl, it is given to those only who show by their sincerity that they are worthy of it, and who give promise of abiding by its dictates. Although faith is called the first principle of the Gospel of Christ, though it be in fact the foundation of all religion, yet even faith is preceded by sincerity of disposition and humility of soul, whereby the word of God may make an impression upon the heart (Rom. 10:17). No compulsion is used in bringing men to a knowledge of God; yet, as fast as we open our hearts to the influences of righteousness, the faith that leads to life eternal will be given us of our Father."--_Articles of Faith_, v:16.

10. Spiritual Symbolism of Eating.--"The idea of eating, as a metaphor for receiving spiritual benefit, was familiar to Christ's hearers, and was as readily understood as our expressions--'devouring a book,' or 'drinking in' instruction. In Isaiah 3:1, the words 'the whole stay of bread,' were explained by the rabbis as referring to their own teaching, and they laid it down as a rule, that wherever, in Ecclesiastes, allusion was made to food or drink, it meant study of the law, and the practise of good works. It was a saying among them--'In the time of the Messiah the Israelites will be fed by Him.' Nothing was more common in the schools and synagogs than the phrases of eating and drinking, in a metaphorical sense. 'Messiah is not likely to come to Israel,' said Hillel, 'for they have already eaten Him'--that is, greedily received His words--'in the days of Hezekiah.' A current conventionalism in the synagogs was that the just would 'eat the Shekinah.' It was peculiar to the Jews to be taught in such metaphorical language. Their rabbis never spoke in plain words, and it is expressly said that Jesus submitted to the popular taste, for 'without a parable spake he not unto them' (Mark 4:34)."--Geikie, _Life and Words of Christ_, vol. i, p. 184.

11. The Crucial Nature of the Discourse.--Commenting on the effect of our Lord's discourse (John 6:26-71), Edersheim (vol. ii, p. 36) says: "Here then we are at the parting of the two ways; and just because it was the hour of decision, did Christ so clearly set forth the highest truths concerning Himself, in opposition to the views which the multitude entertained about the Messiah. The result was yet another and a sorer defection. Upon this many of His disciples went back, and walked no more with Him. Nay, the searching trial reached even unto the hearts of the Twelve. Would they also go away? It was an anticipation of Gethsemane--its first experience. But one thing kept them true. It was the experience of the past. This was the basis of their present faith and allegiance. They could not go back to their old past; they must cleave to Him. So Peter spake it in name of them all: Lord, to whom shall we go? Words of eternal life hast thou! Nay, and more than this, as the result of what they had learned: And we have believed and know that thou art the Holy One of God. It is thus, also, that many of us, whose thoughts may have been sorely tossed, and whose foundations terribly assailed, may have found our first resting-place in the assured, unassailable spiritual experience of the past. Whither can we go for words of eternal life, if not to Christ? If He fails us, then all hope of the eternal is gone. But He has the words of eternal life--and we believed when they first came to us; nay, we know that He is the Holy One of God. And this conveys all that faith needs for further learning. The rest will He show when He is transfigured in our sight. But of these Twelve Christ knew one to be a devil--like that angel, fallen from highest height to lowest depth. The apostasy of Judas had already commenced in his heart. And the greater the popular expectancy and disappointment had been, the greater the reaction and the enmity that followed. The hour of decision was past, and the hand on the dial pointed to the hour of His death."

FOOTNOTES:

[694] Matt. 13:53-58; Mark 6:1-6.
[695] Luke 4:28-30. See pages 179-181.
[696] Pages 254, 274.
[697] Note 2, page 273.
[698] Note 1, end of chapter.
[699] Matt. 10:5-42; Mark 6:7-13; Luke 9:1-5.
[700] Mark 3:14.

[701] Matt. 10:5-42; Mark 6:7-13; Luke 9:1-6.
[702] Note 2, end of chapter.
[703] Matt. 28:19; Mark 16:15. Page 695 herein.
[704] Note 3, end of chapter.
[705] Matt. 10:18-20; compare Mark 13:9; Luke 12:10-12.
[706] Mark 6:7.
[707] John 5; pages 206, 216.
[708] Matt. 11:2-19; Luke 7:18-34; see page 252.
[709] Page 259.
[710] Mark 6:12, 13; Luke 9:10. Note similar testimony of the Seventy, who were sent out at a later time, and who returned rejoicing in the power that had been manifest in their ministry; Luke 10:17.
[711] Note 4, end of chapter.
[712] John 6:5-14; compare Matt. 14:15-21; Mark 6:35-44; Luke 9:12-17.
[713] John 6:4; Matt. 14:19; Mark 6:39.
[714] Note 5, end of chapter.
[715] Matt. 14:22-33; compare Mark 6:45-52; John 6:15-21.
[716] Page 321.
[717] Note 6, end of chapter.
[718] That is to say, "since" or "inasmuch".
[719] Compare Peter's impetuous leap into the sea to reach the resurrected Lord on the shore, John 21:7.
[720] Mark 6:52.
[721] Note that this is the first occurrence of this title in the Synoptic Gospels, as applied to Jesus by mortals; compare an earlier instance of its application by Nathanael, John 1:49.
[722] "Articles of Faith," v:11-13--"Faith a Principle of Power."
[723] Josephus, Wars. iii, 10:7, 8.
[724] Mark 6:53-56; compare Matt. 14:34-36. Note 7, end of chapter.
[725] John 6:22-27.
[726] Note 8, end of chapter.
[727] John 6:32-59.
[728] John 4:13-15; page 174 herein.
[729] Isa. 54:13; Jer. 31:34; Micah 4:2; compare Heb. 8:10; 10:16.
[730] Note 9, end of chapter.
[731] Note 10, end of chapter.
[732] Matt. 26:26-28; Mark 14:22-25; Luke 22:19, 20. Page 596.
[733] John 6:59-71.
[734] Luke 3:16, 17; Matt. 3:11, 12.
[735] Compare this confession (John 6:68, 69) with Peter's later testimony (Matt. 16:16). Note 11, end of chapter.

CHAPTER 22. A PERIOD OF DARKENING OPPOSITION.

Our Lord's last recorded discourse in the synagog at Capernaum, which followed close upon the miracle of feeding the five thousand and that of walking upon the water, marked the beginning of another epoch in the development of His life's work. It was the season of an approaching Passover festival; [736] and at the next succeeding Passover, one year later, as shall be shown, Jesus would be betrayed to His death. At the time of which we now speak, therefore, He was entering upon the last year of His ministry in the flesh. But the significance of the event is other and greater than that of a chronological datum-plane. The circumstance marked the first stage of a turn in the tide of popular regard toward Jesus, which theretofore had been increasing, and which now began to ebb. True, He had been repeatedly criticized and openly assailed by complaining Jews on many earlier occasions; but these crafty and even venomous critics were mostly of the ruling classes; the common people had heard Him gladly, and indeed many of them continued so to do;[737] nevertheless His popularity, in Galilee at least, had begun to wane. The last year of His earthly ministration was inaugurated by a sifting of the people who professed to believe His word, and this process of test, trial, and separation, was to continue to the end.

We are without information as to Jesus having attended this Passover feast; and it is reasonable to infer that in view of the increasing hostility on the part of the rulers, He refrained from going to Jerusalem on the occasion. Conjecture as to whether any of the Twelve went up to the festival is profitless; we are not told. Certain it is that immediately after this time, the detectives and spies, who had been sent from Jerusalem into Galilee to watch Jesus, became more active than ever in their critical espionage. They dogged His footsteps, noted every act, and every instance of omission of traditional or customary observance, and were constantly on the alert to make Him out an offender.

CEREMONIAL WASHINGS, "AND MANY SUCH LIKE THINGS,"[738]

Shortly after the Passover to which allusion has been made, and probably in accordance with a plan decided upon by the Jewish rulers, Jesus was visited by a delegation of Pharisees and scribes who had come from Jerusalem, and who made protest against the disregard of traditional requirements by His followers. It appears that the disciples, and almost certainly the Master Himself, had so far transgressed "the tradition of the elders" as to omit the ceremonial washing of hands before eating; the Pharisaic critics found fault, and came demanding explanation, and justification if such were possible. Mark tells us that the disciples were charged with having eaten with "defiled", or, as the marginal reading gives it, with "common" hands; and he interpolates the following concise and lucid note concerning the custom which the disciples were said to have ignored: "For the Pharisees, and all the Jews, except they wash their hands oft, eat not, holding the tradition of the elders. And when they come from the market, except they wash, they eat not. And many other things there be, which they have received to hold, as the washing of cups, and pots, brasen vessels, and of tables."[739] It should be borne in mind that the offense charged against the disciples was that of ceremonial uncleanness, not physical uncleanliness or disregard of sanitary propriety; they were said to have eaten with common or defiled hands, not specifically with dirty fingers. In all the externals of their man-made religionism, the Jews were insistent on scrupulous exactitude; every possibility of ceremonial defilement was to be carefully guarded against, and the effects thereof had to be counteracted by prescribed washings.[740]

To the question: "Why do thy disciples transgress the tradition of the elders? for they wash not their hands when they eat bread", Jesus gave no direct reply; but asked as a rejoinder: "Why do ye also transgress the commandment of God by your tradition?" To the Pharisaic mind this must have been a very sharp rebuke; for rabbinism held that rigorous compliance with the traditions of the elders was more important than observance of the law itself; and Jesus in His counter question put their cherished traditions as in direct conflict with the commandment of God. Adding to their discomfiture, He cited the prophecy of Isaiah, and applied to them whom He designated hypocrites, the prophet's words: "Well hath Esaias prophesied of you hypocrites, as it is written, This people honoureth me with their lips, but their heart is far from me. Howbeit in vain do they worship me, teaching for doctrines the commandments of men."[741] With deserved severity Jesus carried the lesson home to their consciences, declaring that they had laid aside the commandments of God in order that they might follow the traditions of men.

This accusing affirmation was followed by the citing of an undeniable instance: Moses had voiced the direct commandment of God in saying: "Honour thy father and thy mother," and had proclaimed the ordained penalty in extreme cases of unfilial conduct thus: "Whoso curseth father or mother, let him die";[742] but this law, though given of God direct to Israel, had been so completely superseded that any ungrateful and wicked son could find ready means, which their traditions had made lawful, of escaping all filial obligations, even though his parents were destitute. If a needy father or mother craved help of a son, he had but to say--What you ask of me is Corban--or in other words, an intended gift to God; and he was held to be legally exempt from all requirements to contribute of that substance to the support of his parents. [743] Other obligations could be similarly evaded. To declare that any article of property real or personal, or any part or proportion of one's possessions was "corban," was generally understood as an averment that the property so characterized was dedicated to the temple, or at least was intended to be devoted to ecclesiastical purposes, and would eventually be turned over to the officials, though the donor might continue to hold possession during a specified period, extending even to the end of his life. Property was often declared to be "corban" for other purposes than dedication to ecclesiastical use. The result of such established though utterly unlawful and pernicious traditions was, as Jesus emphatically stated to the Pharisees and scribes, to make the word of God of none effect, and, He added, "Many such like things do ye."

Turning from His titled visitors, He called the people together and proclaimed unto them the truth, as follows: "Hearken unto me every one of you, and understand: There is nothing from without a man, that entering into him can defile him: but the things which come out of him, those are they that defile the man. If any man have ears to hear, let him hear." This was directly in conflict with rabbinical precept and practise; the Pharisees were offended, for they had said that to eat with hands that had not been ritualistically cleansed was to defile the food touched, and in turn to become yet more defiled from the food thus rendered unclean.

The apostles were not sure that they understood the Master's lesson; though couched in plain, non-figurative language, it was to some of them very like a parable, and Peter asked an exposition. The Lord explained that the food one eats is but temporarily part of his body; having served its purpose of nourishing the tissues and supplying energy to the organism, it is eliminated; therefore the food that enters the body through the mouth is of small and transient importance compared with the utterances that issue from the mouth, for these, if evil, are truly defiling. As Jesus set forth: "Those things which proceed out of the mouth come forth from the heart; and they defile the man. For out of the heart proceed evil thoughts, murders, adulteries, fornications, thefts, false witness, blasphemies: these are the things which defile a man; but to eat with unwashen hands defileth not a man."[744]

Some of the disciples asked Jesus whether He knew that the Pharisees had taken offense at His saying; His answer was a further denunciation of Pharisaism: "Every plant, which my heavenly Father hath not planted, shall be rooted up. Let them alone: they be blind leaders of the blind. And if the blind lead the blind, both shall fall into the ditch." There could be no compromise between His doctrine of the kingdom and the corrupt Judaism of the time. The rulers were plotting against His life; if their emissaries chose to take offense at His words, let them be offended and stand the consequences; but blessed would they be if they were not offended because of Him.[745] He had no conciliatory measures to offer those whose inability to understand His meaning was the result of wilful obstinacy, or darkness of mind produced by persistence in sin.

WITHIN THE BORDERS OF TYRE AND SIDON.[746]

Unable to find in Galilee rest, seclusion, or adequate opportunity of instructing the Twelve as He desired to do, Jesus departed with them northward, and journeyed into the coasts or borders of Phenicia, a district commonly known by the names of its prominent cities, Tyre and Sidon. In one of the little towns near the border, the party took lodgings; but the attempt to secure privacy was futile, for the Master's presence "could not be hid." His fame had preceded Him beyond the boundaries of the land of Israel. On earlier occasions, people from the region of Tyre and Sidon had been among His listeners, and some of them had been blessed by His healing mercies.[747]

A woman, hearing of His presence within her own land, came asking a boon. Mark tells us she was a Greek, or more literally a Gentile[748] who spoke Greek, and by nationality a Syro-Phenician; Matthew says she was "a woman of Canaan"; these statements are in harmony, since the Phenicians were of Canaanite descent. The Gospel-historians make clear the fact that this woman was of pagan or heathen birth; and we know that among the peoples so classed the Canaanites were held in particular disrepute by the Jews. The woman cried aloud to Jesus, saying: "Have mercy on me, O Lord, thou son of David; my daughter is grievously vexed with a devil." Her words expressed at once faith in the Lord's power, and a fulness of mother-love, for she implored as though she were the afflicted sufferer. The fact that she addressed Jesus as Son of David demonstrates her belief that He was the Messiah of Israel. At first Jesus refrained from answering her. Undeterred, she pleaded the more, until the disciples besought the Lord saying: "Send her away; for she crieth after us." Their intervention was probably an intercession in her behalf; she could be quieted by the granting of her request; as it was, she was making an undesirable scene, probably on the street, and the Twelve knew well that their Master sought quietude. To them Jesus said: "I am not sent but unto the lost sheep of the house of Israel," and the remark must have reminded them of the restriction under which they had been sent out.[749]

The woman, with importunate desire came near, possibly entering the house; she fell at the Lord's feet and worshiped Him, pleading pitifully, "Lord, help me." To her Jesus said, "It is not meet to take the children's bread, and to cast it to dogs." The words, harsh as they may sound to us, were understood by her in the spirit of the Lord's intent. The original term here translated "dogs" connoted, as the narrative shows, not the vagrant and despized curs elsewhere spoken of in the Bible as typical of a degraded state, or of positive badness,[750] but literally the "little dogs" or domestic pets, such as were allowed in the house and under the table. Certainly the woman took no offense at the comparison, and found therein no objectionable epithet. Instantly she adopted the analogy, and applied it in combined argument and supplication,[751] "Truth, Lord: yet the dogs eat of the crumbs which fall from their masters' table;" or, in the words of Mark's version: "Yes, Lord: yet the dogs under the table eat of the children's crumbs." Her prayer was immediately granted; for Jesus said unto her, "O woman, great is thy faith: be it unto thee even as thou wilt. And her daughter was made whole from that very hour." Mark emphasizes the special recognition of her final plea, and adds: "And when she was come to her house, she found the devil gone out, and her daughter laid upon the bed." The woman's commendable persistency was based on the faith that overcomes apparent obstacles and endures even under discouragement. Her case reminds one of the lesson taught by the Lord on another occasion through the story of the importunate widow.[752]

Many have queried as to why Jesus delayed the blessing. We may not be able to fathom His purposes; but we see that, by the course He adopted, the woman's faith was demonstrated and the disciples were instructed. Jesus impressed upon her that she was not of the chosen people, to whom He had been sent; but His words prefigured the giving of the gospel to all, both Jew and Gentile: "Let the children _first_ be filled" He had said. The resurrected Christ was to be made known to every nation;[753] but His personal ministry as a mortal, as also that of the apostles while He was with them in the flesh, was directed to the house of Israel.[754]

IN THE COASTS OF DECAPOLIS.[755]

We are not told how long Jesus and the Twelve tarried in the land of Tyre and Sidon, nor which portions of the district they traversed. They went thence into the region adjoining the sea of Galilee on the east, "through the midst of the coasts of Decapolis."[756] Though still among semi-pagan peoples, our Lord was greeted by great crowds, amongst whom were many lame, blind, dumb, maimed, and otherwise afflicted; and them He healed. Great was the astonishment of these aliens, "when they saw the dumb to speak, the maimed to be whole, the lame to walk, and the blind to see: and they glorified the God of Israel."

Among the many who were healed was one of whom special mention is made. He was deaf and defective in speech. The people asked the Lord to lay His hands upon the man; but Jesus led him away from the multitude, put His fingers in the man's ears, spat, and touched the man's tongue; then looking upward in prayer, and sighing the while, He uttered a word of command in Aramaic, "Ephphatha, that is, Be opened. And straightway his ears were opened, and the string of his tongue was loosed, and he spake plain." The manner of effecting this cure was different again from the usual mode of our Lord's healing ministrations. It may be that by the finger-touch to the closed ears and to the bound tongue, the man's faith was strengthened and his confidence in the Master's power increased. The people were forbidden to tell abroad what they had witnessed; but the more they were charged the more they published the news. Their conclusion as to Jesus and His works was: "He hath done all things well: he maketh both the deaf to hear, and the dumb to speak."

ANOTHER MEAL IN THE DESERT; OVER FOUR THOUSAND FED.[757]

For three days the glad crowds remained with Jesus and the apostles. Camping out at that season and in that region entailed no great hardship incident to exposure. Their supply of food, however, had become exhausted; and many of them were far from home. Jesus had compassion upon the people, and was loath to send them away fasting, lest they would faint by the way. When He spoke to the disciples on the matter they intimated the impossibility of feeding so great a number, for the entire stock of food at hand comprized but seven loaves and a few little fishes. Had they forgotten the former occasion on which a greater multitude had been fed and filled with but five loaves and two small fishes? Rather let us believe that the disciples remembered well, yet deemed it beyond their duty or privilege to suggest a repetition of the miracle. But the Master commanded; and the people seated themselves on the ground. Blessing and dividing the small provision as before, He gave to the disciples and they distributed to the multitude. Four thousand men, beside women and children, were abundantly fed; and of the broken but uneaten food there remained enough to fill seven baskets. With no semblance of the turbulent enthusiasm that had followed the feeding of the five thousand, this multitude dispersed quietly and returned to their homes, grateful and doubly blessed.

AGAIN BESET BY SIGN-SEEKERS.[758]

Jesus and the apostles returned by boat to the western shore of the lake, and landed near Magdala and Dalmanutha. These towns are understood to have been so close together as to virtually make the latter a suburb of the other. Here the party was met by the ever-vigilant Pharisees, who on this occasion were accompanied by their usually unfriendly rivals, the Sadducees. That the two parties had temporarily laid aside their mutual differences, and had combined their forces in the common cause of opposition to Christ, is a demonstration of the determined purpose of the ecclesiastical authorities to find occasion against Him, and, if possible, destroy Him. Their immediate object was to further alienate the common people, and to counteract the influence of His former teachings with the masses. They set anew the old-time snare of demanding from Him a supernatural sign of His Messiahship, though thrice already had they or others of their kind so attempted to entrap Him, and thrice had they been foiled.[759] Before them, Satan in person had similarly tried and failed.[760] To their present impertinent and impious demand He gave a brief and definite refusal coupled with an exposure of their hypocrisy. This was His reply: "When it is evening, ye say, It will be fair weather: for the sky is red. And in the morning, It will be foul weather today: for the sky is red and lowring. O ye hypocrites, ye can discern the face of the sky; but can ye not discern the signs of the times? A wicked and adulterous generation seeketh after a sign; and there shall no sign be given unto it, but the sign of the prophet Jonas. And he left them, and departed."[761]

THE LEAVEN OF THE PHARISEES AND OF THE SADDUCEES.[762]

Again with the Twelve upon the water, since on the Galilean coast neither peace nor opportunity for effective teaching was found, Jesus directed the vessel's course toward the north-easterly shore. When well out from land, He said to His companions: "Take heed and beware of the leaven of the Pharisees and of the Sadducees," and, as Mark adds, "and of the leaven of Herod." In their hasty departure the disciples had forgotten to take a supply of food; they had with them but a single loaf. They construed His words respecting leaven as a reference to bread, and possibly as a reproof for their neglect. Jesus chided them as of little faith for thinking then of material bread, and refreshed their recollection of the miracles by which the multitudes had been fed, so that their lack of loaves would not further trouble them. Finally they were made to understand that the Master's warning was directed against the false doctrines of the Pharisees and those of the Sadducees, and against the political aspirations of the scheming Herodians.[763]

The party left the boat near the site of the first miraculous feeding of the multitude, and made their way to Bethsaida Julias. A blind man was brought, and Jesus was asked to touch him. He took the sightless one by the hand, led him outside the town, applied saliva to his eyes, laid hands upon him in a ministration, and asked him if he could see. The man answered that he saw dimly, but was unable to distinguish men from trees. Applying His hands to the man's eyes, Jesus told him to look up; the man did so and saw clearly. Bidding him not to enter the town, nor to tell of his deliverance from blindness to any in the place, the Lord sent him away rejoicing. This miracle presents the unique feature of Jesus healing a person by stages; the result of the first ministration was but a partial recovery. No explanation of the exceptional circumstance is given.

THOU ART THE CHRIST.[764]

Accompanied by the Twelve, Jesus continued His way northward to the neighborhood or "coasts" of Cesarea Philippi, an inland city situated near the eastern and principal source of the Jordan, and near the foot of Mount Hermon.[765] The journey afforded opportunity for special and confidential instruction to the apostles. Of them Jesus asked: "Whom do men say that I the Son of man am?" In reply they reported the rumors and popular fancies that had come to their notice. Some people, sharing the superstitious fears of the conscience-stricken Herod Antipas, said that Jesus was John the Baptist returned to life, though such a belief could not have been entertained seriously by many, as John and Jesus were known to have been contemporaries; others said He was Elias, or more exactly, Elijah; still others suggested He was Jeremiah or some other one of the ancient prophets of Israel. It is significant that among all the conceptions of the people as to the identity of Jesus there was no intimation of belief that He was the Messiah. Neither by word nor deed had He measured up to the popular and traditional standard of the expected Deliverer and King of Israel. Fleeting manifestations of evanescent hope that He might prove to be the looked-for Prophet, like unto Moses, had not been lacking; but all such incipient conceptions had been neutralized by the hostile activity of the Pharisees and their kind. To them it was a matter of supreme though evil determination to maintain in the minds of the people the thought of a yet future, not a present, Messiah.

With deep solemnity, and as a soul-searching test for which the Twelve had been in unconscious preparation through many months of close and privileged companionship with their Lord, Jesus asked of them: "But whom say ye that I am?" Answering for all, but more particularly testifying as to his own conviction, Peter, with all the fervor of his soul, voiced the great confession: "Thou art the Christ, the Son of the living God." This was no avowal of mere belief, no expression of a result at which he had arrived by mental process, no solution of a problem laboriously worked out, no verdict based on the weighing of evidence; he spoke in the sure knowledge that knows no question and from which doubt and reservation are as far removed as is the sky from the ground.

"And Jesus answered and said unto him, Blessed art thou, Simon Barjona: for flesh and blood hath not revealed it unto thee, but my Father which is in heaven." Peter's knowledge, which was also that of his brethren, was of a kind apart from all that man may find out for himself; it was a divine bestowal, in comparison with which human wisdom is foolishness and the treasure of earth but dross. Addressing Himself further to the first of the apostles, Jesus continued: "And I say also unto thee, That thou art Peter, and upon this rock I will build my church; and the gates of hell shall not prevail against it. And I will give unto thee the keys of the kingdom of heaven: and whatsoever thou shalt bind on earth shall be bound in heaven: and whatsoever thou shalt loose on earth shall be loosed in heaven."

Through direct revelation from God Peter knew that Jesus was the Christ; and upon revelation, as a rock of secure foundation, the Church of Christ was to be built.[766] Though torrents should fall, floods roll, winds rage, and all beat together upon that structure, it would not, could not, fall, for it was founded upon a rock;[767] and even the powers of hell would be impotent to prevail against it. By revelation alone could or can the Church of Jesus Christ be builded and maintained; and revelation of necessity implies revelators, through whom the will of God may be made known respecting His Church. As a gift from God comes the testimony of Jesus into the heart of man. This principle was comprized in the Master's teachings at Capernaum, that none could come to Him save such as the Father would bring.[768] The Lord's promise, that unto Peter He would give "the keys of the kingdom of heaven," embodies the principle of divine authority in the Holy Priesthood, and of the commission of presidency. Allusion to keys as symbolical of power and authority is not uncommon in Jewish literature, as was well understood in that period and is generally current today.[769] So also the analogies of binding and loosing as indicative of official acts were then usual, as they are now, particularly in connection with judicial functions. Peter's presidency among the apostles was abundantly manifest and generally recognized after the close of our Lord's mortal life. Thus, it was he who spoke in behalf of the Eleven, in the council meeting at which a successor to the traitor Iscariot was chosen; he was the spokesman of his brethren on the occasion of the Pentecostal conversion; it was he who opened the doors of the Church to the Gentiles;[770] and his office of leadership is apparent throughout the apostolic period.

The confession by which the apostles avowed their acceptance of Jesus as the Christ, the Son of the living God, was evidence of their actual possession of the spirit of the Holy Apostleship, by which they were made particular witnesses of their Lord. The time for a general proclamation of their testimony had not arrived, however; nor did it come until after Christ had emerged from the tomb a resurrected, immortalized Personage. For the time being they were charged "that they should tell no man that he was Jesus the Christ." Proclamation of Jesus as the Messiah, particularly if made by the apostles who were publicly known as His most intimate disciples and associates, or open assumption of the Messianic title by Himself, would have aggravated the hostility of the rulers, which had already become a grave interference if not an actual menace to the Savior's ministry; and seditious uprisings against the political government of Rome might easily have resulted. A yet deeper reason for the secrecy enjoined upon the Twelve appears in the fact that the Jewish nation was not prepared to accept their Lord; and to ignore Him through lack of certain knowledge involved a lesser degree of culpability than would have attached to an unpalliated rejection. The particular mission of the apostles at a time then future was to proclaim to all nations Jesus, the crucified and resurrected Christ.

From the time of Peter's confession however, Jesus instructed the Twelve more plainly and with greater intimacy concerning the future developments of His mission, and particularly as touching His appointed death. On earlier occasions He had referred in their hearing to the cross, and to His approaching death, burial and ascension; but the mention in each case was in a measure figurative, and they had apprehended but imperfectly if at all. Now, however, He began to show, and often afterward made plain unto them, "how that he must go unto Jerusalem, and suffer many things of the elders and chief priests and scribes, and be killed, and be raised again the third day."

Peter was shocked at this unqualified declaration, and, yielding to impulse, remonstrated with Jesus, or, as two of the evangelists state, "began to rebuke him," even going so far as to say: "This shall not be unto thee."[771] The Lord turned upon him with this sharp reproof: "Get thee behind me, Satan: thou art an offence unto me: for thou savourest not the things that be of God, but those that be of men." Peter's words constituted an appeal to the human element in Christ's nature; and the sensitive feelings of Jesus were wounded by this suggestion of unfaithfulness to His trust, coming from the man whom He had so signally honored but a few moments before. Peter saw mainly as men see, understanding but imperfectly the deeper purposes of God. Though deserved, the rebuke he received was severe. The adjuration, "Get thee behind me, Satan," was identical with that used against the arch-tempter himself, who had sought to beguile Jesus from the path upon which He had entered,[772] and the provocation in the two instances was in some respects similar—the temptation to evade sacrifice and suffering, though such was the world's ransom, and to follow a more comfortable way.[773] The forceful words of Jesus show the deep emotion that Peter's ill-considered attempt to counsel if not to tempt his Lord had evoked.

Beside the Twelve, who were immediately about the Lord's person, others were nearby; it appears that even in those remote parts, far removed from the borders of Galilee—the habitat of a heathen population, with whom, however, many Jews were intermixed—the people gathered around the Master. These He now called together, and to them and the disciples said: "If any man will come after me, let him deny himself, and take up his cross, and follow me." Here the frightful figure of the cross was again made prominent. There was left no shadow of excuse for the thought that devotion to Christ would not mean denial and privation. He who would save his life at the cost of duty, as Peter had just suggested that Christ should do, would surely lose it in a sense worse than that of physical death; whereas he who stood willing to lose all, even life itself, should find the life that is eternal.

As evincing the soundness of His teachings, Jesus uttered what has since become an inspiring aphorism of life: "For what is a man profited, if he shall gain the whole world, and lose his own soul? or what shall a man give in exchange for his soul?" Whosoever is ashamed of Christ because of His lowly estate, or through offense at His teachings, shall yet find that the Son of Man, when He comes in the glory of the Father, with attending cohorts of angels, will be ashamed of that man. The record of this memorable day in the Savior's life closes with His blessed promise: "Verily I say unto you, There be some standing here, which shall not taste of death, till they see the Son of man coming in his kingdom."[774]

NOTES TO CHAPTER 22.

1. Passover Celebrations Comprized within the Period of Our Lord's Public Ministry.—The dates on which specific acts occurred in the ministry of Jesus are difficult if not impossible to fix, except in few instances; and as heretofore stated and reiterated, even the order of events is often found to be uncertain. It will be remembered that Jesus was in Jerusalem at the time of the Passover soon after His baptism, and that on the visit referred to He forcibly cleared the temple courts of traffickers and their property. This is known as the _first_ Passover during the public life of Jesus. If the unnamed "feast of the Jews" referred to by John (5:1) was a Passover, as many Bible students hold, it marked the close of the year following the cleansing the temple; it is commonly spoken of and written about as the _second_ Passover in the course of our Lord's ministry. Then the Passover near which Jesus fed the five thousand (John 6:4) would be the _third_, and would mark the expiration of two years and a fraction since the baptism of Jesus; it certainly marks the beginning of the last year of the Savior's life on earth.

2. Ceremonial Ablutions.—The numerous washings required by Jewish custom in the time of Christ were admittedly incident to rabbinism and "the tradition of the elders" and not in compliance with the Mosaic law. Under certain conditions, successive washings were prescribed, in connection with which we find mention of "first," "second" and "other" waters, the "second water" being necessary to wash away the "first water," which had become defiled by contact with the "common" hands; and so further with the later waters. Sometimes the hands had to be dipped or immersed; at other times they were to be cleansed by pouring, it being necessary that the water be allowed to run to the wrist or the elbow according to the degree

of supposed defilement; then again, as the disciples of Rabbi Shammai held, only the finger tips, or the fingers up to the knuckles, needed to be wetted under particular circumstances. Rules for the cleansing of vessels and furniture were detailed and exacting; distinct methods applied respectively to vessels of clay, wood, and metal. Fear of unwittingly defiling the hands led to many extreme precautions. It being known that the Roll of the Law, the Roll of the Prophets, and other scriptures, when laid away were sometimes touched, scratched, or even gnawed by mice, there was issued a rabbinical decree, that the Holy Scriptures, or any part thereof comprizing as many as eighty-five letters (the shortest section in the law having just that number), defiled the hands by mere contact. Thus the hands had to be ceremonially cleansed after touching a copy of the scriptures, or even a written passage therefrom.

Emancipation from these and "many such like things" must have been relief indeed. Escape from this thraldom Jesus freely offered, saying: "Come unto me, all ye that labour and are heavy laden, and I will give you rest. Take my yoke upon you, and learn of me; for I am meek and lowly in heart; and ye shall find rest unto your souls. For my yoke is easy, and my burden is light." (Matt. 11:28-30.)

3. "Corban," a Gift.--The law of Moses prescribed rules relating to vows (Lev. 27; Numb. 30). "Upon these rules," says the writer in Smith's _Bible Dict._, "the traditionalists enlarged, and laid down that a man might interdict himself by vow, not only from using for himself, but from giving to another or receiving from him, some particular object whether of food or any other kind whatsoever. The thing thus interdicted was considered as corban. A person might thus exempt himself from any inconvenient obligation under plea of corban. Our Lord denounced practises of this sort (Matt. 15:5; Mark 7:11), as annulling the spirit of the law."

The revised version, Matt. 15:5 is made to read "But ye say, Whosoever shall say to his father or his mother, That wherewith thou mightest have been profited by me is given to God; he shall not honor his father (or, his mother)." The following account of this pernicious custom appears in the _Commentary on The Holy Bible_ edited by Dummelow: "'Corban,' meaning originally a sacrifice or a gift to God, was used in New Testament times as a mere word of vowing, without implying that the thing vowed would actually be offered or given to God. Thus a man would say 'Corban to me is wine for such a time,' meaning that he took a vow to abstain from wine. Or a man would say to a friend 'Corban to me for such a time is whatsoever I might be profited by thee,' meaning that for such a time he vowed that he would receive neither hospitality nor any other benefit from his friend. Similarly, if a son said to his father or mother, 'Corban is whatsoever thou mightest have profited by me' he took a vow not to assist his father or mother in any way, however much they might require it. A vow of this kind was held by the scribes to excuse a man from the duty of supporting his parents, and thus by their tradition they made void the word of God."

4. The "Dogs" that Eat of the Crumbs.--The woman's fervid rejoinder, "Truth, Lord: yet the dogs eat of the crumbs which fall from their masters' table," (Matt. 15:27), is thus commented upon and paraphrased by Trench (_Notes on the Miracles_, p. 271): "The rendering of her answer in our translation is not, however, altogether satisfactory. For, indeed, she accepts the Lord's declaration, not immediately to make exception against the conclusion which He draws from it, but to show how in that very declaration is involved the granting of her petition. 'Saidest thou dogs? It is well; I accept the title and the place; for the dogs have a portion of the meal,--not the first, not the children's portion, but a portion still,--the crumbs which fall from the master's table. In this very putting of the case, Thou bringest us heathen, Thou bringest me, within the circle of the blessings which God, the Great Householder, is ever dispensing to His family. We also belong to His household, though we occupy but the lowest place therein.'"

The Dummelow _Commentary_, on Matt. 15:26, states in part as follows: "The rabbis often spoke of the Gentiles as dogs, e.g. 'He who eats with an idolater is like one who eats with a dog.' ... 'The nations of the world are compared to dogs.' 'The holy convocation belongs to you, not to the dogs.' Yet Jesus in adopting the contemptuous expression slightly softens it. He says not 'dogs,' but 'little dogs,' i.e. household, favorite, dogs; and the woman cleverly catches at the expression, arguing that if the Gentiles are household dogs, then it is only right that they should be fed with the crumbs that fall from their masters' table." Edersheim, referring to the original text, says: "The term means 'little dogs,' or 'house dogs.'"

5. Decapolis.--The name means "the ten cities," and was applied to a region of indefinite boundaries lying mostly on the east of Jordan and southerly from the sea of Galilee. Scythopolis, which Josephus (Wars of the Jews, iii, 9:7) refers to as the largest of the ten cities, was on the west side of the river. There is lack of agreement among historians as to the cities comprized under the name. Biblical mention (Matt. 4:25; Mark 5:20; 7:31) implies a general region rather than a definite area.

6. The Coasts of Cæsarea Philippi.--The term "coast" as it appears in the Bible (authorized, or King James version), is used to connote boundary, limit, or border, and not distinctively a seashore. (For examples see Exo. 10:4, 14, 19; Josh. 15:1, 4; Judg. 11:20; Matt. 2:16, etc.) It is applied therefore to inland areas, and frequently occurs as indicating a vicinity or neighborhood.

Cæsarea Philippi, a town located, as stated in the text, near Mount Hermon at the source of the Jordan, had been enlarged and beautified by Philip the tetrarch, and by him was named Cæsarea in honor of the Roman emperor. It was called Cæsarea Philippi to distinguish it from the already existing Cæsarea, which was situated on the Mediterranean shore of Samaria, and which in later literature came to be known as Cæsarea Palestina. Cæsarea Philippi is believed to be identical with the ancient Baal Gad (Josh. 11:17) and Baal Hermon (Judg. 3:3). It was known as a place of idolatrous worship, and while under Greek sovereignty was called Paneas in recognition of the mythological deity Pan. See Josephus, Ant. xviii, 2:1; this designation persists in the present Arabic name of the place, Banias.

7. Simon Peter and the "Rock" of Revelation.--Simon the son of Jonas, on the occasion of his first recorded interview with Jesus had received from the Lord's lips the distinguishing name-title "Peter," or in the Aramaic tongue "Cephas," the English equivalent of which is "a rock" or "a stone" (John 1:42; see also

page 140 herein). The name was confirmed upon the apostle on the occasion now under consideration (Matt. 16:18). Jesus said to him "thou art Peter," adding, "and upon this rock I will build my church." In the course of the general apostasy subsequent to the ancient apostolic ministry, the Bishop of Rome laid claim to supreme authority as the alleged lineal successor to Peter; and an erroneous doctrine gained currency to the effect that Peter was the "rock" upon which the Church of Christ was founded. Detailed consideration of this inconsistent and infamous claim cannot be undertaken here; it is sufficient to say that a church founded or dependent upon Peter or any other man would be Peter's or the other man's church, and not the Church of Jesus Christ. (See _The Great Apostasy_, chap 9; also B. of M., 3 Nephi 27:1-8; also chapter 40 herein). That upon Peter rested the responsibility of presidency in the ministry, after the ascension of the resurrected Christ, is not questioned; but that he was, even typically, the foundation upon which the Church was built, is at once unscriptural and untrue. The Church of Jesus Christ must authoritatively bear His name, and be guided by revelation, direct and continuous, as the conditions of its building require. Revelation from God to His servants invested with the Holy Priesthood through authorized ordination as was Peter, is the impregnable "rock" upon which the Church is built. (See _Articles of Faith_, xvi,--"Revelation.")

8. Christ's Rebuke to Peter.--In addressing Peter as "Satan," Jesus was obviously using a forceful figure of speech, and not a literal designation; for Satan is a distinct personage, Lucifer, that fallen, unembodied son of the morning (see page 7); and certainly Peter was not he. In his remonstrance or "rebuke" addressed to Jesus, Peter was really counseling what Satan had before attempted to induce Christ to do, or tempting, as Satan himself had tempted. The command, "Get thee behind me, Satan," as directed to Peter, is rendered in English by some authorities "Get thee behind me, tempter." The essential meaning attached to both Hebrew and Greek originals for our word "Satan" is that of an adversary, or "one who places himself in another's way and thus opposes him." (Zenos.) The expression "Thou art an offense unto me" is admittedly a less literal translation than "Thou art a stumbling-block unto me." The man whom Jesus had addressed as Peter--"the rock," was now likened to a stone in the path, over which the unwary might stumble.

9. Some to Live Until Christ Returns.--The Savior's declaration to the apostles and others in the neighborhood of C├ªsarea Philippi, "Verily I say unto you, There be some standing here which shall not taste of death, till they see the Son of man coming in his kingdom," (Matt. 16:28; compare Mark 9:1; Luke 9:27), has occasioned great and diverse comment. The event referred to, that of the Son of Man coming in the glory of His Father attended by the angels, is yet future. At least a partial fulfilment of the prediction is presented in the prolongation of the life of John the apostle, who was there present, and who yet lives in the flesh according to his desire (John 21:20-24; see further B. of M., 3 Nephi 28:1-6; Doc. and Cov. Sec. 7).

10. "Thou Art the Christ."--Peter's solemn and soulful confession of Jesus as the Christ is worded differently by each of the three synoptists. To many the most expressive version is that of Luke: "The Christ of God." On earlier occasions, some or all of the Twelve had acknowledged Jesus Christ to be the Son of God, e.g. following the miracle of walking upon the sea (Matt. 14:33), and again, after the crucial sermon at Capernaum (John 6:69); but it is evident that Peter's upwelling and reverential confession in answer to the Lord's question "But whom say ye that I am?" had a significance, greater in assurance and more exalted in kind, than had any prior expression of his conception concerning his Lord. Yet even the conviction given through direct revelation (Matt. 16:17) did not at the time comprize a comprehensive knowledge of the Savior's mission. Indeed, a fulness of understanding and assurance came to the apostles after the Lord's resurrection (compare Romans 1:4). Nevertheless, Peter's testimony in the land of C├ªsarea Philippi evidences a very exalted attainment. At that stage of the Savior's ministry, the public proclamation of His divine status would have been as the casting of pearls before swine (Matt. 7:6); therefore the Lord instructed the apostles that at that time "they should tell no man that he was Jesus the Christ."

FOOTNOTES:

[736] John 6:4. Note 1, end of chapter.
[737] Mark 12:37.
[738] Matt. 15:1-9; Mark 7:1-13.
[739] As the Oxford marginal note shows "beds" is a more literal rendering than "tables", the couches upon which the eaters reclined at table being meant. See page 261.
[740] Note 2, end of chapter.
[741] Mark 7:6, 7; see also Matt. 15:7-9; Isa. 29:13; compare the words of the resurrected Christ to the prophet Joseph Smith, in the present dispensation, P. of G.P., Joseph Smith, 2:19.
[742] Exo. 20:12; Deut. 5:16; Exo. 21:17; Lev. 20:9.
[743] Note 3, end of chapter.
[744] Matt. 15:10-20; compare Mark 7:14-23.
[745] Matt. 11:6; Luke 7:23; pages 255 and 274 herein.
[746] Matt. 15:21-28; Mark 7:21-30.
[747] Mark 3:8; Luke 6:17.
[748] See marginal reading in Oxford and Bagster Bibles; see also Note 2, page 345.
[749] Matt. 10:5, 6; see also page 328 herein.
[750] Deut. 23:18; 1 Sam. 17:43; 24:14; 2 Sam. 3:8; 16:9; Job 30:1; Matt. 7:6; Philip 3:2; Rev. 22:15.
[751] Note 4, end of chapter.
[752] Luke 18:1-8. Page 436.
[753] Matt. 28:19; Mark 16:15.

[754] Acts 3:25, 26; 13:46-48; Rom. 15:8.
[755] Mark 7:31-37; compare Matt. 15:29-31.
[756] Note 5, end of chapter.
[757] Matt. 15:32-39; Mark 8:1-9.
[758] Matt. 15:29; 16:1-5; Mark 8:10-13.
[759] John 2:18; 6:30; Matt. 12:38.
[760] Matt. 4:6, 7; Luke 4:9-12.
[761] Matt. 16:2-4; compare 12:38-41; pages 155-157 herein.
[762] Matt. 16:6-12; Mark 8:14-21; compare Luke 12:1.
[763] Page 68.
[764] Matt. 16:13-20; Mark 8:27-30; Luke 9:18-21. Note 10, end of chapter.
[765] Note 6, end of chapter.
[766] Note 7, end of chapter.
[767] Compare Matt. 7:24, 25.
[768] John 6:46; compare verses 37, 39, 40.
[769] See Isa. 22:22; Luke 11:52; Rev. 1:18; 3:7; compare Doc. and Cov. 6:28; 7:7; 27:5, 6, 9; 28:7; 42:69; 84:26; etc.
[770] Acts 1:15-26; 2:14-40; chap. 10, compare with 15:7.
[771] Matt. 16:22, 23; Mark 8:32, 33.
[772] Luke 4:8.
[773] Note 8, end of chapter.
[774] Note 9, end of chapter.

CHAPTER 23. THE TRANSFIGURATION.

Of the week following the events last considered, no record is found in the Gospels. We may safely assume that the time was devoted, in part at least, to the further instruction of the Twelve respecting the rapidly approaching consummation of the Savior's mission on earth, the awful circumstances of which the apostles were loath to believe possible. When the week had passed[775] Jesus took Peter, James, and John[776] and with them ascended a high mountain, where they would be reasonably safe from human intrusion.[777] There the three apostles witnessed a heavenly manifestation, which stands without parallel in history; in our Bible captions it is known as the Transfiguration of Christ.[778]

One purpose of the Lord's retirement was that of prayer, and a transcendent investiture of glory came upon Him as He prayed. The apostles had fallen asleep, but were awakened by the surpassing splendor of the scene, and gazed with reverent awe upon their glorified Lord. "The fashion of his countenance was altered, and his raiment was white and glistering." His garments, though made of earth-woven fabric, "became shining, exceeding white as snow; so as no fuller on earth can white them;" "and his face did shine as the sun." Thus was Jesus transfigured before the three privileged witnesses.

With Him were two other personages, who also were in a state of glorified radiance, and who conversed with the Lord. These, as the apostles learned by means not stated though probably as gathered from the conversation in progress, were Moses and Elias, or more literally to us, Elijah; and the subject of their conference with Christ was "his decease which he should accomplish at Jerusalem." As the prophet visitants were about to depart, "Peter said unto Jesus, Master, it is good for us to be here: and let us make three tabernacles; one for thee, and one for Moses, and one for Elias: not knowing what he said." Undoubtedly Peter and his fellow apostles were bewildered, "sore afraid" indeed; and this condition may explain the suggestion respecting the three tabernacles. "He wist not what to say;" yet, though his remark appears confused and obscure, it becomes somewhat plainer when we remember that, at the annual feast of Tabernacles, it was customary to erect a little bower, or booth of wattled boughs, for each individual worshiper, into which he might retire for devotion. So far as there was a purpose in Peter's proposition, it seems to have been that of delaying the departure of the visitants.

The sublime and awful solemnity of the occasion had not yet reached its climax. Even as Peter spake, "behold, a bright cloud overshadowed them: and behold a voice out of the cloud, which said, This is my beloved Son, in whom I am well pleased; hear ye him." It was Elohim,[779] the Eternal Father, who spake; and at the sound of that voice of supreme Majesty, the apostles fell prostrate. Jesus came and touched them, saying, "Arise, and be not afraid." When they looked they saw that again they were alone with Him.

The impression made upon the three apostles by this manifestation was one never to be forgotten; but they were expressly charged to speak of it to no man until after the Savior had risen from the dead. They were puzzled as to the significance of the Lord's reference to His prospective rising from the dead. They had heard with great sorrow, and reluctantly they were being brought to understand it to be an awful certainty, that their beloved Master was to "suffer many things, and be rejected of the elders, and of the chief priests, and scribes, and be killed."[780] Such had been declared to them before, in language devoid of ambiguity and admitting of no figurative construction; and with equal plainness they had been told that Jesus would rise again; but of this latter eventuality they had but dim comprehension. The present reiteration of these teachings seems to have left the three with no clearer understanding of their Lord's resurrection from the dead than they had before. They seem to have had no definite conception as to what was meant by a resurrection; "And they kept that saying with themselves, questioning one with another what the rising from the dead should mean."[781]

The comprehensiveness of the Lord's injunction, that until after His rising from the dead they tell no man of their experiences on the mount, prohibited them from informing even their fellows of the Twelve. Later, after the Lord had ascended to His glory, Peter testified to the Church of the wondrous experience, in this forceful way: "For we have not followed cunningly devised fables, when we made known unto you the power and coming of our Lord Jesus Christ, but were eyewitnesses of his majesty. For he received from God the Father honour and glory, when there came such a voice to him from the excellent glory, This is my beloved Son, in whom I am well pleased. And this voice which came from heaven we heard, when we were with him in the holy mount."[782] And John, reverently confessing before the world the divinity of the Word, the Son of God who had been made flesh to dwell among men, solemnly affirmed: "And we beheld his glory, the glory as of the only begotten of the Father, full of grace and truth."[783]

The divine purpose as shown forth in the Transfiguration may be as incomprehensible to the human mind as is a full conception of the attendant splendor from verbal description; some features of the results achieved are apparent, however. Unto Christ the manifestation was strengthening and encouraging. The prospect of the experiences immediately ahead must naturally have been depressing and disheartening in the extreme. In faithfully treading the path of His life's work, He had reached the verge of the valley of the shadow of death; and the human part of His nature called for refreshing. As angels had been sent to minister unto Him after the trying scenes of the forty days' fast and the direct temptation of Satan,[784] and as, in the agonizing hour of His bloody sweat, He was to be sustained anew by angelic ministry,[785] so at this critical and crucial period, the beginning of the end, visitants from the unseen world came to comfort and support Him. What of actual communication passed in the conference of Jesus with Moses and Elijah is not of full record in the New Testament Gospels.

The voice of His Father, to whom He was the Firstborn in the spirit-world, and the Only Begotten in the flesh, was of supreme assurance; yet that voice had been addressed to the three apostles rather than to Jesus, who had already received the Father's acknowledgment and attestation on the occasion of His baptism. The fullest version of the Father's words to Peter, James, and John is that recorded by Matthew: "This is my beloved Son, in whom I am well pleased; hear ye him." Aside from the proclamation of the Son's divine nature, the Father's words were otherwise decisive and portentous. Moses, the promulgator of the law, and Elijah the representative of the prophets and especially distinguished among them as the one who had not died,[786] had been seen ministering unto Jesus and subservient to Him. The fulfillment of the law and the superseding of the prophets by the Messiah was attested in the command-- Hear ye _Him_. A new dispensation had been established, that of the gospel, for which the law and the prophets had been but preparatory. The apostles were to be guided neither by Moses nor Elijah, but by _Him_, their Lord, Jesus the Christ.

The three selected apostles, "the Man of Rock and the Sons of Thunder" had seen the Lord in glory; and they marveled that such a thing could be at that time, since as they had interpreted the scriptures, it had been predicted that Elijah should precede the Messiah's triumphal advent. As they wended their way down the mountain-side, they asked the Master:[787] "Why then say the scribes that Elias must first come?" Jesus confirmed the prophecy that Elias should first come, that is, before the Lord's advent in glory, which event they had in mind; "But," He added, "I say unto you, That Elias is come already, and they knew him not, but have done unto him whatsoever they listed. Likewise shall also the Son of man suffer of them. Then the disciples understood that he spake unto them of John the Baptist." That John the Baptist would officiate "in the spirit and power of Elias," as the forerunner of the Christ, had been announced by the angel Gabriel to Zacharias,[788] before the Baptist's birth; and that John was _that_ particular Elias had been shown by Jesus in His memorable tribute to the Baptist's fidelity and greatness. That His words would not be generally accepted with understanding is evidenced by the context; Jesus, on that occasion, had said: "And if ye will receive it, this is Elias, which was for to come."[789]

It is not possible that Jesus could have meant that John was the same individual as Elijah; nor could the people have so understood His words, since the false doctrine of transmigration or reincarnation of spirits was repudiated by the Jews.[790] The seeming difficulty is removed when we consider that, as the name appears in the New Testament, "Elias" is used for "Elijah,"[791] with no attempt at distinction between Elijah the Tishbite, and any other person known as Elias. Gabriel's declaration that the then unborn John should manifest "the spirit and power of Elias" indicates that "Elias" is a title of office; every restorer, forerunner, or one sent of God to prepare the way for greater developments in the gospel plan, is an Elias. The appellative "Elias" is in fact both a personal name and a title.

In the present dispensation both the ancient Elias, who belonged to the Abrahamic dispensation and in the spirit of whose office many have officiated in different periods, and also the prophet Elijah, have appeared in person and have conferred their particular and separate authority upon latter-day bearers of the Holy Priesthood, and the keys of the powers exercized by them while on earth are today inherent in the restored Church of Jesus Christ. The authority of Elias is inferior to that of Elijah, the first being a function of the Lesser or Aaronic order of Priesthood, while the latter belongs to the Higher or Melchizedek Priesthood. Malachi's prediction, that before "the great and dreadful day of the Lord" Elijah the prophet would be sent to earth to "turn the heart of the fathers to the children, and the hearts of the children to their fathers,"[792] did not reach fulfilment in the mission of John the Baptist, nor in that of any other "Elias";[793] its complete realization was inaugurated on the third day of April, 1836, when Elijah appeared in the temple at Kirtland, Ohio, and committed to Joseph Smith and Oliver Cowdery the keys of the authority theretofore vested in himself. "The great and dreadful day of the Lord" was not the meridian of time; that awful though blessed period of consummation is yet future, but "near, even at the doors."[794]

NOTES TO CHAPTER 23.

1. Interval Between Time of Peter's Confession and that of the Transfiguration.--Both Matthew (17:1) and Mark (9:2) state that the Transfiguration occurred "after six days" following the time of Peter's great confession that Jesus was the Christ; while Luke (9:28) notes an interval of "about an eight days." It is probable that the six-day period was meant to be exclusive of the day on which the earlier events had occurred and of that on which Jesus and the three apostles retired to the mountain; and that Luke's "about an eight days" was made to include these two days. There is here no ground for a claim of discrepancy.

2. Peter, James, and John who were selected from among the Twelve as the only earthly witnesses of the transfiguration of Christ, had been similarly chosen as witnesses of a special manifestation, that of the raising of the daughter of Jairus (Mark 5:37; Luke 8:51); and, later, the same three were the sole witnesses of our Lord's night agony in Gethsemane (Matt. 26:37; Mark 14:33).

3. Place of the Transfiguration.--The mountain on which the Transfiguration occurred is neither named nor otherwise indicated by the Gospel-writers in such a way as to admit of its positive identification. Mount Tabor, in Galilee, has long been held by tradition as the site, and in the sixth century three churches were erected on its plateau-like summit, possibly in commemoration of Peter's desire to make three tabernacles or booths, one each for Jesus, Moses, and Elijah. Later a monastery was built there. Nevertheless, Mt. Tabor is now rejected by investigators, and Mt. Hermon is generally regarded as the place. Hermon stands near the northerly limits of Palestine, just beyond Cæsarea Philippi, where Jesus is known to have been a week before the Transfiguration. Mark (9:30) distinctly tells us that after His descent from the mount, Jesus and the apostles departed and went through Galilee. Weight of evidence is in favor of Hermon as the Mount of Transfiguration, though nothing that may be called decisive is known in the matter.

4. The Names "Elias" and "Elijah."--The following statement which appears in Smith's _Bible Dictionary_ is supported by authorities in general: "'Elias'" is "the Greek and Latin form of 'Elijah' given in

the Authorized Version of the Apocrypha and New Testament."

5. "The Spirit and Power of Elias."--That John the Baptist, in his capacity as a restorer, a forerunner, or as one sent to prepare the way for a work greater than his own, did officiate as an "Elias" is attested by both ancient and latter-day scripture. Through him water baptism for the remission of sins was preached and administered, and the higher baptism, that of the Spirit, was made possible. True to his mission, he has come in the last dispensation, and has restored by ordination the Priesthood of Aaron, which has authority to baptize. He thus prepared the way for the vicarious labor of baptism for the dead, the authority for which was restored by Elijah, (see page 149 herein), and which is preeminently the work by which the children and the fathers shall be united in an eternal bond.

On the 10th of March, 1844, the Prophet Joseph Smith gave the following exposition of the power of Elias as compared with higher authority: "The spirit of Elias is first, Elijah second, and Messiah last. Elias is a forerunner to prepare the way, and the spirit and power of Elijah is to come after, holding the keys of power, building the temple to the cap-stone, placing the seals of the Melchizedek Priesthood upon the house of Israel, and making all things ready; then Messiah comes to His temple, which is last of all."

"Messiah is above the spirit and power of Elijah, for He made the world, and was that spiritual rock unto Moses in the wilderness. Elijah was to come and prepare the way and build up the kingdom before the coming of the great day of the Lord, although the spirit of Elias might begin it."--_Hist. of the Church_, under date named.

6. Mention of the Lord's Approaching "Decease."--Of the three synoptists, Luke alone makes even brief mention of the matter upon which Moses and Elijah conversed with the Lord at the Transfiguration. The record states that the visitants, who appeared in glory, "spake of his decease which he should accomplish at Jerusalem" (Luke 9:31). It is significant that the _decease_, which the Lord should _accomplish_, not the _death_ that He should _suffer_ or _die_, was the subject of that exalted communion. The Greek word of which "decease" appears as the English equivalent in many of the MSS. of the Gospels, is one connoting "exodus," or "departure," and the word occurring in other early versions signifies glory. So also the Greek original of "accomplish," in the account of the Transfiguration, connotes the successful filling out or completion of a specific undertaking, and not distinctively the act of dying. Both the letter of the record and the spirit in which the recorder wrote indicate that Moses and Elijah conversed with their Lord on the glorious consummation of His mission in mortality--a consummation recognized in the law (personified in Moses) and the prophets (represented by Elijah)--and an event of supreme import, determining the fulfilment of both the law and the prophets, and the glorious inauguration of a new and higher order as part of the divine plan. The _decease_ that the Savior was then so soon to _accomplish_ was the voluntary surrender of His life in fulfilment of a purpose at once exalted and foreordained, not a _death_ by which He would passively _die_ through conditions beyond His control. (See pp. 418, and 662).

FOOTNOTES:

[775] Note 1, end of chapter.
[776] Note 2, end of chapter.
[777] Note 3, end of chapter.
[778] Matt. 17:1-8; Mark 9:2-8; Luke 9:28-36.
[779] Page 38.
[780] Mark 8:31. Note 6, end of chapter.
[781] Mark 9:10.
[782] 2 Peter 1:16-18.
[783] John 1:14.
[784] Matt. 4:11; Mark 1:13.
[785] Luke 22:43; compare John 12:27-28.
[786] 2 Kings 2:11.
[787] Matt. 17:10-13; Mark 9:11-13.
[788] Luke 1:17; pages 77 and 257 herein.
[789] Matt. 11:14.
[790] Edersheim, "Life and Times of Jesus," vol. ii, p. 79.
[791] Note 4, end of chapter.
[792] Mal. 4:5, 6; see page 149 herein.
[793] Note 5, end of chapter.
[794] Doc. and Cov. 110:13-16. See chapter 41, herein.

CHAPTER 24. FROM SUNSHINE TO SHADOW.

Our Lord's descent from the holy heights[795] of the Mount of Transfiguration was more than a physical return from greater to lesser altitudes; it was a passing from sunshine into shadow, from the effulgent glory of heaven to the mists of worldly passions and human unbelief; it was the beginning of His rapid descent into the valley of humiliation. From lofty converse with divinely-appointed ministers, from supreme communion with His Father and God, Jesus came down to a scene of disheartening confusion and a spectacle of demonized dominion before which even His apostles stood in impotent despair. To His sensitive and sinless soul the contrast must have brought superhuman anguish; even to us who read the brief account thereof it is appalling.

HEALING OF YOUTHFUL DEMONIAC.

Jesus and the three apostles returned from the mount on the morrow following the Transfiguration;[796] this fact suggests the assumption that the glorious manifestation had occurred during the night. At or near the base of the mountain the party found the other apostles, and with them a multitude of people, including some scribes or rabbis.[797] There was evidence of disputation and disturbance amongst the crowd; and plainly the apostles were on the defensive. At the unexpected approach of Jesus many of the people ran to meet Him with respectful salutations. Of the contentious scribes He asked: "What question ye with them?" thus assuming the burden of the dispute, whatever it might be, and so relieving the distressed disciples from further active participation. The scribes remained silent; their courage had vanished when the Master appeared. A man, "one of the multitude," gave, though indirectly, the answer. "Master," said he, kneeling at the feet of Christ, "I have brought unto thee my son, which hath a dumb spirit; and wheresoever he taketh him, he teareth him: and he foameth, and gnasheth with his teeth, and pineth away: and I spake to thy disciples that they should cast him out; and they could not."

The disciples' failure to heal the stricken youth had evidently brought upon them hostile criticism, taunts and ridicule from the unbelieving scribes; and their discomfiture must have been intensified by the thought that through them doubt had been cast upon the authority and power of their Lord. Pained in spirit at this--another instance of dearth of faith and consequent lack of power among His chosen and ordained servants--Jesus uttered an exclamation of intense sorrow: "O faithless generation, how long shall I be with you? how long shall I suffer you?" These words, in which there is evident reproof, however mild and pitying it may be, were addressed primarily to the apostles; whether exclusively so or to them and others is of minor importance. As Jesus directed, the afflicted lad was brought nearer; and the tormenting demon, finding himself in the Master's presence, threw his youthful victim into a terrible paroxysm, so that the boy fell to the ground and wallowed in convulsions, the while frothing and foaming at the mouth. With calm deliberation, which contrasted strongly with the eager impatience of the distracted parent, Jesus inquired as to when the malady had first befallen the lad. "Of a child," answered the father, adding, "And ofttimes it hath cast him into the fire, and into the waters, to destroy him." With pathetic eagerness he implored, "If thou canst do anything, have compassion on us and help us." The man spoke of his son's affliction as though shared by himself. "Help us," was his prayer.

To this qualifying expression "If thou canst do anything," which implied a measure of uncertainty as to the ability of the Master to grant what he asked, and this perhaps as in part a result of the failure of the apostles, Jesus replied: "If thou canst believe"; and added, "all things are possible to him that believeth." The man's understanding was enlightened; up to that moment he had thought that all depended upon Jesus; he now saw that the issue rested largely with himself. It is noteworthy that the Lord specified belief rather than faith as the condition essential to the case. The man was evidently trustful, and assuredly fervent in his hope that Jesus could help; but it is doubtful that he knew what faith really meant. He was receptive and eagerly teachable, however, and the Lord strengthened his feeble and uncertain belief. The encouraging explanation of the real need stimulated him to a more abounding trust. Weeping in an agony of hope he cried out: "Lord, I believe;" and then, realizing the darkness of error from which he was just beginning to emerge, he added penitently "help thou mine unbelief."[798]

Looking compassionately upon the writhing sufferer at His feet, Jesus rebuked the demon, thus: "Thou dumb and deaf spirit, I charge thee, come out of him, and enter no more into him. And the spirit cried, and rent him sore, and came out of him: and he was as one dead; insomuch that many said, He is dead. But Jesus took him by the hand, and lifted him up; and he arose;" and as Luke adds, "and delivered him again to his father." The permanency of the cure was assured by the express command that the evil spirit enter no more into the lad;[799] it was no relief from that present attack alone; the healing was permanent.

The people were amazed at the power of God manifested in the miracle; and the apostles who had tried and failed to subdue the evil spirit were disturbed. While on their mission, though away from their Master's helpful presence, they had successfully rebuked and cast out evil spirits as they had received special power and commission to do,[800] but now, during His absence of a day they had found themselves unable. When they had retired to the house, they asked of Jesus, "Why could not we cast him out?" The reply was: "Because of your unbelief;" and in further explanation the Lord said, "Howbeit this kind goeth not out but by prayer and fasting."[801]

Hereby we learn that the achievements possible to faith are limited or conditioned by the genuineness, the purity, the unmixed quality of that faith. "O ye of little faith;" "Where is your faith?" and "Wherefore didst thou doubt?"[802] are forms of admonitory reproof that had been repeatedly addressed to the apostles by the Lord. The possibilities of faith were now thus further affirmed: "Verily I say unto you, If ye have faith as a grain of mustard seed, ye shall say unto this mountain, Remove hence to yonder place; and it shall remove; and nothing shall be impossible unto you."[803] The comparison between effective faith and a grain of mustard seed is one of quality rather than of quantity; it connotes living, virile faith, like unto the seed, however small, from which a great plant may spring,[804] in contrast with a lifeless, artificial imitation, however prominent or demonstrative.

THE LORD'S DEATH AND RESURRECTION AGAIN PREDICTED.[805]

From the locality whereat the last miracle was wrought, Jesus departed with the Twelve, and passed through Galilee toward Capernaum. It is probable that they traveled by the less frequented roads, as He desired that His return should not be publicly known. He had gone into comparative retirement for a season, primarily it seems in quest of opportunity to more thoroughly instruct the apostles in their preparation for the work, which within a few months they would be left to carry on without His bodily companionship. They had solemnly testified that they knew Him to be the Christ; to them therefore He could impart much that the people in general were wholly unprepared to receive. The particular theme of His special and advanced instruction to the Twelve was that of His approaching death and resurrection; and this was dwelt upon again and again, for they were slow or unwilling to comprehend.

"Let these sayings sink down into your ears" was His forceful prelude on this occasion, in Galilee. Then followed the reiterated prediction, spoken in part in the present tense as though already begun in fulfilment: "The Son of man is delivered into the hands of men, and they shall kill him; and after that he is killed, he shall rise the third day." We read with some surprize that the apostles still failed to understand. Luke's comment is: "But they understood not this saying, and it was hid from them, that they perceived it not: and they feared to ask him of that saying." The thought of what the Lord's words might mean, even in its faintest outline, was terrifying to those devoted men; and their failure to comprehend was in part due to the fact that the human mind is loath to search deeply into anything it desires not to believe.

THE TRIBUTE MONEY--SUPPLIED BY A MIRACLE.[806]

Jesus and His followers were again in Capernaum. There Peter was approached by a collector of the temple tax, who asked: "Doth not your Master pay tribute?"[807] Peter answered "Yes." It is interesting to find that the inquiry was made of Peter and not directly of Jesus; this circumstance may be indicative of the respect in which the Lord was held by the people at large, and may suggest the possibility of doubt in the collector's mind as to whether Jesus was amenable to the tax, since priests and rabbis generally claimed exemption.

The annual capitation tax here referred to amounted to half a shekel or a didrachm, corresponding to about thirty-three cents in our money; and this had been required of every male adult in Israel since the days of the exodus; though, during the period of captivity the requirement had been modified.[808] This tribute, as prescribed through Moses, was originally known as "atonement money," and its payment was in the nature of a sacrifice to accompany supplication for ransom from the effects of individual sin. At the time of Christ the annual contribution was usually collected between early March and the Passover. If Jesus was subject to this tax, He was at this time several weeks in arrears.

The conversation between Peter and the tax-collector had occurred outside the house. When Peter entered, and was about to inform the Master concerning the interview, Jesus forestalled him, saying: "What thinkest thou, Simon? of whom do the kings of the earth take custom or tribute? of their own children, or of strangers? Peter saith unto him, Of strangers. Jesus saith unto him, Then are the children free."

Peter must have seen the inconsistency of expecting Jesus, the acknowledged Messiah, to pay atonement money, or a tax for temple maintenance, inasmuch as the temple was the House of God, and Jesus was the Son of God, and particularly since even earthly princes were exempted from capitation dues. Peter's embarrassment over his inconsiderate boldness, in pledging payment for his Master without first consulting Him, was relieved however by Jesus, who said: "Notwithstanding, lest we should offend them, go thou to the sea, and cast an hook, and take up the fish that first cometh up; and when thou hast opened his mouth, thou shalt find a piece of money: that take, and give unto them for me and thee."

The money was to be paid, not because it could be rightfully demanded of Jesus, but lest non-payment give offense and furnish to His opponents further excuse for complaint. The "piece of money," which Jesus said Peter would find in the mouth of the first fish that took his bait, is more correctly designated by the literal translation "stater,"[809] indicating a silver coin equivalent to a shekel, or two didrachms, and therefore the exact amount of the tax for two persons. "That take, and give unto them for me and thee" said Jesus. It is notable that He did not say "for us." In His associations with men, even with the Twelve, who of all were nearest and dearest to Him, our Lord always maintained His separate and unique status, in every instance making the fact apparent that He was essentially different from other men. This is illustrated by His expressions "My Father and your Father," "My God and your God,"[810] instead of our Father and our God. He reverently acknowledged that He was the Son of God in a literal sense that did not apply to any other being.

While the circumstances of the finding of the stater in the fish are not detailed, and the actual accomplishment of the miracle is not positively recorded, we cannot doubt that what Jesus had promised was realized, as otherwise there would appear no reason for introducing the incident into the Gospel narrative. The miracle is without a parallel or even a remotely analogous instance. We need not assume that the stater was other than an ordinary coin that had fallen into the water, nor that it had been taken by the fish in any unusual way. Nevertheless, the knowledge that there was in the lake a fish having a coin in its gullet, that the coin was of the denomination specified, and that that particular fish would rise, and be the first to rise to Peter's hook, is as incomprehensible to man's finite understanding as are the means by which any of Christ's miracles were wrought. The Lord Jesus held and holds dominion over the earth, the sea, and all that in them is, for by His word and power were they made.

The Lord's purpose in so miraculously supplying the money should be studiously considered. The assumption that superhuman power had to be invoked because of a supposed condition of extreme poverty on the part of Jesus and Peter is unwarranted. Even if Jesus and His companions had been actually penniless, Peter and his fellow fishermen could easily have cast their net, and, with ordinary success would have obtained fish enough to sell for the needed amount. Moreover, we find no instance of a miracle wrought by the Lord for personal gain or relief of His own need, however pressing. It appears probable, that by the means employed for obtaining the money, Jesus intentionally emphasized His exceptional reasons for redeeming Peter's pledge that the tax would be paid. The Jews, who did not know Jesus as the Messiah, but only as a Teacher of superior ability and a Man of unusual power, might have taken offense had He refused to pay the tribute required of every Jew. On the other hand, to the apostles and particularly to Peter who had been the mouth-piece of all in the great confession, the payment of the tax in ordinary course and without explanation by Jesus might have appeared as an admission that He was subject to the temple, and therefore less than He had claimed and less than they had confessed Him to be. His catechization of Peter had clearly demonstrated that He maintained His right as the King's Son, and yet would condescend to voluntarily give what could not be righteously demanded. Then, in conclusive demonstration of His exalted status, He provided the money by the utilization of knowledge such as no other man possessed.

AS A LITTLE CHILD.[811]

On the way to Capernaum the apostles had questioned among themselves, as they supposed beyond the Master's hearing; questioning had led to argument, and argument to disputation. The matter about which they were so greatly concerned was as to who among them should be the greatest in the kingdom of heaven. The testimony they had received convinced them beyond all doubt, that Jesus was the long-awaited Christ, and this had been supplemented and confirmed by His unqualified acknowledgment of His Messianic dignity. With minds still tinctured by the traditional expectation of the Messiah as both spiritual Lord and temporal King, and remembering some of the Master's frequent references to His kingdom and the blessed state of those who belonged thereto, and furthermore realizing that His recent utterances indicated a near crisis or climax in His ministry, they surrendered themselves to the selfish contemplation of their prospective stations in the new kingdom, and the particular offices of trust, honor, and emolument each most desired. Who of them was to be prime minister; who would be chancellor, who the commander of the troops? Personal ambition had already engendered jealousy in their hearts.

When they were together with Jesus in the house at Capernaum, the subject was brought up again. Mark tells us that Jesus asked: "What was it that ye disputed among yourselves by the way?" and that they answered not, because, as may be inferred, they were ashamed. From Matthew's record it may be understood that the apostles submitted the question for the Master's decision. The apparent difference of circumstance is unimportant; both accounts are correct; Christ's question to them may have eventually brought out their questions to Him. Jesus, comprehending their thoughts and knowing their unenlightened state of mind on the matter that troubled them, gave them an illustrated lesson. Calling a little child, whom He lovingly took into His arm, He said: "Verily I say unto you, Except ye be converted, and become as little children, ye shall not enter into the kingdom of heaven. Whosoever therefore shall humble himself as this little child, the same is greatest in the kingdom of heaven. And whoso shall receive one such little child in my name receiveth me. But whoso shall offend one of these little ones which believe in me, it were better for him that a millstone were hanged about his neck, and that he were drowned in the depth of the sea." With this lesson we may profitably associate a later teaching, that little children are typical of the kingdom of heaven.[812]

Even the apostles were in need of conversion;[813] respecting the matter at issue their hearts were turned, partly at least, from God and His kingdom. They had to learn that genuine humility is an attribute essential to citizenship in the community of the blessed; and that the degree of humility conditions whatsoever there is akin to rank in the kingdom; for therein the humblest shall be greatest.

Christ would not have had His chosen representatives become childish; far from it, they had to be men of courage, fortitude, and force; but He would have them become childlike. The distinction is important. Those who belong to Christ must become like children in obedience, truthfulness, trustfulness, purity, humility and faith. The child is an artless, natural, trusting believer; the childish one is careless, foolish, and neglectful. In contrasting these characteristics, note the counsel of Paul: "Brethren, be not children in understanding: howbeit in malice be ye children, but in understanding be men."[814] Children as such, and children as types of adults who are true believers, are closely associated in this lesson. Whosoever shall offend, that is cause to stumble or go astray, one such child of Christ, incurs guilt so great that it would have been better for him had he met death even by violence before he had so sinned.

Dwelling upon offenses, or causes of stumbling, the Lord continued: "Woe unto the world because of offences! for it must needs be that offences come; but woe to that man by whom the offence cometh!" Then, repeating some of the precious truths embodied in His memorable Sermon on the Mount, [815] He urged the overcoming of evil propensities whatever the sacrifice. As it is better that a man undergo surgical treatment though he lose thereby a hand, a foot, or an eye, than that his whole body be involved and his life forfeited, so is it commended that he cut off, tear away, or root out from his soul the passions of evil, which, if suffered to remain shall surely bring him under condemnation. In that state his conscience shall gnaw as an undying worm, and his remorse shall be as a fire that cannot be quenched. Every human soul shall be tested as by fire; and as the flesh of the altar sacrifices had to be seasoned with salt, as a type of preservation from corruption,[816] so also the soul must receive the saving salt of the gospel; and that salt must be pure and potent, not a dirty mixture of inherited prejudice and unauthorized tradition that has lost whatever saltness it may once have had. "Have salt in yourselves, and have peace one with another," was the Lord's admonition to the disputing Twelve.[817]

As applicable to children of tender years, and to child-like believers young and old, the Savior gave to the apostles this solemn warning and profound statement of fact: "Take heed that ye despise not one of these little ones; for I say unto you, That in heaven their angels do always behold the face of my Father which is in heaven." The mission of the Christ was presented as that of saving those who are temporarily lost, and who, but for His aid would be lost forever. In elucidation of His meaning, the Teacher presented a parable which has found place among the literary treasures of the world.

THE PARABLE OF THE LOST SHEEP.[818]

"How think ye? if a man have an hundred sheep, and one of them be gone astray, doth he not leave the ninety and nine, and goeth into the mountains, and seeketh that which is gone astray? And if so be that he find it, verily I say unto you, he rejoiceth more of that sheep, than of the ninety and nine which went not astray. Even so it is not the will of your Father which is in heaven, that one of these little ones should perish." In this effective analogy the saving purpose of Christ's mission is made prominent. He is verily the Savior. The shepherd is portrayed as leaving the ninety and nine, pastured or folded in safety we cannot doubt, while he goes alone into the mountains to seek the one that has strayed. In finding and bringing back the wayward sheep, he has more joy than that of knowing the others are yet safe. In a later version of this splendid parable, as addressed to the murmuring Pharisees and scribes at Jerusalem, the Master said of the shepherd on his finding the lost sheep:

"And when he hath found it, he layeth it on his shoulders, rejoicing. And when he cometh home, he calleth together his friends and neighbours, saying unto them, Rejoice with me; for I have found my sheep which was lost. I say unto you, that likewise joy shall be in heaven over one sinner that repenteth, more than over ninety and nine just persons, which need no repentance."[819]

Many have marveled that there should be greater rejoicing over the recovery of one stray sheep, or the saving of a soul that had been as one lost, than over the many who have not been in such jeopardy. In the safe-folded ninety and nine the shepherd had continued joy; but to him came a new accession of happiness, brighter and stronger because of his recent grief, when the lost was brought back to the fold. To this parable in connection with others of analogous import we shall recur in a later chapter.

IN MY NAME.[820]

In continuation of the lesson illustrated by the little child, Jesus said: "Whosoever shall receive this child in my name receiveth me: and whosoever shall receive me receiveth him that sent me: for he that is least among you all, the same shall be great." It may have been Christ's reference to deeds done in His name that prompted John to interject a remark at this point: "Master, we saw one casting out devils in thy name, and he followeth not us: and we forbad him, because he followeth not us. But Jesus said, Forbid him not: for there is no man which shall do a miracle in my name, that can lightly speak evil of me. For he that is not against us is on our part." The young apostle had allowed his zeal for the Master's name to lead to intolerance. That the man who had attempted to do good in the name of Jesus was evidently sincere, and that his efforts were acceptable to the Lord we cannot doubt; his act was essentially different from the unrighteous assumptions for which some others were afterward rebuked;[821] he was certainly a believer in Christ, and may have been one of the class from which the Lord was soon to select and commission special ministers and the Seventy.[822] In the state of divided opinion then existing among the people concerning Jesus, it was fair to say that all who were not opposed to Him were at least tentatively on His side. On other occasions He asserted that those who were not with Him were against Him.[823]

MY BROTHER AND I.[824]

The proper method of adjusting differences between brethren and the fundamental principles of Church discipline were made subjects of instruction to the Twelve. The first step is thus prescribed: "Moreover if thy brother shall trespass against thee, go and tell him his fault between thee and him alone: if he shall hear thee, thou hast gained thy brother." The rule of the rabbis was that the offender must make the first advance; but Jesus taught that the injured one should not wait for his brother to come to him, but go himself, and seek to adjust the difficulty; by so doing he might be the means of saving his brother's soul. If the offender proved to be obdurate, the brother who had suffered the trespass was to take two or three others with him, and again try to bring the transgressor to repentant acknowledgment of his offense; such a course provided for witnesses, by whose presence later misrepresentation would be guarded against.

Extreme measures were to be adopted only after all gentler means had failed. Should the man persist in his obstinacy, the case was to be brought before the Church, and in the event of his neglect or refusal to heed the decision of the Church, he was to be deprived of fellowship, thereby becoming in his relationship to his former associates "as an heathen man and a publican." In such state of non-membership he would be a fit subject for missionary effort; but, until he became repentant and manifested willingness to make amends, he could claim no rights or privileges of communion in the Church. Continued association with the unrepentant sinner may involve the spread of his disaffection, and the contamination of others through his sin. Justice is not to be dethroned by Mercy. The revealed order of discipline in the restored Church is similar to that given to the apostles of old.[825]

The authority of the Twelve to administer the affairs of Church government was attested by the Lord's confirming to them as a body the promise before addressed to Peter: "Verily I say unto you, Whatsoever ye shall bind on earth shall be bound in heaven: and whatsoever ye shall loose on earth shall be loosed in heaven."[826] Through unity of purpose and unreserved sincerity they would have power with God, as witness the Master's further assurance: "Again I say unto you, That if two of you shall agree on earth as touching any thing that they shall ask, it shall be done for them of my Father which is in heaven. For where two or three are gathered together in my name, there am I in the midst of them." Peter here broke in with a question: "Lord, how oft shall my brother sin against me, and I forgive him? till seven times?" He would fain have some definite limit set, and he probably considered the tentative suggestion of seven times as a very liberal measure, inasmuch as the rabbis prescribed a triple forgiveness only.[827] He may have chosen seven as the next number above three having a special Pharisaical significance. The Savior's answer was enlightening: "Jesus saith unto him, I say not unto thee, Until seven times: but, Until seventy times seven." This reply must have meant to Peter as it means to us, that to forgiveness man may set no bounds; the forgiveness, however, must be merited by the recipient.[828] The instruction was made memorable by the following story.

PARABLE OF THE UNMERCIFUL SERVANT.

"Therefore is the kingdom of heaven likened unto a certain king, which would take account of his servants. And when he had begun to reckon, one was brought unto him, which owed him ten thousand talents. But forasmuch as he had not to pay, his lord commanded him to be sold, and his wife, and children, and all that he had, and payment to be made. The servant therefore fell down, and worshipped him, saying, Lord, have patience with me, and I will pay thee all. Then the lord of that servant was moved with compassion, and loosed him, and forgave him the debt. But the same servant went out, and found one of his fellowservants, which owed him an hundred pence: and he laid hands on him, and took him by the throat, saying, Pay me that thou owest. And his fellowservant fell down at his feet, and besought him, saying, Have patience with me, and I will pay thee all. And he would not: but went and cast him into prison, till he should pay the debt. So when his fellowservants saw what was done, they were very sorry, and came and told unto their lord all that was done. Then his lord, after that he had called him, said unto him, O thou wicked servant, I forgave thee all that debt, because thou desiredst me: Shouldest not thou also have had compassion on thy fellowservant, even as I had pity on thee? And his lord was wroth, and delivered him to the tormentors, till he should pay all that was due unto him. So likewise shall my heavenly Father do also unto you, if ye from your hearts forgive not every one his brother their trespasses."[829]

Ten thousand talents are specified as expressive of a sum so great as to put the debtor beyond all reasonable possibility of paying. We may regard the man as a trusted official, one of the king's ministers, who had been charged with the custody of the royal revenues, or one of the chief treasurers of taxes; that he is called a servant introduces no inconsistency, as in an absolute monarchy all but the sovereign are subjects and servants. The selling of the debtor's wife and children and all that he had would not have been in violation of the law in the supposed case, which implies the legal recognition of slavery.[830] The man was in arrears for debt. He did not come before his lord voluntarily but had to be brought. So in the affairs of our individual lives periodical reckonings are inevitable; and while some debtors report of their own accord, others have to be cited to appear. The messengers who serve the summons may be adversity, illness, the approach of death; but, whatever, whoever they are, they enforce a rendering of our accounts.

The contrast between ten thousand talents and a hundred pence is enormous.[831] In his fellowservant's plea for time in which to pay the hundred pence, the greater debtor should have been reminded of the dire straits from which he had just been relieved; the words, "Have patience with me, and I will pay thee all," were identical with those of his own prayer to the king. The base ingratitude of the unmerciful servant justified the king in revoking the pardon once granted. The man came under condemnation, not primarily for defalcation and debt, but for lack of mercy after having received of mercy so abundantly. He, as an unjust plaintiff, had invoked the law; as a convicted transgressor he was to be dealt with according to the law. Mercy is for the merciful. As a heavenly jewel it is to be received with thankfulness and used with sanctity, not to be cast into the mire of undeservedness. Justice may demand retribution and punishment: "With what measure ye mete, it shall be measured to you again."[832] The conditions under which we may confidently implore pardon are set forth in the form of prayer prescribed by the Lord: "Forgive us our debts, as we forgive our debtors."[833]

NOTES TO CHAPTER 24.

1. Faith in Behalf of Others.--The supplication of the agonized father for the benefit of his sorely afflicted son--"Have compassion on us, and help us" (Mark 9:22)--shows that he made the boy's case his own. In this we are reminded of the Canaanite woman who implored Jesus to have mercy on her, though her daughter was the afflicted one (Matt. 15:22; page 354 herein). In these cases, faith was exercized in behalf of the sufferers by others; and the same is true of the centurion who pleaded for his servant and whose faith was specially commended by Jesus (Matt 8:5-10; page 249 herein); of Jairus whose daughter lay dead (Luke 8:41, 42, 49, 50; page 313 herein), and of many who brought their helpless kindred or

friends to Christ and pleaded for them. As heretofore shown, faith to be healed is as truly a gift of God as is faith to heal (page 318); and, as the instances cited prove, faith may be exercized with effect in behalf of others. In connection with the ordinance of administering to the afflicted, by anointing with oil and the laying on of hands, as authoritatively established in the restored Church of Jesus Christ, the elders officiating should encourage the faith of all believers present, that such be exerted in behalf of the sufferer. In the case of infants and of persons who are unconscious, it is plainly useless to look for active manifestation of faith on their part, and the supporting faith of kindred and friends is all the more requisite.

2. Power Developed by Prayer and Fasting.--The Savior's statement concerning the evil spirit that the apostles were unable to subdue--"Howbeit this kind goeth not out but by prayer and fasting"--indicates gradation in the malignity and evil power of demons, and gradation also in the results of varying degrees of faith. The apostles who failed on the occasion referred to had been able to cast out demons at other times. Fasting, when practised in prudence, and genuine prayer are conducive to the development of faith with its accompanying power for good. Individual application of this principle may be made with profit. Have you some besetting weakness, some sinful indulgence that you have vainly tried to overcome? Like the malignant demon that Christ rebuked in the boy, your sin may be of a kind that goeth out only through prayer and fasting.

3. Nothing Impossible to Faith.--Many people have questioned the literal truth of the Lord's declaration that by faith mountains may be removed from their place. Plainly there would have to be a purpose in harmony with the divine mind and plan, in order that faith could be exerted at all in such an undertaking. Neither such a miracle nor any other is possible as a gratification of the yearning for curiosity, nor for display, nor for personal gain or selfish satisfaction. Christ wrought no miracle with any such motive; He persistently refused to show signs to mere sign-seekers. But to deny the possibility of a mountain being removed through faith, under conditions that would render such removal acceptable to God, is to deny the word of God, both as to this specific possibility, and as to the general assurance that "nothing shall be impossible" to him who hath faith adequate to the end desired. It is worthy of note, however, that the Jews in the days of Christ and since often spoke of removing mountains as a figurative expression for the overcoming of difficulties. According to Lightfoot and other authorities a man able to solve intricate problems, or of particular power in argument or acumen in judgment, was referred to as a "rooter up of mountains."

4. The Temple Tribute.--That the tribute money referred to in the text was a Jewish contribution to the temple and not a tax levied by the Roman government, is apparent from the specification of the "didrachma," which in the authorized version is translated "tribute." This coin was equivalent to the half shekel, reckoned "after the shekel of the sanctuary," which was the fixed amount to be paid annually by every male "from twenty years old and above," with the provision that "the rich shall not give more and the poor shall not give less" (Exo. 30:13-15). A tax levied by the political powers would not be designated as the didrachma. Moreover, had the collector who approached Peter been one of the official publicans, he probably would have demanded the tax instead of inquiring as to whether or not the Master was to be counted among the contributors.

Among the many humiliations to which the Jews were subjected in later years, after the destruction of the temple, was the compulsory payment of what had been their temple tribute, to the Romans, who decreed it as a revenue to the pagan temple of Jupiter Capitolinus. Of the emperor Vespasian, Josephus (Wars of the Jews, vii, 6:6) says: That he also laid a tribute wheresoever they were, and enjoined every one of them to bring two drachm |ᵃ every year into the capitol, as they used to pay the same to the temple at Jerusalem.

5. Talents and Pence.--It is evident that by specifying ten thousand talents as the debt due the king, and a hundred pence as that owed by the fellow-servant, the Lord intended to present a case of great disparity and striking contrast. The actual amounts involved are of minor significance in the story. We are not told which variety of talent was meant; there were Attic talents, and both silver and gold talents of Hebrew reckoning; and each differed from the others in value. The Oxford marginal explanation is: "A talent is 750 ounces of silver, which after five shillings the ounce is 187 pounds, ten shillings." This would be in American money over nine and a quarter millions of dollars as the sum of the ten thousand talents. The same authority gives as the value of the penny (Roman) sevenpence half-penny, or fifteen cents, making the second debt equivalent to about fifteen dollars. Comparison with talents mentioned elsewhere may be allowable. Trench says: "How vast a sum it was we can most vividly realize to ourselves by comparing it with other sums mentioned in Scripture. In the construction of the tabernacle, twenty-nine talents of gold were used (Exo. 38:24); David prepared for the temple three thousand talents of gold, and the princes five thousand (1 Chron. 29:4-7); the queen of Sheba presented to Solomon one hundred and twenty talents (1 Kings 10:10); the king of Assyria laid upon Hezekiah thirty talents of gold (2 Kings 18:14); and in the extreme impoverishment to which the land was brought at the last, one talent of gold was laid upon it, after the death of Josiah, by the king of Egypt (2 Chron. 36:3)." Farrar estimates the debt owed to the king as 1,250,000 times that owed by the lesser to the greater debtor.

6. An Assumed Approval of Slavery.--Some readers have assumed that they find in the Parable of the Unmerciful Servant an implied approval of the institution of slavery. The greater debtor, who figures in the story, was to be sold, together with his wife and children and all that he had. A rational consideration of the story as a whole is likely to find at most, in the particular incident of the king's command that the debtor and his family be sold, that the system of buying and selling bondservants, serfs, or slaves, was legally recognized at the time. The purpose of the parable was not even remotely to endorse or condemn slavery or any other social institution. The Mosaic law is explicit in matters relating to bondservants. The "angel of the Lord" who brought to Hagar a message of encouragement and blessing respected the authority

of her mistress (Gen. 16:8, 9). In the apostolic epoch, instruction was directed toward right living under the secular law, not rebellion against the system (Eph. 6:5; Col. 3:22; 1 Tim. 6:1-3; 1 Peter 2:18). Recognition of established customs, institutions, and laws, and proper obedience thereto, do not necessarily imply individual approval. The gospel of Jesus Christ, which shall yet regenerate the world, is to prevail--not by revolutionary assaults upon existing governments, nor through anarchy and violence--but by the teaching of individual duty and by the spread of the spirit of love. When the love of God shall be given a place in the hearts of mankind, when men shall unselfishly love their neighbors, then social systems and governments shall be formed and operated to the securing of the greatest good to the greatest number. Until men open their hearts to the reception of the gospel of Jesus Christ, injustice and oppression, servitude and slavery, in some form or other, are sure to exist. Attempts to extirpate social conditions that spring from individual selfishness cannot be otherwise than futile so long as selfishness is left to thrive and propagate.

FOOTNOTES:

[795] Compare 2 Peter 1:18.
[796] Luke 9:37.
[797] Matt. 17:14-21; Mark 9:14-29; Luke 9:37-42.
[798] Note 1, end of chapter.
[799] Compare Matt. 12:40-45.
[800] Mark 6:12, 13; compare verse 7; also 3:15; Matt. 10:1.
[801] Note 2, end of chapter.
[802] Matt. 14:31; 16:8; Luke 8:25.
[803] Matt. 17:20; compare 21:21; Mark 11:23; Luke 17:6; see also Note 3, end of chapter.
[804] Compare Parable of the Mustard Seed, page 290.
[805] Matt. 17:22-23; Mark 9:30-32; Luke 9:44, 45.
[806] Matt. 17:24-27.
[807] Note 4, end of chapter.
[808] Exo. 30:13; 38:26. Page 171.
[809] See reading in revised version, and in margin of Oxford and Bagster Bibles.
[810] John 20:17.
[811] Matt. 18:1-11; Mark 9:33-37, 42; Luke 9:46-48.
[812] Matt. 19:13-15; Mark 10:13-16; Luke 18:15-17.
[813] Compare Luke 22:32.
[814] 1 Cor. 14:20; compare 13:11; Matt. 11:25; Psa. 131:2.
[815] Page 234.
[816] Mark 9:49, 50; compare Lev. 2:13; Ezek. 43:24.
[817] Mark 9:43-50; compare Matt. 18:8, 9. Page 232 herein.
[818] Matt. 18:12-14; compare Luke 15:3-7 in which occurs a repetition of this impressive parable, as given on a later occasion to Pharisees and scribes at Jerusalem with a somewhat different application.
[819] Luke 15:1-7. See further page 451 herein.
[820] Luke 9:48-50; Mark 9:37-41.
[821] Contrast the instance of the sons of Sceva, Acts 19:13-17.
[822] Compare Luke 9:52; 10:1.
[823] Matt. 12:30; Luke 11:23.
[824] Matt. 18:15-20; compare Luke 17:3, 4.
[825] Compare Doc. and Cov. 20:80; 42:88-93; 98:39-48.
[826] Matt. 18:18; compare 16:19, and John 20:23.
[827] They based this limitation on Amos 1:3 and Job 33:29. In the latter passage, as it appears in the authorized version, the word "oftentimes" is an erroneous rendering of the original, which really signified "twice and thrice."
[828] Compare Luke 17:3, 4.
[829] Matt. 18:23-35.
[830] Compare 2 Kings 4:1; Lev. 25:39.
[831] Note 5, end of chapter.
[832] Matt. 7:1; see also verse 6.
[833] Matt. 6:12; compare Luke 11:4; B. of M., 3 Nephi 13:11; page 240.

Jesus the Christ

CHAPTER 25. JESUS AGAIN IN JERUSALEM.

DEPARTURE FROM GALILEE.[834]

Of our Lord's labors during His brief sojourn in Galilee following His return from the region of C├ªsarea Philippi we have no record aside from that of His instructions to the apostles. His Galilean ministry, so far as the people in general were concerned, had practically ended with the discourse at Capernaum on His return thither after the miracles of feeding the five thousand and walking upon the sea. At Capernaum many of the disciples had turned away from the Master,[835] and now, after another short visit, He prepared to leave the land in which so great a part of His public work had been accomplished.

It was autumn; about six months had passed since the return of the apostles from their missionary tour; and the Feast of Tabernacles was near at hand. Some of the kinsmen of Jesus came to Him, and proposed that He go to Jerusalem and take advantage of the opportunity offered by the great national festival, to declare Himself more openly than He had theretofore done. His brethren, as the visiting relatives are called, urged that He seek a broader and more prominent field than Galilee for the display of His powers, arguing that it was inconsistent for any man to keep himself in comparative obscurity when he wanted to be widely known. "Shew thyself to the world," said they. Whatever their motives may have been, these brethren of His did not advize more extended publicity through any zeal for His divine mission; indeed, we are expressly told that they did not believe in Him.[836] Jesus replied to their presumptuous advice: "My time is not yet come: but your time is alway ready. The world cannot hate you; but me it hateth, because I testify of it, that the works thereof are evil. Go ye up unto this feast: I go not up yet unto this feast; for my time is not yet full come." It was not their prerogative to direct His movements, not to say when He should do even what He intended to do eventually.[837] He made it plain that between their status and His there was essential difference; they were of the world, which they loved as the world loved them; but the world hated Him because of His testimony.

This colloquy between Jesus and His brethren took place in Galilee. They soon started for Jerusalem leaving Him behind. He had not said that He would not go to the feast; but only "I go not up yet unto this feast; for my time is not yet full come." Some time after their departure He followed, traveling "not openly, but as it were in secret." Whether He went alone, or accompanied by any or all of the Twelve, we are not told.

AT THE FEAST OF TABERNACLES.[838]

The agitated state of the public mind respecting Jesus is shown by the interest manifest in Jerusalem as to the probability of His presence at the feast. His brethren, who probably were questioned, could give no definite information as to His coming. He was sought for in the crowds; there was much discussion and some disputation concerning Him. Many people expressed their conviction that He was a good man, while others contradicted on the claim that He was a deceiver. There was little open discussion, however, for the people were afraid of incurring the displeasure of the rulers.

As originally established, the Feast of Tabernacles was a seven day festival, followed by a holy convocation on the eighth day. Each day was marked by special and in some respects distinctive services, all characterized by ceremonies of thanksgiving and praise.[839] "Now about the midst of the feast," probably on the third or fourth day, "Jesus went up into the temple, and taught." The first part of His discourse is not recorded, but its scriptural soundness is intimated in the surprize of the Jewish teachers, who asked among themselves: "How knoweth this man letters, having never learned?" He was no graduate of their schools; He had never sat at the feet of their rabbis; He had not been officially accredited by them nor licensed to teach. Whence came His wisdom, before which all their academic attainments were as nothing? Jesus answered their troubled queries, saying: "My doctrine is not mine, but his that sent me. If any man will do his will, he shall know of the doctrine, whether it be of God, or whether I speak of myself." His Teacher, greater even than Himself, was the Eternal Father, whose will He proclaimed. The test proposed to determine the truth of His doctrine was in every way fair, and withal simple; anyone who would earnestly seek to do the will of the Father should know of himself whether Jesus spoke truth or error.[840] The Master proceeded to show that a man who speaks on his own authority alone seeks to aggrandize himself. Jesus did not so; He honored His Teacher, His Father, His God, not Himself; and therefore was He free from the taint of selfish pride or unrighteousness. Moses had given them the law, and yet, as Jesus affirmed, none of them kept the law.

Then, with startling abruptness, He challenged them with the question, "Why go ye about to kill me?" On many occasions had they held dark counsel with one another as to how they could get Him into their power and put Him to death; but they thought that the murderous secret was hidden within their own circle. The people had heard the seducing assertions of the ruling classes, that Jesus was possessed by a demon, and that He wrought wonders through the power of Beelzebub; and in the spirit of this blasphemous slander, they cried out: "Thou hast a devil: who goeth about to kill thee?"

Jesus knew that the two specifications of alleged guilt on which the rulers were striving most assiduously to convict Him in the popular mind, and so turn the people against Him, were those of Sabbath-breaking and blasphemy. On an earlier visit to Jerusalem He had healed an afflicted man on the Sabbath, and had utterly disconcerted the hypercritical accusers who even then had sought to compass His death.[841] To this act of mercy and power Jesus now referred, saying: "I have done one work, and ye all marvel." Seemingly they were still of unsettled mind, in doubt as to accepting Him because of the miracle or denouncing Him because He had done it on the Sabbath. Then He showed the inconsistency of charging

Him with Sabbath-desecration for such a merciful deed, when the law of Moses expressly allowed acts of mercy, and even required that the mandatory rite of circumcision should not be deferred because of the Sabbath. "Judge not according to the appearance, but judge righteous judgment" said He.

The masses were still divided in their estimate of Jesus, and were moreover puzzled over the indecision of the rulers. Some of the Jerusalem Jews knew of the plan to arrest Him, and if possible to bring Him to death, and the people queried why nothing was done when He was there teaching publicly within reach of the officials. They wondered whether the rulers had not at last come to believe that Jesus was indeed the Messiah. The thought, however, was brushed aside when they remembered that all knew whence He came; He was a Galilean, and from Nazareth, whereas as they had been taught, however wrongly, the advent of the Christ was to be mysterious so that none would know whence He came. Strange it was, indeed, that men should reject Him because of a lack of mystery and miracle in His advent; when, had they known the truth, they would have seen in His birth a miracle without precedent or parallel in the annals of time. Jesus directly answered their weak and faulty reasoning. Crying aloud within the temple courts, He assured them that while they knew whence He came as one of their number, yet they did not know that He had come from God, neither did they know God who had sent Him: "But," He added, "I know him: for I am from him, and he hath sent me." At this reiterated testimony of His divine origin, the Jews were the more enraged, and they determined anew to take Him by force; nevertheless none laid hands upon him "because his hour was not yet come."

Many of the people believed in their hearts that He was of God, and ventured to ask among themselves whether Christ would do greater works than Jesus had done. The Pharisees and chief priests feared a possible demonstration in favor of Jesus, and forthwith sent officers to arrest Him and bring him before the Sanhedrin.[842] The presence of the temple police caused no interruption to the Master's discourse, though we may reasonably infer that He knew the purpose of their errand. He spoke on, saying that He would be with the people but a little while; and that after He had returned to the Father, they would seek Him vainly, for where He would then be they could not come. This remark evoked more bitter discussion. Some of the Jews wondered whether He intended to leave the borders of the land and go among the Gentiles to teach them and the dispersed Israelites.

As part of the temple service incident to the feast, the people went in procession to the Pool of Siloam[843] where a priest filled a golden ewer, which he then carried to the altar and there poured out the water to the accompaniment of trumpet blasts and the acclamations of the assembled hosts.[844] According to authorities on Jewish customs, this feature was omitted on the closing day of the feast. On this last or "great day," which was marked by ceremonies of unusual solemnity and rejoicing, Jesus was again in the temple. It may have been with reference to the bringing of water from the pool, or to the omission of the ceremony from the ritualistic procedure of the great day, that Jesus cried aloud, His voice resounding through the courts and arcades of the temple: "If any man thirst, let him come unto me, and drink. He that believeth on me, as the scripture hath said, out of his belly shall flow rivers of living water."[845]

John, the recorder, remarks parenthetically that this promise had reference to the bestowal of the Holy Ghost, which at that time had not been granted, nor was it to be until after the ascension of the risen Lord.[846]

Again many of the people were so impressed that they declared Jesus could be none other than the Messiah; but others objected, saying that the Christ must come from Bethlehem of Judea and Jesus was known to have come from Galilee.[847] So there was further dissension; and though some wanted Him apprehended, not a man was found who would venture to lay hold on Him.

The police officers returned without their intended prisoner. To the angry demand of the chief priests and Pharisees as to why they had not brought Him, they acknowledged that they had been so affected by His teachings as to be unable to make the arrest. "Never man spake like this man," they said. Their haughty masters were furious. "Are ye also deceived?" they demanded; and further, "Have any of the rulers or of the Pharisees believed on him?" What was the opinion of the common people worth? They had never learned the law, and were therefore accursed and of no concern. Yet with all this show of proud disdain, the chief priests and Pharisees were afraid of the common people, and were again halted in their wicked course.

One voice of mild protest was heard in the assembly. Nicodemus, a member of the Sanhedrin, and the same who had come to Jesus by night to inquire into the new teaching,[848] mustered courage enough to ask: "Doth our law judge any man, before it hear him, and know what he doeth?" The answer was insulting. Maddened with bigotry and blood-thirsty fanaticism, some of his colleagues turned upon him with the savage demand: "Art thou also of Galilee?" meaning, Art thou also a disciple of this Galilean whom we hate? Nicodemus was curtly told to study the scriptures, and he would fail to find any prediction of a prophet arising in Galilee. The anger of these learned bigots had blinded them even to their own vaunted knowledge, for several of the ancient prophets were regarded as Galileans;[849] if, however they had meant to refer only to that Prophet of whom Moses had spoken, the Messiah, they were correct, since all predictions pointed to Bethlehem in Judea as His birthplace. It is evident that Jesus was thought of as a native of Nazareth, and that the circumstances of His birth were not of public knowledge.

GO, AND SIN NO MORE.[850]

After the festivities were over, Jesus went to the temple one morning early; and as He sat, probably in the Court of the Women, which was the usual place of public resort, many gathered about Him and He proceeded to teach them as was His custom. His discourse was interrupted by the arrival of a party of scribes and Pharisees with a woman in charge, who, they said, was guilty of adultery. To Jesus they presented this statement and question: "Now Moses in the law commanded us, that such should be stoned; but what sayest thou?" The submitting of the case to Jesus was a prearranged snare, a deliberate attempt to find or make a cause for accusing Him. Though it was not unusual for Jewish officials to consult rabbis of recognized wisdom and experience when difficult cases were to be decided, the case in point involved no legal complications. The woman's guilt seems to have been unquestioned, though the witnesses required by the statutes are not mentioned as appearing unless the accusing scribes and Pharisees are to be so considered; the law was explicit, and the custom of the times in dealing with such offenders was well known. While it is true that the law of Moses had decreed death by stoning as the penalty for adultery, the infliction of the extreme punishment had lapsed long before the time of Christ. One may reasonably ask why the woman's partner in the crime was not brought for sentence, since the law so zealously cited by the officious accusers provided for the punishment of both parties to the offense.[851]

The question of the scribes and Pharisees, "But what sayest thou?" may have intimated their expectation that Jesus would declare the law obsolete; perhaps they had heard of the Sermon on the Mount, in which many requirements in advance of the Mosaic code had been proclaimed.[852] Had Jesus decided that the wretched woman ought to suffer death, her accusers might have said that he was defying the existing authorities; and possibly the charge of opposition to the Roman government might have been formulated, since power to inflict the death penalty had been taken from all Jewish tribunals; and moreover, the crime with which this woman was charged was not a capital offense under Roman law. Had He said that the woman should go unpunished or suffer only minor infliction, the crafty Jews could have charged Him with disrespect for the law of Moses. To these scribes and Pharisees Jesus at first gave little heed. Stooping down He traced with His finger on the ground; but as He wrote they continued to question Him. Lifting Himself up He answered them, in a terse sentence that has become proverbial: "He that is without sin among you, let him first cast a stone at her." Such was the law; the accusers on whose testimony the death penalty was pronounced were to be the first to begin the work of execution.[853]

Having spoken, Jesus again stooped and wrote upon the ground. The woman's accusers were "convicted by their own conscience"; shamed and in disgrace they slunk away, all of them from the eldest to the youngest. They knew themselves to be unfit to appear either as accusers or judges.[854] What cowards doth conscience make! "When Jesus had lifted up himself, and saw none but the woman, he said unto her, Woman, where are those thine accusers? hath no man condemned thee? She said, No man, Lord. And Jesus said unto her, Neither do I condemn thee: go and sin no more."[855]

The woman was repentant; she remained humbly awaiting the Master's decision, even after her accusers had gone. Jesus did not expressly condone; He declined to condemn; but He sent the sinner away with a solemn adjuration to a better life.[856]

THE LIGHT OF THE WORLD.[857]

Sitting within the temple enclosure in the division known as the Treasury, which was connected with the Court of the Women,[858] our Lord continued His teaching, saying: "I am the light of the world: he that followeth me shall not walk in darkness, but shall have the light of life."[859] The great lamps set up in the court as a feature of the joyful celebration just ended gave point to our Lord's avowal of Himself as the Light of the World. It was another proclamation of His divinity as God and the Son of God. The Pharisees challenged His testimony, declaring it of no worth because He bore record of Himself. Jesus admitted that He testified of Himself, but affirmed nevertheless that what He said was true, for He knew whereof He spoke, whence He came and whither He would go, while they spoke in ignorance. They thought, talked, and judged after the ways of men and the frailties of the flesh; He was not sitting in judgment, but should He choose to judge, then His judgment would be just, for He was guided by the Father who sent Him. Their law required the testimony of two witnesses for the legal determination of any question of fact;[860] and Jesus cited Himself and His Father as witnesses in support of His affirmation. His opponents then asked with contemptuous or sarcastic intent, "Where is thy Father?" The reply was in lofty tone; "Ye neither know me, nor my Father: if ye had known me, ye should have known my Father also." Enraged at their own discomfiture, the Pharisees would have seized Him, but found themselves impotent. "No man laid hands on him; for his hour was not yet come."

THE TRUTH SHALL MAKE YOU FREE.[861]

Again addressing the mixed assemblage, which probably comprized Pharisees, scribes, rabbis, priests, Levites, and lay people, Jesus repeated His former assertion that soon He would leave them, and that whither He went they could not follow; and added the fateful assurance that they would seek Him in vain and would die in their sins. His solemn portent was treated with light concern if not contempt. Some of them asked querulously, "Will he kill himself?" the implication being that in such case they surely would not follow Him; for according to their dogma, Gehenna was the place of suicides, and they, being of the chosen people, were bound for heaven not hell. The Lord's dignified rejoinder was: "Ye are from beneath; I am from above: ye are of this world; I am not of this world. I said therefore unto you, that ye shall die in your sins: for if ye believe not that I am he, ye shall die in your sins."

This reiteration of His distinctive supremacy brought forth the challenging question, "Who art thou?" Jesus replied, "Even the same that I said unto you from the beginning." The many matters on which He might have judged them He refrained from mentioning, but testified anew of the Father, saying: "He that sent me is true; and I speak to the world those things which I have heard of him." Explicit as His earlier explanations had been, the Jews in their gross prejudice "understood not that he spake to them of the

Father." To His Father Jesus ascribed all honor and glory, and repeatedly declared Himself as sent to do the Father's will. "Then said Jesus unto them, When ye have lifted up the Son of man, then shall ye know that I am he, and that I do nothing of myself; but as my Father hath taught me, I speak these things. And he that sent me is with me: the Father hath not left me alone; for I do always those things that please him."

The evident earnestness and profound conviction with which Jesus spoke caused many of His hearers to believe on Him; and these He addressed with the promise that if they continued in that belief, and shaped their lives according to His word, they should be His disciples indeed. A further promise followed: "And ye shall know the truth, and the truth shall make you free." At these words, so rich in blessing, so full of comfort for the believing soul, the people were stirred to angry demonstrations; their Jewish temper was immediately ablaze. To promise them freedom was to imply that they were not already free. "We be Abraham's seed, and were never in bondage to any man: how sayest thou, Ye shall be made free?" In their unbridled fanaticism they had forgotten the bondage of Egypt, the captivity of Babylon, and were oblivious of their existing state of vassalage to Rome. To say that Israel had never been in bondage was not only to convict themselves of falsehood but to stultify themselves wretchedly.

Jesus made it clear that He had not referred to freedom in its physical or political sense alone, though to this conception their false disavowal had been directed; the liberty He proclaimed was spiritual liberty; the grievous bondage from which He would deliver them was the serfdom of sin. To their vaunted boast that they were free men, not slaves, He replied: "Verily, verily, I say unto you, Whosoever committeth sin is the servant of sin." As a sinner, every one of them was in slavery. A bond-servant, Jesus reminded them, was allowed in the master's house by sufferance only; it was not his inherent right to remain there; his owner could send him away at any time, and might even sell him to another; but a son of the family had of his own right a place in his father's home. Now, if the Son of God made them free they would be free indeed. Though they were of Abrahamic lineage in the flesh, they were no heirs of Abraham in spirit or works. Our Lord's mention of His Father as distinct from their father drew forth the angry reiteration, "Abraham is our father", to which Jesus replied: "If ye were Abraham's children, ye would do the works of Abraham. But now ye seek to kill me, a man that hath told you the truth, which I have heard of God: this did not Abraham. Ye do the deeds of your father." In their blind anger they apparently construed this to imply that though they were children of Abraham's household some other man than Abraham was their actual progenitor, or that they were not of unmixed Israelitish blood. "We be not born of fornication" they cried, "we have one Father, even God." Jesus said unto them, "If God were your Father, ye would love me: for I proceeded forth and came from God; neither came I of myself, but he sent me."

They failed to understand because of their stubborn refusal to listen dispassionately. With forceful accusation Jesus told them whose children they actually were, as evinced by the hereditary traits manifest in their lives: "Ye are of your father the devil, and the lusts of your father ye will do. He was a murderer from the beginning, and abode not in the truth, because there is no truth in him. When he speaketh a lie, he speaketh of his own: for he is a liar, and the father of it.[862] And because I tell you the truth, ye believe me not." He challenged them to find sin in Him; and then asked why, if He spake the truth, they so persistently refused to believe Him. Answering His own question, He told them that they were not of God and therefore they understood not the words of God. The Master was unimpeachable; His terse, cogent assertions were unanswerable. In impotent rage the discomfited Jews resorted to invective and calumny. "Say we not well that thou art a Samaritan, and hast a devil?" they shrieked. They had before called Him a Galilean; that appellative was but mildly depreciatory, and moreover was a truthful designation according to their knowledge; but the epithet "Samaritan" was inspired by hate,[863] and by its application they meant to disown Him as a Jew.

The charge that He was a demoniac was but a repetition of earlier slanders. "Jesus answered, I have not a devil; but I honour my Father, and ye do dishonour me." Reverting to the eternal riches offered by His gospel, the Master said: "Verily, verily, I say unto you, If a man keep my saying, he shall never see death." This rendered them the more infuriate: "Now we know that thou hast a devil" they cried, and as evidence of what they professed to regard as His insanity, they cited the fact that great as were Abraham and the prophets they were dead, yet Jesus dared to say that all who kept His sayings should be exempt from death. Did He pretend to exalt Himself above Abraham and the prophets? "Whom makest thou thyself?" they demanded. The Lord's reply was a disclaimer of all self-aggrandizement; His honor was not of His own seeking, but was the gift of His Father, whom He knew; and were He to deny that He knew the Father He would be a liar like unto themselves. Touching the relationship between Himself and the great patriarch of their race, Jesus thus affirmed and emphasized His own supremacy: "Your father Abraham rejoiced to see my day: and he saw it, and was glad." Not only angered but puzzled, the Jews demanded further explanation. Construing the last declaration as applying to the mortal state only, they said: "Thou art not yet fifty years old, and hast thou seen Abraham?" Jesus answered, "Verily, verily, I say unto you, Before Abraham was, I am."

This was an unequivocal and unambiguous declaration of our Lord's eternal Godship. By the awful title I AM He had made Himself known to Moses and thereafter was so known in Israel.[864] As already shown, it is the equivalent of "Yahveh," or "Jahveh," now rendered "Jehovah," and signifies "The Self-existent One," "The Eternal," "The First and the Last."[865] Jewish traditionalism forbade the utterance of the sacred Name; yet Jesus claimed it as His own. In an orgy of self-righteous indignation, the Jews seized upon the stones that lay in the unfinished courts, and would have crushed their Lord, but the hour of His death had not yet come, and unseen of them He passed through the crowd and departed from the temple.

His seniority to Abraham plainly referred to the status of each in the antemortal or preexistent state; Jesus was as literally the Firstborn in the spirit-world, as He was the Only Begotten in the flesh.

Christ is as truly the Elder Brother of Abraham and Adam as of the last-born child of earth.[866]

BODILY AND SPIRITUAL BLINDNESS--SIGHT GIVEN TO A MAN ON THE SABBATH.[867]

At Jerusalem Jesus mercifully gave sight to a man who had been blind from his birth.[868] The miracle is an instance of Sabbath-day healing, of more than ordinary interest because of its attendant incidents. It is recorded by John alone, and, as usual with that writer, his narrative is given with descriptive detail. Jesus and His disciples saw the sightless one upon the street. The poor man lived by begging. The disciples, eager to learn, asked: "Master, who did sin, this man, or his parents, that he was born blind?" The Lord's reply was: "Neither hath this man sinned, nor his parents: but that the works of God should be made manifest in him." The disciples' question implied their belief in a state of moral agency and choice antedating mortality; else, how could they have thought of the man having sinned so as to bring upon himself congenital blindness? We are expressly told that he was born blind. That he might have been a sufferer from the sins of his parents was conceivable.[869] The disciples evidently had been taught the great truth of an antemortal existence. It is further to be seen that they looked upon bodily affliction as the result of personal sin. Their generalization was too broad; for, while as shown by instances heretofore cited,[870] individual wickedness may and does bring physical ills in its train, man is liable to err in his judgment as to the ultimate cause of affliction. The Lord's reply was sufficing; the man's blindness would be turned to account in bringing about a manifestation of divine power. As Jesus explained respecting His own ministry, it was necessary that He do the Father's work in the season appointed, for His time was short. With impressive pertinency as relating to the state of the man who had been in darkness all his days, our Lord repeated the affirmation before made in the temple, "I am the light of the world."

The outward ministration to the blind man was different from the usual course followed by Jesus. "He spat on the ground, and made clay of the spittle, and he anointed the eyes of the blind man with the clay"; and then directed him to go to the pool of Siloam and wash in its waters.[871] The man went, washed, and came seeing. He was evidently a well-known character; many had seen him in his accustomed place begging alms, and the fact that he had been blind from birth was also of common knowledge. When, therefore, it was noised about that he could see, there was much excitement and comment. Some doubted that the man they questioned was the once sightless beggar; but he assured them of his identity, and told how he had been made to see. They brought the man to the Pharisees, who questioned him rigorously; and, having heard his account of the miracle, tried to undermine his faith by telling him that Jesus who had healed him could not be a man of God since He had done the deed on the Sabbath. Some of those who heard demurred to the Pharisaic deduction, and asked: "How can a man that is a sinner do such miracles?" The man was questioned as to his personal opinion of Jesus, and promptly answered: "He is a prophet." The man knew his Benefactor to be more than any ordinary being; as yet, however, he had no knowledge of Him as the Christ.

The inquisitorial Jews were afraid of the result of such a wondrous healing, in that the people would support Jesus whom the rulers were determined to destroy. They assumed it to be possible that the man had not been really blind; so they summoned his parents, who answered their interrogatories by affirming that he was their son, and they knew him to have been born blind; but as to how he had received sight, or through whose ministration, they refused to commit themselves, knowing the rulers had decreed that any one who confessed Jesus to be the Christ should be cast out from the community of the synagog, or, as we would say today, excommunicated from the Church. With pardonable astuteness the parents said of their son: "He is of age; ask him: he shall speak for himself."

Compelled to acknowledge, to themselves at least, that the fact and the manner of the man's restoration to sight were supported by irrefutable evidence, the crafty Jews called the man again, and insinuatingly said unto him: "Give God the praise: we know that this man is a sinner." He replied fearlessly, and with such pertinent logic as to completely offset their skill as cross-examiners: "Whether he be a sinner or no, I know not: one thing I know, that, whereas I was blind, now I see." He very properly declined to enter into a discussion with his learned questioners as to what constituted sin under their construction of the law; of what he was ignorant he declined to speak; but on one matter he was happily and gratefully certain, that whereas he had been blind, now he could see.

The Pharisaical inquisitors next tried to get the man to repeat his story of the means employed in the healing, probably with the subtle purpose of leading him into inconsistent or contradictory statements; but he replied with emphasis, and possibly with some show of impatience, "I have told you already, and ye did not hear:[872] wherefore would ye hear it again? will ye also be his disciples?" They retorted with anger, and reviled the man; the ironical insinuation that they perchance wished to become disciples of Jesus was an insult they would not brook. "Thou art his disciple," said they, "but we are Moses' disciples. We know that God spake unto Moses: as for this fellow, we know not from whence he is." They were enraged that this unlettered mendicant should answer so boldly in their scholarly presence; but the man was more than a match for all of them. His rejoinder was maddening because it flouted their vaunted wisdom, and withal was unanswerable. "Why herein is a marvellous thing," said he, "that ye know not from whence he is, and yet he hath opened mine eyes. Now we know that God heareth not sinners: but if any man be a worshipper of God, and doeth his will, him he heareth. Since the world began was it not heard that any man opened the eyes of one that was born blind. If this man were not of God, he could do nothing."

For such an affront from a layman there was no precedent in all the lore of rabbis or scribes. "Thou wast altogether born in sins, and dost thou teach us?" was their denunciatory though weak and inadequate rejoinder. Unable to cope with the sometime sightless beggar in argument or demonstration, they could at least exercize their official authority, however unjustly, by excommunicating him; and this they promptly did. "Jesus heard that they had cast him out; and when he had found him, he said unto him, Dost thou believe on the Son of God? he answered and said, Who is he, Lord, that I might believe on him? And Jesus said unto him, Thou hast both seen him, and it is he that talketh with thee. And he said, Lord, I believe. And he worshipped him."

In commenting upon the matter Jesus was heard to say that one purpose of His coming into the world was "that they which see not might see; and that they which see might be made blind." Some of the Pharisees caught the remark, and asked in pride: "Are we blind also?" The Lord's reply was a condemnation: "If ye were blind, ye should have no sin: but now ye say, We see; therefore your sin remaineth."

SHEPHERD AND SHEEPHERDER.[873]

"Verily, verily, I say unto you, He that entereth not by the door into the sheep fold, but climbeth up some other way, the same is a thief and a robber. But he that entereth in by the door is the shepherd of the sheep." With these words Jesus prefaced one of His most impressive discourses. The mention of shepherd and sheep must have brought to the minds of His hearers many of the oft-quoted passages from prophets and psalms.[874] The figure is an effective one, and all the more so when we consider the circumstances under which it was used by the Master. Pastoral conditions prevailed in Palestine, and the dignity of the shepherd's vocation was very generally recognized. By specific prophecy a Shepherd had been promised to Israel. David, the king of whom all Israelites were proud, had been taken directly from the sheepfold, and had come with a shepherd's crook in his hand to the anointing that made him royal.

As the Teacher showed, a shepherd has free access to the sheep. When they are folded within the enclosure of safety, he enters at the gate; he neither climbs over nor creeps in.[875] He, the owner of the sheep loves them; they know his voice and follow him as he leads from fold to pasture, for he goes before the flock; while the stranger, though he be the herder, they know not; he must needs drive, for he cannot lead. Continuing the allegory, which the recorder speaks of as a parable, Jesus designated Himself as the door to the sheepfold, and made plain that only through Him could the under-shepherds rightly enter. True, there were some who sought by avoiding the portal and climbing over the fence to reach the folded flock; but these were robbers, trying to get at the sheep as prey; their selfish and malignant purpose was to kill and carry off.

Changing the figure, Christ proclaimed: "I am the good shepherd." He then further showed, and with eloquent exactness, the difference between a shepherd and a hireling herder. The one has personal interest in and love for his flock, and knows each sheep by name, the other knows them only as a flock, the value of which is gaged by number; to the hireling they are only as so many or so much. While the shepherd is ready to fight in defense of his own, and if necessary even imperil his life for his sheep, the hireling flees when the wolf approaches, leaving the way open for the ravening beast to scatter, rend, and kill.

Never has been written or spoken a stronger arraignment of false pastors, unauthorized teachers, self-seeking hirelings who teach for pelf and divine for dollars, deceivers who pose as shepherds yet avoid the door and climb over "some other way," prophets in the devil's employ, who to achieve their master's purpose, hesitate not to robe themselves in the garments of assumed sanctity, and appear in sheep's clothing, while inwardly they are ravening wolves.[876]

With effective repetition Jesus continued: "I am the good shepherd, and know my sheep, and am known of mine. As the Father knoweth me, even so know I the Father: and I lay down my life for the sheep." For this cause was Jesus the Father's Beloved Son--that He was ready to lay down His life for the sake of the sheep. That the sacrifice He was soon to render was in fact voluntary, and not a forfeiture under compulsion, is solemnly affirmed in the Savior's words: "Therefore doth my Father love me, because I lay down my life, that I might take it again. No man taketh it from me, but I lay it down of myself. I have power to lay it down, and I have power to take it again. This commandment have I received of my Father." The certainty of His death and of His subsequent resurrection are here reiterated. A natural effect of His immortal origin, as the earth-born Son of an immortal Sire, was that He was immune to death except as He surrendered thereto. The life of Jesus the Christ could not be taken save as He willed and allowed. The power to lay down His life was inherent in Himself, as was the power to take up His slain body in an immortalized state.[877] These teachings caused further division among the Jews. Some pretended to dispose of the matter by voicing anew the foolish assumption that Jesus was but an insane demoniac, and that therefore His words were not worthy of attention. Others with consistency said "These are not the words of him that hath a devil. Can a devil open the eyes of the blind?" So it was that a few believed, many doubted though partly convinced, and some condemned.

As part of this profound discourse, Jesus said: "And other sheep I have, which are not of this fold: them also I must bring, and they shall hear my voice; and there shall be one fold, and one shepherd."[878] The "other sheep" here referred to constituted the separated flock or remnant of the house of Joseph, who, six centuries prior to the birth of Christ, had been miraculously detached from the Jewish fold in Palestine, and had been taken beyond the great deep to the American continent. When to them the resurrected Christ appeared He thus spake: "And verily, I say unto you, that ye are they of whom I said, other sheep I have which are not of this fold; them also I must bring, and they shall hear my voice; and there shall be one fold, and one shepherd."[879] The Jews had vaguely understood Christ's reference to other sheep as meaning in some obscure way, the Gentile nations; and because of their unbelief and consequent inability to rightly comprehend, Jesus had withheld any plainer exposition of His meaning, for so, He informed the Nephites, had the Father directed. "This much did the Father command me," He explained, "that I should tell unto them, That other sheep I have, which are not of this fold; them also I must bring, and they shall hear my voice; and there shall be one fold, and one shepherd." On the same occasion the Lord declared that there were yet other sheep, those of the Lost, or Ten, Tribes, to whom He was then about to go, and who would eventually be brought forth from their place of exile, and become part of the one blessed fold under the governance of the one supreme Shepherd and King.[880]

NOTES TO CHAPTER 25.

1. The Feast of Tabernacles.--In the order of yearly occurrence this was the third of the great festivals, the observance of which was among the national characteristics of the people of Israel; the others were the Passover, and the feast of Weeks or Pentecost; at each of the three all the males in Israel were required to appear before the Lord in formal celebration of the respective feast (Exo. 23:17). The feast of Tabernacles was also known as the "feast of ingathering" (Exo. 23:16); it was both a memorial and a current harvest celebration. In commemoration of their long journeying in the wilderness following their deliverance from Egypt, in the course of which journey they had to live in tents and improvized booths, the people of Israel were required to observe annually a festival lasting seven days, with an added day of holy convocation. During the week the people lived in booths, bowers, or tabernacles, made of the branches or "boughs of goodly trees" wattled with willows from the brook (Lev. 23:34-43; Numb. 29:12-38; Deut. 16:13-15; 31:10-13). The festival lasted from the 15th to the 22d of the month Tizri, the seventh in the Hebrew calendar, corresponding to parts of our September and October. It was made to follow soon after the annual Day of Atonement which was a time of penitence and affliction of the soul in sorrow for sin (Lev. 23:26-32). The altar sacrifices at the feast of Tabernacles exceeded those prescribed for other festivals, and comprized a daily offering of two rams, fourteen lambs, and a kid as a sin offering, and in addition a varying number of young bullocks, thirteen of which were sacrificed on the first day, twelve on the second, eleven on the third, and so on to the seventh day, on which seven were offered, making in all seventy bullocks (Numb. 29:12-38). Rabbinism invested this number, seventy, and the graded diminution in the number of altar victims, with much symbolical significance not set forth in the law.

At the time of Christ, tradition had greatly embellished many of the prescribed observances. Thus the "boughs of goodly trees," more literally rendered "fruit" (Lev. 23:40), had come to be understood as the citron fruit; and this every orthodox Jew carried in one hand, while in the other he bore a leafy branch or a bunch of twigs, known as the "lulab," when he repaired to the temple for the morning sacrifice, and in the joyous processions of the day. The ceremonial carrying of water from the spring of Siloam to the altar of sacrifice was a prominent feature of the service. This water was mingled with wine at the altar and the mixture was poured upon the sacrificial offering. Many authorities hold that the bringing of water from the pool was omitted on the last or great day of the feast, and it is inferred that Jesus had in mind the circumstance of the omission when He cried: "If any man thirst, let him come unto me, and drink." At night, during the progress of the feast, great lamps were kept burning in the temple courts, and this incident Christ may have used as an objective illustration in his proclamation: "I am the light of the world."

For fuller account see any reliable and comprehensive Bible Dictionary, and Josephus Ant. viii, 4:1; xv, 3:3, etc. The following is an excerpt from Edersheim, _Life and Times of Jesus The Messiah_, vol. ii, p. 158-160: "When the Temple-procession had reached the Pool of Siloam, the priest filled his golden pitcher from its waters. Then they went back to the Temple, so timing it that they should arrive just as they were laying the pieces of the sacrifice on the great altar of burnt-offering, towards the close of the ordinary morning-sacrifice service. A threefold blast of the priests' trumpets welcomed the arrival of the priest as he entered through the Water Gate, which obtained its name from this ceremony, and passed straight into the Court of the Priests.... Immediately after the 'pouring of the water,' the great 'Hallel,' consisting of Psalms 113 to 118 inclusive, was chanted antiphonally, or rather, with responses, to the accompaniment of the flute.... In further symbolism of this Feast, as pointing to the ingathering of the heathen nations, the public services closed with a procession round the altar by the priests.... But on 'the last, the Great Day of the Feast,' this procession of priests made the circuit of the altar, not only once, but seven times, 'as if they were again compassing, but now with prayer, the Gentile Jericho which barred their possession of the promised land.'"

2. The Test of our Lord's Doctrine.--Any man may know for himself whether the doctrine of Christ is of God or not by simply doing the will of the Father (John 7:17). Surely it is a more convincing course than that of relying upon another's word. The writer was once approached by an incredulous student in college, who stated that he could not accept as true the published results of a certain chemical analysis, since the specified amounts of some of the ingredients were so infinitesimally small that he could not believe it possible to determine such minute quantities. The student was but a beginner in chemistry; and with his little knowledge he had undertaken to judge as to the possibilities of the science. He was told to do the things his instructor prescribed, and he should some day know for himself whether the results were true or false. In the senior year of his course, he received for laboratory analysis a portion of the very substance whose composition he had once questioned. With the skill attained by faithful devotion he successfully completed the analysis, and reported results similar to those, which in his inexperience he had thought impossible to obtain. He was manly enough to acknowledge as unfounded his earlier skepticism and rejoiced in the fact that he had been able to demonstrate the truth for himself.

3. The Pool of Siloam.--"The names 'Shiloah' ('Shelah,' Neh. 3:15, 'Siloah' in authorized version) and 'Siloam' are the exact equivalent in Hebrew and Greek, respectively, of 'Silwan' in the modern Arabic name ('Ain Silwan') of the pool at the mouth of El-Wad. All the ancient references agree with this identification (compare Neh. 3:15; Josephus, Wars of the Jews, v, 4:1, 2; 6:1; 9:4; 12:2; ii, 16:2; vi, 7:2; 8:5). In spite of its modern designation as an 'ain' (spring), Siloam is not a spring, but is fed by a tunnel cut through the rock from the Gihon, or Virgin's Fountain."--L. B. Paton, in article "Jerusalem," _Stand. Bible

Dictionary_.

4. Whence was the Messiah to Come?--Many stifled their inward promptings to a belief in Jesus as the Messiah, by the objection that all prophecies relating to His coming pointed to Bethlehem as His birthplace, and Jesus was of Galilee. Others rejected Him because they had been taught that no man was to know whence the Messiah came and they all knew Jesus came from Galilee. The seeming inconsistency is thus explained: The city of David, or Bethlehem in Judea, was beyond question the fore-appointed place of the Messiah's birth; but the rabbis had erroneously taught that soon after birth the Christ Child would be caught away, and after a time would appear as a Man, and that no one would know whence or how He had returned. Geikie (ii, p. 274), citing Lightfoot in part, thus states the popular criticism: "'Do not the rabbis tell us' said some, 'that the Messiah will be born at Bethlehem, but that He will be snatched away by spirits and tempests soon after His birth, and that when He returns the second time no one will know from whence He has come?' But we know this man comes from Nazareth."

5. The Record Relating to the Woman Taken in Adultery.--Some modern critics claim that the verses John 7:53 and 8:1-11 inclusive are out of place as they appear in the authorized or King James version of the Bible, on the grounds that the incident therein recorded does not appear in certain of the ancient manuscript copies of John's Gospel, and that the style of the narrative is distinctive. In some manuscripts it appears at the end of the book. Other manuscripts contain the account as it appears in the English Bible. Canon Farrar pertinently asks (p. 404, note), why, if the incident is out of place or not of John's authorship, so many important manuscripts give place to it as we have it?

6. The Treasury, and Court of the Women.--"Part of the space within the inner courts was open to Israelites of both sexes, and was known distinctively as the Court of the Women. This was a colonnaded enclosure, and constituted the place of general assembly in the prescribed course of public worship. Chambers used for ceremonial purposes occupied the four corners of this court; and between these and the houses at the gates, were other buildings, of which one series constituted the Treasury wherein were set trumpet-shaped receptacles for gifts." (See Mark 12:41-44.)--_The House of the Lord_, pp. 57-58.

7. The Sheepfold.--Dummelow's _Commentary_ says, on John 10:2: "To understand the imagery, it must be remembered that Eastern folds are large open enclosures, into which several flocks are driven at the approach of night. There is only one door, which a single shepherd guards, while the others go home to rest. In the morning the shepherds return, are recognized by the doorkeeper, call their flocks round them, and lead them forth to pasture."

FOOTNOTES:

[834] John 7:1-10.
[835] Page 343.
[836] John 7:5; compare Mark 3:21 in which "friends" is an inaccurate rendition for "kinsmen".
[837] Compare Christ's answer to His mother, John 2:4; see also 7:30; 8:20.
[838] John 7:11-53.
[839] Note 1, end of chapter.
[840] Note 2, end of chapter.
[841] John 5; see pages 206-208 herein.
[842] Page 69.
[843] Note 3, end of chapter.
[844] This was regarded as a literal fulfilment of Isa. 12:3.
[845] John 7:37, 38; compare with the assurance respecting "living water" given to the Samaritan woman, 4:10-15.
[846] John 7:39; compare 14:16, 17, 26; 15:26; 16:7; Luke 24:49; Acts 2:4.
[847] Note 4, end of chapter.
[848] John 3; page 158 herein.
[849] According to many excellent authorities, Jonah, Nahum, and Hosea were all of Galilee; and it is further believed that Elijah also was of Galilean nativity.
[850] John 8:1-11.
[851] Deut. 22:22-27.
[852] Matt. 5:21-48.
[853] Deut. 17:6, 7; also 13:9.
[854] Compare Rom. 2:1, 22; Matt. 7:1, 2; Luke 6:37; 2 Sam. 12:5-7.
[855] John 8:10, 11; compare 5:11. Consider another instance of mercy granted through contrition Luke 7:36-50.
[856] Note 5, end of chapter.
[857] John 8:12-20.
[858] Note 6, end of chapter.
[859] John 8:12; compare 1:4, 5, 9; 3:19; 9:5; 12:35, 36, 46. See also Doc. and Cov. 6:21; 10:58, 70; 11:11; 14:9; 84:45, 46; 88:6-13.
[860] Deut. 17:6; 19:15; Numb. 35:30; Matt. 18:16.
[861] John 8:21-59.
[862] Compare P. of G.P., Moses 4:4; 5:24; B. of M., 2 Nephi 2:18; Doc. and Cov. 10:25; 93:25.
[863] Pages 174, 183.
[864] Exo. 3:14; compare 6:3.
[865] Compare Isa. 44:6; Rev. 1:4, 8; see also John 17:5, 24; Col. 1:17. Page 36 herein.

[866] Page 13.

[867] John 9.

[868] Whether this incident occurred in immediate sequence to the events last considered, or at a later time after the return of Jesus to Jerusalem following an unrecorded departure therefrom, is not stated in the scriptural record. The value of the lesson is not affected by its place in the catalog of our Lord's works.

[869] Exo. 20:5; 34:7; Lev. 26:39; Numb. 14:18; 1 Kings 21:29; compare Ezek. chap. 18.

[870] Pages 192 and 208.

[871] Note 3, end of chapter.

[872] That is, "heed" or "believe".

[873] John 10:1-21.

[874] Note the promise of a Shepherd to Israel, Isa. 40:11; 49:9, 10; Ezek. 34:23; 37:24; compare Jer. 3:15; 23:4; Heb, 13:20; 1 Peter 2:25; 5:4; Rev. 7:17. Read studiously Psalm 23.

[875] Note 7, end of chapter.

[876] Matt. 7:15; compare 24:4, 5, 11, 24; Mark 13:22; Rom. 16:17, 18; Eph. 5:6; Col. 2:8; 2 Peter 2:1-3; 1 John 4:1; Acts 20:29.

[877] Pages 22 and 81.

[878] John 10:16; compare as to "one fold and one shepherd," Ezek. 37:22; Isa. 11:13; Jer. 3:18; 50:4. See "Articles of Faith," xviii,--"The Gathering of Israel."

[879] B. of M., 3 Nephi 15:21; read verses 12-24; see chapter 39 herein.

[880] 3 Nephi 16:1-5.

CHAPTER 26. OUR LORD'S MINISTRY IN PEREA AND JUDEA.

When or under what attendant circumstances our Lord departed from Jerusalem after the Feast of Tabernacles, in the last autumn of His earthly life, we are not told. The writers of the synoptic Gospels have recorded numerous discourses, parables, and miracles, as incidents of a journey toward Jerusalem, in the course of which, Jesus, accompanied by the apostles, traversed parts of Samaria and Perea, and the outlying sections of Judea. We read of Christ's presence in Jerusalem at the Feast of Dedication,[881] between two and three months after the Feast of Tabernacles; and it is probable that some of the events now to be considered occurred during that interval.[882] That Jesus left Jerusalem soon after the Feast of Tabernacles is certain; whether He returned to Galilee, or went only into Perea, possibly with a short detour across the border into Samaria, is not conclusively stated. We shall here as heretofore devote our study primarily to His words and works, with but minor regard to place, time, or sequence.

As the time of His foreknown betrayal and crucifixion drew near, "he steadfastly set his face to go to Jerusalem,"[883] though, as we shall find, He turned northward on two occasions, once when He retired to the region of Bethabara, and again to Ephraim.[884]

HIS REJECTION IN SAMARIA.[885]

Jesus sent messengers ahead, to announce His coming and to prepare for His reception. In one of the Samaritan villages He was refused entertainment and a hearing, "because his face was as though he would go to Jerusalem." Racial prejudice had superseded the obligations of hospitality. This repulse is in unfavorable contrast with the circumstances of His earlier visit among the Samaritans, when He had been received with gladness and entreated to remain; but on that occasion He was journeying not toward but farther from Jerusalem.[886]

The disrespect shown by the Samaritans was more than the disciples could endure without protest. James and John, those Sons of Thunder, were so resentful as to yearn for vengeance. Said they: "Lord, wilt thou that we command fire to come down from heaven, and consume them, even as Elias did?"[887] Jesus rebuked His uncharitable servants thus: "Ye know not what manner of spirit ye are of. For the Son of man is not come to destroy men's lives, but to save them." Repulsed in this village the little company went to another, as the Twelve had been instructed to do under like circumstances.[888] This was but one of the impressive lessons given to the apostles in the matter of tolerance, forbearance, charity, patience, and long-suffering.

Luke gives next place to the incident of three men who were desirous or willing to become disciples of Christ; one of them seems to have been discouraged at the prospect of hardship such as the ministry entailed; the others wished to be temporarily excused from service, one that he might attend the burial of his father, the other that he might first bid his loved ones farewell. This, or a similar occurrence, is recorded by Matthew in another connection, and has already received attention in these pages.[889]

THE SEVENTY CHARGED AND SENT.

The supreme importance of our Lord's ministry, and the shortness of the time remaining to Him in the flesh, demanded more missionary laborers. The Twelve were to remain with Him to the end; every hour of possible instruction and training had to be utilized in their further preparation for the great responsibilities that would rest upon them after the Master's departure. As assistants in the ministry, He called and commissioned the Seventy, and straightway sent them forth,[890] "two and two before his face into every city and place, whither he himself would come." The need of their service was explained in the introduction to the impressive charge by which they were instructed in the duties of their calling. "Therefore said he unto them, The harvest truly is great, but the labourers are few: pray ye therefore the Lord of the harvest, that he would send forth labourers into his harvest."[891]

Many matters on which the Twelve had been instructed prior to their missionary tour were now repeated to the Seventy. They were told that they must expect unfriendly and even hostile treatment; their situation would be as that of lambs among wolves. They were to travel without purse or scrip, and thus necessarily to depend upon the provision that God would make through those to whom they came. As their mission was urgent, they were not to stop on the way to make or renew personal acquaintanceships. On entering a house they were to invoke peace upon it; if the household deserved the gift peace would rest therein, but otherwise the Lord's servants would feel that their invocation was void.[892] To any family by whom they were received they were to impart blessing--healing the afflicted, and proclaiming that the kingdom of God had come nigh unto that house. They were not to go from one house to another seeking better entertainment, nor should they expect or desire to be feasted, but they should accept what was offered, eating that which was set before them, thus sharing with the family. If rejected in any city, they were to depart therefrom, leaving, however, their solemn testimony that the city had turned away from the kingdom of God, which had been brought to its doors, and attesting the same by ridding themselves of the dust of that place.[893] It was not for them to pronounce anathema or curse, but the Lord assured them that such a city would bring upon itself a fate worse than the doom of Sodom.[894] He reminded them that they were His servants, and therefore whoever heard or refused to hear them would be judged as having so treated Him.

They were not restrained, as the Twelve had been, from entering Samaritan towns or the lands of the Gentiles. This difference is consistent with the changed conditions, for now the prospective itinerary of Jesus would take Him into non-Jewish territory, where His fame had already spread; and furthermore,

His plan provided for an extension of the gospel propaganda, which was to be ultimately world-wide. The narrow Jewish prejudice against Gentiles in general and Samaritans in particular was to be discountenanced; and proof of this intent could not be better given than by sending authorized ministers among those peoples. We must keep in mind the progressiveness of the Lord's work. At first the field of gospel preaching was confined to the land of Israel,[895] but the beginning of its extension was inaugurated during our Lord's life, and was expressly enjoined upon the apostles after His resurrection.[896] Duly instructed, the Seventy set out upon their mission.[897]

Mention of the condemnation that would follow wilful rejection of the authorized servants of God aroused in our Lord's mind sad memories of the repulses He had suffered, and of the many unrepentant souls, in the cities wherein He had accomplished so many mighty works. In profound sorrow He predicted the woes then impending over Chorazin, Bethsaida, and Capernaum.[898]

THE SEVENTY RETURN.

Considerable time may have elapsed, weeks or possibly months, between the departure of the Seventy and their return. We are not told when or where they rejoined the Master; but this we know, that the authority and power of Christ had been abundantly manifest in their ministry; and that they had rejoiced in the realization. "Lord," said they, "even the devils are subject unto us through thy name."[899] This testimony was followed by the Lord's solemn statement: "I beheld Satan as lightning fall from heaven." This was said with reference to the expulsion of the rebellious son of the morning, after his defeat by Michael and the heavenly hosts.[900] Commending the Seventy for their faithful labors, the Lord gave them assurance of further power, on the implied condition of their continued worthiness: "I give unto you power to tread on serpents and scorpions, and over all the power of the enemy: and nothing shall by any means hurt you."[901] The promise that they should tread on serpents and scorpions included immunity from injury by venomous creatures if encountered in the path of duty[902] and power to prevail over the wicked spirits that serve the devil, who is elsewhere expressly called the serpent.[903] Great as was the power and authority thus imparted, these disciples were told not to rejoice in such, nor primarily in the fact that evil spirits were subject unto them, but rather because they were accepted of the Lord, and that their names were written in heaven.[904]

The righteous joy of His servants and His contemplation of their faithfulness caused Jesus to rejoice. His happiness found its most appropriate expression in prayer, and thus He prayed: "I thank thee, O Father, Lord of heaven and earth, that thou hast hid these things from the wise and prudent, and hast revealed them unto babes: even so, Father; for so it seemed good in thy sight." Compared with the learned men of the time, such as the rabbis and scribes, whose knowledge served but to harden their hearts against the truth, these devoted servants were as babes in humility, trust, and faith. Such children were and are among the nobles of the kingdom. As in the hours of darkest sorrow, so in this moment of righteous exultation over the faithfulness of His followers, Jesus communed with the Father, to do whose will was His sole purpose.

Our Lord's joy on this occasion is comparable to that which He experienced when Peter had burst forth with the confession of his soul: "Thou art the Christ, the Son of the living God." In solemn discourse Jesus said: "All things are delivered to me of my Father: and no man knoweth who the Son is, but the Father; and who the Father is, but the Son, and he to whom the Son will reveal him." Then in more intimate communion with the disciples He added: "Blessed are the eyes which see the things that ye see: For I tell you, that many prophets and kings have desired to see those things which ye see, and have not seen them; and to hear those things which ye hear, and have not heard them."

WHO IS MY NEIGHBOR?

We have seen that the Pharisees and their kind were constantly on the alert to annoy and if possible disconcert Jesus on questions of law and doctrine, and to provoke Him to some overt utterance or deed.[905] It may be such an attempt that is recorded by Luke in immediate sequence to his account of the joyous return of the Seventy,[906] for he tells us that the "certain lawyer," of whom he speaks, put a question to tempt Jesus. Viewing the questioner's motive with all possible charity, for the basal meaning of the verb which appears in our version of the Bible as "to tempt" is that of putting to test or trial and not necessarily and solely to allure into evil,[907] though the element of entrapping or ensnaring is connoted, we may assume that he wished to test the knowledge and wisdom of the famous Teacher, probably for the purpose of embarrassing Him. Certainly his purpose was not that of sincere search for truth.

This lawyer, standing up among the people who had gathered to hear Jesus, asked: "Master, what shall I do to inherit eternal life?"[908] Jesus replied by a counter question, in which was plainly intimated that if this man, who was professedly learned in the law, had read and studied properly, he should know without asking what he ought to do. "What is written in the law? how readest thou?" The man replied with an admirable summary of the commandments: "Thou shalt love the Lord thy God with all thy heart, and with all thy soul, and with all thy strength, and with all thy mind; and thy neighbour as thyself"[909] The answer was approved. "This do, and thou shalt live" said Jesus. These simple words conveyed a rebuke, as the lawyer must have realized; they indicated the contrast between knowing and doing. Having thus failed in his plan to confound the Master, and probably realizing that he, a lawyer, had made no creditable display of his erudition by asking so simple a question and then answering it himself, he tamely sought to justify himself by inquiring further; "And who is my neighbour?" We may well be grateful for the lawyer's question; for it served to draw from the Master's inexhaustible store of wisdom one of His most appreciated parables.

The story is known as the _Parable of the Good Samaritan_; it runs as follows:

"A certain man went down from Jerusalem to Jericho, and fell among thieves, which stripped him of his raiment, and wounded him, and departed, leaving him half dead. And by chance there came down a certain priest that way: and when he saw him, he passed by on the other side. And likewise a Levite, when he was at the place, came and looked on him, and passed by on the other side. But a certain Samaritan, as he journeyed, came where he was: and when he saw him, he had compassion on him, and went to him, and bound up his wounds, pouring in oil and wine, and set him on his own beast, and brought him to an inn, and took care of him. And on the morrow when he departed, he took out two pence, and gave them to the host, and said unto him, Take care of him; and whatsoever thou spendest more, when I come again, I will repay thee."

Then of the lawyer Jesus asked: "Which now of these three, thinkest thou, was neighbor unto him that fell among the thieves? And he said, He that shewed mercy on him. Then said Jesus unto him, Go, and do thou likewise."[910]

Whatever of motive there may have been in the lawyer's query, "Who is my neighbour?" aside from that of self-justification and a desire to retreat in the best form possible from an embarrassing situation, we may conceive to lie in the wish to find a limitation in the application of the law, beyond which he would not be bound to go. If he had to love his neighbors as he loved himself, he wanted to have as few neighbors as possible. His desire may have been somewhat akin to that of Peter, who was eager to learn just how many times he was required to forgive an offending brother.[911]

The parable with which our Lord replied to the lawyer's question is rich in interest as a story alone, and particularly so as an embodiment of precious lessons. It was withal so true to existing conditions, that, like the story of the sower who went forth to sow, and other parables given by the Lord Jesus, it may be true history as well as parable. The road between Jerusalem and Jericho was known to be infested by highway robbers; indeed a section of the thoroughfare was called the Red Path or Bloody Way because of the frequent atrocities committed thereon. Jericho was prominent as a residence place for priests and Levites. A priest, who, out of respect to his office, if for none other cause, should have been willing and prompt in acts of mercy, caught sight of the wounded traveler and passed by on the far side of the road. A Levite followed; he paused to look, then passed on. These ought to have remembered the specified requirement of the law--that if one saw an ass or an ox fall down by the way, he should not hide himself, but should surely help the owner to lift the creature up again.[912] If such was their duty toward a brother's beast, much greater was their obligation when a brother himself was in so extreme a plight.

Doubtless priest as well as Levite salved his conscience with ample excuse for his inhumane conduct; he may have been in a hurry, or was fearful, perhaps, that the robbers would return and make him also a victim of their outrage. Excuses were easy to find; they spring up as readily and plentifully as weeds by the wayside. When the Samaritan came along and saw the wretched state of the wounded man, he had no excuse for he wanted none. Having done what he could by way of emergency treatment as recognized in the medical practise of the day, he placed the injured one upon his own beast, probably a mule or an ass, and took him to the nearest inn, where he tended him personally and made arrangements for his further care. The essential difference between the Samaritan and the others was that the one had a compassionate heart, while they were unloving and selfish. Though not definitely stated, the victim of the robbers was almost certainly a Jew; the point of the parable requires it to be so. That the merciful one was a Samaritan, showed that the people called heretic and despized by the Jews could excel in good works. To a Jew, none but Jews were neighbors. We are not justified in regarding priest, Levite, or Samaritan as the type of his class; doubtless there were many kind and charitable Jews, and many heartless Samaritans; but the Master's lesson was admirably illustrated by the characters in the parable; and the words of His application were pungent in their simplicity and appropriateness.

MARTHA AND MARY.[913]

On one of His visits to Bethany, a small town about two miles from Jerusalem, Jesus was received at the home where dwelt two sisters, Martha and Mary. Martha was housekeeper, and therefore she assumed responsibility for the proper treatment of the distinguished Guest. While she busied herself with preparations and "was cumbered about much serving," well intended for the comfort and entertainment of Jesus, Mary sat at the Master's feet, listening with reverent attention to His words. Martha grew fretful in her bustling anxiety, and came in, saying: "Lord, dost thou not care that my sister hath left me to serve alone? bid her therefore that she help me." She was talking to Jesus but really at Mary. For the moment she had lost her calmness in undue worry over incidental details. It is reasonable to infer that Jesus was on terms of familiarity in the household, else the good woman would scarcely have appealed to Him in a little matter of domestic concern. He replied to her complaining words with marked tenderness: "Martha, Martha, thou art careful and troubled about many things: but one thing is needful: and Mary hath chosen that good part, which shall not be taken away from her."

There was no reproof of Martha's desire to provide well; nor any sanction of possible neglect on Mary's part. We must suppose that Mary had been a willing helper before the Master's arrival; but now that He had come, she chose to remain with Him. Had she been culpably neglectful of her duty, Jesus would not have commended her course. He desired not well-served meals and material comforts only, but the company of the sisters, and above all their receptive attention to what He had to say. He had more to give them than they could possibly provide for Him. Jesus loved the two sisters and their brother as well.[914] Both these women were devoted to Jesus, and each expressed herself in her own way. Martha was of a practical turn, concerned in material service; she was by nature hospitable and self-denying. Mary, contemplative and more spiritually inclined, showed her devotion through the service of companionship and appreciation.[915]

By inattention to household duties, the little touches that make or mar the family peace, many a woman has reduced her home to a comfortless house; and many another has eliminated the essential elements of home by her self-assumed and persistent drudgery, in which she denies to her dear ones the cheer of her loving companionship. One-sided service, however devoted, may become neglect. There is a time for labor inside the home as in the open; in every family time should be found for cultivating that better part, that one thing needful--true, spiritual development.

ASK, AND IT SHALL BE GIVEN YOU.[916]

"And it came to pass, that, as he was praying in a certain place, when he ceased, one of his disciples said unto him, Lord, teach us to pray." Our Lord's example and the spirit of prayer manifest in His daily life moved the disciples to ask for instruction as to how they should pray. No form of private prayer was given in the law, but formal prayers had been prescribed by the Jewish authorities, and John the Baptist had instructed his followers in the mode or manner of prayer. Responding to the disciples' request, Jesus repeated that brief epitome of soulful adoration and supplication which we call the Lord's Prayer. This He had before given in connection with the Sermon on the Mount.[917] On this occasion of its repetition, the Lord supplemented the prayer by explaining the imperative necessity of earnestness and enduring persistency in praying.

The lesson was made plain by the _Parable of the Friend at Midnight_:

"And he said unto them, Which of you shall have a friend, and   shall go unto him at midnight, and say unto him, Friend, lend me   three loaves; For a friend of mine in his journey is come to me,   and I have nothing to set before him? And he from within shall   answer and say, Trouble me not: the door is now shut, and my   children are with me in bed; I cannot rise and give thee. I say   unto you, Though he will not rise and give him, because he is   his friend, yet because of his importunity he will rise and give   him as many as he needeth."

The man to whose home a friend had come at midnight could not let his belated and weary guest go hungry, yet there was no bread in the house. He made his visitor's wants his own, and pleaded at his neighbor's door as though asking for himself. The neighbor was loath to leave his comfortable bed and disturb his household to accommodate another; but, finding that the man at the door was importunate, he at last arose and gave him what he asked, so as to get rid of him and be able to sleep in peace. The Master added by way of comment and instruction: "_Ask, and it shall be given you; seek, and ye shall find; knock, and it shall be opened unto you._"

The hospitable man in the parable had refused to be repulsed; he kept on knocking until the door was opened; and as a result received what he wanted, found what he had set out to obtain. The parable is regarded by some as a difficult one to apply, since it deals with the selfish and comfort-loving element of human nature, and apparently uses this to symbolize God's deliberate delay. The explanation, however, is clear when the context is duly considered. The Lord's lesson was, that if man, with all his selfishness and disinclination to give, will nevertheless grant what his neighbor with proper purpose asks and continues to ask in spite of objection and temporary refusal, with assured certainty will God grant what is persistently asked in faith and with righteous intent. No parallelism lies between man's selfish refusal and God's wise and beneficent waiting. There must be a consciousness of real need for prayer, and real trust in God, to make prayer effective; and in mercy the Father sometimes delays the granting that the asking may be more fervent. But in the words of Jesus: "If ye then, being evil, know how to give good gifts unto your children: how much more shall your heavenly Father give the Holy Spirit to them that ask him?"

Sometime later Jesus spake another parable, the moral of which is so closely akin to that of the story of the midnight visitor, as to suggest the study of the later lesson here. It is known as the _Parable of the Unjust Judge_, or of the _Importunate Widow_:

"There was in a city a judge, which feared not God, neither   regarded man: And there was a widow in that city; and she came   unto him, saying, Avenge me of mine adversary. And he would not   for a while: but afterward he said within himself, Though I fear   not God, nor regard man; Yet because this widow troubleth me, I   will avenge her, lest by her continual coming she weary   me."[918]

The judge was of wicked character; he denied justice to the widow, who could obtain redress from none other. He was moved to action by the desire to escape the woman's importunity. Let us beware of the error of comparing his selfish action with the ways of God. Jesus did not indicate that as the wicked judge finally yielded to supplication so would God do; but He pointed out that if even such a being as this judge, who "feared not God, neither regarded man," would at last hear and grant the widow's plea, no one should doubt that God, the Just and Merciful, will hear and answer. The judge's obduracy, though wholly wicked on his part, may have been ultimately advantageous to the widow. Had she easily obtained redress she might have become again unwary, and perchance a worse adversary than the first might have oppressed her. The Lord's purpose in giving the parable is specifically stated; it was "to this end, that men ought always to pray, and not to faint."[919]

CRITICISM ON PHARISEES AND LAWYERS.[920]

Varied comment as to the source of our Lord's superhuman powers was aroused afresh by His merciful act of expelling a demon from a man, who, in consequence of this evil possession had been dumb. The old Pharisaic theory, that He cast out devils through the power of "Beelzebub, the chief of the devils," was revived. The utter foolishness of such a conception was demonstrated, as it had been on an earlier occasion to which we have given attention.[921] The spiritual darkness, in which evil men grope for signs, the disappointment and condemnation that await them, and other precious precepts, Jesus elucidated in further discourse.[922]

Then, by invitation He went to the house of a certain Pharisee to dine. Other Pharisees, as also lawyers and scribes, were present. Jesus intentionally omitted the ceremonial washing of hands, which all others in the company scrupulously performed before taking their places at table. This omission caused a murmur of disapproval if not an open expression of fault-finding. Jesus utilized the occasion by voicing a pungent criticism of Pharisaic externalism, which He likened to the cleansing of cups and platters on the outside, while the inside is left filthy. "Fools" said He, "did not he that made that which is without make that which is within also?" In another form we may ask, Did not God who established the outward observances of the law, ordain the inward and spiritual requirements of the gospel also? In response to a question by one of the lawyers, Jesus included them in His sweeping reproof. Pharisees and scribes resented the censure to which they had been subjected, and "began to urge him vehemently, and to provoke him to speak of many things: laying wait for him, and seeking to catch something out of his mouth, that they might accuse him." As our Lord's recorded utterances on this occasion appear also in His final denunciation of Pharisaism, later delivered at the temple, we may well defer further consideration of the matter until we take up in order that notable occurrence.[923]

THE DISCIPLES ADMONISHED AND ENCOURAGED.[924]

Popular interest in our Lord's movements was strong in the region beyond Jordan, as it had been in Galilee. We read of Him surrounded by "an innumerable multitude of people, insomuch that they trode one upon another." Addressing the multitude, and more particularly His disciples, Jesus warned them of the leaven of the Pharisees, which He characterized as hypocrisy.[925] The recent scene at the table of a Pharisee gave special significance to the warning. Some of the precepts recorded in connection with His Galilean ministry were here repeated, and particular stress was laid upon the superiority of the soul to the body, and of eternal life as contrasted with the brief duration of mortal existence.

One man in the company, intent on selfish interests and unable to see beyond the material affairs of life, spoke out saying, "Master, speak to my brother, that he divide the inheritance with me." Jesus promptly refused to act as mediator or judge in the matter. "Man, who made me a judge or a divider over you?" was the Master's rejoinder. The wisdom underlying His refusal to interfere is apparent. As in the case of the guilty woman who had been brought before Him for judgment,[926] so in this instance, He refrained from intervention in matters of legal administration. An opposite course would have probably involved Him in useless disputation, and might have given color to a complaint that He was arrogating to Himself the functions of the legally established tribunals. The man's appeal, however, was made the nucleus of valuable instruction; his clamor for a share in the family inheritance caused Jesus to say: "Take heed, and beware of covetousness: for a man's life consisteth not in the abundance of the things which he possesseth."

This combined admonition and profound statement of truth was emphasized by the _Parable of the Foolish Rich Man_. Thus runs the story:

"The ground of a certain rich man brought forth plentifully: And he thought within himself, saying, What shall I do, because I have no room where to bestow my fruits? And he said, This will I do: I will pull down my barns, and build greater; and there will I bestow all my fruits and my goods. And I will say to my soul, Soul, thou hast much goods laid up for many years; take thine ease, eat, drink, and be merry. But God said unto him, Thou fool, this night thy soul shall be required of thee: then whose shall those things be, which thou hast provided? So is he that layeth up treasure for himself, and is not rich toward God."[927]

The man's abundance had been accumulated through labor and thrift; neglected or poorly-tilled fields do not yield plentifully. He is not represented as one in possession of wealth not rightfully his own. His plans for the proper care of his fruits and goods were not of themselves evil, though he might have considered better ways of distributing his surplus, as for the relief of the needy. His sin was twofold; first, he regarded his great store chiefly as the means of securing personal ease and sensuous indulgence; secondly, in his material prosperity he failed to acknowledge God, and even counted the years as his own. In the hour of his selfish jubilation he was smitten. Whether the voice of God came to him as a fearsome presentiment of impending death, or by angel messenger, or how otherwise, we are not informed; but the voice spoke his doom: "Thou fool, this night thy soul shall be required of thee."[928] He had used his time and his powers of body and mind to sow, reap and garner--all for himself. And what came of it all? Whose should be the wealth, to amass which he had jeopardized his soul? Had he been other than a fool he might have realized as Solomon had done, the vanity of hoarding wealth for another, and he perhaps of uncertain character, to possess.[929]

Turning to the disciples Jesus reiterated some of the glorious truths He had uttered when preaching on the mount,[930] and pointed to the birds of the air, the lilies and grass of the field, as examples of the Father's watchful care; He admonished His hearers to seek the kingdom of God, and, doing so, they should find all needful things added. "Fear not, little flock," He added in tone of affectionate and paternal regard, "for it is your Father's good pleasure to give you the kingdom." They were urged to store their wealth in bags that wax not old,[931] containers suited to the heavenly treasure which, unlike the goods of the foolish rich man, shall not be left behind when the soul is summoned. The man whose treasure is of earth leaves it all at death; he whose wealth is in heaven goes to his own, and death is but the portal to his treasury.

The disciples were admonished to be ever ready, waiting as servants wait at night with lights burning, for their master's return; and, inasmuch as the lord of the household comes at his will, in the early or later watches, if when he comes he finds his faithful servants ready to open immediately to his knock he will honor them as they deserve. So is the Son of Man to come, perhaps when least expected. To a question interjected by Peter as to whether "this parable" was spoken to the Twelve only or to all, Jesus made no direct reply; the answer, however, was conveyed in the continuation of the allegory of contrast between faithful and wicked servants.[932] "Who then is that faithful and wise steward, whom his lord shall make ruler over his household, to give them their portion of meat in due season?" The faithful steward is a good type of the apostles, individually or as a body. As stewards they were charged with the care of the other servants, and of the household; and as to them more had been given than to the others, so of them more would be required; and they would be held to strict accountability for their stewardship.

The Lord then referred feelingly to His own mission, and especially to the dreadful experiences then soon to befall Him, saying: "I have a baptism to be baptised with; and how am I straitened till it be accomplished!" He told again of the strife and dissension that would follow the preaching of His gospel, and dwelt upon the significance of then current events. To those who, ever ready to interpret the signs of the weather, yet remained wilfully blind to the important developments of the times, He applied the caustic epithet, hypocrites![933]

EXCEPT YE REPENT YE SHALL ALL LIKEWISE PERISH.[934]

Some of the people who had been listening to our Lord's discourse reported to Him the circumstances of a tragical event that had taken place, probably but a short time before, inside the temple walls. A number of Galileans had been slain by Roman soldiers, at the base of the altar, so that their blood had mingled with that of the sacrificial victims. It is probable that the slaughter of these Galileans was incident to some violent demonstration of Jewish resentment against Roman authority, which the procurator, Pilate, construed as an incipient insurrection, to be promptly and forcibly quelled. Such outbursts were not uncommon, and the Roman tower or fortress of Antonia had been erected in a commanding position overlooking the temple grounds, and connected therewith by a wide flight of steps, so that soldiers could have ready access to the enclosure at the first indication of turmoil. The purpose of the informants who brought this matter to the attention of Jesus is not stated; but we find probability in the thought that His reference to the signs of the times had reminded them of the tragedy, and that they were inclined to speculate as to the deeper significance of the occurrence. Some may have wondered as to whether the fate of the Galilean victims had befallen them as a merited retribution. Anyway, to some such conception as this Jesus directed His reply. By question and answer He assured them that those who had so been slain were not to be considered as sinners above other Galileans; "But," said He, "except ye repent, ye shall all likewise perish."

Then, referring on His own initiative to another catastrophe, He cited the instance of eighteen persons who had been killed by the fall of a tower at Siloam, and affirmed that these were not to be counted greater sinners than other Jerusalemites. "But," came the reiteration, "except ye repent, ye shall all likewise perish." There were perhaps some who believed that the men upon whom the tower had fallen had deserved their fate; and this conception is the more probable if the generally accepted assumption be correct, that the calamity came upon the men while they were engaged under Roman employ in work on the aqueduct, for the construction of which Pilate had used the "corban" or sacred treasure, given by vow to the temple.[935]

It is not man's prerogative to pass upon the purposes and designs of God, nor to judge by human reason alone that this person or that suffers disaster as a direct result of individual sin.[936] Nevertheless men have ever been prone to so judge. There are many inheritors of the spirit of Job's friends, who assumed his guilt as certain because of the great misfortunes and sufferings that had come upon him. [937] Even while Jesus spake, calamity dark and dire was impending over temple, city and nation; and unless the people would repent and accept the Messiah then in their midst, the decree of destruction would be carried to its dread fulfilment. Hence, as Jesus said, except the people repented they should perish. The imperative need of reformation was illustrated by the _Parable of the Barren Fig Tree_.

"A certain man had a fig tree planted in his vineyard; and he   came and sought fruit thereon, and found none. Then said he unto   the dresser of his vineyard, Behold, these three years I come seeking fruit on this fig tree, and find none: cut it down; why   cumbereth it the ground? And he answering said unto him, Lord,   let it alone this year also, till I shall dig about it, and dung   it: And if it bear fruit, well: and if not, then after that thou   shalt cut it down."[938]

In Jewish literature, particularly in rabbinical lore, the fig tree is of frequent mention as a symbol of the nation. The warning conveyed in the parable is plain; the element of possible escape is no less evident. If the fig tree represents the covenant people, then the vineyard is naturally the world at large, and the dresser of the vineyard is the Son of God, who by personal ministry and solicitous care makes intercession for the barren tree, in the hope that it may yet bear fruit. The parable is of universal application; but so far as it had special bearing upon the Jewish "fig tree" of that time, it was attended by an awful sequel. The Baptist had cried out in warning that the ax was even then in readiness, and every unfruitful tree would be hewn down.[939]

A WOMAN HEALED ON THE SABBATH.[940]

On a certain Sabbath Jesus was teaching in a synagog, of what place we are not told, though it was probably in one of the towns of Perea. There was present a woman who for eighteen years had been suffering from an infirmity that had so drawn and atrophied the muscles as to bend her body so that she could in no wise straighten herself. Jesus called her to Him, and without waiting for petition or request, said simply, "Woman, thou art loosed from thine infirmity." These words He accompanied by the laying-on of hands, a feature of His healing ministrations not always performed. She was healed forthwith and stood erect; and, acknowledging the source of the power by which she had been released from her bonds, glorified God in a fervent prayer of thanksgiving. Doubtless many of the beholders rejoiced with her; but there was one whose soul was stirred by indignation only; and he, the ruler of the synagog. Instead of addressing himself to Jesus, of whose power he may have been afraid, he vented his ill feeling upon the people, by telling them there were six days in which men ought to work, and that on those days they who wished to be healed should come, but not on the Sabbath. The rebuke was ostensibly directed to the people, especially to the woman who had received the blessing, but in reality against Jesus; for if there were any element of work in the healing it had been done by Him, not by the woman nor by others. Upon the ruler of the synagog the Lord turned with direct address: "Thou hypocrite, doth not each one of you on the sabbath loose his ox or his ass from the stall, and lead him away to watering? And ought not this woman, being a daughter of Abraham, whom Satan hath bound, lo, these eighteen years, be loosed from this bond on the sabbath day?"

It may be inferred that the woman's affliction had been more deeply seated than in the muscles; for Luke who was himself a physician[941] tells us she "had a spirit of infirmity," and records the significant words of the Lord to the effect that Satan had held her bound for eighteen years. But whatever her ailment, whether wholly physical or in part mental and spiritual, she was freed from her bonds. Again was the Christ triumphant; His adversaries were shamed into silence, while the believers rejoiced. The rebuke to the ruler of the synagog was followed by a brief discourse in which Jesus gave to these people some of the teachings before delivered in Galilee; these included the parables of the mustard seed and the leaven.[942]

WILL MANY OR FEW BE SAVED?[943]

Continuing His journey toward Jerusalem, Jesus taught in many of the cities and towns of Perea. His coming had probably been announced by the Seventy, who had been sent to prepare the people for His ministry. One of those who had been impressed by His doctrines submitted this question: "Lord, are there few that be saved?" Jesus replied: "Strive to enter in at the strait gate: for many, I say unto you, will seek to enter in, and shall not be able."[944] The counsel was enlarged upon to show that neglect or procrastination in obeying the requirements for salvation may result in the soul's loss. When the door is shut in judgment many will come knocking, and some will plead that they had known the Lord, having eaten and drunk in His company, and that He had taught upon their streets; but to them who had failed to accept the truth when offered the Lord shall say: "I tell you, I know you not whence ye are; depart from me, all ye workers of iniquity." The people were warned that their Israelitish lineage would in no wise save them, for many who were not of the covenant people would believe and be saved, while unworthy Israelites would be thrust out.[945] So is it that "There are last which shall be first, and there are first which shall be last."

JESUS WARNED OF HEROD'S DESIGN.[946]

On the day of the discourse last noted, certain Pharisees came to Jesus with this warning and advice: "Get thee out, and depart hence: for Herod will kill thee."[947] We have heretofore found the Pharisees in open hostility to the Lord, or secretly plotting against Him; and some commentators regard this warning as another evidence of Pharisaic cunning--possibly intended to rid the province of Christ's presence, or designed to drive Him toward Jerusalem, where He would be again within easy reach of the supreme tribunal. Ought we not to be liberal and charitable in our judgment as to the intent of others? Doubtless there were good men in the fraternity of Pharisees,[948] and those who came informing Christ of a plot against His life were possibly impelled by humane motives, and may even have been believers at heart. That Herod had designs against our Lord's liberty or life appears most probable in the answer Jesus made. He received the information in all seriousness, and His comment thereon is one of the strongest of His utterances against an individual. "Go ye," said He, "and tell that fox, Behold, I cast out devils, and I do cures to day and to morrow, and the third day I shall be perfected." The specifying of today, tomorrow, and the third day, was a means of expressing the present in which the Lord was then acting, the immediate future, in which He would continue to minister, since, as He knew, the day of His death was yet several months distant, and the time at which his earthly work would be finished and He be perfected. He placed beyond doubt the fact that He did not intend to hasten His steps, neither cut short His journey nor cease His labors through fear of Herod Antipas, who for craft and cunning was best typified by a sly and murderous fox. Nevertheless it was Christ's intention to go on, and soon in ordinary course He would leave Perea, which was part of Herod's domain, and enter Judea; and at the foreknown time would make His final entry into Jerusalem, for in that city was He to accomplish his sacrifice. "It cannot be," He explained, "that a prophet perish out of Jerusalem."

The awful reality that He, the Christ, would be slain in the chief city of Israel wrung from Him the pathetic apostrophe over Jerusalem, which was repeated when for the last time His voice was heard within the temple walls.[949]

NOTES TO CHAPTER 26.

1. Christ's Ministry Following His Final Withdrawal From Galilee.--John tells us that when Jesus went from Galilee to Jerusalem to attend the Feast of Tabernacles, He went "not openly, but as it

were in secret" (7:10). It appears improbable that the numerous works recorded by the synoptic writers as features of our Lord's ministry, which extended from Galilee through Perea, into Samaria and parts of Judea, could have attended that special and, as it were secret, journey, at the time of the Feast of Tabernacles. The lack of agreement among writers as to the sequence of events in Christs' life is wide. A comparison of the "Harmonies" published in the most prominent Bible Helps (see e.g. Oxford and Bagster "Helps") exemplifies these divergent views. The subject-matter of our Lord's teachings maintains its own intrinsic worth irrespective of merely circumstantial incidents. The following excerpt from Farrar (_Life of Christ_, chap. 42) will be of assistance to the student, who should bear in mind, however, that it is professedly but a tentative or possible arrangement. "It is well known that the whole of one great section in St. Luke--from 9:51 to 18:30--forms an episode in the Gospel narrative of which many incidents are narrated by this Evangelist alone, and in which the few identifications of time and place all point to one slow and solemn progress from Galilee to Jerusalem (9:51; 13:22; 17:11; 10:38). Now after the Feast of Dedication our Lord retired into Perea, until He was summoned thence by the death of Lazarus (John 10:40, 42; 11:1-46); after the resurrection [raising] of Lazarus, He fled to Ephraim (11:54); and He did not leave His retirement at Ephraim until He went to Bethany, six days before His final Passover (12:1).

"This great journey, therefore, from Galilee to Jerusalem, so rich in occasions which called forth some of His most memorable utterances, must have been either a journey to the Feast of Tabernacles or to the Feast of Dedication. That it could not have been the former may be regarded as settled, not only on other grounds, but decisively because that was a rapid and secret journey, this an eminently public and leisurely one.

"Almost every inquirer seems to differ to a greater or less degree as to the exact sequence and chronology of the events which follow. Without entering into minute and tedious disquisitions where absolute certainty is impossible, I will narrate this period of our Lord's life in the order which, after repeated study of the Gospels, appears to me to be the most probable, and in the separate details of which I have found myself again and again confirmed by the conclusions of other independent inquirers. And here I will only premise my conviction--

"1. That the episode of St. Luke up to 18:30, mainly refers to a single journey, although unity of subject, or other causes, may have led the sacred writer to weave into his narrative some events or utterances which belong to an earlier or later epoch.

"2. That the order of the facts narrated even by St. Luke alone is not, and does not in any way claim to be, strictly chronological; so that the place of any event in the narrative by no means necessarily indicates its true position in the order of time.

"3. That this journey is identical with that which is partially recorded in Matt. 18:1; 20:16; Mark 10:1-31.

"4. That (as seems obvious from internal evidence) the events narrated in Matt. 20:17-28; Mark 10:32-45; Luke 18:31-34, belong not to this journey but to the last which Jesus ever took--the journey from Ephraim to Bethany and Jerusalem."

2. Jesus at the Home in Bethany.--Some writers (e.g. Edersheim) place this incident as having occurred in the course of our Lord's journey to Jerusalem to attend the Feast of Tabernacles; others (e.g. Geikie) assume that it took place immediately after that feast; and yet others (e.g. Farrar) assign it to the eve of the Feast of Dedication, nearly three months later. The place given it in the text is that in which it appears in the scriptural record.

3. Shall but Few be Saved?--Through latter-day revelation we learn that graded conditions await us in the hereafter, and that beyond salvation are the higher glories of exaltation. The specified kingdoms or glories of the redeemed, excepting the sons of perdition, are the Celestial, the Terrestrial, and the Telestial. Those who obtain place in the Telestial, the lowest of the three, are shown to be "as innumerable as the stars in the firmament of heaven, or as the sand upon the seashore." And these shall not be equal, "For they shall be judged according to their works, and every man shall receive according to his own works, his own dominion, in the mansions which are prepared. And they shall be servants of the Most High, but where God and Christ dwell they cannot come, worlds without end." See Doc. and Cov. 76:111, 112; read the entire section; see also _The Articles of Faith_ xxii:16-27; and p. 601 herein.

FOOTNOTES:

[881] John 10:22.
[882] Note 1, end of chapter.
[883] Luke 9:51.
[884] John 10:40; 11:54.
[885] Luke 9:51-56.
[886] John 4:4-42; page 176 herein.
[887] Luke 9:54; compare 2 Kings 1:10, 12.
[888] Matt. 10:23.
[889] Luke 9:57-62; see pages 305-307 herein.
[890] Luke 10:1-12.
[891] Compare Matt. 9:37, 38; see also John 4:35.
[892] Edersheim (vol. ii, p. 138) says: "The expression 'if the son of peace be there' is a Hebraism, equivalent to 'if the house be worthy' (compare Matt. 10:13) and refers to the character of the head of the house and the tone of the household."
[893] Compare Matt. 10:14; page 329 herein.

[894] Compare the charge given the Seventy with that of the Twelve, Matt. 10:5-42; Mark 6:7-11; Luke 9:1-5; see page 328 herein.

[895] Matt. 10:5, 6; 15:24.

[896] Matt. 28:19; Mark 16:15.

[897] Doc. and Cov. 107:25; 124:137-140; see also "Articles of Faith," xi:20, 28. The special office of the Seventy has been reestablished in the restored Church; and in this, the last dispensation, many quorums of Seventy are maintained for the work of the ministry. The office of the Seventy is one belonging to the Higher or Melchizedek Priesthood.

[898] Luke 10:13-15; compare Matt. 11:20-24; see page 258 herein.

[899] Luke 10:17.

[900] Rev. 9:1; 12:8, 9; see pages 6 and 7 herein.

[901] Luke 10:19; read verses 20-24.

[902] Compare Mark 16:18; Acts 28:5.

[903] Rev. 12:9; 20:2; compare Gen. 3:1-4, 14, 15.

[904] Compare Rev. 13:8; 20:12; 21:27.

[905] Compare Mark 12:13; see also Luke 11:53, 54.

[906] Luke 10:25-37.

[907] Compare Gen. 22:1.

[908] Compare Matt. 19:16; Mark 10:17; Luke 18:18.

[909] Luke 10:27; compare Deut. 6:5, and Lev. 19:18; see also Matt. 22:35-40.

[910] Luke 10:30-37.

[911] Matt. 18:21, 22; compare Luke 17:4; page 392 herein.

[912] Deut. 22:4; compare. Exo. 23:5.

[913] Luke 10:38-42. Note 2, end of chapter.

[914] John 11:5.

[915] Compare John 12:2, 3.

[916] Luke 11:1-13.

[917] Pages 238-241.

[918] Luke 18:2-5; read verses 1, and 6-8. See also Doc. and Cov. 101:81-94.

[919] Luke 18:1; compare 21:36; Rom. 12:12; Eph. 6:18; Col. 4:2; 1 Thess. 5:17.

[920] Luke 11:37-54.

[921] Luke 11:14-28; see page 265 herein.

[922] Luke 11:29-36; see page 270 herein.

[923] Matt. 23; see chapter 31 herein.

[924] Luke 12:1-12.

[925] Page 359.

[926] Page 404.

[927] Luke 12:14-21.

[928] Compare the fate that overtook Nebuchadnezzar, while the words of boastful pride were yet in his mouth (Dan. 4:24-33); and that of Belshazzar, before whose eyes appeared the hand of destiny in the midst of his riotous feast; in that night was the king's soul required of him. (Dan. 5.)

[929] Eccles. 2:18, 19; compare succeeding verses; see also Psa. 39:6: 49:6-20; Job 27: 16, 17.

[930] Luke 12:22-31; compare Matt. 6:25-34.

[931] Compare Matt. 6:20.

[932] Luke 12:35-48.

[933] Luke 12:49-57; compare Matt. 10:34-37.

[934] Luke 13:1-5.

[935] Josephus, Wars ii, 9:4; also page 352 herein.

[936] Compare John 9:2, 3; also page 413 herein.

[937] Job 4:7; 8:2-14, 20; 22:5.

[938] Luke 13:6-9.

[939] Luke 3:9.

[940] Luke 13:11-17.

[941] Colos. 4:14.

[942] Luke 13:19-21; see pages 290, 291 herein.

[943] Luke 13:23-30. Note 3, end of chapter.

[944] Compare Matt. 7:13.

[945] Compare Matt. 7:23; 8:11, 12; 19:30; Mark 10:31.

[946] Luke 13:31-33.

[947] In the revised version the last clause reads "for Herod would fain kill thee."

[948] Paul the apostle had been a Pharisee of the most pronounced type. (Acts 23:6; 26:5.)

[949] Luke 13:34, 35: compare Matt. 23:37-39.

CHAPTER 27. CONTINUATION OF THE PEREAN AND JUDEAN MINISTRY.

IN THE HOUSE OF ONE OF THE CHIEF PHARISEES.[950]

On a certain Sabbath Jesus was a guest at the house of a prominent Pharisee. A man afflicted with dropsy was there; he may have come with the hope of receiving a blessing, or possibly his presence had been planned by the host or others as a means of tempting Jesus to work a miracle on the holy day. The exercize of our Lord's healing power was at least thought of if not openly intimated or suggested, for we read that "Jesus answering spake unto the lawyers and Pharisees, saying, Is it lawful to heal on the Sabbath day?"[951] No one ventured to reply. Jesus forthwith healed the man; then He turned to the assembled company and asked: "Which of you shall have an ass or an ox fallen into a pit, and will not straightway pull him out on the sabbath day?"[952] The learned expositors of the law remained prudently silent.

Observing the eager activity of the Pharisee's guests in securing for themselves prominent places at table, Jesus instructed them in a matter of good manners, pointing out not only the propriety but the advantage of decent self-restraint. An invited guest should not select for himself the seat of honor, for some one more distinguished than he may come, and the host would say: "Give this man place." Better is it to take a lower seat, then possibly the lord of the feast may say: "Friend, go up higher." The moral follows: "For whosoever exalteth himself shall be abased; and he that humbleth himself shall be exalted."[953]

This festive gathering at the house of the chief Pharisee included persons of prominence and note, rich men and officials, leading Pharisees, renowned scholars, famous rabbis and the like. Looking over the distinguished company, Jesus said: "When thou makest a dinner or a supper, call not thy friends, nor thy brethren, neither thy kinsmen, nor thy rich neighbours; lest they also bid thee again, and a recompence be made thee. But when thou makest a feast, call the poor, the maimed, the lame, the blind: And thou shalt be blessed; for they cannot recompense thee: for thou shalt be recompensed at the resurrection of the just." This bit of wholesome advice was construed as a reproof; and some one attempted to relieve the embarrassing situation by exclaiming: "Blessed is he that shall eat bread in the kingdom of God."[954] The remark was an allusion to the great festival, which according to Jewish traditionalism was to be a feature of signal importance in the Messianic dispensation. Jesus promptly turned the circumstance to good account by basing thereon the profoundly significant _Parable of the Great Supper_:

"A certain man made a great supper, and bade many: And sent his servant at supper time to say to them that were bidden, Come; for all things are now ready. And they all with one consent began to make excuse. The first said unto him, I have bought a piece of ground, and I must needs go and see it: I pray thee have me excused. And another said, I have bought five yoke of oxen, and I go to prove them: I pray thee have me excused. And another said, I have married a wife, and therefore I cannot come. So that servant came, and shewed his lord these things. Then the master of the house being angry said to his servant, Go out quickly into the streets and lanes of the city, and bring in hither the poor, and the maimed, and the halt, and the blind. And the servant said, Lord, it is done as thou hast commanded, and yet there is room. And the lord said unto the servant, Go out into the highways and hedges, and compel them to come in, that my house may be filled. For I say unto you, That none of those men which were bidden shall taste of my supper."[955]

The story implies that invitations had been given sufficiently early to the chosen and prospective guests; then on the day of the feast a messenger was sent to notify them again, as was the custom of the time. Though called a supper, the meal was to be a sumptuous one; moreover, the principal meal of the day was commonly spoken of as supper. One man after another declined to attend, one saying: "I pray thee have me excused"; another: "I cannot come." The matters that engaged the time and attention of those who had been bidden, or as we would say, invited, to the feast, were not of themselves discreditable, far less sinful; but to arbitrarily allow personal affairs to annul an honorable engagement once accepted was to manifest discourtesy, disrespect and practical insult toward the provider of the feast. The man who had bought a field could have deferred the inspection; he who had just purchased cattle could have waited a day to try them under the yoke; and the newly married man could have left his bride and his friends for the period of the supper that he had promised to attend. Plainly none of these people wanted to be present. The master of the house was justly angry. His command to bring in the poor and the maimed, the halt and the blind from the city streets must have appealed to those who listened to our Lord's recital as a reminiscence of His counsel given a few minutes before, concerning the kind of guests a rich man could invite with profit to his soul. The second sending out of the servant, this time into the highways and hedges outside the city walls, to bring in even the country poor, indicated boundless benevolence and firm determination on the householder's part.

Explication of the parable was left to the learned men to whom the story was addressed. Surely some of them would fathom its meaning, in part at least. The covenant people, Israel, were the specially invited guests. They had been bidden long enough aforetime, and by their own profession as the Lord's own had agreed to be partakers of the feast. When all was ready, on the appointed day, they were severally summoned by the Messenger who had been sent by the Father; He was even then in their midst. But the cares of riches, the allurement of material things, and the pleasures of social and domestic life had engrossed them; and they prayed to be excused or irreverently declared they could not or would not come. Then the gladsome invitation was to be carried to the Gentiles, who were looked upon as spiritually poor, maimed, halt, and blind. And later, even the pagans beyond the walls, strangers in the gates of the holy city, would be bidden to the supper. These, surprized at the unexpected summons, would hesitate, until by gentle urging and effective assurance that they were really included among the bidden guests, they would feel themselves constrained or compelled to come. The possibility of some of the discourteous ones arriving later, after they had attended to their more absorbing affairs, is indicated in the Lord's closing words: "For I say unto you, That none of those men which were bidden shall taste of my supper."

COUNTING THE COST.[956]

As had been in Galilee, so was it in Perea and Judea--great multitudes attended the Master whenever He appeared in public. When once a scribe has presented himself as a disciple, offering to follow wherever the Master led, Jesus had indicated the self-denial, privation and suffering incident to devoted service, with the result that the man's enthusiasm was soon spent.[957] So now to the eager multitude Jesus applied a test of sincerity. He would have only genuine disciples, not enthusiasts of a day, ready to desert His cause when effort and sacrifice were most needed. Thus did He sift the people: "If any man come to me, and hate not his father, and mother, and wife, and children, and brethren, and sisters, yea, and his own life also, he cannot be my disciple. And whosoever doth not bear his cross, and come after me, cannot be my disciple." Literal hatred toward one's family was not specified as a condition of discipleship; indeed a man who indulges hatred or any other evil passion is a subject for repentance and reformation. The preeminence of duty toward God over personal or family demands on the part of one who had assumed the obligations of a disciple was the precept.[958]

As Jesus pointed out, it is good common-sense to count well the cost before one enters upon a great undertaking, even in ordinary affairs. A man who wishes to build, say a tower or a house, tries to determine, before he begins the work, what the expense will be; otherwise he may be able to do no more than lay the foundation; then, not only will he find himself a loser, for the unfinished structure will be of no service, but people may laugh at his lack of prudent forethought. So also a king, finding his realm menaced by hostile invaders, does not rush into battle recklessly; he first tries to ascertain the strength of the enemy's forces; and then, if the odds against him be too great, he sends an embassage to treat for peace. "So likewise," said Jesus to the people around Him, "whosoever he be of you that forsaketh not all that he hath, he cannot be my disciple." All who entered His service would be expected to maintain their self-sacrificing devotion. He wanted no disciples who would become like salt that had spoiled, unsavory and useless. "He that hath ears to hear, let him hear."[959]

SALVATION FOR "PUBLICANS AND SINNERS"--ILLUSTRATIVE PARABLES.[960]

The Pharisees in Galilee had intolerantly criticized Jesus because of His friendly and helpful ministry among the publicans and their associates, who were disparagingly classed together as "publicans and sinners."[961] He had replied to these uncharitable aspersions by saying that a physician is most needed by them that are sick, and that He had come to call sinners to repentance. The Judean Pharisees raised a similar complaint, and were particularly virulent when they saw that "all the publicans and sinners" drew near to hear Him. He met their murmurs by presenting a number of parables, designed to show the incumbent duty of trying to recover the lost, and the joy of success in such God-like endeavor. The first of the series of parables was that of the _Lost Sheep_; this we have considered in connection with its earlier delivery in the course of instruction to the disciples in Galilee.[962] Its application in the present instance, however, is somewhat different from that of its former presentation. The lesson on this later occasion was directed to the self-seeking Pharisees and scribes who personified the theocracy, and whose bounden duty it should have been to care for the strayed and the lost. If the "publicans and sinners," whom these ecclesiasts so generally contemned, were nearly as bad as they were represented to be, if they were men who had broken through the close-hedged path of the law and had become in a measure apostate, they were the ones toward whom the helping hand of missionary service could be best extended. In no instance of Pharisaic slur upon, or open denunciation of, these "publicans and sinners," do we find Jesus defending their alleged evil ways; His attitude toward these spiritually sick folk was that of a devoted physician: His concern over these strayed sheep was that of a loving shepherd whose chief desire was to find them out and bring them back to the fold. This neither the theocracy as a system nor its officials as individual ministers even attempted to do. The shepherd, on finding the sheep that was lost, thinks not at the time of reprimand or punishment; on the contrary, "when he hath found it, he layeth it on his shoulders, rejoicing. And when he cometh home, he calleth together his friends and neighbours, saying unto them: Rejoice with me; for I have found my sheep which was lost."

A direct application of the parable appears in the Lord's concise address to the Pharisees and scribes: "I say unto you, that likewise joy shall be in heaven over one sinner that repenteth, more than over ninety and nine just persons, which need no repentance." Were they the ninety and nine, who, by self-estimation had strayed not, being "just persons, which need no repentance?" Some readers say they catch this note of just sarcasm in the Master's concluding words. In the earlier part of the story, the Lord Himself appears as the solicitous Shepherd, and by plain implication His example is such as the theocratic leaders ought to emulate. Such a conception puts the Pharisees and scribes in the position of shepherds rather than of sheep. Both explications are tenable; and each is of value as portraying the status and duty of professing servants of the Master in all ages.

Without break in the narrative, the Lord passed from the story of the lost sheep to the _Parable of the Lost Coin_.

"Either what woman having ten pieces of silver, if she lose one piece, doth not light a candle, and sweep the house, and seek diligently till she find it? And when she hath found it, she calleth her friends and her neighbours together, saying, Rejoice with me; for I have found the piece which I had lost. Likewise, I say unto you, there is joy in the presence of the angels of God over one sinner that repenteth."

Between this parable and that of the lost sheep there are certain notable differences, though the lesson in each is in general the same. The sheep had strayed by its own volition; the coin[963] had been dropped, and so was lost as a result of inattention or culpable carelessness on the part of its owner. The woman, discovering her loss institutes a diligent search; she sweeps the house, and perhaps learns of dirty corners, dusty recesses, cobwebby nooks, to which she had been oblivious in her self-complacency as an outwardly clean and conventional housewife. Her search is rewarded by the recovery of the lost piece, and is incidentally beneficial in the cleansing of her house. Her joy is like that of the shepherd wending his way homeward with the sheep upon his shoulders--once lost but now regained.

The woman who by lack of care lost the precious piece may be taken to represent the theocracy of the time, and the Church as an institution in any dispensational period; then the pieces of silver, every one a genuine coin of the realm, bearing the image of the great King, are the souls committed to the care of the Church; and the lost piece symbolizes the souls that are neglected and, for a time at least, lost sight of, by the authorized ministers of the Gospel of Christ. These cogent illustrations were followed by one yet richer in imagery and more impressively elaborate in detail. It is the never to be forgotten _Parable of the Prodigal Son_.[964]

"And he said, A certain man had two sons; And the younger of them said to his father, Father, give me the portion of goods that falleth to me. And he divided unto them his living. And not many days after the younger son gathered all together, and took his journey into a far country, and there wasted his substance with riotous living. And when he had spent all, there arose a mighty famine in that land; and he began to be in want. And he went and joined himself to a citizen of that country; and he sent him into his fields to feed swine. And he would fain have filled his belly with the husks that the swine did eat: and no man gave unto him. And when he came to himself, he said, How many hired servants of my father's have bread enough and to spare, and I perish with hunger! I will arise and go to my father, and will say unto him, Father, I have sinned against heaven, and before thee, And am no more worthy to be called thy son: make me as one of thy hired servants. And he arose, and came to his father. But when he was yet a great way off, his father saw him, and had compassion, and ran, and fell on his neck, and kissed him. And the son said unto him, Father, I have sinned against heaven, and in thy sight, and am no more worthy to be called thy son. But the father said to his servants, Bring forth the best robe, and put it on him; and put a ring on his hand, and shoes on his feet: And bring hither the fatted calf, and kill it; and let us eat, and be merry: For this my son was dead, and is alive again; he was lost, and is found. And they began to be merry. Now his elder son was in the field: and as he came and drew nigh to the house, he heard musick and dancing. And he called one of the servants, and asked what these things meant. And he said unto him, Thy brother is come; and thy father hath killed the fatted calf, because he hath received him safe and sound. And he was angry, and would not go in: therefore came his father out, and intreated him. And he answering said to his father, Lo, these many years do I serve thee, neither transgressed I at any time thy commandment: and yet thou never gavest me a kid, that I might make merry with my friends: But as soon as this thy son was come, which hath devoured thy living with harlots, thou hast killed for him the fatted calf. And he said unto him, Son, thou art ever with me, and all that I have is thine. It was meet that we should make merry, and be glad: for this thy brother was dead, and is alive again; and was lost, and is found."

The demand of the younger son for a portion of the patrimony even during his father's lifetime, is an instance of deliberate and unfilial desertion; the duties of family cooperation had grown distasteful to him, and the wholesome discipline of the home had become irksome. He was determined to break away from all home ties, forgetful of what home had done for him and the debt of gratitude and duty by which he was morally bound. He went into a far country, and, as he thought, beyond the reach of the father's directing influence. He had his season of riotous living, of unrestrained indulgence and evil pleasure, through it all wasting his strength of body and mind, and squandering his father's substance; for what he had received had been given as a concession and not as the granting of any legal or just demand. Adversity came upon him, and proved to be a more effective minister for good than pleasure had been. He was reduced to the lowest and most menial service, that of herding swine, which occupation, to a Jew, was the extreme of degradation. Suffering brought him to himself. He, the son of honorable parentage, was feeding pigs and eating with them, while even the hired servants at home had good food in plenty and to spare. He realized not alone his abject foolishness in leaving his father's well-spread table to batten with hogs, but the unrighteousness of his selfish desertion; he was not only remorseful but repentant. He had sinned against his father and against God; he would return, confess his sin, and ask, not to be reinstated as a son, but to be allowed to work as a hired servant. Having resolved he delayed not, but immediately set out to find his long way back to home and father.

The father became aware of the prodigal's approach and hastened to meet him. Without a word of condemnation, the loving parent embraced and kissed the wayward but now penitent boy, who, overcome by this undeserved affection, humbly acknowledged his error, and sorrowfully confessed that he was not worthy to be known as his father's son. It is noteworthy that in his contrite confession he did not ask to be accepted as a hired servant as he had resolved to do; the father's joy was too sacred to be thus marred, he would please his father best by placing himself unreservedly at that father's disposal. The rough garb of poverty was discarded for the best robe; a ring was placed on his finger as a mark of reinstatement; shoes told of restored sonship, not of employment as a hired servant. The father's glad heart could express itself only in acts of abundant kindness; a feast was made ready; for was not the son, once counted as dead now alive? Had not the lost been found again?

So far the story sustains a relation of close analogy to the two parables that preceded it in the same discourse; the part following introduces another important symbolism. No one had complained at the recovery of the stray sheep nor at the finding of the lost coin; friends had rejoiced with the finder in each case. But the father's happiness at the return of the prodigal was interrupted by the grumbling protest of the elder son. He, on approaching the house, had observed the evidences of festal joy; and, instead of entering as was his right, had inquired of one of the servants as to the cause of the unusual rejoicing. On learning that his brother had returned and that the father had prepared a festival in honor of the event, this elder son grew angry, and churlishly refused to enter the house even after his father had come out and entreated him. He cited his own faithfulness and devotion to the routine labor of the farm, to which claim of excellence the father did not demur; but the son and heir reproached his father for having failed to give him so much as a kid with which to make merry with his friends; while now that the wayward and spendthrift son had come back the father had killed for him even the fatted calf. There is significance in the elder one's designation of the penitent as "this thy son," rather than "my brother." The elder son, deafened by selfish anger, refused to hear aright the affectionate assurance; "Son, thou art ever with me, and all that I have is thine," and with heart hardened by unbrotherly resentment he stood unmoved by the emotional and loving outburst, "this thy brother was dead, and is alive again; and was lost, and is found."

We are not justified in extolling the virtue of repentance on the part of the prodigal above the faithful, plodding service of his brother, who had remained at home, true to the duties required of him. The devoted son was the heir; the father did not disparage his worth, nor deny his deserts. His displeasure over the rejoicing incident to the return of his wayward brother was an exhibition of illiberality and narrowness; but of the two brothers the elder was the more faithful, whatever his minor defects may have been. The particular point emphasized in the Lord's lesson, however, had to do with his uncharitable and selfish weaknesses.

Pharisees and scribes, to whom this masterpiece of illustrative incident was delivered, must have taken to themselves its personal application. They were typified by the elder son, laboriously attentive to routine, methodically plodding by rule and rote in the multifarious labors of the field, without interest except that of self, and all unwilling to welcome a repentant publican or a returned sinner. From all such they were estranged; such a one might be to the indulgent and forgiving Father, "this thy son," but never to them, a brother. They cared not who or how many were lost, so long as they were undisturbed in heirship and possession by the return of penitent prodigals. But the parable was not for them alone; it is a living perennial yielding the fruit of wholesome doctrine and soul-sustaining nourishment for all time. Not a word appears in condonation or excuse for the prodigal's sin; upon that the Father could not look with the least degree of allowance;[965] but over that sinner's repentance and contrition of soul, God and the household of heaven rejoiced.

The three parables which appear in the scriptural record as parts of a continuous discourse, are as one in portraying the joy that abounds in heaven over the recovery of a soul once numbered among the lost, whether that soul be best symbolized by a sheep that had wandered afar, a coin that had dropped out of sight through the custodian's neglect, or a son who would deliberately sever himself from home and heaven. There is no justification for the inference that a repentant sinner is to be given precedence, over a righteous soul who has resisted sin; were such the way of God, then Christ, the one sinless Man, would be surpassed in the Father's esteem by regenerate offenders. Unqualifiedly offensive as is sin, the sinner is yet precious in the Father's eyes, because of the possibility of his repentance and return to righteousness. The loss of a soul is a very real and a very great loss to God. He is pained and grieved thereby, for it is His will that not one should perish.[966]

DISCIPLES INSTRUCTED BY PARABLE.

Addressing Himself more directly to the disciples present, who on this occasion probably comprized in addition to the apostles, many believers, including even some of the publicans, Jesus spake the _Parable of the Unrighteous Steward_.[967]

"And he said also unto his disciples, There was a certain rich   man, which had a steward; and the same was accused unto him that   he had wasted his goods. And he called him, and said unto him,   How is it that I hear this of thee? give an account of thy   stewardship; for thou mayest be no longer steward. Then the   steward said within himself, What shall I do? for my lord taketh   away from me the stewardship: I cannot dig; to beg I am ashamed.   I am resolved what to do, that, when I am put out of the   stewardship, they may receive me into their houses. So he called   every one of his lord's debtors unto him, and said unto the   first, How much owest thou unto my lord? And he said, An hundred measures of oil. And he said unto him, Take thy bill, and sit   down quickly, and write fifty. Then said he to another, And how   much owest thou? And he said, An hundred measures of wheat. And   he said unto him, Take thy bill, and write fourscore. And the   lord commended the unjust steward, because he had done wisely: for the children of this world are in their generation wiser   than the children of light."

The three preceding parables show forth their lessons through the relationship of close analogy and intimate similarities; this one teaches rather by its contrast of situations. The steward in the story was the duly authorized agent of his employer, holding what we would call the power-of-attorney to act in his master's name.[968] He was called to account because a report of his wastefulness and lack of care had reached the master's ears. The steward did not deny his guilt, and forthwith he received notice of dismissal. Considerable time would be required for making up his accounts preparatory to turning the stewardship over to his successor. This interval, during which he remained in authority, he determined to use so far as possible to his own advantage, even though he wrought further injustice to his master's interests. He contemplated the condition of dependence in which he would soon find himself. Through unthrift and extravagance he had failed to lay by any store from his earnings; he had wasted his own and his lord's substance. He felt that he was unfit for hard manual labor; and he would be ashamed to beg, particularly in the community in which he had been a lavish spender and a man of influence. With the desire to put others under some obligation to himself so that when he was deposed he could the more effectively appeal to them, he called his lord's debtors and authorized them to change their bonds, bills of sale, or notes of hand, so as to show a greatly decreased indebtedness. Without doubt these acts were unrighteous; he defrauded his employer, and enriched the debtors through whom he hoped to be benefited. Most of us are surprized to know that the master, learning what his far-seeing though selfish and dishonest steward had done, condoned the offense and actually commended him for his foresight, "because he had done wisely" as our version reads, or "because he had done prudently" as many scholars aver to be the better rendering.

In pointing the moral of the parable Jesus said:[969] "For the children of this world are in their generation wiser than the children of light. And I say unto you, Make to yourselves friends of the mammon of unrighteousness; that, when ye fail, they may receive you into everlasting habitations." Our Lord's purpose was to show the contrast between the care, thoughtfulness, and devotion of men engaged in the money-making affairs of earth, and the half hearted ways of many who are professedly striving after spiritual riches. Worldly-minded men do not neglect provision for their future years, and often are sinfully eager to amass plenty; while the "children of light," or those who believe spiritual wealth to be above all earthly possessions, are less energetic, prudent, or wise. By "mammon of unrighteousness" we may understand material wealth or worldly things. While far inferior to the treasures of heaven, money or that which it represents may be the means of accomplishing good, and of furthering the purposes of God. Our Lord's admonition was to utilize "mammon" in good works, while it lasted, for some day it shall fail, and only the results achieved through its use shall endure.[970] If the wicked steward, when cast out from his master's house because of unworthiness, might hope to be received into the homes of these whom he had favored, how much more confidently may they who are genuinely devoted to the right hope to be received into the everlasting mansions of God! Such seems to be part of the lesson.

It was not the steward's dishonesty that was extolled; his prudence and foresight were commended, however; for while he misapplied his master's substance, he gave relief to the debtors; and in so doing he did not exceed his legal powers, for he was still steward though he was morally guilty of malfeasance. The lesson may be summed up in this wise: Make such use of your wealth as shall insure you friends hereafter. Be diligent; for the day in which you can use your earthly riches will soon pass. Take a lesson from even the dishonest and the evil; if they are so prudent as to provide for the only future they think of, how much more should you, who believe in an eternal future, provide therefor! If you have not learned wisdom and prudence in the use of "unrighteous mammon," how can you be trusted with the more enduring riches? If you have not learned how to use properly the wealth of another, which has been committed to you as steward, how can you expect to be successful in the handling of great wealth should such be given you as your own? Emulate the unjust steward and the lovers of mammon, not in their dishonesty, cupidity, and miserly hoarding of the wealth that is at best but transitory, but in their zeal, forethought, and provision for the future. Moreover, let not wealth become your master; keep it to its place as a servant, for, "No servant can serve two masters: for either he will hate the one, and love the other; or else he will hold to the one, and despise the other. Ye cannot serve God and mammon."

DERISION OF THE PHARISEES MET; ANOTHER ILLUSTRATIVE PARABLES.[971]

The Pharisees, who were covetous, or more precisely stated, who were lovers of money,[972] overheard the foregoing instructions to the disciples, and openly scoffed at the Teacher and the lesson. What did this Galilean, who owned nothing but the clothes He wore, know about money or the best way of administering wealth? Our Lord's reply to their words of derision was a further condemnation. They knew all the tricks of the business-world, and could outdo the unrighteous steward in crafty manipulation; and yet so successfully could they justify themselves before men as to be outwardly honest and straightforward; furthermore, they made ostentatious display of a certain type of simplicity, plainness, and self-denial, in which external observances they asserted superiority over the luxury-loving Sadducees; they had grown arrogantly proud of their humility, but God knew their hearts, and the traits and practises they most esteemed were an abomination in His sight. They posed as custodians of the law and expounders of the prophets. The "law and the prophets" had been in force until the Baptist's time, since which the gospel of the kingdom had been preached, and people were eager to enter it[973] though the theocracy strove mightily to prevent. The law had not been invalidated; easier were it that heaven and earth pass away than that one tittle of the law fail of fulfilment;[974] yet those Pharisees and scribes had tried to nullify the law. In the matter of divorce, for example, they, by their unlawful additions and false interpretations, had condoned even the sin of adultery.

The Master gave as a further lesson the _Parable of the Rich Man and Lazarus.

"There was a certain rich man, which was clothed in purple and fine linen, and fared sumptuously every day: And there was a certain beggar named Lazarus, which was laid at his gate, full of sores, And desiring to be fed with the crumbs which fell from the rich man's table: moreover the dogs came and licked his sores. And it came to pass, that the beggar died, and was carried by the angels into Abraham's bosom: the rich man also died, and was buried; And in hell he lift up his eyes, being in torments, and seeth Abraham afar off, and Lazarus in his bosom. And he cried and said, Father Abraham, have mercy on me, and send Lazarus, that he may dip the tip of his finger in water, and cool my tongue; for I am tormented in this flame. But Abraham said, Son, remember that thou in thy lifetime receivedst thy good things, and likewise Lazarus evil things: but now he is comforted, and thou art tormented. And beside all this, between   us and you there is a great gulf fixed: so that they which would pass from hence to you cannot; neither can they pass to us, that   would come from thence. Then he said, I pray thee therefore,   father, that thou wouldest send him to my father's house: For I   have five brethren; that he may testify unto them, lest they   also come into this place of torment. Abraham saith unto him,   They have Moses and the prophets; let them hear them. And he   said, Nay, father Abraham; but if one went unto them from the   dead, they will repent. And he said unto him, If they hear not Moses and the prophets, neither will they be persuaded, though   one rose from the dead."[975]

The afflicted beggar is honored with a name; the other is designated simply as "a certain rich man."[976] The two are presented as the extremes of contrast between wealth and destitution. The rich man was clothed in the costliest attire, purple and fine linen; and his every-day fare was a sumptuous feast. Lazarus had been brought to the gates of the rich man's palace, and there left, a helpless mendicant, his body covered with sores. The rich man was attended by servitors ready to gratify his slightest desire; the poor beggar at his gates had neither companions nor attendants except the dogs, which like himself waited for the refuse from the rich man's table. Such is the picture of the two in life. An abrupt change of scene brings into view the same two on the far side of the veil that hangs between the here and the hereafter. Lazarus died; no mention is made of his funeral; his festering body was probably thrown into a pauper's grave; but angels bore his immortal spirit into Paradise, the resting place of the blessed and commonly known in the figurative lore of the rabbis as Abraham's bosom. The rich man also died; his burial was doubtless an elaborate affair, but we read not of any angelic escort receiving his spirit. In hell he lifted up his eyes and saw, afar, Lazarus at peace in the abode of Abraham.

As a Jew the man had often boasted of having Abraham for his father; and now the wretched spirit appealed to the patriarch of his race by the paternal address, "Father Abraham," and asked only the boon of a single drop of water to be placed on his parched tongue; this he prayed that Lazarus, the erstwhile beggar, might bring. The reply throws light on certain conditions existing in the spirit world, though as in the use of parables generally, the presentation is largely figurative. Addressing the poor tormented spirit as "Son," Abraham reminded him of all the good things he had kept for himself on earth, whilst Lazarus had lain a suffering, neglected beggar at his gates; now by the operation of divine law, Lazarus had received recompense, and he, retribution. Moreover, to grant his pitiful request was impossible, for between the abode of the righteous where Lazarus rested and that of the wicked where he suffered "there is a great gulf fixed," and passage between the two is interdicted. The next request of the miserable sufferer was not wholly selfish; in his anguish he remembered those from whom he had been separated by death, fain would he save his brothers from the fate he had met; and he prayed that Lazarus be sent back to earth to visit the ancestral home, and warn those selfish, pleasure-seeking, and yet mortal brothers, of the awful doom awaiting them except they would repent and reform. There may have been in this petition an insinuation that had he been sufficiently warned he would have done better, and would have escaped the torment. To the reminder that they had the words of Moses and the prophets, which they should obey, he replied that if one went to them from the dead they would surely repent. Abraham answered that if they would not heed Moses and the prophets neither would "they be persuaded, though one rose from the dead."

In any attempt to interpret the parable as a whole or definitely apply any of its parts, we should bear in mind that it was addressed to the Pharisees as an instructive rebuke for the derision and scorn with which they had received the Lord's warning concerning the dangers attending servitude to mammon. Jesus employed Jewish metaphors, and the imagery of the parable is such as would most directly appeal to the official expounders of Moses and the prophets. While as a practise it would be critically unfair to deduce doctrinal principles from parabolic incidents, we cannot admit that Christ would teach falsely even in parable; and therefore we accept as true the portrayal of conditions in the world of the disembodied. That righteous and unrighteous dwell apart during the interval between death and resurrection is clear. Paradise, or as the Jews like to designate that blessed abode, "Abraham's bosom," is not the place of final glory, any more than the hell to which the rich man's spirit was consigned is the final habitation of the condemned. [977] To that preliminary or intermediate state, however, men's works do follow them;[978] and the dead shall surely find that their abode is that for which they have qualified themselves while in the flesh. The rich man's fate was not the effect of riches, nor was the rest into which Lazarus entered the resultant of poverty. Failure to use his wealth aright, and selfish satisfaction with the sensuous enjoyment of earthly things to the exclusion of all concern for the needs or privations of his fellows, brought the one under condemnation; while patience in suffering, faith in God and such righteous life as is implied though not expressed, insured happiness to the other. The proud self-sufficiency of the rich man, who lacked nothing that wealth could furnish, and who kept aloof from the needy and suffering, was his besetting sin. The aloofness of the Pharisees, on which indeed they prided themselves, as their very name, signifying "separatists," expressed, was thus condemned. The parable teaches the continuation of individual existence after death, and the relation of cause to effect between the life one leads in mortality and the state awaiting him beyond.

UNPROFITABLE SERVANTS.[979]

From the Pharisees, Jesus turned to His disciples and admonished them to diligence. Having cautioned them against unguarded utterances or actions at which others might take offense, He proceeded to impress the absolute necessity of unselfish devotion, toleration and forgiveness. The apostles, realizing the whole-souled service required of them, implored the Lord, saying: "Increase our faith." They were shown that faith was less fitly reckoned in terms of quantity than by test of quality; and the analogy of the mustard seed was again invoked. "And the Lord said, If ye had faith as a grain of mustard seed, ye might say unto this sycamine tree, Be thou plucked up by the root, and be thou planted in the sea; and it should obey you."[980] Their faith could best be gaged by obedience and untiring service.

This was emphasized by the _Parable of the Unprofitable Servants.

"But which of you, having a servant plowing or feeding cattle,   will say unto him by and by, when he is come from the field, Go   and sit down to meat? And will not rather say unto him, Make ready wherewith I may sup, and gird thyself, and serve me, till   I have eaten and drunken; and afterward thou shalt eat and   drink? Doth he thank that servant because he did the things that   were commanded him? I trow not. So likewise ye, when ye shall   have done all those things which are commanded you, say, We are   unprofitable servants: we have done that which was our duty to   do."

The servant might well feel that after a day's work in the field he is entitled to rest; but on reaching the house he finds other demands made upon him. The master has a right to the servant's time and attention; such was among the conditions under which the servant had been engaged; and while his employer might thank him or give some substantial reward, the servant cannot demand such recompense. So the apostles, who had given themselves entirely up to their Master's service, were not to hesitate nor demur, whatever the effort or sacrifice required. The best they could do would be no more than their duty required; and, without regard to the Master's estimate of their worth, they were to account themselves as unprofitable servants.[981]

TEN LEPERS HEALED.[982]

In the course of His journey toward Jerusalem Jesus "passed through the midst of Samaria and Galilee." Ten men afflicted with leprosy approached, probably they came as near as the law permitted, yet they were afar off. These men were of mixed nationality; the plague under which they suffered in common had made them companions in distress. They cried aloud "Jesus, Master, have mercy on us." The Lord answered: "Go shew yourselves unto the priests."[983] This instruction implied their ultimate healing; obedience would be the test of their faith. None who had been leprous could be lawfully restored to community life until pronounced clean by a priest. The stricken ten hastened to obey the Lord's command, "and it came to pass, that, as they went, they were cleansed."[984] One of the ten turned back, and with loud voice glorified God; then he prostrated himself at the feet of Christ, giving thanks. We are told that the grateful one was a Samaritan, from which we infer that some or all of the others were Jews. Pained over the lack of gratitude on the part of the nine, Jesus exclaimed: "Were there not ten cleansed? but where are the nine? There are not found that return to give glory to God, save this stranger." And to the cleansed Samaritan, still worshiping at His feet, the Lord said: "Arise, go thy way: thy faith hath made thee whole." Doubtless the nine who came not back were obedient to the strict letter of the Lord's command; for He had told them to go to the priests; but their lack of gratitude and their failure to acknowledge the power of God in their restoration stand in unfavorable contrast with the spirit of the one; and he was a Samaritan. The occurrence must have impressed the apostles as another evidence of acceptability and possible excellence on the part of aliens, to the disparagement of Jewish claims of superiority irrespective of merit.

THE PHARISEE AND THE PUBLICAN.[985]

"And he spake this parable unto certain which trusted in themselves that they were righteous, and despised others:

"Two men went up into the temple to pray; the one a Pharisee,   and the other a publican. The Pharisee stood and prayed thus   with himself, God, I thank thee, that I am not as other men are, extortioners, unjust, adulterers, or even as this publican. I   fast twice in the week, I give tithes of all that I possess. And   the publican, standing afar off, would not lift up so much as   his eyes unto heaven, but smote upon his breast, saying, God be   merciful to me a sinner. I tell you, this man went down to his house justified rather than the other: for every one that   exalteth himself shall be abased; and he that humbleth himself   shall be exalted."

We are expressly told that this parable was given for the benefit of certain ones who trusted in their self-righteousness as an assurance of justification before God. It was not addressed to the Pharisees nor to the publicans specifically. The two characters are types of widely separated classes. There may have been much of the Pharisaic spirit of self-complacency among the disciples and some of it even among the Twelve. A Pharisee and a publican went up to the temple to pray. The Pharisee prayed "with himself"; his words can hardly be construed as a prayer to God. That he stood while praying was not an impropriety, for the standing attitude was usual in prayer; the publican also stood. The Pharisee thanked God that he was so much better than other men; he was true to his class, a separatist who looked with disdain upon all who were not like him. That he was not like "this publican" was made a point of special thanksgiving. His boast, that he fasted twice a week and gave tithes of all that he possessed, was a specification of worthiness above what was required by the law as then administered; he thus implied that God was his debtor.[986] The publican, standing afar off, was so oppressed by his consciousness of sin and his absolute need of divine help, that he cast down his eyes and smote upon his breast, craving mercy as a penitent sinner. The Pharisee departed, justified in his own conscience and before man, prouder than ever; the other went down to his house justified before God though still a despized publican. The parable is applicable to all men; its moral was summed up in a repetition of our Lord's words spoken in the house of the chief Pharisee: "For every one that exalteth himself shall be abased; and he that humbleth himself shall be exalted."[987]

ON MARRIAGE AND DIVORCE.[988]

While wending His way by short stages toward Jerusalem, and while still "beyond" or on "the farther side" of Jordan, and therefore in Perean territory, Jesus was met by a body of Pharisees, who had come with the deliberate purpose of inciting Him to say or do something on which they could base an accusation. The question they had agreed to submit related to marriage and divorce, and no subject had been more vehemently contested in their own schools and among their own rabbis.[989] The crafty questioners may have hoped that Jesus would denounce the adulterous state in which Herod Antipas was then living, and so bring upon Himself the fury of Herodias, to which the Baptist had already died a victim. "Is it lawful for a man to put away his wife for every cause?" they asked. Jesus cited the original and eternal law of God in the matter; and indicated the only rational conclusion to be drawn therefrom: "Have ye not read, that he which made them at the beginning made them male and female, and said, For this cause shall a man leave father and mother, and shall cleave to his wife: and they twain shall be one flesh? Wherefore they are no more twain, but one flesh. What therefore God hath joined together, let not man put asunder."[990] God had provided for honorable marriage, and had made the relation between husband and wife paramount even to that of children to parents; the severing of such a union was an invention of man, not a command of God. The Pharisees had a ready rejoinder: "Why did Moses then command to give a writing of divorcement, and to put her away?" Be it remembered that Moses had not commanded divorce, but had required that in case a man should separate from his wife he give her a bill of divorcement.[991] Jesus made this fact plain, saying: "Moses because of the hardness of your hearts suffered you to put away your wives: but from the beginning it was not so."

The higher requirement of the gospel followed: "And I say unto you, Whosoever shall put away his wife, except it be for fornication, and shall marry another, committeth adultery: and whoso marrieth her which is put away doth commit adultery."[992] The Mosaic provision had been but permissive, and was justified only because of existing unrighteousness. Strict compliance with the doctrine enunciated by Jesus Christ is the only means by which a perfect social order can be maintained. It is important to note, however, that in His reply to the casuistical Pharisees, Jesus announced no specific or binding rule as to legal divorces; the putting away of a wife, as contemplated under the Mosaic custom, involved no judicial investigation or action by an established court. In our Lord's day the prevailing laxity in the matter of marital obligation had produced a state of appalling corruption in Israel; and woman, who by the law of God had been made a companion and partner with man, had become his slave. The world's greatest champion of woman and womanhood is Jesus the Christ.[993]

The Pharisees retired foiled in purpose and convicted in conscience. The Lord's strict construction of the marriage bond was startling even to some of the disciples; these came to Him privately, saying that if a man was so bound it would be better not to marry at all. Such a broad generalization the Lord disapproved except so far as it might apply in special cases. True, there were some who were physically incapacitated for marriage; others voluntarily devoted themselves to a celibate life, and some few adopted celibacy "for the kingdom of heaven's sake," that thereby they might be free to render all their time and energy to the Lord's service. But the disciples' conclusion that "it is not good to marry" was true only in the exceptional instances stated. Marriage is honorable;[994] for neither man without woman nor woman without man can be perfect in the Lord's sight.[995]

JESUS AND THE LITTLE ONES.[996]

The next event of record is one of surpassing sweetness, rich in precept and invaluable in example. Mothers brought their little children to Jesus, reverently desiring that the lives of those little ones be brightened by a sight of the Master and be blessed by a touch of His hand or a word from His lips. The circumstance appears in appropriate sequence to that of the Lord's instructions concerning the sacredness of marriage and the sanctity of the home. The disciples, zealous that their Master be not troubled unnecessarily, and conscious of the continuous demands on His time and attention, rebuked those who had so ventured to trespass. Even the disciples seem to have been yet under the influence of the traditional conception that women and children were of inferior status, and that for such to seek the Lord's attention was an act of presumption. Jesus was displeased over the misdirected zeal of His followers, and rebuked them. Then He uttered that memorable sentence of infinite tenderness and divine affection: "_Suffer the little children to come unto me, and forbid them not: for of such is the kingdom of God._" Taking the children one by one into His arms, He laid His hands upon them and blessed them.[997] Then said He: "Verily I say unto you, Whosoever shall not receive the kingdom of God as a little child, he shall not enter therein."[998]

ONE THING THOU LACKEST.[999]

Jesus was accosted on the way by a young man, who came running to meet or overtake Him, and who knelt at His feet, inquiring: "Good Master, what shall I do that I may inherit eternal life?" The question was asked in earnestness; the questioner was in very different spirit from that of the lawyer who made a similar inquiry with the purpose of tempting the Master.[1000] Jesus said: "Why callest thou me good? there is none good but one, that is, God." This remark was no denial of sinlessness on the Savior's part; the young man had called Him "good" by way of polite compliment rather than in recognition of His Godship, and Jesus declined to acknowledge the distinction when applied in that sense. The Lord's remark must have deepened the young man's conception as to the seriousness of his question. Then said Jesus: "If thou wilt enter into life, keep the commandments." To the further inquiry, as to which commandments were meant, Jesus cited the prohibitions against murder, adultery, theft, and the bearing of false witness, and the requirements as to honoring parents, and loving one's neighbor as one's self. In simplicity and without pride or sense of self-righteousness, the young man said: "All these things have I kept from my youth up: what lack I yet?" His evident sincerity appealed to Jesus, who looked upon him lovingly and said: "One thing thou lackest: go thy way, sell whatsoever thou hast, and give to the poor, and thou shalt have treasure in heaven: and come, take up the cross, and follow me."[1001]

The young man was disappointed and saddened. He had probably expected to hear the great Teacher prescribe some one special observance, by which excellence could be achieved. Luke tells us that the young man was a ruler; this may mean that he was a presiding official in the local synagog or possibly a Sanhedrist. He was well versed in the law, and had been strict in obedience thereto. He desired to advance in good works and make clear his title to an eternal heritage. But the Master prescribed what he had least expected; "And he was sad at that saying, and went away grieved: for he had great possessions." In his way, he yearned for the kingdom of God, yet more devotedly he loved his great possessions. To give up wealth, social position, and official distinction, was too great a sacrifice; and the necessary self-denial was a cross too heavy for him to bear, even though treasure in heaven and life eternal were offered him. Love of worldly things was this man's besetting weakness; Jesus diagnosed his case and prescribed a suitable remedy. We are not warranted in saying that the same treatment would be best in all cases of spiritual defection; but where the symptoms indicate the need, it may be employed with confidence as to the cure.

Gazing sorrowfully upon the retreating figure of the wealthy young ruler Jesus said to the disciples: "Verily I say unto you, That a rich man shall hardly enter into the kingdom of heaven." To impress the lesson more thoroughly He applied one of the figurative proverbs of the age, and said: "It is easier for a camel to go through the eye of a needle, than for a rich man to enter into the kingdom of God."[1002] At this statement the disciples were amazed. "Who then can be saved?" they wondered. Jesus understood their perplexity, and encouraged them with the assurance that with God all things are possible. Thus were they given to understand that while wealth is a means of temptation to which many succumb, it is no insuperable obstacle, no insurmountable barrier, in the way of entrance to the kingdom. Had the young ruler followed the advice called forth by his inquiry, his possession of riches would have made possible to him meritorious service such as few are able to render. Willingness to place the kingdom of God above all material possessions was the one thing he lacked.[1003] Everyone of us may pertinently ask, What do I lack?

THE FIRST MAY BE LAST, AND THE LAST FIRST.[1004]

The sorrowful departure of the rich young ruler, whose great possessions were so much a part of his life that he could not give them up at the time, though we may hope that he afterward did, brought forth from Peter an abrupt question, which revealed the course of his thoughts and aspirations: "Behold, we have forsaken all, and followed thee; what shall we have therefore?" Whether he spoke for himself alone, or by his use of the plural "we" meant to include all the Twelve, is uncertain and unimportant. He was thinking of the home and family he had left, and a longing for them was pardonable; he was thinking also of boats and nets, hooks and lines, and the lucrative business for which such things stood. All these he had forsaken; what was to be his reward? Jesus answered: "Verily I say unto you, That ye which have followed me, in the regeneration when the Son of man shall sit in the throne of his glory, ye also shall sit upon twelve thrones, judging the twelve tribes of Israel." It is doubtful that Peter or any other of the Twelve had ever conceived of so great a distinction. The day of regeneration, when the Son of Man shall sit on the throne of His glory, as Judge and King, is even yet future; but in that day, those of the Lord's Twelve who endured to the end shall be enthroned as judges in Israel. The further assurance was given that "every one that hath forsaken houses, or brethren, or sisters, or father, or mother, or wife, or children, or lands, for my name's sake, shall receive an hundredfold, and shall inherit everlasting life." Rewards of such transcendent worth could scarcely be reckoned or their meaning comprehended. Lest those to whom they were promised might count too surely upon successful attainment, to the neglect of effort, and become proud withal, the Lord added this profound precept of caution: "But many that are first shall be last; and the last shall be first."

It was the text of the sermon known to us as the _Parable of the Laborers_.[1005] Hear it:

"For the kingdom of heaven is like unto a man that is an   householder, which went out early in the morning to hire   labourers into his vineyard. And when he had agreed with the   labourers for a penny a day, he sent them into his vineyard. And   he went out about the third hour, and saw others standing idle   in the marketplace, and said unto them:

"Go ye also into the vineyard, and whatsoever is right I will   give you. And they went their way. Again he went out about the   sixth and ninth hour, and did likewise. And about the eleventh   hour he went out, and found others standing idle, and saith unto   them, Why stand ye here all the day idle? They say unto him,   Because no man hath hired us. He saith unto them, Go ye also   into the vineyard; and whatsoever is right, that shall ye   receive. So when even was come, the lord of the vineyard saith   unto his steward, Call the labourers, and give them their hire,   beginning from the last unto the first. And when they came that   were hired about the eleventh hour, they received every man a   penny. But when the first came, they supposed that they should   have received more; and they likewise received every man a   penny. And when they had received it, they murmured against the   goodman of the house, saying, These last have wrought but one   hour, and thou hast made them equal unto us, which have borne   the burden and heat of the day. But he answered one of them, and   said, Friend, I do thee no wrong: didst not thou agree with me   for a penny? Take that thine is, and go thy way: I will give   unto this last, even as unto thee. Is it not lawful for me to do   what I will with mine own? Is thine eye evil, because I am good? So the last shall be first, and the first last: for many be   called, but few chosen."

The procedure of a householder going into the marketplace to hire laborers was common to the time and place, and is still an ordinary occurrence in many lands. The first to be hired in the course of the story made a definite bargain as to wages. Those who were employed at nine, twelve, and three o'clock respectively went willingly without agreement as to what they were to receive; so glad were they to find a chance to work that they lost no time in specifying terms. At five o'clock in the afternoon or evening, when but a single hour of the working day remained, the last band of laborers went to work, trusting to the master's word that whatever was right they should receive. That they had not found work earlier in the day was no fault of theirs; they had been ready and willing, and had waited at the place where employment was most likely to be secured. At the close of the day, the laborers came for their wages; this was in accordance with law and custom, for it had been established by statute in Israel that the employer should pay the servant, hired by the day, before the sun went down.[1006] Under instructions, the steward who acted as paymaster began with those who had been engaged at the eleventh hour; and to each of them he gave a denarius, or Roman penny, worth about fifteen cents in our money, and the usual wage for a day's work. This was the amount for which those who began earliest had severally bargained; and as these saw their fellow-workers, who had served but an hour, receive each a penny, they probably exulted in the expectation of receiving a wage proportionately larger, notwithstanding their stipulation. But each of them received a penny and no more. Then they complained; not because they had been underpaid, but because the others had received a full day's pay for but part of a day's work. The master answered in all kindness, reminding them of their agreement. Could he not be just to them and charitable to the rest if he so chose? His money was his own, and he could give of it as he liked. Were those grumblers justified in their evil displeasure because their master was charitable and good? "So," said Jesus, passing directly from the story to one of the lessons it was designed to teach, "the last shall be first, and the first last: for many be called, but few chosen."[1007]

The parable was plainly intended for the edification of the Twelve. It was called out by Peter's question, "What shall we have therefore?" It stands as truly in force today as when it was delivered by the Master, as a rebuke of the bargaining spirit in the Lord's work. God needs workers, and such as will labor faithfully and effectively are welcomed into the vineyard. If, before beginning they insist on the stipulation of a wage, and this be agreed to, each shall receive his penny provided he has not lost his place through idleness or transgression. But those who diligently labor, knowing that the Master will give to them whatever is right, and with thought for the work rather than for the wage, shall find themselves more bountifully enriched. A man may work for wages and yet not be a hireling. Between the worthy hired servant and the hireling there is the difference that distinguishes the shepherd from the sheep herder.[1008] Was there not a suggestion of the hireling's spirit in the query of even the first of the apostles, "What shall we have therefore?" The Twelve had been called into service early in the Savior's ministry; they had responded to the call, without promise of even a penny; they were yet to feel the burden and heat of the day; but they were solemnly cautioned against attempt or desire to fix their reward. The Master shall judge as to the deserts of each servant; the wage at best is a free gift; for on the basis of strict accounting who of us is not in debt to God? The last called is as likely as the first to prove unworthy. No general reversal is implied whereby all the late comers shall be advanced and all the early workers demoted. "Many that are first shall be last" was the Lord's statement, and by implication we may understand that not all the last, though some of them, may be counted among the first. Of the many called or permitted to labor in the vineyard of the Lord, few may so excel as to be chosen for exaltation above their fellows. Even the call and ordination to the Holy Apostleship is no guarantee of eventual exaltation in the celestial kingdom. Iscariot was so called and placed among the first; now, verily he is far below the last in the kingdom of God.

NOTES TO CHAPTER 27.

1. Rich Men and Their Stewards.--"'A certain rich man had a steward,' We learn here, incidentally, how evenly balanced are the various conditions of life in a community, and how little of substantial advantage wealth can confer on its possessor. As your property increases, your personal control over it diminishes; the more you possess the more you must entrust to others. Those who do their own work are not troubled with disobedient servants; those who look after their own affairs, are not troubled with unfaithful overseers."--Arnot's _Parables of our Lord_, p. 454.

2. The Mammon of Unrighteousness.--The revised version of Luke 16:9, reads: "And I say unto you, Make to yourselves friends by means of the mammon of unrighteousness, that, when it shall fail, they may receive you into the eternal tabernacles." The Lord's counsel to the disciples was to so use worldly wealth as to accomplish good thereby, that when "it," i.e. all earthly possessions, fail, they would have friends to welcome them into "the eternal tabernacles" or heavenly mansions. In studying a parable based on contrasts, such as this one is, care must be exercized not to carry too far any one point of analogy. Thus, we cannot reasonably gather that Jesus intended even to intimate that the prerogative of receiving any soul into the "eternal tabernacles" or excluding therefrom, rests with those who on earth had been benefited or injured through that person's acts, except so far as their witness to his deeds may be taken into account in the final judgment. The whole parable is full of wisdom for him who is in search of such; to the hypercritical mind it may appear inconsistent, as so it did appear to the Pharisees who derided Jesus for the story He had told. Luke 16:14 is rendered in the revised version, "And the Pharisees, who were lovers of money, heard all these things; and they scoffed at him."

3. Lazarus and Dives.--Of all our Lord's recorded parables this is the only one in which a

personal name is applied to any of the characters. The name "Lazarus" used in the parable was also the true name of a man whom Jesus loved, and who, subsequent to the delivery of this parable, was restored to life after he had lain for days in the tomb. The name, a Greek variant of Eleazar, signifies "God is my help." In many theological writings, the rich man of this parable is called Dives, but the name is not of scriptural usage. "Dives" is a Latin adjective meaning "rich." Lazarus the brother of Martha and Mary (John 11:1, 2, 5) is one of three men mentioned by name as subjects of our Lord's beneficent miracles; the other two are Bartimeus (Mark 10:46) and Malchus (John 18:10). Commenting on the fact that our Lord gave a name to the beggar but left the rich man nameless in the parable, Augustine (in Sermon xli) suggestively asks: "Seems He not to you to have been reading from that book where He found the name of the poor man written, but found not the name of the rich; for that book is the Book of Life?"

4. Divergent Views Concerning Divorce.--In relation to the different opinions upon this subject among Jewish authorities in the time of Christ, Geikie (vol. ii, p. 347-8) says: "Among the questions of the day fiercely debated between the great rival schools of Hillel and Shammai, no one was more so than that of divorce. The school of Hillel contended that a man had a right to divorce his wife for any cause he might assign, if it were no more than his having ceased to love her, or his having seen one he liked better, or her having cooked a dinner badly. The school of Shammai, on the contrary, held that divorce could be issued only for the crime of adultery, and offences against chastity. If it were possible to get Jesus to pronounce in favor of either school, the hostility of the other would be roused, and hence, it seemed a favorable chance for compromising Him." The following from Dummelow's _Commentary_, dealing with Matt. 5:32, is further illustrative: "Rabbi Akiba (Hillelite) said, 'If a man sees a woman handsomer than his own wife he may put her [his wife] away, because it is said, If she find not favor in his eyes.' The school of Hillel said 'If the wife cook her husband's food ill, by over-salting or over-roasting it, she is to be put away.' On the other hand Rabbi Jochanan (a Shammaite) said 'The putting away of a wife is odious.' Both schools agreed that a divorced wife could not be taken back.... Rabbi Chananiah said 'God has not subscribed His name to divorces, except among Israelites, as if He had said: I have conceded to the Israelites the right of dismissing their wives; but to the Gentiles I have not conceded it.' Jesus retorts that it is not the privilege but the infamy and reproach of Israel, that Moses found it necessary to tolerate divorce."

5. Jesus the Ennobler of Woman.--Geikie thus paraphrases part of Christ's reply to the Pharisee's question concerning divorce, and comments thereon. "'I say, therefore, that whoever puts away his wife, except for fornication, which destroys the very essence of marriage by dissolving the oneness it had formed, and shall marry another, commits adultery; and whoever marries her who is put away for any other cause commits adultery, because the woman is still, in God's sight, wife of him who had divorced her.' This statement was of far deeper moment than the mere silencing of malignant spies. It was designed to set forth for all ages the law of His New Kingdom in the supreme matter of family life. It swept away for ever from His Society the conception of woman as a mere toy or slave of man, and based true relations of the sexes on the eternal foundation of truth, right, honor, and love. To ennoble the House and the Family by raising woman to her true position was essential to the future stability of His Kingdom, as one of purity and spiritual worth. By making marriage indissoluble, He proclaimed the equal rights of woman and man within the limits of the family, and, in this, gave their charter of nobility to the mothers of the world. For her nobler position in the Christian era, compared with that granted her in antiquity, woman is indebted to Jesus Christ."--_Life and Words of Christ_, vol. ii, p. 349.

6. The Blessing of Children.--When Christ, a resurrected Being, appeared among the Nephites on the western continent, He took the children, one by one, and blessed them; and the assembled multitude saw the little ones encircled as with fire, while angels ministered unto them. (3 Nephi 17:11-25.) Through modern revelation the Lord has directed that all children born in the Church be brought for blessing to those who are authorized to administer this ordinance of the Holy Priesthood. The commandment is as follows: "Every member of the church of Christ having children, is to bring them unto the elders before the church, who are to lay their hands upon them in the name of Jesus Christ, and bless them in His name." (Doc. and Cov. 20:70.) Accordingly, it is now the custom in the Church to bring the little ones to the Fast-day service in the several wards, at which they are received one by one into the arms of the elders, and blessed, names being given them at the same time. The father of the child, if he be an elder, is expected to participate in the ordinance.

The blessing of children is in no sense analogous to, far less is it a substitution for, the ordinance of baptism, which is to be administered only to those who have come to years of understanding, and who are capable of repentance. As the author has written elsewhere, "Some point to the incident of Christ blessing little children, and rebuking those who would forbid the little ones coming unto Him, (Matt. 19:13; Mark 10:13; Luke 13:15) as an evidence in favor of infant baptism; but, as has been tersely said:--'From the action of Christ's blessing infants, to infer they are to be baptized, proves nothing so much as that there is a want of better argument; for the conclusion would with more probability be derived thus: Christ blessed infants, and so dismissed them, but baptized them not; therefore infants are not to be baptized.'"--The author, _Articles of Faith_, vi:14. See paragraphs 11-17 in same lecture.

7. The Camel and the Needle's Eye.--In comparing the difficulty of a rich man entering the kingdom with that of a camel passing through the eye of a needle, Jesus used a rhetorical figure, which, strong and prohibitory as it appears in our translation, was of a type familiar to those who heard the remark. There was a "common Jewish proverb, that a man did not even in his dreams see an elephant pass through the eye of a needle" (Edersheim). Some interpreters insist that a rope, not a camel, was mentioned by Jesus, and these base their contention on the fact that the Greek word _kamelos_ (camel) differs in but a single letter from _kamilos_ (rope), and that the alleged error of substituting "camel" for "rope" in the scriptural text is chargeable to the early copyists. Farrar (p. 476) rejects this possible interpretation on the

ground that proverbs involving comparisons of a kind with that of a camel passing through the eye of a needle are common in the Talmud.

It has been asserted that the term "needle's eye" was applied to a small door or wicket set in or alongside the great gates in the walls of cities; and the assumption has been raised that Jesus had such a wicket in mind when He spoke of the seeming impossibility of a camel passing through a needle's eye. It would be possible though very difficult for a camel to squeeze its way through the little gate, and it could in no wise do so except when relieved of its load and stripped of all its harness. If this conception be correct, we may find additional similitude between the fact that the camel must first be unloaded and stripped, however costly its burden or rich its accoutrement, and the necessity of the rich young ruler, and so of any man, divesting himself of the burden and trappings of wealth, if he would enter by the narrow way that leadeth into the kingdom. The Lord's exposition of His saying is all-sufficient for the purposes of the lesson: "With men this is impossible, but with God all things are possible." (Matt. 19:26.)

8. Undue Concern as to Wages in the Lord's Service.—The instructive and inspiring Parable of the Laborers was called forth by Peter's question of self-interest—"What shall we have therefore?" In tender mercy the Lord refrained from directly rebuking His impulsive servant for undue concern as to the wage to be expected; but He turned the incident to excellent purpose by making it the text of a valuable lesson. The following treatment by Edersheim (vol. ii, p. 416) is worth consideration. "There was here deep danger to the disciples: danger of lapsing into feelings akin to those with which the Pharisees viewed the pardoned publicans, or the elder son in the parable his younger brother; danger of misunderstanding the right relations, and with it the very character of the kingdom, and of work in and for it. It is to this that the Parable of the Laborers in the Vineyard refers. The principle which Christ lays down is, that, while nothing done for Him shall lose its reward, yet, from one reason or another, no forecast can be made, no inferences of self-righteousness may be drawn. It does not by any means follow, that most work done—at least, to our seeing and judging—shall entail a greater reward. On the contrary, 'many that are first shall be last; and the last shall be first.' Not _all_, nor yet always and necessarily, but 'many.' And in such cases no wrong has been done; there exists no claim, even in view of the promises of due acknowledgment of work. Spiritual pride and self assertion can only be the outcome either of misunderstanding God's relation to us, or else of a wrong state of mind towards others—that is, it betokens mental or moral unfitness. Of this the Parable of the Laborers is an illustration.... But, while illustrating how it may come that some who were first are last, and how utterly mistaken or wrong is the thought that they must necessarily receive more than others, who, seemingly, have done more—how, in short, work for Christ is not a ponderable quantity, so much for so much, nor yet we be the judges of when and why a worker has come—it also conveys much that is new, and, in many respects, most comforting."

FOOTNOTES:

[950] Luke 14:1-24.
[951] The question is identical with that asked of Jesus in the synagog at Capernaum preliminary to the healing of the man with the withered hand (Matt. 12:10).
[952] Exo. 23:5; Deut. 22:4; Luke 13:15.
[953] Compare Matt. 23:12; Luke 1:52; 18:14; James 4:6; 1 Peter 5:5.
[954] Compare Matt. 8:11; Rev. 19:9. The expression "eat bread" is a Hebraism, signifying eating in full as at a feast rather than partaking of bread only.
[955] Luke 14:16-24. Compare the parable relating to the marriage of the king's son (Matt. 22:2-10); study points of resemblance and difference between the two and the distinctive lessons of each. See page 536.
[956] Luke 14:25-35.
[957] Matt. 8:19, 20; compare Luke 9:57, 58; page 305 herein.
[958] Compare the requirement under the Mosaic administration, Deut. 13:6-11; and note the application of the principle to the apostles, Matt. 10:37-39.
[959] Compare Matt. 5:13; Mark 9:50
[960] Luke 15.
[961] Matt. 9:10-13; Mark 2:15-17; Luke 5:29-32. See page 193 herein.
[962] Matt. 18:12-14. See page 389 herein.
[963] That the lost piece of silver was a coin, and not a piece of unstamped bullion nor an ornament, is apparent from the original, "drachma," a silver coin. See page 384 herein.
[964] Luke 15:11-32.
[965] Compare Doc. and Cov. 1:31; B. of M., Alma 45:16.
[966] Compare Matt. 18:14; P. of G.P., Moses 1:39.
[967] Luke 16:1-8.
[968] Note 1, end of chapter.
[969] Luke 16:9-13.
[970] Note 2, end of chapter.
[971] Luke 16:14-31.
[972] Note 2, end of chapter.
[973] Revised version, Luke 16:16: "The law and the prophets were until John; from that time the gospel of the kingdom of God is preached, and every man entereth violently into it."
[974] Compare Matt. 5:18; see page 233 herein.
[975] Luke 16:19-31.

[976] Note 3, end of chapter.

[977] Compare B. of M., Alma 40:11-14; see "Articles of Faith," xxi, Note 5. "The Intermediate State of the Soul."

[978] Rev. 14:13.

[979] Luke 17:1-10.

[980] Compare Matt. 17:20; 21:21; Mark 9:23; 11:23; see page 381 herein.

[981] Compare Job 22:3; 35:7.

[982] Luke 17:11-19. Many writers treat this occurrence as having immediately followed the repulse of Jesus and the apostles in a certain Samaritan village (Luke 9:52-56). We give it place in the order followed by Luke, the sole recorder of the two incidents.

[983] Compare Lev. 13:2; 14:2; see also page 189 herein.

[984] Compare case of Naaman the Syrian, 2 Kings 5:14.

[985] Luke 18:9-14. Luke's narrative, the order of which we have followed in the events succeeding Christ's departure from Jerusalem after the Feast of Tabernacles, includes our Lord's reply to the Pharisee's question as to "when the kingdom of God should come," and additions thereto (17:20-37); these matters were afterward treated with greater fulness in a discourse near Jerusalem (Matt. 24) and will be considered in connection with that later event. The Parable of the Importunate Widow (Luke 18:1-7) has already received attention, (page 436).

[986] Note to what blasphemous extreme the doctrine of supererogation, or excess of merit, was carried by the papacy in the 13th century; see "The Great Apostasy," 913-15.

[987] Compare Luke 14:11.

[988] Matt. 19:3-12; see also Mark 10:2-12. This subject is introduced by Matthew and Mark directly preceding that of Christ blessing little children; which latter is recorded by Luke next after the Parable of the Pharisee and the Publican. We therefore turn from Luke's record to the accounts given by the other synoptic writers.

[989] Note 4, end of chapter.

[990] Compare Gen. 1:27; 2:24; 5:2; Eph. 5:31.

[991] Deut. 24:1-4.

[992] Compare Matt. 5:32; Luke 16:18; see also 1 Cor. 7:10-13.

[993] Note 5, end of chapter.

[994] Compare Heb. 13:4.

[995] Compare 1 Cor. 11:11.

[996] Mark 10:13-16; compare Matt. 19:13-15; Luke 18:15-17.

[997] Compare B. of M., 3 Nephi 17:11-25. See Note 6, end of chapter.

[998] Page 386.

[999] Matt. 19:16-26; Mark 10:17-27; Luke 18:18-30.

[1000] Luke 10:25; page 429 herein.

[1001] This is Mark's record, (10:21) which is the most detailed of the three accounts.

[1002] Note 7, end of chapter.

[1003] Consider the lessons of the parables of the Hidden Treasure, and the Pearl of Great Price, pages 292-4.

[1004] Matt. 19:27-30; Mark 10:28-31; Luke 18:28-30.

[1005] Matt. 20:1-16. The parable is the outgrowth of the events immediately preceding it. Matt. 19:27-30 should be read as part of the narrative continued in chap. 20. The existing division into chapters is unfortunate.

[1006] Deut. 24:15.

[1007] The concluding clause, "for many be called but few chosen," is omitted from the revised version. Note 8, end of chapter.

[1008] Page 416.

Jesus the Christ

CHAPTER 28. THE LAST WINTER.

AT THE FEAST OF DEDICATION.[1009]

Jesus returned to Jerusalem in time to attend the Feast of Dedication during the last winter of His earthly life. This feast, like that of Tabernacles, was one of national rejoicing, and was celebrated annually for a period of eight days beginning on the 25th of Chislev,[1010] which corresponds in part to our December. It was not one of the great feasts prescribed by Mosaic statute, but had been established in 164 or 163 B.C. at the time of the rededication of the Temple of Zerubbabel following the rehabilitation of the sacred structure after its profane desecration by Antiochus Epiphanes, the pagan king of Syria.[1011] While the festival was in progress, Jesus went to the temple and was seen walking in the part of the enclosure known as Solomon's Porch.[1012] His presence soon became known to the Jews, who came crowding about Him in unfriendly spirit, ostensibly to ask questions. Their inquiry was: "How long dost thou make us to doubt? If thou be the Christ, tell us plainly," The mere asking of such a question evidences the deep and disturbing impression which the ministry of Christ had produced among the official classes and the people generally; in their estimation, the works he had wrought appeared as worthy of the Messiah.

The Lord's reply was indirect in form, though in substance and effect incisive and unmistakable. He referred them to His former utterances and to His continued works. "I told you," He said, "and ye believed not: the works that I do in my Father's name, they bear witness of me. But ye believe not, because ye are not of my sheep, as I said unto you. My sheep hear my voice, and I know them, and they follow me: And I give unto them eternal life; and they shall never perish, neither shall any man pluck them out of my hand. My Father, which gave them me, is greater than all; and no man is able to pluck them out of my Father's hand. I and my Father are one." The reference to what had been before told was a reminder of His teachings on the occasion of an earlier sojourn among them, when He had proclaimed Himself as the I AM, who was older and greater than Abraham, and of His other proclamation of Himself as the Good Shepherd.[1013]

He could not well answer their inquiry by a simple unqualified affirmation, for by such He would have been understood as meaning that He claimed to be the Messiah according to their conception, the earthly king and conqueror for whom they professed to be looking. He was no such Christ as they had in mind; yet was He verily Shepherd and King to all who would hear His words and do His works; and to such He renewed the promise of eternal life and the assurance that no man could pluck them out of His own or the Father's hand. To this doctrine, both exalted and profound in scope, the casuistical Jews could offer no refutation, nor could they find therein the much desired excuse for open accusation; our Lord's concluding sentence, however, stirred the hostile throng to frenzy. "I and my Father are one" was His solemn declaration.[1014] In their rage they scrambled for stones wherewith to crush Him. Owing to the unfinished state of the temple buildings, there were probably many blocks and broken fragments of rock at hand; and this was the second murderous attempt upon our Lord's life within the purlieus of His Father's House.[1015]

Fearless, and with the compelling calmness of more than human majesty, Jesus said: "Many good works have I shewed you from my Father; for which of those works do ye stone me?" They angrily retorted: "For a good work we stone thee not; but for blasphemy; and because that thou, being a man, makest thyself God."[1016] Plainly they had found no ambiguity in His words. He then cited to them the scriptures, wherein even judges empowered by divine authority are called gods,[1017] and asked: "Is it not written in your law, I said, Ye are gods? If he called them gods, unto whom the word of God came, and the scripture cannot be broken: say ye of him, whom the Father hath sanctified, and sent into the world, Thou blasphemest; because I said, I am the Son of God?" Then, reverting to the first avouchment that His own commission was of the Father who is greater than all, He added: "If I do not the works of my Father, believe me not. But if I do, though ye believe not me, believe the works: that ye may know, and believe, that the Father is in me, and I in him."[1018] Again the Jews sought to take Him, but were foiled by means not stated; He passed from their reach and departed from the temple.

OUR LORD'S RETIREMENT IN PEREA.[1019]

The violent hostility of the Jews in Jerusalem, the headquarters of the theocracy, was such that Jesus withdrew from the city and its neighborhood. The day for His sacrifice had not yet come, and while His enemies could not kill Him until He allowed Himself to be taken into their hands, His work would be retarded by further hostile disturbances. He retired to the place at which John the Baptist had begun his public ministry, which is probably also the place of our Lord's baptism. The exact location is not specified; it was certainly beyond Jordan and therefore in Perea. We read that Jesus abode there, and from this we gather that He remained in one general locality instead of traveling from town to town as had been His custom. People resorted to Him even there, however, and many believed on Him. The place was endeared to those who had gone to hear John and to be baptized by him;[1020] and as these recalled the impassioned call to repentance, the stirring proclamation of the kingdom by the now murdered and lamented Baptist, they remembered his affirmation of One mightier than himself, and saw in Jesus the realization of that testimony. "John," they said, "did no miracle: but all things that John spake of this man were true."

The duration of this sojourn in Perea is nowhere recorded in our scriptures. It could not have lasted more than a few weeks at most. Possibly some of the discourses, instructions, and parables already treated as following the Lord's departure from Jerusalem after the Feast of Tabernacles in the preceding autumn, may chronologically belong to this interval. From this retreat of comparative quiet, Jesus returned to Judea in response to an earnest appeal from some whom He loved. He left the Bethany of Perea for the Judean Bethany, where dwelt Martha and Mary.[1021]

LAZARUS RESTORED TO LIFE.[1022]

Lazarus, the brother of Mary and Martha, lay ill in the family home at Bethany of Judea. His devoted sisters sent a messenger to Jesus, with the simple announcement, in which, however, we cannot fail to recognize a pitiful appeal: "Lord, behold, he whom thou lovest is sick." When Jesus received the message, He remarked: "This sickness is not unto death, but for the glory of God, that the Son of God might be glorified thereby." This was probably the word carried back to the sisters, whom Jesus loved. Lazarus had died in the interval; indeed he must have expired soon after the messenger had started with the tidings of the young man's illness. The Lord knew that Lazarus was dead; yet He tarried where He was for two days after receiving the word; then He surprized the disciples by saying: "Let us go into Judea again." They sought to dissuade the Master by reminding Him of the recent attempt upon His life at Jerusalem, and asked wonderingly, "Goest thou thither again?" Jesus made clear to them that He was not to be deterred from duty in the time thereof, nor should others be; for as He illustrated, the working day is twelve hours long; and during that period a man may walk without stumbling, for he walks in the light, but if he let the hours pass and then try to walk or work in darkness, he stumbles. It was then His day to work, and He was making no mistake in returning to Judea.

He added: "Our friend Lazarus sleepeth; but I go, that I may awake him out of sleep." The simile between death and sleep was as common among the Jews as with us;[1023] but the disciples construed the saying literally, and remarked that if the sick man was sleeping it would be well with him. Jesus set them right. "Lazarus is dead," He said, and added, "And I am glad for your sakes that I was not there, to the intent ye may believe; nevertheless let us go unto him." It is evident that Jesus had already decided to restore Lazarus to life; and, as we shall see, the miracle was to be a testimony of our Lord's Messiahship, convincing to all who would accept it. A return to Judea at that time was viewed by at least some of the apostles with serious apprehension; they feared for their Master's safety, and thought that their own lives would be in peril; nevertheless they did not hesitate to go. Thomas boldly said to the others: "Let us also go, that we may die with him."

Arriving on the outskirts of Bethany, Jesus found that Lazarus "had lain in the grave four days already."[1024] The bereaved sisters were at home, where had gathered, according to custom, friends to console them in their grief. Among these were many prominent people, some of whom had come from Jerusalem. Word of the Master's approach reached Martha first, and she hastened to meet Him. Her first words were: "Lord, if thou hadst been here, my brother had not died." It was an expression of anguish combined with faith; but, lest it appear as lacking in trust, she hastened to add: "But I know, that even now, whatsoever thou wilt ask of God, God will give it thee." Then said Jesus in words of assuring tenderness: "Thy brother shall rise again." Perhaps some of the Jews who had come to comfort her had said as much, for they, the Sadducees excepted, believed in a resurrection; and Martha failed to find in the Lord's promise anything more than a general assurance that her departed brother should be raised with the rest of the dead. In natural and seemingly casual assent she remarked: "I know that he shall rise again in the resurrection at the last day." Then said Jesus: "I am the resurrection, and the life: he that believeth in me, though he were dead, yet shall he live: And whosoever liveth and believeth in me shall never die. Believest thou this?"

The sorrowing woman's faith had to be lifted and centered in the Lord of Life with whom she was speaking. She had before confessed her conviction that whatever Jesus asked of God would be granted; she had to learn that unto Jesus had already been committed power over life and death. She was hopefully expectant of some superhuman interposition by the Lord Jesus in her behalf, yet she knew not what that might be. Apparently at this time she had no well-defined thought or even hope that He would call her brother from the tomb. To the Lord's question as to whether she believed what He had just said, she answered with simple frankness; all of it she was not able to understand; but she believed in the Speaker even while unable to fully comprehend His words. "Yea, Lord," she said, "I believe that thou art the Christ, the Son of God, which should come into the world."

Then she returned to the home, and with precaution of secrecy on account of the presence of some whom she knew to be unfriendly to Jesus, said to Mary: "The Master is come, and calleth for thee." Mary left the house in haste. The Jews who had been with her thought that she had been impelled by a fresh resurgence of grief to go again to the grave, and they followed her. When she reached the Master, she knelt at His feet, and gave expression to her consuming sorrow in the very words Martha had used: "Lord, if thou hadst been here, my brother had not died." We cannot doubt that the conviction so voiced had been the burden of comment and lamentation between the two sisters--if only Jesus had been with them they would not have been bereft of their brother.

The sight of the two women so overcome by grief, and of the people wailing with them, caused Jesus to sorrow, so that He groaned in spirit and was deeply troubled. "Where have ye laid him?" He asked; and Jesus wept. As the sorrowing company went toward the tomb, some of the Jews, observing the Lord's emotion and tears, said: "Behold how he loved him!" but others, less sympathetic because of their prejudice against Christ, asked critically and reproachfully: "Could not this man, which opened the eyes of the blind, have caused that even this man should not have died?" The miracle by which a man blind from birth had been made to see was very generally known, largely because of the official investigation that had followed the healing.[1025] The Jews had been compelled to admit the actuality of the astounding occurrence; and the question now raised as to whether or why One who could accomplish such a wonder could not have preserved from death a man stricken with an ordinary illness, and that man one whom He seemed to have dearly loved, was an innuendo that the power possessed by Jesus was after all limited, and of uncertain or capricious operation. This manifestation of malignant unbelief caused Jesus again to groan with sorrow if not indignation.[1026]

The body of Lazarus had been interred in a cave, the entrance to which was closed by a great block of stone. Such burial-places were common in that country, natural caves or vaults hewn in the solid rock being used as sepulchres by the better classes of people. Jesus directed that the tomb be opened. Martha, still unprepared for what was to follow, ventured to remonstrate, reminding Jesus that the corpse had been four days immured, and that decomposition must have already set in.[1027] Jesus thus met her objection: "Said I not unto thee, that, if thou wouldest believe, thou shouldest see the glory of God?" This may have had reference both to His promise spoken to Martha in person--that her brother should rise again--and to the message sent from Perea--that the illness of Lazarus was not unto final death at that time, but for the glory of God and that the Son of God might be glorified thereby.

The stone was removed. Standing before the open portal of the tomb, Jesus looked upward and prayed: "Father, I thank thee that thou hast heard me. And I knew that thou hearest me always: but because of the people which stand by I said it, that they may believe that thou hast sent me." He did not ask the Father for power or authority; such had already been given Him; but He gave thanks, and in the hearing of all who stood by acknowledged the Father and expressed the oneness of His own and the Father's purposes. Then, with a loud voice He cried: "Lazarus, come forth." The dead man heard that voice of authoritative command; the spirit straightway reentered the tabernacle of flesh, the physical processes of life were resumed; and Lazarus, again alive, came forth. His freedom of motion was limited, for the grave clothes hampered his movements, and his face was still bound by the napkin by which the lifeless jaw had been held in place. To those who stood near, Jesus said: "Loose him, and let him go."

The procedure throughout was characterized by deep solemnity and by the entire absence of every element of unnecessary display. Jesus, who when miles away and without any ordinary means of receiving the information knew that Lazarus was dead, doubtless could have found the tomb; yet He inquired: "Where have ye laid him?" He who could still the waves of the sea by a word could have miraculously effected the removal of the stone that sealed the mouth of the sepulchre; yet He said: "Take ye away the stone." He who could reunite spirit and body could have loosened without hands the cerements by which the reanimated Lazarus was bound; yet He said: "Loose him, and let him go." All that human agency could do was left to man. In no instance do we find that Christ used unnecessarily the superhuman powers of His Godship; the divine energy was never wasted; even the material creation resulting from its exercize was conserved, as witness His instructions regarding the gathering up of the fragments of bread and fish after the multitudes had been miraculously fed.[1028]

The raising of Lazarus stands as the third recorded instance of restoration to life by Jesus. [1029] In each the miracle resulted in a resumption of mortal existence, and was in no sense a resurrection from death to immortality. In the raising of the daughter of Jairus, the spirit was recalled to its tenement within the hour of its quitting; the raising of the widow's son is an instance of restoration when the corpse was ready for the grave; the crowning miracle of the three was the calling of a spirit to reenter its body days after death, and when, by natural processes the corpse would be already in the early stages of decomposition. Lazarus was raised from the dead, not simply to assuage the grief of mourning relatives; myriads have had to mourn over death, and so myriads more shall have to do. One of the Lord's purposes was that of demonstrating the actuality of the power of God as shown forth in the works of Jesus the Christ, and Lazarus was the accepted subject of the manifestation; just as the man afflicted with congenital blindness had been chosen to be the one through whom "the works of God should be made manifest."[1030]

That the Lord's act of restoring Lazarus to life was of effect in testifying to His Messiahship is explicitly stated.[1031] All the circumstances leading up to final culmination in the miracle contributed to its attestation. No question as to the actual death of Lazarus could be raised, for his demise had been witnessed, his body had been prepared and buried in the usual way, and he had lain in the grave four days. At the tomb, when he was called forth, there were many witnesses, some of them prominent Jews, many of whom were unfriendly to Jesus and who would have readily denied the miracle had they been able. God was glorified and the divinity of the Son of Man was vindicated in the result.

THE HIERARCHY GREATLY AGITATED OVER THE MIRACLE.[1032]

As in connection with most of our Lord's public acts--while some of those who heard and saw were brought to believe in Him, others rejected the proffered lesson and reviled the Master--so with this mighty work--some were stirred to faith and others went their ways each with mind darkened and spirit more malignant than ever. Some of those who had seen the dead man raised to life went immediately and reported the matter to the rulers, whom they knew to be intensely hostile toward Jesus. In the parable we have recently studied, the spirit of the rich man pleaded from his place of anguish that Lazarus, the once pitiable beggar, be sent from paradise to earth, to warn others of the fate awaiting the wicked, to which appeal Abraham replied: "If they hear not Moses and the prophets, neither will they be persuaded, though one rose from the dead."[1033] Now a Lazarus had been in reality raised from the dead, and many of the Jews rejected the testimony of his return and refused to believe in Christ through whom alone death is overcome. The Jews tried to get Lazarus into their power that they might kill him and, as they hoped, silence forever his testimony of the Lord's power over death.[1034]

The chief priests, who were mostly Sadducees, and the Pharisees with them assembled in council to consider the situation created by this latest of our Lord's great works. The question they discussed was: "What do we? for this man doeth many miracles. If we let him thus alone, all men will believe on him: and the Romans shall come and take away both our place and nation." As stated by themselves, there was no denying the fact of the many miracles wrought by Jesus; but instead of earnestly and prayerfully investigating as to whether these mighty works were not among the predicted characteristics of the Messiah, they thought only of the possible effect of Christ's influence in alienating the people from the established theocracy, and of the fear that the Romans, taking advantage of the situation, would deprive the hierarchs of their "place" and take from the nation what little semblance of distinct autonomy it still possessed. Caiaphas, the high priest,[1035] cut short the discussion by saying: "Ye know nothing at all." This sweeping assertion of ignorance was most likely addressed to the Pharisees of the Sanhedrin; Caiaphas was a Sadducee. His next utterance was of greater significance than he realized: "Nor consider that it is expedient for us, that one man should die for the people, and that the whole nation perish not." John solemnly avers that Caiaphas spake not of himself, but by the spirit of prophecy, and that thus: "He prophesied that Jesus should die for that nation; and not for that nation only, but that also he should gather together in one the children of God that were scattered abroad." But a few years after Christ had been put to death, for the salvation of the Jews and of all other nations, the very calamities which Caiaphas and the Sanhedrin had hoped to avert befell in full measure; the hierarchy was overthrown, the temple destroyed, Jerusalem demolished and the nation disrupted. From the day of that memorable session of the Sanhedrin, the rulers increased their efforts to bring about the death of Jesus, by whatever means they might find available. They issued a mandate that whosoever knew of His whereabouts should give the information to the officials, that they might promptly take Him into custody.[1036]

JESUS IN RETIREMENT AT EPHRAIM.[1037]

The hostility of the ecclesiastical rulers became so great that Jesus once more sought retirement in a region sufficiently far from Jerusalem to afford Him security from the watchful and malignant eyes of His powerful and openly avowed enemies. But a few weeks of mortal life remained to Him, and the greater part of this brief period had to be devoted to the further instruction of the apostles. He prudently withdrew from the vicinity of Bethany and "went thence unto a country near to the wilderness, into a city called Ephraim, and there continued with his disciples." Thus did our Lord spend the rest of the winter and probably the early days of the succeeding spring. That His retreat was private if not practically secret is suggested by John's statement that "Jesus therefore walked no more openly among the Jews"; and further indication is found in the fact that although the chief priests and Pharisees had virtually set a price upon His head, no man gave information as to His whereabouts. The place of this last retirement is not definitely known; it is generally thought to be the locality elsewhere called Ephrain and Ephron,[1038] which lay a little less than twenty miles northerly from Jerusalem. Equally uncertain is the duration of our Lord's abode there. When He emerged again into public notice, it was to enter upon His solemn march toward Jerusalem and the cross.

NOTES TO CHAPTER 28.

1. Origin of the Feast of Dedication.--Concerning the second temple, known as the Temple of Zerubbabel, the author has written elsewhere: "Of the later history of this temple the biblical record gives but few details; but from other sources we learn of its vicissitudes. In connection with the Maccabean persecution the House of the Lord was profaned. A Syrian king, Antiochus Epiphanes, captured Jerusalem (168 to 165 B.C.) and perpetrated blasphemous outrage against the religion of the people. He plundered the temple and carried away its golden candlestick, its golden altar of incense, its table of shewbread, and even tore down the sacred veils, which were of fine linen and scarlet. His malignity was carried so far that he purposely desecrated the altar of sacrifice by offering swine thereon, and erected a heathen altar within the sacred enclosure. Not content with the violation of the temple, this wicked monarch had altars erected in the towns, and ordered the offering of unclean beasts upon them. The rite of circumcision was forbidden on pain of death, and the worship of Jehovah was declared a crime. As a result of this persecution many of the Jews apostatized, and declared that they belonged to the Medes and Persians--the nations from whose dominion they had been delivered by the power of God.... Then in the year 163 B.C. the House was rededicated; and the occasion was remembered in annual festival thereafter under the name of the Feast of Dedication."--_The House of the Lord_, pp. 51-53. According to Josephus (Ant. xii, 7:7) the festival came to be known as The Lights; and brilliant illumination both of the temple and of dwellings, was a feature of the celebration. Traditional accounts say that eight days had been set as the duration of the feast, in commemoration of a legendary miracle by which the consecrated oil in the only jar found intact, and bearing the unbroken seal of the high priest, had been made to serve for temple purposes through eight days, which time was required for the ceremonial preparation of a new supply.

2. Solomon's Porch.--This name had been applied to the eastern colonnade or row of porticoes within the temple enclosure, in recognition of a tradition that the porch covered and included a portion of the original wall belonging to the Temple of Solomon. See _The House of the Lord_, pp. 55-57.

3. The Oneness of Christ and the Father.--The revised version gives for John 10:30: "I and the Father are one" instead of "I and my Father are one." By "the Father" the Jews rightly understood the Eternal Father, God. In the original Greek "one" appears in the neuter gender, and therefore expresses oneness in attributes, power, or purpose, and not a oneness of personality which would have required the masculine form. For treatment of the unity of the Godhead, and the separate personality of each Member,

see _Articles of Faith_, ii, 20-24.

4. The Place of our Lord's Retirement.--Jesus went "beyond Jordan into the place where John at first baptized" (John 10:40). This was probably Bethabara (1:28), which is called Bethany in some of the earliest manuscripts and is so designated in the latest revised version. Care must be taken not to confuse this Perean Bethany with the Bethany in Judea, the home of Martha and Mary, which was within two miles of Jerusalem.

5. Lazarus in the Tomb Four Days.--On the very probable assumption that the journey from Bethany in Judea to the place where Jesus was, in Perea, would require one day, Lazarus must have died on the day of the messenger's departure; for this day and the two days that elapsed before Jesus started toward Judea, and the day required for the return, would no more than cover the four days specified. It was and still is the custom in Palestine as in other oriental countries to bury on the day of death.

It was the popular belief that on the fourth day after death the spirit had finally departed from the vicinity of the corpse, and that thereafter decomposition proceeded unhindered. This may explain Martha's impulsive though gentle objection to having the tomb of her brother opened four days after his death (John 11:39). It is possible that the consent of the next of kin was required for the lawful opening of a grave. Both Martha and Mary were present, and in the presence of many witnesses assented to the opening of the tomb in which their brother lay.

6. Jesus Groaned in Spirit.--The marginal readings for "he groaned in the spirit" (John 11:33) and "again groaning in himself" (v. 38), as given in the revised version, are "was moved with indignation in the spirit" and "being moved with indignation in himself." All philological authorities agree that the words in the original Greek express sorrowful indignation, or as some aver, anger, and not alone a sympathetic emotion of grief. Any indignation the Lord may have felt, as intimated in verse 33, may be attributed to disapproval of the customary wailing over death, which as vented by the Jews on this occasion, profaned the real and soulful grief of Martha and Mary; and His indignation, expressed by groaning as mentioned in verse 38, may have been due to the carping criticism uttered by some of the Jews as recorded in verse 37.

7. Caiaphas, High Priest that Year.--John's statement that Caiaphas was high priest "that same year" must not be construed as meaning that the office of high priest was of a single year's tenure. Under Jewish law the presiding priest, who was known as the high priest, would remain in office indefinitely; but the Roman government had arrogated to itself the appointive power as applying to this office; and frequent changes were made. This Caiaphas, whose full name was Josephus Caiaphas, was high priest under Roman appointment during a period of eleven years. To such appointments the Jews had to submit, though they often recognized as the high priest under their law, some other than the "civil high priest" appointed by Roman authority. Thus we find both Annas and Caiaphas exercizing the authority of the office at the time of our Lord's arrest and later. (John 18:13, 24; Acts 4:6; compare Luke 3:2.) Farrar (p. 484, note) says: "Some have seen an open irony in the expression of St. John (11:49) that Caiaphas was high priest 'that same year,' as though the Jews had got into this contemptuous way of speaking during the rapid succession of priests--mere phantoms set up and displaced by the Roman fiat--who had in recent years succeeded each other. There must have been at least five living high priests, and ex-high priests at this council--Annas, Ismael Ben Phabi, Eleazar Ben Haman, Simon Ben Kamhith, and Caiaphas, who had gained his elevation by bribery."

8. Divinely Appointed Judges Called "gods."--In Psalm 82:6, judges invested by divine appointment are called "gods." To this scripture the Savior referred in His reply to the Jews in Solomon's Porch. Judges so authorized officiated as the representatives of God and are honored by the exalted title "gods." Compare the similar appellation applied to Moses (Exo. 4:16; 7:1). Jesus Christ possessed divine authorization, not through the word of God transmitted to Him by man, but as an inherent attribute. The inconsistency of calling human judges "gods," and of ascribing blasphemy to the Christ who called Himself the Son of God, would have been apparent to the Jews but for their sin-darkened minds.

FOOTNOTES:

[1009] John 10:22-39.
[1010] Also rendered Kisleu, Chisleu, and Cisleu. See Zech. 7:1.
[1011] Josephus, Antiquities, xii, 5:3-5. See Ezra 6:17, 18; also Note 1, end of chapter.
[1012] Note 2, end of chapter.
[1013] John 8:58; and 10:11; see also pages 411 and 416 herein.
[1014] Revised version gives "I and the Father." See Note 3, end of chapter.
[1015] John 8:59. Page 412.
[1016] Concerning blasphemy see pages 191 and 269, also page 629.
[1017] Psa. 82, particularly verses 1 and 6. Note 8, end of chapter.
[1018] A better rendering of the last verse is: "But if I do them [i.e. the Father's works], though ye believe not me, believe the works; that ye may know and understand that the Father is in me, and I in the Father."--(Revised version.)
[1019] John 10:40-42.
[1020] Pages 121-124.
[1021] Note 4, end of chapter.
[1022] John 11:1-46.
[1023] Compare Matt. 9:24; Mark 5:39; Luke 8:52; Job 14:12; 1 Thess. 4:14.
[1024] Note 5, end of chapter.
[1025] John 9; see page 412 herein.

[1026] Note 6, end of chapter.
[1027] Note 5, end of chapter.
[1028] John 6:12; Matt. 15:37; see pages 334 and 358 herein.
[1029] Matt. 9:23-25; Luke 7:11-17; pages 251 and 313 herein.
[1030] John 9:3.
[1031] John 12:9-11, 17.
[1032] John 11:46-54.
[1033] Luke 16:31; page 466 herein.
[1034] John 12:10.
[1035] Note 7, end of chapter.
[1036] John 11:57.
[1037] John 11:54.
[1038] 2 Chron. 13:19; Josh. 15:9.

CHAPTER 29. ON TO JERUSALEM.

JESUS AGAIN FORTELLS HIS DEATH AND RESURRECTION.[1039]

Each of the three synoptic writers has made record of this last journey to Jerusalem and of occurrences connected therewith. The deep solemnity of the developments now so near at hand, and of the fate He was setting out to meet so affected Jesus that even the apostles were amazed at His absorption and evident sadness; they fell behind in amazement and fear. Then He paused, called the Twelve about Him, and in language of absolute plainness, without metaphor or simile, He said: "Behold, we go up to Jerusalem, and all things that are written by the prophets concerning the Son of man shall be accomplished. For he shall be delivered unto the Gentiles, and shall be mocked, and spitefully entreated, and spitted on: And they shall scourge him, and put him to death: and the third day he shall rise again."

It is to us an astounding fact that the Twelve failed to comprehend His meaning; yet Luke unqualifiedly affirms: "And they understood none of these things: and this saying was hid from them, neither knew they the things which were spoken." This avouchment of the Savior's approaching death and resurrection spoken in confidential certainty to the Twelve was the third of its kind; and still they could not bring themselves to accept the awful truth.[1040] According to Matthew's account, they were told of the very manner by which the Lord should die--that the Gentiles should crucify Him; yet they understood not. To them there was some dreadful incongruity, some dire inconsistency or inexplicable contradiction in the sayings of their beloved Master. They knew Him to be the Christ, the Son of the living God; and how could such a One be brought into subjection and be slain? They could not fail to realize that some unprecedented development in His life was impending; this they may have vaguely conceived to be the crisis for which they had been waiting, the open proclamation of His Messianic dignity, His enthronement as Lord and King. And such indeed was to be, though in a manner far different from their anticipations. The culminating prediction--that on the third day He would rise again--seems to have puzzled them the most; and, at the same time, this assurance of ultimate triumph may have made all intermediate occurrences appear as of but secondary and transitory import. They persistently repelled the thought that they were following their Lord to the cross and the sepulchre.

THE QUESTION OF PRECEDENCE AGAIN.[1041]

Notwithstanding all the instructions the apostles had received concerning humility, and though they had before them the supreme example of the Master's life and conduct, in which the fact that service was the only measure of true greatness was abundantly demonstrated, they continued to dream of rank and honor in the kingdom of the Messiah. Perhaps because of the imminence of the Master's triumph, with which they all were particularly impressed at this time though ignorant of its real significance, certain of the Twelve appealed to the Lord in the course of this journey with a most ambitious request. The petitioners were James and John, though according to Matthew's record their mother[1042] was the first to ask. The request was that when Jesus came into possession of His kingdom, He would so signally honor the aspiring pair as to install them in seats of eminence, one on His right hand, the other on His left. Instead of sharply rebuking such presumption, Jesus gently but impressively asked: "Are ye able to drink of the cup that I shall drink of, and to be baptized with the baptism that I am baptized with?" The answer was full of self-confidence inspired by ignorant misapprehension. "We are able," they replied. Then said Jesus: "Ye shall drink indeed of my cup, and be baptized with the baptism that I am baptized with: but to sit on my right hand, and on my left, is not mine to give, but it shall be given to them for whom it is prepared of my Father."

The ten apostles were indignant at the two brothers, possibly less through disapproval of the spirit that had prompted the petition than because the two had forestalled the others in applying for the chief posts of distinction. But Jesus, patiently tolerant of their human weaknesses, drew the Twelve around Him, and taught them as a loving father might instruct and admonish his contentious children. He showed them how earthly rulers, such as princes among the Gentiles, domineer over their subjects, manifesting lordship and arbitrarily exercizing the authority of office. But it was not to be so among the Master's servants; whoever of them would be great must be a servant indeed, willingly ministering unto his fellows; the humblest and most willing servant would be the chief of the servants. "For even the Son of man came not to be ministered unto, but to minister, and to give his life a ransom for many."[1043]

SIGHT RESTORED TO THE BLIND NEAR JERICHO.[1044]

In the course of His journey Jesus came to Jericho, at or near which city He again exerted His wondrous power in opening the eyes of the blind. Matthew states that two sightless men were made to see, and that the miracle was enacted as Jesus was leaving Jericho; Mark mentions but one blind man, whom he names Bartimeus or the son of Timeus, and agrees with Matthew in saying that the healing was effected when Jesus was departing from the city; Luke specifies but one subject of the Lord's healing mercy, "a certain blind man," and chronicles the miracle as an incident of Christ's approach to Jericho. These slight variations attest the independent authorship of each of the records, and the apparent discrepancies have no direct bearing upon the main facts, nor do they detract from the instructional value of the Lord's work. As we have found to be the case on an earlier occasion, two men were mentioned though but one figures in the circumstantial accounts.[1045]

The man who is more particularly mentioned, Bartimeus, sat by the wayside, asking alms.

Jesus approached, accompanied by the apostles, many other disciples, and a great multitude of people, probably made up largely of travelers on their way to Jerusalem to attend the Passover festival, the time for which was about a week ahead. Hearing the tramp of so great a company the sightless beggar inquired what it all meant, and was answered, "Jesus of Nazareth passeth by." Eager lest the opportunity of gaining the Master's attention be lost, he immediately cried in a loud voice: "Jesus, thou son of David, have mercy on me." His appeal, and particularly his use of the title, Son of David, show that he knew of the great Teacher, had confidence in His power to heal and faith in Him as the promised King and Deliverer of Israel.[1046] Those who were in advance of Jesus in the company tried to silence the man, but the more they rebuked him the louder and more persistently did he cry: "Thou son of David, have mercy on me." Jesus halted in His course and directed that the man be brought to Him. Those who but a moment before would have stopped the blind man's yearning appeal, now that the Master had noticed him were eager to be of service. To the sightless one they brought the glad word: "Be of good comfort, rise; he calleth thee"; and he, casting aside his outer garment lest it hinder, came in haste to Christ. To the Lord's question, "What wilt thou that I shall do unto thee?" Bartimeus answered: "Lord, that I may receive my sight." Then Jesus spake the simple words of power and blessing: "Receive thy sight: thy faith hath saved thee." The man, full of gratitude and knowing that nothing short of divine interposition could have opened his eyes, followed his Benefactor, glorifying God in heartfelt prayers of thanksgiving, in which many of those who had witnessed the miracle fervently joined.

ZACCHEUS, THE CHIEF AMONG THE PUBLICANS.[1047]

Jericho was a city of considerable importance; among its resident officials was a staff of publicans, or collectors of customs, and of these the chief was Zaccheus,[1048] who had grown rich from the revenues of office. He had doubtless heard of the great Galilean who hesitated not to mingle with publicans, detested though they were by the Jews in general; he may have known, also, that Jesus had placed one of this publican class among the most prominent of the disciples. That Zaccheus was a Jew is indicated by his name, which is a variant of "Zacharias," with a Greek or Latin termination; he must have been particularly obnoxious to his people on account of his advanced status among the publicans, all of whom were in Roman employ. He had a great desire to see Jesus; the feeling was not one of mere curiosity; he had been impressed and set thinking by the things he had heard about this Teacher from Nazareth. But Zaccheus was a little man, and could not ordinarily see over the heads of others; so he ran ahead of the company and climbed a tree alongside the road. When Jesus reached the place, to the great surprize of the man in the tree He looked up and said: "Zaccheus, make haste, and come down; for to day I must abide at thy house." Zaccheus came down with haste, and joyfully received the Lord as his guest. The multitude by whom Jesus had been accompanied appear to have been generally friendly toward Him; but at this turn of affairs they murmured and criticized, saying that the Master "was gone to be guest with a man that is a sinner"; for all publicans were sinners in Jewish eyes, and Zaccheus admitted that the opprobrium in his case was possibly deserved. But having seen and conversed with Jesus, this chief among the publicans believed and was converted. As proof of his change of heart Zaccheus then and there voluntarily vowed unto the Lord to make amends and restitution if it were found that he owed such. "Behold, Lord," he said, "the half of my goods I give to the poor; and if I have taken anything from any man by false accusation, I restore him fourfold." These were works meet for repentance. The man realized that he could not change his past; but he knew he could in part at least atone for some of his misdeeds. His pledge to restore in fourfold measure whatever he had wrongfully acquired was in line with the Mosaic law as to restitution, but far in excess of the recompense required.[1049] Jesus accepted the man's profession of repentance, and said: "This day is salvation come to this house, forsomuch as he also is a son of Abraham." Another stray sheep had been returned to the fold; another lost treasure had been found; another wayward son had come back to the Father's house.[1050] "For the Son of man is come to seek and to save that which was lost."

UNTO EVERY ONE THAT HATH SHALL BE GIVEN.[1051]

As the multitude approached Jerusalem, Jesus being in their midst, expectation ran high as to what the Lord would do when He reached the capital of the nation. Many of those with Him were looking for a proclamation of His royal authority and "they thought that the kingdom of God should immediately appear." Jesus told them a story; we call it the _Parable of the Pounds_:

"A certain nobleman went into a far country to receive for himself a kingdom, and to return. And he called his ten servants, and delivered them ten pounds, and said unto them, Occupy till I come. But his citizens hated him, and sent a message after him, saying, We will not have this man to reign over us. And it came to pass, that when he was returned, having received the kingdom, then he commanded these servants to be called unto him, to whom he had given the money, that he might know how much every man had gained by trading. Then came the first, saying, Lord, thy pound hath gained ten pounds. And he said unto him, Well, thou good servant: because thou hast been faithful in a very little, have thou authority over ten cities. And the second came, saying, Lord, thy pound hath gained five pounds. And he said likewise to him, Be thou also over five cities. And another came, saying, Lord, behold, here is thy pound, which I have kept laid up in a napkin: For I feared thee, because thou art an austere man: thou takest up that thou layedst not down, and reapest that thou didst not sow. And he saith unto him, Out of thine own mouth will I judge thee, thou wicked servant. Thou knewest that I was an austere man, taking up that I laid not down, and reaping that I did not sow: Wherefore then gavest not thou my money into the bank, that at my coming I might have required mine own with usury? And he said unto them that stood by, Take from him the pound, and give it to him that hath ten pounds. (And they said unto him, Lord, he hath ten pounds.) For I say unto you, That unto every one which hath shall be given; and from him that hath not, even that he hath shall be taken away from him. But those mine enemies, which would not that I should reign over them, bring hither, and slay them before me."

Both the circumstances of the story and the application of the parable were more readily apparent to the Jewish multitude than they are to us. The departure of a certain nobleman from a vassal province to the court of the suzerain to seek investiture of kingly authority, and the protest of the citizens over whom he asserted the right to reign, were incidents of Jewish history still fresh in the minds of the people to whom Christ spoke.[1052] The explication of the parable is this: The people were not to look for an immediate establishment of the kingdom in temporal power. He who would be king was pictured as having departed for a far country from which he would assuredly return. Before leaving he had given to each of his servants a definite sum of money; and by their success in using this he would judge of their fitness to serve in offices of trust. When he returned he called for an accounting, in the course of which the cases of three servants are specified as types. One had so used the pound as to gain ten pounds; he was commended and received a reward such as only a sovereign could give, the governorship of ten cities. The second servant, with equal capital had increased it only five fold; he was properly rewarded in proportion by appointment as governor over five cities. The third gave back what he had received, without increase, for he had failed to use it. He had no reason and only a very poor excuse to offer for his dereliction. In justice he was severely reprimanded, and the money was taken from him. When the king directed that the pound so forfeited by the unfaithful servant be given to him who already had ten, some surprize was manifest amongst those who stood by; but the king explained, that "unto every one that hath shall be given," for such a one uses to advantage the means entrusted to his care, while "from him that hath not, even that he hath shall be taken away from him"; for he has demonstrated his utter unfitness to possess and use aright. This part of the parable, while of general application, must have appealed to the apostles as particularly apt; for each of them had received in trust an equal endowment through ordination, and each would be required to account for his administration.

The fact is apparent that Christ was the nobleman who was to be invested with the authority of kingship, and who would return to require the accounting at the hands of His trusted servants.[1053] But many of the citizens hated Him and would protest His investiture, saying they would not have Him to reign over them.[1054] When He does return in power and authority, these rebellious citizens shall surely receive the punishment they deserve.[1055]

IN THE HOUSE OF SIMON THE LEPER.[1056]

Six days before the Feast of the Passover, that is to say before the day on which the paschal lamb was to be eaten,[1057] Jesus arrived at Bethany, the home town of Martha and Mary, and of Lazarus who had recently died and been restored to life. The chronology of events during the last week of our Lord's life supports the generally accepted belief that in this year, the fourteenth day of Nisan, on which the Passover festival began, fell on Thursday; and this being so, the day on which Jesus reached Bethany was the preceding Friday, the eve of the Jewish Sabbath. Jesus fully realized that this was the last He would live to see in mortality. The Gospel-writers have drawn a veil of reverent silence over the events of that day. It appears that Jesus passed His last Sabbath in retirement at Bethany. The journey afoot from Jericho had been no easy walk, for the road ascended to an altitude of nearly three thousand feet, and was withal otherwise a toilsome way.

On Saturday,[1058] probably in the evening after the Sabbath had passed, a supper was spread for Jesus and the Twelve in the house of Simon the leper. No other mention of this man, Simon, appears in scripture. If he was living at the time our Lord was entertained in the house known by his name, and if he was present, he must have been previously healed of his leprosy, as otherwise he could not have been allowed within the town, far less to be one of a festal company. It is reasonable to think that the man had once been a victim of leprosy and had come to be currently known as Simon the leper, and that he was one among the many sufferers from this dread disease who had been healed through the Lord's ministrations.

Martha was in charge of the supper arrangements on this memorable occasion, and her sister Mary was with her, while Lazarus sat at table with Jesus. Many have assumed that the house of Simon the leper was the family home of the two sisters and Lazarus, in which case it is possible that Simon was the father of the three; but of such relationship we have no proof.[1059] There was no attempt to secure unusual privacy at this supper. Such occasions were customarily marked by the presence of many uninvited lookers-on in that time; and we are not surprized to learn, therefore, that many people were there and that they had come "not for Jesus' sake only, but that they might see Lazarus also, whom he had raised from the dead." Lazarus was a subject of much interest and doubtless of curiosity among the people; and at the time of his privileged and intimate association with Jesus in Bethany, the chief priests were plotting to put him to death, on account of the effect his restoration had had upon the people, many of whom believed on Jesus because of the miracle.

That supper in Bethany was an event never to be forgotten. Mary, the more contemplative and spiritually minded of the two sisters, she who loved to sit at the feet of Jesus and listen to His words, and who had been commended for having so chosen the one needful thing, which her more practical sister lacked,[1060] brought from among her treasures an alabaster cruse containing a pound of costly spikenard ointment; she broke the sealed flask[1061] and poured its fragrant contents upon the head and feet of her Lord, and wiped His feet with her loosened tresses.[1062] To anoint the head of a guest with ordinary oil was to do him honor; to anoint his feet also was to show unusual and signal regard; but the anointing of head and feet with spikenard, and in such abundance, was an act of reverential homage rarely rendered even to kings.[1063] Mary's act was an expression of adoration; it was the fragrant outwelling of a heart overflowing with worship and affection.

But this splendid tribute of a devout woman's love was made the cause of disagreeable protest. Judas Iscariot, treasurer of the Twelve, but dishonest, avaricious, and small-souled in character, vented his grumbling complaint, saying: "Why was not this ointment sold for three hundred pence, and given to the poor?"[1064] His seeming solicitude for the poor was all hypocrisy. He was a thief and lamented that he had not been given the precious ointment to sell, or that the price had not been turned into the bag of which he was the self-interested custodian. Mary's use of the costly unguent had been so lavish that others beside Judas had let their surprize grow into murmuring; but to him is attributed the distinction of being the chief complainer. Mary's sensitive nature was pained by the ungracious words of disapproval; but Jesus interposed, saying: "Why trouble ye the woman? for she hath wrought a good work upon me." Then in further rebuke and by way of solemn instruction He continued; "For ye have the poor always with you; but me ye have not always. For in that she hath poured this ointment on my body, she did it for my burial. Verily I say unto you, Wheresoever this gospel shall be preached in the whole world, there shall also this, that this woman hath done, be told for a memorial of her."

We are left without certain information as to whether Mary knew that within a few days her beloved Lord would be in the tomb. She may have been so informed in view of the hallowed intimacy between Jesus and the family; or she may have gathered from the remarks of Christ to the apostles that the sacrifice of His life was impending; or perhaps by inspired intuition she was impelled to render the loving tribute by which her memory has been enshrined in the hearts of all who know and love the Christ. John has preserved to us this remark of Jesus in the rebuke called forth by the grumbling Iscariot: "Let her alone; against the day of my burying hath she kept this"; and Mark's version is likewise suggestive of definite and solemn purpose on Mary's part: "She is come aforehand to anoint my body to the burying."

CHRIST'S TRIUMPHAL ENTRY INTO JERUSALEM.[1065]

While still in Bethany or in the neighboring village of Bethphage, and according to John's account on the next day after the supper at Simon's house, Jesus directed two of His disciples to go to a certain place, where, He told them, they would find an ass tied, and with her a colt on which no man had ever sat. These they were to bring to Him. If stopped or questioned they were to say the Lord had need of the animals. Matthew alone mentions both ass and colt; the other writers specify the latter only; most likely the mother followed as the foal was led away, and the presence of the dam probably served to keep the colt tractable. The disciples found all to be as the Lord had said. They brought the colt to Jesus, spread their coats on the gentle creature's back, and set the Master thereon. The company started toward Jerusalem, Jesus riding in their midst.

Now, as was usual, great numbers of people had come up to the city many days before the beginning of the Passover rites, in order that they might attend to matters of personal purification, and make good their arrears in the offering of prescribed sacrifices. Though the great day, on which the festival was to be inaugurated, was yet four days ahead, the city was thronged with pilgrim crowds; and among these much questioning had arisen as to whether Jesus would venture to appear publicly in Jerusalem during the feast, in view of the well-known plans of the hierarchy to take Him into custody. The common people were interested in every act and movement of the Master; and word of His departure from Bethany sped ahead of Him; so that by the time He began the descent from the highest part of the road on the flank of the Mount of Olives, great crowds had gathered about Him. The people were jubilant over the spectacle of Jesus riding the holy city; they spread out their garments, and cast palm fronds and other foliage in His path, thus carpeting the way as for the passing of a king. For the time being He was their king, and they His adoring subjects. The voices of the multitude sounded in reverberating harmony: "Blessed be the King that cometh in the name of the Lord: peace in heaven, and glory in the highest"; and again: "Hosanna to the son of David: Blessed is he that cometh in the name of the Lord; Hosanna in the highest."[1066]

But amidst all this jubilation, Jesus was sad as He came in sight of the great city wherein stood the House of the Lord; and He wept, because of the wickedness of His people, and of their refusal to accept Him as the Son of God; moreover He foresaw the awful scenes of destruction before which both city and temple were soon to fall. In anguish and tears, He thus apostrophized the doomed city: "If thou hadst known, even thou, at least in this thy day, the things which belong unto thy peace! but now they are hid from thine eyes. For the days shall come upon thee, that thine enemies shall cast a trench about thee, and compass thee round, and keep thee in on every side, And shall lay thee even with the ground, and thy children within thee; and they shall not leave in thee one stone upon another; because thou knewest not the time of thy visitation." The multitude was increased by tributary crowds who fell in with the imposing procession at every crossway; and the shouts of praise and homage were heard inside the city while the advancing company was yet far from the walls. When the Lord rode through the massive portal and actually entered the capital of the Great King, the whole city was thrilled. To the inquiry of the uninformed, "Who is this?" the multitude shouted: "This is Jesus, the prophet of Nazareth of Galilee." It may be that the Galilean pilgrims were first to answer and loudest in the gladsome proclamation; for the proud Judeans held Galilee in low esteem, and on this day, Jesus of Galilee was the most prominent personage in Jerusalem. The Pharisees, resentful of the honors thus shown to One whom they had long plotted to destroy, impotently condoled with one another over the failure of all their nefarious schemes, saying: "Perceive ye how ye prevail nothing? behold, the world is gone after him." Unable to check the surging enthusiasm of the multitudes, or to silence the joyous acclamations, some of the Pharisees made their way through the throngs until they reached Jesus, and to Him they appealed, saying: "Master, rebuke thy disciples." But the Lord "answered and said unto them, I tell you that, if these should hold their peace, the stones would immediately cry out"[1067]

Dismounting, He entered afoot the temple enclosure; shouts of adulation greeted Him there. Chief priests, scribes, and Pharisees, the official representatives of the theocracy, the hierarchy of Judaism, were incensed; there was no denying the fact that the people were rendering Messianic honors to this troublesome Nazarene; and that too within the very purlieus of the temple of Jehovah.

The purpose of Christ in thus yielding Himself for the day to the desires of the people and accepting their homage with kingly grace may not be fully comprehended by us of finite mind. That the occasion was no accidental or fortuitous happening, of which He took advantage without preconceived intention, is evident. He knew beforehand what would be, and what He would do. It was no meaningless pageantry; but the actual advent of the King into His royal city, and His entry into the temple, the house of the King of kings. He came riding on an ass, in token of peace, acclaimed by the Hosanna shouts of multitudes; not on a caparisoned steed with the panoply of combat and the accompaniment of bugle blasts and fanfare of trumpets. That the joyous occasion was in no sense suggestive of physical hostility or of seditious disturbance is sufficiently demonstrated by the indulgent unconcern with which it was viewed by the Roman officials, who were usually prompt to send their legionaries swooping down from the fortress of Antonia at the first evidence of an outbreak; and they were particularly vigilant in suppressing all Messianic pretenders, for false Messiahs had arisen already, and much blood had been shed in the forcible dispelling of their delusive claims. But the Romans saw nothing to fear, perhaps much to smile at, in the spectacle of a King mounted upon an ass, and attended by subjects, who, though numerous, brandished no weapons but waved instead palm branches and myrtle sprigs. The ass has been designated in literature as "the ancient symbol of Jewish royalty," and one riding upon an ass as the type of peaceful progress.

Such triumphal entry of Jesus into the chief city of the Jews would have been strikingly inconsistent with the general tenor of His ministry in its early stages. Even the intimation that He was the Christ had been made with guarded care, if at all; and every manifestation of popular regard in which He might have figured as a national leader had been suppressed. Now, however, the hour of the great consummation was near at hand; the public acceptance of the nation's homage, and the acknowledgment of both kingly and Messianic titles, constituted an open and official proclamation of His divine investiture. He had entered city and temple in such royal state as befitted the Prince of Peace. By the rulers of the nation He had been rejected and His claims derided. The manner of His entry should have appealed to the learned teachers of the law and the prophets; for Zechariah's impressive forecast, the fulfilment of which the evangelist, John, finds in the events of this memorable Sunday,[1068] was frequently cited among them: "Rejoice greatly, O, daughter of Zion; shout, O, daughter of Jerusalem: behold, thy King cometh unto thee: he is just, and having salvation; lowly, and riding upon an ass, and upon a colt, the foal of an ass."[1069]

CERTAIN GREEKS VISIT CHRIST.[1070]

Among the multitudes who came to Jerusalem at the time of the annual Passover were people of many nations. Some of these, though not of Jewish descent, had been converted to Judaism; they were admitted to the temple precincts, but were not allowed to pass beyond the court of the Gentiles.[1071] Sometime during our Lord's last week of mortal life, possibly on the day of His royal entry into the city, [1072] certain Greeks, who were evidently numbered among the proselytes since they had come "to worship at the feast," sought an interview with Jesus. Imbued with a becoming sense of decorum they hesitated to directly approach the Master, and applied instead to Philip, one of the apostles, saying: "Sir, we would see Jesus." Philip consulted with Andrew, and the two then informed Jesus, who, as we may reasonably infer from the context though the fact is not explicitly stated, graciously received the foreign visitors and imparted to them precepts of the utmost worth. It is evident that the desire of these Greeks to meet the Master was not grounded on curiosity or other unworthy impulse; they earnestly wished to see and hear the Teacher whose fame had reached their country, and whose doctrines had impressed them.

To them Jesus testified that the hour of His death was near at hand, the hour in which "the Son of man should be glorified." They were surprised and pained by the Lord's words, and possibly they inquired as to the necessity of such a sacrifice. Jesus explained by citing a striking illustration drawn from nature: "Verily, verily, I say unto you, Except a corn of wheat fall into the ground and die, it abideth alone: but if it die, it bringeth forth much fruit;"[1073] The simile is an apt one,--and at once impressively simple and beautiful. A farmer who neglects or refuses to cast his wheat into the earth, because he wants to keep it, can have no increase; but if he sow the wheat in good rich soil, each living grain may multiply itself many fold, though of necessity the seed must be sacrificed in the process. So, said the Lord, "He that loveth his life shall lose it; and he that hateth his life in this world shall keep it unto life eternal." The Master's meaning is clear; he that loves his life so well that he will not imperil it, or, if need be, give it up, in the service of God, shall forfeit his opportunity to win the bounteous increase of eternal life; while he who esteems the call of God as so greatly superior to life that his love of life is as hatred in comparison, shall find the life he freely yields or is willing to yield, though for the time being it disappear like the grain buried in the soil; and he shall rejoice in the bounty of eternal development. If such be true of every man's existence, how transcendently so was it of the life of Him who came to die that men may live? Therefore was it necessary that He die, as He had said He was about to do; but His death, far from being life lost, was to be life glorified.

VOICE FROM HEAVEN.[1074]

The realization of the harrowing experiences upon which He was about to enter, and particularly the contemplation of the state of sin, which made His sacrifice imperative, so weighed upon the Savior's mind that He sorrowed deeply. "Now is my soul troubled," He groaned; "and what shall I say?" He exclaimed in anguish. Should He say, "Father, save me from this hour" when as He knew "for this cause" had He come "unto this hour?" To His Father alone could He turn for comforting support, not to ask relief from, but strength to endure, what was to come; and He prayed: "Father, glorify thy name." It was the rising of a mighty Soul to meet a supreme issue, which for the moment had seemed to be overwhelming. To that prayer of renewed surrender to the Father's will, "Then came there a voice from heaven, saying, I have both glorified it, and will glorify it again."

The voice was real; it was no subjective whisper of comfort to the inner consciousness of Jesus, but an external, objective reality. People who were standing by heard the sound, and interpreted it variously; some said it was thunder; others, of better spiritual discernment, said: "An angel spake to him"; and some may have understood the words as had Jesus. Now fully emerged from the passing cloud of enveloping anguish, the Lord turned to the people, saying: "This voice came not because of me, but for your sakes." And then, with the consciousness of assured triumph over sin and death, He exclaimed in accents of divine jubilation, as though the cross and the sepulchre were already of the past: "Now is the judgment of this world: now shall the prince of this world be cast out." Satan, the prince of the world was doomed.[1075] "And I," the Lord continued, "if I be lifted up from the earth, will draw all men unto me." John assures us that this last utterance signified the manner of the Lord's death; the people so understood, and they asked an explanation of what seemed to them an inconsistency, in that the scriptures, as they had been taught to interpret the same, declared that the Christ was to abide forever,[1076] and now He who claimed to be the Messiah, the Son of Man, averred that He must be lifted up. "Who is this Son of man?" they asked. Mindful as ever not to cast pearls where they would not be appreciated, the Lord refrained from a direct avowal, but admonished them to walk in the light while the light was with them, for darkness would surely follow; and as He reminded them, "he that walketh in darkness knoweth not whither he goeth." In conclusion the Lord admonished them thus: "While ye have light, believe in the light, that ye may be the children of light."[1077]

At the close of this discourse Jesus departed from the people "and did hide himself from them." The record of the first day of what has come to be known as the week of our Lord's passion[1078] is thus concluded by Mark: "And when he had looked round about upon all things, and now the eventide was come, he went out unto Bethany with the twelve."[1079]

NOTES TO CHAPTER 29.

1. The Mother of James and John.--The mother of these two sons of Zebedee (Matt. 20:20; compare 4:21) is generally understood to have been the Salome mentioned as one of the women present at the crucifixion (Mark 15:40; compare Matt. 27:56 in which "the mother of Zebedee's children" is mentioned, and the name "Salome" is omitted), and one of those who arrived first at the tomb on the morning of the resurrection (Mark 16:1). From the fact that John mentions the mother of Jesus and "his mother's sister" (19:25) and omits mention of Salome by name, some expositors hold that Salome was the sister of Mary the mother of Jesus; and therefore the Savior's aunt. This relationship would make James and John cousins to Jesus. While the scriptural record does not disprove this alleged kinship, it certainly does not affirm the same.

2. Jericho.--This was an ancient city, lying north-easterly from Jerusalem, a little less than fifteen miles in a straight line. In the course of the exodus it was captured by the people of Israel through a miraculous interposition of divine power. (Josh. 6). The productiveness of the region is indicated by the descriptive appellation "city of palm trees" (Deut. 34:3; Judg. 1:16; 3:13; 2 Chron. 28:15). The name Jericho means "place of fragrance." Its climate was semi-tropical, a consequence of its low altitude. It lay in a valley several hundred feet below the level of the Mediterranean; this explains Luke's statement (19:28) that after Jesus had spoken the Parable of the Pounds when on the way from Jericho, "he went before, ascending up to Jerusalem." In the time of Christ, Jericho was an important city; and the abundance of its commercial products, particularly balsam and spices, led to the maintenance of a customs office there, over which Zaccheus seems to have presided.

3. The Nobleman and the Kingdom.--The local setting of the part of the Parable of the Pounds that relates to a certain nobleman going into a far country to receive for himself a kingdom, had its parallel in history. Archelaus, who by the will of his father, Herod the Great, had been named king of the Jews, set out for Rome to ask of the emperor the confirmation of his royal status. He was opposed by a protest from the people. On the utilization of this circumstance in the parable, Farrar (p. 493, note) says: "A nobleman going into a far country to receive a kingdom would be utterly unintelligible, had we not fortunately known that this was done both by Archelaus and by Antipas (Jos. Ant. xvii, 9:4). And in the case of Archelaus the Jews had actually sent to Augustus a deputation of fifty, to recount his cruelties and oppose his claims, which, though it failed at the time, was subsequently successful (Josephus, Ant. xvii, 13:2). Philipus defended the property of Archelaus, during his absence, from the encroachments of the Proconsul Sabinus. The magnificent palace which Archelaus had built at Jericho (Jos. Ant. xvii, 13:1) would naturally recall these circumstances to the mind of Jesus, and the parable is another striking example of the manner in which He utilized the most ordinary circumstances around Him, and made them the bases of His highest teachings. It is also another unsuspected indication of the authenticity and truthfulness of the Gospels."

4. "We Will Not Have this Man to Reign Over Us."--On this phase of the parable, Trench

(_Miracles_, p. 390) very aptly remarks: "Twice before He had gone to receive His kingdom, this very declaration found formal utterance from their lips,--once when they cried to Pilate, 'We have no king but C├ªsar'; and again when they remonstrated with him, 'Write not, The King of the Jews' (John 19:15, 21; compare Acts 17:7). But the stricter fulfilment of these words is to be found in the demeanor of the Jews after His ascension, their fierce hostility to Christ in His infant Church (Acts 12:3; 13:45; 14:18; 17:5; 18:6; 22:22; 23:12; 1 Thes. 2:15)."

5. The Day of the Supper at Bethany.--John places this event as having occurred on the day following Christ's arrival in Bethany, for as we see from 12:12, the triumphal entry into Jerusalem took place on the next day after the supper, and, as stated in the text, Jesus most probably reached Bethany on Friday. The joyous processional into Jerusalem did not occur on the day following Friday, for that was the Jewish Sabbath. Matthew (26:2-13) and Mark (14:1-9) give place to the incident of the supper after the record of the triumphal entry and other events, from which some have drawn the inference that these two writers place the supper two days before the Passover. This inference lacks confirmation. In this matter the chronological order given by John appears to be the true one.

6. The Family Home at Bethany.--The home of Martha, Mary, and Lazarus appears to have been the usual abiding place of Jesus when He was in Bethany. Undoubtedly He was on terms of very close and affectionate acquaintanceship with all members of the family, even before the miraculous raising of Lazarus from the dead, and, this supremely blessed occurrence must have intensified into worshipful reverence the esteem in which our Lord had been held in that household. As to whether this home was identical with the house of Simon the leper, the scriptural record does not state. John, who gives a fairly detailed account of the supper served by Martha, makes no mention of Simon or his house. It is noticeable that the synoptic writers say very little about this home in Bethany. Farrar has aptly remarked (p. 483): "We seem to trace in the Synoptists a special reticence about the family at Bethany. The house in which they take a prominent position is called 'the house of Simon the leper'; Mary is called simply 'a woman' by St. Matthew and St. Mark (Matt. 26:6, 7; Mark 14:3); and St. Luke contents himself with calling Bethany 'a certain village' (Luke 10:38), although he was perfectly aware of the name (Luke 19:29)."

7. Spikenard Ointment.--This was among the most highly prized of oriental unguents. That with which Mary anointed Jesus is described by Matthew and Mark as "very precious," and by John as "very costly." In the original the adjective "pistic" appears; this is translated by some as meaning "liquid," but by others as signifying "genuine." There were many inferior imitations of the real spikenard, or nard; and we are left without a doubt that Mary's precious gift was of the best. The plant from which the fragrant extract is obtained is a species of bearded grass indigenous in India. Spikenard is mentioned in Song of Solomon 1:12; 4:13, 14.

8. Hosanna!--"Hosanna" is a Greek form of the Hebrew expression for "Save us now," or "Save, we pray," which occurs in the original of Psalm 118:25. It occurs nowhere in the English Bible except in the acclamations of the people at Christ's triumphal entry into Jerusalem, and in the joyous shouts of children in the temple (Matt. 21:9, 15). Note the rendering of the "Hosanna Shout" in the restored Church of Christ in the current dispensation on occasions of particular rejoicing before the Lord (see the _House of the Lord_, pp. 120, 150, 210). "Hallelujah," literally rendered, means "Praise ye Jehovah." It occurs in the Greek form "Alleluia" in Rev. 19:1, 3, 4, 6.

9. The First Day in Passion Week.--A comparison of the accounts of the Lord's triumphal entry into Jerusalem, and of certain events following, as recorded by the three synoptists, shows at least a possibility of discrepancy as to sequence. It appears certain that Jesus visited the temple grounds on the day of the royal advent into the city. From Matthew 21:12 and Luke 19:45 and the context preceding these passages, the inference has been drawn that the second clearing of the temple occurred on the day of the processional entry; while others interpret Mark 11:11 and 15 as meaning that the event took place on a later day. The question is admittedly an open one; and the order of presentation followed in the text is one of convenience of treatment based on rational probability.

FOOTNOTES:

[1039] Matt. 20:17-19; Mark 10:32-34; Luke 18:31-34.

[1040] The earlier predictions were: (1) that spoken shortly before the Transfiguration (Matt. 16:21; Mark 8:31), and (2) that which followed, in Galilee, (Matt. 17:22, 23; Mark 9:31; compare Luke 9:44).

[1041] Matt. 20:20-28; Mark 10:35-45.

[1042] Note 1, end of chapter.

[1043] For earlier lessons on the greatness of humility see pages 386 and 471; for the significance of the title, Son of Man, see pages 142-144.

[1044] Matt. 20:30-34; Mark 10:46-52; Luke 18:35-43.

[1045] See account of the two demoniacs, Matt. 8:28, compare Mark 5:1, Luke 8:27. See also page 310 herein.

[1046] Compare Matt. 9:27; 15:22; page 85 herein.

[1047] Luke 19:1-10.

[1048] Note 2, end of chapter.

[1049] Exo. 22:1-9.

[1050] Compare pages 389 and 454 to 461.

[1051] Luke 19:11-27.

[1052] Note 3, end of chapter.

[1053] Compare Mark 13:34.

[1054] Note 4, end of chapter.

[1055] Comparison of similarities and differences between this parable and that of the Talents (Matt. 25:14-30) will be made in chapter 32, pages 580-584.

[1056] John 12:1-8; Matt. 26:6-13; Mark 14:3-9.

[1057] See Exo. 12:1-10; also page 112 herein.

[1058] Note 5, end of chapter.

[1059] Note 6, end of chapter.

[1060] Luke 10:40-42; page 432 herein.

[1061] The better rendering is "cruse" or "flask" instead of "box." See revised version.

[1062] This occurrence must not be confused with that of an earlier anointing of Jesus by a penitent sinner in the house of Simon the Pharisee (Luke 7:36-50) in Galilee. See page 262 herein.

[1063] Note 7, end of chapter.

[1064] Three hundred pence or Roman denarii would be approximately equal in value to forty-five dollars.

[1065] Matt. 21:1-11; Mark 11:1-11; Luke 19:29-44; John 12:12-19.

[1066] Note 8, end of chapter.

[1067] Compare Hab. 2:11.

[1068] The Sunday before Easter is annually celebrated by many Christian sects as Palm Sunday, in commemoration of our Lord's triumphal entry into Jerusalem.

[1069] Zech. 9:9.

[1070] John 12:20-26.

[1071] See "House of the Lord," pages 56, 57.

[1072] John records this event in immediate sequence to the Lord's triumphal entry, though without any specific indication of the time of its occurrence.

[1073] Compare 1 Cor. 15:36.

[1074] John 12:27-36.

[1075] Compare John 14:30; 16:11.

[1076] See e.g. Isa. 9:7; Dan. 7:14, 27; Ezek. 37:25.

[1077] Compare John 1:9; 3:19; 8:12; 9:5; 12:46; see page 407.

[1078] Acts 1:3.

[1079] Mark 11:11. Note 9, end of chapter.

CHAPTER 30. JESUS RETURNS TO THE TEMPLE DAILY.

AN INSTRUCTIVE INCIDENT ON THE WAY.[1080]

On the morrow, which, as we reckon, was Monday, the second day of Passion week, Jesus and the Twelve returned to Jerusalem and spent the greater part of the day at the temple. The start from Bethany was an early one, and Jesus hungered by the way. Looking ahead He saw a fig tree that differed from the rest of the many fig trees of the region in that it was in full leaf though the season of fruit had not yet come.[1081] It is well known that the fruit-buds of a fig-tree appear earlier than do the leaves, and that by the time the tree is in full foliage the figs are well advanced toward maturity. Moreover, certain species of figs are edible while yet green; indeed the unripe fruit is relished in the Orient at the present time. It would be reasonable, therefore, for one to expect to find edible figs even in early April on a tree that was already covered with leaves. When Jesus and His party reached this particular tree, which had rightly been regarded as rich in promise of fruit, they found on it nothing but leaves; it was a showy, fruitless, barren tree. It was destitute even of old figs, those of the preceding season, some of which are often found in spring on fruitful trees. Jesus pronounced upon that tree the sentence of perpetual barrenness. "No man eat fruit of thee hereafter forever" He said according to Mark's account; or, as Matthew records the judgment, "Let no fruit grow on thee henceforward for ever." The latter writer tells us in immediate sequence that "presently the fig tree withered away"; but the former makes it appear that the effect of the curse was not observed until the following morning, when, as Jesus and the apostles were once again on the way between Bethany and Jerusalem, they saw that the fig tree had withered and dried from the roots up. Peter called attention to the blasted tree, and, addressing Jesus, exclaimed: "Master, behold, the fig tree which thou cursedst is withered away."

Applying the lesson of the occasion, Jesus said, "Have faith in God"; and then He repeated some of His former assurances as to the power of faith, by which even mountains may be removed, should there be need of such miraculous accomplishment, and through which, indeed, any necessary thing may be done. The blighting of a tree was shown to be small in comparison with the greater possibilities of achievement through faith and prayer. But to so achieve one must work and pray without reservation or doubt, as the Lord thus made plain: "Therefore I say unto you, What things soever ye desire, when ye pray, believe that ye receive them, and ye shall have them." Prayer must be acceptable unto God to be effective; and it follows that he who desires to accomplish any work through prayer and faith must be fit to present himself before the Lord in supplication; therefore Jesus again instructed the apostles saying: "And when ye stand praying, forgive, if ye have ought against any: that your Father also which is in heaven may forgive you your trespasses. But if ye do not forgive, neither will your Father which is in heaven forgive your trespasses."[1082]

The blighting of the barren fig tree is regarded by many as unique among the recorded miracles of Christ, from the fact that while all the others were wrought for relief, blessing, and beneficent purposes generally, this one appears as an act of judgment and destructive execution, Nevertheless in this miracle the Lord's purpose is not hidden; and the result, while fatal to a tree, is of lasting blessing to all who would learn and profit, by the works of God. If no more has been accomplished by the miracle than the presenting of so impressive an object lesson for the instructions that followed, that smitten tree has proved of greater service to humanity than have all the fig orchards of Bethphage.[1083] To the apostles the act was another and an indisputable proof of the Lord's power over nature, His control of natural forces and all material things, His jurisdiction over life and death. He had healed multitudes; the wind and the waves had obeyed His words; on three occasions He had restored the dead to life; it was fitting that He should demonstrate His power to smite and to destroy. In manifesting His command over death, He had mercifully raised a maiden from the couch on which she had died, a young man from the bier on which he was being carried to the grave, another from the sepulchre in which he had been laid away a corpse; but in proof of His power to destroy by a word He chose a barren and worthless tree for His subject. Could any of the Twelve doubt, when, a few days later they saw Him in the hands of vindictive priests and heartless pagans, that did He so will He could smite His enemies by a word, even unto death? Yet not until after His glorious resurrection did even the apostles realize how truly voluntary His sacrifice had been.

But the fate that befell the barren fig tree is instructive from another point of view. The incident is as much parable as miracle. That leafy tree was distinguished among fig trees; the others offered no invitation, gave no promise; "the time of figs was not yet"; they, in due season would bring forth fruit and leaves; but this precocious and leafy pretender waved its umbrageous limbs as in boastful assertion of superiority. For those who responded to its ostentatious invitation, for the hungering Christ who came seeking fruit, it had naught but leaves. Even for the purposes of the lesson involved, we cannot conceive of the tree being blighted primarily because it was fruitless, for at that season the other fig trees were bare of fruit also; it was made the object of the curse and the subject of the Lord's instructive discourse, because, having leaves, it was deceptively barren. Were it reasonable to regard the tree as possessed of moral agency, we would have to pronounce it a hypocrite; its utter barrenness coupled with its abundance of foliage made of it a type of human hypocrisy.

The leafy, fruitless tree was a symbol of Judaism, which loudly proclaimed itself as the only true religion of the age, and condescendingly invited all the world to come and partake of its rich ripe fruit; when in truth it was but an unnatural growth of leaves, with no fruit of the season, nor even an edible bulb held over from earlier years, for such as it had of former fruitage was dried to worthlessness and made repulsive in its worm-eaten decay. The religion of Israel had degenerated into an artificial religionism, which in pretentious show and empty profession outclassed the abominations of heathendom. As already pointed out in these pages, the fig tree was a favorite type in rabbinical representation of the Jewish race, and the Lord had before adopted the symbolism in the Parable of the Barren Fig Tree, that worthless growth which did but cumber the ground.[1084]

SECOND CLEARING OF THE TEMPLE.[1085]

Within the temple grounds Jesus was filled with indignation at the scene of tumult and desecration which the place presented. Three years before, at Passover time, He had been wrought up to a high state of righteous anger by a similar exhibition of sordid chaffering within the sacred precincts, and had driven out the sheep and oxen and forcibly expelled the traders and the money-changers and all who were using His Father's house as a house of merchandize.[1086] That was near the beginning of His public labor, and the vigorous action was among the first of His works to attract general attention; now, within four days of the cross, He cleared the courts again by casting out all "them that sold and bought in the temple, and overthrew the tables of the moneychangers, and the seats of them that sold doves"; nor would He suffer any to carry their buckets and baskets through the enclosure, as many were in the habit of doing, and so making the way a common thoroughfare. "Is it not written," He demanded of them in wrath, "My house shall be called of all nations the house of prayer? but ye have made it a den of thieves." On the former occasion, before He had declared or even confessed His Messiahship, He had designated the temple as "My Father's house"; now that He had openly avowed Himself to be the Christ, He called it "My house." The expressions are in a sense synonymous; He and the Father were and are one in possession and dominion. The means by which the later expulsion was accomplished are not stated; but it is plain that none could withstand His authoritative command; He acted in the strength of righteousness, before which the forces of evil had to give way.

His wrath of indignation was followed by the calmness of gentle ministry; there in the cleared courts of His house, blind and lame folk came limping and groping about Him, and He healed them. The anger of the chief priests and scribes was raging against Him; but it was impotent. They had decreed His death, and had made repeated efforts to take Him, and there He sat within the very area over which they claimed supreme jurisdiction, and they were afraid to touch Him because of the common people, whom they professed to despize yet heartily feared--"for all the people were very attentive to hear him."

The rage of the officials was further aggravated by a touching incident, which seems to have accompanied or to have immediately followed His merciful healing of the afflicted folk at the temple. Children saw what He did; with their innocent minds yet unsullied by the prejudice of tradition and their sight yet undarkened by sin, they perceived in Him the Christ, and burst forth into praise and worship in a hymn that was heard by the angels: "Hosanna to the son of David." With ill-concealed anger the temple officials demanded of Him: "Hearest thou what these say?" They probably expected Him to disclaim the title, or possibly hoped that He would reassert His claim in a manner that would afford excuse for legal action against Him, for to most of them the Son of David was the Messiah, the promised King. Would He clear Himself of the blasphemy that attached to the unjustified acknowledgment of so awful a dignity? Jesus answered, with an implied rebuke for their ignorance of the scriptures: "Yea; have ye never read, Out of the mouth of babes and sucklings thou hast perfected praise?"[1087]

It was now Monday evening; Jesus left the city and retired again to Bethany, where He lodged. This course was a prudent one, in view of the determination of the rulers to get Him into their power provided they could do so without arousing the people. This they could not accomplish by day, for wherever He appeared He was the center of a multitude; but had He remained in Jerusalem over night the vigilant emissaries of the hierarchy might have succeeded in taking Him, unless He withstood them by some miraculous action. Near as was His hour, it had not yet struck; and He would be made captive only as He permitted Himself, a voluntary victim, to be taken into the hands of His enemies.

CHRIST'S AUTHORITY CHALLENGED BY THE RULERS.[1088]

On the following day, that is on Tuesday, He returned to the temple with the Twelve, passing the withered fig tree on the way and impressing the moral of the combined miracle and parable as we have already seen. As He taught in the sacred place, preaching the gospel to all who would hear, the chief priests with a number of scribes and elders came upon Him in a body. They had been debating about Him over night, and had resolved on at least one step; they would challenge His authority for what He had done the day before. They were the guardians of the temple, both the material structure and the theocratic system for which the holy edifice stood; and this Galilean, who permitted Himself to be called the Christ and defended those who so acclaimed Him, had for the second time ignored their authority within the temple walls and in the presence of the common people over whom they lorded so arrogantly. So this official deputation, with plans matured, came to Him saying: "By what authority doest thou these things? and who gave thee this authority?" This action was doubtless a preliminary step in a preconcerted attempt to suppress the activities of Jesus, both of word and deed, within the temple precincts. It will be remembered that after the first cleansing of the temple, the Jews had angrily demanded of Jesus a sign by which they might judge the question of His divine commission;[1089] and it is significant that on this latter occasion no sign was asked, but instead thereof, a specific avowal as to the authority He possessed and by whom it had been given Him. A three years' course of miracle and teaching was known to them; on the yesterday blind and lame had been healed inside the temple walls; and Lazarus, the living testimony of the Lord's power over death and the grave was before them. To ask a further sign would have been to flagrantly expose themselves to the ridicule of the people.

They knew what authority the Lord claimed; their question was of sinister purpose. Jesus did not condescend to voice an answer in which they could possibly find further excuse for antagonizing Him; but He availed Himself of a method very common among themselves--that of countering one question with another. "And Jesus answered and said unto them, I also will ask you one thing, which if ye tell me, I in like wise will tell you by what authority I do these things. The baptism of John, whence was it? from heaven, or of men?" They consulted among themselves as to what answer would best serve to extricate them from an embarrassing position; no mention is made of any attempt to ascertain the truth and reply accordingly; they were thoroughly nonplussed. Should they answer that John's baptism was of God, Jesus would probably demand of them why then they had not believed in the Baptist, and why they did not accept John's testimony concerning Himself. On the other hand, should they aver that John had no divine authority to preach and baptize, the people would turn against them, for the martyred Baptist was revered by the masses as a prophet. In spite of their boasted learning, they answered as puzzled school-boys might do when they perceive hidden difficulties in what at first seemed but a simple problem. "We cannot tell" said they. Then Jesus replied "Neither tell I you by what authority I do these things."

Chief priests, scribes, and elders of the people were outwitted and humiliated. The tables were completely turned upon them; Jesus, whom they had come to question, became the examiner; they a class of cowed and unwilling listeners. He the ready instructor, and the multitude interested observers. With little likelihood of immediate interruption the Master proceeded in calm deliberation to relate to them a series of three splendid stories, each of which they felt applied to themselves with incisive certainty. The first of the narrations we call the _Parable of the Two Sons_.

"But what think ye? A certain man had two sons; and he came to the first, and said, Son, go work today in my vineyard. He answered and said, I will not: but afterward he repented, and went. And he came to the second, and said likewise. And he answered and said, I go, sir: and went not. Whether of them twain did the will of his father? They say unto him, The first. Jesus saith unto them, Verily I say unto you, That the publicans and the harlots go into the kingdom of God before you. For John came unto you in the way of righteousness, and ye believed him not; but the publicans and the harlots believed him: and ye, when ye had seen it, repented not afterward, that ye might believe him."[1090]

The opening sentence, "But what think ye?" was a call to close attention. It implied a question soon to follow; and that proved to be: Which of the two sons was the obedient one? There was but one consistent answer, and they had to give it, however loath. The application of the parable followed with convicting promptness. They, the chief priests, scribes, Pharisees and elders of the people, were typified by the second son, who, when told to labor in the vineyard answered so assuredly, but went not, though the vines were running to wild growth for want of pruning, and such poor fruit as might mature would be left to fall and rot upon the ground. The publicans and sinners upon whom they vented their contempt, whose touch was defilement, were like unto the first son, who in rude though frank refusal ignored the father's call, but afterward relented and set to work, repentantly hoping to make amends for the time he had lost and for the unfilial spirit he had shown.[1091] Publicans and sinners, touched in their hearts by the clarion call to repentance, had flocked to the Baptist in the wilderness with the earnest inquiry: "Master, what shall we do?"[1092] John's call had been to no particular class; but while self-confessed sinners had repented and sought baptism at his hands, those very Pharisees and elders of the people had rejected his testimony and had hypocritically sought to ensnare him.[1093] Through the parable Jesus answered His own question as to whether the baptism of John was of God or of man. The Lord's affirmation, "Verily I say unto you, That the publicans and the harlots go into the kingdom of God before you," was condemnatory of the corrupt though sanctimonious polity of the hierarchy throughout. It was not wholly without intimation of possible reformation, however. He did not say that the repentant sinners should enter, and the priestly hypocrites stand forever excluded; for the latter there was hope if they would but repent, though they would have to follow, not lead, in the glorious procession of the redeemed. In a continuation of the same discourse the Lord presented the _Parable of the Wicked Husbandmen_, as follows:

"Hear another parable: There was a certain householder, which planted a vineyard, and hedged it round about, and digged a winepress in it, and built a tower, and let it out to husbandmen, and went into a far country: And when the time of the fruit drew near, he sent his servants to the husbandmen, that they might receive the fruits of it. And the husbandmen took his servants, and beat one, and killed another, and stoned another. Again, he sent other servants more than the first: and they did unto them likewise. But last of all he sent unto them his son, saying, They will reverence my son. But when the husbandmen saw the son, they said among themselves, This is the heir; come, let us kill him, and let us seize on his inheritance. And they caught him, and cast him out of the vineyard, and slew him. When the lord therefore of the vineyard cometh, what will he do unto those husbandmen? They say unto him, He will miserably destroy those wicked men, and will let out his vineyard unto other husbandmen, which shall render him the fruits in their seasons."[1094]

Again the Jews were compelled to make answer to the great question with which the parable dealt, and again by their answer they pronounced judgment upon themselves. The vineyard, broadly speaking, was the human family, but more specifically the covenant people, Israel; the soil was good and capable of yielding in rich abundance; the vines were choice and had been set out with care; and the whole vineyard was amply protected with a hedge, and suitably furnished with winepress and tower.[1095] The husbandmen could be none other than the priests and teachers of Israel, including the ecclesiastical leaders who were then and there present in an official capacity. The Lord of the vineyard had sent among the people prophets authorized to speak in His name; and these the wicked tenants had rejected, maltreated, and, in many instances, cruelly slain.[1096] In the more detailed reports of the parable we read that when the first servant came, the cruel husbandmen "beat him and sent him away empty"; the next they wounded "in the head, and sent him away shamefully handled"; another they murdered and all who came later were brutally mistreated, and some of them were killed. Those wicked men had used the vineyard of their Lord for personal gain, and had rendered no part of the vintage to the lawful Owner. When the Lord sent other messengers, "more than the first," or in other words, greater than the earlier ones, the most recent example being John the Baptist, the husbandmen rejected them with evil determination more pronounced than ever. At last the Son had come in person; His authority they feared as that of the lawful heir, and with malignity almost beyond belief, they determined to kill Him that they might perpetuate their unworthy possession of the vineyard and thenceforward hold it as their own.

Jesus carried the story without break from the criminal past to the yet more tragic and awful future, then but three days distant; and calmly related in prophetic imagery, as though already fulfilled, how those evil men cast the well beloved Son out of the vineyard and slew Him. Unable to evade the searching question as to what the Lord of the vineyard would naturally and righteously do to the wicked husbandmen, the Jewish rulers gave the only pertinent answer possible--that He would surely destroy those wretched sinners, and let out His vineyard to tenants who were more honest and worthy.

Suddenly changing the figure, "Jesus saith unto them, Did ye never read in the scriptures, The stone which the builders rejected, the same is become the head of the corner: this is the Lord's doing, and it is marvellous in our eyes? Therefore say I unto you, The kingdom of God shall be taken from you, and given to a nation bringing forth the fruits thereof. And whosoever shall fall on this stone shall be broken; but on whomsoever it shall fall, it will grind him to powder."[1097] There could be no misapprehension as to the Lord's meaning; the rejected Stone which was eventually to have chief place, "the head of the corner," in the edifice of salvation, was Himself, the Messiah. To some that Stone would be a cause of stumbling; wo unto them, for thereby would they be broken, and only through repentance and works of righteousness could they even in part recover; but upon others, those who would persist in their opposition, the Stone would fall in judgment; and wo, wo to them, for beneath it they would be destroyed as though ground to powder.[1098] From them, the leaders, and from the people who followed their unholy precepts and foul example, the kingdom of God was about to be taken, and would in time be given to the Gentiles, who, the Lord affirmed, would prove more worthy than Israel had been. We gather from Luke's account that in contemplation of this awful penalty, "they," whether priestly rulers or common people we are not told, exclaimed in despair, "God forbid!"

As the chief priests and Pharisees realized the completeness of their discomfiture and the extent of the humiliation to which they had been subjected in the eyes of the people, they were incensed beyond measure, and even attempted to lay hold on Jesus there in the temple; but the sympathies of the multitude were so unmistakably in His favor that the angry ecclesiasts desisted. The people in general, while not prepared to openly proclaim Him as the Christ, knew that He was a prophet of God, and their dread of official displeasure and possible penalty did not deter them from friendly demonstrations.

Jesus resumed His teaching by relating the _Parable of the Royal Marriage Feast_.

"And Jesus answered and spake unto them again by parables, and said, The kingdom of heaven is like unto a certain king, which made a marriage for his son, And sent forth his servants to call them that were bidden to the wedding: and they would not come. Again, he sent forth other servants, saying, Tell them which are bidden, Behold, I have prepared my dinner: my oxen and my fatlings are killed, and all things are ready: come unto the marriage. But they made light of it, and went their ways, one to his farm, another to his merchandise: And the remnant took his servants, and entreated them spitefully, and slew them. But when the king heard thereof, he was wroth: and he sent forth his armies, and destroyed those murderers, and burned up their city. Then saith he to his servants, The wedding is ready, but they which were bidden were not worthy. Go ye therefore into the highways, and as many as ye shall find, bid to the marriage. So those servants went out into the highways, and gathered together all as many as they found, both bad and good: and the wedding was furnished with guests."[1099]

The invitation of a king to his subjects is equivalent to a command. The marriage feast was no surprize event, for the selected guests had been bidden long aforetime; and, in accordance with oriental custom were notified again on the opening day of the festivities,[1100] which, according to Hebrew customs, would be understood as extending over a period of seven or fourteen days; in this case of a marriage in the royal family the greater duration would be assumed. Many of the bidden guests refused to come when formally summoned; and of the tolerant king's later and more pressing message they made light and went their ways, while the most wicked turned upon the servants who brought the royal summons, mistreated them cruelly, and some of them they killed. It is plainly evident that the refusal to attend the king's feast was a deliberate rebellion against the royal authority and a personal indignity against both the reigning sovereign and his son. It was as much a duty as an honor for loyal subjects to attend the marriage festival of the prince, whom we cannot err in regarding as the lawful heir to the throne, and therefore the one who might some day reign over them. The turning away by one man to his farm and by another to his merchandize is in part an evidence of their engrossment in material pursuits to the utter disregard of their sovereign's will; but it signifies further an effort to deaden their troubled consciences by some absorbing occupation; and possibly also a premeditated demonstration of the fact that they placed their personal affairs above the call of their king. The monarch executed a terrible retribution upon his rebellious subjects. If the parable was intended to be an allegorical presentation of actual events, it passes at this point from the story of the past to that of the future, for the destruction of Jerusalem postdates by several decades the death of Christ. Finding the guests who had some claim on the royal invitation to be utterly unworthy, the king sent out his servants again, and these gathered in from the highways and cross-roads, from the byways and the lanes, all they could find, irrespective of rank or station, whether rich or poor, good or bad; "and the wedding was furnished with guests."

The great feast by which the Messianic reign was to be ushered in was a favorite theme of jubilant exposition in both synagog and school; and exultation ran high in the rabbinical dictum that none but the children of Abraham would be among the blessed partakers. The king in the parable is God; the son whose marriage was the occasion of the feast is Jesus, the Son of God; the guests who were bidden early, yet who refused to come when the feast was ready, are the covenant people who rejected their Lord, the Christ; the later guests, who were brought in from the streets and the roads, are the Gentile nations, to whom the gospel has been carried since its rejection by the Jews; the marriage feast is symbolical of the glorious consummation of the Messiah's mission.[1101]

All students of the subject must have noted the points of resemblance by which this parable is related to that of the great supper;[1102] fewer perhaps have considered the differences between the two. The earlier story was told in the house of one of the chief Pharisees, probably in some town in Perea; the later one was related within the temple, after Pharisaic opposition to Christ had reached its height. The first is of simpler plot and of gentler climax. The neglect of the invited guests in the first story was accompanied by excuses in which some approach to polite apology appears; the refusal of those bidden in the second parable was markedly offensive, and was coupled with outrageous abuse and murder. The host in one instance was a wealthy though private citizen, in the other the giver of the feast was a king. In the first, the occasion was one of ordinary though abundant entertainment; in the second, the determining time was that of the appointed marriage of the royal heir. Retribution in the first instance was limited to exclusion from the banquet; in the latter the individual punishment was death, which was followed by the punitive example of the city's destruction.

Our account of the royal marriage feast is not yet complete; the story already considered is supplemented by the following:

"And when the king came in to see the guests, he saw there a man   which had not on a wedding garment: And he saith unto him,   Friend, how camest thou in hither not having a wedding garment?   And he was speechless. Then said the king to the servants, Bind   him hand and foot, and take him away, and cast him into outer   darkness; there shall be weeping and gnashing of teeth. For many   are called, but few are chosen."

The lessons embodied in this section of the parable may be advantageously considered apart from those of the first division. As was befitting his dignity, the king came into the banquet hall after the guests had taken their places in orderly array. His immediate detection of one who was without the prescribed garment implies a personal scrutiny of the guests. One may be led to inquire, how, under the circumstances of hurried summoning, the several guests could have suitably attired themselves for the feast. The unity of the narrative requires that some provision had been made whereby each one who properly applied was given the garment prescribed by the king's command, and in keeping with the established custom at court. That the unrobed guest was guilty of neglect, intentional disrespect, or some more grievous offense, is plain from the context. The king at first was graciously considerate, inquiring only as to how the man had entered without a wedding garment. Had the guest been able to explain his exceptional appearance, or had he any reasonable excuse to offer, he surely would have spoken; but we are told that he remained speechless. The king's summons had been freely extended to all whom his servants had found; but each of them had to enter the royal palace by the door; and before reaching the banquet room, in which the king would appear in person, each would be properly attired; but the deficient one, by some means had entered by another way; and not having passed the attendant sentinels at the portal, he was an intruder, of a kind with the man to whom the Lord had before referred as a thief and a robber because, not entering by the door, he had climbed up some other way.[1103] The king gave a command, and his ministers[1104] bound the offender and cast him forth from the palace into outer darkness, where the anguish of remorse caused weeping and gnashing of teeth.

As summary and epilogue of the three great parables constituting this series, the Lord spake these words of solemn import: "For many are called, but few are chosen."[1105] Each of the parables has its own wealth of wisdom; and the three are as one in declaring the great truth that even the children of the covenant will be rejected except they make good their title by godly works; while to the heathen and the sinners the portals of heaven shall open, if by repentance and compliance with the laws and ordinances of the gospel they shall merit salvation.

The story of the royal marriage feast was the last of our Lord's parables delivered publicly to a mixed audience. Two others were spoken to the apostles, as they sat in solemn converse with the Lord on the Mount of Olives after the public ministry of Christ had been brought to a close.

NOTES TO CHAPTER 30.

1. Fig Tree.--"The fig tree is very common in Palestine (Deut. 8:8). Its fruit is a well known and highly esteemed article of food. In the East this is of three kinds; (1) the early fig, ripening about the end of June; (2) the summer fig, ripening in August; (3) the winter fig, larger and darker than No. 2, hanging and ripening late on the tree, even after the leaves were shed, and sometimes gathered in the spring. The blossoms of the fig tree are within the receptacle or so-called fruit, and not visible outwardly; and this fruit begins to develop before the leaves. Hence the fig tree which had leaves before the usual time might naturally have been expected to have also some figs on it (Mark 11:13); but it was not true to its pretensions." (Smith's _Comp. Bible Dict_.)

2. The Two Sons in the Parable.--Although this excellent parable was addressed to the chief priests, scribes, and elders, who had come in hostile spirit to demand of Christ the credentials of His authority, its lesson is of universal application. The two sons are yet alive in every human community--the

one openly boastful of his sin, the other a hypocritical pretender. Jesus did not commend the rough refusal of the first son of whom the father made a righteous demand for service; it was his subsequent repentance attended by works that made him superior to his brother who had made fair promise but had kept it not. There are many today who boast that they make no profession of religion, nor pretense of godly life. Their frankness will not mitigate their sins; it simply shows that a certain species of hypocrisy is not prominent among their numerous offenses; but that a man is innocent of one vice, say that of drunkenness, in no wise diminishes his measure of guilt if he be a liar, a thief, an adulterer, or a murderer. Both the sons in the parable were grievous sinners; but the one turned from his evil ways, which theretofore he had followed with flagrant openness, while the other continued in dark deeds of sin, which he sought to cover by a cloak of hypocrisy. Let no man think that because he becomes intoxicated at the public bar he is any the less a drunkard than is he who swallows the "beverage of hell" in comparative privacy, though the latter be both drunkard and hypocrite. For these sins, as for all others, genuine repentance is the only saving antidote. 3. Israel Symbolized by Vineyard and Vines.--The aptness of our Lord's representation of Israel as a vineyard could not have escaped the perception of the Jews, to whom Old Testament similes of analogous form were familiar figures. Notable among others is the striking picture presented by Isaiah (5:1-7), in which the well provided vineyard is shown as producing wild grapes only, for which grievous disappointment of his expectations the owner determined to break down the wall, remove the hedge, and leave the vineyard to its fate of abandonment. The explication of the parable is thus given: "For the vineyard of the Lord of hosts is the house of Israel, and the men of Judah his pleasant plant: and he looked for judgment, but behold oppression; for righteousness, but behold a cry." The worthlessness of a vine save only for its fruit was set forth by the Lord through His prophet Ezekiel (15:2-5); and truly it is so, that the wood of the grape plant is fit for nothing but burning; the whole vine as wood is inferior to a branch from a forest tree (verse 3). And Israel is represented as such a vine, precious if but fruitful, otherwise nothing but fuel and that of poor quality. The psalmist sang of the vine that Jehovah had brought out of Egypt and which, planted with care and hedged about, had flourished even with goodly boughs; but the favor of the Lord had been turned from the vine, and it had been left desolate (Psalm 80:8-16). For further allusions see Isa. 27:2-6; Jer. 2:21; Ezek. 19:10-14; Hosea 10:1.

4. The Call to the Marriage Feast.--The calling of the guests who had been bidden aforetime is thus commented upon by Trench (_Parables_, pp. 175-6): "This summoning of those already bidden, was, and, as modern travellers attest, is still, quite in accordance with Eastern manners. Thus Esther invites Haman to a banquet on the morrow (Esth. 5:8), and when the time has actually arrived, the chamberlain comes to usher him to the banquet (6:14). There is, therefore, no slightest reason why we should make '_them that were bidden_' to mean them that were now _to be bidden_; such an interpretation not merely violating all laws of grammar, but the higher purpose with which the parable was spoken; for our Lord, assuming that the guests had been invited long ago, does thus remind His hearers that what He brought, if in one sense new, was in another a fulfilment of the old; that He claimed to be heard, not as one suddenly starting up, unconnected with aught which had gone before but as Himself 'the end of the law,' to which it had been ever tending, the birth with which the whole Jewish dispensation had been pregnant, and which alone should give a meaning to it all. In His words, '_them that were bidden_,' is involved the fact that there was nothing abrupt in the coming of His kingdom, that its rudiments had a long while before been laid, that all to which His adversaries clung as precious in their past history was prophetic of blessings now actually present to them in Him. The original invitation, which had now come to maturity, reached back to the foundation of the Jewish commonwealth, was taken up and repeated by each succeeding prophet, as he prophesied of the crowning grace that should one day be brought to Israel (Luke 10:24; 1 Pet. 1:12), and summoned the people to hold themselves in a spiritual readiness to welcome their Lord and their King."

5. Servants and Ministers.--According to good philological authority, "ministers" or "ministering attendants" is a more literal rendering of the original than "servants" in Matt. 22:13. In the earlier verses 3, 4, 6, 8, 10, of the same chapter, "servants" or "servitors" best expresses the meaning of the original. The distinction is significant, as it implies an important difference of station between the servants who were sent out to bid the people to the feast, and the ministers in immediate attendance upon the king. The first are typical of God's servants who proclaim His word in the world; the latter symbolize the angels who shall execute His judgments on the wicked by gathering out from His kingdom all things that offend. Compare Matt. 13:30, 39, 41; Doc. and Cov. 86:5.

6. The Called and the Chosen.--Edersheim's reflections upon this subject follow in part (vol. ii, pp. 429, 430): "The King entered to see His guests, and among them he descried one who had not on a wedding garment.... As the guests had been travelers, and as the feast was in the King's palace, we cannot be mistaken in supposing that such garments were supplied in the palace to all who sought them. And with this agrees the circumstance, that the man so addressed 'was speechless.' His conduct argued utter insensibility as regarded that to which he had been called--ignorance of what was due the King, and what became such a feast. For, although no previous state of preparedness was required of the invited guests, all being bidden, whether good or bad, yet the fact remained that, if they were to take part in the feast they must put on a garment suited to the occasion. All are invited to the gospel feast; but they who will partake of it must put on the King's wedding garment of evangelical holiness. And whereas it is said in the parable that only one was descried without this garment, this is intended to teach, that the King will not only generally view His guests, but that each will be separately examined, and that no one--no, not a single individual--will be able to escape discovery amidst the mass of guests, if he has not the wedding garment. In short, in that day of trial, it is not a scrutiny of churches, but of individuals in the Church.... The call comes to all; but it may be outwardly accepted, and a man may sit down to the feast, and yet he may not be chosen to partake of the feast, because he has not the wedding garment of converting, sanctifying grace.

Jesus the Christ

And so, one may be thrust even from the marriage board into the darkness without, with its sorrow and anguish. Thus, side by side, yet wide apart, are these two--God's call and God's choice. The connecting link between them is the wedding garment, freely given in the Palace. Yet, we must seek it, ask it, put it on. And as here also, we have, side by side, God's gift and man's activity. And still, to all time, and to all men, alike in its warning, teaching, and blessing, is it true: 'Many are called, but few chosen!' Many words of related meaning, both Hebrew and Greek, are translated 'garment' in our English Bible. The Greek original in the mention of the wedding garment is _enduma_; this does not occur in other Bible passages as the original of 'garment.' The noun is related to the Greek verb _enduein_, 'to put on, as a garment.' Compare Luke 24:49, 'until ye be endued with power from on high.'"

FOOTNOTES:

[1080] Matt. 21:18-22; Mark 11:12-14, 20-26.
[1081] Note 1, end of chapter.
[1082] Page 240.
[1083] "Bethphage," the name of a village close to Bethany, and therefore near to the Mount of Olives, means "house of figs." See mention, Matt. 21:1; Mark 11:1; Luke 19:29. "Bethany" signifies "house of dates." For "house" in the literal translation we may read "place."
[1084] Luke 13:6-9; page 443 herein.
[1085] Matt. 21:12, 13: Mark 11:15-17; Luke 19:45, 46.
[1086] John 2:14-17; pages 153-158 herein.
[1087] Matt. 21:16; compare Psalm 8:2; see also Matt. 11:25; 1 Cor. 1:27.
[1088] Matt. 21:23-27; Mark 11:27-33; Luke 20:1-8.
[1089] John 2:18-21; page 156 herein.
[1090] Matt. 21:28-32.
[1091] Note 2, end of chapter.
[1092] Luke 3:12; compare 7:29; see page 123 herein.
[1093] Matt. 3:7.
[1094] Matt. 21:33-41; compare Mark 12:1-9; Luke 20:9-16.
[1095] Note 3, end of chapter.
[1096] Compare Luke 11:47, 48; Matt. 23:29-33.
[1097] Matt. 21:42-44; see also Mark 12:10, 11; Luke 20:17, 18; compare Psalm 118:22; Isa. 28:16; Acts 4:11; Eph. 2:20; 1 Peter 2:6, 7.
[1098] Compare Dan. 2:44, 45; Isa. 60:12.
[1099] Matt. 22:1-10.
[1100] Note 4, end of chapter.
[1101] Compare Matt. 25:10; 2 Cor. 11:2; Eph. 5:32; Rev. 19:7; 21:2, 9.
[1102] Luke 14:16-24; page 450 herein.
[1103] Compare page 416.
[1104] Note 5, end of chapter.
[1105] Matt. 22:14; compare 20:16; see page 481. Note 6, end of chapter.

Jesus the Christ

CHAPTER 31. THE CLOSE OF OUR LORD'S PUBLIC MINISTRY.

A CONSPIRACY OF PHARISEES AND HERODIANS.[1106]

The Jewish authorities continued unceasingly active in their determined efforts to tempt or beguile Jesus into some act or utterance on which they could base a charge of offense, under either their own or Roman law. The Pharisees counseled together as to "how they might entangle him in his talk"; and then, laying aside their partisan prejudices, they conspired to this end with the Herodians, a political faction whose chief characteristic was the purpose of maintaining in power the family of the Herods,[1107] which policy of necessity entailed the upholding of the Roman power, upon which the Herods depended for their delegated authority. The same incongruous association had been entered into before in an attempt to provoke Jesus to overt speech or action in Galilee; and the Lord had coupled the parties together in His warning to the disciples to beware of the leaven of both.[1108] So, on the last day of our Lord's teaching in public, Pharisees and Herodians joined forces against Him; the one watchful for the smallest technical infringement of the Mosaic law, the other alert to seize upon the slightest excuse for charging Him with disloyalty to the secular powers. Their plans were conceived in treachery, and put into operation as the living embodiment of a lie. Choosing some of their number who had not before appeared in personal antagonism to Jesus, and who were supposed to be unknown to Him, the chief conspirators sent these with instructions to "feign themselves just men, that they might take hold of his words, that so they might deliver him unto the power and authority of the governor."

This delegation of hypocritical spies came asking a question, in pretended sincerity, as though they were troubled in conscience and desired counsel of the eminent Teacher. "Master," said they with fawning duplicity, "we know that thou art true, and teachest the way of God in truth, neither carest thou for any man: for thou regardest not the person of men." This studied tribute to our Lord's courage and independence of thought and action was truthful in every word; but as uttered by those fulsome dissemblers and in their nefarious intent, it was egregiously false. The honeyed address, however, by which the conspirators attempted to cajole the Lord into unwariness, indicated that the question they were about to submit was one requiring for its proper answer just such qualities of mind as they pretendingly attributed to Him.

"Tell us therefore," they continued, "What thinkest thou? Is it lawful to give tribute unto C├ªsar, or not?" The question had been chosen with diabolic craft; for of all acts attesting compulsory allegiance to Rome that of having to pay the poll-tax was most offensive to the Jews. Had Jesus answered "Yes," the guileful Pharisees might have inflamed the multitude against Him as a disloyal son of Abraham; had His answer been "No," the scheming Herodians could have denounced Him as a promoter of sedition against the Roman government. Moreover the question was unnecessary; the nation, both rulers and people had settled it, however grudgingly, for they accepted and circulated among themselves the Roman coinage as a common medium of exchange; and it was a criterion of recognition among the Jews that to make current the coins of any sovereign was to acknowledge his royal authority. "But Jesus perceived their wickedness, and said, Why tempt ye me, ye hypocrites?" All their artful expressions of false adulation were countered by the withering epithet "hypocrites." "Shew me the tribute money," He commanded, and they produced a penny--a Roman denarius bearing the effigy and name of Tiberius C├ªsar, emperor of Rome. "Whose is this image and superscription?" He asked. They answered "C├ªsar's." "Then saith he unto them, Render therefore unto C├ªsar the things which are C├ªsar's; and unto God the things that are God's.[1109]

The reply was a masterly one by whatever standard we gage it; it has become an aphorism in literature and life. It swept away any lingering thought or expectation that in the mind of Him who had so recently ridden into Jerusalem as King of Israel and Prince of Peace, there was even the semblance of aspiration for earthly power or dominion. It established for all time the one righteous basis of relationship between spiritual and secular duties, between church and state. The apostles in later years builded upon this foundation and enjoined obedience to the laws of established governments.[1110]

One may draw a lesson if he will, from the association of our Lord's words with the occurrence of C├ªsar's image on the coin. It was that effigy with its accompanying superscription that gave special point to His memorable instruction, "Render therefore unto C├ªsar the things which are C├ªsar's." This was followed by the further injunction: "and unto God the things that are God's." Every human soul is stamped with the image and superscription of God, however blurred and indistinct the lines may have become through the corrosion or attrition of sin;[1111] and as unto C├ªsar should be rendered the coins upon which his effigy appeared, so unto God should be given the souls that bear His image. Render unto the world the stamped pieces that are made legally current by the insignia of worldly powers, and give unto God and His service, yourselves--the divine mintage of His eternal realm.

Pharisees and Herodians were silenced by the unanswerable wisdom of the Lord's reply to their crafty question. Try as they would, they could not "take hold of his words," and they were put to shame before the people who were witnesses to their humiliation. Marveling at His answer, and unwilling to take the chance of further and possibly greater embarrassment, they "left him, and went their way." Nevertheless these perverted Jews persisted in their base and treacherous purpose, as appears nowhere more glaringly evident than in their utterly false accusation before Pilate--that Jesus was guilty of "forbidding to give tribute to C├ªsar, saying that he himself is Christ a King."[1112]

SADDUCEES QUESTION ABOUT THE RESURRECTION.[1113]

Next, the Sadducees tried to discomfit Jesus by propounding what they regarded as an involved if not indeed a very difficult question. The Sadducees held that there could be no bodily resurrection, on which point of doctrine as on many others, they were the avowed opponents of the Pharisees.[1114] The question submitted by the Sadducees on this occasion related directly to the resurrection, and was framed to discredit the doctrine by a most unfavorable and grossly exaggerated application thereof. "Master," said the spokesman of the party, "Moses said, If a man die, having no children, his brother shall marry his wife, and raise up seed unto his brother. Now there were with us seven brethren: and the first, when he had married a wife, deceased, and, having no issue, left his wife unto his brother: Likewise the second also, and the third, unto the seventh. And last of all the woman died also. Therefore in the resurrection whose wife shall she be of the seven? for they all had her." It was beyond question that the Mosaic law authorized and required that the living brother of a deceased and childless husband should marry the widow with the purpose of rearing children to the name of the dead, whose family lineage would thus be legally continued. [1115] Such a state of affairs as that presented by the casuistical Sadducees, in which seven brothers in succession had as wife and left as childless widow the same woman, was possible under the Mosaic code relating to levirate marriages; but it was a most improbable instance.

Jesus stopped not, however, to question the elements of the problem as presented to Him; whether the case was assumed or real mattered not, since the question "Whose wife shall she be?" was based on an utterly erroneous conception. "Jesus answered and said unto them, Ye do err, not knowing the scriptures, nor the power of God. For in the resurrection they neither marry, nor are given in marriage, but are as the angels of God in heaven." The Lord's meaning was clear, that in the resurrected state there can be no question among the seven brothers as to whose wife for eternity the woman shall be, since all except the first had married her for the duration of mortal life only, and primarily for the purpose of perpetuating in mortality the name and family of the brother who first died. Luke records the Lord's words as follows in part: "But they which shall be accounted worthy to obtain that world, and the resurrection from the dead, neither marry, nor are given in marriage: Neither can they die any more: for they are equal unto the angels; and are the children of God, being the children of the resurrection." In the resurrection there will be no marrying nor giving in marriage; for all questions of marital status must be settled before that time, under the authority of the Holy Priesthood, which holds the power to seal in marriage for both time and eternity. [1116]

From the case presented by His treacherous questioners, Jesus turned to the actuality of the resurrection, which was involved in and implied by the inquiry. "But as touching the resurrection of the dead," said He, "have ye not read that which was spoken unto you by God, saying, I am the God of Abraham, and the God of Isaac, and the God of Jacob? God is not the God of the dead, but of the living." This was a direct assault upon the Sadducean doctrine of negation concerning the literal resurrection of the dead. The Sadducees were distinctively the zealous upholders of the law, wherein Jehovah affirms Himself to be the God of Abraham, Isaac, and Jacob;[1117] yet they denied the possible resurrection of these patriarchs, and made the exalted title, under which the Lord had revealed Himself to Moses, valid only during the brief mortal existence of the progenitors of the Israelitish nation. The declaration that Jehovah is not the God of the dead but of the living was an unanswerable denunciation of the Sadducean perversion of scripture; and with solemn finality the Lord added: "Ye therefore do greatly err." Certain of the scribes present were impressed by the incontrovertible demonstration of the truth, and exclaimed with approbation: "Master, thou hast well said." The proud Sadducees were confuted and silenced; "and after that they durst not ask him any question at all."

THE GREAT COMMANDMENT.[1118]

The Pharisees, covertly rejoicing over the discomfiture of their rivals, now summoned courage enough to plan another attack of their own. One of their number, a lawyer, by which title we may understand one of the scribes who was distinctively also a professor of ecclesiastical law, asked: "Which is the first commandment of all?" or, as Matthew states the question: "Master, which is the great commandment in the law?" The reply was prompt, incisive, and so comprehensive as to cover the requirements of the law in their entirety. With the imperative call to attention with which Moses had summoned Israel to hear and heed,[1119] the very words of which were written on the phylacteries[1120] which the Pharisees wore as frontlets between their eyes, Jesus answered: "Hear, O Israel; The Lord our God is one Lord: And thou shalt love the Lord thy God with all thy heart, and with all thy soul, and with all thy mind, and with all thy strength: this is the first commandment. And the second is like, namely this, Thou shalt love thy neighbour as thyself. There is none other commandment greater than these." Matthew's wording of the concluding declaration is: "On these two commandments hang all the law and the prophets."

The philosophic soundness of the Lord's profound generalization and comprehensive summarizing of the "law and the prophets"[1121] will appeal to all students of human nature. It is a common tendency of man to reach after, or at least to inquire after and marvel about, the superlative. Who is the greatest poet, philosopher, scientist, preacher or statesman? Who stands first and foremost in the community, the nation, or even, as the apostles in their aspiring ignorance asked, in the kingdom of heaven? Which mountain overtops all the rest? Which river is the longest or the largest? Such queries are ever current. The Jews had divided and subdivided the commandments of the law, and had supplemented even the minutest subdivision with rules of their own contriving. Now came the Pharisee asking which of all these requirements was the greatest.[1122] To love God with all one's heart and soul and mind is to serve Him and keep all His commandments. To love one's neighbor as one's self is to be a brother in the broadest and, at the same time, the most exacting sense of the term. Therefore the commandment to love God and man is the greatest, on the basis of the simple and mathematical truth that the whole is greater than any part. What need of the decalog could there be if mankind would obey this first and great and all-embracing commandment? The Lord's reply to the question was convincing even to the learned scribe who had acted as spokesman for his Pharisaic colleagues. The man was honest enough to admit the righteousness and wisdom on which the reply was grounded, and impulsively he voiced acceptance, saying, "Well, Master, thou hast said the truth: for there is one God; and there is none other but he: And to love him with all the heart, and with all the understanding, and with all the soul, and with all the strength, and to love his neighbour as himself, is more than all whole burnt offerings and sacrifices." Jesus was no whit less prompt than the well-intending scribe in acknowledging merit in the words of an opponent; and to the man He gave the encouraging assurance: "Thou art not far from the kingdom of God." As to whether the scribe remained firm in purpose and eventually gained entrance into that blessed abode, the scriptural record is silent.

JESUS TURNS QUESTIONER.[1123]

Sadducees, Herodians, Pharisees, lawyers, and scribes, all had in turn met discomfiture and defeat in their efforts to entangle Jesus on questions of doctrine or practise, and had utterly failed to incite Him to any act or utterance on which they could lawfully charge Him with offense. Having so effectually silenced all who had ventured to challenge Him to debate, either covertly or with open intent, that "no man after that durst ask him any question," Jesus in turn became the aggressive interrogator. Turning to the Pharisees, who had clustered together for greater facility in consultation, Jesus began a colloquy which proceeded as follows:

"What think ye of Christ? whose son is he? They say unto him, The son of David. He saith unto them, How then doth David in spirit call him Lord, saying, The Lord said unto my Lord, Sit thou on my right hand, till I make thine enemies thy footstool? If David then call him Lord, how is he his son?" The Lord's citation of David's jubilant and worshipful song of praise, which, as Mark avers, Jesus said was inspired by the Holy Ghost, had reference to the Messianic psalm[1124] in which the royal singer affirmed his own reverent allegiance, and extolled the glorious reign of the promised King of kings, who is specifically called therein "a priest forever after the order of Melchizedek."[1125] Puzzling as was the unexpected question to the erudite Jews, we fail to perceive in it any inexplicable difficulty, since to us, less prejudiced than they who lived in expectation of a Messiah who would be David's son only in the sense of family descent and royal succession in the splendor of temporal rule, the eternal Godship of the Messiah is a fact demonstrated and undeniable. Jesus the Christ is the Son of David in the physical way of lineage by which both Jesus and David are sons of Jacob, Isaac, Abraham, and Adam. But while Jesus was born in the flesh as late in the centuries as the "meridian of time"[1126] He was Jehovah, Lord and God, before David, Abraham, or Adam was known on earth.[1127]

WICKED SCRIBES AND PHARISEES DENOUNCED.[1128]

The humiliating defeat of the Pharisaic party was made all the more memorable and bitter by the Lord's final denunciation of the system, and His condemnation of its unworthy representatives. Addressing Himself primarily to the disciples, yet speaking in the hearing of the multitude, He directed the attention of all to the scribes and Pharisees, who, He pointed out, occupied the seat of Moses as doctrinal expounders and official administrators of the law, and who were therefore to be obeyed in their authoritative rule; but against their pernicious example the disciples were forcefully warned. "All therefore whatsoever they bid you observe, that observe and do," said the Lord, "but do not ye after their works; for they say, and do not." Distinction between due observance of official precept and the personal responsibility of following evil example, though it be that of men high in authority, could not have been made plainer. Disobedience to law was not to be excused because of corruption among the law's representatives, nor was wickedness in any individual to be condoned or palliated because of another's villainy.

In explanation of the caution He so openly blazoned against the vices of the rulers, the Lord continued: "For they bind heavy burdens and grievous to be borne, and lay them on men's shoulders; but they themselves will not move them with one of their fingers." Rabbinism had practically superseded the law in the substitution of multitudinous rules and exactions, with conditional penalties; the day was filled with traditional observances by which even the trivial affairs of life were encumbered; yet from bearing these and other grievous burdens hypocritical officials could find excuse for personal exemption.

Their inordinate vanity and their irreverent assumption of excessive piety were thus stigmatized: "But all their works they do for to be seen of men: they make broad their phylacteries,[1129] and enlarge the borders of their garments, and love the uppermost rooms at feasts, and the chief seats in the synagogues, and greetings in the markets, and to be called of men, Rabbi, Rabbi." The high-sounding title, Rabbi, signifying Master, Teacher, or Doctor, had eclipsed the divinely recognized sanctity of priesthood; to be a rabbi of the Jews was regarded as vastly superior to being a priest of the Most High God.[1130] "But be not ye called Rabbi," said Jesus to the apostles and the other disciples present, "for one is your Master, even Christ; and all ye are brethren. And call no man your father upon the earth: for one is your Father, which is in heaven. Neither be ye called masters: for one is your Master, even Christ."[1131]

Those upon whom would rest the responsibility of building the Church He had founded were not to aspire to worldly titles nor the honors of men; for those chosen ones were brethren, and their sole purpose should be the rendering of the greatest possible service to their one and only Master. As had been so strongly impressed on earlier occasions, excellence or supremacy in the apostolic calling, and similarly in the duties of discipleship or membership in the Church of Christ, was and is to be achieved through humble and devoted service alone; therefore said the Master again, "he that is greatest among you shall be your servant. And whosoever shall exalt himself shall be abased; and he that shall humble himself shall be exalted."

From the mixed multitude of disciples and unbelievers, comprizing many of the common people who listened in glad eagerness to learn,[1132] Jesus turned to the already abashed yet angry rulers, and deluged them with a veritable torrent of righteous indignation, through which flashed the lightning of scorching invective, accompanied by thunder peals of divine anathema.

"But woe unto you, scribes and Pharisees, hypocrites! for ye shut up the kingdom of heaven against men: for ye neither go in yourselves, neither suffer ye them that are entering to go in." The Pharisaic standard of piety was the learning of the schools; one unversed in the technicalities of the law was accounted as unacceptable to God and veritably accursed.[1133] By their casuistry and perverted explications of scripture they confused and misled the "common people," and so stood as obstacles at the entrance to the kingdom of God, refusing to go in themselves and barring the way to others.

"Woe unto you, scribes and Pharisees, hypocrites! for ye devour widows' houses, and for a pretence make long prayer: therefore ye shall receive the greater damnation."[1134] The avarice of the Jewish hierarchy in our Lord's lifetime was an open scandal. By extortion and unlawful exaction under cover of religious duty the priestly rulers had amassed an enormous treasure,[1135] of which the contributions of the poor, and the confiscation of property, including even the houses of dependent widows, formed a considerable proportion; and the perfidy of the practise was made the blacker by the outward pretense of sanctity and the sacrilegious accompaniment of wordy prayer.

"Woe unto you, scribes and Pharisees, hypocrites! for ye compass sea and land to make one proselyte, and when he is made, ye make him twofold more the child of hell than yourselves." It is possible that this woe was directed more against the effort to secure proselytes to Pharisaism than that of converting aliens to Judaism; but as the latter was thoroughly degraded and the former disgustingly corrupt, the application of our Lord's denunciation to either or both is warranted. Of the Jews who strove to make proselytes it has been said that "out of a bad heathen they made a worse Jew." Many of their converts soon became perverts.

"Woe unto you, ye blind guides, which say, Whosoever shall swear by the temple, it is nothing; but whosoever shall swear by the gold of the temple, he is a debtor! Ye fools and blind: for whether is greater, the gold, or the temple that sanctifieth the gold? And, Whosoever shall swear by the altar, it is nothing; but whosoever sweareth by the gift that is upon it, he is guilty. Ye fools and blind: for whether is greater, the gift, or the altar that sanctifieth the gift? Whoso therefore shall swear by the altar, sweareth by it, and by all things thereon. And whoso shall swear by the temple, sweareth by it, and by him that dwelleth therein. And he that shall swear by heaven, sweareth by the throne of God, and by him that sitteth thereon." Thus did the Lord condemn the infamous enactments of the schools and the Sanhedrin concerning oaths and vows; for they had established or endorsed a code of rules, inconsistent and unjust, as to technical trifles by which a vow could be enforced or invalidated. If a man swore by the temple, the House of Jehovah, he could obtain an indulgence for breaking his oath; but if he vowed by the gold and treasure of the Holy House, he was bound by the unbreakable bonds of priestly dictum. Though one should swear by the altar of God, his oath could be annulled; but if he vowed by the corban gift or by the gold upon the altar,[1136] his obligation was imperative. To what depths of unreason and hopeless depravity had men fallen, how sinfully foolish and how wilfully blind were they, who saw not that the temple was greater than its gold, and the altar than the gift that lay upon it! In the Sermon on the Mount the Lord had said "Swear not at all";[1137] but upon such as would not live according to that higher law, upon those who persisted in the use of oaths and vows, the lesser and evidently just requirement of strict fidelity to the terms of self-assumed obligations was to be enforced, without unrighteous quibble or inequitable discrimination.

"Woe unto you, scribes and Pharisees, hypocrites! for ye pay tithe of mint and anise and cummin, and have omitted the weightier matters of the law, judgment, mercy, and faith: these ought ye to have done, and not to leave the other undone. Ye blind guides, which strain at a gnat, and swallow a camel." The law of the tithe had been a characteristic feature of the theocratic requirements in Israel from the days of Moses; and the practise really long antedated the exodus. As literally construed, the law required the tithing of flocks and herds, fruit and grain,[1138] but by traditional extension all products of the soil had been included. The conscientious tithing of all one's possessions, even pot-herbs and other garden produce, was approved by the Lord; but He denounced as rank hypocrisy the observance of such requirements as an excuse for neglecting the other duties of true religion. The reference to "the weightier matters of the law" may have been an allusion to the rabbinical classification of "light" and "heavy" requirements under the law; though it is certain the Lord approved no such arbitrary distinctions. To omit the tithing of small things, such as mint leaves, and sprigs of anise and cummin, was to fall short in dutiful observance; but to ignore the claims of judgment, mercy, and faith, was to forfeit one's claim to blessing as a covenant child of God. By a strong simile, the Lord stigmatized such inconsistency as comparable to one's scrupulous straining at a gnat while figuratively willing to gulp down a camel.[1139]

"Woe unto you, scribes and Pharisees, hypocrites! for ye make clean the outside of the cup and of the platter, but within they are full of extortion and excess. Thou blind Pharisee, cleanse first that which is within the cup and platter, that the outside of them may be clean also."[1140] Pharisaic scrupulosity in the ceremonial cleansing of platters and cups, pots and brazen vessels, has been already alluded to. Cleanliness the Lord in no wise depreciated; His shafts of disapprobation were aimed at the hypocrisy of maintaining at once outward spotlessness and inward corruption. Cups and platters though cleansed to perfection were filthy before the Lord if their contents had been bought by the gold of extortion, or were to be used in pandering to gluttony, drunkenness or other excess.

"Woe unto you, scribes and Pharisees, hypocrites! for ye are like unto whited sepulchres, which indeed appear beautiful outward, but are within full of dead men's bones, and of all uncleanness. Even so ye also outwardly appear righteous unto men, but within ye are full of hypocrisy and iniquity." It was an awful figure, that of likening them to whitewashed tombs, full of dead bones and rotting flesh. As the dogmas of the rabbis made even the slightest contact with a corpse or its cerements, or with the bier upon which it was borne, or the grave in which it had been lain, a cause of personal defilement, which only ceremonial washing and the offering of sacrifices could remove, care was taken to make tombs conspicuously white, so that no person need be defiled through ignorance of proximity to such unclean places; and, moreover, the periodical whitening of sepulchres was regarded as a memorial act of honor to the dead. But even as no amount of care or degree of diligence in keeping bright the outside of a tomb could stay the putrescence going on within, so no externals of pretended righteousness could mitigate the revolting corruption of a heart reeking with iniquity. Jesus had before compared Pharisees with unmarked graves, over which men inadvertently walked and so became defiled though they knew it not;[1141] on the occasion now under consideration He denounced them as whitened tombs, flauntingly prominent, but sepulchres nevertheless.

"Woe unto you, scribes and Pharisees, hypocrites! because ye build the tombs of the prophets, and garnish the sepulchres of the righteous, And say, If we had been in the days of our fathers, we would not have been partakers with them in the blood of the prophets. Wherefore ye be witnesses unto yourselves, that ye are the children of them which killed the prophets." National pride, not wholly unlike patriotism, had for centuries expressed itself in formal regard for the burial crypts of the ancient prophets, many of whom had been slain because of their righteous and fearless zeal. Those modern Jews were voluble to disavow all sympathy with the murderous deeds of their progenitors, who had martyred the prophets, and ostentatiously averred that if they had lived in the times of those martyrdoms they would have been no participators therein, yet by such avouchment they proclaimed themselves the offspring of those who had shed innocent blood.

With scorching maledictions the Lord thus consigned them to their fate: "Fill ye up then the measure of your fathers. Ye serpents, ye generation of vipers, how can ye escape the damnation of hell? Wherefore, behold, I send unto you prophets, and wise men, and scribes: and some of them ye shall kill and crucify; and some of them shall ye scourge in your synagogues, and persecute them from city to city: That upon you may come all the righteous blood shed upon the earth, from the blood of righteous Abel unto the blood of Zacharias son of Barachias, whom ye slew between the temple and the altar. Verily I say unto you, All these things shall come upon this generation." To their sanctimonious asseverations of superiority over their fathers who had slain Jehovah's envoys, Jehovah Himself replied by predicting that they would dye their hands in the blood of prophets, wise men, and righteous scribes, whom He would send amongst them; and thus would they prove themselves literal sons of murderers, and murderers themselves, so that upon them should rest the burden of all the righteous blood that had been shed for a testimony of God, from righteous Abel to the martyred Zacharias.[1142] That dread fate, outlined with such awful realism, was to be no eventuality of the distant future; every one of the frightful woes the Lord had uttered was to be realized in that generation.

THE LORD'S LAMENTATION OVER JERUSALEM.[1143]

Concerning scribes, Pharisees, and Pharisaism, Jesus had uttered His last word. Looking from the temple heights out over the city of the great King, soon to be abandoned to destruction, the Lord was obsessed by emotions of profound sorrow. With the undying eloquence of anguish He broke forth in such a lamentation as no mortal father ever voiced over the most unfilial and recreant of sons.

"O Jerusalem, Jerusalem, thou that killest the prophets, and stonest them which are sent unto thee, how often would I have gathered thy children together, even as a hen gathereth her chickens under her wings, and ye would not! Behold, your house is left unto you desolate. For I say unto you, Ye shall not see me henceforth, till ye shall say, Blessed is he that cometh in the name of the Lord." Had Israel but received her King, the world's history of post-meridian time would never have been what it is. The children of Israel had spurned the proffered safety of a protecting paternal wing; soon the Roman eagle would swoop down upon them and slay. The stupendous temple, which but a day before the Lord had called "My house," was now no longer specifically His; "Your house," said He, "is left unto you desolate." He was about to withdraw from both temple and nation; and by the Jews His face was not again to be seen, until, through the discipline of centuries of suffering they shall be prepared to acclaim in accents of abiding faith, as some of them had shouted but the Sunday before under the impulse of an erroneous conception, "Blessed is he that cometh in the name of the Lord."

A WIDOW'S GIFT.[1144]

From the open courts Jesus moved over toward the colonnaded treasury of the temple, and there He sat, seemingly absorbed in a revery of sorrow. Within that space were thirteen chests, each provided with a trumpet-shaped receptacle; and into these the people dropped their contributions for the several purposes indicated by inscriptions on the boxes. Looking up, Jesus observed the lines of donors, of all ranks and degrees of affluence and poverty, some depositing their gifts with evident devoutness and sincerity of purpose, others ostentatiously casting in great sums of silver and gold, primarily to be seen of men. Among the many was a poor widow, who with probable effort to escape observation dropped into one of the treasure-chests two small bronze coins known as mites; her contribution amounted to less than half a cent in American money. The Lord called His disciples about Him, directed their attention to the poverty-stricken widow and her deed, and said: "Verily I say unto you, That this poor widow hath cast more in, than all they which have cast into the treasury: For all they did cast in of their abundance; but she of her want did cast in all that she had, even all her living."

In the accounts kept by the recording angels, figured out according to the arithmetic of heaven, entries are made in terms of quality rather than of quantity, and values are determined termined on the basis of capability and intent. The rich gave much yet kept back more; the widow's gift was her all. It was not the smallness of her offering that made it especially acceptable, but the spirit of sacrifice and devout intent with which she gave. On the books of the heavenly accountants that widow's contribution was entered as a munificent gift, surpassing in worth the largess of kings. "For if there be first a willing mind, it is accepted according to that a man hath, and not according to that he hath not."[1145]

CHRIST'S FINAL WITHDRAWAL FROM THE TEMPLE.

Our Lord's public discourses and the open colloquies in which He had participated with professionals and priestly officials, in the course of His daily visits to the temple during the first half of Passion week, had caused many of the chief rulers, beside others, to believe on Him as the veritable Son of God; but the fear of Pharisaic persecution and the dread of excommunication from the synagog[1146] deterred them from confessing the allegiance they felt, and from accepting the means of salvation so freely offered. "They loved the praise of men more than the praise of God."[1147]

It may have been while Jesus directed His course for the last time toward the exit portal of the one-time holy place that He uttered the solemn testimony of His divinity recorded by John.[1148] Crying with a loud voice to priestly rulers and the multitude generally, He said: "He that believeth on me, believeth not on me, but on him that sent me. And he that seeth me seeth him that sent me." Allegiance to Himself was allegiance to God; the people were plainly told that to accept Him was in no degree a weakening of their adherence to Jehovah, but on the contrary a confirmation thereof. Repeating precepts of earlier utterance, He again proclaimed Himself the light of the world, by whose rays alone mankind might be delivered from the enveloping darkness of spiritual unbelief. The testimony He left with the people would be the means of judgment and condemnation to all who wilfully rejected it. "For," said He in solemn finality, "I have not spoken of myself; but the Father which sent me, he gave me a commandment, what I should say, and what I should speak. And I know that his commandment is life everlasting; whatsoever I speak therefore, even as the Father said unto me, so I speak."

DESTRUCTION OF THE TEMPLE PREDICTED.[1149]

As Jesus was departing from the enclosure wherein stood what once had been the House of the Lord, one or more of the disciples called His attention to the magnificent structures, the massive stones, the colossal columns, and the lavish and costly adornment of the several buildings. The Lord's answering comment was an unqualified prophecy of the utter destruction of the temple and everything pertaining to it. "Verily I say unto you, There shall not be left here one stone upon another, that shall not be thrown down." Such was the definite and dire prediction. Those who heard were dumbfounded; neither by question nor other response did they attempt to elicit more. The literal fulfilment of that awful portent was but an incident in the annihilation of the city less than forty years later.

With the Lord's final departure from the temple, which probably occurred in the afternoon of the Tuesday of that last week, His public ministry was brought to its solemn ending. Whatever of discourse, parable, or ordinance was to follow, would be directed only to the further instruction and investiture of the apostles.

NOTES TO CHAPTER 31.

1. The Image on the Coin.--The Jews had an aversion for images or effigies in general, the use of which they professed to hold as a violation of the second commandment. Their scruples, however, did not deter them from accepting coins bearing the effigies of kings, even though these monarchs were pagans. Their own coins bore other devices, such as plants, fruits, etc., in place of a human head; and the Romans had condescendingly permitted the issue of a special coinage for Jewish use, each piece bearing the name but not the effigy of the monarch. The ordinary coinage of Rome was current in Palestine, however.

2. Submission to Secular Authority.--Governments are instituted of God, sometimes by His direct interposition, sometimes by His permission. When the Jews had been brought into subjection by Nebuchadnezzar, king of Babylon, the Lord commanded through the prophet Jeremiah (27:4-8) that the people render obedience to their conqueror, whom He called His servant; for verily the Lord had used the pagan king to chastize the recreant and unfaithful children of the covenant. The obedience so enjoined included the payment of taxes and extended to complete submission. After the death of Christ the apostles taught obedience to the powers that be, which powers, Paul declared "are ordained of God." See Rom. 13:1-7; Titus 3:1; 1 Tim. 2:1-3; see also 1 Peter 2:13, 14. Through the medium of modern revelation, the Lord has required of His people in the present dispensation, obedience to and loyal support of the duly established and existing governments in all lands. See Doc. and Cov. 58:21-22; 98:4-6; and section 134 throughout. The restored Church proclaims as an essential part of its belief and practise: "We believe in being subject to kings, presidents, rulers, and magistrates, in obeying, honoring, and sustaining the law." See _Articles of Faith_, xxiii.

3. Marriage for Eternity.--Divine revelation in the dispensation of the fulness of times has made

plain the fact, that contracts of marriage, as indeed all other agreements between parties in mortality, are of no validity beyond the grave, except such contracts be ratified and validated by the duly established ordinances of the Holy Priesthood. Sealing in the marriage covenant for time and eternity, which has come to be known as celestial marriage, is an ordinance established by divine authority in the restored Church of Jesus Christ. See the author's treatment of this subject in _Articles of Faith_, xxiv, 18-24; and _House of the Lord_, under "Sealing in Marriage," pp. 101-109.

4. Divisions and Subdivisions of the Law.--"The Rabbinical schools, in their meddling, carnal, superficial spirit of word-weaving and letter-worship, had spun large accumulations of worthless subtlety all over the Mosaic law. Among other things they had wasted their idleness in fantastic attempts to count, and classify, and weigh, and measure all the separate commandments of the ceremonial and moral law. They had come to the sapient conclusion that there were 248 affirmative precepts, being as many as the members in the human body, and 365 negative precepts, being as many as the arteries and veins, or the days of the year: the total being 613, which was also the number of letters in the decalog. They arrived at the same result from the fact that the Jews were commanded (Numb. 15:38) to wear fringes (_tsitsith_) on the corners of their _tallith_, bound with a thread of blue; and as each fringe had eight threads and five knots, and the letters of the word _tsitsith_ make 600, the total number of commandments was, as before 613. Now surely, out of such a large number of precepts and prohibitions, _all_ could not be of quite the same value; some were 'light' (_kal_), and some were 'heavy' (_kobhed_). But which? and what was the greatest commandment of all? According to some Rabbis, the most important of all is that about the _tephillin_ and the _tsitsith_, the fringes and phylacteries; and 'he who diligently observes it is regarded in the same light as if he had kept the whole Law.'

"Some thought the omission of ablutions as bad as homicide; some that the precepts of the Mishna were all 'heavy'; those of the Law were some 'heavy' and some 'light.' Others considered the _third_ to be the greatest commandment. None of them had realized the great principle, that the wilful violation of one commandment is the transgression of all (James 2:10), because the object of the entire Law is the spirit of _obedience to God_. On the question proposed by the lawyer the Shammaites and Hillelites were in disaccord, and, as usual, both schools were wrong: the Shammaites, in thinking that mere trivial external observances were valuable, apart from the spirit in which they were performed, and the principle which they exemplified; the Hillelites, in thinking that _any_ positive command could in itself be unimportant, and in not seeing that great principles are essential to the due performance of even the slightest duties."--Farrar, _Life of Christ_, chap. 52.

5. Phylacteries and Borders.--Through a traditional interpretation of Exo. 13:9 and Deut. 6:8, the Hebrews adopted the custom of wearing phylacteries, which consisted essentially of strips of parchment on which were inscribed in whole or in part the following texts: Exo. 13:2-10 and 11-17; Deut. 6:4-9, and 11:13-21. Phylacteries were worn on the head and arm. The parchment strips for the head were four, on each of which one of the texts cited above was written. These were placed in a cubical box of leather measuring from 1/2 inch to 1-1/2 inches along the edge; the box was divided into four compartments and one of the little parchment rolls was placed in each. Thongs held the box in place on the forehead between the eyes of the wearer. The arm phylactery comprized but a single roll of parchment on which the four prescribed texts were written; this was placed in a little box which was bound by thongs to the inside of the left arm so as to be brought close to the heart when the hands were placed together in the attitude of devotion. The Pharisees wore the arm phylactery above the elbow, while their rivals, the Sadducees, fastened it to the palm of the hand (see Exo. 13:9). The common people wore phylacteries only at prayer time; but the Pharisees were said to display them throughout the day. Our Lord's reference to the Pharisees' custom of making broad their phylacteries had reference to the enlarging of the containing box, particularly the frontlet. The size of the parchment strips was fixed by rigid rule.

The Lord had required of Israel through Moses (Numb. 15:38) that the people attach to the border of their garment a fringe with a ribbon of blue. In ostentatious display of assumed piety, the scribes and Pharisees delighted to wear enlarged borders to attract public attention. It was another manifestation of hypocritical sanctimoniousness.

6. Ecclesiastical Titles.--Our Lord severely condemned the seeking after titles as insignia of rank in His service. Nevertheless He named the Twelve whom He chose, Apostles; and in the Church founded by Himself the offices of Evangelist, High Priest, Pastor, Elder, Bishop, Priest, Teacher, and Deacon were established (see _Articles of Faith_, xi:1-4). It was the empty man-made title that attached to the individual, not the authorized title of office to which men were called through authoritative ordination, to which the Lord affixed the seal of His disapproval. Titles of office in the Holy Priesthood are of too sacred a character to be used as marks of distinction among men. In the restored Church in the current dispensation, men are ordained to the Priesthood and to the several offices comprized within both the Lesser or Aaronic, and the Higher or Melchizedek Priesthood; but though one be thus made an Elder, a Seventy, a High Priest, a Patriarch or an Apostle, he should not court the usage of the title as a mere embellishment of his name. (See "The Honor and Dignity of Priesthood" by the author in _Improvement Era_, Salt Lake City, March, 1914.)

Chas. F. Deems, in _The Light of the Nations_, pp. 583-4, says in speaking of the irreverent use of ecclesiastical titles: "The Pharisees loved also the highest places in the synagogs, and it gratified their vanity to be called Teacher, Doctor, Rabbi. Against these Jesus warned His disciples. They were not to love to be called Rabbi, a title which occurs in three forms, _Rab_, Teacher, Doctor; _Rabbi_, My Doctor or Teacher; _Rabboni_, My great Doctor. Nor were they to call any man 'Father,' in the sense of granting him any infallibility of judgment or power over their consciences.... 'Papa,' as the simple Moravians call their great man, Count Zinzendorf: 'Founder,' as Methodists denominate good John Wesley; 'Holy Father in God,' as bishops are sometimes called; 'Pope,' which is the same as 'Papa'; 'Doctor of Divinity,' the Christian equivalent of the Jewish 'Rabbi,' are all dangerous titles. But it is not the employment of a name which Jesus denounces, it is the spirit of vanity which animated the Pharisees, and the servile spirit which the employment of titles is apt to engender. Paul and Peter spoke of themselves as spiritual fathers. Jesus teaches that positions in the societies of his followers, such as should afterward be formed, were not to be regarded as dignities, but rather as services; that no man should seek them for the honor they might confer, but for the field of usefulness they might afford; and that no man should lead off a sect, there being but one leader; and that the whole body of believers are brethren, of whom God is the Father."

The writer last quoted very properly disparages aspirations, stimulated by vanity and self-righteous assumption, to the use of the title "Reverend" as applied to men.

7. Seven or Eight Woes?--Some of the early Mss. of the Gospels omit verse 14 from Matt. 23. Such omission reduces the number of specific utterances beginning "Woe unto you" from eight to seven. There is no question as to the appearance in the original of the passages in Mark 12:40 and Luke 20:47, which are one in meaning with Matt. 23:14.

8. The Temple Treasure.--In connection with the incident of the widow's mites, Edersheim (vol. ii, pp. 387-8) writes: "Some might come with appearance of self-righteousness, some even with ostentation, some as cheerfully performing a happy duty. 'Many that were rich cast in much'--yes, very much, for such was the tendency that a law had to be enacted forbidding the gift to the Temple of more than a certain proportion of one's possessions. And the amount of such contributions may be inferred by recalling the circumstance, that at the time of Pompey and Crassus, the Temple treasury, after having lavishly defrayed every possible expenditure, contained in money nearly half a million, and precious vessels to the value of nearly two millions sterling." See also Josephus, Antiquities xiv, 4:4; 7:1, 2.

9. Zacharias the Martyr.--In referring to the martyrs of ante-meridian time the Lord is recorded as having used the expression "from the blood of righteous Abel unto the blood of Zacharias son of Barachias, whom ye slew between the temple and the altar" (Matt. 23:35). The Old Testament as at present compiled, contains no mention of a martyr named Zacharias son of Barachias, but does chronicle the martyrdom of Zechariah son of Jehoiada (2 Chron. 24:20-22). "Zechariah" and "Zacharias" are equivalent names. It is the opinion of most Bible scholars that the Zacharias referred to in Matthew's record is Zechariah son of Jehoiada. In the Jewish compilation of Old Testament scriptures, the murder of Zechariah appears as the last recorded martyrdom; and the Lord's reference to the righteous men who had been slain, from Abel to Zechariah or Zacharias, may have been a sweeping inclusion of all the martyrs down to that time, from first to last. However, we have a record of Zechariah son of Berechiah (Zech. 1:1, 7), and this Berechiah was the son of Iddo. Then again, Zechariah son of Iddo is mentioned (Ezra 5:1); but, as is elsewhere found in the older scriptures, the grandson is called the son. The Old Testament does not number this Zechariah among the martyrs, but traditional accounts (Whitby's citation of the Targum) say that he was killed "in the day of propitiation." That the Lord referred to a late and probably the latest of the recorded martyrdoms is probable; and it is equally evident that the case was well known among the Jews. It is likely that a fuller account appeared in scriptures current among the Jews at the time of Christ but since lost. See Note 4, page 119.

10. Destruction of the Temple.--"For thirty or more years after the death of Christ, the Jews continued the work of adding to and embellishing the temple buildings. The elaborate design conceived and projected by Herod had been practically completed; the Temple was well-nigh finished, and, as soon afterward appeared, was ready for destruction. Its fate had been definitely foretold by the Savior Himself. Commenting on a remark by one of the disciples concerning the great stones and the splendid buildings on the Temple hill, Jesus had said, 'Seest thou these great buildings? There shall not be left one stone upon another, that shall not be thrown down.' (Mark 13:1, 2; see also Matt. 24:1, 2; Luke 21:5, 6.) This dire prediction soon found its literal fulfilment. In the great conflict with the Roman legions under Titus, many of the Jews had taken refuge within the Temple courts, seemingly hoping that there the Lord would again fight the battles of His people and give them victory. But the protecting presence of Jehovah had long since departed therefrom and Israel was left a prey to the foe. Though Titus would have spared the Temple, his legionaries, maddened by the lust of conflict, started the conflagration and everything that could be burned was burned. The slaughter of the Jews was appalling; thousands of men, women and children were ruthlessly butchered within the walls, and the temple courts were literally flooded with human blood. This event occurred in the year 70 A.D.; and according to Josephus, in the same month and on the same day of the month as that on which the once glorious Temple of Solomon had fallen a prey to the flames kindled by the king of Babylon. (Josephus, Wars of the Jews, vi, 4:5, 8. For a detailed and graphic account of the destruction of the Temple see chapters 4 and 5 in their entirety.) Of the Temple furniture the golden candlestick and the table of shewbread from the Holy Place were carried by Titus to Rome as trophies of war; and representations of these sacred pieces are to be seen on the arch erected to the name of the victorious general. Since the destruction of the splendid Temple of Herod no other structure of the kind, no Temple, no House of the Lord as the terms are used distinctively, has been reared on the eastern hemisphere."--_The House of the Lord_, pp. 61, 62.

Josephus ascribes the destruction of the Temple of Herod to the anger of God, and states that the devouring flames "took their rise from the Jews themselves, and were occasioned by them." The soldier who applied the torch to the Holy House, which had remained intact while fire raged in the courts, is regarded by the historian as an instrument of divine vengeance. We read (Wars, vi, 4:5): "One of the soldiers, without staying for any orders, and without any concern or dread upon him at so great an undertaking, and being hurried on by a certain divine fury, snatched somewhat out of the materials that were on fire, and being lifted up by another soldier, he set fire to a golden window, through which there was a passage to the rooms that were round the Holy House, on the north side of it. As the flames went upward the Jews made a great clamor, such as so mighty an affliction required."

FOOTNOTES:

[1106] Matt. 22:15-22; Mark 12:13-17; Luke 20:19-26.
[1107] Page 68.
[1108] Mark 3:6; 8:15.
[1109] Note 1, end of chapter.
[1110] Note 2, end of chapter.
[1111] Pages 12, 13.
[1112] Luke 23:2. Page 633.
[1113] Matt. 22:23-33; Mark 12:18-27; Luke 20:27-38.
[1114] Pages 65, 72.
[1115] Deut. 25:5.
[1116] Note 3, end of chapter.
[1117] Gen. 28:13; Exo. 3:6, 15.
[1118] Matt. 22:34-40; Mark 12:28-34.
[1119] Deut. 6:4, 5.
[1120] Note 5, page 565.
[1121] Compare page 245.
[1122] Note 4, end of chapter.
[1123] Matt. 22:41-46; Mark 12:35-37; Luke 20:41-44.
[1124] Psalm 110.
[1125] Psalm 110:4; compare Heb. 5:6; 6:20; 7:17, 21.
[1126] Chapter 6.
[1127] Chapters 4 and 5.
[1128] Matt. 23; Mark 12:38-40; Luke 20:45-47; compare Luke 11:39-52.
[1129] Note 5, end of chapter.
[1130] Pages 63, 71.
[1131] Note 6, end of chapter.
[1132] Mark 12:37.
[1133] John 7:49; compare 9:34.
[1134] Note 7, end of chapter.
[1135] Note 8, end of chapter.
[1136] Page 352.
[1137] Matt. 5:33-37; page 235 herein.
[1138] Lev. 27:30; Numb. 18:21; Deut. 12:6; 14:22-28. See also the author's "The Law of the Tithe"; 20 pp., 1914.
[1139] The revised version, generally admitted the more nearly correct, reads "strain out the gnat" instead of "strain at a gnat."
[1140] Compare Luke 11:39, 40; Mark 7:4; page 437 herein.
[1141] Luke 11:44.
[1142] Note 9, end of chapter.
[1143] Matt. 23:37-39; compare Luke 13:34, 35.
[1144] Mark 12:41-44; Luke 21:1-4.
[1145] 2 Cor. 8:12.
[1146] John 12:42; compare 7:13; 9:22.
[1147] John 12:43; compare 5:44.
[1148] John 12:44-50.
[1149] Matt. 24:1, 2; Mark 13:1, 2; Luke 21:5, 6. Note 10, end of chapter.

Jesus the Christ

CHAPTER 32. FURTHER INSTRUCTION TO THE APOSTLES.

PROPHECIES RELATING TO THE DESTRUCTION
OF JERUSALEM AND THE LORD'S FUTURE ADVENT.[1150]

In the course of His last walk from Jerusalem back to the beloved home at Bethany, Jesus rested at a convenient spot on the Mount of Olives, from which the great city and the magnificent temple were to be seen in fullest splendor, illumined by the declining sun in the late afternoon of that eventful April day. As He sat in thoughtful revery He was approached by Peter and James, John and Andrew, of the Twelve, and to them certainly, though probably to all the apostles, He gave instruction, embodying further prophecy concerning the future of Jerusalem, Israel, and the world at large. His fateful prediction--that of the temple buildings not one stone would be left upon another--had caused the apostles to marvel and fear; so they came privately requesting explanation. "Tell us," said they, "when shall these things be? and what shall be the sign of thy coming, and of the end of the world?" The compound character of the question indicates an understanding of the fact that the destruction of which the Lord had spoken was to be apart from and precedent to the signs that were to immediately herald His glorious advent and the yet later ushering in of the consummation commonly spoken of then and now as "the end of the world." An assumption that the events would follow in close succession is implied by the form in which the question was put.

The inquiry referred specifically to time--when were these things to be? The reply dealt not with dates, but with events; and the spirit of the subsequent discourse was that of warning against misapprehension, and admonition to ceaseless vigilance. "Take heed that no man deceive you" was the first and all-important caution; for within the lives of most of those apostles, many blaspheming imposters would arise, each claiming to be the Messiah. The return of Christ to earth as Lord and Judge was more remote than any of the Twelve realized. Before that glorious event, many wonderful and appalling developments would be witnessed, among the earliest of which would be wars and rumors of wars, caused by nation rising against nation and kingdom against kingdom, to the dread accompaniment of famines, pestilences, and earthquakes in many places; yet all these would be but the beginning of the sorrow or travail to follow.

They, the apostles, were told to expect persecution, not only at the hands of irresponsible individuals, but at the instance of the officials such as they who were at that moment intent on taking the life of the Lord Himself, and who would scourge them in the synagogs, deliver them up to hostile tribunals, cite them before rulers and kings, and even put some of them to death--all because of their testimony of the Christ. As they had been promised before, so again were they assured, that when they would stand before councils, magistrates, or kings, the words they should speak would be given them in the hour of their trial, and therefore they were told to take no premeditative thought as to what they should say or how they should meet the issues confronting them; "for," said the Master, "it is not ye that speak, but the Holy Ghost."[1151] Even though they found themselves despized and hated of men, and though they were to suffer ignominy, torture, and death, yet as to their eternal welfare they were promised such security that by comparison they would lose not so much as a hair of their heads. In consoling encouragement the Lord bade them possess their souls in patience.[1152] In face of all trials and even the direst persecution, it was incumbent upon them to persevere in their ministry, for the divine plan provided and required that the gospel of the kingdom be preached amongst all nations. Their labors would be complicated and opposed by the revolutionary propaganda of many false prophets, and differences of creed would disrupt families, and engender such bitterness that brothers would betray one another, and children would rise against their parents, accusing them of heresies and delivering them up to death. Even among those who had professed discipleship to Christ many would be offended and hatred would abound; love for the gospel would wax cold, and iniquity would be rampant among men; and only those who would endure to the end of their lives could be saved.

From this circumstantial forecast of conditions then directly impending, the Lord passed to other developments that would immediately precede the destruction of Jerusalem and the total disruption of the Jewish nation. "When ye therefore shall see the abomination of desolation, spoken of by Daniel the prophet, stand in the holy place," said He, according to Matthew's account, and virtually so also as stated by Mark, or "when ye shall see Jerusalem compassed with armies" as Luke writes, "then know that the desolation thereof is nigh." This was a specific sign that none could misunderstand. Daniel the prophet had foreseen the desolation and abominations thereof, which comprized the forcible cessation of temple rites, and the desecration of Israel's shrine by pagan conquerors.[1153]

The realization of Daniel's prophetic vision was to be heralded by the encompassing of Jerusalem by armies. Then all who would escape should make haste; from Judea they should flee to the mountains; he who was on the housetop would have no time to take his goods, but should hasten down by the outer steps and flee; he who was in the field would better leave without first returning to his house even for his clothes. Terrible, indeed, would that day be for women hampered by the conditions incident to approaching maternity, or the responsibility of caring for their suckling babes. All would do well to pray that their flight be not forced upon them in winter time; nor on the Sabbath, lest regard for the restrictions as to Sabbath-day travel, or the usual closing of the city gates on that day, should diminish the chances of escape. The tribulations of the time then foreshadowed would prove to be unprecedented in horror and would never be paralleled in all their awful details in Israel's history; but in mercy God had decreed that the dreadful period should be shortened for the sake of the elect believers, otherwise no flesh of Israel would be saved alive. Multitudes were to fall by the sword; other hosts were to be led away captive, and so be scattered amongst all nations; and Jerusalem, the pride and boast of degenerate Israel, should be "trodden down of the Gentiles, until the times of the Gentiles be fulfilled." In every frightful detail was the Lord's prediction brought to pass, as history avouches.[1154]

After the passing of those terrible times, and thence onward for a period of unspecified duration, Satan would deceive the world through false doctrines, spread by evil men masquerading as ministers of God, who would continue to cry "Lo, here is Christ; or, lo, he is there"; but against all such the Twelve were put on their guard, and through them and other teachers, whom they would call and ordain, would the world be warned. Deceiving prophets, emissaries of the devil, would be active, some alluring people into the deserts, and impelling them to hermit lives of pernicious asceticism, others insisting that Christ could be found in the secret chambers of monastic seclusion; and some of them showing forth through the power of Satan, such signs and wonders as "to seduce, if it were possible, even the elect"; but of all such scheming of the prince of evil, the Lord admonished His own: "Believe it not"; and added, "take ye heed; behold I have foretold you all things."[1155]

In the day of the Lord's advent in glory and vengeance, no man shall be in doubt; there shall be no chance of conflicting claims by contending sects, "For as the lightning cometh out of the east, and shineth even unto the west; so shall also the coming of the Son of man be."[1156] The gathering of Israel in the last days was pictured as the flocking of eagles to the place where the body of the Church would be established.[1157]

The chronological order of the predicted occurrences so far considered in this wonderful discourse on things to come, is clear; first there was to be a period of virulent persecution of the apostles and the Church of which they would be in charge; then the destruction of Jerusalem, with all the horrors of merciless warfare to follow; and this in turn was to be succeeded by a long period of priestcraft and apostasy with bitter sectarian dissension and cruel persecution of the righteous. The brief reference to the non-localized, universal phenomena, by which His advent is to be signalized, is a parenthetical demonstration of the false claims as to where Christ would be found; later the Lord passed to distinctive and unquestionable reference to the circumstances of His then and yet future advent. Following the age of man-made creeds, and unauthorized ministry characteristic of the great apostasy, marvelous occurrences are to be manifested through the forces of nature, and the sign of the Son of Man shall ultimately appear, one accompanying feature of which shall be the completion of the gathering of the elect from all parts of the earth to the places appointed.

The duty that Jesus enjoined upon the apostles as of first importance throughout all the coming scenes of sorrow, suffering and turmoil, was that of vigilance. They were to pray, watch, and work, diligently and with unwavering faith. The lesson was illustrated by a masterly analogy, which, under the broadest classification, may be called a parable. Directing their attention to the fig tree and other trees which flourished on the sunny slopes of Olivet, the Master said: "Behold the fig tree, and all the trees; when they now shoot forth, ye see and know of your own selves that summer is now nigh at hand. So likewise ye, when ye see these things come to pass, know ye that the kingdom of God is nigh at hand." Of the fig tree in particular the Lord remarked: "When his branch is yet tender, and putteth forth leaves, ye know that summer is nigh." This sign of events near at hand was equally applicable to the premonitory conditions which were to herald the fall of Jerusalem and the termination of the Jewish autonomy, and to the developments by which the Lord's second advent shall be immediately preceded.

The next declaration in the order of the evangelical record reads: "Verily I say unto you, This generation shall not pass, till all these things be fulfilled." This may be understood as applying to the generation in which the portentous happenings before described would be realized. So far as the predictions related to the overthrow of Jerusalem, they were literally fulfilled within the natural lifetime of several of the apostles and of multitudes of their contemporaries; such of the Lord's prophecies as pertain to the heralding of His second coming are to be brought to pass within the duration of the generation of some who witness the inauguration of their fulfilment. The certainty of fulfilment was emphasized by the Lord in the profound affirmation: "Heaven and Earth shall pass away, but my words shall not pass away."[1158]

All speculation concerning the time of the Lord's appearing, whether based on assumption, deduction, or calculation of dates, was forestalled by Christ's averment: "But of that day and that hour knoweth no man, no, not the angels which are in heaven, neither the Son, but the Father."[1159] That His advent in power and glory is to be sudden and unexpected to the unobserving and sinful world, but in immediate sequence to the signs which the vigilant and devout may read and understand, was made plain by comparison with the prevailing social conditions of Noah's time, when in spite of prophecy and warning the people had continued in their feasting and merry-making, in marrying and giving in marriage, until the very day of Noah's entrance into the ark, "And knew not until the flood came, and took them all away; so shall also the coming of the Son of man be."

In the last stages of the gathering of the elect, the ties of companionship shall be quickly severed; of two men laboring in the field, or of two women engaged side by side in household duties, the faithful one shall be taken and the sinner left. "Watch therefore," was the solemn behest, "for ye know not what hour your Lord doth come." In explication of this admonishment, the Lord condescended to compare the suddenness and secrecy of His coming to the movements of a night-prowling thief; and pointed out, that if a householder had certain knowledge as to the time of a burglar's predetermined visit, he would remain on vigilant watch; but because of uncertainty he may be found off his guard, and the thief may enter and despoil the home.

Again likening the apostles to duly appointed stewards in a great household,[1160] the Lord spoke of Himself as the householder, saying: "The Son of man is as a man taking a far journey, who left his house, and gave authority to his servants, and to every man his work, and commanded the porter to watch. Watch ye therefore: for ye know not when the master of the house cometh, at even, or at midnight, or at the cockcrowing, or in the morning: Lest coming suddenly he find you sleeping. And what I say unto you I say unto all, Watch." But if the steward grow negligent because of his master's long absence, and give himself up to feasting and unlicensed pleasure, or become autocratic and unjust toward his fellow-servants, his lord shall come in an hour when least expected, and shall consign that wicked servant to a place among the hypocrites, where he shall weep bitter tears of remorse, and gnash his teeth in impotent despair.[1161]

THE NEED OF WATCHFULNESS AND DILIGENCE ILLUSTRATED BY PARABLES.

To more indelibly impress upon the apostles, and, through their subsequent ministry, upon the world, the absolute need of unceasing watchfulness and unwavering diligence in preparation for the coming of the Lord in judgment, Jesus depicted in parables the prospective condition of mankind in the last times. The first of these illustrative portrayals is the _Parable of the Ten Virgins_. The only report of it we have is that given by Matthew,[1162] as follows:

"Then shall the kingdom of heaven be likened unto ten virgins, which took their lamps, and went forth to meet the bridegroom. And five of them were wise, and five were foolish. They that were foolish took their lamps, and took no oil with them: but the wise took oil in their vessels with their lamps. While the bridegroom tarried, they all slumbered and slept. And at midnight there was a cry made, Behold, the bridegroom cometh; go ye out to meet him. Then all those virgins arose, and trimmed their lamps. And the foolish said unto the wise, Give us of your oil; for our lamps are gone out. But the wise answered, saying, Not so; lest there be not enough for us and you: but go ye rather to them that sell, and buy for yourselves. And while they went to buy, the bridegroom came; and they that were ready went in with him to the marriage: and the door was shut. Afterward came also the other virgins, saying, Lord, Lord, open to us. But he answered and said, Verily I say unto you, I know you not. Watch therefore, for ye know neither the day nor the hour wherein the Son of man cometh."

The story itself is based on oriental marriage customs, with which the Lord's attentive listeners were familiar. It was and yet is common in those lands, particularly in connection with marriage festivities among the wealthy classes, for the bridegroom to go to the home of the bride, accompanied by his friends in processional array, and later to conduct the bride to her new home with a larger body of attendants composed of groomsmen, bridesmaids, relatives and friends. As the bridal party progressed, to the accompaniment of gladsome music, it was increased by little groups who had gathered in waiting at convenient places along the route, and particularly near the end of the course where organized companies came forth to meet the advancing procession. Wedding ceremonies were appointed for the evening and night hours; and the necessary use of torches and lamps gave brilliancy and added beauty to the scene.

In the parable ten maidens were waiting to welcome and join in with the bridal company, the time of whose arrival was uncertain. Each had her lamp attached to the end of a rod so as to be held aloft in the festal march; but of the ten virgins five had wisely carried an extra supply of oil, while the other five, probably counting on no great delay, or assuming that they would be able to borrow from others, or perchance having negligently given no thought at all to the matter, had no oil except the one filling with which their lamps had been supplied at starting. The bridegroom tarried, and the waiting maidens grew drowsy and fell asleep. At midnight, the forerunners of the marriage party loudly proclaimed the bridegroom's approach, and cried in haste: "Go ye out to meet him." The ten maidens, no longer sleepy, but eagerly active, set to work to trim their lamps; then the wise ones found use for the oil in their flasks, while the thoughtless five bewailed their destitute condition, for their lamps were empty and they had no oil for replenishment. They appealed to their wiser sisters, asking a share of their oil; but these declined; for, in a time of such exigency, to give of their store would have been to render themselves unfit, inasmuch as there was oil enough for their own lamps only. Instead of oil they could impart only advice to their unfortunate sisters, whom they directed to go to the nearest shop and buy for themselves. While the foolish virgins were away in quest of oil, the wedding party passed into the house wherein the feast was provided, and the door was shut against all tardy comers. In time the unwise maidens, too late to participate in the processional entry, called from without, pleading for admittance; but the bridegroom refused their request, and disclaimed all acquaintanceship with them, since they had not been numbered among his attendants or those of the bride.

The Bridegroom is the Lord Jesus; the marriage feast symbolizes His coming in glory, to receive unto Himself the Church on earth as His bride.[1163] The virgins typify those who profess a belief in Christ, and who, therefore, confidently expect to be included among the blessed participants at the feast. The lighted lamp, which each of the maidens carried, is the outward profession of Christian belief and practise; and in the oil reserves of the wiser ones we may see the spiritual strength and abundance which diligence and devotion in God's service alone can insure. The lack of sufficient oil on the part of the unwise virgins is analogous to the dearth of soil in the stony field, wherein the seed readily sprouted but soon withered away. [1164] The Bridegroom's coming was sudden; yet the waiting virgins were not held blamable for their surprize at the abrupt announcement, but the unwise five suffered the natural results of their unpreparedness. The refusal of the wise virgins to give of their oil at such a critical time must not be regarded as uncharitable; the circumstance typifies the fact that in the day of judgment every soul must answer for himself; there is no way by which the righteousness of one can be credited to another's account; the doctrine of supererogation is wholly false.[1165] The Bridegroom's condemnatory disclaimer, "I know you not," was equivalent to a declaration that the imploring but neglectful ones, who had been found unready and unprepared, did not know Him.[1166]

The application of the parable and its wealth of splendid suggestion are summarized in a masterly manner by the Lord's impressive adjuration: "Watch therefore, for ye know neither the day nor the hour wherein the Son of man cometh." The fulfilment of the predictions enshrined in this precious parable is yet future, but near. In 1831 the Lord Jesus Christ revealed anew the indications by which the imminence of His glorious advent may be perceived. Through the mouth of His prophet Joseph Smith He thus spake: "And at that day, when I shall come in my glory, shall the parable be fulfilled which I spake concerning the ten virgins: for they that are wise and have received the truth, and have taken the Holy Spirit for their guide, and have not been deceived; verily I say unto you, they shall not be hewn down and cast into the fire, but shall abide the day, and the earth shall be given unto them for an inheritance; and they shall multiply and wax strong, and their children shall grow up without sin unto salvation, for the Lord shall be in their midst, and his glory shall be upon them, and he will be their King and their Lawgiver."[1167]

Still discoursing in solemn earnestness to the apostles as the evening shadows gathered about the Mount of Olives, the Lord delivered the last of His recorded parables. We call it the _Parable of the Entrusted Talents_.[1168]

"For the kingdom of heaven is as a man travelling into a far country, who called his own servants, and delivered unto them his goods. And unto one he gave five talents, to another two, and to another one; to every man according to his several ability; and straightway took his journey. Then he that had received the five talents went and traded with the same, and made them other five talents. And likewise he that had received two, he also gained other two. But he that had received one went and digged in the earth, and hid his lord's money. After a long time the lord of those servants cometh, and reckoneth with them. And so he that had received five talents came and brought other five talents, saying, Lord, thou deliveredst unto me five talents: behold, I have gained beside them five talents more. His lord said unto him, Well done, thou good and faithful servant: thou hast been faithful over a few things, I will make thee ruler over many things: enter thou into the joy of thy lord. He also that had received two talents came and said, Lord, thou deliveredst unto me two talents: behold, I have gained two other talents beside them. His lord said unto him, Well done, good and faithful servant; thou hast been faithful over a few things, I will make thee ruler over many things: enter thou into the joy of thy lord. Then he which had received the one talent came and said, Lord, I knew thee that thou art an hard man, reaping where thou hast not sown, and gathering where thou hast not strawed: And I was afraid, and went and hid thy talent in the earth: lo, there thou hast that is thine. His lord answered and said unto him, Thou wicked and slothful servant, thou knewest that I reap where I sowed not, and gather where I have not strawed: Thou oughtest therefore to have put my money to the exchangers, and then at my coming I should have received mine own with usury. Take therefore the talent from him, and give it unto him which hath ten talents. For unto every one that hath shall be given, and he shall have abundance: but from him that hath not shall be taken away even that which he hath. And cast ye the unprofitable servant into outer darkness: there shall be weeping and gnashing of teeth."

Some of the resemblances between this parable and that of the Pounds[1169] appear on even a casual reading; significant differences are discovered by comparison and study. The earlier parable was spoken to a mixed multitude in the course of our Lord's last journey from Jericho to Jerusalem; the later one was given in privacy to the most intimate of His disciples in the closing hours of the last day of His public preaching. The two should be studied together. In the story of the Pounds, an equal amount of capital is given to each of the servants, and men's diverse ability to use and apply, with commensurate results in reward or penalty, is demonstrated; in that of the Entrusted Talents, the servants receive different amounts, "every man according to his several ability"; and equal diligence, though shown in one instance by great gain and in the other by small but proportionate increase, is equally rewarded. Unfaithfulness and negligence are condemned and punished in both.

In the parable now under consideration, the master is presented as delivering his wealth into the hands of his own servants, literally, bondservants;[1170] they, as well as the possessions held by them in trust were his. Those servants had no rights of actual ownership, nor title of permanent proprietorship in the treasure committed to their care; all they had, the time and opportunity to use their talents, and they themselves, belonged to their lord. We cannot fail to perceive even in the early incidents of the story that the Master of the servants was the Lord Jesus; the servants, therefore, were the disciples and more particularly the apostles, who, while of equal authority through ordination in the Holy Priesthood, as specifically illustrated by the earlier parable of the Pounds, were of varied ability, of diverse personality, and unequal generally in nature and in such accomplishments as would be called into service throughout their ministry. The Lord was about to depart; He would return only "after a long time"; the significance of this latter circumstance is in line with that expressed through the parable of the Ten Virgins in the statement that the Bridegroom tarried.

At the time of reckoning, the servants who had done well, the one with his five talents, the other with his two, reported gladly, conscious as they were of having at least striven to do their best. The unfaithful servant prefaced his report with a grumbling excuse, which involved the imputation of unrighteousness in the Master. The honest, diligent, faithful servants saw and reverenced in their Lord the perfection of the good qualities which they possessed in measured degree; the lazy and unprofitable serf, afflicted by distorted vision, professed to see in the Master his own base defects. The story in this particular, as in the other features relating to human acts and tendencies, is psychologically true; in a peculiar sense men are prone to conceive of the attributes of God as comprizing in augmented degree the dominant traits of their own nature.

Both the servant who had been entrusted with five talents and he who had received but two were equally commended, and, as far as we are told, were equally recompensed. The talents bestowed upon each were the gift of his Lord, who knew well whether that servant was capable of using to better advantage one, two, or five. Let no one conclude that good work of relatively small scope is less necessary or acceptable than like service of wider range. Many a man who has succeeded well in business with small capital would have failed in the administration of vast sums; so also in spiritual achievements "there are diversities of gifts, but the same Spirit."[1171] Of the man endowed with many talents greater returns were expected; of the one-talented man relatively little was required, yet in that little he failed.[1172] At the least he could have delivered the money to the bank, through which it would have been kept in circulation to the benefit of the community, and would have earned interest meanwhile. Likewise, in the spiritual application, a man possessed of any good gift, such as musical ability, eloquence, skill in handicraft, or the like, ought to use that gift to the full, that he or others may be profited thereby: but should he be too neglectful to exercize his powers in independent service, he may assist others to profitable effort, by encouragement if by nothing more.

Who can doubt in the spirit of the Lord's teaching, that had the man been able to report the doubling of his single talent, he would have been as cordially commended and as richly recompensed as were his more highly endowed and faithful fellows? It is notable that to the charge of unrighteousness made by the unfaithful servant, the Lord deigns no refutation; the spirit of the reply was the same as that expressed in the earlier parable: "Out of thine own mouth will I judge thee, thou wicked servant."[1173] The unworthy man sought to excuse himself by the despicable but all too common subterfuge of presumptuously charging culpability in another, and in this instance, that other was his Lord. Talents are not given to be buried, and then to be dug up and offered back unimproved, reeking with the smell of earth and dulled by the corrosion of disuse. The unused talent was justly taken from him who had counted it as of so little worth, and was given to one, who, although possessing much, would use the additional gift to his own profit, to the betterment of his fellows, and to the glory of his Lord.

THE INEVITABLE JUDGMENT.[1174]

The Lord had uttered His last parable. In words of plainness, though suffused with the beauty of effective simile, He impressed upon the listening disciples the certainty of judgment by which the world shall be visited in the day of His appearing. Then shall the wheat be segregated from the tares,[1175] and the sheep divided from the goats. "When the Son of man shall come in his glory, and all the holy angels with him, then shall he sit upon the throne of his glory: And before him shall be gathered all nations: and he shall separate them one from another, as a shepherd divideth his sheep from the goats: And he shall set the sheep on his right hand, but the goats on the left." Unto those on His right hand the King shall give commendation and blessing, bestowing a rich recompense for their good works, as attested by the hungry they had fed, the thirsty to whom they had given drink, the stranger they had lodged, the naked they had clothed, the sick to whom they had ministered, the prisoners they had visited and encouraged, all of which mercies are accredited to them as having been rendered to their Lord in person. The blessed company, overwhelmed by the plenitude of the King's bounty, of which they regard themselves as undeserving, will fain disclaim the merit attributed to them; "And the King shall answer and say unto them, Verily I say unto you, Inasmuch as ye have done it unto one of the least of these my brethren, ye have done it unto me."

Unto them who wait on the left in terrified expectancy, the King shall recount their several deficiencies, in that they had given Him neither food nor drink, shelter nor clothing despite His need; neither had they visited Him though ill, nor ministered unto His wants when He lay in a prison cell. In the desperation of anguish these shall ask when and where they had had such opportunity of comforting Him, and He shall answer, "Verily I say unto you, Inasmuch as ye did it not to one of the least of these, ye did it not to me." The righteous shall be welcomed with "Come ye blessed of my Father"; the wicked shall hear the awful sentence, "Depart from me ye cursed." Eternal life is the inestimable reward; everlasting punishment the unfathomable doom.[1176]

Viewing as one discourse the two parables and the teaching that directly followed, we find in it such unity of subject and thoroughness of treatment as to give to the whole both beauty and worth beyond the sum of these qualities exhibited in the several parts. Vigilant waiting in the Lord's cause, and the dangers of unreadiness are exemplified in the story of the virgins; diligence in work and the calamitous results of sloth are prominent features of the tale of the talents. These two phases of service are of reciprocal and complementary import; it is as necessary at times to wait as at others to work. The lapse of a long period, as while the Bridegroom tarried, and as during the Master's absence in "a far country,"[1177] is made plain throughout as intervening between the Lord's departure and His return in glory. The absolute certainty of the Christ coming to execute judgment upon the earth, in the which every soul shall receive according to his deserts, is the sublime summary of this unparalleled discourse.

ANOTHER SPECIFIC PREDICTION OF THE LORD'S DEATH.

Following the instructions to the apostles at the resting place on Olivet, and probably in the course of the continued walk toward Bethany that evening, Jesus reminded the Twelve of the awful fate awaiting Him, and specified the time of His betrayal and the manner of His death. "Ye know," He said, "that after two days is the feast of the passover, and the Son of man is betrayed to be crucified."[1178]

NOTES TO CHAPTER 32.

1. Early Fulfilment of the Lord's Prophecies.--As to the literal fulfilment of the Lord's predictions relating to the times immediately following His ascension and down to the destruction of Jerusalem, the

student must be referred to scriptural and other history. Only a brief summary of the most notable events can be attempted here.

On the matter of wars and rumors or threats of wars, see Josephus, Antiquities xviii, ch. 9, and Wars, ii, ch. 10. The latter reference is to the account of the decree issued by Caligula, that his statue be set up and duly reverenced in the temple, in consequence of which the Jews protested so strenuously that war was declared against them, but was averted by the death of the emperor. Concerning the death of Caligula, Josephus remarks that it "happened most happily for our nation in particular, which would have almost utterly perished, if he had not been suddenly slain." Other threats of war against the Jews were severally made by the emperors Claudius and Nero.

Nation rose against nation, as for example, in the assault of Greeks and Syrians upon the Jews, in the course of which 50,000 Jews were slain at Selucia on the Tigris, and 20,000 at C sarea, 13,000 at Scythopolis, and 2,500 at Ascalon. Famine and its attendant pestilence prevailed during the reign of Claudius, (41-54 A.D.) and such had been specifically predicted by inspiration, through Agabus (Acts 11:28). The famine was very severe in Palestine (Josephus, Antiquities, xx, ch. 2). Earthquakes were of alarming frequency and of unusual severity, between the death of Christ and the destruction of Jerusalem, particularly in Syria, Macedonia, Campania, and Achia. See Tacitus, _Annals_, books xii and xiv; and for account of violent seismic disturbances at Rome, see Suetonius in his _Life of Galba_. Josephus (Wars iv, ch. 4) records a particularly severe earthquake that disrupted parts of Judea, and was accompanied by "amazing concussions and bellowings of the earth--a manifest indication that some destruction was coming upon men." The portent of "fearful sights and great signs" from heaven, as recorded by Luke was realized in the phenomenal events chronicled by Josephus (Preface to "Wars").

Of the persecution that befell the apostles and others, and of their arraignment before rulers, Dr. Adam Clarke, in his commentary on passages in Matt 24, says: "We need go no farther than the Acts of the Apostles for the completion of these particulars. Some were delivered to councils, as Peter and John (Acts 4:5). Some were brought before rulers and kings, as Paul before Gallio (18:12); before Felix (ch. 24); before Festus and Agrippa (ch. 25). Some had utterance and wisdom which their adversaries were not able to resist; so Stephen (6:10), and Paul who made even Felix himself tremble (24:25). Some were imprisoned, as Peter and John (4:3). Some were beaten, as Paul and Silas (16:23). Some were put to death, as Stephen (7:59); and James the brother of John (12:2). But if we look beyond the book of the Acts of the Apostles, to the bloody persecutions under Nero, we shall find these predictions still more amply fulfilled; in these, numberless Christians fell, besides those two champions of the faith, Peter and Paul. And it was, as says Tertullian, a war against the very name of Christ; for he who was called Christian had committed crime enough in bearing the name to be put to death. So true were our Savior's words that they should be hated of all men for His Name's sake."

Among the false prophets, and men who claimed to be the duly accredited ministers of Christ, were Simon Magus who drew many people after him (Acts 8:9, 13, 18-24; see also _The Great Apostasy_, 7:1, 2), Menander, Dositheus, and Theudas, and the false apostles referred to by Paul (2 Cor. 11:13) and others, such as Hymeneus and Philetus (2 Tim. 2:17, 18). Dummelow's _Commentary_ applies here the record by Josephus concerning "a body of wicked men, who deceived and deluded the people under pretense of divine inspiration, who prevailed with the multitude to act like madmen, and went before them into the wilderness, pretending that God would there show them the signals of victory." Compare 2 Peter 2:1; 1 John 2:18; 4:1. That the love of many did wax cold, both before and after the destruction of Jerusalem, is attested by the facts of the world-wide apostasy, which was the result of corruption within and persecution from without the Church (see _The Great Apostasy_, chaps. 3-9).

The preaching of the gospel of the kingdom "in all the world" was no less truly an essential characteristic of the apostolic period than it is of the current or last dispensation. The rapid spread of the gospel and the phenomenal growth of the Church under the direction of the apostles of old, is recorded as one of the marvels of history (_Great Apostasy_, 1:21, and citation of Eusebius). Paul, writing about thirty years after Christ's ascension, affirms that the gospel had already been carried to every nation, and "preached to every creature under heaven" (Col. 1:23, compare verse 6).

The "abomination of desolation" cited by the Lord from the prophecy by Daniel was strictly fulfilled in the investment of Jerusalem by the Roman army (compare Luke 21:20, 21). To the Jews the ensigns and images of the Romans were a disgusting abomination. Josephus (Wars vi, ch. 6) states that the Roman ensigns were set up inside the temple and that the soldiery offered sacrifices before them.

The warning to all to flee from Jerusalem and Judea to the mountains when the armies would begin to surround the city was so generally heeded by members of the Church, that according to the early Church writers not one Christian perished in the awful siege (see Eusebius, _Eccles. Hist._, book iii, ch. 5). The first siege by Gallus was unexpectedly raised, and then, before the armies of Vespasian arrived at the walls, all Jews who had faith in the warning given by Christ to the apostles, and by these to the people, fled beyond Jordan, and congregated mostly at Pella (compare Josephus, Wars ii, ch. 19).

As to the unprecedented horrors of the siege, which culminated in the utter destruction of Jerusalem and the temple, see Josephus, Wars vi, chaps. 3 and 4. That historian estimates the number slain in Jerusalem alone as 1,100,000 and in other cities and rural parts a third as many more. For details see Josephus, Wars ii, chaps. 18, 20; iii, 2, 7, 8, 9; iv, 1, 2, 7, 8, 9; vii, 6, 9, 11. Many tens of thousands were taken captive, to be afterward sold into slavery, or to be slain by wild beasts, or in gladiatorial combat in the arena for the amusement of Roman spectators.

In the course of the siege, a wall was constructed about the entire city, thus fulfilling the Lord's prediction (Luke 19:43), "thine enemies shall cast a trench about thee," in which, by the admittedly better translation, "bank" or "palisade" should appear instead of "trench". In September A.D. 70 the city fell into the hands of the Romans; and its destruction was afterward made so thorough that its site was plowed up. Jerusalem was "trodden down of the Gentiles", and ever since has been under Gentile dominion, and so shall continue to be "until the times of the Gentiles be fulfilled." (Luke 21:24.)

2. In the Deserts and in Secret Chambers.--The 24th chapter of Matthew, and its parallel scriptures in Mark 13 and Luke 21, may be the more easily understood if we bear in mind that the Lord therein speaks of two distinct events, each a consummation of long ages of preparation, and the first a prototype of the second. Many of the specific predictions are applicable both to the time preceding or at the destruction of Jerusalem, and to developments of succeeding time down to the second coming of Christ. The passage in Matt. 24:26 may be given this two-fold application. Josephus tells of men leading others away into the desert, saying under pretended inspiration that there should they find God; and the same historian mentions a false prophet who led many into the secret chambers of the temple during the Roman assault, promising them that there would the Lord give them deliverance. Men, women, and children followed this fanatical leader, and were caught in the holocaust of destruction, so that 6,000 of them perished in the flames (Josephus, Wars vi, ch. 5). Concerning an application of the Lord's precepts to later times and conditions, the author has elsewhere written (_The Great Apostasy_, 7:22-25): One of the heresies of early origin and rapid growth in the Church was the doctrine of antagonism between body and spirit, whereby the former was regarded as an incubus and a curse. From what has been said this will be recognized as one of the perversions derived from the alliance of Gnosticism with Christianity. A result of this grafting in of heathen doctrines was an abundant growth of hermit practises, by which men sought to weaken, torture, and subdue their bodies, that their spirits or "souls" might gain greater freedom. Many who adopted this unnatural view of human existence retired to the solitude of the desert, and there spent their time in practises of stern self-denial and in acts of frenzied self-torture. Others shut themselves up as voluntary prisoners, seeking glory in privation and self-imposed penance. It was this unnatural view of life that gave rise to the several orders of recluses, hermits, and monks.

Think you not that the Savior had such practises in mind, when, warning the disciples of the false claims to sanctity that would characterize the times then soon to follow, He said: "Wherefore if they shall say unto you. Behold he [Christ] is in the desert, go not forth: behold, he is in the secret chambers, believe it not"?

3. The Time of Christ's Advent Not Known.--The Lord's statement that the time of His advent in glory was unknown to man, and that the angels knew it not, "neither the Son", but that it was known to the Father only, appears plain and unambiguous notwithstanding many and conflicting commentaries thereon. Jesus repeatedly affirmed that His mission was to do the will of the Father; and it is evident that the Father's will was revealed to Him from time to time. While in the flesh He laid no claim to omniscience; though whatever He willed to know He learned through the medium of communication with the Father. Christ had not asked to know what the Father had not intimated His readiness to reveal, which, in this instance, was the day and hour of the Son's appointed return to earth as a glorified, resurrected Being. We need not hesitate to believe that at the time Jesus delivered to the apostles the discourse under consideration, He was uninformed on the matter; for He so states. In the last interview between Christ and the apostles immediately before His ascension (Acts 1:6, 7) they asked "Lord, wilt thou at this time restore again the kingdom to Israel? And he said unto them, It is not for you to know the times or the seasons, which the Father hath put in his own power." Nor has the date of the Messianic consummation been since revealed to any man; though even now, the fig tree is rapidly putting forth its leaves, and he who hath eyes to see and a heart to understand knows that the summer of the Lord's purpose is near at hand.

4. The False Doctrine of Supererogation.--Among the pernicious fallacies promulgated as authorized dogmas by the apostate church during the long period of spiritual darkness following the close of the apostolic ministry, was the awful enormity known as the doctrine of supererogation. As stated by Mosheim (_Eccl. Hist._ Cent. xii, part ii, ch. 3:4) the dreadful doctrine was formulated in the thirteenth century as follows: "That there actually existed an immense treasure of _merit_, composed of the pious deeds and virtuous actions which the saints had performed _beyond what was necessary for their own salvation_, and which were therefore applicable to the benefit of others; that the guardian and dispenser of this precious treasure was the Roman pontiff, and that of consequence he was empowered to assign to such as he thought proper a portion of this inexhaustible source of merit, suitable to their respective guilt, and sufficient to deliver them from the punishment due to their crimes." Concerning the fallacy of this doctrine the author has written (_The Great Apostasy_, 9:15), in this wise: "This doctrine of supererogation is as unreasonable as it is unscriptural and untrue. Man's individual responsibility for his acts is as surely a fact as is his agency to act for himself. He will be saved through the merits and by the atoning sacrifice of our Redeemer and Lord; and his claim upon the salvation provided is strictly dependent on his compliance with the principles and ordinances of the gospel as established by Jesus Christ. Remission of sins and the eventual salvation of the human soul are provided for; but these gifts of God are not to be purchased with money. Compare the awful fallacies of supererogation and the blasphemous practise of assuming to remit the sins of one man in consideration of the merits of another, with the declaration of the one and only Savior of mankind: 'But I say unto you that every idle word that men shall speak, they shall give an account thereof in the day of judgment.'" If conclusions as to doctrine may be drawn from our Lord's parables, the parable of the Ten Virgins affords refutation of the Satanic suggestion that one man's sin may be neutralized by another's righteousness. We know no supererogation but that of the Lord Jesus Christ, through whose merits salvation is placed within the reach of all men.

5. "This Generation."--Consult any reliable unabridged dictionary of the English language for evidence of the fact that the term "generation," as connoting a period of time, has many meanings, among which are "race, kind, class." The term is not confined to a body of people living at one time. Fausett's _Bible

Cyclopedia, Critical and Expository_, after citing many meanings attached to the word, says: "In Matthew 24:34 'this generation shall not pass (viz. the Jewish race, of which the generation in Christ's days was a sample in character; compare Christ's address to the "generation," 23:35, 36, in proof that "generation" means at times the whole Jewish race) till all these things be fulfilled'--a prophecy that the Jews shall be a distinct people still when He shall come again."

FOOTNOTES:

[1150] Matt. 24:3-51; Mark 13:3-37: Luke 21:5-35. Compare P. of G.P., Joseph Smith, 1.
[1151] Mark 13:11; compare Matt. 10:19, 20; Luke 12:11, 12; 21:14, 15.
[1152] Luke 21:19; compare Doc. and Cov. 101:38.
[1153] Dan. 9:27.
[1154] Note 1, end of chapter.
[1155] Note 2, end of chapter.
[1156] Matt. 24:27; compare Luke 17:22-24.
[1157] The "body," as that of the Church, is rendered "carcase" in both authorized and revised versions. For the application of the figure--of eagles gathering about a carcase--to the assembling of scattered Israel, see P. of G.P., Joseph Smith, 1:27, where we read: "so likewise shall mine elect be gathered from the four quarters of the earth." Among Bible scholars, a favorite interpretation of the passage, "For wheresoever the carcase is, there will the eagles be gathered together," is that Christ was likening unto eagles (revised version "vultures") the angels that shall come with Him to execute judgment upon mankind, and unto a carcase the corruption of sin. See Matt. 24:28; compare Luke 17:37.
[1158] Matt. 24:35; compare 5:18; Mark 13:31; Luke 21:33; compare 16:17; see also Heb. 1:10, 11; 2 Peter 3:7-10; Rev. 21:1. Note 5, end of chapter.
[1159] This is Mark's version; in the parallel passage Matt. 24:36, the words "neither the Son" are not found in the King James text, but do appear in the revised version. See Note 3, end of chapter.
[1160] Page 441.
[1161] Matt. 24:45-51; Mark 13:34-37; Luke 21:34-36, compare 12:35-48.
[1162] Matt. 25:1-13.
[1163] Compare Rev. 21:2, 9; 22:17; see also Matt. 9:15; John 3:29.
[1164] See Parable of the Sower, Matt. 13:5, 6, 20, 21; page 282 herein.
[1165] Note 4, end of chapter.
[1166] Compare John 10:14.
[1167] Doc. and Cov. 45:56-59; see also 63:53, 54.
[1168] Matt. 25:14-30.
[1169] Luke 19:12-27; see also page 508 herein.
[1170] Margin, revised version.
[1171] 1 Cor. 12:4; study the entire chapter.
[1172] Luke 12:48.
[1173] Luke 19:22; compare Matt. 12:37.
[1174] Matt. 25:31-46.
[1175] Matt. 13:24-30; page 286 herein. [1176] Page 286.
[1177] The revised version reads "another country" instead of "a far country," in Matt. 25:14.
[1178] Matt. 26:2.

CHAPTER 33. THE LAST SUPPER AND THE BETRAYAL.

PRIESTLY CONSPIRATORS AND THE TRAITOR.

As the time for the annual Feast of the Passover approached, and particularly during the two days immediately preceding the beginning of the festival, the chief priests, scribes, and elders of the people, in short the Sanhedrin and the entire priestly party, conspired persistently together as to the best manner of taking Jesus into custody and putting Him to death. At one of these gatherings of evil counsel, which was held at the palace of the high priest, Caiaphas,[1179] it was decided that Jesus should be taken by subtlety if possible, as the probable effect of an open arrest would be an uprising of the people. The rulers feared especially an outbreak by the Galileans, who had a provincial pride in the prominence of Jesus as one of their countrymen, and many of whom were then in Jerusalem. It was further concluded and for the same reasons, that the Jewish custom of making impressive examples of notable offenders by executing public punishment upon them at times of great general assemblages, be set aside in the case of Jesus; therefore the conspirators said: "Not on the feast day, lest there be an uproar among the people."[1180]

On earlier occasions they had made futile attempts to get Jesus into their hands;[1181] and they were naturally dubious as to the outcome of their later machinations. At this juncture they were encouraged and gladdened in their wicked plots by the appearance of an unexpected ally. Judas Iscariot, one of the Twelve, sought an audience with these rulers of the Jews, and infamously offered to betray his Lord into their hands.[1182] Under the impulse of diabolic avarice, which, however, was probably but a secondary element in the real cause of his perfidious treachery, he bargained to sell his Master for money, and chaffered with the priestly purchasers over the price of the Savior's blood. "What will ye give me?" he asked; "and they covenanted with him for thirty pieces of silver."[1183] This amount, approximately seventeen dollars in our money, but of many times greater purchasing power with the Jews in that day than now with us, was the price fixed by the law as that of a slave; it was also the foreseen sum of the blood-money to be paid for the Lord's betrayal.[1184] That the silver was actually paid to Judas, either at this first interview or at some later meeting between the traitor and the priests, is demonstrated by after events. [1185]

He had pledged himself to the blackest deed of treachery of which man is capable, and from that hour he sought the opportunity of superseding his infamous promise by its more villainous fulfilment. We are yet to be afflicted by other glimpses of the evil-hearted Iscariot in the course of this dread chronicle of tragedy and perdition; for the present let it be said that before Judas sold Christ to the Jews, he had sold himself to the devil; he had become Satan's serf, and did his master's bidding.

THE LAST SUPPER.

The day preceding the eating of the passover lamb had come to be known among the Jews as the first day of the feast of unleavened bread,[1186] since on that day all leaven had to be removed from their dwellings, and thereafter for a period of eight days the eating of anything containing leaven was unlawful. On the afternoon of this day, the paschal lambs were slain within the temple court, by the representatives of families or companies who were to eat together; and a portion of the blood of each lamb was sprinkled at the foot of the altar of sacrifice by one of the numerous priests on duty for the day. The slain lamb, then said to have been sacrificed, was borne away to the appointed gathering place of those by whom it was to be eaten. During the first of the days of unleavened bread, which in the year of our Lord's death appears to have fallen on Thursday,[1187] some of the Twelve inquired of Jesus where they should make preparations for the paschal meal.[1188] He instructed Peter and John to return to Jerusalem, and added: "Behold, when ye are entered into the city, there shall a man meet you, bearing a pitcher of water; follow him into the house where he entereth in. And ye shall say unto the goodman of the house, The Master saith unto thee, Where is the guest chamber, where I shall eat the passover with my disciples? And he shall shew you a large upper room furnished: there make ready. And they went, and found as he had said unto them: and they made ready the passover."

In the evening, Thursday evening as we reckon time, but the beginning of Friday according to the Jewish calendar,[1189] Jesus came with the Twelve, and together they sat down to the last meal of which the Lord would partake before His death. Under strain of profound emotion, "He said unto them, With desire I have desired to eat this passover with you before I suffer: for I say unto you, I will not any more eat thereof, until it be fulfilled in the kingdom of God. And he took the cup, and gave thanks, and said, Take this, and divide it among yourselves: for I say unto you, I will not drink of the fruit of the vine, until the kingdom of God shall come." The pronouncing of a blessing by the host upon a cup of wine, which was afterward passed round the table to each participant in turn, was the customary manner of beginning the Passover supper. At this solemn meal Jesus appears to have observed the essentials of the Passover procedure; but we have no record of His compliance with the many supernumerary requirements with which the divinely established memorial of Israel's deliverance from bondage had been invested by traditional custom and rabbinical prescription. As we shall see, the evening's proceedings in that upper room comprized much beside the ordinary observance of an annual festival.

The supper proceeded under conditions of tense sadness. As they ate, the Lord sorrowfully remarked: "Verily I say unto you, One of you which eateth with me shall betray me." Most of the apostles fell into a state of introspection; and one after another exclaimed: "Is it I?" "Lord, is it I?" It is pleasing to note that each of those who so inquired was more concerned with the dread thought that possibly he was an offender, however inadvertently so, than as to whether his brother was about to prove himself a traitor.

Jesus answered that it was one of the Twelve, then and there eating with Him from the common dish, and continued with the terrifying pronouncement: "The Son of man indeed goeth, as it is written of him: but woe to that man by whom the Son of man is betrayed! good were it for that man if he had never been born." Then Judas Iscariot, who had already covenanted to sell his Master for money, and who at this moment probably feared that silence might arouse suspicion against himself, asked with a brazen audacity that was veritably devilish: "Master, is it I?" With cutting promptness the Lord replied: "Thou hast said."[1190]

There was further cause of sorrow to Jesus at the supper. Some of the Twelve had fallen into muttering dispute among themselves over the matter of individual precedence,[1191] possibly as to the order in which they should take their places at table, over which triviality scribes and Pharisees as well as the Gentiles often quarreled;[1192] and again the Lord had to remind the apostles that the greatest of them all was he who most willingly served his fellows. They had been taught before; yet now, at this late and solemn hour, they were suffused with vain and selfish ambition. In sorrowful earnestness the Lord pleaded with them, asking who is greater, he that sits at the table, or he that serves? And the obvious reply He supplemented by the statement: "But I am among you as he that serveth." With loving pathos He added: "Ye are they which have continued with me in my temptations;"[1193] and then He assured them that they should lack neither honor nor glory in the kingdom of God, for if they proved faithful they should be appointed to thrones as the judges of Israel. For those of His chosen ones who were true to Him, the Lord had no feeling less than that of love, and of yearning for their victory over Satan and sin.

THE ORDINANCE OF THE WASHING OF FEET[1194]

Leaving the table, the Lord laid aside His outer garments and girded Himself with a towel as an apron; then having provided Himself with a basin and a supply of water, He knelt before each of the Twelve in turn, washed his feet, and wiped them with the towel. When He reached Peter, that impulsive apostle protested, saying: "Lord, dost thou wash my feet?" That the proceeding was something more than mere service for personal comfort, and more than an object-lesson of humility, appears in the Lord's words to Peter--"What I do thou knowest not now; but thou shalt know hereafter." Peter, failing to understand, objected yet more vehemently; "Thou shalt never wash my feet," he exclaimed. Jesus answered: "If I wash thee not, thou hast no part with me." Then, with even greater impetuosity than before, Peter implored as he stretched forth both feet and hands, "Lord, not my feet only, but also my hands and my head." He had gone to the other extreme, insisting, though ignorantly and unthinkingly, that things be done his way, and failing yet to see that the ordinance had to be administered as the Lord willed. Again correcting His well-intending though presumptuous servant, Jesus said to him: "He that is washed needeth not save to wash his feet, but is clean every whit: and ye are clean, but not all." Each of them had been immersed at baptism; the washing of feet was an ordinance pertaining to the Holy Priesthood, the full import of which they had yet to learn. [1195]

Having resumed His garments and returned to His place at the table, Jesus impressed the significance of what he had done, saying: "Ye call me Master and Lord: and ye say well; for so I am. If I then, your Lord and Master, have washed your feet; ye also ought to wash one another's feet. For I have given you an example, that ye should do as I have done to you. Verily, verily, I say unto you, The servant is not greater than his lord; neither he that is sent greater than he that sent him. If ye know these things, happy are ye if ye do them."[1196]

THE SACRAMENT OF THE LORD'S SUPPER.[1197]

While Jesus with the Twelve still sat at table, He took a loaf or cake of bread, and having reverently given thanks and by blessing sanctified it, He gave a portion to each of the apostles, saying: "Take, eat; this is my body"; or, according to the more extended account, "This is my body which is given for you: this do in remembrance of me." Then, taking a cup of wine, He gave thanks and blessed it, and gave it unto them with the command: "Drink ye all of it; for this is my blood of the new testament, which is shed for many for the remission of sins. But I say unto you, I will not drink henceforth of this fruit of the vine, until that day when I drink it new with you in my Father's kingdom."[1198] In this simple but impressive manner was instituted the ordinance, since known as the Sacrament of the Lord's Supper. The bread and wine, duly consecrated by prayer, become emblems of the Lord's body and blood, to be eaten and drunk reverently, and in remembrance of Him.

The proceedings at the institution of this sacred rite were afterward revealed to Paul the apostle, whose recorded testimony as to its establishment and sanctity is in accord with the accounts given by the Gospel-writers.[1199] As shall be hereinafter shown, the ordinance was instituted by the Lord among the Nephites, on the western continent, and has been reestablished in the present dispensation.[1200] During the dark ages of apostasy, unauthorized changes in the administration of the Sacrament were introduced, and many false doctrines as to its meaning and effect were promulgated.[1201]

THE BETRAYER GOES OUT INTO THE NIGHT.[1202]

In saying to the Twelve, whose feet He had washed, "Ye are clean," the Lord had specified an exception by His after remark, "but not all." John, the recorder, takes care to explain that Jesus had in mind the traitor, and, "therefore said he, Ye are not all clean." The guilty Iscariot had received without protest the Lord's service in the washing of his recreant feet, though after the ablution he was spiritually more filthy than before. When Jesus had again sat down, the burden of His knowledge concerning the treacherous heart of Judas again found expression. "I speak not of you all," He said, "I know whom I have chosen: but that the scripture may be fulfilled, He that eateth bread with me hath lifted up his heel against me."[1203] The Lord was intent on impressing the fact of His foreknowledge as to what was to come, so that when the terrible development was an accomplished fact, the apostles would realize that thereby the scriptures had been fulfilled. Troubled in spirit, He reiterated the dreadful assertion that one of those present would betray Him. Peter made signs to John, who occupied the place next to Jesus and was at that moment leaning his head on the Lord's breast, that he ask which of them was the traitor. To John's whispered inquiry the Lord replied: "He it is, to whom I shall give a sop, when I have dipped it."

There was nothing unusual for a person at table, particularly the host, to dip a piece of bread into the dish of gravy or savory mixture, and hand it to another. Such action on the part of Jesus attracted no general attention. He dipped the morsel of bread and gave it to Judas Iscariot, with the words: "That thou doest, do quickly." The others understood the Lord's remark as an instruction to Judas to attend to some duty or go upon some errand of ordinary kind, perhaps to purchase something for the further celebration of the Passover, or to carry gifts to some of the poor, for Judas was the treasurer of the party and "had the bag." But Iscariot understood. His heart was all the more hardened by the discovery that Jesus knew of his infamous plans, and he was maddened by the humiliation he felt in the Master's presence. After the sop, which he had opened his mouth to receive from the Lord's hand, "Satan entered into him" and asserted malignant mastership. Judas went out immediately, abandoning forever the blessed company of his brethren and the Lord. John chronicles the traitor's departure with the terse and ominous remark, "and it was night."

DISCOURSE FOLLOWING THE SUPPER.

The departure of Judas Iscariot appears to have dissipated to some degree the cloud of utter sadness by which the little company had been depressed; and our Lord Himself was visibly relieved. As soon as the door had closed upon the retreating deserter, Jesus exclaimed, as though His victory over death had been already accomplished: "Now is the Son of man glorified, and God is glorified in him." Addressing the Eleven in terms of parental affection, He said: "Little children, yet a little while I am with you. Ye shall seek me: and as I said unto the Jews, Whither I go, ye cannot come; so now I say to you. A new commandment I give unto you, That ye love one another; as I have loved you, that ye also love one another. By this shall all men know that ye are my disciples, if ye have love one to another."[1204] The law of Moses enjoined mutual love among friends and neighbors;[1205] but the new commandment, by which the apostles were to be governed, embodied love of a higher order. They were to love one another as Christ loved them; and their brotherly affection was to be a distinguishing mark of their apostleship, by which the world would recognize them as men set apart.

The Lord's reference to His impending separation from them troubled the brethren. Peter put the question, "Lord, whither goest thou?" Jesus answered: "Whither I go, thou canst not follow me now; but thou shalt follow me afterwards. Peter said unto him, Lord, why cannot I follow thee now? I will lay down my life for thy sake." Peter seems to have realized that his Master was going to His death; yet, undeterred, he asserted his readiness to follow even that dark way rather than be separated from his Lord. We cannot doubt the earnestness of Peter's purpose nor the sincerity of his desire at that moment. In his bold avowal, however, he had reckoned with the willingness of his spirit only, and had failed to take into full account the weakness of his flesh. Jesus, who knew Peter better than the man knew himself, thus tenderly reproved his excess of self-confidence: "Simon, Simon, behold, Satan hath desired to have you, that he may sift you as wheat: but I have prayed for thee, that thy faith fail not: and when thou art converted, strengthen thy brethren." The first of the apostles, the Man of Rock, yet had to be converted, or as more precisely rendered, "turned again";[1206] for as the Lord foresaw, Peter would soon be overcome, even to the extent of denying his acquaintanceship with Christ. When Peter stoutly declared again his readiness to go with Jesus, even into prison or to death, the Lord silenced him with the remark: "I tell thee, Peter, the cock shall not crow this day, before that thou shalt thrice deny that thou knowest me."

The apostles had to be prepared to meet a new order of things, new conditions and new exigencies; persecution awaited them, and they were soon to be bereft of the Master's sustaining presence. Jesus asked of them: "When I sent you without purse, and scrip, and shoes, lacked ye anything? And they said, Nothing. Then said he unto them, But now, he that hath a purse, let him take it, and likewise his scrip: and he that hath no sword, let him sell his garment, and buy one. For I say unto you, that this that is written must yet be accomplished in me, And he was reckoned among the transgressors: for the things concerning me have an end." The Lord was soon to be numbered among the transgressors, as had been foreseen;[1207] and His disciples would be regarded as the devotees of an executed criminal. In the mention of purse, scrip, shoes, and sword, some of the brethren caught at the literal meaning, and said, "Lord, behold, here are two swords," Jesus answered with curt finality, "It is enough," or as we might say, "Enough of this." He had not intimated any immediate need of weapons, and most assuredly not for His own defense. Again they had failed to fathom His meaning; but experience would later teach them.[1208]

For such information as we have concerning the last discourse delivered by Jesus to the apostles before His crucifixion, we are indebted to John alone among the Gospel-writers; and every reader is advized to study with care the three chapters in which these sublime utterances are preserved for the enlightenment of mankind.[1209] Observing the sorrowful state of the Eleven, the Master bade them be of good cheer, grounding their encouragement and hope on faith in Himself. "Let not your heart be troubled," He said, "ye believe in God, believe also in me." Then, as though drawing aside the veil between the earthly and the heavenly state and giving His faithful servants a glimpse of conditions beyond, He continued: "In my

Father's house are many mansions; if it were not so, I would have told you. I go to prepare a place for you. And if I go and prepare a place for you, I will come again, and receive you unto myself; that where I am, there ye may be also. And whither I go ye know, and the way ye know."[1210] Thus in language simple and plain the Lord declared the fact of graded conditions in the hereafter, of variety of occupation and degrees of glory, of place and station in the eternal worlds.[1211] He had affirmed His own inherent Godship, and through their trust in Him and obedience to His requirements would they find the way to follow whither He was about to precede them. Thomas, that loving, brave, though somewhat skeptical soul, desiring more definite information ventured to say: "Lord, we know not whither thou goest; and how can we know the way?" The Lord's answer was a reaffirmation of His divinity; "I am the way, the truth, and the life: no man cometh unto the Father, but by me. If ye had known me, ye should have known my Father also: and from henceforth ye know him, and have seen him."

At this point Philip interposed with the request, "Lord, shew us the Father, and it sufficeth us." Jesus answered with pathetic and mild reproof: "Have I been so long time with you, and yet hast thou not known me, Philip? he that hath seen me hath seen the Father; and how sayest thou then, Shew us the Father?" He was grieved by the thought that His nearest and dearest friends on earth, those upon whom He had conferred the authority of the Holy Priesthood, should be yet ignorant of His absolute oneness with the Father in purpose and action. Had the Eternal Father stood amongst them, in Person, under the conditions there existing, He would have done as did the Well Beloved and Only Begotten Son, whom they knew as Jesus, their Lord and Master. So absolutely were the Father and the Son of one heart and mind, that to know either was to know both; nevertheless the Father could be reached only through the Son. So far as the apostles had faith in Christ, and did His will, should they be able to do the works that Christ in the flesh had done, and even greater things, for His mortal mission was of but a few hours further duration, and the unfolding of the divine plan of the ages would call for yet greater miracles than those wrought by Jesus in the brief period of His ministry.

For the first time the Lord directed His disciples to pray in His name to the Father, and assurance of success in righteous supplication was given in these words: "And whatsoever ye shall ask in my name, that will I do, that the Father may be glorified in the Son. If ye shall ask any thing in my name, I will do it."[1212] The name of Jesus Christ was to be thenceforth the divinely established talisman by which the powers of heaven could be invoked to operate in any righteous undertaking.

The Holy Ghost was promised to the apostles; He would be sent through Christ's intercession, to be to them "another Comforter," or as rendered in later translations, "another Advocate" or "Helper," even the Spirit of Truth, who, though the world would reject Him as they had rejected the Christ, should dwell with the disciples, and in them even as Christ then dwelt in them and the Father in Him. "I will not leave you comfortless," Jesus assured the brethren, "I will come to you. Yet a little while, and the world seeth me no more; but ye see me: because I live, ye shall live also. At that day ye shall know that I am in my Father, and ye in me, and I in you."[1213] This was followed by the assurance that Christ though unknown by the world would manifest Himself to those who loved Him and kept His commandments.

Judas Thaddeus, otherwise known as Lebbeus,[1214] "not Iscariot," as the recorder is careful to particularize, was puzzled over the untraditional and un-Jewish thought of a Messiah who would be known but to the chosen few and not to Israel at large; and he asked: "Lord, how is it that thou wilt manifest thyself unto us, and not unto the world?" Jesus explained that His and the Father's companionship was attainable only by the faithful. He further cheered the apostles by the promise that when the Comforter, the Holy Ghost, whom the Father would send in the name of the Son, would come to them, He would teach them further, and would bring to their remembrance the teachings they had received from the Christ. The distinct personality of each member of the Godhead, Father, Son, and Holy Ghost, is here again plainly shown.[1215] Comforting the yet troubled disciples, Jesus said: "Peace I leave with you, my peace I give unto you"; and that they might realize that this meant more than the conventional salutation of the times, for "Peace be with you" was an every-day greeting among the Jews, the Lord affirmed that He gave that invocation in a higher sense, and "not as the world giveth." Again bidding them put aside their grief and be not afraid, Jesus added: "Ye have heard how I said unto you, I go away, and come again unto you. If ye loved me, ye would rejoice, because I said, I go unto the Father: for my Father is greater than I." The Lord made clear to His servants that He had told them these things beforehand, so that when the predicted events came to pass the apostles would be confirmed in their faith in Him, the Christ. He had time to say but little more, for the next hour would witness the beginning of the supreme struggle; "the prince of this world cometh," He said, and with triumphal joy added, "and hath nothing in me."[1216]

In superb allegory the Lord thus proceeded to illustrate the vital relationship between the apostles and Himself, and between Himself and the Father, by the figure of a vine-grower, a vine, and its branches:[1217] "I am the true vine, and my Father is the husbandman. Every branch in me that beareth not fruit he taketh away: and every branch that beareth fruit, he purgeth it,[1218] that it may bring forth more fruit." A grander analogy is not to be found in the world's literature. Those ordained servants of the Lord were as helpless and useless without Him as is a bough severed from the tree. As the branch is made fruitful only by virtue of the nourishing sap it receives from the rooted trunk, and if cut away or broken off withers, dries, and becomes utterly worthless except as fuel for the burning, so those men, though ordained to the Holy Apostleship, would find themselves strong and fruitful in good works, only as they remained in steadfast communion with the Lord. Without Christ what were they, but unschooled Galileans, some of them fishermen, one a publican, the rest of undistinguished attainments, and all of them weak mortals? As branches of the Vine they were at that hour clean and healthful, through the instructions and authoritative ordinances with which they had been blessed, and by the reverent obedience they had manifested.

"Abide in me," was the Lord's forceful admonition, else they would become but withered boughs.

"I am the vine," He added in explication of the allegory "ye are the branches: He that abideth in me, and I in him, the same bringeth forth much fruit: for without me ye can do nothing. If a man abide not in me, he is cast forth as a branch, and is withered; and men gather them, and cast them into the fire, and they are burned. If ye abide in me, and my words abide in you, ye shall ask what ye will, and it shall be done unto you. Herein is my Father glorified, that ye bear much fruit: so shall ye be my disciples." Their love for one another was again specified as an essential to their continued love for Christ.[1219] In that love would they find joy. Christ had been to them an exemplar of righteous love from the day of their first meeting; and He was about to give the supreme proof of His affection, as foreshadowed in His words, "Greater love hath no man than this, that a man lay down his life for his friends." And that those men were the Lord's friends was thus graciously affirmed; "Ye are my friends, if ye do whatsoever I command you. Henceforth I call you not servants; for the servant knoweth not what his lord doeth: but I have called you friends; for all things that I have heard of my Father I have made known unto you." This intimate relationship in no sense modified the position of Christ as their Lord and Master, for by Him they had been chosen and ordained; and it was His will that they should so live that whatever they asked in the name of the holy friendship which He acknowledged should be granted them of the Father.

They were again told of the persecutions that awaited them, and of their apostolic calling as special and individual witnesses of the Lord.[1220] That the world then did, and would yet more intensely hate them was a fact they had to face; but they were to remember that the world had hated their Master before them, and that they had been chosen and by ordination had been set apart from the world; therefore they must not hope to escape the world's hatred. The servant was not greater than his master, nor the apostle than his Lord, as on general principles they knew, and as they had been specifically told. They that hated them hated the Christ; and they that hated the Son hated the Father; great shall be the condemnation of such. Had the wicked Jews not closed their eyes and stopped their ears to the mighty works and gracious words of the Messiah, they would have been convinced of the truth, and the truth would have saved them; but they were left without cloak or excuse for their sin; and Christ affirmed that in their evil course had the scriptures been fulfilled in that they had hated Him without a cause.[1221] Then, reverting to the great and cheering promise of support through the coming of the Holy Ghost, the Lord said: "But when the Comforter is come, whom I will send unto you from the Father, even the Spirit of truth, which proceedeth from the Father, he shall testify of me: and ye also shall bear witness, because ye have been with me from the beginning."

These things had Jesus declared unto them that they might not "be offended," or in other words, taken by surprize, misled, and caused to doubt and stumble by the unprecedented events then impending. The apostles were forewarned of persecution, of their expulsion from the synagogs, and of a time in which hatred against them should be so bitter and the Satanic darkness of mind and spirit so dense that whosoever succeeded in killing one of them would profess that his foul deed had been done in God's service. In view of their overwhelming sorrow at the Lord's departure, He sought again to cheer them, saying: "Nevertheless I tell you the truth; It is expedient for you that I go away: for if I go not away, the Comforter will not come unto you; but if I depart, I will send him unto you."

The assured descent of the Holy Ghost, through whom they should be made strong to meet every need and emergency, was the inspiring theme of this part of the Lord's discourse. Many things which Christ yet had to say to His apostles, but which they were at that time unable to understand, the Holy Ghost would teach them. "Howbeit," said Jesus, "when he, the Spirit of truth, is come, he will guide you into all truth: for he shall not speak of himself; but whatsoever he shall hear, that shall he speak: and he will shew you things to come. He shall glorify me: for he shall receive of mine, and shall shew it unto you. All things that the Father hath are mine: therefore said I, that he shall take of mine, and shall shew it unto you."[1222]

Turning again to the matter of His departure, then so near as to be reckoned by hours, the Lord said, in amplified form of what He had before affirmed: "A little while, and ye shall not see me: and again, a little while, and ye shall see me, because I go to the Father."[1223] The apostles pondered and some questioned among themselves as to the Lord's meaning, yet so deep was the solemnity of the occasion that they ventured no open inquiry. Jesus knew of their perplexity and graciously explained that they would soon weep and lament while the world rejoiced; this had reference to His death; but He promised that their sorrow should be turned into joy; and this was based on His resurrection to which they should be witnesses. He compared their then present and prospective state to that of a woman in travail, who in the after joy of blessed motherhood forgets her anguish. The happiness that awaited them would be beyond the power of man to take away; and thenceforth they should ask not of Christ alone, but of the Father in Christ's name; "And," said the Lord, "in that day ye shall ask me nothing. Verily, verily, I say unto you, Whatsoever ye shall ask the Father in my name, he will give it you. Hitherto have ye asked nothing in my name: ask, and ye shall receive, that your joy may be full."[1224] They were to be advanced to such honor and exalted recognition that they should approach the Father in prayer direct, but in the name of the Son; for they were beloved of the Father because they had loved Jesus, the Son, and had accepted Him as One sent by the Father. The Lord again solemnly averred: "I came forth from the Father, and am come into the world: again, I leave the world, and go to the Father." The disciples were gratified at this plain avouchment, and exclaimed: "Lo, now speakest thou plainly, and speakest no proverb. Now are we sure that thou knowest all things, and needest not that any man should ask thee: by this we believe that thou camest forth from God." Their satisfaction threatened danger through over-confidence; and the Lord cautioned them, saying, that in an hour then close they should all be scattered, every man to his own, leaving Jesus alone, except for the Father's presence. In the same connection He told them that before the night had passed every one of them would be offended because of Him, even as it had been written: "I will smite the shepherd, and the sheep of the flock shall be scattered abroad."[1225] Peter, the most vehement of all in his protestations, had been told, as we have seen, that by cock-crow that night he would have thrice denied his Lord; but all of them had declared they would be faithful whatever the trial.[1226] In further affirmation of the material actuality of His resurrection, Jesus promised the apostles that after He had risen from the grave He would go before them into Galilee.[1227]

In conclusion of this last and most solemn of the discourses delivered by Christ in the flesh, the Lord said: "These things I have spoken unto you, that in me ye might have peace. In the world ye shall have tribulation: but be of good cheer; I have overcome the world."[1228]

THE CONCLUDING PRAYER.

The impressive discourse to the apostles was followed by a prayer such as could be addressed to none but the Eternal Father, and such as none but the Son of that Father could offer.[1229] It has been called, and not inappropriately, the Lord's High-Priestly Prayer. In it Jesus acknowledged the Father as the source of His power and authority, which authority extends even to the giving of eternal life to all who are worthy: "And this is life eternal, that they might know thee the only true God, and Jesus Christ, whom thou hast sent." By way of reverent report as to the work assigned Him, the Son said: "I have glorified thee on the earth: I have finished the work which thou gavest me to do. And now, O Father, glorify thou me with thine own self with the glory which I had with thee before the world was." With unfathomable love the Lord pleaded for those whom the Father had given Him, the apostles then present, who had been called out from the world, and who had been true to their testimony of Himself as the Son of God. Of them but one, the son of perdition, had been lost. In the fervor of devoted supplication, the Lord pleaded:

"I pray not that thou shouldest take them out of the world, but   that thou shouldest keep them from the evil. They are not of the   world, even as I am not of the world. Sanctify them through thy truth: thy word is truth. As thou hast sent me into the world,   even so have I also sent them into the world. And for their   sakes I sanctify myself, that they also might be sanctified   through the truth. Neither pray I for these alone, but for them   also which shall believe on me through their word; that they all   may be one; as thou, Father, art in me, and I in thee, that they   also may be one in us: that the world may believe that thou hast   sent me. And the glory which thou gavest me I have given them;   that they may be one, even as we are one: I in them, and thou in   me, that they may be made perfect in one; and that the world may   know that thou hast sent me, and hast loved them, as thou hast   loved me. Father, I will that they also, whom thou hast given   me, be with me where I am; that they may behold my glory, which   thou hast given me: for thou lovedst me before the foundation of   the world. O righteous Father, the world hath not known thee: but I have known thee, and these have known that thou hast sent   me. And I have declared unto them thy name, and will declare it: that the love wherewith thou hast loved me may be in them, and I   in them." When they had sung a hymn, Jesus and the Eleven went out to the Mount of Olives.[1230]

THE LORD'S AGONY IN GETHSEMANE.[1231]

Jesus and the eleven apostles went forth from the house in which they had eaten, passed through the city gate, which was usually left open at night during a public festival, crossed the ravine of the Cedron, or more accurately Kidron, brook, and entered an olive orchard known as Gethsemane,[1232] on the slope of Mount Olivet. Eight of the apostles He left at or near the entrance, with the instruction: "Sit ye here, while I go and pray yonder"; and with the earnest injunction: "Pray that ye enter not into temptation." Accompanied by Peter, James and John, He went farther; and was soon enveloped by deep sorrow, which appears to have been, in a measure, surprizing to Himself, for we read that He "began to be sore amazed, and to be very heavy." He was impelled to deny Himself the companionship of even the chosen three; and, "Saith he unto them, My soul is exceeding sorrowful, even unto death: tarry ye here, and watch with me. And he went a little farther, and fell on his face, and prayed, saying, O my Father, if it be possible, let this cup pass from me: nevertheless not as I will, but as thou wilt." Mark's version of the prayer is: "Abba, Father, all things are possible unto thee; take away this cup from me: nevertheless not what I will, but what thou wilt."[1233]

This part of His impassioned supplication was heard by at least one of the waiting three; but all of them soon yielded to weariness and ceased to watch. As on the Mount of Transfiguration, when the Lord appeared in glory, so now in the hour of His deepest humiliation, these three slumbered. Returning to them in an agony of soul Jesus found them sleeping; and addressing Peter, who so short a time before had loudly proclaimed his readiness to follow the Lord even to prison and death, Jesus exclaimed: "What, could ye not watch with me one hour? Watch and pray, that ye enter not into temptation"; but in tenderness added, "the spirit indeed is willing, but the flesh is weak." The admonition to the apostles to pray at that time lest they be led into temptation may have been prompted by the exigencies of the hour, under which, if left to themselves, they would be tempted to prematurely desert their Lord.

Aroused from slumber the three apostles saw the Lord again retire, and heard Him pleading in agony: "O my Father, if this cup may not pass away from me, except I drink it, thy will be done." Returning a second time He found those whom He had so sorrowfully requested to watch with Him sleeping again, "for their eyes were heavy"; and when awakened they were embarrassed or ashamed so that they wist not what to say. A third time He went to His lonely vigil and individual struggle, and was heard to implore the Father with the same words of yearning entreaty. Luke tells us that "there appeared an angel unto him from heaven, strengthening him"; but not even the presence of this super-earthly visitant could dispel the awful anguish of His soul. "And being in an agony he prayed more earnestly: and his sweat was as it were great drops of blood falling down to the ground."[1234]

Peter had had a glimpse of the darksome road which he had professed himself so ready to tread; and the brothers James and John knew now better than before how unprepared they were to drink of the cup which the Lord would drain to its dregs.[1235]

When for the last time Jesus came back to the disciples left on guard, He said: "Sleep on now, and take your rest: behold, the hour is at hand, and the Son of man is betrayed into the hands of sinners." There was no use of further watching; already the torches of the approaching band conducted by Judas were observable in the distance. Jesus exclaimed: "Rise, let us be going: behold, he is at hand that doth betray me." Standing with the Eleven, the Lord calmly awaited the traitor's coming.

Christ's agony in the garden is unfathomable by the finite mind, both as to intensity and cause. The thought that He suffered through fear of death is untenable. Death to Him was preliminary to resurrection and triumphal return to the Father from whom He had come, and to a state of glory even beyond what He had before possessed; and, moreover, it was within His power to lay down His life voluntarily.[1236] He struggled and groaned under a burden such as no other being who has lived on earth might even conceive as possible. It was not physical pain, nor mental anguish alone, that caused Him to suffer such torture as to produce an extrusion of blood from every pore; but a spiritual agony of soul such as only God was capable of experiencing. No other man, however great his powers of physical or mental endurance, could have suffered so; for his human organism would have succumbed, and syncope would have produced unconsciousness and welcome oblivion. In that hour of anguish Christ met and overcame all the horrors that Satan, "the prince of this world"[1237] could inflict. The frightful struggle incident to the temptations immediately following the Lord's baptism[1238] was surpassed and overshadowed by this supreme contest with the powers of evil.

In some manner, actual and terribly real though to man incomprehensible, the Savior took upon Himself the burden of the sins of mankind from Adam to the end of the world. Modern revelation assists us to a partial understanding of the awful experience. In March 1830, the glorified Lord, Jesus Christ, thus spake: "For behold, I, God, have suffered these things for all, that they might not suffer if they would repent, but if they would not repent, they must suffer even as I, which suffering caused myself, even God, the greatest of all, to tremble because of pain, and to bleed at every pore, and to suffer both body and spirit: and would that I might not drink the bitter cup and shrink-- nevertheless, glory be to the Father, and I partook and finished my preparations unto the children of men."[1239]

From the terrible conflict in Gethsemane, Christ emerged a victor. Though in the dark tribulation of that fearful hour He had pleaded that the bitter cup be removed from His lips, the request, however oft repeated, was always conditional; the accomplishment of the Father's will was never lost sight of as the object of the Son's supreme desire. The further tragedy of the night, and the cruel inflictions that awaited Him on the morrow, to culminate in the frightful tortures of the cross, could not exceed the bitter anguish through which He had successfully passed.

THE BETRAYAL AND THE ARREST.[1240]

During the period of the Lord's last and most loving communion with the Eleven, Judas had been busy in his treacherous conspiracy with the priestly authorities. It is probable that the determination to make the arrest that night was reached when Judas reported that Jesus was within the city walls and might easily be apprehended. The Jewish rulers assembled a body of temple guardsmen or police, and obtained a band of Roman soldiers under command of a tribune; this band or cohort was probably a detachment from the garrison of Antonia commissioned for the work of the night on requisition of the chief priests.[1241] This company of men and officers representing a combination of ecclesiastical and military authority, set forth in the night with Judas at their head, intent on the arrest of Jesus. They were equipped with lanterns, torches, and weapons. It is probable that they were first conducted to the house in which Judas had left his fellow apostles and the Lord, when the traitor had been dismissed; and that finding the little company had gone out, Judas led the multitude to Gethsemane, for he knew the place, and knew also that "Jesus ofttimes resorted thither with his disciples."

While Jesus was yet speaking to the Eleven whom He had roused from slumber with the announcement that the betrayer was at hand, Judas and the multitude approached. As a preconcerted sign of identification the recreant Iscariot, with treacherous duplicity, came up with a hypocritical show of affection, saying, "Hail, master," and profaned his Lord's sacred face with a kiss.[1242] That Jesus understood the treacherous significance of the act appears in His pathetic, yet piercing and condemning reproach: "Judas, betrayest thou the Son of man with a kiss?" Then, applying the title with which the other apostles had been honored, the Lord said: Friend, do that for which thou art come.[1243] It was a reiteration of the behest given at the supper table, "That thou doest, do quickly."

The armed band hesitated, though their guide had given the signal agreed upon. Jesus walked toward the officers, with whom stood Judas, and asked, "Whom seek ye?" To their reply, "Jesus of Nazareth," the Lord rejoined: "I am he." Instead of advancing to take Him, the crowd pressed backward, and many of them fell to the ground in fright. The simple dignity and gentle yet compelling force of Christ's presence proved more potent than strong arms and weapons of violence. Again He put the question, "Whom seek ye?" and again they answered, "Jesus of Nazareth." Then said Jesus: "I have told you that I am he; if therefore ye seek me, let these go their way." The last remark had reference to the apostles, who were in danger of arrest; and in this evidence of Christ's solicitude for their personal safety, John saw a fulfilment of the Lord's then recent utterance in prayer, "Of them which thou gavest me have I lost none."[1244] It is possible that had any of the Eleven been apprehended with Jesus and made to share the cruel abuse and torturing humiliation of the next few hours, their faith might have failed them, relatively immature and untried as it then was; even as in succeeding years many who took upon themselves the name of Christ yielded to persecution and went into apostasy.[1245]

When the officers approached and seized Jesus, some of the apostles, ready to fight and die for their beloved Master, asked, "Lord, shall we smite with the sword?" Peter, waiting not for a reply, drew his sword and delivered a poorly aimed stroke at the head of one of the nearest of the crowd, whose ear was severed by the blade. The man thus wounded was Malchus, a servant of the high priest. Jesus, asking liberty of His captors by the simple request, "Suffer ye thus far,"[1246] stepped forward and healed the injured man by a touch. Turning to Peter the Lord rebuked his rashness, and commanded him to return the sword to its scabbard, with the reminder that "all they that take the sword shall perish with the sword." Then, to show the needlessness of armed resistance, and to emphasize the fact that He was submitting voluntarily and in accordance with foreseen and predicted developments, the Lord continued: "Thinkest thou that I cannot now pray to my Father, and he shall presently give me more than twelve legions of angels? But how then shall the scriptures be fulfilled, that thus it must be?"[1247] And further, "the cup which my Father hath given me, shall I not drink it?"[1248]

But, though surrendering Himself unresistingly, Jesus was not unmindful of His rights; and to the priestly officials, chief priests, captain of the temple guard, and elders of the people who were present, He voiced this interrogative protest against the illegal night seizure: "Are ye come out as against a thief with swords and staves for to take me? I sat daily with you teaching in the temple, and ye laid no hold on me. But all this was done, that the scriptures of the prophets might be fulfilled." Luke records the Lord's concluding words thus: "but this is your hour, and the power of darkness." Unheeding His question, and without deference to His submissive demeanor, the captain and the officers of the Jews bound Jesus with cords and led Him away, a Prisoner at the mercy of His deadliest enemies.

The eleven apostles, seeing that resistance was useless, not only on account of disparity of numbers and supply of weapons but chiefly because of Christ's determination to submit, turned and fled. Every one of them forsook Him, even as He had foretold. That they were really in jeopardy is shown by an incident preserved by Mark alone. An unnamed young man, aroused from sleep by the tumult of the marching band, had sallied forth with no outer covering but a linen sheet. His interest in the arrest of Jesus and his close approach caused some of the guardsmen or soldiers to seize him; but he broke loose and escaped leaving the sheet in their hands.

NOTES TO CHAPTER 33.

1. The Day of the Passover Feast.--Controversy has been rife for many centuries as to the day of the passover feast in the week of our Lord's death. That He was crucified on Friday, the day before the Jewish Sabbath, and that He rose a resurrected Being on Sunday, the day following the Sabbath of the Jews, are facts attested by the four Gospel-writers. From the three synoptists we infer that the last supper occurred on the evening of the first day of unleavened bread, and therefore at the beginning of the Jewish Friday. That the Lord's last supper was regarded by Himself and the apostles as a passover meal appears from Matt. 26:2, 17, 18, 19 and parallel passages, Mark 14:14-16; Luke 22:11-13; as also from Luke 22:7, 15. John, however, who wrote after the synoptists and who probably had their writings before him, as is indicated by the supplementary character of his testimony or "Gospel", intimates that the last supper of which Jesus and the Twelve partook together occurred before the Feast of the Passover (John 13:1, 2); and the same writer informs us that on the following day, Friday, the Jews refrained from entering the Roman hall of judgment, lest they be defiled and so become unfit to eat the Passover (18:28). It should be remembered that by common usage the term "Passover" was applied not only to the day or season of the observance, but to the meal itself, and particularly to the slain lamb (Matt. 26:17; Mark 14:12, 14, 16; Luke 22:8, 11, 13, 15; John 18:28; compare 1 Cor. 5:7). John also specifies that the day of the crucifixion was "the preparation of the passover" (19:14), and that the next day, which was Saturday, the Sabbath, "was an high day" (verse 31), that is a Sabbath rendered doubly sacred because of its being also a feast day.

Much has been written by way of attempt to explain this seeming discrepancy. No analysis of the divergent views of Biblical scholars on this subject will be attempted here; the matter is of incidental importance in connection with the fundamental facts of our Lord's betrayal and crucifixion; for brief summaries of opinions and concise arguments the student may be referred to Smith's _Comprehensive Bible Dictionary_, article "Passover"; Edersheim's _Life and Times of Jesus the Messiah_, pp. 480-2, and 566-8; Farrar's _Life of Christ_, Appendix, Excursus 10; Andrews' _Life of our Lord_, and Gresswell's _Dissertations_. Suffice it here to say that the apparent inconsistency may be explained by any of several assumptions. Thus, first, and very probably, the Passover referred to by John, for the eating of which the priests were desirous of keeping themselves free from Levitical defilement, may not have been the supper at which the paschal lamb was eaten, but the supplementary meal, the Chagigah. This later meal, the flesh part of which was designated as a sacrifice, had come to be regarded with veneration equal to that attaching to the paschal supper. Secondly; it is held by many authorities on Jewish antiquities that before, at, and after the time of Christ, two nights were devoted yearly to the paschal observance, during either of which the lamb might be eaten, and that this extension of time had been made in consideration of the increased population, which necessitated the ceremonial slaughtering of more lambs than could be slain on a single day; and in this connection it is interesting to note that Josephus (Wars, vi, ch. 9:3) records the number of lambs slain at a single Passover as 256,500. In the same paragraph, Josephus states that the lambs had to be slain between the ninth and the eleventh hour (3 to 5 p.m.). According to this explanation, Jesus and the

Twelve may have partaken of the passover meal on the first of the two evenings, and the Jews who next day feared defilement may have deferred their observance until the second. Thirdly; the Lord's last paschal supper may have been eaten earlier than the time of general observance, He knowing that night to be His last in mortality. Supporters of this view explain the message to the man who provided the chamber for the last supper, "My time is at hand" (Matt. 26:18) as indicating a special urgency for the passover observance by Christ and the apostles, before the regularly appointed day. Some authorities assert that an error of one day had crept into the Jewish reckoning of time, and that Jesus ate the passover on the true date, while the Jews were a day behind. If "the preparation of the passover" (John 19:14) on Friday, the day of Christ's crucifixion, means the slaughtering of the paschal lambs, our Lord, the real sacrifice of which all earlier altar victims had been but prototypes, died on the cross while the passover lambs were being slain at the temple.

2. Did Judas Iscariot Partake of the Sacrament of the Lord's Supper?--This question cannot be definitely answered from the brief accounts we have of the proceedings at the last supper. At best, only inference, not conclusion, is possible. According to the records made by Matthew and Mark, the Lord's announcement that there was a traitor among the Twelve was made early in the course of the meal; and the institution of the Sacrament occurred later. Luke records the prediction of treachery as following the administering of the sacramental bread and wine. All the synoptists agree that the Sacrament of the Lord's Supper was administered before the sitting at the ordinary meal had broken up; though the Sacrament was plainly made a separate and distinct feature. John (13:2-5) states that the washing of feet occurred when supper was ended, and gives us good reason for inferring that Judas was washed with the rest (verses 10, 11), and that he later (verses 26-30) went out into the night for the purpose of betraying Jesus. The giving of a "sop" to Judas (verses 26, 27) even though supper was practically over, is not inconsistent with John's statement that the supper proper was ended before the washing of feet was performed; the act does not appear to have been so unusual as to cause surprize. To many it has appeared plausible, that because of his utter baseness Judas would not be permitted to participate with the other apostles in the holy ordinance of the Sacrament; others infer that he was allowed to partake, as a possible means of moving him to abandon his evil purpose even at that late hour, or of filling his cup of iniquity to overflowing. The writer's personal opinion is based on the last conception.

3. Washing of Feet.--The ordinance of the washing of feet was reestablished through revelation December 27, 1832. It was made a feature of admission to the school of the prophets, and detailed instructions relating to its administration were given (see Doc. and Cov. 88:140, 141). Further direction as to the ordinances involving washing were revealed January 19, 1841 (see Doc. and Cov. 124:37-39).

4. Discontinuity of the Lord's Last Discourse to the Apostles.--It is certain that part of the discourse following the last supper was delivered in the upper room where Christ and the Twelve had eaten; it is possible that the latter portion was spoken and the prayer offered (John 15, 16, 17) outdoors as Jesus and the Eleven wended their way toward the Mount of Olives. The 14th chapter of John ends with "Arise, let us go hence"; the next chapter opens with another section of the discourse. From Matt 26:30-35, and Mark 14:26-31 we may infer that the prediction of Peter's denial of his Lord was made as the little company walked from the city to the mount. On the other hand, John (18:1) states that "When Jesus had spoken these words", namely, the whole discourse, and the concluding prayer, "he went forth with his disciples over the brook Cedron." Not one of our Lord's sublime utterances on that night of solemn converse with His own, and of communion between Himself and the Father, is affected by the circumstance of place.

5. Gethsemane.--The name means "oil-press" and probably has reference to a mill maintained at the place for the extraction of oil from the olives there cultivated. John refers to the spot as a garden, from which designation we may regard it as an enclosed space of private ownership. That it was a place frequented by Jesus when He sought retirement for prayer, or opportunity for confidential converse with the disciples, is indicated by the same writer (John 18:1, 2).

6. The Bloody Sweat.--Luke, the only Gospel-writer who mentions sweat and blood in connection with our Lord's agony in Gethsemane, states that "his sweat was as it were great drops of blood falling down to the ground" (22:44). Many critical expositors deny that there was an actual extrusion of blood, on the grounds that the evangelist does not positively affirm it, and that the three apostles, who were the only human witnesses, could not have distinguished blood from sweat falling in drops, as they watched from a distance in the night, even if the moon, which at the passover season was full, had been unobscured. Modern scripture removes all doubt. See Doc. and Cov. 19:16-19 quoted in the text (page 613), also 18:11. See further a specific prediction of the bloody sweat, B. of M., Mosiah 3:7.

7. "Suffer Ye thus Far."--Many understand these words, uttered by Jesus as He raised His hand to heal the wounded Malchus, to have been addressed to the disciples, forbidding their further interference. Trench (_Miracles_, 355) considers the meaning to be as follows: 'Hold now; thus far ye have gone in resistance, but let it be no further; no more of this.' The disputed interpretation is of little importance as to the bearing of the incident on the events that followed.

8. The Cup as a Symbol.--Our Lord's frequent mention of His foreseen sufferings as the cup of which the Father would have Him drink (Matt. 26:39, 42; Mark 14:36; Luke 22:42; John 18:11; compare Matt. 20:22; Mark 10:38; 1 Cor. 10:21) is in line with Old Testament usage of the term "cup" as a symbolic expression for a bitter or poisonous potion typifying experiences of suffering. See Psa. 11:6; 75:8; Isa. 51:17, 22; Jer. 25:15, 17; 49:12. In contrast, the opposite meaning is attached to the use of the term in some passages, e.g. Psa. 16:5; 23:5; 116:13; Jer. 16:7.

FOOTNOTES:

[1179] Matt. 26:3-5; see also Mark 14:1; Luke 22:1, 2.
[1180] Revised version of Matt. 26:5 reads: "Not during the feast, lest there be a tumult among the people."
[1181] John 7:30, 44, 45-53; 11:47-57.
[1182] Matt. 26:14-16; Mark 14:10, 11; Luke 22:3-6.
[1183] Matt. 26:15. The revised version reads: "And they weighed unto him thirty pieces of silver." Compare Zech. 11:12.
[1184] Exo. 21:32; Zech. 11:12, 13.
[1185] Matt. 27:3-10.
[1186] Matt. 26:17.
[1187] Note 1, end of chapter.
[1188] Matt. 26:17-19; Mark 14:12-16; Luke 22:7-13.
[1189] It should be remembered that the Jews counted their days as beginning at sunset, not, as with us, at midnight.
[1190] Note 2, end of chapter.
[1191] Luke 22:24-30.
[1192] Luke 14:7-11; see page 449 herein.
[1193] Luke 22:28; see page 133 herein.
[1194] John 13:1-20.
[1195] Note 3, end of chapter.
[1196] The Lord's expression "neither he that is sent greater than he that sent him" (John 13:16) is more correctly rendered "neither the apostle than he that sent him" (revised version, margin); see pages 228, 229 herein.
[1197] Matt. 26:26-29; Mark 14:22-25; Luke 22:19, 20.
[1198] In the revised version we read "covenant" instead of "testament" in Matt. 26:28, and in parallel passages.
[1199] 1 Cor. 11:23-34.
[1200] B. of M., 3 Nephi 18:6-11; Doc. and Cov. 20:75; see also the "Articles of Faith," ix.
[1201] See "The Great Apostasy" 8:15-19.
[1202] John 13:18-30.
[1203] Compare Psalm 41:9.
[1204] John 13:31-34.
[1205] Lev. 19:18.
[1206] So reads the revised version of Luke 22:32.
[1207] Isa. 53:12; compare Mark 15:28.
[1208] Read John 13:36-38; Luke 22:31-38; compare Matt. 26:31-35; Mark 14: 27-31.
[1209] John, chaps. 14, 15, 16.
[1210] John 14:1-4.
[1211] See "The Articles of Faith," iv:28, 29; and xxii:16-27.
[1212] John 14:13, 14; compare 16:24.
[1213] John 14:15-20; compare verse 26; and 15:26.
[1214] Matt. 10:3, and Luke 6:16; also page 224 herein.
[1215] See "Articles of Faith," ii:20-24; page 127 herein.
[1216] John 14:22-31.
[1217] John 15:1-8.
[1218] Revised version, "cleanseth it."
[1219] John 15:9-17.
[1220] John 15:18-27.
[1221] Verse 25; compare Psalms 35:19; 69:4; 109:3.
[1222] John 16:13-15; read verses 1-15.
[1223] John 16:16; compare 7:33; 13:33; 14:19.
[1224] John 16:17, 23, 24; read verses 17-28.
[1225] Matt. 26:31; Mark 14:27; compare Zech. 13:7; see also Matt. 11:6.
[1226] Matt. 26:31-35; Mark 14:29-31.
[1227] Matt. 26:32; Mark 14:28; compare 16:7.
[1228] John 16:33.
[1229] John 17.
[1230] Note 4, end of chapter.
[1231] Matt. 26:36-46; Mark 14:32-42; Luke 22:39-46.
[1232] Note 5, end of chapter.
[1233] "Abba" is expressive of combined affection and honor, and signifies "Father." It is applied to the Eternal Father by Jesus in the passage above, and by Paul (Rom. 8:15; Gal. 4:6).
[1234] Note 6, end of chapter.
[1235] John 13:37; Matt. 20:22; Mark 10:38, 39.
[1236] John 5:26, 27; and 10:17, 18; also page 418 herein.
[1237] John 14:30.
[1238] Page 127.

[1239] Doc. and Cov. 19:16-19; compare 18:11. See also B. of M., 2 Nephi 9:5, 7, 21; Mosiah 3:7-14; 15:12; Alma 7:11-13; 11:40; 22:14; 34:8-15; 3 Nephi 11:11; 27:14, 15; and chapter 4 herein.

[1240] Matt. 26:47-56; Mark 14:43-52; Luke 22:47-53; John 18:1-12.

[1241] "Cohort," a term descriptive of a Roman body, and "military tribune" are more literal renderings of the Greek original than "band" and "captain" in John 18:3, 12. See revised version, margin.

[1242] The Greek text of Matt. 26:49, and Mark 14:45 clearly implies that Judas "kissed him much," that is many times, or effusively. See margin of revised version. [1243] This is a more nearly correct translation than "wherefore art thou come?" in the common version. See revised version. Matt. 26:50.

[1244] John 18:9; compare 17:12.

[1245] See "The Great Apostasy," chaps. 4 and 5.

[1246] Note 7, end of chapter.

[1247] Compare Isa. 53:8.

[1248] Note 8, end of chapter.

CHAPTER 34. THE TRIAL AND CONDEMNATION.

THE JEWISH TRIAL.

From Gethsemane the bound and captive Christ was haled before the Jewish rulers. John alone informs us that the Lord was taken first to Annas, who sent Him, still bound, to Caiaphas, the high priest; [1249] the synoptists record the arraignment before Caiaphas only.[1250] No details of the interview with Annas are of record; and the bringing of Jesus before him at all was as truly irregular and illegal, according to Hebrew law, as were all the subsequent proceedings of that night. Annas, who was father-in-law to Caiaphas, had been deposed from the high-priestly office over twenty years before; but throughout this period he had exerted a potent influence in all the affairs of the hierarchy.[1251] Caiaphas, as John is careful to remind us, "was he, which gave counsel to the Jews, that it was expedient that one man should die for the people."[1252]

At the palace of Caiaphas, the chief priests, scribes, and elders of the people were assembled, in a meeting of the Sanhedrin, informal or otherwise, all eagerly awaiting the result of the expedition led by Judas. When Jesus, the object of their bitter hatred and their predetermined victim, was brought in, a bound Prisoner, He was immediately put upon trial in contravention of the law, both written and traditional, of which those congregated rulers of the Jews professed to be such zealous supporters. No legal hearing on a capital charge could lawfully be held except in the appointed and official courtroom of the Sanhedrin. From the account given in the fourth Gospel we infer that the Prisoner was first subjected to an interrogative examination by the high priest in person.[1253] That functionary, whether Annas or Caiaphas is a matter of inference, inquired of Jesus concerning His disciples and His doctrines. Such a preliminary inquiry was utterly unlawful; for the Hebrew code provided that the accusing witnesses in any cause before the court should define their charge against the accused, and that the latter should be protected from any effort to make him testify against himself. The Lord's reply should have been a sufficient protest to the high priest against further illegal procedure. "Jesus answered him, I spake openly to the world; I ever taught in the synagogue, and in the temple, whither the Jews always resort; and in secret have I said nothing. Why askest thou me?--ask them which heard me, what I have said unto them: behold, they know what I said." This was a lawful objection against denying to a prisoner on trial his right to be confronted by his accusers. It was received with open disdain; and one of the officers who stood by, hoping perhaps to curry favor with his superiors, actually struck Jesus a vicious blow,[1254] accompanied by the question, "Answerest thou the high priest so?" To this cowardly assault the Lord replied with almost superhuman gentleness:[1255] "If I have spoken evil, bear witness of the evil: but if well, why smitest thou me?" Combined with submissiveness, however, this constituted another appeal to the principles of justice; if what Jesus had said was evil, why did not the assailant accuse Him; and if He had spoken well, what right had a police officer to judge, condemn, and punish, and that too in the presence of the high priest? Law and justice had been dethroned that night.

"Now the chief priests, and elders, and all the council, sought false witness against Jesus, to put him to death."[1256] Whether "all the council" means a legal quorum, which would be twenty-three or more, or a full attendance of the seventy-two Sanhedrists, is of small importance. Any sitting of the Sanhedrin at night, and more particularly for the consideration of a capital charge, was directly in violation of Jewish law. Likewise was it unlawful for the council to consider such a charge on a Sabbath, a feast day, or on the eve of any such day. In the Sanhedrin, every member was a judge; the judicial body was to hear the testimony, and, according to that testimony and nought else, render a decision on every case duly presented. The accusers were required to appear in person; and they were to receive a preliminary warning against bearing false witness. Every defendant was to be regarded and treated as innocent until convicted in due course. But in the so-called trial of Jesus, the judges not only sought witnesses, but specifically tried to find false witnesses. Though many false witnesses came, yet there was no "witness" or testimony against the Prisoner, for the suborned perjurers failed to agree among themselves; and even the lawless Sanhedrists hesitated to openly violate the fundamental requirement that at least two concordant witnesses must testify against an accused person, for, otherwise, the case had to be dismissed.

That Jesus was to be convicted on some charge or other, and be put to death, had been already determined by the priestly judges; their failure to find witnesses against Him threatened to delay the carrying out of their nefarious scheme. Haste and precipitancy characterized their procedure throughout; they had unlawfully caused Jesus to be arrested at night; they were illegally going through the semblance of a trial at night; their purpose was to convict the Prisoner in time to have Him brought before the Roman authorities as early as possible in the morning--as a criminal duly tried and adjudged worthy of death. The lack of two hostile witnesses who would tell the same falsehoods was a serious hindrance. But, "at the last came two false witnesses, and said, This fellow said, I am able to destroy the temple of God, and to build it in three days." Others, however, testified: "We heard him say, I will destroy this temple that is made with hands, and within three days I will build another made without hands."[1257] And so, as Mark observes, even in this particular their "witness" or testimony did not agree. Surely in a case at bar, such discrepancy as appears between "I am able to" and "I will," as alleged utterances of the accused, is of vital importance. Yet this semblance of formal accusation was the sole basis of a charge against Christ up to this stage of the trial. It will be remembered that in connection with the first clearing of the temple, near the commencement of Christ's ministry, He had answered the clamorous demand of the Jews for a sign of His authority by saying "Destroy this temple, and in three days I will raise it up." He spoke not at all of Himself as the one who would destroy; the Jews were to be the destroyers, He the restorer. But the inspired writer is particular to explain that Jesus "spake of the temple of his body," and not at all of those buildings reared by man.

[1258]
One may reasonably inquire as to what serious import could be attached to even such a declaration as the perjured witnesses claimed to have heard from the lips of Christ. The veneration with which the Jews professed to regard the Holy House, however wantonly they profaned its precincts, offers a partial but insufficient answer. The plan of the conspiring rulers appears to have been that of convicting Christ on a charge of sedition, making Him out to be a dangerous disturber of the nation's peace, an assailant of established institutions, and consequently an inciter of opposition against the vassal autonomy of the Jewish nation, and the supreme dominion of Rome.[1259]
The vaguely defined shadow of legal accusation produced by the dark and inconsistent testimony of the false witnesses, was enough to embolden the iniquitous court. Caiaphas, rising from his seat to give dramatic emphasis to his question, demanded of Jesus: "Answerest thou nothing? what is it which these witness against thee?" There was nothing to answer. No consistent or valid testimony had been presented against Him; therefore He stood in dignified silence. Then Caiaphas, in violation of the legal proscription against requiring any person to testify in his own case except voluntarily and on his own initiative, not only demanded an answer from the Prisoner, but exercized the potent prerogative of the high-priestly office, to put the accused under oath, as a witness before the sacerdotal court. "And the high priest answered and said unto him, I adjure thee by the living God, that thou tell us whether thou be the Christ, the Son of God."[1260] The fact of a distinct specification of "the Christ" and "the Son of God" is significant, in that it implies the Jewish expectation of a Messiah, but does not acknowledge that He was to be distinctively of divine origin. Nothing that had gone before can be construed as a proper foundation for this inquiry. The charge of sedition was about to be superseded by one of greater enormity--that of blasphemy.
[1261]
To the utterly unjust yet official adjuration of the high priest, Jesus answered: "Thou hast said: nevertheless I say unto you: Hereafter shall ye see the Son of man sitting on the right hand of power, and coming in the clouds of heaven." This expression "Thou hast said" was equivalent to--I am what thou hast said.[1262] It was an unqualified avowal of divine parentage, and inherent Godship. "Then the high priest rent his clothes, saying, He hath spoken blasphemy; what further need have we of witnesses? behold, now ye have heard his blasphemy. What think ye? They answered and said, He is guilty of death."[1263]
Thus the judges in Israel, comprizing the high priest, the chief priests, the scribes and elders of the people, the Great Sanhedrin, unlawfully assembled, decreed that the Son of God was deserving of death, on no evidence save that of His own acknowledgment. By express provision the Jewish code forbade the conviction, specifically on a capital charge, of any person on his own confession, unless that was amply supported by the testimony of trustworthy witnesses. As in the Garden of Gethsemane Jesus had voluntarily surrendered Himself, so before the judges did He personally and voluntarily furnish the evidence upon which they unrighteously declared Him deserving of death. There could be no crime in the claim of Messiahship or divine Sonship, except that claim was false. We vainly search the record for even an intimation that inquiry was made or suggested as to the grounds upon which Jesus based His exalted claims. The action of the high priest in rending his garments was a dramatic affectation of pious horror at the blasphemy with which his ears had been assailed. It was expressly forbidden in the law that the high priest rend his clothes;[1264] but from extra-scriptural writings we learn that the rending of garments as an attestation of most grievous guilt, such as that of blasphemy, was allowable under traditional rule.[1265] There is no indication that the vote of the judges was taken and recorded in the precise and orderly manner required by the law.
Jesus stood convicted of the most heinous offense known in Jewry. However unjustly, He had been pronounced guilty of blasphemy by the supreme tribunal of the nation. In strict accuracy we cannot say that the Sanhedrists sentenced Christ to death, inasmuch as the power to authoritatively pronounce capital sentences had been taken from the Jewish council by Roman decree. The high-priestly court, however, decided that Jesus was worthy of death, and so certified when they handed Him over to Pilate. In their excess of malignant hate, Israel's judges abandoned their Lord to the wanton will of the attendant varlets, who heaped upon Him every indignity their brutish instincts could suggest. They spurted their foul spittle into His face;[1266] and then, having blindfolded Him, amused themselves by smiting Him again and again, saying the while: "Prophesy unto us, thou Christ, Who is he that smote thee?" The miscreant crowd mocked Him, and railed upon Him with jeers and taunts, and branded themselves as blasphemers in fact.
[1267]
The law and the practise of the time required that any person found guilty of a capital offense, after due trial before a Jewish tribunal, should be given a second trial on the following day; and at this later hearing any or all of the judges who had before voted for conviction could reverse themselves; but no one who had once voted for acquittal could change his ballot. A bare majority was sufficient for acquittal, but more than a majority was required for conviction. By a provision that must appear to us most unusual, if all the judges voted for conviction on a capital charge the verdict was not to stand and the accused had to be set at liberty; for, it was argued, a unanimous vote against a prisoner indicated that he had had no friend or defender in court, and that the judges might have been in conspiracy against Him. Under this rule in Hebrew jurisprudence the verdict against Jesus, rendered at the illegal night session of the Sanhedrists, was void, for we are specifically told that "they all condemned him to be guilty of death."[1268]
Apparently for the purpose of establishing a shadowy pretext of legality in their procedure, the Sanhedrists adjourned to meet again in early daylight. Thus they technically complied with the requirement--that on every case in which the death sentence had been decreed the court should hear and judge a second time in a later session--but they completely ignored the equally mandatory provision that the second trial must be conducted on the day following that of the first hearing. Between the two sittings on

consecutive days the judges were required to fast and pray, and to give the case on trial calm and earnest consideration.

Luke, who records no details of the night trial of Jesus, is the only Gospel-writer to give place to a circumstantial report of the morning session. He says: "And as soon as it was day, the elders of the people and the chief priests and the scribes came together, and led him into their council."[1269] Some Biblical scholars have construed the expression, "led him into their council," as signifying that Jesus was condemned by the Sanhedrin in the appointed meeting-place of the court, viz. Gazith or the Hall of Hewn Stones, as the law of the time required; but against this we have the statement of John that they led Jesus directly from Caiaphas to the Roman hall of judgment.[1270]

It is probable, that at this early daylight session, the irregular proceedings of the dark hours were approved, and the details of further procedure decided upon. They "took counsel against Jesus to put him to death"; nevertheless they went through the form of a second trial, the issue of which was greatly facilitated by the Prisoner's voluntary affirmations. The judges stand without semblance of justification for calling upon the Accused to testify; they should have examined anew the witnesses against Him. The first question put to Him was, "Art thou the Christ? tell us." The Lord made dignified reply: "If I tell you, ye will not believe: and if I also ask you, ye will not answer me, nor let me go. Hereafter shall the Son of man sit on the right hand of the power of God." Neither did the question imply nor the answer furnish cause for condemnation. The whole nation was looking for the Messiah; and if Jesus claimed to be He, the only proper judicial action would be that of inquiring into the merit of the claim. The crucial question followed immediately: "Art thou then the Son of God? And he said unto them, Ye say that I am. And they said, What need we any further witness? for we ourselves have heard of his own mouth."[1271]

Jehovah was convicted of blasphemy against Jehovah. The only mortal Being to whom the awful crime of blasphemy, in claiming divine attributes and powers, was impossible, stood before the judges of Israel condemned as a blasphemer. The "whole council," by which expression we may possibly understand a legal quorum, was concerned in the final action. Thus ended the miscalled "trial" of Jesus before the high-priest and elders[1272] of His people. "And straightway in the morning the chief priests held a consultation with the elders and scribes and the whole council, and bound Jesus, and carried him away, and delivered him to Pilate."[1273] During the few hours that remained to Him in mortality, He would be in the hands of the Gentiles, betrayed and delivered up by His own.[1274]

PETER'S DENIAL OF HIS LORD.[1275]

When Jesus was taken into custody in the Garden of Gethsemane, all the Eleven forsook Him and fled. This is not to be accounted as certain evidence of cowardice, for the Lord had indicated that they should go.[1276] Peter and at least one other disciple followed afar off; and, after the armed guard had entered the palace of the high priest with their Prisoner, Peter "went in, and sat with the servants to see the end." He was assisted in securing admittance by the unnamed disciple, who was on terms of acquaintanceship with the high priest. That other disciple was in all probability John, as may be inferred from the fact that he is mentioned only in the fourth Gospel, the author of which characteristically refers to himself anonymously.[1277]

While Jesus was before the Sanhedrists, Peter remained below with the servants. The attendant at the door was a young woman; her feminine suspicions had been aroused when she admitted Peter, and as he sat with a crowd in the palace court she came up, and having intently observed him, said: "Thou also wast with Jesus of Galilee." But Peter denied, averring he did not know Jesus. Peter was restless; his conscience and the fear of identification as one of the Lord's disciples troubled him. He left the crowd and sought partial seclusion in the porch; but there another maid spied him out, and said to those nearby: "This fellow was also with Jesus of Nazareth"; to which accusation Peter replied with an oath: "I do not know the man."

The April night was chilly, and an open fire had been made in the hall or court of the palace. Peter sat with others at the fire, thinking, perhaps, that brazen openness was better than skulking caution as a possible safeguard against detection. About an hour after his former denials, some of the men around the fire charged him with being a disciple of Jesus, and referred to his Galilean dialect as evidence that he was at least a fellow countryman with the high priest's Prisoner; but, most threatening of all, a kinsman of Malchus, whose ear Peter had slashed with the sword, asked peremptorily: "Did not I see thee in the garden with him?" Then Peter went so far in the course of falsehood upon which he had entered as to curse and swear, and to vehemently declare for the third time, "I know not the man." As the last profane falsehood left his lips, the clear notes of a crowing cock broke upon his ears,[1278] and the remembrance of his Lord's prediction welled up in his mind. Trembling in wretched realization of his perfidious cowardice, he turned from the crowd and met the gaze of the suffering Christ, who from the midst of the insolent mob looked into the face of His boastful, yet loving but weak apostle. Hastening from the palace, Peter went out into the night, weeping bitterly. As his later life attests, his tears were those of real contrition and true repentance.

CHRIST'S FIRST APPEARANCE BEFORE PILATE.

As we have already learned, no Jewish tribunal had authority to inflict the death penalty; imperial Rome had reserved this prerogative as her own. The united acclaim of the Sanhedrists, that Jesus was deserving of death, would be ineffective until sanctioned by the emperor's deputy, who at that time was Pontius Pilate, the governor, or more properly, procurator, of Judea, Samaria, and Idumea. Pilate maintained his official residence at Cæsarea,[1279] on the Mediterranean shore; but it was his custom to be present in Jerusalem at the times of the great Hebrew feasts, probably in the interest of preserving order, or of promptly quelling any disturbance amongst the vast and heterogeneous multitudes by which the city was thronged on these festive occasions. The governor with his attendants was in Jerusalem at this momentous Passover season. Early on Friday morning, the "whole council," that is to say, the Sanhedrin, led Jesus, bound, to the judgment hall of Pontius Pilate; but with strict scrupulosity they refrained from entering the hall lest they become defiled; for the judgment chamber was part of the house of a Gentile, and somewhere therein might be leavened bread, even to be near which would render them ceremonially unclean. Let every one designate for himself the character of men afraid of the mere proximity of leaven, while thirsting for innocent blood!

In deference to their scruples Pilate came out from the palace; and, as they delivered up to him their Prisoner, asked: "What accusation bring ye against this man?" The question, though strictly proper and judicially necessary, surprized and disappointed the priestly rulers, who evidently had expected that the governor would simply approve their verdict as a matter of form and give sentence accordingly; but instead of doing so, Pilate was apparently about to exercize his authority of original jurisdiction. With poorly concealed chagrin, their spokesman, probably Caiaphas, answered: "If he were not a malefactor, we would not have delivered him up unto thee." It was now Pilate's turn to feel or at least to feign umbrage, and he replied in effect: Oh, very well; if you don't care to present the charge in proper order, take ye him, and judge him according to your law; don't trouble me with the matter. But the Jews rejoined: "It is not lawful for us to put any man to death."

John the apostle intimates in this last remark a determination on the part of the Jews to have Jesus put to death not only by Roman sanction but by Roman executioners;[1280] for, as we readily may see, had Pilate approved the death sentence and handed the Prisoner over to the Jews for its infliction, Jesus would have been stoned, in accordance with the Hebrew penalty for blasphemy; whereas the Lord had plainly foretold that His death would be by crucifixion, which was a Roman method of execution, but one never practised by the Jews. Furthermore, if Jesus had been put to death by the Jewish rulers, even with governmental sanction, an insurrection among the people might have resulted, for there were many who believed on Him. The crafty hierarchs were determined to bring about His death under Roman condemnation.

"And they began to accuse him, saying, We found this fellow perverting the nation, and forbidding to give tribute to C┤ᵉsar, saying that he himself is Christ a King."[1281] It is important to note that no accusation of blasphemy was made to Pilate; had such been presented, the governor, thoroughly pagan in heart and mind, would probably have dismissed the charge as utterly unworthy of a hearing; for Rome with her many gods, whose number was being steadily increased by current heathen deification of mortals, knew no such offense as blasphemy in the Jewish sense. The accusing Sanhedrists hesitated not to substitute for blasphemy, which was the greatest crime known to the Hebrew code, the charge of high treason, which was the gravest offense listed in the Roman category of crimes. To the vociferous accusations of the chief priests and elders, the calm and dignified Christ deigned no reply. To them He had spoken for the last time--until the appointed season of another trial, in which He shall be the Judge, and they the prisoners at the bar.

Pilate was surprized at the submissive yet majestic demeanor of Jesus; there was certainly much that was kingly about the Man; never before had such a One stood before him. The charge, however, was a serious one; men who claimed title to kingship might prove dangerous to Rome; yet to the charge the Accused answered nothing. Entering the judgment hall, Pilate had Jesus called.[1282] That some of the disciples, and among them almost certainly John, also went in, is apparent from the detailed accounts of the proceedings preserved in the fourth Gospel. Anyone was at liberty to enter, for publicity was an actual and a widely proclaimed feature of Roman trials.

Pilate, plainly without animosity or prejudice against Jesus, asked: "Art thou the King of the Jews? Jesus answered him, Sayest thou this thing of thyself, or did others tell it thee of me?" The Lord's counter-question, as Pilate's rejoinder shows, meant, and was understood to mean, as we might state it: Do you ask this in the Roman and literal sense--as to whether I am a king of an earthly kingdom--or with the Jewish and more spiritual meaning? A direct answer "Yes" would have been true in the Messianic sense, but untrue in the worldly signification; and "No" could have been inversely construed as true or untrue. "Pilate answered, Am I a Jew? Thine own nation and the chief priests have delivered thee unto me: what hast thou done? Jesus answered, My kingdom is not of this world: if my kingdom were of this world, then would my servants fight, that I should not be delivered to the Jews: but now is my kingdom not from hence. Pilate therefore said unto him, Art thou a king then? Jesus answered, Thou sayest that I am a king. To this end was I born, and for this cause came I into the world, that I should bear witness unto the truth. Every one that is of the truth heareth my voice."

It was clear to the Roman governor that this wonderful Man, with His exalted views of a kingdom not of this world, and an empire of truth in which He was to reign, was no political insurrectionist; and that to consider Him a menace to Roman institutions would be absurd. Those last words--about truth-- were of all the most puzzling; Pilate was restive, and perhaps a little frightened under their import. "What is truth?" he rather exclaimed in apprehension than inquired in expectation of an answer, as he started to leave the hall. To the Jews without he announced officially the acquittal of the Prisoner. "I find in him no fault at all" was the verdict.

But the chief priests and scribes and elders of the people were undeterred. Their thirst for the blood of the Holy One had developed into mania. Wildly and fiercely they shrieked: "He stirreth up the people, teaching throughout all Jewry, beginning from Galilee to this place." The mention of Galilee suggested to Pilate a new course of procedure. Having confirmed by inquiry that Jesus was a Galilean, he determined to send the Prisoner to Herod, the vassal ruler of that province, who was in Jerusalem at the time.[1283] By this action Pilate hoped to rid himself of further responsibility in the case, and moreover, Herod, with whom he had been at enmity, might be placated thereby.

CHRIST BEFORE HEROD.[1284]

Herod Antipas, the degenerate son of his infamous sire, Herod the Great,[1285] was at this time tetrarch of Galilee and Perea, and by popular usage, though without imperial sanction, was flatteringly called king. He it was who, in fulfilment of an unholy vow inspired by a woman's voluptuous blandishments, had ordered the murder of John the Baptist. He ruled as a Roman vassal, and professed to be orthodox in the observances of Judaism. He had come up to Jerusalem, in state, to keep the feast of the Passover. Herod was pleased to have Jesus sent to him by Pilate; for, not only was the action a gracious one on the part of the procurator, constituting as after events proved a preliminary to reconciliation between the two rulers,[1286] but it was a means of gratifying Herod's curiosity to see Jesus, of whom he had heard so much, whose fame had terrified him, and by whom he now hoped to see some interesting miracle wrought. [1287]

Whatever fear Herod had once felt regarding Jesus, whom he had superstitiously thought to be the reincarnation of his murdered victim, John the Baptist, was replaced by amused interest when he saw the far-famed Prophet of Galilee in bonds before him, attended by a Roman guard, and accompanied by ecclesiastical officials. Herod began to question the Prisoner; but Jesus remained silent. The chief priests and scribes vehemently voiced their accusations; but not a word was uttered by the Lord. Herod is the only character in history to whom Jesus is known to have applied a personal epithet of contempt. "Go ye and tell that fox" He once said to certain Pharisees who had come to Him with the story that Herod intended to kill Him.[1288] As far as we know, Herod is further distinguished as the only being who saw Christ face to face and spoke to Him, yet never heard His voice. For penitent sinners, weeping women, prattling children, for the scribes, the Pharisees, the Sadducees, the rabbis, for the perjured high priest and his obsequious and insolent underling, and for Pilate the pagan, Christ had words--of comfort or instruction, of warning or rebuke, of protest or denunciation--yet for Herod the fox He had but disdainful and kingly silence. Thoroughly piqued, Herod turned from insulting questions to acts of malignant derision. He and his men-at-arms made sport of the suffering Christ, "set him at nought and mocked him"; then in travesty they "arrayed him in a gorgeous robe and sent him again to Pilate."[1289] Herod had found nothing in Jesus to warrant condemnation.

CHRIST AGAIN BEFORE PILATE.[1290]

The Roman procurator, finding that he could not evade further consideration of the case, "called together the chief priests and the rulers and the people," and "said unto them, Ye have brought this man unto me, as one that perverteth the people: and, behold, I, having examined him before you, have found no fault in this man touching those things whereof ye accuse him; No, nor yet Herod: for I sent you to him; and, lo, nothing worthy of death is done unto him. I will therefore chastise him, and release him." Pilate's desire to save Jesus from death was just and genuine; his intention of scourging the Prisoner, whose innocence he had affirmed and reaffirmed, was an infamous concession to Jewish prejudice. He knew that the charge of sedition and treason was without foundation; and that even the framing of such an accusation by the Jewish hierarchy, whose simulated loyalty to C⊦sar was but a cloak for inherent and undying hatred, was ridiculous in the extreme; and he fully realized that the priestly rulers had delivered Jesus into his hands because of envy and malice.[1291]

It was the custom for the governor at the Passover season to pardon and release any one condemned prisoner whom the people might name. On that day there lay in durance, awaiting execution, "a notable prisoner, called Barabbas," who had been found guilty of sedition, in that he had incited the people to insurrection, and had committed murder. This man stood convicted of the very charge on which Pilate specifically and Herod by implication had pronounced Jesus innocent, and Barabbas was a murderer in addition. Pilate thought to pacify the priests and people by releasing Jesus as the subject of Passover leniency; this would be a tacit recognition of Christ's conviction before the ecclesiastical court, and practically an endorsement of the death sentence, superseded by official pardon. Therefore he asked of them: "Whom will ye that I release unto you? Barabbas, or Jesus which is called Christ?" There appears to have been a brief interval between Pilate's question and the people's answer, during which the chief priests and elders busied themselves amongst the multitude, urging them to demand the release of the insurrectionist and murderer. So, when Pilate reiterated the question: "Whether of the twain will ye that I release unto you?" assembled Israel cried "Barabbas." Pilate, surprized, disappointed, and angered, then asked: "What shall I do then with Jesus which is called Christ? They all say unto him, Let him be crucified. And the governor said, Why, what evil hath he done? But they cried out the more, saying, Let him be crucified."

The Roman governor was sorely troubled and inwardly afraid. To add to his perplexity he received a warning message from his wife, even as he sat on the judgment seat: "Have thou nothing to do with that just man: for I have suffered many things this day in a dream because of him." Those who know not God are characteristically superstitious. Pilate feared to think what dread portent his wife's dream might presage. But, finding that he could not prevail, and foreseeing a tumult among the people if he persisted in the defense of Christ, he called for water and washed his hands before the multitude--a symbolic act of disclaiming responsibility, which they all understood--proclaiming the while: "I am innocent of the blood of this just person: see ye to it." Then rose that awful self-condemnatory cry of the covenant people: "His blood be on us and on our children." History bears an appalling testimony to the literal fulfilment of that dread invocation.[1292] Pilate released Barabbas, and gave Jesus into the custody of the soldiers to be scourged.

Scourging was a frightful preliminary to death on the cross. The instrument of punishment was a whip of many thongs, loaded with metal and edged with jagged pieces of bone. Instances are of record in which the condemned died under the lash and so escaped the horrors of living crucifixion. In accordance with the brutal customs of the time, Jesus, weak and bleeding from the fearful scourging He had undergone, was given over to the half-savage soldiers for their amusement. He was no ordinary victim, so the whole band came together in the Pretorium, or great hall of the palace, to take part in the diabolical sport. They stripped Jesus of His outer raiment, and placed upon Him a purple robe.[1293] Then with a sense of fiendish realism they platted a crown of thorns, and placed it about the Sufferer's brows; a reed was put into His right hand as a royal scepter; and, as they bowed in a mockery of homage, they saluted Him with: "Hail, King of the Jews!" Snatching away the reed or rod, they brutally smote Him with it upon the head, driving the cruel thorns into His quivering flesh; they slapped Him with their hands, and spat upon Him in vile and vicious abandonment.[1294]

Pilate had probably been a silent observer of this barbarous scene. He stopped it, and determined to make another attempt to touch the springs of Jewish pity, if such existed. He went outside, and to the multitude said: "Behold, I bring him forth to you, that ye may know that I find no fault in him." This was the governor's third definite proclamation of the Prisoner's innocence. "Then came Jesus forth, wearing the crown of thorns, and the purple robe. And Pilate saith unto them, Behold the man!"[1295] Pilate seems to have counted on the pitiful sight of the scourged and bleeding Christ to soften the hearts of the maddened Jews. But the effect failed. Think of the awful fact--a heathen, a pagan, who knew not God, pleading with the priests and people of Israel for the life of their Lord and King! When, unmoved by the sight, the chief priests and officers cried with increasing vindictiveness, "crucify him, crucify him," Pilate pronounced the fatal sentence, "Take ye him and crucify him," but added with bitter emphasis: "I find no fault in him."

It will be remembered that the only charge preferred against Christ before the Roman governor was that of sedition; the Jewish persecutors had carefully avoided even the mention of blasphemy, which was the offense for which they had adjudged Jesus worthy of death. Now that sentence of crucifixion had been extorted from Pilate, they brazenly attempted to make it appear that the governor's mandate was but a ratification of their own decree of death; therefore they said: "We have a law, and by our law he ought to die, because he made himself the Son of God." What did it mean? That awe-inspiring title, Son of God, struck yet deeper into Pilate's troubled conscience. Once more he took Jesus into the judgment hall, and in trepidation asked, "Whence art thou?" The inquiry was as to whether Jesus was human or superhuman. A direct avowal of the Lord's divinity would have frightened but could not have enlightened the heathen ruler; therefore Jesus gave no answer. Pilate was further surprized, and perhaps somewhat offended at this seeming disregard of his authority. He demanded an explanation, saying: "Speakest thou not unto me? knowest thou not that I have power to crucify thee, and have power to release thee?" Then Jesus replied: "Thou couldest have no power at all against me, except it were given thee from above: therefore he that delivered me unto thee hath the greater sin." The positions were reversed; Christ was the Judge, and Pilate the subject of His decision. Though not found guiltless, the Roman was pronounced less culpable than he or those who had forced Jesus into his power, and who had demanded of him an unrighteous committal.

The governor, though having pronounced sentence, yet sought means of releasing the submissive Sufferer. His first evidence of wavering was greeted by the Jews with the cry, "If thou let this man go, thou art not Cæsar's friend: whosoever maketh himself a king speaketh against Cæsar." Pilate took his place in the judgment seat, which was set up in the place of the Pavement, or Gabbatha, outside the hall. He was resentful against those Jews who had dared to intimate that he was no friend of Cæsar, and whose intimation might lead to an embassy of complaint being sent to Rome to misrepresent him in exaggerated accusation. Pointing to Jesus, he exclaimed with unveiled sarcasm: "Behold your King!" But the Jews answered in threatening and ominous shouts: "Away with him, away with him, crucify him." In stinging reminder of their national subjugation, Pilate asked with yet more cutting irony, "Shall I crucify your King?" And the chief priests cried aloud: "We have no king but Cæsar."

Even so was it and was to be. The people who had by covenant accepted Jehovah as their King, now rejected Him in Person, and acknowledged no sovereign but Cæsar. Cæsar's subjects and serfs have they been through all the centuries since. Pitiable is the state of man or nation who in heart and spirit will have no king but Cæsar![1296]

Wherein lay the cause of Pilate's weakness? He was the emperor's representative, the imperial procurator with power to crucify or to save; officially he was an autocrat. His conviction of Christ's blamelessness and his desire to save Him from the cross are beyond question. Why did Pilate waver, hesitate, vacillate, and at length yield contrary to his conscience and his will? Because, after all, he was more slave than freeman. He was in servitude to his past. He knew that should complaint be made of him at Rome, his corruption and cruelties, his extortions and the unjustifiable slaughter he had caused would all be brought against him. He was the Roman ruler, but the people over whom he exercized official dominion delighted in seeing him cringe, when they cracked, with vicious snap above his head, the whip of a threatened report about him to his imperial master, Tiberius.[1297]

JUDAS ISCARIOT.[1298]

When Judas Iscariot saw how terribly effective had been the outcome of his treachery, he became wildly remorseful. During Christ's trial before the Jewish authorities, with its associated humiliation and cruelty, the traitor had seen the seriousness of his action; and when the unresisting Sufferer had been delivered up to the Romans, and the fatal consummation had become a certainty, the enormity of his crime filled Judas with nameless horror. Rushing into the presence of the chief priests and elders, while the final preparations for the crucifixion of the Lord were in progress, he implored the priestly rulers to take back the accursed wage they had paid him, crying in an agony of despair: "I have sinned, in that I have betrayed the innocent blood." He may have vaguely expected a word of sympathy from the conspirators in whose wickedly skilful hands he had been so ready and serviceable a tool; possibly he hoped that his avowal might stem the current of their malignancy, and that they would ask for a reversal of the sentence. But the rulers in Israel repulsed him with disgust. "What is that to us?" they sneered, "see thou to that." He had served their purpose; they had paid him his price; they wished never to look upon his face again; and pitilessly they flung him back into the haunted blackness of his maddened conscience. Still clutching the bag of silver, the all too real remembrancer of his frightful sin, he rushed into the temple, penetrating even to the precincts of priestly reservation, and dashed the silver pieces upon the floor of the sanctuary.[1299] Then, under the goading impulse of his master, the devil, to whom he had become a bond-slave, body and soul, he went out and hanged himself.

The chief priests gathered up the pieces of silver, and in sacrilegious scrupulosity, held a solemn council to determine what they should do with the "price of blood." As they deemed it unlawful to add the attainted coin to the sacred treasury, they bought with it a certain clay-yard, once the property of a potter, and the very place in which Judas had made of himself a suicide; this tract of ground they set apart as a burial place for aliens, strangers, and pagans. The body of Judas, the betrayer of the Christ, was probably the first to be there interred. And that field was called "Aceldama, that is to say, The field of blood."[1300]

NOTES TO CHAPTER 34.

1. Annas, and His Interview with Jesus.--"No figure is better known in contemporary Jewish history than that of Annas; no person deemed more fortunate or successful, but also none more generally execrated than the late high priest. He had held the pontificate for only six or seven years; but it was filled by not fewer than five of his sons, by his son-in-law Caiaphas, and by a grandson. And in those days it was, at least for one of Annas' disposition, much better to have been than to be high priest. He enjoyed all the dignity of the office, and all its influence also, since he was able to promote to it those most closely connected with him. And while they acted publicly, he really directed affairs, without either the responsibility or the restraints which the office imposed. His influence with the Romans he owed to the religious views which he professed, to his open partisanship of the foreigner, and to his enormous wealth.... We have seen what immense revenues the family of Annas must have derived from the Temple booths, and how nefarious and unpopular was the traffic. The names of those bold, licentious, unscrupulous, degenerate sons of Aaron were spoken with whispered curses. Without referring to Christ's interference with that Temple-traffic, which, if His authority had prevailed, would of course have been fatal to it, we can understand how antithetic in every respect a Messiah, and such a Messiah as Jesus, must have been to Annas.... No account is given of what passed before Annas. Even the fact of Christ's being first brought to him is only mentioned in the fourth Gospel. As the disciples had all forsaken Him and fled, we can understand that they were in ignorance of what actually passed, till they had again rallied, at least so far, that Peter and 'another disciple', evidently John, 'followed Him into the palace of the high priest'--that is, into the palace of Caiaphas, not of Annas. For as, according to the three synoptic Gospels, the palace of the high priest Caiaphas was the scene of Peter's denial, the account of it in the fourth Gospel must refer to the same locality, and not to the palace of Annas."--Edersheim, _Life and Times of Jesus the Messiah_; vol. 2, pp. 547-8.

2. Christ's Forbearance when Smitten.--That Jesus maintained His equanimity and submissiveness even under the provocation of a blow dealt by a brutish underling in the presence of the high priest, is confirmatory of our Lord's affirmation that He had "overcome the world" (John 16:33). One cannot read the passage without comparing, perhaps involuntarily, the divine submissiveness of Jesus on this occasion, with the wholly natural and human indignation of Paul under somewhat similar conditions at a later time (Acts 23:1-5). The high priest Ananias, displeased at Paul's remarks, ordered someone who stood by to smite him on the mouth. Paul broke forth in angry protest: "God shall smite thee, thou whited wall: for sittest thou to judge me after the law, and commandest me to be smitten contrary to the law?" Afterward he apologized, saying that he knew not that it was the high priest who had given the command that he be smitten. See _Articles of Faith_, xxiii, II, and Note 1 following the same lecture; and Farrar's _Life and Works of St. Paul_, pp. 539-540.

3. High Priests and Elders.--These titles as held by officials of the Jewish hierarchy in the time of Christ must not be confused with the same designations as applied to holders of the Higher or Melchizedek Priesthood. The high priest of the Jews was the presiding priest; he had to be of Aaronic descent to be a priest at all; he became high priest by Roman appointment. The elders, as the name indicates, were men of mature years and experience, who were appointed to act as magistrates in the towns, and as judges in the ecclesiastical tribunals, either in the Lesser Sanhedrins of the provinces, or in the Great Sanhedrin at Jerusalem. The term "elder" as commonly used among the Jews in the days of Jesus had no closer relation to eldership in the Melchizedek Priesthood than had the title "scribe". The duties of Jewish high priests and elders combined both ecclesiastical and secular functions; indeed both offices had come to be in large measure political perquisites. See "Elder" in Smith's _Bible Dictionary_. From the

departure of Moses to the coming of Christ, the organized theocracy of Israel was that of the Lesser or Aaronic Priesthood, comprizing the office of priest, which was confined to the lineage of Aaron, and the lesser offices of teacher and deacon, which were combined in the Levitical order. See "Orders and Offices in the Priesthood" by the author in _The Articles of Faith_, xi:13-24.

4. Illegalities of the Jewish Trial of Jesus.--Many volumes have been written on the so-called trial of Jesus. Only a brief summary of the principal items of fact and law can be incorporated here. For further consideration reference may be made to the following treatments: Edersheim, _Life and Times of Jesus the Messiah_; Andrews, _Life of Our Lord_; Dupin, _Jesus before Caiaphas and Pilate_; Mendelsohn, _Criminal Jurisprudence of the Ancient Hebrews_; Salvador, _Institutions of Moses_; Innes, _The Trial of Jesus Christ_; Maimonides, _Sanhedrin_; MM. Lemann, _Jesus before the Sanhedrin_; Benny, _Criminal Code of the Jews_; and Walter M. Chandler, of the New York Bar, _The Trial of Jesus from a Lawyer's Standpoint_. The last named is a two volume work treating respectively, "The Hebrew Trial" and "The Roman Trial", and contains citations from the foregoing and other works.

Edersheim (vol. 2, pp. 556-8) contends that the night arraignment of Jesus in the house of Caiaphas was not a trial before the Sanhedrin, and notes the irregularities and illegalities of the procedure as proof that the Sanhedrin could not have done what was done that night. With ample citations in corroboration of the legal requirements specified, the author says: "But besides, the trial and sentence of Jesus in the palace of Caiaphas would have outraged every principle of Jewish criminal law and procedure. Such causes could only be tried, and capital sentence pronounced, in the regular meeting-place of the Sanhedrin, not, as here, in the high priest's palace; no process, least of all such an one, might be begun in the night, nor even in the afternoon, although if the discussion had gone on all day, sentence might be pronounced at night. Again, no process could take place on Sabbaths or feast-days, or even on the eves of them, although this would not have nullified proceedings; and it might be argued on the other side, that a process against one who had seduced the people should preferably be carried on, and sentence executed, on public feast-days, for the warning of all. Lastly, in capital causes there was a very elaborate system of warning, and cautioning witnesses; while it may safely be affirmed that at a regular trial Jewish judges, however prejudiced, would not have acted as the Sanhedrists and Caiaphas did on this occasion.... But although Christ was not tried and sentenced in a formal meeting of the Sanhedrin, there can, alas! be no question that His condemnation and death were the work, if not of the Sanhedrin, yet of the Sanhedrists--of the whole body of them ('all the council') in the sense of expressing what was the judgment and purpose of all the supreme council and leaders of Israel, with only very few exceptions. We bear in mind that the resolution to sacrifice Christ had for some time been taken."

The purpose in quoting the foregoing is to show on acknowledged and eminent authority, some of the illegalities of the night trial of Jesus, which, as shown by the above, and by the scriptural record, was conducted by the high priest and "the council" or Sanhedrin, in admittedly irregular and unlawful manner. If the Sanhedrists tried and condemned, yet were not in session as the Sanhedrin, the enormity of the proceeding is, if possible, deeper and blacker than ever.

In Chandler's excellent work (vol. I, "The Hebrew Trial"), the record of fact in the case, and the Hebrew criminal law bearing thereon are exhaustively considered. Then follows an elaborate "Brief", in which the following points are set forth in order.

"_Point 1: The Arrest of Jesus was illegal_", since it was effected by night, and through the treachery of Judas, an accomplice, both of which features were expressly forbidden in the Jewish law of that day.

"_Point 2: The private examination of Jesus before Annas or Caiaphas was illegal_"; for (1) it was made by night; (2) the hearing of any cause by a 'sole judge' was expressly forbidden; (3) as quoted from Salvador, 'A principle perpetually reproduced in the Hebrew scriptures relates to the two conditions of publicity and liberty.'

"_Point 3: The indictment against Jesus was, in form, illegal._ 'The entire criminal procedure of the Mosaic code rests upon four rules: certainty in the indictment; publicity in the discussion; full freedom granted to the accused; and assurance against all dangers or errors of testimony'--Salvador, p. 365. 'The Sanhedrin did not and could not originate charges; it only investigated those brought before it'--Edersheim, vol. I, p. 309. 'The evidence of the leading witnesses constituted the charge. There was no other charge; no more formal indictment. Until they spoke and spoke in the public assembly, the prisoner was scarcely an accused man,'--Innes, p. 41. 'The only prosecutors known to Talmudic criminal jurisprudence are the witnesses to the crime. Their duty is to bring the matter to the cognizance of the court, and to bear witness against the criminal. In capital cases they are the legal executioners also. Of an official accuser or prosecutor there is nowhere any trace in the laws of the ancient Hebrews.'-- Mendelsohn, p. 110.

"_Point 4: The proceedings of the Sanhedrin against Jesus were illegal because they were conducted at night._ 'Let a capital offense be tried during the day, but suspend it at night,'--Mishna, Sanhedrin 4:1. 'Criminal cases can be acted upon by the various courts during daytime only, by the Lesser Sanhedrions from the close of the morning service till noon, and by the Great Sanhedrion till evening.'--Mendelsohn, p. 112.

"_Point 5: The proceedings of the Sanhedrin against Jesus were illegal because the court convened before the offering of the morning sacrifice._ 'The Sanhedrin sat from the close of the morning sacrifice to the time of the evening sacrifice,'--Talmud, Jer. San. 1:19. 'No session of the court could take place before the offering of the morning sacrifice'.--MM. Lemann, p. 109. 'Since the morning sacrifice was offered at the dawn of day, it was hardly possible for the Sanhedrin to assemble until the hour after that time,'--Mishna, Tamid, ch. 3.

"_Point 6: The proceedings against Jesus were illegal because they were conducted on the day preceding a Jewish Sabbath; also on the first day of unleavened bread and the eve of the Passover._ 'They shall not judge on the eve of the Sabbath nor on that of any festival.'--Mishna, San. 4:1. 'No court of justice in Israel was permitted to hold sessions on the Sabbath or any of the seven Biblical holidays. In cases of capital crime, no trial could be commenced on Friday or the day previous to any holiday, because it was not lawful either to adjourn such cases longer than over night, or to continue them on the Sabbath or holiday.'--Rabbi Wise, 'Martyrdom of Jesus', p. 67.

"_Point 7: The trial of Jesus was illegal because it was concluded within one day._ 'A criminal case resulting in the acquittal of the accused may terminate the same day on which the trial began. But if a sentence of death is to be pronounced, it cannot be concluded before the following day.'--Mishna, San. 4:1.

"_Point 8: The sentence of condemnation pronounced against Jesus by the Sanhedrin was illegal because it was founded upon His uncorroborated confession._ 'We have it as a fundamental principle of our jurisprudence that no one can bring an accusation against himself. Should a man make confession of guilt before a legally constituted tribunal, such confession is not to be used against him unless properly attested by two other witnesses,'--Maimonides, 4:2. 'Not only is self-condemnation never extorted from the defendant by means of torture, but no attempt is ever made to lead him on to self-incrimination. Moreover, a voluntary confession on his part is not admitted in evidence, and therefore not competent to convict him, unless a legal number of witnesses minutely corroborate his self-accusation.'--Mendelsohn, p. 133.

"_Point 9: The condemnation of Jesus was illegal because the verdict of the Sanhedrin was unanimous._ 'A simultaneous and unanimous verdict of guilt rendered on the day of the trial has the effect of an acquittal.'--Mendelsohn, p. 141. 'If none of the judges defend the culprit, i.e., all pronounce him guilty, having no defender in the court, the verdict of guilty was invalid and the sentence of death could not be executed.'--Rabbi Wise, 'Martyrdom of Jesus', p. 74.

"_Point 10: The proceedings against Jesus were illegal in that: (1) The sentence of condemnation was pronounced in a place forbidden by law; (2) The high priest rent his clothes; (3) The balloting was irregular._ 'After leaving the hall Gazith no sentence of death can be passed upon any one soever,'--Talmud, Bab. 'Of Idolatry' 1:8. 'A sentence of death can be pronounced only so long as the Sanhedrin holds its sessions in the appointed place.'--Maimonides, 14. See further Levit. 21:10; compare 10:6. 'Let the judges each in his turn absolve or condemn.'--Mishna, San. 15:5. 'The members of the Sanhedrin were seated in the form of a semicircle, at the extremity of which a secretary was placed, whose business it was to record the votes. One of these secretaries recorded the votes in favor of the accused, the other those against him.'--Mishna, San. 4:3. 'In ordinary cases the judges voted according to seniority, the oldest commencing; in a capital case the reverse order was followed.'--Benny, p. 73.

"_Point 11: The members of the Great Sanhedrin were legally disqualified to try Jesus._ 'Nor must there be on the judicial bench either a relation or a particular friend, or an enemy of either the accused or of the accuser.'--Mendelsohn, p. 108. 'Nor under any circumstances was a man known to be at enmity with the accused person permitted to occupy a position among the judges.'--Benny, p. 37.

"_Point 12: The condemnation of Jesus was illegal because the merits of the defense were not considered._ 'Then shalt thou enquire, and make search, and ask diligently.'--Deut. 13:14. 'The judges shall weigh the matter in the sincerity of their conscience.'--Mishna, San. 4:5. 'The primary object of the Hebrew judicial system was to render the conviction of an innocent person impossible. All the ingenuity of the Jewish legists was directed to the attainment of this end.'--Benny, p. 56."

Chandler's masterly statements of fact and his arguments on each of the foregoing points are commended to the investigator. The author tersely avers: "The pages of human history present no stronger case of judicial murder than the trial and crucifixion of Jesus of Nazareth, for the simple reason that all forms of law were outraged and trampled under foot in the proceedings instituted against Him." (p. 216.)

5. "His Blood be on us, and on Our Children."--Edersheim (vol. 2, p. 578) thus forcefully comments on the acknowledgment of responsibility for the death of Christ: "The Mishna tells us that, after the solemn washing of hands of the elders and their disclaimer of guilt, priests responded with this prayer: 'Forgive it to thy people Israel, whom thou hast redeemed, O Lord, and lay not innocent blood upon thy people Israel.' But here, in answer to Pilate's words, came back that deep, hoarse cry: 'His blood be upon us,' and--God help us!--'on our children.' Some thirty years later, and on that very spot, was judgment pronounced against some of the best in Jerusalem; and among the 3,600 victims of the governor's fury, of whom not a few were scourged and crucified right over against the Pretorium, were many of the noblest of the citizens of Jerusalem. (Josephus, Wars, xiv, chap. 8:9). A few years more, and hundreds of crosses bore Jewish mangled bodies within sight of Jerusalem. And still have these wanderers seemed to bear, from century to century, and from land to land, that burden of blood; and still does it seem to weigh 'on us and on our children'."

6. "We Have no King but Cæsar."--"With this cry Judaism was, in the person of its representatives, guilty of denial of God, of blasphemy, of apostasy. It committed suicide; and ever since has its dead body been carried in show from land to land, and from century to century,--to be dead and to remain dead, till He come a second time, who is the resurrection and the life."--Edersheim, vol. 2, p. 581.

7. The Underlying Cause of Pilate's Surrender to the Jewish Demands.--Pilate knew what was right but lacked the moral courage to do it. He was afraid of the Jews, and more afraid of hostile influence at Rome. He was afraid of his conscience, but more afraid of losing his official position. It was the policy of Rome to be gracious and conciliatory in dealing with the religions and social customs of conquered nations. Pontius Pilate had violated this liberal policy from the early days of his procuratorship. In utter disregard of the Hebrew antipathy against images and heathen insignia, he had the legionaries enter Jerusalem at night, carrying their eagles and standards decorated with the effigy of the emperor. To the Jews this act was a defilement of the Holy City. In vast multitudes they gathered at Cæsarea, and petitioned the procurator that

the standards and other images be removed from Jerusalem. For five days the people demanded and Pilate refused. He threatened a general slaughter, and was amazed to see the people offer themselves as victims of the sword rather than relinquish their demands. Pilate had to yield (Josephus, Ant. xviii, chap. 3:1; also Wars, ii, chap. 9:2, 3). Again he gave offense in forcibly appropriating the Corban, or sacred funds of the temple, to the construction of an aqueduct for supplying Jerusalem with water from the pools of Solomon. Anticipating the public protest of the people, he had caused Roman soldiers to disguise themselves as Jews; and with weapons concealed to mingle with the crowds. At a given signal these assassins plied their weapons and great numbers of defenceless Jews were killed or wounded (Josephus, Ant. xviii, chap. 3:2; and Wars, ii, chap. 9:3, 4). On another occasion, Pilate had grossly offended the people by setting up in his official residence at Jerusalem, shields that had been dedicated to Tiberius, and this "less for the honor of Tiberius than for the annoyance of the Jewish people." A petition signed by the ecclesiastical officials of the nation, and by others of influence, including four Herodian princes, was sent to the emperor, who reprimanded Pilate and directed that the shields be removed from Jerusalem to C┟ᵃsarea (Philo. De Legatione ad Caium; sec. 38).

These outrages on national feeling, and many minor acts of violence, extortion and cruelty, the Jews held against the procurator. He realized that his tenure was insecure, and he dreaded exposure. Such wrongs had he wrought that when he would have done good, he was deterred through cowardly fear of the accusing past.

8. Judas Iscariot.--Today we speak of a traitor as a "Judas" or an "Iscariot". The man who made the combined name infamous has been for ages a subject of discussion among theologians and philosophers, and in later times the light of psychological analysis has been turned upon him. German philosophers were among the earliest to assert that the man had been judged in unrighteousness, and that his real character was of brighter tint than that in which it had been painted. Indeed some critics hold that of all the Twelve Judas was the one most thoroughly convinced of our Lord's divinity in the flesh; and these apologists attempt to explain the betrayal as a deliberate and well-intended move to force Jesus into a position of difficulty from which He could escape only by the exercize of His powers of Godship, which, up to that time, He had never used in His own behalf.

We are not the invested judges of Judas nor of any other; but we are competent to frame and hold opinions as to the actions of any. In the light of the revealed word it appears that Judas Iscariot had given himself up to the cause of Satan while ostensibly serving the Christ in an exalted capacity. Such a surrender to evil powers could be accomplished only through sin. The nature and extent of the man's transgressions through the years are not told us. He had received the testimony that Jesus was the Son of God; and in the full light of that conviction he turned against his Lord, and betrayed Him to death. Modern revelation is no less explicit than ancient in declaring that the path of sin is that of spiritual darkness leading to certain destruction. If the man who is guilty of adultery, even in his heart only, shall, unless he repents, surely forfeit the companionship of the Spirit of God, and "shall deny the faith", and so the voice of God hath affirmed (see Doc. and Cov. 63:16), we cannot doubt that any and all forms of deadly sin shall poison the soul and, if not forsaken through true repentance, shall bring that soul to condemnation. For his trained and skilful servants, Satan will provide opportunities of service commensurate with their evil ability. Whatever the opinion of modern critics as to the good character of Judas, we have the testimony of John, who for nearly three years had been in close companionship with him, that the man was a thief (12:6); and Jesus referred to him as a devil (6:70), and as "the son of perdition" (17:12). See in this connection Doc. and Cov. 76:41-48.

That the evil proclivities of Judas Iscariot were known to Christ is evidenced by the Lord's direct statement that among the Twelve was one who was a devil; (John 6:70; compare 13:27; Luke 22:3); and furthermore that this knowledge was His when the Twelve were selected is suggested by the words of Jesus: "I know whom I have chosen", coupled with the explanation that in the choice He had made would the scriptures be fulfilled. As the sacrificial death of the Lamb of God was foreknown and foretold so the circumstances of the betrayal were foreseen. It would be contrary to both the letter and spirit of the revealed word to say that the wretched Iscariot was in the least degree deprived of freedom or agency in the course he followed to so execrable an end. His was the opportunity and privilege common to the Twelve, to live in the light of the Lord's immediate presence, and to receive from the source divine the revelation of God's purposes. Judas Iscariot was no victim of circumstances, no insensate tool guided by a superhuman power, except as he by personal volition gave himself up to Satan, and accepted a wage in the devil's employ. Had Judas been true to the right, other means than his perfidy would have operated to bring the Lamb to the slaughter. His ordination to the apostleship placed him in possession of opportunity and privilege above that of the uncalled and unordained; and with such blessed possibility of achievement in the service of God came corresponding capability to fall. A trusted and exalted officer of the government can commit acts of treachery and treason such as are impossible to the citizen who has never learned the secrets of State. Advancement implies increased accountability, even more literally so in the affairs of God's kingdom than in the institutions of men.

There is an apparent discrepancy between the account of Judas Iscariot's death given by Matthew (27:3-10) and that in Acts (1:16-20). According to the first, Judas hanged himself; the second states that he fell headlong, "and all his bowels gushed out." If both records be accurate, the wretched man probably hanged himself, and afterward fell, possibly through the breaking of the cord or the branch to which it was attached. Matthew says the Jewish rulers purchased the "field of blood"; the writer of the Acts quotes Peter as saying that Judas bought the field with the money he had received from the priests. As the ground was bought with the money that had belonged to Iscariot, and as this money had never been formally taken back by the temple officials, the field bought therewith belonged technically to the estate of

Judas. The variations are of importance mainly as showing independence of authorship. The accounts agree in the essential feature, that Judas died a miserable suicide.

Concerning the fate of the "sons of perdition," the Lord has given a partial but awful account through a revelation dated February 16, 1832: "Thus saith the Lord, concerning all those who know my power, and have been made partakers thereof, and suffered themselves, through the power of the devil, to be overcome, and to deny the truth and defy my power--They are they who are the sons of perdition, of whom I say that it had been better for them never to have been born, For they are vessels of wrath, doomed to suffer the wrath of God, with the devil and his angels in eternity; Concerning whom I have said there is no forgiveness in this world nor in the world to come, Having denied the Holy Spirit after having received it, and having denied the Only Begotten Son of the Father--having crucified him unto themselves and put him to an open shame. These are they who shall go away into the lake of fire and brimstone, with the devil and his angels, And the only ones on whom the second death shall have any power.... Wherefore, he saves all except them: they shall go away into everlasting punishment, which is endless punishment, which is eternal punishment, to reign with the devil and his angels in eternity, where their worm dieth not, and the fire is not quenched, which is their torment; And the end thereof, neither the place thereof, nor their torment, no man knows. Neither was it revealed, neither is, neither will be revealed unto man, except to them who are made partakers thereof: Nevertheless I, the Lord, show it by vision unto many, but straightway shut it up again: Wherefore the end, the width, the height, the depth, and the misery thereof, they understand not, neither any man except them who are ordained unto this condemnation."-- Doc. and Cov. 76:31-37, 44-48.

FOOTNOTES:

[1249] John 18:13, 24.
[1250] Matt. 26:57; Mark 14:53; Luke 22:54.
[1251] Note 1, end of chapter.
[1252] John 18:14; compare 11:49, 50.
[1253] John 18:19-23.
[1254] The common text of John 18:22, says that the man "struck Jesus with the palm of his hand," that is to say slapped Him; such an act added humiliating insult to violence; the marginal reading of the revised version is "with a rod." There is lack of agreement on this point in the early Mss.
[1255] Note 2, end of chapter.
[1256] Matt. 26:59-61; Mark 14:55-59.
[1257] Matt. 26:61 and Mark 14:58.
[1258] John 2:18-22; see pages 156, 157 herein.
[1259] Note the accusation reported to Pilate that Jesus was guilty of "perverting the nation," Luke 23:2.
[1260] Matt. 26:63-66; compare Mark 14:61-64.
[1261] Pages 191, 201.
[1262] Compare Mark 14:62.
[1263] Matt. 26:65, 66. Revised version reads: "He is worthy of death," and gives in margin a yet more literal rendering: "liable to" death.
[1264] Lev. 21:10.
[1265] Josephus, Wars, ii, 15:2, 4; also 1 Maccabees 11:71.
[1266] Matt. 26:67; Mark 14:65; compare Luke 18:32; see also Isa. 50:6.
[1267] Matt. 26:68; Luke 22:62-65.
[1268] Mark 14:64.
[1269] Luke 22:66.
[1270] John 18:28.
[1271] Luke 22:66-71.
[1272] Note 3, end of chapter.
[1273] Mark 15:1; compare Matt. 27:1, 2; John 18:28.
[1274] Note 4, end of chapter, gives further details of the unlawful irregularities of the Jewish trial of Jesus.
[1275] Matt. 26:58, 69-75; Mark 14:54, 66-72; Luke 22:54-62; John 18:15-18, 25-27.
[1276] John 18:8, 9; page 615 herein.
[1277] John 1:35, 40; 13:23; 19:26; 20:2; 21:7, 20, 24.
[1278] Observe that Mark, who alone states that the Lord said to Peter "before the cock crow twice, thou shalt deny me thrice," (14:30) records a first crowing of the cock after Peter's first denial (v. 68) and a second crowing after the third denial (v. 72).
[1279] Cæsarea Palestina, not Cæsarea Philippi.
[1280] John 18:28-32.
[1281] Luke 23:2.
[1282] John 18:33-38; compare Matt. 27:11; Mark 15:2; Luke 23:3, 4.
[1283] Luke 23:5-7.
[1284] Luke 23:8-12.
[1285] Pages 110, 118; see also page 106.
[1286] Luke 23:12.
[1287] Matt. 14:1; Mark 6:14; Luke 9:7, 9.
[1288] Luke 13:31, 32; page 446 herein.

[1289] Luke 23:11. Revised version reads, "arraying him in gorgeous apparel." Clarke ("Commentaries") and many other writers assume that the robe was white, that being the usual color of dress amongst the Jewish nobility.

[1290] Luke 23:13-25; Matt. 27:15-31; Mark 15:6-20; John 18:39, 40; 19:1-16.

[1291] Matt. 27:18; Mark 15:10.

[1292] Note 5, end of chapter.

[1293] Matthew says "scarlet," Mark and John say "purple."

[1294] Compare Luke 18:32.

[1295] "Ecce Homo."

[1296] Note 6, end of chapter.

[1297] Note 7, end of chapter.

[1298] Matt. 27:3-10; compare Acts 1:16-20.

[1299] Revised version of Matt. 27:5 reads, "And he cast down the pieces of silver into the sanctuary" instead of "in the temple," signifying that he flung the money into the Porch of the Holy House, as distinguished from the outer and public courts.

[1300] Acts 1:19; Matt. 27:8. Note 8, end of chapter.

CHAPTER 35. DEATH AND BURIAL.

ON THE WAY TO CALVARY.[1301]

Pontius Pilate, having reluctantly surrendered to the clamorous demands of the Jews, issued the fatal order; and Jesus, divested of the purple robe and arrayed in His own apparel, was led away to be crucified. A body of Roman soldiers had the condemned Christ in charge; and as the procession moved out from the governor's palace, a motley crowd comprizing priestly officials, rulers of the Jews, and people of many nationalities, followed. Two convicted criminals, who had been sentenced to the cross for robbery, were led forth to death at the same time; there was to be a triple execution; and the prospective scene of horror attracted the morbidly minded, such as delight to gloat over the sufferings of their fellows. In the crowd, however, were some genuine mourners, as shall be shown. It was the Roman custom to make the execution of convicts as public as possible, under the mistaken and anti-psychological assumption, that the spectacle of dreadful punishment would be of deterrent effect. This misconception of human nature has not yet become entirely obsolete.

The sentence of death by crucifixion required that the condemned person carry the cross upon which he was to suffer. Jesus started on the way bearing His cross. The terrible strain of the preceding hours, the agony in Gethsemane, the barbarous treatment He had suffered in the palace of the high priest, the humiliation and cruel usage to which He had been subjected before Herod, the frightful scourging under Pilate's order, the brutal treatment by the inhuman soldiery, together with the extreme humiliation and the mental agony of it all, had so weakened His physical organism that He moved but slowly under the burden of the cross. The soldiers, impatient at the delay, peremptorily impressed into service a man whom they met coming into Jerusalem from the country, and him they compelled to carry the cross of Jesus. No Roman or Jew would have voluntarily incurred the ignominy of bearing such a gruesome burden; for every detail connected with the carrying out of a sentence of crucifixion was regarded as degrading. The man so forced to walk in the footsteps of Jesus, bearing the cross upon which the Savior of the world was to consummate His glorious mission, was Simon, a native of Cyrene. From Mark's statement that Simon was the father of Alexander and Rufus we infer that the two sons were known to the evangelist's readers as members of the early Church, and there is some indication that the household of Simon the Cyrenian came to be numbered with the believers.[1302]

Among those who followed or stood and watched the death-procession pass, were some, women particularly, who bewailed and lamented the fate to which Jesus was going. We read of no man who ventured to raise his voice in protest or pity; but on this dreadful occasion as at other times, women were not afraid to cry out in commiseration or praise. Jesus, who had been silent under the inquisition of the priests, silent under the humiliating mockery of the sensual Herod and his coarse underlings, silent when buffeted and beaten by the brutal legionaries of Pilate, turned to the women whose sympathizing lamentations had reached His ears, and uttered these pathetic and portentous words of admonition and warning: "Daughters of Jerusalem, weep not for me, but weep for yourselves, and for your children. For, behold, the days are coming, in the which they shall say, Blessed are the barren, and the wombs that never bare, and the paps which never gave suck. Then shall they begin to say to the mountains, Fall on us; and to the hills, Cover us. For if they do these things in a green tree, what shall be done in the dry?" It was the Lord's last testimony of the impending holocaust of destruction that was to follow the nation's rejection of her King. Although motherhood was the glory of every Jewish woman's life, yet in the terrible scenes which many of those there weeping would live to witness, barrenness would be accounted a blessing; for the childless would have fewer to weep over, and at least would be spared the horror of seeing their offspring die of starvation or by violence; for so dreadful would be that day that people would fain welcome the falling of the mountains upon them to end their sufferings.[1303] If Israel's oppressors could do what was then in process of doing to the "Green Tree," who bore the leafage of freedom and truth and offered the priceless fruit of life eternal, what would the powers of evil not do to the withered branches and dried trunk of apostate Judaism?

Along the city streets, out through the portal of the massive wall, and thence to a place beyond but yet nigh unto Jerusalem, the cortege advanced. The destination was a spot called Golgotha, or Calvary, meaning "the place of a skull."[1304]

CRUCIFIXION.[1305]

At Calvary the official crucifiers proceeded without delay to carry into effect the dread sentence pronounced upon Jesus and upon the two criminals. Preparatory to affixing the condemned to the cross, it was the custom to offer each a narcotic draught of sour wine or vinegar mingled with myrrh and possibly containing other anodyne ingredients, for the merciful purpose of deadening the sensibility of the victim. This was no Roman practise, but was allowed as a concession to Jewish sentiment. When the drugged cup was presented to Jesus He put it to His lips, but having ascertained the nature of its contents refused to drink, and so demonstrated His determination to meet death with faculties alert and mind unclouded.

Then they crucified Him, on the central cross of three, and placed one of the condemned malefactors on His right hand, the other on His left. Thus was realized Isaiah's vision of the Messiah numbered among the transgressors.[1306] But few details of the actual crucifixion are given us. We know however that our Lord was nailed to the cross by spikes driven through the hands and feet, as was the Roman method, and not bound only by cords as was the custom in inflicting this form of punishment among some other nations. Death by crucifixion was at once the most lingering and most painful of all forms of execution. The victim lived in ever increasing torture, generally for many hours, sometimes for days. The spikes so cruelly driven through hands and feet penetrated and crushed sensitive nerves and quivering tendons, yet inflicted no mortal wound. The welcome relief of death came through the exhaustion caused by intense and unremitting pain, through localized inflammation and congestion of organs incident to the strained and unnatural posture of the body.[1307]

As the crucifiers proceeded with their awful task, not unlikely with roughness and taunts, for killing was their trade and to scenes of anguish they had grown callous through long familiarity, the agonized Sufferer, void of resentment but full of pity for their heartlessness and capacity for cruelty, voiced the first of the seven utterances delivered from the cross. In the spirit of God-like mercy He prayed: "_Father, forgive them; for they know not what they do._" Let us not attempt to fix the limits of the Lord's mercy; that it would be extended to all who in any degree could justly come under the blessed boon thereof ought to be a sufficing fact. There is significance in the form in which this merciful benediction was expressed. Had the Lord said, "I forgive you," His gracious pardon may have been understood to be but a remission of the cruel offense against Himself as One tortured under unrighteous condemnation; but the invocation of the Father's forgiveness was a plea for those who had brought anguish and death to the Father's Well Beloved Son, the Savior and Redeemer of the world. Moses forgave Miriam for her offense against himself as her brother; but God alone could remit the penalty and remove the leprosy that had come upon her for having spoken against Jehovah's high priest.[1308]

It appears that under Roman rule, the clothes worn by a condemned person at the time of execution became the perquisites of the executioners. The four soldiers in charge of the cross upon which the Lord suffered distributed parts of His raiment among themselves; and there remained His coat,[1309] which was a goodly garment, woven throughout in one piece, without seam. To rend it would be to spoil; so the soldiers cast lots to determine who should have it; and in this circumstance the Gospel-writers saw a fulfilment of the psalmist's prevision: "They parted my garments among them, and upon my vesture did they cast lots."[1310]

To the cross above the head of Jesus was affixed a title or inscription, prepared by order of Pilate in accordance with the custom of setting forth the name of the crucified and the nature of the offense for which he had been condemned to death. In this instance the title was inscribed in three languages, Greek, Latin, and Hebrew, one or more of which would be understood by every observer who could read. The title so exhibited read: "_This is Jesus the King of the Jews_"; or in the more extended version given by John "_Jesus of Nazareth the King of the Jews_."[1311] The inscription was read by many, for Calvary was close to the public thoroughfare and on this holiday occasion the passers-by were doubtless numerous. Comment was aroused; for, if literally construed, the inscription was an official declaration that the crucified Jesus was in fact King of the Jews. When this circumstance was brought to the attention of the chief priests, they excitedly appealed to the governor, saying: "Write not, The King of the Jews; but that he said, I am King of the Jews. Pilate answered, What I have written I have written." Pilate's action in so wording the title, and his blunt refusal to permit an alteration, may have been an intended rebuff to the Jewish officials who had forced him against his judgment and will to condemn Jesus; possibly, however, the demeanor of the submissive Prisoner, and His avowal of Kingship above all royalty of earth had impressed the mind if not the heart of the pagan governor with a conviction of Christ's unique superiority and of His inherent right of dominion; but, whatever the purpose behind the writing, the inscription stands in history as testimony of a heathen's consideration in contrast with Israel's ruthless rejection of Israel's King.[1312]

The soldiers whose duty it was to guard the crosses, until loitering death would relieve the crucified of their increasing anguish, jested among themselves, and derided the Christ, pledging Him in their cups of sour wine in tragic mockery. Looking at the title affixed above the Sufferer's head, they bellowed forth the devil-inspired challenge: "If thou be the king of the Jews, save thyself." The morbid multitude, and the passers-by "railed on him, wagging their heads, and saying, Ah, thou that destroyest the temple, and buildest it in three days, save thyself, and come down from the cross." But worst of all, the chief priests and the scribes, the elders of the people, the unvenerable Sanhedrists, became ring-leaders of the inhuman mob as they gloatingly exulted and cried aloud: "He saved others; himself he cannot save. If he be the King of Israel, let him now come down from the cross, and we will believe him. He trusted in God; let him deliver him now, if he will have him: for he said, I am the Son of God."[1313] Though uttered in ribald mockery, the declaration of the rulers in Israel stands as an attestation that Christ had saved others, and as an intended ironical but a literally true proclamation that He was the King of Israel. The two malefactors, each hanging from his cross, joined in the general derision, and "cast the same in his teeth." One of them, in the desperation incident to approaching death, echoed the taunts of the priests and people: "If thou be Christ, save thyself and us."

The dominant note in all the railings and revilings, the ribaldry and mockery, with which the patient and submissive Christ was assailed while He hung, "lifted up" as He had said He would be,[1314] was that awful "If" hurled at Him by the devil's emissaries in the time of mortal agony; as in the season of the temptations immediately after His baptism it had been most insidiously pressed upon Him by the devil himself.[1315] That "If" was Satan's last shaft, keenly barbed and doubly envenomed, and it sped as with the fierce hiss of a viper. Was it possible in this the final and most dreadful stage of Christ's mission, to make Him doubt His divine Sonship, or, failing such, to taunt or anger the dying Savior into the use of His superhuman powers for personal relief or as an act of vengeance upon His tormentors? To achieve such a victory was Satan's desperate purpose. The shaft failed. Through taunts and derision, through blasphemous challenge and diabolical goading, the agonized Christ was silent.

Then one of the crucified thieves, softened into penitence by the Savior's uncomplaining fortitude, and perceiving in the divine Sufferer's demeanor something more than human, rebuked his railing fellow, saying: "Dost not thou fear God, seeing thou art in the same condemnation? And we indeed justly; for we receive the due reward of our deeds: but this man hath done nothing amiss." His confession of guilt and his acknowledgment of the justice of his own condemnation led to incipient repentance, and to faith in the Lord Jesus, his companion in agony. "And he said unto Jesus, Lord, remember me when thou comest into thy kingdom."[1316] To the appeal of penitence the Lord replied with such a promise as He alone could make: "Verily I say unto thee, To day shalt thou be with me in paradise."[1317]

Among the spectators of this, the greatest tragedy in history, were some who had come in sympathy and sorrow. No mention is found of the presence of any of the Twelve, save one, and he, the disciple "whom Jesus loved," John the apostle, evangelist, and revelator; but specific record is made of certain women who, first at a distance, and then close by the cross, wept in the anguish of love and sorrow. "Now there stood by the cross of Jesus his mother, and his mother's sister, Mary the wife of Cleophas, and Mary Magdalene."[1318]

In addition to the women named were many others, some of whom had ministered unto Jesus in the course of His labors in Galilee, and who were among those that had come up with Him to Jerusalem. [1319] First in point of consideration among them all was Mary, the mother of Jesus, into whose soul the sword had pierced even as righteous Simeon had prophesied.[1320] Jesus looking with tender compassion upon His weeping mother, as she stood with John at the foot of the cross, commended her to the care and protection of the beloved disciple, with the words, "_Woman, behold thy son!_" and to John, "_Behold thy mother!_" The disciple tenderly led the heart-stricken Mary away from her dying Son, and "took her unto his own home," thus immediately assuming the new relationship established by his dying Master.

Jesus was nailed to the cross during the forenoon of that fateful Friday, probably between nine and ten o'clock.[1321] At noontide the light of the sun was obscured, and black darkness spread over the whole land. The terrifying gloom continued for a period of three hours. This remarkable phenomenon has received no satisfactory explanation from science. It could not have been due to a solar eclipse, as has been suggested in ignorance, for the time was that of full moon; indeed the Passover season was determined by the first occurrence of full moon after the spring equinox. The darkness was brought about by miraculous operation of natural laws directed by divine power. It was a fitting sign of the earth's deep mourning over the impending death of her Creator.[1322] Of the mortal agony through which the Lord passed while upon the cross the Gospel-scribes are reverently reticent.

At the ninth hour, or about three in the afternoon, a loud voice, surpassing the most anguished cry of physical suffering issued from the central cross, rending the dreadful darkness. It was the voice of the Christ: "_Eloi, Eloi, lama sabachthani?_ which is, being interpreted, My God, my God, why hast thou forsaken me?_" What mind of man can fathom the significance of that awful cry? It seems, that in addition to the fearful suffering incident to crucifixion, the agony of Gethsemane had recurred, intensified beyond human power to endure. In that bitterest hour the dying Christ was alone, alone in most terrible reality. That the supreme sacrifice of the Son might be consummated in all its fulness, the Father seems to have withdrawn the support of His immediate Presence, leaving to the Savior of men the glory of complete victory over the forces of sin and death. The cry from the cross, though heard by all who were near, was understood by few. The first exclamation, _Eloi_, meaning _My God_, was misunderstood as a call for Elias.

The period of faintness, the conception of utter forsakenness soon passed, and the natural cravings of the body reasserted themselves. The maddening thirst, which constituted one of the worst of the crucifixion agonies, wrung from the Savior's lips His one recorded utterance expressive of physical suffering. "_I thirst_" He said. One of those who stood by, whether Roman or Jew, disciple or skeptic, we are not told, hastily saturated a sponge with vinegar, a vessel of which was at hand, and having fastened the sponge to the end of a reed, or stalk of hyssop, pressed it to the Lord's fevered lips. Some others would have prevented this one act of human response, for they said: "Let be, let us see whether Elias will come to save him." John affirms that Christ uttered the exclamation, "I thirst," only when He knew "that all things were now accomplished"; and the apostle saw in the incident a fulfilment of prophecy.[1323]

Fully realizing that He was no longer forsaken, but that His atoning sacrifice had been accepted by the Father, and that His mission in the flesh had been carried to glorious consummation, He exclaimed in a loud voice of holy triumph: "_It is finished!_" In reverence, resignation, and relief, He addressed the Father saying: "_Father, into thy hands I commend my spirit._"[1324] He bowed His head, and voluntarily gave up His life.

Jesus the Christ was dead. His life had not been taken from Him except as He had willed to permit. Sweet and welcome as would have been the relief of death in any of the earlier stages of His suffering from Gethsemane to the cross, He lived until all things were accomplished as had been appointed. In the latter days the voice of the Lord Jesus has been heard affirming the actuality of His suffering and death, and the eternal purpose thereby accomplished. Hear and heed His words: "For, behold, the Lord your Redeemer suffered death in the flesh; wherefore he suffered the pain of all men, that all men might repent and come unto him."[1325]

IMPORTANT OCCURRENCES BETWEEN THE LORD'S DEATH AND BURIAL.

The death of Christ was accompanied by terrifying phenomena. There was a violent earthquake; the rocks of the mighty hills were disrupted, and many graves were torn open. But, most portentous of all in Judaistic minds, the veil of the temple which hung between the Holy Place and the Holy of Holies[1326] was rent from top to bottom, and the interior, which none but the high priest had been permitted to see, was thrown open to common gaze. It was the rending of Judaism, the consummation of the Mosaic dispensation, and the inauguration of Christianity under apostolic administration.

The Roman centurion and the soldiers under his command at the place of execution were amazed and greatly affrighted. They had probably witnessed many deaths on the cross, but never before had they seen a man apparently die of his own volition, and able to cry in a loud voice at the moment of dissolution. That barbarous and inhuman mode of execution induced slow and progressive exhaustion. The actual death of Jesus appeared to all who were present to be a miracle, as in fact it was. This marvel, coupled with the earthquake and its attendant horrors, so impressed the centurion that he prayed to God, and solemnly declared: "Certainly this was a righteous man." Others joined in fearsome averment: "Truly this was the Son of God." The terrified ones who spoke and those who heard left the place in a state of fear, beating their breasts, and bewailing what seemed to be a state of impending destruction.[1327] A few loving women, however, watched from a distant point, and saw all that took place until the Lord's body was laid away.

It was now late in the afternoon; at sunset the Sabbath would begin. That approaching Sabbath was held to be more than ordinarily sacred for it was a high day, in that it was the weekly Sabbath and a paschal holy day.[1328] The Jewish officials, who had not hesitated to slay their Lord, were horrified at the thought of men left hanging on crosses on such a day, for thereby the land would be defiled;[1329] so these scrupulous rulers went to Pilate and begged that Jesus and the two malefactors be summarily dispatched by the brutal Roman method of breaking their legs, the shock of which violent treatment had been found to be promptly fatal to the crucified. The governor gave his consent, and the soldiers broke the limbs of the two thieves with cudgels. Jesus, however, was found to be already dead, so they broke not His bones. Christ, the great Passover sacrifice, of whom all altar victims had been but suggestive prototypes, died through violence yet without a bone of His body being broken, as was a prescribed condition of the slain paschal lambs.[1330] One of the soldiers, to make sure that Jesus was actually dead, or to surely kill Him if He was yet alive, drove a spear into His side, making a wound large enough to permit a man's hand to be thrust thereinto.[1331] The withdrawal of the spear was followed by an outflow of blood and water,[1332] an occurrence so surprizing that John, who was an eye-witness, bears specific personal testimony to the fact, and cites the scriptures thereby fulfilled.[1333]

THE BURIAL.[1334]

A man known as Joseph of Arimathea, who was at heart a disciple of Christ, but who had hesitated to openly confess his conversion through fear of the Jews, desired to give the Lord's body a decent and honorable interment. But for some such divinely directed intervention, the body of Jesus might have been cast into the common grave of executed criminals. This man, Joseph, was "a counsellor; and he was a good man, and a just." It is expressly said of him that he "had not consented to the counsel and deed of them"; from which statement we infer that he was a Sanhedrist and had been opposed to the action of his colleagues in condemning Jesus to death, or at least had refrained from voting with the rest. Joseph was a man of wealth, station, and influence. He went in boldly unto Pilate and begged the body of Christ. The governor was surprized to learn that Jesus was already dead; he summoned the centurion and inquired as to how long Jesus had lived on the cross. The unusual circumstance seems to have added to Pilate's troubled concern. He gave command and the body of Christ was delivered to Joseph.

The body was removed from the cross; and in preparing it for the tomb Joseph was assisted by Nicodemus, another member of the Sanhedrin, the same who had come to Jesus by night three years before, and who at one of the conspiracy meetings of the council had protested against the unlawful condemnation of Jesus without a hearing.[1335] Nicodemus brought a large quantity of myrrh and aloes, about a hundredweight. The odorous mixture was highly esteemed for anointing and embalming, but its cost restricted its use to the wealthy. These two revering disciples wrapped the body of Jesus in clean linen, "with the spices, as the manner of the Jews is to bury"; and then laid it in a new sepulchre, hewn in the rock. The tomb was in a garden, not far from Calvary, and was the property of Joseph. Because of the nearness of the Sabbath the interment had to be made with haste; the door of the sepulchre was closed, a large stone was rolled against it;[1336] and thus laid away the body was left to rest. Some of the devoted women, particularly Mary Magdalene, and "the other Mary," who was the mother of James and Joses, had watched the entombment from a distance; and when it was completed "they returned, and prepared spices and ointments; and rested the sabbath day according to the commandment."

THE SEPULCHRE GUARDED.[1337]

On the day following the "preparation," that is to say on Saturday, the Sabbath and "high-day,"[1338] the chief priests and Pharisees came in a body to Pilate, saying: "Sir, we remember that that deceiver said, while he was yet alive, After three days I will rise again. Command therefore that the sepulchre be made sure until the third day, lest his disciples come by night, and steal him away, and say unto the people, He is risen from the dead: so the last error shall be worse than the first." It is evident that the most inveterate of the human enemies of Christ remembered His predictions of an assured resurrection on the third day after His death. Pilate answered with terse assent: "Ye have a watch: go your way, make it as sure as ye can." So the chief priests and Pharisees satisfied themselves that the sepulchre was secure by seeing that the official seal was affixed at the junction of the great stone and the portal, and that an armed guard was placed in charge.

NOTES TO CHAPTER 35.

1. Simon the Cyrenian.--Simon, upon whom the cross of Jesus was laid, was a member of the Jewish colony in northern Africa, which had been established nearly three centuries before the birth of Christ by Ptolemeus Lagi, who transported thither great numbers of Jews from Palestine (Josephus, Antiquities, xii, chap. 1). Cyrene, the home of Simon, was in the province of Libya; its site is within the present boundaries of Tunis. That the African Jews were numerous and influential is evidenced by the fact that they maintained a synagog in Jerusalem (Acts 6:9) for the accommodation of such of their number as visited the city. Rufus and his mother are mentioned in friendly reference by Paul over a quarter of a century after the death of Christ (Romans 16:13). If this Rufus be one of the sons of Simon named by Mark (15:21), as tradition indicates, it is probable that Simon's family was prominently identified with the Primitive Church. As to whether Simon had become a disciple before the crucifixion, or was converted through his compulsory service in bearing the Lord's cross, or became a member of the Church at a later date, we are not definitely told.

2. Christ's Words to the Daughters of Jerusalem.--"The time would come, when the Old Testament curse of barrenness (Hosea 9:14) would be coveted as a blessing. To show the fulfilment of this prophetic lament of Jesus it is not necessary to recall the harrowing details recorded by Josephus (Wars, vi, 3:4), when a frenzied mother roasted her own child, and in the mockery of desperateness reserved the half of the horrible meal for those murderers who daily broke in upon her to rob her of what scanty food had been left her; nor yet other of those incidents, too revolting for needless repetition, which the historian of the last siege of Jerusalem chronicles. But how often, these many centuries, must Israel's women have felt that terrible longing for childlessness, and how often must the prayer of despair for the quick death of falling mountains and burying hills rather than prolonged torture (Hosea 10:8), have risen to the lips of Israel's sufferers! And yet, even so, these words were also prophetic of a still more terrible future (Rev. 6:10). For, if Israel had put such flame to its 'green tree' how terribly would the divine judgment burn among the dry wood of an apostate and rebellious people, that had so delivered up its Divine King, and pronounced sentence upon itself by pronouncing it upon Him!"--Edersheim, _Life and Times of Jesus the Messiah_ vol. 2, p. 588.

Concerning the prayer that mountains fall to crush and hide, Farrar (_Life of Christ_, p. 645, note), says: "These words of Christ met with a painfully literal illustration when hundreds of the unhappy Jews at the siege of Jerusalem hid themselves in the darkest and vilest subterranean recesses, and when, besides those who were hunted out, no less than two thousand were killed by being buried under the ruins of their hiding places." A further fulfilment may be yet future. Consult Josephus, Wars, vi. 9:4. See also Hos. 9:12-16; 10:8; Isa. 2:10; compare Rev. 6:16.

3. "The Place of a Skull."--The Aramaic Hebrew name "Golgotha", the Greek "Kranion", and the Latin "Calvaria" or, as Anglicized, "Calvary", have the same meaning, and connote "a skull". The name may have been applied with reference to topographical features, as we speak of the brow of a hill; or, if the spot was the usual place of execution, it may have been so called as expressive of death, just as we call a skull a death's head. It is probable that the bodies of executed convicts were buried near the place of death; and if Golgotha or Calvary was the appointed site for execution, the exposure of skulls and other human bones through the ravages of beasts and by other means, would not be surprizing; though the leaving of bodies or any of their parts unburied was contrary to Jewish law and sentiment. The origin of the name is of as little importance as are the many divergent suppositions concerning the exact location of the spot.

4. Crucifixion.--"It was unanimously considered the most horrible form of death. Among the Romans also the degradation was a part of the infliction, and the punishment if applied to freeman was only used in the case of the vilest criminals.... The criminal carried his own cross, or at any rate a part of it. Hence, figuratively, _to take, take up_ or _bear one's cross_ is _to_ endure suffering, affliction, or shame_ like a criminal on his way to the place of crucifixion (Matt. 10:38; 16:24; Luke 14:27, etc.). The place of execution was outside the city (1 Kings 21:13; Acts 7:58; Heb. 13:12), often in some public road or other conspicuous place. Arrived at the place of execution, the sufferer was stripped naked, the dress being the perquisite of the soldiers (Matt. 27:35). The cross was then driven into the ground, so that the feet of the condemned were a foot or two above the earth, and he was lifted upon it; or else stretched upon it on the ground and then lifted with it." It was the custom to station soldiers to watch the cross, so as to prevent the removal of the sufferer while yet alive. "This was necessary from the lingering character of the death, which sometimes did not supervene even for three days, and was at last the result of gradual benumbing and starvation. But for this guard, the persons might have been taken down and recovered, as was actually done in the case of a friend of Josephus.... In most cases the body was suffered to rot on the cross by the action of sun and rain, or to be devoured by birds and beasts. Sepulture was generally therefore forbidden; but in consequence of Deut. 21:22, 23, an express national exception was made in favor of the Jews (Matt. 27:58). This accursed and awful mode of punishment was happily abolished by Constantine." Smith's _Bible Dict._

5. Pilate's Inscription--"The King of the Jews."--No two of the Gospel-writers give the same wording of the title or inscription placed by Pilate's order above the head of Jesus on the cross; the meaning, however, is the same in all, and the unessential variation is evidence of individual liberty among the recorders. It is probable that there was actual diversity in the trilingual versions. John's version is followed in the common abbreviations used in connection with Roman Catholic figures of Christ: J. N. R. J.; or, inasmuch as "I" used to be an ordinary equivalent of "J",--I. N. R. I.--"Jesus of Nazareth, King [Rex] of the Jews."

6. The Women at the Cross.--"According to the authorized version and revised version, only three women are named, but most modern critics hold that four are intended. Translate, therefore, 'His

mother, and His mother's sister, (i.e. Salome, the mother of the evangelist [John]); and Mary the wife of Cleophas; and Mary Magdalene.'"--Taken from Dummelow's commentary on John 19:25.

7. The Hour of the Crucifixion.--Mark (15:25) says: "And it was the third hour and they crucified him"; the time so specified corresponds to the hour from 9 to 10 a.m. This writer and his fellow synoptists, Matthew and Luke, give place to many incidents that occurred between the nailing of Christ to the cross and the sixth hour or the hour from 12 noon to 1 p.m. From these several accounts it is clear that Jesus was crucified during the forenoon. A discrepancy plainly appears between these records and John's statement (19:14) that it was "about the sixth hour" (noon) when Pilate gave the sentence of execution. All attempts to harmonize the accounts in this particular have proved futile because the discrepancy is real. Most critics and commentators assume that "about the sixth hour" in John's account is a misstatement, due to the errors of early copyists of the manuscript Gospels, who mistook the sign meaning 3rd for that signifying 6th.

8. The Physical Cause of Christ's Death.--While, as stated in the text, the yielding up of life was voluntary on the part of Jesus Christ, for He had life in Himself and no man could take His life except as He willed to allow it to be taken, (John 1:4; 5:26; 10:15-18) there was of necessity a direct physical cause of dissolution. As stated also the crucified sometimes lived for days upon the cross, and death resulted, not from the infliction of mortal wounds, but from internal congestion, inflammations, organic disturbances, and consequent exhaustion of vital energy. Jesus, though weakened by long torture during the preceding night and early morning, by the shock of the crucifixion itself, as also by intense mental agony, and particularly through spiritual suffering such as no other man has ever endured, manifested surprizing vigor, both of mind and body, to the last. The strong, loud utterance, immediately following which He bowed His head and "gave up the ghost", when considered in connection with other recorded details, points to a physical rupture of the heart as the direct cause of death. If the soldier's spear was thrust into the left side of the Lord's body and actually penetrated the heart, the outrush of "blood and water" observed by John is further evidence of a cardiac rupture; for it is known that in the rare instances of death resulting from a breaking of any part of the wall of the heart, blood accumulates within the pericardium, and there undergoes a change by which the corpuscles separate as a partially clotted mass from the almost colorless, watery serum. Similar accumulations of clotted corpuscles and serum occur within the pleura. Dr. Abercrombie of Edinburgh, as cited by Deems (_Light of the Nations_, p. 682), "gives a case of the sudden death of a man aged seventy-seven years, owing to a rupture of the heart. In his case 'the cavities of the pleura contained _about three pounds of fluid_, but the lungs were sound.'" Deems also cites the following instance: "Dr. Elliotson relates the case of a woman who died suddenly. 'On opening the body the pericardium was found distended with _clear serum_, and a very large coagulum of blood, which had escaped through a spontaneous rupture of the aorta near its origin, without any other morbid appearance.' Many cases might be cited, but these suffice." For detailed treatment of the subject the student may be referred to Dr. Wm. Stroud's work _On the Physical Cause of the Death of Christ_. Great mental stress, poignant emotion either of grief or joy, and intense spiritual struggle are among the recognized causes of heart rupture.

The present writer believes that the Lord Jesus died of a broken heart. The psalmist sang in dolorous measure according to his inspired prevision of the Lord's passion: "Reproach hath broken my heart; and I am full of heaviness: and I looked for some to take pity, but there was none; and for comforters, but I found none. They gave me also gall for my meat; and in my thirst they gave me vinegar to drink." (Psalm 69:20, 21; see also 22:14.)

9. The Request that Christ's Tomb be Sealed.--Many critics hold that the deputation called upon Pilate on Saturday evening, after the Sabbath had ended. This assumption is made on the ground that to do what these priestly officials did, in personally supervizing the sealing of the tomb, would have been to incur defilement, and that they would not have so done on the Sabbath. Matthew's statement is definite--that the application was made on "the next day, that followed the day of the preparation." The preparation day extended from sunset on Thursday to the beginning of the Sabbath at sunset on Friday.

FOOTNOTES:

[1301] Matt. 27:31-33; Mark 15:20-22; Luke 23:26-33; John: 16, 17.
[1302] Note 1, end of chapter.
[1303] Note 2, end of chapter.
[1304] Note 3, end of chapter.
[1305] Matt. 27:34-50; Mark 15:23-37; Luke 23:33-46; John 19:18-30.
[1306] Isa. 53:12; compare Mark 15:28; Luke 22:37.
[1307] Note 4, end of chapter.
[1308] Numb. 12.
[1309] Revised version, marginal reading, "tunic."
[1310] Matt. 27:35; Mark 15:24; Luke 23:34; John 19:23,24; compare Psa. 22:18.
[1311] Note 5, end of chapter.
[1312] Pages 85 and 89.
[1313] Matt. 27:42, 43. The clause "if he be the King of Israel" in verse 42 of the common text is admittedly a mistranslation; it should read "He is the King of Israel." See revised version; also Edersheim, vol. 2, p. 596; compare Mark 15:32.
[1314] John 3:14; 8:28; 12:32.
[1315] Matt. 4:3, 6; see pages 130, 137 herein.

[1316] Luke 23:42; the revised version reads "when thou comest in thy kingdom."

[1317] See chapter 36, following.

[1318] John 19:25; compare Matt. 27:55, 56; Mark 15:40, 41; Luke 23:48, 49. See Note 6, end of chapter.

[1319] See references last cited; and Luke 8:2, 3; also page 264 herein.

[1320] Luke 2:34, 35; page 97 herein.

[1321] Mark 15:25; see Note 7, end of chapter.

[1322] Compare P. of G.P., Moses 7:37, 40, 48, 49, 56.

[1323] John 19:28; compare Psa. 69:21.

[1324] The Gospel writers leave us in some uncertainty as to which of the last two utterances from the cross.--"It is finished," and "Father, into thy hands I commend my spirit," was spoken first.

[1325] Doc. and Cov. 18:11; revelation given in June 1829; see also 19:16-19, and page 613 herein.

[1326] See "The House of the Lord," pages 59, 60.

[1327] Matt. 27:51-54; Mark 15:38, 39; Luke 23:47-49.

[1328] John 19:31-37.

[1329] Deut. 21:23.

[1330] Exo. 12:46; Numb. 9:12; Psa. 34:20; John 19:36; 1 Cor. 5:7.

[1331] John 20:27; B. of M., 3 Nephi 11:14, 15.

[1332] Note 8, end of chapter.

[1333] John 19:34-37; compare Psa. 22:16, 17; Zech. 12:10; Rev. 1:7. [1334] Matt. 27:57-61; Mark 15:42-47; Luke 23:50-56; John 19:38-42.

[1335] John 3:1, 2; 7:50; see pages 158 and 404 herein.

[1336] See revised version, Mark 15:46.

[1337] Matt. 27:62-66.

[1338] Note 9, end of chapter.

CHAPTER 36. IN THE REALM OF DISEMBODIED SPIRITS.

Jesus the Christ died in the literal sense in which all men die. He underwent a physical dissolution by which His immortal spirit was separated from His body of flesh and bones, and that body was actually dead. While the corpse lay in Joseph's rock-hewn tomb, the living Christ existed as a disembodied Spirit. We are justified in inquiring where He was and what were His activities during the interval between His death on the cross and His emergence from the sepulchre with spirit and body reunited, a resurrected Soul. The assumption that most naturally suggests itself is that He went where the spirits of the dead ordinarily go; and that, in the sense in which while in the flesh He had been a Man among men, He was, in the disembodied state a Spirit among spirits. This conception is confirmed as a fact by scriptural attestation.

As heretofore shown[1339] Jesus Christ was the chosen and ordained Redeemer and Savior of mankind; to this exalted mission He had been set apart in the beginning, even before the earth was prepared as the abode of mankind. Unnumbered hosts who had never heard the gospel, lived and died upon the earth before the birth of Jesus. Of those departed myriads many had passed their mortal probation with varying degrees of righteous observance of the law of God so far as it had been made known unto them, but had died in unblamable ignorance of the gospel; while other multitudes had lived and died as transgressors even against such moiety of God's law to man as they had learned and such as they had professed to obey. Death had claimed as its own all of these, both just and unjust. To them went the Christ, bearing the transcendently glorious tidings of redemption from the bondage of death, and of possible salvation from the effects of individual sin. This labor was part of the Savior's foreappointed and unique service to the human family. The shout of divine exultation from the cross, "It is finished," signified the consummation of the Lord's mission in mortality; yet there remained to Him other ministry to be rendered prior to His return to the Father.

To the penitent transgressor crucified by His side, who reverently craved remembrance when the Lord should come into His kingdom,[1340] Christ had given the comforting assurance: "Verily I say unto thee, Today shalt thou be with me in paradise." The spirit of Jesus and the spirit of the repentant thief left their crucified bodies and went to the same place in the realm of the departed.[1341] On the third day following, Jesus, then a resurrected Being, positively stated to the weeping Magdalene: "I am not yet ascended to my Father." He had gone to paradise but not to the place where God dwells. Paradise, therefore, is not Heaven, if by the latter term we understand the abode of the Eternal Father and His celestialized children.[1342] Paradise is a place where dwell righteous and repentant spirits between bodily death and resurrection. Another division of the spirit world is reserved for those disembodied beings who have lived lives of wickedness and who remain impenitent even after death. Alma, a Nephite prophet, thus spake of the conditions prevailing among the departed:

"Now concerning the state of the soul between death and the resurrection. Behold, it has been made known unto me, by an angel, that the spirits of all men, as soon as they are departed from this mortal body; yea, the spirits of all men, whether they be good or evil, are taken home to that God who gave them life. And then shall it come to pass that the spirits of those who are righteous, are received into a state of happiness, which is called paradise; a state of rest; a state of peace, where they shall rest from all their troubles and from all care, and sorrow, &c. And then shall it come to pass, that the spirits of the wicked, yea, who are evil; for behold, they have no part nor portion of the Spirit of the Lord; for behold, they chose evil works rather than good; therefore the spirit of the devil did enter into them, and take possession of their house; and these shall be cast out into outer darkness; there shall be weeping, and wailing, and gnashing of teeth; and this because of their own iniquity; being led captive by the will of the devil. Now this is the state of the souls of the wicked: yea, in darkness, and a state of awful, fearful, looking for the fiery indignation of the wrath of God upon them; thus they remain in this state, as well as the righteous in paradise, until the time of their resurrection."[1343]

While divested of His body Christ ministered among the departed, both in paradise and in the prison realm where dwelt in a state of durance the spirits of the disobedient. To this effect testified Peter nearly three decades after the great event: "For Christ also hath once suffered for sins, the just for the unjust, that he might bring us to God, being put to death in the flesh, but quickened by the Spirit: By which also he went and preached unto the spirits in prison; Which sometime were disobedient, when once the longsuffering of God waited in the days of Noah, while the ark was a preparing, wherein few, that is, eight souls were saved by water."[1344]

The disobedient who had lived on earth in the Noachian period are especially mentioned as beneficiaries of the Lord's ministry in the spirit world. They had been guilty of gross offenses, and had wantonly rejected the teachings and admonitions of Noah, the earthly minister of Jehovah. For their flagrant sin they had been destroyed in the flesh, and their spirits had endured in a condition of imprisonment, without hope, from the time of their death to the advent of Christ, who came as a Spirit amongst them. We are not to assume from Peter's illustrative mention of the disobedient antediluvians that they alone were included in the blessed opportunities offered through Christ's ministry in the spirit realm; on the contrary, we conclude in reason and consistency that all whose wickedness in the flesh had brought their spirits into the prison house were sharers in the possibilities of expiation, repentance, and release. Justice demanded that the gospel be preached among the dead as it had been and was to be yet more widely preached among the living. Let us consider the further affirmation of Peter, as part of his pastoral admonition to the members of the Primitive Church: "Who shall give account to him that is ready to judge the quick and the dead. For this cause was the gospel preached also to them that are dead, that they might be judged according to men in the flesh, but live according to God in the spirit."[1345]

That Jesus knew, while yet in the body, that His mission as the universal Redeemer and Savior of the race would not be complete when He came to die is sufficiently demonstrated by His words to the casuistical Jews, following the Sabbath day healing at Bethesda: "Verily, verily, I say unto you, The hour is coming, and now is, when the dead shall hear the voice of the Son of God: and they that hear shall live. For as the Father hath life in himself; so hath he given to the Son to have life in himself; and hath given him authority to execute judgment also, because he is the Son of man. Marvel not at this: for the hour is coming, in the which all that are in the graves shall hear his voice, and shall come forth; they that have done good, unto the resurrection of life; and they that have done evil, unto the resurrection of damnation."[1346] The solemn truth, that through the atonement of Christ salvation would be made possible to the dead as well as to the living, was revealed to the prophets centuries before the meridian of time. Isaiah was permitted to foresee the fate of the ungodly, and the state prepared for haughty and rebellious offenders against righteousness; but the dread vision was in part brightened by the deliverance that had been provided. "And it shall come to pass in that day, that the Lord shall punish the host of the high ones that are on high, and the kings of the earth upon the earth. And they shall be gathered together, as prisoners are gathered in the pit, and shall be shut up in the prison, and after many days shall they be visited."[1347] To the same mighty prophet was shown the universality of the Savior's atoning victory, as comprizing the redemption of Jew and Gentile, living and dead; and convincingly he voiced the word of revelation: "Thus saith God the Lord, he that created the heavens, and stretched them out; he that spread forth the earth, and that which cometh out of it; he that giveth breath unto the people upon it, and spirit to them that walk therein: I the Lord have called thee in righteousness, and will hold thine hand, and will keep thee, and give thee for a covenant of the people, for a light of the Gentiles; to open the blind eyes, to bring out the prisoners from the prison, and them that sit in darkness out of the prison house."[1348]

David, singing the praises of the Redeemer whose dominion should extend even to the souls in hell, shouted in joy at the prospect of deliverance: "Therefore my heart is glad, and my glory rejoiceth: my flesh also shall rest in hope. For thou wilt not leave my soul in hell; neither wilt thou suffer thine Holy One to see corruption. Thou wilt shew me the path of life: in thy presence is fulness of joy; at thy right hand there are pleasures for evermore."[1349]

From these and other scriptures it is evident that the ministry of Christ among the disembodied was foreseen, predicted, and accomplished. The fact that the gospel was preached to the dead necessarily implies the possibility of the dead accepting the same and availing themselves of the saving opportunities thereof. In the merciful providence of the Almighty, provision has been made for vicarious service by the living for the dead, in the ordinances essential to salvation; so that all who in the spirit-world accept the word of God as preached to them, develop true faith in Jesus Christ as the one and only Savior, and contritely repent of their transgressions, shall be brought under the saving effect of baptism by water for the remission of sins, and be recipients of the baptism of the Spirit or the bestowal of the Holy Ghost.[1350] Paul cites the principle and practise of baptism by the living for the dead as proof of the actuality of the resurrection: "Else what shall they do which are baptized for the dead, if the dead rise not at all? why are they then baptized for the dead?"[1351] Free agency, the divine birthright of every human soul, will not be annulled by death. Only as the spirits of the dead become penitent and faithful will they be benefited by the vicarious service rendered in their behalf on earth.

Missionary labor among the dead was inaugurated by the Christ; who of us can doubt that it has been continued by His authorized servants, the disembodied, who while in the flesh had been commissioned to preach the gospel and administer in the ordinances thereof through ordination in the Holy Priesthood? That the faithful apostles who were left to build up the Church on earth following the departure of its divine Founder, that other ministers of the word of God ordained to the Priesthood by authority in the Primitive as well as in the Latter-day Church, have passed from ministerial service among mortals to a continuation of such labor among the disembodied, is so abundantly implied in scripture as to be made a certainty. They are called to follow in the footsteps of the Master, ministering here among the living, and beyond among the dead.

The victory of Christ over death and sin would be incomplete were its effects confined to the small minority who have heard, accepted, and lived the gospel of salvation in the flesh. Compliance with the laws and ordinances of the gospel is essential to salvation. Nowhere in scripture is a distinction made in this regard between the living and the dead. The dead are those who have lived in mortality upon earth; the living are mortals who yet shall pass through the ordained change which we call death. All are children of the same Father, all to be judged and rewarded or punished by the same unerring justice, with the same interposition of benign mercy. Christ's atoning sacrifice was offered, not alone for the few who lived upon the earth while He was in the flesh, nor for those who were to be born in mortality after His death, but for all inhabitants of earth then past, present, and future. He was ordained of the Father to be a judge of both quick and dead;[1352] He is Lord alike of living and dead,[1353] as men speak of dead and living, though all are to be placed in the same position before Him; there will be but a single class, for all live unto Him.[1354] While His body reposed in the tomb, Christ was actively engaged in the further accomplishment of the Father's purposes, by offering the boon of salvation to the dead, both in paradise and in hell.

NOTES TO CHAPTER 36.

1. Paradise.--The scriptures prove that at the time of the final judgment every man will stand before the bar of God, clothed in his resurrected body, and this, irrespective of his condition of righteousness or guilt. While awaiting resurrection, disembodied spirits exist in an intermediate state, of happiness and rest or of suffering and suspense, according to the course they have elected to follow in

mortality. Reference to paradise as the abode of righteous spirits between the time of death and that of the resurrection is made by the prophet Nephi (2 Nephi 9:13), by a later prophet of the same name (4 Nephi 14), by Moroni (Moroni 10:34); as also by Alma whose words are quoted in the text (Alma 40:12, 14). New Testament scripture is of analogous import (Luke 23:43; 2 Cor. 12:4; Rev. 2:7). The word "paradise" by its derivation through the Greek from the Persian, signifies a pleasant place, or a place of restful enjoyment. (See _The Articles of Faith_, xxi, note 5). By many the terms "hades" and "sheol" are understood to designate the place of departed spirits, comprizing both paradise and the prison realm; by others the terms are applied only to the latter, the place of the wicked, which is apart from paradise, the abode of the just.

The assumption that the gracious assurance given by Christ to the penitent sinner on the cross was a remission of the man's sins, and a passport into heaven, is wholly contrary to both the letter and spirit of scripture, reason, and justice. Confidence in the efficacy of death-bed professions and confessions on the basis of this incident is of the most insecure foundation. The crucified malefactor manifested both faith and repentance; his promised blessing was that he should that day hear the gospel preached in paradise; in the acceptance or rejection of the word of life he would be an agent unto himself. The requirement of obedience to the laws and ordinances of the gospel as an essential to salvation was not waived, suspended, or superseded in his case.

2. The Scripture Relating to Christ Among the Spirits in Prison.--The revised version of 1 Peter 3:18-20 reads: "Because Christ also suffered for sins once, the righteous for the unrighteous, that he might bring us to God; being put to death in the flesh, but quickened in the spirit; in which also he went and preached unto the spirits in prison, which aforetime were disobedient, when the longsuffering of God waited in the days of Noah, while the ark was a preparing, wherein few, that is eight souls were saved through water." This is regarded by scholars as a closer approach to accuracy in translation than the common version. Certain important differences between the two versions will appear to the studious reader. The common version of the latter part of verse 18 and the whole of verse 19 reads: "being put to death in the flesh, but quickened by the spirit: By which also he went and preached unto the spirits in prison." The revised text expresses the true thought that Christ was quickened, that is to say, was active, in His own spirit state, although His body was inert and in reality dead at the time; and that _in_ that disembodied state He went and preached to the disobedient spirits. The later reading fixes the time of our Lord's ministry among the departed as the interval between His death and resurrection.

FOOTNOTES:

[1339] Chapters 2 and 3 herein.
[1340] Page 659.
[1341] Note 1, end of chapter.
[1342] Note the distinction made by Paul 2 Cor. 12:2-4.
[1343] B. of M., Alma 40:11-14.
[1344] 1 Peter 3:18-20; see Note 2, end of chapter.
[1345] 1 Peter 4:5, 6. See Note 2, end of chapter.
[1346] John 5:25-29; see also page 210 herein.
[1347] Isa. 24:21, 22.
[1348] Isa. 42:5-7.
[1349] Psalm 16:9-11.
[1350] See page 124 herein; also "The Articles of Faith," vii:18-33; and "The House of the Lord," pages 63-93.
[1351] 1 Cor. 15:29; see also "House of the Lord," p. 92.
[1352] Acts 10:42; 2 Tim. 4:1; 1 Peter 4:5.
[1353] Rom. 14:9.
[1354] Luke 20:36, 38; "The Articles of Faith," vii:18.

CHAPTER 37. THE RESURRECTION AND THE ASCENSION.

CHRIST IS RISEN.

Saturday, the Jewish Sabbath, had passed, and the night preceding the dawn of the most memorable Sunday in history was well nigh spent, while the Roman guard kept watch over the sealed sepulchre wherein lay the body of the Lord Jesus. While it was yet dark, the earth began to quake; an angel of the Lord descended in glory, rolled back the massive stone from the portal of the tomb, and sat upon it. His countenance was brilliant as the lightning, and his raiment was as the driven snow for whiteness. The soldiers, paralyzed with fear, fell to the earth as dead men. When they had partially recovered from their fright, they fled from the place in terror. Even the rigor of Roman discipline, which decreed summary death to every soldier who deserted his post, could not deter them. Moreover, there was nothing left for them to guard; the seal of authority had been broken, the sepulchre was open, and empty.[1355]

At the earliest indication of dawn, the devoted Mary Magdalene and other faithful women set out for the tomb, bearing spices and ointments which they had prepared for the further anointing of the body of Jesus. Some of them had been witnesses of the burial, and were conscious of the necessary haste with which the corpse had been wrapped with spicery and laid away by Joseph and Nicodemus, just before the beginning of the Sabbath; and now these adoring women came early to render loving service in a more thorough anointing and external embalmment of the body. On the way as they sorrowfully conversed, they seemingly for the first time thought of the difficulty of entering the tomb. "Who shall roll us away the stone from the door of the sepulchre?" they asked one of another. Evidently they knew nothing of the seal and the guard of soldiery. At the tomb they saw the angel, and were afraid; but he said unto them: "Fear not ye: for I know that ye seek Jesus, which was crucified. He is not here: for he is risen, as he said. Come, see the place where the Lord lay. And go quickly, and tell his disciples that he is risen from the dead; and, behold, he goeth before you into Galilee; there shall ye see him: lo, I have told you."[1356]

The women, though favored by angelic visitation and assurance, left the place amazed and frightened. Mary Magdalene appears to have been the first to carry word to the disciples concerning the empty tomb. She had failed to comprehend the gladsome meaning of the angel's proclamation "He is risen, as he said"; in her agony of love and grief she remembered only the words "He is not here," the truth of which had been so forcefully impressed by her own hasty glance at the open and tenantless tomb. "Then she runneth, and cometh to Simon Peter, and to the other disciple, whom Jesus loved, and saith unto them, They have taken away the Lord out of the sepulchre, and we know not where they have laid him."

Peter, and "that other disciple" who, doubtless, was John, set forth in haste, running together toward the sepulchre. John outran his companion, and on reaching the tomb stooped to look in, and so caught a glimpse of the linen cerements lying on the floor; but the bold and impetuous Peter rushed into the sepulchre, and was followed by the younger apostle. The two observed the linen grave-clothes, and lying by itself, the napkin that had been placed about the head of the corpse. John frankly affirms that having seen these things, he believed, and explains in behalf of himself and his fellow apostles, "For as yet they knew not the scripture, that he must rise again from the dead."[1357]

The sorrowful Magdalene had followed the two apostles back to the garden of the burial. No thought of the Lord's restoration to life appears to have found place in her griefstricken heart; she knew only that the body of her beloved Master had disappeared. While Peter and John were within the sepulchre, she had stood without, weeping. After the men had left she stooped and looked into the rock-hewn cavern. There she saw two personages, angels in white; one sat "at the head, and the other at the feet, where the body of Jesus had lain." In accents of tenderness they asked of her: "Woman, why weepest thou?" In reply she could but voice anew her overwhelming sorrow: "Because they have taken away my Lord, and I know not where they have laid him." The absence of the body, which she thought to be all that was left on earth of Him whom she loved so deeply, was a personal bereavement. There is a volume of pathos and affection in her words, "They have taken away my Lord."

Turning from the vault, which, though at that moment illumined by angelic presence, was to her void and desolate, she became aware of another Personage, standing near. She heard His sympathizing inquiry: "Woman, why weepest thou? whom seekest thou?" Scarcely lifting her tearful countenance to look at the Questioner, but vaguely supposing that He was the caretaker of the garden, and that He might have knowledge of what had been done with the body of her Lord, she exclaimed: "Sir, if thou have borne him hence, tell me where thou hast laid him, and I will take him away." She knew that Jesus had been interred in a borrowed tomb; and if the body had been dispossessed of that resting place, she was prepared to provide another. "Tell me where thou hast laid him," she pleaded.

It was Jesus to whom she spake, her beloved Lord, though she knew it not. One word from His living lips changed her agonized grief into ecstatic joy. "Jesus saith unto her, Mary." The voice, the tone, the tender accent she had heard and loved in the earlier days lifted her from the despairing depths into which she had sunk. She turned, and saw the Lord. In a transport of joy she reached out her arms to embrace Him, uttering only the endearing and worshipful word, "Rabboni," meaning My beloved Master. Jesus, restrained her impulsive manifestation of reverent love, saying, "Touch me not[1358] for I am not yet ascended to my Father," and adding, "but go to my brethren, and say unto them, I ascend unto my Father, and your Father; and to my God, and your God."[1359]

To a woman, to Mary of Magdala, was given the honor of being the first among mortals to behold a resurrected Soul, and that Soul, the Lord Jesus.[1360] To other favored women did the risen Lord next manifest Himself, including Mary the mother of Joses, Joanna, and Salome the mother of the apostles James and John. These and the other women with them had been affrighted by the presence of the angel at the tomb, and had departed with mingled fear and joy. They were not present when Peter and John entered the vault, nor afterward when the Lord made Himself known to Mary Magdalene. They may have returned later, for some of them appear to have entered the sepulchre, and to have seen that the Lord's body was not there. As they stood wondering in perplexity and astonishment, they became aware of the presence of two men in shining garments, and as the women "bowed down their faces to the earth" the angels said unto them: "Why seek ye the living among the dead? He is not here, but is risen: remember how he spake unto you when he was yet in Galilee, saying, The Son of man must be delivered into the hands of sinful men, and be crucified, and the third day rise again. And they remembered his words."[1361] As they were returning to the city to deliver the message to the disciples, "Jesus met them, saying, All hail. And they came and held him by the feet, and worshipped him. Then said Jesus unto them, Be not afraid: go tell my brethren that they go into Galilee, and there shall they see me."[1362]

One may wonder why Jesus had forbidden Mary Magdalene to touch Him, and then, so soon after, had permitted other women to hold Him by the feet as they bowed in reverence. We may assume that Mary's emotional approach had been prompted more by a feeling of personal yet holy affection than by an impulse of devotional worship such as the other women evinced. Though the resurrected Christ manifested the same friendly and intimate regard as He had shown in the mortal state toward those with whom He had been closely associated, He was no longer one of them in the literal sense. There was about Him a divine dignity that forbade close personal familiarity. To Mary Magdalene Christ had said: "Touch me not; for I am not yet ascended to my Father." If the second clause was spoken in explanation of the first, we have to infer that no human hand was to be permitted to touch the Lord's resurrected and immortalized body until after He had presented Himself to the Father. It appears reasonable and probable that between Mary's impulsive attempt to touch the Lord, and the action of the other women who held Him by the feet as they bowed in worshipful reverence, Christ did ascend to the Father, and that later He returned to earth to continue His ministry in the resurrected state.

Mary Magdalene and the other women told the wonderful story of their several experiences to the disciples, but the brethren could not credit their words, which "seemed to them as idle tales, and they believed them not."[1363] After all that Christ had taught concerning His rising from the dead on that third day,[1364] the apostles were unable to accept the actuality of the occurrence; to their minds the resurrection was some mysterious and remote event, not a present possibility. There was neither precedent nor analogy for the stories these women told--of a dead person returning to life, with a body of flesh and bones, such as could be seen and felt--except the instances of the young man of Nain, the daughter of Jairus, and the beloved Lazarus of Bethany, between whose cases of restoration to a renewal of mortal life and the reported resurrection of Jesus they recognized essential differences. The grief and the sense of irreparable loss which had characterized the yesterday Sabbath, were replaced by profound perplexity and contending doubts on this first day of the week. But while the apostles hesitated to believe that Christ had actually risen, the women, less skeptical, more trustful, knew, for they had both seen Him and heard His voice, and some of them had touched His feet.

A PRIESTLY CONSPIRACY OF FALSEHOOD.[1365]

When the Roman guardsmen had sufficiently recovered from fright to make their precipitate departure from the sepulchre, they went to the chief priests, under whose orders they had been placed by Pilate,[1366] and reported the supernatural occurrences they had witnessed. The chief priests were Sadducees, of which sect or party a distinguishing feature was the denial of the possibility of resurrection from the dead. A session of the Sanhedrin was called, and the disturbing report of the guard was considered. In the spirit in which these deceiving hierarchs had tried to kill Lazarus for the purpose of quelling popular interest in the miracle of his restoration to life, they now conspired to discredit the truth of Christ's resurrection by bribing the soldiers to lie. These were told to say "His disciples came by night, and stole him away while we slept"; and for the falsehood they were offered large sums of money. The soldiers accepted the tempting bribe, and did as they were instructed; for this course appeared to them the best way out of a critical situation. If they were found guilty of sleeping at their posts, immediate death would be their doom;[1367] but the Jews encouraged them by the promise: "If this come to the governor's ears, we will persuade him and secure you." It must be remembered that the soldiers had been put at the disposal of the chief priests, and presumably therefore were not required to report the details of their doings to the Roman authorities.

The recorder adds that until the day of his writing, the falsehood of Christ's body having been stolen from the tomb by the disciples was current among the Jews. The utter untenability of the false report is apparent. If all the soldiers were asleep--a most unlikely occurrence inasmuch as such neglect was a capital offense--how could they possibly know that any one had approached the tomb? And, more particularly, how could they substantiate their statement even if it were true, that the body was stolen and that the disciples were the grave-robbers?[1368] The mendacious fiction was framed by the chief priests and elders of the people. Not all the priestly circle were parties to it however. Some, who perhaps had been among the secret disciples of Jesus before His death, were not afraid to openly ally themselves with the Church, when, through the evidence of the Lord's resurrection, they had become thoroughly converted. We read that but a few months later "a great company of the priests were obedient to the faith."[1369]

CHRIST WALKS AND TALKS WITH TWO OF THE DISCIPLES.[1370]

During the afternoon of that same Sunday, two disciples, not of the apostles, left the little band of believers in Jerusalem and set out for Emmaus, a village between seven and eight miles from the city. There could be but one topic of conversation between them, and on this they communed as they walked, citing incidents in the Lord's life, dwelling particularly upon the fact of His death through which their hopes of a Messianic reign had been so sadly blighted, and marveling deeply over the incomprehensible testimony of the women concerning His reappearance as a living Soul. As they went, engrossed in sorrowful and profound discourse, another Wayfarer joined them; it was the Lord Jesus, "but their eyes were holden that they should not know him." In courteous interest, He asked: "What manner of communications are these that ye have one to another, as ye walk, and are sad?" One of the disciples, Cleopas by name, replied with surprize tinged with commiseration for the Stranger's seeming ignorance: "Art thou only a stranger in Jerusalem, and hast not known the things which are come to pass there in these days?" Intent on drawing from the men a full statement of the matter by which they were so plainly agitated, the unrecognized Christ asked, "What things?" They could not be reticent. "Concerning Jesus of Nazareth" they explained, "which was a prophet mighty in deed and word before God and all the people: and how the chief priests and our rulers delivered him to be condemned to death, and have crucified him." In sorrowful mood they went on to tell how they had trusted that the now crucified Jesus would have proved to be the Messiah sent to redeem Israel; but alas! this was the third day since He had been slain. Then, with brightening countenances, yet still perplexed, they told of certain women of their company who had astonished them that morning by saying that they had visited the sepulchre early and had discovered that the Lord's body was not there, but, "that they had also seen a vision of angels, which said that he was alive." Moreover, others beside the women had gone to the tomb, and had verified the absence of the body but had not seen the Lord.

Then Jesus, gently chiding His fellow travelers as foolish men and slow of heart in their hesitating acceptance of what the prophets had spoken, asked impressively, "Ought not Christ to have suffered these things, and to enter into his glory?" Beginning with the inspired predictions of Moses, He expounded to them the scriptures, touching upon all the prophetic utterances concerning the Savior's mission. Having continued with the two men to their destination Jesus "made as though he would have gone further," but they urged Him to tarry with them, for the day was already far spent. He so far acceded to their hospitable entreaty as to enter the house, and, as soon as their simple meal was prepared, to seat Himself with them at the table. As the Guest of honor, He took the loaf, "blessed it and brake, and gave to them." There may have been something in the fervency of the blessing, or in the manner of breaking and distributing the bread, that revived memories of former days; or, possibly, they caught sight of the pierced hands; but, whatever the immediate cause, they looked intently upon their Guest, "and their eyes were opened, and they knew him; and he vanished out of their sight." In a fulness of joyful wonderment they rose from the table, surprized at themselves for not having recognized Him sooner. One said to the other, "Did not our heart burn within us, while he talked with us by the way, and while he opened to us the scriptures?" Straightway they started to retrace their steps and hastened back to Jerusalem to confirm by their witness what, before, the brethren had been slow to believe.

RISEN LORD APPEARS TO THE DISCIPLES IN JERUSALEM AND EATS IN THEIR PRESENCE.[1371]

When Cleopas and his companion reached Jerusalem that night, they found the apostles and other devoted believers assembled in solemn and worshipful discourse within closed doors. Precautions of secrecy had been taken "for fear of the Jews." Even the apostles had been scattered by the arrest, arraignment, and judicial murder of their Master; but they and the disciples in general rallied anew at the word of His resurrection, as the nucleus of an army soon to sweep the world. The two returning disciples were received with the joyous announcement, "The Lord is risen indeed, and hath appeared to Simon." This is the sole mention made by the Gospel-writers of Christ's personal appearance to Simon Peter on that day. The interview between the Lord and His once recreant but now repentant apostle must have been affecting in the extreme. Peter's remorseful penitence over his denial of Christ in the palace of the high priest was deep and pitiful; he may have doubted that ever again would the Master call him His servant; but hope must have been engendered through the message from the tomb brought by the women, in which the Lord sent greetings to the apostles, whom for the first time He designated as His brethren,[1372] and from this honorable and affectionate characterization Peter had not been excluded; moreover, the angel's commission to the women had given prominence to Peter by particular mention.[1373] To the repentant Peter came the Lord, doubtless with forgiveness and loving assurance. The apostle himself maintains a reverent silence respecting the visitation, but the fact thereof is attested by Paul as one of the definite proofs of the Lord's resurrection.[1374]

Following the jubilant testimony of the assembled believers, Cleopas and his fellow traveler told of the Lord's companionship with them on the Emmaus road, of the things He had taught them, and of the manner in which He had become known unto them in the breaking of bread. As the little company communed together, "Jesus himself stood in the midst of them, and saith unto them, Peace be unto you." They were affrighted, supposing with superstitious dread that a ghost had intruded amongst them. But the Lord comforted them, saying "Why are ye troubled? and why do thoughts arise in your hearts? Behold my hands and my feet, that it is I myself: handle me, and see; for a spirit hath not flesh and bones, as ye see me have." Then He showed them the wounds in His hands and feet and side. "They yet believed not for joy," which is to say, they thought the reality, to which they all were witnesses, too good, too glorious, to be true. To further assure them that He was no shadowy form, no immaterial being of tenuous substance, but a living Personage with bodily organs internal as well as outward, He asked "Have ye here any meat?" They gave Him a piece of a broiled fish and other food,[1375] which He took "and did eat before them."

These unquestionable evidences of their Visitant's corporeity calmed and made rational the minds of the disciples; and now that they were composed and receptive the Lord reminded them that all things that had happened to Him were in accordance with what He had told them while He had lived amongst them. In His divine presence their understanding was quickened and enlarged so that they comprehended as never before the scriptures--the Law of Moses, the books of the prophets and the psalms--concerning Him. That His now accomplished death was a necessity, He attested as fully as He had predicted and affirmed the same aforetime. Then He said unto them: "Thus it is written, and thus it behoved Christ to suffer, and to rise from the dead the third day: and that repentance and remission of sins should be preached in his name among all nations, beginning at Jerusalem. And ye are witnesses of these things." Then were the disciples glad. As He was about to depart the Lord gave them His blessing, saying "Peace be unto you: as my Father hath sent me, even so send I you." This specification of men sent by authority points directly to the apostles; "And when he had said this, he breathed on them, and saith unto them, Receive ye the Holy Ghost: whose soever sins ye remit, they are remitted unto them; and whose soever sins ye retain, they are retained,"[1376]

DOUBTING THOMAS.[1377]

When the Lord Jesus appeared in the midst of the disciples on the evening of the Resurrection Sunday, one of the apostles, Thomas, was absent. He was informed of what the others had witnessed, but was unconvinced; even their solemn testimony, "We have seen the Lord," failed to awaken an echo of faith in his heart. In his state of mental skepticism he exclaimed: "Except I shall see in his hands the print of the nails, and put my finger into the print of the nails, and thrust my hand into his side, I will not believe." Caution and charity must attend our judgment in any conclusion as to the incredulous attitude of this man. He could scarcely have doubted the well attested circumstance of the empty sepulchre, nor the veracity of Mary Magdalene and the other women as to the presence of angels and the Lord's appearing, nor Peter's testimony nor that of the assembled company; but he may have regarded the reported manifestations as a series of subjective visions; and the absence of the Lord's body may have been vaguely considered as a result of Christ's supernatural restoration to life followed by a bodily and final departure from earth. It was the corporeal manifestation of the risen Lord, the exhibition of the wounds incident to crucifixion, the invitation to touch and feel the resurrected body of flesh and bones, to which Thomas demurred. He had no such definite conception of the resurrection as would accord with a literal acceptance of the testimony of his brethren and sisters who had seen, heard, and felt.

A week later, for so the Jewish designation, "after eight days," is to be understood, therefore on the next Sunday, which day of the week afterward came to be known to the Church as the "Lord's Day" and to be observed as the Sabbath in place of Saturday, the Mosaic Sabbath,[1378] the disciples were again assembled, and Thomas was with them. The meeting was held within closed and, presumably, guarded doors, for there was danger of interference by the Jewish officers. "Then came Jesus, the doors being shut, and stood in the midst, and said, Peace be unto you. Then saith he to Thomas, Reach hither thy finger, and behold my hands; and reach hither thy hand, and thrust it into my side: and be not faithless, but believing."

The skeptical mind of Thomas was instantly cleansed, his doubting heart was purified; and a conviction of the glorious truth flooded his soul. In contrite reverence he bowed before his Savior, the while exclaiming in worshipful acknowledgment of Christ's Deity: "My Lord and my God." His adoration was accepted, and the Savior said: "Thomas, because thou hast seen me, thou hast believed: blessed are they that have not seen, and yet have believed."

AT THE SEA OF GALILEE.[1379]

The angel at the sepulchre and the risen Christ Himself had severally sent word to the apostles to go into Galilee, where the Lord would meet them as He had said before His death.[1380] They deferred their departure until after the week following the resurrection, and then once again in their native province, they awaited further developments. In the afternoon of one of those days of waiting, Peter said to six of his fellow apostles, "I go a fishing"; and the others replied, "We also go with thee." Without delay they embarked on a fishing boat; and though they toiled through the night, the net had been drawn in empty after every cast. As morning approached they drew near the land, disappointed and disheartened. In the early dawn they were hailed from the shore by One who asked: "Children, have ye any meat?"[1381] They answered "No." It was Jesus who made the inquiry, though none in the boat recognized Him. He called to them again, saying: "Cast the net on the right side of the ship, and ye shall find. They cast therefore, and now they were not able to draw it for the multitude of fishes." They did as directed and the result was so surprizing as to appear to them miraculous; it must have aroused memories of that other remarkable draught of fishes, in the taking of which their fishermen's skill had been superseded; and at least three witnesses of the earlier miracle were now in the boat.[1382]

John, quick to discern, said to Peter, "It is the Lord"; and Peter, impulsive as ever, hastily girt his fisher's coat about him and sprang into the sea, the sooner to reach land and prostrate himself at his Master's feet. The others left the vessel and entered a small boat in which they rowed to shore, towing the heavily laden net. On the land they saw a fire of coals, with fish broiling thereon, and alongside a supply of bread. Jesus told them to bring of the fish they had just caught, to which instruction the stalwart Peter responded by dashing into the shallows and dragging the net to shore. When counted, the haul was found to consist of a hundred and fifty-three great fishes; and the narrator is careful to note that "for all there were so many, yet was not the net broken."

Then Jesus said "Come and dine"; and as the Host at the meal, He divided and distributed the bread and fish. We are not told that He ate with His guests. Everyone knew that it was the Lord who so hospitably served; yet on this, as on all other occasions of His appearing in the resurrected state, there was about Him an awe-inspiring and restraining demeanor. They would have liked to question Him, but durst not. John tells us that this was the "third time that Jesus shewed himself to his disciples, after that he was risen from the dead"; by which we understand the occasion to have been the third on which Christ had manifested Himself to the apostles, in complete or partial assembly; for, including also the appearing to Mary Magdalene, to the other women, to Peter, and to the two disciples on the country road, this was the seventh recorded appearance of the risen Lord.

When the meal was finished, "Jesus saith to Simon Peter, Simon, son of Jonas, lovest thou me more than these?" The question, however tenderly put, must have wrung Peter's heart, coupled as it was with the reminder of his bold but undependable protestation, "Though all men shall be offended because of thee, yet will I never be offended",[1383] followed by his denial that he had ever known the Man.[1384] To the Lord's inquiry Peter answered humbly, "Yea, Lord; thou knowest that I love thee." Then said Jesus, "Feed my lambs." The question was repeated; and Peter replied in identical words, to which the Lord responded, "Feed my sheep." And yet the third time Jesus asked, "Simon, son of Jonas, lovest thou me?" Peter was pained and grieved at this reiteration, thinking perhaps that the Lord mistrusted him; but as the man had three times denied, so now was he given opportunity for a triple confession. To the thrice repeated question, Peter answered: "Lord, thou knowest all things; thou knowest that I love thee. Jesus saith unto him. Feed my sheep."

The commission "Feed my sheep" was an assurance of the Lord's confidence, and of the reality of Peter's presidency among the apostles. He had emphatically announced his readiness to follow his Master even to prison and death. Now, the Lord who had died said unto him: "Verily, verily; I say unto thee, When thou wast young, thou girdest thyself, and walkedst whither thou wouldst: but when thou shalt be old, thou shalt stretch forth thy hands, and another shall gird thee, and carry thee whither thou wouldst not." John informs us that the Lord so spake signifying the death by which Peter should find a place among the martyrs; the analogy points to crucifixion, and traditional history is without contradiction as to this being the death by which Peter sealed his testimony of the Christ.

Then said the Lord to Peter, "Follow me." The command had both immediate and future significance. The man followed as Jesus drew apart from the others on the shore; yet a few years and Peter would follow his Lord to the cross. Without doubt Peter comprehended the reference to his martyrdom, as his writings, years later, indicate.[1385] As Christ and Peter walked together, the latter, looking backward, saw that John was following, and inquired: "Lord, and what shall this man do?" Peter wished to peer into the future as to his companion's fate--was John also to die for the faith? The Lord replied: "If I will that he tarry till I come, what is that to thee? follow thou me." It was an admonition to Peter to look to his own course of duty, and to follow the Master, wherever the road should lead.

Concerning himself, John adds: "Then went this saying abroad among the brethren, that that disciple should not die: yet Jesus said not unto him, He shall not die; but, If I will that he tarry till I come, what is that to thee?" That John still lives in the embodied state, and shall remain in the flesh until the Lord's yet future advent, is attested by later revelation.[1386] In company with his martyred and resurrected companions, Peter and James, the "disciple whom Jesus loved" has officiated in the restoration of the Holy Apostleship in this the dispensation of the fulness of times.

OTHER MANIFESTATIONS OF THE RISEN LORD IN GALILEE.[1387]

Jesus had designated a mountain in Galilee whereon He would meet the apostles; and thither the Eleven went. When they saw Him at the appointed place, they worshiped Him. The record adds "but some doubted," by which may be implied that others beside the apostles were present, among whom were some who were unconvinced of the actual corporeity of the resurrected Christ. This occasion may have been that of which Paul wrote a quarter of a century later, concerning which he affirms that Christ "was seen of above five hundred brethren at once," of whom, though some had died, the majority remained at the time of Paul's writing, living witnesses to his testimony.[1388]

To those assembled on the mount Jesus declared: "All power is given unto me in heaven and in earth." This could be understood as nothing less than an affirmation of His absolute Godship. His authority was supreme, and those who were commissioned of Him were to minister in His name, and by a power such as no man could give or take away.

FINAL COMMISSION AND THE ASCENSION.

Throughout the forty days following His resurrection, the Lord manifested Himself at intervals to the apostles, to some individually and to all as a body,[1389] and instructed them in "the things pertaining to the kingdom of God."[1390] The record is not always specific and definite as to time and place of particular events; but as to the purport of the Lord's instructions during this period there exists no cause for doubt. Much that He said and did is not written,[1391] but such things as are of record, John assures his readers, "are written, that ye might believe that Jesus is the Christ, the Son of God; and that believing ye might have life through his name."[1392]

As the time of His ascension drew nigh, the Lord said unto the eleven apostles: "Go ye into all the world, and preach the gospel to every creature. He that believeth and is baptized shall be saved; but he that believeth not shall be damned. And these signs shall follow them that believe; In my name shall they cast out devils; they shall speak with new tongues; they shall take up serpents; and if they drink any deadly thing, it shall not hurt them; they shall lay hands on the sick, and they shall recover."[1393] In contrast with their earlier commission, under which they were sent only "to the lost sheep of the house of Israel,"[1394] they were now to go to Jew and Gentile, bond and free, to mankind at large, of whatever nation, country, or tongue. Salvation, through faith in Jesus the Christ, followed by repentance and baptism, was to be freely offered to all; the rejection of the offer thenceforth would bring condemnation. Signs and miracles were promised to "follow them that believe," thus confirming their faith in the power divine; but no intimation was given that such manifestations were to precede belief, as baits to catch the credulous wonder-seeker.

Assuring the apostles anew that the promise of the Father would be realized in the coming of the Holy Ghost, the Lord instructed them to remain in Jerusalem, whither they had now returned from Galilee, until they would be "endued with power from on high";[1395] and He added: "For John truly baptized with water; but ye shall be baptized with the Holy Ghost not many days hence."[1396]

In that last solemn interview, probably as the risen Savior led the mortal Eleven away from the city toward the old familiar resort on the Mount of Olives, the brethren, still imbued with their conception of the kingdom of God as an earthly establishment of power and dominion, asked of Him, "Lord, wilt thou at this time restore again the kingdom to Israel?" Jesus answered, "It is not for you to know the times or the seasons, which the Father hath put in his own power. But ye shall receive power, after that the Holy Ghost is come upon you: and ye shall be witnesses unto me both in Jerusalem, and in all Judea, and in Samaria, and unto the uttermost part of the earth."[1397] Their duty was thus defined and emphasized: "Go ye therefore, and teach all nations, baptizing them in the name of the Father, and of the Son, and of the Holy Ghost: teaching them to observe all things whatsoever I have commanded you: and, lo, I am with you alway, even unto the end of the world. Amen."[1398]

When Christ and the disciples had gone "as far as to Bethany," the Lord lifted up His hands, and blessed them; and while yet He spake, He rose from their midst, and they looked upon Him as He ascended until a cloud received Him out of their sight. While the apostles stood gazing steadfastly upward, two personages, clothed in white apparel, appeared by them; these spake unto the Eleven, saying: "Ye men of Galilee, why stand ye gazing up into heaven? this same Jesus, which is taken up from you into heaven, shall so come in like manner as ye have seen him go into heaven."[1399]

Worshipfully and with great joy the apostles returned to Jerusalem, there to await the coming of the Comforter. The Lord's ascension was accomplished; it was as truly a literal departure of a material Being as His resurrection had been an actual return of His spirit to His own corporeal body, theretofore dead. With the world abode and yet abides the glorious promise, that Jesus the Christ, the same Being who ascended from Olivet in His immortalized body of flesh and bones, shall return, descending from the heavens, in similarly material form and substance.

NOTES TO CHAPTER 37.

1. Precise Time and Manner of Christ's Emergence from the Tomb Not Known.--Our Lord definitely predicted His resurrection from the dead on the third day, (Matt. 16:21; 17:23; 20:19; Mark 9:31; 10:34; Luke 9:22; 13:32; 18:33), and the angels at the tomb (Luke 24:7), and the risen Lord in Person (Luke 24:46) verified the fulfilment of the prophecies; and apostles so testified in later years (Acts 10:40; 1 Cor. 15:4). This specification of the third day must not be understood as meaning after three full days. The Jews began their counting of the daily hours with sunset; therefore the hour before sunset and the hour following belonged to different days. Jesus died and was interred during Friday afternoon. His body lay in the tomb, dead, during part of Friday (first day), throughout Saturday, or as we divide the days, from sunset Friday to sunset Saturday, (second day), and part of Sunday (third day). We know not at what hour between Saturday sunset and Sunday dawn He rose.

The fact that an earthquake occurred, and that the angel of the Lord descended and rolled the stone from the portal of the tomb in the early dawn of Sunday--for so we infer from Matt. 28:1, 2--does not prove that Christ had not already risen. The great stone was rolled back and the inside of the sepulchre exposed to view, so that those who came could see for themselves that the Lord's body was no longer there; it was not necessary to open the portal in order to afford an exit to the resurrected Christ. In His immortalized state He appeared in and disappeared from closed rooms. A resurrected body, though of tangible substance, and possessing all the organs of the mortal tabernacle, is not bound to earth by gravitation, nor can it be hindered in its movements by material barriers. To us who conceive of motion only in the directions incident to the three dimensions of space, the passing of a solid, such as a living body of flesh and bones, through stone walls, is necessarily incomprehensible. But that resurrected beings move in accordance with laws making such passage possible and to them natural, is evidenced not only by the instance of the risen Christ, but by the movements of other resurrected personages. Thus, in September, 1823, Moroni, the Nephite prophet who had died about 400 A.D., appeared to Joseph Smith in his chamber, three times during one night, coming and going without hindrance incident to walls or roof, (see P. of G.P., Joseph Smith 2:43; also _The Articles of Faith_, i:15-17). That Moroni was a resurrected man is shown by his corporeity manifested in his handling of the metallic plates on which was inscribed the record known to us as the Book of Mormon. So also resurrected beings possess the power of rendering themselves visible or invisible to the physical vision of mortals.

2. Attempts to Discredit the Resurrection Through Falsehood.--The inconsistent assertion that Christ had not risen but that His body had been stolen from the tomb by the disciples, has been sufficiently treated in the text. The falsehood is its own refutation. Unbelievers of later date, recognizing the palpable absurdity of this gross attempt at misrepresentation, have not hesitated to suggest other hypotheses, each

of which is conclusively untenable. Thus, the theory based upon the impossible assumption that Christ was not dead when taken from the cross, but was in a state of coma or swoon, and that He was afterward resuscitated, disproves itself when considered in connection with recorded facts. The spear-thrust of the Roman soldier would have been fatal, even if death had not already occurred. The body was taken down, handled, wrapped and buried by members of the Jewish council, who cannot be thought of as actors in the burial of a living man; and so far as subsequent resuscitation is concerned, Edersheim (vol. 2, p. 626) trenchantly remarks: "Not to speak of the many absurdities which this theory involves, it really shifts--if we acquit the disciples of complicity--the fraud upon Christ Himself." A crucified person, removed from the cross before death and subsequently revived, could not have walked with pierced and mangled feet on the very day of his resuscitation, as Jesus did on the road to Emmaus. Another theory that has had its day is that of unconscious deception on the part of those who claimed to have seen the resurrected Christ, such persons having been victims of subjective but unreal visions conjured up by their own excited and imaginative condition. The independence and marked individuality of the several recorded appearings of the Lord disprove the vision theory. Such subjective visual illusions as are predicated by this hypothesis, presuppose a state of expectancy on the part of those who think they see; but all the incidents connected with the manifestations of Jesus after His resurrection were directly opposed to the expectations of those who were made witnesses of His resurrected state.

The foregoing instances of false and untenable theories regarding the resurrection of our Lord are cited as examples of the numerous abortive attempts to explain away the greatest miracle and the most glorious fact of history. The resurrection of Jesus Christ is attested by evidence more conclusive than that upon which rests our acceptance of historical events in general. Yet the testimony of our Lord's rising from the dead is not founded on written pages. To him who seeks in faith and sincerity shall be given an individual conviction which shall enable him to reverently confess as exclaimed the enlightened apostle of old: "Thou art the Christ, the Son of the living God." Jesus, who is God the Son, is not dead. "I know that my Redeemer liveth." (Job 19:25.)

3. Recorded Appearances of Christ Between Resurrection and Ascension.--
1. To Mary Magdalene, near the sepulchre (Mark 16:9, 10; John 20:14).
2. To other women, somewhere between the sepulchre and Jerusalem (Matt. 28:9).
3. To two disciples on the road to Emmaus (Mark 16:12; Luke 24:13).
4. To Peter, in or near Jerusalem (Luke 24:34; 1 Cor. 15:5).
5. To ten of the apostles and others at Jerusalem (Luke 24:36; John 20:19).
6. To the eleven apostles at Jerusalem (Mark 16:14; John 20:26).
7. To the apostles at the Sea of Tiberias, Galilee, (John 21).
8. To the eleven apostles on a mountain in Galilee (Matt. 28:16).
9. To five hundred brethren at once (1 Cor. 15:6); locality not specified, but probably in Galilee.
10. To James (1 Cor. 15:7). Note that no record of this manifestation is made by the Gospel-writers.
11. To the eleven apostles at the time of the ascension, Mount of Olives, near Bethany (Mark 16:19; Luke 24:50, 51).

The Lord's manifestations of Himself to men subsequent to the ascension will be considered later.

FOOTNOTES:

[1355] Matt. 28:1-4, see also verse 11.
[1356] Matt. 28:5-7; compare Mark 16:1-7; Luke 24:1-8; John 20:1-2.
[1357] John 20:1-10.
[1358] Revised version, "Take not hold on me" (margin).
[1359] John 20:11-17.
[1360] Mark 16:9.
[1361] Luke 24:3-8.
[1362] Matt. 28:9, 10.
[1363] Luke 24:9-11; compare Mark 16:9-13.
[1364] Note 1, end of chapter.
[1365] Matt. 28:11-15.
[1366] Matt. 27:65, 66; page 665 herein.
[1367] Compare Acts 12:19.
[1368] Note 2, end of chapter.
[1369] Acts 6:7; compare John 12:42.
[1370] Luke 24:13-32; compare Mark 16:12.
[1371] Luke 24:33-48; John 20:19-23.
[1372] Matt. 28:10; John 20:17.
[1373] Mark 16:7.
[1374] 1 Cor. 15:5.
[1375] The words "and of an honeycomb" (Luke 24:42) are omitted from the revised version, and by many authorities are declared to be a spurious addition to the original text.
[1376] John 20:21-23.
[1377] John 20:24-29; compare Mark 16:14.
[1378] Rev. 1:10; compare Acts 20:7; 1 Cor. 16:2.

[1379] John 21:1-23.
[1380] Matt 28:10; Mark 16:7; compare Matt. 26:32, Mark 14:28.
[1381] The noun of address, "Children" is equivalent to our modern use of "Sirs," "Men" or "Lads." It was quite in harmony with the vernacular.
[1382] Luke 5:4-10; also page 198 herein.
[1383] Matt. 26:33; Mark 14:29; compare Luke 22:33; John 13:37; p. 600 herein.
[1384] Matt. 26:70, 72, 74; also page 629 herein.
[1385] Peter 1:14.
[1386] Doc. and Cov. Sec. 7; compare B. of M., 3 Nephi 28:1-12.
[1387] Matt. 28:16-18.
[1388] 1 Cor. 15:6.
[1389] Note 3, end of chapter.
[1390] Acts 1:3.
[1391] John 20:30; compare 21:25 remembering that the latter passage may have reference to occurrences both before and after the Lord's death.
[1392] John 20:31.
[1393] Mark 16:15-18.
[1394] Matt. 10:5, 6.
[1395] "Clothed with power from on high" according to revised version, Luke 24:49.
[1396] Acts 1:5; see also Luke 24:49; and compare John 14:16, 17, 26; 15:26; 16:7, 13.
[1397] Acts 1:7, 8; compare Matt. 24:36; Mark 13:32.
[1398] Matt. 28:19, 20.
[1399] Acts 1:9-11; see also Luke 24:50, 51.

CHAPTER 38. THE APOSTOLIC MINISTRY.

MATTHIAS ORDAINED TO THE APOSTLESHIP.[1400]

After witnessing the Lord's ascension from Olivet, the eleven apostles returned to Jerusalem filled with joy and thoroughly suffused with the spirit of adoring worship. Both in the temple and in a certain upper room, which was their usual place of meeting, they continued in prayer and supplication, often in association with other disciples, including Mary the mother of the Lord, some of her sons, and the little sisterhood of faithful women who had ministered to Jesus in Galilee and had followed Him thence to Jerusalem and to Calvary.[1401] The disciples, most of whom had been dispersed by the tragic events of that last and fateful Passover, had gathered again, with renewed and fortified faith, about the great fact of the Lord's resurrection. Christ had become "the firstfruits of them that slept," "the first begotten of the dead," and "the firstborn" of the race to rise from death to immortality.[1402] They knew that not only had the grave been compelled to give up the body of their Lord, but that a way had been provided for the striking of the fetters of death from every soul. Immediately following the resurrection of the Lord Jesus, many righteous ones who had slept in the tomb had been resurrected, and had appeared in Jerusalem, revealing themselves unto many.[1403] The universality of the resurrection of the dead was soon to become a prominent feature of apostolic teaching.

The first official act undertaken by the apostles was the filling of the vacancy in the council of the Twelve, occasioned by the apostasy and suicide of Judas Iscariot. Sometime between the ascension of Christ and the feast of Pentecost, when the Eleven and other disciples, in all about a hundred and twenty, were together "with one accord in prayer and supplication," Peter laid the matter before the assembled Church, pointing out that the fall of Judas had been foreseen,[1404] and citing the psalmist's invocation: "Let his habitation be desolate, and let no man dwell therein: and his bishoprick let another take,"[1405] Peter affirmed the necessity of completing the apostolic quorum; and he thus set forth the qualifications essential in the one who should be ordained to the Holy Apostleship: "Wherefore of these men which have companied with us all the time that the Lord Jesus went in and out among us, beginning from the baptism of John, unto that same day that he was taken up from us, must one be ordained to be a witness with us of his resurrection." Two faithful disciples were nominated by the Eleven, Joseph Barsabas and Matthias. In earnest supplication the assembly besought the Lord to indicate whether either of these men, and if so which, was to be chosen for the exalted office; then, "they gave forth their lots; and the lot fell upon Matthias; and he was numbered with the eleven apostles."

The proceeding throughout is deeply significant and instructive. The Eleven fully realized that on them lay the responsibility, and in them was vested the authority, to organize and develop the Church of Christ; that the council or quorum of the apostles was limited to a membership of twelve; and that the new apostle, like themselves, must be competent to testify in special and personal witness concerning the earthly ministry, death, and resurrection of the Lord Jesus. The selection of Matthias was accomplished in a general assembly of the Primitive Church; and while the nominations were made by the apostles, all present appear by implication to have had a voice in the matter of installation. The principle of authoritative administration through common consent of the membership, so impressively exemplified in the choosing of Matthias, was followed, a few weeks later, by the selection of "seven men of honest report, full of the Holy Ghost and wisdom," who having been sustained by the vote of the Church, were set apart to a special ministry by the laying-on of the apostles' hands.[1406]

THE BESTOWAL OF THE HOLY GHOST.[1407]

At the time of Pentecost, which fell on the fiftieth day after the Passover,[1408] and therefore, at this particular recurrence, about nine days after Christ's ascension, the apostles "were all with one accord in one place," engaged in their customary devotions, and waiting, as instructed, until they would be endowed with a particular bestowal of power from on high.[1409] The promised baptism by fire and the Holy Ghost befell them on that day. "Suddenly there came a sound from heaven as of a rushing mighty wind, and it filled all the house where they were sitting. And there appeared unto them cloven tongues like as of fire, and it sat upon each of them. And they were all filled with the Holy Ghost, and began to speak with other tongues, as the Spirit gave them utterance."

The "sound from heaven as of a rushing mighty wind" was heard abroad;[1410] and a multitude gathered about the place. The visible manifestation of "cloven tongues like as of fire," by which each of the Twelve was invested, was seen by those within the house, but apparently not by the gathering crowds. The apostles spoke to the multitude, and a great miracle was wrought, by which "every man heard them speak in his own language"; for the apostles, now richly gifted, spake in many tongues, as the Holy Ghost, by whom they had been endowed, gave them utterance. There were present men from many lands and of many nations, and their languages were diverse. In amazement some of them said: "Behold, are not all these which speak Galileans? And how hear we every man in our own tongue, wherein we were born?" While many were impressed by the preternatural ability of the brethren, others in mocking tones said the men were drunken. This instance of Satanic prompting to inconsiderate speech is especially illustrative of inconsistency and rash ineptitude. Strong drink gives to no man wisdom; it steals away his senses and makes of him a fool.

Then Peter, as the president of the Twelve, stood up and proclaimed in behalf of himself and his brethren: "Ye men of Judea, and all ye that dwell at Jerusalem, be this known unto you, and hearken to my words: for these are not drunken, as ye suppose, seeing it is but the third hour of the day." It was the

Jewish custom, particularly on festival days, to abstain from food and drink until after the morning service in synagog, which was held about the third hour, or nine o'clock in the forenoon. The apostle cited ancient prophecy embodying the promise of Jehovah that He would pour out His Spirit upon all flesh, so that wonders would be wrought, even as those there present witnessed.[1411] Then boldly did Peter testify of Jesus of Nazareth, whom he characterized as "a man approved of God among you by miracles and wonders and signs, which God did by him in the midst of you, as ye yourselves also know;" and, reminding them, in accusing earnestness, of the awful crime to which they had been in some degree parties, he continued: "Him, being delivered by the determinate counsel and foreknowledge of God, ye have taken, and by wicked hands have crucified and slain: whom God hath raised up, having loosed the pains of death: because it was not possible that he should be holden of it." Citing the inspired outburst of the psalmist, who had sung in jubilant measure of the soul that should not be left in hell, and of the flesh that should not see corruption, he showed the application of these scriptures to the Christ; and fearlessly affirmed: "This Jesus hath God raised up, whereof we all are witnesses. Therefore being by the right hand of God exalted, and having received of the Father the promise of the Holy Ghost, he hath shed forth this, which ye now see and hear." With increasing fervency, fearing neither derision nor violence, and driving home to the hearts of his enthralled listeners the fearful fact of their guilt, Peter proclaimed as in voice of thunder: "Therefore let all the house of Israel know assuredly, that God hath made that same Jesus, whom ye have crucified, both Lord and Christ."

The power of the Holy Ghost could not be resisted; to every earnest soul it carried conviction. They that heard were pricked in their hearts, and in contrition cried out to the apostles: "Men and brethren, what shall we do?" Now that they were prepared for the message of salvation, it was given without reserve. "Repent," answered Peter, "and be baptized every one of you in the name of Jesus Christ for the remission of sins, and ye shall receive the gift of the Holy Ghost. For the promise is unto you, and to your children, and to all that are afar off, even as many as the Lord our God shall call."

To the apostles' testimony, to the exhortation and warning, the people responded with profession of faith and repentance. Their joy was comparable to that of the spirits in prison, to whom the disembodied Christ had borne the authoritative word of redemption and salvation. Those who repented and confessed their belief in Christ at that memorable Pentecost were received into the Church by baptism, to the number of about three thousand. That their conversion was genuine and not the effect of a passing enthusiasm, that they were literally born again through baptism into a newness of life, is evidenced by the fact that they endured in the faith--"and they continued steadfastly in the apostles' doctrine and fellowship, and in breaking of bread, and in prayers." So devoted were these early converts, so richly blessed with the outpouring of the Holy Ghost was the Church in those days, that the members voluntarily disposed of their individual possessions and had all things in common. To them faith in the Lord Jesus Christ was of greater worth than the wealth of earth.[1412] Among them, there was nothing called "mine" or "thine," but all things were theirs in the Lord.[1413] Signs and wonders followed the apostles, "and the Lord added to the church daily such as should be saved."

Through the bestowal of the Holy Ghost the apostles had become changed men. As made clear to them by the Spirit of Truth, the scriptures constituted a record of preparation for the events to which they were special and ordained witnesses. Peter, who but a few weeks earlier had quailed before a serving-maid, now spoke openly, fearing none. Seeing once a lame beggar at the Gate Beautiful which led into the temple court, he took the afflicted one by the hand, saying: "Silver and gold have I none; but such as I have give I thee: In the name of Jesus Christ of Nazareth rise up and walk."[1414] The man was healed and leaped in the exuberance of his newly found strength; then he went with Peter and John into the temple, praising God aloud. An amazed crowd, which grew to include about five thousand men, gathered around the apostles in Solomon's Porch; and Peter, observing their wonderment, seized on the occasion to preach to them Jesus the Crucified. He ascribed all praise for the miracle to the Christ whom the Jews had delivered up to be slain, and in unambiguous accusation declared: "The God of Abraham, and of Isaac, and of Jacob, the God of our fathers, hath glorified his Son Jesus; whom ye delivered up, and denied him in the presence of Pilate, when he was determined to let him go. But ye denied the Holy One and the Just, and desired a murderer to be granted unto you; and killed the Prince of life, whom God hath raised from the dead; whereof we are witnesses." In merciful recognition of the ignorance in which they had sinned, he exhorted them to expiatory penitence, crying: "Repent ye therefore, and be converted, that your sins may be blotted out, when the times of refreshing shall come from the presence of the Lord; and he shall send Jesus Christ, which before was preached unto you: whom the heaven must receive until the times of restitution of all things, which God hath spoken by the mouth of all his holy prophets since the world began." There was no encouragement to a belief that their sins could be annulled by wordy profession; a due season of repentance was their privilege, if so be they would believe.

As Peter and John thus testified, the priests and the captain of the temple, together with the ruling Sadducees, came upon them toward evening, and put them in prison to await the action of the judges next day.[1415] On the morrow they were arraigned before Annas, Caiaphas, and other officials, who demanded of them by what power or in whose name they had healed the lame man. Peter, impelled by the power of the Holy Ghost, answered: "Be it known unto you all, and to all the people of Israel, that by the name of Jesus Christ of Nazareth, whom ye crucified, whom God raised from the dead, even by him doth this man stand here before you whole. This is the stone which was set at nought of you builders, which is become the head of the corner. Neither is there salvation in any other: for there is none other name under heaven given among men, whereby we must be saved."[1416]

The hierarchy learned to their consternation that the work they had sought to destroy through the crucifixion of Jesus Christ was spreading now as it had never spread before. In desperation they commanded the apostles, "Not to speak at all nor teach in the name of Jesus." But Peter and John answered boldly: "Whether it be right in the sight of God to hearken unto you more than unto God, judge ye. For we cannot but speak the things which we have seen and heard." This rejoinder of righteous defiance the priestly rulers dared not openly resent; they had to content themselves with threats.

The Church grew with surprizing rapidity; "believers were the more added to the Lord, multitudes both of men and women." So abundantly was the gift of healing manifest through the ministrations of the apostles that as formerly to Christ, now to them, the people flocked, bringing their sick folk and those possessed of evil spirits; and all were healed. So great was the faith of the believers that they laid their afflicted ones on couches in the streets, "that at the least the shadow of Peter passing by might overshadow some of them."[1417]

The high priest and his haughty Sadducean associates caused the apostles to be again arrested and thrown into the common prison. But that night the angel of the Lord opened the dungeon doors and brought the prisoners forth, telling them to go into the temple and further proclaim their testimony of the Christ. This the apostles did, and were so engaged when the Sanhedrin assembled to put them on trial. The officers who were sent to bring the prisoners to the judgment hall returned, saying: "The prison truly found we shut with all safety, and the keepers standing without before the doors; but when we had opened, we found no man within." As the judges sat in impotent consternation, an informer appeared with the word that the men they wanted were at that moment preaching in the courts. The captain and his guard arrested the apostles a third time, and brought them in, but without violence, for they feared the people. The high priest accused the prisoners by question and affirmation: "Did not we straitly command you that ye should not teach in this name? and, behold, ye have filled Jerusalem with your doctrine, and intend to bring this man's blood upon us." Yet, how recently had those same rulers led the rabble in the awful imprecation, "His blood be on us, and on our children."[1418]

Peter and the other apostles, undaunted by the august presence, and undeterred by threatening words or actions, answered with the direct counter-charge that they who sat there to judge were the slayers of the Son of God. Ponder well the solemn affirmation: "We ought to obey God rather than men. The God of our fathers raised up Jesus, whom ye slew and hanged on a tree. Him hath God exalted with his right hand to be a Prince and a Saviour, for to give repentance to Israel, and forgiveness of sins. And we are his witnesses of these things; and so is also the Holy Ghost, whom God hath given to them that obey him."

Closing, locking, bolting their hearts against the testimony of the Lord's own, the chief priests, scribes, and elders of the people counseled together as to how they could put these men to death. There was at least one honorable exception among the murderously inclined councilors. Gamaliel, who was a Pharisee and a noted doctor of the law, the teacher of Saul of Tarsus afterward known through conversion, works, and divine commission, as Paul the apostle,[1419] rose in the council, and having directed that the apostles be removed from the hall, warned his colleagues against the injustice they had in mind. He cited the cases of men falsely claiming to have been sent of God, everyone of whom had come to grief with utter and most ignominious failure of his seditious plans; so would these men come to nought if the work they professed proved to be of men; "But," added the dispassionate and learned doctor, "if it be of God, ye cannot overthrow it; lest haply ye be found even to fight against God."[1420] Gamaliel's advice prevailed for the time being, to the extent of causing the apostles' lives to be spared; but the council, in contravention of justice and propriety, had the prisoners beaten. Then the brethren were discharged with the renewed injunction that they speak not in the name of Jesus. They went out rejoicing that they were counted worthy to suffer stripes and humiliation in defense of the Lord's name; and daily, both in the temple, and by house to house visitation, they valiantly taught and preached Jesus the Christ. Converts to the Church were not confined to the laity; a great company of the priests swelled the number of the disciples, who multiplied greatly in Jerusalem.[1421]

STEPHEN THE MARTYR; HIS VISION OF THE LORD.[1422]

First among the "seven men of honest report" who were set apart under the hands of the apostles to administer the common store of the Church community, was Stephen, a man eminent in faith and good works, through whom the Lord wrought many miracles. He was zealous in service, aggressive in doctrine, and fearless as a minister of Christ. Some of the foreign Jews, who maintained a synagog in Jerusalem, engaged Stephen in disputation, and being unable "to resist the wisdom and the spirit by which he spake," conspired to have him charged with heresy and blasphemy. He was brought before the council on the word of men suborned to witness against him; and these averred that they had "heard him speak blasphemous words against Moses, and against God." The perjured accusers further testified that he had repeatedly spoken blasphemously against the temple, and the law, and had even declared that Jesus of Nazareth would some day destroy the temple, and change the Mosaic ceremonies. The charge was utterly false in spirit and fact, though possibly in a sense partly true in form; for, judging by what we have of record concerning Stephen's character and works, he was a zealous preacher of the word as a world religion, through which the exclusiveness and alleged sanctity of Jerusalem as the holy city and of the now desecrated temple as the earthly abiding-place of Jehovah, would be abrogated; furthermore he seems to have realized that the law of Moses had been fulfilled in the mission of the Messiah.

When the Sanhedrists looked upon him, his face was illumined, and they saw it "as it had been the face of an angel." In answer to the charge, he delivered an address, which on critical analysis appears to have been extemporaneous, nevertheless it is strikingly logical and impressive in argument. The delivery was abruptly terminated, however, by a murderous assault.[1423] In effective epitome Stephen traced the history of the covenant people from the time of Abraham down, showing that the patriarchs, and in turn

Moses and the prophets, had lived and ministered in progressive preparation for the development of which those present were witnesses. He pointed out that Moses had foretold the coming of a Prophet, who was none other than Jehovah, whom their fathers had worshipped in the wilderness, before the tabernacle, and later in the temple; but, he affirmed, "the most High dwelleth not in temples made with hands," the most gorgeous of which could be but small to Him who said: "Heaven is my throne, and earth is my footstool."[1424]

It is plain to be seen that Stephen's speech was not one of vindication, and far from a plea in his own defense; it was a proclamation of the word and purposes of God by a devoted servant who had no thought for personal consequences. In forceful arraignment he thus addressed his judges: "Ye stiffnecked and uncircumcised in heart and ears, ye do always resist the Holy Ghost: as your fathers did, so do ye. Which of the prophets have not your fathers persecuted? and they have slain them which shewed before of the coming of the Just One; of whom ye have been now the betrayers and murderers." Maddened at this direct accusation, the Sanhedrists "gnashed on him with their teeth." He knew that they thirsted for his blood; but, energized by the Holy Ghost, he looked steadfastly upward, and exclaimed in rapture: "Behold I see the heavens opened, and the Son of man standing on the right hand of God."[1425] This is the first New Testament record of a manifestation of Christ to mortal eyes by vision or otherwise, subsequent to His ascension. The priestly rulers cried aloud, and stopped their ears to what they chose to regard as blasphemous utterances; and, rushing upon the prisoner with one accord, they hurried him outside the city walls and stoned him to death. True to his Master, he prayed: "Lord Jesus, receive my spirit"; and then, crushed to earth, he cried with a loud voice: "Lord, lay not this sin to their charge. And when he had said this, he fell asleep."

So died the first martyr for the testimony of the risen Christ. He was slain by a mob comprizing chief priests, scribes, and elders of the people. What cared they that no sentence had been pronounced against him, or that they were acting in reckless defiance of Roman law? Devout men bore the mangled body to its burial; and all the disciples lamented greatly. Persecution increased, and members of the Church were scattered through many lands, wherein they preached the gospel and won many to the Lord. The blood of Stephen the martyr proved to be rich and virile seed, from which sprang a great harvest of souls.[1426]

CHRIST MANIFESTS HIMSELF TO SAUL OF TARSUS, LATER KNOWN AS PAUL, THE APOSTLE.

Among the disputants who, when defeated in discussion, conspired against Stephen and brought about his death, were Jews from Cilicia.[1427] Associated with them was a young man named Saul, a native of the Cilician city of Tarsus. This man was an able scholar, a forceful controversialist, an ardent defender of what he regarded as the right, and a vigorous assailant of what to him was wrong. Though born in Tarsus he had been brought to Jerusalem in early youth and had there grown up a strict Pharisee and an aggressive supporter of Judaism. He was a student of the law under the tutelage of Gamaliel, one of the most eminent masters of the time[1428] and had the confidence of the high priest.[1429] His father, or perhaps an earlier progenitor, had acquired the rank of Roman citizenship, and Saul was a born heir to that distinction. Saul was a violent opponent of the apostles and the Church, and had made himself a party to the death of Stephen by openly consenting thereunto and by holding in personal custody the garments of the false witnesses while they stoned the martyr.

He wrought havoc in the Church by entering private houses and haling thence men and women suspected of belief in the Christ, and these he caused to be cast into prison.[1430] The persecution in which he took so prominent a part caused a scattering of the disciples throughout Judea, Samaria, and other lands; though the apostles remained and continued their ministry in Jerusalem.[1431] Not content with local activity against the Church, "Saul, yet breathing out threatenings and slaughter against the disciples of the Lord, went unto the high priest, and desired of him letters to Damascus to the synagogues, that if he found any of this way, whether they were men or women, he might bring them bound unto Jerusalem."[1432]

As Saul and his attendants neared Damascus they were halted by an occurrence of awe-inspiring grandeur.[1433] At noontide there suddenly appeared a light far exceeding the brightness of the sun, and in this dazzling splendor the whole party was enveloped, so that they fell to the ground in terror. In the midst of the unearthly glory, a sound was heard, which to Saul alone was intelligible as an articulate voice; he heard and understood the reproving question spoken in the Hebrew tongue: "Saul, Saul, why persecutest thou me?" In trepidation he inquired: "Who art thou, Lord?" The reply sounded the heart of Saul to its depths: "I am Jesus of Nazareth, whom thou persecutest"; and continued, as in sympathetic consideration of the persecutor's situation and the renunciation that would be required of him: "It is hard for thee to kick against the pricks."[1434] The enormity of his hostility and enmity against the Lord and His people filled the man's soul with horror, and in trembling contrition he asked: "Lord, what wilt thou have me to do?" The reply was: "Arise, and go into the city, and it shall be told thee what thou must do." The brilliancy of the heavenly light had blinded Saul. His companions led him into Damascus, where, at the house of Judas, in the street called Straight, he sat in darkness for three days, during which period he neither ate nor drank.

There lived in that city a faithful disciple named Ananias, to whom the Lord spake, instructing him to visit Saul and minister unto him that he might be healed of his blindness. Ananias was astonished at the commission, and ventured to remind the Lord that Saul was a notorious persecutor of the saints, and had come at that time to Damascus to arrest and put in bonds all believers. But the Lord answered: "Go thy way: for he is a chosen vessel unto me, to bear my name before the Gentiles, and kings, and the children of Israel: for I will shew him how great things he must suffer for my name's sake." Ananias went to Saul, laid his hands upon the penitent sufferer, saying: "Brother Saul, the Lord, even Jesus, that appeared unto thee in the way as thou camest, hath sent me, that thou mightest receive thy sight, and be filled with the Holy Ghost." The physical obstruction to vision was removed; scaly particles fell from the eyes of Saul, and his sight was restored. Without delay or hesitation, he was baptized. When strengthened by food he communed with the disciples at Damascus and straightway began to preach in the synagogs, declaring Jesus to be the Son of God.[1435]

When Saul returned to Jerusalem, the disciples were doubtful of his sincerity, they having known of him as a violent persecutor; but Barnabas, a trusted disciple, brought him to the apostles, told of his miraculous conversion and testified of his valiant service in preaching the word of God. He was received into fellowship, and afterward was ordained under the hands of the apostles.[1436] His Hebrew name, Saul, was in time substituted by the Latin Paulus, or as to us, Paul.[1437] In view of his commission to carry the Gospel to the Gentiles, the use of his Roman name may have been of advantage, and particularly so as he was a Roman citizen and therefore could claim the rights and exemptions attaching to the status of citizenship.[1438]

It is no part of our present purpose to follow even in outline the labors of the man thus peremptorily and miraculously called into the ministry; the fact of Christ's personal manifestations to him is the sole subject of present consideration. While in Jerusalem Paul was blessed with a visual manifestation of the Lord Jesus, accompanied by the giving of specific instructions. His own testimony is to this effect: "While I prayed in the temple, I was in a trance; and saw him saying unto me, Make haste, and get thee quickly out of Jerusalem: for they will not receive thy testimony concerning me." In explanation of his rejection by the people, Paul confessed his evil past, saying, "Lord, they know that I imprisoned and beat in every synagogue them that believed on thee: and when the blood of thy martyr Stephen was shed, I also was standing by, and consenting unto his death, and kept the raiment of them that slew him." To this the Lord replied: "Depart; for I will send thee far hence unto the Gentiles."[1439] Once again, as he lay a prisoner in the Roman castle, the Lord stood by him in the night, and said: "Be of good cheer, Paul: for as thou hast testified of me in Jerusalem, so must thou bear witness also at Rome."[1440]

Paul's personal witness that he had seen the resurrected Christ is explicit and emphatic. With his enumeration of some of the risen Lord's appearances he associates his own testimony, as addressed to the Corinthian saints, in this wise: "For I delivered unto you first of all that which I also received, how that Christ died for our sins according to the scriptures; and that he was buried, and that he rose again the third day according to the scriptures: and that he was seen of Cephas, then of the Twelve: after that, he was seen of above five hundred brethren at once; of whom the greater part remain unto this present, but some are fallen asleep. After that, he was seen of James; then of all the apostles. And last of all he was seen of me also, as of one born out of due time. For I am the least of the apostles, that am not meet to be called an apostle, because I persecuted the church of God."[1441]

CLOSE OF THE APOSTOLIC MINISTRY--THE REVELATION THROUGH JOHN.

The period of apostolic ministry continued until near the close of the first century of our era, approximately sixty to seventy years from the time of the Lord's ascension. In the course of that epoch the Church experienced both prosperity and vicissitude. At first the organized body increased in membership and influence in a manner regarded as phenomenal, if not miraculous.[1442] The apostles and the many other ministers who labored under their direction in graded positions of authority strove so effectively to spread the word of God, that Paul writing approximately thirty years after the ascension affirmed that the gospel had already been carried to every nation, or, to use his words, "preached to every creature under heaven."[1443] Through the agency of the Holy Ghost Christ continued to direct the affairs of His Church on the earth; and His mortal representatives, the apostles, traveled and taught, healed the afflicted, rebuked evil spirits, and raised the dead to a renewal of life.[1444]

We are without record of any direct or personal appearance of Christ to mortals between the manifestations to Paul and the revelation to John on the isle of Patmos. Tradition confirms John's implication that he had been banished thither "for the word of God, and for the testimony of Jesus Christ."[1445] He avers that what he wrote, now known as the book of Revelation, is "The Revelation of Jesus Christ, which God gave unto him, to shew unto his servants things which must shortly come to pass; and he sent and signified it by his angel unto his servant John."[1446] The apostle gives a vivid description of the glorified Christ as seen by him: and of the Lord's words he made record as follows: "Fear not; I am the first and the last: I am he that liveth, and was dead; and, behold, I am alive for evermore, Amen; and have the keys of hell and of death."[1447] John was commanded to write to each of the seven churches, or branches of the Church of Christ, then existing in Asia, administering reproof, admonition and encouragement, as the condition of each required.

The final ministry of John marked the close of the apostolic administration in the Primitive Church. His fellow apostles had gone to their rest, most of them having entered through the gates of martyrdom, and although it was his special privilege to tarry in the flesh until the Lord's advent in glory, [1448] he was not to continue his service as an acknowledged minister, known to and accepted by the Church. Even while many of the apostles lived and labored, the seed of apostasy had taken root in the Church and had grown with the rankness of pernicious weeds. This condition had been predicted, both by Old Testament prophets[1449] and by the Lord Jesus.[1450] The apostles also spake in plain prediction of the growth of the apostasy all too grievously apparent to them as then in progress.[1451] Personal manifestations of the Lord Jesus to mortals appear to have ceased with the passing of the apostles of old, and were not again witnessed until the dawn of the Dispensation of the Fulness of Times.

NOTES TO CHAPTER 38.

1. Presiding Authority and Common Consent.--"Another instance of official action in choosing and setting apart men to special office in the Church arose soon after the ordination of Matthias. It appears that one feature of the Church organization in early apostolic days was a common ownership of material things, distribution being made according to need. As the members increased, it was found impracticable for the apostles to devote the necessary attention and time to these temporal matters, so they called upon the members to select seven men of honest report, whom the apostles would appoint to take special charge of these affairs. These men were set apart by prayer and by the laying on of hands. The instance is instructive as showing that the apostles realized their possession of authority to direct in the affairs of the Church, and that they observed with strictness the principle of common consent in the administration of their high office. They exercized their priestly powers in the spirit of love, and with due regard to the rights of the people over whom they were placed to preside."--The author, _The Great Apostasy_, 1:19.

2. Pentecost.--The name means "fiftieth" and was applied to the Jewish feast that was celebrated fifty days after the second day of unleavened bread, or the Passover day. It is also known as "the feast of weeks" (Exo. 34:22; Deut. 16:10), because according to the Hebrew style, it fell seven weeks, or a week of weeks, after the Passover; as "the feast of harvest" (Exo. 23:16); and as "the day of the first-fruits" (Numb. 28:26). Pentecost was one of the great feasts in Israel, and was of mandatory observance. Special sacrifices were appointed for the day, as was also an offering suitable to the harvest season, comprising two leavened loaves made of the new wheat; these were to be waved before the altar and then given to the priests (Lev. 23:15-20). Because of the unprecedented events that characterized the first Pentecost after our Lord's ascension, the name has become current in Christian literature as expressive of any great spiritual awakening or unusual manifestation of divine grace.

3. Having All Things in Common.--No condition recorded of the early apostolic ministry expresses more forcefully the unity and devotion of the Church in those days than does the fact of the members establishing a system of common ownership of property (Acts 2:44, 46; 4:32-37; 6:1-4). One result of this community of interest in temporal things was a marked unity in spiritual matters; they "were of one heart and of one soul." Lacking nothing, they lived in contentment and godliness. Over thirty centuries earlier the people of Enoch had rejoiced in a similar condition of oneness, and their attainments in spiritual excellence were so effective that "the Lord came and dwelt with his people ... And the Lord called his people Zion, because they were of one heart and one mind, and dwelt in righteousness; and there was no poor among them." (P. of G.P., Moses 7:16-18.) The Nephite disciples grew in holiness, as "they had all things common among them, every man dealing justly, one with another." (B. of M., 3 Nephi 26:19; see also 4 Nephi 1:2-3.) A system of unity in material affairs has been revealed to the Church in this current dispensation, (Doc. and Cov. 82:17, 18; 51:10-13, 18; 104:70-77), to the blessings of which the people may attain as they learn to replace selfish concern by altruism, and individual advantage by devotion to the general welfare.--See _The Articles of Faith_, xxiv:13-15.

4. Saul's Conversion.--The sudden change of heart by which an ardent persecutor of the saints was so transformed as to become a true disciple, is to the average mind a miracle. Saul of Tarsus was a devoted student and observer of the law, a strict Pharisee. We find no intimation that he ever met or saw Jesus during the Lord's life in the flesh; and his contact with the Christian movement appears to have been brought about through disputation with Stephen. In determining what he would call right and what wrong the young enthusiast was guided too much by mind and too little by heart. His learning, which should have been his servant, was instead his master. He was a leading spirit in the cruel persecution of the first converts to Christianity; yet none can doubt his belief that even in such he was rendering service to Jehovah (compare John 16:2). His unusual energy and superb ability were misdirected. As soon as he realized the error of his course, he turned about, without counting risk, cost, or the certainty of persecution and probable martyrdom. His repentance was as genuine as had been his persecuting zeal. All through his ministry he was tortured by the past (Acts 22:4, 19, 20; 1 Cor. 15:9; 2 Cor. 12:7; Gal. 1:13); yet he found a measure of relief in the knowledge that he had acted in good conscience (Acts 26:9-11). It was "hard for him to kick against the pricks" (revised version "goad," Acts 9:5; 26:14) of tradition, training, and education; yet he hesitated not. He was a chosen instrument for the work of the Lord (Acts 9:15); and promptly he responded to the Master's will. Whatever of error Saul of Tarsus had committed through youthful zeal, Paul the apostle gave his all--his time, talent, and life--to expiate. He was preeminently the Lord's apostle to the Gentiles; and this opening of the doors to others than Jews was the main contention between himself and Stephen. In accordance with the divine and fateful purpose, Paul was called to do the work, in opposition to which he had been a participant in the martyrdom of Stephen. At the Lord's word of direction Paul was ready to preach Christ to the Gentiles; only by a miracle could the Jewish exclusiveness of Peter and the Church generally be overcome (Acts 10; and 11:1-18).

5. Rapid Growth of the Primitive Church.--Eusebius, who wrote in the early part of the fourth century, speaking of the first decade after the Savior's ascension, says: "Thus, then, under a celestial influence and cooperation, the doctrine of the Savior, like the rays of the sun, quickly irradiated the whole world. Presently, in accordance with divine prophecy, the sound of His inspired evangelists and apostles had gone throughout all the earth, and their words to the ends of the world. Throughout every city and village, like a replenished barn floor, churches were rapidly abounding and filled with members from every people. Those who, in consequence of the delusions that had descended to them from their ancestors, had been fettered by the ancient disease of idolatrous superstition, were now liberated by the power of Christ, through the teachings and miracles of His messengers."--(Eusebius, _Eccles. Hist._, Book I, ch. 3.)

6. Patmos.--A small island in the Icarian section of the Aegean Sea. Dr. John R. Sterret writes of

it in the _Standard Bible Dictionary_ as follows: "A volcanic island of the Sporades group, now nearly treeless. It is characterized by an indented coast and has a safe harbor. By the Romans it was made a place of exile for the lower class of criminals. John, the author of 'Revelation' was banished thither by Domitian, 94 A.D. According to tradition he lived there at hard labor for eighteen months."

7. The Holy Ghost Given.--In answer to a question as to whether the Holy Ghost was received by the apostles at or before Pentecost, a statement was published by the First Presidency of the Church on February 5, 1916 (see _Deseret News_ of that date), from which statement the following excerpts are taken: "The answer to this question depends upon what is meant by 'receiving' the Holy Ghost. If reference is made to the promise of Jesus to His apostles about the endowment or gift of the Holy Ghost by the presence and ministration of the 'personage of Spirit,' called the Holy Ghost by revelation (Doc. and Cov. 130:22), then the answer is, it was not until the day of Pentecost that the promise was fulfilled. But the divine essence called the Spirit of God, or Holy Spirit, or Holy Ghost, by which God created or organized all things, and by which the prophets wrote and spoke, was bestowed in former ages, and inspired the apostles in their ministry long before the day of Pentecost.... We read that Jesus, after His resurrection, breathed upon His disciples and said, 'Receive ye the Holy Ghost.' But we also read that He said, 'Behold, I send the promise of my Father upon you: but tarry ye in the city of Jerusalem, until ye be endued with power from on high' (John 20:22; Luke 24:49). We read further: 'For the Holy Ghost was not yet given; because that Jesus was not yet glorified.' (John 7:39.) Thus the promise was made, but the fulfilment came after, so that the Holy Ghost sent by Jesus from the Father did not come in person until the day of Pentecost, and the cloven tongues of fire were the sign of His coming."

FOOTNOTES:

[1400] Acts 1:15-26.
[1401] Luke 24:52,53; Acts 1:12-14.
[1402] 1 Cor. 15:20; Rev. 1:5; Colos. 1:18.
[1403] Matt. 27:52, 53.
[1404] Acts 1:16; compare Psalm 41:9; see also John 13:18.
[1405] Acts 1:20. The revised version substitutes on a preponderance of authority "office" or, (marginal reading), "overseership," for the erroneous rendering "bishoprick" in the common version. Compare Psalm 109:8.
[1406] Acts 6:1-6; Note 1, end of chapter.
[1407] Acts 2:1-41. Note 7, end of chapter.
[1408] Note 2, end of chapter.
[1409] Luke 24:49; Acts 1:4, 5, 8.
[1410] Acts 2:6, in a better rendering than that of the common text (see revised version) reads: "And when this sound was heard, the multitude came together."
[1411] Joel 2:28, 29; compare Zech. 12:10.
[1412] Note 3, end of chapter.
[1413] Acts 2:44-46; 4:32-37; 6:1-4.
[1414] Acts 3:6; read the entire chapter.
[1415] Acts 4:1-22.
[1416] Acts 4:8-12; compare Psalm 118:22; Isa. 28:16; Matt. 21:42.
[1417] Acts 5:12-17.
[1418] Matt. 27:25; compare 23:35; see pages 638 and 648 herein.
[1419] Acts 22:3.
[1420] Acts 5:33-40.
[1421] Acts 6:7.
[1422] Acts 6:8-15; and 7.
[1423] Acts 7:1-53.
[1424] Isa. 66:1, 2; see also Matt. 5:34, 35; 23:22.
[1425] Acts 7:56. Note this exceptional application of the title, Son of Man, to Christ by anyone other than Himself. See page 142 herein.
[1426] Acts 8:4; 11:19.
[1427] Acts 6:9.
[1428] Acts 22:3; compare 5:34; page 708 herein.
[1429] In view of Saul's social status and recognized ability, many believe him to have been a member of the Sanhedrin; but for this assumption we find no definite warrant in scripture.
[1430] Acts 7:58; 8:1-3.
[1431] Acts 8:1.
[1432] Acts 9:1, 2. Observe that "way" here used for the first time to connote the gospel or religion of Christ, occurs frequently in Acts (16:17; 18:25, 26; 19:9, 23; 22:4; 24:14, 22).
[1433] Three versions of this manifestation and its immediate results appear in Acts (9:3-29; 22:6-16; and 26:12-18): the first is the historian's narrative, while the others are given as reports of Saul's own words.
[1434] Note 4, end of chapter.
[1435] Note 4, end of chapter.
[1436] Acts 9:26-28; 13:2, 3.
[1437] Acts 13:9.

[1438] Acts 16:37-40; 22:25-28; 23:27; 25:11; 26:32; 28:19.
[1439] Acts 22:17-21.
[1440] Acts 23:11.
[1441] 1 Cor. 15:3-9.
[1442] Note 5, end of chapter.
[1443] Col. 1:23; see verse 6; also "The Great Apostasy," 1:20, 21.
[1444] Acts 9:36-43.
[1445] Rev. 1:9; see Note 6, end of chapter.
[1446] Rev. 1:1; read the whole chapter.
[1447] Rev. 1:10-20.
[1448] Page 694 herein.
[1449] Isa. 24:1-6; Amos. 8:11, 12.
[1450] Matt. 24:4, 5, 10-13, 23-26.
[1451] Acts 20:17-31, particularly 29, 30; 1 Tim. 4:1-3; 2 Tim. 4:1-4; 2 Thess. 2:3, 4, 7, 8; 2 Peter 2:1-3, read the entire chapter and observe its application to conditions in the world today; Jude 3, 4, 17-19; Rev. 13:4, 6-9; 14:6, 7. See "The Great Apostasy," chapter 2.

CHAPTER 39. MINISTRY OF THE RESURRECTED CHRIST ON THE WESTERN HEMISPHERE.

By considering the apostolic ministry in immediate sequence to our study of the Lord's ascension from the Mount of Olives, we have departed from the chronological order of the several personal manifestations of the risen Savior to mortals; for very soon after His final farewell to the apostles in Judea He visited His "other sheep," not of the eastern fold, whose existence He had affirmed in that impressive sermon concerning the Good Shepherd and His sheep.[1452] Those other sheep who were to hear the Shepherd's voice and eventually be made part of the united fold, were the descendants of Lehi who, with his family and a few others, had left Jerusalem 600 B.C. and had crossed the great deep to what we now know as the American continent, whereon they had grown to be a mighty though a divided people.[1453]

THE LORD'S DEATH SIGNALIZED BY GREAT CALAMITIES ON THE AMERICAN CONTINENT.

As already set forth in these pages, the birth of Jesus at Bethlehem had been made known to the Nephite nation on the western hemisphere by divine revelation; and the glad event had been marked by the appearance of a new star, by a night devoid of darkness so that two days and the night between had been as one day, and by other wonderful occurrences, all of which had been predicted through the prophets of the western world.[1454] Samuel the Lamanite, who through faithfulness and good works had become a prophet, mighty in word and deed, duly chosen and commissioned of God, had coupled with his predictions of the glorious occurrences that were to mark the birth of Christ, prophecies of other signs--of darkness, terror, and destruction--by which the Savior's death on the cross would be signalized.[1455] Every prophetic word concerning the phenomena that were to attend the Lord's birth had been fulfilled; and many people had been brought thereby to believe in Christ as the promised Redeemer; but, as is usual with those whose belief rests on miracles, many among the Nephites "began to forget those signs and wonders which they had heard, and began to be less and less astonished at a sign or a wonder from heaven, insomuch that they began to be hard in their hearts, and blind in their minds, and began to disbelieve all which they had heard and seen."[1456]

Thirty and three years had sped their course since the illumined night and the other signs of Messiah's advent; then, on the fourth day of the first month, or, according to our calendar, during the first week of April, in the thirty-fourth year, there arose a great and terrible tempest, with thunderings, lightnings, and both elevations and depressions of the earth's surface, so that the highways were broken up, mountains were sundered, and many cities were utterly destroyed by earthquake, fire, and the inrush of the sea. For three hours the unprecedented holocaust continued; and then thick darkness fell, in the which it was found impossible to kindle a fire; the awful gloom was like unto the darkness of Egypt[1457] in that its clammy vapors could be felt. This condition lasted until the third day, so that a night a day and a night were as one unbroken night, and the impenetrable blackness was rendered the more terrible by the wailing of the people, whose heart-rending refrain was everywhere the same, "O that we had repented before this great and terrible day."[1458]

Then, piercing the darkness, came a Voice,[1459] before which the frightful chorus of human lamentation was silenced; "Wo, wo, wo unto this people" resounded throughout the land. The Voice proclaimed increasing woes except the people should repent. Destruction had befallen because of wickedness, and the devil was then laughing over the number of the dead and the retributive cause of their destruction. The extent of the dread calamity was detailed; cities that had been burned with their inhabitants, others that had sunk into the sea, yet others buried in the earth, were enumerated; and the divine reason for this widespread destruction was plainly set forth--that the wickedness and abominations of the people might be hidden from the face of the earth. Those who had lived to hear were declared to be the more righteous of the inhabitants; and to them hope was offered on conditions of more thorough repentance and reformation.

The identity of the Voice was thus made known: "Behold, I am Jesus Christ the Son of God. I created the heavens and the earth, and all things that in them are. I was with the Father from the beginning. I am in the Father, and the Father in me; and in me hath the Father glorified his name." The Lord commanded that the people should no longer serve Him with bloody sacrifices and burnt offerings; for the law of Moses was fulfilled; and thenceforth the only acceptable sacrifice would be the broken heart and the contrite spirit; and such should never be rejected. The humble and repentant Lord would receive as His own. "Behold," He said, "for such I have laid down my life, and have taken it up again; therefore repent, and come unto me ye ends of the earth, and be saved."

The Voice ceased; and through the space of many hours of continuing darkness vociferous lamentations were hushed, for the people were convicted of their guilt and silently wept in astonishment over what they had heard, and in hopeful anticipation of the salvation that had been offered. A second time the Voice was heard, as in sorrow over those who had refused to accept the Savior's succor; for often had He protected them, more often would He have so done had they been willing, and yet in the future would He cherish them, "as a hen gathereth her chickens under her wings" if they would repent and live in righteousness. On the morning of the third day the darkness dispersed, seismic disturbances ceased, and the storms abated. As the pall was lifted from the land the people saw how profound had been the convulsions of earth, and how great had been their loss of kindred and friends. In their contrition and humiliation they remembered the predictions of the prophets, and knew that the mandate of the Lord had been executed upon them.[1460]

Christ had risen; and following Him many of the righteous dead on the western continent rose from their graves, and appeared as resurrected, immortalized beings among the survivors of the land-wide destruction; even as in Judea many of the saints had been raised immediately after the resurrection of Christ.[1461]

FIRST VISITATION OF JESUS CHRIST TO THE NEPHITES.[1462]

About six weeks or more after the events last considered,[1463] a great multitude of the Nephites had assembled at the temple in the land called Bountiful,[1464] and were earnestly discoursing with one another over the great changes that had been wrought in the land, and particularly concerning Jesus Christ, of whose atoning death the predicted signs had been witnessed in all their tragic details. The prevailing spirit of the assembly was that of contrition and reverence. While thus congregated they heard a sound as of a Voice from above; but both a first and a second utterance were to them unintelligible. As they listened with rapt intentness, the Voice was heard a third time, and it said unto them: "_Behold my beloved Son, in whom I am well pleased, in whom I have glorified my name: hear ye him._"[1465]

While gazing upward in reverent expectation, the people beheld a Man, clothed in a white robe, who descended and stood among them. He spake, saying: "Behold, I am Jesus Christ, whom the prophets testified shall come into the world; and behold, I am the light and the life of the world; and I have drunk out of that bitter cup which the Father hath given me, and have glorified the Father in taking upon me the sins of the world, in the which I have suffered the will of the Father in all things from the beginning." The multitude prostrated themselves in adoration for they remembered that their prophets had foretold that the Lord would appear among them after His resurrection and ascension.[1466]

As He directed, the people arose, and one by one came to Him, and did see and feel the prints of the nails in His hands and feet, and the spear-wound in His side. Moved to adoring utterance, with one accord they cried: "Hosanna! blessed be the name of the Most High God!" then, falling at the feet of Jesus, they worshiped Him.

Summoning Nephi and eleven others to approach, the Lord gave them authority to baptize the people after His departure, and prescribed the mode of baptism with particular injunction against disputation in the matter or alteration of the given form, as witness the Lord's words:

"Verily I say unto you, that whoso repenteth of his sins through your words, and desireth to be baptized in my name, on this wise shall ye baptize them: behold, ye shall go down and stand in the water, and in my name shall ye baptize them. And now behold, these are the words which ye shall say, calling them by name, saying, Having authority given me of Jesus Christ, I baptize you in the name of the Father, and of the Son, and of the Holy Ghost. Amen. And then shall ye immerse them in the water, and come forth again out of the water. And after this manner shall ye baptize in my name, for behold, verily I say unto you, that the Father, and the Son, and the Holy Ghost are one; and I am in the Father, and the Father in me, and the Father and I are one. And according as I have commanded you thus shall ye baptize. And there shall be no disputations among you, as there hath hitherto been; neither shall there be disputations among you concerning the points of my doctrine, as there hath hitherto been."[1467]

The people in general, and particularly the Twelve, chosen as stated, were impressively warned against contention over matters of doctrine, the spirit of which was declared to be of the devil, "who is the father of contention." The doctrine of Jesus Christ was set forth in simple yet comprehensive summary in these words:

"Behold, verily, verily, I say unto you, I will declare unto you my doctrine. And this is my doctrine, and it is the doctrine which the Father hath given unto me; and I bear record of the Father and the Father beareth record of me, and the Holy Ghost beareth record of the Father and me, and I bear record that the Father commandeth all men: everywhere, to repent and believe in me; And whoso believeth in me, and is baptized, the same shall be saved; and they are they who shall inherit the kingdom of God. And whoso believeth not in me, and is not baptized, shall be damned."[1468]

Repentance, and humility akin to that of the innocent trusting child were the prerequisites for baptism, without which none could inherit the kingdom of God. With the incisiveness and simplicity that had characterized His teachings in Palestine, the Lord thus instructed His newly chosen Twelve:

"Verily, verily, I say unto you, that this is my doctrine, and whoso buildeth upon this, buildeth upon my rock, and the gates of hell shall not prevail against them. And whoso shall declare more or less than this, and establish it for my doctrine, the same cometh of evil, and is not built upon my rock, but he buildeth upon a sandy foundation, and the gates of hell standeth open to receive such, when the floods come and the winds beat upon them. Therefore go forth unto this people, and declare the words which I have spoken unto the ends of the earth."[1469]

Then, turning to the multitude, Jesus admonished them to give heed to the teachings of the Twelve, and continued with a discourse embodying the sublime principles He had taught among the Jews in the Sermon on the Mount.[1470] The Beatitudes, the Lord's Prayer, and the same splendid array of ennobling precepts are set forth, and the same wealth of effective comparison and apt illustration appear, in both Matthew's and Nephi's versions of this unparalleled address; but a significant difference is observed in every reference to the fulfilment of the Mosaic law; for where the Jewish scriptures record the Lord's words as pointing to a fulfilment then incomplete, the corresponding expressions in the Nephite account are in the past tense, the law having been already fulfilled in its entirety through the death and resurrection of Christ. Thus, to the Jews Jesus had said: "Till heaven and earth pass, one jot or one tittle shall in no wise pass from the law, till all be fulfilled"; but to the Nephites: "For verily I say unto you, one jot nor one tittle hath not passed away from the law, but in me it hath all been fulfilled."[1471]

Many marveled over this matter, wondering what the Lord would have them do concerning the law of Moses; "for they understood not the saying that old things had passed away, and that all things had become new." Jesus, conscious of their perplexity, proclaimed in plainness that He was the Giver of the law, and that by Him had it been fulfilled and therefore abrogated. His affirmation is particularly explicit:

"Behold I say unto you, that the law is fulfilled that was given   unto Moses. Behold, I am he that gave the law, and I am he who   covenanted with my people Israel: therefore, the law in me is fulfilled, for I have come to fulfil the law; therefore it hath   an end. Behold, I do not destroy the prophets, for as many as   have not been fulfilled in me, verily I say unto you, shall all   be fulfilled. And because I said unto you, that old things hath   passed away, I do not destroy that which hath been spoken concerning things which are to come. For behold, the covenant   which I have made with my people is not all fulfilled; but the   law which was given unto Moses, hath an end in me."[1472]

Addressing Himself to the Twelve He affirmed that never had the Father commanded Him to inform the Jews concerning the existence of the Nephites, except indirectly by mention of other sheep not of the Jewish fold; and as, "because of stiffneckedness and unbelief," they had failed to comprehend His words, the Father had commanded Him to say no more with reference either to the Nephites or to the third fold--comprizing "the other tribes of the house of Israel, whom the Father hath led away out of the land." To the Nephite disciples Jesus taught many other matters that had been withheld from the Jews, who through unfitness to receive had been left in ignorance. Even the Jewish apostles had wrongly supposed that those "other sheep" were the Gentile nations, not realizing that the carrying of the gospel to the Gentiles was part of their particular mission, and oblivious to the fact that never would Christ manifest Himself in person to those who were not of the house of Israel. Through the promptings of the Holy Ghost and under the ministrations of men commissioned and sent would the Gentiles hear the word of God; but to the personal manifestation of the Messiah they were ineligible.[1473] Great, however, will be the Lord's mercies and blessings to the Gentiles who accept the truth, for unto them the Holy Ghost shall bear witness of the Father and of the Son; and all of them who comply with the laws and ordinances of the gospel shall be numbered in the house of Israel. Their conversion and enfoldment with the Lord's own will be as individuals, and not as nations, tribes, or peoples.[1474]

The adoring multitude, numbering about two thousand five hundred souls, thought that Jesus was about to depart; and they tearfully yearned to have Him remain. He comforted them with the assurance that He would return on the morrow, and admonished them to ponder upon the things He had taught, and to pray in His name to the Father for understanding. He had already informed the Twelve, and now stated to the people, that He would show Himself and minister "unto the lost tribes of Israel, for they are not lost unto the Father, for he knoweth whither he hath taken them." Voicing the compassion He felt, the Lord directed the people to fetch their afflicted ones, the lame, halt, maimed, blind and deaf, the leprous, and the withered; and when these were brought He healed them, every one. Then, as He commanded, parents brought their little children, and placed them in a circle around Him. The multitude bowed in prayer; and Jesus prayed for them; "And," wrote Nephi, "no tongue can speak, neither can there be written by any man, neither can the hearts of men conceive so great and marvellous things as we both saw and heard Jesus speak; and no one can conceive of the joy which filled our souls at the time we heard him pray for us unto the Father." The prayer being ended, Jesus bade the multitude arise; and joyfully He exclaimed: "Blessed are ye because of your faith. And now behold, my joy is full." Jesus wept. Then He took the children, one by one, and blessed them, praying unto the Father for each.

"And when he had done this he wept again, and he spake unto the   multitude, and saith unto them, behold your little ones. And as   they looked to behold, they cast their eyes towards heaven, and   they saw the heavens open, and they saw angels descending out of   heaven as it were, in the midst of fire; and they came down and   encircled those little ones about, and they were encircled about   with fire; and the angels did minister unto them."[1475]

The Lord Jesus sent for bread and wine, and caused the people to sit down. The bread He brake and blessed, and gave thereof to the Twelve; these, having eaten, distributed bread to the multitude. The wine was blessed, and all partook, the Twelve first, and afterward the people. With impressiveness similar to that attending the institution of the Sacrament of the Lord's Supper among the apostles in Jerusalem, Jesus made plain the sanctity and significance of the ordinance, saying that authority for its future administration would be given; and that it was to be participated in by all who had been baptized into fellowship with Christ, and was always to be observed in remembrance of Him, the bread being the sacred emblem of His body, the wine the token of His blood that had been shed. By express commandment, the Lord forbade the sacrament of bread and wine to all but the worthy; "For," He explained, "whoso eateth and drinketh my flesh and blood unworthily, eateth and drinketh damnation to his soul; therefore if ye know that a man is unworthy to eat and drink of my flesh and blood, ye shall forbid him." But the people were forbidden to cast out from their assemblies those from whom the Sacrament was to be withheld, if so be they would but repent and seek fellowship through baptism.[1476]

The necessity of prayer was explicitly emphasized by the Lord, the commandment to pray being given to the Twelve and to the multitude separately. Individual supplication, family devotions, and congregational worship were thus enjoined:

"Therefore ye must always pray unto the Father in my name; and   whatsoever ye shall ask the Father in my name, which is right,   believing that ye shall receive, behold it shall be given unto   you. Pray in your families unto the Father, always in my name,   that your wives and your children may be blessed. And behold, ye   shall meet together oft, and ye shall not forbid any man from   coming unto you when ye shall meet together, but suffer them   that they may come unto you, and forbid them not; but ye shall   pray for them, and shall not cast them out; and if it so be that   they come unto you oft, ye shall pray for them unto the Father,   in my name."[1477]

The Lord then touched with His hand each of the Twelve, investing them, in words unheard by others, with power to confer the Holy Ghost by the imposition of hands upon all repentant and baptized believers.[1478] As he finished the ordination of the Twelve, a cloud overshadowed the people, so that the Lord was hidden from their sight; but the twelve disciples "saw and did bear record that he ascended again into heaven."

CHRIST'S SECOND VISITATION TO THE NEPHITES.[1479]

On the morrow a yet greater multitude assembled in expectation of the Savior's return. Throughout the night messengers had spread the glorious tidings of the Lord's appearing, and of His promise to again visit His people. So great was the assembly that Nephi and his associates caused the people to separate into twelve bodies, to each of which one of the disciples was assigned to impart instruction and to lead in prayer. The burden of supplication was that the Holy Ghost should be given unto them. Led by the chosen disciples the whole vast concourse approached the water's edge, and Nephi, going first, was baptized by immersion; he then baptized the eleven others whom Jesus had chosen. When the Twelve had come forth out of the water, "they were filled with the Holy Ghost, and with fire. And behold, they were encircled about as if it were fire; and it came down from heaven, and the multitude did witness it, and do bear record; and angels did come down out of heaven, and did minister unto them. And it came to pass that while the angels were ministering unto the disciples, behold, Jesus came and stood in the midst, and ministered unto them."[1480]

Thus Jesus appeared in the midst of the disciples and ministering angels. At His command the Twelve and the multitude knelt in prayer; and they prayed unto Jesus, calling Him their Lord and their God. Jesus separated Himself by a little space, and in humble attitude prayed, saying in part: "Father, I thank thee that thou hast given the Holy Ghost unto these whom I have chosen; and it is because of their belief in me, that I have chosen them out of the world. Father, I pray thee that thou wilt give the Holy Ghost unto all them that shall believe in their words." The disciples were yet fervently praying to Jesus when He returned to them; and as He looked upon them with merciful and approving smile, they were glorified in His presence, so that their countenances and their apparel shone with a brilliancy like unto that of the face and garments of the Lord, even so that "there could be nothing on earth so white as the whiteness thereof." A second and a third time Jesus retired and prayed unto the Father; and while the people comprehended the meaning of His prayer, they confessed and bare record that "so great and marvellous were the words which he prayed, that they cannot be written, neither can they be uttered by man." The Lord rejoiced in the faith of the people, and to the disciples He said: "So great faith have I never seen among all the Jews; wherefore I could not shew unto them so great miracles, because of their unbelief. Verily I say unto you, there are none of them that have seen so great things as ye have seen; neither have they heard so great things as ye have heard."[1481] Then the Lord administered the Sacrament in manner as on the yesterday; but both the bread and the wine were provided without human aid. The sanctity of the ordinance was thus expressed: "He that eateth this bread, eateth of my body to his soul, and he that drinketh of this wine, drinketh of my blood to his soul, and his soul shall never hunger nor thirst, but shall be filled."

This was followed by instructions concerning the covenant people, Israel, of whom the Nephites were a part, and of the relation they would bear to the Gentile nations in the future development of the divine purpose. Jesus declared Himself to be that Prophet whose coming Moses had foretold, and the Christ of whom all the prophets had testified. The temporary supremacy of the Gentiles, whereby the further scattering of Israel would be accomplished, and the eventual gathering of the covenant people, were predicted, with frequent reference to the inspired utterances of Isaiah bearing thereon.[1482] The future of Lehi's descendants was pictured as a dwindling in unbelief through iniquity; in consequence of which the Gentiles would grow to be a mighty people on the western continent, even though that land had been given as an ultimate inheritance to the house of Israel. The establishment of the then future but now existent American nation, characterized as "a free people," was thus foretold and God's purpose therein explained: "For it is wisdom in the Father that they should be established in this land, and be set up as a free people by the power of the Father, that these things might come forth from them unto a remnant of your seed, that the covenant of the Father may be fulfilled which he hath covenanted with his people, O house of Israel."[1483]

As a sign of the time in which the gathering of the several branches of Israel from their long dispersion should take place, the Lord specified the prosperity of the Gentiles in America, and their agency in bringing the scriptures to the degraded remnant of Lehi's posterity or the American Indians.[1484] It was made plain that all Gentiles who would repent, and accept the gospel of Christ through baptism, should be numbered among the covenant people and be made partakers of the blessings incident to the last days, in which the New Jerusalem would be established on the American continent. The joyful account of gathered Israel as Jehovah had given it aforetime through the mouth of His prophet Isaiah, was repeated by the resurrected Jehovah to His Nephite flock.[1485] Admonishing them to ponder the words of the prophets, which were of record amongst them, and to give heed to the new scriptures He had made known, and especially commanding the Twelve to teach the people further concerning the things He had expounded, the Lord informed them of the revelations given through Malachi, and directed that the same be written.[1486]

The prophecies so reiterated by Him who had inspired Malachi to utterance, were at that time obviously of the future, and are even yet unfulfilled in their entirety. The advent of the Lord, to which these scriptures testify, is yet future; but that the time is now near--that "great and dreadful day of the Lord"--is attested by the fact that Elijah who was to come before that day, has appeared in the discharge of his particular commission--that of turning the hearts of the living children to their dead progenitors, and the hearts of the departed fathers to their still mortal posterity.[1487]

The personal ministry of Christ on the occasion of this second visitation lasted three days, during which He gave the people many scriptures, such as had been before given unto the Jews, for so the Father had commanded; and He expounded unto them the purposes of God, from the beginning until the time at which Christ shall return in His glory; "And even unto the great and last day, when all people, and all kindreds, and all nations and tongues shall stand before God, to be judged of their works, whether they be good or whether they be evil; if they be good, to the resurrection of everlasting life; and if they be evil, to the resurrection of damnation, being on a parallel, the one on the one hand, and the other on the other hand, according to the mercy, and the justice, and the holiness which is in Christ, who was before the world began." In merciful ministration He healed their afflicted folk, and raised a man from the dead. At later but unspecified times, He showed Himself among the Nephites, and "did break bread oft, and bless it, and give it unto them."[1488]

After His second ascension from among them, the spirit of prophecy was manifest among the people, and this extended even to children and babes, many of whom spake of marvelous things, as the Spirit gave them utterance. The Twelve entered upon their ministry with vigor, teaching all who would hear, and baptizing those who, through repentance, sought communion with the Church. Upon all who thus complied with the requirements of the gospel, the Holy Ghost was bestowed; and those so blessed lived together in love, and were called the Church of Christ.[1489]

CHRIST'S VISITATION TO HIS CHOSEN TWELVE AMONG THE NEPHITES.[1490]

Under the administration of the twelve ordained disciples the Church grew and prospered in the land of Nephi.[1491] The disciples, as special witnesses of the Christ, traveled, preached, taught, and baptized all who professed faith and showed forth repentance. On a certain occasion the Twelve were assembled in "mighty prayer and fasting," seeking instruction on a particular matter which, notwithstanding the Lord's injunction against contention, had given rise to disputation among the people. As they supplicated the Father in the Son's name, Jesus appeared amongst them, and asked: "What will ye that I shall give unto you?" Their answer was: "Lord, we will that thou wouldst tell us the name whereby we shall call this church; for there are disputations among the people concerning this matter." They had provisionally called the community of baptized believers the Church of Christ; but, apparently this true and distinguishing name had not been generally accepted without question.

"And the Lord said unto them, Verily, verily, I say unto you,   why is it that the people should murmur and dispute because of   this thing? Have they not read the scriptures, which say ye must take upon you the name of Christ, which is my name? for by this   name shall ye be called at the last day; and whoso taketh upon   him my name, and endureth to the end, the same shall be saved at   the last day; therefore whatsoever ye shall do, ye shall do it   in my name; therefore ye shall call the church in my name; and   ye shall call upon the Father in my name, that he will bless the   church for my sake; And how be it my church, save it be called   in my name? for if a church be called in Moses' name, then it be Moses' church; or if it be called in the name of a man, then it   be the church of a man; but if it be called in my name, then it   is my church, if it so be that they are built upon my gospel.   Verily I say unto you, that ye are built upon my gospel;   therefore ye shall call whatsoever things ye do call, in my   name; therefore if ye call upon the Father, for the church, if   it be in my name, the Father will hear you; and if it so be that   the church is built upon my gospel, then will the Father shew   forth his own works in it; but if it be not built upon my   gospel, and is built upon the works of men, or upon the works of   the devil, verily I say unto you, they have joy in their works   for a season, and by and by the end cometh, and they are hewn   down and cast into the fire, from whence there is no return; for   their works do follow them, for it is because of their works   that they are hewn down; therefore remember the things that I   have told you."[1492]

In such wise did the Lord confirm as an authoritative bestowal, the name which, through inspiration, had been assumed by His obedient children, _The Church of Jesus Christ_. The Lord's explanation as to the one and only Name by which the Church could be appropriately known is cogent and convincing. It was not the church of Lehi or Nephi, of Mosiah or Alma, of Samuel or Helaman; else it should have been called by the name of the man whose church it was, even as today there are churches named after men;[1493] but being the Church established by Jesus Christ, it could properly bear none other name than His.

Jesus then reiterated to the Nephite Twelve many of the cardinal principles He had before enunciated to them and to the people at large; and commanded that His words be written, excepting certain exalted communications which He forbade them to write. The importance of preserving as a priceless treasure the new scriptures He had given was shown, with assurance that in heaven records were kept of all things done by divine direction. The Twelve were told that they were to be the judges of their people; and in view of such investiture they were admonished to diligence and godliness.[1494] The Lord was made glad by the faith and ready obedience of the Nephites amongst whom He had ministered; and to the twelve special witnesses He said: "And now behold, my joy is great, even unto fulness, because of you, and also this generation; yea, and even the Father rejoiceth, and also all the holy angels, because of you and this generation; for none of them are lost. Behold, I would that ye should understand; for I mean them who are now alive of this generation; and none of them are lost; and in them I have fulness of joy." His joy, however, was mingled with sorrow because of the apostasy into which the later generations would fall; this He foresaw as a dire condition that would attain its climax in the fourth generation from that time.[1495]

THE THREE NEPHITES.

In loving compassion the Lord spoke unto the twelve disciples, one by one, asking: "What is it that ye desire of me, after that I am gone to the Father?"[1496] All but three expressed the desire that they might continue in the ministry until they had reached a goodly age, and then in due time be received by the Lord into His kingdom. To them Jesus gave blessed assurance, saying: "After that ye are seventy and two years old, ye shall come unto me in my kingdom, and with me ye shall find rest." He turned to the three who had reserved the request they ventured not to express;

"And he said unto them, Behold, I know your thoughts, and ye   have desired the thing which John, my beloved, who was with me   in my ministry, before that I was lifted up by the Jews, desired of me; therefore more blessed are ye, for ye shall never taste   of death, but ye shall live to behold all the doings of the   Father, unto the children of men, even until all things shall be   fulfilled, according to the will of the Father, when I shall   come in my glory, with the powers of heaven; and ye shall never   endure the pains of death; but when I shall come in my glory, ye   shall be changed in the twinkling of an eye from mortality to   immortality: and then shall ye be blessed in the kingdom of my   Father."[1497]

The blessed three were assured that in the course of their prolonged life they should be immune to pain, and should know sorrow only as they grieved for the sins of the world. For their desire to labor in bringing souls unto Christ as long as the world should stand, they were promised an eventual fulness of joy, even like unto that to which the Lord Himself had attained. Jesus touched each of the nine who were to live and die in the Lord, but the three who were to tarry till He would come in His glory He did not touch. "And then he departed."

A change was wrought in the bodies of the Three Nephites, so that, while they remained in the flesh, they were exempt from the usual effects of physical vicissitude. The heavens were opened to their gaze; they were caught up, and saw and heard unspeakable things. "And it was forbidden them that they should utter; neither was it given unto them power that they could utter the things which they saw and heard." Though they lived and labored as men among their fellows, preaching, baptizing, and conferring the Holy Ghost upon all who gave heed to their words, the enemies to the truth were powerless to do them injury. Somewhat later than a hundred and seventy years after the Lord's last visitation, malignant persecution was waged against the Three. For their zeal in the ministry they were cast into prison; but "the prisons could not hold them, for they were rent in twain." They were incarcerated in underground dungeons; "But they did smite the earth with the word of God, insomuch that by his power they were delivered out of the depths of the earth; and therefore they could not dig pits sufficient to hold them." Thrice they were cast into a furnace of fire, but received no harm; and three times were they thrown into dens of ravenous beasts, but, "behold they did play with the beasts, as a child with a suckling lamb, and received no harm."[1498] Mormon avers that in answer to his prayers the Lord had made known unto him that the change wrought upon the bodies of the Three, was such as to deprive Satan of all power over them, and that "they were holy, and that the powers of the earth could not hold them; and in this state they were to remain until the judgment day of Christ; and at that day they were to receive a greater change, and to be received into the kingdom of the Father to go no more out, but to dwell with God eternally in the heavens."[1499] For nearly three hundred years, and possibly longer, the Three Nephites ministered visibly among their fellows; but as the wickedness of the people increased these special ministers were withdrawn, and thereafter manifested themselves only to the righteous few. Moroni, the last prophet of the Nephites, when engaged in completing the record of his father, Mormon, and adding thereto matters of his own knowledge, wrote concerning these three disciples of the Lord, that they "did tarry in the land until the wickedness of the people was so great, that the Lord would not suffer them to remain with the people; and whether they be upon the face of the land no man knoweth. But behold, my father and I have seen them, and they have ministered unto us."[1500] Their ministry was to be extended to Jews and Gentiles, amongst whom they labor unrecognized as of ancient birth; and they are sent unto the scattered tribes of Israel, and to all nations, kindreds, tongues and peoples, from whom they have brought and are bringing many souls unto Christ, "that their desire may be fulfilled, and also because of the convincing power of God which is in them."[1501]

GROWTH OF THE CHURCH FOLLOWED BY THE APOSTASY OF THE NEPHITE NATION.

The Church of Jesus Christ developed rapidly in the land of Nephi, and brought to its faithful adherents unprecedented blessings. Even the hereditary animosity between Nephites and Lamanites was forgotten; and all lived in peace and prosperity. So great was the unity of the Church that its members owned all things in common, and "therefore they were not rich and poor, bond and free, but they were all made free, and partakers of the heavenly gift."[1502] Populous cities replaced the desolation of ruin that had befallen at the time of the Lord's crucifixion. The land was blessed, and the people rejoiced in righteousness. "And it came to pass that there was no contention in the land, because of the love of God which did dwell in the hearts of the people. And there were no envyings, nor strifes, nor tumults, nor whoredoms, nor lyings, nor murders, nor any manner of lasciviousness; and surely there could not be a happier people among all the people who had been created by the hand of God."[1503] Nine of the twelve special witnesses chosen by the Lord passed at appointed times to their rest, and others were ordained in their stead. The state of blessed prosperity and of common ownership continued for a period of a hundred and sixty-seven years; but soon thereafter came a most distressing change. Pride displaced humility, display of costly apparel superseded the simplicity of happier days; rivalry led to contention, and thence the people "did have their goods and their substance no more common among them, and they began to be divided into classes, and they began to build up churches unto themselves, to get gain, and began to deny the true church of Christ."[1504] Man-made churches multiplied, and persecution, true sister to intolerance, became rampant. The red-skinned Lamanites reverted to their degraded ways, and developed a murderous hostility against their white brothers; and all manner of corrupt practises became common among both nations. For many decades the Nephites retreated before their aggressive foes, making their way north-eastward through what is now the United States. About 400 A.D. the last great battle was fought near the hill Cumorah;[1505] and the Nephite nation became extinct.[1506] The degenerate remnant of Lehi's posterity, the Lamanites or American Indians, have continued until this day. Moroni, the last of the Nephite prophets, hid away the record of his people in the hill Cumorah, whence it has been brought forth by divine direction in the current dispensation. That record is now before the world translated through the gift and power of God, and published to the edification of all nations, as the BOOK OF MORMON.

NOTES TO CHAPTER 39.

1. The Land Bountiful.--This comprized the northerly part of South America, extending to the Isthmus of Panama. On the north it was bounded by the Land of Desolation, which embraced Central America, and, in later Nephite history, an indefinite extent north of the Isthmus. The South American continent in general is called, in the Book of Mormon, the Land of Nephi.

2. The Jewish and Nephite Versions of the "Sermon on the Mount."--As indicated in the text, one of the most impressive contrasts between the Sermon on the Mount and the virtual repetition of the discourse by our Lord on the occasion of His visit to the Nephites, is that of prediction concerning the fulfilment of the law of Moses in the first delivery, and unqualified affirmation in the second that the law had been fulfilled. Among the Beatitudes certain differences appear, in each of which the Nephite sermon is more explicit. Thus, instead of, "Blessed are the poor in spirit" (Matt. 5:3), we read, "Blessed are the poor in spirit who come unto me" (3 Nephi 12:3). Instead of, "Blessed are they which do hunger and thirst after righteousness; for they shall be filled" (Matt.), we read, "And blessed are all they who do hunger and thirst after righteousness, for they shall be filled with the Holy Ghost" (Nephi). Instead of, "for righteousness' sake," (Matt.) we have "for my name's sake," (Nephi). For the difficult passage, "Ye are the salt of the earth: but if the salt have lost his savour, wherewith shall it be salted?" (Matt.), we have the clearer expression, "I give unto you to be the salt of the earth; but if the salt shall lose its savor, wherewith shall the earth be salted?" (Nephi). And, as already noted, in place of "one jot or one tittle shall in no wise pass from the law, till all be fulfilled" (Matt.), we have "one jot nor one tittle hath not passed away from the law, but in me it hath all been fulfilled" (Nephi). Variations in succeeding verses are incident to this prospective fulfilment (Matt.), and affirmed accomplishment (Nephi). Instead of the strong analogy concerning the plucking out of an offending eye, or the severing of an evil hand (Matt.), we find: "Behold, I give unto you a commandment, that ye suffer none of these things to enter into your heart; for it is better that ye should deny yourselves of these things, wherein ye will take up your cross, than that ye should be cast into hell" (Nephi). Following the illustrative instances of the gospel requirements superseding those of the law, the Nephite record presents this splendid summation: "Therefore those things which were of old time, which were under the law in me, are all fulfilled. Old things are done away, and all things have become new; therefore I would that ye should be perfect even as I, or your Father who is in heaven is perfect."

In Matthew's report of the sermon, little distinction is made between the precepts addressed to the multitude in general, and the instructions given particularly to the Twelve. Thus, Matt. 6:25-34 was spoken inferentially to the apostles; for they and not the people were to lay aside all worldly pursuits; in the sermon delivered to the Nephites the distinction is thus made clear: "And now it came to pass that when Jesus had spoken these words, he looked upon the twelve whom he had chosen, and said unto them, Remember the words which I have spoken. For behold, ye are they whom I have chosen to minister unto this people. Therefore I say unto you, take no thought for your life, what ye shall eat, or what ye shall drink; nor yet for your body, what ye shall put on. Is not the life more than meat, and the body than raiment?" etc. (See 3 Nephi 13:25-34). Matt 7 opens with "Judge not that ye be not judged," without intimation as to its general or special application; 3 Nephi 14 begins "And now it came to pass that when Jesus had spoken these words, he turned again to the multitude, and did open his mouth unto them again, saying, Verily, verily, I say unto you, judge not, that ye be not judged." A careful, verse-by-verse comparison between the Sermon on the Mount as recorded by Matthew, and the risen Lord's discourse to His people on the western continent is earnestly recommended to every student.

3. Baptisms Among the Nephites After the Lord's Visitation.--We read that before the second appearing of Christ to the Nephites, the chosen Twelve were baptized (3 Nephi 19:10-13). These men had doubtless been baptized before, for Nephi had been empowered not only to baptize but to ordain others to the requisite authority for administering baptism (3 Nephi 7:23-26). The baptism of the disciples on the morn of the Savior's second visit, was in the nature of a rebaptism, involving a renewal of covenants, and confession of faith in the Lord Jesus.

It is possible that in the earlier Nephite baptisms some irregularity in mode or impropriety in the spirit of administering the ordinance may have arisen; for, as we have seen the Lord enjoined upon the people in connection with the instructions concerning baptism that disputations must cease. (3 Nephi 11:28-33.)

As to second or later baptisms, the author has written elsewhere (see _The Articles of Faith_, vii:12-17) practically as follows. Rebaptisms recorded in scripture are few, and in each instance the special circumstances justifying the action are apparent. Thus, we read of Paul baptizing certain disciples at Ephesus, though they had already been immersed after the manner of John's baptism. But in this case the apostle was evidently unconvinced that the baptism had been solemnized by due authority, or that the believers had been properly instructed as to the import of the ordinance. When he tested the efficacy of their baptism by asking "Have ye received the Holy Ghost since ye believed?" they answered him, "We have not so much as heard whether there be any Holy Ghost." Then asked he in seeming surprize, "Unto what then were ye baptized? and they said, Unto John's baptism. Then said Paul, John verily baptized with the baptism of repentance, saying unto the people, that they should believe on him which should come after him, that is, on Christ Jesus. When they heard this, they were baptized in the name of the Lord Jesus." (See Acts 19:1-6.)

In the Church today a repetition of the baptismal rite on an individual is allowable under certain specific conditions. Thus, if one, having entered the Church by baptism, withdraws from it, or is excommunicated therefrom, and afterward repents and desires to regain his standing in the Church, he can do so only through baptism. However, such is a repetition of the initiatory ordinance as previously administered. There is no ordinance of "rebaptism" in the Church distinct in nature, form, or purpose, from other baptism; and, therefore, in administering baptism to a subject who has been formerly baptized, the form of the ceremony is exactly the same as in first baptisms.

FOOTNOTES:

[1452] John 10:16; compare B. of M., 3 Nephi 15:17-21; page 416 herein.
[1453] See pages 49, 55 herein.
[1454] Pages 49-52.
[1455] Helaman 14:14-27.
[1456] 3 Nephi 2:1.
[1457] Exo. 10:21-23.
[1458] 3 Nephi 8:5-25; compare Helaman 14:20-27.
[1459] 3 Nephi chap. 9.
[1460] 3 Nephi, chap. 10.
[1461] Helaman 14:25; 3 Nephi 23:7-13; compare Matt. 27:52, 53.
[1462] 3 Nephi, chaps. 11-18 inclusive.
[1463] 3 Nephi 10:18. Bear in mind that Christ's ascension took place forty days after His resurrection.
[1464] Note 1, end of chapter.
[1465] 3 Nephi 11:7; compare Matt. 3:17; Mark 1:11; Luke 9:35; P. of G.P., Joseph Smith 2:17.
[1466] 3 Nephi 11:12; compare 1 Nephi 12:6; 2 Nephi 26:1, 9; Alma 16:20.
[1467] 3 Nephi 11:23-28; compare Doc. and Cov. 20:72-74.
[1468] 3 Nephi 11:31-34; compare Mark 16:15, 16; see also John 12:48.
[1469] 3 Nephi 11:39-41.
[1470] 3 Nephi, chaps. 12, 13, 14; compare Matt. chaps. 5, 6, 7.
[1471] Matt. 5:18, and 3 Nephi 12:18; compare 46, 47; 15:2-10; and 9:17-20. See Note 2, end of chapter.
[1472] 3 Nephi 15:4-8. See pages 234, 373, 374 herein.
[1473] 3 Nephi 15:11-24.
[1474] 3 Nephi 16:4-20.
[1475] 3 Nephi 17:23-24; read entire chapter.
[1476] 3 Nephi 18:1-14, 27-34; compare 1 Cor. 11:23-30. For the prescribed manner of administering the Sacrament, see Moroni, chaps. 4 and 5; compare Doc. and Cov. 20:75-79.
[1477] 3 Nephi 18:19-23.
[1478] 3 Nephi 18:36, 37; Moroni 2:1-3.
[1479] 3 Nephi, chaps. 19-25, and 26:1-5.
[1480] Note 3, end of chapter.
[1481] 3 Nephi, chap. 19:35, 36; read the entire chapter.
[1482] 3 Nephi, chap. 20; see references to Isaiah given therein.
[1483] 3 Nephi 21:4.
[1484] 3 Nephi 21:1-7; for prophecies concerning subsequent events see remainder of chapter.
[1485] 3 Nephi, chap. 22; compare Isa. chap. 54.
[1486] 3 Nephi, chaps. 24 and 25; compare Malachi, chap. 3 and 4.
[1487] Doc. and Cov. 110:13-16. Elijah appeared in the Kirtland Temple April 3, A.D. 1836, and committed to the Church the keys of authority for vicarious work in behalf of the dead. See chapter 41 herein, page 775.
[1488] 3 Nephi 26:4, 5, 13-15.
[1489] 3 Nephi 26:14-21.
[1490] 3 Nephi, chaps. 26, 27, and 28:1-12.
[1491] Note 1, end of chapter.
[1492] 3 Nephi 27:4-12.
[1493] E.g. of Calvin, Luther, Wesley; see also "The Great Apostasy," 10:21, 22.
[1494] Note the assurance of a similar commission promised the Jewish apostles: Matt. 19:28; Luke 22:30. See also 1 Nephi 12:9.
[1495] 3 Nephi 27:32 and references given therewith.
[1496] 3 Nephi 28:1; read verses 1-12.

[1497] 3 Nephi 28:6-8; see page 694 herein.
[1498] 3 Nephi 28:13-23; compare 4 Nephi 1:14, 29-33.
[1499] 3 Nephi 28:39, 40.
[1500] Mormon 8:10, 11; see also 3 Nephi 28:26-32, 36-40, 4 Nephi 1:14, 37; Ether 12:17.
[1501] 3 Nephi 28:27-32.
[1502] 4 Nephi 1:3; read 1:23; see pages 705 and 718 herein.
[1503] 4 Nephi 1:15, 16.
[1504] 4 Nephi 1:25, 26.
[1505] Near Manchester, Ontario county, New York.
[1506] See Mormon, chapters 1-9; and Moroni, chapter 10.

CHAPTER 40. THE LONG NIGHT OF APOSTASY.

For over seventeen hundred years on the eastern hemisphere, and for more than fourteen centuries on the western, there appears to have been silence between the heavens and the earth.[1507] Of direct revelation from God to man during this long interval, we have no authentic record. As already shown, the period of apostolic ministry on the eastern continent probably terminated before the dawn of the second century of the Christian era. The passing of the apostles was followed by the rapid development of a universal apostasy as had been foreseen and predicted.[1508]

In the accomplishment of this great falling away, external and internal causes cooperated. Among the disintegrating forces acting from without, the most effective was the persistent persecution to which the saints were subjected, incident to both Judaistic and pagan opposition. Vast numbers who had professed membership and many who had been officers in the ministry deserted the Church; while a few were stimulated to greater zeal under the scourge of persecution. The general effect of opposition from the outside--of external causes of decline in faith and works considered as a whole--was the defection of individuals, resulting in a widespread _apostasy from the Church_. But immeasurably more serious was the result of internal dissension, schism and disruption, whereby an absolute _apostasy of the Church_ from the way and word of God was brought about.

Judaism was the earliest oppressor of Christianity, and became the instigator and abettor of the succeeding atrocities incident to pagan persecution. Open and vigorous hostility of the Roman powers against the Christian Church became general during the reign of Nero, (beginning about 64 A.D.), and continued with occasional respites of a few months or even years at a time to the close of Diocletian's reign (about 305 A.D.). The inhuman cruelty and savage barbarity to which were subjected those who dared profess the name of Christ during these centuries of heathen domination are matters of accepted history. [1509] When Constantine the Great came to the throne in the first quarter of the fourth century, a radical change was inaugurated in the attitude of the state toward the church. The emperor straightway made the so-called Christianity of the time the religion of his realm; and zealous devotion to the church became the surest recommendation to imperial favor. But the church was already in great measure an apostate institution and even in crude outline of organization and service bore but remote resemblance to the Church of Jesus Christ, founded by the Savior and builded through the instrumentality of the apostles. Whatever vestiges of genuine Christianity may have possibly survived in the church before, were buried beyond the sight of man by the abuses that followed the elevation of the churchly organization to secular favor through the decree of Constantine. The emperor, even though unbaptized, made himself the head of the church, and priestly office was more sought after than military rank or state preferment. The spirit of apostasy, by which the church had become permeated before Constantine threw about it the mantle of imperial protection and emblazoned it with the insignia of state, now was roused to increased activity as the leaven of Satan's own culture flourished under the conditions most favorable for such fungoid growth.

The bishop of Rome had already asserted supremacy over his fellows in the episcopate; but when the emperor made Byzantium his capital, and renamed it in his own honor, Constantinople, the bishop of that city claimed equality with the Roman pontiff. The claim was contested; the ensuing dissension divided the church; and the disruption has persisted until the present day, as is evidenced by the existing distinction between the Roman Catholic and the Greek Catholic churches.

The Roman pontiff exercised secular as well as spiritual authority; and in the eleventh century arrogated to himself the title of _Pope_, signifying _Father_, in the sense of paternal ruler in all things. During the twelfth and thirteenth centuries the temporal authority of the pope was superior to that of kings and emperors; and the Roman church became the despotic potentate of nations, and an autocrat above all secular states. Yet this church, reeking with the stench of worldly ambition and lust of dominance, audaciously claimed to be the Church established by Him who affirmed: "My kingdom is not of this world." The arrogant assumptions of the Church of Rome were not less extravagant in spiritual than in secular administration. In her loudly asserted control over the spiritual destinies of the souls of men, she blasphemously pretended to forgive or retain individual sins, and to inflict or remit penalties both on earth and beyond the grave. She sold permission to commit sin and bartered for gold charters of indulgent forgiveness for sins already done. Her pope, proclaiming himself the vicar of God, sat in state to judge as God Himself; and by such blasphemy fulfilled the prophecy of Paul following his warning in relation to the awful conditions antecedent to the second coming of the Christ: "Let no man deceive you by any means: for that day shall not come, except there come a falling away first, and that man of sin be revealed, the son of perdition; Who opposeth and exalteth himself above all that is called God, or that is worshipped; so that he as God sitteth in the temple of God, shewing himself that he is God."[1510]

In her unrestrained abandon to the license of arrogated authority, the Church of Rome hesitated not to transgress the law of God, change the ordinances essential to salvation, and ruthlessly break the everlasting covenant, thereby defiling the earth even as Isaiah had foretold.[1511] She altered the ordinance of baptism, destroying its symbolism and associating with it imitations of pagan rites; she corrupted the Sacrament of the Lord's Supper and befouled the doctrine thereof by the vagary of _transubstantiation_;[1512] she assumed to apply the merits of the righteous to the forgiveness of the sinner in the unscriptural and wholly repellent dogma of _supererogation_; she promoted idolatry in most seductive and pernicious forms; she penalized the study of the holy scriptures by the people at large; she enjoined an unnatural state of celibacy upon her clergy; she revelled in unholy union with the theories and sophistries of men, and so adulterated the simple doctrines of the gospel of Christ as to produce a creed rank with superstition and heresy; she promulgated such perverted doctrines regarding the human body as to make the divinely formed tabernacle of flesh appear as a thing fit only to be tortured and contemned; she proclaimed it an act of virtue insuring rich reward to lie and deceive if thereby her own interests might be subserved; and she so thoroughly departed from the original plan of Church organization as to make of herself a spectacle of ornate display, fabricated by the caprice of man.[1513]

The most important of the internal causes by which the apostasy of the Primitive Church was brought about may be thus summarized: (1) The corrupting of the simple doctrines of the gospel of Christ by admixture with so-called philosophic systems. (2) Unauthorized additions to the prescribed rites of the Church and the introduction of vital alterations in essential ordinances. (3) Unauthorized changes in Church organization and government.[1514]

Under the tyrannous repression incident to usurped and unrighteous domination by the Roman church, civilization was retarded and for centuries was practically halted in its course. The period of retrogression is known in history as the Dark Ages. The fifteenth century witnessed the movement known as the Renaissance or Revival of Learning; there was a general and significantly rapid awakening among men, and a determined effort to shake off the stupor of indolence and ignorance was manifest throughout the civilized world. By historians and philosophers the revival has been regarded as an unconscious and spontaneous prompting of the "spirit of the times"; it was a development predetermined in the Mind of God to illumine the benighted minds of men in preparation for the restoration of the gospel of Jesus Christ, which was appointed to be accomplished some centuries later.[1515]

With the renewal of intellectual activity and effort in material betterment, there came, as a natural and inevitable accompaniment, protest and revolt against the ecclesiastical tyranny of the age. The Albigenses in France had risen in insurrection against churchly despotism during the thirteenth century; and in the fourteenth, John Wickliffe of Oxford University had boldly denounced the corruption of the Roman church and clergy, and particularly the restrictions imposed by the papal hierarchy on the popular study of the scriptures. Wickliffe gave to the world a version of the Holy Bible in English. These manifestations of independent belief and action the papal church sought to repress and punish by force. The Albigenses had been subjected to inhuman cruelties and unrestrained slaughter. Wickliffe was the subject of severe and persistent persecution; and though he died in his bed the vindictiveness of the Roman church was unsated until she had caused his body to be exhumed and burned and the ashes scattered abroad. John Huss and Jerome of Prague were prominent on the continent of Europe in agitation against papal despotism, and both fell martyrs to the cause. Though the church had become apostate to the core, there were not lacking men brave of heart and righteous of soul, ready to give their lives to the furtherance of spiritual emancipation.

A notable revolt against the papacy occurred in the sixteenth century, and is known as the Reformation. This movement was begun in 1517 by Martin Luther, a German monk; and it spread so rapidly as soon to involve the whole domain of popedom. Formal _protests_ against the despotism of the papal church were formulated by the representatives of certain German principalities and other delegates at a diet or general council held at Spires A.D. 1529; and the reformers were thenceforth known as _Protestants_. An independent church was proposed by John, Elector of Saxony, a constitution for which was prepared at his instance by Luther and his colleague, Melanchthon. The Protestants were discordant. Being devoid of divine authority to guide them in matters of church organization and doctrine, they followed the diverse ways of men, and were rent within while assailed from without. The Roman church, confronted by determined opponents, hesitated at no extreme of cruelty. The court of the Inquisition, which had been established in the latter part of the fifteenth century under the infamously sacrilegious name of the "Holy Office," became intoxicated with the lust of barbarous cruelty in the century of the Reformation, and inflicted indescribable tortures on persons secretly accused of heresy.

In the early stages of the Reformation instigated by Luther, the king of England, Henry VIII, declared himself a supporter of the pope, and was rewarded by a papal bestowal of the distinguishing title "Defender of the Faith." Within a few years, this same British sovereign was excommunicated from the Roman church, because of impatient disregard of the pope's authority in the matter of Henry's desire to divorce Queen Catherine so that he could marry one of her maids. The British parliament, in 1534, passed the Act of Supremacy, by which the nation was declared free from all allegiance to papal authority. By Act of Parliament the king was made the head of the church within his own dominions. Thus was born the Church of England, a direct result of the licentious amours of a debauched and infamous king. With blasphemous indifference to the absence of divine commission, with no semblance of priestly succession, an adulterous sovereign created a church, provided therein a "priesthood" of his own, and proclaimed himself supreme administrator in all matters spiritual.

With the conflict between Catholicism and Protestantism in Great Britain the student of history is familiar. Suffice it here to say that the mutual hatred of the two contending sects, the zeal of their respective adherents, their professed love of God and devotion to Christ's service, were chiefly signalized by the sword, the ax, and the stake. Revelling in the realization of at least a partial emancipation from the tyranny of priestcraft, men and nations debauched their newly acquired liberty of thought, speech, and action, in a riot of abhorrent excess. The mis-called Age of Reason, and the atheistical abominations culminating in the French Revolution stand as ineffaceable testimony of what man may become when glorying in his denial of God.

Is it to be wondered at, that from the sixteenth century onward, churches of man's contriving have multiplied with phenomenal rapidity? Churches and churchly organizations professing Christianity as their creed have come to be numbered by hundreds. On every side is heard in this day, "Lo, here is Christ" or "Lo, there." There are sects named from the circumstances of their origin--as the Church of England; others after their famous founders or promoters--as Lutheran, Calvinist, Wesleyan; some are known by peculiarities of doctrine or plan of administration--as Methodist, Presbyterian, Baptist, Congregationalist;

but down to the third decade of the nineteenth century there was no church on earth affirming name or title as the Church of Jesus Christ. The only organization called a church existing at that time and venturing to assert claim to authority by succession was the Catholic church, which for centuries had been apostate and wholly bereft of divine authority or recognition. If the "mother church" be without a valid priesthood, and devoid of spiritual power, how can her offspring derive from her the right to officiate in the things of God? Who would dare to affirm that man can originate a priesthood which God is bound to honor and acknowledge? Granted that men may and do create among themselves societies, associations, sects, and even "churches" if they choose so to designate their organizations; granted that they may prescribe rules, formulate laws, and devize plans of operation, discipline, and government, and that all such laws, rules, and schemes of administration are binding upon those who assume membership--granted all these rights and powers--whence can such human institutions derive the authority of the Holy Priesthood, without which there can be no Church of Christ?[1516]

The apostate condition of Christendom has been frankly admitted by many eminent and conscientious representatives of the several churches, and by churches as institutions. Even the Church of England acknowledges the awful fact in her official declaration of degeneracy, as set forth in the "_Homily Against Peril of Idolatry_," in these words:

"So that laity and clergy, learned and unlearned, all ages, sects, and degrees of men, women, and children of whole Christendom--an horrible and most dreadful thing to think--have been at once drowned in abominable idolatry; of all other vices most detested of God, and most damnable to man; and that by the space of eight hundred years and more."[1517]

Let it not be concluded that through the night of the universal apostasy, long and dark as it was, God had forgotten the world. Mankind had not been left wholly to itself. The Spirit of God was operative so far as the unbelief of men permitted. John the apostle, and the Three Nephite disciples,[1518] were ministering among men, though unknown. But through the centuries of spiritual darkness men lived and died without the administration of a contemporary apostle, prophet, elder, bishop, priest, teacher, or deacon. Whatever of the form of Godliness existed in the churches of human establishment was destitute of divine power. The time foreseen by the inspired apostle had fully come--mankind in general refused to endure sound doctrine, but, having itching ears, did they heap to themselves teachers, after their own lusts, and verily had they turned away their ears from the truth to follow after fables.[1519] The first quarter of the nineteenth century witnessed the cumulative fulfilment of the conditions predicted through the prophet Amos: "Behold, the days come, saith the Lord God, that I will send a famine in the land, not a famine of bread, nor a thirst for water, but of hearing the words of the Lord: And they shall wander from sea to sea, and from the north even to the east, they shall run to and fro to seek the word of the Lord, and shall not find it."[1520]

Throughout the period of apostasy the windows of heaven had been shut toward the world, so as to preclude all direct revelation from God, and particularly any personal ministration or theophany of the Christ. Mankind had ceased to know God; and had invested the utterances of prophets and apostles of old, who had known Him, with a pall of mystery and fancy, so that the True and the Living God was no longer believed to exist; but in His place the sectaries had tried to conceive of an incomprehensible being, devoid of "body, parts, or passions," an immaterial nothing.[1521]

But it had been determined in the councils of heaven, that after many centuries of benighted ignorance the world should be illumined anew by the light of truth. Through the operation of the genius of intelligence, which is the Spirit of Truth, the soul of the race had been undergoing a preparation, like unto the deep plowing of a field, for the planting of the gospel afresh. The principle of the mariner's compass was revealed by the Spirit; the material embodiment thereof was invented by man; and by its aid the unknown oceans were explored. Toward the end of the fifteenth century Columbus was led by the inspiration of God to the discovery of the New World, whereon dwelt the degenerate posterity of Lehi, a dark-skinned remnant of the house of Israel--the American Indians. In due time the good ships _Mayflower_ and _Speedwell_ brought to the western world the Pilgrim Fathers, as the vanguard of a host escaping from exile and seeking a new home wherein they could worship according to the dictates of their consciences. The coming of Columbus and the later immigration of the Puritan Pilgrims had been predicted nearly six hundred years before Christ; their respective missions had been as truly appointed unto them as has been the sending of any prophet with a message to deliver and a work to do.[1522] The war between the American Colonies and the Mother Country, and the victorious issue thereof in the emancipation of the American nation once and forever from monarchial rule, had been foretold as further steps in preparation for the restoration of the gospel. Time was allowed for the establishment of a stable government, for the raising up of men chosen and inspired to frame and promulgate the Constitution of the United States, which promises to every man a full measure of political and religious freedom. It was not meet that the precious seed of the restored gospel be thrown upon unplowed soil, hardened by intolerance, and fit to produce only thorns of bigotry and rank weeds of mental and spiritual serfdom. The gospel of Jesus Christ is the embodiment of liberty; it is the truth that shall make free every man and every nation who will accept and obey its precepts.

At the appointed time, the Eternal Father and His Son Jesus the Christ appeared to man upon the earth, and inaugurated the Dispensation of the Fulness of Times.

NOTES TO CHAPTER 40.

1. Cessation of Revelation on the Western Hemisphere.--"The eastern world had lost this knowledge of the Lord earlier than the western hemisphere. Upon the land of North America, four hundred years after the birth of our Savior and Master, there stood at least one man who knew the Lord God

Almighty as a distinct personality, a Being capable of communicating Himself to man. That man was Moroni, the son of Mormon, whose testimony abides now and must abide through all the ages to come."-- George Q. Cannon, _Life of Joseph Smith_, p. 21. See B. of M., Moroni 10:27-34.

2. Results of the Great Apostasy Divinely Overruled for Eventual Good.--The thoughtful student cannot fail to see in the progress of the great apostasy and its results the existence of an overruling power operating toward eventual good, however mysterious its methods. The heart-rending persecutions to which the saints were subjected in the early centuries of our era, the anguish, the torture, the bloodshed incurred in defense of the testimony of Christ, the rise of an apostate church, blighting the intellect and leading captive the souls of men--all these dread conditions were foreknown to the Lord. While we cannot say or believe that such exhibitions of human depravity and blasphemy of heart were in accordance with the divine will, certainly God willed to permit full scope to the free agency of man, in the exercize of which agency some won the martyr's crown, and others filled the flagon of their iniquity to overflowing. Not less marked is the divine permission in the revolts and rebellions, in the revolutions and reformations, that developed in opposition to the darkening influence of the apostate church. Wickliffe and Huss, Luther and Melanchthon, Zwingli and Calvin, Henry VIII in his arrogant assumption of priestly authority, John Knox in Scotland, Roger Williams in America--these and a host of others builded better than they knew, in that their efforts laid in part the foundation of the structure of religious freedom and liberty of conscience--and this in preparation for the restoration of the gospel as had been divinely predicted.--_The Great Apostasy_, 10:19, 20.

3. Declaration of a General Apostasy by the Church of England.--The _Book of Homilies_, from which the quotation given in the text is taken, was published about the middle of the sixteenth century. The official proclamation of a universal apostasy was made prominently current, for the Homilies were "appointed to be read in churches" in lieu of sermons under certain conditions. In the statement cited, the Church of England solemnly avers that a state of apostasy affecting all ages, sects, and degrees throughout whole Christendom, had prevailed for eight hundred years prior to the establishment of the church making the declaration. That this affirmation remains effective today, as both confession and profession of the Church of England, appears from the fact that the homily "Against Peril of Idolatry" and certain other homilies are specifically ratified and endorsed, and withal prescribed "to be read in Churches by the Ministers diligently and distinctly that they may be understanded of the people." See "Articles of Religion" xxxv, in current issues of Church of England, _Book of Common Prayer_.

4. The "Creed of Athanasius."--At the Council of Nice, convoked by the emperor Constantine, 325 A.D., a formal statement of belief concerning the Godhead was adopted. Later a modification was issued, known as the "Creed of Athanasius," and though the authorship is questioned, the creed has a place in the ritual of some of the Protestant churches. No more conclusive evidence that men had ceased to know God need be adduced than the Athanasian Creed. As confessed by the Church of England in this day, and as published in the official ritual (see _Prayer Book_) "The Creed of Saint Athanasius" is this: "We worship one God in Trinity, and Trinity in Unity; neither confounding the Persons: nor dividing the Substance. For there is one Person of the Father, another of the Son: and another of the Holy Ghost. But the Godhead of the Father, of the Son, and of the Holy Ghost, is all one: the Glory equal, the Majesty co-eternal. Such as the Father is, such is the Son: and such is the Holy Ghost. The Father uncreate, the Son uncreate: and the Holy Ghost uncreate. The Father incomprehensible, the Son incomprehensible: and the Holy Ghost incomprehensible. The Father eternal, the Son eternal: and the Holy Ghost eternal. And yet they are not three eternals: but one eternal. As also there are not three incomprehensibles, nor three uncreated: but one uncreated, and one incomprehensible. So likewise the Father is Almighty, the Son Almighty: and the Holy Ghost Almighty. And yet they are not three Almighties: but one Almighty. So the Father is God, the Son is God: and the Holy Ghost is God. And yet they are not three Gods: but one God. So likewise the Father is Lord, the Son Lord, and the Holy Ghost Lord. And yet not three Lords: but one Lord."

Then follows this strange confession of what is at once required by "Christian verity," and forbidden by the "Catholick Religion": "For like as we are compelled by the Christian verity: to acknowledge every Person by himself to be God and Lord; so are we forbidden by the Catholick Religion: to say, There be three Gods, or three Lords."

5. The Mission of Columbus and Its Results.--Unto Nephi, son of Lehi, was shown the future of his people, including the degeneracy of a branch thereof, afterward known as Lamanites and in modern times as American Indians. The coming of a man from among the Gentiles, across the deep waters, was revealed in such plainness as to positively identify that man with Columbus; and the coming of other Gentiles to this land, out of captivity, is equally explicit. The revelation is thus recorded by Nephi to whom it was given: "And it came to pass that I looked and beheld many waters; and they divided the Gentiles from the seed of my brethren. And it came to pass that the angel said unto me, Behold the wrath of God is upon the seed of thy brethren. And I looked and beheld a man among the Gentiles who was separated from the seed of my brethren by the many waters; and I beheld the Spirit of God, that it came down and wrought upon the man; and he went forth upon the many waters, even unto the seed of my brethren, who were in the promised land. And it came to pass that I beheld the Spirit of God, that it wrought upon other Gentiles; and they went forth out of captivity, upon the many waters." (1 Nephi 13:10-13). The establishment of a great Gentile nation on the American continent, the subjugation of the Lamanites or Indians, the war between the newly established nation and Great Britain, or "their mother Gentiles," and the victorious outcome of that struggle for independence, are set forth with equal clearness in the same chapter.

FOOTNOTES:

[1507] Note 1, end of chapter.

[1508] No extended account of the apostasy of the Primitive Church can be attempted here; the reader is referred to special works treating this important subject. See the author's "The Great Apostasy, considered in the Light of Scriptural and Secular History," a work of 176 pages.

[1509] See "The Great Apostasy," chaps. 4 and 5.

[1510] 1 Thess. 2:3, 4.

[1511] Isa. 24:5.

[1512] The false doctrine of "transubstantiation" is to the effect that the bread and wine administered as emblems of Christ's flesh and blood in the Sacrament of the Lord's Supper are transmuted by priestly consecration into the actual flesh and blood of Jesus Christ. See "The Great Apostasy," 8:16-19. As to "supererogation" see page 590 herein.

[1513] "The Great Apostasy," chaps. 6, 7, 8.

[1514] "The Great Apostasy," 6:14, 15; for comprehensive treatment of the subject see chapters 6 to 9 inclusive.

[1515] Note 2, end of chapter.

[1516] This paragraph is in part a paraphrase of "The Great Apostasy," 10:21, 22.

[1517] Note 3, end of chapter.

[1518] Pages 694 and 738.

[1519] See 2 Tim. 4:1-4; also "The Great Apostasy," 2:30.

[1520] Amos. 8:11, 12.

[1521] See Church of England "Book of Common Prayer," "Articles of Religion" i. Note 4, end of chapter.

[1522] See B. of M., 1 Nephi 13:10-13. Note 5, end of chapter.

CHAPTER 41. PERSONAL MANIFESTATIONS OF GOD THE ETERNAL FATHER AND OF HIS SON JESUS CHRIST IN MODERN TIMES.

A NEW DISPENSATION.

In the year of our Lord 1820 there lived at Manchester, Ontario county, state of New York, a worthy citizen named Joseph Smith. His household comprized his wife and their nine children. The third son and fourth child of the family was Joseph Smith Jr., who at the time of which we speak was in his fifteenth year. In the year specified, New York and adjacent states were swept by a wave of intense agitation in religious matters; and unusual zeal was put forth by ministers of the numerous rival sects to win converts to their respective folds. The boy Joseph was profoundly affected by this intense excitement, and was particularly puzzled and troubled over the spirit of confusion and contention manifest through it all. As our present subject has to do with him specifically, and in view of the transcendent importance of his testimony to the world, his own account of what ensued is given herewith.

"Some time in the second year after our removal to Manchester, there was in the place where we lived an unusual excitement on the subject of religion. It commenced with the Methodists, but soon became general among all the sects in that region of country. Indeed, the whole district of country seemed affected by it, and great multitudes united themselves to the different religious parties, which created no small stir and division amongst the people, some crying, 'Lo, here!' and others, 'Lo, there!' Some were contending for the Methodist faith, some for the Presbyterian, and some for the Baptist.

"For notwithstanding the great love which the converts to these different faiths expressed at the time of their conversion, and the great zeal manifested by the respective clergy, who were active in getting up and promoting this extraordinary scene of religious feeling, in order to have everybody converted, as they were pleased to call it, let them join what sect they pleased--yet when the converts began to file off, some to one party and some to another, it was seen that the seemingly good feelings of both the priests and the converts were more pretended than real; for a scene of great confusion and bad feeling ensued; priest contending against priest, and convert against convert; so that all their good feelings one for another, if they ever had any, were entirely lost in a strife of words and a contest about opinions.

"I was at this time in my fifteenth year. My father's family was proselyted to the Presbyterian faith, and four of them joined that church, namely--my mother Lucy; my brothers Hyrum and Samuel Harrison; and my sister Sophronia.

"During this time of great excitement, my mind was called up to serious reflection and great uneasiness; but though my feelings were deep and often poignant, still I kept myself aloof from all these parties, though I attended their several meetings as often as occasion would permit. In process of time my mind became somewhat partial to the Methodist sect, and I felt some desire to be united with them; but so great were the confusion and strife among the different denominations, that it was impossible for a person young as I was, and so unacquainted with men and things, to come to any certain conclusion who was right and who was wrong.

"My mind at times was greatly excited, the cry and tumult were so great and incessant. The Presbyterians were most decided against the Baptists and Methodists, and used all the powers of either reason or sophistry to prove their errors, or, at least, to make the people think they were in error. On the other hand, the Baptists and Methodists in their turn were equally zealous in endeavoring to establish their own tenets and disprove all others.

"In the midst of this war of words and tumult of opinions, I often said to myself, What is to be done? Who of all these parties are right; or, are they all wrong together? If any one of them be right, which is it, and how shall I know it?

"While I was laboring under the extreme difficulties caused by the contests of these parties of religionists, I was one day reading the Epistle of James, first chapter and fifth verse, which reads: _If any of you lack wisdom, let him ask of God, that giveth to all men liberally, and upbraideth not; and it shall be given him._

"Never did any passage of scripture come with more power to the heart of man than this did at this time to mine. It seemed to enter with great force into every feeling of my heart. I reflected on it again and again, knowing that if any person needed wisdom from God, I did; for how to act I did not know, and unless I could get more wisdom than I then had, I would never know; for the teachers of religion of the different sects understood the same passages of scripture so differently as to destroy all confidence in settling the question by an appeal to the Bible.

"At length I came to the conclusion that I must either remain in darkness and confusion, or else I must do as James directs, that is, ask of God. I at length came to the determination to 'ask of God,' concluding that if He gave wisdom to them that lacked wisdom, and would give liberally, and not upbraid, I might venture.

"So, in accordance with this, my determination to ask of God, I retired to the woods to make the attempt. It was on the morning of a beautiful, clear day, early in the spring of eighteen hundred and twenty. It was the first time in my life that I had made such an attempt, for amidst all my anxieties I had never as yet made the attempt to pray vocally.

"After I had retired to the place where I had previously designed to go, having looked around me, and finding myself alone, I kneeled down and began to offer up the desires of my heart to God. I had scarcely done so, when immediately I was seized upon by some power which entirely overcame me, and had such an astonishing influence over me as to bind my tongue so that I could not speak.

Thick darkness gathered around me, and   it seemed to me for a time as if I were doomed to sudden destruction.

"But, exerting all my powers to call upon God to deliver me out   of the power of this enemy which had seized upon me, and at the   very moment when I was ready to sink into despair and abandon myself to destruction--not to an imaginary ruin, but to the   power of some actual being from the unseen world, who had such   marvelous power as I had never before felt in any being--just at   this moment of great alarm, I saw a pillar of light exactly over   my head, above the brightness of the sun, which descended   gradually until it fell upon me.

"It no sooner appeared than I found myself delivered from the   enemy which held me bound. When the light rested upon me I saw   two personages, whose brightness and glory defy all description,   standing above me in the air. One of them spake unto me, calling   me by name, and said, pointing to the other--_This is my beloved   Son, hear him!_

"My object in going to inquire of the Lord was to know which of   all the sects was right, that I might know which to join. No   sooner, therefore, did I get possession of myself, so as to be   able to speak, than I asked the personages who stood above me in   the light, which of all the sects was right--and which I should   join.

"I was answered that I must join none of them, for they were all   wrong; and the personage who addressed me said that all their   creeds were an abomination in his sight; that those professors were all corrupt; that 'they draw near to me with their lips,   but their hearts are far from me; they teach for doctrines the   commandments of men, having a form of godliness, but they deny   the power thereof.'

"He again forbade me to join with any of them; and many other   things did he say unto me, which I cannot write at this time.   When I came to myself again, I found myself lying on my back, looking up into heaven.

"Some few days after I had this vision, I happened to be in   company with one of the Methodist preachers, who was very active   in the before mentioned religious excitement; and, conversing with him on the subject of religion, I took occasion to give him   an account of the vision which I had had. I was greatly   surprised at his behavior; he treated my communication not only   lightly, but with great contempt, saying, it was all of the   devil, that there were no such things as visions or revelations   in these days; that all such things had ceased with the   apostles, and that there would never be any more of them.

"I soon found, however, that my telling the story had excited a   great deal of prejudice against me among professors of religion,   and was the cause of great persecution, which continued to increase; and though I was an obscure boy, only between fourteen   and fifteen years of age, and my circumstances in life such as   to make a boy of no consequence in the world, yet men of high   standing would take notice sufficient to excite the public mind   against me, and create a bitter persecution; and this was common   among all the sects--all united to persecute me.

"It caused me serious reflection then, and often has since, how   very strange it was that an obscure boy, of a little over   fourteen years of age, and one, too, who was doomed to the   necessity of obtaining a scanty maintenance by his daily labor,   should be thought a character of sufficient importance to   attract the attention of the great ones of the most popular   sects of the day, and in a manner to create in them a spirit of   the most bitter persecution and reviling. But strange or not, so   it was, and it was often the cause of great sorrow to myself.

"However, it was nevertheless a fact that I had beheld a vision.   I have thought since, that I felt much like Paul, when he made   his defense before King Agrippa, and related the account of the vision he had when he saw a light, and heard a voice; but still   there were but few who believed him; some said he was dishonest,   others said he was mad; and he was ridiculed and reviled. But   all this did not destroy the reality of his vision. He had seen   a vision, he knew he had, and all the persecution under heaven   could not make it otherwise; and though they should persecute   him unto death, yet he knew, and would know to his latest   breath, that he had both seen a light, and heard a voice   speaking unto him, and all the world could not make him think or   believe otherwise.

"So it was with me. I had actually seen a light, and in the   midst of that light I saw two personages, and they did in   reality speak to me; and though I was hated and persecuted for   saying that I had seen a vision, yet it was true; and while they   were persecuting me, reviling me, and speaking all manner of   evil against me falsely for so saying, I was led to say in my   heart: Why persecute me for telling the truth? I have actually   seen a vision, and who am I that I can withstand God, or why   does the world think to make me deny what I have actually seen?   For I had seen a vision; I knew it, and I knew that God knew it,   and I could not deny it, neither dared I do it, at least I knew   that by so doing I would offend God, and come under   condemnation.

"I had now got my mind satisfied so far as the sectarian world   was concerned; that it was not my duty to join with any of them,   but to continue as I was until further directed. I had found the testimony of James to be true, that a man who lacked wisdom   might ask of God, and obtain, and not be upbraided."[1523]

In this wise was ushered in the Dispensation of the Fulness of Times.[1524] The darkness of the long night of apostasy was dispelled; the glory of the heavens once more illumined the world; the silence of centuries was broken; the voice of God was heard again upon the earth. In the spring of A.D. 1820 there was one mortal, a boy not quite fifteen years old, who knew as well as that he lived, that the current human conception of Deity as an incorporeal essence of something possessing neither definite shape nor tangible substance was as devoid of truth in respect to both the Father and the Son as its statement in formulated creeds was incomprehensible. The boy Joseph knew that both the Eternal Father and His glorified Son,

the spot that had been shown him in vision. By the aid of a lever he removed a large stone, which proved to be the cover of a stone box wherein lay the plates and other articles described by Moroni. The angel appeared at the place, and forbade Joseph to remove the contents of the box at that time. The young man replaced the massive stone lid and left the spot.

Four years later, the plates, the Urim and Thummim, and the breastplate were delivered into Joseph's keeping by the angel Moroni. This Moroni, who now came as a resurrected being, was the last survivor of the Nephite nation; he had completed the record, and then shortly before his death had hidden away the same in the hill Cumorah, whence it was brought forth through his instrumentality and delivered to the modern prophet and seer, Joseph Smith, September 22, 1827. That record, or, strictly speaking a part thereof, is now accessible to all; it has been translated through divine instrumentality and is now published in many languages as the Book of Mormon.[1530]

THE AARONIC PRIESTHOOD CONFERRED BY JOHN THE BAPTIST.

On the 15th of May, 1829, Joseph Smith and his scribe in the work of translating the Nephite record, Oliver Cowdery, retired to a secluded glade to pray. Their special purpose was to inquire of the Lord concerning the ordinance of baptism for the remission of sins, some account of which they had found on the plates. Joseph writes:

"While we were thus employed, praying and calling upon the Lord,   a messenger from heaven descended in a cloud of light, and   having laid his hands upon us, he ordained us, saying:

"_Upon you my fellow servants, in the name of Messiah, I confer   the Priesthood of Aaron, which holds the keys of the ministering   of angels, and of the Gospel of repentance, and of baptism by immersion for the remission of sins; and this shall never be   taken again from the earth, until the sons of Levi do offer   again an offering unto the Lord in righteousness."_[1531]

The angelic visitor stated that his name was John, the same who is designated in the New Testament, John the Baptist; and that he had acted in ordaining the two under the direction of Peter, James, and John, who held the keys of the Higher or Melchizedek Priesthood. He explained that the Aaronic Priesthood did not comprize "the power of laying on hands for the gift of the Holy Ghost";[1532] but he predicted that the Higher Priesthood, having this power, would be conferred later. By his express direction, Joseph baptized Oliver, and the latter in turn baptized Joseph, by immersion in water.

THE MELCHIZEDEK PRIESTHOOD CONFERRED BY PETER, JAMES, AND JOHN.

Shortly after their ordination to the Lesser or Aaronic Priesthood, Joseph Smith and Oliver Cowdery were visited by the presiding apostles of old, Peter, James, and John, who conferred upon them the Melchizedek Priesthood and ordained them to the Holy Apostleship. In a later revelation the Lord Jesus thus specifically acknowledges the respective ordinations as having been done by His will and commandment:

"Which John I have sent unto you, my servants, Joseph Smith,   jun., and Oliver Cowdery, to ordain you unto this first   priesthood which you have received, that you might be called and ordained even as Aaron.... And also with Peter, and James, and   John, whom I have sent unto you, by whom I have ordained you and   confirmed you to be apostles, and especial witnesses of my name,   and bear the keys of your ministry, and of the same things which   I revealed unto them: Unto whom I have committed the keys of my   kingdom, and a dispensation of the gospel for the last times;   and for the fulness of times, in the which I will gather   together in one all things, both which are in heaven, and which are on the earth."[1533]

ESTABLISHMENT OF THE CHURCH OF JESUS CHRIST OF LATTER-DAY SAINTS.

On the sixth day of April A.D. 1830, the Church of Jesus Christ of Latter-day Saints was formally organized, at Fayette, Seneca county, New York, in accordance with the secular law governing the establishment of religious associations. The persons actually participating in the organization numbered but six, such being the minimum required by law in such an undertaking; many others were present however, some of whom had already received the ordinance of baptism for the remission of sins. By revelation to Joseph Smith, the Lord had previously specified the day on which the organization was to be effected, and had made known His plan of Church government--with detailed instructions as to the requisite conditions for membership; the indispensability of baptism by immersion, and the precise manner in which the initiatory ordinance was to be administered; the manner of confirming baptized believers as members of the Church; the duties of elders, priests, teachers, and deacons in the Church; the exact procedure to be followed in the administration of the Sacrament of the Lord's Supper; the order of Church discipline, and the method of transferring members from one branch to another.[1534] The baptized converts present at the organization were called upon to express their acceptance or rejection of Joseph Smith and Oliver Cowdery as elders in the Church; and in accordance with the unanimous vote in the affirmative the ordination or setting apart of these two men as respectively first and second elder in the new organization was performed. [1535]

While the Book of Mormon had been in course of translation, particularly during the two years immediately preceding the organization of the Church, several revelations had been given through Joseph the prophet and seer, relating to the work of translation and to the preparatory labor necessary to the establishment of the Church as an institution among men. The Author of these several revelations declared Himself definitely to be Jesus Christ, God, the Son of God, the Redeemer, the Light and Life of the World,

Alpha and Omega, Christ the Lord, the Lord and Savior.[1536] As early as A.D. 1829, the calling of the Twelve Apostles was indicated, and appointment was made for the searching out of the Twelve who should stand before the world as special witnesses of the Christ; these were subsequently ordained to the Holy Apostleship, and the council or quorum of the Twelve has been recognized, and instructions concerning their exalted duties have been given, in numerous revelations of later dates.[1537]

In such manner has the Church of Jesus Christ been reestablished upon the earth, with all the powers and authority pertaining to the Holy Priesthood as committed by the Lord Jesus to His apostles in the period of His personal ministry. The inauguration of a new dispensation of the gospel, with a restoration of the Priesthood, was absolutely necessary; since through the apostasy of the Primitive Church there lived not a man empowered to speak or administer in the name of God or His Christ. John the Revelator saw in his vision of the last days an angel bringing anew "the everlasting gospel to preach unto them that dwell on the earth, and to every nation, and kindred, and tongue, and people, saying with a loud voice, Fear God, and give glory to him; for the hour of his judgment is come: and worship him that made heaven, and earth, and the sea, and the fountains of waters."[1538]

Such an angelic embassage would have been but a needless and empty display, and therefore an impossibility, had the everlasting gospel remained upon the earth with its powers of priesthood perpetuated by succession. The scriptural assurances of a restoration in the last days through direct bestowal from the heavens is conclusive proof of the actuality of the universal apostasy. Moroni came to Joseph Smith as "a messenger sent from the presence of God," and delivered a record containing "the fulness of the everlasting gospel," as it had been imparted to the Lord's people in ancient times; and the world-wide distribution of the Book of Mormon, and of other publications embodying the revealed word in modern times, and the ministry of thousands who labor in the authority of the Holy Priesthood combine as the loud voice addressed to every nation, crying: "Fear God, and give glory to him; for the hour of his judgment is come."

FURTHER COMMUNICATIONS FROM THE HEAVENS TO MAN.

Following the organization of the Church as heretofore described, direct communication between the Lord Jesus Christ and His prophet Joseph was frequent, as the needs of the Church required. Numerous revelations were given, and these are accessible to all who will read.[1539] A marvelous manifestation was granted to the prophet and his associate in the presidency of the Church, Sidney Rigdon, the record of which appears as follows:

"We, Joseph Smith, jun., and Sidney Rigdon, being in the Spirit on the sixteenth of February, in the year of our Lord, one thousand eight hundred and thirty-two, by the power of the Spirit our eyes were opened and our understandings were enlightened, so as to see and understand the things of God--even those things which were from the beginning before the world was, which were ordained of the Father, through his Only Begotten Son, who was in the bosom of the Father, even from the beginning, of whom we bear record, and the record which we bear is the fulness of the gospel of Jesus Christ, who is the Son, whom we saw and with whom we conversed in the heavenly vision; For while we were doing the work of translation, which the Lord had appointed unto us, we came to the twenty-ninth verse of the fifth chapter of John, which was given unto us as follows. Speaking of the resurrection of the dead, concerning those who shall hear the voice of the Son of Man, and shall come forth; they who have done good in the resurrection of the just, and they who have done evil in the resurrection of the unjust. Now this caused us to marvel, for it was given unto us of the Spirit; and while we meditated upon these things, the Lord touched the eyes of our understandings and they were opened, and the glory of the Lord shone round about; and we beheld the glory of the Son, on the right hand of the Father, and received of his fulness; and saw the holy angels, and they who are sanctified before his throne, worshiping God, and the Lamb, who worship him for ever and ever. And now, after the many testimonies which have been given of him, this is the testimony last of all, which we give of him, that he lives; for we saw him, even on the right hand of God, and we heard the voice bearing record that he is the Only Begotten of the Father--that by him and through him, and of him the worlds are and were created, and the inhabitants thereof are begotten sons and daughters unto God."[1540]

The vision was followed by further revelation both through sight and hearing; and the Lord showed unto His servants and proclaimed aloud the fate of the wicked and the characteristic features of the varied degrees of glory provided for the souls of mankind in the hereafter. The several states of graded honor and exaltation pertaining to the telestial, the terrestrial, and the celestial kingdoms were revealed, and the ancient scriptures relating thereto were illumined with the new light of simplicity and literalness.[1541]

PERSONAL APPEARING OF THE LORD JESUS CHRIST IN THE KIRTLAND TEMPLE.

In less than three and a half years after its organization the Church began the erection of the first temple of modern times at Kirtland, Ohio. The work was undertaken in compliance with a revelation from the Lord requiring this labor at the hands of His people. The Church membership was small; the people were in poverty; the period was one of determined opposition and relentless persecution.[1542] Be it understood that to the Latter-day Saints a temple is more than chapel, church, tabernacle, or cathedral; it is no place of common assembly even for purposes of congregational worship, but an edifice sacred to the ordinances of the Holy Priesthood--distinctively and essentially a House of the Lord. The temple at Kirtland stands today, a substantial and stately building; but it is no longer in possession of the people who reared it by unmeasured sacrifice of time, substance, and effort extending through years of self-denial and suffering.

Its corner-stones were laid July 23, 1833, and the completed structure was dedicated March 27, 1836. The dedicatory service was made ever memorable by a Pentecostal outpouring of the Spirit of the Lord accompanied by the visible presence of angels. In the evening of the same day the several quorums of priesthood assembled in the house, and a yet greater manifestation of divine power and glory was witnessed. On the succeeding Sunday--April 3, 1836--after a service of solemn worship, including the administration of the Lord's Supper, the prophet Joseph and his counselor, Oliver Cowdery, retired for prayer within the veils enclosing the platform and pulpit reserved for the presiding authorities of the Melchizedek Priesthood. They bear this solemn testimony to the personal appearing of the Lord Jesus Christ at that time and place:

"The veil was taken from our minds, and the eyes of our understanding were opened. We saw the Lord standing upon the breast work of the pulpit, before us, and under his feet was a paved work of pure gold in color like amber. His eyes were as a flame of fire, the hair of his head was white like the pure snow, his countenance shone above the brightness of the sun, and his voice was as the sound of the rushing of great waters, even the voice of Jehovah, saying--I am the first and the last, I am he who liveth, I am he who was slain, I am your advocate with the Father. Behold, your sins are forgiven you, you are clean before me, therefore lift up your heads and rejoice, let the hearts of your brethren rejoice, and let the hearts of all my people rejoice, who have, with their might, built this house to my name. For behold, I have accepted this house, and my name shall be here, and I will manifest myself to my people in mercy in this house, Yea, I will appear unto my servants, and speak unto them with mine own voice, if my people will keep my commandments, and do not pollute this holy house, Yea the hearts of thousands and tens of thousands shall greatly rejoice in consequence of the blessings which shall be poured out, and the endowment with which my servants have been endowed in this house; and the fame of this house shall spread to foreign lands, and this is the beginning of the blessing which shall be poured out upon the heads of my people. Even so. Amen."[1543]

After the Savior's withdrawal, the two mortal prophets were visited by glorified beings, each of whom had officiated on earth as a specially commissioned servant of Jehovah, and now came to confer the authority of his particular office upon Joseph and Oliver, thus uniting all the powers and authorities of olden dispensations in the restored Church of Christ, which characterizes the last and greatest dispensation of history. This is the record:

"After this vision closed, the heavens were again opened unto us, and Moses appeared before us, and committed unto us the keys of the gathering of Israel from the four parts of the earth, and the leading of the ten tribes from the land of the north. After this, Elias appeared, and committed the dispensation of the gospel of Abraham, saying, that in us, and our seed, all generations after us should be blessed. After this vision had closed, another great and glorious vision burst upon us, for Elijah the prophet, who was taken to heaven without tasting death, stood before us, and said--Behold, the time has fully come, which was spoken of by the mouth of Malachi, testifying that he (Elijah) should be sent before the great and dreadful day of the Lord come, to turn the hearts of the fathers to the children, and the children to the fathers, lest the whole earth be smitten with a curse. Therefore the keys of this dispensation are committed into your hands, and by this ye may know that the great and dreadful day of the Lord is near, even at the doors."[1544]

JESUS THE CHRIST IS WITH HIS CHURCH TODAY.

Right gloriously has the Lord brought about a fulfilment of the promises uttered through the mouths of His holy prophets in by-gone ages--to restore the gospel with all its former blessings and privileges; to bestow anew the Holy Priesthood with authority to administer in the name of God; to reestablish the Church bearing His name and founded upon the rock of divine revelation; and to proclaim the message of salvation to all nations, kindreds, tongues, and peoples. In spite of persecution both mobocratic and judicially sanctioned, in spite of assaults, drivings, and slaughter, the Church has developed with marvelous rapidity and strength since the day of its organization. Joseph, the prophet, and his brother Hyrum, the patriarch of the Church, were brutally slain as martyrs to the truth at Carthage, Illinois, June 27, 1844. But the Lord raised up others to succeed them; and the world learned in part and yet shall know beyond all question that the Church so miraculously established in the last days is not the church of Joseph Smith nor of any other man, but in literal verity, the Church of Jesus Christ. The Lord has continued to make known His mind and will through prophets, seers, and revelators whom He has successively chosen and appointed to lead His people; and the voice of divine revelation is heard in the Church today. As provided for in its revealed plan and constitution, the Church is blessed by the ministry of prophets, apostles, high priests, patriarchs, seventies, elders, bishops, priests, teachers, and deacons.[1545] The spiritual gifts and blessings of old are again enjoyed in rich abundance.[1546] New scriptures, primarily directed to present duties and current developments in the purposes of God, yet which illuminate and make plain in simplicity the scriptures of old, have been given to the world through the channel of the restored priesthood; and other scriptures shall yet be written. The united membership of the Church proclaims:

"We believe all that God has revealed, all that He does now reveal, and we believe that He will yet reveal many great and important things pertaining to the Kingdom of God."[1547]

The predicted gathering of Israel from their long dispersion is in progress under the commission given by the Lord through Moses. The "mountain of the Lord's house" is already established in the top of the mountains, and all peoples flow unto it; while the elders of the Church go forth among the nations, saying: "Come ye, and let us go up to the mountain of the Lord, to the house of the God of Jacob; and he will teach us of his ways, and we will walk in his paths: for out of Zion shall go forth the law, and the word of the Lord from Jerusalem."[1548]

Within sacred temples, the living are officiating vicariously in behalf of the dead; and the hearts of mortal children are turned with affectionate concern toward their departed ancestors, while disembodied hosts are praying for the success of their posterity, yet in the flesh, in the service of salvation.[1549] The saving gospel is offered freely to all, for so hath its Author commanded. Through the medium of the press, and by the personal ministrations of men invested with the Holy Priesthood whom the Church sends out by thousands, this Gospel of the Kingdom is today preached throughout the world. When such witness among the nations is made complete, "then shall the end come"; and the nations "shall see the Son of Man coming in the clouds of heaven, with power and great glory."[1550]

NOTES TO CHAPTER 41.

1. The Dispensation of the Fulness of Times.--"Now the thing to be known is, what the fulness of times means, or the extent and authority thereof. It means this, that the dispensation of the fulness of times is made up of all the dispensations that ever have been given since the world began, until this time. Unto Adam first was given a dispensation. It is well known that God spake to him with His own voice in the garden, and gave him the promise of the Messiah. And unto Noah also was a dispensation given; for Jesus said, 'As it was in the days of Noah, so shall it be also in the days of the coming of the Son of Man;' and as the righteous were saved then, and the wicked destroyed, so it will be now. And from Noah to Abraham, and from Abraham to Moses, and from Moses to Elias, and from Elias to John the Baptist, and from then to Jesus Christ, and from Jesus Christ to Peter, James, and John, the Apostles all having received in their dispensation by revelation from God, to accomplish the great scheme of restitution, spoken by all the holy Prophets since the world began; the end of which is, the dispensation of the fulness of times, in which all things shall be fulfilled that have been spoken of since the earth was made."--See _Millennial Star_, vol. 16, p. 220.

2. Limitations of the Aaronic Priesthood.--After conferring the Lesser or Aaronic Priesthood upon Joseph Smith and Oliver Cowdery, the officiating angel, who had been known while a mortal being as John the Baptist, explained that the authority he had imparted did not extend to the laying-on of hands for the bestowal of the Holy Ghost, the latter ordinance being a function of the Higher or Melchizedek Priesthood. Consider the instance of Philip, (not the apostle Philip), whose ordination empowered him to baptize, though a higher authority than his was requisite for the conferring of the Holy Ghost; and consequently the apostles Peter and John went down to Samaria to officiate in the case of Philip's baptized converts (Acts 8:5, 12-17). See Doc. and Cov. 20:41, 46.

3. Priesthood and Office Therein.--It is important to know that although Joseph Smith and Oliver Cowdery had been ordained to the Holy Apostleship, and therefore to a fulness of the Melchizedek Priesthood, by Peter, James, and John, it was necessary that they be ordained as elders in the Church. When they received the Melchizedek Priesthood from the three ancient apostles, there was no organized Church of Jesus Christ, and consequently no need of Church officers, such as elders, priests, teachers, or deacons. As soon as the Church was established, officers were chosen therein and these were ordained to the requisite office or grade in the Priesthood. Moreover, the principle of common consent in the conduct of Church affairs was observed in this early action of the members in voting to sustain the men nominated for official positions, and has continued to be the rule of the Church to this day. It is pertinent to point out further that in conferring upon Joseph and Oliver the Aaronic Priesthood, John the Baptist did not ordain them to the office of priest, teacher, or deacon. These three offices are included in the Aaronic, as are the offices of elder, seventy, high priest, etc., in the Melchizedek Priesthood. Read Doc. and Cov. 20:38-67; _The Articles of Faith_, xi.

4. Modern Temples.--The Lord's gracious promise given in the Kirtland Temple--to appear unto His servants at times then future, and to speak unto them with His own voice, provided the people would keep His commandments and not pollute that holy house--has been in no wise abrogated nor forfeited through the enforced relinquishment of the Kirtland Temple by the Latter-day Saints. The people were compelled to flee before the fury of mobocratic persecution; but they hastened to erect another and yet more splendid sanctuary at Nauvoo, Illinois, and were again dispossessed by lawless mobs. In the valleys of Utah the Church has erected four great temples, each more stately than the last; and in these holy houses the sacred ordinances pertaining to salvation and exaltation of both the living and the dead are in uninterrupted progress. The temples of the present dispensation, at the time of the present writing designated according to location, are those of Kirtland, Ohio; Nauvoo, Illinois; St. George, Logan, Manti, and Salt Lake City, Utah; Cardston, Canada, and Laie, Hawaii. See _The House of the Lord_, pp. 63-232.

5. Consistency of the Church's Claim to Authority.--The proofs of order and system in the restoration of authority to officiate in particular functions pertaining to the priesthood are striking, and go to prove the continued validity, beyond the grave, of authoritative ordination on earth. The keys of the Aaronic order, comprizing authority to baptize for the remission of sins, were brought by John the Baptist, who had been especially commissioned in that order of priesthood in the time of Christ. The apostleship, comprizing all powers inherent in the Melchizedek Priesthood, was restored by the presiding apostles of old, Peter, James, and John. Then, as has been seen, Moses conferred the authority to prosecute the work of gathering; and Elijah, who, not having tasted death, held a peculiar relation to both the living and the dead, delivered the authority of vicarious ministry for the departed. To these appointments by heavenly authority should be added that given by Elias, who appeared to Joseph Smith and Oliver Cowdery, and "committed the dispensation of the gospel of Abraham." It is evident, then, that the claims made by the Church with respect to its authority are complete and consistent as to the source of the powers professed and the

channels through which such have been delivered again to earth. Scripture and revelation, both ancient and modern, support as an unalterable law the principle that no one can delegate to another an authority which the giver does not possess.

6. Cessation of the Melchizedek Administration in Ancient Times.--The Higher or Melchizedek Priesthood was held by the patriarchs from Adam to Moses. Aaron was ordained to the priest's office, as were his sons; but that Moses held superior authority is abundantly shown (Numb. 12:1-8). After Aaron's death his son Eleazar officiated in the authority of the Lesser Priesthood; and even Joshua had to take counsel and authority from him (Numb. 27:18-23). From the ministry of Moses to that of Jesus Christ, the Lesser Priesthood alone was operative upon the earth, excepting only the instances of specially delegated authority of the higher order such as is manifest in the ministrations of certain chosen prophets, Isaiah, Jeremiah, Ezekiel, and others. It is evident that these prophets, seers, and revelators were individually and specially commissioned; but it appears that they had not authority to call and ordain successors, for in their time the Higher Priesthood was not existent on earth in an organized state with duly officered quorums. Not so with the Aaronic and Levitical Priesthood, however. The matter is made particularly plain through latter-day revelation. See Doc. and Cov. 84:23-28; read the entire section; also _The House of the Lord_ pp. 235-238.

FOOTNOTES:

[1523] P. of G.P., Joseph Smith 2:5-26; also "History of the Church of Jesus Christ of Latter-day Saints," vol. 1, pp. 2-8.

[1524] Eph. 1:9, 10. Note 1, end of chapter.

[1525] See page 151 herein; Note 5, end of chapter.

[1526] For earlier instances, see pages 126, 371, and 725.

[1527] P. of G.P., Joseph Smith 2:29-54, 59; also "History of the Church," vol. 1, pp. 10-16, 18.

[1528] P. of G.P., Joseph Smith 2:28.

[1529] P. of G.P., Joseph Smith 2:36-41; and "History of the Church," vol. 1. pp. 12, 13.

[1530] See B. of M., Mormon 6:6; Moroni 10:2.

[1531] P. of G.P., Joseph Smith 2:68, 69; Doc. and Cov. sec. 13; "History of the Church," vol. 1, p. 39.

[1532] Notes 2 and 6. end of chapter.

[1533] Doc. and Cov. 27: 8, 12, 13.

[1534] Doc. and Cov. sec. 20.

[1535] Doc. and Cov. 20:2, 3; compare 21:11; see also "History of the Church." vol. 1, pp. 40, 41. Note 3, end of chapter.

[1536] Doc. and Cov. sections 5, 6, 8, 10-12, 14-20.

[1537] Doc. and Cov. 18:27, 31-36; 20:38-44; 84:63, 64; 95:4; 107:23-25; 112:1, 14, 21; 118; 124:127-130.

[1538] Rev. 14:6, 7.

[1539] See Doctrine and Covenants, and "History of the Church."

[1540] Doc. and Cov. 76:11-24; also "History of the Church" under date specified.

[1541] See Doc. and Cov. 76:25-119; also "The Articles of Faith," iv:29; and xxii:18-27.

[1542] See "The House of the Lord," pages 114-123.

[1543] Doc. and Cov. 110:1-10; also "History of the Church" under date specified. Note 4, end of chapter.

[1544] Doc. and Cov. 110:11-16. Note 5, end of chapter. [1545] See "Plan of Government in the Restored Church," in "The Articles of Faith," xi:13-32.

[1546] See "Spiritual Gifts" in "The Articles of Faith," xii.

[1547] No. 9 of "The Articles of Faith of the Church of Jesus Christ of Latter-day Saints."

[1548] Isa. 2:2, 3; compare Micah 4:1, 2; see also Doc. and Cov. 29:8.

[1549] See "The House of the Lord," pp. 63-109.

[1550] P. of G.P., Joseph Smith 1:31, 36; compare Matt 24:14, 30.

CHAPTER 42. JESUS THE CHRIST TO RETURN.

THE LORD'S SECOND ADVENT PREDICTED IN ANCIENT SCRIPTURE.

"Ye men of Galilee, why stand ye gazing up into heaven? this same Jesus, which is taken up from you into heaven, shall so come in like manner as ye have seen him go into heaven."[1551] So spake the white-robed angels to the eleven apostles as the resurrected Christ ascended from their midst on Olivet. The scriptures abound in predictions of the Lord's return.

By the "second advent" we understand not the personal appearing of the Son of God to a few, such as His visitation to Saul of Tarsus, to Joseph Smith in 1820, and again in the Kirtland Temple in 1836; nor later manifestations to His worthy servants as specifically promised;[1552] but His yet future coming in power and great glory, accompanied by hosts of resurrected and glorified beings, to execute judgment upon the earth and to inaugurate a reign of righteousness.

The prophets of both hemispheres, who lived prior to the meridian of time, said comparatively little concerning the Lord's second coming; their souls were too full of the merciful plan of redemption associated with the Savior's birth into mortality to permit them to dwell upon the yet more distant consummation appointed for the last days. Certain of them, however, were permitted to behold in vision the working out of the divine purposes even to the end of time; and these testified with unsurpassed fervency concerning the glorious coming of Christ in the final dispensation. Enoch, the seventh from Adam, prophesied saying, "Behold the Lord cometh with ten thousands of his saints, to execute judgment upon all."[1553] In a more extended account of the Lord's revelations to Enoch than is included in the Bible, we read that after this righteous prophet had been shown the scenes of Israel's history, down to and beyond the death, resurrection and ascension of Jesus Christ, he pleaded with God, saying: "I ask thee if thou wilt not come again on the earth. And the Lord said unto Enoch: As I live, even so will I come in the last days, in the days of wickedness and vengeance, to fulfil the oath which I have made unto you concerning the children of Noah.... And it came to pass that Enoch saw the day of the coming of the Son of Man, in the last days, to dwell on the earth in righteousness for the space of a thousand years."[1554] Isaiah, in rapturous contemplation of the eventual triumph of righteousness, exclaimed: "Say to them that are of a fearful heart, Be strong, fear not: behold, your God will come with vengeance, even God with a recompence; he will come and save you"; and again: "Behold, the Lord God will come with strong hand, and his arm shall rule for him: behold, his reward is with him, and his work before him."[1555] The conditions specified were not realized in the earthly life of the Redeemer; moreover the context clearly shows that the prophet's words are applicable to the last days only--the time of the ransomed of the Lord, the time of restitution, and of the triumph of Zion.

Of all Biblical scriptures relating to our subject, the utterances of the Christ Himself in the course of His earthly ministry are most direct and certain. Many of these we have already considered in the narrative of the Savior's life; the few following are sufficient for present demonstration. "For the Son of man shall come in the glory of his Father with his angels; and then he shall reward every man according to his works."[1556] To the apostles and the people generally He proclaimed: "Whosoever therefore shall be ashamed of me and of my words in this adulterous and sinful generation; of him also shall the Son of man be ashamed, when he cometh in the glory of his Father with the holy angels."[1557] When a bound prisoner before proud Caiaphas, Jesus answered the unlawful adjuration of the corrupt high priest, by affirming: "I say unto you, Hereafter shall ye see the Son of man sitting on the right hand of power, and coming in the clouds of heaven."[1558]

The apostles had been so impressed with the Master's assurance that He would return to earth in power and glory, that they eagerly questioned as to the time and signs of His coming.[1559] He stated explicitly, though at the time they failed to comprehend Him, that many great events would intervene between His departure and return, including the long era of darkness associated with the apostasy.[1560] But as to the certainty of His advent in glory, as Judge, and Lord, and King, Jesus left no excuse for dubiety in the minds of His apostles. After the ascension, throughout the course of apostolic administration, the future coming of the Lord was preached with earnest emphasis.[1561]

Book of Mormon prophecies concerning the advent of the Lord in the last days are specific and definite. On the occasion of His appearing to the Nephites on the American continent shortly after His ascension from the Mount of Olives, Christ preached the gospel to assembled multitudes; "And he did expound all things, even from the beginning until the time that he should come in his glory"; and the events to follow, "even unto the great and last day."[1562] In granting the wish of the three Nephite disciples who desired to continue their ministry in the flesh throughout the generations to come, the Lord said unto them:

"Ye shall live to behold all the doings of the Father, unto the children of men, even until all things shall be fulfilled, according to the will of the Father, when I shall come in my glory, with the powers of heaven; And ye shall never endure the pains of death; but when I shall come in my glory, ye shall be changed in the twinkling of an eye from mortality to immortality: and then shall ye be blessed in the kingdom of my Father."[1563]

THE COMING OF THE LORD PROCLAIMED THROUGH MODERN REVELATION.

To the Church of Jesus Christ, restored and reestablished in these the last days, the word of the Lord has come repeatedly, declaring the actuality of His second advent and the nearness of that glorious yet dreadful event. But a few months after the Church was organized, the voice of Jesus Christ was heard, admonishing the elders to vigilance and proclaiming as follows:

"For the hour is nigh, and the day soon at hand when the earth is ripe: and all the proud, and they that do wickedly, shall be as stubble, and I will burn them up, saith the Lord of Hosts, that wickedness shall not be upon the earth; for the hour is nigh, and that which was spoken by mine apostles must be fulfilled; for as they spoke so shall it come to pass; for I will reveal myself from heaven with power and great glory, with all the hosts thereof, and dwell in righteousness with men on earth a thousand years, and the wicked shall not stand."[1564] In the month following, the Lord gave instructions to certain elders, concluding with these portentous words:

"Wherefore, be faithful, praying always, having your lamps trimmed and burning, and oil with you, that you may be ready at the coming of the Bridegroom: for behold, verily, verily, I say unto you, that I come quickly. Even so. Amen."[1565]

Again we read in a later revelation:

"And blessed are you because you have believed; and more blessed are you because you are called of me to preach my gospel, to lift up your voice as with the sound of a trump, both long and loud, and cry repentance unto a crooked and perverse generation, preparing the way of the Lord for his second coming; for behold, verily, verily, I say unto you, the time is soon at hand, that I shall come in a cloud with power and great glory, and it shall be a great day at the time of my coming, for all nations shall tremble."[1566]

The Lord Jesus addressed a general revelation to His Church in March 1831, through which His earlier predictions uttered to the Twelve shortly before His betrayal were made plain, and the assurances of His glorious coming were thus reiterated:

"Ye look and behold the fig-trees, and ye see them with your eyes, and ye say when they begin to shoot forth, and their leaves are yet tender, that summer is now nigh at hand; even so it shall be in that day when they shall see all these things, then shall they know that the hour is nigh. And it shall come to pass that he that feareth me shall be looking forth for the great day of the Lord to come, even for the signs of the coming of the Son of man: And they shall see signs and wonders, for they shall be shown forth in the heavens above, and in the earth beneath; and they shall behold blood, and fire, and vapors of smoke; and before the day of the Lord shall come, the sun shall be darkened, and the moon be turned into blood, and stars fall from heaven; and the remnant shall be gathered unto this place, and then they shall look for me, and, behold, I will come; and they shall see me in the clouds of heaven, clothed with power and great glory, with all the holy angels; and he that watches not for me shall be cut off."[1567]

So near is the consummation that the intervening period is called "today"; and, in applying this time designation in the year 1831, the Lord said:

"Behold, now it is called today (until the coming of the Son of man), and verily it is a day of sacrifice, and a day for the tithing of my people; for he that is tithed shall not be burned (at his coming); For after today cometh the burning: this is speaking after the manner of the Lord; for verily I say, tomorrow all the proud and they that do wickedly shall be as stubble; and I will burn them up, for I am the Lord of hosts: and I will not spare any that remain in Babylon. Wherefore, if ye believe me, ye will labor while it is called today."[1568]

THE TIME AND ACCOMPANIMENTS OF THE LORD'S COMING.

The date of the future advent of Christ has never been revealed to man. To the inquiring apostles who labored with the Master, He said: "But of that day and hour knoweth no man, no, not the angels of heaven, but my Father only."[1569] In the present age, a similar declaration has been made by the Father: "I, the Lord God, have spoken it, but the hour and the day no man knoweth, neither the angels in heaven, nor shall they know until he comes."[1570] Only through watchfulness and prayer may the signs of the times be correctly interpreted and the imminence of the Lord's appearing be apprehended. To the unwatchful and the wicked the event will be as sudden and unexpected as the coming of a thief in the night. [1571] But we are not left without definite information as to precedent signs. Biblical prophecies bearing upon this subject we have heretofore considered.[1572] As later scriptures affirm: "Before the great day of the Lord shall come, Jacob shall flourish in the wilderness, and the Lamanites shall blossom as the rose. Zion shall flourish upon the hills and rejoice upon the mountains, and shall be assembled together unto the place which I have appointed."[1573] War shall become so general that every man who will not take arms against his neighbor must of necessity flee to the land of Zion for safety.[1574] Ephraim shall assemble in Zion on the western continent, and Judah shall be again established in the east; and the cities of Zion and Jerusalem shall be the capitals of the world empire, over which Messiah shall reign in undisputed authority. The Lost Tribes shall be brought forth from the place where God has hidden them through the centuries and receive their long deferred blessings at the hands of Ephraim. The people of Israel shall be restored from their scattered condition.[1575]

In addressing the elders of His Church in 1832, the Lord urged upon them the imperative need of devoted diligence, and said:

"Abide ye in the liberty wherewith ye are made free; entangle not yourselves in sin but let your hands be clean, until the Lord come; For not many days hence and the earth shall tremble and reel to and fro as a drunken man, and the sun shall hide his face, and shall refuse to give light, and the moon shall be bathed in blood, and the stars shall become exceeding angry, and shall cast themselves down as a fig that falleth from off a fig tree. And after your testimony cometh wrath and indignation upon the people; For after your testimony cometh the testimony of earthquakes, that shall cause groanings in the midst of her, and men shall fall upon the ground, and shall not be able to stand. And also cometh the testimony of the voice of thunderings, and the voice of lightnings, and the voice of tempests, and the voice of the waves of the sea, heaving themselves beyond their   bounds. And all things shall be in commotion; and surely, men's   hearts shall fail them; for fear shall come upon all people; And   angels shall fly through the midst of heaven, crying with a loud   voice, sounding the trump of God, saying, Prepare ye, prepare   ye, O inhabitants of the earth; for the judgment of our God is   come: behold, and lo! the Bridegroom cometh, go ye out to meet   him."[1576]

A characteristic of present-day revelation is the reiteration of the fact that the event is nigh at hand, "even at the doors." The fateful time is repeatedly designated in scripture, "the great and dreadful day of the Lord."[1577] Fearful indeed will it be to individuals, families, and nations, who have so far sunk into sin as to have forfeited their claim to mercy. The time is not that of the final judgment--when the whole race of mankind shall stand in the resurrected state before the bar of God--nevertheless it shall be a time of unprecedented blessing unto the righteous and of condemnation and vengeance upon the wicked.[1578] With Christ shall come those who have already been resurrected; and His approach shall be the means of inaugurating a general resurrection of the righteous dead, while the pure and just who are still in the flesh shall be instantaneously changed from the mortal to the immortal state and shall be caught up with the newly resurrected to meet the Lord and His celestial company, and shall descend with Him. To this effect did Paul prophesy: "Even so them also which sleep in Jesus will God bring with him.... For the Lord himself shall descend from heaven with a shout, with the voice of the archangel, and with the trump of God: and the dead in Christ shall rise first: Then we which are alive and remain shall be caught up together with them in the clouds, to meet the Lord in the air."[1579] Compare the promise made to the Three Nephites: "And ye shall never endure the pains of death; but when I shall come in my glory, ye shall be changed in the twinkling of an eye from mortality to immortality."[1580] Of the superlative glories awaiting the righteous when the Lord shall come, we have received in this day a partial description as follows: "And the face of the Lord shall be unveiled; and the saints that are upon the earth, who are alive, shall be quickened, and be caught up to meet him."[1581] The heathen nations shall be redeemed and have part in the first resurrection.[1582]

THE KINGDOM OF HEAVEN TO COME.

The coming of Christ in the last days, accompanied by the apostles of old[1583] and by the resurrected saints, is to mark the establishment of the Kingdom of Heaven upon earth. The faithful apostles who were with Jesus in His earthly ministry are to be enthroned as judges of the whole house of Israel; [1584] they will judge the Nephite Twelve, who in turn will be empowered to judge the descendants of Lehi, or that branch of the Israelitish nation which was established upon the western continent.[1585]

While the expressions "Kingdom of God" and "Kingdom of Heaven" are used in the Bible synonymously or interchangeably, later revelation gives to each a distinctive meaning. The Kingdom of God is the Church established by divine authority upon the earth; this institution asserts no claim to temporal rule over nations; its sceptre of power is that of the Holy Priesthood, to be used in the preaching of the gospel and in administering its ordinances for the salvation of mankind living and dead. The Kingdom of Heaven is the divinely ordained system of government and dominion in all matters, temporal and spiritual; this will be established on earth only when its rightful Head, the King of kings, Jesus the Christ, comes to reign. His administration will be one of order, operated through the agency of His commissioned representatives invested with the Holy Priesthood. When Christ appears in His glory, and not before, will be realized a complete fulfilment of the supplication: "Thy kingdom come. Thy will be done in earth, as it is in heaven."

The Kingdom of God has been established among men to prepare them for the Kingdom of Heaven which shall come; and in the blessed reign of Christ the King shall the two be made one. The relationship between them has been revealed to the Church in this wise:

"Hearken, and lo, a voice as of one from on high, who is mighty   and powerful, whose going forth is unto the ends of the earth,   yea, whose voice is unto men--Prepare ye the way of the Lord,   make his paths straight. The keys of the kingdom of God are   committed unto man on the earth, and from thence shall the   gospel roll forth unto the ends of the earth, as the stone which   is cut out of the mountain without hands shall roll forth, until   it has filled the whole earth; Yea, a voice crying--Prepare ye the way of the Lord, prepare ye the supper of the Lamb, make   ready for the Bridegroom; Pray unto the Lord, call upon his holy   name, make known his wonderful works among the people; Call upon   the Lord, that his kingdom may go forth upon the earth, that the   inhabitants thereof may receive it, and be prepared for the days   to come, in the which the Son of man shall come down in heaven,   clothed in the brightness of his glory, to meet the kingdom of   God which is set up on the earth; Wherefore may the kingdom of   God go forth, that the kingdom of heaven may come, that thou, O   God, mayest be glorified in heaven so on earth, that thy enemies   may be subdued for thine is the honour, power and glory, for ever and ever. Amen."[1586]

THE MILLENNIUM.

The inauguration of Christ's reign on earth is to be the beginning of a period that shall be distinct in many important particulars from all precedent and subsequent time; and the Lord shall reign with His people a thousand years. The government of individuals, communities and nations throughout this Millennium is to be that of a perfect theocracy, with Jesus the Christ as Lord and King. The more wicked part of the race shall have been destroyed; and during the period Satan shall be bound "that he should deceive the nations no more, till the thousand years should be fulfilled"; while the just shall share with

Christ in rightful rule and dominion. The righteous dead shall have come forth from their graves, while the wicked shall remain unresurrected until the thousand years be past.[1587] Men yet in the flesh shall mingle with immortalized beings; children shall grow to maturity and then die in peace or be changed to immortality "in the twinkling of an eye."[1588] There shall be surcease of enmity between man and beast; the venom of serpents and the ferocity of the brute creation shall be done away, and love shall be the dominant power of control. Among the earliest revelations on the subject is that given to Enoch; and in this the return of that prophet and his righteous people with Christ in the last days was thus assured:

"And the Lord said unto Enoch: Then shalt thou and all thy city   meet them there, and we will receive them into our bosom, and   they shall see us; and we will fall upon their necks, and they shall fall upon our necks, and we will kiss each other; And   there shall be mine abode, and it shall be Zion, which shall   come forth out of all the creations which I have made; and for   the space of a thousand years the earth shall rest. And it came   to pass that Enoch saw the day of the coming of the Son of Man,   in the last days, to dwell on the earth in righteousness for the   space of a thousand years."[1589]

In these latter days the Lord has thus spoken, requiring preparation for the Millennial era, and describing in part the glories thereof:

"And prepare for the revelation which is to come, when the veil   of the covering of my temple, in my tabernacle, which hideth the   earth, shall be taken off, and all flesh shall see me together. And every corruptible thing, both of man, or of the beasts of   the field, or of the fowls of the heavens, or of the fish of the   sea, that dwell upon all the face of the earth, shall be   consumed; And also that of element shall melt with fervent heat;   and all things shall become new, that my knowledge and glory may dwell upon all the earth. And in that day the enmity of man, and   the enmity of beasts, yea, the enmity of all flesh, shall cease   from before my face. And in that day whatsoever any man shall   ask, it shall be given unto him. And in that day Satan shall not   have power to tempt any man. And there shall be no sorrow   because there is no death. In that day an infant shall not die   until he is old, and his life shall be as the age of a tree, and   when he dies he shall not sleep, (that is to say in the earth,)   but shall be changed in the twinkling of an eye, and shall be   caught up, and his rest shall be glorious. Yea, verily I say unto you, in that day when the Lord shall come, he shall reveal   all things."[1590]

The Millennium is to precede the time designated in scriptural phrase "the end of the world." When the thousand years are passed, Satan shall be loosed for a little season, and the final test of man's integrity to God shall ensue. Such as are prone to impurity of heart shall yield to temptation while the righteous shall endure to the end.[1591] A revelation to this effect was given the Church in 1831, in part as follows:

"For the great Millennium, of which I have spoken by the mouth   of my servants, shall come; For Satan shall be bound, and when   he is loosed again, he shall only reign for a little season, and then cometh the end of the earth; And he that liveth in   righteousness shall be changed in the twinkling of an eye, and   the earth shall pass away so as by fire; And the wicked shall go   away into unquenchable fire, and their end no man knoweth on   earth, nor ever shall know, until they come before me in judgment. Hearken ye to these words: Behold, I am Jesus Christ,   the Saviour of the world. Treasure these things up in your   hearts, and let the solemnities of eternity rest upon your   minds."[1592]

THE CELESTIAL CONSUMMATION.

The vanquishment of Satan and his hosts shall be complete. The dead, small and great, all who have breathed the breath of life on earth, shall be resurrected--every soul that has tabernacled in flesh, whether good or evil--and shall stand before God, to be judged according to the record as written in the books.[1593] So shall be brought to glorious consummation the mission of the Christ. "Then cometh the end, when he shall have delivered up the kingdom to God, even the Father; when he shall have put down all rule and all authority and power. For he must reign, till he hath put all enemies under his feet. The last enemy that shall be destroyed is death. For he hath put all things under his feet."[1594] Then shall the Lord Jesus "deliver up the kingdom, and present it unto the Father spotless, saying--I have overcome and have trodden the wine-press alone, even the winepress of the fierceness of the wrath of Almighty God. Then shall he be crowned with the crown of his glory, to sit on the throne of his power to reign for ever and ever."[1595] The earth shall pass to its glorified and celestialized condition, an eternal abode for the exalted sons and daughters of God.[1596] Forever shall they reign, kings and priests to the Most High, redeemed, sanctified, and exalted through their Lord and God JESUS THE CHRIST.

NOTES TO CHAPTER 42.

1. Enoch, spoken of by Jude as "the seventh from Adam." was the father of Methuselah. In Genesis 5:24 we read: "And Enoch walked with God; and he was not; for God took him." From the Lord's revelation to Moses we learn that Enoch was a mighty man, favored of God because of his righteousness, and a leader of and revelator to his people. Through his agency a city was built, the inhabitants of which excelled in righteous living to such an extent that they were of one heart and one mind and had no poor among them. It was called the City of Holiness or Zion. The residue of the race were all corrupt in the sight of the Lord. Enoch and his people were taken from the earth and are to return with Christ at His coming. (P. of G.P., Moses 7:12-21, 68, 69; compare Doc. and Cov. 45:11, 12.)

2. Heathen in the First Resurrection.--"And then shall the heathen nations be redeemed, and they that knew no law shall have part in the first resurrection; and it shall be tolerable for them." (Doc. and

Cov. 45:54.) Such is the word of the Lord with respect to those benighted peoples who live and die in ignorance of the laws of the gospel. This affirmation is sustained by other scriptures, and by a consideration of the principles of true justice according to which humanity is to be judged. Man shall be accounted blameless or guilty according to his deeds as interpreted in the light of the law under which he is required to live. It is inconsistent with our conception of a just God to believe Him capable of inflicting condemnation upon any one for non-compliance with a requirement of which the person had no knowledge. Nevertheless, the laws of the gospel cannot be suspended even in the case of those who have sinned in darkness and ignorance; but it is reasonable to believe that the plan of redemption shall afford such benighted ones an opportunity of learning the laws of God; and, as fast as they so learn, will obedience be required on pain of the penalty. See _Articles of Faith_, xxi:33.

3. Regeneration of the Earth.--In speaking of the graded and progressive glories provided for His creations, and of the laws of regeneration and sanctification, the Lord has thus spoken through revelation in the present dispensation: "And again, verily I say unto you, the earth abideth the law of a celestial kingdom, for it filleth the measure of its creation, and transgresseth not the law. Wherefore it shall be sanctified; yea, notwithstanding it shall die, it shall be quickened again, and shall abide the power by which it is quickened, and the righteous shall inherit it." (Doc. and Cov. 88:25, 26.) This appointed change, by which the earth shall pass to the condition of a celestialized world, is referred to in numerous scriptures as the institution of "a new heaven and a new earth" (Rev. 21:1, 3, 4; B. of M., Ether 13:9; Doc. and Cov. 29:23).

FOOTNOTES:

[1551] Acts 1:11.

[1552] Pages 713, 715, 761, and 774; see also Doc. and Cov. 110:8; compare 36:8; 42:36; 97:15, 16; 109:5; 124:27; 133:2.

[1553] Jude 14, 15; compare Gen. 5:18; see next reference following.

[1554] P. of G.P., Moses 7:59, 60, 65. Note 1, end of chapter.

[1555] Isa. 35:4; and 40:10; see also Psalms 50:3; Mal. 3:1; 4:5, 6; compare Note 1 on page 149 herein.

[1556] Matt. 16:27.

[1557] Mark 8:38; compare Luke 9:26.

[1558] Matt. 26:64.

[1559] Matt. 24:3; Mark 13:26; Luke 21:7; Acts 1:6; compare page 149 herein.

[1560] Matt. 24; see chapters 32 and 40 herein.

[1561] See Acts 3:20, 21; 1 Cor. 4:5; 11:26; Philip. 3:20; 1 Thess. 1:10; 2:19; 3:13; 4:15-18; 2 Thess. 2:1, 8; 1 Tim. 6:14, 15; Titus 2:13; James 5:7, 8; 1 Peter 1:5-7; 4:13; 1 John 2:28; 3:2; Jude 14, etc.

[1562] B. of M., 3 Nephi 26:3, 4.

[1563] B. of M., 3 Nephi 28:7, 8; see also 29:2.

[1564] Doc. and Cov. 29:9-11.

[1565] Doc. and Cov. 33:17, 18.

[1566] Doc. and Cov. 34:4-8.

[1567] Doc. and Cov. 45:37-44; compare this section with Matt. 24, and Luke 21:5-36. See also Doc. and Cov. 49:23-28.

[1568] Doc. and Cov. 64:23-25.

[1569] Matt. 24:36; compare Mark 13:32-37; see pages 575, 696 herein.

[1570] Doc. and Cov. 49:7; the context shows that the words are those of the Father.

[1571] Thess. 5:2; 2 Peter 3:10; compare Matt. 24:43, 44; 25:13; Luke 12:39, 40; page 575 herein.

[1572] Page 573.

[1573] Doc. and Cov. 49:24, 25.

[1574] Doc. and Cov. 45:68-71.

[1575] Doc. and Cov. 133:7-14, 21-35; "Articles of Faith," xviii and xix.

[1576] Doc. and Cov. 88:86-92.

[1577] Doc. and Cov. 110:14, 16; compare Joel 2:31; Mal. 4:5; B. of M., 3 Nephi 25:5.

[1578] Doc and Cov. 29:11-17.

[1579] 1 Thess. 4:14-17.

[1580] B. of M., 3 Nephi 28:8; see page 738 herein.

[1581] Doc. and Cov. 88:95-98.

[1582] Note 2, end of chapter.

[1583] Doc. and Cov. 29:12.

[1584] Doc. and Cov. 29:12; compare Matt. 19:28; Luke 22:30; page 479 herein.

[1585] B. of M., 3 Nephi 27:27; compare 1 Nephi 12:9, 10; Mormon 3:18. 19.

[1586] Doc. and Cov. 65. For a fuller treatment of this subject as also the distinction between Church and Kingdom, see "Articles of Faith," xx:16-26.

[1587] Rev. 20:1-6; compare Doc. and Cov. 43:18.

[1588] Doc. and Cov. 63:50-51; 101:30; compare 1 Cor. 15:51-57.

[1589] P. of G.P., Moses 7:63-65.

[1590] Doc. and Cov. 101:23-32; compare Isa. 65:17-25 and 11:6-9; see also Doc. and Cov. 29:11, 22; 43:30; 63:51.

[1591] Rev. 20:7-15.

[1592] Doc and Cov. 43:30-34. See also "Articles of Faith," xx:27-31.
[1593] Rev. 20:11-15.
[1594] 1 Cor. 15:24-27.
[1595] Doc. and Cov. 76:107, 108.
[1596] Note 3, end of chapter.

Made in the USA
Middletown, DE
10 August 2020

RIDE FROM WITHIN

RIDE FROM WITHIN

Use Tai Chi Principles to Awaken Your Natural Balance and Rhythm

James Shaw

with Christopher Bray
and Charlene Strickland

J.A. ALLEN
LONDON

First published in Great Britain in 2005

ISBN 0 85131 923 8

J.A. Allen
An imprint of Robert Hale Ltd.
Clerkenwell House
45/47 Clerkenwell Green
London EC1R 0HT

The author has made every effort to obtain releases from all persons appearing in the photographs used in this book and all photographers. In some cases, however, the persons and photographers identities and whereabouts were unknown. Should any names become available, they will be credited in future editions, assuming permission is granted.

Disclaimer of Liability
The authors and publisher shall have neither liability nor responsibility to any person or entity with respect to any loss or damage caused or alleged to be caused directly or indirectly by the information contained in this book. While the book is as accurate as the authors can make it, there may be errors, omissions, and inaccuracies.

Illustration Credits
Photos: Dean Goodwin (page 6); Kristi Smythe (pages 26, 55, 57–60, 105, 110, 134–5, 161 top and bottom right); James Shaw (28, 181); Joe Torrino (pages 38–9, 45, 47, 52–3, 70–1, 91–2 right, 103, 107–8, 122–3, 125, 127–8, 130, 133, 139, 141, 143, 147, 151–2, 155, 159–160, 161 bottom left, 193); Merrily Veatch (pages 40, 92 left, 93); Mandy Lorraine, courtesy of Betsy Steiner (page 176); phelpsphotos.com, courtesy of Betsy Steiner (pages 186, 192, 203, 210)
Line Art: James Shaw (page 3); Brenda Gountis (pages 19, 21, 25–6, 84, 86–8, 101, 112, 119, 144, 148, 177, 180, 188, 194, 199, 211); Heather Mansfield (pages 246–250)

Book design by Carrie Fradkin
Cover design by Heather Mansfield
Typeface: Rotis Sans, Rotis Serif, Modern No. 20, and Syntax

Printed in China

10 9 8 7 6 5 4 3 2 1

To my son Liam

Born one month after the agreement was made to write this book and inspiring me to take the first step of the journey into the life of my wildest dreams. The love I feel for you fills me in a way that I never dreamed possible. It is that abundance of love that moves me through the fears and doubts that come with living wild dreams. I hope, in turn, I inspire you to live your dreams.

And to my parents Edward & Alice Shaw

My mom, who gave me my first and greatest gift: life. You have been a shining example of how to live and embrace the adventure of Life. We've come a long way from the miracle of tenth-grade English class.

My dad: We had far too short a time together in this life. I feel your presence near me often and I hope I've made you proud.

"A good traveler has no fixed plans
and is not intent on arriving."

—Lao Tzu, *Tao Te Ching*

Table of Contents

Preface

True wisdom endures and remains timelessly relevant. You are about to begin a profound journey of learning and discovery in which you will encounter a 4,000-year-old art that is still wise, still relevant, and entirely vital.

In centuries past, horse ownership and training, as well as instruction in riding, were often limited to society's elite. Today these pursuits have become accessible to people from all walks of life, and an ever-growing number of riders now have the opportunity to experience the unparalleled sensations of flow, strength, and connection that one can feel upon the back of a horse—an astoundingly beautiful and powerful animal.

In ancient China, Tai Chi was only available to the elite. Today, Tai Chi has become widely accessible and millions of people now practice this art. Tai Chi unifies the body, mind, and spirit in a series of flowing movements that align the posture, breath, and the inner and outermost being. This ancient art offers a path to becoming more completely alive and more fully conscious.

Bringing together horsemanship and Tai Chi makes great sense and provides riders with a wonderful opportunity. Tai Chi can open the doors to deep experiences for horsemen, both on and off the horse. Learning to ride well requires us to be conscious equestrians, but this means that we must first be *self*-conscious. *To become one with your horse you must first become one with yourself*—this is the journey of this book.

On this voyage, your mind and breath will take you deep into your body's center, to discover the origins of connection as well as those of disconnection—the imbalances and tensions that separate you from your inner self and from your horse. You will also find the roots of power, which you will learn to apply to your riding. You will become more centered in your body and calm in your mind. Most importantly, you will gain control over your breathing, so that you stay connected in mind and body.

As you gain Tai Chi skills and experiences and apply them to your riding, you will find your horsemanship becoming not just more skilled, but more deeply satisfying on a level that transcends language and even time. You and your horse will simply be.

Note to the Reader

Why and How to Use This Book

To guide you along the path of mind, breath, and body, I introduce the fundamentals of Tai Chi in the early chapters and then include a variety of exercises in chapters 3 through 6. These chapters form a program, with exercises building upon the teachings and personal experiences you have just learned. In chapter 6, you'll apply the skills and awareness you've gained from the exercises to your riding.

Using step-by-step instruction and pictures, I coach you through the essentials of Tai Chi for the equestrian. The exercises generally include both unmounted and mounted versions. The unmounted exercises are based on Tai Chi forms, specifically adapted to prepare you for in-the-saddle exercises. On pages 240–243 in the *Appendix* you can see a detailed summary of all the exercises, which outlines their purpose, the routine to be followed, and when to move on.

The exercises are presented as follows:
Riding Goals list the goals of each exercise and the benefits that will carry over to your riding.
Function previews how the exercise will change your mind, breath, and body.
Intent suggests ways to use your mind to help you focus on the exercise.
Step-by-Step gives you a breakdown of the movements.
You'll find instructions for both unmounted and mounted phases. Some exercises are only on the ground, although you'll carry over these new abilities into the saddle.
Ah-Ha! shares insights about what you'll experience when you practice correctly. These feelings let you know you're succeeding.
Ability Transition includes tips to keep you advancing. Practicing an exercise helps you make progress.
Reminders present cautions to help you avoid the pitfalls that I most commonly see when people are learning a new movement.
James On Your Shoulder provides you, on occasion, with supplementary ideas to help improve your practice and enrich your understanding of it. Think of me as standing right behind you, or sitting behind you as you ride, offering suggestions and inspiration.

Benefits You'll Experience through the Exercise Program

Benefit	What You'll Experience
• Improved mind–body connection	All your actions will be directed by your mind. You will begin to sense what your horse is going to do before it happens.
• Enhanced mobility in all your joints	The movement in your body will become smoother, more sensitive, and better controlled, and your range of motion will increase.
• Heightened sensitivity	You will feel more of your horse's movements in your seat and hands and be able to adjust to those changes without over compensating.
• Relaxed, consistent breathing	You will always know where your breath is and that you are not holding it.
• Expanded awareness	You will hear, feel, and see more when you're riding, leading to a deeper connection with your horse.
• Improved balance	You will discover and change imbalances in you and your horse before they adversely affect your connection.
• Improved health	With regular practice, you will feel stronger in your body and calmer in your mind. You will experience improved energy and endurance.

Tai Chi and Horsemanship

1

N THIS FIRST CHAPTER, I LAY THE GROUNDWORK for the rest of this book. You learn about what Tai Chi—both as a philosophy and a martial art—offers you as a rider, and you are introduced to the systems of thinking underlying Tai Chi, including Yin and Yang, Tao, and Tai Chi's connection with horsemanship. In addition, you learn what enrichments you can expect from making Tai Chi part of your riding practice.

Tai Chi: Riding with Life's Energy, Connecting with Your Horse

Through Tai Chi you will achieve a true connection by learning to *join centers* with your horse. When joined, you match the rhythm of your center to that of your horse. You actively control the movements of your entire body, not just your arms and legs. You develop your balance independent of your horse. If you rely on your horse for balance, your horse is in control of your center; if your horse relies on you for his balance, then you are in control of your horse's center.

Tai Chi teaches you to stay centered by controlling your position and motion. Control grows from a strengthened mind-body foundation, in which you develop a perfect state of awareness. This awareness allows you to detect instantly any change of balance, either in yourself or your horse, and compensate for it without ever losing your rhythm. Your mind directs your body, and your body follows. You soon discover that your mind directs not only your body, but also your horse.

Tai Chi as a *philosophy* or *spiritual practice* abounds with unseen forces and energies that are often difficult to comprehend or explain. Tai Chi as a *martial art*, in contrast, is bound by well-known and well-understood laws of physics. I assume that the natural laws of physics apply to riding, and that is the perspective from which I have written this book. I have, however, seen things happen while working with a horse and rider that are difficult to explain in exclusively scientific terms.

Chi means "energy" or "life force," and in Tai Chi, you direct the flow of your chi with your mind. Because some practitioners of Tai Chi believe that there are no limits to the mind's capabilities, they also believe that this art can extend beyond what we can explain through our usual understanding of our everyday world. While this book will limit its approach and instructions to the world of natural law, I can confidently tell you that you are very likely to find your practice of Tai Chi occasionally going beyond ordinary experience. Rather than label these experiences or debate their nature, I suggest we simply enjoy them as part of the daily miracle that we call life. We will discuss chi in much greater depth in the next chapter.

The Yin Yang Perspective

From Tai Chi, which means, literally, "great ultimate," arise Yin and Yang, the fundamental, equal and opposite forces that underlie the ever-changing cycles of the universe. Complementary and inseparable, these two powers constantly balance each other. Everything in the universe derives its existence from the balanced interaction of Yin and Yang. You can see this interaction in the apparent opposites in our world—summer and winter, night and day, hot and cold, male and female.

The idea of balancing two natural forces has been a constant throughout Chinese history, whether it refers to the way of the universe, the martial art of Tai Chi, or the balance between horse and rider. The idea of Yin and Yang is also at the foundation of this book and my teaching method. By applying this theory to riding, you can discover a wealth of information and techniques to improve your connection with the horse.

When I look at a horse and rider, I see them as one organic whole—one whole in which two separate entities or forces can join synergistically, and the whole becomes greater than the sum of its parts. If there is an imbalance in either part, the whole is imbalanced. By changing one, we change the other. When the two join in balance, there is a flow and power like that of a great river moving through a mountain gorge.

The Tai Chi symbol is often referred to as the Yin and Yang. The Yin (soft, female, light) and Yang (hard, male, heavy) applies not only to horse and rider but also to the entire human body. Tai Chi Master Chang San-Feng wrote in the *Tai Chi Classics*, "When the entire body is integrated with all parts connected together, it becomes a vast connection of positive and negative energy units. Each positive and negative unit should be connected to every other unit and permitted no interruption among them."

For example, when moving forward, the *front* of your body is considered positive or Yang, and the *back* negative or Yin. Furthermore, if you are pushing your hand forward with the palm out, the palm is considered Yang, and the back of the hand Yin. In relationship to the whole arm, the hand is Yang, and the arm Yin. If the left hand is moving forward (Yang), the right hand is Yin. Neither positive nor negative can act independently; all body parts and all movements are relative.

Yin and Yang: A Horse Story

I was once asked by a friend to come out to her barn and help her horse's movement: his inside hind foot was not tracking up, that is, not stepping forward far enough to fall in the foot print of the inside front.

As I stood in the middle of the arena watching her and a magnificent stallion circle

The Chinese character Chi, meaning breath energy, life force, and air.

The Tai Chi symbol, more commonly known as the Yin and Yang symbol, represents the principle of balance in the universe.

around me, my first thought was, "How incredibly connected they both are." My second thought was, "How can I help improve the trot of a world-class rider and equally talented horse?" The answer was to see them as Yin and Yang on a small scale and know that they were bound by the same natural laws.

My next thought was that if there were more weight to the inside of the circle, it could cause the horse to put his hind foot down sooner, not allowing it to travel as far forward. I had to find out whether or not this added weight came from the rider or the horse.

Applying the theory of Yin and Yang, I reasoned that if one side is heavy the other must be light, so I asked my friend to imagine a 5-pound weight in her outside hand as she rode on the circle. Within one revolution, the inside hind foot of her horse moved a full 6 inches forward and was now tracking up beautifully.

The rider's success was directly related to her ability to weight her hand subtly without compromising the fluid motion of the rest of her body. That's not an easy task at the walk, let alone at the trot. The insight that directed us to the root of the problem and the solution was an understanding of Yin and Yang principles.

Tao

If Yin and Yang are the parts, the Tao is the whole. "Tao" means many things to many people, and its meaning goes beyond words. Ancient texts describe the Tao tangentially, developing their definitions through sayings, stories, and allegories. The concept of Tao is difficult to fathom with a Western mind. For me, defining the Tao is like asking someone from the West to describe God definitively. What would she say? "He/She/It is every-where, the beginning and the end, the cause and director of all life"?

The following words describing Tao were inscribed on a Ming rock dated 1556. In trying to grasp the concept of Tao, it may be helpful to replace the word "Tao" with "God." Read it with an open mind and a God of your own understanding.

> Vast indeed is the Ultimate Tao,
> Spontaneously itself, apparently without acting,
> End of all ages and beginning of all ages,
> Existing before Earth and existing before Heaven,
> Silently embracing the whole of time,

Continuing uninterrupted through all eons,
In the east it taught Father Confucius,
In the west it converted the Golden man [the Buddha],
Taken as pattern by a hundred kings,
Transmitted by generations of sages,
It is the ancestor of all doctrines,
The mystery beyond all mysteries.[1]

Lao Tzu, a contemporary of Confucius, was keeper of the imperial archives at Loyang in the province of Honan in the sixth century BC. Acknowledging the profundity of this concept, Lao Tzu said, "The Tao that can be told is not the eternal Tao."

According to ancient legend, as Lao Tzu was riding off into the desert to die, sick at heart at the ways of men, he was persuaded to write down his teachings for posterity. The work he created, the *Tao Te Ching*, captures the essence of Taoism in only five thousand words. For over 2500 years this book has been one of the greatest influences on Chinese thought and culture.

Tai Chi exercise is born of the Yin and Yang, and "The mother of Yin and Yang is Tao." Lao Tzu put it this way in the *Tao Te Ching*:

The Tao that can be told is not the eternal Tao.
The name that can be named is not the eternal name.
The nameless is the beginning of heaven and earth.
The named is the mother of ten thousand things.[2]

I interpret that passage in this way:

The Tao that can be told is not the eternal Tao.
The name that can be named (Tai Chi) is not the eternal name (Tao).
The nameless (Tao) is the beginning of heaven and earth (Yin and Yang).
The named (Tai Chi) is the mother of ten thousand things (Universe).

Lao Tzu continues:

Under heaven and earth all can see beauty as beauty only because there is ugliness.
All can know good as good only because there is evil.
Therefore having and not having arise together.

1 Rawson, Philip and Legeza, Laszlo. *Tao: The Chinese Philosophy of Time and Change*. London: Thames and Hudson, 1973.

2 Feng, Gia-Fu, and English, Jane, trans. *Tao Te Ching*. New York: Random House, 1972.

Difficult and easy complement each other.
Long and short contrast each other.
High and low rest upon each other.
Voice and sound harmonize each other.
Front and back follow one another.

Tai Chi, Horsemanship, and the Laws of Nature

Tai Chi and horsemanship share a long, rich history. Horsemanship dates back approximately 6000 years, and horses played important and revered roles in the feudal society of ancient China. Over thousands of years, the dynasties of the Shang, Chou, Han,

Ming horse

T'ang, Ming, Ch'ing and others created a rich and splendid culture. They all developed the arts and sciences, and they all waged war. Throughout these millennia, horses helped the dynasties thrive, in peace and in war, and stories and images of horses are woven into the fabric of Chinese culture. Their high esteem is reflected in the honor accorded them by their burial in royal tombs dating from the 14th century BC.

Horsemanship, like Tai Chi, embodies centuries of wisdom passed from generation to generation, perpetuated by masters instructing students, the best of whom become the next generation's masters. In this way, the tenets of horsemanship have survived, inculcated through direct instruction and codified in classic manuals such as Xenophon's *The Art of Horsemanship*, written over 2000 years ago, or Pluvinel's *Le Maneige Royal*, written almost 400 years ago. In this way, knowledge of the art, as well as its humanity, has survived across time.

The forms of Tai Chi relate closely to the practice of horsemanship. A skilled rider communicates thoughts that become the actions of the horse. Horsemanship and Tai Chi also share concepts of mind and body control. Through the practice of Tai Chi, you learn to take advantage of, and stay in harmony with, the laws of nature. The influence of these forces on you and your horse should not be underestimated. Whether you recognize them or not, these forces and your response to them determine whether or not you are in or out of rhythm with your horse. Because you can't escape these laws of physics, you need to learn how to use them to enhance your riding—and that is what we will do in chapter 2. But first, I want to introduce the four principal forces affecting you as a rider: they are *gravity*, *momentum*, *tension*, and *centripetal force*.

Gravity

When talking about natural laws, gravity is the king. Ever-present and unyielding, gravity can be either your tiring nemesis or your tireless friend. Understanding gravity is the first step to making it your friend.

Most people have spent their entire lives moving within this constant force without ever fully understanding its effects on human movement and health. Space travel, for example, has proven that gravity has a positive effect on our bones. During periods of extended weightlessness, when skeletons no longer have to resist gravity, an astronaut's bones lose density and strength. Gravity provides us with continual, necessary exercise.

Life on earth requires us to "stand up to" the constant force of gravity, and we use our bones and muscles to accomplish this. If we align our skeletons with the force of gravity, then our bones can passively support much of our weight and our muscles have an easier job, as they only have to work to maintain the alignment of our skeleton. If we lose that alignment, then our muscles have to work harder to support us because they are forced to actively carry some of the load that our bones can carry passively.

You already know this intuitively: if you have to pick up something heavy, you pick it up closer to your body (in alignment with your spine, thereby maximizing the load on your bones), not out at arm's length, where the effort becomes almost entirely muscular.

In the same way, riding starts with your foundation, with "picking up," supporting, and balancing your body. To achieve this balance in the saddle, you employ your muscles and skeleton. The more you maintain the alignment of your skeleton, the less muscular effort you must use for balance, which translates into less tension and fatigue and more relaxation and better connection with your horse. You can then take advantage of the tremendous power of *momentum*.

Momentum

Using momentum is the key to being able to direct your horse's force, which is far greater than your own, with minimal effort. The relationship between you and momen-

Tai Chi means "the great ultimate." It is both a Chinese martial art and a way of life. Among the ancient Chinese arts, Tai Chi was an internal art, a metaphysical concept. Master Chang San-Feng wrote in the *Tai Chi Classics*, "Tai Chi became the invisible power that guided the movements of Chinese history for thousands of years. It gave tremendous impetus to that fabulous culture, showing its influence in areas ranging from medicine to diet, from art to economics." Tai Chi is a discipline inspired by the Taoist philosophy. As philosophies of idealism, both Tai Chi and Taoism unite the body with the mind, so the individual lives in harmony with nature.

The author practicing Tai Chi

While no one knows exactly when Tai Chi coalesced into a formal system, most historians date its founding to approximately 2000 BC. The art has grown and evolved in different ways, shaped by its practitioners. Tai Chi has often been affected by political systems, such as when authoritarian regimes saw Tai Chi as a weapon and developed it as a fighting art for nobles and warriors. Taoists and other intellectuals, however, remaining independent of the political structures of the dynasties, emphasized Tai Chi's more metaphysical aspects. The Taoist monk Chang San-Feng, for example, established in AD 1200 an internal system of pure art, in contrast to the external, martial art practiced by the ruling class. Regardless of each practice's emphasis or origins, the pedagogy was similar: masters tutored students who became disciples of the art, and some of these students went on to become masters themselves.

Under the Ch'ing (Manchu) dynasty (AD 1644–1912), Tai Chi was a sophisticated and highly developed art that continued to evolve both as a martial art and as an intellectual discipline that included the philosophy of natural harmony. During this period, three principal styles of Tai Chi emerged: the original Chen style and two offshoots, the Yang and Wu. The Yang style was founded by Yang Lu-Chang, a famous martial arts master. Yang instructed Chuan You, whose son, Master Wu Chian-chuan (1870–1940) went on to found the Wu style.

The Wu style focuses on smooth, even, continuous motions, and it is the inspiration for Tai Chi for the equestrian. Master Wu himself established the connection between Tai Chi and riding: "[Wu] was also good at horse-riding and shooting and could hide himself under the saddle of a horse or stand on his head on the back of a horse when it was running fast."[3]

When the nearly 300-year-old Ch'ing dynasty ended in 1912 with the founding of the Republic of China, Tai Chi evolved once again. The Yang and Wu styles became available to the public through the Athletic Research Institute in Peking, where Master Wu became one of the teachers. In 1928, Master Wu moved to Shanghai to continue his teachings, and in 1935 he founded the Chian-chuan Taichichuan Association. The Association has helped to spread the Wu style throughout China and around the world.

Common to all these styles are the *forms*, a sequence of slow movements that incorporate aspects of the martial arts, body soundness, and meditation. In a form, the student joins deliberate movements with a tranquility of mind, and action follows thought.

3 Ma Yueh-liang, et al. *Wu Style Tai Chi Chuan*, Berkeley: North Atlantic Books, 2002.

tum is like that between waves and the ocean. The energy (momentum) of a wave created by a hurricane can travel thousands of miles before it crashes into the shore-line. The energy does not move or transport the water itself these thousands of miles; the energy moves *through* the water. Waves of momentum created by the horse move through your body. When you relax, becoming "fluid" (like water!), you allow the wave of horse-generated energy to move through you, unrestricted by tension, and your body remains quiet and still.

As a rider, you can harness the power of momentum. You give your most effective aids when you take advantage of your own momentum. Think about giving an aid with your seat while trotting. The most advantageous time to apply the aid is when the momentum of your body, dropping with the saddle (the horse's center), reaches the lowest point in the fall of your "joined centers." If you give the aid too early, you cut its effectiveness dramatically. Without momentum on your side, you must use your leg to drive the horse on; what should have been the joined forward flow of energy now becomes, instead, the disjointed movements of a horse and rider pair that are no longer in full harmony.

To tap into the power of your momentum you must first match the rhythm of your body to that of your horse. Without this harmony of motion, you will lack the timing necessary to take advantage of the innate power of your momentum.

Just as a lack of timing works against the effortless application of momentum in your riding, unnecessary *tension* in your body works to keep you separated from the power of your horse. This is one of those cases of "If it (the horse's power) is not working for you, it's working against you."

Tension

Tension is the condition of exerting force against one's self, pitting one muscle against another. Tension is apparent when you are "holding" yourself in balance, or when you brace any part of your body prior to giving an aid.

Tension disrupts and disconnects the body from the natural power of momentum. Momentum cannot flow through tense muscles, though it will move *past* tense muscles regardless. Again think of a wave moving through the ocean. When the wave encounters an iceberg (tension), the wave does not flow through it. Instead the wave lifts, tilts, and jostles the berg as it moves past.

Waves of momentum moving through a tense body upset its balance in the same way. The unbalanced body then becomes even tenser, including the seat, thereby reducing the rider's effectiveness, and leaving the rider even more vulnerable to further unbalancing by the next wave of energy from the horse. The solution to this deteriorating situation is first to align your bones. This will reduce the tension in your body and relax your mind. As a result, you will recover your natural balance and ride in relaxation—both mentally and physically. A relaxed mind creates a state of calmness in which your mind is acutely aware of your body. And, a relaxed body has muscles that are free of any unnecessary tension.

Thus far we have looked at the role of gravity that pulls on us constantly, momentum that generates power we can harness, tension that can interfere with our connection with the horse, and now we'll look at the last major force that influences our riding: *centripetal force.*

Centripetal Force

A fundamental law of physics observes that objects travel forward in a straight line at constant speed unless acted on by another force. When centripetal (center-seeking) force is applied to an object traveling in a straight line, the object begins to move on a circle rather than straight ahead. For example, when a parent holds a child's hands and spins the child in a circle, the parent not only moves the child forward, but also pulls the child in. This "pulling in" is centripetal force. Its complement is centrifugal (center-fleeing) force—the "pulling out" force exerted on the parent by the child.

When you and your horse ride a circle, your horse plays the role of the parent, and you the child. On a left lead, for instance, with every stride, your horse not only carries you forward, but also pulls you a little to the left and inside. When he does this over and over again, you complete a circle.

As a rider, however, you may feel more that you are "falling to the outside" than being "pulled to the inside." Because your body's constant tendency is to move straight ahead, while your horse is moving ahead and to the inside, you are, relative to your horse, "falling to the outside."

Regardless of whether we focus on the physics or your perceptions, centripetal force is always at work when you and your horse turn—and it may unbalance you. Using Tai

Chi, you do not need to fight centripetal force; you learn to compensate for it and maintain your soft, balanced seat—your foundation. (For a more in-depth look at centripetal force, see page 213.)

Tai Chi, You, and Your Horse

As you have already begun to learn, Tai Chi is about developing your self and then using that more developed self to enhance your riding. Your improvement as a rider will affect your horse's performance. You won't try to change your horse *directly*, but rather *indirectly* by changing your balance. In my experience, the horse changes dramatically when the rider's balance improves.

Before we go on, let's consider your current situation. While there are many levels at which you and I may communicate with horses—mentally, physically, and spiritually—the moment that you climb on your horse's back, none of those forms of communication speaks louder than the physical. Do you move in harmony and rhythm with your horse? Or, do you sense that through imbalance and tension you get in the way of his natural balance and flow? Are you asking your horse for one thing with your mind and spirit, but telling him something else with your body?

When you ride, you may confront challenges that feel like problems. Can you identify with any of these?

- A lack of harmony or feeling out of rhythm with your horse.
- Conflicts that feel like a tug-o-war, either physical or mental.
- Flashes of connecting with your horse that seem to vanish as soon as you realize they've occurred.
- Fear that your horse may misbehave.
- Fear that you may fall and possibly be injured.
- Frustration because your horse is not listening to you.

In the chapters that follow, I'll investigate ways to diffuse these issues. Tai Chi will help you solve your problems, improve your riding, and develop a more intimate relationship with your horse.

Instructions and Rider Insights

Each chapter of this book contains a series of comfortable, straightforward steps in which you will learn Tai Chi techniques that enable you, regardless of your current riding level or discipline, to advance. At first these exercises may seem a bit daunting, yet as I guide you through the simple, step-by-step instructions, I can assure you that you *will learn*—at the levels of mind, body, and spirit.

In addition to me as your guide, in *Rider Insights* you will hear the helpful stories of many other riders with whom I've worked. These riders faced the same issues you face, and they'll share their experiences with you.

Before we begin, listen to several other riders who have also started down this same path.

> *Rider Insight, Laura: "I can't tell you how cool it was! I had an epiphany. My body fell into place just as James said it would, and I was riding an awesome canter half-pass. Even better, as my body assimilated the information, I now found that I also had a plan for doing groundwork with this supple and willing little horse for the next three months. I have had the pleasure of riding with many wonderful and insightful riding instructors, but I never expected that my next enlightenment would happen under the tutelage of a martial artist."*

> *Rider Insight, Dian: "I have been taking lessons with James for almost three years. In that time, my entire concept of the art of riding has changed through the practice of Tai Chi. James shares with his students his teachings of inner balance and harmonies with the horse. He's taught me how to use my internal energy and economy of motion in relationship to my horse so that we truly move as one. It has been a joyful series of 'enlightenments' for me."*

> *Rider Insight, Susan: "I met James at a national riding event in Columbus, Ohio. When I was told I'd be riding in two Tai Chi clinics, I wasn't sure what to expect. I had no previous knowledge of Tai Chi. After working with James for about fifteen minutes, I began to understand what he was trying to achieve. By the end of the second day I was amazed at the difference in my body. I was moving much better with Thor. I was able to sit his trot without my body and legs becoming stiff. My only regret is that we live on opposite sides of the country. I could really benefit from more instruction from James."*

What Tai Chi Offers You

Incorporating Tai Chi into your riding and life offers you many rewards. As you pursue a softer, gentler approach to riding, you will:

- subtly change your position, creating a change in the horse
- soften your position for a truly independent seat, so your body and its movement will become relaxed and free of unnecessary tension
- feel yourself meld with your horse's rhythm

Tai Chi also helps you improve your general health. You will:

- increase your lung capacity
- stir your chi through your internal organs and enhance their functioning
- combat the effects of osteoporosis, as your bones direct the force of gravity in your body
- release stress down through your body to the ground, thus healing many stress-related diseases.

What's Next

In chapter 2, "Fundamentals of Tai Chi: An Ancient Art, A New Perspective," I will look at the principles underlying all the exercises ahead in the book. This will provide a basis for seeing the coherent system of knowledge that connects the many facets of Tai Chi.

Fundamentals of Tai Chi

An Ancient Art, A New Perspective

2

THIS CHAPTER INTRODUCES THE FUNDAMENTALS that underlie the exercises appearing later in the book. These fundamentals include Eight Principles that will guide our practice, as well as the "anatomy" of Tai Chi: the three Dain Tians, the fourteen meridians, and the Eight Gates, all of which direct how energy is held and moved throughout the body.

The Eight Principles

The training exercises and forms taught in this book are drawn from many different styles of internal arts, each emphasizing different motions and goals. Some are done for health and healing, others for meditation, and still others as a martial arts practice. The common thread that they all share is a set of underlying principles as described in the ancient Tai Chi classics, which describe each principle and teach its correct practice. Some of these principles translate into very clear and concise directions. Others are less direct, presenting concepts of one's relationship to nature, and they may seem esoteric if not vague. I suggest that if you seek the meanings of the latter with an open mind, you will discover ways in which they apply to riding.

I will do my best to relate each principle's meaning and application to riding. You also need to remember that any one person's experience and knowledge is limited—hence the saying, "Art is long, and life is short." With this in mind, please don't limit the meaning and application of these principles to your riding by your initial comprehension of their meaning. Your comprehension of them, like mine, will continue to grow throughout your practice.

1 Use the mind, not force

In all exercises, it is imperative that your mind directs all action. At no time do you want to fall victim to the unconscious actions of your body. If your mind does not direct the movement of your body, those movements will be rigid and out of rhythm. Inevitably this lack of rhythm leads to the use of force rather than sensitivity. Your conscious mind directs your *intent* (see p. 34), and your body follows. The body is limited by physics, but the mind can be developed infinitely beyond the limits of time and space.

2 Never oppose force with force

Tai Chi assumes a force bigger and stronger than you is trying to upset your balance—whether it be the conscious intent of an opponent or the unconscious action of your horse.

Whether mounted or on the ground, to confront the strength of a horse directly with your own strength is to lose. The result of this kind of battle can be seen in the bent and twisted body of many an old cowboy who spent decades opposing the force of horses. You will never be bigger or stronger than your horse. Using force is to lose not only the battle, but also the war.

3 Yield and overcome

Rather than oppose force with force, yield and overcome. This philosophy is best represented in an old Chinese story.

In a violent storm a mighty oak tree—tall, strong, and known its rigidity—stood against the mighty wind with all its strength. In the same storm a bamboo tree with its long and slender stalks was blown over to the ground as it yielded to the force of the storm. After the storm passed, the seemingly weak and fragile bamboo bounced back and once again reached to the sky. The majestic oak, which had tried to stand strong against the gale, lay uprooted with branches torn from its trunk.

4 Balance like a scale

When you practice, stand with your posture balanced like a scale. Your state of balance should be as sensitive as that of a scale, so that the slightest change of balance in either you or your horse will be detected. When you move, your movements should revolve effortlessly like turning a wheel.

Let your whole body move in harmony. As you compensate for the ever-changing balance of you and your horse, your movement should flow and circulate ceaselessly and without interruption.

Just as the movement of the wheel starts at the hub, so should all the movement of your body originate from your center. The slightest movement of your fingers in a rein aid should be connected to your center (seat). This principle involves a lifetime of thought and application.

5 Seek stillness in motion

This principle initially refers to maintaining a calm state of mind while your body is in motion, but as with all of our practice, it can lead to deeper and more profound experiences: "The water of the spring is clear, like crystal. The water of the pond is deep and placid. Your mind should be like that of the pond and your spirit like the spring."

I have experienced this feeling of stillness while riding when completely connected to my horse and we are moving together in one rhythmic flow, neither opposing nor resisting each other's force. I become aware of the sensation of being still while everything in my peripheral vision is moving. It's a calm and almost surrealistic feeling. It is much like standing in the middle of a moving carousel and perceiving that you are standing still while the world moves around you.

The ability to move all parts of your body as one coordinated unit is at the heart of this principle. You'll experience this state of stillness in motion and motion in stillness in the *Walking Backward* exercise in chapter 3 (see p. 62).

6 Be heavy and light

The root of heaviness is lightness. When you can be soft and pliable, and then, at will, hard and strong so that no force can upset your balance, you have mastered your internal energy, or chi.

Your mind controls and directs your chi, and chi can only flow through a calm and relaxed body. To achieve this, you must first calm and relax your breathing.

7 Focus and expand

Guard against developing tunnel vision, which leads to a narrowed view and decreased perceptivity. Remember that you want to increase your focus by expanding your awareness.

For example, if you are constantly looking down at your horse's head, you decrease your sensitivity to the rest of his body. Or, when riding on a circle, if you are not as aware of the center of the circle as you are the circumference on which you are trying to ride, it will be nearly impossible to ride a "perfect" circle. This does not mean that you must look in two directions at once, but rather that you should see the big picture.

8 Remember that art is long, life is short

More a philosophy than a principle, this saying reminds us that there is no end to learning the secrets of our art. My teacher after forty years of daily practice in Tai Chi once told me, "James, I still need to relax my fingers more." When I keep this in mind, it helps me to not become discouraged and frustrated when I have an off day or my discipline is less than I expect from myself.

Dain Tians

The *Dain Tians* are gathering places of energy and force within the body. You have three:

• The upper Dain Tian in the center of your head
• The middle Dain Tian at the center of your chest
• The lower Dain Tian behind your navel

When I refer to the Dain Tian and don't specify which one, I'm referring to the lower Dain Tian.

Visualize your lower Dain Tian as a gyroscope, encompassing 360 degrees of moving parts inside your body, including all the joints of your pelvis, and your lumbar and sacral spine.

Your Dain Tian is your center. *Every motion starts in your center.*

Visualize the area of the lower Dain Tian as if it were a gyroscope.

Meridians

Traditional Chinese medicine teaches that the body has fourteen meridians or channels:

• The Lung
• The Large Intestine
• The Stomach
• The Spleen
• The Heart
• The Small Intestine
• The Bladder
• The Kidney
• The Pericardium
• The Triple Warmer
• The Gall Bladder
• The Liver
• The Front and the Back Meridians (Rue and Due)

On all the meridians, there are a series of points. Each of these points can be manipulated to restrict or enhance the flow of chi through them. These are the points in which acupuncturists place needles or where acupressurists apply finger pressure to treat imbalances, ailments, or diseases. See the *Appendix*, p. 250, for a chart of the meridians.

Putting It All Together

Thus far we have discussed the *Eight Principles*, which describe a philosophy of employing chi for maximal benefit. We have also discussed the *Dain Tians* and *meridians*, which could be said to describe an "anatomy of chi," that is, the places in which chi gathers and the channels though which it moves. So, we have a spirit in which to work, and the energy and pathways with which to work. Now we need a system to control this energy. That control is provided by means of the *Eight Gates*. These gates control the rider's chi, and when the rider is well connected with the horse, the rider's gates also influence the horse's chi and movement.

The Eight Gates

The Eight Gates control the flow of the essential life force—chi—in the body. The gates are an integral part of the path we're traveling to develop our Tai Chi knowledge and skills, which we can then use to enhance our horsemanship. Each gate can be opened only with your mind, and opening the gates changes your body, changes your motion, and builds your awareness.

In addition to controlling the flow of your chi through the meridians within your body, the gates also affect the flow of chi between you and your horse. When all the gates are opened, the energy of you and your horse combine and are in harmony. When horse and rider are moving as one, energy is pumped through the Eight Gates, energizing your body as well as your horse's. As a pair you become one fluid energy, allowing for seamless transitions and nearly effortless aids.

When the gates are closed, they restrict or inhibit the synergistic flow of energy between horse and rider. When closed, the horse's energy is not allowed to flow through your body, so it effectively disconnects you from your horse.

By opening these gates, you will make subtle changes in your riding and increase the connection with your body and your horse. You'll use the gates in the exercises throughout the book.

Learning to open these gates on the ground is essential to opening them later while riding. The opening of a gate is a subtle relaxation and expansion of a particular area of your body. You open a gate first by visualization, which is then followed by directing and focusing your breath. While you are on the ground, the result of this opening is subtle; while riding, the result is profound.

Here are two stories that demonstrate what riders can achieve by opening their gates:

Rider Insight, Sue: While I was working with Sue, an advanced dressage rider, I coached her both on the ground and mounted to open Gate 7: The Upper Pass. The moment she opened this gate, her mare collected and softened to a level they had never achieved before. More important than the actual physical change in both was the deeper feeling of connection she felt with her horse.

Sue had owned this mare a long time, and always felt that somehow she was in the way of her own riding. She knew that her horse was capable of a higher level, but she just didn't know how to get it. For Sue, the lesson ended in tears of joy. She left with not only some new riding tools, but also a deeper bond with an old friend.

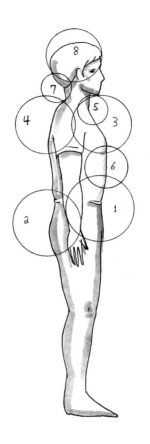

The Eight Gates

1 The Dain Tian (lower)

2 The Ming Meng

3 The Front of the Heart

4 The Back of the Heart

5 The Chi Who (right and left)

6 The Liver and Spleen

7 The Upper Pass
  (at the base of the skull)

8 The Crown

Rider Insight, Carrie: A young girl, Carrie, was ready to get rid of her horse because, even though she loved him, she could not control his energy and she felt that he was always running out from under her. (This was a gaited horse, very energetic and beautiful. With two big headstrong egos, they mirrored each other perfectly.) We worked together for two days to open her Gate 2: the Ming Meng, and Gates 3 and 4: the Front and Back of the Heart gates. As the gates opened, more of the horse's energy came up into Carrie, enabling her to join with and control the energy of her horse without having to "squish" it down.

Again the greatest effect of the opening of these gates was the release of emotional frustration that Carrie felt toward her horse—and the fact that he was no longer for sale.

Opening the Eight Gates

This section lists the gates and the effects of each gate being either opened or closed. While there are tangible physical motions that precede the opening of all the gates, these motions alone are not enough. Your mind must first direct that the gate open; only then can the physical change in your body actually open the gate. Remember that in Tai Chi there are no limits to the development of the mind. The only limits are the ones that we place on ourselves. (See *Appendix,* p. 245, for diagrams of human skeletal and muscular anatomy.)

Gate 1: The Dain Tian

Where: As I mentioned, there are three major Dain Tians (gathering places of energy) in Chinese medicine. We will concentrate on the lower in this book. The lower Dain Tian is located inside the body approximately 2 inches below the navel. The lower Dain Tian is also known as the "chi bank," because it is believed to be the area in which the chi resides.

Opened: When opened, this gate allows your breath to drop into your abdomen, effectively lowering your center of gravity. It relaxes your hips and abdomen, creating a deeper, more solid seat. With practice you can use the opening and closing of Gate 1 to initiate a halt or walk.

Closed: Riding with the Dain Tian closed inhibits your breathing and creates tension in your waist and hips. This tightness leads to your feeling of riding *on* the horse, not *with* the horse. When the rider's Dain Tian opens, the horse's topline immediately softens and he relaxes. The strides become lighter and the head lowers.

The abdominal breathing techniques in the following chapters are the initial key to opening the lower Dain Tian.

Exercises used to facilitate the opening of the Dain Tian: *Heaven and Earth* (p. 106), *Counting Your Breath* (p. 97), and *Wall Sitting* (p. 59).

Gate 2: The Ming Meng

Where: The Ming Meng is located on your spine in your lower back, directly behind the navel. *Gate 2: The Ming Meng* is also referred to as the "gate of life" because it is the first gate to be energized and is the gate where chi flows into and up the spinal cord.

Opened: Opening Gate 2: The Ming Meng allows for a further expansion of your lower back and deepening of your breath. This gate's opening enables your lower lumbar region to move more freely, thus deepening the seat. When your lower body is relaxed and centered, the balance of your upper body is easier to maintain. The muscles of your upper back and chest can relax and therefore allow for the opening of the heart gates.

Opening the Ming Meng creates more "throughness" in the horse by engaging the hind end while lightening the forehand. Your new balance means the horse does not have to divide his energy and focus between balancing you and moving freely forward. Opening the Ming Meng puts the rider's center deep into the pelvis (rather than up in the chest). Only if the center is in the Ming Meng can the rider be in self-carriage, and until the rider is in self-carriage, the horse cannot be in self-carriage.

Closed: If you keep the Ming Meng closed while riding, you experience tightening of the lower back and restriction of breath. In the horse, it restricts the motion of the hind end and leads to tightness in the withers.

Exercises used to facilitate the opening of the Ming Meng are: *Horse Stance and Wall Sitting* (p. 56), *Walking Backward* (p. 62), *Heaven and Earth* (p. 106), and *Open the Ming Meng* (p. 99).

Gate 3: The Front of the Heart

Opened: Opening *Gate 3: The Front of the Heart* helps relax your chest and lower your shoulders, and so keeps your elbows down. This, in turn, quiets your hands. You will feel more of your horse, because the energy can move up through your Ming Meng and Dain Tian into your heart and upper body, out through your arms to your hands, and back into the horse via the reins. This is *connection.* It is impossible to ride with your front heart gate open and carry negative thoughts or emotions. Negative states directly affect your horse's trust in you and his willingness to collect.

> *Rider Insight, Sue:* "When my front heart gate opened, I suddenly realized that my energy and motion moving up from my lower body was for the first time no longer hitting a 'wall' at the level of my heart. Suddenly my horse and I became one single energy unit. It was no longer my smaller mass riding my horse's larger

mass—his 1200 pounds and my 140. My entire sense of mass disappeared, and I could lift his back with my intent and creativity rather than with effort and work."

I believe in a higher level of communication between horse and rider than merely the physical act of riding. When connected, the horse will follow your intent. Your intent is created in your mind and projected through your heart when your front heart gate is open. *Only through an open heart can you communicate your intent to your horse.*

Exercises to facilitate opening the heart: *Heaven and Earth* (p. 62), *Spread Your Chest* (p. 126), *Spread Your Wings* (p. 131), and *Bend with an Arch* (p. 154).

Gate 4: The Back of the Heart

Opened: Opening *Gate 4: The Back of the Heart* further relaxes your upper back and neck muscles. This relaxation allows your thoracic and cervical vertebrae to move more freely with the rhythm of the horse. Opening the Back of the Heart also lengthens the reach of your arms, so that your elbows can stay bent and pointing down without pulling on the reins. This position allows your shoulders, elbows, wrists, and fingers to act as shock absorbers between the horse's mouth and the movements in your body.

> *Rider Insight, Trish:* "Thank you for the awesome experience I had during your clinic. The breakthroughs I had affected not only my work with horses but other areas of my life as well. You were so right in your assessment of me being a very closed person. I don't allow very much to come into me, so asking me to open my heart was huge for me. Opening from the back has made it all possible.
>
> "Since the clinic I have found I react differently when Nick, my very sensitive Thoroughbred, spooks. I am quieter, calmer, and can focus through the upset and go back to work faster. I have also noticed a change in his attitude toward me. He seems to be easier to get along with on the ground. Maybe that is just my change in (heart) attitude toward him. I'm learning to trust on a deeper level."

Closed: When the Back of your Heart is closed, your muscles are holding your upper spine in place and resisting the motion of the horse to maintain balance. This is often the root cause of shoulder tension and tightness in the neck. You transfer this tightness through your arms and hands to the horse. Your horse reflects the tightness through stiffness in his neck and chest.

When you ride with your heart closed (left), the reins function like ropes tied high in a tree: they have great leverage, and using this advantage, your horse can easily uproot your seat. Opening the Back of the Heart (right) is like moving the rope down to the trunk of the tree: the leverage is decreased and your seat is strong and rooted.

The reason so many riders keep the Back of the Heart closed is that the tension created acts as an anchor or brace for the arms and hands to pull from. This anchor leads to a false sense of centered strength that becomes apparent when the rider is pulled forward out of her seat by a small tug of the horse's head.

Holding in the upper back (heart gate closed) causes you to use your trapezius and rhomboid muscles to maintain balance. It leads to a disconnection between your upper body and seat.

Riding with a closed heart restricts the ability of your chest and abdomen to expand during inhalation, inhibiting your body's rhythm. Opening the Back of the Heart causes your latissimus dorsi muscles to engage. In doing so, you're physically connecting the reins to your seat through your bones and muscles.

Riding with an open heart releases tension in the horse's neck and shoulders. It allows for more complete collection and opens the path for communicating thought and intent.

The back's larger muscles and their attachments to the spine, shoulder, and upper arm (humerus), properly used in relaxation (left), and improperly used (right)—note the raised shoulder and jutting elbow.

Exercises to facilitate opening Gate 4: The Back of the Heart: *Wall Sitting* (p. 59), and *Embracing the Moon* (p. 102).

Gate 5: The Chi Who (Right and Left)
Where: Gate 5: The Chi Who (right and left sides) are located just below the collarbones in line between the nipples and ear lobes. To locate one, hold your arm out to your side at shoulder level, and form an "OK" sign with your index finger and thumb. Bend your arm at the elbow until your hand touches your chest. The center of the circle created by your fingers marks the location of the Chi Who (see photo).

Opened: Opening the Chi Who gates directly affects the softness and sensitivity of your hands to the bit. It plays a major role in stabiliz-

The location of the Chi Who gate, just below the collarbone.

ing the upper body during trot and canter. Opening the Chi Who relaxes and releases tension in the muscles of the chest and neck, allowing the head to move in rhythm with the rest of your body and the horse. When your trapezius, deltoids, and pectoral muscles are relaxed and your latissimus dorsi muscles are engaged, you allow your shoulders to move independently of your spine (see *Appendix*, p. 245, for anatomy chart). Your shoulders act as shock absorbers between your torso and the horse's mouth.

If you observe very advanced riders from behind, it looks as though their spine is moving up and down with the rise and fall of the horse's body, but the shoulders remain at relatively the same level as the spine moves

The rider's position is the same as a Tai Chi master's on the ground.

between them. I first observed this independence in the German dressage rider Klaus Balkenhol during the 1996 Olympics in Atlanta. His position on the horse was the same as a Tai Chi master's would be on the ground (see drawings).

With Gate 5: the Chi Who open, it is impossible to use the front of your chest to brace against the horse's pulling on the reins. If you do brace—thereby closing the Chi Who—you may find yourself being jerked out of the saddle by the horse, which disconnects the two of you. You'd also allow the horse to halt or fall out of his gait.

Looking at the same scenario—this time with an open Chi Who—when the horse pulls on the reins, the force travels up through the bones of your arms. As the force travels up your arms, it is transferred into the latissimus dorsi muscles, which then take the force down to the lower half of your back and seat. The force effectively pulls you deeper into your mount. If, in the moment that the horse pulls against the reins, you tighten the muscles of your chest and shoulders, the force is transferred through the shoulders to the upper back and neck via the trapezius muscles. It is then a matter of relative strength; the horse, being bigger and stronger, always wins this tug-o-war.

Closed: With the Chi Who closed, you will rely on the muscles of your upper body to hold yourself in balance. This is not a particular problem at the walk. However, as soon as the motion becomes bigger, your muscles have to work harder to hold your mass over your now moving center (seat). Soon your shoulders come up, your elbows go out, and your abdomen tightens. This all happens unconsciously as your body goes into self-preservation mode in an attempt to literally *hold itself* in balance.

I see these symptoms in many beginning and intermediate riders. This is not to say that all, or even most, advanced riders open their Chi Who, but they just become better at hiding the effects of riding with it closed. In advanced riders, the signs of a closed Chi Who are seen as tightness in the muscles of the jaw and the front of the neck. This tightness is the result of having to *hold* the head balanced over the upper body much in the same way the beginner holds her upper body over her center.

I suggest two ways of relaxing the jaw and neck. The first approach you can try is to smile, but if the Chi Who is closed, the smiling will not last and soon your neck and jaw will tighten again. The second, deeper approach, opening *Gate 7: The Upper Pass* and *Gate 8: The Crown* is addressed a little later in this section.

A closed Gate 6: The Liver and Spleen (left) and the soft and yielding abdomen of an open Gate 6 (right).

Opening the Upper Pass and the Crown gates helps you maintain your head and neck in a relaxed and aligned position that helps, in turn, to keep the Chi Who open. All gates are integrated, part of a path, and thus action on one affects the others.

Exercises to facilitate opening Gate 5: The Chi Who: *Neck Turns* (p. 121), *Spread Your Chest* (p. 126), and *Spread Your Wings* (p. 131).

Gate 6: The Liver and Spleen

Where: The Liver and Spleen gates are located, as you'd guess, near the liver (right side) and spleen (left side)—that is, just below the rib cage in line with the nipples. While these are two, separate gates, I'm counting them as one for these reasons:

1 They are both opened in the same way. In fact, it is nearly impossible to open one and not the other.

2 They are mirror images of each other, and the left and right serve the same function, namely, transferring energy back to the horse laterally.

These two gates should be the last two you try to open, as inexperience keeping the other gates open while focusing on these will often shut all of your gates.

Opened: The opening of Gate 6: The Liver and Spleen creates an incredible connection between you and your horse during lateral work. When open, these gates allow the horse's energy to move from the horse's hindquarters through your abdomen, with no restriction or blocks, into your hand. To open these gates, you must first be able to relax your abdomen completely as you'll learn in the abdominal breathing exercises in chapter 4. You can then use your intent to soften and expand the gate while inhaling in order to ensure that this region of your abdomen is completely relaxed.

Often, when I watch a rider performing lateral work, such as half-pass or shoulder-in, I see a great deal of resistance in the abdomen just below the rib cage. This resistance arises when the horse's body moves forward and to the side, and the rider's center moves out of rhythm with her upper body. Unconsciously, she tightens the abdomen and her upper body gets pulled along with the center. Remember, all this happens without a thought and in a fraction of a second, but that is enough to break the rhythm and upset the combined balance of horse and rider.

With The Liver and Spleen gates opened, they act to make your center bigger and more sensitive while creating a true connection between your seat and upper body. When I ride, it feels as if the horse's energy or force moves first through the open gate a moment prior to my seat and abdomen moving. Energetically, it is as if the horse leads the gate, and the gate leads the body. Physically, it feels like riding a wave that starts in the horse. Let's say the right hind moves through my right seat bone and hip—it's then transferred diagonally through the abdomen and out the spleen (left) gate.

Exercises to facilitate opening Gate 6: The Liver and Spleen: *Hold the Sky with Both Hands* (p. 138), and *Thrust Palm in Bow Stance* (p. 146).

Gate 7: The Upper Pass

Where: Gate 7: The Upper Pass is located at the base of the skull, where the head and spine come together, and is where the chi passes from the lower body into the head.

Opened: When the Upper Pass gate is opened, your mind is clear and focused, and you ride with a heightened sense of awareness.

There are more than seven muscles that either attach or pass through the Upper Pass. When you use the outermost of these muscles to hold your head in balance, the pass is closed and tension is present. Opening the Upper Pass engages the innermost muscles to connect your head and spine. These muscles are smaller postural muscles that by design were meant to hold up the bones against gravity. They can be engaged without hindering the motion and rhythm of the head, neck, and spine. Therefore, they allow your head to stay balanced and the outermost muscles to remain soft and sensitive. The bigger and more open the Upper Pass, the easier it is to balance the head without using the larger muscles of your neck, shoulders, and upper back.

The energy that empowers your intent comes through the Upper Pass. With your skull and neck in the proper position, you open the Upper Pass with your mind or your intent. I visualize it opening like a shutter of a camera—it spirals open.

My Riding Insight: While working with a dressage competitor, I noticed that her whole body looked relaxed except for her jaw and neck. This made it very difficult for her to smile while riding. I knew that she was not making a conscious choice not to smile, but nevertheless, soon after I would remind her to smile, it would disappear. Knowing that the tension in the muscles of her neck, face, and upper back was there to hold her head in balance, we looked for another way to keep her head balanced and in rhythm with the rest of her body and her horse.

I remembered that in my own riding, when I opened my Upper Pass and expanded my Crown my head felt light and floating (not light-headed, but physically light) I took a moment to explain the idea of opening the Upper Pass and Crown, and then we gave it a try in the saddle. After a few moments of moving her awareness to the Upper Pass, it opened. Immediately her neck and jaw softened, her shoulders dropped slightly, and the smile on her face was beautiful and effortless. What I did not expect was that the sound of the horse's hooves hitting the ground became very soft, and he seemed to get bigger and rounder.

Exercises to facilitate opening Gate 7: The Upper Pass: *Walking Backward* (p. 62), and *Neck Turns* (p. 121).

Gate 8: The Crown

Where: Gate 8: The Crown is located at the top of your head. Think of where a crown would sit; the Crown gate is the entire area that a crown would cover. The opening of this gate is often associated with enlightenment. Creativity—your seventh sense—enters through the Crown gate. In Eastern healing arts this area is referred to as the Crown chakra.

Opened: The Crown gate is opened primarily with your intent. That is, you consciously focus your intent on the area and see it opening. Visualize it opening like the petals of a flower opening with the morning sun.

Opening this gate is said to increase your conscious contact with the divine. My own experience is that when I open my Crown, I always feel a chill of energy run down and then up my spine. It is usually such a strong sensation that it makes me shiver for a moment.

As with all the Eight Gates, it is not enough to merely "think" the gate open. Your intent must be supported by the proper position of your body. For your Crown to open you must "suspend the top of your head"—aligning your head and center with the heavens above. Classical Tai Chi asserts that suspending of the head has the effect of promoting one's spirit and preventing one from being heavy and clumsy.

To suspend the head correctly, keep your chin slightly inward and straighten your neck. Your eyes gaze slightly below the horizon—lowered approximately 25 degrees, which, when mounted means that you look ahead between the horse's ears. In this traditional riding posture, your head is lifted as if it were suspended from the heavens by a thread.

Position your head by sensing—not by using force—and avoid any muscle tension in your neck. This position must be maintained regardless of the movement of the rest of your body. When your crown is suspended, it acts to lift your head in such a way as to bring your chin down lightly and lift the head from the vertebrae in the neck. In short, it balances your head on your spine. I've noticed that riders at the higher levels, often on big, strong, and highly energetic horses, tend to hold the head in balance with the muscles in the neck, which creates tension in the jaw and front of the neck.

A dressage competitor that I was working with learned to remove the tension in her face and neck simply by suspending her head and smiling. The impact on her horse was amazing, as he gave his back completely and seemed to float through his strides.

Exercises to facilitate opening Gate 8: The Crown: *Standing Meditation* (p. 37), *Walking Backward* (p. 62), *Neck Turns* (p. 121), and *Lift a Single Iron Arm* (p. 158).

What's Next

In the next chapter, "Your Mind: Awakening Self-Awareness and the Creative Mind," we will begin to lay the foundation of all the work to come by exploring awareness and the mind-body connection that is essential to enhancing *everything* we do, both on and off the horse.

Your Mind

Awakening Self-Awareness and the Creative Mind

IN THIS CHAPTER, YOU WILL DISCOVER a deeper level of awareness of your body that precedes the mind-body connection. You will experience being in a truly balanced state, both mind *and* body. You will see how small changes in your body's alignment and movement can create huge differences in your ability to relax and stay balanced. This makes your horse's job of supporting you much easier. This first series of exercises, based on traditional Tai Chi forms, offers you a simple way to expand your awareness and help develop your mind-body connection.

Unified Learning

To begin any new endeavor without first unifying mind and body by becoming aware of your physical state is at best inefficient. Self-awareness is the first step toward unifying your mind and body. Without self-awareness, you will be trapped in your old ways of thinking and moving. Realize that out of a twenty-four-hour day, you may ride for two hours, sleep for eight, and the other fourteen you're in old habits. The exercises will help you identify your own habits of imbalance on the ground, where they are more easily discovered. At the same time, the exercises will teach you a new and more balanced way to move. Remember that bad habits don't just go away—they must be deliberately replaced.

> "We must go beyond thought, go beyond visualization, go beyond imagination, and actually open a part of the mind that is usually closed and untapped in most people."
>
> (Deng Ming-Dao, from *365 Tao Daily Meditations*)

To build your awareness, you will explore the relationship between balance and tension, gravity and structural alignment, breath and intent. During these exercises, you will be asked to reflect back to the principles from chapter 2, and apply your knowledge of them to enhance your experience and understanding of your body in stillness and in motion. You will become aware of your strengths. You will learn more effectively on the ground, so all the exercises start with ground work. The knowledge you gain you'll later apply directly to your riding and your relationship to your horse.

Permission to Learn

Have you ever watched a young child who is learning to walk? Her parents step back and encourage her to come toward them. Her intent is to move forward, even if her legs are unsure. She staggers forward following her intent. Without being taught, she has taken her first steps. When she develops her motor skills, she never has to think about walking. It just happens, with or without her awareness. In a sense we first learn to walk by stumbling. When it's time to learn something new, do you still give yourself permission to stumble?

Sensing and Intent

One of the most powerful and often misunderstood tools available to you while riding is your *intent*. Intent is a *stretching of your mind toward a certain goal or object*. Proper use of your intent allows you to see and prepare for changes prior to the actual change. Whether the change is in the horse's gait or asking for collection, your intent projects what you envision or create in your mind.

Here's a story that demonstrates the power of intent. Once, while working with a dressage trainer on a young horse, I asked her to extend her trot as she reached a pre-arranged spot in the arena. While she approached the mark, I watched as she asked for extension. Within three strides she achieved an extended trot, and we thought, "Pretty good for a young horse." I then asked her what her focus was prior to giving the aid. She said that she was paying close attention to the horse in anticipation of the correct time to give the aid for extended trot. Reminding me of her horse's youth, she added that he rarely, if ever, responded to her aids in the moment she applied them.

Prior to her second attempt, I asked her do two things: (1) to see the extension of the trot in her mind's eye long before the two reached their spot, and (2) rather than focus on her horse as she gave the aids, to focus her intent on being light and balanced in the saddle. Now the two achieved the desired trot within one stride. On their next pass, their trot extended the moment they passed through the desired spot. The difference was that her intent was clear and in the right place prior to giving the physical aids. Because the rider focused on her own body position and balance, her horse could do the same.

Consider the horse's experience of this same situation: have you ever tried to complete a task with someone breathing down your neck, ready to correct any mistake you might make? It's nerve-racking to say the least, and it's not a situation apt to help you perform at your best. I believe that when the rider above used her intent to create a clear picture of the desired trot in her mind prior to asking for it, the horse was able to understand the goal without any physical communication.

A gifted equine dentist once told me that the moment he sets foot on a property, every horse there can sense any fear, anger, frustration, or anxiety he has held in his body. Before any horse allows him to do his work, he must remove those emotions. By the way, he performs all his work without the use of drugs to numb his patients, and they relax and melt into him with complete trust as he is working. It seems that even if you are unaware of it, your intent is at work. You'll explore and experience intent through the *Walking Backward* exercise later in this chapter.

With the understanding that your intent is constantly at work, it is of vital importance to know what you are projecting. Rather than trying to identify many so-called "negative" emotions that may show up with you at the barn on any given day, you will let them go and replace them by focusing on the body. A quiet, calm mind is the only place to develop and explore this tool.

Your mind's eye—also called the third eye or your "inner" eye—is a versatile tool in riding. When you open your mind's eye, you can progress from being a good rider, who's wise in the techniques of horsemanship, to being an enlightened equestrian. You'll employ this sense—this "knowing" yourself and your horse as one—whenever you handle your horse on the ground or ride him. Chapter 6 further develops heightening this sense.

Safety

In each exercise, remember to follow safety procedures. Choose an open area, without any hazards or obstacles like jumps or cavaletti. In the saddle, have a friend assist you, possibly by holding the horse while he's standing still, and certainly to longe you in a corral or round pen. If you're riding in an enclosed area and you know your horse well, you can ride with the reins dropped.

The First and Only Rule: Smile and Breathe!

This is the book's only rule, and it applies to all the exercises. Smile and breathe—it's good to be alive! Riding is fun. Tai Chi will enhance the pleasures you share with your horse.

And here's another reason for smiling: you relax and soften. Look at a young rider—when her pony misbehaves, she laughs and relaxes. When you're relaxed and your horse rears or spooks, think of what happens: instead of tensing—which communicates more anxiety to your horse—your body softens. You reconnect with your horse to counteract the rearing or spooking.

So, smile and breathe. Practice seriously—but don't be too serious when you practice!

Standing Meditation

Riding Goal: Balance

Your goals are to develop a new awareness and understanding of balance in *Standing Meditation* on the ground. Later you will carry this learning with you onto the horse, where you will experience and develop a state of quiet stillness in the saddle, which I call *Sitting Meditation*. This exercise teaches you the different roles the bones, muscles, and mind play in maintaining your balance.

Function

This exercise has three important functions: it introduces and teaches you to achieve true balance; it defines the roles of your muscles and bones in maintaining balance; and it leads to discovery of your body's inherent strengths and weaknesses.

Intent

You'll use your mind to observe the changes in your body as you alter your alignment. This exercise is the first step to learning how to listen to your body. In classic Tai Chi forms this situation is known as *wu ji* or "double-weighted." This is the only time in a Tai Chi form that your weight remains distributed 50/50 in both feet. At all other times you pass through 50/50 weight distribution as you move from one position to the next. During this exercise you feel what it is like to move your body with your mind. This will be your introduction to the principle of using your mind, not force.

Step-by-Step

1 Stand in a shoulder-width parallel stance. Your legs are straight, neither locked nor bent. Your knees are relaxed. Your arms hang naturally at your sides, with the hands relaxed.

Stand with your feet parallel to each other, that is, they point directly forward and are neither pigeon-toed nor splayed.

Here's how to check that your feet are shoulder-width: keeping the ball of your left foot in place, swing your left heel 90 degrees toward the toes of your right foot. When your left foot is perpendicular to the right, you should see a space of one fist between the heel of your left foot and the toes of your right.

James On Your Shoulder

Smiling is the best way to relax over 100 muscles in and around your face. Also, it's very hard to hold on to negative thoughts while smiling. I believe that a horse is well aware of your mental state, and a negative mind will not achieve positive results. Have you ever had to spend a long period of time around negative people? How did it feel? If you had a choice, would you stay in their company? Would you feel connected with them? Your horse would give, I believe, similar answers.

Steps 1 and 2

Steps 4 and 6: If your weight is in your heels (left) allow it to move to the balls of your feet (right).

2 Look forward to the horizon. Smile and breathe.

3 Next, suspend your head as if it were held from above by a silken thread, or you can imagine the crown of your head floating upward. This idea and visualization acts to put your head and neck in proper alignment, without creating undue tension in the muscles of your neck.

Try to imagine that you are just a skeleton with no muscles to hold up your bones. How would you have to align your bones to keep them standing?

4 Now become aware of where your weight is in your feet. How is that weight distributed? Equally between the two feet, or more in one foot or the other? Evenly within your feet, or with more weight to the inside or outside? More weight in your heels, or more weight in the balls of your feet? Make a mental note of what you find because this has an important connection to your riding: where your weight is in your feet on the ground tells you where your weight is in your seat in the saddle. We'll return to this in the mounted portion of this exercise. For now, simply focus your mind on the balls of your feet. Put 100 percent of your focus and concentration there.

Most people stand with their weight back in the heel of the foot (see photo). In that position, you lack structural alignment and you have less strength. When you stand with your weight in your heels, you are at the "end of your rope" as far as balance is concerned. Why? Because the slightest push on your chest will send you backward out of balance with very little chance to recover.

5 Now move your attention to your breathing. Take two or three deep, slow breaths, and with every breath relax a little more.

6 Become aware of your body, and check your weight: has it shifted into the balls of your feet? If your weight is still in your heels, allow it to move into the balls of your feet.

Next, we will adapt the work we've been doing on the ground to being on the horse.

Exploring Weight, Balance, and Strength

Try this test with a friend. Stand with your weight back in your heels. Have a friend push gently on your chest with one hand as if to push you backward (top photo).

Notice how you react. Do you tense your muscles in an attempt to hold your position? Do you push your hips forward toward your friend? Do you hold your breath? Do your arms or elbows come up? Does your chin drop and your eyes look down? Before you fall will you grab onto your friend's arms?

In the saddle, your horse serves as your friend. When you begin to lose your alignment, all these same things are likely to happen. They are *symptoms* of imbalance, not *causes*.

Now stand with your weight in the balls of your feet and relax all your muscles. Have your friend slowly push again (bottom photo).

Notice how much more strength you have to resist the push. Can you relax your muscles, especially your gluteals and quadriceps? Can you continue breathing? While your friend pushes, can you drop more weight into your feet? The point of this practice is not that you won't be pushed over; the point is that when you are properly aligned, maintaining your balance is much easier, even when your body is being moved by an outside force.

There are two principles behind allowing your weight to move: (1) all motion is directed by your mind; and (2) your body will seek perfect balance on its own *if you relax*. When the weight drops through your bones into the balls of your feet, you are in true structural alignment. You are balanced. In this position, listen to your body. Do you sense any tension you can now release? When your body is not in structural alignment, your muscles must hold a certain amount of tension to support the misalignment, often resulting in an assortment of predispositions for strains and injuries. After achieving proper alignment, the muscle may still hold this tension as a result of training or habit. Structurally aligned bones will allow you to let go of the tension in your muscles. In return, you will feel stronger and more grounded in this stance.

Sitting Meditation

If you have not just done *Standing Meditation*, return to the beginning of that exercise (p. 37) and tune yourself into the quiet, relaxed, strong, and balanced state that you can achieve. When done, keep that feeling in mind, and then begin *Sitting Meditation*.

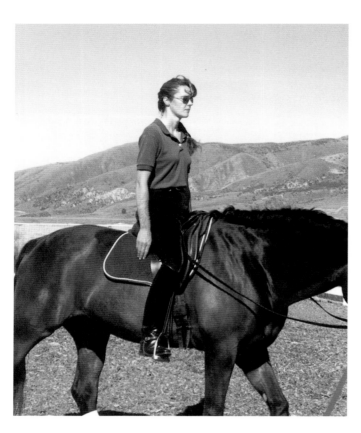

Step-by-Step

1 Mount your horse and remain at the halt.

2 Look forward to the horizon. Smile and breathe.

3 Expand your crown upward. Visualize your head lifting, so you feel like you're floating upward. Feel the lift through all of your vertebrae, not just the top of your spine. That is, feel that the floating comes from expanding the small space between every vertebra in your spine, not from trying to stretch your neck up.

4 Relaxed and focused in the saddle, now become aware of where your weight is in your seat bones. Focus your mind on these bones. Try to feel what I call the "bone-to-leather connection." Put 100 percent of your focus and concentration there.

5 Earlier, I said that where your weight is in your feet mirrors where your weight is in your seat bones. Is this true for you? Where is your weight in your seat bones?

Just as most people stand with their weight back in their heels, most riders place their weight back in their seat bones. And just as when most people shift their weight forward to the balls of their feet they initially report that they feel as if they're leaning forward, most riders, when they move their weight to the center of their seat bones, report that they're leaning forward. While this impression is entirely normal, it's also inaccurate: you've actually found your center. With time, this position will feel "normal"—not to mention stronger, more supple, and better connected with your horse.

6 Again, focus on your "bone-to-leather" connection. Visualize your seat bones. How big are they? As big as golf balls? Tennis balls? See them and feel them. Where is your weight in that sphere you are envisioning?

7 Now move your attention to your breathing. Take two or three deep, slow breaths, and with every breath relax a little more.

8 Smile and sit quietly on your horse. Appreciate the relaxed, deep balanced seat you have right now. Your goal is to have this seat whenever you ride.

Ah-Ha!

When you are in *Standing Meditation*, with your bones aligned to support your body against gravity, you will feel heavier. As we have discussed, when you first experience being in true alignment, you may feel as if you are leaning forward, a sensation that will go away with time, as you get used to your new balance. Most of us have been living behind our center for all of our adult life, and we've become comfortable with and accustomed to our imbalance.

Here's a little test you can easily do to check your alignment. While in *Standing Meditation*, have a friend push straight down on your shoulders. You should feel the added force drop though your body into the ground, without having to tense or resist the force. If you are not in alignment, you will tighten the muscles of your abdomen, making it harder to breathe. At the same time, your hips will push forward to negotiate the added load, and the muscles of your lower back will tighten to compensate for the misalignment of your spine. Your body will respond in the same way when riding as your horse moves and gravity pushes down on you—unless you are properly aligned to negotiate the force.

Ability Transition

Throughout your day, you will begin to catch yourself with your weight in your heels. Weight in your heels will start to feel unbalanced. You will also notice that when your weight is centered, you need to use your muscles less to hold your body upright. You will start to hear your body like never before. You will recognize when you are overusing your muscles to compensate for misalignment. Remember that over your lifetime, you have trained your muscles to compensate for your structural misalignment.

Reminder

This exercise is used primarily to build your awareness of balance and how a lack of balance creates tension in your body. You have begun to develop the roadmap to a place of quiet connection with your horse. You have embarked upon a path, which is a pattern of initiating movement by using your mind, breath, and body.

In a Tai Chi form, the only time your weight is distributed 50/50 between your two feet is at the beginning and the end of the form. The same should be true for your riding. Your weight is only 50/50 in your seat bones when your horse is standing still and square. At any other moment, your weight is in transition. Balance in riding is not static, but dynamic and ever-shifting. The weight in your seat bones passes through this 50/50 point, but is never held or caught there. Whether in Tai Chi or riding, your goal is fluidity.

Side Step

Riding Goal: Balance

You will learn how to shift your weight effectively from one seat bone to another without negatively affecting your center and balance. You will ride more effectively by doing less.

Function

Side Step increases your ability to use your pelvis to negotiate your balance between the top and bottom of your body. This ability relieves tension in your lower back and teaches you to move your body as one whole unit. You'll develop a new understanding of your body alignment and balance.

This exercise builds on the awareness you experienced in *Standing Meditation*. You'll discover how you compensate for lack of structural alignment and how this compensation may interfere with your communication with the horse.

Intent

Imagine that the ball of your foot is a stake driven deep into the ground. That stake is the root of your balance while shifting your weight. Focus deep into your pelvis. Only then can you begin to move muscles consciously that up until now have only worked unconsciously.

Step-by-Step

1 Begin in *Standing Meditation.*

2 Now move your two feet slightly closer together, in preparation for the next step.

3 Step out to the side into a shoulder-width parallel stance without leaning to one side. You'll step and then shift your weight from one foot to the other. Move your left or right foot out into the shoulder-width parallel stance, without looking down. Ask yourself if your feet are parallel and a shoulder-width apart. What is the answer?

4 Now look down and compare the positions of your feet with where you thought they would be. If your feet aren't placed where you expected, reposition them to the correct position. Take a moment to experience what that position feels like.

Sometimes we think we know where our body is, but upon honest investigation we find it's not where we thought it was. For example, many times while working with a rider at the rising trot, I'll ask her if she thinks she is straight during the brief sitting phase. Most often she says, "Yes." When I tell her that actually she's leaning forward, she usually doesn't believe it. I must then employ onlookers to help me convince her that what she thinks is straight is not. As we continue to work and she is finally able to sit straight, she says that she feels as if she is leaning backward. It takes time and help to overcome this false knowing. A videotape is very helpful in this situation and can save a great deal of time and frustration.

5 Step back into the beginning position (with your feet closer together).

6 Step out once again into a shoulder-width stance. This time notice if you must lean to one side to take the step.

Of the riders I have worked with, I would say that 99 percent must lean to move one foot. This may not seem like a big deal in riding, but remember that how you have trained yourself to move on the ground is how you move in the saddle.

If you have to lean to pick up and reposition your foot—in other words to shift your weight—then you will do the same thing to some extent when you shift your weight from one seat bone to another. Most riders are unaware of this lean in the saddle, but I assure you that your horse is not.

To shift your weight without leaning, you must use your pelvis. *Side Step* helps you learn to move your pelvis directly, rather than first tensing it and your (stationary) supporting leg and then moving your center over the tensed leg by leaning in order to lighten the foot you want to lift.

7 Try this: take a deep breath and relax your abdomen. Imagine all your weight pouring like sand into the ball of your right foot. With this clearly in your mind, stretch your tailbone down as if there were a large, heavy weight attached to it. This is known as "dropping the tailbone." Note this is not tucking the tailbone under or pushing it forward as in a pelvic thrust.

Step 2 *Step 3* *Step 5* *Step 6*

8 As your tailbone drops, bend your left leg slightly at the knee and feel your leg becoming lighter and lighter. When 100 percent of your weight has shifted from your left leg into your right—no sooner—you may step out to the side.

This shift may seem like a very simple task, but there is a wealth of knowledge contained in this very unassuming exercise. The movement in the pelvis necessary to step out without leaning is the same movement used in a sitting trot to follow the motion of your horse. To develop this conscious movement is the difference between a good sitting trot and a great sitting trot.

Step 7 *Step 8*

Ah-Ha!

You will start to feel your weight shift inside your body before you perform any outside movement. You're engaging yourself, just as your horse engages his hindquarters. You will become increasingly aware of smaller and smaller percentages of weight shift. As you step, you will feel as if you are growing taller, or the crown of your head is stretching upward.

Ability Transition

Throughout your day you will increasingly catch yourself whenever you slip back into your old habit of leaning with your spine to initiate movement—rather than engaging your pelvis and moving from your center. Stop, pause, take a deep breath, and then move correctly—from your center.

In the saddle, you will be able to shift your weight and negotiate the movement of your horse through your body more efficiently and with less effort.

Reminder

Take your time and really listen to your body. Look for tension and unnecessary contractions of your muscles. Use your breath to help relax your body and let go of tension.

Wrist Shaking

Riding Goals: Balance, Relaxation, Body Control

You will gain a new awareness of your balance and what your horse may feel when compensating for your lack of balance. You will learn to stay relaxed in mind and body while riding. This relaxation in turn allows the horse to move more freely without constantly having to adjust for your imbalance. This freer movement increases both horse and rider endurance, because both of you are using less muscle to achieve greater results.

Function

The exercise develops a new understanding of body alignment and balance. When done properly, this exercise helps you to use and move your body as a coherent whole. You experience bouncing that helps relax and warm up all the joints and connective tissues of your body. This exercise helps you understand how body, mind, and breath can be used to refine balance and relaxation. Also, it teaches how a slight imbalance in your body leads to unnecessary fatigue and tension.

Intent

During *Wrist Shaking*, use your mind primarily to monitor muscle tension and breathing. However, this exercise requires your mind to stay calm and attentive to the smallest of changes in your body. Practice *Wrist Shaking* after learning *Standing Meditation*.

Step-by-Step

As with most of our work, you'll build on the awareness created from previous exercises. Review the Ability Transition on p. 41 and p. 46 before starting this exercise.

1 Start in *Standing Meditation*.

2 Begin slowly bouncing on the balls of your feet. Your heels should come completely off the ground during the bounce. At no time should

Step 2

you lose your connection to the ground through the balls of your feet. Let your arms hang relaxed at your sides, elbows straight and not locked. Your wrists should be relaxed so that the motion of your body up and down shakes and flexes your wrists. The exercise creates a rhythmic motion in your body as you bounce. Feel your arms as pendulums; let them swing. Let your wrists flex. As you bounce, you will become immediately aware of your balance or lack of it.

3 It is important to continue bouncing for at least one minute, and then stop.

Ask yourself, "Where is my weight? Where is my breath?" If you are like most people, your weight probably shifted back in your body to where it is normally while standing (in the heels). In this position, you are misaligned and must therefore tighten various muscles to compensate for this misalignment. This tension is then transferred into your abdomen as it attempts to hold your center over your feet. For this reason, it may be difficult to maintain deep abdominal breathing while doing the exercise.

By this time you should be acutely aware of how a very small imbalance in your body is multiplied when you add motion to it. Were your calf muscles working hard? Did you feel how, when you lost your balance, your muscles immediately tightened to try and regain it? And after a very short time, did you feel that muscle begin to ache?

Take a moment and put yourself in your horse's shoes. Think of how much muscle he must use to compensate for your lack of balance. Remember the imbalance you have on the ground you have in the saddle—the only difference is you don't feel it, but your horse does. With this in mind, how many times have you thought that your horse was being naughty or "he just doesn't like to go to the right," when actually he was compensating for your imbalance that impedes his ability to move freely and respond to your aids? Don't feel bad, because the solution is at hand, or at your feet.

4 Now start to bounce again. This time start very slowly, by just lifting your heels off the ground.

5 Relax your calf muscles and let your heels drop back down.

6 Repeat this action several times until you can "let go" with your muscles and your heels drop with a thud to the ground.

Notice that your imbalance usually occurs when you're lifting up, not when you drop.

Are you using too many muscles to lift your body? If so, this will pull you out of alignment.

7 Try a few seconds of abdominal breathing before you lift your heels off the ground. Inhale as you lift your heels off the ground and exhale as you drop. Within a few tries, you should feel lighter on the lift and heavier on the drop.

8 Begin to bounce again. Compare your balance with the beginning of the exercise. Is your balance significantly better than in the beginning?

After you've stopped the bouncing, focus your mind on your hands. Listen to them for one minute.

Do you feel the sensation of electricity or tingling in them? What you feel is your chi.

Focus all your intent toward this sensation. Can you feel it moving? Does it move up your arms? Can you feel it in the balls of your feet?

This is a great warm-up and can be done before and after you ride. Try this one in the morning when you first wake up, to help shake off the sleep and start your day balanced.

> *Rider Insight, Lolly:* Lolly had experienced carpal tunnel syndrome for fifteen
> years. When she practiced Wrist Shaking, *she felt fire shooting down her wrists*
> *and out her fingertips. She was experiencing the stretching and relaxing of her*
> *tendons and muscles as they moved through the restricted area in her wrist. Doing*
> *this exercise, along with a few others in this book, helped her regain strength and*
> *range of motion in her hands and wrists. (She tells her full story in chapter 8, p. 227.)*

Ah-Ha!

With practice you will be able to bounce longer without getting tired. You will be able to maintain deep abdominal breathing throughout. The sense of well-being and calm attained by focusing on the chi will come sooner and last longer.

Tai Chi masters say that the chi is directed only by the mind and will go where the mind goes. Also, great healing properties have been accredited to the manipulation of chi. I would ask you to diligently practice listening to the chi every time you do this exercise.

Many marvelous and mysterious powers have been given to the development and mastery of one's own chi. There are stories of Tai Chi masters throwing their chi out beyond their own bodies to knock over opponents without physically touching them. I cannot attest to the validity of these claims, because I have never seen any of these feats in person. However, I do know that I can focus on the sensation created by this exercise for a long period of time. When I finish this exercise, I feel a deep sensation of calm and clarity.

Ability Transition

The knowledge gained about your balance, weight distribution, and breath will begin to become apparent throughout the day and when you ride. You will be able to make adjustments in your body to maintain your balance before the tension sets in your muscles.

Reminder

When done regularly, this simple exercise will reveal a lifetime of knowledge about your body and balance.

Sink and Circulate the Chi

Riding Goals: Balance, Relaxation

When your breath is relaxed, even, and fluid, your horse can feel it, and he also will relax.

Function

This exercise teaches you to harmonize your breath and motion into one conscious flow. It teaches you how to continue breathing throughout a ride, regardless of the horse's behavior. Most riders tend to hold their breath just prior to giving an aid, if only for a moment. This holding causes the body to tense. Your horse can feel this tension and must compensate for it.

Intent

In this exercise, as with all the movements in this book, your mind directs the breath and the body. You also use your mind to create or remind yourself of certain positive feelings that help change your physical body. For instance, while opening your arms in the initial motions of this form, I suggest imagining that you are welcoming an old friend or loved one to your home. The energy is light and open, just as the movement should be.

Step-by-Step

1 Begin in *Standing Meditation.*

2 Slowly raise your arms up and out to your sides, keeping your palms faced forward and your thumbs pointed up. Continue to lift your arms in an arcing motion until your hands are at ear level.

3 While keeping your elbows in the same spot, relax and bend your elbows so that your hands circle up, around, and down past your face. Now your palms are facing down, with your hands at about chin level and 12 inches in front of you. Note that your elbows remain slightly bent.

Step 1: Two views

James On Your Shoulder

Find the rotation of your arm within the larger movement of the circles. When your breath matches the motion and you feel a tingling sensation in your hands during the exercise, you are circulating chi.

Visualize the chi moving from your center (your lower Dain Tian), back and upward through your spine up to your head. Your chi then moves back down the front of your body and returns to your center.

4 Continue to lower your hands as if you were pushing down on a ball filled with helium. This movement, in fact the entire exercise, should be soft and fluid; *even while in motion, create a feeling of stillness.*

5 As your hands reach your waist, roll each humerus (upper arm), which will cause your elbows to drop back to your sides. At the same time rotate your wrists, so that your palms now face up and are in front of your Dain Tian.

6 Pause in this position and take two or three slow abdominal breaths. With each breath expand the sphere of energy originating in your Dain Tian until you have filled a large ball of energy that now rests in your hands.

7 Slowly raise your arms up in front of your body, keeping your wrists and elbows slightly bent. Your arms should rise as if someone were lifting them by a string that is attached at your wrists. Continue lifting your arms until they are at the level of your heart and the middle Dain Tian.

Step 2

Step 3

Step 4

Steps 5 and 6

Step 7

8 Draw your hands toward your body by slowly bending and dropping your elbows simultaneously, until your hands are approximately one fist length in front of your chest. The palms of your hands should face downward at approximately 45 degrees.

9 Slowly and gently push your palms outward until your elbows are nearly straight.

10 Slowly allow your arms to drop down to the sides of your body, back into the beginning position.

Mounted

Repeat the above motions while on the longe line, in the round pen, or while at the walk in an arena. Notice how your horse relaxes. Pay attention to his breathing as you allow the slow, circular, rhythmic motion to relax your breath and body (see photos).

You are opening *Gate 4: The Back of the Heart*. You already do things in your life that open this gate. When you hug someone you love, you spread your shoulder blades as you wrap your arms around them. You're also softening *Gate 3: The Front of the Heart*.

You make your arms rounder and couple their motion with your breath. Feel like you expand in your back: imagine that you have a tiny purple dot between your shoulders—now you make it bigger by expanding between your shoulders.

When you open your gates, your horse will feel it. He will be more likely to collect and round his back under you. When your gates are closed, your horse won't come up into you.

Ah-Ha!

When you lift your arms correctly, they will feel light—even weightless. This feeling happens when you maintain proper structural alignment throughout the motion and use only the muscles necessary to lift your arms.

Ability Transition

You will notice that your breathing becomes deeper and slower as you practice. As your mind, breath, and body begin to move in harmony, you may experience a sense of calm and well-being. The circling of your arms will feel bigger and rounder with practice.

Performing the steps for Sink and Circulate the Chi while mounted.

Reminder

Do not force your breath down. You want the breath to sink deep into the abdomen naturally; forcing it down will create tension in your body. Force creates tension, and this is the habit you're trying to break by retraining yourself. So, breathe with ease and relaxation. When you breathe in, imagine you are smelling a flower.

Horse Stance and Wall Sitting

Riding Goals: Awareness, Position/Seat, Body Control

This exercise trains you to ride with the muscles of the backs of your legs and gluteus muscles relaxed. When these muscles are tightened, their attachment point at your pelvis is tight and hard, which restricts the fluid motion of your pelvis and separates you from your saddle and horse.

Function

This exercise teaches you to breathe continuously, gently, and deeply into your abdomen while strengthening the muscles in your legs and abdomen. While it is absolutely necessary for you to use certain muscles in your legs and abdomen while riding, you don't need to employ all the muscles in those areas. In fact, the overuse of certain dominant muscles in these areas leads to restricted motion in your hips and lower back, which in turn separates you from your horse. This exercise helps you identify which muscles are unnecessarily, unconsciously engaged while in a riding position. It also teaches you how to "let go of" and relax those muscles, while using only the muscles necessary for balance.

In addition, you'll also learn to move your lower lumbar region independently of the rest of your body. This will change your balance, and this new motion, originating in your center, will help you sit the trot and canter.

Intent

The exercise trains your mind to stay focused and calm when your body begins to tire. Through focus and awareness, you use your mind to direct your breath down into your abdomen and lower back (your Ming Meng).

Step-by-Step

There are two parts to this exercise:

Part One: *Horse Stance* builds an understanding of what happens in your body unconsciously while in a riding position, which typically leads to a separation of horse and rider.

Part Two: *Wall Sitting* trains your body to move more effectively while in the *Horse Stance* position.

Horse Stance

1 You'll start from a standing position. I would like you to put yourself into—as closely as you can—the position you are in while riding.

Take your time. Close your eyes and see yourself on your horse, and really make sure you are in your riding position. Ask yourself, "Are my legs bent enough? Is my back straight? Where are my elbows; my hands?" Take a few moments to feel your body in this position and become aware of any tension in your body. Is there tightness in your lower back? Are your legs straining to support your weight in this position? Is your abdomen relaxed? Is your breathing shallow and up in your chest?

2 Now try and let go of the tension. Relax and don't change the position, but just try to relax into it. Chances are if you begin to relax for a moment, it will not last. Very soon your body will likely become tense. This happens because you're inherently in a structurally weak position. I'll explain the reasons why.

Look down at the space between your knees and ask yourself, "Is my horse really that skinny?" Approximately 99 percent of the thousands of riders I've worked with stand with their knees far too close together when I ask them to assume their riding position. You may think that all you have to do is move your knees out a bit, or you say, "My knees go where the width of my horse puts them." You would be correct as long as you were on the ground, but things change when you mount your horse. On your horse, you ask him not only to support your weight, but also make up for your imbalances. I believe that your stance is crucial, and it plays a major role in keeping you from a soft and connected seat.

Begin in your riding position with your legs bent and your back straight. Check if your knees are too close together by placing two fingers on your seat bones, as described in Step 3.

3 Try this little experiment: assume your riding position with your knees closer together, and with two fingers reach back under your seat and place your fingers on your seat bones. Can you feel the muscles and tendons that lie over the top of the bones? No? That's because in this position the muscles and tendons are relaxed and not in use. This relaxation would be great if this were truly the position you were in while riding.

Step 5

Now, while keeping your fingers on your seat bones, push your knees out into the position that the width of your horse puts them in. Notice how the muscles and tendons tighten and push your fingers away from the bone. This tightening is what happens when you sit in the saddle and your horse moves your knees apart. It pushes you out of the saddle with tension between you and the horse. Most riders unconsciously compensate for this by arching their lower back, putting their body out of alignment. Arching your back completely compromises your structural support and balance.

5 Take another moment and play with this position. See how by moving your knees and arching your back, you not only change the state of the muscles and tendons in your seat but you also affect your balance.

6 In this *Horse Stance*, have a friend softly push on your chest. Are you easily pushed out of balance?

Feel how your body tenses against the push. Having a friend push against you simulates the effects of an outside force applied to your position. The pushing produces the same reaction in your body that the movement of the horse underneath you creates when you sit in a weak position. Notice that as the push is continued, your body attempts to maintain balance in the same way it does when riding out of balance. You immediately hold your breath and tense up, your elbows begin to rise, and either your chest pushes forward or your hips move forward toward your friend. When this happens your lower back will tighten and your hands squeeze. The last thing you will do in an attempt to keep from falling is to reach out and grab your friend's arms—just as you tend to "grab" or hold the reins when things go poorly in the saddle.

Caution

This initial position is extremely important to this exercise being effective and safe. An incorrect starting position will result in undue stress upon your knees and back.

Now let's work on developing a better Horse Stance. For this exercise, you will need a sturdy, flat wall to sit back against, with a floor that is level and not slippery.

1 Stand with your back to the wall. Place your heels approximately 12 to 15 inches away from the wall. To find the optimum position: (a) place your right heel against the wall; (b) reach down and place your right fist on the floor in front of the toes of your right foot—the side of your fist away from the wall now marks where you should place your right heel; (c) stand back up and move your right heel to this location, moving your left foot the same distance from the wall; (d) place your feet one shoulder-width apart and parallel to each other.

2 Slowly sit back against the wall and lower your body so that your thighs are parallel to the ground. Your upper and lower legs should form a 90-degree angle. Your hands rest on your knees, which are directly over your feet. Your back is flat against the wall.

3 Rest the back of your head against the wall. Take a moment in this position to feel your body. What muscles are you using? Is your breath relaxed and deep?

4 Slowly roll your tailbone off the wall so that your lower back (your Ming Meng) pushes back into the wall. At the same time, roll your shoulders forward away from the wall so that more of your lower back presses into the wall.

5 Hold this position for two full deep breaths. As you inhale, direct your breath with your mind down into your lower back. Think of your abdomen as a balloon, expanding out in all directions.

Step 2

Step 4

6 Slowly lean back with your shoulders as you allow your tailbone to move back against the wall. Feel the arch in your lower spine return to its resting position as it pulls your lower back away from the wall.

7 Repeat Steps 4 through 6 until the motion is clean and fluid (review the Eight Principles, p. 16). As your body becomes stronger and more relaxed with the movement, increase the length of time you're in the "pulled-away-from-the-wall" position.

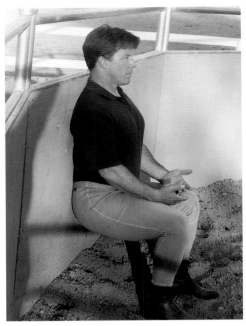

Step 6

Ah-Ha!

For many of you, the first thing you will feel is a burning in your thighs. This is a good thing. It means that the right muscles are at work. Your thighs are the root of your waist, and they need to be strong and tension-free. Any unnecessary tension in the thighs leads to restricted motion in the pelvis.

As you pull your shoulders and tailbone away from the wall, you will feel the muscle on the inside of your upper leg down near your knee start to work. Again, this is good. This muscle, the vastus medialus, helps stabilizes your knee and upper leg while riding. If you use your whole thigh to stabilize your leg, you only succeed in squeezing the horse and restricting the movement of your pelvis.

Ability Transition

When you practice, you will find that it becomes easier to keep your abdominal breathing slow and deep. It is my experience that when I control my breath, I control my body and mind. When I first began training in this exercise, I noticed a sort of mental panic when I felt the burn in my legs in this stance. It was not my muscles that were giving out, but my mind. The minute I began to focus on the burn, I lost focus on my breath, which disconnected me from the rest of my body.

Be sure that you aren't dropping, tucking, or tilting your tailbone. You are moving your spine and pelvis. See the related exercise in chapter 4, *Open the Ming Meng* (p. 99).

As with most of the exercises in this book, there are many levels of teachings. Remember that the great treasures lie just under the surface of these seemingly simple forms. While riding you will start to notice that your center moves more, yet you will feel more balanced and centered.

Reminder

If you feel any pain in your knees or back, stop immediately and check your position and alignment. In the beginning, don't try to do too many repetitions or hold the position for an extended period of time.

Mounted

Practice this exercise before a ride to warm up the muscles of your spine and legs.

When you ride at the posting trot, apply the feeling of the *Horse Stance*. Think about your legs and their position in the sitting and rising phases of your posting. Actively remember the feeling of support you felt in your legs, seat, and back during *Wall Sitting*: an awareness of muscular presence in your legs; an awareness of softness in your seat; and an awareness of a back free of all tension. Your goal is to carry the awareness you gained on the wall over to sitting in the saddle. Don't surrender your structural alignment for a soft seat. Be soft, but achieve this through balanced alignment rather than muscular effort.

Walking Backward

Riding Goals: Awareness, Balance, Body Control, Influencing the Horse

This exercise has two main goals:

First, you will develop coordination in your body by walking backward—the opposite of what you are accustomed to. All the muscles that usually play the dominant role in walking and riding will need to follow the lead of your less-used muscles. This motion develops balance and sensitivity of both the individual muscles and your body as a whole.

Second, you will learn to trust all your senses, not just your eyes. Most of us only believe what we can see. This is apparent in the majority of riders that I have observed who spend a considerable amount of time looking down at the horse to see if they have changed leads, collected, or are posting on the correct diagonal. These riders often continue to look at the horse, even after their instructor has pointed out and proven to them how unstable and weak the body is with the head down. This is simply a bad habit that we need to overcome by retraining.

Function

This exercise's most important function is to increase your awareness of the power of your intent. It also builds a certain level of trust between mind and body. By moving in the direction opposite of where you are looking, and not allowing yourself to look back, you force your body to trust what your mind knows. On completing this exercise you will experience a change in your reality and perception of your environment and how your intent has the power to move everything you see.

Intent

Use your mind to manipulate your intent and perception. When you first stop walking backward, everything you see will appear to be moving toward you. This may challenge your balance at first, but you will use your mind to imagine you are floating an inch off the ground, and instead of being pushed over, you will feel as if you are floating and bringing your environment to you. This technique can be used to perfect the timing of your transitions. It's one of the most powerful exercises I've ever experienced.

Step-by-Step

The actual exercise is very simple—you walk backward for at least five minutes.

1 Stand in an empty riding arena or any quiet place where you can see the entire path on which you will be walking.

It helps if the place is familiar to you. It is very important before you begin walking that you can look and see there is nothing to trip over or fall down into.

2 Start walking backward. There are two things you must do while walking backward: (a) Keep your head straight forward, resisting the temptation to look back over your shoulder to see where you are going. You have already seen for yourself that there is nothing to trip you up. Trust yourself, and develop your other senses.

(b) When you step backward, try to keep your feet parallel and shoulder-width apart at all times. This will help to develop the weaker muscles in the legs and enhance your balance.

3 After walking for at least five minutes stop and focus on what you see. Is everything in sight moving toward you, knocking you off balance? Do you feel as though you are losing your balance backward?

4 Now change your focus and align your body into *Standing Meditation.*

5 Expand your crown upward. Imagine that you are floating an inch off the ground in perfect structural alignment.

Does it now seem as if you are flying or floating toward any point you choose in your field of vision?

6 Stand for one minute or longer and experience this new reality.

Later in the book, you will recreate this experience while riding. The experience will aid in the timing of transitions from one gait to another.

Ah-Ha!

With a little practice, you will be able to call up this incredible focus at will. You will find that when you stop walking and stand in place, you will immediately begin to float.

Ability Transition

As you walk more and more, your stride will become smoother and longer and you'll develop a rhythmic gait to your movement.

Reminder

Don't look back. Fight the urge to look, because this ability to focus will later help you to not look down while riding. Keep your feet parallel while walking.

> *Rider Insight, Trish:* "*The best part of the weekend was the* Walking Backward *exercise. It was so powerful for me because I have a tendency to rush into things. Recognizing the world was moving toward me instead of me rushing to get to something was incredible. Now when I feel myself get impatient, I remember that it's out there waiting to happen and I can refocus and be intentional about whatever it is I'm waiting for. It has sparked some interesting conversations with my friends, who have pointed out that maybe I don't have to wait—whatever I am looking for is right there ready to happen, and I just have to reach out for it. However I look at it, the exercise has helped me to relax and start to move in the professional and personal directions I want, rather than spinning my wheels and going nowhere fast.*"

Walking backward makes some people feel giddy. One person told me she was transported back to mind-bending feelings she experienced in the 1960s, and she asked, "Is this legal?"

Summary

You've begun to experience the effortless mind-body connection in this first series of exercises. You're *born* with this mind-body connection. Watch an infant respond to someone tickling her toe. Her whole body moves.

Two Types of Mind

There are two types of mind: the sensing or spiritual mind (yi) and the intellectual, analytical mind (shen). The exercises in this chapter help you experience your yi mind, feeling your body rather than intellectualizing about what you're doing. The more you think about your motion, the greater chance you'll get "stuck" thinking it out rather than allowing yourself to experience sensations.

"Don't try to understand yourself with physical seeing."

(adapted from Deng Ming-Dao, from *365 Tao Daily Meditations*)

Use your mind's eye to see within your body as well as outside the body. Remember how you felt before you experienced *Walking Backward*, and then what you felt after. This exercise helps you open up your third eye, because your intent is behind you. This same experience—this faith—will apply to the exercises to come. You'll be able to visualize the effects of the exercises. It's not just faith alone, but also the other tools you'll apply. Every aspect of each exercise has a physical reality, and a physical change takes place that you can measure.

Remember this image, and realize that you, too, always possess that connection. With time and practice, the satisfying moments of deep mind-body connection will come more quickly and last longer.

You'll find it's a challenge to maintain the mind-body connection, because it's easy to be pulled out of this state by distracting thoughts, physical bad habits, or being startled. As you practice, you may even experience moments that frighten you. Don't worry about these reactions; they're entirely normal. Just relax and keep working.

These exercises also started to make you aware of your breath and your intent. Now you have begun to use your breath as the vehicle that takes your mind into your body. By becoming mindful of your breath, you'll prolong and maintain that connection.

In the exercises to come, you'll build on your new awareness of mind and body. You will develop mindfulness of your breath. Your breath and your intent are your most versatile and powerful tools in riding.

The awareness gained from *Walking Backward* prepares you for the subtleties of future exercises, which include using your breath to maintain your own awareness and posture as well as to influence your horse. You will then learn to use your intent to visualize a change in your body prior to it happening—for instance when changing gaits. It's necessary for you to visualize it before it happens. By visualizing, I don't mean developing your logical understanding. This work with mind and body is actually a form of meditation.

What's Next

In chapter 4: "Expanding Our Perspective: Tai Chi's Healing Path and the Gift of the Horse," we will continue to build the foundation of the rest of the book. We will do this foundation work both physically—for instance, doing the first of a series of therapeutic *Laing Gong* exercises—and intellectually, as we consider a variety of perspectives on riding, including balance, injury, and control. We will look at strategies to working with forces larger than ourselves (such as our horses), and finally we'll briefly discuss Tai Chi and other Asian arts.

Expanding Our Perspective

Tai Chi's Healing Path and the Gift of the Horse

4

IN THIS CHAPTER I AM GOING TO CONSIDER A NUMBER of influences on horsemanship to which you might not ordinarily give much thought—but all of which can have a profound effect on your well-being and your riding. These influences range from the psychological to the physical.

Horse as Mirror, Horse as Healer

Horses are a perfect mirror of what is going on inside the rider physically and emotionally. When you are sitting on your horse, his movement is a natural reflection of your own state of physical balance. The horse's attitude and disposition is an accurate reflection of a rider's emotional and spiritual state.

Native American tradition teaches that Great Spirit first placed the animals upon the earth as our teachers. They are closer to nature than the "two-leggeds." The medicine of Horse is that of the healer, and its symbolism is progress of psyche and inner spirit. The horse is incapable of lying. This makes him a very honest partner who offers us an opportunity for learning to be more truthful with others and ourselves.

Let's explore more of the background teachings of *Ride from Within.*

Laing Gong Exercises

Laing Gong is a complete set of therapeutic exercises designed to unblock and create a strong flow of internal energy (chi) throughout the body. This flow is essential to our health and longevity; *Laing Gong* means, in fact, "ultimate health exercise." Beyond the general health benefits of these exercises are gains of particular interest to riders: Laing Gong enhances range of motion in your joints while maintaining the structural balance essential in riding, and through Laing Gong, you develop highly sensitive control of your physical body as well as focus and concentration of the mind.

These exercises are the best way I know of quickly and effectively increasing your body's ability to ride. Remember there is a vital difference between knowing, understanding, and visualizing, and being able to do something physically; your goal is to learn to ride better, not just think about riding better. These exercises will be part of your ongoing work to take what you learn mentally and bring that learning into action in your body.

The Ideas Behind Laing Gong

Your chi meridians and channels function like hoses through which chi flows, much like water in a garden hose. The stretching done in Laing Gong blocks the flow of chi in the meridians—like squeezing a garden hose in the middle—creating back pressure. Upon releasing the stretch, the trapped chi surges forward with much more force than it would naturally have on its own. This surge of chi flushes the meridian, dislodging any blockages. Because of the back pressure created, it is important not to hold the stretch of any Laing Gong exercises for more than one second so as not to damage the meridians. I call this the one-second stretch rule, and I'll remind you of this from time to time. (See chart of meridians in the *Appendix,* p. 250)

You can feel chi in your body in a number ways—as heat, as a pins-and-needles sensation, or even the sensation of electricity moving through the arm. Do not be frightened by these sensations—they are natural and healing. In the beginning, the sensations may be strong. With repeated practice, the intensity of these sensations generally subsides, as the channels have been opened and the chi now flows more freely.

Laing Gong exercises are simple movements designed to unblock your chi. They will help you feel the energy that powers your entire body. Laing Gong is divided into six series. Each series contains six exercises. Each series focuses on healing and strengthening specific areas of the body.

- Series 1–Neck and Shoulders
- Series 2–Back
- Series 3–Hips, Knees, and Ankles
- Series 4–Joints
- Series 5–Tendons and Connective Tissue
- Series 6–Healing Internal Disorders

You'll practice Laing Gong exercises on the ground and from the saddle in the coming chapters. On the next page is an exercise I suggest you practice now.

Laing Gong Palm and Fist

The largest concentration of acupressure and acupuncture points on any given meridian is located from the finger tips to just behind the wrist. The hands reveal tension in the body by the way the fingers move and are held in relaxation. The following exercise will help you understand the precise yet simple movement of the Laing Gong forms and how there is more to each exercise than first meets the eye.

Step-by-Step

1 Hold your hand open with the fingers together and pointing away from your body. The thumb should be at a 90-degree angle from the fingers. The back of the hand and the forearm create a straight line.

2 Holding the hand in this position, feel what is going on. Do you feel tension in the fingers, thumb, wrist, or forearm? Breathe. Relax. Take a moment and let go of the unnecessary tension. The fingers and the thumb should feel as if they are stretching away from the palm of the hand. With the hand held in this manner, the center of the palm (see photo) should be slightly concave and soft.

Steps 1 and 2

3 Slowly close the opened hand into a fist by rolling your fingers down into the palm of the hand and at the same time close the thumb over the outside of your fingers to form the Laing Gong fist. The fist is not clenched; do not squeeze it tight.

4 Once again search for unwanted tension. Is your fist tight? Are the muscles in your forearm tense? If there is tension, let go of it. As you release the tension, does the flatness of the back of the hand and forearm change?

5 Repeat this slow closing and opening of the palm to a fist several times. Find a rhythm in the stretching out of the thumb and fingers from the palm. With just a little practice you will begin to feel energy pumping into your hand. Remember to follow the one-second stretch rule.

Steps 3 and 4: Two views

The main goal of this exercise is for you to begin to see how much unnecessary tension you create when you move—even when performing the simplest of tasks. Once you become aware of this tension, practicing the exercise then teaches you to let go of it and move with greater ease.

Laing Gong exercises also help develop your ability for independent motion, such as moving your spine without moving your limbs. You'll be better able to follow the motion of your horse in your trunk without setting your arms and legs into motion. Every motion is generated from your center, so you can create motion in the horse from inside your body while the outside remains quiet.

The Horse's Natural Balance

Horses move in natural balance, as you see when watching your horse at liberty. Natural balance is distinct from purely athletic balance. Natural balance precedes athletic balance; it is innate in all horses and derives from their integral connection to the natural world, to the earth.

All horses, just like any other sort of athlete, vary in their talent. Some horses move in better athletic balance than others—both at liberty and under saddle. Every horse has to learn how to move in athletic balance when carrying a rider—this is one of the most important skills that a trainer can help a horse develop. Because this book focuses on riders, let's assume that you're riding a trained horse that can move in athletic balance while carrying a rider.

When we change our focus to the rider, I find that the majority of riders tend to unbalance their horses. I have never seen a horse that has less balance than his rider. Your horse compensates for your imbalance—he supports your imbalance and in doing so becomes imbalanced himself.

> *Rider Insight, Judy: While attending one of my clinics, Judy became aware during the groundwork just how restricted the movement of her body had become. She had injured her back four years earlier, and she said that she had only been relatively pain-free for the last year. However, her horse's back was now so tender and sore that he could barely tolerate her sitting in the saddle. Judy could not trace the horse's problems to any disease, injury, or accident. She had owned the horse since birth and was a good, loving owner. She had sought chiropractic help,*

Tai Chi's Internal and External Forces

Americans tend to think of Tai Chi as a slow-motion "health" exercise. What they often don't realize is that Tai Chi is a martial art. In Tai Chi for the equestrian, the secrets of its power are hidden in its motions. The motions of a Tai Chi form are actually martial arts techniques strung together based on a series of attack and counter maneuvers. While I will not focus on the martial aspect of each motion, I will explore the underlying forces that are at the heart of how Tai Chi works.

changed the horse's feed, and used massage. She was considering retiring him if it meant keeping him out of pain.

I cautiously suggested that her horse might have developed his back problems by compensating for hers. After watching the two ride for a few minutes, it was clear that the lack of movement and rigidity in Judy's body was causing the horse to brace against Judy's force. This caused him to hold with muscles that should be relaxed in movement, and therefore created misalignment in his spine. Many horses would not have tolerated this unfair balancing act and simply would have resisted being ridden at all.

By our working on Judy's body movement and breathing, she was able to improve her balance and relax her horse. By no means can Tai Chi "fix" a problem years in the making in a one-hour session—it takes a lot of consistent work to cure such an issue of balance. The good news is that Judy is no longer treating her horse's symptoms and has discovered the root cause of his pain.

Let's say, over time, you've slowly lost your natural balance. Bad habits moved in and have disturbed your original, natural alignment. You may have forgotten what it feels like to be well-aligned and balanced—both naturally and athletically. The good news is that you can still regain these abilities and feelings.

Use the exercises in this book both on the ground and on your horse; they will help you develop your natural balance and your athletic balance. Remember that your goals are physical and spiritual. Don't underestimate the power of the horse as healer.

When you understand how Tai Chi works as a martial art, you can begin to see its direct relationship with riding. Understanding the difference between internal and external force is essential. In classic Tai Chi thought, internal energy is synonymous with chi, and its application in force is called *fah jing. Fah* means "to project" and *jing* means "internal power."

Internal Force

Internal force refers to the way you generate power through your entire body. Your internal forces produce your position and keep your body in rhythm. You create internal force and direct it from the center (your Dain Tian) of your body.

> "The internal energy should be extended, and vibrate like the beat of a drum. The spirit should be condensed in toward the center of your body."
>
> *(Tai Chi Classics)*

For your purposes, consider internal force as any motion originating from your center directed by your mind. The motion works in harmony with the natural laws described in chapter 2. You direct your internal forces, starting with your mind directing your breath. You breathe through your abdomen, and you gain control of your center (see *Dain Tians,* p. 19).

As you sit on the horse, you redirect or influence the internal force of the horse with your internal force. This is the meaning of joining energy. Ideally when you sit relaxed, aligned, and balanced, your horse will move by using only his natural, internal energy, rather than having to use external force or strength.

External Force

External force is any power you create using muscle to move an isolated part of your body, such as when you squeeze your thighs to hold yourself onto the saddle or pull back on the reins with your arms by tensing your shoulders and tightening the biceps.

External force disconnects one part of your body from the rest through tension. When the motion of any part of your body does not move in concert with the overall flow of momentum in the body as a whole, it becomes disconnected and your power is fragmented. For example, picture yourself riding and maintaining your center over the horse's center (joined). You are moving your whole body in rhythmic waves of force. However, when you apply a leg aid, you tighten—and tense—your thigh to produce the aid. In creating that force, you have disconnected your thigh from the flow of momentum and natural power of the body.

Remember when you use external force, whether it's to maintain your own balance or influence your horse, you disconnect from the greater flow of your combined energy. Not only do you disrupt the natural rhythm of your body, but you also interfere with the horse's natural rhythm.

You are the horse's "guest." You sit on his weakest point—the center of his spine—suspended between his structural supports, his legs—by only the strength of his muscles. You sit in the saddle and govern his movements through your influence.

Rider-Based Issues

Injuries and Compensation

Most people have at some time in their life been injured, and if so, their bodies carry the memories of these past traumas. Some people are conscious of these memories; others are not. Whether conscious or not, everyone who has been injured compensates for the injury to one degree or another.

If you have been hurt, you may find that in compensating you create imbalance, misalignment, and stress in your body. You compensate both mentally and physically, and both types directly affect your horse. Here are some real examples from friends and students of mine.

One friend, who had been riding only a few years, was on the trail when her horse spooked and bolted. She held on as best she could for nearly a quarter mile, until she was thrown as her horse turned to miss a fence. She was very lucky that she escaped with only a few bruised ribs when her body came to a stop against the fence. Her horse ran off and was not found for three days. He was also fine—a bit scratched up and dirty, but none the worse for wear.

I first began to work with the two of them in an indoor arena, and they looked relaxed and moved quite well together. Then we moved to the outdoor arena, which had no fence, just a rail on the ground defining the edges.

The rider became tense and tight in her upper body, and she began to hunch over her horse. The entire change in her physical body was because she was afraid to lose control, and this is certainly understandable. The problem was that the position of her body created not the connection and confidence she wanted, but exactly the opposite: disconnection and fear. I could tell by watching her horse that he was reacting to her position and fear by becoming distracted, and increasingly paying more attention to what was "out there" than to her. She was a good example of how emotional compensation affects the body.

Asian Healing Arts

Traditional Chinese medicine is based on the concept that chi is the animating force of life, and without it there is no life. Practitioners believe that everything contains chi—plants, animals, rocks, and air—and that there is a free flow of chi through all things in the universe. Sickness is the result of either a lack of chi or its stagnation. The goal of acupuncture and acupressure is to stimulate and move this chi through the body. Acupuncture uses needles applied to specific points on the chi meridians in the body to move your unseen life force. Acupressure uses finger pressure or massage to stimulate chi flow.

You and Your Horse: Food for Thought

Finish these sentences to help you assess your strengths and weaknesses:

I can ride _____ minutes a day.

I have _____ (more/less) energy after I ride than before I started.

My horse feels _____ (tense/relaxed) when I start to ride.

When my horse shies, I react by _____.

When I see myself ride in photographs or videos, I am smiling ___ percent of the time.

Now answer yes or no:

When my horse evades my aids, I become more active with my hands, legs, and seat.

When I half-halt my horse, I tense up.

I am aware of my body's breathing when I ride.

I am aware of my body's rhythm when I ride.

I am aware of my horse's breathing when I ride.

An example of physical compensation is that of a cowboy I worked with, who had been living with mild but constant back pain for years. He was in his fifties and rode mostly for pleasure by this time in his life. During a weekend lesson, I noticed he always rode with one hand on the reins and one hand firmly placed on his thigh. When I asked him why, he said it was just comfortable and a habit. Upon further investigation I learned of his back pain, and we came to discover that his hand on his thigh was really a way to brace his back against the motion of the horse.

The problem as I saw it was that his bracing was actually prolonging the back injury by protecting it. By keeping one hand on his thigh, he was actually bypassing his spine. The force created by the movement of his horse was transferred through his arm and hand into his leg and then into his seat. Pretty smart on his part! In bypassing the spine, his lower back did not have to negotiate the force down through it, and it remained tight and rigid. This compensation strategy kept the area "safe," but it also kept it from healing. Only through relaxing the smaller muscles of the lumbar can they move, heal, gain strength, and begin at another level to trust the brain again.

Innate Fear of Falling

We all have an innate fear of falling. Unless we have trained ourselves to overcome this fear, we carry it with us on and off the horse. I'm not suggesting that everyone who rides should first learn how to fall, although for some it would definitely help. However, I do believe that it is beneficial to understand how your body reacts to and compensates for this fear.

If you begin to lose your balance, your body immediately starts to tense up and you hold your breath. This tension is the body's attempt to hold itself in balance. Unfortunately, if you were not in alignment when you began to lose your balance, you have already compromised your structural support and you cannot rebalance yourself. Your next reaction is to reach out to hold onto something or someone, in an attempt to keep from falling further. If that is of no avail, you continue to fall and the last thing your body does before hitting the ground is to close its eyes—and then, thud.

In the saddle, if you begin to lose your balance even slightly, your body reacts with tension. This tightening of the abdomen (to protect the internal organs) causes you to hold your breath. If that does the trick and you catch your balance, no big deal. You just have to remember to breathe and let go of the tension in your abdomen and torso, and within a few strides you may regain your connection with your horse. If you cannot catch your balance, you next try to reach out to regain it. Typically your elbows jut out, your hands come up and out, and you push your head forward.

Practitioners of martial arts such as Tai Chi recognized early on the inevitability of falling and hitting the ground, and they realized that the only thing they truly had any control over was how they hit the ground. There is a saying in martial arts: "I'm not interested in hitting or kicking an opponent—I'm interested in capturing his spine. It is then just a matter of steps before he hits the ground. And the ground never misses and hits much harder than I."

In your own riding watch for the patterns of tensing and movement associated with the fear of falling. Realize that balance is the key to preventing falling in the first place, and Tai Chi can help you gain the alignment that underlies improved balance.

Control Issues

> *Rider Insight, Jenny:* "*Lack of power: that is our dilemma. If I just could get my horse to listen, to go where I tell her, to behave while I'm grooming her, to pay attention to my aids, and to stop scratching and pulling on the bit. Then I could focus on me, my breath, my body.*"

Some riders are under the illusion that their horses are in their lives for them to control. They feel that if they gain control over their horses, it will empower them in other areas of their lives where they feel out of control.

Horses *are* in our lives to empower and heal us, but not through our controlling them. No person is bigger and stronger than a horse, and without the advantage of tack most people could never ride. Horses are a gift, and our teachers, if we choose to listen.

Remember that the horse's gift to man is *healing*. Horses help you get inside yourself. They have the ability to expose your greatest weaknesses and strengths. You probably take better care of your horse than you do yourself. Your horse puts you in touch with your unconditional love and compassion. If you listen, he lets you know when you're carrying anger, frustration, and fear. By spending a few hours with your horse, you can let go of negative emotions. The next time you doubt the healing nature of the horse, spend a day at a therapeutic riding center and see the gift in action.

The whole of this book deals with the unintentional, unconscious disconnection of mind and body and how to regain this connection. This disconnectedness separates us not only from our true divine nature but also from our fellow man and woman. It keeps our eyes fixed on the symptoms as it distracts us from the root causes of our pain. If not for the gift of the horse, some of us would go through our lives never knowing we were separated from ourselves.

Your Horse as a Larger, Stronger Force

Your horse probably weighs between 900 and 1200 pounds. Stand beside him, and notice how much bigger and longer his head is than your head. Feel the size of his

Tai Chi and Other Asian Arts

You'll find similarities among Tai Chi, yoga, and transcendental meditation. I see hundreds of similarities, because all were developed to improve the human mind–body connection. Each discipline recognizes that this connection is vital when on the path of spiritual development. The goals of these arts are the same. The difference is that Tai Chi is bound by martial laws.

The history of riding as well as Tai Chi finds its roots in the martial arts. Cross country, dressage and jumping all developed from battle. You ride to the battle, you fight while mounted on your horse, and you ride back. Consider the great mounted battles of the past where there were as many as 80,000 warriors on each side. What chaos—what a challenge!

In the midst of this confusion, a warrior had to control his horse from his center because he held a sword in one hand and a shield in the other. He didn't rely on the reins to guide the horse. To survive, he had to control his horse's motion from his center. This concept might seem a bit much for those of you who enjoy a leisurely weekend trail ride. Nonetheless, the concepts in this book and their applications to riding have been proven over centuries of mounted warfare. Empires were built and conquered on the backs of horses by skilled warriors who understood the necessity of being one with their horse.

chest—the horse's lungs are huge. They fill most of his chest cavity, which can measure 72 inches, or 6 feet, around. If you saw a photograph of the two of you from the back, you'd see that his haunches are gigantic in comparison to yours! If you were dealing with a human of these proportions, I'm quite sure there would be much less telling and commanding and a lot more asking and listening.

When your horse moves, he must manage a tremendous amount of momentum due to his great weight. This momentum is a force that you can never stop with strength alone; at best you can only influence it. This limitation is demonstrated particularly clearly in jumping: once the horse has left the ground there is very little you can do until the horse lands.

Similarly, in the middle of a canter pirouette when the horse is at the apex of his upward motion, you can influence the way he comes to the ground, but you certainly can't stop the horse from coming down. The reason I point out the obvious in these examples is that as riders we sometimes believe that we always control the movements of our horse. In other words, we always lead, when in fact there are times that the best we can do is follow.

Power

Any horse can easily out-walk, out-jog, and outrun you. A horse can pull much more than his own massive weight. He can jump higher and farther than any human. The horse can also resist you in many ways, due to his superior size and strength. He can halt his forward impulsion, balk completely, back up, choose his own direction, rear, buck, or even lie down and refuse to get up.

In the saddle, you typically only feel his power when he pulls against your rein contact or bulges against your leg aid. On the ground, you are more likely to experience his awesome power, such as on those occasions where he might push you against a wall, or throw his weight back against the pressure of a lead rope.

Because horses are generous creatures, they allow you to mount them and direct them in activities like dressage, jumping, reining, and barrel racing. His size and strength, partnered with your skill and tact, make you and your horse partners in equestrian sport.

Your horse is an external force, separate from you but in many ways closer to the "supreme ultimate" that is Tai Chi. The horse moves with chi. He moves more in harmony with the universe, with fewer distractions than you. Your horse gives you a great rhythm to connect with—you feel the grace and power and are better for the experience. Consider your horse your teacher.

Summary

Now you have had your first taste of Laing Gong, the healing exercises that I will return to in chapter 6 in much greater depth. You have also explored some of the physical, psychological, and spiritual aspects of working with horses and riding. All this is food for thought for the curious equestrian. Let your curiosity draw you into all the work in this book. There is a great deal of fascinating work in the coming chapters.

What's Next

In chapter 5, "Your Breath: Learning to Breathe and Connect with Your Horse," you will deepen your understanding of Tai Chi by delving into one of its most fundamental tools: breath. Breath awareness and control is central to Tai Chi's goals of cultivating and balancing the flow of life force—chi—in your bodies. While this may sound mysterious or impractical, all the exercises in the next chapter have a direct application to riding—as well as, of course, enhancing your general health.

Your Breath

5

Learning to Breathe and Connect with Your Horse

THOUSANDS OF YEARS AGO IN CHINA, Taoist monks formulated the idea of an ultimate underlying power in the universe. They believed that this unseen power was responsible for life and order on earth and in the heavens. They called this power Chi, which means air, energy, motion, and power. Chi is the mother of Yin and Yang, and flows ceaselessly between two opposites; this flow joins the positive and negative at every level in the universe, and it is in this connection that we can find balance.

In Tai Chi we refer to chi as our internal energy. Tai Chi seeks to increase and balance the chi in our bodies through meditation and through movement. The exercises and breathing techniques in this chapter will engage

Breath and intent: the mind directs breath down into the abdomen where it is energized and stirs the chi (red arrows), and then directs the movement of the chi throughout the body (purple arrows).

your mind and body in both. When I use the word "meditation," I simply mean to focus on one thing with a calm and open mind. And, when I use the word "movement," I am speaking not just of the movement of your limbs, but also the movement of your breath.

Breathing is a perfect metaphor for life. Breathing *is* life. Breath is what we have in common with everything—the balance of nature and its pairing of Yin and Yang. For example, we share a perfectly complementary respiration with plants: they take in the carbon dioxide we exhale and produce oxygen; we take in the oxygen they give off and produce carbon dioxide.

And here's another example of Yin and Yang: there are only two breaths that don't come in pairs—your first and your last. At all other times, they are parts of a whole: inhalation and exhalation.

Breathing is for the most part an unconscious act. Thank goodness for that, because if we had to remember to breathe, most of us would not be here to read this book. You breathe in and out over 23,000 times a day. That's a lot of opportunity for practice and change.

Breathing is your body's natural metronome. Breathing sets the rhythm of your body, and rhythm is the key to timing. Without it you leave timing to chance, and timing is the key to transitions in speed, direction, and gait.

When you truly connect with your breath, your breathing synchronizes with your horse. Many times while I'm working with a rider on moving her breath down into the belly, as her breath drops, I hear the horse let out a sigh of relaxation. As you know, I often refer to the horse as your greatest teacher. If you listen to how your horse is breathing at any given gait, it will be a clue as to how you should breathe at that same gait.

If you're not in control of your breath, you're not in complete control of your body and balance. The question I most commonly ask riders is, "Where is your breath?" I ask this to remind them of the importance of breathing—especially when learning, because often when we are trying hard to do some new task, we tend to hold our breath. When you hold your breath you are cut off from your body. The exercises in this chapter help you discover where your breath is and how to better control your breathing.

Expanding Your Center through Breathing

You use your breath as a tool to expand your center. Physically, you can expand (increase the volume of) your center, your Dain Tian, by breathing. Abdominal breathing effectively expands your center, thereby making it easier to stay balanced. As your diaphragm pushes down on your internal organs, you learn to let go with the external muscles around your abdomen and pelvis. This letting go allows for freer movement of your joints in those areas, making it easier to stay with your horse.

Imagine your center is a balloon that expands as you breathe air down into it.

You can't expand your center with force, and you can't develop muscles to expand your center. As far as your muscles are concerned, expanding your center means letting go of the tension held in your abdomen, and one of the most effective ways to release this tension is through abdominal breathing. Your center, you may be surprised to learn, can extend outside your body because your center incorporates not just bone and muscle but also breathe, awareness, and intent, all of which can expand into the space around you.

Chinese Tai Chi master Ma Yueh-liang, who was an expert in "Push Hands" (a two-man form of sparring in Tai Chi), said, "How can I be defeated when I can put my center behind you? How can you ever uproot me when my center is bigger than both of us, and it's behind you?" Ma Yueh-liang had 60 years of daily training. He was able to stand on one leg, and no one could uproot him. Imagine how balanced you'd be if you could put your center under your horse, or if you expanded your center so much that it encompassed you and your horse.

You can only expand your center through abdominal breathing and developing that combination of awareness and intent that I discussed in chapter 2. One of your goals is to transform your everyday breathing to match an old saying in Tai Chi: "Breathe in as if you're smelling a flower; breathe out as if you're playing a flute."

As an infant, you naturally breathed from your abdomen. Unfortunately, at around age five or six, you—like most children—probably began to breathe up in your chest. The good news is that you knew how to breathe into the belly once a long time ago, and now you just need to relearn, to remember how.

Abdominal breathing is also your first key to opening your gates. The first two you can open with breath are those of your center, Gate 1: The Dain Tian, and Gate 2: The Ming Meng. By opening these gates you begin to stimulate the flow of chi in the body and start to release the tension that separates you from your horse. Think about the power of air (chi). Air penetrates the strongest fortress. You've probably learned to try to protect yourself by holding your body like a fortress, with your muscles tense and locked up. You've built up armor on your outside. In that state, even with bodywork and massage it's difficult to get behind the armor in order to help you relax. Breathing will help you get in behind the walls that you have built and expand your body from within. Use your intent to drop your breath down into your abdomen. Imagine a tube that enables you to send your breath to your abdomen, just as you see in the drawing on page 88.

You'll practice *opening all your gates* in the breathing exercises. Envision the gates lined up, one behind the other. You open them sequentially: you open the first to get to the second, the second to get to the third, and so on. That is, you open Gate 1: The Dain Tian before you open Gate 2: The Ming Meng, and with the opening of the Ming Meng you can then open Gate 3: The Front of the Heart. It progresses in this way through all Eight Gates. When your last gate, Gate 8: The Crown, is open, you can return to the Dain Tian and open it even more, then expand the Ming Meng more, and so on. One gate's opening or expansion makes possible the opening or expansion of the next.

Once you have become proficient at opening the Eight Gates in sequence through breathing and intent, you will no longer have to open them in sequence. With experience, you will be able to open any gate at any time by just asking with your intent. *Opening the gates* is a series of awarenesses, of realizations—and of these there is no end.

As I mentioned earlier, although my Tai Chi teacher, Wen Mei Yu has been practicing for 40 years, she says we can always let go of more. "Even after all these years," she told me one day, "I need to relax my fingers more." You can always move to another more subtle, more powerful, level.

Influencing the Horse with Your Breath

On the path of mind, breath, and body, breathing is the way you introduce the mind to the body to develop a more conscious mind-body connection. Your breath also connects you with your horse. Your breath is the first thing your horse hears, a wordless whisper, one of the subtle ways you communicate with your horse. Breathing may tell the horse more than your physical body does. When you're approaching a transition, do you hold your breath? If you do, you immediately begin to tense your body, and in doing so, you tell the horse that something is worrisome—and because he's a sensitive flight animal, he may prepare to run. At the very least you are distracting him from the task of being your graceful and balanced partner.

Inhale and bring your breath down into your abdomen, which should expand out from the spine in all directions, just as when you inflate an ordinary balloon it expands symmetrically. Asymmetrical expansion indicates the presence of tension.

When the wind blows a leaf into your arena, do you typically react by holding your breath? If you're startled, you breathe high and short into your chest—and so does your horse! When anything goes wrong and you hold your breath, you tell your horse that something bad *is* going on. Your fear may never disappear completely, but by keeping your breath down and relaxed you can lower your center into the horse for greater security. You exhale when the surprise is over. It's the sigh of relief, a natural relaxant. The sigh is you letting go.

Tension can also have internal causes, including fear, anger, resentment, stress, and frustration. When you come to the barn, check in with yourself before you ride to see if you carried any of these negative emotions in with you. If you did, release them before you ride by doing a brief warm-up of *Standing Meditation* (p. 37) and *Abdominal Breathing*, a new exercise I'll describe on page 90.

Regardless of the tension's origin, are you aware of the moments when you hold your breath? Rarely is it enough for me to say to a rider, "You're holding your breath." Remembering to breathe deeply is far easier to think about than to do. For most riders there is a pattern to their breath-holding. My experience from working with hundreds of riders is that they hold their breath when going into a transition or when the horse does not respond favorably to an aid.

Let's look at this a little closer and ask yourself if this could be you. You approach the transition and inhale and hold your breath when you begin to give the aid for the next gait. It could be that you hold it because you've tensed your muscles in giving the aid and in doing so you've lost your balance a bit. (And remember that most riders hold their breath as soon as they begin to lose their balance.) Or, perhaps you inhale and hold your breath because you're never sure of what your horse's response will be to an aid, and so you brace for a possible overreaction. In either case, when you've completed the transition and realize that you weren't breathing, you exhale to relax.

Here's a test: take a deep breath, hold your breath, and listen to your body. Hold your breath as long as you possibly can, and feel the tension rise up in your body. Tension rises—relaxation sinks. Have you ever felt this same sensation while riding?

Because tension rises in your body, to relax you must let go of tension. Tension doesn't disappear. It seeks ground, just as electricity seeks the easiest path to earth. Imagine tension—like electricity—traveling down through your bones. Whether you are on your feet or mounted, abdominal breathing helps direct the released tension down through your body to the ground.

The automatic nature of breathing is both a strength and a weakness: because you don't have to think about it, you are not aware of its power. To change your breathing, you have to bring it out of the unconscious mind and into the conscious mind. If you're 50 years old, you've likely experienced over 45 years of shallow breathing. Changing your breathing will require daily practice.

Breath and Spirit

Breath is the root of spirituality. Nearly all religious sects use song as a means to praise or become closer to their creator. Have you ever sung in a choir? You focus on your breath, and you are connected to your body when you sing. That unconscious connection occurs because you sing from the abdomen. When monks chant, their song enables them to become completely present and fully conscious—and the vehicle to this place is the breath. Breath engages the conscious mind with unconscious intent. When you breathe from the abdomen, you are closer to nature.

Abdominal Breathing

Riding Goals: Relaxation, Awareness

The goal of this exercise is to be in constant control of your breath while mounted. Your goal is to move your breath into the abdomen, and in order to do so, your abdomen must become relaxed without sacrificing your structural alignment. When you relax, your lower back, pelvis, and spine will move freely within your center. In return, this freer movement deepens the seat and allows you to match the rhythm of the horse. Matching the horse's rhythm is another way of becoming one with your horse. When you ride in this way, your horse has to spend much less energy and focus balancing you on his back. When you match your horse, you allow him to move more freely and effectively in any gait.

Function

Abdominal breathing expands your thoracic cavity downward. The benefits of deep abdominal breathing are many. Here are a few—you'll discover more with time.

- Increased vital capacity of the heart and lungs
- Greater unity of mind and body
- Smoother, more rhythmic body motions
- Reduced stress, especially in the lower back and shoulders
- Deeper, natural relaxation and released tension
- Freer, unlocked energy centers (gates) within the body
- Fewer injuries

Intent

Use your mind to direct your breath down into your Dain Tian, and then locate and identify any tension in your body. Use your mind to "think in"—to direct or see with your mind the intended action of your body (or bodies, such as you and your horse) a moment prior to manifesting the physical action.

Step-by-Step

Unmounted

1 Begin in *Standing Meditation* so that you can enter the exercise from a quiet, centered place (p. 37).

2 Place your hands in front of your abdomen with your palms facing your body. Create a diamond shape with your fingers by placing the tips of the thumbs together and the tips of your index fingers together.

3 Place your thumbs on your belly button, and your palms against your abdomen.

4 Exhale completely while gently "sucking in" your stomach. Focus your mind on the space inside the diamond, and feel your hands against your belly.

Steps 2 and 3

5 Inhale, and use your mind to direct your breath down into the abdomen. You will feel your belly pushing out against your hands as you breathe in.

6 Exhale, and repeat. Try to take long, smooth, deep breaths. As you exhale, feel your stomach return to its relaxed state.

In the beginning, practice abdominal breathing for one minute at a time. As you become successful at expanding your abdomen by inhaling and filling your lungs completely, you may increase the time to suit your needs. Five minutes of abdominal breathing while in *Standing Meditation* is a wonderful way to release stress in your body and mind prior to riding.

The Simplicity and Power of Breath

The fluidity on horseback that you can achieve through abdominal breathing exemplifies all the Eight Principles we discussed earlier:

- Use the mind, not force
- Never oppose force with force
- Yield and overcome
- Balance like a scale
- Seek stillness in motion
- Be heavy and light
- Focus and expand
- Remember that art is long, life is short.

Western culture tends to value the complex. Breath is overlooked because of its apparent simplicity. Tai Chi understands the profound power of the simple.

Step 2

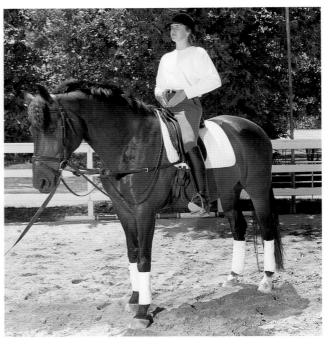

Step 4

Mounted

As you may have already discovered from your groundwork, retraining the way you breathe takes a great deal of focus and concentration. You have to be able to focus completely on your breath and body while you practice; you don't want to be distracted by your horse. Therefore, begin the exercise with your horse either in a round pen or on the longe line. Because horses react, sometimes strongly, to the rider's breath, you'll need a friend to direct your horse. Your hands will then be free of the reins and you'll be free to concentrate.

1 Begin in *Sitting Meditation* (p. 40).

2 Start at the walk (later you'll progress to the trot and canter). While walking on a 20-meter circle or the perimeter of a round pen, become aware of where your breath is in your body. Is it up in your chest or down in your belly? Your arms should

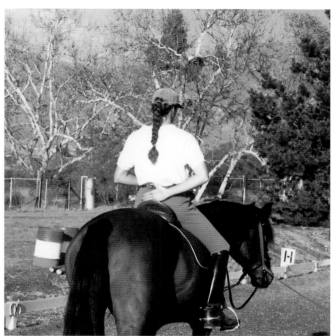

Step 9 and 10: Two views

hang at your sides. Allow the motion of the horse and gravity to lengthen your arms, and feel the weight of your arms pulling your shoulders down.

3 Form a "diamond" with your hands, just as you did in the unmounted portion of this exercise. Place your thumbs on your belly button with your palms lying against your abdomen.

4 Focus your mind on the space inside the "diamond." Use your mind to direct your breath down into your abdomen.

5 As you inhale, feel your belly push out against your hands. As you exhale, feel your stomach shrink away from your hands.

6 Repeat this exercise completing at least 3 circles.

When you're sitting well with your breath dropped down in your abdomen, the motion of your horse will often feel bigger and rounder. Your hips and upper body may now be moving more rhythmically.

James On Your Shoulder

Imagine your breath dropping down into your pelvic girdle and groin area. Feel these areas relax and expand. Your breath should be smooth and natural— don't force it. Think about allowing the motion of the horse to help move your breath down.

7 At this time briefly turn your attention to your horse. Do you feel that he is more relaxed and moving more freely underneath you? Your horse's breathing pattern may have changed, having become more regular and relaxed.

8 Change direction and practice this exercise making at least 3 circles in the new direction.

9 After you have had some success breathing into your belly, move your inside hand behind your back, placing the backside of the hand against your lower back (the Ming Meng). Your outside hand remains on your belly. Through your hands, feel whether or not your lower back expands as you breathe in. Remember that the abdomen can expand away from the center of the body in all directions just as a balloon can expand in all directions.

10 With your hands still in place—front and back—walk 2 complete circles. Feel the movement of your body.

Focus your mind on the area under your hand on your lower back. Imagine that area filling with air and becoming soft. In the beginning, it might help if you round your lower back to make room for the breath. Rounding the lower back can create freedom of movement in the lumbar area of the spine. Can you feel your spine being moved by the horse? Feel how the horse moves you. Can you feel the moments where you can move your seat without interfering with the rhythm of your horse?

You won't hold the position of rounding your back. To find your center, you must first define the outside edges, and this is an outside edge. The origins of this rounding come from the abdomen and lumbar, not the tailbone or seat. This is not tucking or pulling the tailbone under. Without the ability to move the lower spine independently of the rest of the spine, most riders will tuck the tailbone in an attempt to round or soften the lower back. You may want to return to *Wall Sitting* (p. 59) to help you develop a more independent motion of the lower lumbar spine.

11 When you are able to incorporate *Abdominal Breathing* successfully at the walk, try it at the trot and canter. Ideally, you will be working on a longe line so that your hands will be free to feel your body. If you are in a round pen and must hold the reins, alternate the hand holding the reins to free the other hand to feel your body.

Ah-Ha!

As you begin to drop your breath, you will feel more stable and relaxed. You will become more aware of unnecessary tension in the body and be able to release it as you exhale. Your mind will become clearer and your body will feel lighter.

Your Dain Tian is the home of your chi. A good belly laugh opens your Dain Tian, so ask a friend to tell you a good joke while you ride. When you laugh, you relax and don't try so hard to hold your position. Laugh on your horse, and it changes your seat.

I also recommend riding bareback at the walk. You can gain so much: a better sense of the horse's movement and rhythm; a better sense of your own movement and rhythm; and an ever-increasing general sense of confidence on horseback, coupled with an ever-diminishing sense of fear of riding or falling.

> *Rider Insight, Silke: Silke experienced severe back pain. When she rode her young Friesian stallion, she realized she was holding her spine rigid and tight. When she started focusing on her breathing, she was able to relax her lower back. She worked on breathing both on and off the horse. After she'd completed three sessions of breathing while mounted, she found her pain had disappeared.*

Ability Transition

Throughout the day, you will begin to catch yourself whenever you hold your breath. With a little experience, you will notice that this holding is always preceded by physical or emotional stress. As abdominal breathing becomes natural, you will find yourself thinking less and feeling more.

Reminder

Remember that you breathe in and out over 23,000 times a day. Your body may not be used to the larger amount of oxygen abdominal breathing supplies to your lungs, and it is common in the first days of practice to feel a bit light-headed or dizzy. Do not be alarmed, because your body will soon get used to the increased oxygen, and the light-headedness will disappear.

Many of my students, after having practiced a few days, have a breakthrough while lying in bed just before they fall asleep. Up until now, breathing for most of you has been an unconscious habit. Now I am asking you to make a conscious effort to change the manner in which you breathe. When you master abdominal breathing, you'll find it an exciting accomplishment and it will become an automatic function of your body. You'll no longer have to think about it, because it will happen naturally.

You may be concerned about keeping the appearance of a flat, hard stomach, even while breathing from the belly. The strength training to get those "abs" works your exterior muscles. You can make your muscles so taut that they won't expand, but to breathe from the abdomen, your muscles must be elastic so that they can relax. There is a balance that must be reached—hard flat abs that aren't flexible are the equivalent of being muscle-bound in the abdomen.

Counting Your Breath

Riding Goals: Rhythm, Awareness

Your horse hears your breath. When you are not in control of your breath, you are not in control of your horse. *Counting Your Breath* helps you gain control of your breath, which in turn creates your rhythm.

Function

Counting Your Breath increases your awareness of your own body and the horse's. You will find the rhythm of your breath, and the rhythm of your breath—its cadence—sets the rhythm of your body. When you are more connected to your own body and its natural rhythm, you allow the horse to find his own rhythm.

Intent

Counting the breath demands the complete attention of your mind on your body. This attention develops your focus and concentration.

Step-by-Step

Mounted

As with *Abdominal Breathing*, this exercise is most effective if done in a round pen or on a longe line. Ask a friend for assistance so that you can concentrate on the exercise while he or she directs your horse.

1 Begin in *Sitting Meditation.*

2 Start at the walk. For the first few minutes, just focus on your breath. Are you breathing from the abdomen? If not, allow yourself the time to drop your breath down to your belly.

3 Count the number of breaths you take on a complete circle. To keep things consistent, count one inhalation and the accompanying exhalation as one breath.

How many did you take? Say the number out loud to yourself or your longe partner.

4 Repeat the counting for 2 more circles. Did the number of breaths you took change? The more relaxed and connected you become with your body, the fewer breaths you will take on the circle.

5 Now you'll repeat the counting at the trot. As you ask for the trot, notice whether you are breathing in or out.

It is not the inhaling or exhaling that is important; it is your awareness that's important.

6 Count the number of breaths you take on a complete circle again, and say the number out loud to yourself or your longe partner. Notice how the rhythm of your breath changes at the trot in comparison to the walk.

Ah-Ha!

You will realize that you are breathing in rhythm with your motion.

Ability Transition

As you practice this exercise, you will be less prone to becoming distracted or losing track of the count, and the number of breaths you take will decrease as your lung capacity increases and breathing relaxes.

Reminder

Throughout this and all the breathing exercises, don't force a change in your breathing patterns. In the saddle, you should feel relaxed and calm. Allow your breath to drop lower into your belly.

Open the Ming Meng

Open the Ming Meng teaches you to let go of tension in your lower back through abdominal breathing.

Function

The exercise opens the Ming Meng, which relaxes and engages the lower lumbar region of your back, allowing your seat to move more freely with the horse. *Opening the Ming Meng* also allows the energy of the horse to move up through your seat into the rest of your body.

Intent

Use your mind to direct your breath into your lower back area. Expand and open the Ming Meng, inviting your horse's energy up.

Step-by-Step

Unmounted

Before starting this exercise, review *Wall Sitting* (p. 59). The practice of wall sitting introduces you to the physical motion of opening the Ming Meng. Combining that knowledge with your intent is the key to learning how to *Open the Ming Meng* while standing or riding your horse.

1 Begin in *Standing Meditation*.

2 Practice a few deep abdominal breaths to relax the belly. (Review, if necessary, *Abdominal Breathing*, p. 90.)

3 Slowly and completely exhale all the air from your lungs while you slightly "suck in" your gut.

4 Slowly begin to inhale into your abdomen, allowing your belly to expand. As your belly expands, move your intent to your lower back. While continuing to inhale, slightly round your lower back (the same motion as in *Wall Sitting*), and allow your

back to expand with your breath. It will feel as if your tailbone is dropping toward the ground.

You may find it helpful to imagine a weight attached by a string to your tailbone that helps pull it down. However, this visualization sometimes causes riders to try to force the tailbone to drop—this is not correct. Dropping of the tailbone is the *result* of expanding and moving the lumbar region, not the cause. During the mounted portion of this exercise it is impossible to move your tailbone down without causing a great deal of tension in your thighs and seat. On the other hand, moving the lumbar region with your intent is effortless and this is your goal.

5 Exhale and let your belly and back shrink and contract.

6 Repeat Steps 1 through 5 until your back expands freely with your breath and intent.

Mounted

You will do the mounted practice of this exercise at the walk. I suggest riding in a large arena so that you won't have to divert your attention to changing direction because you're running out of space. Riding along a straight trail also works well. If neither are available, that's okay—just be aware of the distractions that will pull your intent away from your body.

1 Begin in *Sitting Meditation*.

2 Walk forward and take a few deep abdominal breaths. Allow your belly to relax and expand with each inhalation.

3 Exhale completely and become aware of the sucking in of your belly. If the exhalation causes you to tense up in your back or abdomen, repeat Steps 2 and 3 until you are completely relaxed in your body while breathing.

4 As you inhale and your belly begins to expand, move your intent to your lower back (the Ming Meng). Use your intent and breath to allow the lower back to relax and expand.

Use your intent to combine the experience of *Wall Sitting* and the groundwork portion of this exercise. As your Ming Meng opens, you will feel more connection with the horse through your seat. You may experience some discomfort in your seat bones until they've become accustomed to staying in complete contact with the leather of the saddle.

When I first started riding and was experimenting with the opening of the Ming Meng, I experienced an innate fear of letting go with my lower back. Upon investigation I found this fear had nothing to do with my back, but it had to do with my front, with the anatomical differences between men and women. When any rider lets go and opens the Ming Meng there will be more contact, both front and back, with the saddle. For men this can occasionally produce great discomfort, particularly at the trot and canter. The first step in overcoming this problem is to purchase riding attire that provides maximum support. The second step is to continue to develop a more centered and secure seat, and all the exercises in this book will help you with that.

Ah-Ha!

You will begin to experience the sensation of your intent moving your breath in your body. You will feel the skin covering your lower back stretching with the expansion. Imagine the skin of a balloon stretching as it inflates.

Ability Transition

When your body has become familiar with this newfound movement, you will begin to be able to open the Ming Meng by simply willing it open. You will couple the experience and ability developed on the ground and direct it with your intent.

Reminder

Forcing the Ming Meng open is not possible, and trying to do so is very counterproductive. If you aren't successful, don't worry. Relax and review the groundwork, including *Counting Your Breath* (p. 97), to build a stronger foundation. Eventually your breath will fill your abdomen like water poured into a glass, the gathering energy filling you from the bottom up, not from the top down.

Embracing the Moon

Riding Goals: Position, Seat

Embracing the Moon will teach you to train your breath to move down into the abdomen while keeping your upper body relaxed, engaged, and open. This form allows the horse more freedom of motion in his front end. It puts your upper body, arms, and wrists into the optimum alignment for holding the reins, and it creates a higher awareness and sensitivity in your hands.

Function

This exercise teaches you to use your arms, chest, and upper back in a more balanced and effective manner, while developing consistent abdominal breathing. It keeps you from bracing with your chest.

Intent

You'll envision a large sphere embraced within your arms. Imagine that your arms are supported by and held round by the sphere. With every breath, your arms become lighter and rounder. After learning the exercise's movements, focus your mind on the area inside the sphere within your arms. Imagine your breath filling the sphere and expanding it until it encompasses your whole body.

Step-by-Step

Unmounted

1 Begin in *Standing Meditation.*

2 Next perform *Sink and Circulate the Chi* (p. 51). Remember to breathe from the abdomen.

3 Slowly lift your arms out to your sides. Bring your hands to shoulder level, keeping your thumbs up and your palms facing forward. Pause and imagine that you are about to hug a loved one. Your arms should be slightly bent at the elbows. Think wrapping, not grabbing!

Steps 1 and 2   *Step 3*

Steps 4 and 5: Two views

4 Circle your still-bent arms to the front of your body until your hands are approximately two fists apart, at shoulder level. As your arms sweep forward, rotate your wrists so that by the time your hands come near each other, your thumbs are now pointed down and your palms facing forward. Feel this motion originating in your back, not your shoulders.

5 Pause in this position and complete 2 or 3 cycles of abdominal breathing.

6 Slowly lower your hands back to your sides, following the same path in which you raised them.

Mounted

The exercise works best when practiced on a longe line or in a round pen. Ask a friend for assistance so that you can concentrate on the exercise while he or she directs your horse.

1 Repeat the same motions and breathing patterns in the saddle as you did on the ground. Note that the photographs show a slightly more advanced version of the exercise; the hands have been brought to the front with the palms facing the rider. Some people find it easier to open their backs in this version, but you must also be careful to keep your shoulders completely relaxed.

2 Practice for at least 2 full circles.

3 After you have completed the circles, let your elbows drop slowly to your sides and let your hands drop softly as if holding the reins.

Ah-Ha!

The front of your chest will be soft and your upper back will feel expanded. You may feel a sensation like heat or pins and needles in your hands.

Ability Transition

As you become familiar with the motions, explore the rotation of your arms within the larger motion of the embrace. The rotation helps keep tension from finding a home in your shoulders and neck.

You will notice that your breath begins to fill your body from the belly up. With time, your breath will expand your lower back and then move up to fill your upper back, where it will open Gate 4: The Back of the Heart. When the mind and body connect through these motions, the Front and Back of the Heart gates are opened.

Learn to open Gate 3: The Front of your Heart by imagining how you hug someone. It may not be easy for you to open the Front of the Heart, because in riding, you protect your front. Think about the feeling of drawing back the string of a bow; do this on both sides of your body. Let go of the muscles.

Drop your sternum. Let your breath travel down to your abdomen, then back, and up, and around your upper back. Visualize a circle opening and expanding. You don't expand your heart up and out as though inhaling strongly, like a soldier sucking in a big breath when coming to attention. This is expansion through relaxation. You cannot use force.

Think of opening your Dain Tian, Ming Meng, and Back of the Heart gates as a progression. You might imagine a series of circles painted on your skin; now expand each circle, one after the other.

Reminder

Let the rhythm of your horse at the walk help slow and deepen your breath. Don't force the movement of your breath, but direct it with your mind. Pay close attention to your shoulders, and do not hold the position so long that you create tension in them. Think of the breath filling your abdomen as supporting your shoulders.

Step 1: Two views

Heaven and Earth

Riding Goals: Relaxation, Awareness

Heaven and Earth teaches you to breathe from your abdomen in a rhythmic manner while moving your arms and eyes. When done in the saddle, this exercise aids in relaxing you and your horse.

Function

The exercise develops your ability to control and manipulate the breath to maintain balance and rhythm while in the saddle.

Intent

Use your mind to direct the movement of your breath within your body. As you look upward and your palms face the heavens, imagine that your arms reach out and embrace the heavens. As you scoop down, imagine that your hands go deep into the ground and pull the energy of the earth into your body. You may then release the energy up into the heavens as you raise your arms again. As my teacher would say, "We become the bridge that joins heaven and earth."

Also observe with your mind the changes in your horse as your breath relaxes and becomes deeper and more rhythmic.

Step-by-Step

Unmounted

The general rule for breathing in this exercise is that when your arms are moving up or out, you breathe in; when your arms are moving down or in, you breathe out. The objective is to create an even rhythm of breathing in which to explore the possibilities of expanding and contracting the body from the inside out.

Your breath should be soft and smooth, never held or forced. Your breath should set the pace of the exercise.

1 Begin in *Standing Meditation*.

Step 3   *Step 4*

2 From *Standing Meditation,* you may push your heels out by pivoting on the balls of your feet so that your feet are slightly pigeon-toed (not shown in these photos). This position helps relax the muscles of your lower back.

3 Raise both hands in front of you until arms are shoulder level, with your elbows slightly bent and your palms facing downward.

There is a rotation of your arms that causes your palms to face down. The rotation is created from the shoulder, not the elbow.

During the entire *Heaven and Earth* exercise, your head and eyes follow your hands. As you move your head, be sure to use only your neck, and not your upper back.

4 Circle your arms out to the sides and down in an arcing motion. Continue the movement until your hands are in front of your Dain Tian (at your waist) with the palms facing upward. Your fingertips should point at each other and be approximately 6 inches apart.

Step 5

Step 6

Step 7

5 Slowly raise your hands, palms up, toward your chest, maintaining the distance between them.

6 As your hands pass in front of your face, rotate your hands outward and continue raising your arms, pushing your palms, now facing up, sending energy toward the sky (Heaven). Follow your hands aloft with your eyes.

7 Release your arms and let them arc down. Relax your shoulders, your arms, and your hands. Let them travel down and return to your Dain Tian in a scooping motion, with the palms facing up (having gathered energy from Earth).

8 Repeat Steps 4, 5, and 6 for a total of 3 repetitions. On the last repetition, let your hands drop to your sides.

Mounted

Practice this exercise while riding at the walk on a loose rein or longe line. Ask a friend for assistance so that you can concentrate on the exercise while he or she directs your horse.

Ah-Ha!

You will notice that both your belly and lower back expand with your inhalation. You will feel your shoulders relax as your arms rotate.

While in the saddle, you may observe that your horse stops walking when your head begins to move. When this happens, it is most likely because your seat has tightened slightly and stopped moving with the horse. Consider this response a good thing, because it proves how easily you're distracted from your seat and how a subtle change in your body affects your horse. Learn how to change this in Ability Transition next.

Ability Transition

As you practice *Heaven and Earth*, you will notice that your motions seem to become bigger and rounder. This change happens when the muscles in your chest and arms begin to relax while in motion. The rotation of the arms plays a vital role in the relaxation of the entire body.

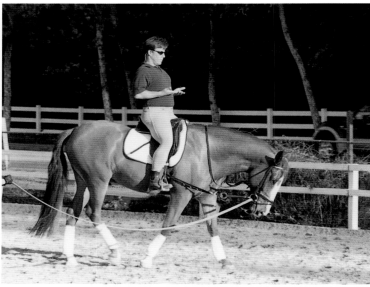

Performing the steps for Heaven and Earth while mounted.

Reminder

While you practice, search your body for tension and then ask yourself what the cause is. Is it because you lost your balance and are now working to hold yourself in position? Or is the tension there in the form of an old habit? In either case, search within the form for the moment that the tension is born. When you find it, you can then discover the root cause of your tension and retrain yourself—preventing the tension from reappearing in your body.

Remember that you start the *unmounted* phase of every exercise from *Standing Meditation*, in complete relaxation and balance. And you start the *mounted* phase of every exercise from *Sitting Meditation*, again, in complete relaxation and balance. You want to maintain this balance throughout the form and throughout your ride. To constantly be letting go of tension is not true balance. Discovering, changing, and flowing through the moments when tension is born—*before it takes hold*—is true balance and the essence of Tai Chi.

Breathing to a Halt or Walk

Riding Goals: Rhythm, Awareness, Influencing the Horse

This exercise teaches you that your horse listens to your breath. You can use your breath to slow the motion of your pelvis and communicate a halt to the horse.

Function

You move your center forward, so your weight drops into your seat bones. This exercise also helps you in the half-halt, where you communicate to get the horse's attention. Your breath is a convincing aid. By using your breath, you will only need to give one-quarter of the aid that you previously gave to get a halt.

Intent

Think about sitting down to get the halt. Look at the ground 20 feet in front of you, and imagine that you bring the ground straight up into a wall in front of you. Raise the ground like a drawbridge.

Step-by-Step

Unmounted

1 Begin in *Standing Meditation.*

2 Sit down in a chair and practice abdominal breathing.

3 Fill your abdomen with air, and expand it forward. That feeling will be your halt. With abdominal breathing, your center shifts forward when you inhale. In riding, this means that your center shifts forward so more weight drops into the front of your seat bones. This change is very subtle and can hardly be seen from the outside of the body. You're experiencing a physical change of your center.

4 Exhale and sense your center shifting backward.

Mounted

1 Begin in *Sitting Meditation.*

2 Walk your horse on a straight line.

3 Breathe into and expand your Dain Tian forward. As you expand your belly, you drop more of your weight to the front of your seat bones. This slows the movement in your pelvis, signaling your horse to halt.

Feel the influence your breath has on the motion of your pelvis.

Ah-Ha!

You will notice with practice that your horse begins to halt as soon as you start your inhale. When you use your breath, your horse listens. When you exhale, more weight drops into the back of your seat bones—use this reaction as a driving aid.

Ability Transition

Remember that though your horse may be big, he is sensitive. Drop your weight to the front of the saddle by ounces, not by pounds. Abdominal breathing changes the volume of your center. In changing the volume, you change the distribution of weight over your seat bones. This slight weight shift directed by your breath is a powerful yet subtle tool.

Reminder

Many riders fail to drop the weight to the front of the saddle. They bring their energy (breath) up into the chest, so that the chest—not the center—becomes the root of the halt. Then, when they pull the reins to halt, the horse resists and pulls the rider's seat bones up. The result is the opposite of sitting down to stop. Remember, too, that your horse is also learning. It will take time and practice for both of you to get used to this new communication.

A Culture of Harmony

When I ask riders, "Where is your breath," many don't know. Everything in the universe is controlled by an underlying rhythm. In riding, rhythm is the key to timing. Now that you're mindful of your breath's timing, you've started to tune in to your horse's breathing as well. Your breath can harmonize with your horse's breath, so the two of you can truly join centers.

The horse has a rhythm to his breathing. Look for your horse's breath. His breathing will communicate his physical and mental state, so you can sense his attitude moment by moment.

Horses are sensitive to our breathing. Over the years I have found that when I breathe, the horse breathes. The first few times it happened I thought it was a coincidence, but with time I've found it happens too regularly to be just a coincidence. I have also found that when the rider exhales and relaxes, the horse exhales and relaxes, too.

You can control the rhythm of your breath to match your horse's rhythm. Start by enhancing your perception of how your horse breathes. From the ground, observe how he inhales and exhales at rest and at the walk.

From the saddle, pay attention to his breathing at the trot. At the canter, your horse will take bigger breaths and exhale more loudly. You'll notice that he breathes in rhythm with his stride. Listen to the rhythm of the horse's breath at the canter; it should be smooth and rhythmic.

Summary

All these exercises introduced you to the power of breathing. It's natural not to think about breathing all the time. Once you've retrained your breath, you can forget about it because you will have created a new awareness and positive habits of breathing.

There's a Taoist saying, "Work is done, then forgotten. Therefore it lasts forever." All this breath training is a means to an end. The end is to have breathing become uncon-

scious and correct. Breathing is a powerful tool to be used consciously when necessary and one that never unconsciously works against you. Tai Chi examines the ways
of nature in order to become closer to it. Babies breathe correctly, and they don't
think about it. A newborn colt knows how to walk, trot, and canter, and he doesn't
think about it. That's what I want you to do—think less, feel more, and always know
where your breath is.

What's Next

In chapter 6, "Your Body: Enhancing Your Movement and Power," we will work with a
set of nine more Laing Gong exercises in order to develop enhanced mobility.

Your Body

Enhancing Your Movement and Power

THERE IS A FANTASTIC SYNERGY that can occur between mind, breath, and body. Having focused on mind and breath in earlier chapters, now we will focus on body, in concert with mind and breath.

The goal of this chapter is to train your body to move in a new way, from the inside out. We will use your innate physical abilities to relax and to be aware of your body and couple them with exercises that expand your range of motion and develop your strength. From this training you will gain "enhanced mobility."

Enhanced Mobility

Enhanced mobility is the ability to move

    a) through an increased range of motion,

    b) with greater control and strength, and

    c) with your abdomen and back in relaxed, structural alignment.

Enhanced mobility is based upon *internal* strength (mind, breath, alignment, and balance), not *external* strength (muscles acting in isolation). All the exercises in this chapter work to help you develop enhanced mobility that will assist you as you negotiate the forces at play when riding.

There are three sets of forces in action when you ride: those developed by the horse (his momentum); those transferred from the horse to you (your momentum); and those within your body (your own muscular effort). Of these, you only have control of the last. By developing enhanced mobility, you are better able to move any part of your body without being overwhelmed by the greater force of the horse or by your own momentum. Enhanced mobility optimizes your ability to remain connected to your horse *and* to move independently of him. Paradoxically, only when you can remain independent of your horse, can you really join centers with him. Learning to ride in this way is an unending process because you and your horse must find your center again every time you ride.

Balance without Force

When you ride, you are dealing with a force bigger and stronger than you. You must learn to deal with the horse's potentially unbalancing movement. If you rely on strength, you're using your force to try to oppose the force of the horse. This approach has three problems: (1) the horse is far stronger than you; (2) using force inhibits a joint's flexibility; (3) using force produces injuries. In the course of your life, you may only oppose bigger stronger forces with force for so long before your body begins to pay the price.

Up until now I've talked about mind-body unity and moving the body as a whole. When you are training for enhanced mobility, you isolate a joint and a muscle group and discover how to use less muscular effort to get more effective motion by applying the principles of Tai Chi.

Root Causes

Riders often mistake the symptom of a problem as its cause, and then they treat only the symptom. In doing so, you may alter the symptom, but your cure will be ineffective because the root cause will remain unchanged. If you discover a specific physical problem, examine its root. Investigate and dig for the internal cause of an external symptom. What is your body telling you?

For example, the "elbows out" position (a symptom) can be the consequence of being immobile in your spine (root cause). This immobility means that you cannot absorb the horse's motion and you are thrown out of balance, which causes more tension and rigidity. You bring your elbows out to your sides to help yourself regain your balance, much as a tightrope walker holds a long pole for balance. Telling yourself to drop your elbows is no more helpful than telling the tightrope walker to drop her balance pole. In reality, you both need to make proactive, internal (root) adjustments that will enhance your balance.

Enhanced Mobility Training: Laing Gong

This chapter's nine exercises are all derived from *Laing Gong*, the set of therapeutic exercises introduced in chapter 4. The ultimate goal of these exercises is to train your body's muscles to work together, so your body moves as one—a cohesive unit of mind-body, muscle-bone, and inside-outside. In order to accomplish this complex and ambitious aim, I will break down the training into more easily learned exercises. The first three exercises address the neck and shoulders; the last six address the back, pelvis, and spine.

Please note that these exercises should always be performed while standing; their mechanics require you to stand and support your body against gravity using your bones instead of muscular effort. Of course, the mounted adaptations of these exercises are performed sitting—but you are still supporting yourself as you sit in the sort of self-carriage you learned in *Sitting Meditation* (p. 40).

Neck Turns

Riding Goals: Position/Seat, Relaxation

An enhanced awareness of balance is the first step in becoming truly aligned with the horse. You'll improve your posture and seat, and relax your body to relax the horse. The goal is to keep your head in balance over your shoulders and torso without causing undue tension in your neck and shoulder muscles.

Function

Neck Turns develops truly independent use of your head and neck. You'll be able to move your head and neck in a relaxed manner, without engaging any other muscle in your body. The exercise also helps to release tension in your neck and shoulders.

Intent

Imagine that the crown of your head is suspended from above and your whole body is as light as a feather. The more you turn your head, the taller you become. Visualize the smallest muscles in your neck moving your head, as the larger ones relax and allow your head to turn without restriction.

Step-by-Step

Unmounted

1 Begin in *Standing Meditation* (p. 37).

2 Place your hands on your hips, with your fingers pointing forward. Your legs are straight, not locked and not bent.

3 Slowly turn your head to the left, making sure it stays level as you turn. Don't look down or up. This is the first movement of the 4-part movement in which you'll turn your head left, right, up, and down.

4 When you feel you are at the end of your range of motion, stretch a little farther for just one second. Remember to keep your head straight. Don't sacrifice the position of your head to stretch further. Lock your knees and straighten your body during the one-second stretch period; do this for each of the 4 directions you'll turn.

Step 2

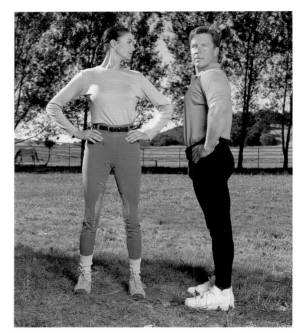

Step 3

5 Release the tension and return to the center—that is, the starting position, with your head over your body in relaxed natural alignment.

6 Turn your head to the right and stretch for one second, remembering to keep your head straight, then return to the center. Remember to lock your knees and straighten your body during the one-second stretch period.

7 Lift your chin to the sky as you stretch for one second, and then return to the center.

Be sure you don't arch your back while lifting your head. You should lift your chin rather than tilt your head back. By focusing on lifting the chin, you exercise the highest vertebra in your neck. Control of this area is essential for true balance.

8 Bring your chin down to your chest, stretch for one second, and return to the starting position.

9 Repeat the exercise 4 times.

Step 6

Step 7

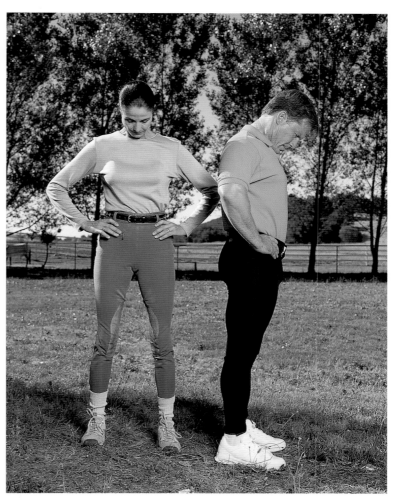

Step 8

Mounted

Practice *Neck Turns* while riding at the walk on a loose rein or longe line. Ask a friend for assistance so that you can concentrate on the exercise while he or she directs your horse. A partner is also helpful in giving you feedback on the correctness of your position, which often varies from what you think and feel.

You may want to start this exercise at the halt, and then work at the walk. After you are comfortable with it at the walk, move into the trot and canter. The steps are the same for the mounted work as they are for the groundwork. Keep these thoughts in mind as you work:

- While turning your head, avoid tightening the muscles in your neck. Tightening them will interfere with the balance of your head over your body, which will in turn cause you to tense in order to balance yourself. Such tension will decrease the fluid movement of your spine, and your horse may stop or move poorly—not the desired result, but certainly useful feedback from your equine partner.
- When you stretch your chin to the sky, imagine that you are stretching upward and slightly forward. Otherwise you may find yourself slightly behind your center and the movement of your horse. If you fall behind the motion, your lower back will tighten and drop more weight into the back of your seat, which can cause your horse to accelerate. Falling behind can also create a tremendous amount of stress in your lower back.
- When stretching the chin to the chest pay attention not to lean forward as your chin and eyes go down. If you do, your horse may let you know by coming to a halt.

Ah Ha!

Notice how much your balance depends on where you are looking. Soon you will be able to look away and remain completely aware of your center. This exercise is great for increasing your awareness of the overall rhythm of your body and how the smallest unbalanced movement can completely alter that rhythm.

You should feel as if your head can rotate on an axis. Your shoulders will not rise, and you will feel an even stretch on both sides of the neck with no "kinks." You may experience a tingling sensation up the back of your neck and over the top of your head, as you open and expand your crown.

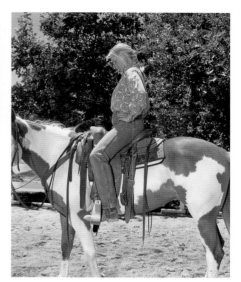

Performing Neck Turns while mounted

Ability Transition

With practice you will significantly increase the range of motion of your head and neck. You will also begin to catch yourself holding your head in a poor position at different times during the day, and you'll be able to realign and relax your head and neck before tension sets in.

Reminder

Remember to hold the stretch for only one second. Holding it longer does not increase the benefit. The goal in all these exercises is to develop a slow, even, balanced motion with a complete awareness of your body. Take your time; don't hurry. There are no shortcuts to achieving good results.

Make sure you are completely balanced throughout the exercise at the walk before trying it at the trot.

Use this as a mounted warm-up every time you ride. You will be amazed how much more you'll get out of your training if you take the time to warm up first.

Spread Your Chest

Riding Goals: Position/Seat, Rhythm, Influencing the Horse

Spread Your Chest develops the enhanced mobility of your shoulders and chest necessary for increasing the sensitivity of your hands. It helps soften your chest, shoulders, and upper back. And finally, the exercise will help you maintain the rhythm of your seat and your connection with the horse.

The mounted version of this exercise enhances your ability to balance your upper body. It also teaches you to recognize and release tension in your arms, chest, and shoulders.

Function

Spreading your chest teaches you to move energy through your neck and shoulders down the back and into your seat; this helps you keep your upper body free from the tension that leads to fatigue. It can also help prevent chronic injuries of the neck and shoulders.

You may experience some popping or cracking noises in your shoulder joints. Don't be alarmed—it is natural for the body to make noise as the muscles, tendons, and ligaments stretch, realign, and heal. However, if you have had any shoulder injuries, you must use caution in doing this exercise. You may experience some discomfort in the shoulder while performing the stretch, but it should not be painful. Only you can determine the difference between discomfort and pain. In any case, you should feel no pain after completing the exercise. Often we have to move through and past discomfort in order to heal an old injury.

The position and alignment of your bones during all the Laing Gong exercises is of vital importance. Only with proper position can you realize the tremendous healing nature of these exercises.

Intent

Imagine that your arms are stretching out from your spine, not just from your shoulders. Feel a sensation of heat moving out of your arms—use your mind to push heat out to your hands and then out beyond your fingertips.

As you become familiar with the motion, look at one hand, but focus your mind on the other; this concentration will engage both hemispheres of your brain simultaneously and increase awareness.

Steps 2 and 3   *Step 4*

Unmounted

1 Begin in *Standing Meditation.*

2 Stretch your arms straight down in front of your body, with your right palm on top of the back of the left hand. Lock your elbows; they remain locked throughout the exercise. Remember to hold your fingers together and thumbs out.

3 Your eyes and head look down at your right hand.

4 Raise your paired arms straight forward and up, until they are directly over your head. Keep your eyes on your right hand.

Steps 6, 7, and 8   *Step 9*

5 Stretch your arms up by bringing your shoulders to your ears for one second as you extend your fingers toward the sky.

6 Move your arms back past your head as you separate your hands, and push your arms out and back in a circular motion.

7 Keep your palms facing up by rotating the upper arm, not the forearm.

8 Follow your right hand with your eyes and head.

9 Continue to move your arms in a circular motion—back, out, and down. As your hands drop below the level of your shoulders, let the upper arm rotate forward while the arms return to the beginning position, but now with the left hand on top.

10 Repeat for your left side.

11 Once to the right and once to the left form one complete repetition. Do at least 4 repetitions.

Mounted

Practice *Spread Your Chest* while riding at the walk on a loose rein or longe line. Ask a friend for assistance.

1 Begin in *Sitting Meditation* (p. 40).

2 Riding at the walk, begin the exercise just as you would on the ground.

Notice how your body reacts to the movement of the horse as you begin to circle your arms back and out. Remember to keep your eyes on one hand—first on one side, and then on the other as you repeat the movement.

This form can create strong sensations in your arms and hands. You may feel a tingling or heat. It's not uncommon to experience a feeling of electricity shooting through your arms.

While mounted, you may even experience a feeling I can only describe as riding with an open heart—it will feel as if your horse's energy moves up through your body into your heart.

Physically, when the muscles of your chest and shoulders are relaxed, they soften and allow your spine to move more freely, and this enables you to maintain the alignment of your upper body over your center.

Ability Transition

When you gain control and flexibility in your neck and shoulders, the sensation of heat will subside and so should any "noise" in your shoulders. While you continue to practice on and off the horse, you will notice that your arms and shoulders will be more relaxed. You will feel the horse's mouth through your arms and chest, not just with your hands. With time, you'll feel your horse's mouth in your whole upper body. You'll monitor and control this connection using the Back of the Heart gate.

Reminder

As always, move softly, and gently keep your eyes on your hand throughout the form. Pay close attention to your back. It should be straight, not arched. Arching your back

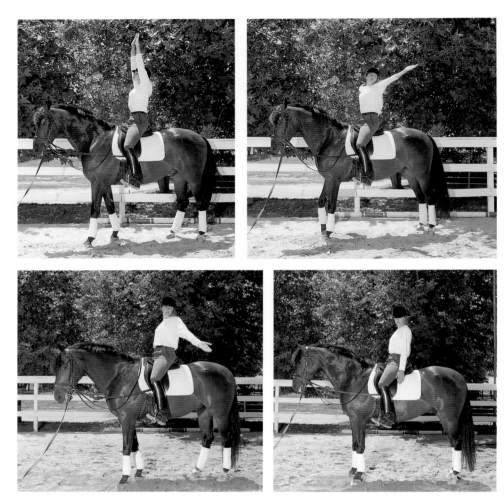

Performing Spread Your Chest while mounted

in this exercise inhibits the range of motion of your shoulders and takes you out of structural alignment. Arching creates the illusion of flexibility in the shoulders by moving the whole chest and shoulder. Remember that the goal is a smooth, correct, controlled motion.

Spread Your Wings

Riding Goals: Balance, Rhythm

Spread Your Wings develops enhanced mobility in your shoulders and neck, which will enable you to keep your head balanced without undue tension. When your head is balanced, you allow the horse to move with more freedom. By opening your shoulder joints and the accompanying meridians, you will increase the sensitivity of your hands and fingers—helping you improve your communication with your horse.

Function

You'll develop the ability to move your arms and shoulders with minimal use of your upper trapezius muscles. You will also use your latissimus dorsi muscles to hold your shoulders down. (For anatomical references, see the *Appendix*, p. 245.) This independent movement allows your shoulders and energy to stay down, so you don't raise your center of gravity while raising your arms. This exercise also helps you learn to use your upper body while keeping your seat. A good seat is vital to maintaining the circuit that brings energy from the earth, up through the horse, into your seat, up through your body and out the reins to the horse, where it travels back down to the earth to begin the cycle again.

Intent

Focus your eyes and mind on your elbows. Imagine stretching your elbows out and away from your body while drawing large circles in the air with your elbows. As you become familiar with the motion, look at one elbow but focus your mind on the other. This focus will engage both hemispheres of your brain simultaneously and increase your awareness.

Step-by-Step

Unmounted

1 Begin in *Standing Meditation*.

James On Your Shoulder

This motion is much easier to master on the ground than in the saddle, so develop your skills doing the unmounted version before doing the exercise mounted.

2 Place your hands on your hips with your thumbs forward. Turn your head and look at your right elbow, as I am in the photo. Pull your elbows back and up, stretching the front of your chest open, while keeping your shoulders down and your palms close at your sides. Your eyes and head continue to follow the position of your right elbow.

3 Continue to lift your elbows back and up until they are higher than your shoulders. Keep your palms close to your body as your bent arms continue circling up. Circle your elbows toward the front of your body, allowing your hands to rise up to and through your armpits to the front of your chest.

4 The backs of your palms are now facing each other. Your wrists and fingers should be soft and relaxed. Your elbows should be higher than your wrists and your shoulders (trapezius muscles) should be relaxed and down.

Remember to follow the path of your right elbow with your eyes, but to keep your attention on the left elbow.

5 Using your wrist as a pivot point, allow your elbows to drop down and your palms to face forward—but not quite straight forward: your hands should be positioned as though you were holding a large ball in front of your face.

6 Relax your shoulders and elbows, while you allow your arms to return to the beginning position.

7 Repeat and focus this time on your left elbow.

8 Once to the right and once to the left form one complete repetition. Do at least 4 repetitions.

Mounted

The mounted version of *Spread Your Wings* is the virtually the same as the ground version. Practice it while riding at the walk on a loose rein or longe line. Ask a friend for assistance.

1 Begin in *Sitting Meditation.*

2 Do the exercise at the walk. Pay close attention to your seat while rotating your elbows. You will know immediately if you tighten the trapezius muscles because

Step 1

Step 2

Step 3

Step 4

Step 5

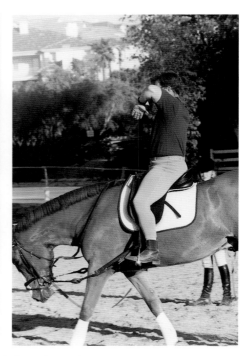

Performing Spread Your Wings while mounted, various views

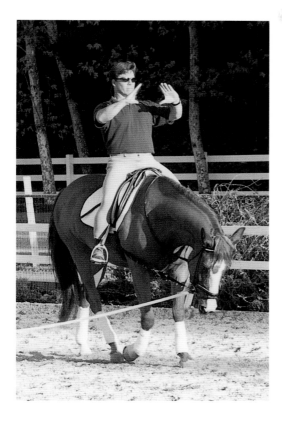

your seat will tighten and you'll start to lose your balance backward and brace your lower back.

Have a friend watch the arm you are not looking at. Ask her to make sure that the motion of both your arms is the same.

Ah-Ha!

You should feel no tension in your neck or hands. The motion will become smooth and relaxed throughout. With practice, you will recognize the moment you engage unnecessary muscles in your shoulders and neck, and you'll be able to release them before they affect your balance or your connection with your horse.

Ability Transition

At some point you will learn to lift your elbows without raising your shoulders and creating any unnecessary tension that restricts motion. Your armpits will feel "empty," or completely without tension. While riding, this new ability will allow your head to move freely in rhythm with the horse, rather than requiring you to hold your head in place by tightening the muscles of your neck and shoulders. The exercise will also help you keep your shoulders and elbows down and relaxed.

Let me remind you of a story I mentioned earlier, as now you're doing an exercise that can help you achieve similar results. I studied a videotape of Olympic Gold Medalist Klaus Balkenhol's winning dressage test. At one point he cantered away from the camera down the centerline, giving you a perfect view of his back. His shoulders and spine seemed to be detached from one another. His spine moved up and down with the motion of the horse, but his shoulders remained still. This independent motion can only happen when the upper back and shoulders are completely relaxed and the spine is aligned naturally.

Interesting, too, was Balkenhol's overall profile: from the side, his posture looked more like that of a boxer, with the upper back full and slightly more rounded than the rigidly held, upright position I often see in even very accomplished riders. The tape showed a rider with all his gates open, moving in harmony with his horse and enjoying a beautiful ride.

Reminder

Move softly and gently. Breathe as you move, and support your elbows from below rather than lifting them with the trapezius muscles. Remember that any tension in your arms will show up in your hands. Think about keeping your armpits empty.

The Biomechanics of a Laing Gong Exercise

For riders interested in the biomechanics of Laing Gong, let's take a look at *Spread Your Chest* (p. 126).

There are six possible muscle actions involved in your upper limbs and shoulder joints:

1 Adduction

2 Abduction

3 Extension

4 Flexion

5 Medial rotation

6 Lateral rotation

Spread Your Chest includes all six motions. One muscle or group of muscles begins the motion, and then these muscles surrender to another group for the next part of the motion; this muscle group, in turn, surrenders to a following group, and so on, until the motion is completed. We often get energetically trapped in a motion by dominant muscles that can't let go sufficiently to allow the smaller, more sensitive muscles to take over.

In *Spread Your Chest*, for example, you need to use your trapezius to lift your shoulder blades, and the pectorals and deltoids to raise your arms. At some point you let go of the trapezius while continuing to use the pectorals. At some point above the height of your shoulder, the pectorals have to let go to allow the deltoids to take over the motion. To continue into the rotation back, the trapezius muscles need to relax again to allow the rhomboids to take over. The rhomboids then move the shoulder blades back, bringing along with them your shoulders and arms (see diagram on p. 247).

Hold the Sky with Both Hands

Riding Goals: Balance, Awareness, Position/Seat

Hold the Sky with Both Hands teaches you an effective way to transfer weight from one side of your seat to the other without creating tightness. When you ride with an aligned and evenly weighted seat, you often solve the problem of the horse's shoulders popping out or falling in while riding through a turn. The exercise can also be helpful in keeping the horse's haunches in line. Last, it is one of the best exercises I know for stretching and developing balance muscles in your lower back.

Function

You further develop your understanding of your body alignment and balance. You increase the flexibility of your lower lumbar vertebrae, abdomen, and waist, while maintaining structural balance. In the exercise, you shift weight into one or the other seat bone, while creating no tension in your seat or legs. When you lean to one side and maintain a straight spine the movement originates in the lower lumbar.

Intent

While performing this exercise, imagine your spine being completely fused together except for the last two vertebrae just above your pelvis. Use your mind not only to direct the lean but also to listen to what your muscles around your spine are saying.

Step-by-Step

Unmounted

1 Begin in *Standing Meditation.*

2 Lace your fingers together, palms down in front of your body. You are in the center position for the exercise. Look down at your hands.

3 Raise your hands up directly over your head, with your elbows locked. Swing your palms from facing down, to facing forward, to facing up. Stretch your hands to the sky by bringing your shoulders to your ears.

Step 2

Step 3

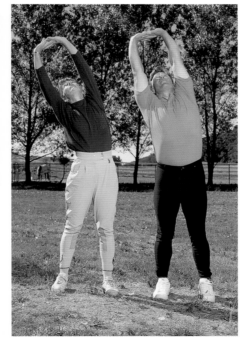

Step 4

Step 6

Hold the Sky with Both Hands (cont.)

James On Your Shoulder

Are you breathing? Use your breath to help let go with your muscles. Your breath may be used as a "negotiator" between mind and muscle.

4 Lean to the left, while keeping your spine straight. Drop your breath deep into your abdomen before you start the lean. Exhale slowly as you lean.

Your head should travel only 2 to 6 inches to the side. Focus on doing the motion well, not in trying to lean as far as you can.

Focus your intent through your palms, which should be stretching upward through the whole exercise. Keep your shoulders to your ears during the lean.

The bend should come from as low as possible in your spine. Be sure to keep your hips stationary and your spine straight. You should feel this stretch in your lower back and hips.

Listen to the muscles in your lower back. Did they tighten without the consent of your mind? If so, direct them with your mind to relax.

5 Return to center position.

6 Repeat the exercise, this time leaning to the right.

7 Once to the left and once to the right form one complete repetition. Do at least 4 repetitions.

Mounted

Practice *Hold the Sky with Both Hands* first at the halt and then at the walk while on a loose rein or longe line. Ask a friend for assistance.

1 Begin in *Sitting Meditation.*

2 Repeat the unmounted Steps 2 through 6 while mounted.

The leaning movement is especially subtle when mounted; you need only lean far enough to move your head approximately one to 2 inches to the side (versus 2 to 6 inches when unmounted). Experiment and see how much you can accomplish moving your nose only one-half inch to the side.

The shift of weight created by your lean may cause your horse to adjust his stride to maintain balance. If you are leaning to the inside of the circle, your shift should make it easier for your horse to turn. However, if you lean to the outside of the circle, you may challenge your horse's balance because you're sending your horse a mixed message: your intent is telling your horse to ride on a circle; your seat bones are telling him to turn out of that circle. This is why it's best in the beginning to do this exercise from the halt. Refer back to the Riding Goals on page 138.

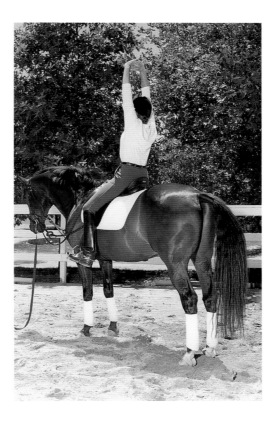

Performing Hold the Sky with Both Hands while mounted

Ah-Ha!

Feel as if you are moving your spine as a whole, with the motion originating in your lower lumbar vertebrae. While unmounted, as you practice you will find that with very little lean, you will feel a greater and greater shift of weight in your feet. You will slowly develop control of the smallest muscles in your back. They may feel a little sore after practice in the beginning. This is natural and is a good thing.

Ability Transition

Your goal is to have your bend come entirely from your lower lumbar vertebrae.

The sensitivity and strength of your seat lie in your lower back and abdomen, which are both enhanced by this exercise. When you gain control over these areas, you will be able to give aids using less effort and your horse will respond sooner, bringing you another step closer to your goal of riding with greater effectiveness. This is also in keeping with the first Principle: *Use the mind, not force* (see p. 16).

Hip Circles

Riding Goals: Position/Seat, Body Control

Hip Circles develops strength and sensitivity in your hips (pelvis). Moving your hips enables you to follow the lateral motion of the horse's hindquarters without surrendering the structural alignment of your upper body.

You receive the force created by your horse through your seat, and your pelvis is the primary director of that force through your own body. If, from lack of flexibility, you do not direct this force effectively, it pushes you out of center (the combined center of you and your horse). When this happens, your horse must compensate, and his movement is inhibited. You may be unaware of your own role in your horse's diminished performance.

Function

Your pelvis lies at the center of your body. When it is tight and inflexible, the rest of your body must compensate for this lack of motion in ways that sometimes cause injuries, most often to the back, knees, and ankles. This exercise develops enhanced mobility in the pelvis, hip joints, and the lower lumbar vertebrae. It is an excellent form for healing back injuries.

Intent

Use your mind to keep your spine straight during the motions. Listen for unnecessary tension in your body.

Step-by-Step

Unmounted

1 Begin in *Standing Meditation* and place your hands on your hips, with your thumbs forward.

2 Push your hips out to the right, while keeping your spine and your legs straight. This is the first step in the diamond pattern in which you'll be moving your hips.

Steps 1 and 2

Step 3   *Step 4*   *Step 5*

3 Push your hips forward while supporting your upper body with your hands. Your hands help keep your spine straight.

4 Push to the left side while maintaining your structural alignment, still supporting your upper body with your hands.

5 Push your hips backward while keeping your head, neck, and spine in a straight line.

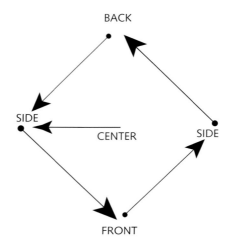

Step 6: Diamond Pattern of Hip Circles

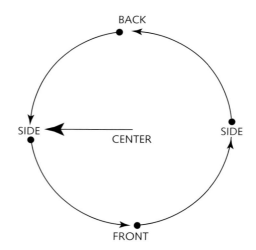

Step 7: Circular Pattern of Hip Circles

6 Move your hips in the diamond pattern one more time, completing 2 repetitions.

7 Move your hips in a circular pattern for the last 2 repetitions.

Ah-Ha!

When done correctly you will feel no tension in the lower back. Also, you will be able to maintain deep abdominal breathing throughout the exercise.

Ability Transition

As with all these exercises, the feelings you have in your body will change with time and practice. You might first feel the stretch in your hip on the side you are pushing toward. In time, the stretch may move up into your rib area or down into your thigh.

Enhanced mobility in the pelvis will help your riding. You will be more flexible and move in greater balance. As a result, you will need less time to warm up, and you'll find you have more energy—as will your horse, because he will be spending less energy compensating for your stiffness and imbalance.

Reminder

Be sure to move your hips out from under your upper body, rather than just leaning to the side, front, and back with your upper body. When done correctly, if you look down during the stretch, you should see that a line dropped straight down from your nose never falls outside your stance. If the exercise is done incorrectly, you place a tremendous stress on your lower back.

Thrust Palm in Bow Stance

Riding Goals: Position/Seat, Body Control, Relaxation

This form helps you develop the ability to give aids using your seat and legs while maintaining your upper body's balance. Proficiency in this form will help you keep your horse's outside shoulder from falling out.

Function

Thrust Palm in Bow Stance helps you develop enhanced mobility in your pelvis. It trains your upper body to move independently of your lower body. You gain a new understanding of body alignment and balance, and you unblock the six meridians in your legs and the six in your arms.

Intent

Imagine that you are suspended by a thread from the crown of your head. Imagine that your legs and feet are stone and cannot move. Focus on stretching your fingers beyond your body. Do not lean forward from the hips as you stretch.

Imagine that a pole runs through your body, from the base of your skull down through your torso and pelvis, and then into the ground. When you turn your pelvis, you turn the pole.

Step-by-Step

1 Begin in *Standing Meditation.*

2 Move your feet apart to a double shoulder-width stance with your feet parallel. Place your hands on your hips.

3 Hold your head straight, with your eyes forward. Relax your abdominals and gluteus muscles.

4 Pivot your right foot, on the heel, 90 degrees to the right. This will create a right angle between your two feet.

5 Bend your right leg forward, bringing your right knee over the toes of your right foot while you straighten your left leg.

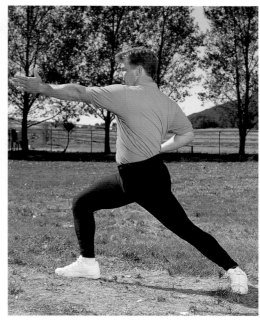

Steps 2 and 3   *Step 6*   *Step 7*

6 Turn your pelvis, waist, shoulders, and head to the right, so that your torso now faces in the same direction that your right toes are pointing toward.

Initiate the turn from your pelvis. Your goal is to rotate the entire torso as a unit, not simply twist at the waist.

Keep your back straight and vertical. Do not lean forward.

Your left leg is straight, and both feet are flat on the ground.

7 Push your left hand forward, reaching in the direction that your right toes are pointing. As your left hand moves forward from your waist, form a Laing Gong palm, while your right hand, which remains at your right hip, forms a Laing Gong fist (see p. 70). Stretch your left arm and palm as far forward as possible by turning your waist; this will pull your pelvis around a little more and rotate the head of your femur in your hip joint. Hold this stretch for one second or less.

Keep your right knee directly over your toes, your left knee locked, and your left leg straight. The relative position of your knees and feet does not change during the stretch.

As your pelvis turns, the femur of your straight leg rotates slightly. Let your leg rotate as one unit, from your hip all the way down to the ankle of your back foot. This foot should remain flat on the ground throughout the movement. Doing so develops your ability to keep your feet actively quiet while riding.

As you keep your right knee over your toes, feel your weight traveling down into the ground through the ball of your foot.

8 Return to the beginning position and repeat to the left.

There is no mounted version of this exercise. When you are sitting in the saddle, the saddle and the horse prevent you from turning your pelvis completely, limiting the root motion of the form.

The ability to move your pelvis and femur independently of one another is essential to good riding, as it enables you to give aids without losing your connection with your horse. The mobility you gain from this exercise will enable you to give aids with your seat while keeping your legs quiet, and aids with your legs without disturbing your seat.

Ah-Ha!

You will feel a stretch in the hip and thigh of the leg that you hold straight, also across your middle and lower back. When you hold your back in the proper position, you will feel your body spring back to the pre-stretch position.

Ability Transition

As you gain experience with this form, you will notice that the origin of the motion is your pelvis and that everything moves from there. You will feel the stretch in different parts of your body. In the beginning, you may feel most of the stretch in the hips. With time, you'll feel it in your rib cage and the underlying muscles of your abdomen.

Reminder

Remember to keep three things straight in this form: your back, your arm, and your outstretched leg. Be sure to keep the knee of your forward leg over your toes during the stretch. It's common while focusing on the opposing arm and hand to let the knee pull back as you push your hand out, but this backing motion will take away from the stretch in the hips. Also, do not lean forward from the waist while stretching. And, as always, this exercise is designed to align your bones in such a way that they take the force of gravity through your body into the ground. Therefore, being in the correct position prior to the stretch is of paramount importance.

Hold Knee to Chest

Riding Goals: Balance, Awareness, Position/Seat

Hold Knee to Chest teaches you a more effective way to transfer weight from one side of your seat to the other without creating tightness in your seat.

Function

You'll develop enhanced mobility in your lower lumbar vertebrae, abdomen, pelvis, legs, and knees. You will strengthen your legs and improve your balance, while learning how to breathe from the abdomen regardless of body position. The exercise increases your focus and concentration while you are in motion.

Intent

Use your mind to focus *beyond* your body, which, paradoxically, helps you develop a heightened awareness of your actual body position. The root of heaviness is lightness. Before you begin this exercise, imagine that the leg you will lift and your upper body are light as a feather—and the leg you will stand on goes deep into the ground and is as heavy as if it were made of stone.

Step-by-Step

1 Begin in *Standing Meditation*. Place your hands on your hips.

2 Inhale and slowly begin to shift your weight into your left foot as you step forward onto the heel of your right foot. Simultaneously lift your arms straight out in front of you and swing them up until they are directly over your head. Hold your elbows locked. Keep your palms faced in and your fingers pointed up.

3 Stretch your fingers to the sky by bringing your shoulders to your ears.

4 Continue to move your weight forward until 95 percent of your weight is balanced on your right foot. Keep the ball and toes of your left foot on the ground and lift up the heel of the left.

This movement is done while inhaling and should be smooth and fluid throughout.

Step 1

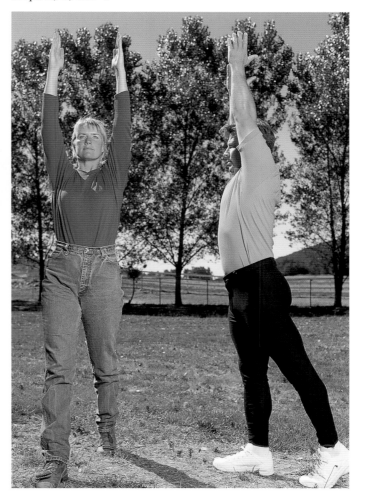

James On Your
Shoulder

Stand straight and light.
Imagine that you are being
held from above by a
thread attached to the top
of your head.

5 Without moving forward, allow the last 5 percent of your weight to sink down into your right leg and foot, as if it were sinking through your body and into the ground. Exhale, and at the same time slowly lift your left leg up in front of your body with your knee bent and your toes relaxed and pointing down.

Remember, do not hold your breath. You should be exhaling before you begin to move your body and shift your weight.

6 Circle your arms out and down from over your head, bringing your hands together around your raised knee. Lift the raised knee to your chest.

7 Pull your left knee tight to your body as you let the last bit of breath leave your lungs. Don't force it. Let the stretch help you exhale.

Steps 5 and 6

8 Slowly release your knee and let your left leg stretch down and back to its original position. Allow your toes to touch the ground first, then the ball of your foot with the heel still off the ground. (You will feel a stretch in the foot.) As your left foot touches down, swing your arms back up over your head, palms facing in and fingers stretched to the sky. Allow your whole body to stretch, from toes to fingertips.

9 Continue to shift your weight back into your left foot as your heel comes down. When 100 percent of your weight has shifted into your left foot, step back with the right foot, putting yourself back into a shoulder-width parallel stance. At the same time, drop your arms straight down in front of you until they have returned to their original position.

10 Repeat for the opposite side, this time stepping forward with the left foot and raising your right knee to your chest.

11 Once to the right and once to the left form one complete repetition. Do at least 4 repetitions.

NOTE: This is another exercise for which there is no safe or practical *mounted* version. You will, however, take your new balance and flexibility with you when you ride.

Ah-Ha!

You should eventually feel that your whole body is relaxed during the exercise, and that all your limb movements start and stop at the same time. You will also breathe smoothly and continuously throughout.

Ability Transition

Drop your breath deep into your abdomen before you take the step forward. Exhale slowly as you shift your weight. In the beginning you may lose your balance, wobble, and have to put your leg down to keep from falling. This is natural. Remember that to find and develop your balance, you must first define your imbalance. Only then do you have a scale with which to measure your improvement.

Focus your intent up through your hands as they are stretching to the sky. As you practice and develop your skills, you will notice that you move your upper body very little to shift a great deal of weight. Less and less of your motion will be visible and external; more and more of it will be invisible and internal.

Hold Knee to Chest exercise develops your ability to control your weight and balance as you move both forward and backward as well as to the side. You do this sort of balancing on a micro-muscular scale, and these skills are invaluable for producing transitions, flying-lead changes, and especially big, energetic trots and canters. When done with the proper dedication and effort, this exercise produces tremendous results.

Reminder

Remember, your horse must compensate for your lack of balance when he's supporting you. Any wobble or slight imbalance of yours is felt many-fold by your sensitive horse.

Bend with an Arch

Bend with an Arch helps you gain enhanced mobility in your spine. Your spine is a key element in enabling you to stay balanced over your horse, which then allows the horse to move more freely within his own body.

Function

The exercise enhances your understanding of body alignment and balance. It trains you to keep your spine straight and extended while moving it as one unit. At the same time, it also develops your ability to move your arms, shoulders, and legs independently of your spine. This enhances your ability to remain balanced while you give aids, thereby directing your horse without interfering with him. As with most of these exercises, when done correctly you will feel a very strong sensation of energy rushing through your body as you reach the final position.

Intent

Try visualizing your body as two steel poles stacked end on end. The bottom pole includes your legs; the upper pole includes your torso and head. The poles are hinged at your waist. As you bend, the two poles remain perfectly straight. Only the hinge (your waist) moves.

When you raise your arms, imagine that they are being pulled by your fingertips out and away from your body. Move your awareness from your spine out through your arms into your fingertips.

Step-by-Step

Unmounted

1 Begin in *Standing Meditation.*

2 Lay one hand over the back of your other hand with your fingertips pointed straight down. Tip your head down and look at the backs of your hands.

Step 2

Step 3: Two views

Step 4: Two views

Step 5

Step 6

Step 7

Step 8

3 Lift your arms up, swinging them forward and up directly over your head. Stretch your arms up to the sky by bringing your shoulders to your ears, while keeping your elbows locked.

4 Lower your straightened arms to the sides until your hands, palms up, are at shoulder level. Your back should be arched as much as possible and should remain so throughout the form. Again, stretch your fingers out away from your spine as if someone were gently pulling them.

5 Bend forward from the waist as far as you can without losing any of the arch in your back. As you bend forward, allow your bottom to push back slightly, and let your arms, which remain straight, rotate so that your palms face the ground when you finish the bending motion. Remember that all motion begins from the center; that is, you start the bend by moving your hips back.

6 Drop your arms down toward the ground, crossing your palms. Check that your back is still well arched.

7 Without lifting your body, raise your arms up until they stretch out in front of your head.

8 While maintaining this arms-forward position, lift your torso up, keeping the arch in your back. Raise your body up until you are standing tall, with your arms over your head and your hands stretching to the sky, as in Step 3.

9 Relax your arms and allow them to drop down to your sides, with your palms touching your thighs.

10 Do 3 repetitions.

Mounted

There is no safe way to do this entire exercise mounted, but you can take portions of it into the saddle. The positions in Steps 3 and 4 are great to practice while mounted. They will help you connect your whole body in alignment.

Ah-Ha!

When *Bend with an Arch* is done correctly, you should feel no stress in your back while bending or lifting your body. However, you will feel a tremendous stretch in the backs of your legs and in your gluteus muscles. When you lift your body, use all the muscles in the back of your legs to bring your torso up. At the end of the exercise, while you are dropping your arms, you will feel an overwhelming rush of energy throughout your entire body. This is an excellent opportunity to feel the energy we all possess.

Ability Transition

With practice, the flexibility of your legs and spine will increase and you will develop a greater awareness of your posture, alignment, and balance. After I finish this form, I move with much less tension and have a clearer state of mind.

Reminder

The most important thing to remember in this exercise is to keep your back arched throughout. To arch the back completely you must engage all the smaller muscles that support the individual vertebrae. Any break in the arch becomes the weak link in your structure, and injury may occur. With this in mind, bend only as far as you can without surrendering your arch. This sounds simple, but you would be surprised to know how many people are unaware of when they let go of the arch. Please listen closely to your spine!

Lift a Single Iron Arm

Riding Goals: Balance, Position/Seat

Lift a Single Iron Arm helps you control the left and right vertical balance of your body, ensuring even weight aids in the saddle. When you sit, is your weight even in the saddle? Or, are you heavier on one side than the other? Most of us are one-sided, and this imbalance has a negative effect on the horse's performance.

Function

This exercise engages all the muscles on one side of your spine while allowing the muscles of the opposite side to remain relaxed. Rarely in your daily life do you use one side of the spinal muscles independently of the other side. The exercise's motions make us aware of what would otherwise be an unconscious imbalance. *Lift a Single Iron Arm* works to eliminate one-sidedness by retraining your body to move in harmony between the left and right sides of the spine.

Intent

Hold the arm you lift as straight as an iron rod. There should be no bend whatsoever in your arm from shoulder to fingertips as it is being raised over your head. When pushing your palm toward the sky, feel the stretch from the heel of your foot all the way up through your body to your palm. It should feel as if someone is pulling up on your palm from above, and let that entire side of your body yield to the force. In your mind, completely detach the left side of your body from the right. While you push up one side and feel its lightness, let the other side relax and feel its heaviness.

Step-by-Step

Unmounted

1 Begin in *Standing Meditation.*

2 Slowly lift your left arm straight out to your side with the palm facing down. Your right arm slowly bends at the elbow as you place the back of your right hand against the small of your back.

Step 1

Step 2

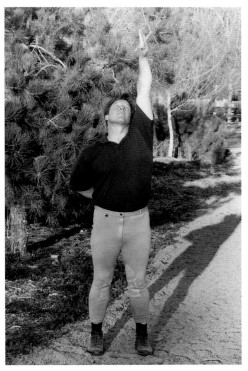

Steps 3 and 4

3 Continue to raise your left arm until your hand is directly over your head with your fingers pointing straight up. With your head and eyes, follow the movement of your hand from shoulder level to the stretch position over your head.

Be sure not to let the shoulder of this arm rise with tension. Keep your head and neck straight and the shoulder soft and relaxed.

4 Slowly bring this shoulder toward your ear. Keep your back hand relaxed and the same shoulder down. In other words, don't let the push and stretch of one side create tension in the other.

5 In your raised arm, turn your palm up, so your hand and wrist form a right angle.

6 Point your fingers back at a 45-degree angle, while keeping your hand and wrist in the position in Step 5.

7 Push your palm toward the sky, stretching it upward.

8 Relax your left arm and slowly bring the arm back down, following the same path it took going up, and place it at the small of your back.

9 As your left hand drops below your shoulder, straighten your right arm, swinging your right hand from the small of your back down to your side. The left hand swings in to the small of your back just after the right hand has swung out.

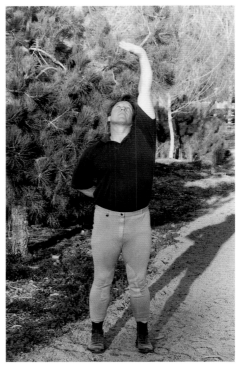

Steps 5, 6, and 7

10 Now your right arm becomes the "iron arm" and swings up, repeating the palm push on the right side. Repeat Steps 2 through 10.

11 Once with the left and once with the right form one complete repetition. Do at least 4 repetitions.

Mounted

Practice *Lift a Single Iron Arm* while riding at the walk on a loose rein or longe line. Ask a friend for assistance.

1 Begin with *Sitting Meditation.*

2 After feeling the connection with your horse, follow the same steps outlined in the unmounted version.

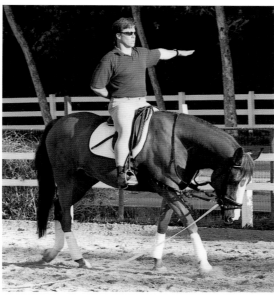

Performing Lift a Single Iron Arm while mounted

Step 5 for both right and left arms: Two views

Ah-Ha!

With practice you will begin to feel the muscles on the relaxed side of your spine letting go before you begin to push your raised palm upward. You will also feel the stretch taking place farther and farther down your spine. Eventually you will feel, in the *unmounted* version, the stretch along the full length of your body, from heel to palm.

Ability Transition

As you develop increasingly enhanced mobility, you may move the hand behind you higher up your back. This more elevated position will relax the shoulder and open the front of the shoulder joint for improved circulation and sensitivity.

Reminder

While pushing the palm up, bring your shoulder to your ear, not the ear to the shoulder. Your spine should be held perfectly straight during the entire exercise. Tilting your head to one side not only takes away from the healing nature of this form, but it also creates or reinforces poor structural alignment.

Summary

In this chapter we have explored a profound territory, a place where you have learned to improve your health and develop your athleticism using Laing Gong. Every time you use these healing exercises, you develop more enhanced mobility in many joints crucial to riding. If you have encountered any difficulties, such as stiffness or pain, I hope you have now clearly identified the root problems and the exercises that can help you heal yourself and overcome these challenges.

You have learned how to move differently—from your quiet center in relaxation rather than through force—and you have become more physically self-aware, so that you can continue to recognize any future "errors" such as tightness, straining, and imbalance. These errors are simply bad habits, or patterns, which you can now identify. When you encounter them, stop, relax, and breathe. Congratulate yourself for noticing the problem, and begin again, watching for the point at which you begin to enter the old pattern. Use your intent and breath to escape that pattern and develop a new pattern, one founded in enhanced mobility. New patterns and lasting change do not come overnight, so you will need to use these exercises with diligence over an extended period of time. Remember what my teacher told me: "There is always a deeper level of relaxation and connection with your body."

Take heart as you work, and know that you have begun to transform your world forever. As one of my mentors regularly reminds me, "We have the power to change the world at anytime by simply changing our perception."

What's Next

In chapter 7, "Application: Bringing It All Together in the Saddle," your focus will shift to riding. You'll work on the quality of the gaits, transitions, bending, lateral work, jumping, and more. Your goal will be to apply to your riding the enhanced mobility you've been developing in this chapter, as well as the enhanced awareness you've developed in the earlier chapters.

Application

Bringing It All Together in the Saddle

NOW YOU CAN APPLY THE MIND, BREATH, and body skills you've been learning to riding situations. In this chapter, you'll encounter questions to expand your awareness. I ask you to remember experiences from previous chapters, and I explain and show you how they can be used now as tools to enhance your riding.

Practice seriously—but
don't be too serious when
you practice!

Your mind is the general,
your awareness the guide.

Remember it all starts
with a smile.

Ride from Your Center

As you continue to practice the exercises in this book, I can promise that you'll experience the following:

• Your body will increasingly act as one cohesive unit with all your aids coming from your center. Taking advantage of your innate strengths and working with the laws of nature (gravity, momentum, and centripetal force), you'll make your horse responsive to the slightest changes in your body.

• You will experience a connection like never before with your horse. You will know that your horse is your greatest teacher, and that *he* has picked *you* as a student.

• With clear intent you will project transitions out in front of you and your horse. From a foundation of smooth, rhythmic breathing, your timing will be flawless; transitions will appear as if there was a silent agreement made by you and your horse to change at a predetermined spot.

These are my promises. I do not take them lightly. I have seen them come true for hundreds of riders.

This is simple, but not easy. The letting go of old ideas and habits is a challenge—mentally, physically, and even emotionally. You may experience joy and fear, laughter and tears. All of these are common, and healthy. In all of this, remember that words will get you no closer to your truth. You will need to practice on and off your horse.

Ride from your center. Abdominal breathing changes the volume of your center, making it bigger, and therefore easier for you to stay balanced. Remember your breath is the vehicle that takes your mind into your body and to your center. Therefore, always know where your breath is. Without it, nothing can change—and with it, nothing is impossible. Your horse can feel a fly on his rump, and he can feel when you hold your breath.

Having a Conversation with Your Horse

When you're in the saddle you need to have a give and take with your horse. It's a conversation, not a lecture. Conversations require that you listen as well as speak, and you can't listen if you're always speaking. This is the basis of a respectful relationship. Some of us do prefer to lecture and lead, but you can't do this all the time. And I

The Most Helpful Question

What is my most fundamental and helpful question for you?

"Where is your breath?"

Search your body with a quiet, calm mind. Maybe you'll find it up high in your chest; maybe it'll be down deep in your belly. In either case, your mind will be focused inward. You'll be connected in mind and body. With a heightened awareness and sensitivity developed by the exercises in previous chapters, you'll move your body with enhanced mobility.

But don't always wait for me to ask you this question. Make it your own! At any time—while exercising or riding, or while just going to the post office or market—you will always benefit from asking yourself this most helpful question: "Where is my breath?"

would suggest that what you get in these situations is compliance, but is that all you want from your horse? If so, you're missing a profound opportunity.

As you've come so far in this book, which sees the horse as our greatest teacher, I will assume that you are interested in having a conversation with your horse. In fact, you do this any time that you join centers with him.

Let's also be clear about what I am *not* suggesting: passivity. When you ride, you *actively* direct your horse. You are responsible for both the horse and yourself. You are leading, but you're not *only* leading.

Practically speaking, any time you attempt to join centers with a force greater than yourself you can't just lead—you're not in a position of power and you will be overwhelmed. (Remember the first three Principles of Tai Chi: *Use the mind, not force*; *Never oppose force with force*; and, *Yield and overcome*.)

Given that you must direct your horse—having him walk, trot, canter, jump—how do you do this while maintaining a conversation with your horse? You *follow, match, and lead.*

Strength as Weakness

Your strengths can trap you and limit your progress. It is human nature to want to "put your best foot forward." It's easy to rely on your strengths, but it takes courage to look at and develop your weaknesses.

For example, if you have a beautiful trot but it takes you a few strides after the transition to "settle in" to this trot, then the transition represents your greatest opportunity for improvement. Practicing transitions will be hard. It will demand dropping out of what is comfortable (the trot), only to return to the uncomfortable over and over again.

With thoughtful consideration of the Tai Chi principles and your newly acquired sensitivity of mind and body, you're ready to take on this challenge. If you persevere and continue the work you've begun in this book, I am confident that you will make the leap to the next level in your riding.

Follow—Match—Lead

Perhaps the quickest way to explain *follow—match—lead* is by example. While this approach applies to all riding situations, here's how it works when you ride a posting trot:

1 You *follow* when the rising energy from the horse's hind legs lifts you out of the saddle;

2 you *match* when you reach the height of your posting; and

3 you *lead* when you sit and apply your driving aid.

Follow—match—lead can be applied to any energy that moves in rhythm, in waves or circles of force. The concept itself is a continuous cycle, constant and yet ever-changing. You are always in one of these three states, and you always move through them in this order.

Sometimes this concept is difficult to feel while riding, and this is often because the speed at which the cycle is revolving is too fast; we don't have enough time to feel the phases and react. This is one of the reasons we usually learn a new movement at a slow speed. As children, we walk before we run. As riders, we walk before we trot. If when you are riding you can't feel the energy cycles, relax and don't worry. With practice you will learn how to follow, match, and lead at this gait, too. At these moments it is enough to "know" in your mind that you are still part of this flow of energy—most likely just following. And surprisingly enough, knowing that you can not always lead often has a calming effect on the mind.

Let's look at this cycle in more detail:

Follow

The horse moves, and you allow him to influence you at that moment. He sets the rhythm, and your body follows him. You follow him, relaxed and listening. You may follow his motion for a half-second, or for ten seconds. Once you've relaxed and followed, you're ready to match.

Match

Now you are connected with the horse's motion, and your mind, breath, and body match him. You're not ahead of or behind the motion, but synchronized and neutral. You are relaxed in your body. Your mind is calm and aware. You are ready to lead.

Lead

You are the directing partner, and you lead your horse by indicating direction, speed, and impulsion. You communicate with your aids within his rhythm. Now that you've communicated your intent, you follow the greater force of the horse.

Returning to our earlier analogy to a conversation:

• when your horse is speaking, you are listening (*following*);

• then there is a moment of quiet (*matching*); and finally,

• when you are speaking (*leading*), your horse is listening.

The conversation flows on and on.

Practically, you already know that aids are most effective when they are precise and brief. After giving the aid, you then need to listen (by following and then matching) in order to assess your horse's response. If the horse did not respond as you wished, you give another aid—lead again. (Of course, this assumes that you are giving the correct aids at the right time.) As you and your horse improve, you'll spend more and more of your time matching, and less and less of your time following or leading. The next time you ride, think about identifying which state you're in, and when you move into another state.

How do you learn to follow, match, and lead? Just as the rhythm of your breath is the key to timing in your body, so is breath the key to maintaining the connection between you and your horse. All the work you have done so far in this book has prepared you to be with your horse in this way.

Let's look at another example of *follow—match—lead*: jumping.

You lead in the approach, match, in the takeoff, and follow over the fence. Now, decompose that sequence into a more detailed, second-by-second series of states:

- When you're approaching the jump, you're leading, and you're directing the horse's attention to the fence.

- Then you follow and match, sensing his response—if he's focused, you can stay matched. If you sense him starting to consider an evasion, you lead again, then follow and match as you assess his response.

  If you need to adjust your striding, you lead, and then return to following and matching.

- As soon as he takes off, he leads, and you follow and then match him in the air and through the landing.

Remember that if you are leading, your horse is following. If you are following, your horse is leading.

Now, consider your own riding. Whether over fences or on the flat, ask yourself these questions:

- Am I always trying to lead?

- Do I follow too often, and let my horse lead me?

Tai Chi's Connection with Follow—Match—Lead

In the discussion of *follow—match—lead*, you may have noticed its underlying complementary nature: it involves, like Yin and Yang, a circular, flowing exchange. You never oppose the force of the horse. Through follow, match, and lead, you redirect the force of the horse from your center.

Expand your awareness, become enlightened, and anything is possible. Otherwise, you will remain trapped in your old ways of thinking and moving. If you continue to do the work you've been learning in this book, you will become enlightened, and you will learn more deeply and quickly.

Does "enlightenment" sound too grandiose or unattainable? Here's another saying from the *Tao Te Ching*: "Knowing others is wisdom. Knowing yourself is enlightenment."

When I first went to Wen Mei Yu, my first Tai Chi teacher, and asked to study with her, she turned me down, saying, "You have too many bad habits. In fact, you have the best bad habits I've ever seen." I came to understand how they permeated my whole body. I had practiced for years noticing only the outside of my body, never looking deeper and never addressing my weaknesses.

Can any rider gain enlightenment? Yes, it's possible, even necessary, because your bad habits don't go away on the horse. You, like all of us, need to retrain yourself to use your body well. You will need to free yourself from fear and let go of old habits. You will have to overcome barriers of mind, desire, willingness, and intent. You will have to be vigilant because as soon as your awareness fades, your unconscious habits will drift back in to fill the space. Enlightenment, and better riding, are won through many, many small efforts, day after day. As Lao Tzu wrote: "A good traveler has no fixed plans, and is not intent on arriving."

Probably the good riders you admire are wise. And the best riders are enlightened. They've earned that knowledge through years of practice. You, too, can know the wisdom of riding a horse and become enlightened by knowing your own body.

Developing Your Program

The exercises in the previous chapters are excellent riding warm-ups. Do the ground versions of these forms before you ride. Once you've learned them, all these exercises take less than twenty minutes. Pick your four favorites, or perhaps your four least favorites (to develop your weaknesses), and do them before you saddle your horse. Once you're on your horse, repeat the *mounted* versions.

Just before you mount up, ask yourself these questions:

- Do I release my stress and tension before I ride?
- Am I communicating unnecessary tension and stress to my horse?
- Do I remember that my horse also needs to shift into his work?
- Do I always warm him up and cool him down?

It's nearly impossible to keep the mind–body connection continuous and unbroken. And it's also difficult to keep the stresses and fears of the world and society out of your mind and body. You can, however, reduce these tension-creating distractions within a few minutes by using these exercises as warm-ups prior to riding. You and your horse will be happier and more productive.

Intent

In the coming sections I'll focus on the trot, canter, transitions, bending, and lateral work. Before you start, ask yourself, "Who knows how to canter better—my horse or I? Who was born knowing how to canter?" I ask these questions because all too often I see riders whose horse is not moving well, and so they think that they should teach their horse how to move. This may, in fact, be true. But before we assume it is, let's also make explicit what this assumes. It assumes that your horse is sound, that your saddle and bit fit well, that you ride balanced, centered, and connected with your horse, and that you have sufficient knowledge to teach him. If you're unsure of how you'd assess any of these, seek professional help from your veterinarian, chiropractor, farrier, saddle-fitter, riding instructor, or horse trainer. Let's assume that you've passed all these tests with flying colors, and now return to you, your horse, and using intent.

Using *follow—match—lead*, you will ask (lead) and then follow. To guide your horse in these movements, you

- must be clear in your intent before you commit to an aid, and
- must move your body from its center with your mind.

Your intent leads your horse.

First, feel where you're going. Put your mind there and then let the body follow. In the *Side Step* exercise (p. 43), you practiced engaging your intent, and letting your body follow. You "melted" the muscles in front of your body. You didn't move until 100 percent of your weight was shifted.

Practice this same pattern in your mounted work. Without clear intent you will move awkwardly, without good timing, and without full body unity. Your horse will never quite know what you are asking for, and in your frustration you will very likely "over aid" and use force. Force always creates a separation between you and your horse. Often your horse will actively avoid your forced direction in an attempt to relieve the discomfort you're causing.

Intent and Jumping

You can project your intent out in front of you at any given moment. With a little experience and practice, you can even place your intent in two places at one time. In fact, there are no limits to where and how you project your intent. For example, in a jumping round, you may in the same moment be completely aware of the state of your body while projecting your intent out beyond an upcoming jump. It is the same as putting your mind into the balls of your feet prior to letting your weight move forward (see *Standing Meditation*, p. 37).

You've probably heard the saying, "Throw your heart over the fence, and your horse will follow." With your focus out beyond the jump, your awareness is heightened and your horse is reassured about where the two of you are headed. Your expanded awareness makes your sensitivity acute, and therefore you experience no need to micromanage your position and your horse. Remember it's your horse that is going to jump the fence, not you.

The exercises coming up in this chapter follow a slightly different format from those in earlier chapters. You'll find an "Opening the Gates" section that will connect each exercise back to your earlier work on the Eight Gates.

Aids from Your Center

Only when your center is loosened can you move with agility and coordination. It is as if your center is the hub of a wheel that's constantly rotating. All motion begins at the center.

With a loosened center, you can "talk" to your horse using a whisper instead of a loud voice. Most of us never learned how to move from the center. Instead of using the core muscles in the body to move your center, we tend to use the bigger, dominant muscles of our limbs and torso to pull our center this way and that.

Here's a little test.

1 If you're not sitting, sit.

2 Move your left seat bone forward in your chair.

How easy was it? Did you have to think about how to do it? Did you pull your seat forward with your left thigh, or did you push with your gluteus muscles? Did your weight shift to the left? Did you clench or brace any muscles? Did you hold your breath as you attempted to move your seat?

All of the above results are symptoms—symptoms that disconnect you from your horse. If you were riding, how much connection with the horse would you have given up to simply move your seat bone forward?

1 Try it again. Only this time I would like you to become aware of your belly button, which is a useful landmark for locating our center.

2 Now move your belly button to the right by turning your waist to the right. Feel your left seat bone move forward as your center—belly button—moves to the right. Notice the ease in which you move your seat bones when shift your focus to moving your center.

You may be accustomed to shifting your weight by leaning, and by pushing and pulling from outside your center. The approach throughout this book, however, is to move from inside our center. When we move in this way we move with less effort and more fluidity and speed. Moving your belly button can become a highly effective focal point for directing your primary aids while staying connected with your horse.

The belly button idea is one of many techniques you'll learn in this chapter to help you stay centered and free of tension while riding. Your aids will effortlessly redirect your horse when they are directed from your center. When you join centers with your horse, "your" center includes the horse's. You can redirect the horse by simply moving your own center because you and your horse share a joined center.

In classical Tai Chi, students are challenged to discover how to redirect the force of 1000 pounds using only 4 ounces of force. While you're probably tempted to think that this feat is almost impossible, you need to realize that you are already well on your way to possessing these skills.

Refining the Walk

At the walk you can develop your skills of awareness, breathing, and intent. Because the walk is the slowest gait, you have time to go through the checklist of mind, breath, and body. You can identify and address the root cause of what you do in the saddle. In addition, you'll learn how to energize your horse's walk.

Before You Mount

Revisit the *Horse Stance* (p. 56). Push your knees out and feel the tendons under your seat bones tighten. Now arch your lower back and feel the tendons soften. Realize that you are in a very weak position, one that you want to avoid. Breathe deeply and slowly and soften your lower back. Fix this by redirecting your breath toward the lower back so you expand and open the Ming Meng.

Step-by-Step

1 When you mount, begin in *Sitting Meditation* (p. 40). Where is your breath? If it's not already in your Dain Tian, direct it with your mind down into your Dain Tian. Search for tension in your body and ask yourself why it is there. Let tension drop through your bones, down through the horse, and into the ground.

2 When you are completely relaxed and aware, then signal your horse to walk. As your horse moves forward underneath you, listen to your body. Again, are you arching your back in an effort to "sit up straight"? If you are, you now know that you are adversely affecting your structural alignment. You are blocking the energy of the horse at your waist and putting weight on the horse's forehand through the leverage created by your stiff spine.

3 Instead of sitting up straight, fill your belly with your breath. This "filling" acts to support a straight and sensitive spine without restricting your ability to move with your horse. You're opening Gate 1: The Dain Tian.

4 After you feel your abdomen relax and expand, move your attention to your lower back and allow your breath to fill and soften it. You're opening Gate 2: The Ming Meng.

5 Feel how your horse moves underneath you; feel the power of his movement and how your body moves with the force.

Your horse is always moving you, because he's bigger and stronger. Keep your head and eyes up—don't look down at the horse.

Now is the time to connect with your horse, not to direct him. You can connect with his rhythmic motion. Instructors of therapeutic riding rely on that motion to help their riders. The horse's rhythm is your ally. All riding is therapeutic: the horse's action is like a massage that helps you move your body and regain natural mobility.

Maintain your structural integrity. Let the rhythm of your horse teach you how to move. Join with that rhythm. At this point, your goal should be to let go, not "to do something." Excess body motion affects the horse's stride—for instance, making him tense and quick in his front legs. Relax. Let yourself be moved. Breathe. Follow.

Ask a friend to watch your upper body movement. Are you "pushing" toward the pommel of the saddle, with too much forward movement, and not the same motion in the back?

Move your awareness to your center; see if you can find the left-right rise and fall of the horse's hindlegs. This vertical motion combined with the constant forward motion of you and your horse acts to create a figure-eight shaped motion in your center (see drawing).

Think of your pelvis moving inside a sphere, which is your center (your expanded center—don't forget that your joining centers with your horse). Rather than focusing on your horse's movement, search inside your center and locate that three-dimensional, figure-eight motion. Your relaxed and following seat allows the energy of the horse to move through you in this pattern. When you have become aware of the motion inside, you are truly connected with your horse. Realize that once again you have used the path of mind, breath, and body to connect with your horse.

James On Your Shoulder

Remember the first and only rule, "Smile."

When you want to know what your horse is doing, feel, don't look. Trust that you can sense everything you need to know about your horse without using your eyes.

A figure-eight motion in your center.

6 Walk a circle, and investigate the cadence of your breath. Are you taking one long breath in, accompanied by one long breath out? Or, do you inhale on a count like, "*in* one, two; *out* one, two"?

Find the relationship between the cadence of your breath and the strides of your horse. How many steps does your horse take while you're inhaling, and how many while you're exhaling? By changing the cadence or rhythm of your breathing you can influence your horse's gait. Slow, deep breaths tell the horse to relax and lengthen his strides, decreasing his tempo. Quicker, more energetic breaths pick up the horse's tempo.

7 Quicken the rhythm of your breath. Don't change the depth of your breathing, but just try to take in the same amount of air a little faster.

For example, instead of inhaling and exhaling on a two-count, inhale on a three-count, and exhale to a four-count. Play with this exercise until you experience how you can refine your horse's walk simply by exercising your breath. Be careful not to use your leg on the horse while practicing this exercise. The goal is to develop your breath as a riding aid. The goal is not a spirited, energized walk, but the quality of the walk that results from using this aid.

CAUTION: Don't hyperventilate. If you begin to feel light-headed, you are trying too hard. Relax and slow your respiration until you feel centered, and then try again taking shorter breaths.

8 As your horse's gait quickens, so does the figure-eight motion in your center. Imagine that the eight is getting bigger and moving a little faster.

Remember that your breath is merely an aid in creating the mind–body connection. Once connected, the motion of your center influences your horse most. The figure eight is a great tool that allows you to focus on your center without tightening up. Practice changing the shape of the eight. How does your center affect the tempo and energy of your horse?

9 See if you can get more motion in your lower back. Can you relax more and expand your lower back so that you can actually feel the force of the horse's hind end move through your Ming Meng toward the front of your body? When this happens, it will feel as if your lumbar vertebrae are stretched open as if suspended from above. This is an extremely effective method for healing a sore back and loosening a tight lower back.

Opening the Gates

At the walk, you are concerned with three gates: The Dain Tian, Ming Meng, and the Back of the Heart. By directing your breath into these areas, you soften and expand your body—opening the gates. The ability to open any of the Eight Gates while riding depends on your practice on the ground. Without sufficient time spent discovering and becoming aware of these areas, your work on the horse will be greatly hampered.

Review these exercises to help open the Dain Tian, Ming Meng, and the Back of the Heart:

- *Abdominal Breathing* (p. 90)
- *Open the Ming Meng* (p. 99)
- *Thrust Palm in Bow Stance* (p. 146)

> *Rider Insight, Cindy:* "When I learned to open the two lower gates, it felt as if I were riding inside my horse. As soon as I let go with the back of my heart, I felt as if I were riding on a big squishy ball instead of a saddle."

Reminder

If you don't feel connected, go back to *Counting Your Breath* (p. 97).

If you feel tight, revisit these exercises to unlock your body:

- *Embracing the Moon* (p. 102)
- *Hold the Sky with Both Hands* (p. 138)
- *Neck Turns* (p. 121)
- *Spread Your Chest* (p. 126)

Because you practiced these exercises on the ground, your body will remember them and the awareness will follow you into the saddle. If you haven't done these on the ground, don't expect them to work magically on the horse. There are no shortcuts.

In a similar way, there are no shortcuts on your horse either. For example, the beginning of a great trot starts with the end of a great walk. In your upward transition, you must end with a great walk to experience a seamless transition upward into the trot. You take these abilities into the trot and canter, where the motion is bigger. You learn them at the walk, because you can't effectively learn them at the faster, more energetic gaits. The bigger the movement, the harder it is to release and let go of the tension that binds the body.

Using Observation to See Energy Moving

The idea of seeing energy might conjure up visions of metaphysical and New Age followers gazing into auras and looking at colors and light. While I believe that some people really do see forms of energy that most of us miss, the energy that I'm describing can be seen by everyone who knows where to look—as I'll explain in a moment.

While most of us cannot explain the mechanics of gravity, we sense it and can anticipate its effects (a suspended ball, for instance, will drop when released). While riders might not be able to explain the mechanics of energy flows between horse and rider, we can sense and anticipate its effects (a connected walk, for instance, will propel our center through a figure-eight pattern).

Because we've lived with gravity since birth, we have developed a deep, largely unconscious sense of its effects. None of us has, in contrast, spent nearly as much time on horseback—for many of us it's a relatively brief encounter perhaps two or three times a week—so it's no wonder that we are less sensitive and skilled at seeing these horse-rider energy flows.

When I look at horse and rider I see them as one organic whole. Your two separate energies combine to make one force greater than the sum of your two parts. The way that I see the movement of energy move from the horse into the rider and back into the horse is first by watching the way the wrinkles of your clothing move as you ride. It's the same way that I can be sitting inside a building and know without any doubt that the wind is blowing outside by observing the undulating movements of a flag. By paying close attention to how the wrinkles move, I can see how the energy of your horse is moving through you.

For example, if I'm watching you at the trot, I might see the wrinkles in the back of your shirt roll horizontally upward from your lower back (Ming Meng), traveling straight up and out the neck of your shirt. This tells me that the energy of your horse is not being redirected back into the whole—you and your horse—but is instead being lost out the top of your head.

See for yourself. Watch the wrinkles in the shirt of a rider who is one with her horse. You will see the wrinkles move up toward the upper back—when they reach Gate 4: The Back of the Heart, the wrinkles dissipate out toward the shoulders, where they disappear. This motion of the wrinkles tells me that the rider's energy has been redirected at Gate 4, forward out Gate 3: The Front of the Heart, and down the arms through the reins back to the horse.

Watch the rhythm of the horse in the rider's shirt wrinkles. If the two are connected, there will be a common rhythm between the movement of the horse's tail and the rider's clothing. If the rider you are watching wears her hair in a ponytail, look for the movement of the ponytail in relation to the horse's tail and mane.

The movement of the wrinkles in the rider's shirt mirrors the internal flow of energy through his body.

Refining the Walk (cont.)

Root Problems

Usually you are more concerned with the horse than yourself; this outward focus distracts you from your part of the union with your horse. Your body goes into a sort of autopilot, where tension can run rampant. For instance, this tension may lead you to hold your breath. Or, if you are breathing, you might breathe high into a tight chest. In an attempt to get a more energetic walk or to push your horse forward, you may be tempted to use force to contort, push, and pull with your seat. Underlying all these symptoms is a single root problem—not relaxing and breathing deep into your abdomen.

If you find yourself in this tense predicament, don't get caught up by the situation. Take a good, deep belly breath. Relax. Just start again—hit your own "reset" button by returning to the beginning of the exercise. If you still find yourself becoming tense, return to the unmounted exercises. Remember that all the time you spend in the unmounted exercises is an investment—not time lost from riding. Working on the ground gives you an opportunity to focus on your mind, breath, and body without any distractions. These exercises then pay dividends when you ride. Please don't think of the unmounted exercises as something to graduate from.

To improve your riding at the walk, review these two exercises:

- *Hold the Sky with Both Hands*, for moving your spine as a single unit (p. 138)
- *Thrust Palm in Bow Stance*, for creating independent motion of your torso and pelvis (p. 146)

Smooth, Invisible Transitions

Your riding goal should be to think a transition and have your horse respond by executing your thought. This effortless harmony can become real. You've probably seen riding masters who can ride any horse and stay connected with the horse's every action, and all the while they ride without any obvious aids. Keep those images in mind.

The key to seamless transitions is timing. Without it, your transitions are left to chance. I have observed many riders whose walk, trot, and canter are beautiful, but their transitions are disjointed. For example, I often see walk-trot transitions in which the rider asks for a transition and then struggles for two or three strides, until the horse gets the message and picks up the trot. Typically, I see this pattern repeated with nearly every transition, upward or downward.

In these situations, the rider, within the first moments of asking for and not getting the trot, tenses and begins to overuse aids that are ineffective mainly because of their inappropriate timing, nothing else. As the rider pushes, pulls, and adjusts, the only thing that's accomplished is putting her body into an unbalanced position. Now the horse faces two challenges: unclear aids and an unbalanced and unbalancing rider. Remember that when you're giving an aid, you are leading (*follow—match—lead*). *An unbalanced rider cannot lead the horse to anything but an unbalanced state.*

At this point, several things can happen:

- The horse and rider can continue in imbalance, or
- they can recover balance by relaxing back into a walk, or
- the horse can take over the lead, make the transition and establish the trot, and then the rider can follow and match—in essence recovering her balance thanks to the horse.

But this whole struggle is entirely avoidable.

The problem starts before any physical aid is given; it starts in the rider's mind. Most transitions are asked for at a specific point predetermined by the rider or trainer, such as a letter in a dressage arena, a cone in the reining pen, or some other landmark. When the transition point is defined in this way, it is nearly impossible to maintain a rhythmic connection with the horse as you approach "The Spot." Predetermining the exact point or spot of transition creates in the mind an invisible vertical plane in time and space at which the transition must take place. It's much like running up to a stream to jump over it and realizing when you get closer that you are on the wrong lead to jump. You adjust by taking half- or stutter-steps in an attempt to get the right lead. This throws your body out of rhythm and usually results in a weak—and wet—jump.

When you use a specific spot to plan your transitions, this self-imposed starting line often causes you to barge into your transitions regardless of whether or not you and your horse are ready. In this case, the problem lays in your perception, not your ability; that is, you have forced your timing and fouled yourself up.

Step-by-Step

Here's the technique I use to help create seamless and effortless transitions.

1 Assuming that you and your horse are well warmed up, pick a spot in the arena where you would like to have the transition take place.

2 Envision a sphere large enough to contain both you and your horse and see that sphere surrounding the spot where the transition will happen.

Now there is no longer a line, but rather an area in which you perform the transition. It's important to *see* it, not just *think* it. I personally envision a large soap bubble for my sphere, like the ones I blew as a child. I see all the colors of the rainbow swirling inside its shimmering surface.

3 Next, close your eyes and see and feel a perfect trot in your mind's eye. You and your horse move in complete harmony, as if you were trotting on air.

4 Open your eyes and look again at the bubble, and see that perfect trot happening inside the bubble. With your intent you project what you created in your mind forward into the sphere, so now the perfect trot waits for you and your horse to ride into it.

Instead of having to focus on a tense, thin line in space, you can now focus on entering the bubble from a balanced and quiet walk, completely ready to follow your horse into the perfect trot that awaits you. By taking a few moments to change your perception and expand your awareness, you can achieve amazing results in your transitions.

Opening the Gates

You'll use three gates in the process of creating and projecting the trot: Gate 3: The Front of the Heart, Gate 7: The Upper Pass, and Gate 8: The Crown. Open the Upper Pass and Crown to create the trot in your mind's eye. I think of it like a movie projector. Your mind's eye is the film—the image of the trot you envision; the Upper Pass is the lens, focusing this image forward, keeping it clear and real; and the Crown is the light source that projects the image. Now, to carry this metaphor just a bit further, we need to direct that image to a particular place. Your *open heart* and your *intent* direct the created image to the sphere.

Reminder

If you haven't practiced *Walking Backward* (p. 62), you are missing an important experience that is necessary in order to make this technique effective. Remember that the power of this technique comes from expanding your awareness to change your perception.

Your mind, breath, and body must be connected at the walk before you attempt a walk-trot transition. If you have trouble using this technique, return to the unmounted exercises to build your skills and awareness.

Upward Transition: Walk to Trot

You have probably experienced those gratifying moments when your horse flowed from walk to trot, or from trot to walk. The transitions were calm, with one gait rolling into the next with no bouncing or undue effort. You can help yourself have transitions like this all the time by first projecting your intent and then staying focused on your body. Your horse will feel subtle adjustments instead of "loud" aids. You'll relive that moment of perfection, following the path of mind, breath, and body.

Before You Ask

The walk-trot transition can be executed in a moment when your timing is correct. As you project your intent into the coming trot, however, ride the walk you're still in.

On a physical level, a smooth transition starts at the last stride of the gait leading into it. To enjoy a good walk-trot transition, ride that last walk step with the same quality of rhythm and impulsion as the previous steps. Be entirely physically present and aware of every moment in the walk. Savor it! Taste it as you would a fine wine—without rushing, enjoying it for what it is, rather than anticipating the taste of what you're going to eat or drink next.

As you maintain this intense physical connection with the walk, mentally use your intent to envision and project your perfect trot. There is no contradiction here: physically, you're entirely present in the moment; mentally, you're anticipating the coming trot. Remember the exercise *Walking Backward* (p. 62), in which you experienced the power and independence of your physical body and your intent.

Most of the transition problems I see arise because riders *abandon the walk before the transition*. They slip into a no-man's land—neither walk nor trot—and lose their connection with their horse.

Maintain your "bone-to-leather" connection in your seat. Stay with your horse. Inhale when you think of the trot. Exhale when you ask.

Make your aid clear and concise. I see riders whose horses have been aided to dullness, and usually it's because the rider's body gets in the way. Could this be you? Don't let your body get in the way of clear communication.

In giving an aid with your outside leg, did you move your upper body out, up, and away from your leg that applied the aid? Think back to your experience of *Side Step* (p. 43). Did you lean to take the step? If yes, then you're now seeing that same movement habit here in the trot transition. Don't lean with your body to get your outside leg back, otherwise your horse will have to compensate for your shifting weight before he can respond to your aid.

Don't leave your body's position entering the transition to chance. I'll repeat my most fundamental question: "Where is your breath?" When asking for the trot, are you breathing in or out? Experiment and determine whether your horse changes gaits better when you're inhaling or exhaling.

Step-by-Step

1 When you mount, begin in *Sitting Meditation*. Complete your normal warm-up.

2 For the first round, try asking for the transition while inhaling. The very first communication with your horse when asking for the trot should be your breath. Breathe in and expand the space under your rib cage. Expand the Ming Meng. You get an instant connection for the transition. Your body will be ready to receive the change in force in your horse's gait as he picks up the trot.

3 Lead your body with your mind. Use your intent to create the trot you want; project it in front of you. Don't worry about moving your body into that trot—your horse will do that for you. By projecting your intent forward, you have created the new space into which you and your horse will move. Let your body remain quiet, correct, and ready to lead.

Listen to your body, and feel whether or not you tense your seat when you prepare for the change. Do you hold your breath? If so, think about exhaling into the trot.

4 Give your aid. As your horse picks up the trot, you pick up your breath. You have now changed the rhythm and your breathing must follow. Find the new rhythm of

The figure-eight motion in your center at the trot.

your breath. It will be dictated by the bigger motion of the horse in your body.

Revisit the figure-eight pattern you practiced in *Refining the Walk* (p. 176). That figure eight is still there, only now because of the suspension present in the trot it follows a more vertical ellipse with a kind of over-the-top-feeling rather than the flatter, more horizontal plane it follows at the walk (see drawing).

Opening the Gates

Begin the transition by energizing Gate 8: The Crown and Gate 2: The Ming Meng. In the last moments of the walk, pay close attention to the Ming Meng, keeping it open throughout the transition. The power of the horse rising into your body can cause you to tighten your heart. Exhaling into the transition will help you avoid any such tightening and help you maintain your connection into the trot.

Reminder

Remember that your breath is a powerful and versatile tool. You may find that you have better transitions while exhaling rather than inhaling. Whatever the case may be, your fluid, rhythmic breathing is the key to staying connected with the horse through transitions. I recommend that you take the time to discover the treasures hidden in this exercise. Your goal should not be getting the trot, but understanding the transition.

Root Causes

Concentrating on leg and rein aids pulls us out of awareness of our center. Remember that all change comes from our center. Check yourself for over-reliance on these external aids. Are you perhaps using them to help you balance? Breathe and shift your focus to your center as you quiet these aids.

Downward Transition: Trot to Walk to Halt

You've followed the mind, breath, and body path to the upward transition. Now you'll use the same aids to transition down to the walk and then the halt. You may want to refer back to your earlier work in *Breathing to a Halt or Walk* (p. 112).

In transitioning down to a walk from the trot, your center must lead—as it must in any transition. The motion and rhythm of your pelvis must slow without disconnecting from your horse. The most frequent root cause of this disconnection is tensing the muscles around the seat. This tensing is known as holding or bracing.

Bracing changes the movement of your pelvis and can cause you to bounce to a walk—not what we want. The aid I often see in this transition is the rider holding her breath as she tightens her abdominal muscles to slow the pelvis. This tightening or squeezing with the abs and bracing in the lower back (Ming Meng) does slow the pelvis, by restricting the movement of the lower lumbar. If you do this, you cut yourself in half energetically, and you cannot redirect the horse's energy down to the walk.

Instead, use your breath to slow your pelvis without tightening the lower back. Breathe down deep into your belly and as your diaphragm pushes down, your visceral cavity expands, changing its volume with the pressure. This change in pressure slows your pelvis without restricting its motion through holding with the external muscles of your abdomen. You need those external muscles to be soft and sensitive to negotiate the changing rhythm in your body as your horse slows to the walk. Holding your breath negates your aid and disconnects you from your horse.

Before You Ask

Slowing your horse with your body alone is ineffective. First, think about the transition: clarify your intent, and let your body go where your mind has already gone.

Expand your awareness outward. Think of the exercise *Walking Backward* (p. 62), in which you experienced your environment moving independently. Use this experience to see your riding environment slowing down and coming to a walk.

Imagine your Ming Meng gate closing slightly. This will slow the movement in your lower back and open your Dain Tian. In this state the weight of your body will fall slightly forward in your seat and slow your pelvis.

James On Your Shoulder

Don't get frustrated if you can't breathe into the walk from the trot on your first try. Feel your breath sink into your abdomen and imagine it sinking down through your body into your horse. Awareness is the start.

Opening the heart gates at the trot prior to getting the walk can be a challenge. It requires letting go of fear. Fear in all its forms closes the heart; in fact, it slams it closed. Most of us have built up armor in the form of a closed heart. We have done so to protect ourselves and now it keeps us separated from our horse. Deep healing and connection can take place when we let go of our old fears.

Step-by-Step

1 Put your mind into your center. As you trot, feel the motion of your center and connect with it before you slow it. Use your mind's eye to see your pelvic bone: see its rocking in relationship to the rhythm of your breath.

2 When your mind and body are connected through your breath, your horse will walk when you ask. Ask as you exhale, letting this be your first aid. During the down transition your motion may be slightly ahead of your horse. You need, therefore, to redirect your energy down into your horse through the Dain Tian. If you don't, you'll be pushed forward out of your seat, and your weight will fall onto the horse's forehand.

In addition, you can compensate for the transition by keeping the Back of the Heart gate open throughout. I think of it like an open parachute slowing down my upper body. This opening helps to redirect the momentum down through your spine into your seat, rather than forward through the Front of the Heart gate, again pushing you forward.

Ideally, you'll have both your heart gates open, and this will help your upper body to be balanced, and your hands quiet and sensitive. All of this allows your seat to remain soft and deep and keeps you from bouncing forcefully down on the horse's back. Opening the front heart gate also helps open the Chi Who gates, and their opening enhances the strength and sensitivity of the hands and arms.

Opening the Gates

Closing the Ming Meng slightly while keeping the Back of the Heart and Dain Tian wide open will help your down transitions. Keeping the Back of the Heart open helps you avoid tightening and getting pushed forward in the saddle. This tightening often originates in using the reins to slow the horse.

If you're having trouble keeping the front heart gate open, try this: reach up with one arm and place your hand on top of your head; keep your elbow pointing out to the side. This position opens the Chi Who gate (below your collarbone), and this, in turn, helps open the front heart gate. Now gently lower your arm and retake the reins, paying close attention all the while to maintain the softness in the Chi Who. If you have a tendency to brace in your chest and shoulders, you will feel the tension return to the heart and Chi Who as soon as the arm drops. It's simply a bad habit, and you now have the tools to change it.

Reminder

Remember the more your pelvis moves, the less your upper body moves. Your lower lumbar moves and dissipates the motion of your upper body. If you brace in the chest, everything else moves. Holding on with your seat, you fight physics. Surrender your center and spine to the rhythm of the horse.

Go back to *Spread Your Chest* (p. 126), and practice the exercise with this new awareness of tightness in your chest. This exercise creates the enhanced mobility in your shoulders that will enable you to join with the power of the horse so that he can't jerk his head down to pull you forward.

You have tremendous power in the subtle rotation of the humerus bone in your upper arm. With your humerus rotated, you enable the force from the reins to be passed through your arm, into the latissimus dorsi, and down to your seat. Rather than tightening your upper body and leaning back on the reins, just use a slight rotation of your upper arm. (See anatomical diagrams in the *Appendix*, p. 245.)

Root Causes

The root cause of many down-transition problems is bracing in the torso. First observe yourself carefully; do you tighten in this way? If so, keep track of the rhythm of your breath. Focus on breathing and relaxing so that you stay connected with your horse.

Revisiting the Trot

To ride the trot—sitting or posting, collected or lengthened—you apply the knowledge you've gained at the walk. The mechanics of the horse's two-beat gait affects your position and the way in which you ride.

At the trot, think of your spine moving like a flag in the wind. The flag moves in rolls as the force of the wind passes *through* it. When you have relaxed control of your joints, your limbs can stay still and sensitive as your spine rolls and moves with the energy of the horse. In Tai Chi, this is the principle of yield and overcome.

Before You Mount

Practice *Wall Sitting* (p. 59), in which you push your lower back into the wall. That same feeling should lead the sitting phase of your posting trot.

If we look at the movement and rhythm of the pelvis at the rising trot, we can say that it's two-beat: 1-up, 1-down; 1-up, 1-down. Your pelvis is in the saddle only every other beat. Once you sit the trot, your pelvis's rhythm doubles, as you must absorb every beat. To help you sit better, you need to relax all the muscles that you were using to balance and move yourself while posting.

Step-by-Step

1 While at the trot you want to engage your lower lumbar to help you sit straight and strong. When sitting, if you expand your lower back, opening the Ming Meng gate, you can maintain your connection with your horse (see "correct" photo).

For many riders, their main problem in the trot is their inability to surrender the spine fully to the motion of the horse. Usually a closed Ming Meng and a tight, braced lower back are the root causes. Many riders end up with a lower back braced in an accentuated arch, which cuts their body in half energetically. Rather than allowing the energy of the horse to move freely up their spine, the energy meets resistance in their lower or middle back. This resistance causes the upper part of their body to become unstable as the full force of the horse pushes against the resistance.

Your goal is to allow the lower lumbar to move. Use your mind and breath to soften your lower back.

At the posting trot, most riders do not sit truly straight and erect during the sitting phase. Their upper body is nearly always leaning slightly forward, and this misalignment prevents their bones from transferring energy through their bodies in relaxation (see "incorrect" photo). For instance, gravity still pulls the rider down, but due to this misalignment, the force doesn't travel into their seat to make their seat aids powerful. Without a deep connection in the seat, they resort to overusing their legs as a means of gaining impulsion in the horse.

The root of power for your legs, however, is not your seat, but your lower back. You must tighten your lower back to use your legs. Now your lower back becomes even tighter and your seat even more disconnected, and your position deteriorates even further into tension. As you can see, holding the lower back has a snowballing effect and it traps you in a weakened position.

2 When you are posting and you begin to drop your seat to the saddle, expand your lower back. Look ahead, imagining something in the sky like a soaring hawk or a string of balloons. Ride to the hawk or balloons. Allow your crown to float upward. And smile!

Step 1: Correct (left): the rider's lower lumbar is released and moving freely with the force of the horse, resulting in harmony and smooth, rhythmic motion. (Note: the rider's head position is too forward— a remnant of her compensatory mechanism to counterbalance her formerly closed back that will disappear as the rider next learns to open her crown.)

Incorrect (right): this rider's misalignment (leaning forward) locks the lower back, closes the Ming Meng, and the horse's energy enters the rider's body percussively, resulting in disharmony, unbalance, and a jolting ride.

Ride to the Balloons

One of the biggest challenges many riders have is keeping their heads up and their eyes off the horse. Looking down puts the head and neck in a weak and unhealthy position as far as structural balance is concerned. In this position, it is impossible to maintain the fluid rhythm of the spine while riding. With the head down, you must hold it balanced with the muscles of the neck and upper back, creating tension in the neck and shoulders of not only the rider, but the horse. To break this habit of looking down, I ask the rider to imagine a string of balloons floating in the air approximately 15 feet ahead of them. I ask them to tell me how many balloons are in the bunch and what colors they are. Look up and forward—ride to the balloons.

This visualization helps you focus on something other than your horse and it engages your imagination and intent. Experiment with it; play with it. See if it helps you place your head in the right position through relaxation rather than direct muscular effort.

3 When you are posting and you begin to drop your seat to the saddle, then your Ming Meng gate should expand and soften. Breathe in, expanding your lower back. This acts to release the muscle holding your spine. Yes, it's easier said than done, I know. You can apply the technique of counting the cadence at the trot to help in the timing of letting go with your lower back.

4 As you sit more erect, you can sit longer and deeper, so your horse really lifts you into the next posting phase. When you rise, lead the motion of your body using your awareness of opening your Dain Tian. In my mind, as I'm riding the posting trot, I experience a series of openings and closings of the Dain Tian and Ming Meng.

To help in the timing and rhythm at the trot, it may also be helpful to think of it in terms of *follow—match—lead*. When the horse lifts you, you are following. You rise and near the top of the motion, you've matched the rhythm. You sit and make contact with the saddle, and you lead. The cycle is then repeated throughout the trot.

Remember it is most effective to give aids when you are leading, which also means that your horse is following.

5 To build the energy of your trot, take deeper and quicker breaths. You're changing your intent, toward bigger and rounder strides. Your horse responds, so his strides become deeper and stronger, bigger and rounder.

You can also drive the horse by "bouncing" your breath off the ground. Visualize sending your breath down through the horse into the ground, when it then rebounds to you up through the horse's energized motion.

6 When you near the corner of the ring, expand your crown and lean from your lower lumbar. This is the same feeling as in *Hold the Sky with Both Hands* (p. 138). You should feel more weight on your inside seat bone. Your weight shifts and cues your horse to turn.

Opening the Gates

To help your trot work, you open these four gates: the Dain Tian, Ming Meng, Front of the Heart, and Back of the Heart. Opening the gates allows the energy of the horse to move through you without creating resistance.

> *Rider Insight, Margaret:* "I asked James if he could show me how I could encourage my horse to increase his suspension. He said to open up and receive his energy and movement. When I did this at the top of his stride (uppermost moment of suspension), it encouraged his back to lift, which created a definite increase in suspension and softness in my horse. The idea of receiving his energy rather than manipulating it was astronomically effective. Of course much of the reason that I could understand and execute James's instructions was due to our earlier unmounted work. The opening of the heart, front and back, greatly increased my capacity to feel the horse."

The Dain Tian and Ming Meng are directly responsible for maintaining a deep and active seat. They form the foundation necessary to open the heart. Opening the heart makes room for and invites the horse up into you. As you explore the relationship between opening and closing these gates and the movement of your horse, remember that it all starts with your breath and your intent.

The Constantly Changing Center

When riding, there is only one time that your weight should remain distributed 50/50 left and right in your seat: when your horse is at the halt with his feet square and parallel. At all other times, when the horse is moving, your weight is constantly shifting. Your center is actually a sphere that is constantly moving and changing. Trying to hold fast to a point that we call the center is impossible. To define your center you need to know where the outside edges lie.

Buddha said that entire answers lie in the middle ground—and to know the middle you must know the edges.

To enhance your balance, you want to redefine your outside edges and bring them closer together. In Tai Chi, as in riding, your balance cannot depend on a stationary position. It must be alive and moving—and always within your center.

Realize that the horse's center is also moving with the forward motion of the trot. To keep your centers joined, you pass through the center where both of you meet. When you ride in a posting trot imagine yourself passing through the center with each stride, so you're not trying to hold your center still. Think of letting your center breathe.

Exercises that you can use to open these gates and enhance your trot work include:

- *Open the Ming Meng* (p. 99)
- *Thrust Palm in Bow Stance* (p. 146)
- *Bend with an Arch* (p. 154)
- *Hip Circles* (p. 142)
- *Lift a Single Iron Arm* (p. 158)

All these exercises help you soften your lower lumbar and gain enhanced mobility in your spine. By practicing these exercises, you will be able to more reliably open your gates.

Reminder

If you tighten up those muscles around your spine, you won't be able to stay flexible enough to stay connected to your horse and his motion. Your seat will be weakened, and you will need to overuse your muscles to maintain your position. Because of your resulting rigidity, you won't be able to take advantage of the natural power that originates in your center. You then make up for this weakness by relying on more leg aids and spurs, because your horse is not getting the message from your seat.

The structural aspects of the trot relate back to *Sitting Meditation*. When your horse stands immobile, you can sit and focus on the awareness you gained in that exercise. See how opening your Ming Meng helps your horse move up into you.

Root Causes

Here is a list of symptoms that I see at the trot:

- Your head pushes forward or is constantly looking down.
- Your elbows are out and up.
- Your seat is bouncing, and your legs swing.
- You grip with your legs.
- Your upper body is not quiet.
- Your horse is constantly tugging on the reins.
- You must use your legs to keep the horse moving forward.

All these symptoms derive from a single root cause: an inability to move the lower lumbar region of the spine independently of the rest of the spine or the lower body. This inflexibility prevents the rider from having a connected seat. This lack of ability is apparent if you need to lean your upper body backward or forward to enhance the use of your seat. Leaning gives you leverage, and this extra power may make you feel safe. However, leaning also reduces your sensitivity to the movement of the horse—the connection that you seek.

Bending on the Circle

Whenever you bend your horse on a circle, turn him on the forehand, or turn him on the haunches, you can apply the tools of mind, breath, and body. Technically, to bend your horse, you move either your left or right seat bone forward. Moving the left seat bone forward bends the horse to the left; moving the right seat bone forward bends the horse to the right. This bends the horse but does not mean that he moves on a circle.

On the circle, you must shift your weight slightly to the inside seat bone. This causes your horse to step under your shifted center and move on the circle. If this is not the procedure you follow to ride a circle or turn a corner, chances are you need to apply an inside rein aid on every stride. You probably also find it necessary to keep your outside leg slightly back and on the horse to prevent the haunches from drifting out. All this activity makes for a very busy rider and a distracted horse. Once again, all these are symptoms of the root cause of not moving from your center.

Before You Mount

Earlier, I introduced moving your center from your belly button. Let's revisit that feeling, so you can transfer it to the saddle. You'll do less and get more response from your horse.

1 Sit in a hard, flat chair so that you feel your seat bones against the seat. Your feet should be flat on the ground; let your elbows rest at your sides.

2 Try moving your right seat bone forward, as if you were going to bend your horse. Was the motion effortless? Or did you struggle to find the muscles to move your seat bone?

3 Try it again, and listen closely to your body to determine what muscles you had to engage to move that seat bone forward.

Chances are one or more of these things happened:

• you had to pull with one leg and push with the other, causing one knee to move forward and one back;

• you pushed with the gluteus muscles and pulled with the abdominals—and in doing so, you tightened your lower back and abdomen.

4 Try it yet again, and consider these questions.

- When you moved your seat bone, did your weight remain equal in each seat bone?
- Did you lift one side of your body in order to lighten the seat bone that you wanted to move?
- Did you lean back to the left to move the right seat bone?
- Did your head and chest stay still or move forward instead of your seat bone?

Remember that moving your seat bone forward bends the horse.

As you investigate your movements, remember that you probably move in the same way in the saddle, whether you're aware of it or not—it's an established movement habit, one that we're trying to retrain and improve. If your habit includes any tension or unbalancing, remember too that your horse has to compensate for these problems.

EYES LOOK HERE •

HORSE'S SHOULDER
RIDER'S SHOULDER
RIDER'S HIP
HORSE'S HIP

THE **3** CIRCLES REPRESENT:
① RIDER
② HORSE'S HIND
③ HORSE'S WITHERS

When riding your horse on a circle, your shoulders should be aligned with the horse's shoulders, and your hips should be aligned with the horse's hips.

5 Once again, move your left seat bone forward, but this time do it by turning your belly button to the *right* (the outside of your imagined circle). As your left seat bone moves forward, you'll also notice that your right seat bone moves back. Keep your seat bones equally weighted (50/50). And keep your feet flat on the ground and your spine upright and relaxed.

Follow the path of mind, breath, and body. Focus your mind on your center. Relax your abdomen and let your breath expand the Dain Tian and Ming Meng.

6 Now reverse—that is, turn your waist (belly button/center) to the left, and notice that your right seat bone moves forward. You've just reversed your horse's bend.

7 Once again, listen again to your body as you make these moves. What muscles did you use to move? Did you feel the same tension as you did the first time I asked you to move your seat bone forward? Isn't it easier to turn your belly button than move your seat bone forward?

Practice this motion in the chair until you can move, breathe, and feel your center with ease. Your goal is a relaxed reorientation to the outside of your center—from which all motion comes—in order to move your inside seat bone forward, thereby bending your horse to the inside. Also important in this exercise is keeping your shoulders quiet, relaxed and independent of your center.

The drawing on page 199 illustrates the important goal you are aiming for: orient your shoulders and hips independently of each other, but in alignment with the horse's hips and shoulders. *When riding your horse on the circle or through a corner, your hips should match the horse's hips, and your shoulders match the horse's shoulders.*

Step-by-Step

1   When you mount, begin in *Sitting Meditation*. Complete your normal warm-up.

2   Walk your horse on a straight line. To move the horse onto a circle you are going to do two things, which are entirely independent of one another: you are going to *bend the horse from your center* (turning your belly button to what will be the outside of the circle), and *shift your weight into the seat bone you moved forward* (the inside seat bone).

3   To prove the independence of these two aids to yourself, move your right seat bone forward (by turning your center, your belly button, to the left) *while keeping the weight evenly distributed in your two seat bones.* Your horse will bend to the right but should continue to travel forward in a straight line.

4   Next, shift your weight slightly into the right (forward) seat bone. Your horse, already bent to the right, should now start to circle to the right as well. The most effective way to shift your weight without tensing is by leaning with a straight spine, just as you did in the exercise *Hold the Sky with Both Hands* (p. 138).

Weighting one seat bone or the other causes the horse to step under your now shifted center. This weighting creates the circle—not the bending. Weighting makes it easy for the horse, and it's the kindest thing you can do. He won't have to work against himself, trying to walk a circle in which you are pulling on the inside rein every stride to remind him to keep his head to the inside.

To ride an integrated, coherent circle, with rider and horse joined, do the following:

- Point your belly button to the outside (bringing your inside seat bone forward) to bend your horse to the inside; and,
- shift your weight slightly to the inside seat bone by leaning to the inside with a straight spine. (The leaning movement is subtle: your nose should move 2 inches or less to the inside; try to move it only one-half inch!) And,
- align your shoulders to match your horse's shoulders.

5 Check your alignment: you and your horse align corresponding body parts. Just think: *shoulders to shoulders; hips to hips.* Are your shoulders relaxed and aligned with your horse's? If not, relax, breathe, and let them align. (It's at moments such as this that all your groundwork pays off handsomely.)

6 As you continue to walk on a circle, project your intent forward and a little to the inside of your horse.

7 Pick up a trot. Imagine me standing in the center of your circle. Look at me while you keep your belly button turned away from me.

Move your seat without tightening your abdomen, seat, or legs. Move from the inside, using your internal muscles, and don't think about the seat bones. In this position your pelvis is free to move with the horse. This relaxed position also frees your legs to move independently, allowing you to give aids in rhythm with the horse's movements.

How did your horse respond? Remember, he's your professor, your best teacher. Most horses will lower their head and turn easily. The horse's spine does bend. He won't need a constant rein aid because he has truly bent through his whole body, not just moved his head to the inside.

In the beginning, it's easier to move your head and chest to the outside with your belly button, turning your whole body as one unit. But on the horse, you'll have to bring your head and shoulders into alignment with the horse's shoulders while maintaining the position of the belly button to the outside of the circle.

Opening the Gates

While riding on the circle, keep the Dain Tian and Ming Meng open. This requires a lot of practice on the ground and in the saddle in order to be able to do this effortlessly.

James On Your Shoulder

Pointing your belly button is the most effective and effortless way to move one seat bone forward and the other one back. Moving your belly button takes very little muscle effort, because you turn from your center. Your legs are relaxed, your gluteus muscles soft, and your abdomen and lower back relaxed. In this position, you can effectively follow the rhythm of the horse and adhere to all the previous principles and natural laws.

Your seat bones are fused together by your pelvis. They are like opposite spokes on a wheel. A balanced, efficient, and even way of moving them both is to move your center, which is like moving the hub of the wheel to move the spokes.

If you turn your center with your first two gates closed, you will close the heart gates, which will, in turn, cause the upper body to tense, bringing your chest, shoulders, and head to the outside.

> *Rider Insight, Linda:* "At first I didn't get the idea of turning the belly button. After a little bit of practice I was amazed at how easily my horse was moving on the circle. His head was low and I could feel his back moving up into my seat. It was like riding on a big, soft ball. Leading with my belly button into corners has made all the difference in the world in staying 'through' in the corners."

Reminder

Your goal is to turn—to move your seat bones—without affecting the structural alignment of your spine. You free up the push and pull in your legs, and release the push of gluteus muscles and the pull of abdominal muscles, which work in pairs. You also free up your lower back and open the Ming Meng. Guard against unconsciously tightening up your lower back.

Root Causes

The biggest challenge in turning your belly button is to turn *only* your belly button—keeping your shoulders still. If you can't do this on the ground, you won't be able to do it in the saddle, so practice on the ground. Repeat the unmounted portion of this exercise—Before You Mount on page 198, and practice *Thrust Palm in Bow Stance* (p. 146) to help you gain this mobility.

Canter

With its three-beat count and huge forward motion, the canter produces the greatest amount of energy of all the gaits we will work with in this book. The suspension, rise, and drop inherent in the movement of the horse's center will provide the best opportunity for you to practice your newly acquired skills.

The circular force and the slower, deeper rhythm of the canter makes it possible to feel as if you are riding *inside* your horse's center. As your centers join, you will feel the energy of the horse through your body and be challenged to redirect it through your gates.

My Riding Insight: While being longed at the canter on my trainer's very wonderful stallion, I first felt the concept of follow—match—lead.

It was as if time had slowed down and I was moving in a quiet stillness, feeling every footfall of my partner. My trainer observed that our breaths became synchronized. I began to let go of the tension in my body. As I did so, the horse began to fill up into me. I could feel the power of the horse moving through every gate in my body. I was reminded by my trainer to smile, and as I did it opened the Upper Pass and Crown gates in my head. With these gates open, I needed only to think the circle bigger and it got bigger. As I thought of collection, the horse collected. We had achieved a connection that I had only heard of before. (It's important to note that at that time I had only been riding for two years, and hadn't ridden at all for about five months.)

It was just about this time that I felt the horse drop out from under me as if he had stepped in a huge hole. I wasn't sure what had happened, and we continued to canter. My trainer seemed concerned and began to reel us in on the longe line. What had happened was that the horse had bucked and kicked.

In reviewing the video, the horse's hind feet were nearly as high as my head when he kicked. However, in this state of oneness, with all my gates open, I was able to stay effortlessly connected to his center through all his movements, including the bucking. This is a state that you, too, can ride in.

I don't intend to teach a "how-to-canter" lesson. The lesson will be "how to become one at the canter."

Before You Mount

Review *Smooth, Invisible Transitions* (p. 183). You're going to re-enter that giant bubble.

Let's also briefly review the horse's three-beat movement in the canter:

- On the first beat, the horse steps under with his outside hind and propels himself (and you) up and forward.
- In the second beat, the diagonal pair (inside hind and outside fore) comes through, further lifting horse and rider toward the apex of the motion, which occurs between the second and third beats.
- On the third beat, the inside fore comes through, sending the horse into the suspension phase, during which his body falls to its lowest point before beginning to rise again with the first beat of the next stride.

Step-by-Step

1 When you mount, begin in *Sitting Meditation*. Complete your normal warm-up.

2 Ride your best walk or trot right through its last stride before the transition to canter. The quality of your canter depends on your transition. Use your intent to project yourself into the canter as you did earlier in the walk-trot transition. Visualize that large bubble where the canter is already happening, and flow into the transition.

I think of the beginning of the canter is like taking off on a large wave or dropping over the edge of a very steep ski run. If you hesitate in your body or mind, you will be left behind from the very start and have to play catch-up with a very large energy. That's not an easy task.

To examine my first analogy, think of riding a canter as if you were going to ride a 10-foot ocean wave. If your weight is slightly back and the canter starts big, you will be left behind. In an attempt to catch up, you'll probably arch your back and push your hips forward. This, in turn, causes you to tighten your abdomen and hold your breath. This tension is immediately transferred to the horse, who often falls out of the canter because of it. Don't inhale and hold your breath.

3 Take a deep breath and exhale. Your breath tells the horse that you are changing.

4 When you enter the sphere of the transition, you should be inhaling deep into the belly with the Dain Tian and Ming Meng open. Open the Back of the Heart gate, expanding your shoulder blades. Your chest should be soft and slightly dropped with your armpits empty.

5 Ask for the canter with your leg, paying close attention to your abdomen. Keep it relaxed, soft and following as your horse picks up the canter.

6 On the second canter beat, you continue to feel the energy rise from the hindquarters of the horse. Allow it to enter your body through the Ming Meng and travel up into the Back of the Heart, and then to the Front of the Heart.

7 At this point your horse's back will start to drop away. Again, maintain that relaxed, soft center whose expansion and stretching will allow you to follow the horse's back as it drops down from your center.

8 As the horse's inside fore comes through, you enter the suspension phase. During this phase, the Front of the Heart should be completely open. Opening this gate helps to project your intent forward and keep your body light and balanced.

9 Before the horse begins the next canter stride, exhale and drop the energy in your heart down your front to the Dain Tian and back to the horse. You are now ready to repeat the cycle.

Receive the force of the horse through your lower back, let it move into the upper body, and then fall back down your front, where it returns to your horse. This circulation of the horse's energy will help keep you from hollowing your lower back. Some hollowing—emptying of the lower back—is natural, but too much acts to cut your body in half energetically, preventing the flow of energy between you and your horse. Your upper body falls out of rhythm with your center and the horse. In addition, a hollowed back makes you rigid, and this causes your falling motion to end in collision with the horse's back. This impact discomforts and unbalances the horse, as well as disconnects you, making it all the harder for you to join the horse's rising motion which has already begun as he completes the suspension phase and begins the next canter stride.

10 Breathe and relax as the next canter stride begins. Maintain your posture and send you and your horse forward with your clear, focused intent.

11 If you're cantering on a circle, be sure to turn your belly button to the outside to bend your horse effortlessly.

When you are cantering on a circle, the horse's increased speed creates a much stronger sense of centripetal force than you felt on a similar size circle at the trot. Instead of getting caught up in the tension of "trying to stay on," simply relax and turn your belly button to the outside to stay with your horse. Turning in this way—bending from your center—also places both your legs in a perfect inside-forward and outside-back position.

If your horse is not really bent, you will have to use the inside rein at least once in every stride. As the horse's inside front leg impacts the ground and begins to transfer his force forward by pushing off, his head and neck will try to straighten if the spine is not bent. This is when you will pull with the rein to bring his head back on the circle. This constant focus on the rein creates tension in your arm and shoulder and causes the Chi Who gate on that side to close. The result inhibits the sensitivity of your hand and creates tension in your upper body.

Reminder

Tension in your body gives outside forces of gravity, momentum, and centripetal force something to "push" against. Instead employ these forces as your allies in the canter by aligning your bones, deepening your breath, and connecting to the rhythm of your horse. This allows you to relax and let energy flow through you, just as an ocean wave's tremendous energy passes quietly through open water but becomes a crashing, violent force when it meets resistance, such as a shoreline. Be like the water. If you carry tension in your body, you become like the shoreline, and all these allies become opponents.

Opening the Gates

Cantering involves opening all the Eight Gates. You know that the first four gates—the Dain Tian, Ming Meng, and the Back and Front of the Heart—are first on the list to open. They are truly your foundation. To connect completely with the bigger energy of the canter, it is also necessary to open the Upper Pass, Crown, and Chi Who gates.

While the Chi Who (left and right) are opened primarily by softening the chest and emptying the armpits, you open the Upper Pass and Crown more through your intent than any physical action. Smiling and suspending the crown are the keys that unlock the gate, but your intent pushes it open.

Up until now I haven't addressed Gate 6: The Liver and Spleen. The dropping of the horse's back at the canter is an ideal time to feel the Liver and Spleen gate opening and closing. When the horse drops away, you allow your abdomen to stretch. When your pelvis drops, following the horse's back, the Liver and Spleen gate opens. If you do not squeeze with your abdominal muscles when your horse lifts you up, your gates stay open. The rolling motion of the canter can have a massaging effect on your internal organs if these gates remain soft and open.

When you ride with Gate 6 open, your horse's forehand becomes incredibly light and responsive. You can feel the front feet of your horse as if there were a string connecting each hoof with your gut.

Exercises that help at the canter include:

- *Walking Backward* (p. 62)
- *Open the Ming Meng* (p. 99)
- *Hip Circles* (p. 142)
- *Spread Your Wings* (p. 131)
- *Hold the Sky with Both Hands* (p. 138)
- *Thrust Palm in Bow Stance* (p. 146)

Root Causes

Problems that I see at the canter include:
- Riders brace in the upper body.
- Riders bounce in the seat.
- Riders hold their abdomen tight and bear down. Their breath shortens and comes up high into the chest. The shoulder blades pinch together, and the chin comes down and in toward the chest. They lean the upper body (not the full, straight spine) to the inside of the cantering circle, so they're not structurally aligned to deal with the centripetal force of the horse's motion.

All these symptoms derive from not maintaining a balanced, connected center with your horse.

Tai Chi at the Horse Show

One of the great side benefits of developing the path of mind, breath, and body is how the skills you gain can help you at shows and performances—anywhere those butterflies end up in your stomach. Try to remember the last time you competed in a dressage test, rode in an exposition, or performed in front of a crowd. Did you feel anxious? Do you know why you were nervous?

My Riding Insight: Perhaps you're a bit like me—the moment before I'm "on," I wonder if I should be performing. Did I skip a day of training? Am I sufficiently prepared? Thoughts like these are unproductive and can in no way enhance your performance. The only thing they do is take you out of the present moment and distract you from your body and breath.

During my martial arts career I had the opportunity to perform publicly at least four times a year for fourteen years. While working a full-time job and practicing my art six days a week, four to six hours a day after work, I often ran out of time to practice the extra forms for demonstration. So, I began practicing in my head; I would go through the entire form, motion by motion in my mind, usually at my lunch break or before I went to sleep at night.

The problem with this practice was that a form that might take ten minutes to complete in real time would take only seconds in my head. I realized that I was only thinking about the form, not actually doing it. As a result, when I returned to physically practicing the form, I would find myself arriving at moments when I didn't know whether or not I had just left out a huge piece of the form. If I didn't think at all, it was fine—I had done the forms so many times that my body knew what to do regardless of whether or not my mind was present. In some martial arts, achieving this state of "no mind" is a good thing, but in Tai Chi it is not, in which the goal is complete mind–body connection. I had to come up with another mental rehearsal technique.

My solution was to continue to practice in my mind, but to move in concert with my breath, so that I was doing the form in real time instead of just thinking about it. I realized two things while working this way: (1) I could not stay focused through the whole form without being distracted by some random thought; and (2) there were times that I held my breath, usually just prior to difficult motions or motions that I did not fully understand. These were both valuable experiences: the former taught me that my concentration needed to improve, and the latter pointed out to me just what sections I needed to work on. While somewhat painful to encounter, our weaknesses always give us our greatest learning opportunities.

This type of mental practice is an invaluable self-teaching method. Try it the next time you're going to compete.

Sit at the in-gate of the arena or wherever you're going to perform. In your mind's eye see yourself perform the entire test, jumping round, or pattern.

Breathe yourself through from start to finish. Do you start by inhaling or exhaling? Where is your breath when you ride right in front of the judge? Make that transition? Begin the tempi changes? Halt and salute? Are you smiling, or is your face tense? Are you clenching your jaw? Envision the performance as fully as possible.

Repeat your mind's eye performance, noting your start time.

When you are done, note the time, determine how long your "performance" took, and compare this time to the actual performance time. Ask yourself, "Did I get distracted? Where did I hold my breath? Did I speed up through sections that I do not completely understand or that I find difficult?"

I have found that this type of practice actually improved my performances more quickly than just repeating the physical motions over and over. Until you can do your test, course, or pattern in your mind in real time, you don't know the routine through and through. This technique is invaluable in getting off a learning plateau and reaching the next level in understanding yourself and your art.

Lateral Movements

The same techniques and abilities you learned to bend your horse are also used to perform lateral movements such as leg-yield, shoulder-in, and half-pass. The one change is that you don't hold your center (your belly button) in a static position—instead, it moves rhythmically with your horse. You need flexible, independent control of your shoulders and pelvis, as you need to align your shoulders with the horse's shoulders and your hips with the horse's hips. The exercise *Thrust Palm in Bow Stance* (p. 146) is extremely helpful for gaining this mobility.

In lateral work, your center is your primary aid, and your leg is the support aid. They work in harmony with each other. You lead with your center, follow with your leg, allow the horse to move through, and follow the horse. This all happens within one stride, and you repeat the process in the next stride. The movement of your center feels like an oblong figure eight, with the bigger side moving in the direction the horse is going (see drawing).

The principle of *follow—match—lead* is never more apparent than it is here.

The opening and closing of Gate 6: The Liver and Spleen strongly affects the fluidity and "throughness" of this technique. The opening of the gate leads you into and through the motion.

Opening the Gates

Allow the Liver and Spleen gate to soften and expand so that energy flows from the hind end of the horse through your torso and back into the horse's forehand. It is common for riders to resist the force coming from the horse at their rib cage. This happens when they tighten their upper abdominal muscles as the force pushes up into their torso. The result is excess movement in the upper body, which in turn means that their upper body tenses and resists the horse's movement. This creates imbalance in the rider that causes further tensing, and it interferes with the horse's motion.

As in the canter, it is impossible to open Gate 6: The Liver and Spleen gate if the Front and Back of the Heart gates are not already open. The liver and spleen are located below your ribs, on either side of your body. You open Gate 6 by letting go with your upper abdominal muscles and allowing the force of the horse's step to move through your body. The muscles involved are both involuntary and voluntary. By breathing deep into the belly, you let go of the voluntary muscles. The movement of the horse will aid in relaxing the involuntary muscles. Rarely in your everyday life do you think about using these muscles. They open when you laugh, and they slam shut when you cough or sneeze.

The figure-eight movement of energy in lateral work

You can also open Gate 6 through massage. When open, the outer muscles are soft, so you can push your fingers into your body under your rib cage. Your diaphragm is up inside there. You can feel it push down and out if you breathe into the Dain Tian.

Your seat receives the horse's energy through the open Ming Meng. Your seat then redirects this energy out either the Liver (right) or Spleen (left) gate, depending on your direction. If you leg-yield to the left, you receive most of the horse's power up through your right seat bone. It's transferred through the Ming Meng diagonally through your center and then into your spleen (left) gate. The energy is then sent out through the opened gate and projected back into the horse. It's a circular motion, a flow of energy. Use your intent to lead with the open gate in the direction you're moving. With practice, you can refine this work, opening and closing the Ming Meng to create a half-halt that's accomplished primarily with your breath.

If you have a dominant side—and for many riders this is their right side—you must surrender it. For example, if you're right dominant, you need to open the left gate and project the energy through, thereby pulling your right side through. Similarly, your intent moves your body and your horse, and it too pulls you through, instead of pushing.

Jumping

Your center and the horse's center should match in the air over a fence. To achieve this harmony, in the takeoff imagine propelling your center over the fence. Use the same strategy that you used to create smooth and effortless transitions; that is, use your *intent*. By creating and seeing in your mind's eye the perfect jump, and then projecting it to a sphere that encompasses the entire jump area, you will be able to focus (mind) on your timing (breath) and your balance (body).

Step-by-Step

1 When you approach a jump, ask yourself whether or not you are inhaling or exhaling, or even holding your breath. Remember that your breathing sets your rhythm, and rhythm is the key to perfect timing.

2 In working with jumpers of various skill levels, I've found that the most effective breathing pattern is to inhale as the horse begins to drop his force into the ground, just prior to pushing off. This is a good example of "the root of lightness is heaviness."

3 As the horse and you leave the ground, start the exhaling and continue until just before landing on the other side.

4 Inhale as you land. Remember to breathe deep into your abdomen, opening the Dain Tian and Ming Meng.

If you allow your breath to stay up in your chest, you create a very high center away from your horse's center. Chest breathing is a bit like strapping a 20-pound weight to your chest and then trying to jump. In addition, if you hold your breath while jumping, it locks your body into a rigid position and decreases your ability to stay in balance with your horse. Such imbalance causes heavier landings that are hard on both bodies.

Eventually, you will be able to breath in this way over jumps effortlessly and unconsciously, and your connection with your horse will be sustained throughout your jumping round. At this point, you may then start to project your intent out beyond the jump itself.

5 To start, pick a point well past the jump to keep your eyes focused on—perhaps 20 to 30 yards out. If that is not possible because of a turn in the course, then focus on where the upcoming turn will take place.

When I work in person with someone, I stand 20 yards beyond the jump and have the rider keep eye contact with me as she approaches, jumps, and lands. The whole time we both smile and keep our hearts open. The resulting jumps are typically quiet and light.

Opening the Gates

In jumping it's essential that you open the Ming Meng, Front and Back of the Heart, Crown, and Upper Pass gates, and you need to project your intent forward. Jumping is the ultimate realization of "where the mind goes the body follows." More than any other form of riding, jumping demands lightness and thoroughness.

A balanced jumping seat demands that your pelvis be pushed back slightly. In this position, your lower back and thighs support more of the weight of your body. You can use your lower back without becoming tense and rigid. Avoid rigidity by keeping your breath down and the Ming Meng open, so you allow the energy of the horse to move up through you as he jumps.

Reminder

Remember that any resistance to the flow of energy is actually pushing against it. Such resistance is oftentimes the root cause of back pain in jumpers. With the Ming Meng open, the Back of the Heart can be open during the jump. You'll keep your upper body light, which in return will minimize the possibility of your weight crashing into the horse's forehand upon landing. Notice that the gates we are focusing on—Ming Meng, Heart, Crown, Upper Pass—all open upward during a jump and help to create suspension in your body. You'll float with your horse over the fence.

Practical Physics: Negotiating Centripetal Force

Earlier in the book we briefly discussed centripetal force (p. 11), the potentially unbalancing lateral force you experience whenever you turn or ride a circle. Now I'd like to revisit this subject and explain the forces at play and show you how the skills you have been learning can help you compensate for these forces and ride better turns and circles.

Here's a more detailed summary of the physics involved:

1 Our starting point is inertia, the property Newton described in his First Law of

Motion: unless acted on by a force, objects in motion travel straight ahead at an unchanging speed, and objects at rest remain at rest.

2 A moving object's "quantity of motion" is called its momentum*.

3 Thus, we have moving objects, with measurable momentum, tending to travel straight ahead unless acted on by a force. If we use a moving car as an example, that force can be with the motion of the car (acceleration), against the motion of the car (braking), or lateral to the motion of the car (turning). The last of these is centripetal force.

4 When you apply centripetal (center-seeking) force to an object traveling in a straight line, the object's path is altered from straight ahead to ahead but at an angle.

* Momentum (p) is defined as $p = mv$, that is, an object's momentum is its mass times its velocity.

If the centripetal force is maintained, these moments of the object moving forward at a small angle add up—first to produce a turn, and eventually to produce a full circle.

The "sharpness" of the turn and the size of the circle depend on the relative influences of momentum (the "quantity of motion" proceeding straight ahead) and centripetal force (pushing or pulling sideways on the object).

Returning to the example of the car, you know that the more sharply you turn the steering wheel, the more sharply the car turns. This is because the car's tires, when turned more sharply, push against the pavement at a greater angle, deflecting the car from its straight path to one forward at an angle. The tires push the car sideways, making it turn, and creating centripetal force.

When you're a passenger riding in the car your inertia (tendency to move straight forward) and momentum are constant—until the car turns. As the car turns left, for instance, you are "thrown" against the right door—in reality, your body keeps traveling straight ahead until it collides with the interior of the car, which is moving left. Once you're pressed against the passenger door, the car keeps pulling you left as it continues to turn; the car is exerting a centripetal force (force toward the center of the turn) on you.

To summarize: in a turn forward momentum is deflected from a straight line to forward at an angle by the application of lateral (centripetal) force.

5 Now, let's look at these same physics, but with you on your horse:

a) First, your horse accelerates you from a standstill up to the speed of your chosen gait; from this you gain your forward motion, momentum, and inertia—the tendency to keep moving forward at the same speed and direction.

b) Second, when your horse turns he not only carries you forward, but also exerts a lateral, centripetal force on you, pushing you toward the circle's center a little bit with every stride. The horses hooves, pushing off against the ground at an angle, are like the car's turned tires. As a result, you and your horse move forward at an angle, and if you do this for a sufficient number of strides, you complete a circle.

6 Many riders, when asked about the forces they sense while riding a circle, report not that they feel centripetal force "pushing them to the inside," but rather that they are "falling to the outside." Why?

Inertia is a property of all moving objects and your body's tendency is always to move straight ahead. Because your horse is turning—moving forward at an angle—you and your horse are simply on diverging paths: he is moving forward and to the inside, and you are moving straight ahead, which, relative to your horse, is to his outside. As your horse "disappears" out from underneath you, you feel you are falling to the outside.

7 Two factors increase centripetal force: increasing your speed, and making the circle smaller. Practically speaking, most riders begin to notice centripetal force and inertia (even if they would not use these terms) when trotting a circle of 10 meters or less, or cantering a circle of 20 meters or less.

Regardless of the speed at which you sense these forces and what they "feel like" to you, the physical reality is that your body must negotiate both inertia and centripetal force when riding a turn or circle.

8 Given these physics, now let's look at the situation practically:

You're riding a circle, sitting in a saddle that's moving forward and pulling you to the inside, and your body as a whole is traveling straight forward. You can't ignore either force. How do you reconcile them physically? You can negotiate a physical compromise in many different ways—with ease or with a struggle.

Most of our instinctual responses are not helpful and they generally involve tension.

(Tension in your body is always an excellent clue; it's a signal that you're using an ineffective strategy.) These unproductive responses include:

- leaning into the turn
- collapsing the inside hip
- gripping with the legs
- hanging on the inside rein

All of these approaches have two unfortunate consequences to varying degrees: they disconnect you from your horse, and they cause your horse to compensate for you in ways that inhibit his movement.

As you know by now, on the mind–breath–body path we are following in our work, we always seek to move in concert with the principles of Tai Chi. We will, therefore, look for a relaxed, balanced solution: use the mind, not force; never oppose force with force; yield and overcome; balance like a scale; seek stillness in motion; be heavy and light; focus and expand.

You have far better options than tensing or struggling; use the tools you learned in *Bending on the Circle* (p. 198).

> a) turn your belly button to the outside, bringing your inside seatbone forward and aligning your hips with the horse's hips;
> b) shift your weight onto the inside seatbone;
> c) align your shoulders with the horse's shoulders; and,
> d) relax and use your body to join and balance these two alignments and the forces associated with each.

When you sit in this way, your body exhibits a fascinating wisdom from the standpoint of physics:

- by turning your belly button to the outside, you align your pelvis with your body's inertia, which always travels straight ahead, perpetually leaving the circle; and
- by turning your shoulders to the inside, you align them with the path you are traveling on with the horse, which is your momentum as deflected by centripetal force.

In short, your body is simultaneously aligned with both of the physical influences affecting you when you ride a circle! And because you are doing this in centered, balanced relaxation, you have achieved an artful compromise.

This "double-alignment" that you've accomplished is subtle when a rider is on a large circle; that is, the centripetal component is modest compared to your straight-line momentum, and your shoulders only need to shift a little to the inside.

If we watch a rider in a canter pirouette, however, we can more easily see these two forces at work because they are more nearly equal:

- the centripetal component is greatly increased because the radius of the pirouette is so small (decreasing the radius of a turn or circle increases the centripetal effect); and,
- the forward momentum of the rider is much less in the pirouette.

Responding to these two forces, the rider is now more visibly aligned in two different directions. The rider's shoulders are turned further to the inside of the rider's pelvis, sometimes so much so that the rider almost seems to be looking back over her inside shoulder.

Now when you watch other riders on a circle, look at the alignment of their pelvis versus their shoulders. Can you see these forces interacting? How are they using their bodies to negotiate these conflicting energies? Are they relaxed or tense? And don't forget to ask yourself all these same questions when you ride a circle.

These techniques don't negate centripetal force and momentum—nothing can—but they do allow you to respond in relaxation rather than with force. You align your bones to exactly balance the forces. Struggling against physics with muscular effort is replaced by going with the motion in relaxed alignment, which creates a base from which you have independent control of your legs, arms, and hands to guide your horse as needed with aids.

Summary

This chapter has pulled together information from the entire book. It asked you to use your breath with relaxed attention, to focus your mind with clear intent, and to move your body with enhanced mobility, and then draw all those abilities together to use them while riding. No set of instructions in this chapter is long, but as you can sense, you can spend a lifetime practicing them without boredom, without repetition—and

Coping with Diversions

The greatest benefit derived from using your breath to gain access to your body and its hidden abilities is that it keeps you absolutely present in your body—and this presence is the basis of awareness, and it takes absolute awareness to retrain your body, create new habits, and leave behind old habits. Any distraction that diverts your awareness will allow an old habit to slip back in.

Being in the moment is of vital importance. You must practice keeping your focus on you, not the horse. This is not to say that you are not aware of what your horse is doing, quite the contrary. When you are completely present, all your senses are heightened, and you will be able to feel even the slightest change in your horse without ever having to look down.

If and when your horse acts up or does something that you did not ask for, do not automatically look down at your horse, as if that will change things or make him listen. Instead, ask yourself, "Did I have anything to do with my horse's action? Did I unknowingly hold my breath, or tighten somewhere in my body? Did I ask for this change?" This is not to say that your horse never misbehaves or acts entirely on his own, but we want to be clear on what our role may have been.

without perfection. Awareness, health, and joy are our ultimate goals—and what better partner could you have on this journey than your horse?

What's Next

In chapter 8, "The Road Continues: Health and Tai Chi," I will look in greater detail at the health benefits of practicing Tai Chi. In addition, I have included a section called "Frequent Questions and Answers," in which I share my answers to questions that I often hear in clinics.

The Road Continues

8

Health and Tai Chi

THE JOURNEY WE HAVE BEGUN IN THIS BOOK may suggest questions and areas for further study. Here, I'll share more information about how Tai Chi can improve your well-being, and also address some of the questions and concerns that I most often hear from riders.

Healing Aspects of Tai Chi

Tai Chi is a three-in-one exercise of the mind, chi (breath), and body. Chinese medicine, too, recognizes this same interrelationship of mind, chi, and body. The philosophy underlying traditional Chinese medicine asserts the importance of balancing various opposing, but complementary, natural forces or energies—Yin and Yang—in the macrocosm of the universe, as well as in the microcosm that is the human being. All illness and disease are seen as the result of an imbalance of these forces known as chi. Traditional Chinese medicine encompasses many techniques to balance chi in the body in order to attain health and longevity. Acupressure, acupuncture, herbal medicine, Tai Chi, chi gong, and a complete dietetic system all take this same integrated and balanced approach to creating and maintaining optimal health and spirituality.

In Chinese medicine the environment in which you live, the foods you eat, and the exercises you do are all essential to maintaining your health. There is a saying in Chinese medicine: "A healthy fish cannot long swim in dirty water."

This chapter addresses only a small part of the healing process of Chinese medicine. Tai Chi is no quick fix to your health problems. The environment of your body took a long time to pollute. It did not happen overnight, but over your lifetime. With earnest practice, proper movement of the body, and correct breathing, you can enhance your health.

You have used abdominal breathing to help lower your center of balance and connect the mind with the body. This type of breathing can also bring significant health gains, including an increased lung capacity that promotes the exchange of gases in the body. In addition, abdominal breathing acts as an internal massage of the organs of the visceral cavity, including the kidneys, stomach, bladder, colon, large and small intestine, liver, and spleen. The daily movement of these organs helps balance and maintain their health.

Studies in the U.S. and China show that the practice of Tai Chi promotes health of the nervous system due to the calming effect it has on the cerebral cortex. The cerebral cortex links all activities in the human body through the central nervous system. This effect can be beneficial in the control of chronic diseases such as hypertension and peptic ulcers. In addition, these calming effects ripple throughout the nervous system and beyond; studies have demonstrated that Tai Chi practice is linked to the reduction of chemicals responsible for the body's production of adrenaline (a precursor for heart disease), and a decrease in the levels of stored lactic acid.

My own teacher, Wen Mei Yu, was first directed to Tai Chi at the age of seventeen as a means of healing a chronic ulcer. Within nine months the ulcer was gone. There are numerous studies proving the beneficial effects of Tai Chi for various systems in the body. I encourage you to research on your own the many resources available for your particular needs. See the bibliography on page 252 for some suggested reading.

The healing effects of Tai Chi are inherent in its practice. In order to make these health gains you need not focus your attention on them. You will heal yourself by simply "doing" the practice. Create the time and space for your own practice. What more meaningful, more empowering gift could you possibly give yourself?

Motion Meditation

As a healing art, Tai Chi balances and promotes the flow of chi in the body. If there is a lack of chi (energy), the combination of movements, increased oxygen intake, and stimulation of the Dain Tian increases your vital energy. If you have an overabundance of chi up in the head, which may be seen as hyperactivity or compulsive thinking, the forms balance the chi and calm the mind. The flowing movements of the body directed by the mind create with practice what is known as "motion meditation." Just as the body's systems benefit from the therapeutic motion, the mind benefits from the calming effect of focusing exclusively on the form.

After a time of regular practice, you may feel as if your mind is actually observing your body's movement rather than dictating it. Often when I complete my Tai Chi practice I realize that I have completely lost my sense of time, and I'm not sure whether I have been practicing for one hour or three hours. This is not an *out-of-body* experience, but rather a completely *in-body* experience.

Troubleshooting Your Own Riding and Health

The human body needs to be moved and used within the laws of nature to sustain health. Many of the injuries we sustain are caused by either abuse (meaning literally "use that causes injury") or by trying to use the body without regard for the natural laws. For example, not warming up before you ride is an example of abuse, and using brute strength against a far stronger force (your horse) is an example of working outside the natural laws.

Below I will help you identify the possible root causes for a variety of injuries, symptoms, and problems common in riding. I provide short- and long-term solutions, referring you to exercises from the previous chapters that will be helpful in healing yourself or resolving the problem.

Riding Problems and Tai Chi Exercise Solutions

Lower back pain after riding

Possible Root Causes and Effects

Bracing in the abdomen and lower back abuses the small muscles in the lumbar region of the spine.

When you hold tension in your spine, it acts as a lever against the lower lumbar region and pelvis. This effect creates a tremendous amount of potentially damaging force.

Short Term Strategies

Exercises: *Hold the Sky with Both Hands*; *Horse Stance*; *Thrust Palm in Bow Stance*; *Bend with an Arch*; *Hip Circles*

Long Term Strategies

Keep the Ming Meng and Dain Tian gates open while riding. Always seek a rhythmic and fluid movement in your spine.

Neck or shoulder pain during or after riding

Possible Root Causes and Effects

Misalignment of the head over the neck.
Overdependence on the trapezius muscles for strength and balance in the upper body.

Short Term Strategies

Exercises: *Neck Turns*; *Lift a Single Iron Arm*; *Spread Your Wings*; *Spread Your Chest*

Long Term Strategies

Keep the Chi Who and Front and Back of the Heart gates open while riding. Learn to engage the latissimus dorsi muscles of your back while riding, to allow the force applied on your body to travel down the spine and into your seat back to the horse.

Holding your breath while riding

Possible Root Causes and Effects

Lack of balance; fear of falling; or bracing in the abdomen.

Short Term Strategies

Exercises: *Abdominal Breathing*; *Counting Your Breath*; *Open the Ming Meng*

Find your structural alignment in the saddle.

Long Term Strategies

At least three times a day become aware of your breath and take a deep abdominal breath. In other words, on a daily basis be mindful of your breath. Remember holding your breath is a symptom, and there is always a reason: look for the cause that *precedes* your holding it.

Constantly looking down at your horse to "see" if he's done what you've asked

Possible Root Causes and Effects

Misalignment of upper body over the center, causing your head to move forward to maintain balance.

Poor mind-body connection so you must "see to believe."

Short Term Strategies

Exercises: *Neck Turns; Lift a Single Iron Arm; Spread Your Chest; Sitting Meditation; Wrist Shaking; Side Step; Walking Backward*

Long Term Strategies

Use your mind to direct your body. Become aware of your peripheral vision and start to see more. Expand your awareness. Open Gate 8: The Crown and Gate 7: The Upper Pass. Smile and see the balloons.

Your lateral work on one side is significantly better than the other

Possible Root Causes and Effects

One side of the body is dominant over the other, and you are twisting or holding in the spine to compensate for imbalance.

Short Term Strategies

Exercises: *Hold the Sky with Both Hands; Hold Knee to Chest; Walking Backward; Wall Sitting*

Long Term Strategies

Practice, through abdominal breathing techniques, the opening and closing of Gate 6: The Liver and Spleen. Pay close attention to the role your mind plays in your body's left and right dominance. It's as though one side of the body takes over in an attempt to make up for the apparent weakness in the other side.

This role of dominance is often hard to let go of, even after the balance is returned. Is one side of your body not allowing the other side to lead?

If the right side is dominant, but it's now the left side's turn to lead, you may have to focus more on letting go with the right than leading with the left.

Your horse does not change gaits when you ask, or he takes a few strides to pick up the new gait

Possible Root Causes and Effects

Lack of intent.
Holding your breath as you enter the transition.
Lack of structural balance is making your aids unclear.

Short Term Strategies

Exercises: *Abdominal Breathing; Counting Your Breath; Walking Backward*
Review all the *Opening Your Gates* and *Intent* sections in chapter 7.

Long Term Strategies

Become aware throughout your day what you project. For example, do you project negative outcomes for future events, or do you hope for and expect the best? Are you sure your horse is going to spook at the place he "always" does before you get there?

Notice throughout the day how your intent affects your breathing. When you are anticipating a negative result, does your breath shorten and stay high in your chest?

Be sure you are not throwing away a good walk to make your transition to the trot. See *Smooth, Invisible Transitions* in chapter 7.

While riding on a circle you: (1) drift in or out from the circumference of the circle; (2) find yourself hanging or leaning off to one side or the other of the saddle; or (3) constantly need to use the inside rein to keep your horse's head on the circle

Possible Root Causes and Effects
Looking into the center of the circle without regard for the outside of the circle.
Leaning the upper body into the circle rather than actually bending the horse.
Using just the leg and rein to ride a circle.

Short Term Strategies
Exercises: *Embracing the Moon; Heaven and Earth*
Review *Practical Physics* (p. 213) and *Bending on the Circle* (p. 198).

Long Term Strategies
Practice leading by using Gate 6: The Liver and Spleen; if going to the left, use the spleen; if going to the right, use the liver.

Your horse does not track up at the walk or trot

Possible Root Causes and Effects
Bracing in the lower back.
Riding with Gates 3 and 4, the Front and Back of the Heart gates closed.
Not being in rhythm with the horse.

Any of these cause your center to move behind the center of the horse. Because your two centers are joined, if your center moves back, so does your horse's. In order to stay in balance he has to shorten his stride. The further you move the center back, the shorter his stride has to be.

A second reason that a horse may not track up is that your weight is slightly off-center to the left or the right. This condition will cause the horse's hoof to fall sooner under the side that is heavier. This is common while riding on a circle, although often overlooked.

Short Term Strategies
Exercises: *Open the Ming Meng; Embracing the Moon; Heaven and Earth; Walking Backward*

Review *Smooth, Invisible Transitions* (p. 183) and *Bending on the Circle* (p. 198)

Long Term Strategies
Keep Gate 8: the Crown; Gate 7: the Upper Pass; and Gates 3 and 4: the Heart gates open, and project your intent out and up. Look at the balloons, as described on page 194.

Make sure when riding on a circle that you allow your horse to bend and that you're not leaning to the inside of the circle more than necessary. See *Bending on a Circle* (p. 198).

Relieving Stress with Tai Chi

It is well known that stress is a killer—maybe more so than we truly understand. Stress enters the body through the mind. If it is not recognized and addressed at that moment, it will move into the body and find a home. Once in the body, it becomes much more difficult to dislodge and move out.

Stress of the mind becomes tension in the body. This tension seems to take up residence in the most fragile rooms in the body, such as the neck, spine, and lower back. It then begins to apply its force to the nerves, pushing and pulling until ultimately stopping you in your tracks.

I often think that the scenario described here is actually the body's last defense against a driven mind that pushes you forward, dragging the body along without regard for your well-being and needs. My good friend and mentor, Dr. Syng Ku Yu, founder of the International Finger Pressure Institute in Pomona, California, says there are three things needed for great health. In order of importance, these include (1) replenishing and rejuvenating sleep; (2) a healthy diet that includes more vegetables than meat; and (3) exercise. So, the number one factor in creating and maintaining health is quality sleep. The number one killer of quality sleep is stress.

In the East they say the body is your temple, and your mind is the main gate to the temple. Tai Chi addresses stress at the gate as well as in the temple. The slow, light, and relaxed movements of the whole body must be directed by the mind, not forced. This slow-motion dance requires and facilitates the brain's control and balance of the body. It is as if the body teaches the brain to slow down. The body leads the mind into a calm focus that insulates it from random thoughts and disorder. In this state of mind and body, you feel a sense of well-being and euphoria. This state, gained whenever we practice, provides a respite from our hurried life—this is the sanctuary of Tai Chi.

Rider Insights about Healing

I'd like to share the stories of three riders.

Rider Insight, Lolly: "I've dealt with carpal tunnel syndrome in both wrists for nearly fifteen years, and my right hand is more severely affected. As this condition set in, simple tasks that involved thumb or wrist strength, such as holding a pen to write, and all gripping actions became increasingly difficult and painful. I was losing flexibility and range of motion. My doctor gave me two options—surgery or braces. So I began wearing the braces at night, but they were cumbersome and uncomfortable, and they did very little for me. If I slept without the braces, however, my sleep was interrupted several times each night by severe numbness and aching that went from my fingertips to my shoulders. I could relieve these symptoms by hanging one arm at a time over the side of the bed to help the circulation to return, but this 'cure' was itself disruptive to my sleep. I still didn't want to have surgery, but I began to feel that I was running out of options.*

"Then I met James Shaw while attending his Tai Chi for Equestrians clinic. Upon discovering his knowledge of the Chinese healing arts, and his genuinely friendly and caring manner, I knew he could offer me some suggestions. James led me through an exercise—Wrist Shaking—that nearly dropped me to my knees. I'm not a person overly sensitive to pain. I've delivered two healthy, robust boys through natural childbirth without drugs. I always thought if I could endure that, I could endure just about anything. But this exercise was quite extraordinary.

"James led me through the exercise three or four times. As my familiarity with the motions increased, I was able to put more effort into being more precise. As I released the energy from my arms as James instructed, it felt as though fire shot down my wrists and out my fingertips. That's when my knees started to buckle and I nearly cried out from the pain. James explained this pain was due to the tendons in my arms stretching and then relaxing, similar to the stretching and relaxing of a rubber band. He explained that wearing the braces only immobilized the tendons, which was just the opposite of what needed to be done.

"That initial pain was worth it. One year later I am not wearing braces; my hands and forearms do not go numb nor do they ache. The strength and range of motion in my forearms and wrists has returned. I did continue to wear the braces for a few nights after the clinic. During my daily activities I felt no pain, but a warm tingling in my hands and forearms that was pleasant, which indicated to me that healing was taking place. I decided to stop wearing the braces and I found that the numbness and pain was greatly reduced, eventually just fading away completely. I am so grateful that I met James. I am convinced that without his techniques my hands and arms would have just continued to become more weakened, stiff, and painful until I could have no longer done what I love to do—work with my Haflingers."

Rider Insight, Silke: "I have been riding for thirty years, and due to the amount of riding I have done, my back has suffered tremendously. For the last five years I have had to rely heavily on painkillers on a daily basis. I went to James's clinic without expectations. What I got was priceless. With the help of James's breathing techniques I was able to relax my lower back while riding, and my pain has since disappeared. I have not taken painkillers since that weekend in November 2000."

Rider Insight, Anne: "My husband Ed attended your clinic this past weekend and could not say enough about how much he enjoyed it. He asked if you might send him the tape of your healing movements that you showed him at the clinic. He had not been able to turn his head at all, to either side prior to the clinic, without experiencing great pain. And with just the short time you spent working with him, he is now pain-free and the range of motion in his neck and shoulders has increased dramatically."

Tai Chi and Longevity

I'll share some guidelines for older riders. One of the goals of Tai Chi is to attain longevity and live in an "eternal spring"—when life awakens anew from its winter slumber, soft and bending, vigorously stretching to the light.

In the many years that I have been traveling and working with equestrians, what most touches and saddens my heart is seeing a rider whose body is bent, stiffened, and plagued with pain from years of riding against the greater force of the horse. Just as one of the most important goals of Tai Chi is longevity in life, one of the most important goals of this book is to supply riders of all ages with the tools for longevity in riding. I believe that I will ride better at 70 than I do at 40, and I expect to have more energy when I finish a ride than before I started. My own Tai Chi teacher, who's now in her seventies, practices daily and maintains a rigorous teaching schedule.

The slow, rhythmic nature of the forms creates grace and balance in the body of all who practice, old or young. The curative benefits are well-known and have been the focus of many studies. In those who practice regularly, the strength of the bones and muscles are increased, and the functions of the metabolic, cardiovascular, and respiratory systems are improved. It is the nature of Tai Chi, as well as the human body, to have the bones carry the force of gravity and any other outside force applied to the body, through the body into the earth, our supreme support. In doing so, the bones are strengthened throughout your lifetime. In addition, Tai Chi practitioners enjoy improved balance and agility. A 1995 Washington University School of Medicine study concluded that Tai Chi practice decreases the likelihood of fall-related injuries in the elderly by as much as 25 percent.

There are many studies that I could cite that demonstrate that Tai Chi is one of the best forms of exercise to improve your life and riding. But my wish is that you prove it to yourself through the practice of the art.

My words get you no closer to your truth. If you or someone you know suffers from the difficulties that arise from an aging body trapping a young mind, please introduce them to the exercises in this book or find a Tai Chi class near you. You *can* turn back the clock; it's never too late.

Selecting a Teacher

I have been a student for virtually my whole life, and I have been a teacher for more than twenty-five years. I offer these guidelines in selecting a teacher:

1 Always have a teacher who has a teacher.

2 There are only three things a student can give to a Master (teacher): practice, service, and money. If, at any time, either service or money becomes more important than practice, the teacher has lost his way, and the student should move on.

These two simple rules can save you time, money, and heartache.

Frequent Questions and Answers

In this section, I'll address some of the questions I frequently get asked in my clinics about Tai Chi and horsemanship, and about Tai Chi as a martial art.

When I'm riding and everything is going well, it is easy to stay in balance. When things aren't going quite so well, I start to try to get it right again and it all falls apart. Is there a place that I can look to in my body to find that balance again?

Yes, there is such a place in your body: your *center.* This is a very interesting question not in the sense that you were balanced, lost your balance, and then found it difficult to regain. To me the word "try" is the key to understanding the root cause of this difficulty. Often it is the trying that keeps us out of center.

We bring all our habits, unconscious and conscious, to the saddle. If, in trying to regain your balance, you forget and slip into your unconscious habits and away from the connection you obviously had when "things were going well," you will only frustrate yourself and your horse. Remember that the *path* is mind–breath–body. The *result* is a balanced connection with your horse, not the other way around. You need to be able to let go of what you had—whether near balance, or complete imbalance—in order to find a new, real balance. What's crucial to remember is that balance comes *after* establishing the union of mind, breath, and body.

This is actually very simple—not easy, but simple. You must stay present in your body and return to the path: first you find your breath, next move it down into your center, then find your rhythm—and *then* you can find your balance.

We ride with our minds as well as our bodies, and the two are inseparable. One influences the other for better or for worse. If your horse is acting up and your focus is exclusively on his behavior, you cannot focus on your body—you are disconnected. On the other hand, if you become too focused on the position of your body on the outside, your mind detaches and becomes unaware of what is going on inside your body. You lose connection not only with your body, but also with your horse.

I am right-handed, and when I track left, my left seat doesn't contact my horse correctly—as though on the left side I have no horse to sit on. What's going on and how do I fix this?

The root of this problem is in the left/right imbalance in your body. Your right side is the dominate side, and it therefore unconsciously wants to control and lead. When tracking left the left side of the body must lead, and the right side must follow. The solution is to let go and release the right side in order to help the left to take over and lead. Controlling this sort of release is difficult until you first gain conscious control of the body in this area. You can gain this control by practicing these exercises unmounted: *Spread Your Chest* (p. 126), *Thrust Palm in Bow Stance* (p. 146), and *Hip Circles* (p. 142).

When this challenge comes up on horseback, you can work on this as follows, using the path of mind–breath–body. First, become aware of the tension in the right side of your body. Second, soften and release this tension through abdominal breathing; visualize it dropping down through the bones of your body, then down through your horse, and finally into the ground. Now track left and turn your belly button to the right as you move to the left. This places the left side of your body in the lead position and moves the right back slightly to follow.

My horse is constantly falling out of the gait he's in. Why does this happen?

I have seen this happen many times and I have heard the rider claim that her horse is lazy and does not like to work. I believe that in most cases the horse is more confused than lazy, and he would love to work if the rider's weight was not constantly shifting forward onto the horse's forehand.

Let me explain: I often see a rider ask for the trot from a poorly balanced position. When the horse responds and picks up the trot, the rider is ill-prepared to follow the new larger motion of the animal. If, through habit she is slightly ahead of the horse's movement (she does this to feel safe), the added momentum caused by the horse's increased motion pushes her body weight even more forward. If her weight drops to the front of her seat, it slows the movement in the pelvis, thus telling the horse to stop or slow. On the other hand, if through tension her weight does not drop down, it must then go up and forward, getting transferred through leverage into the horse's forehand, causing discomfort and a mixed message. The horse, not surprisingly, often falls out of the gait at this point.

Now, I'm sure that there are times when the horse is a problem. My focus is always on the rider. Only after I'm sure it's not the rider do I look to the horse.

My horse has a habit of jerking his head and neck forward, trying to pull against me.

Your horse jerks you forward to get your weight off his back. There may be other reasons for this pulling, but for our purposes we will assume the root problem is in your seat.

When you sit on a horse's back you take on a great responsibility because you're sitting on the horse's weakest part, right in the middle of his spine, and directly over his center. Structurally, that's the weakest part of his body. He has more structural strength over his feet at the withers and hindquarters.

Think about the mechanics of your position on the horse. You sit in a comfortable place. The horse has greater strength and motion at the shoulders and hips. You're joining centers at the place of least motion on the horse's spine. This is the nature of the center—that it moves the least and every motion that comes from the center moves out from the center.

Many times I have seen riders get pulled out of the saddle as the horse throws his head forward, jerking the reins. When the rider loses her seat, it allows the horse to stop. The rider then sits back into the saddle and tells the horse to walk, then trot, and the jerking starts immediately. Somehow the blame gets put on the horse, when in my opinion the cause is the rider's seat. Of course if this action and reaction continues for any length of time, it can become a habit in the horse. Whether or not this pulling has become routine, the solution lies in the rider's seat.

I have been having trouble getting my horse to collect. What's wrong?

When a horse collects and rounds his back, the spine is softened and he is more comfortable to sit on. A horse will only do this if the rider's seat allows it in a manner that's comfortable for the horse. If your seat is not soft, it will constantly push against the horse's back at the wrong moments, and he will not offer his back in collection. Too often I see a rider using the reins, spurs, and whip in an effort to aid in collection before the rider is truly ready, meaning that her position is in opposition to the horse's back. As you know, horses' backs are sensitive. The horse will give you his back when your invitation to him is equally sensitive.

The required "sensitive" invitation involves more than just having a mechanically correct seat. You must have centered yourself and then joined centers with your horse by *opening your gates*. It is my experience that a horse will only connect with you to the degree that you can open your Eight Gates. The rider's gates correspond to the horse's. Your Heart gates align with your upper back, and so do the horse's. If they are closed, the horse's will also be closed. Once you open, he can open, and his back will come to you.

I've seen riders who are quite accomplished at opening all the gates except their Front and Back of the Heart gates. This is usually tied to protecting themselves emotionally in other areas of their lives. When they let go of the fear of being hurt and really open their hearts to the horse, the level of collection and connection that follows is remarkable.

I have a hard time sitting trot extensions. What do you suggest?

The extended trot creates a great deal of energy coming up through the horse's back, and it also increases the time that you must follow. (Review *Follow—Match—Lead*, p. 168.) These changes often cause the rider to "hold on," and in doing so, close the Back of the Heart gate as the breath rises in the body. Note that the holding may only affect the breath and not be seen in the physical body as clenching or tightening. The holding in the body is hidden in the cervical–thoracic junction of the spine. The key here is to open the Back of the Heart by expanding the breath back and out. By so doing you can allow the latissimus dorsi muscles to hold the shoulders down, pulling the energy back into the seat. Your goal is to expand and connect with your horse rather than tighten and push away.

I have a green horse. How can Tai Chi benefit my training?

I have many students whose job entails starting young green horses. The greatest bene-fit of Tai Chi for them is the sense of calm and physical balance gained from the prac-tice of this program. If there is one thing a young horse needs, it's a leader both on the ground and in the saddle. The key to developing a relationship of mutual respect on the ground is clear communication without force, and the same is true in the saddle. Tai Chi provides the training for clear, balanced communication without force.

My horse is hot. How can Tai Chi affect him?

The most direct way that Tai Chi helps a hot horse is through the calm and controlled abdominal breathing you develop. When you're on the back of a hot horse, very often your breath is short and up high in your chest. Breathing in this way brings your energy up, and this brings the horse's up as well. By staying calm and balanced, you can direct the heat of the horse in a positive, controlled direction.

Are there variations of Tai Chi?

Yes, there are many different styles of Tai Chi taught in the U.S. Some styles are more physically demanding than others, such as the Chen and Wu styles. Other styles are taught as a motion-meditation or a no-impact form of exercise. Whatever style you choose, your teacher should be able to demonstrate and explain the martial applica-tion of all the postures. This basis is what makes the practice real and it works to improve your riding skill. Otherwise, the movements are just another form of exercise.

How can I learn Tai Chi—should I take a class?

There is no substitute for a great teacher. There are many books and videotapes avail-able (my video, *Tai Chi for the Equestrian*, being one of them), but just as in riding, you must acquire the feel of it all by practicing, which I believe is best done in person with an instructor. Books and tapes are helpful references, for motions, underlying principles, and history; they can be valuable supplements to one-on-one or a group instruction.

Do I need a trained Tai Chi instructor to incorporate Tai Chi into my riding?

No, not necessarily. With the help of this book, you should be able to take what you learn and apply it successfully to your riding. However, if you are interested in "really" learning Tai Chi—that is, learning it for more than solely using it in your riding program—then yes, I would encourage you to find a qualified Tai Chi instructor in your area.

Can Tai Chi cause injury?

While the slow and relaxed nature of the movements of Tai Chi rarely causes injuries, there is always the possibility for something unexpected to happen. The most common complaint is that of a sore back after a long period of practice. I have found through my own experience and that of others that back pain usually involves two factors: (1) there is a preexisting condition in the back, and (2) the positions are not being done properly.

If the proper alignment of the bones is not maintained, the stress of gravity will inevitably take its toll on the back. Old injuries and developed compensations in the body can be healed and retrained through the practice of Tai Chi. I would recommend that you follow the guidance of an experienced teacher.

I'm a disabled rider. How can I adapt the exercises?

I have had the pleasure of working with many handicapped and disabled riders, and together we've had great success at modifying motions to suit individual needs. While I can't say specifically how to modify any one particular exercise for every person's disability, here are some guidelines to follow.

Always focus on slow, deep breathing directed by the mind.

I once worked with a group of disabled riders in Washington state. One of the riders suffered from cerebral palsy. The left side of her body was greatly affected, so much so that she could not lift her arm and had minimal movement in the fingers and hand on that side. For the exercise *Thrust Palm in Bow Stance* (p. 146). I asked her just to imagine that her left arm was raised and the palm pushing out. She did so, and as she returned to the center position, her eyes were lit up and her face was full of excitement. She told me that she could feel the electricity flowing through her arm and into her hand as she focused and directed her mind and chi.

All of the upper body motions may be done from a wheelchair.

Most of the mounted work can be done by a disabled rider if closely directed by a qualified handicapped riding instructor. I have also had the pleasure of meeting and working with a riding instructor and horseman who, as a result of injury, lost the use of his legs fifteen years ago. Almost immediately he "got back on the horse," and he has learned how to ride without the use of his legs. That means that he rides from his center. Without the leverage and active weight supplied by the muscles in his legs, all his aids must come from his seat. Although our language is slightly different, through conversation we have discovered that he has done on his own out of necessity many of the things that I have taught you. By learning and following the principles and theories in this book, you can ride more by doing less.

How does Tai Chi differ from Yoga?

There are far more similarities between Tai Chi and yoga than there are differences. Both focus the mind exclusively on the body and develop mind and body harmony through movement and breath control. Both seek to create and move that invisible life force energy within the human body. In Tai Chi it's called chi, and in yoga, it's called prana.

The major difference between the two is that Tai Chi is a martial art and therefore bound by different laws. During the practice of Tai Chi, you are always aware that there is an opponent trying to uproot your balance by any means possible. So in Tai Chi practice you never negate gravity by sitting or lying on the ground. In a form, you also never use gravity alone to stretch the body. You always use an opposing muscle group to create the stretch. Yoga is a fantastic mind and body exercise that I myself practice. Remember, variety is the spice of life, or as the Buddha said, "Many roads lead to enlightenment."

Acknowledgments

I'd like to thank the people of Trafalgar Square Publishing: Caroline Robbins, Publisher, and Martha Cook, Managing Editor, for their patience and support from the beginning—and most of all, for asking me to write this book.

Chris Bray, writer/editor and friend: thank you for your hours editing and your research in and out of the saddle. Your personal experience of the work has added greatly to this book. Thanks to Charlene Strickland, writer/editor.

My sisters, Becky Stanzyk and Cynthia Thomas, for your unconditional love and guidance throughout my whole life.

My good friends and riding instructors:
Dr. Susan Connors: from day one you have embraced and made this work your own, and by doing so, have taken it to a level I would not have reached without you. Thank you for your guidance, knowledge and most of all friendship.

Missy Hicks, Gayle Smith, Kay Kamish, Suzi Hoffman Peacock, Jute Heinerson, Alexander Kurland: thank you for unselfishly sharing your knowledge of riding and horses with me and for letting me in. We've only scratched the surface. Linda Rogers, for your early support of my work and our friendship.

Betsy Steiner, my friend and teacher: thank you for all you have done and continue to do for me. You introduced me to riding with our first article, and before I ever sat on a horse you foresaw the benefits of Tai Chi for the riding world. I am forever grateful.

My Lau Kune Do Brothers: Joseph Lavitt, Dan Brewer, George Gains, Chris Hendrix, Fred Payne—who never lowered the bar and taught me that when the mind and body are exhausted, it is the Spirit that endures the last miles.

Richard Tsim, for your early guidance on this journey and for providing the sanctuary of the temple in which I, and countless others, could grow to our own heights.

Wen Mei-Yu, for sharing with me your incredible knowledge of the inner workings of Tai Chi and being a living example that grace, beauty, and power arise from the same source deep within the human spirit.

Tim Cartmel, one of the greatest martial artists and teachers I've had the pleasure to meet—thanks for keeping it all very real.

Paul Wiederman: thank you, my brother, for being a constant source of creative inspiration and encouragement. See you at Boodle Hole.

Bill W., Dr. Bob, and friends, for picking me up at the bottom and giving me the spiritual tools by which to live this new life.

Janice Bear, for her mystic foresight and the gift of "walking backward."

Mary Trost: thank you for your constant love and support of me at every level.

Dr. Syng Ku Yu, for sharing your life's work of healing with me and encouraging me to follow my own path.

Cele and Tony Nobel, for your constant love and support from the very start. Thank you, oh "Keepers of the Tree."

Sharon Shaw: You were the first to say, "You can do this, and it will be great." Thank you for your love and encouragement.

My four-legged "Masters": these are the true masters of riding and healing. Thank you for choosing me and enriching my life beyond compare.

There are many more people to whom I owe a dept of gratitude, especially all who have participated in my workshops, clinics, and lectures. I wouldn't be able to do this work without you.

Appendix A

Summary of Exercises in This Book

Summary of Exercises

Chapter 1: Tai Chi and Horsemanship
Lays the groundwork for applying Tai Chi to riding.

Chapter 2: Fundamentals of Tai Chi: An Ancient Art, A New Perspective
Introduces the Eight Principles that guide Tai Chi practice and the Eight Gates that affect the flow of chi in the rider's body.

Chapter 3: Your Mind: Awakening Self-Awareness and the Creative Mind

Exercises	Purpose	Routine	When to Move On
Standing Meditation and Sitting Meditation	The most basic position in which to develop the mind/body connection while maintaining structural alignment of the bones. Practicing these exercises plants the seed of quiet awareness that all other exercises build on.	These exercises can be practiced any time you have a moment to focus inward and should be practiced for a few minutes every morning before you start your day. I recommend 2 to 5 minutes of *Standing Meditation* before you ride for at least 2 weeks, after that, the time it takes to get the benefit can be achieved in less than a minute.	After 2 weeks of practice and when you have felt the change in your body described in the Ah Ha! section of this exercise.
Side Step	*Side Step* first challenges you to maintain the mind/body connection achieved in *Standing Meditation* while moving your body. The slow, subtle shift of weight that takes place by engaging the pelvis not only creates sensitivity of the seat, but also brings to the surface the unconscious physical limitations of the pelvis that you will overcome through practice.	Initially, *Side Step* should be practiced 5 times every time you do *Standing Meditation*. During your first 2 weeks of practice you will most likely find yourself practicing the shift of weight throughout your day—this is the intent. Moving in this way should become a part of your life, not just something you do as an exercise before you ride. When this happens, you may reduce the practice to just before you ride.	After 2 weeks of practice and when you have felt the change in your body described in the Ah Ha! section of this exercise.
Wrist Shaking	The purpose of this exercise is two-fold: (1) to make you aware of the internal energy of the body (chi), and (2) to help you check your progress in the physical balancing of your body in regard to the inseparable role the bones and muscles play in maintaining balance in motion.	A few moments of *Wrist Shaking* after *Side Step* is sufficient in the first 2 weeks. Remember, *Wrist Shaking* is done to check your progress in your overall mind/body balance.	After 2 weeks of practice and when you have felt the change in your body described in the Ah Ha! section of this exercise.

(left margin: Tai Chi)

Exercises	Purpose	Routine	When to Move On
Sink and Circulate the Chi	The purpose of this exercise is to begin to match the movements of your body with the rhythm of your breath while maintaining the mind/body connection.	5 repetitions of *Sink and Circulate the Chi* after *Wrist Shaking* is sufficient during the first 2 weeks. With this amount of practice you will begin to find that you are connecting your breath to the movements of your body throughout your day. Bravo!	After 2 weeks of practice and when you have felt the change in your body described in the Ah Ha! section of this exercise.
Horse Stance and Wall Sitting	The purpose of this exercise is to develop leg strength and train the body to open the second gate (Ming Meng) while negotiating the force of gravity through the body.	I recommend doing 5 repetitions every day. If this is too much, I would recommend that it be done a minimum of 3 repetitions, 3 times a week. This is one of the most valuable exercises in this book; I also realize it's the most physically challenging. If you do it, you will be able to access your Ming Meng in a very short time.	After 2 weeks of practice and when you have felt the change in your body described in the Ah Ha! section of this exercise.
Walking Backward	This exercise teaches you to move with balance and rhythm.	Do this exercise as often as possible, or at least 3 times a week for one month. Performing the exercise for 5 to 15 minutes at a time is ideal.	This exercise should become a part of your routine for the rest of your life.

*(Left margin label: Tai Chi)*

Chapter 4: Expanding Our Perspective: Tai Chi's Healing Path and the Gift of the Horse

Exercises	Purpose	Routine	When to Move On
Laing Gong Palm and Fist	This seemingly simple exercise is contained in every Laing Gong exercise except one (*Hold the Sky with Both Hands*). It functions to pump chi throughout the arms and hands. It is very effective at reducing the amount of tension that is unconsciously held in the hand. This exercise is also used to start to heal pain and stiffness in the hands.	To start, spend a few minutes a day practicing opening and closing the hand into the Laing Gong Palm and Fist. The time varies with each person, but with practice you should very soon see a change in the color of the palm, that is, white spots will appear in the palm and fingers.	Practice until you can easily open the hand, keep the fingers together, and "hollow" the palm of the hand.

*(Left margin label: Laing Gong)*

Chi Gong

Exercises	Purpose	Routine
Abdominal Breathing	The purpose of this exercise is to retrain the body to allow for the expansion of the center (abdomen). The exercise also lowers the rider's center of balance from the chest to the waist, and it teaches you to open the first gate (Dain Tian).	As with all the breath work in this chapter, you can practice anytime you become aware of your breath. After becoming competent with the exercise, 5 repetitions, 3 times a day is a good start. This should be completed in about one minute's time. When mounted, try spending the first few minutes of your time in the saddle focused on this breathing. Keep doing this exercise until you catch yourself breathing correctly more often than not. The goal of all breath work is to not have to think about it.
Counting Your Breath	The purpose of this exercise is to bring into the conscious mind the rhythm of your breath and learn how it affects your movement.	Anytime during the day that you become aware of your breath, spend a few moments finding your rhythm by counting your breath. When mounted, practice for one minute after completing *Abdominal Breathing.*
Open the Ming Meng	This exercise creates free movement in the lower back and spine. The exercise also teaches you to open the second gate (Ming Meng).	Practice anytime you become aware of your breath. After becoming competent with the exercise, 5 repetitions, 3 times a day is a good start. Try *Open the Ming Meng* at night before you go to sleep while lying on your back in bed. Many people have found this to be effective. This should be completed in about one minute's time. In the saddle, do 5 minutes of focused practice every time you ride.
Embracing the Moon	This exercise connects the upper body to the lower body. The exercise removes tension from the chest and arms, and teaches you to open the third and fourth gates (the *Front and Back of the Heart*).	As with all the breath work in this chapter, you can practice anytime you become aware of your breath. After becoming competent with the exercise, 5 repetitions, 3 times a day is a good start. This should be completed in about 2 to 3 minutes time.
Heaven and Earth	This exercise teaches you to use the upper body while staying connected to the lower. The exercise also connects you to the earth and heavens energetically, and it trains the mind to keep the first four gates open while moving.	
Breathing to a Halt or Walk	The purpose of this exercise is to begin to actively use your breath as an aid.	

Chapter 6: Your Body: Enhancing Your Movement and Power

Laing Gong

Exercises	Purpose	Routine
Neck Turns	Heals the neck and shoulders.	For all these Laing Gong exercises: After learning the movements, try to complete 200 repetitions within 2 weeks—that is, 7 repetitions every morning and every evening for 2 weeks.
Spread Your Chest	Heals the neck and shoulders.	
Spread Your Wings	Heals the neck and shoulders.	
Hold the Sky with Both Hands	Heals the lower back.	
Hip Circles	Heals the lower back and hips.	
Thrust Palm in Bow Stance	Heals the lower back and hips.	
Hold Knee to Chest	Heals the lower back and hips.	
Bend with an Arch	Heals the lower back and hips.	
Lift a Single Iron Arm	Heals the lower back and shoulders.	

Chapter 7: Application: Bringing It All Together in the Saddle

Teaches you to apply what you've learned to the gaits, transitions, bending, lateral movements, and jumping.

Chapter 8: The Road Continues: Health and Tai Chi

Shows how to use Tai Chi to improve your health, and includes frequently asked questions and answers.

Appendix B

Anatomical Diagrams

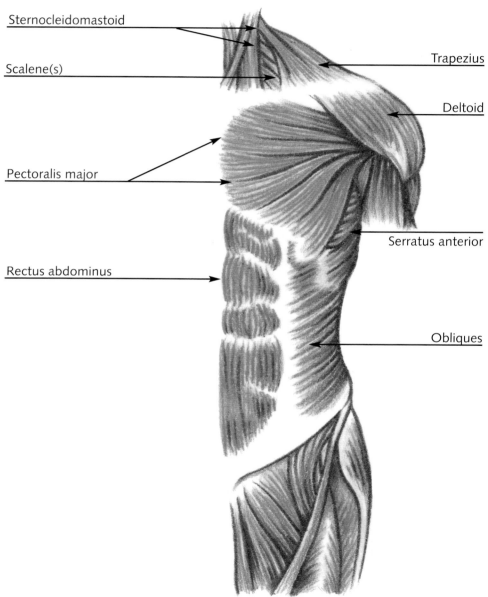

Sternocleidomastoid

Scalene(s)

Pectoralis major

Rectus abdominus

Trapezius

Deltoid

Serratus anterior

Obliques

Muscles of the Anterior Torso

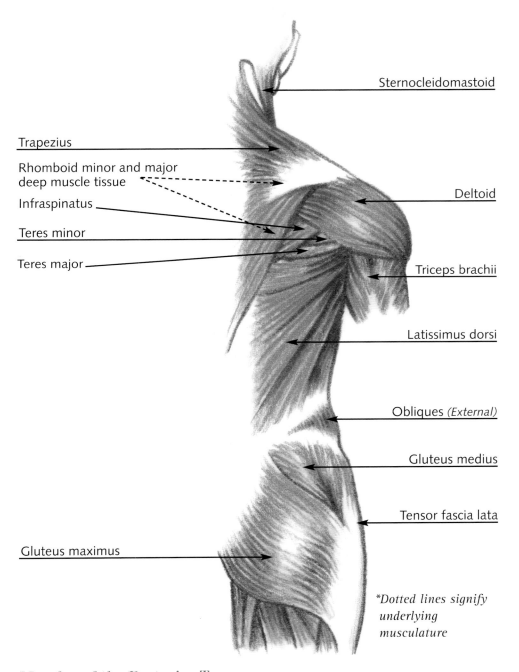

Sternocleidomastoid

Trapezius

Rhomboid minor and major
deep muscle tissue

Deltoid

Infraspinatus

Teres minor

Teres major

Triceps brachii

Latissimus dorsi

Obliques *(External)*

Gluteus medius

Tensor fascia lata

Gluteus maximus

*Dotted lines signify
underlying
musculature*

Muscles of the Posterior Torso

Supraspinatus

Infraspinatus

Teres minor

Teres major

Latissimus dorsi

Anconeus

Extensor carpi ulnaris

Extensor digiti minimi

Extensor retinaculum

Deltoid

Triceps brachii

Brachialis

Brachioradialis

Extensor digitorum

Extensor carpi radialis longus

Abductor pollicis longus

Extensor pollicis brevis

Muscles of the Posterior Arm

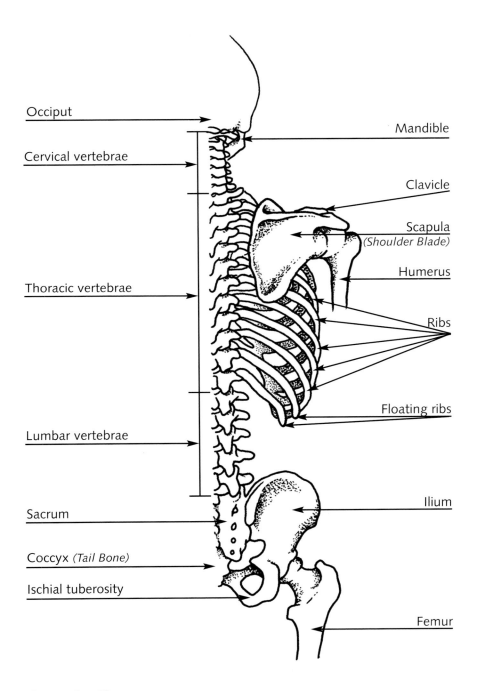

Occiput

Cervical vertebrae

Thoracic vertebrae

Lumbar vertebrae

Sacrum

Coccyx (Tail Bone)

Ischial tuberosity

Mandible

Clavicle

Scapula
(Shoulder Blade)

Humerus

Ribs

Floating ribs

Ilium

Femur

Posterior Torso

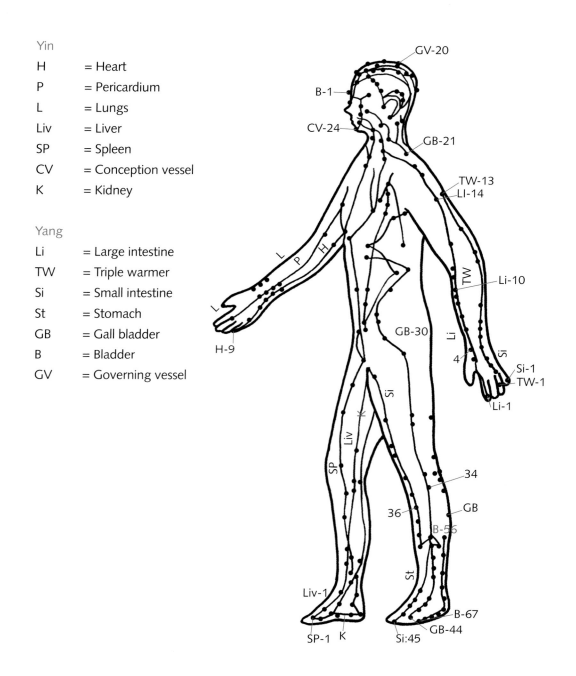

Yin

H	= Heart
P	= Pericardium
L	= Lungs
Liv	= Liver
SP	= Spleen
CV	= Conception vessel
K	= Kidney

Yang

Li	= Large intestine
TW	= Triple warmer
Si	= Small intestine
St	= Stomach
GB	= Gall bladder
B	= Bladder
GV	= Governing vessel

GV-20
B-1
CV-24
GB-21
TW-13
LI-14
Li-10
GB-30
Si-1
TW-1
Li-1
H-9
34
36
GB
B-56
Liv-1
B-67
GB-44
SP-1 K
Si:45

Yin and Yang Meridians

Appendix C

Resources

Web Sites

www.shawtaichi.com

This is my own web site; you can find out more about me and my work here including upcoming clinics and events, videos, and more. (You can also contact me directly at taishawchi@aol.com.)

www.shenwu.com

Tim Cartmell's web site, the best martial artist I've ever seen. Tim has had a great influence on my teaching. He teaches the truth without any secrets or mysticism. Tim's site also has a great deal of information on various martial arts and links to other resources.

www.thinkfit.com

Paul Widerman's web site, creator of Smart Bells™, an innovative replacement for dumb bells. If you need to increase your strength, Smart Bells™ are the way to go.

www.wenmeiyu.com

Wen Mei Yu is a Tai Chi Grandmaster and my teacher. She is a great inspiration as a martial artist and a person. There are many links from this web site to the world of Tai Chi and other martial arts.

Bibliography and Further Reading

Andrews, Ted. *Animal Speak*. St. Paul, Minnesota: Llewellyn Publications, 1993.

Benfield, Harriet, L.Ac., and Korngold, Efrem, L.Ac., O.M.D. *Between Heaven and Earth: A Guide to Chinese Medicine*. New York: Ballantine Books, 1991.

Berk, William R. *Chinese Healing Arts*. Unique Publications, 1986.

Cartmell, Tim. *Effortless Combat Throws*. High View Publications, 1996.

Choa Kok Sui. *Advanced Pranic Healing*. York Beach, Maine: Samuel Weiser, Inc., 1995.

Collinge, William, Ph.D. *Subtle Energy*. New York: Warner Books, 1998.

Deng Ming-Dao. *365 Tao Daily Meditations*. San Francisco: Harper Collins, 1992.

Loa Tsu. *Tao Te Ching*. Translated by Gia-Fu Feng and Jane English. New York: Random House, 1972.

Miyamoto Musashi. *The Book of Five Rings*. Translated by Thomas Cleary. Boston: Shambhala Publications, 1993.

Rawson, Philip, and Legeza, Laszlo. *Tao: The Chinese Philosophy of Time and Change*. London: Thames and Hudson, 1973.

Schusdziarra, H, M.D., and Schusdziarra, V. *An Anatomy of Riding*. Breakthrough Publications, Inc., 1978.

Storm, Hyemeyohsts. *Seven Arrows*. New York: Ballantine Books, 1972.

Sun Tzu. *The Art of War*. Translated by Samuel B. Griffith. Oxford: Oxford University Press, 1971.

Swift, Sally. *Centered Riding*. North Pomfret, Vermont: Trafalgar Square Publishing, 1985.

Thich Nhat Hanh. *Breath! You Are Alive*. Berkeley: Parallax Press, 1996.

Thich Nhat Hanh. *The Miracle of Mindfulness*. Boston: Beacon Press, 1975.

Waysun Liao. *Tai Chi Classics*. Boston: Shambhala Publications, 1990.

Wu Ying-hua, and Ma Yueh-liang. *Wu Style Taichichuan*. Shanghai Book Company, 1993.

Xie Peiqi. *Guiding Energy Sitting Meditations*. Toronto: Traditional Studies Press, 1995.

Yeshi Donden. *Health Through Balance: An Introduction to Tibetan Medicine*. Ithaca, New York: Snow Lion Publications, 1986.

Index